S0-AZU-006

Glencoe

Teacher Wraparound Edition

Writer's Choice

GRAMMAR and COMPOSITION

GRADE 9

Before him stretched the long, laborious road, dry
FREEWRITE
"I know why the cage bird sings, ah me,
when his wing is bruised and his bosom sore,--
when he beats his bars and he would be free;"
cyberspa
"He clasps the crag with crooked hands."

Mc
Graw
Hill

Glencoe

ACKNOWLEDGMENTS

Grateful acknowledgment is given authors, publishers, photographers, museums, and agents for permission to reprint the following copyrighted material. Every effort has been made to determine copyright owners. In case of any omissions, the Publisher will be pleased to make suitable acknowledgments in future editions.

Cover (Maya Angelou) ©Deborah Feingold/Corbis; (Scrabble tiles) Jeffrey Coolidge/Getty Images; (bkgd) Gerry Charm/SuperStock **vi** The Estate of John Lennon, 1989; **vii** Courtesy Bernice Stienbaum Gallery, New York; **viii** *The Starry Night,* (1889). Vincent Van Gogh. Collection, the Museum of Modern Art, NY. Acquired through the Lillie P. Bliss Foundation; **ix** The Brooklyn Museum, gift of the Ernest Erickson Foundation; **x** Courtesy the Chapingo Chapel of the National School of Agriculture and the Instituto Nacional de Bellas Artes, Mexico; **xi** File photo; **xii** PhotoDisc, Inc.; **xiii** P. and G. Bowater/The Image Bank; **xiv** ©1985, the Estate of Keith Haring; **xv** (t) file photo, (b) the Telegraph Colour Library/FPG; **xvi** Kent Fleming/Lifestyles; **xvii** (t)file photo; **xx** ©1990 Thames & Hudson, Ltd., London. Photo by David Lavender; **xxi** (t) Courtesy of the Lilly Library, Indiana University, Bloomington, Indiana, (b) PhotoDisc, Inc.; **xxii** © 1986 Courtesy of Collier, Macmillan Publishers, London. Photo by Ralph J. Brunke; **xxiii** Scala/Art Resource, NY; **xxiv** Photodisc, Inc; **xxv** Stella, Frank. *Katsura.* Collection, The Museum of Modern Art, New York. Acquired through Mr. and Mrs. Victor Ganz; **xxxi-1** Edward Owens/Art Resource, NY.

Acknowledgments continued on page 974.

The **Facing the Blank Page** feature in this book was prepared in collaboration with the writers and editors of *TIME*.

The McGraw·Hill Companies

Glencoe

Send all inquiries to:
Macmillan/McGraw-Hill • Glencoe/McGraw-Hill
8787 Orion Place
Columbus, OH 43240-4027

ISBN: 978-0-07-888773-4 (Teacher Wraparound Edition)
MHID: 0-07-888773-9 (Teacher Wraparound Edition)
ISBN: 978-0-07-888772-7 (Student Edition)
MHID: 0-07-888772-0 (Student Edition)

Printed in the United States of America.

2 3 4 5 6 7 8 9 10 DOW 12 11 10 09

Contents

Teacher Wraparound Edition

Welcome to *Writer's Choice*

Congratulations! By opening this book, you've taken an important step toward helping your students become **better writers and communicators**. The pages that follow help you see at a glance the features of the *Writer's Choice* Student Edition, the Teacher Wraparound Edition, and the program's additional resources.

The Benefits of *Writer's Choice*

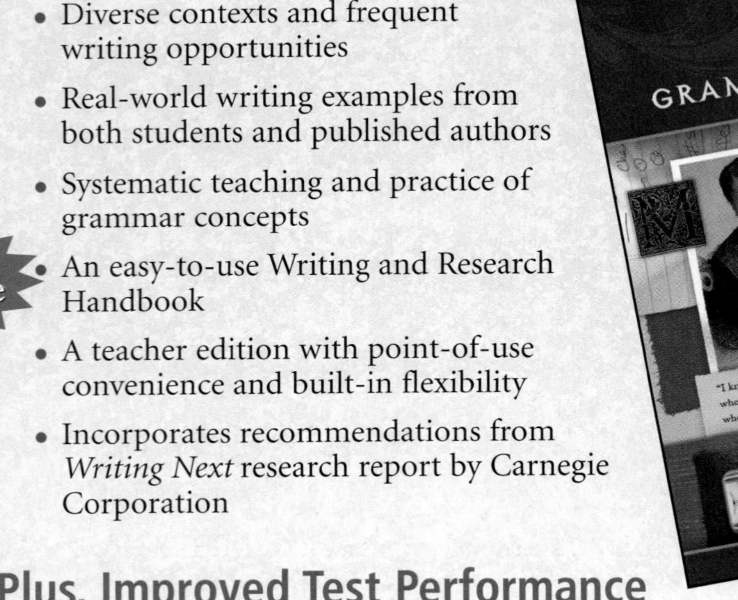
Quick Reference

- An integrated approach to language arts
- Concise lessons that target key skills
- Diverse contexts and frequent writing opportunities
- Real-world writing examples from both students and published authors
- Systematic teaching and practice of grammar concepts
- An easy-to-use Writing and Research Handbook
- A teacher edition with point-of-use convenience and built-in flexibility
- Incorporates recommendations from *Writing Next* research report by Carnegie Corporation

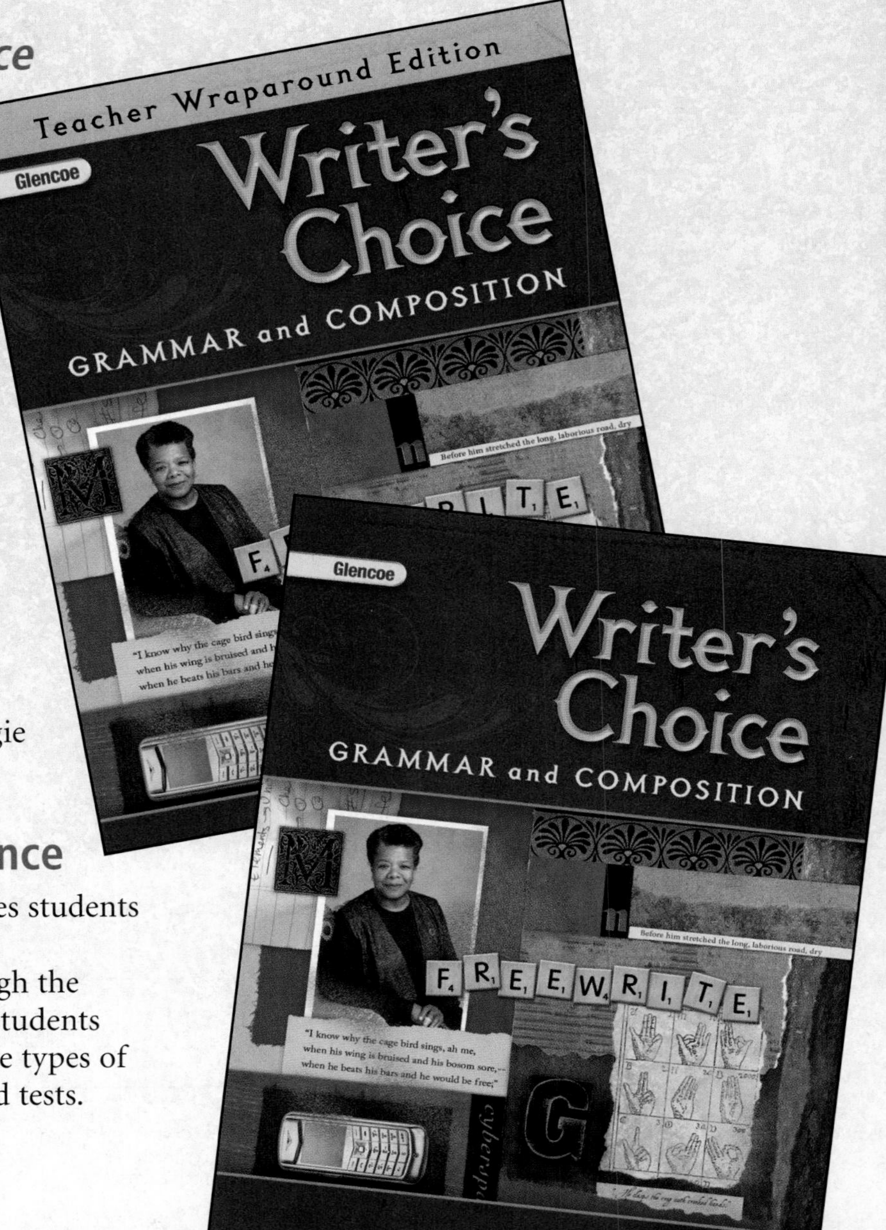
Teacher Wraparound Edition
Glencoe
Writer's Choice
GRAMMAR and COMPOSITION
Glencoe
Writer's Choice
GRAMMAR and COMPOSITION
FREEWRITE
"I know why the cage bird sings, ah me,
when his wing is bruised and his bosom sore,—
when he beats his bars and he would be free;"
Before him stretched the long, laborious road, dry

Plus, Improved Test Performance

The **Taking Tests** unit of *Writer's Choice* gives students the strategies and the practice they need to become better test-takers. Working through the **Standardized Test Practice** pages will help students become comfortable with the format and the types of items they will typically face on standardized tests.

Targeted Writing Instruction, Modeling, and Practice

In **Part 1: Composition,** students will learn how to apply the writing process to various modes of writing. Grammar and other language arts skills are integrated into each lesson.

Real Writers at Work

A four-page **Writing in the Real World** case study launches each composition unit. This **behind-the-scenes glimpse of the writing process** offers students a model of good writing practices.

The **writing process,** as practiced by professional writers, presents a clear map for working through a piece of writing.

Targeted visuals provide access to writing skills for students who learn best visually.

Real-life examples offer models for students and provide answers to the difficult question "When am I ever going to use this?"

Thoughtful **analysis questions** prompt readers to question and think about what makes good writing.

Grammar Links provide practice on a grammar, usage, or mechanics issue related to the writing examples.

Writing in the Real World

Media Connection — Magazine Article

As both a freelance writer and writing teacher, Lorenzo Chavez has lots of experience with the writing process. Chavez writes feature stories, or "human interest" stories, that cover a large range of topics. Below is an excerpt from a feature he wrote for *Vista,* a magazine for Hispanic readers inserted in about twenty Sunday newspapers nationwide.

The Quest for Hispanic Roots

by Lorenzo Chavez

For 15 years, Mickey Garcia has searched quietly for clues to a lost treasure buried in history books, church records and dusty family albums. The Texan's "treasure" is her family history, a unique link with the past that may help her gain a better understanding of her Latin roots.

"Some of my Mexican cousins think I'm crazy," she says from her suburban Houston home. "They think: 'What in the world does she want with all these dead people?'"

Whether out of cultural pride, simple curiosity or legal necessity, Latinos like Garcia are actively tracing their ancestral roots for clues to their Hispanic identity.

Since the 1977 telecast of Alex Haley's *Roots* sparked interest in family history, Hispanics have enthusiastically joined other Americans in the rush to the libraries.

Mexican Americans in particular, especially in the Southwest, are tracing generations of family roots. The historical records of immigrants from Cuba, Puerto Rico and South America—more recent, by comparison—are still evolving.

Genealogical societies, libraries and universities in southern Texas eagerly compile church and civil records relating to pioneers who explored and settled the border.

largest and most successful Hispanic family reunion ever held in the United States.

Through that warm summer weekend, they gathered at the 5,000-acre Laguna Seca ranch to celebrate their surname and to honor Salvador Vela and Leonor Zamora, who carried their children across the Rio Grande from Reynosa, Mexico, to McAllen in the late 1800s.

A book published last December, "Four Generations of Velas," was the result of ten years of research by those immigrants' descendants. . . .

Spanish surnames are more accessible than non-Spanish sur-

Writing in the Real World

World from the 15th to the 19th centuries.

Amateur and professional researchers should be grateful for that bureaucratic system, which required three copies of every document. . . . The copies were kept by the local officials, the regional governor and the Crown. Catholic church records also helped unify the Hispanic world, says Ryskamp.

"Most people who get interested in genealogy are two or three generations removed from their mother country," Ryskamp notes. "Economically, they are middle-class or above. I expect the interest to grow in the next 10 to 20 years as the Hispanic population makes greater economic gains. . . ."

Meanwhile, Mickey Garcia continues searching for names and dates. She has traced her mother's family to the early 1700's, but remains "stuck" in the 1880's with the paternal branch of the tree.

"You have to be interested," Garcia explains. "One of my ancestors was married three times and ended up with 21 children. And in 1833 a lot of my relatives died of cholera. That makes for a lot of 'added research.'"

"To be a good genealogist you have to be a good detective," sums up Ryskamp, the California lawyer. "You never know what you are going to find."

A Writer's Process

Prewriting
Collecting the Facts

Chavez will tell you that ideas for feature stories are everywhere, in fact, there are "just too many," laughed Chavez. And, of course, you have to be alert and open to ideas. The idea for Chavez's story on family histories, "The Quest for Hispanic Roots," came from *Vista* readers. Over the years, hundreds of *Vista* readers had written in to "Rootsearch," a popular genealogy column devoted to tracing family histories. With so many readers writing in to the column, the *Vista* staff

cover in the allotted space of 1,500 words, or about six pages in *Vista* magazine. Chavez then gathered the facts by looking for answers to these questions: Why do people search for their pasts? What libraries or associations can help?

It took Chavez about a week to get the answers. Some information came from newspaper clippings, but most of it came through the thirty or forty phone calls he made to libraries and researchers.

Vela family reunion

Writing in the Real World 55

Writing in the Real World

Drafting
Telling the Story

After his interviews, Chavez had twenty pages of notes, several taped conversations, a few newspaper clips, and a head full of ideas. Before sitting down at the computer, Chavez reminded himself of the people he was writing for. His audience was a "middle-aged to older generation, people of Mexican descent, mostly retirees, who have spare time and an interest in history and politics." To engage his readers, Chavez had to put himself in their shoes and anticipate questions they might ask.

Now Chavez was ready to write. To grab the reader, he used an anecdote about Mickey Garcia, a Texas genealogist who researches family histories. He portrayed Garcia as a treasure hunter. "She's searching for a valuable thing—not gold, but a family history," Chavez said. "I used that [approach] because I didn't want to frighten the reader by saying this was a long, time-consuming, arduous task."

From there Chavez stitched the story together using quotes, descriptions, and explanations about what sparked people's interest in genealogy. He introduced top researchers, described huge family reunions, and explained how to find family records.

Revising
Making Necessary Changes

Chavez wrote a rough draft in three days. "It was messy, but I knew I had everything I wanted there," he said. Now he was ready to revise.

At this stage, Chavez began working on a printout of his story instead of working at the computer. On hard copy, he could spot problems more clearly. "If the lead is too long, you can see it—the paragraph is all gray. No one is going to get through that first paragraph," he explains.

Editing
Bringing in Style

Chavez began editing his story by checking his facts, spelling, and grammar. "If you have poor spelling and grammar or the facts are wrong, the reader will ask, 'Why should I read this guy? He doesn't know what he's talking about.'"

After that, Chavez worked to improve his style. He rewrote dull sentences to make them bold and active. He varied sentence lengths to create rhythm, so the story sounded interesting, not monotonous. Finally, he checked to be sure the story had some mystery. "You can't put all the information at the top or the reader doesn't have anything to look forward to," Lorenzo said. "You have to have some suspense, something pushing the reader forward."

Finally, Chavez turned his copy over to staff editors who reviewed his work before publication. His editors, he said, catch mistakes and other problems because they have a fresh point of view.

56 Unit 2 The Writing Process

Examining Writing in the Real World

Analyzing the Media Connection

Discuss the following questions about the article on pages 54–55.

1. For what audience did Chavez write his feature story?
2. In what ways does Chavez direct the article to the interests of his readers?
3. Chavez describes the Vela family reunion that 1,500 family members attended. How effective was this anecdote?
4. Why do you think Chavez opens the story by focusing on the family search of one woman, Mickey Garcia? Why does he return to Garcia at the closing?
5. Chavez includes some history about Spanish and Mexican migration. What do you think his reason is for including this information?

Analyzing A Writer's Process

Discuss these questions about Lorenzo Chavez's writing process.

1. How was the topic for Chavez's article selected?
2. What sources of facts did Chavez use for his story? What are some other possible sources he might have used?
3. Before he started to draft his story, what did Chavez need to know about his audience?
4. Why did Chavez revise on a printout rather than on the computer?
5. Why does Chavez take extra care to check his spelling and grammar?

Grammar Link

Vary sentence lengths.

Lorenzo Chavez writes that he varied sentence lengths to create rhythm, so the story sounded interesting, not monotonous. You can vary sentence lengths by using a variety of sentence patterns: simple, compound, complex, and compound-complex.

Revise each item below by combining each pair of simple sentences in two different ways. Add or change words or phrases as needed.

1. Feature story ideas are everywhere. Ideas often come from news articles.
2. Chavez writes for *Vista* magazine. *Vista* is targeted to Hispanic readers.
3. Chavez interviewed genealogists. He collected taped conversations.
4. Chavez improved his draft. He changed words and sentences.
5. Genealogists share their research findings. There are many genealogical societies.

See Lessons 13.3 and 13.4, pages 541–544.

Writing in the Real World 37

Focused Four-Page Lessons

You won't find long-winded writing about writing in *Writer's Choice.* Literature models, student models, and instructional visuals combine to **show rather than just tell.**

Literature Models supply students with models for good writing. Thoughtful callouts prompt students to analyze how published authors use the strategies being taught in the lesson.

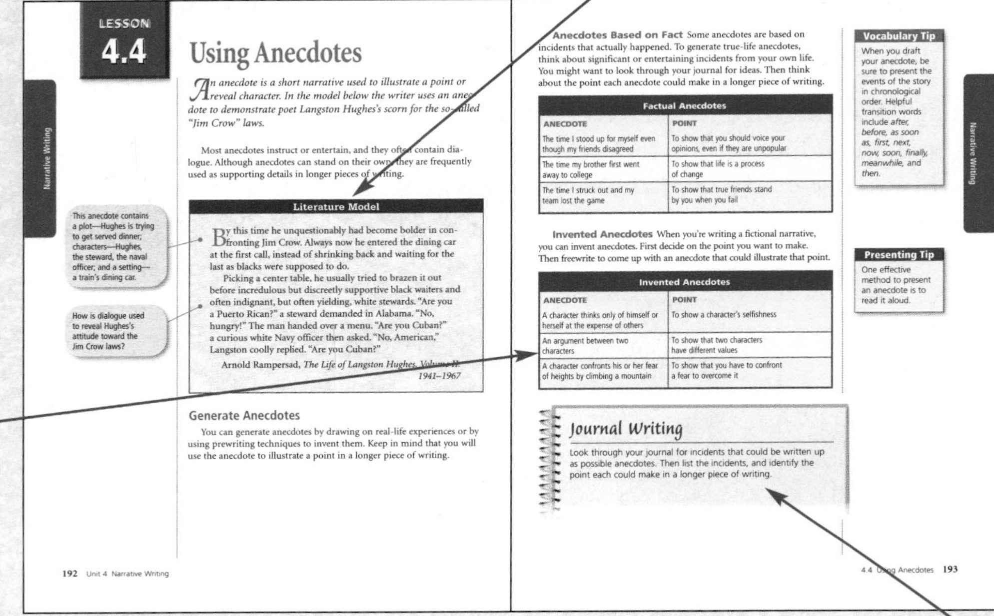

LESSON 4.4

Using Anecdotes

An anecdote is a short narrative used to illustrate a point or reveal character. In the model below the writer uses an anecdote to demonstrate poet Langston Hughes's scorn for the so-called "Jim Crow" laws.

Most anecdotes instruct or entertain, and they often contain dialogue. Although anecdotes can stand on their own, they are frequently used as supporting details in longer pieces of writing.

This anecdote contains a plot—Hughes is trying to get served dinner; characters—Hughes, the steward, the naval officer; and a setting—a train's dining car.

How is dialogue used to reveal Hughes's attitude toward the Jim Crow laws?

Literature Model

By this time he unquestionably had become bolder in confronting Jim Crow. Always now he entered the dining car at the first call, instead of shrinking back and waiting for the last as blacks were supposed to do.

Picking a center table, he usually tried to brazen it out before incredulous but discreetly supportive black waiters and often indignant, but often yielding, white stewards. "Are you a Puerto Rican?" a steward demanded in Alabama. "No, hungry!" The man handed over a menu. "Are you Cuban?" a curious white Navy officer then asked. "No, American," Langston coolly replied. "Are you Cuban?"

Arnold Rampersad, *The Life of Langston Hughes, Volume II: 1941–1967*

Generate Anecdotes

You can generate anecdotes by drawing on real-life experiences or by using prewriting techniques to invent them. Keep in mind that you will use the anecdote to illustrate a point in a longer piece of writing.

192 Unit 4 Narrative Writing

Anecdotes Based on Fact Some anecdotes are based on incidents that actually happened. To generate true-life anecdotes, think about significant or entertaining incidents from your own life. You might want to look through your journal for ideas. Then think about the point each anecdote could make in a longer piece of writing.

Factual Anecdotes

ANECDOTE	POINT
The time I stood up for myself even though my friends disagreed	To show that you should voice your opinions, even if they are unpopular
The time my brother first went away to college	To show that life is a process of change
The time I struck out and my team lost the game	To show that true friends stand by you when you fail

Invented Anecdotes When you're writing a fictional narrative, you can invent anecdotes. First decide on the point you want to make. Then freewrite to come up with an anecdote that could illustrate that point.

Invented Anecdotes

ANECDOTE	POINT
A character thinks only of himself or herself at the expense of others	To show a character's selfishness
An argument between two characters	To show that two characters have different values
A character confronts his or her fear of heights by climbing a mountain	To show that you have to confront a fear to overcome it

Journal Writing

Look through your journal for incidents that could be written up as possible anecdotes. Then list the incidents, and identify the point each could make in a longer piece of writing.

Vocabulary Tip

When you draft your anecdote, be sure to present the events of the story in chronological order. Helpful transition words include *after, before, as soon as, first, next, now, soon, finally, meanwhile,* and *then.*

Presenting Tip

One effective method to present an anecdote is to read it aloud.

4.4 Using Anecdotes 193

Illustrations, graphs, and charts make information visual and easy to grasp. Also, fine art in many styles and from many cultures inspires writing and discussion.

Student models illustrate how student writers put into practice the lessons being taught.

Journal Writing activities midway through each lesson prompt students to "write to learn."

Prewriting Tip

If you are writing about yourself, you might ask family members to discuss their early memories of you. Their stories could supply you with useful anecdotes.

Decide Where and How to Use Anecdotes

Once you have an anecdote, you need to consider whether or not to use it to make a specific point in a longer piece of writing. To help you decide, ask yourself the questions in the chart below.

Questions to Determine the Usefulness of an Anecdote

1. Does this anecdote make the point I want to make?
2. Does the anecdote advance the narrative?
3. Is the anecdote brief, yet meaningful?
4. Does the anecdote instruct or entertain?

In Jennifer Tuck's short story "My Grandmother's House," the narrator dreads returning to her grandmother's house after her grandmother dies. As a little girl, she had been afraid of the house because it was so large and dark. This anecdote reveals, however, on one particular occasion her grandmother helped her overcome her fears.

What does the anecdote reveal about the narrator's grandmother?

Notice that the anecdote could stand on its own as a brief narrative, complete with plot, setting, and characters.

Student Model

I had been sitting on the porch for nearly an hour when my grandmother came out, quietly letting the screen door creak on its old rusty hinges and then sigh as it came to rest against the crooked door frame Grandpa was always saying he would fix.

"Why don't you come inside?" she said. "We are going to eat dinner soon and I would hate to think of sitting at the table without you."

"I'm afraid." I barely whispered this shameful feeling, and stared straight down at my untied shoes.

"That's OK. I was afraid when we first moved here, too. You just have to remember that this house is a lot like your house, only there's love from many families here instead of just our own. Did you ever stop to wonder who could have lived here before? There must be so many memories within these walls!"

We talked on and on and gradually my fear began to fade. When my mother called us inside, I didn't hesitate for an instant before following my grandmother inside.

Jennifer Tuck, Central High School, Manchester, New Hampshire
First appeared in *Merlyn's Pen: The National Magazine of Student Writing*

194 Unit 4 Narrative Writing

4.4 Writing Activities

Write an Anecdote

Your English class is collecting an anecdote from each class member for a get-to-know-your-classmates project. The collection will be distributed to all of the students in the class. Write an anecdote that reveals something about your personality. You may choose to write about a time when you made a fool of yourself in front of someone you wanted to impress, or a time when your sense of humor helped relieve an unpleasant situation. You might choose to reveal another aspect of your personality.

PURPOSE To write an anecdote that reveals something about yourself
AUDIENCE The members of your class
LENGTH 3–4 paragraphs

WRITING RUBRICS To write an effective anecdote, you should

- be sure your anecdote supports your point
- include significant details regarding character, setting, and plot

Cross-Curricular Activity

FINE ART Look at the painting. What ideas for anecdotes does it suggest? Freewrite or list to generate ideas for anecdotes and for the points they could illustrate.

Joan Brown, *After the Alcatraz Swim #3,* 1976

Grammar Link

Use comparative and superlative forms of adjectives and adverbs correctly.

Comparative adjectives and adverbs compare two things—for example, Langston Hughes's becoming "bolder" in confronting Jim Crow. *Superlative forms* of adjectives and adverbs compare more than two things.

Complete each sentence below with the correct form of the word in parentheses.

1. After some time, Langston Hughes entered the dining car ________ than he first had. (courageously)
2. Who were ________ (amazed): the white stewards or the black waiters?
3. Perhaps ________ of all were the fellow passengers Hughes encountered in the dining cars. (surprised)
4. Some passengers moved to the ________ corner of the dining car when they saw the poet approach. (far)
5. They showed ________ what they thought than did those passengers who just ignored Hughes. (clearly)

See Lessons 18.1–18.3, pages 659–664.

Listening and Speaking

COOPERATIVE LEARNING With a classmate, create a dialogue based on your responses to the painting to the left and present it to the class as a dramatic reading.

Writing Online For more writing and grammar practice, go to glencoe.com and enter QuickPass code WC97727p1.

4.4 Using Anecdotes 195

Writing Activities provide prompts and rubrics related to the lesson. Grammar Links provide practice. Other activities show alternative ways of working with the topic.

Scaffolded Instruction of the Writing Process

For each mode of writing, the **Writing Process in Action** pages walk students through the recursive steps of prewriting, drafting, revising, editing, and publishing a piece of writing.

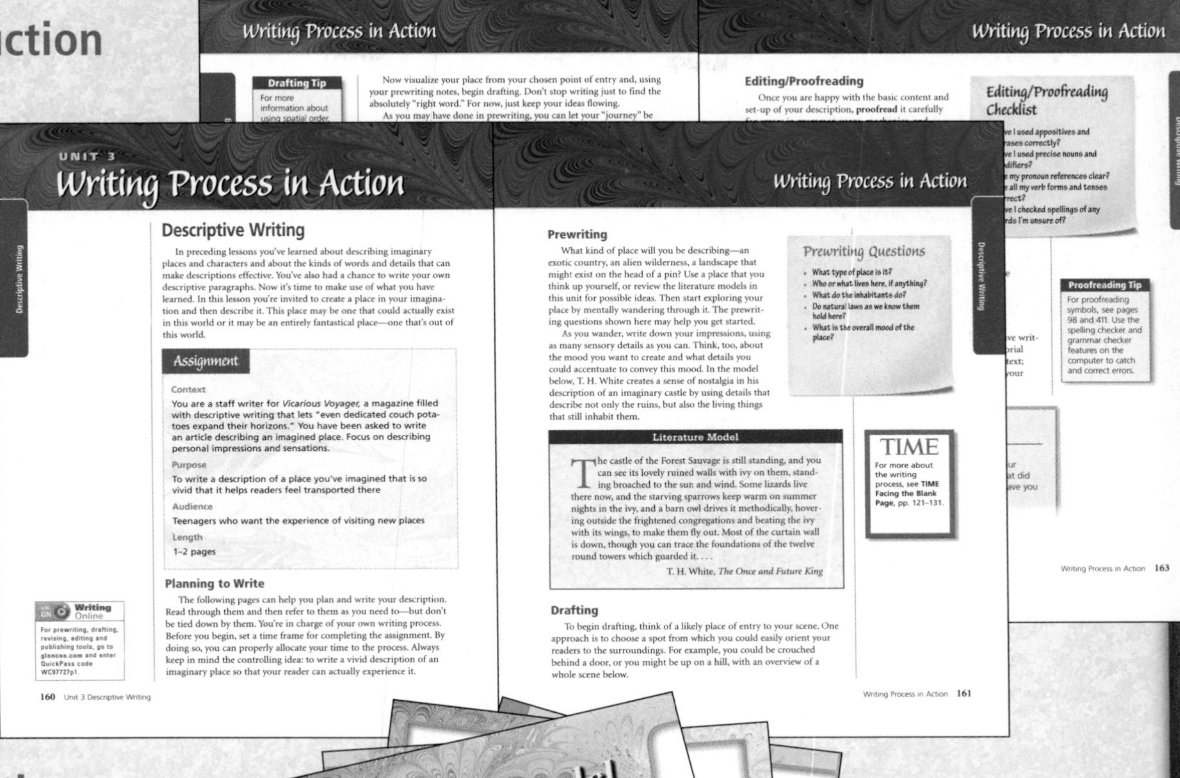

UNIT 3

Writing Process in Action

Descriptive Writing

In preceding lessons you've learned about describing imaginary places and characters and about the kinds of words and details that can make descriptions effective. Now you've also had a chance to write your own descriptive paragraphs. Now it's time to make use of what you have learned. In this lesson you're invited to create a place in your imagination and then describe it. This place may be one that could actually exist in this world or it may be an entirely fantastical place—one that's out of this world.

Assignment

Context
You are a staff writer for *Vicarious Voyager*, a magazine filled with descriptive writing that lets "even dedicated couch potatoes expand their horizons." You have been asked to write an article describing an imagined place. Focus on describing personal impressions and sensations.

Purpose
To write a description of a place you've imagined that is so vivid that it helps readers feel transported there

Audience
Teenagers who want the experience of visiting new places

Length
1–2 pages

Planning to Write

The following pages can help you plan and write your description. Read through them and then refer to them as you need to—but don't be tied down by them. You're in charge of your own writing process. Before you begin, set a time frame for completing the assignment. By doing so, you can properly allocate your time to the process. Always keep in mind the controlling idea: to write a vivid description of an imaginary place so that your reader can actually experience it.

Writing Online
For prewriting, drafting, revising, editing and publishing tools, go to glencoe.com and enter QuickPass code WC97727p1.

160 Unit 3 Descriptive Writing

Writing Process in Action

Prewriting

What kind of place will you be describing—an exotic country, an alien wilderness, a landscape that might exist on the head of a pin? Use a place that you think up yourself, or review the literature models in this unit for possible ideas. Then start exploring your place by mentally wandering through it. The prewriting questions shown here may help you get started.

As you wander, write down your impressions, using as many sensory details as you can. Think, too, about the mood you want to create and what details you could accentuate to convey this mood. In the model below, T. H. White creates a sense of nostalgia in his description of an imaginary castle by using details that describe not only the ruins, but also the living things that still inhabit them.

Prewriting Questions
- What type of place is it?
- Who or what lives here, if anything?
- What do the inhabitants do?
- Do natural laws as we know them hold here?
- What is the overall mood of the place?

Literature Model

The castle of the Forest Sauvage is still standing, and you can see its lovely ruined walls with ivy on them, standing broached to the sun and wind. Some lizards live there now, and the starving sparrows keep warm on summer nights in the ivy, and a barn owl drives it methodically, hovering outside the frightened congregations and beating the ivy with its wings, to make them fly out. Most of the curtain wall is down, though you can trace the foundations of the twelve round towers which guarded it. . . .

T. H. White, *The Once and Future King*

TIME
For more about the writing process, see TIME Facing the Blank Page, pp. 121–131.

Drafting

To begin drafting, think of a likely place of entry to your scene. One approach is to choose a spot from which you could easily orient your readers to the surroundings. For example, you could be crouched behind a door, or you might be up on a hill, with an overview of a whole scene below.

Writing Process in Action 161

The Reading/Writing Connection

Literature Models by contemporary authors mirror the mode of writing taught in each unit. Discussion questions and a related writing activity follow each selection.

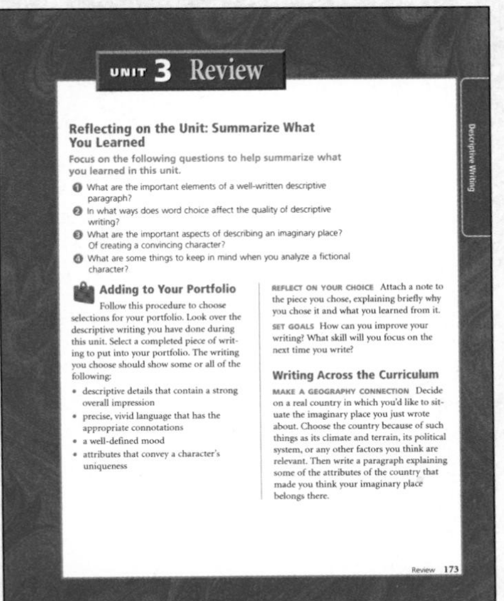

UNIT 3 Review

Reflecting on the Unit: Summarize What You Learned

Focus on the following questions to help summarize what you learned in this unit.

1. What are the important elements of a well-written descriptive paragraph?
2. In what ways does word choice affect the quality of descriptive writing?
3. What are the important aspects of describing an imaginary place? Of creating a convincing character?
4. What are some things to keep in mind when you analyze a fictional character?

Adding to Your Portfolio

Follow this procedure to choose selections for your portfolio. Look over the descriptive writing you have done during this unit. Select a completed piece of writing to put into your portfolio. The writing you choose should show some or all of the following:

- descriptive details that contain a strong overall impression
- precise, vivid language that has the appropriate connotations
- a well-defined mood
- attributes that convey a character's uniqueness

REFLECT ON YOUR CHOICE Attach a note to the piece you chose, explaining briefly why you chose it and what you learned from it.

SET GOALS How can you improve your writing? What skill will you focus on the next time you write?

Writing Across the Curriculum

MAKE A GEOGRAPHY CONNECTION Decide on a real country in which you'd like to situate the imaginary place you just wrote about. Choose the country because of such things as its climate and terrain, its political system, or any other factors you think are relevant. Then write a paragraph explaining some of the attributes of the country that made you think your imaginary place belongs there.

Review 173

Authentic Assessment of Writing Skills

Unit Review questions, activities, and portfolio selections give you the opportunity to assess students' knowledge and skills.

Systematic Grammar Instruction with Extensive Practice

Based on a define-explain-model approach and strongly supported with extensive practice-and-apply exercises, **Part 2: Grammar, Usage, and Mechanics** provides the solid foundation your students need.

Short Targeted Lessons

Each Part 2 lesson focuses on a single grammar, usage, or mechanics concept. Each lesson presents **clear, direct teaching** and provides exercises for practice.

Exercises give students the chance to practice what they've learned.

A **definition** or **rule** clearly states the concept being taught.

Examples, often in graphic form, illustrate the concept.

Elaboration further explains and refines the concept.

17.2 Pronouns with and as Appositives

- Use the nominative case for a pronoun that is in apposition to a subject or a predicate nominative.

The judges, **she** and **Mrs. Chiu,** will have a difficult task. [*Judges* is the subject of the sentence.]

The winners were the pianists, **Linda** and **he.** [*Pianists* is the predicate nominative.]

- Use the objective case for a pronoun that is in apposition to a direct object, an indirect object, or an object of a preposition.

The audience cheered their favorite performers, **Darnell** and **her.** [*Performers* is the direct object.]

The director gave the stage crew, **Lee** and **him,** special thanks. [*Crew* is the indirect object.]

The judges explained the rules to both groups, **them** and **us.** [*Groups* is the object of the preposition *to.*]

- When a pronoun is followed by an appositive, choose the case of the pronoun that would be correct if the appositive were omitted.

We violinists hope one day to play in a concert hall. [*We* is the correct form because *we* is the subject of the sentence.]

The music teacher handed the scores to **us musicians.** [*Us* is the correct form because *us* is the object of the preposition *to.*]

Exercise 3 Using Pronouns with and as Appositives

For each sentence in the following paragraph, write on your paper the correct pronoun from the pair in parentheses.

Making a Movie

[1]The writers, Lawrence Kasdan and (she/her), were willing to revise the script. [2]The director worked well with the leads, Harrison Ford and (she/her). [3]The two cinematographers, Gordon Willis and (him/he), were both efficient and creative. [4](We/Us) young actors were lucky to work with such a fine team. [5]There is no question that working on this film had a positive effect on (we/us) beginners.

Using Pronouns Correctly

17.2 Pronouns with and as Appositives 635

Exercise 4 Using Pronouns with and as Appositives

For each of the following sentences, write on your paper the correct personal pronoun from the pair in parentheses.

The Game of Golf

1. The first lecturers, Anna and (I/me), explained to the class that golf was popularized by King James IV of Scotland and his granddaughter, Mary.
2. The two of them, James IV and (she/her), helped to introduce the game to sports enthusiasts in England and France.
3. We then mentioned that (we/us) Americans often do well in professional tournaments.
4. Michelle Wie and (he/him), two very successful contemporary golfers, earn top salaries.
5. Tiger Woods and (she/her), two golf masters, were two recent winners of major golf tournaments.
6. Then the class asked golf experts Anna and (I, me) some questions about the game.
7. Two students, (he/him) and Larry, wanted to know how many Americans actually play the game.
8. (She, Her) and I, the experts, mentioned that the game is enjoyable for all age groups, both older people and (we/us) youngsters, because it emphasizes skill rather than strength.
9. We gave two students, Gayle and (he/him), a putter and a ball.
10. Both of us, Anna and (I, me), felt that our lecture to the class had gone very well.

Exercise 5 Using Pronouns in Sentences

On your paper, complete the following sentences by replacing each blank with a personal pronoun that makes sense.

Impressionism

1. We art lovers, Claire and ______, have learned to appreciate the contribution made by Auguste Renoir to the art style known as Impressionism.
2. Two leaders in Impressionism were Monet and ______ .
3. The first Impressionist exhibit showcased Degas, Cézanne, and ______ .
4. Viewers were highly critical of the work by Renoir and ______ .
5. Critics were not pleased by ______ using mauve shadows.
6. The painters were derisively called Impressionists because of *Impression, Sunrise,* by Monet, which later became one of ______ more famous paintings.
7. The artists, Renoir and ______, were undaunted by the negative criticism.
8. Although Edouard Manet was never part of the group, he was a good friend of ______.
9. Renoir and ______ sometimes painted together.
10. The Impressionists have left a valuable legacy for ______ art lovers.

Using Pronouns Correctly

636 Unit 17 Using Pronouns Correctly

Comprehensive Grammar Assessment

Grammar Reviews at the end of each unit allow you to assess students' learning in a comprehensive and meaningful way.

A **Literature Model** shows students how a published author handles the concepts covered in the unit.

Exercises assess students' understanding of the concepts taught in the unit.

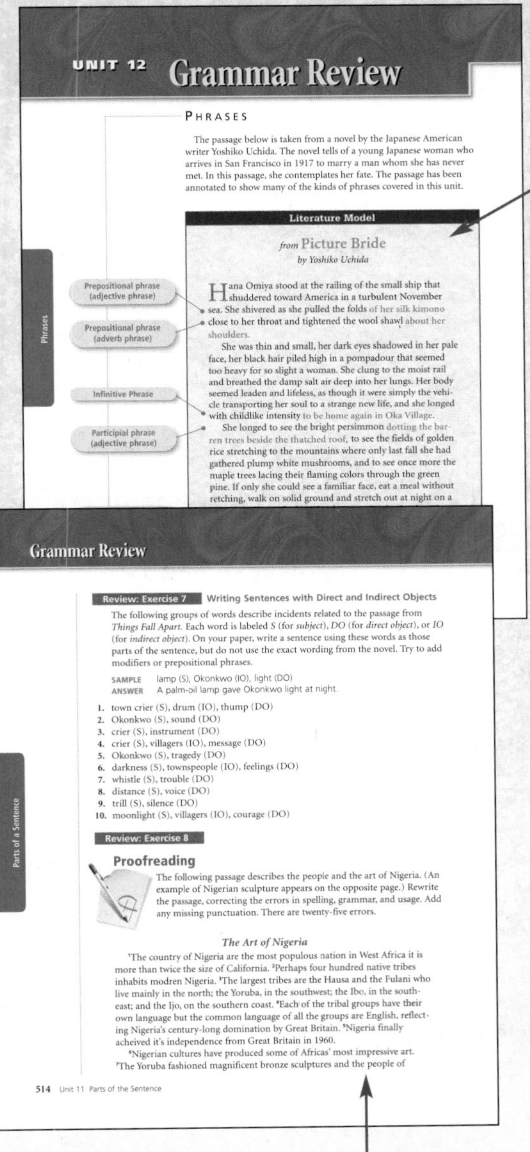

UNIT 12 **Grammar Review**

PHRASES

The passage below is taken from a novel by the Japanese American writer Yoshiko Uchida. The novel tells of a young Japanese woman who arrives in San Francisco in 1917 to marry a man whom she has never met. In this passage, she contemplates her fate. The passage has been annotated to show many of the kinds of phrases covered in this unit.

Literature Model

from Picture Bride
by Yoshiko Uchida

Hana Omiya stood at the railing of the small ship that shuddered toward America in a turbulent November sea. She shivered as she pulled the folds of her silk kimono close to her throat and tightened the wool shawl about her shoulders.

She was thin and small, her dark eyes shadowed in her pale face, her black hair piled high in a pompadour that seemed too heavy for so slight a woman. She clung to the moist rail and breathed the damp salt air deep into her lungs. Her body seemed leaden and lifeless, as though it were simply the vehicle transporting her soul to a strange new life, and she longed with childlike intensity to be home again in Oka Village.

She longed to see the bright persimmon dotting the barren trees beside the thatched roof, to see the fields of golden rice stretching to the mountains where only last fall she had gathered plump white mushrooms, and to see once more the maple trees lacing their flaming colors through the green pine. If only she could see a familiar face, eat a meal without retching, walk on solid ground and stretch out at night on a

Grammar Review

Review: Exercise 7 Writing Sentences with Direct and Indirect Objects

The following groups of words describe incidents related to the passage from *Things Fall Apart.* Each word is labeled *S* (for *subject*), *DO* (for *direct object*), or *IO* (for *indirect object*). On your paper, write a sentence using these words as those parts of the sentence, but do not use the exact wording from the novel. Try to add modifiers or prepositional phrases.

SAMPLE lamp (S), Okonkwo (IO), light (DO)
ANSWER A palm-oil lamp gave Okonkwo light at night.

1. town crier (S), drum (IO), thump (DO)
2. Okonkwo (S), sound (DO)
3. crier (S), instrument (DO)
4. crier (S), villagers (IO), message (DO)
5. Okonkwo (S), tragedy (DO)
6. darkness (S), townspeople (IO), feelings (DO)
7. whistle (S), trouble (DO)
8. distance (S), voice (DO)
9. trill (S), silence (DO)
10. moonlight (S), villagers (IO), courage (DO)

Review: Exercise 8

Proofreading

The following passage describes the people and the art of Nigeria. (An example of Nigerian sculpture appears on the opposite page.) Rewrite the passage, correcting the errors in spelling, grammar, and usage. Add any missing punctuation. There are twenty-five errors.

The Art of Nigeria

[1]The country of Nigeria are the most populous nation in West Africa it is more than twice the size of California. [2]Perhaps four hundred native tribes inhabits modren Nigeria. [3]The largest tribes are the Hausa and the Fulani who live mainly in the north; the Yoruba, in the southwest; the Ibo, in the southeast; and the Ijo, on the southern coast. [4]Each of the tribal groups have their own language but the common language of all the groups are English, reflecting Nigeria's century-long domination by Great Britain. [5]Nigeria finally acheived it's independence from Great Britain in 1960.

[6]Nigerian cultures have produced some of Africas' most impressive art. [7]The Yoruba fashioned magnificent bronze sculptures and the people of

514 Unit 11 Parts of the Sentence

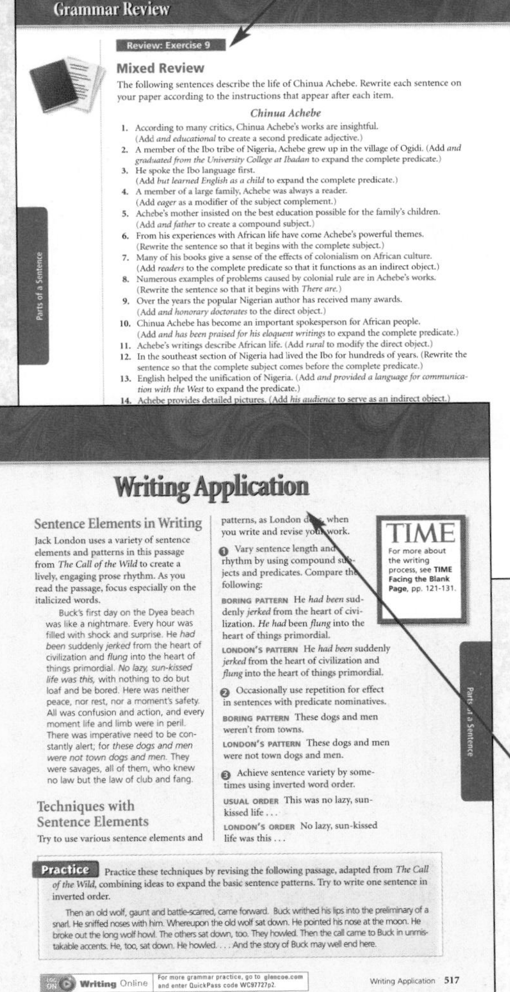

Grammar Review

Review: Exercise 9

Mixed Review

The following sentences describe the life of Chinua Achebe. Rewrite each sentence on your paper according to the instructions that appear after each item.

Chinua Achebe

1. According to many critics, Chinua Achebe's works are insightful. (Add *and educational* to create a second predicate adjective.)
2. A member of the Ibo tribe of Nigeria, Achebe grew up in the village of Ogidi. (Add *and graduated from the University College at Ibadan* to expand the complete predicate.)
3. He spoke the Ibo language first. (Add *but learned English as a child* to expand the complete predicate.)
4. A member of a large family, Achebe was always a reader. (Add *eager* as a modifier of the subject complement.)
5. Achebe's mother insisted on the best education possible for the family's children. (Add *and father* to create a compound subject.)
6. From his experiences with African life have come Achebe's powerful themes. (Rewrite the sentence so that it begins with the complete subject.)
7. Many of his books give a sense of the effects of colonialism on African culture. (Add *readers* to the complete predicate so that it functions as an indirect object.)
8. Numerous examples of problems caused by colonial rule are in Achebe's works. (Rewrite the sentence so that it begins with *There are.*)
9. Over the years the popular Nigerian author has received many awards. (Add *and honorary doctorates* to the direct object.)
10. Chinua Achebe has become an important spokesperson for African people. (Add *and has been praised for his eloquent writings* to expand the complete predicate.)
11. Achebe's writings describe African life. (Add *rural* to modify the direct object.)
12. In the southeast section of Nigeria had lived the Ibo for hundreds of years. (Rewrite the sentence so that the complete subject comes before the complete predicate.)
13. English helped the unification of Nigeria. (Add *and provided a language for communication with the West* to expand the predicate.)
14. Achebe provides detailed pictures. (Add *his audience* to serve as an indirect object.)

Writing Application

Sentence Elements in Writing

Jack London uses a variety of sentence elements and patterns in this passage from *The Call of the Wild* to create a lively, engaging prose rhythm. As you read the passage, focus especially on the italicized words.

Buck's first day on the Dyea beach was like a nightmare. Every hour was filled with shock and surprise. He *had been* suddenly *jerked* from the heart of civilization and *flung* into the heart of things primordial. *No lazy, sun-kissed life was this,* with nothing to do but loaf and be bored. Here was neither peace, nor rest, nor a moment's safety. All was confusion and action, and every moment life and limb were in peril. There was imperative need to be constantly alert; for *these dogs and men were not town dogs and men.* They were savages, all of them, who knew no law but the law of club and fang.

Techniques with Sentence Elements

Try to use various sentence elements and patterns, as London does, when you write and revise your work.

1. Vary sentence length and rhythm by using compound subjects and predicates. Compare the following:

BORING PATTERN He *had been* suddenly *jerked* from the heart of civilization. *He had* been *flung* into the heart of things primordial.

LONDON'S PATTERN He *had been* suddenly *jerked* from the heart of civilization and *flung* into the heart of things primordial.

2. Occasionally use repetition for effect in sentences with predicate nominatives.

BORING PATTERN These dogs and men weren't from towns.

LONDON'S PATTERN These dogs and men were not town dogs and men.

3. Achieve sentence variety by sometimes using inverted word order.

USUAL ORDER This was no lazy, sun-kissed life . . .

LONDON'S ORDER No lazy, sun-kissed life was this . . .

TIME For more about the writing process, see **TIME Facing the Blank Page**, pp. 121-131.

Practice Practice these techniques by revising the following passage, adapted from *The Call of the Wild,* combining ideas to expand the basic sentence patterns. Try to write one sentence in inverted order.

Then an old wolf, gaunt and battle-scarred, came forward. Buck writhed his lips into the preliminary of a snarl. He sniffed noses with him. Whereupon the old wolf sat down. He pointed his nose at the moon. He broke out the long wolf howl. The others sat down, too. They howled. Then the call came to Buck in unmistakable accents. He, too, sat down. He howled. . . . And the story of Buck may well end here.

LOG ON Writing Online For more grammar practice, go to glencoe.com and enter QuickPass code WC97727p2.

Writing Application 517

A **proofreading exercise** gives students the editing practice they need to become good writers.

The **Writing Application** helps students connect grammar, usage, and mechanics concepts with good writing and good literature.

A "Tool Kit" of Real-World Skills

Part 3: Resources and Skills provides instruction, examples, and practice in research, vocabulary, spelling, study skills, test-taking, listening and speaking, viewing and representing, and using electronic resources.

Clear Instruction

Easy-to-read text and graphics connect students' interests with what they need to know.

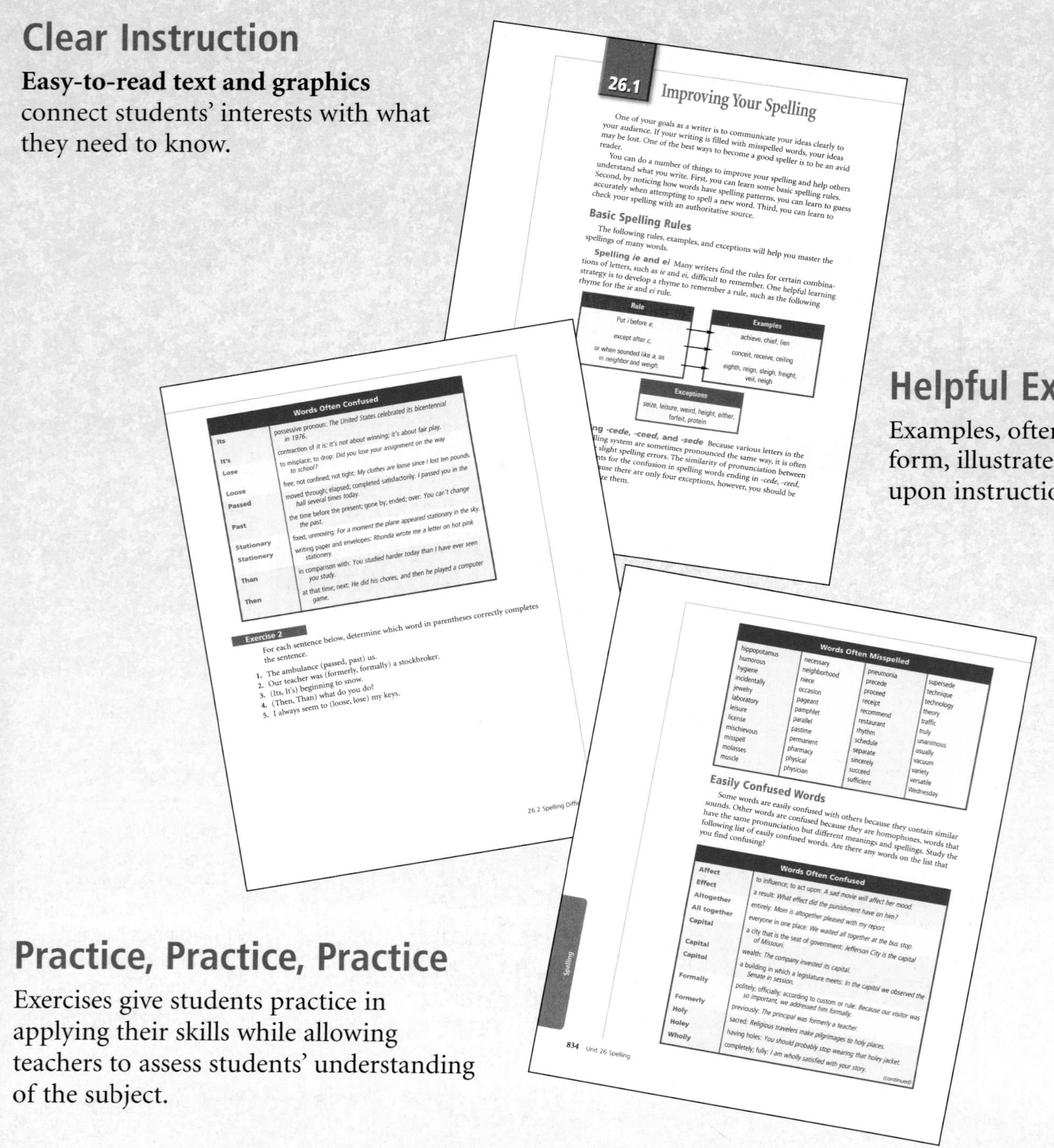

26.1 Improving Your Spelling

One of your goals as a writer is to communicate your ideas clearly to your audience. If your writing is filled with misspelled words, your ideas may be lost. One of the best ways to become a good speller is to be an avid reader.

You can do a number of things to improve your spelling and help others understand what you write. First, you can learn some basic spelling rules. Second, by noticing how words have spelling patterns, you can learn to guess accurately when attempting to spell a new word. Third, you can learn to check your spelling with an authoritative source.

Basic Spelling Rules

The following rules, examples, and exceptions will help you master the spellings of many words.

Spelling *ie* and *ei* Many writers find the rules for certain combinations of letters, such as *ie* and *ei*, difficult to remember. One helpful learning strategy is to develop a rhyme to remember a rule, such as the following rhyme for the *ie* and *ei* rule.

Rule	Examples
Put *i* before *e*,	achieve, chief, lien
except after *c*,	conceit, receive, ceiling
or when sounded like *a*, as in *neighbor* and *weigh*.	eighth, reign, sleigh, freight, veil, neigh

Exceptions
seize, leisure, weird, height, either, forfeit, protein

ng -cede, -ceed, and -sede Because various letters in the
lling system are sometimes pronounced the same way, it is often
slight spelling errors. The similarity of pronunciation between
nts for the confusion in spelling words ending in *-cede, -ceed,*
ause there are only four exceptions, however, you should be
ze them.

Words Often Confused	
Its	possessive pronoun: *The United States celebrated its bicentennial in 1976.*
It's	contraction of *it is*: *It's not about winning; it's about fair play.*
Lose	to misplace; to drop: *Did you lose your assignment on the way to school?*
Loose	free; not confined; not tight: *My clothes are loose since I lost ten pounds.*
Passed	moved through; elapsed; completed satisfactorily: *I passed you in the hall several times today.*
Past	the time before the present; gone by; ended; over: *You can't change the past.*
Stationary	fixed; unmoving: *For a moment the plane appeared stationary in the sky.*
Stationery	writing paper and envelopes: *Rhonda wrote me a letter on hot pink stationery.*
Than	in comparison with: *You studied harder today than I have ever seen you study.*
Then	at that time; next: *He did his chores, and then he played a computer game.*

Exercise 2

For each sentence below, determine which word in parentheses correctly completes the sentence.

1. The ambulance (passed, past) us.
2. Our teacher was (formerly, formally) a stockbroker.
3. (Its, It's) beginning to snow.
4. (Then, Than) what do you do?
5. I always seem to (loose, lose) my keys.

26.2 Spelling Diffi

Words Often Misspelled			
hippopotamus	necessary	pneumonia	supersede
humorous	neighborhood	precede	technique
hygiene	niece	proceed	technology
incidentally	occasion	receipt	theory
jewelry	pageant	recommend	traffic
laboratory	pamphlet	restaurant	truly
leisure	parallel	rhythm	unanimous
license	pastime	schedule	usually
mischievous	permanent	separate	vacuum
misspell	pharmacy	sincerely	variety
molasses	physical	succeed	versatile
muscle	physician	sufficient	Wednesday

Easily Confused Words

Some words are easily confused with others because they contain similar sounds. Other words are confused because they are homophones, words that have the same pronunciation but different meanings and spellings. Study the following list of easily confused words. Are there any words on the list that you find confusing?

Words Often Confused	
Affect	to influence; to act upon: *A sad movie will affect her mood.*
Effect	a result: *What effect did the punishment have on him?*
Altogether	entirely: *Mom is altogether pleased with my report.*
All together	everyone in one place: *We waited all together at the bus stop.*
Capital	a city that is the seat of government: *Jefferson City is the capital of Missouri.*
Capital	wealth: *The company invested its capital.*
Capitol	a building in which a legislature meets: *In the capitol we observed the Senate in session.*
Formally	politely; officially; according to custom or rule: *Because our visitor was so important, we addressed him formally.*
Formerly	previously: *The principal was formerly a teacher.*
Holy	sacred: *Religious travelers make pilgrimages to holy places.*
Holey	having holes: *You should probably stop wearing that holey jacket.*
Wholly	completely; fully: *I am wholly satisfied with your story.*

(continued)

Spelling

834 Unit 26 Spelling

Helpful Examples

Examples, often in graphic form, illustrate and expand upon instruction.

Practice, Practice, Practice

Exercises give students practice in applying their skills while allowing teachers to assess students' understanding of the subject.

Taking Standardized Tests

While the entire *Writer's Choice* program has been designed to help students gain the skills and knowledge they need to achieve on standardized tests, the **Taking Tests** unit in particular helps students prepare for these tests.

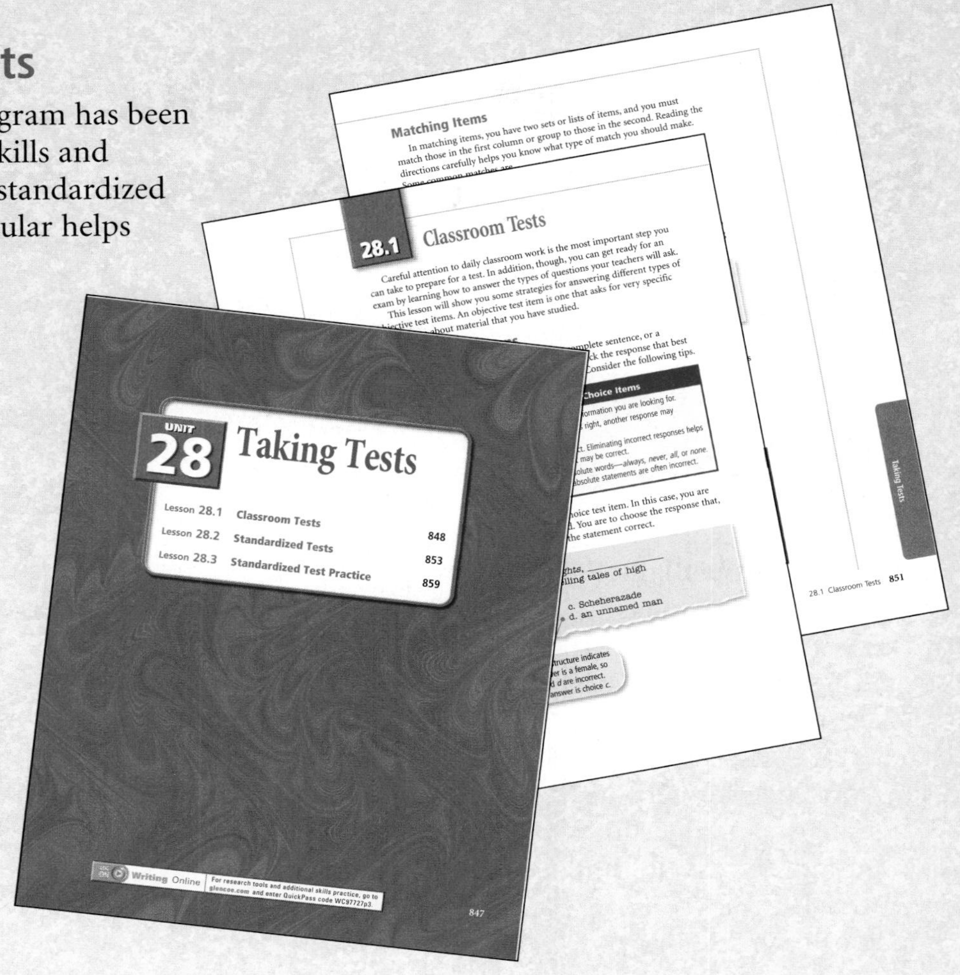

UNIT 28 Taking Tests

Writing Online For research tools and additional skills practice, go to glencoe.com and enter QuickPass code WC97727p3.

847

Effective Test Preparation

The unit begins with **proven test-taking strategies** and an explanation of the types of items and formats most commonly used in standardized tests.

Standardized Test Practice

Read each passage. Some sections are underlined. The underlined sections may be one of the following:

- Incomplete sentences
- Run-on sentences
- Correctly written sentences that should be combined
- Correctly written sentences that do not need to be rewritten

Choose the best way to write each underlined section and mark the letter for your answer. If the underlined section needs no change, mark the choice "Correct as is" on your paper.

A visit to New York City may feel overwhelming. To someone who has never been there before. (1) The buildings appear to go on for miles. In fact, Manhattan is only a little more than 22 square miles in area.

Running beneath New York's surface, the subway system is a vast transportation network. This network contains 772 miles of active track. (2) It is the largest underground transportation system in the world. The first subway was constructed in 1870 by Alfred Ely Beach, who was also the inventor of the typewriter. (3) Of course, there are many different ways to get around town in New York. The subway, however, is often the fastest option, it gets you where you need to go without the worry of traffic. (4)

1 A A visit to New York City overwhelming to someone who has never been there before.
B A visit to New York City may feel overwhelming to someone. Who has never been there before.
C A visit to New York City may feel overwhelming to someone who has never been there before.
D Correct as is

2 F Running beneath New York's surface, the subway system is a vast transportation network that contains 772 miles of active track.
G Running beneath New York's surface, the subway system and a vast transportation network contain 772 miles of active track.
H Running beneath New York's surface, the subway system is a vast transportation network, and this transportation network contains 772 miles of active track.
J Running beneath New York's surface, the subway system is a vast transportation network, and the subway system also containing 772 miles of active track.

3 A The first subway was constructed in 1870 by Alfred Ely Beach, he was also the inventor of the typewriter.
B The first subway was constructed in 1870 by Alfred Ely Beach. Who was also the inventor of the typewriter.
C The first subway constructing in 1870 by Alfred Ely Beach, who also the inventor of the typewriter.
D Correct as is

4 F The subway, however, is often the fastest option. Getting you where you need to go without the worry of traffic.
G The subway, however, is often the fastest option, getting you where you need to go without the worry of traffic.
H The subway, however, is often the fastest option getting you where you need to go. Without the worry of traffic.
J Correct as is

866 Unit 28 Taking Tests

Standardized Test Practice

On October 2, 1800, Nat Turner was born as an enslaved person, it was in Virginia. (1) Thirty-one years later, he would be known as one of the bravest enslaved people in history when he led the Southampton Slave Revolt.

Nat Turner had grown increasingly angry with the way that his people were treated in the South. It was an early morning in August of 1831. Nat Turner decided to rebel against slavery in his community. (2) He recruited seventy fellow enslaved men and, together, they marched through the streets of Southampton. The revolt lasted two days. Before the Virginia Militia finally put an end to it. (3) Nat Turner escaped, but was captured two months later. Although Nat Turner was not able to put an end to slavery with his revolt, he did make an important contribution toward freedom for enslaved peoples. (4)

1 A On October 2, 1800, Nat Turner was born an enslaved person. In Virginia.
B On October 2, 1800, Nat Turner was born an enslaved person in Virginia.
C On October 2, 1800. Nat Turner was born an enslaved person in Virginia.
D Correct as is

2 F It was an early morning in August of 1831 if Nat Turner decided to rebel against slavery in his community.
G Nat Turner decided to in 1831 to rebel on an early August morning against slavery in his community.
H It was an early morning in August of 1831, when Nat Turner decided to rebel against slavery in his community.
J Early morning 1831 when Nat Turner in August decided to rebel against slavery in his community.

3 A The revolt lasted two days before the Virginia Militia finally put an end to it.
B The revolt lasted. Two days before the Virginia Militia finally put an end to it.
C The revolt lasted two days before. The Virginia Militia finally put an end to it.
D Correct as is

4 F Although Nat Turner. Was not able to put an end to slavery with his revolt, he did make an important contribution toward freedom for enslaved peoples.
G He did make an important contribution toward freedom for enslaved peoples, then Nat Turner was not able to put an end to slavery with his revolt.
H Although Nat Turner was not able to put an end to slavery with his revolt. He did make an important contribution toward freedom for enslaved peoples.
J Correct as is

28.3 Standardized Test Practice 867

Extensive Test Practice

Exercises that mimic the format and content of standardized writing tests provide students with practice in answering items on sentence structure, usage, and mechanics.

Special Features: Enrichment and Remediation

Writer's Choice has many outstanding features to support and extend students' learning. From real-world advice to real-time remediation, these features maximize students' potential.

Writing Advice from the Pros

TIME **Facing the Blank Page** shows how professional writers and editors at TIME magazine practice each stage of the writing process. Thoughtful discussion questions, relevant writing assignments, and questions prompting students to think about their own writing conclude each section.

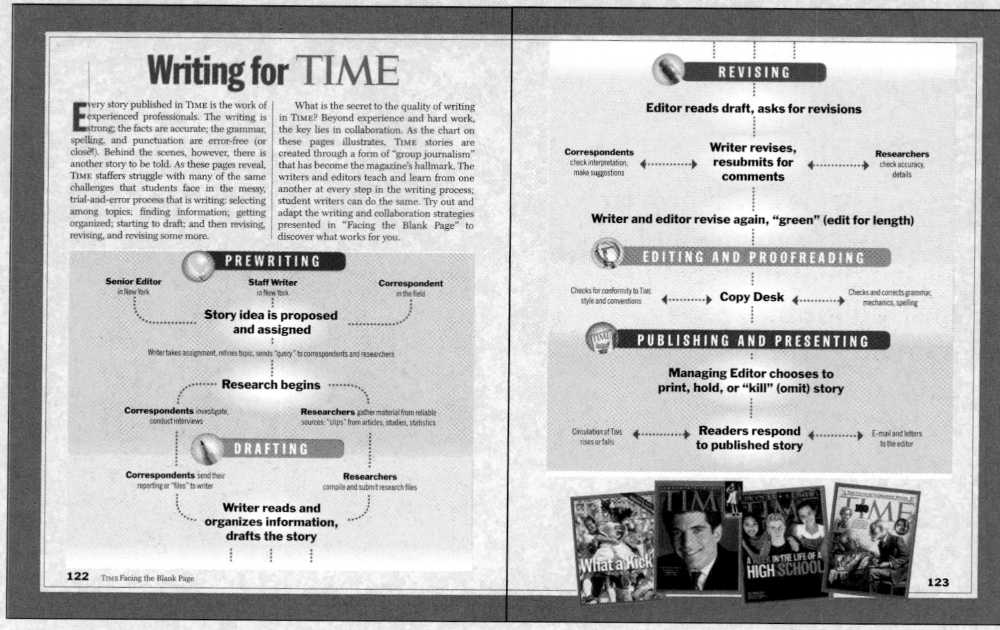

Writing for TIME

Every story published in TIME is the work of experienced professionals. The writing is strong; the facts are accurate; the grammar, spelling, and punctuation are error-free (or close!). Behind the scenes, however, there is another story to be told. As these pages reveal, TIME staffers struggle with many of the same challenges that students face in the messy, trial-and-error process that is writing: selecting among topics; finding information; getting organized; starting to draft; and then revising, revising, and revising some more.

What is the secret to the quality of writing in TIME? Beyond experience and hard work, the key lies in collaboration. As the chart on these pages illustrates, TIME stories are created through a form of "group journalism" that has become the magazine's hallmark. The writers and editors teach and learn from one another at every step in the writing process; student writers can do the same. Try out and adapt the writing and collaboration strategies presented in "Facing the Blank Page" to discover what works for you.

122 TIME Facing the Blank Page

123

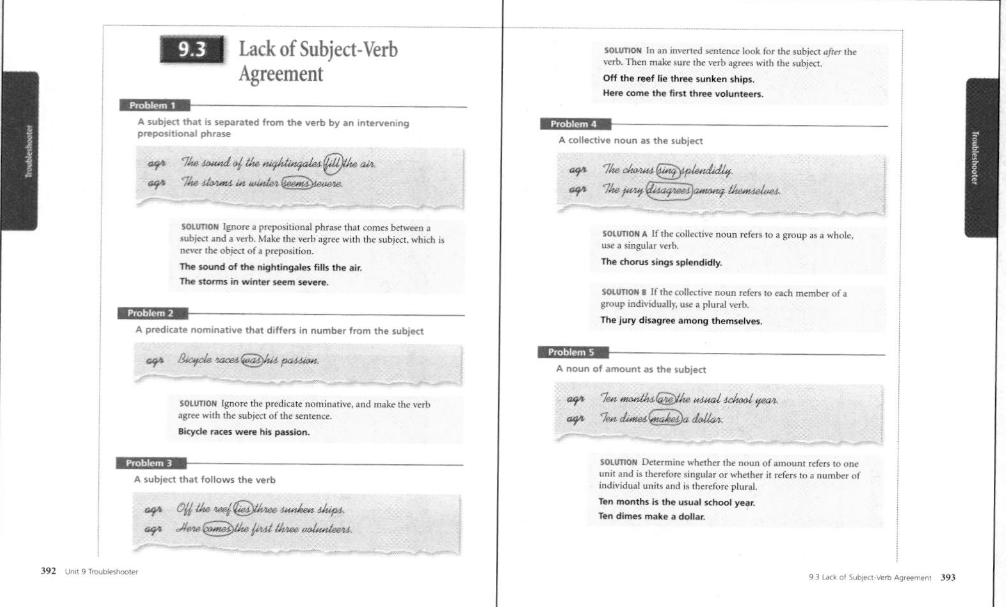

9.3 Lack of Subject-Verb Agreement

Problem 1

A subject that is separated from the verb by an intervening prepositional phrase

agr *The sound of the nightingales fill the air.*
agr *The storms in winter seems severe.*

SOLUTION Ignore a prepositional phrase that comes between a subject and a verb. Make the verb agree with the subject, which is never the object of a preposition.

The sound of the nightingales fills the air.
The storms in winter seem severe.

Problem 2

A predicate nominative that differs in number from the subject

agr *Bicycle races was his passion.*

SOLUTION Ignore the predicate nominative, and make the verb agree with the subject of the sentence.

Bicycle races were his passion.

Problem 3

A subject that follows the verb

agr *Off the reef lies three sunken ships.*
agr *Here comes the first three volunteers.*

392 Unit 9 Troubleshooter

SOLUTION In an inverted sentence look for the subject *after* the verb. Then make sure the verb agrees with the subject.

Off the reef lie three sunken ships.
Here come the first three volunteers.

Problem 4

A collective noun as the subject

agr *The chorus sing splendidly.*
agr *The jury disagrees among themselves.*

SOLUTION A If the collective noun refers to a group as a whole, use a singular verb.

The chorus sings splendidly.

SOLUTION B If the collective noun refers to each member of a group individually, use a plural verb.

The jury disagree among themselves.

Problem 5

A noun of amount as the subject

agr *Ten months are the usual school year.*
agr *Ten dimes makes a dollar.*

SOLUTION Determine whether the noun of amount refers to one unit and is therefore singular or whether it refers to a number of individual units and is therefore plural.

Ten months is the usual school year.
Ten dimes make a dollar.

9.3 Lack of Subject-Verb Agreement 393

Fixes for Common Errors

Teachers see certain errors again and again in student writing. **Troubleshooter** offers solutions to the most common of these errors, including fragments, run-ons, and lack of subject-verb agreement.

Writing for Work

Lessons on topics such as writing a business letter, conducting interviews, and creating multimedia presentations introduce students to the specialized skills of **Business and Technical Writing.**

Fun Facts About Language

Wordworks takes a humorous look at how we use and misuse our language. Unique one-page lessons give students an enjoyable way to study words and language development.

Easy-to-Reference Writing Guide

The **Writing and Research Handbook** provides tips for writing good sentences, paragraphs, and compositions. It offers instruction on using the 6+1 Trait® model and tools to help students conduct and document research.

A Teacher Edition with Point-of-Use Convenience

The **Teacher Wraparound Edition** accommodates a diversity of teachers and learners with an easy-to-use format. Each lesson plan has four parts: Focus, Teach, Assess, and Close. The margins offer additional information and strategies to help you meet the varied needs of your students.

Teach provides varied strategies for customizing the lesson and addressing the needs of basic, average, and advanced learners.

Focus sets clear objectives for learning writing, thinking, and listening and speaking skills. It also provides a daily language activity and motivating activity to jump-start your lesson.

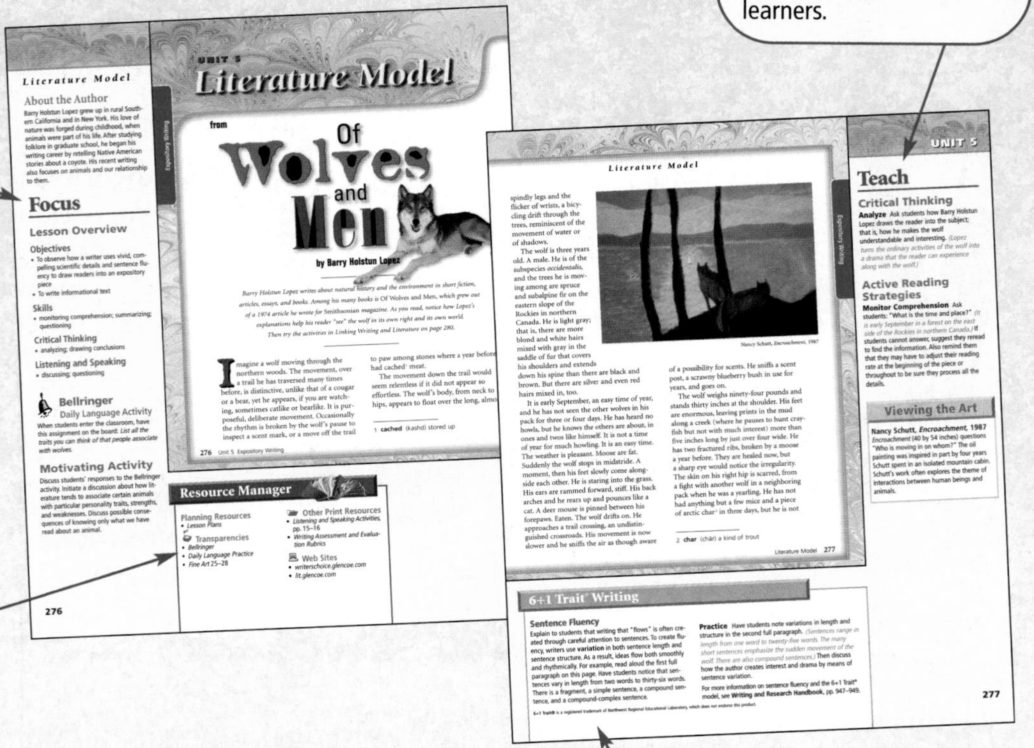

The **Resource Manager** lists ancillaries that extend and support the lesson.

6+1 Trait® Writing notes help students identify and practice the seven traits of effective writing: ideas, organization, voice, word choice, sentence fluency, conventions, and presentation.

A **Two-Minute Skill Drill** provides quick skill practice and challenges students to actively apply lesson concepts.

Strategies and background information support critical thinking, cooperative learning, cultural diversity, cross-curricular connections, fine art, technology, and civic literacy. They provide help to English language learners and less-proficient readers and offer enrichment and extension ideas for advanced students.

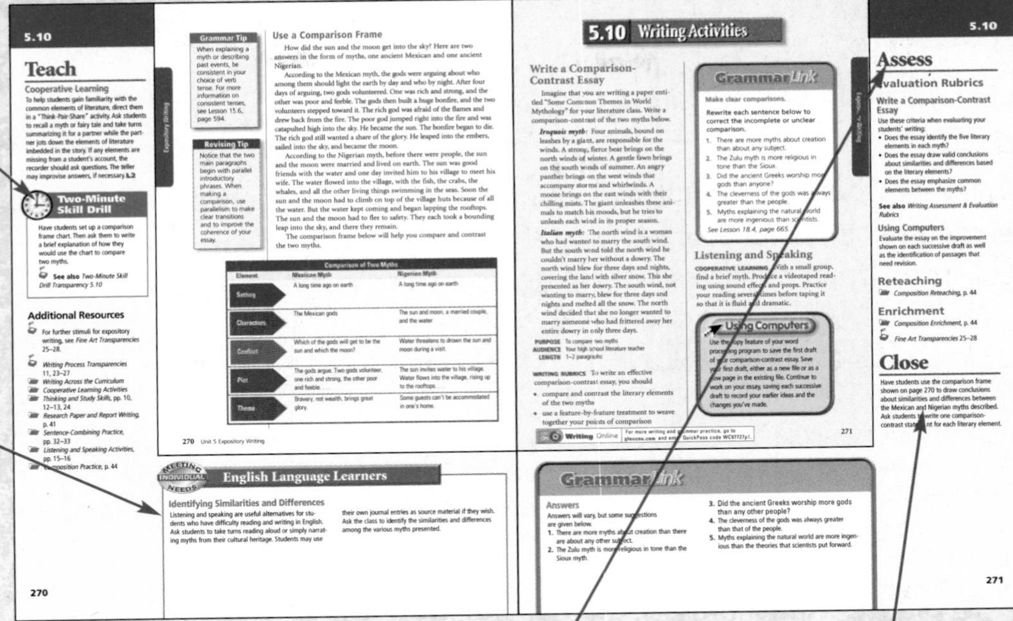

Assess presents Evaluation Rubrics to help you critique and assess student writing.

Close gives tips for reviewing, applying, and extending the lesson.

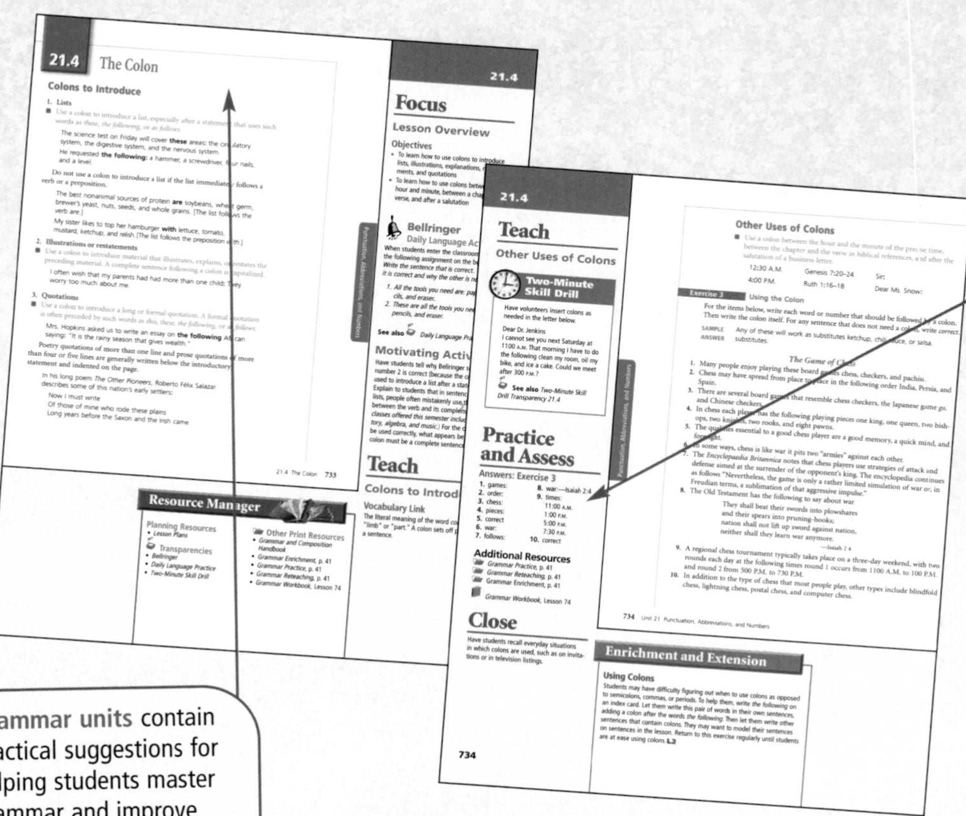

Answers to all grammar exercises are conveniently located in the margin, at the point of use.

Grammar units contain practical suggestions for helping students master grammar and improve their writing.

Program Resources That Expand Your Teaching Options

Writer's Choice and its ancillary resources deliver **comprehensive, research-based language arts instruction.** Whatever your teaching style or students' learning needs may be, there are program resources that are right for you.

Timesaving Teacher Resources

- TeacherWorks CD-ROM
- ExamView Assessment Suite CD-ROM (Testmaker)
- Presentation Plus! CD-ROM
- Lesson Plans (print version)
- Block Scheduling Guide
- Teaching Transparencies: Writing Process, Bellringer Activities, Daily Language, Fine Art, and Two-Minute Skill Drill
- Spanish Resources Binder
- Vocabulary Power Puzzlemaker software glencoe.com

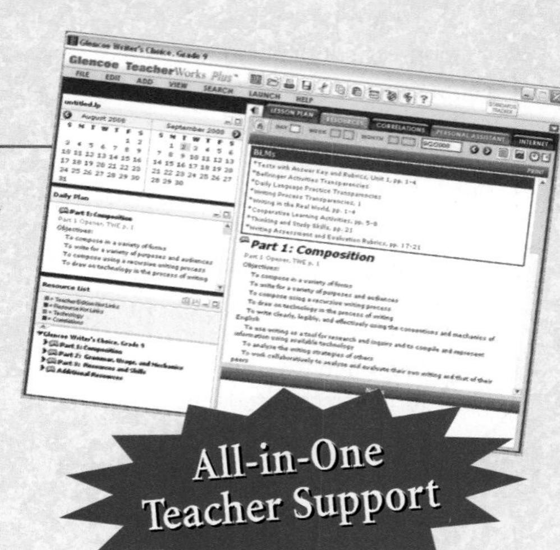

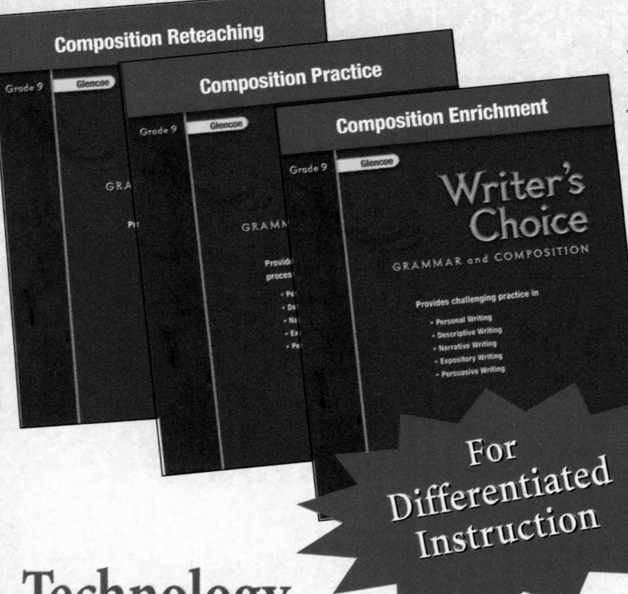

Writing

- Composition Reteaching, Composition Practice, and Composition Enrichment
- Research Paper and Report Writing
- Style and Documentation Sourcebook for Writers
- Business and Technical Writing Activities
- Sentence-Combining Practice
- Writing Across the Curriculum
- Writing in the Real World
- Revising with Style blackline masters

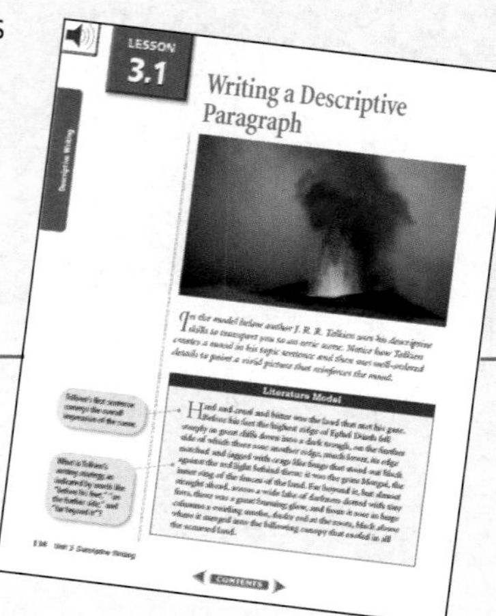

Technology

- StudentWorks CD-ROM
- Revising with Style CD-ROM
- Sentence Diagraming CD-ROM
- Interactive Grammar and Language Workbook CD-ROM
- Mindjogger Videoquizzes
- TechConnect Online
- Writer's Choice Online Student Edition: **glencoe.com**
- Writer's Choice Web site: **glencoe.com**
- Glencoe Literature Web site: **glencoe.com**

Assessment

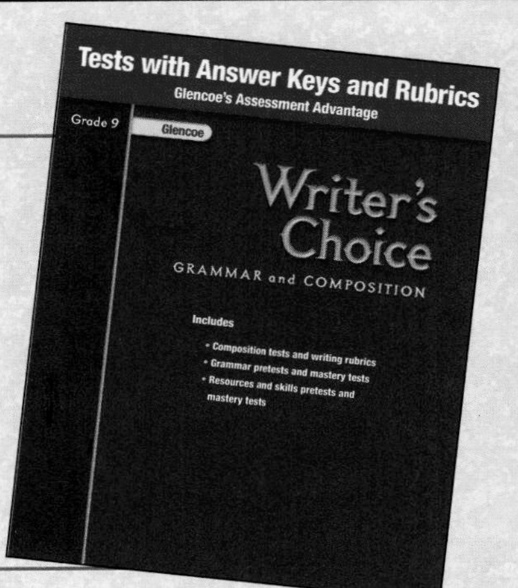

- Tests with Answer Keys and Rubrics
- Taking Standardized Tests
- Writing Assessment and Evaluation Rubrics
- *ExamView Assessment Suite* CD-ROM (Testmaker)
- Interactive Tutor: Self-Assessment CD-ROM

Integrated Language Arts

- inTIME magazine
- Humanities Across TIME
- Listening and Speaking Activities
- Viewing and Representing Activities
- Glencoe Literature Library
- Thinking and Study Skills
- Literature Library Teacher Resource
- Cooperative Learning Activities

Grammar

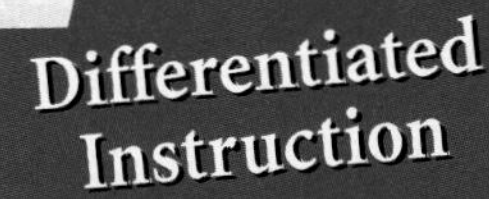

- Grammar Reteaching, Grammar Practice, and Grammar Enrichment
- Grammar and Language Workbook
- Grammar and Composition Handbook
- Grammar Practice Workbook
- Sentence Diagraming blackline masters

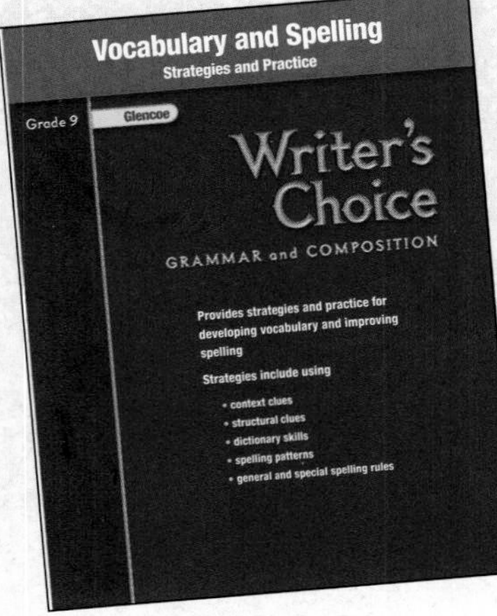

Vocabulary and Spelling

- Vocabulary and Spelling Strategies and Practice
- Spelling Power
- Vocabulary Power

Dinah Zike's FOLDABLES™ for *Writer's Choice*

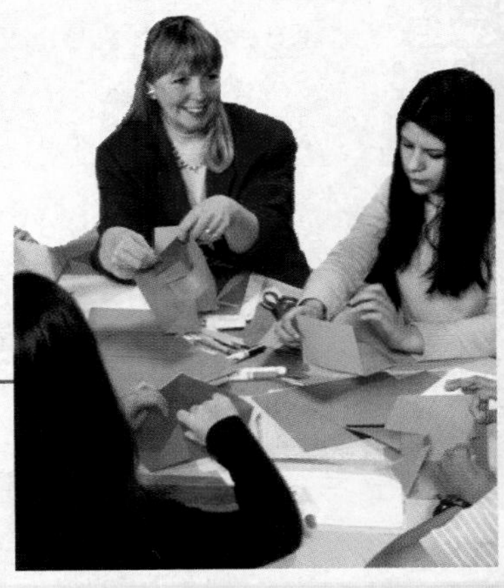

Only *Writer's Choice* gives you the power of FOLDABLES™! ***Dinah Zike's FOLDABLES™ for* Writer's Choice** shows students how to use three-dimensional interactive graphic organizers to **organize** information, **review** concepts, and **assess** their knowledge.

Integrating Writing, Grammar, and Other Language Skills

Time-saver

The **Weekly Planner** saves you time by suggesting one way to **organize** the lessons in *Writer's Choice* into a yearlong course of instruction. Research suggests that students learn best when the language arts are **integrated.** The Weekly Planner is color coded to show you how to meaningfully integrate

Part 1 Composition

Part 2 Grammar, Usage, and Mechanics

Part 3 Resources and Skills

Differentiated Homework Options

The Weekly Planner lists several key grammar and composition resources you can use as homework for learners of different levels:

- **Reteaching** for basic learners
- **Practice** for average learners
- **Enrichment** for advanced learners

Key resources for improving language and thinking skills for learners of all levels appear under **Mixed Abilities.**

Assessment Opportunities

Tests with Answer Key and Rubrics (also available as *Exam View Assessment Suite/Testmaker* software) provides you with **Pretests** and **Mastery Tests** to gauge your students' progress in a unit. For selected composition units, the resource provides three tests:

- **Choice A** } writing tests you can use as
- **Choice B** } either pretests or mastery tests
- **Composition Objective Test** multiple-choice mastery test

Customized Lesson Plans

Keep in mind that this Weekly Planner is only a suggestion. *Writer's Choice* helps you adjust lesson plans to your instructional needs in several ways.

- The Teacher Wraparound Edition lists additional resources at point of use and in Resource Manager boxes.
- The ***TeacherWorks***™ **CD-ROM** helps you customize your own lesson plans in a calendar format.

	Lessons	Key Resources
WEEK 1 Personal Writing & Parts of Speech	**Part 1 Composition** **Unit 1 Personal Writing** Unit 1 Writing in the Real World, pp. 4–7 1.1 Writing to Discover, pp. 8–11 1.2 Keeping a Journal, pp. 12–15 1.3 Writing a Personal Essay, pp. 16–19 **Part 2 Grammar, Usage, and Mechanics** **Unit 10 Parts of Speech** 10.1 Nouns, pp. 439–445 10.2 Pronouns, pp. 446–451 10.3 Verbs, pp. 452–460	**Classroom Activities** **Nonfiction Reading and Writing** *inTIME,* pp. 1, 6–9, 27 **Differentiated Homework Options** **Reteaching** *Composition Reteaching,* pp. 1–3 *Grammar Reteaching,* pp. 1–4 **Practice** *Composition Practice,* pp. 1–3 *Grammar Practice Workbook,* pp. 1–4 **Enrichment** *Composition Enrichment,* pp. 1–3 *Grammar Enrichment,* pp. 1–4 **Mixed Abilities** *Grammar and Language Workbook,* Lessons 1–7, 52–57 *Vocabulary and Spelling Strategies and Practice,* p. 1 **Assessment** *Tests with Answer Key and Rubrics,* pp. 1–2, 35–36 *ExamView Assessment Suite* CD-ROM
WEEK 2 Personal Writing & Parts of Speech	**Part 1 Composition** 1.4 Writing Autobiography, pp. 20–23 1.5 Writing a Poem, pp. 24–27 1.6 Keeping a Reader-Response Journal, pp. 28–31 1.7 Writing About Biography, pp. 32–35 **Part 2 Grammar, Usage, and Mechanics** 10.4 Adjectives, pp. 461–466 10.5 Adverbs, pp. 467–472	**Classroom Activities** **Nonfiction Reading and Writing** *inTIME,* pp. 26, 42, 46 **Differentiated Homework Options** **Reteaching** *Composition Reteaching,* pp. 4–7 *Grammar Reteaching,* pp. 5–6 **Practice** *Composition Practice,* pp. 4–7 *Grammar Practice Workbook,* pp. 5–6 **Enrichment** *Composition Enrichment,* pp. 4–7 *Grammar Enrichment,* pp. 5–6 **Mixed Abilities** *Grammar and Language Workbook,* Lessons 8–9
WEEK 3 Personal Writing & Parts of Speech	**Part 1 Composition** Unit 1 Writing Process in Action, pp. 36–39 Unit 1 Literature Model, pp. 40–50 Unit 1 Review, p. 51 **Part 2 Grammar, Usage, and Mechanics** 10.6 Prepositions, pp. 473–474 10.7 Conjunctions, pp. 475–480 10.8 Interjections, p. 481 Unit 10 Grammar Review, pp. 482–493	**Classroom Activities** **Technology** *Revising with Style* CD-ROM **Differentiated Homework Options** **Reteaching** *Composition Reteaching,* p. 8 *Grammar Reteaching,* pp. 7–8 **Practice** *Composition Practice,* p. 8 *Grammar Practice Workbook,* pp. 7–8 **Enrichment** *Composition Enrichment,* p. 8 *Grammar Enrichment,* pp. 7–8 **Mixed Abilities** *Grammar and Language Workbook,* Lessons 10–11, 18; Unit 1 Review; Cumulative Review: Unit 1 *Vocabulary and Spelling Strategies and Practice,* p. 7 **Assessment** *Tests with Answer Key and Rubrics,* pp. 3–4, 37–38 *ExamView Assessment Suite* CD-ROM

	Lessons	Key Resources
WEEK 4 Study Skills	**Part 3 Resources and Skills** **Unit 27 Study Skills** 27.1 Taking Notes in Class, pp. 837–838 27.2 Studying Outside of Class, pp. 838–842 27.3 Learning from Graphics, pp. 843–846	**Differentiated Homework Options** **Mixed Abilities** *Thinking and Study Skills,* pp. 2–4, 8, 18, 30–32, 34–36, 39–40 **Assessment** *Tests with Answer Key and Rubrics,* pp. 103–106 *ExamView Assessment Suite* CD-ROM
WEEK 5 The Writing Process & Parts of the Sentence	**Part 1 Composition** **Unit 2 The Writing Process** Unit 2 Writing in the Real World, pp. 54–57 2.1 Overview of the Writing Process, pp. 58–61 2.2 Prewriting: Getting Started, pp. 62–67 2.3 Prewriting: Identifying Purpose and Audience, pp. 68–71 2.4 Prewriting: Gathering Information, pp. 72–75 **Part 2 Grammar, Usage, and Mechanics** **Unit 11 Parts of the Sentence** 11.1 Simple Subjects and Simple Predicates, p. 495 11.2 Complete Subjects and Complete Predicates, pp. 496–497 11.3 Compound Subjects and Compound Predicates, pp. 498–500	**Classroom Activities** **Nonfiction Reading and Writing** *inTIME,* p. 15 **Differentiated Homework Options** **Reteaching** *Composition Reteaching,* pp. 9–12 *Grammar Reteaching,* p. 9 **Practice** *Composition Practice,* pp. 9–12 *Grammar Practice Workbook,* p. 9 **Enrichment** *Composition Enrichment,* pp. 9–12 *Grammar Enrichment,* p. 9 **Mixed Abilities** *Grammar and Language Workbook,* Lessons 12–14 *Vocabulary and Spelling Strategies and Practice,* p. 2 **Assessment** *Tests with Answer Key and Rubrics,* pp. 5–6, 39–40 *ExamView Assessment Suite* CD-ROM
WEEK 6 The Writing Process & Parts of the Sentence	**Part 1 Composition** 2.5 Drafting: Turning Notes into Paragraphs, pp. 76–79 2.6 Drafting: Writing Unified Paragraphs, pp. 80–83 2.7 Drafting: Ordering the Details, pp. 84–87 2.8 Drafting: Writing Coherent Paragraphs, pp. 88–91 **Part 2 Grammar, Usage, and Mechanics** 11.4 Order of Subject and Predicate, pp. 501–503 11.5 Complements, pp. 504–509 Unit 11 Grammar Review, pp. 510–517	**Differentiated Homework Options** **Reteaching** *Composition Reteaching,* pp. 13–16 *Grammar Reteaching,* pp. 10–12 **Practice** *Composition Practice,* pp. 13–16 *Grammar Practice Workbook,* pp. 10–12 **Enrichment** Composition Enrichment, pp. 13–16 Grammar Enrichment, pp. 9–12 **Mixed Abilities** *Grammar and Language Workbook,* Lessons 15–17; Unit 2 Review; Cumulative Review: Units 1–2 **Assessment** *Tests with Answer Key and Rubrics,* pp. 41–42 *ExamView Assessment Suite* CD-ROM
WEEK 7 The Writing Process & Phrases	**Part 1 Composition** 2.9 Revising: Improving Paragraphs, pp. 92–95 2.10 Editing/Proofreading: Final Checking, pp. 96–99 2.11 Publishing/Presenting: Sharing Writing, pp. 100–103 2.12 Explaining Theme, pp. 104–107 **Part 2 Grammar, Usage, and Mechanics** **Unit 12 Phrases** 12.1 Prepositional Phrases, pp. 519–520 12.2 Appositives and Appositive Phrases, pp. 521–522 12.3 Verbals and Verbal Phrases, pp. 523–527	**Classroom Activities** **Nonfiction Reading and Writing** *inTIME,* pp. 3–5 **Differentiated Homework Options** **Reteaching** *Composition Reteaching,* pp. 17–20 *Grammar Reteaching,* pp. 13–17 **Practice** *Composition Practice,* pp. 17–20 *Grammar Practice Workbook,* pp. 13–17 **Enrichment** *Composition Enrichment,* pp. 17–20 *Grammar Enrichment,* pp. 13–17

	Lessons	Key Resources
WEEK 7 *continued*		**Mixed Abilities** *Grammar and Language Workbook,* Lessons 18–22 **Assessment** *Tests with Answer Key and Rubrics,* pp. 7–8, 45–46 *ExamView Assessment Suite* CD-ROM
WEEK 8 **The Writing Process & Phrases**	**Part 1 Composition** Unit 2 Writing Process in Action, pp. 108–111 Unit 2 Literature Model, pp. 112–119 Unit 2 Review, p. 120 **Part 2 Grammar, Usage, and Mechanics** Unit 12 Grammar Review, pp. 528–537	**Classroom Activities** **Technology** *Revising with Style* CD-ROM **Differentiated Homework Options** **Mixed Abilities** *Grammar and Language Workbook,* Unit 3 Review; Cumulative Review: Units 1–3 *Vocabulary and Spelling Strategies and Practice,* p. 8 **Assessment** *Tests with Answer Key and Rubrics,* pp. 7–8, 45–46 *ExamView Assessment Suite* CD-ROM
WEEK 9 **The English Language**	**Part 3 Resources and Skills** **Unit 22 The English Language** 22.1 English in Our Time, pp. 783–784 Wordworks: Eponyms, p. 785 22.2 Conquest and Conversion, pp. 786–787 Wordworks: Spoonerisms, p. 788 22.3 A Conqueror from France, pp. 789–790 Wordworks: Puns and Tom Swifties, p. 791 22.4 Commerce, Culture, and Settlement, pp. 792–793 Wordworks: Euphemisms, p. 794 22.5 New Technology and Ideas, pp. 795–796 Wordworks: Slang, p. 797	**Differentiated Homework Options** **Mixed Abilities** *Vocabulary and Spelling Strategies and Practice,* pp. 37, 79–82 **Assessment** *Tests with Answer Key and Rubrics,* pp. 83–86 *ExamView Assessment Suite* CD-ROM
WEEK 10 TIME **Facing the Blank Page, Descriptive Writing, & Clauses and Sentence Structure**	**Part 1 Composition** TIME **Facing the Blank Page,** pp. 121–131 **Unit 3 Descriptive Writing** Unit 3 Writing in the Real World, pp. 134–137 3.1 Writing a Descriptive Paragraph, pp. 138–143 **Part 2 Grammar, Usage, and Mechanics** **Unit 13 Clauses and Sentence Structure** 13.1 Main Clauses, p. 539 13.2 Subordinate Clauses, p. 540 13.3 Simple and Compound Sentences, pp. 541–542	**Differentiated Homework Options** **Reteaching** *Composition Reteaching,* p. 21 *Grammar Reteaching,* p. 18 **Practice** *Composition Practice,* p. 21 *Grammar Practice Workbook,* p. 18 **Enrichment** *Composition Enrichment,* p. 21 *Grammar Enrichment,* p. 18 **Mixed Abilities** *Grammar and Language Workbook,* Lessons 23–24 *Vocabulary and Spelling Strategies and Practice,* p. 3 **Assessment** *Tests with Answer Key and Rubrics,* pp. 9–10, 47–48 *ExamView Assessment Suite* CD-ROM

	Lessons	Key Resources
WEEK 11 **Descriptive Writing & Clauses and Sentence Structure**	**Part 1 Composition** 3.2 Using Descriptive Language, pp. 144–147 3.3 Describing an Imaginary Place, pp. 148–151 3.4 Describing an Imaginary Person, pp. 152–155 **Part 2 Grammar, Usage, and Mechanics** 13.4 Complex and Compound-Complex Sentences, pp. 543–544 13.5 Adjective Clauses, pp. 545–547 13.6 Adverb Clauses, pp. 548–549 13.7 Noun Clauses, pp. 550–551 13.8 Four Kinds of Sentences, p. 552 13.9 Sentence Fragments, pp. 553–554 13.10 Run-on Sentences, pp. 555–557 Unit 13 Grammar Review, pp. 558–569	**Differentiated Homework Options** **Reteaching** *Composition Reteaching,* pp. 22–24 *Grammar Reteaching,* pp. 19–24 **Practice** *Composition Practice,* pp. 22–24 *Grammar Practice Workbook,* pp. 19–24 **Enrichment** *Composition Enrichment,* pp. 22–24 *Grammar Enrichment,* pp. 18–24 **Mixed Abilities** *Grammar and Language Workbook,* Lessons 8, 25–32, 54; Unit 4 Review; Cumulative Review: Units 1–4 **Assessment** *Tests with Answer Key and Rubrics,* pp. 49–50 *ExamView Assessment Suite* CD-ROM
WEEK 12 **Descriptive Writing & Diagraming Sentences**	**Part 1 Composition** 3.5 Analyzing Character Descriptions, pp. 155–159 Unit 3 Writing Process in Action, pp. 160–163 Unit 3 Literature Model, pp. 164–172 Unit 3 Review, p. 173 **Part 2 Grammar, Usage, and Mechanics** **Unit 14 Diagraming Sentences** 14.1 Diagraming Simple Sentences, pp. 571–573 14.2 Diagraming Simple Sentences with Phrases, pp. 574–576 14.3 Diagraming Sentences with Clauses, pp. 577–579	**Classroom Activities** **Technology** *Revising with Style* CD-ROM *Sentence Diagraming* CD-ROM **Differentiated Homework Options** **Reteaching** *Composition Reteaching,* pp. 25–26 **Practice** *Composition Practice,* pp. 25–26 **Enrichment** *Composition Enrichment,* pp. 25–26 **Mixed Abilities** *Grammar and Language Workbook,* Lessons 33–35 Vocabulary and Spelling Strategies and Practice, p. 9 **Assessment** *Tests with Answer Key and Rubrics,* pp. 11–12, 51–54 *ExamView Assessment Suite* CD-ROM
WEEK 13 **Using Dictionaries, Vocabulary, & Spelling**	**Part 3 Resources and Skills** **Unit 24 Using Dictionaries** 24.1 General Dictionaries, pp. 812–816 24.2 Thesauruses, pp. 816–817 **Unit 25 Vocabulary** 25.1 Building Vocabulary, pp. 819–822 25.2 Recognizing Parts of a Word, pp. 823–826 **Unit 26 Spelling** 26.1 Improving Your Spelling, pp. 828–833 26.2 Spelling Difficult Words, pp. 833–835	**Classroom Activities** **Cooperative Learning** *Listening and Speaking Activities,* pp. 5–6 **Differentiated Homework Options** **Mixed Abilities** *Vocabulary and Spelling Strategies and Practice,* pp. 18–49 **Assessment** *Tests with Answer Key and Rubrics,* pp. 91–102 *ExamView Assessment Suite* CD-ROM

	Lessons	Key Resources
WEEK 14 **Narrative Writing & Verb Tenses and Voice**	**Part 1 Composition** **Unit 4 Narrative Writing** Unit 4 Writing in the Real World, pp. 176–179 4.1 Writing Simple Narratives, pp. 180–183 4.2 Developing Conflict in Narrative, pp. 184–187 4.3 Writing Dialogue, pp. 188–189 **Part 2 Grammar, Usage, and Mechanics** **Unit 15 Verb Tenses and Voice** 15.1 Principal Parts of Verbs, p. 581 15.2 Regular and Irregular Verbs, pp. 582–585 15.3 Tenses of Verbs, pp. 586–588	**Classroom Activities** **Nonfiction Reading and Writing** *inTIME,* p. 48 **Differentiated Homework Options** **Reteaching** *Composition Reteaching,* pp. 27–29 *Grammar Reteaching,* p. 25 **Practice** *Composition Practice,* pp. 27–29 *Grammar Practice Workbook,* p. 25 **Enrichment** *Composition Enrichment,* pp. 27–29 *Grammar Enrichment,* p. 25 **Mixed Abilities** *Grammar and Language Workbook,* Lessons 36–38 Vocabulary and Spelling Strategies and Practice, p. 4 **Assessment** *Tests with Answer Key and Rubrics,* pp. 13–14, 55–56 *ExamView Assessment Suite* CD-ROM
WEEK 15 **Narrative Writing & Verb Tenses and Voice**	**Part 1 Composition** 4.4 Using Anecdotes, pp. 192–195 4.5 Writing a Sports Narrative, pp. 196–199 4.6 Writing About Suspense, pp. 200–203 4.7 Analyzing Point of View in a Narrative, pp. 204–207 **Part 2 Grammar, Usage, and Mechanics** 15.4 Perfect Tenses, pp. 589–591 15.5 Progressive and Emphatic Forms, pp. 592–593	**Classroom Activities** **Nonfiction Reading and Writing** *inTIME,* pp. 11, 16–17 **Differentiated Homework Options** **Reteaching** *Composition Reteaching,* pp. 30–33 *Grammar Reteaching,* p. 26 **Practice** *Composition Practice,* pp. 30–33 *Grammar Practice Workbook,* p. 26 **Enrichment** *Composition Enrichment,* pp. 30–33 *Grammar Enrichment,* p. 28 **Mixed Abilities** *Grammar and Language Workbook,* Lessons 39, 41
 **WEEK 16** **Narrative Writing & Verb Tenses and Voice**	**Part 1 Composition** Unit 4 Writing Process in Action, pp. 208–211 Unit 4 Literature Model, pp. 212–220 Unit 4 Review, p. 221 **Part 2 Grammar, Usage, and Mechanics** 15.6 Compatibility of Tenses, pp. 594–595 15.7 Voice of Verbs, pp. 596–597 Unit 15 Grammar Review, pp. 598–607	**Classroom Activities** **Technology** *Revising with Style* CD-ROM **Differentiated Homework Options** **Reteaching** *Composition Reteaching,* p. 34 *Grammar Reteaching,* p. 27 **Practice** *Composition Practice,* p. 34 *Grammar Practice Workbook,* p. 27 **Enrichment** *Composition Enrichment,* p. 34 *Grammar Enrichment,* pp. 26–27 **Mixed Abilities** *Grammar and Language Workbook,* Lessons 42–43; Unit 6 Review; Cumulative Review: Units 1–6 *Vocabulary and Spelling Strategies and Practice,* p. 10 **Assessment** *Tests with Answer Key and Rubrics,* pp. 15–16, 57–58 *ExamView Assessment Suite* CD-ROM

	Lessons	Key Resources
WEEK 17 Library Resources & Electronic Resources	**Part 3 Resources and Skills** **Unit 23 Library Resources** 23.1 Library Arrangement, pp. 799–800 23.2 Locating Books and Other Resources, pp. 801–805 23.3 How to Search for Periodicals, pp. 806–808 23.4 Using Reference Sources, pp. 808–810 **Unit 31 Electronic Resources** 31.1 Word Processing and the Writing Process, pp. 906–908 31.2 Learning with Technology, pp. 909–911 31.3 Communicating Visually, pp. 912–914 31.4 Producing in Multimedia, pp. 915–917	**Differentiated Homework Options** **Mixed Abilities** *Thinking and Study Skills,* pp. 6–7, 11 *Vocabulary and Spelling Strategies and Practice,* pp. 18–22 **Assessment** *Tests with Answer Key and Rubrics,* pp. 87–90, 119–122 *ExamView Assessment Suite* CD-ROM
WEEK 18 Expository Writing & Subject-Verb Agreement	**Part 1 Composition** **Unit 5 Expository Writing** Unit 5 Writing in the Real World, pp. 224–227 5.1 Explaining and Informing, pp. 228–231 5.2 Going into Detail, pp. 232–235 5.3 Explaining How To . . . , pp. 236–239 5.4 Explaining Cause and Effect, pp. 240–243 5.5 Classifying a Subject, pp. 244–247 **Part 2 Grammar, Usage, and Mechanics** **Unit 16 Subject-Verb Agreement** 16.1 Intervening Prepositional Phrases, pp. 609–610 16.2 Agreement with Linking Verbs, p. 611 16.3 Agreement in Inverted Sentences, pp. 612–613 16.4 Agreement with Special Subjects, pp. 614–615	**Classroom Activities** **Nonfiction Reading and Writing** *inTIME,* pp. 30, 31, 34–35, 39–41 *Research Paper and Report Writing,* pp. 43–48 **Differentiated Homework Options** **Reteaching** *Composition Reteaching,* pp. 35–39 *Grammar Reteaching,* p. 28 **Practice** *Composition Practice,* pp. 35–39 *Grammar Practice Workbook,* pp. 28–29 **Enrichment** *Composition Enrichment,* pp. 35–39 *Grammar Enrichment,* pp. 28–29 **Mixed Abilities** *Grammar and Language Workbook,* Lessons 1, 45–48 Vocabulary and Spelling Strategies and Practice, p. 5 **Assessment** *Tests with Answer Key and Rubrics,* pp. 17–18, 59–60 *ExamView Assessment Suite* CD-ROM
WEEK 19 Expository Writing & Subject-Verb Agreement	**Part 1 Composition** 5.6 Comparing and Contrasting, pp. 248–251 5.7 Writing with Graphics, pp. 252–255 5.8 Writing a Feature Article, pp. 256–261 5.9 Answering an Essay Question, pp. 262–267 **Part 2 Grammar, Usage, and Mechanics** 16.5 Agreement with Compound Subjects, pp. 616–617 16.6 Intervening Expressions, p. 618 16.7 Indefinite Pronouns as Subjects, pp. 619–621	**Classroom Activities** **Nonfiction Reading and Writing** *inTIME,* pp. 12–14, 24–25, 32–33, 44–45 **Differentiated Homework Options** **Reteaching** *Composition Reteaching,* pp. 40–43 *Grammar Reteaching,* p. 29 **Practice** *Composition Practice,* pp. 40–43 *Grammar Practice Workbook,* p. 29 **Enrichment** *Composition Enrichment,* pp. 40–43 *Grammar Enrichment,* p. 29 **Mixed Abilities** *Grammar and Language Workbook,* Lessons 49–51

	Lessons	Key Resources
WEEK 20 **Expository Writing & Subject-Verb Agreement**	**Part 1 Composition** 5.10 Comparing and Contrasting Two Myths, pp. 268–271 Unit 5 Writing Process in Action, pp. 272–275 Unit 5 Literature Model, pp. 276–280 Unit 5 Review, p. 281 **Part 2 Grammar, Usage, and Mechanics** Unit 16 Grammar Review, pp. 622–631	**Classroom Activities** **Technology** *Revising with Style* CD-ROM **Differentiated Homework Options** **Reteaching** *Composition Reteaching,* pp. 44–45 **Practice** *Composition Practice,* pp. 44–45 **Enrichment** *Composition Enrichment,* pp. 44–45 **Mixed Abilities** *Grammar and Language Workbook,* Unit 7 Review; Cumulative Review: Units 1–7 *Vocabulary and Spelling Strategies and Practice,* p. 11 **Assessment** *Tests with Answer Key and Rubrics,* pp. 19–20, 61–62 *ExamView Assessment Suite* CD-ROM
WEEK 21 **Listening and Speaking**	**Part 3 Resources and Skills** **Unit 29 Listening and Speaking** 29.1 Listening Effectively, pp. 885–887 29.2 Speaking Effectively, pp. 888–891 29.3 Participating in Groups, pp. 891–892 29.4 Conducting Interviews, p. 892	**Classroom Activities** **Cooperative Learning** *Listening and Speaking Activities,* pp. 1–3, 10–11, 14–17 **Differentiated Homework Options** **Mixed Abilities** *Thinking and Study Skills,* p. 34 **Assessment** *Tests with Answer Key and Rubrics,* pp. 111–114 *ExamView Assessment Suite* CD-ROM
WEEK 22 **Persuasive Writing & Using Pronouns Correctly**	**Part 1 Composition** **Unit 6 Persuasive Writing** Unit 6 Writing in the Real World, pp. 284–287 6.1 Writing Persuasively, pp. 288–291 6.2 Using Evidence Effectively, pp. 292–295 **Part 2 Grammar, Usage, and Mechanics** **Unit 17 Using Pronouns Correctly** 17.1 Case of Personal Pronouns, pp. 633–634 17.2 Pronouns with and as Appositives, pp. 635–636 17.3 Pronouns After *Than* and *As,* p. 637 17.4 *Who* and *Whom* in Questions and Subordinate Clauses, pp. 638–639	**Classroom Activities** **Nonfiction Reading and Writing** *inTIME,* pp. 10, 22, 28–29, 43, 47, 49 **Differentiated Homework Options** **Reteaching** *Composition Reteaching,* pp. 46–47 *Grammar Reteaching,* pp. 30–32 **Practice** *Composition Practice,* pp. 46–47 *Grammar Practice Workbook,* pp. 30–32 **Enrichment** *Composition Enrichment,* pp. 46–47 *Grammar Enrichment,* pp. 30–32 **Mixed Abilities** *Grammar and Language Workbook,* Lessons 52–54 *Vocabulary and Spelling Strategies and Practice,* p. 6 **Assessment** *Tests with Answer Key and Rubrics,* pp. 21–22, 63–64 *ExamView Assessment Suite* CD-ROM

	Lessons	Key Resources
WEEK 23 **Persuasive Writing & Using Pronouns Correctly**	**Part 1 Composition** 6.3 Checking Reasoning, pp. 296–299 6.4 Using Language to Advantage, pp. 300–303 6.5 Writing an Editorial, pp. 304–307 6.6 Writing a Movie Review, pp. 308–311 **Part 2 Grammar, Usage, and Mechanics** 17.5 Pronoun-Antecedent Agreement, pp. 640–644	**Classroom Activities** **Nonfiction Reading and Writing** *inTIME*, pp. 18–21, 23, 36–38 **Differentiated Homework Options** **Reteaching** *Composition Reteaching*, pp. 48–51 *Grammar Reteaching*, p. 33 **Practice** *Composition Practice*, pp. 48–51 *Grammar Practice Workbook*, p. 33 **Enrichment** *Composition Enrichment*, pp. 48–51 *Grammar Enrichment*, p. 33 **Mixed Abilities** *Grammar and Language Workbook*, Lesson 55
WEEK 24 **Persuasive Writing & Using Pronouns Correctly**	**Part 1 Composition** Unit 6 Writing Process in Action, pp. 312–315 Unit 6 Literature Model, pp. 316–320 Unit 6 Review, p. 321 **Part 2 Grammar, Usage, and Mechanics** 17.6 Clear Pronoun Reference, pp. 645–647 Unit 17 Grammar Review, pp. 648–657	**Classroom Activities** **Technology** *Revising with Style* CD-ROM **Differentiated Homework Options** **Reteaching** *Composition Reteaching*, p. 52 *Grammar Reteaching*, p. 34 **Practice** *Composition Practice*, p. 52 *Grammar Practice Workbook*, p. 34 **Enrichment** *Composition Enrichment*, p. 52 *Grammar Enrichment*, p. 34 **Mixed Abilities** *Grammar and Language Workbook*, Lessons 56–58; Unit 8 Review; Cumulative Review: Units 1–8 *Vocabulary and Spelling Strategies and Practice*, p. 12 **Assessment** *Tests with Answer Key and Rubrics*, pp. 23–24, 65–66 *ExamView Assessment Suite* CD-ROM
WEEK 25 **Viewing and Representing**	**Part 3 Resources and Skills** **Unit 30 Viewing and Representing** 30.1 Examining Visual Messages, pp. 894–898 30.2 Evaluating Media Messages, pp. 899–901 30.3 Producing Media Messages, pp. 902–904	**Classroom Activities** **Cooperative Learning** *Viewing and Representing Activities* **Assessment** *Tests with Answer Key and Rubrics*, pp. 117–120 *ExamView Assessment Suite* CD-ROM

	Lessons	Key Resources
WEEK 26 **Research Paper Writing & Using Modifiers Correctly**	**Part 1 Composition** **Unit 7 Research Paper Writing** 7.1 Prewriting: Planning and Researching, pp. 324–329 7.2 Prewriting: Outlining, pp. 330–333 **Part 2 Grammar, Usage, and Mechanics** **Unit 18 Using Modifiers Correctly** 18.1 The Three Degrees of Comparison, pp. 659–660 18.2 Irregular Comparisons, pp. 661–662 18.3 Double Comparisons, pp. 663–664 18.4 Incomplete Comparisons, p. 665	**Classroom Activities** **Nonfiction Reading and Writing** *Research Paper and Report Writing,* pp. 1–17 **Differentiated Homework Options** **Reteaching** *Grammar Reteaching,* p. 35 **Practice** *Grammar Practice Workbook,* pp. 35–36 **Enrichment** *Grammar Enrichment,* pp. 35–36 **Mixed Abilities** *Grammar and Language Workbook, Lessons* 59–61 **Assessment** *Tests with Answer Key and Rubrics,* pp. 25–26, 67–68 *ExamView Assessment Suite* CD-ROM
WEEK 27 **Research Paper Writing & Using Modifiers Correctly**	**Part 1 Composition** 7.3 Drafting, pp. 334–337 7.4 Citing Sources, pp. 338–343 **Part 2 Grammar, Usage, and Mechanics** 18.5 *Good* or *Well; Bad* or *Badly,* pp. 666–667 18.6 Double Negatives, pp. 668–669 18.7 Misplaced and Dangling Modifiers, pp. 670–675	**Classroom Activities** **Nonfiction Reading and Writing** *Research Paper and Report Writing,* pp. 18–27 **Differentiated Homework Options** **Reteaching** *Grammar Reteaching,* pp. 36–37 **Practice** *Grammar Practice Workbook,* p. 37 **Enrichment** *Grammar Enrichment,* pp. 36–37 **Mixed Abilities** *Grammar and Language Workbook,* Lessons 62–64
WEEK 28 **Research Paper Writing & Using Modifiers Correctly**	**Part 1 Composition** 7.5 Revising, pp. 344–347 7.6 Editing and Presenting: A Model Paper, pp. 348–349 Unit 7 Student Model, pp. 350–356 Unit 7 Review, p. 357 **Part 2 Grammar, Usage, and Mechanics** Unit 18 Grammar Review, pp. 676–685	**Classroom Activities** **Nonfiction Reading and Writing** *Research Paper and Report Writing,* pp. 28–35 **Technology** *Revising with Style* CD-ROM **Differentiated Homework Options** **Mixed Abilities** *Grammar and Language Workbook,* Unit 9 Review; Cumulative Review: Units 1–9 **Assessment** *Tests with Answer Key and Rubrics,* pp. 27–28, 69–70 *ExamView Assessment Suite* CD-ROM
WEEK 29 **Taking Tests**	**Part 3 Resources and Skills** **Unit 28 Taking Tests** 28.1 Classroom Tests, pp. 848–852 28.2 Standardized Tests, pp. 853–858 28.3 Standardized Test Practice, pp. 859–883	**Classroom Activities** **Assessment Practice** *Taking Standardized Tests* **Differentiated Homework Options** **Mixed Abilities** *Thinking and Study Skills,* pp. 24, 39–40 **Assessment** *Tests with Answer Key and Rubrics,* pp. 107–110 *ExamView Assessment Suite* CD-ROM

	Lessons	Key Resources
WEEK 30 **Sentence Combining & Usage Glossary**	**Part 1 Composition** **Unit 8 Sentence Combining** Style Through Sentence Combining, pp. 360–364 8.1 Description, pp. 365–368 8.2 Narration, pp. 369–372 **Part 2 Grammar, Usage, and Mechanics** **Unit 19 Usage Glossary** 19.0 Usage Glossary, pp. 687–701 Unit 19 Grammar Review, pp. 702–709	**Differentiated Homework Options** **Mixed Abilities** *Grammar and Language* Workbook, Lessons 65–69; Unit 10 Review; Cumulative Review: Units 1–10 **Assessment** *Tests with Answer Key and Rubrics,* pp. 71–74 *ExamView Assessment Suite* CD-ROM
WEEK 31 **Sentence Combining & Capitalization**	**Part 1 Composition** 8.3 Exposition, pp. 373–376 8.4 Persuasion, pp. 377–380 8.5 Literature Exercises, pp. 381–385 **Part 2 Grammar, Usage, and Mechanics** **Unit 20 Capitalization** 20.1 Capitalization of Sentences, pp. 711–712 20.2 Capitalization of Proper Nouns, pp. 713–719 20.3 Capitalization of Proper Adjectives, pp. 720–723 Unit 20 Grammar Review, pp. 724–729	**Differentiated Homework Options** **Reteaching** *Grammar Reteaching,* pp. 38–39 **Practice** *Grammar Practice Workbook,* pp. 38–39 **Enrichment** *Grammar Enrichment,* p. 39 **Mixed Abilities** *Grammar and Language Workbook,* Lessons 2, 70–72; Unit 11 Review; Cumulative Review: Units 1–11 **Assessment** *Tests with Answer Key and Rubrics,* pp. 75–78 *ExamView Assessment Suite* CD-ROM
WEEK 32 **Troubleshooter**	**Part 1 Composition** **Unit 9 Troubleshooter** 9.1 Sentence Fragment, pp. 388–389 9.2 Run-on Sentence, pp. 390–391 9.3 Lack of Subject-Verb Agreement, pp. 392–395 9.4 Lack of Pronoun-Antecedent Agreement, pp. 396–397 9.5 Lack of Clear Pronoun Reference, pp. 398–399 9.6 Shift in Pronoun, p. 400 9.7 Shift in Verb Tense, p. 401 9.8 Incorrect Verb Tense or Form, pp. 402–403 9.9 Misplaced or Dangling Modifier, pp. 404–405 9.10 Missing or Misplaced Possessive Apostrophe, pp. 406–407 9.11 Missing Commas with Nonessential Element, pp. 408–409 9.12 Missing Commas in a Series, pp. 410–411	**Differentiated Homework Options for Review** **Mixed Abilities** *Grammar and Language Workbook,* Lessons 31–32, 36–37, 42, 44–51, 55–58, 64, 76–83, 89

	Lessons	Key Resources
WEEK 33 **Business and Technical Writing & Punctuation, Abbreviations, and Numbers**	**Part 1 Composition** **Business and Technical Writing** Business Letters, pp. 413–420 **Part 2 Grammar, Usage, and Mechanics** **Unit 21 Punctuation, Abbreviations, and Numbers** 21.1 The Period, p. 731 21.2 The Exclamation Point, p. 732 21.3 The Question Mark, p. 732 21.4 The Colon, pp. 733–734 21.5 The Semicolon, pp. 735–737 21.6 The Comma, pp. 738–748 21.7 The Dash, p. 749	**Differentiated Homework Options** **Reteaching** *Grammar Reteaching,* pp. 40–48 **Practice** *Grammar Practice Workbook,* pp. 40–48 **Enrichment** *Grammar Enrichment,* pp. 40–48 **Mixed Abilities** *Business and Technical Writing Activities,* pp. 3–6 *Grammar and Language Workbook,* Lessons 73–84 **Assessment** *Tests with Answer Key and Rubrics,* pp. 31–32, 79–80 *ExamView Assessment Suite* CD-ROM
WEEK 34 **Business and Technical Writing & Punctuation, Abbreviations, and Numbers**	**Part 1 Composition** Memos, E-mail, and Applications, pp. 421–424 Using the Computer as a Writing Tool, pp. 425–430 **Part 2 Grammar, Usage, and Mechanics** 21.8 Parentheses, pp. 750–751 21.9 Quotation Marks, pp. 752–756 21.10 Italics (Underlining) , pp. 757–758 21.11 The Apostrophe, pp. 759–761 21.12 The Hyphen, pp. 762–764 21.13 Abbreviations, pp. 765–767 21.14 Numbers and Numerals, pp. 768–771	**Differentiated Homework Options** **Reteaching** *Grammar Reteaching,* pp. 48–52 **Practice** *Grammar Practice Workbook,* pp. 48–52 **Enrichment** *Grammar Enrichment,* pp. 47, 49–52 **Mixed Abilities** *Business and Technical Writing Activities,* pp. 7–16 *Grammar and Language Workbook,* Lessons 86–92
WEEK 35 **Business and Technical Writing & Punctuation, Abbreviations, and Numbers**	**Part 1 Composition** Technical Writing, pp. 431–433 Collaborative Writing in the Business World, pp. 434–437 **Part 2 Grammar, Usage, and Mechanics** Unit 21 Grammar Review, pp. 772–779	**Differentiated Homework Options** **Mixed Abilities** *Business and Technical Writing Activities,* pp. 17–22 *Grammar and Language Workbook,* Unit 12 Review; Cumulative Review: Units 1–12 **Assessment** *Tests with Answer Key and Rubrics,* pp. 33–34, 81–82 *ExamView Assessment Suite* CD-ROM

Confidence and Competence in Writing

William Strong

Professor of Secondary Education at Utah State University, Director of the Utah Writing Project, and member of the National Writing Project Advisory Board

For many of our students—and perhaps even for us—the blank page inspires a queasy sensation, a primitive *fear.* Do we have anything to say? Will words come? Will we sound stupid? Doubts like these remind us that writing is hard work as well as an audaciously public act. Our words stand by themselves, naked to the scrutiny of others. No wonder we are tentative!

> ***Our words stand by themselves, naked to the scrutiny of others. No wonder we are tentative!***

How Do We Improve Writing Confidence?

The following strategies can help students overcome their writing roadblocks and improve their writing confidence.

1. Have students *write frequently.* Keeping a journal or a learning log that is not graded helps students improve their fluency and reduce their writing anxiety.
2. *Guide students* through the writing process. Suggest strategies such as "talking through" ideas with others to promote ownership of ideas and careful reasoning.
3. Create a *supportive environment.* According to Sarah Freedman in NCTE Research Report No. 23 (1987), "allowing students time and support while they work to communicate their ideas" (160) is a distinguishing characteristic of successful teachers.
4. *Respond positively* to students' writing. Praise encourages students to keep trying.

How Do We Improve Writing Competence?

According to George Hillocks in *Research on Written Composition* (NCTE/ERIC, 1986), the most effective teaching emphasizes "structured problem-solving activities, with clear objectives, planned to enable students to deal with similar problems in composing" (247). Three teaching practices have proven to be highly effective:

1. inquiry teaching (e.g., focusing on a concrete data set and involving students in one or two strategies)
2. the use of grading scales, explicit criteria, and specific questions to guide individual or group work
3. sentence-combining practice

Beyond these research-based recommendations, we can improve students' writing competence by sharing drafts-in-progress, by modeling response strategies, and by teaching skills in context rather than in isolation. Moreover, by encouraging students to evaluate their own products in portfolios, we put the responsibility for learning where it should be—with students themselves.

Students become hooked when text itself becomes their teacher—infinitely flexible, patient, and recursive. Then the blank page seems not so much a threat as an engaging array of options, each waiting to be explored.

Writer's Choice Delivers!

- Explicit instruction in the writing process
- Frequent and varied writing opportunities
- Realistic writing prompts with real-world contexts
- Collaborative Writing activities that allow students to work together to plan, draft, revise, and edit
- Focused writing criteria and evaluation rubrics
- Questions for self-evaluation and prompts for portfolio building
- A whole unit's practice in sentence combining

Integrating the Language Arts

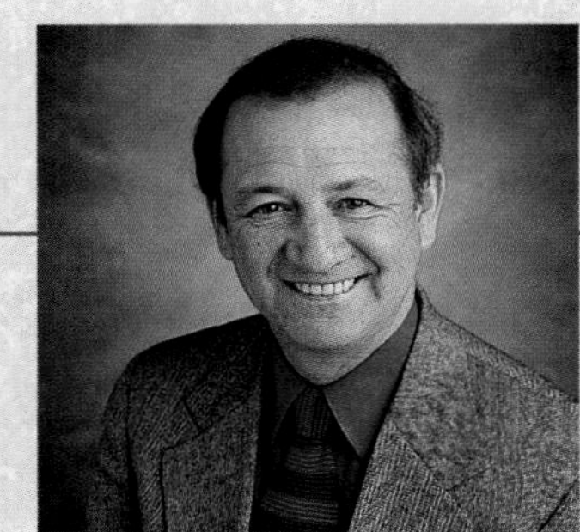

Denny Wolfe
Professor of English Education at Old Dominion University in Norfolk, Virginia; Director of the Tidewater Virginia Writing Project

Why Integrate the Language Arts?

As English teachers, we have a unique responsibility: to assist students in their growth toward language maturity. Specifically, we must help students read, write, speak, and listen capably and effectively. If we're successful, students learn to think critically and imaginatively.

Reading, writing, speaking, and listening are complementary processes. That is, growth in any one enhances growth in the others. During and after reading and writing, for example, the exchange of perceptions through further oral and written activities broadens and deepens students' understanding. A curriculum designed to help students achieve both *oracy* (speaking and listening competence) and *literacy* (reading and writing competence) fosters total language growth.

Making language work for students is like making cars work for drivers.

Think of learning how to drive. Competent drivers manage a variety of tasks simultaneously—steering, using the brake, paying attention to road signs. Cars won't work for drivers unless they learn to perform these tasks in concert. Making language work for students is like making cars work for drivers. To become truly competent readers,writers, listeners, and speakers, students must recognize that all language processes are interdependent, more meaningful when used together. We as teachers must lead them to this recognition.

How Can We Integrate the Language Arts?

We can help students integrate skills by drawing together two worlds: the world of literature (fiction and nonfiction) and the world of students' experience. Activities such as the following accomplish this objective:

- Discuss a topic (such as sunsets) in general terms before writing something specific about it (such as a memorable experience students associate with a particular sunset)
- Read or listen to a literary or informational text about the topic (such as a poem about sunsets or an article explaining why the sun appears to change color)
- Relate the text to their own experience in discussion or journal writing as a precursor to fuller reflections in a formal piece of writing or oral presentation (such as an analysis of the poem or a report on puzzling natural phenomena)

When students engage in experiences that integrate reading, writing, speaking, and listening, they gain a sense of the wholeness of English. They develop a sense of community as they talk together, share perceptions from their reading, and respond to each other's writing. In short, they grow toward full language maturity and become better, more imaginative thinkers.

Writer's Choice Delivers!

- Cooperative Learning—reading, writing, speaking, listening, and thinking toward common goals
- Writing Applications, Grammar Links, and Troubleshooter solutions that integrate composition and grammar
- Listening and Speaking Activities that integrate listening and speaking with composition lessons
- Annotated Student and Literature Models that illustrate exemplary writing
- Literature-based Grammar Reviews

Cultural Diversity

Arnold Webb
Senior Research Associate, Research for Better Schools, Philadelphia, Pennsylvania

What Is Cultural Diversity?

Cultural diversity is one of those terms that we educators tend to believe we all use in the same way.

But what educators consider to be meaningful cultural diversity in our classrooms ranges from fostering a common culture to celebrating different cultures. Hard-core adherents to each of these views believe strongly that their approach is the only viable way to channel the dynamic cultural and ethnic mix in our classrooms into areas that support and strengthen our democratic society.

But as Asa Hilliard reminds us, we do not need "to choose between (cultural) commonality and uniqueness." In truth, both are essential. We must provide an environment in which children can understand the world around them and their place in that society as citizens and upholders of democratic precepts and ideals. We cannot do this, however, without empowering all children to recognize and value their individual worth. For many children, that empowerment can occur only when their educational environment provides opportunities for them to appreciate how their heritage contributes to their land of origin and to the American dream.

How Do We Strike the Right Balance?

How do we teachers strike a balance between providing youngsters with a positive sense of self-worth through pride in their cultural heritage and engendering appreciation of our unique shared culture as Americans? We might begin by responding candidly to these questions:

- What do I know about the culture of my students?
- How is this knowledge utilized in my planning and teaching?
- Does the curriculum I teach reflect the truths of a pluralistic society? In what ways?
- What opportunities are provided in my classroom for children to know, understand, and relate to classmates from other backgrounds and cultures?
- What skills are my students learning that enable them to contribute positively to our society?

Whatever our answers, in the final analysis, we teachers must be responsive to the needs and exigencies of our changing society. For example, the 2000 Census reveals that one of every four Americans is a person of color. Cultural and ethnic diversity is endemic. We can shy away from its impact to our detriment, or we can build upon its strengths to our and our students' benefit.

Writer's Choice Delivers!

- Student Advisory Board-approved instruction that reflects the needs and interests of a variety of students
- Cultural Diversity and Civic Literacy annotations in the Teacher Wraparound Edition
- Media Connections that exemplify a variety of social roles and contributions
- Student Models, Literature Models, photographs, and fine art that reflect cultural variety and the truths of a pluralistic society

Differentiated Instruction

Bonnie S. Sunstein
Associate Professor of English and Education, College of Education, University of Iowa

and Dan-Ling Fu
Professor, School of Teaching and Learning, College of Education, University of Florida

How Can We Teach Writing to Students Who Have Difficulty with Language?

Much has been written recently about creating curriculum that begins with students' abilities rather than their disabilities or disadvantages. A coherent writing plan based on personal choice can enable students to connect what they already know with new skills and knowledge.

1. *Start with the students.* Let them freely put their ideas on paper. Once students have something to say and reasons to say it, they have the incentive to construct meaningful sentences using standard conventions.
2. *Students need to talk first and then write.* Composition theorists and researchers have taught us that meaningful speech must come before the written word (James Moffett, James Britton, Gordon Wells). Students who don't have a chance to speak the language or listen to others using it won't be able to write it. Students need to tell their stories, and they need to be inspired by listening to the stories of others' inspiration. In a language-rich classroom, no opportunity for talk is a waste.
3. *To have control of language, students need to choose what they say.* The work of Eleanor Duckworth and Donald Graves has taught us that when students gather their own ideas, they will have reason to work toward reshaping those ideas for others.
4. *When students write, we need to highlight the conventions they already know how to use.* Intuitively, students use many of the narrative and analytical conventions we teach. We must help students name, record, and document those conventions.
5. *Students need a supportive, literate community.* Students with language difficulties need to spend time in school with people who want to read and write. In Mike Rose's words, they must "enter the conversation." When we assume that they are members of a literate community (Nancie Atwell, Mike Rose), they begin to function as one.

> ***A coherent writing plan based on personal choice can enable students to connect what they already know with new skills and knowledge.***

Writer's Choice Delivers!

- Short manageable lessons to meet specific writing needs and goals
- A wide variety of writing prompts offering different degrees of guidance
- Journal writing and portfolio keeping
- Alternative strategies for basic and advanced students and for English Language Learners (Teacher's Wraparound Edition)
- *Practice, Reteaching,* and *Enrichment* workbooks meet individual needs

Journal Writing

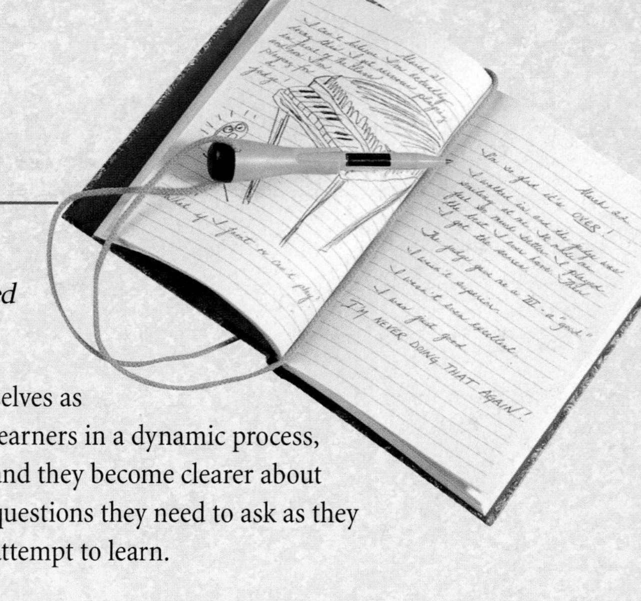

Sharyn Lowenstein
Associate Professor and Director of the Center for Community-Based Learning, Lasell College, Newton, Massachusetts

What Can Students Learn from Journal Writing?

Journal writing is very close to inner speech—we're actually thinking without having to translate for others. Journals help students develop thinking and writing skills in several ways.

- **Students become aware of what is on their minds.** Journals give students a chance to complain, express frustration, and change their minds. Once they express themselves, they are often able to concentrate on other academic tasks.
- **Students retrieve significant memories through free association.** Journal writing gives students permission to wander; often these wanderings allow them to recapture memories that can be mined for content-area writing assignments.
- **Students evaluate their own learning.** When students keep journals that are focused on project-related work, they learn to analyze their problem-solving behaviors. By reviewing their journals, they keep track of the various approaches they tried, identify their challenges, and appreciate their successes. Students come to see themselves as learners in a dynamic process, and they become clearer about questions they need to ask as they attempt to learn.

How Do Both Teachers and Students Benefit from Journal Writing?

Toby Fulwiler and others have written extensively about journal use in the class. Teachers can assign students journal writing to

- contemplate the day's lesson
- summarize class discussion
- articulate confusion
- anticipate new information
- synthesize or evaluate material

Journals written in class help teachers evaluate and adapt instruction as well as assess students' knowledge about a subject. Journals written outside class help individualize lessons and, in effect, extend instruction.

Journals help students incubate ideas without students having to evaluate the ideas. The journal can be a safe place to "play" with ideas, topics, and approaches. Writing from several perspectives helps students develop their arguments so their papers will ultimately become more convincing. Journal writing in class also helps quieter students and students who need more time to process information.

When all students keep journals (and especially if the teacher keeps a journal too), the class is taking writing risks together. Their shared experience contributes to a sense of community that enhances learning.

Writer's Choice Delivers!

- Instruction for journal writing that includes models of journals from both student and published authors
- Journal writing prompts in each composition lesson
- One unit focused on personal writing to help students learn to express thoughts, retrieve memories, and evaluate learning
- Writing Process in Action features with suggestions for journal writing

Portfolios

Bonnie S. Sunstein

Associate Professor of English and Education, College of Education, University of Iowa

What Are Portfolios?

Once the exclusive hallmark of artists, musicians, heads of state, and financiers, portfolios can now be found in colorful and energetic varieties in schools and colleges across the country. The word *portfolio* derives from the Latin *portare* (to carry) and *fogli* (leaves or sheets of paper). With homage to their heritage, all portfolios "carry" representative "leaves" of paper for the display of their owners' work.

Some portfolios hold samples of students' *best* work. Deciding what's best becomes a negotiation between a teacher and a student in which both consider what is important in writing. A "best" paper might be the one with the least errors or the one that most clearly fulfills the teacher's assignment. But a "best" paper might also be the one in which the student took a risk, worked out a nagging question, or researched and synthesized a new idea. This paper might not have followed the assignment exactly, but it might represent a new depth of thought.

How Can Portfolios Help Students, Teachers, and Schools?

Portfolios help us evaluate where we've been, assess where we are, and project where we want to go next. They facilitate evaluation and assessment for students, teachers, and schools.

- A collection of writing over time can offer **students** insights as they write reflectively about their own learning. They provide opportunities for metacognition as students think about their own thinking and document it. Students become authorities in judging what is good or bad about their work.
- Portfolios enable **teachers** to include students in the evaluation process. In addition, a teacher's own portfolio can include written reflections on the time devoted to students and to personal literacy.
- With portfolios, **whole classes** can view progress over time and make more informed decisions about curriculum coverage.
- For **school systems,** large-scale use of portfolios can offer new information and raise questions that have never been asked before.

Portfolios are not simply writing folders redone; they are documented collections of literary decisions made at certain times by certain people. They reflect our philosophies of reflection, evaluation, and learning. Portfolio keeping is decision making, and making decisions involves asking tough questions—of teachers and students—about their values in writing and reading.

Writer's Choice Delivers!

- Portfolio and reflecting ideas at the end of every composition unit
- Writing portfolios for collecting student work
- Writing activities that point the way at each stage of the writing process
- Rubrics for self-evaluation with every Writing Process in Action
- Unit reviews that help students ask the right questions about their work

Writing to Learn

Denny Wolfe

Professor of English Education at Old Dominion University in Norfolk, Virginia; Director of the Tidewater Virginia Writing Project

Why Teach Students to Write to Learn?

Traditionally only half of the power of writing has been exploited in our schools. We typically ask students to write for the purpose of telling us what they've learned about various subjects or about writing itself. But the other half of the power of writing is quite different. It is the writing we do primarily for ourselves. It is the writing we do to find out what we know and do not know. This is ungraded writing, writing not meant to be judged by an audience. Admitting this kind of writing into our classrooms can work to improve students' learning.

The point is that writing briefly to inquire, clarify, interpret, define, decide, explore—even play—can be a fertile tool for teaching and learning.

How Can We Help Students Write to Learn?

Some students believe that the only writing worth doing is the writing that teachers grade, but if we want students to improve as writers, they must write far more than we can

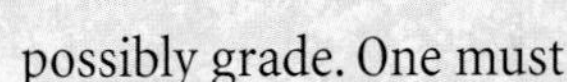

possibly grade. One must write *a lot* to hone the craft of writing. Response to writing is necessary, but not to *all* writing.

Teachers can encourage students to practice ungraded writing in the following ways.

- **In-class Surveys** Ask students to write for a few minutes about where the class ended yesterday or what they learned today.
- **Summaries and Questions** Ask students to summarize their reading or to write a question for class discussion.
- **Journal Writing** Ask students to keep a daily journal, which can be a source of ideas for writing assignments.

The point is that writing briefly to inquire, clarify, interpret, define, decide, explore—even play—can be a fertile tool for teaching and learning.

How Do Students Benefit from Writing to Learn?

When students write for themselves, they discover knowledge, ask questions, find gaps in their understanding, and surprise themselves by acquiring new attitudes. Writing for the sake of inventing, investigating, and discovering makes one reflective, introspective, and curious—qualities that help define good learners. Finally, as students become more comfortable and able language users, the writing we *do* grade becomes more pleasurable to read.

Writer's Choice Delivers!

- Individual lessons covering such topics as Keeping a Learning Log, Writing to Learn, and Keeping a Reader-Response Journal
- Journal writing activities in every composition lesson
- Annotated models, Media Connections, and literature selections that invite student response
- Engaging writing and cross-curricular assignments
- Writing Process in Action lessons with extended modeling and guidance

Thinking and Writing

Carol Booth Olson
Director of the UCI Writing Project and a faculty member in the Department of Education at the University of California, Irvine

What Are the Premises About Thinking That Can Inform the Teaching of Writing?

Writing is a mode of thinking. Writers must generate ideas, plan the process of writing, translate thought into print, revise what they have articulated, and evaluate the effectiveness of their efforts. In short, writers tap all of the levels of Bloom's taxonomy of the cognitive domain.

If thinking and writing are connected, then a number of premises about thinking can and should inform the teaching of writing.

- **Thinking is developmental.** Thinking is an evolving process that grows with maturity and experience. A developmental writing curriculum should *start where the kids are,* tap what Howard Gardner calls "areas of potential" (linguistic, musical, logical-mathematical, kinesthetic, etc.), and build bridges from the student's personal experience to the world of school. Instruction should be challenging, but goals should be attainable.
- **Thinking is progressive.** As Piaget observed, the mind is better able to make cognitive leaps when learning moves from the concrete to the abstract. A writing curriculum should move progressively from concrete descriptive and narrative writing to more-abstract expository writing.
- **Thinking is cumulative and recursive.** Teachers who use a process model of composition should invite students to continually revisit what they have written. A writing curriculum should be scaffolded in such a way that students must go back to prior learning before moving forward to the next assignment.
- **Thinking is fostered, not taught.** Hilda Taba concludes that "how people think may depend largely on the kinds of 'thinking experience' they have had." Writing is one of the most complex and challenging thinking experiences a teacher can provide.
- **Thinking as well as writing must be practiced.** Teachers need to provide students with guided practice in a range of thinking and writing tasks so students develop a repertoire of problem-solving strategies that they can apply to future thinking/writing challenges.

If thinking and writing are connected, then a number of premises about thinking can and should inform the teaching of writing.

Writer's Choice Delivers!

- An organizational structure that moves from more-concrete to more-abstract modes of writing and thinking
- A consistent emphasis on the writing process, including Media Connections that exemplify how real-world writers use a recursive writing process
- Assignments that allow students to draw on personal experiences and cross-curricular interests
- Journal writing lessons in every composition lesson that encourage reflexivity
- Reflecting and Adding to Your Portfolio features in unit reviews that help students think about their writing
- A multiplicity of writing and thinking opportunities

Cooperative Learning

Judith Summerfield
Professor of English and Director of Freshman Year Initiative, Queens College, City University of New York

What is Cooperative Learning?

Cooperative learning is a new name for the old adage "Two heads are better than one." And nowhere is cooperative learning better than in the classroom. One of the gifts we can give to our students is the time to write and the time to read their writing to their peers and listen to the writing of others.

But "How?" you ask—when classes are large and there is so much else to do. It might be useful to think about cooperative learning in two ways: (1) *whole-class activity* and (2) *small-group work.*

How Can a Whole-Class Activity Be Cooperative?

Here's how it might work.

1. Write William Carlos Williams's "The Red Wheelbarrow" on the board. Give students ten minutes to write new poems patterned after the poem. Each poem should begin with "So much depends upon" and contain two images. (You write too.)
2. Have students read their poems to the class.
3. See what happens.

Being willing to "see what happens"—to allow for the happy accidents that arise when writers write—turns your class into a writing class. When I used the Williams exercise recently in a literature class after students had read the Williams poem, there were loud protests. Rather than allow this energy to dissipate, I *used* it. I asked students to take out their writers' notebooks and imitate Williams's poem, using the form "So much depends upon" + two images. Then they all read their poems aloud. I believe that what they gained through their own writing was an appreciation for what can be said in such a short confined space. The class cooperative turned us all into poets.

How Is Small-Group Work Cooperative?

Students gather in pairs, trios, quartets, or quintets, depending upon the task. The tasks must be *carefully planned and defined.* Students can use one another, as writers do, to plan or brainstorm, to throw ideas around, to share drafts, or to edit or proofread. Students realize that they can make things happen on the page and that a page can be turned into a portfolio of their own writing or a collection of the class writings—the ultimate cooperative venture.

Writer's Choice Delivers!

- Cooperative learning activities such as brainstorming, peer response, problem solving, and group researching and presenting
- Instruction in and opportunities for peer editing
- Writing conferences as part of every Writing Process in Action
- Additional cooperative learning activities in the Teacher Wraparound Edition

Sentence Combining and the Writing Process

William Strong
Professor of Secondary Education at Utah State University, Director of the Utah Writing Project, and a member of the National Writing Project Advisory Board

What Is the Role of Sentence Combining in Writing Instruction?

Our focus on what students do when they compose has led many teachers to use sentence combining (SC) in their classes. Research has shown that SC can be twice as effective as free writing as a means of improving the quality of student compositions.

Practice in SC can benefit students in a variety of ways. Students learn to

- say more in fewer words
- write more-varied sentences
- master sentence fluency

To explain the value of these skills, George Hillocks suggests SC practice may provide "writers with systematic knowledge of syntactic possibilities, the access of which allows them to sort through alternatives in their heads as well as on paper and to choose those which are most apt" (150).

SC can be implemented in the classroom through two methods.

- **Cued, or Signaled, Exercises** By working with clusters of sentences out of context, students learn to make transformations with ease. Such exercises provide support for English language learners or others needing a direct structured approach to sentence construction.
- **Whole-Discourse Models** When combining sentences in paragraph-length texts of descriptive, narrative, or expository writing, students make decisions in context.

Because SC is essentially a revising activity, students should understand that its aim is to help them construct *better* sentences, not merely longer ones.

Because sentence combining is essentially a revising activity, students should understand that its aim is to help them construct better *sentences, not merely longer ones.*

How Does Sentence Combining Improve Students' Writing Style?

SC practice provides a no-risk context in which students can explore stylistic options, make mistakes, and learn from their mistakes. Doing exercises orally, either with the entire class or in small groups, is a particularly effective activity. Inviting students to compare their sentences with those of other class members and to make decisions about which sentences they prefer builds skill and confidence. When teachers publicly praise various stylistic improvements, such as the use of parallelism or sentence variety, students are encouraged to explore more possibilities. Finally, challenging students to compare their style with the style of a professional writer can lead to insights and surprises.

Writer's Choice Delivers!

- Opportunities for both whole-discourse sentence combining and cued, or signaled, exercises
- A Sentence combining unit in each book that includes instruction and exercises for descriptive, narrative, expository, and persuasive writing
- *Sentence Combining* Practice blackline masters provide signaled as well as unsignaled exercises

Assessment

Charles R. Duke
Dean of Reich College of Education, Appalachian State University

What Is Assessment?

Assessment of student writing can take two forms.

- **Formative evaluation** consists of questions about the writing process and comments intended to assist the writer in achieving his or her purpose.
- **Summative evaluation** judges the writer's finished composition against established standards and usually results in a recorded grade.

What Is the Role of Formative Evaluation?

For teachers to use assessment effectively in conjunction with the writing process, both formative and summative evaluation are necessary, but the most important, when working with young writers, is the formative. Formative evaluation performs two important functions.

- **Diagnosis** assesses the writer's competence at any stage of the writing process and provides feedback designed to help the writer move to the next stage. Teachers must pay close attention to the *signals in students' composing processes* and avoid passing summative judgments early in the writing process. Instead, teachers play the role of collaborator, responding to drafts as readers, not judges, and providing responses that help the writers clarify meaning and purpose.
- Feedback allows student writers to work together to clarify meaning and purpose in their writing. Peer response groups can be helpful because they enlarge the writer's audience and free teachers from reading many early drafts, thus enabling them to offer concise, focused feedback in brief one-to-one conferences.

Since not all writers develop at the same pace, writing options based upon diagnosis of a student's abilities, needs, and interests should be offered.

Writer's Choice Delivers!

- Support for both formative and summative evaluation
- Writing rubrics on Writing Activities pages and in Writing Process in Action features
- Instruction in peer editing and response
- Opportunities for writing conferences in all Writing Process in Action features
- Adding to Your Portfolio activities in every unit review
- Evaluation rubrics in the Teacher Wraparound Edition
- *Writing Assessment and Evaluation Rubrics* ancillary

How Can Teachers Best Prepare for Summative Evaluation?

A useful way of preparing to grade students' writing is to establish **writing portfolios,** which can include students' commentaries and self-evaluations of their progress. If teachers have established a classroom where **formative evaluation** has been an ongoing activity, then **summative evaluation** should emerge as a final assessment of the ability of teachers and students to collaborate in the writing process.

Technology

Barbara King-Shaver
Supervisor of English, South Brunswick High School, Monmouth Junction, New Jersey; Adjunct Faculty Member, Rutgers University Graduate School of Education

How Does Technology Aid in the Writing Process?

In an era of word processors, e-mail and instant messaging, and near-universal access to the Internet in public schools (U.S. Department of Education, National Center for Education Statistics, "Internet Access in U.S. Public Schools and Classrooms: 1994–2002," 2003), students have never had so many tools at their disposal for becoming better writers. At each stage of the writing process, these technologies greatly accelerate and extend what students had been able to do with pen and paper and a library card.

Students have never had so many tools at their disposal for becoming better writers.

Prewriting Students who freewrite using a word processor have less tendency to stop and edit what they have written, so they develop fluency and generate ideas more quickly. Students who use Internet search engines to find information can quickly explore potential topics for writing. E-mail and instant messaging allow students to brainstorm outside the classroom.

Drafting With a word processor, the ease with which students can later revise frees them from having to correct mistakes while drafting.

Revising The cut, copy, and paste functions of a word processor let students remove or rearrange whole sentences or paragraphs in one or two simple steps. Students can easily share their work with teachers and peers, either by printing out copies or by sending e-mail attachments. Teachers and peers can use editing tools to indicate where revisions are needed.

Editing and Proofreading Word processors contain editing tools such as spelling and grammar checkers. Online, students can find dictionaries, thesauri, grammar references, and style guides that will help them identify errors.

Publishing and Presenting Students using word processors can print out clean, presentable copies of their writing. Teachers can post student work on classroom Web pages to increase students' potential audience.

How Does Technology Aid Assessment?

Technology makes assessment more efficient. Since results of computer-based tests can be instantaneous, teachers can tell right away whether to review lessons or to move ahead. A typical computer-based test may also include features that allow teachers to monitor students' progress more easily.

Writer's Choice Delivers!

- An Electronic Resources unit that covers word processing, Internet usage, and multimedia projects
- Using Computers notes and Technology Tips
- Writing prompts and online support at **glencoe.com**
- Interactive exercises with *Revising with Style* CD-ROM
- Pretests, posttests, and the option to customize with *ExamView* Assessment Suite CD-ROM
- Online instruction in technology and language arts skills with *TechCONNECT*

Improving Writing and Other Skills with Foldables™

by Dinah Zike, M.Ed., Creator of Foldables™

Foldables™, *my three-dimensional interactive graphic organizers, have been shown by teachers and students to enhance students' comprehension by tapping into kinesthetic learning abilities. Students fold paper, cut tabs, write, and manipulate what they have made in order to* ***organize*** *information;* ***review*** *skills, concepts, and strategies; and* ***assess*** *their knowledge.*

Using Dinah Zike's Foldables™ in Writing and English/Language Arts Classes

Glencoe/McGraw-Hill shares my vision that Foldables can play an important role in students' learning. The regular use of these manipulatives will help students to master essential writing and other English/language arts skills by

- focusing on the **steps of the writing process** and on the specific requirements of various types of writing
- recognizing and classifying **parts of speech** and other **grammatical structures**
- building **vocabulary**
- developing **research skills** and **listening and speaking skills**

Using Foldables Makes Learning Easy and Enjoyable

Anyone who has paper, scissors, and maybe a stapler or some glue can use **Foldables** in the classroom. Just follow the illustrated step-by-step directions. These directions have been tested with teachers and students to make sure that they are easy to use and simple to understand for both students and teachers. Look at the sample below (and try it yourself!). On the following reproducible pages (T43–T48), you'll find additional Foldables that you can use with lessons from *Writer's Choice.*

Learning Objective: to recognize and classify types of nouns

Students focus on the purpose of the assignment.

On this Foldable you can list all the nouns in a set of sentences and identify them according to type.

Step 1. Place a sheet of paper in front of you so that the long side is at the top. Fold the paper in half from side to side.
Step 2. Then fold it in half from side to side again, making four columns.
Step 3. Fold down about an inch at the top of the paper.
Step 4. Unfold the paper and draw lines along the folds. In the section at the top of each column, write the labels ***Common, Proper, Concrete,*** and ***Abstract.***
Step 5. As you read each sentence, list the nouns in the correct column. Remember that some nouns can be placed in more than one column.

Students practice following step-by-step directions.

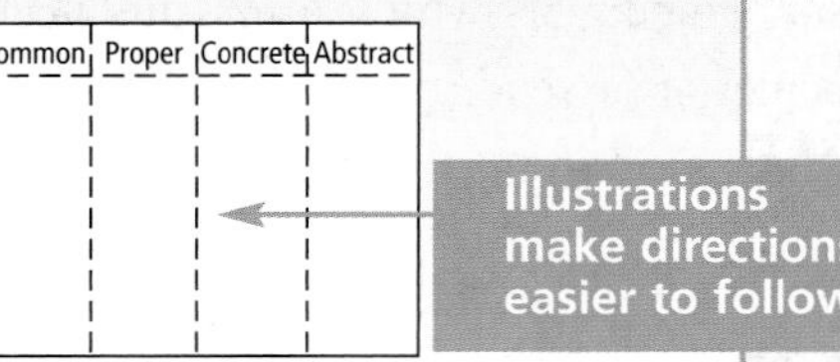

Illustrations make directions easier to follow.

Compare-and-Contrast Writing

Learning objective: to prepare for compare-and-contrast writing by identifying similarities and differences between two subjects

Use the following Foldable to help you generate ideas for a piece of writing in which you compare and contrast two subjects.

Step 1. Place a sheet of paper in front of you so that the long side is at the top. Fold the paper in half from top to bottom.

1

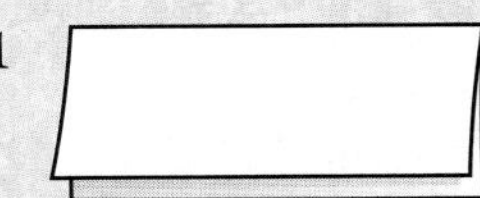

Step 2. Fold the paper into thirds.

2

Step 3. Unfold the last fold and draw ovals, making sure that the ovals overlap in the middle section.

Step 4. Cut through the top layer of paper along the fold lines. This will make three tabs.

3, 4

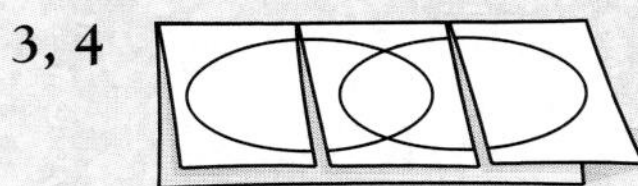

Step 5. On the left tab, write a label for the first subject being compared and contrasted. On the right tab, write a label for the second subject. Write the label ***Both*** in the middle tab where the ovals overlap.

5, 6

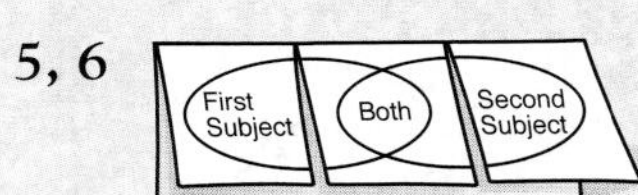

Step 6. Under the left tab, jot down characteristics that are unique to the first subject. Under the right tab, jot down characteristics that are unique to the second subject. Under the middle tab, jot down characteristics that the two subjects share.

You may use this Foldable with writing in a variety of genres—including descriptive writing, expository writing, and persuasive writing—as long as your writing activity involves comparing and contrasting two subjects. The subjects may be persons, places, things, events, ideas, qualities—almost anything that you want to compare.

Persuasive Writing

Learning objective: to develop support for a claim in persuasive writing

As you work on a piece of persuasive writing, use the following Foldable to help you track the kinds of evidence you use for support.

Step 1. Stack three sheets of paper with the top edges about an inch apart. Be sure to keep the edges straight.

1

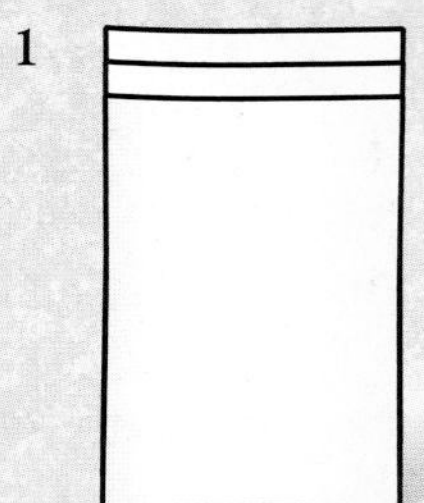

Step 2. Fold up the bottom edges of the paper to form six tabs, five of which will be the same size.

Step 3. When the top five tabs are the same size, crease the fold to hold the tabs in place and staple the sheets together along the crease.

2

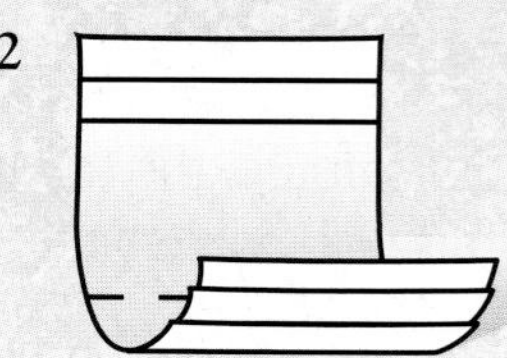

Step 4. Turn the sheets so that the stapled edge is at the top. On the top tab, write the claim you wish to make. Label the five remaining tabs ***Facts, Statistics, Examples/Incidents, Opinions,*** and ***Reasons.***

Step 5. Take notes on your Foldable as you collect evidence to support your claim. Under each tab, write down at least two pieces of evidence of the kind labeled on the tab.

3, 4, 5, 6

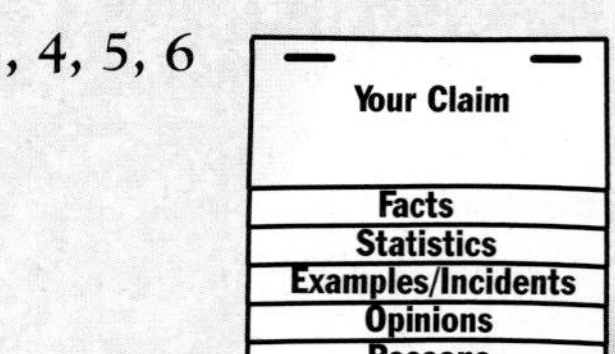

Step 6. Mark with an asterisk (*) what you think are the most persuasive pieces of evidence. Be sure to include them as support for your claim in your first draft.

By changing the labels, you can adapt this simple Foldable for several other types of writing. For example, you can use this Foldable to help you write a personal narrative about an event in your life. Just write your name on the top tab. Then change the remaining tabs to read ***What?, Where?, When?, Why?,*** and ***How?*** Record your answers to these questions under the tabs. Then refer to your answers as you prepare an outline for your narrative.

Research Paper Writing

Learning objective: to generate and answer questions for research

As you work on a research paper, use the following Foldable to help you identify what you know, what you might want to know, and what you learned about your research topic.

Step 1. Place a sheet of paper in front of you so that the long side is at the top. Fold the top of the paper down, stopping about an inch from the bottom.

1

Step 2. Fold the paper into thirds from side to side as shown.

2

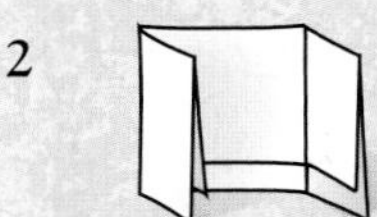

Step 3. Unfold the paper. Then, along both folds, cut the top layer only. This will make three tabs.

3

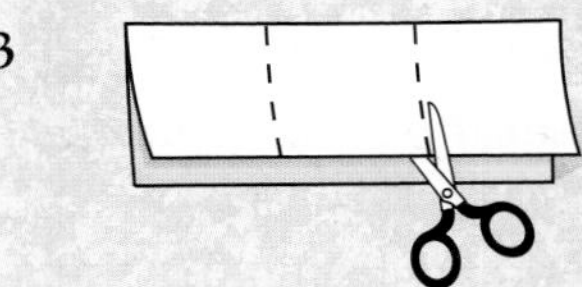

Step 4. Write the title of your research topic along the bottom of the page. Label the tabs ***Know, Want to Know,*** and ***Learned.***

Step 5. Before you begin your research, write what you already know about the topic under the left tab and what you want to know under the middle tab.

4, 5, 6

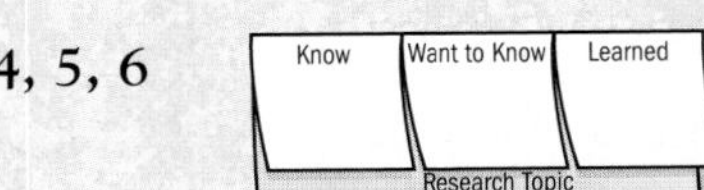

Step 6. As you find information on your research topic, jot down notes in your own words about what you learned under the right tab. Then use your notes to guide your writing of your research paper.

By changing the labels, you can adapt this simple Foldable for several other types of writing. For example, you can use this Foldable to help you write persuasively, as in an editorial. Just write the topic along the bottom of the page. Then change the tab labels to read (from left to right) ***My Opinion, Supporting Facts,*** and ***Reasons.***

Kinds of Sentences

Learning objective: to understand and write four types of sentences

To help you review the four types of sentences, use the following Foldable.

Step 1. Draw a mark at the midpoint of a sheet of paper along the long side. Then fold the top and bottom edges in to touch the midpoint.

1

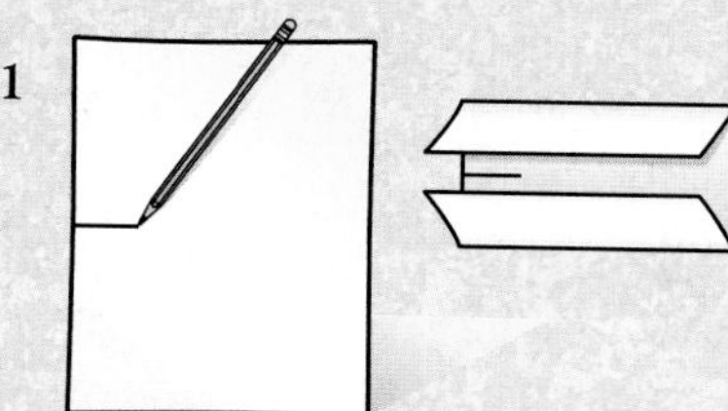

Step 2. Fold the paper in half from side to side.

2

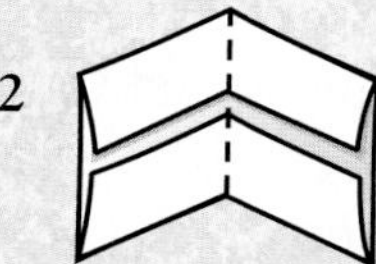

Step 3. Turn the paper vertically. Unfold it and cut along the inside fold lines to form four tabs.

3

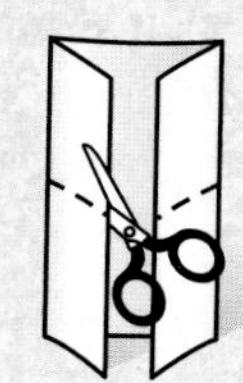

Step 4. Label the tabs ***Simple, Compound, Complex,*** and ***Compound-Complex.***

Step 5. Under each tab, write a definition of the type of sentence and write an example of that type of sentence.

4, 5

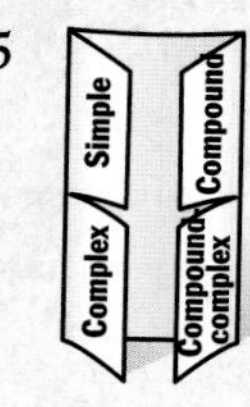

By changing the labels on the tabs, you can use this Foldable with lessons from *Writer's Choice* as follows:

- to classify four kinds of sentences according to whether they are declarative, imperative, exclamatory, or interrogative
- to review compound nouns, possessive nouns, collective nouns, and appositives
- to identify action verbs, linking verbs, transitive verbs, and intransitive verbs

Building Vocabulary

Learning objective: to expand vocabulary by recording new words

Use the following Foldable for recording new words that you come across as you read or listen.

Step 1. Place a sheet of paper in front of you with the long side at the top.

Step 2. Fold the top of the paper down and the bottom up to divide the paper into thirds.

Step 3. Turn the paper vertically, unfold, and label the columns ***Word, Root,*** and ***Prefixes/Suffixes.***

Step 4. Fill in the chart for each new word you come across during the day. (Keep in mind that not every new word you come across will have all of the parts.)

1, 2

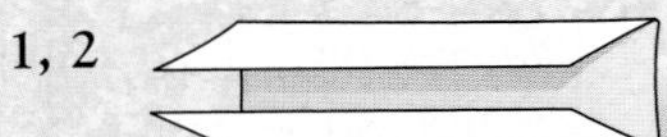

3, 4

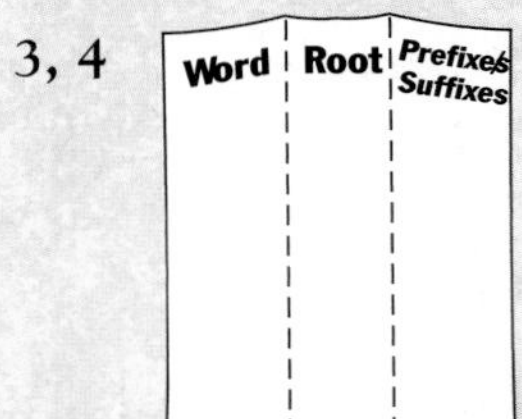

Check your understanding of the words by using them in original sentences that you write on the back of the chart or on a separate sheet of paper.

Facts and Opinions

Learning objective: to identify facts and opinions in writing or in oral presentations

Use this Foldable to help you to read and listen critically.

Step 1. Place a piece of paper in front of you with the long side at the top. Fold the paper in half from top to bottom.

1
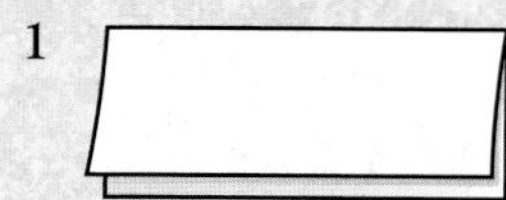

Step 2. Turn the paper and fold down one inch from the top.

2

Step 3. Unfold the paper and draw a line along the one-inch fold. Label the left column ***Facts*** and the right column ***Opinions.***

Step 4. As you read or listen to a speech or a radio commercial, write the facts in the column labeled ***Facts*** and the opinions in the column labeled ***Opinions.***

3, 4
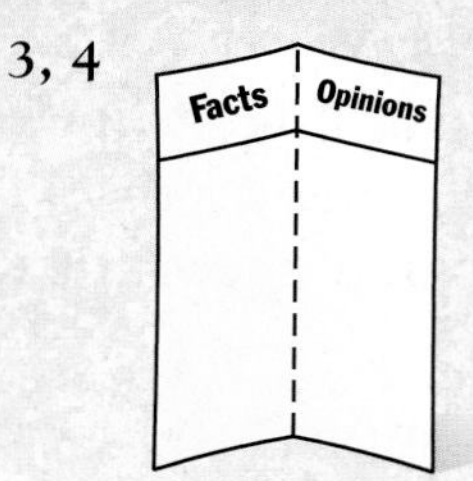

By changing the labels, you can adapt this Foldable for several other uses. For example, you might use it to list the ***Pros*** and ***Cons*** of an argument.

Glencoe

Writer's Choice

GRAMMAR and COMPOSITION

GRADE 9

Before him stretched the long, laborious road, dry
FREEWRITE
"I know why the cage bird sings, ah me,
when his wing is bruised and his bosom sore,--
when he beats his bars and he would be free;"

McGraw Hill Glencoe

ACKNOWLEDGMENTS

Grateful acknowledgment is given authors, publishers, photographers, museums, and agents for permission to reprint the following copyrighted material. Every effort has been made to determine copyright owners. In case of any omissions, the Publisher will be pleased to make suitable acknowledgments in future editions.

Cover (Maya Angelou) ©Deborah Feingold/Corbis; (Scrabble tiles) Jeffrey Coolidge/Getty Images; (bkgd) Gerry Charm/SuperStock **vi** The Estate of John Lennon, 1989; **vii** Courtesy Bernice Stienbaum Gallery, New York; **viii** *The Starry Night,* (1889). Vincent Van Gogh. Collection, the Museum of Modern Art, NY. Acquired through the Lillie P. Bliss Foundation; **ix** The Brooklyn Museum, gift of the Ernest Erickson Foundation; **x** Courtesy the Chapingo Chapel of the National School of Agriculture and the Instituto Nacional de Bellas Artes, Mexico; **xi** File photo; **xii** PhotoDisc, Inc.; **xiii** P. and G. Bowater/The Image Bank; **xiv** ©1985, the Estate of Keith Haring; **xv** (t) file photo, (b) the Telegraph Colour Library/FPG; **xvi** Kent Fleming/Lifestyles; **xvii** (t)file photo; **xx** ©1990 Thames & Hudson, Ltd., London. Photo by David Lavender; **xxi** (t) Courtesy of the Lilly Library, Indiana University, Bloomington, Indiana, (b) PhotoDisc, Inc.; **xxii** © 1986 Courtesy of Collier, Macmillan Publishers, London. Photo by Ralph J. Brunke; **xxiii** Scala/Art Resource, NY; **xxiv** Photodisc, Inc; **xxv** Stella, Frank. *Katsura.* Collection, The Museum of Modern Art, New York. Acquired through Mr. and Mrs. Victor Ganz; **xxxi-1** Edward Owens/Art Resource, NY.

Acknowledgments continued on page 974.

The **Facing the Blank Page** feature in this book was prepared in collaboration with the writers and editors of *TIME.*

The McGraw-Hill Companies

Glencoe

Send all inquiries to:
Macmillan/McGraw-Hill • Glencoe/McGraw-Hill
8787 Orion Place
Columbus, OH 43240-4027

ISBN: 978-0-07-888772-7
MHID: 0-07-888772-0

ii

PROGRAM CONSULTANTS

Mark Lester is Professor of English Emeritus at Eastern Washington University. He served as Chair of the Department of English at Eastern University and Chair of the Department of English as a Second Language at the University of Hawaii. He is the author of *Grammar and Usage in the Classroom* (Allyn & Bacon, 2000), co-author of *A Commonsense Guide to Grammar and Usage* (Bedford/St. Martin's 2006), *Essential ESL Grammar* (McGraw-Hill, 2008), and of numerous other professional books and articles.

Sharon O'Neal is Associate Professor at the College of Education, Texas State University–San Marcos, where she teaches reading instruction. She was formerly Director of Reading and Language Arts of the Texas Education Agency and has authored, and contributed to, numerous articles and books on reading instruction and teacher education.

Jacqueline Jones Royster is Professor of English and Executive Dean of the Colleges of Arts and Sciences at The Ohio State University. Her professional interests include the rhetorical history of women of African descent, the development of literacy, and contexts and processes related to the teaching of writing. In addition to her many years of teaching writing, directing writing programs and writing centers, and serving as a leader in several English professional organizations, she is also the author of numerous articles in literacy studies, and several books, among them: *Traces of a Stream: Literacy and Social Change Among African American Women; Critical Inquiries: Readings on Culture and Community; and Calling Cards: Theory and Practice in the Study of Race, Gender, and Culture.*

William Strong is Professor of Secondary Education at Utah State University, Director of the Utah Writing Project, and a member of the National Writing Project Advisory Board. A nationally known authority on the teaching of composition, he is the author of many volumes, including *Coaching Writing: The Power of Guided Practice* (Heinemann, 2001) and *Writing Incisively: Do-It-Yourself Prose Surgery* (McGraw-Hill, 1991).

Jeffrey Wilhelm, a middle and high school English teacher for thirteen years, is currently Associate Professor of English Education at Boise State University, where he specializes in adolescent literacy, with research interests including gender and literacy, technology and literacy, and assisting struggling readers and writers. He is the founding director of the Maine Writing Project and Boise State Writing Project. He has authored fifteen books on literacy and education and has won the NCTE Promising Research Award for *You Gotta BE the Book* and the Russell Award for Distinguished Research for *Reading Don't Fix No Chevys.*

Denny Wolfe, a former high school English teacher and department chair, is Professor of English Education Emeritus, Director of the Tidewater Virginia Writing Project, and Director of the Center for Urban Education at Old Dominion University in Norfolk, Virginia. Author of more than seventy-five articles and books on teaching English, Dr. Wolfe is a frequent consultant to schools and colleges on the teaching of English language arts.

iii

Advisors

Michael Angelotti
Professor of Instructional Leadership and Academic Curriculum, English/Literacy Education
College of Education
University of Oklahoma

Larry Beason
Associate Professor of English and Director of Freshman Composition Program
University of South Alabama

Charles Duke
Dean of Reich College of Education
Appalachian State University

Carol Booth Olson
Director
University of California, Irvine, Writing Project

Willis L. Pitkin
Professor of English
Utah State University

Judith Summerfield
Professor of English and Director of Freshman Year Initiative
Queens College
City University of New York

Bonnie S. Sunstein
Associate Professor of English and Education
College of Education
University of Iowa

Educational Reviewers

Janice Brown
Houston ISD
Houston, Texas

Lenore Croudy
Flint Community School
Flint, Michigan

John A. Grant
St. Louis Public Schools
St. Louis, Missouri

Vicki Haker
Mead Junior High School
Mead, Washington

Frederick G. Johnson
Georgia Department of Education
Atlanta, Georgia

Sterling C. Jones Jr.
Detroit Public Schools
Detroit, Michigan

Barry Kincaid
Raytown School District
Kansas City, Missouri

Evelyn G. Lewis
Newark Public Schools
Newark, New Jersey

M. DeAnn Morris
Crescenta Valley High School
La Crescenta, California

Anita Moss
University of North Carolina
Charlotte, North Carolina

Ann S. O'Toole
Chesterfield County Schools
Richmond, Virginia

Suzanne Owens
Glendale High School
Glendale, California

Sally P. Pfeifer
Lewis and Clark High School
Spokane, Washington

Marie Rogers
Independence High School
Charlotte, North Carolina

Barbara Schubert
Santa Clara County Office of Education
San Jose, California

Ronnie Spilton
Chattahoochee High School
Alpharetta, Georgia

Robert Stolte
Huntington Beach High School
Huntington Beach, California

Student Advisory Board

The Student Advisory Board was formed in an effort to ensure student involvement in the development of *Writer's Choice.* The editors wish to thank members of the board for their enthusiasm and dedication to the project. The editors also wish to thank the many student writers whose models appear in this book.

iv

BOOK OVERVIEW

Part 1 Composition

Part 2 Grammar, Usage, and Mechanics

Part 3 Resources and Skills

Reference Section

v

CONTENTS

Part 1 Composition

vi

vii

Vincent van Gogh, *The Starry Night,* 1889

viii

UNIT 3

Descriptive Writing 132

ix

UNIT 4 Narrative Writing

x

MEDIA Connection
First Set up the bath for safety.
Second Gather the materials.
cotton
K-9 Shampoo
Then While water is running, put cotton in the dog's ears.

xi

xii

xiii

UNIT 8 Sentence Combining

Keith Haring, *Untitled,* 1985

Part 2 Grammar, Usage, and Mechanics

xv

UNIT 11 Parts of the Sentence ... 494

UNIT 12 Phrases ... 518

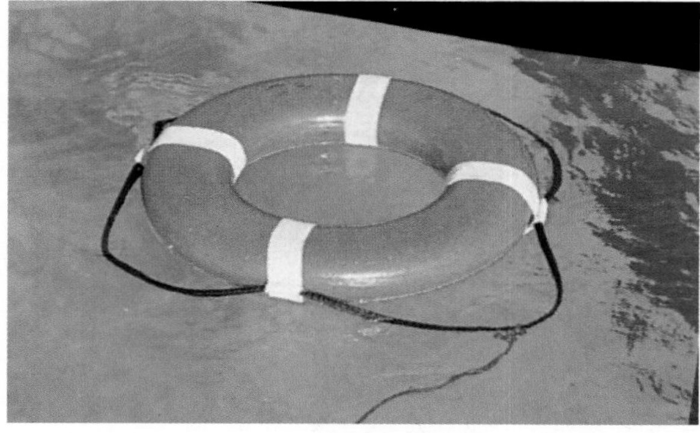

xvi

xvii

xviii

xix

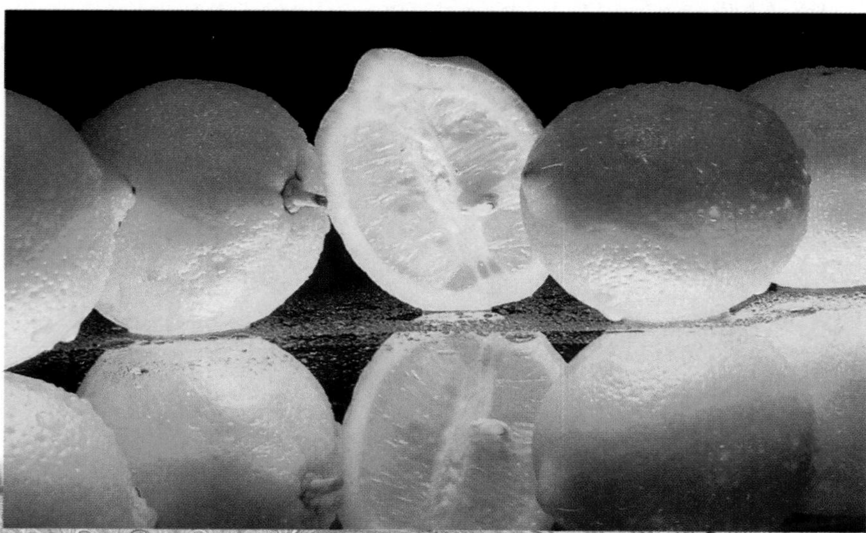

xx

UNIT 21 Punctuation, Abbreviations, and Numbers 730

xxi

Part 3 Resources and Skills

xxii

xxiii

xxiv

UNIT 28 Taking Tests

UNIT 29 Listening and Speaking

UNIT 30 Viewing and Representing

Reference Section *Fast answers to questions about writing, research, and language*

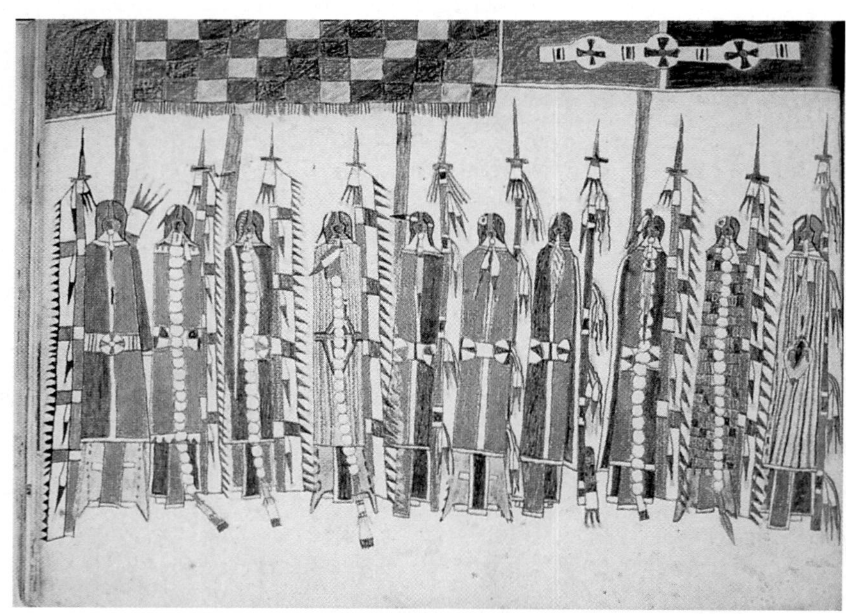

xxvi

LITERATURE MODELS

Composition Models

Each literature selection is an extended example of the mode of writing taught in the unit.

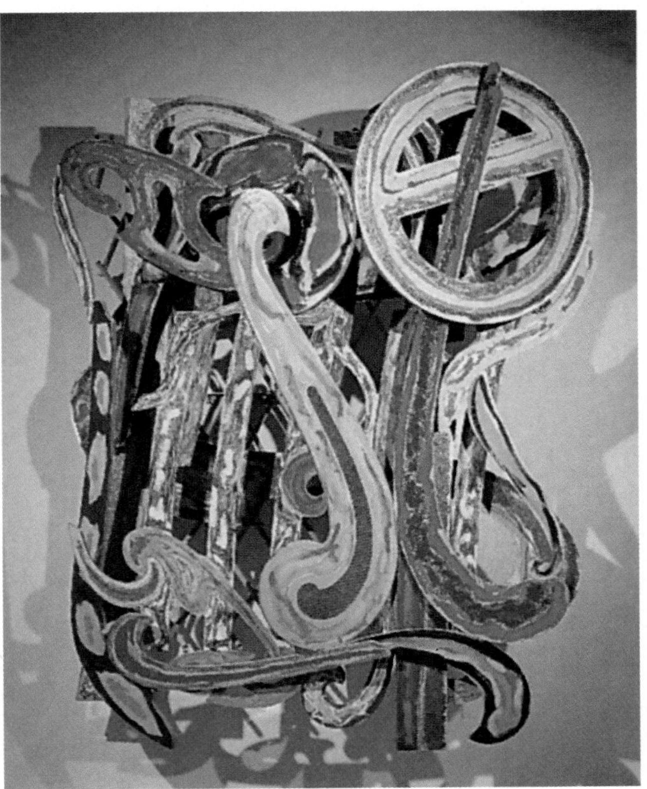

Skill Models

Excerpts from outstanding works of fiction and nonfiction exemplify specific writing skills.

xxvii

LITERATURE MODELS

Skill Models *continued*

Language Models

Each Grammar Review uses excerpts to link grammar, usage, or mechanics to literature.

xxviii

FINE ART

Fine art—paintings, drawings, photos, and sculpture—is used to teach as well as to stimulate writing ideas.

xxix

GLENCOE

Writer's Choice

Grammar and Composition

Welcome to Writer's Choice!

Your writing and your choices are what this book is all about. Take a few minutes to get to know each of the book's four main parts: Composition; Grammar, Usage, and Mechanics; Resources and Skills; and the Writing and Research Handbook.

Part 1

Composition

How do you become a better writer? By writing! Four-page lessons give you the strategies you need to improve your writing skills. Each lesson focuses on a specific writing problem or task, offers clear instruction, shows models of effective writing, and—most importantly—provides a variety of writing activities for you to practice what you've learned.

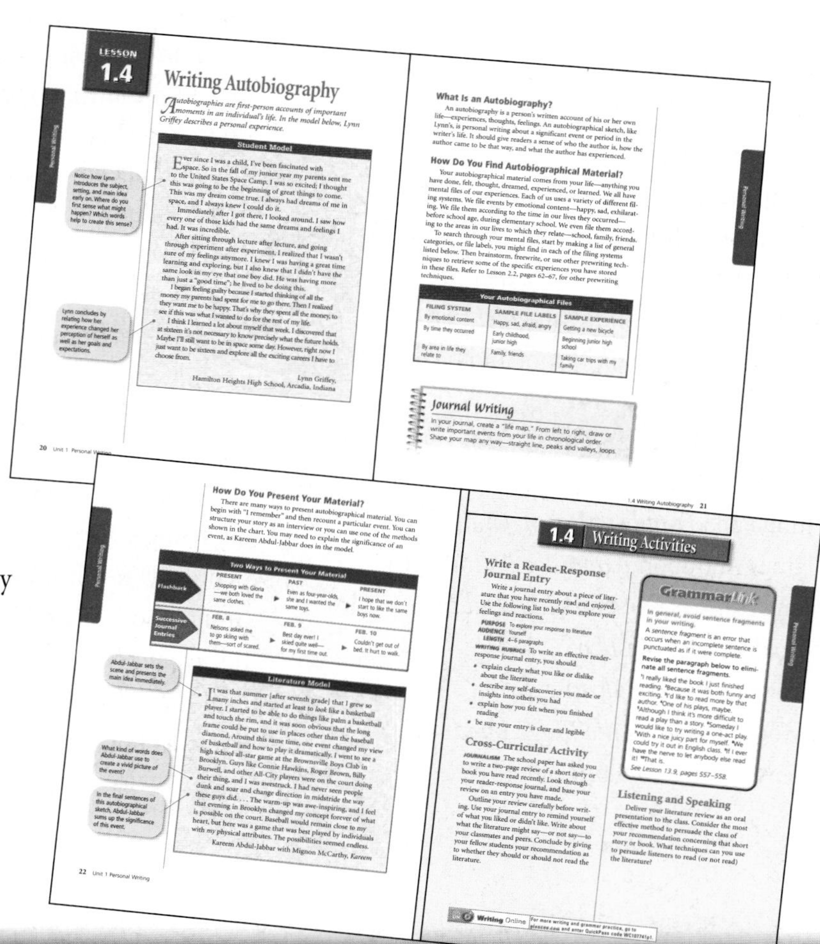

Part 2

Grammar, Usage, and Mechanics

Short focused lessons make learning grammar easy. Rules and definitions teach you the basics, while examples and literature models show you how the concepts are used in real-life writing.

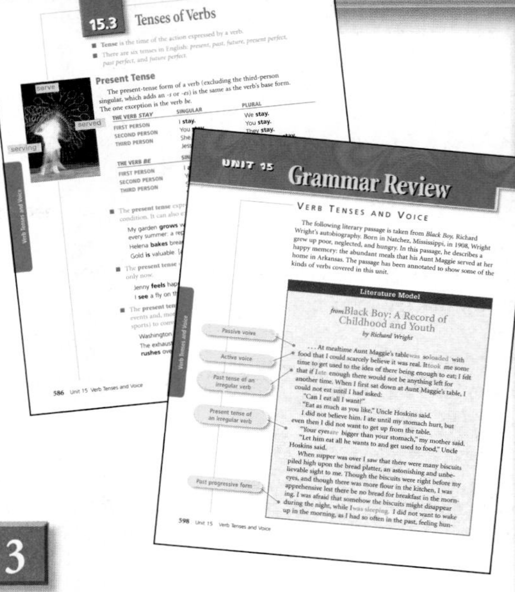

15.3 Tenses of Verbs

- Tense is the time of the action expressed by a verb.
- There are six tenses in English: *present, past, future, present perfect, past perfect,* and *future perfect.*

Present Tense

The present-tense form of a verb (excluding the third-person singular, which adds an *-s* or *-es*) is the same as the verb's base form. The one exception is the verb *be.*

THE VERB STAY	SINGULAR	PLURAL
FIRST PERSON	I **stay.**	We **stay.**
SECOND PERSON	You	You **stay.**
THIRD PERSON	She	They **stay.**

586 Unit 15 Verb Tenses and Voice

UNIT 15 **Grammar Review**

VERB TENSES AND VOICE

The following literary passage is taken from *Black Boy,* Richard Wright's autobiography. Born in Natchez, Mississippi, in 1908, Wright grew up poor, neglected, and hungry. In this passage, he describes a happy memory: the abundant meals that his Aunt Maggie served at her home in Arkansas. The passage has been annotated to show some of the kinds of verbs covered in this unit.

Literature Model

from Black Boy: A Record of Childhood and Youth

by Richard Wright

. . . At mealtime Aunt Maggie's table was so loaded with food that I could scarcely believe it was real. It took me some time to get used to the idea of there being enough to eat; I felt that if I ate enough there would not be anything left for another time. When I first sat down at Aunt Maggie's table, I could not eat until I had asked:

"Can I eat all I want?"

"Eat as much as you like," Uncle Hoskins said.

I did not believe him. I ate until my stomach hurt, but even then I did not want to get up from the table.

"Your eyes are bigger than your stomach," my mother said.

"Let him eat all he wants to and get used to food," Uncle Hoskins said.

When supper was over I saw that there were many biscuits piled high upon the bread platter, an astonishing and unbelievable sight to me. Though the biscuits were right before my eyes, and though there was more flour in the kitchen, I was apprehensive lest there be no bread for breakfast in the morning. I was afraid that somehow the biscuits might disappear during the night, while I was sleeping. I did not want to wake up in the morning, as I had so often in the past, feeling hun-

598 Unit 15 Verb Tenses and Voice

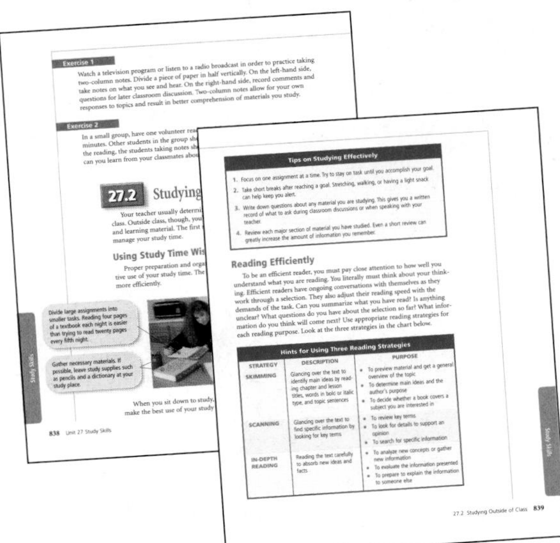

Exercise 1

Watch a television program or listen to a radio broadcast in order to practice taking two-column notes. Divide a piece of paper in half vertically. On the left-hand side, take notes on what you see and hear. On the right-hand side, record comments and questions for later classroom discussion. Two-column notes allow for your own responses to topics and result in better comprehension of materials you study.

Exercise 2

27.2 Studying

838 Unit 27 Study Skills

Tips on Studying Effectively

1. Focus on one assignment at a time. Try to stay on task until you accomplish your goal.
2. Take short breaks after reaching a goal. Stretching, walking, or having a light snack can help keep you alert.
3. Write down questions about any material you are studying. This gives you a written record of what to ask during classroom discussions or when speaking with your teacher.
4. Review each major section of material you have studied. Even a short review can greatly increase the amount of information you remember.

Reading Efficiently

To be an efficient reader, you must pay close attention to how well you understand what you are reading. You literally must think about your thinking. Efficient readers have ongoing conversations with themselves as they work through a selection. They also adjust their reading speed with the demands of the task. Can you summarize what you have read? Is anything unclear? What questions do you have about the selection so far? What information do you think will come next? Use appropriate reading strategies for each reading purpose. Look at the three strategies in the chart below.

Hints for Using Three Reading Strategies

STRATEGY	DESCRIPTION	PURPOSE
SKIMMING	Glancing over the text to identify main ideas by reading chapter and lesson titles, words in bold or italic type, and topic sentences	• To preview material and get a general overview of the topic • To determine main ideas and the author's purpose • To decide whether a book covers a subject you are interested in
SCANNING	Glancing over the text to find specific information by looking for key terms	• To review key terms • To look for details to support an opinion • To search for specific information
IN-DEPTH READING	Reading the text carefully to absorb new ideas and facts	• To analyze new concepts or gather new information • To evaluate the information presented • To prepare to explain the information to someone else

27.2 Studying Outside of Class 839

Part 3

Resources and Skills

Would you like to improve your study skills, learn how to give a speech, or get better at taking tests? The lessons in this part give you the skills you need to do all these things and more. Each lesson is complete, concise, and easy to use.

WRITING AND RESEARCH HANDBOOK

This user-friendly handbook gives explanations, examples, and tips to help you write strong sentences, paragraphs, compositions, and research papers. Use it whenever you get stuck!

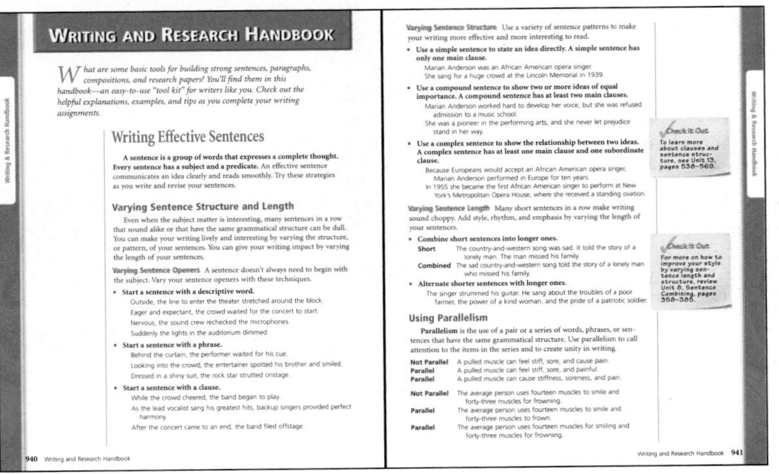

WRITING AND RESEARCH HANDBOOK

What are some basic tools for building strong sentences, paragraphs, compositions, and research papers? You'll find them in this handbook—an easy-to-use "tool kit" for writers like you. Check out the helpful explanations, examples, and tips as you complete your writing assignments.

Writing Effective Sentences

A sentence is a group of words that expresses a complete thought. Every sentence has a subject and a predicate. An effective sentence communicates an idea clearly and reads smoothly. Try these strategies as you write and revise your sentences.

Varying Sentence Structure and Length

Even when the subject matter is interesting, many sentences in a row that sound alike or that have the same grammatical structure can be dull. You can make your writing lively and interesting by varying the structure, or pattern, of your sentences. You can give your writing impact by varying the length of your sentences.

Varying Sentence Openers A sentence doesn't always need to begin with the subject. Vary your sentence openers with these techniques.

- **Start a sentence with a descriptive word.**
  Outside, the line to enter the theater stretched around the block.
  Eager and expectant, the crowd waited for the concert to start.
  Nervous, the sound crew rechecked the microphones.
  Suddenly the lights in the auditorium dimmed.
- **Start a sentence with a phrase.**
  Behind the curtain, the performer waited for his cue.
  Looking into the crowd, the entertainer spotted his brother and smiled.
  Dressed in a shiny suit, the rock star strutted onstage.
- **Start a sentence with a clause.**
  While the crowd cheered, the band began to play.
  As the lead vocalist sang his greatest hits, backup singers provided perfect harmony.
  After the concert came to an end, the band filed offstage.

940 Writing and Research Handbook

Varying Sentence Structure Use a variety of sentence patterns to make your writing more effective and more interesting to read.

- **Use a simple sentence to state an idea directly. A simple sentence has only one main clause.**
  Marian Anderson was an African American opera singer.
  She sang for a huge crowd at the Lincoln Memorial in 1939.
- **Use a compound sentence to show two or more ideas of equal importance. A compound sentence has at least two main clauses.**
  Marian Anderson worked hard to develop her voice, but she was refused admission to a music school.
  She was a pioneer in the performing arts, and she never let prejudice stand in her way.
- **Use a complex sentence to show the relationship between two ideas. A complex sentence has at least one main clause and one subordinate clause.**
  Because Europeans would accept an African American opera singer, Marian Anderson performed in Europe for ten years.
  In 1955 she became the first African American singer to perform at New York's Metropolitan Opera House, where she received a standing ovation.

Varying Sentence Length Many short sentences in a row make writing sound choppy. Add style, rhythm, and emphasis by varying the length of your sentences.

- **Combine short sentences into longer ones.**
  Short The country-and-western song was sad. It told the story of a lonely man. The man missed his family.
  Combined The sad country-and-western song told the story of a lonely man who missed his family.
- **Alternate shorter sentences with longer ones.**
  The singer strummed his guitar. He sang about the troubles of a poor farmer, the power of a kind woman, and the pride of a patriotic soldier.

Using Parallelism

Parallelism is the use of a pair or a series of words, phrases, or sentences that have the same grammatical structure. Use parallelism to call attention to the items in the series and to create unity in writing.

Not Parallel A pulled muscle can feel stiff, sore, and cause pain.
Parallel A pulled muscle can feel stiff, sore, and painful.
Parallel A pulled muscle can cause stiffness, soreness, and pain.

Not Parallel The average person uses fourteen muscles to smile and forty-three muscles for frowning.
Parallel The average person uses fourteen muscles to smile and forty-three muscles to frown.
Parallel The average person uses fourteen muscles for smiling and forty-three muscles for frowning.

Check It Out To learn more about clauses and sentence structure, see Unit 13, pages 538–569.

Check It Out For more on how to improve your style by varying sentence length and structure, review Unit 8, Sentence Combining, pages 358–385.

Writing and Research Handbook 941

PART 1

Composition

Objectives

The units in Part 1 guide students in their development toward becoming effective, confident writers. Throughout these units, students will be asked

- to compose in a variety of forms
- to write for a variety of purposes and audiences
- to compose using a recursive writing process
- to draw on technology in the process of writing
- to write clearly, legibly, and effectively using the conventions and mechanics of English
- to use writing as a tool for research and inquiry and to compile and represent information using available technology
- to analyze the writing strategies of others
- to work collaboratively to analyze and evaluate their own writing and that of their peers

Viewing the Art

Vincent van Gogh (1853–1890) is one of the world's greatest post-Impressionist painters. His paintings and drawings are among the world's best-known and most expensive works of art. In this painting of willows, the crowns have been pollarded, or pruned severely, to stimulate denser growth.

Interpret and Analyze Use the following questions for discussion:

- What does Van Gogh's choice of this subject suggest about his perspective on what merits capturing on canvas?
- Are the trunks or the sun the focal point in this painting?
- What mood is conveyed by the dominant color in this painting?

Vincent van Gogh, Pollard Willows and Setting Sun, 1888

"What perils that tangle of trees and underbrush might hold for him did not concern Rainsford just then."

—Richard Connell
"The Most Dangerous Game"

Resource Manager

Use the following resources to customize your teaching of the units in Part 1.

Planning Resources

- *Lesson Plans*
- *Block Scheduling*

Transparencies

- *Bellringer*
- *Daily Language Practice*
- *Fine Art*
- *Two-Minute Skill Drill*
- *Writing Process*

Other Print Resources

- *Business and Technical Writing Activities*
- *Composition Enrichment*
- *Composition Practice*
- *Composition Reteaching*
- *Cooperative Learning Activities*
- *Dinah Zike's Foldables™ for Writer's Choice*
- *Glencoe Literature Library*
- *Grammar and Composition Handbook*
- *Grammar Workbook*
- *inTime*
- *Listening and Speaking Activities*
- *Research Paper and Report Writing*
- *Sentence-Combining Practice*
- *Spelling Power*
- *Style and Documentation Source-book for Writers*
- *Taking Standardized Tests*

PART 1

Composition

- *Tests with Answer Key and Rubrics*
- *Thinking and Study Skills*
- *Vocabulary Power*
- *Writing Across the Curriculum*
- *Writing Assessment and Evaluation Rubrics*
- *Writing in the Real World*

Software
- *Interactive Grammar and Language Workbook*
- *Presentation Plus!*
- *Revising with Style*
- *Testmaker*
- *Vocabulary Power Puzzlemaker*

Video
- *MindJogger Videoquizzes*

Web Site
- *glencoe.com*

Discussing the Quotation

The quotation is from "The Most Dangerous Game," a short story by Richard Connell (1893–1949). Discuss the quotation with the class, and ask students how they would interpret the author's meaning. How might the sense of uncertainty and expectation voiced by the author be connected to starting a writing project?

Writing Prompt Write a brief explanation of how Connell's words, coupled with the images of the willows and setting sun, can be seen to connect to the process of composition.

UNIT 1

Viewing the Art

The photograph of wrapped presents suggests a sense of wonder as well as mystery. The sparkling ribbon and wrapping paper attract attention, while also concealing the contents of each package. In much the same way, personal writing combines the best of both elements—the mystery of filling an empty page with the thrill of finishing a composition.

Interpret and Analyze Use the following questions for discussion:

- How would you describe the mood of this photograph? What effect do the design and colors of the wrapping paper have on the mood?
- There is an old saying that "you can't judge a book by its cover." How might this saying relate to the message of the photograph?

Discussing the Quotation

The quotation comes from "Rules of the Game," a short story by Amy Tan (b. 1952). Discuss the quotation with the class, and ask students how they would interpret the author's meaning. What importance do you think the author places on the specific package she selects? How might the wrapping paper have influenced her decision?

Writing Prompt Write a brief explanation of how Tan's words, coupled with the image of the wrapped presents, can be seen to connect to personal writing.

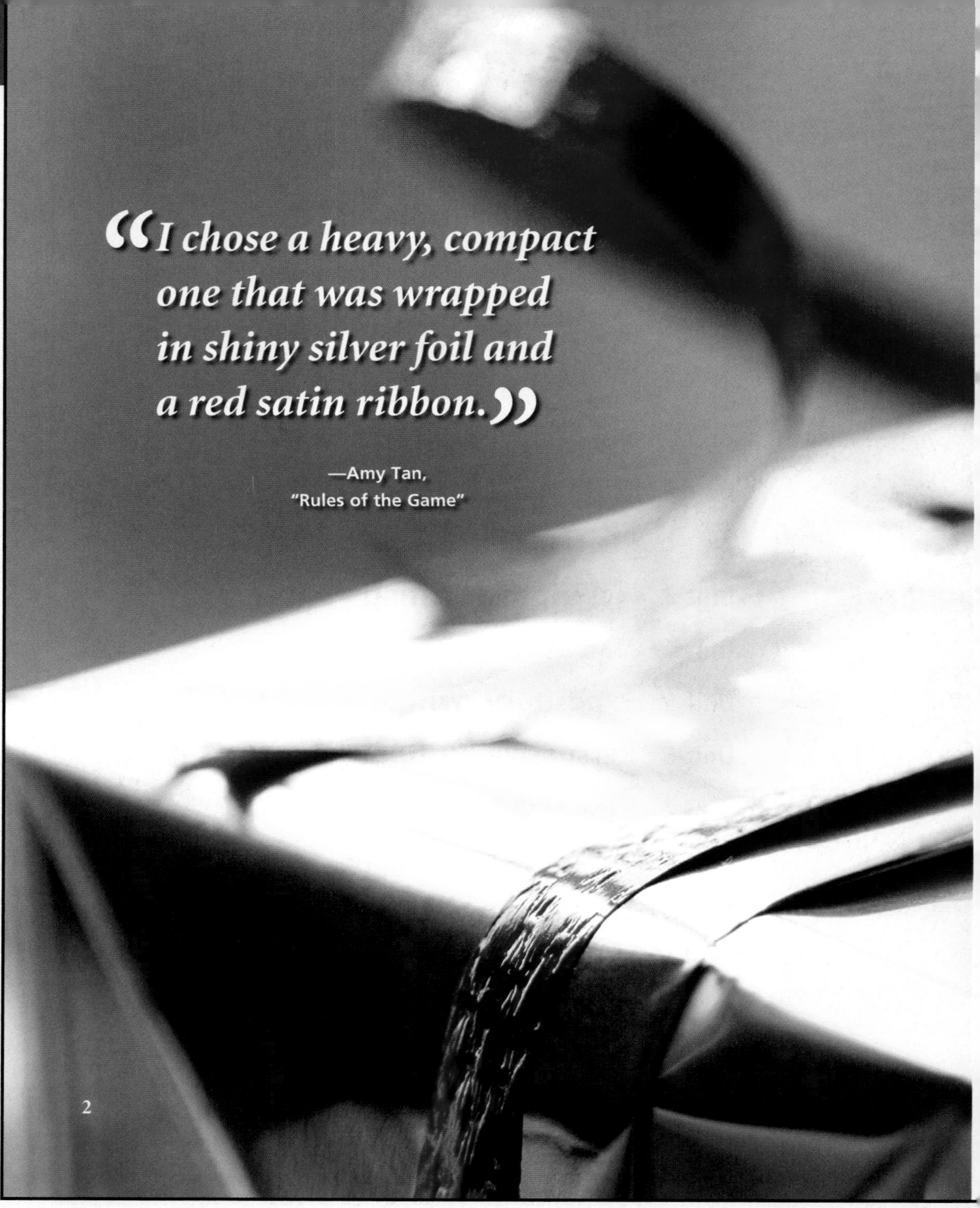

"I chose a heavy, compact one that was wrapped in shiny silver foil and a red satin ribbon."

—Amy Tan, "Rules of the Game"

2

Resource Manager

Planning Resources
- *Lesson Plans*
- *Block Scheduling*

Transparencies
- *Bellringer*
- *Daily Language Practice*
- *Fine Art*
- *Two-Minute Skill Drill*
- *Writing Process*

Other Print Resources
- *Composition Enrichment*
- *Composition Practice*
- *Composition Reteaching*
- *Cooperative Learning Activities*
- *Glencoe Literature Library*
- *Grammar and Composition Handbook*
- *Grammar Workbook*
- *Listening and Speaking Activities*
- *Sentence-Combining Practice*
- *Tests with Answer Key and Rubrics*
- *Thinking and Study Skills*
- *Writing Across the Curriculum*
- *Writing Assessment and Evaluation Rubrics*
- *Writing in the Real World*

UNIT 1

Personal Writing

3

Objectives

- To help students, through example and instruction, develop an understanding of themselves through personal writing
- To focus on various applications of personal writing, including journals, personal essays, autobiographies, poetry, and reader-response logs
- To apply the techniques learned to writing an autobiography

ASSESSMENT OPTIONS

Tests with Answer Key & Rubrics
Unit 1 Choice A Test, p. 1
Unit 1 Choice B Test, p. 2
Unit 1 Composition Objective Test, pp. 3–4

Testmaker
Unit 1 Choice A Test
Unit 1 Choice B Test
Unit 1 Composition Objective Test

You may wish to administer either the Unit 1 Choice A Test or the Unit 1 Choice B Test as a pretest.

Key to Ability Levels

L1 Level 1 activities are within the basic ability range of students.

L2 Level 2 activities are within the ability range of average students.

L3 Level 3 activities are more challenging activities.

Video
- *MindJogger Videoquizzes*

Software
- *Presentation Plus!*
- *Revising with Style*
- *Testmaker*

Web Site
- *glencoe.com*

Focus

Lesson Overview

Objectives
- To examine the use of personal writing in a real-life situation
- To learn how to use personal writing to share thoughts, feelings, and experiences

Skills
- discussing; analyzing; writing personal letters

Critical Thinking
- recalling events; making inferences; relating details; analyzing reactions

Listening and Speaking
- discussing; informal speaking; evaluating; questioning

Bellringer
Daily Language Activity

When students enter the classroom, have this assignment on the board: Write a response to the following question: *When is it preferable to write a letter rather than to speak to someone in person or by phone?*

Grammar Link to the Bellringer

Have students review what they wrote for the Bellringer activity above. Encourage them to rewrite it incorporating these subordinate clauses: *when I write; when I telephone; when someone lives far away; since phoning can be expensive.*

See also  *Daily Language Practice*

Motivating Activity

Discuss students' responses to the Bellringer activity. Then ask these questions:
- Is there a "proper" way to write a letter?
- What do you like and dislike about letter writing?

Writing in the Real World

Personal Writing

A letter to Gwendolyn Brooks by Sandra Cisneros

Writing about your own thoughts, feelings, and experiences is called personal writing. Personal writing can either be kept confidential or be shared. Personal letters can help you communicate with someone, teach you something about yourself, and stimulate new ideas. Novelist Sandra Cisneros wrote the letter shown on the next page to her friend Gwendolyn Brooks, Pulitzer Prize winner and poet laureate of Illinois.

Author Sandra Cisneros

Cisneros begins her letter by describing the wind over the mesa.

Resource Manager

Planning Resources
- *Lesson Plans*

Transparencies
- *Bellringer*
- *Daily Language Practice*
- *Writing Process 1*

Other Print Resources
- *Cooperative Learning Activities,* pp. 5–8
- *Thinking and Study Skills,* p. 21
- *Writing Assessment and Evaluation Rubrics*
- *Writing in the Real World,* pp. 1–4

A Writer's Process

Prewriting

Getting the Idea

The letter to Gwendolyn Brooks was written by Sandra Cisneros as she was about to go on a book tour to promote her new book *Woman Hollering Creek*. She says, "For some reason, I always tour with Brooks's book *Maud Martha*. That morning I'd read one of the stories. I thought, 'I should tell Ms. Brooks how much I like her book.'" Cisneros had not written to Brooks for a long time, but she says, "I wanted her to know how happy her book made me at this moment and how important it's been to me."

Everyone who sits down to do some personal writing approaches it in his or her own personal style. For Cisneros, being free to be herself is important. The author says her letters are "not the kind of conversations you have when you're dressed in your suit, but the kind you have sitting at your kitchen table wearing your pajamas, talking to someone who's very dear to you."

Even the writing tools that Cisneros uses set a cozy mood for her writing. She says she often writes her letters on "pretty paper, that delicious creamy kind with texture. Not intimidating paper, but paper you can do anything on. I'm very fussy about my pens and my papers."

March 5th, 1991

Dear Ms. Brooks,

It is what Winnie the Pooh would call a blustery day here. Or what Miss Emily would designate a wind like a bugle. From over and over the mesas, snapping dust and terrifying trees.

I am in my pajamas though it's past mid-day but I like my leisure to dream a little longer when I am asleep, and continue dreaming on paper when I am awake. I am rereading your wonderful MAUD MARTHA again, a copy you gave me, and which I am very grateful to have. I remember when I first discovered that book, in the American library in Sarajevo, across from the famous river where the archduke was shot that started a world war. And it was there too that I read T.S. Eliot's collected poems. If you go to Sarajevo, and look at the chapter on PRACTICAL CATS you'll see a cherry stain on one of the pages--because I was reading the book on the opposite bank of the river, under a row of cherry trees in front of my American friend Ana's apartment house, and at the moment I was reading about one of Eliot's cats--the Rum Tum Tigger?--a wind shook a cherry loose that landed with a startled plop on the page. And my heart gave a little jump too because the book wasn't mine. A wine-colored stain against the thick creamy pages.

I mean to teach it one day along with other books that use a series of short inter-related stories. Perhaps with Ermilo Abreu Gomez's CANEK and Nellie Campobello's CARTUCHO albeit the translation of both is crooked. The form fascinates. And I'd done as much with MANGO STREET, though I hadn't met your MAUD yet. Perhaps I was "recollecting the things to come."

Ms. Brooks, please know I haven't quite disappeared altogether from the land. I've been migrant professor these past years, guest writer-in-residence at UC Berkeley, UC Irvine, the Univ. of Michigan at Ann Arbor and now here for one semester. All for the sake of protecting my writer self. Some years dipped low and some reeled to high heaven. But now the days are good to me. I have a new book due out from Random (see enclosed reviews) and I have sold my little house on Mango to the big house of Vintage. Both books slated for this April. And it seems my life is in a whirl like the wind outside my window today. Everything shook and snapped and wind-washed and fresh, and, yes, that is how it should be.

I only wanted to say this to you today. That your book gives me such pleasure. That I admire it terribly. I think of you often, Ms. Brooks, and your spirit is with me always.

un abrazo fuerte, fuerte,

Sandra

Sandra Cisneros

Personal Writing

Teach

Reading Media

Have students preview the title and focus of the Media Connection on page 4. Discuss the purpose and audience of personal writing, pointing out that every writer uses a different tone or perspective to communicate with an audience. Remind students that they use personal details every day when they are speaking or sharing stories with friends. Have students read the article.

Discussion Prompts

- Even though personal letters can be chatty and informal, do you think the best letters are dashed off or carefully conceived and written? Why?
- How can personal writing help you make new discoveries about yourself, your life, and your heritage?
- Sandra Cisneros ends her letter with a Spanish phrase *un abrazo fuerte, fuerte,* which literally means "a big hug, strong, strong." What original phrases could you substitute for the commonly used *love* or *sincerely*? What would be lost if Cisneros concluded her letter with a more standard closing?

Cultural Connections

Making New Discoveries

Sandra Cisneros calls herself a "migrant professor," referring to the migrant field workers who share her Hispanic heritage. In her writing Cisneros draws upon her personal experiences as a Mexican American growing up in the United States. By writing about these experiences, she makes new discoveries about her life and her culture.

Teach

Discussion Prompts

- Cisneros says, ". . . you can start a letter from whatever comes into your head." What are some good ways to get ideas to come into your head?
- Why do you think Cisneros believes that letter writing more accurately reflects her life than any other kind of writing, including journal writing?
- How can letter writing reveal to you hidden aspects of yourself?
- What do you think Cisneros means when she says that she uses letter writing as a "'runway' to the creative writing process"?

Additional Resources

 *Writing Process Transparencies* 1
 *Writing in the Real World,* pp. 1–4
 *Cooperative Learning Activities*
Thinking and Study Skills, p. 21

Assess

Analyzing the Media Connection

1. Cisneros starts her letter in a friendly way by quoting Winnie the Pooh on the weather.
2. ". . . in the American library in Sarajevo, across from the famous river where the archduke was shot that started a world war."
3. Cisneros provides sharp images of the wind over the mesas ("snapping dust and terrifying trees").

Drafting

Fresh Discoveries

When you write a letter to a dear friend, says Cisneros, "You are blessing your recipient with your confidence, allowing [her or him] to follow your inner meanderings and showing a part of you that perhaps no one else has seen."

Cisneros had recently moved to New Mexico when she began her letter to Gwendolyn Brooks. "When I get to a new place, I like to sift through the events that are affecting me. I don't know how I feel about them until I write letters. Now, [people] talk about the sky in New Mexico, but they never mention the wind. The wind here just rolls out and bangs porch doors open. I've never seen anything like it."

Cisneros often revises her letters.

So Cisneros opened her letter to Gwendolyn Brooks by talking about the wind in New Mexico. As Cisneros says, "People don't realize that you can start a letter from whatever comes into your head."

In the course of drafting a letter, Cisneros may discover deeper, hidden aspects of herself. She calls letter writing her "way of meditating, of listening inside my heart to how I'm being affected by the outside world. The heart of who you are comes out when you truly write."

This writer considers her letters to be a much more accurate reflection of her life than any other kind of record, including her journal, which she uses primarily as a place to write "shorthand" notes to herself.

Cisneros says, "In my letters, I can plunge right into that deeper level where my poems come from. Unless you talk for a very long time to someone you know very well, you can't reach that level. I often surprise myself by what I pull up. Then I make copies of my letters and they become longer journal entries."

Revising/Editing

Runways

Although Cisneros often writes her drafts by hand, she says, "Then I need to get to a typewriter, I need to see it typed to do the editing."

Even after she mails a letter, Cisneros keeps marking the copy she makes for herself. She says she often uses a letter as a "runway" to the creative writing process.

She says, "Sometimes I'll go through copies of my letters and I'll underline with a marker some nugget I'm going to save to reuse. When I'm stuck with a story, I might go through all my old letters and just read. I'll ask, 'Where can I put this?' Sometimes I start by writing a letter and then realize I've got a story. Other times, as I'm writing a story, I'll have a character rant or rave or whine or howl or laugh or swoon, and I'll realize that was really a letter to someone, but it's not going to get sent and it doesn't matter."

She continues, "I might use part of this letter to Gwendolyn Brooks in an essay that would include the anecdote of the cherry stain. What this letter particularly sparked for me was how I would like [to teach] the book *Maud Martha* in a course."

interNET CONNECTION

Using Community Resources

Encourage students who do not have access to a computer with a modem at home or in school to use the equipment available at many local libraries. Students can use the Internet to write and send personal e-mail letters to people in other parts of the country or world who share a common interest, hobby, or talent. Students may want to copy "nuggets" from their letters with word processing software and paste them into their journals for future writing projects.

Examining Writing in the Real World

Analyzing the Media Connection

Discuss these questions about the letter on page 5.

1. How does Cisneros's language signal that she is writing a friendly letter rather than a formal one?
2. What words does Cisneros use to place the reader by the river in Sarajevo?
3. How does Cisneros's language create a vivid sense of the place where she currently lives?
4. What images in her letter might contribute to a story Cisneros might later write?
5. How well do you think Sandra Cisneros knows Gwendolyn Brooks? Use evidence in the letter to support your answer.

Analyzing a Writer's Process

Discuss these questions about Sandra Cisneros's writing process.

1. What inspired Cisneros to write to Gwendolyn Brooks?
2. How might Cisneros's choice of writing materials influence her writing process? Would the letter be the same if she did all of the writing on her computer?
3. In what way does Cisneros feel that writing a personal letter helps her learn about herself?
4. How does Cisneros use her letters as a source of ideas for her other writing?
5. In her letter to Gwendolyn Brooks, what details does Cisneros include that help you understand her feelings?

GrammarLink

Use subordinate clauses to create variety in sentence structure.

A **subordinate clause** has a subject and a predicate, but it cannot stand alone as a sentence. It must be attached to a main clause to make sense.

I am in my pajamas ***though it's past mid-day. . . .***

Use each subordinate clause below in a sentence. Start by thinking whom or what the clause might describe.

1. who moved away last year
2. after I had finished supper
3. although I have a desk in my room
4. before I was halfway through
5. when I get a chance

See Lesson 13.2, page 540.

Personal Writing

4. Answers will vary. Possible answers: [wind] "snapping dust and terrifying trees;" a cherry-stained book page; "some years dipped low and some reeled to high heaven"
5. Answers will vary. Students may comment that Cisneros knows Brooks well enough to share her feelings in a long informal letter, yet she also shows respectful admiration of the older writer.

Analyzing a Writer's Process

1. Cisneros admired one of Brooks' books, *Maud Martha,* and wanted to tell the author how much it meant to her.
2. Writing on "pretty paper . . . with texture" may inspire her to write a more personal letter. Students may suggest that letters composed on the computer are more impersonal and less poetic.
3. She discovers thoughts and feelings that she hadn't realized before.
4. Cisneros goes through copies of her letters and underlines images or characters that she might use in a story or poem.
5. Answers will vary. Possible answers: "I like . . . to continue dreaming on paper when I am awake"; "my heart gave a little jump too because the book wasn't mine."

Reteaching

Remind students that they can use details about what they hear, smell, feel, or taste to begin a letter. They can begin with an image or a description that expresses their state of mind.

Enrichment

Ask students to select material from their letters that they can use in a short story, poem, or essay. If possible, have students post their contributions to a class Web site, where material can be downloaded, performed, or discussed in small groups.

Close

Have students discuss how to use the process described in the Media Connection to write a letter to a close friend.

GrammarLink

Answers

Answers will vary, but suggestions are given below.

1. My best friend, who moved . . .
2. . . . supper, I did my homework.
3. . . . my room, I often do my homework at the kitchen table.
4. . . . through, my father wanted to set the table for dinner.
5. . . . a chance, I'm going to organize my desk so I can use it again.

Focus

Lesson Overview

Objectives

- To understand and appreciate how self-discovery can happen in many ways
- To learn how to get started writing about yourself by asking personal questions
- To generate personal writing using one's own experiences, feelings, memories, observations, and reactions

Skills

- asking questions; learning by writing; writing about yourself

Critical Thinking

- recalling; identifying; analyzing; summarizing; defining and clarifying

Listening and Speaking

- note taking; discussing; questioning

Bellringer

Daily Language Activity

When students enter the classroom, have this assignment on the board: *List several characteristics that you think are special about yourself. You may include heritage, personality traits, interests, or other notable facts of your own choosing.*

Grammar Link to the Bellringer

Ask students to rewrite their Bellringer lists as paragraphs. Check each paragraph for inappropriate verb-tense changes.

See also *Daily Language Practice*

Motivating Activity

Discuss students' responses to the Bellringer activity. Tell students that personal writing does not have to "follow the rules" with complete sentences and correct punctuation. It is often better to just start writing by putting down anything that comes to mind. Remind students to focus on the topic—in this case themselves—rather than on writing correctly.

Personal Writing

LESSON 1.1

Writing to Discover

Self-discovery can happen in many ways. Former Beatle John Lennon expressed his identity in this self-portrait. N. Scott Momaday, in the model below, writes to discover something about himself.

John Lennon, *Self Portrait*

Literature Model

Oh I feel so dumb . . . I don't know how to be a Kiowa Indian my grandmother lives in a house . . . only it doesn't have lights . . . and you have to carry wood in from the wood pile . . . but that isn't what makes it Indian its my grandma the way she is the way she looks her hair in braids the clothes somehow yes the way she talks she doesn't speak English so well . . . wait I know why it's an Indian house because . . . there is Indian stuff all around blankets and shawls bows and arrows everyone there . . . talks Kiowa and the old people wear Indian clothes . . . and there is laughing Indians laugh a lot and they sing oh yes they love to sing . . . there are drums too and it goes on through the night *that's* Indian . . .

N. Scott Momaday, *The Names*

What uncertainties does Momaday give voice to here? In your opinion, for whom is this written?

Recalling specific details of sights and sounds helps Momaday deal with his uncertainties.

Resource Manager

Planning Resources

- *Lesson Plans*

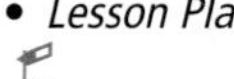

Transparencies

- *Bellringer*
- *Daily Language Practice*
- *Fine Art* 1–6
- *Two-Minute Skill Drill*
- *Writing Process* 1

Other Print Resources

- *Composition Enrichment,* p. 1
- *Composition Practice,* p. 1
- *Composition Reteaching,* p. 1
- *Cooperative Learning Activities,* pp. 5–8
- *Listening and Speaking Activities,* pp. 9, 19, 20
- *Thinking and Study Skills,* pp. 13, 21
- *Writing Across the Curriculum*
- *Writing Assessment and Evaluation Rubrics*

Learn by Writing

Asking personal questions is one way to get started writing about yourself. In the model on page 8, Momaday probably began with questions about his Kiowa heritage and then found answers as he recalled experiences, feelings, and observations. You can review elements of your own life to learn more about who you are, as the diagram below illustrates.

Personal Questions Chart (with Sample Answers)

Q. What are some of the central things that make me *me?*
A. African American, teenager, oldest kid in my family, member of soccer team

Q. How do I feel as a typical day goes on?
A. I usually feel pretty good; too much homework gets me down, though. I feel warm and secure at home but free and more myself with my friends.

Q. What kinds of lessons have I learned recently?
A. I've learned about friendship, about dating, and about being a good sport in soccer.

Q. What do I enjoy most?
A. I like hanging out with friends, playing soccer, watching TV, and, believe it or not, my world history class.

Some sources for personal writing

Observations Our dog, Sparky, is getting pretty old. He sleeps most of the time and doesn't play catch anymore.

Reactions I get so angry when Mom expects me to babysit my little sister, Mandy.

Memories Oatmeal always reminds me of breakfasts with my grandmother.

Experiences The first time Alissa and I went downtown alone, we got lost.

Feelings I feel completely in control when I strike out a batter.

Journal Writing

John Lennon's self-portrait on page 8 emphasizes three features: his hair, his nose, and his eyeglasses. In your journal, draw a simple sketch of yourself. Emphasize three simple attributes, either physical characteristics or personality traits. Then write to answer this question: What does your self-portrait reveal about who you are?

Teach

Using the Model

Momaday's writing in the model on page 8 is introspective, and he uses a free-flowing style that many students may find difficult. You may wish to read the model aloud to help students understand it. **L2**

Cooperative Learning

Ask students to create a cluster diagram like the one shown on this page, filling in their own observations, memories, experiences, feelings, and reactions. Then divide the class into small groups for a round-robin activity. Have each student take turns sharing his or her diagram with group members. The group should then discuss how the student could use the items in the diagram to start writing. **L2**

Journal Writing Tip

Identifying Attributes Before they begin the journal writing activity, remind students that an attribute can refer to a physical characteristic, a personality trait, or both at the same time. For example, a lopsided grin might indicate a missing front tooth and a cheerful disposition. Encourage students to have fun determining their attributes.

Teach

Using the Model

Point out that McCann is very honest about her feelings. Also, by using words like "yeehah," she makes her writing sound authentic. **L2**

Getting Started

For a free-association word game, select a word or phrase that will have some personal meaning to students (such as *family, homework, mall*), and invite them to talk about whatever personal responses the word triggers. When you end the game, have students freewrite ideas for five minutes. **L3**

Two-Minute Skill Drill

List these verbs on the board. Have students write the past tense of each.

come	go	like
live	is	move
run	get	am
bring	have	think

See also *Two-Minute Skill Drill Transparency 1.1*

Additional Resources

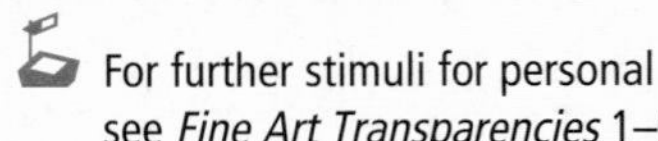

For further stimuli for personal writing, see *Fine Art Transparencies* 1–6.

- *Writing Process Transparencies* 1
- *Writing Across the Curriculum*
- *Cooperative Learning Activities*
- *Thinking and Study Skills*, pp. 13, 21
- *Listening and Speaking Activities*, pp. 9, 19, 20

Write About Yourself

Whatever your sources, often the easiest way to begin personal writing is simply to begin—let your thoughts run free and write whatever comes to mind. Don't worry about spelling or grammar. Set a definite time limit—say, ten minutes—and keep writing until the time is up. If you get stuck, write anything, even "I'm stuck!" Just keep going. Before you know it, a word will spark a memory or another idea, and you'll be on your way. In the process, you may clarify your thoughts and even discover something about yourself. The chart below shows how this might happen.

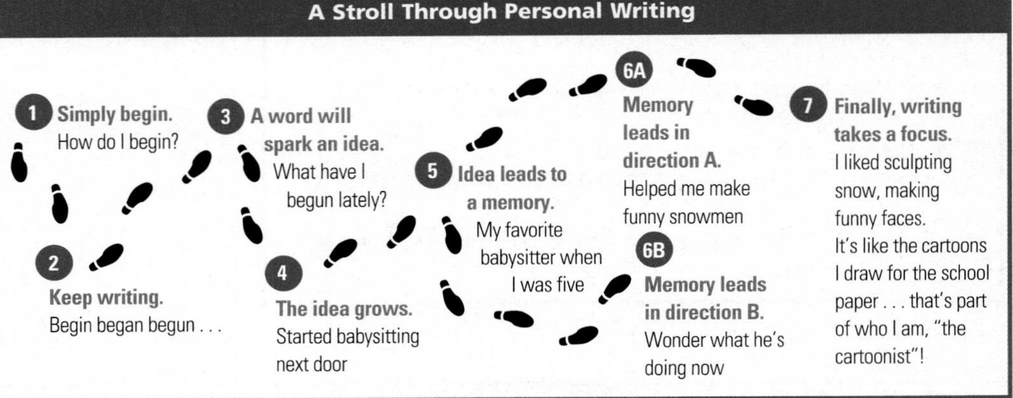

A Stroll Through Personal Writing
1 Simply begin. How do I begin?
2 Keep writing. Begin began begun . . .
3 A word will spark an idea. What have I begun lately?
4 The idea grows. Started babysitting next door
5 Idea leads to a memory. My favorite babysitter when I was five
6A Memory leads in direction A. Helped me make funny snowmen
6B Memory leads in direction B. Wonder what he's doing now
7 Finally, writing takes a focus. I liked sculpting snow, making funny faces. It's like the cartoons I draw for the school paper . . . that's part of who I am, "the cartoonist"!

Your experiences, feelings, memories, observations, and reactions are your best sources for personal writing. See what student Vallery McCann learned about herself.

How would you assess the honesty of Vallery's writing? Does it sound authentic?

This journal entry helps Vallery think about plans for her future. What plans might you write about?

Student Model

Well, today is a milestone in my life. Yeehah. Three years ago today I was ending an old life and beginning a new one, & I didn't even know it. The freedom I have today is incredible. I am not ashamed of me. I have gotten to know myself. I was thinking on my way to school today maybe the difference between a romantic relationship & a friendship is that in a friendship the only commitment is unconditional love. I'm getting ready to graduate. Life looms ahead. I'm finding myself believing in education. I want to teach and give that opportunity of freedom to others. So today is my third anniversary drug free! I will not back down! I am free!

Vallery McCann, Hamilton Heights High School, Arcadia, Indiana

Meeting Individual Needs: English Language Learners

Using Visual Prompts

Encourage students to bring in or collect family photos as a way to stimulate ideas for their writing. Partners might tell each other about memories triggered by the photos, writing down key words in English or their primary language. These key words can serve as nuclei for writing projects.

1.1 Writing Activities

Freewrite About Yourself

Choose one of the following opening phrases, or use one of your own, to write about freely for five minutes. Remember, keep writing. If you get stuck, repeat a word over and over until something else comes to you.

- If only I could . . .
- The one word that best describes me is . . .
- I would never give up my . . .
- No one knows that I . . .
- The one thing I would like to change about myself is . . .

PURPOSE Self-discovery
AUDIENCE Yourself
LENGTH 3–4 paragraphs

WRITING RUBRICS To freewrite effectively about yourself, you should

- let your thoughts run free and simply begin writing whatever comes to mind
- write without stopping to reread, rephrase, or rethink what you are saying
- set a definite time limit

Cross-Curricular Activity

SOCIAL STUDIES Spend several minutes writing a paragraph or two about your community. Include answers to some of the following questions:

- How does the size of your community affect you?
- Do your friends and neighbors share a similar cultural background, or is the neighborhood very mixed? What have you learned from the neighborhood's culture?
- How have the schools and other institutions in your neighborhood affected you?
- How do the characteristics of your community contribute to making you the kind of person you are?

Grammar*Link*

When you write, avoid shifting verb tenses for no reason.

Revise each sentence below to make the verb tenses consistent.

1. We went to the movies yesterday, and we see a double feature.
2. Sam's birthday party will be next week; it was a bowling party.
3. That school bus goes along Main Street and turned right on Linden.
4. When I got to school, I meet my friend before science class.
5. Pat likes this book because she enjoyed the author's style.

See Lesson 15.6, page 594.

Personal Writing

LOG ON **Writing** Online | For more writing and grammar practice, go to glencoe.com and enter QuickPass code WC97727p1.

Assess

Evaluation Rubrics

Freewrite About Yourself

Use the following criteria to evaluate your students' writing:

- Does the writing contain details that are personally relevant to the student's life?
- Does the writing sound natural?

Cross-Curricular Activity

Use these criteria when evaluating your students' writing. The writing should

- contain the student's own observations, memories, experiences, feelings, and reactions.
- contain some facts about the size, population, and nature of the community.
- draw conclusions about what the student learned from growing up in his or her community.

See also *Writing Assessment & Evaluation Rubrics*

Viewing and Representing

Evaluate student work on the following: creativity in describing self; appropriately illustrated map; link between map and writing.

Reteaching

Composition Reteaching, p.1.

Enrichment

Composition Enrichment, p.1.

Close

Invite students to tell what they have discovered about themselves during the writing they did in this lesson. Encourage students to share their thoughts with the class.

Grammar*Link*

Answers

1. saw
2. will be
3. turns (*or* went)
4. met (*or* get)
5. liked (*or* enjoys)

Avoiding Tense Shifts Encourage students to review their writing in the Writing Activities. Have them check each sentence for inappropriate shifts in verb tense.

Viewing the Art

John Lennon, *Self Portrait,* 1968
John Lennon (1940–1980) helped compose most of the Beatles' popular lyrics. Many reflected the group's own experiences and struck a chord with young people. The self-portrait on page 8 appears on the cover of the soundtrack album for *Imagine,* a biographical film of Lennon's life.

Focus

Lesson Overview

Objectives

- To define the purpose of a writer's journal
- To identify different kinds of journals such as diaries, learning logs, scrapbooks, or writer's journals
- To learn how to keep a journal

Skills

- generating ideas for journals; evaluating approaches

Critical Thinking

- evaluating ideas; making inferences; analyzing experiences

Listening and Speaking

- discussing; evaluating; questioning

Bellringer

Daily Language Activity

When students enter the classroom, have this assignment on the board: *List reasons a person might keep a journal.*

Grammar Link to the Bellringer

Discuss the reasons students wrote for keeping a journal. (The most common reason may be to record daily events.) Ask students to correct the pronouns in the following sentences that describe a daily event.

Dad and me went to the store today.
The clerk gave Dad and I a receipt.

See also 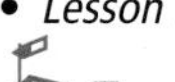 *Daily Language Practice*

Motivating Activity

Explain that in this lesson, students will learn more about keeping journals. Point out that while most journal writers write only for themselves, some journals, such as Anne Frank's, have been published and read widely. Ask students why the public would be interested in reading other people's journals. Ask students whose journals they would like to read.

LESSON 1.2

Keeping a Journal

A writer's journal can be a place to examine feelings, record daily events, or try out new ideas. During World War II, thirteen-year-old Anne Frank and her family were forced to hide in a cramped attic to avoid capture by the Nazis. Frank's journal became her refuge during those terrible times.

Notice that Frank dates the journal entry.

Frank is first inspired to write by thoughts of sensory details—"cold on their faces," "smelling fresh air."

Frank uses this brief journal entry to ask important questions, give herself advice, and vent her feelings. In your opinion, what is the value of such expression?

Literature Model

Friday, 24 December 1943

When someone comes in from outside, with the wind in their clothes and the cold on their faces, then I could bury my head in the blankets to stop myself thinking: "When will we be granted the privilege of smelling fresh air?" And because I must not bury my head in the blankets, but the reverse—I must keep my head high and be brave, the thoughts will come not once, but oh, countless times. Believe me, if you have been shut up for a year and a half, it can get too much for you some days . . . . Cycling, dancing, whistling, looking out into the world, feeling young, to know that I'm free—that's what I long for; still, I mustn't show it. . . . I sometimes ask myself, "Would anyone, either Jew or non-Jew understand this about me, that I am simply a young girl badly in need of some rollicking fun?" I don't know, and I couldn't talk about it to anyone.

from *Anne Frank: The Diary of a Young Girl*

Why Keep a Journal?

Keeping a journal is like thinking out loud—on paper. In your journal, you might record daily events, but you also are free to follow an idea wherever it leads. By writing about your experiences, reactions, and observations, you can make discoveries about yourself and the world.

Resource Manager

Planning Resources

- *Lesson Plans*

Transparencies

- *Bellringer*
- *Daily Language Practice*
- *Fine Art* 1–6
- *Two-Minute Skill Drill*
- *Writing Process* 1

Other Print Resources

- *Composition Enrichment,* p. 2
- *Composition Practice,* p. 2
- *Composition Reteaching,* p. 2
- *Cooperative Learning Activities,* pp. 5–8
- *Listening and Speaking Activities,* pp. 9, 19, 20
- *Thinking and Study Skills,* pp. 10, 29, 30
- *Writing Across the Curriculum*
- *Writing Assessment and Evaluation Rubrics*

Student Model

It just dawned on me! In only five days my sister will be nineteen years old! The last year of teen-agism. What happened to the little girl who would play Barbies with me, to my best friend who had been by my side for the last sixteen years? I miss her so much! Growing up can really hurt. It really is painful how everyone must part and make their separate way.

Kimberly Daniel, Jefferson Davis High School, Montgomery, Alabama

Freewriting can go wherever the writer's mind goes. Notice how Kimberly even makes up a word—"teen-agism."

Kimberly expresses an important lesson about growing up and moving on. Perhaps she'll develop this idea more fully later.

You can choose from a number of different kinds of journals, each with a different purpose. A diary, for example, is a personal record of daily events that the writer doesn't usually plan to share. A student may also keep a learning log to record thoughts and impressions of classes.

A journal can also serve as a writer's journal—that is, a source for ideas to inspire your writing. These might be brief notes on writing ideas, a collection of words or phrases, even news clippings, jokes, or photographs. Here's a story idea that came from one student's journal.

Student Model

I was thinking about something rather funny the other day. I wondered what it would be like to have grown old overnight and pass up all the hardships of life (develop this as the opening of my story). I would already be retired and I wouldn't have to worry about finishing school or getting a job . . . I would be able to go places and do things without having to worry about getting somewhere on time (give examples and go into more detail) . . . (All of this could be developed into a story about a boy who has grown old and finds out . . . that he has missed the best parts of life.)

Matthew Porter, Jefferson Davis High School, Montgomery, Alabama

Do you find Matthew's idea for writing interesting?

Notice how Matthew uses his writing to come up with a concrete idea for a story. This can work for you too.

Journal Writing

Compare the two student models on this page. What do they reveal about their writers? What kinds of materials are included in each? Record your reactions in your own journal.

Teach

Using the Models

Ask students how keeping a diary might help a person cope with stress and problems. In Anne Frank's case, her journal was her only tool to cope with the loss of her personal freedom.

Tell the class that sometimes reading another person's ideas can spark the reader's own. Ask students to suggest some variations on either Kimberly's or Matthew's ideas. **L2**

Generating Ideas

Remind students that it is not uncommon to have trouble coming up with an idea for a writing assignment. Initiate a discussion about where to look for ideas. Then point out the value of reading other people's writing in order to find writing ideas of one's own. **L2**

Two-Minute Skill Drill

Write this on the board: Complete the sentences with *I, me,* or *my.*

It was a gift for you and____.

Sara and____went camping.

She gave____her old backpack.

See also *Two-Minute Skill Drill Transparency 1.2*

Journal Writing Tip

Comparing Remind students to consider each writer's goal and how the goal will affect what is included in the writing. A goal can reveal as much about a writer as the subject matter itself.

Teach

Keeping a Scrapbook

A scrapbook is another form of journal keeping. Students who are visually-oriented may like the idea of collecting photos, ticket stubs, and programs from sports events or concerts, as well as the postcards and letters they receive. For inclusion in the scrapbook, students could write a brief description of each item and a note about its meaning. **L2**

Exploring Different Forms of Expression

Challenge students to experiment with different forms of expression when they write in their journals. They might find that doodles, cartoons, poetry, foreign phrases, or even mathematical equations will help them express their ideas. **L3**

Additional Resources

For further stimuli for journal writing, see *Fine Art Transparencies* 1–6.

Writing Process Transparencies 1

Writing Across the Curriculum

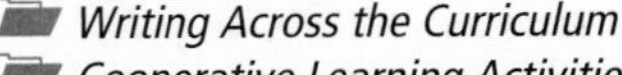

Cooperative Learning Activities

Thinking and Study Skills, pp. 10, 29–30

Listening and Speaking Activities, pp. 9, 19, 20

Composition Practice, p. 2

How Do You Keep a Journal?

Journal writing has no set rules. You just need to find a system that works for you. Here are some tips that might help you get started on your own journal.

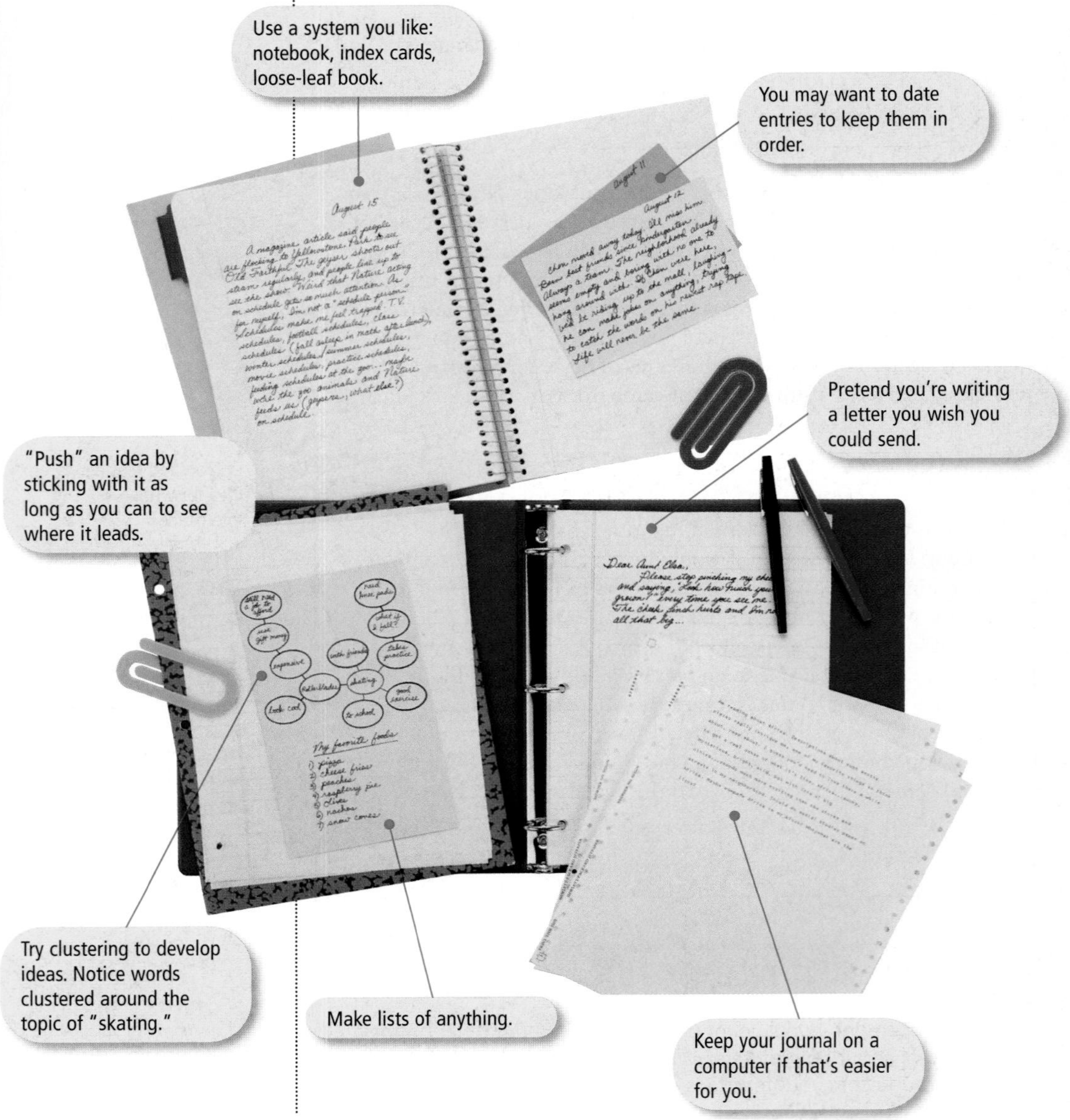

Use a system you like: notebook, index cards, loose-leaf book.

You may want to date entries to keep them in order.

Pretend you're writing a letter you wish you could send.

"Push" an idea by sticking with it as long as you can to see where it leads.

Try clustering to develop ideas. Notice words clustered around the topic of "skating."

Make lists of anything.

Keep your journal on a computer if that's easier for you.

MEETING INDIVIDUAL NEEDS

English Language Learners

Keeping a Journal

Students who are learning English may feel overwhelmed by the prospect of keeping a journal in English. Tell these students that if they have difficulty expressing a particular emotion or idea in English, they should feel free to express it in their primary language. Later, after they have become more comfortable or proficient in English, they might review their journals and try to translate their writing into English.

1.2 Writing Activities

Write a Journal Entry

Look through this book to find a painting that interests you. Create a journal entry based on that painting. Write, for example, about what you see in the painting. Does it evoke any memories? Any feelings or ideas for writing?

PURPOSE To free-associate from a painting
AUDIENCE Yourself
LENGTH 1–3 paragraphs

WRITING RUBRICS To write an effective journal entry, you should

- let one idea lead to another
- date your entry
- write about experiences, reactions, observations

Listening and Speaking

From a published journal, log, or diary of your choice, select a passage that describes an event that was important to the writer. Read the passage aloud with as much feeling as you can. Record your reading, and replay the passage several times. Then, in your journal, describe your impressions of the reading. Consider the following questions:

- How did the writer convey the importance of the experience?
- How well were you able to interpret the passage as the author might have?
- If you were an actor playing the writer, would the audience understand the meaning and importance of the passage?

Grammar*Link*

In personal writing, be sure you use the correct pronoun, *I* or *me*, in a compound subject or object.

Use *I* or *me* to complete each sentence below.

1. Dan and _____ are working on a history project.
2. His grandfather has sent some old family documents for him and _____ to use.
3. My sister drove Dan and _____ to the main library on Saturday.
4. He and _____ each used the computer and microfiche to locate information.
5. Our adviser told Dan and _____ that we can exhibit our project in the media center.

See Lesson 17.1, page 633.

Writing Online | For more writing and grammar practice, go to **glencoe.com** and enter QuickPass code WC97727p1.

Assess

Evaluation Rubrics

Write a Journal Entry

Use these criteria when evaluating your students' journal entries:

- Is the entry based on the painting?
- Does one idea lead to another?
- Does it convey personal reactions?
- Does it contain possible writing ideas?

See also *Writing Assessment & Evaluation Rubrics*

Cross-Curricular Activity

Travel may include local journeys or journeys of the mind. If you evaluate or review students' journal writing, look for evidence that students learned something about themselves from the travel experience.

Reteaching

Composition Reteaching, p. 2

Enrichment

Composition Enrichment, p. 2

Fine Art Transparencies 1–6

Close

Have students discuss the differences and similarities between writing in a personal journal and writing in a learning log or writer's journal. When would they want to write in each kind of journal?

Grammar*Link*

Answers

1. I
2. me
3. me
4. I
5. me

Focus

Lesson Overview

Objectives

- To define the purpose of a personal essay
- To learn how to develop a personal essay by selecting an appropriate topic and composing a thesis statement
- To learn how to make a personal essay come to life by using vivid details, effective word choice, and interesting examples

Skills

- selecting a topic; developing a thesis statement; making an essay interesting

Critical Thinking

- analyzing information; defining and clarifying ideas; stating a main idea

Listening and Speaking

- discussing; interviewing; note taking; evaluating; questioning

Bellringer

Daily Language Activity

When students enter the classroom, have this assignment on the board: *List five things or topics that are important to you in some way.*

Grammar Link to the Bellringer

Have students use the five topics from the Bellringer activity in sentences and underline the verbs. Then have them replace each underlined verb, if possible, with a more vivid or expressive verb.

See also *Daily Language Practice*

Motivating Activity

Discuss students' responses to the Bellringer activity. Then explain that in this lesson they will learn to write a personal essay on a topic of interest to them. The essay will be about something they have knowledge of, but not about them personally.

LESSON 1.3

Writing a Personal Essay

A personal essay offers opinions about something the writer has experienced or takes a personal interest in. In the model below, Robert Fulghum tells why he thinks certain household experiences are crucial to growing up.

Literature Model

After the dishes are washed and the sink rinsed out, there remains in the strainer at the bottom of the sink what I will call, momentarily, some "stuff." A rational, intelligent, objective person would say that this is simply a mixture of food particles too big to go down the drain. . . . But any teenager who has been dragooned into washing dishes knows this explanation is a lie. That stuff in the bottom of the strainer is toxic waste—deadly poison—a danger to health. In other words, about as icky as icky gets.

One of the . . . reasons I had . . . respect for my mother when I was thirteen was because she would reach into the sink with her bare hands—BARE HANDS—and pick up that lethal gunk and drop it into the garbage. . . .

Never mind what any parent or objective adult might tell me, I knew that the stuff in the sink drainer was lethal. . . .

But now. Now, I am a grown-up. And have been for some time. And I imagine making a speech to a high school graduating class. . . . I would give them this list of things that grown-ups do: clean the sink strainer . . . clean up the floor when the baby throws strained spinach, clean ovens and grease traps and roasting pans. . . . I'd tell the graduates that when they can do these things, they will be adults. Some of the students might not want to go on at this point. But they may as well face the truth . . . Being an adult *is* dirty work.

But someone has to do it.

Robert Fulghum, *It Was on Fire When I Lay Down on It*

What effect do words like "toxic" and "icky" have on you? What other words contribute to Fulghum's vivid, humorous picture?

Why do you suppose Fulghum saved the main point for the end of his piece?

Resource Manager

Planning Resources

- *Lesson Plans*

Transparencies

- *Bellringer*
- *Daily Language Practice*
- *Fine Art* 1–6
- *Two-Minute Skill Drill*
- *Writing Process* 1

Other Print Resources

- *Composition Enrichment, p. 3*
- *Composition Practice,* p. 3
- *Composition Reteaching,* p. 3
- *Cooperative Learning Activities,* pp. 5–8
- *Listening and Speaking Activities,* pp. 9, 19, 20
- *Thinking and Study Skills,* pp. 12, 21
- *Writing Across the Curriculum*
- *Writing Assessment and Evaluation Rubrics*

What Is a Personal Essay?

A personal essay expresses your viewpoint about a subject you have experienced—a subject other than yourself. The personal essay is not directly about you. You may write your personal essay in a traditional essay format—introduction, body paragraphs, and conclusion—or you may write it in a freer way, following your own train of thought. As you write your essay, you can follow Fulghum's example and use humorous anecdotes and exaggeration to express your views.

What Can I Write About?

If you have an assigned topic, explore the aspects that especially intrigue you. Otherwise, write about whatever interests you.

Select a Topic Your journal, newspapers, and magazines are sources of essay ideas. Here are two other ways to find a topic.

Freewriting

Write freely to find a topic. Write on whatever we want...write on write on write on...right on! Old slang phrase. Not totally awesome or even groovy--more tubular? Slang words mean different things. "Bad" means good (drove Dad crazy with that one!) Where did all those words come from? (requires research) What does slang do for me? Why slang? with friends? with adults? It'S LANG uage isn't it? TOPIC!

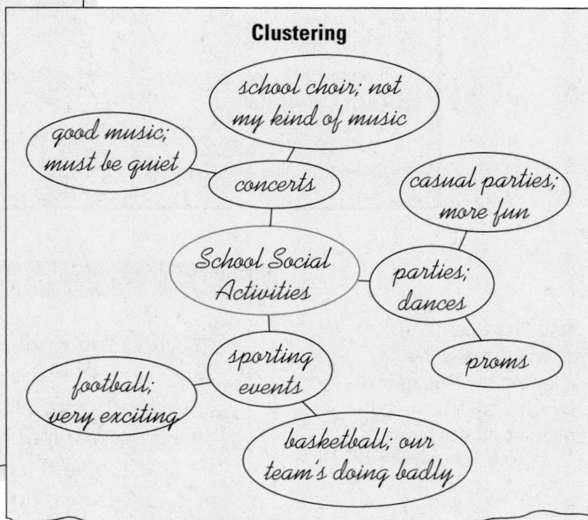

Journal Writing

In your journal, try creating a cluster diagram to help you think of an essay topic. Begin with a base word about something that interests you and see where you end up. If you need help getting started, look around the room, and write the name of an object.

Teach

Using the Model

Ask students what words in the model on page 16 contribute to the mock-serious view Fulghum has of what it means to be an adult (*stuff, dragooned,* and *BARE HANDS*). Point out that the use of quotation marks and capital letters contributes to his humorous tone.

By placing his thesis last, Fulghum leaves the reader thinking about it. Let students know that this tactic works well here because his point is a serious one that might get lost in his humorous presentation. **L2**

Cooperative Learning

Have each student work with a partner. While one student talks about an interesting topic, the other should listen and ask questions to clarify the speaker's views. Allow the partners five or ten minutes to talk, and then ask them to exchange roles. **L2**

Two-Minute Skill Drill

List these verbs on the board and have students write a more vivid verb for each.

go	walk	think
run	look	

See also *Two-Minute Skill Drill Transparency 1.3*

Journal Writing Tip

Representing Before students begin representing their ideas on the cluster diagram, remind them to leave plenty of space around their central topic so that they can explore more offbeat avenues of thought.

Teach

Using the Model

Ask students to identify some of the vivid details Keshia White uses to make her essay come to life. See if students can suggest other approaches they might use to further enliven the essay. Then ask them if Keshia's essay would be as interesting if she had made her main point at the beginning. **L2**

Choosing a Topic

Students who have trouble with open-ended choices may have difficulty finding an essay topic. Point out that topics can often be found in simple ways, such as by looking at photographs or talking to someone. You may want to suggest that students choose one or two subjects listed in the cluster diagram they created in their journals. **L2**

Additional Resources

For further stimuli for personal writing, see *Fine Art Transparencies* 1–6.

Writing Process Transparencies 1
Writing Across the Curriculum
Cooperative Learning Activities
Thinking and Study Skills, pp. 12, 21
Listening and Speaking Activities, pp. 9, 19, 20
Composition Practice, p. 3

Compose a Thesis Statement A thesis statement conveys your main point. It may also explain how you intend to support your main point. To develop a thesis statement, ask yourself questions about your topic. Focus on a specific aspect of the subject; then condense the subject to a basic statement. Consider Fulghum's thesis statement: "Being an adult *is* dirty work."

How Can I Make My Essay Come to Life?

By letting your enthusiasm for your topic influence your choice of words and details, you can make your essay lively. Support your thesis statement with vivid details and examples. Use these tips and model.

How Can I Make My Essay Interesting?

TIP	EXAMPLE
Answer offbeat questions about the subject.	What might views on this subject have been a hundred years ago? A hundred years ago, people might have thought that . . .
Include personal anecdotes.	I won my first carnival goldfish when . . .
Pretend to be a reporter covering a news story.	We are at the local video arcade to . . .
Compare your topic to something familiar and fun.	Doing algebra problems is a little like working out crossword puzzles.

Notice how Keshia expresses herself by following her own train of thought instead of using traditional essay form.

Like Fulghum, Keshia presents her main point at the end of the essay.

Student Model

Don't You Know Me?
Our smiles are simple smiles. As we both sit down next to each other we realize that smile that was shared will probably be the first and last between us. Even though we go to the same school and have the same classes, we're two different people with two different images to uphold. Hers is the jet set world of witty conversation, the latest styles, and dates. The purse, the walk, and the friends she keeps tell her lifestyle and identity. The buzzing in the halls, the shared glances between them let you know you are the outsider looking in.

As we step off the bus we put on our "masks" for the stage we'll be on. One's mask is a little bit brighter, the other one's dull, but each a character just the same.

Keshia White, Hyde Park Career Academy, Chicago, Illinois

English Language Learners

Choosing Words

Students who are less proficient in English may need extra assistance in choosing precise, vivid verbs. You might, at this point, teach them to use a thesaurus. Provide some common verbs (such as *like, want, walk, go*). Ask students to think of more specific substitutes for each. Then have them look up each word in a thesaurus to see what additional substitute words they can find. Remind students that they should use these substitutes in their writing only if they have a firm understanding of the words' definitions. A thesaurus does not take the place of a dictionary but can be used in conjunction with one.

1.3 Writing Activities

Write a Personal Essay

On a topic of your own choosing, write a personal essay that could be published in your school or hometown newspaper.

PURPOSE To express your viewpoint on a topic that interests you
AUDIENCE Adult and teenage newspaper readers
LENGTH 3–4 paragraphs

WRITING RUBRICS To write an effective personal essay, you should

- include a thesis statement
- use vivid details and examples
- compose complete and logical sentences

Viewing and Representing

In a small group, study and discuss the painting below. Consider how the same artist might have painted your street if he had used you or your neighbors as subjects, and write an essay about this topic.

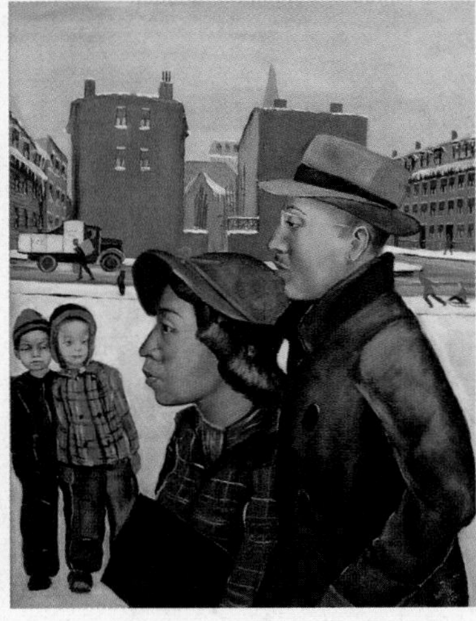

Allan Crite, *Harriet and Leon,* 1941

GrammarLink

Use strong, specific verbs to make your personal writing clear and effective.

In each sentence, replace the general verb with one that is more precise.

1. The student volunteers worked all day at the new community center.
2. Some cleaned floors and windows.
3. Others moved lumber and cinder blocks from the yard into the meeting room.
4. Most of the students like the results of the day's efforts.
5. Only a few spoke about the difficulty of the work.

See Lesson 10.3, pages 452–460.

Cross-Curricular Activity

GOVERNMENT Attend a meeting of the student council, school board, city council, or other local governing body. Obtain a copy of the agenda and use it as a guide to the issues under discussion. Listen to ways in which participants on all sides of the issues frame their arguments. Divide a sheet of paper into two columns. Write statements "for" a position in one column and "against" in the other.

After the meeting, look over your lists. Choose a potential thesis and rewrite it so that you could develop it to reflect your personal approach to the issue.

Writing Online For more writing and grammar practice, go to glencoe.com and enter QuickPass code WC97727p1.

Assess

Evaluation Rubrics

Write a Personal Essay

Use these criteria when evaluating your students' writing:

- Is the thesis statement clear?
- Does the essay express the student's point of view?
- Are the verbs vivid?
- Do personal anecdotes support assertions?

See also *Writing Assessment & Evaluation Rubrics*

Viewing and Representing

Evaluate the essay on the following: creativity; vivid verbs; coherence in overall impression; support of the main point

Reteaching

Composition Reteaching, p. 3

Enrichment

Composition Enrichment, p. 3

Fine Art Transparencies 1–6

Close

Discuss the power of language. In 1989, author Salman Rushdie was forced into hiding by death threats he received following the publication of his novel *The Satanic Verses.* Ask students if they think writers are responsible for their readers' reactions to their words. Should censorship laws be designed to protect readers or writers?

GrammarLink

Answers

Answers will vary. Suggestions:

1. . . . labored . . .
2. . . . scrubbed . . .
3. . . . hauled . . .
4. . . . are satisfied with . . .
5. . . . complained . . .

Viewing the Art

Allan Crite, *Harriet and Leon,* 1941

Ask students if the painting by African American artist Allan Crite could be said to have a thesis statement. (One interpretation could be that the children are curious about their adult neighbors.) The 35-by-30-inch oil painting hangs in the Boston Anthenaeum.

Focus

Lesson Overview

Objectives

- To define the purpose of an autobiography
- To learn how to obtain autobiographical material from various sources
- To learn two methods for presenting autobiographical material
- To write an autobiographical sketch

Skills

- choosing topics; using details to convey the essence of a personal experience

Critical Thinking

- recalling; classifying; relating

Listening and Speaking

- discussing; listening to an autobiographical sketch

Bellringer

Daily Language Activity

When students enter the classroom, have this assignment on the board: *Write a short paragraph that starts with this phrase:*

My first memory is . . .

Grammar Link to the Bellringer

Ask students to share their paragraphs. Explain that this type of personal writing is called autobiography. Point out that the phrase you wrote on the board is a sentence fragment. Ask students to tell how they turned it into a complete sentence.

See also  *Daily Language Practice*

Motivating Activity

Ask students if they have ever had an experience that changed or somehow influenced the course of their lives. Encourage students to discuss what their experience taught them and how it changed them. Tell students that such an experience could be material for an autobiographical sketch.

Personal Writing

LESSON 1.4

Writing Autobiography

Autobiographies are first-person accounts of important moments in an individual's life. In the model below, Lynn Griffey describes a personal experience.

Student Model

Ever since I was a child, I've been fascinated with space. So in the fall of my junior year my parents sent me to the United States Space Camp. I was so excited; I thought this was going to be the beginning of great things to come. This was my dream come true. I always had dreams of me in space, and I always knew I could do it.

Immediately after I got there, I looked around. I saw how every one of those kids had the same dreams and feelings I had. It was incredible.

After sitting through lecture after lecture, and going through experiment after experiment, I realized that I wasn't sure of my feelings anymore. I knew I was having a great time learning and exploring, but I also knew that I didn't have the same look in my eye that one boy did. He was having more than just a "good time"; he lived to be doing this.

I began feeling guilty because I started thinking of all the money my parents had spent for me to go there. Then I realized they want me to be happy. That's why they spent all the money, to see if this was what I wanted to do for the rest of my life.

I think I learned a lot about myself that week. I discovered that at sixteen it's not necessary to know precisely what the future holds. Maybe I'll still want to be in space some day. However, right now I just want to be sixteen and explore all the exciting careers I have to choose from.

Lynn Griffey,
Hamilton Heights High School, Arcadia, Indiana

Notice how Lynn introduces the subject, setting, and main idea early on. Where do you first sense what might happen? Which words help to create this sense?

Lynn concludes by relating how her experience changed her perception of herself as well as her goals and expectations.

Resource Manager

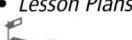

Planning Resources

- *Lesson Plans*

 Transparencies

- *Bellringer*
- *Daily Language Practice*
- *Fine Art* 1–6
- *Two-Minute Skill Drill*
- *Writing Process* 1

Other Print Resources

- *Composition Enrichment,* p. 4
- *Composition Practice,* p. 4
- *Composition Reteaching,* p. 4
- *Cooperative Learning Activities,* pp. 5–8
- *Listening and Speaking Activities,* pp. 9, 19, 20
- *Thinking and Study Skills,* pp. 2, 5, 8
- *Writing Across the Curriculum*
- *Writing Assessment and Evaluation Rubrics*

What Is an Autobiography?

An autobiography is a person's written account of his or her own life—experiences, thoughts, feelings. An autobiographical sketch, like Lynn's, is personal writing about a significant event or period in the writer's life. It should give readers a sense of who the author is, how the author came to be that way, and what the author has experienced.

How Do You Find Autobiographical Material?

Your autobiographical material comes from your life—anything you have done, felt, thought, dreamed, experienced, or learned. We all have mental files of our experiences. Each of us uses a variety of different filing systems. We file events by emotional content—happy, sad, exhilarating. We file them according to the time in our lives they occurred—before school age, during elementary school. We even file them according to the areas in our lives to which they relate—school, family, friends.

To search through your mental files, start by making a list of general categories, or file labels, you might find in each of the filing systems listed below. Then brainstorm, freewrite, or use other prewriting techniques to retrieve some of the specific experiences you have stored in these files. Refer to Lesson 2.2, pages 62–67, for other prewriting techniques.

Your Autobiographical Files

FILING SYSTEM	SAMPLE FILE LABELS	SAMPLE EXPERIENCE
By emotional content	Happy, sad, afraid, angry	Getting a new bicycle
By time they occurred	Early childhood, junior high	Beginning junior high school
By area in life they relate to	Family, friends	Taking car trips with my family

Journal Writing

In your journal, create a "life map." From left to right, draw or write important events from your life in chronological order. Shape your map any way—straight line, peaks and valleys, loops.

Teach

Using the Model

Ask students how far they had read into the model on page 21 when they knew that Lynn Griffey's feelings about space were going to change as a result of her experience with the space camp. (almost immediately) Point out the phrase *I thought this was going to be the beginning.* Ask how the word *thought,* in particular, alerts the reader that a transformation will follow. Note that Griffey first describes her experience at the space camp and then draws conclusions based on the experience. **L2**

Filing Ideas

Some students may benefit from using a more concrete autobiographical filing system, created out of shoeboxes or other containers. After students have collected containers, suggest that they label them with headings, such as "Favorite Memories" or "Things That Make Me Laugh," and then fill the boxes with ideas appropriate to the headings. Encourage students to look through the boxes to find a topic for an autobiographical sketch. **L1**

Journal Writing Tip

Gathering Information Suggest that students freewrite to compile a list of important events before they begin creating their life map. Then suggest that they focus on the most important events in their lives.

1.4

Teach

Using the Model

Ask students to identify the action verbs Kareem Abdul-Jabbar uses in the following: *I had never seen people dunk and soar and change direction in midstride.* Discuss how they help the reader experience the moment. **L2**

Interviewing Family Members

Ask students to choose a significant event in their lives. Tell them to interview family and friends to see what they remember about it. Discuss how an interview can help someone see an event from another perspective. **L3**

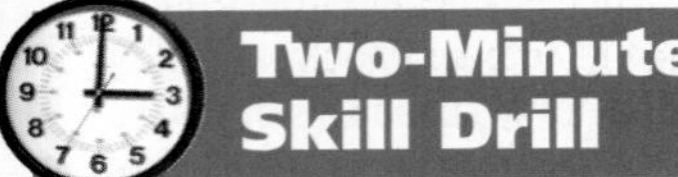

Ask students to demonstrate how to use flashbacks to present autobiographical material. Tell them to write one flashback in the present tense and one in the past tense.

See also *Two-Minute Skill Drill Transparency 1.4*

Additional Resources

For further stimuli for personal writing, see *Fine Art Transparencies* 1–6.

- *Writing Process Transparencies* 1
- *Writing Across the Curriculum*
- *Cooperative Learning Activities*
- *Thinking and Study Skills,* pp. 2, 5, 8
- *Listening and Speaking Activities,* pp. 9, 19, 20
- *Composition Practice,* p. 4

Personal Writing

How Do You Present Your Material?

There are many ways to present autobiographical material. You can begin with "I remember" and then recount a particular event. You can structure your story as an interview or you can use one of the methods shown in the chart. You may need to explain the significance of an event, as Kareem Abdul-Jabbar does in the model.

Two Ways to Present Your Material

	PRESENT		PAST		PRESENT
Flashback	Shopping with Gloria—we both loved the same clothes.	▶	Even as four-year-olds, she and I wanted the same toys.	▶	I hope that we don't start to like the same boys now.
	FEB. 8		**FEB. 9**		**FEB. 10**
Successive Journal Entries	Nelsons asked me to go skiing with them—sort of scared.	▶	Best day ever! I skied quite well—for my first time out.	▶	Couldn't get out of bed. It hurt to walk.

Literature Model

Abdul-Jabbar sets the scene and presents the main idea immediately.

It was that summer [after seventh grade] that I grew so many inches and started at least to *look* like a basketball player. I started to be able to do things like palm a basketball and touch the rim, and it was soon obvious that the long frame could be put to use in places other than the baseball diamond. Around this same time, one event changed my view of basketball and how to play it dramatically. I went to see a high school all-star game at the Brownsville Boys Club in Brooklyn. Guys like Connie Hawkins, Roger Brown, Billy Burwell, and other All-City players were on the court doing their thing, and I was awestruck. I had never seen people dunk and soar and change direction in midstride the way these guys did. . . . The warm-up was awe-inspiring, and I feel that evening in Brooklyn changed my concept forever of what is possible on the court. Baseball would remain close to my heart, but here was a game that was best played by individuals with *my* physical attributes. The possibilities seemed endless.

Kareem Abdul-Jabbar with Mignon McCarthy, *Kareem*

What kind of words does Abdul-Jabbar use to create a vivid picture of the event?

In the final sentences of this autobiographical sketch, Abdul-Jabbar sums up the significance of this event.

MEETING INDIVIDUAL NEEDS

English Language Learners

Preparing to Write

Pair students who are learning English with students who are fluent in English. Encourage students who are learning English to tell their autobiographical story to their partners. If students encounter difficulty with vocabulary words or concepts, the fluent English speaker can suggest language that will help get the thought across in a clear manner. Encourage students to make notes to use when they begin writing their autobiographical stories.

1.4 Writing Activities

Write an Autobiographical Sketch

Think of an event or period in your life that you feel had an impact on the kind of person you are now. You might remember making or losing a friend, visiting a new place, or learning a new skill or sport. Once you have chosen a topic, decide on the most effective technique to tell your story.

PURPOSE To tell about an important event in your life
AUDIENCE Classmates and teacher
LENGTH 5–6 paragraphs

WRITING RUBRICS To write an effective autobiographical sketch, you should

- provide all the information your readers will need
- explain why the episode you are describing had such an effect on you
- tell what happened; don't just comment on it
- write in complete sentences

Using Computers

You may wish to present your autobiographical sketch to family members or friends. Word processing, presentation, and Web page design software offer abundant options for composing documents and presentations. Such software allows you to import scanned photographs, sound clips, and even video.

GrammarLink

In general, avoid sentence fragments in your writing.

A **sentence fragment** is an incomplete sentence that is punctuated as a complete sentence.

Ever since I was a child. (fragment)
I've been fascinated with space.
Ever since I was a child, I've been fascinated with space. (complete sentence)

Change each sentence fragment below to form a complete sentence.

I want to make my career in music. [1]Because I love playing trumpet. I play in the band and orchestra. [2]And the jazz band too. Next I want to learn to play the French horn. [3]Maybe during summer vacation. [4]If my job leaves me enough time to practice. My parents say I should plan a different career. [5]Something dependable, like accounting or teaching. We'll see.

See Lesson 13.9, pages 553–554.

Viewing and Representing

CREATING A TIMELINE Imagine you will live to be one hundred years old. On drawing paper, create a fictional timeline that charts those hundred years. Highlight the important events.

LOG ON **Writing Online** For more writing and grammar practice, go to glencoe.com and enter QuickPass code WC97727p1.

Assess

Evaluation Rubrics

Write an Autobiographical Sketch

Use these criteria when evaluating your students' writing:

- Did the student use incidents from his or her own life?
- Did the student explain the significance of a feeling or experience?
- Is the material presented in a lively manner?

See also *Writing Assessment & Evaluation Rubrics*

Using Computers

Students who use computers may wish to organize their autobiographical material on disk files. They can create a separate folder or subdirectory for each of their major headings (for example, Emotional Events), and then create files within that folder (Happy, Sad, Angry). This system allows a file to be stored with related files for more convenient retrieval.

Reteaching

Composition Reteaching, p. 4

Enrichment

Composition Enrichment, p. 4

Close

Ask students why they think people like to read autobiographies. (They may hope to gain some new insight that will help them in their own lives. They may want to learn about life in another time and place.)

GrammarLink

Answers

Answers will vary, but a suggestion is given below.

I want to make my career in music because I love playing trumpet. I play in the band, the orchestra, and the jazz band, too. Next, I want to learn to play the French horn. Maybe I'll do that during summer vacation if my job leaves me enough time to practice. My parents say I should plan a different career. They think I should do something that is more dependable like accounting or teaching. We'll see.

Focus

Lesson Overview

Objectives

- To define two forms of poetry
- To identify and use five poetic devices
- To write a poem that expresses personal feelings

Skills

- writing traditional and free-verse poetry; using poetic devices; comparing forms of poetry

Critical Thinking

- analyzing; comparing; contrasting

Listening and Speaking

- discussing; evaluating

Bellringer
Daily Language Activity

When students enter the classroom, have this assignment on the board: *Read the lines written below. In a few sentences, identify what kind of writing it is and how you know.* (It is poetry. It rhymes.)

I had a little nut tree,
Nothing would it bear
But a silver nutmeg
And a golden pear.

Grammar Link to the Bellringer

Ask students to rewrite the poem, omitting the adjectives. (*little, nut, silver, golden*) Lead students in a discussion of how the use of precise adjectives can alter a poem.

See also  *Daily Language Practice*

Motivating Activity

Ask students to substitute adjectives for the ones in the poem above. How does the poem's mood change when the adjectives change? Tell students that in this lesson they will learn about poetry that rhymes and poetry that does not.

LESSON 1.5

Writing a Poem

Whether rhymed or unrhymed, poems often convey personal feelings through the use of strong, precise language.

Langston Hughes wanted to express his feelings about his people, African Americans. Notice how powerfully he does so—and with so few words—in this brief poem.

This free-verse poem does not have regular rhyme or rhythm patterns, but the repetition gives it a rhythmic feeling.

Literature Model

My People

The night is beautiful,
So the faces of my people.

The stars are beautiful,
So the eyes of my people.

Beautiful, also, is the sun.
Beautiful, also, are the souls of my people.

Langston Hughes

Poetry as Self-Expression

Effective poets like Hughes put together words to create sounds and images that express much more than what the words alone actually say. Such sounds and images help poets actively engage their readers' memories, emotions, and imaginations.

Traditional and Free Verse

In free verse such as Hughes's poem, there are no set patterns of rhyme or rhythm. More traditional poems, however, do follow set rhyme and rhythm patterns. Compare the following humorous poem with Hughes's poem. Read each poem aloud. Notice the regular rhyming and rhythmic patterns in "Song of the Open Road" and the freer form and style of "My People."

Resource Manager

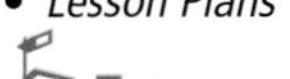

Planning Resources

- *Lesson Plans*

Transparencies

- *Bellringer*
- *Daily Language Practice*
- *Fine Art* 1–6
- *Two-Minute Skill Drill*
- *Writing Process* 1

Other Print Resources

- *Composition Enrichment,* p. 5
- *Composition Practice,* p. 5
- *Composition Reteaching,* p. 5
- *Cooperative Learning Activities,* pp. 5–8
- *Listening and Speaking Activities,* pp. 9, 19, 20
- *Thinking and Study Skills,* pp. 16, 31–32
- *Writing Across the Curriculum*
- *Writing Assessment and Evaluation Rubrics*

Literature Model

Song of the Open Road

I think that I shall never see
A billboard lovely as a tree.
Indeed, unless the billboards fall
I'll never see a tree at all.

Ogden Nash

The Special Language of Poetry

The language of poetry is one of vivid sounds and images. Just think of how Langston Hughes's images of night, stars, and sun linger and overlap with the images of his people's faces, eyes, and souls. Poets create such memorable pictures with a variety of techniques such as those explained in this chart.

Some Poetic Devices

Device	Definition	Example
Sensory detail	A detail that appeals to one of the senses: sight, touch, taste, smell, or hearing	Slivers of frosty grass crunched underfoot.
Simile	A comparison between two unlike things, using the words *like* or *as*	Sleep, like a soft, dark blanket, comforted him.
Metaphor	A comparison between two unlike things, without using the words *like* or *as*	Her dress was a pink cloud of crepe.
Personification	The giving of human qualities to objects, animals, or things	Flowers saluted the morning sun.
Sound effect	A pattern of sound (e.g., rhyme, rhythm, repetition) used to help create an image	The raspy snarl of a motorcycle awakened him.

Journal Writing

Find a single word in one of the poems in this lesson or in the list of examples above and use it as the center for brainstorming. Generate associations, in the form of words or phrases, with this word as fast as you can. Then use some of your associations to create a brief poem.

Teach

Using the Models

Some students may be familiar with the traditional verse modeled by Ogden Nash's poem, "Song of the Open Road," but may have difficulty perceiving any rhythm in Langston Hughes's poem, "My People." Ask several volunteers to read aloud the latter. Encourage them to exaggerate what they think gives the poem its rhythmic feeling; for example, standardizing the length of pauses at commas or periods, or using the same tone of voice for emphasis of repeated words such as *beautiful*, or phrases such as *of my people*. **L2**

Promoting Discussion

Invite students to recite Mother Goose rhymes they learned as children. Then point out that simple rhymes are also often used in songs and commercial jingles. Ask students why they think this is so. Does rhyming make the words easier to remember? Why is that particularly desirable in children's poetry and in advertising? **L2**

Prewriting Poetry

Ask students to write down the reactions and feelings that come to mind when they think about their school. Overall, what mood is expressed? Does the mood suggest any obvious comparisons? Are there any obvious rhymes? **L2**

Journal Writing Tip

Metaphorical Relationships Point out that a poet uses metaphors to make the reader think about the likeness between two ideas or objects. Encourage students to come up with metaphors that express their own insights.

1.5

Teach

Using the Model

Invite a volunteer to describe how Langston Hughes gave structure to his free verse poem "My People" on page 24. (through repetition of words and phrases) Point out that Heather Robertson uses the same technique in "Intimate Calm." Ask what Robertson repeated in her poem. (the word *with*) Point out that by beginning several lines with the word *with,* Robertson draws readers into her sense of inner peacefulness. **L2**

Two-Minute Skill Drill

List the terms below on the board. Ask students to identify which three poetic devices are modeled in the poems on this page.

sensory detail
simile
metaphor
personification
sound effect

See also *Two-Minute Skill Drill Transparency 1.5*

Additional Resources

For further stimuli for personal writing, see *Fine Art Transparencies* 1–6.

- *Writing Process Transparencies* 1
- *Writing Across the Curriculum*
- *Cooperative Learning Activities*
- *Listening and Speaking Activities,* pp. 9, 19, 20
- *Thinking and Study Skills,* pp. 16, 31–32
- *Composition Practice,* p. 5

Personal Writing

Forms of Poetry

Literature Model

There was a young person from Perth
Who was born on the day of his birth.
He was married, they say,
On his wife's wedding day
And died when he quitted this earth.

Anonymous

Like most limericks, this one begins "There was a . . ." and ends with a funny or unusual rhyming line.

Like most traditional haiku, this one has five syllables in lines 1 and 3 and seven in line 2.

Literature Model

Butterfly, these words
from my brush are not flowers,
only their shadows.

Soseki

With a partner, read these poems aloud. Notice the limerick's rhyming pattern and the haiku's syllable pattern. Following is a free verse poem.

Student Model

Intimate Calm

There—
With the soft rays of the lamp
Resting on the pallid walls
And the earthen carpet—
With the falling leaves and the dark, dewy dusk
Enveloping me
Like my grandmother's familiar afghan—
With the comforting sounds of the television
Capturing my attention with its witty charm—
With the beautiful willowing wisps
Of my brother's laughter in the kitchen
With my body
Propped against my favorite pillow
Sunken into the billowing cushions
Curled like the kitten
Asleep in my lap
Underneath that familiar yarn
Which conceals the memories of my mother's mother—
I lay
With a peaceful mind—
Eating refried beans

Heather Robertson,
Jefferson Davis High School, Montgomery, Alabama

Why do you suppose Heather chose to repeat the word "with" at the beginning of several lines?

The repetition of the *k* and hard *c* sound provides a rhythm to these two lines.

MEETING INDIVIDUAL NEEDS

Less Proficient Readers

Reading for Understanding

Have less proficient readers follow in their books as you read aloud the poems on this page. When you have finished the readings, lead students in a discussion of the humor in the limerick, the imagery in the haiku, and the absence of punctuation in the free verse. Encourage students to reread the poems to help them answer each other's questions. You may prompt discussion with such questions as, *Why is the limerick funny? What are the shadows mentioned in the haiku? Where does* "Intimate Calm" *take place?* **L1**

1.5 Writing Activities

Write Your Own Poem

Try freewriting to come up with an idea for a poem. Begin by focusing on a subject about which you have strong feelings. Underline any words or phrases that are especially descriptive of your topic or your feelings about it. Use some or all of the underlined items as you write your poem.

PURPOSE To write an original poem
AUDIENCE Students and teachers
LENGTH 5–15 lines

WRITING RUBRICS To write an effective poem, you should

- use poetic devices such as those listed on the chart on page 25
- decide whether rhyme or free verse will be more effective
- use sensory detail and clear language to convey your feelings

Listening and Speaking

READING POETRY ALOUD In a small group, select two favorite poems. Practice reading them aloud, paying attention to the patterns of sound, where the emphasis falls in each line, and the mood created by the poet. Discuss afterward why the poems you chose are important to you.

Cross-Curricular Activity

ART In a small group, brainstorm to create a list of ideas for a poem about what you see in the painting on this page. Use some of the poetic techniques discussed in this lesson (similes, metaphors, personification). Imagine that you are the central figure in the painting. What do you see? What are you thinking about? Write your own poem; then, meet again as a group to share and discuss your poems.

Rufino Tamayo, *Hombre Ante el Infinito* (*Man Contemplates Infinity*), 1950

Grammar*Link*

Use precise adjectives to bring your sentences to life.

Notice how Heather Robertson, in her poem "Intimate Calm," uses precise *adjectives* to create vivid images:

pallid *walls;* ***billowing*** *cushions*

Revise the lines below by adding vivid adjectives to modify nouns.

1. two people standing on a hillside overlooking a lake
2. a baby sleeping in its stroller
3. the chair in the dentist's office, surrounded by tools and equipment
4. wind in the trees outside the cabin
5. a potted plant on the table near the window

See Lesson 10.4, pages 461–466.

 **Writing** Online — For more writing and grammar practice, go to glencoe.com and enter QuickPass code WC97727p1.

Personal Writing

Assess

Evaluation Rubrics

Write Your Own Poem

Use these criteria when evaluating your students' writing:

- Some or all descriptive words or phrases in the freewriting are underlined.
- The poem has a pattern. If it is traditional verse, it adheres to the appropriate rhyme or rhythm structure.

See also *Writing Assessment & Evaluation Rubrics*

Cross-Curricular Activity

Remind students to follow appropriate guidelines for brainstorming sessions. Students may find a peer review of their first drafts helpful.

Reteaching

Composition Reteaching, p. 5

Enrichment

Composition Enrichment, p. 5.

Fine Art Transparencies 1–6

Close

Ask students to summarize what they learned about poetry in the lesson. Invite volunteers to share their summaries and then lead a discussion of poetry as a means of self-expression.

Grammar*Link*

Answers

Answers will vary. Suggestions:

1. smiling people, grassy hillside, looking-glass lake
2. exhausted baby, well-traveled stroller
3. battered chair, ancient dentist's decrepit office, mysterious tools and equipment
4. gentle wind, tall trees, tiny cabin
5. gigantic potted plant, rickety table, open window

Viewing the Art

Rufino Tamayo, *Hombre Ante el Infinito (Man Contemplates Infinity),* 1950

Rufino Tamayo's vision of a person's place in the cosmos reflects pre-Hispanic mythology. The 37-by-53-inch oil painting hangs in the Musées Royaux des Beaux Arts in Brussels, Belgium.

Focus

Lesson Overview

Objectives

- To define the purpose of a reader-response journal
- To develop new ways of responding to reading
- To record creative personal responses to literature in a reader-response journal

Skills

- writing descriptive details; discussing; specifying details

Critical Thinking

- predicting; analyzing; recalling; evaluating

Speaking and Listening

- note taking; interviewing; evaluating

Bellringer
Daily Language Activity

When students enter the classroom, have this assignment on the board: *Write down the name of a book, movie, or TV program about which you and a friend disagreed.*

Grammar Link to the Bellringer

Have students write a sentence about any title they chose for the Bellringer activity. Then ask them to identify any pronouns in their title.

See also *Daily Language Practice*

Motivating Activity

Initiate a discussion about the real-life responses people have made to a work of literature or to a film. Some people have been inspired to pursue a career in medicine, for example, because they admired a doctor in a story. Others have imitated the acts of heroism or kindness they have read about or seen on the screen. Ask students if a particular work has ever influenced them strongly.

Personal Writing

LESSON 1.6

WRITING ABOUT LITERATURE

Keeping a Reader-Response Journal

A reader-response journal is a place where you can record your reactions to what you are reading.

When Mitchell Kittlaus, a student from Illinois, finished reading Katherine Mansfield's story "The Doll's House," he was prompted to write in his reader-response log. Read the "letter-to-the-character" letter Mitchell wrote. See what it was that impressed him about the character Kezia.

Student Model

Dear Kezia,

I admire you greatly for the courage you displayed. . . . You took a big risk by inviting the Kelvey girls into your court-yard to see the doll house. Do not be intimidated by your aunt's punishment. Although you should obey your elders, it was right of you to question their negative opinion of the Kelveys. If you do not understand their attitude, take the initiative to talk with your parents and relatives, so that together you can discuss their views. You may not agree with what they believe, but it is important that you fully comprehend their feelings.

I also respect you for the kindness that you showed to Lil and Else Kelvey. It is always easier to hurt someone's feelings by acting in an inconsiderate way, especially when such thoughtless behavior is encouraged by one's peers. . . .

I encourage you to continue to keep an open mind in your relations with others. People should only be judged by the content of their character. Hopefully, you can set a positive example for others to follow.

Mitchell Kittlaus,
Evanston Township High School, Evanston, Illinois

What word choices in Mitchell's letter suggest the degree of his involvement in the story?

Mitchell expresses his personal feelings about the story's main incident.

Resource Manager

Planning Resources

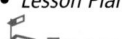

- *Lesson Plans*

Transparencies

- *Bellringer*
- *Daily Language Practice*
- *Fine Art* 1–6
- *Two-Minute Skill Drill*
- *Writing Process* 1

Other Print Resources

- *Composition Enrichment,* p. 6
- *Composition Practice,* p. 6
- *Composition Reteaching,* p. 6
- *Cooperative Learning Activities,* pp. 5–8
- *Listening and Speaking Activities,* pp. 9, 19, 20
- *Thinking and Study Skills,* pp. 5, 20–21
- *Writing Across the Curriculum*
- *Writing Assessment and Evaluation Rubrics*

Respond Personally

A reader-response journal can be a special section in a larger personal journal or a journal in itself. In a reader-response journal, you can write about what interests, puzzles, angers, or even bores you about your reading. The journal can help you keep track of what's going on in the work you are reading. More importantly it can help you relate your reading to your own life. For example, you might write about similarities you find between a character's view of life and your own.

Respond Creatively

Think of new ways to respond to your reading. You might write a letter of encouragement (or complaint) to the main character. You could rewrite a scene from a play to make it take place in your home town. Some of these ideas may inspire you to write your own creative pieces.

Responding to What You Read

IDEA	SAMPLE
1. Write a news flash.	Flash! Three local children disappeared last night from their backyard. Relatives say the three had been talking about time travel just prior to their disappearance. (response to *A Wrinkle in Time* by Madeleine L'Engle)
2. Imagine yourself as a main character.	Here I am shipwrecked on a deserted island with just a bunch of other boys my own age. I'd better make a plan for survival. (response to *Lord of the Flies* by William Golding; the photo on the right is from a movie based on that novel)
3. Write about the character visiting your home.	As Mrs. Luella Bates Washington Jones came through the door, she filled our living room with her powerful presence. (response to "Thank You, M'am" by Langston Hughes)

In your reader-response journal, you could suggest what might have happened if two characters had never met or if one event hadn't taken place. What if the setting were changed? Be creative in finding ways to write about your reading.

Journal Writing

Choose a book or story you have read recently. In your journal, respond to the story in any way you wish.

Teach

Using the Model

Point out that the fact that Mitchell Kittlaus's response is a letter to a character in a story demonstrates his strong involvement in that story. Kezia has come to life for him, and he speaks to her directly. Mitchell's admiration for the character is reflected by phrases such as "I admire you" and "I also respect you." It is also clear that Kittlaus empathizes with Kezia when he tells her, "You took a big risk." He even gives Kezia advice for the future: "I encourage you to continue to keep an open mind." **L1**

Cooperative Learning

Have students form groups of five or six. Suggest that they exchange the first reader-response entries they wrote in their journals with a group member for peer editing. Ask peer editors to look for responses that are not clarified by supporting details from the literature. Remind peer editors to make positive comments about each entry—what the editor liked about the response and what it revealed about its author. **L1**

Journal Writing Tip

Activating Prior Knowledge Tell students who have difficulty choosing literary works that they may need to jog their memory by looking through the class's literature anthology or their bookshelf at home. When they find a favorite piece, they can leaf through it to recall details that will help them explain why they've chosen the piece.

Teach

Making Predictions

Suggest that making predictions is another form of reader response. For example, a reader might predict an answer to the following question: *What will happen to the characters ten years after the story ends?* Remind students that to make their predictions more than guesses they should use their own knowledge plus all available information in the work they are responding to. **L1**

Speaking and Listening

Divide students into groups for discussion of books on sports, science fiction, or animals. Then ask them to bring to class any books or articles they've enjoyed on their chosen subjects to share with the rest of the group. **L1**

Two-Minute Skill Drill

Ask students to list three forms of reader responses they might find in newspapers, on TV, or in another form of communication.

See also *Two-Minute Skill Drill Transparency 1.6*

Additional Resources

For further stimuli for personal writing, see *Fine Art Transparencies* 1–6.

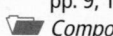

Writing Process Transparencies 1
Writing Across the Curriculum
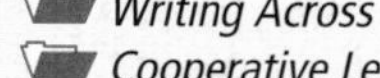
Cooperative Learning Activities
Thinking and Study Skills, pp. 5, 20–21
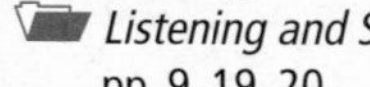
Listening and Speaking Activities, pp. 9, 19, 20
Composition Practice, p. 6

Respond to Learn About Yourself

An important part of any story, novel, play, essay, or poem is what you, the reader, bring to it. When you reflect on it in light of your personal experiences and impressions, literature can actually change you.

Keeping a reader-response journal gives you a chance to think more about a work of literature—to consider the relevance of the story or poem to your own life. What do you think about . . . ? How would you change it to make it more real? What if . . . ? Would you have done what the characters did?

By considering these kinds of questions, you come to a new, deeper understanding of the story. Michelle Kalski learns about herself by responding to Shel Silverstein's poem "Reflection" in two different ways.

Reflection

Each time I see the Upside-Down Man
Standing in the water,
I look at him and start to laugh,
Although I shouldn't oughtter.
For maybe in another world
Another time
Another town,
Maybe HE is right side up
And I am upside down.

Shel Silverstein

Student Model

Just a reflection of myself.
Or so it seems.
What stares back is a person
Full of peace and at ease.
A backward image of me.

Dear Mr. Silverstein,

Finally, someone has managed to step into the world of a reflection. As a curious youngster, I was always fascinated with reflections and looked for ways to prove that the person in the pool of water or the mirror was somehow different than me. I thought it was wonderful of you to reveal the idea of a reflection being in the world right side up.

Michelle Kalski,
Evanston Township High School, Evanston, Illinois

Notice how Michelle relates Silverstein's poem to her own life by telling of a childhood fascination of hers.

MEETING INDIVIDUAL NEEDS

English Language Learners

Practicing Freewriting

Students who have difficulty writing in English may find freewriting an accessible form of reader response. Suggest that they choose one of the questions in the second paragraph on this page and use it to freewrite about a work of literature for five minutes. Students may then wish to underline those thoughts that most strongly express their reaction to the work.

1.6 Writing Activities

Write a Reader-Response Journal Entry

Read the poem below and the Langston Hughes poem on page 24. Then choose one of them or a poem of your own choosing. Respond to the poem you select in a creative way as you would in a reader-response journal.

Old Mary

My last defense
Is the present tense.

It little hurts me now to know
I shall not go

Cathedral-hunting in Spain
Nor cherrying in Michigan or Maine.

Gwendolyn Brooks

PURPOSE To explore your reactions to a poem
AUDIENCE Yourself
LENGTH 1–3 paragraphs

WRITING RUBRICS To write a memorable reader-response journal entry, you should

- explain how the literature selection relates to your life
- describe the feelings and new ideas it evokes
- express yourself in complete, logical sentences

Viewing and Representing

CREATING A COMIC STRIP In your reader response journal, respond to a favorite story by drawing a multipaneled comic strip. Illustrate key scenes from the story. Draw yourself as a character in the story. Present your comic strip to a group of classmates and discuss its effectiveness.

Using Computers

If you are entering your reader-response entries into a computer file, you will need some way to identify your entries for retrieval. A good plan is to date each entry. Or you might add a code word, such as *poems* or the author's name. Then you can use the Search function to retrieve a particular entry.

Grammar*Link*

When using pronouns, do not shift person or number without a good reason.

Supply appropriate pronouns in the following sentences.

1. I especially like reading science fiction, where ______ appreciate the combination of fact and fantasy.
2. When one reads a play, ______ must visualize the action of the characters.
3. We enjoyed his poetry because ______ can clearly understand his feelings.
4. If you don't like the major characters in a book, it is hard for ______ to take much interest in what happens to ______.
5. They love Agatha Christie's stories because ______ never tire of her characters.

See Lesson 17.5, pages 640–641.

LOG ON **Writing** Online — For more writing and grammar practice, go to glencoe.com and enter QuickPass code WC97727p1.

Assess

Evaluation Rubrics

Write a Reader-Response Journal Entry

Use these criteria when evaluating your students' writing:

- Does the response tell how the poem reflects the student's personal experiences and impressions?
- Does the response include a description of the feelings the poem suggests?
- Did the student state agreement or disagreement with the poem's main idea?

See also *Writing Assessment & Evaluation Rubrics*

Viewing and Representing

Evaluate the comic strip by the organization of the story, the relationship between the panels and key scenes from the story, and the creativity of the presentation.

Reteaching

Composition Reteaching, p. 6

Enrichment

Composition Enrichment, p. 6

Close

Ask students to choose a book they have recently read or are presently reading. Tell them to write a review of the book of their choice in one or two paragraphs.

Grammar*Link*

Answers

1. I
2. one
3. we
4. you, them
5. they

Focus

Lesson Overview

Objectives

- To learn how to respond personally to biographical material by relating events in the subject's life to one's own life
- To identify different formats for responding personally to a biography
- To learn how to know the subject of a biography by conducting an imaginary interview

Skills

- relating events to one's personal experiences

Critical Thinking

- classifying; relating; comparing; identifying

Listening and Speaking

- discussing; interviewing; informal speaking

Bellringer

Daily Language Activity

When students enter the classroom, have this assignment on the board. *Choose two real people you admire. Then write a sentence explaining your choices. Make the two people you chose the subject of the sentence.*

Grammar Link to the Bellringer

Tell students that when the subject of a sentence is a compound that refers to two people or things and is joined by *and,* the verb must be plural. Encourage students to check their sentences to see if they needed a plural verb.

See also *Daily Language Practice*

Motivating Activity

Ask students to name a famous person with whom they closely identify. Then find out why they feel drawn to that particular person. What do they have in common with the person? What do they admire about the person? Tell students that expressing their personal response to someone else's life will help them better understand that person and themselves.

Personal Writing

LESSON 1.7

WRITING ABOUT LITERATURE

Writing About Biography

When you are reading a biography, one way to respond is to relate events in the subject's life to your own life. Shella Calamba does this in the model below.

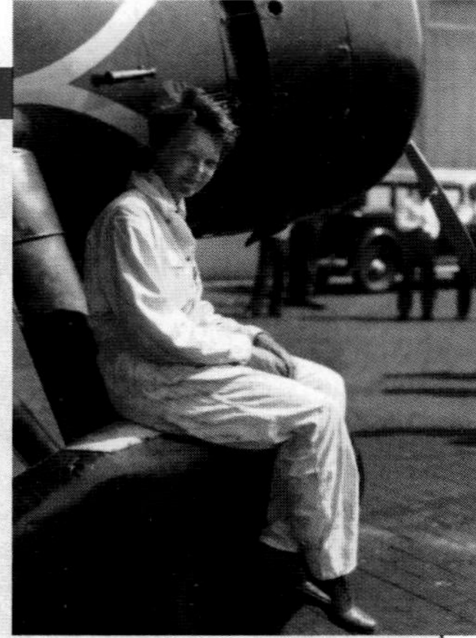

Amelia Earhart, 1933

Student Model

I never thought Amelia Earhart and I could have so much in common. Although, as a little girl, I was outfitted in frilly doll dresses and constantly reminded to be "ladylike," I, like Amelia, preferred to do things that were branded as "tomboy" activities, such as climbing trees, which was hard, but feasible, while wearing a pink dress. Amelia's roller coaster project reminded me of my own skateboard dashes down a hill in sledding fashion. As Amelia did, I, too, often employ the phrase "because I want to," to justify actions that may seem inane or highly psychotic to others.

Not only did Amelia's childhood remind me of mine, she also made me think of a friend from grammar school who dreams of becoming a pilot. She will undoubtedly be forced to deal with sexism in pursuing her goal, but I think reading Amelia's biography would prevent her from being discouraged in achieving her ambitions. Even by today's standards, what Amelia accomplished was remarkable and unprecedented by any man or woman. However, Amelia is not someone to be admired exclusively by pilots. Her courage, determination, and persistence set an inspiring example for anyone with a dream.

Shella Calamba,
Lincoln Park High School, Chicago, Illinois

What words signal the many comparisons between Shella and Amelia in the first paragraph?

Shella shows the relevance of the biography to others in today's world, moving from personal meanings to more general ones.

Resource Manager

Planning Resources

- *Lesson Plans*

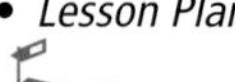

Transparencies

- *Bellringer*
- *Daily Language Practice*
- *Fine Art* 1–6
- *Two-Minute Skill Drill*
- *Writing Process* 1

Other Print Resources

- *Composition Enrichment,* p. 7
- *Composition Practice,* p. 7
- *Composition Reteaching,* p. 7
- *Cooperative Learning Activities,* pp. 5–8
- *Listening and Speaking Activities,* pp. 9, 19, 20
- *Thinking and Study Skills,* pp. 11, 24, 31–32
- *Writing Assessment and Evaluation Rubrics*

Respond Personally to a Biography

When you respond personally to a biography, you are responding to the subject of the biography and to his or her world. You can try to get to know the subject by focusing your reader-response journal entries on the subject's attitudes, values, and behavior. What does the subject care about? What motivates her or him in life? Relate your discoveries to your own life. Do you care about the same kinds of things as the subject? What qualities does the subject have that you admire? What do the subject's accomplishments teach you about your own life?

The chart below shows some ways you can respond personally to a biography. Try any of the following suggestions or come up with other ways of thinking about a biography's subject.

Some Formats for Responding to Biography

FORMAT	EXAMPLE
Write a skit showing how the person might act in a new and unusual situation.	Ben Franklin at an electrical plant
Write an encouraging letter helping the subject with a problem.	To Mohandas Gandhi encouraging his efforts to win independence for India
Write an editorial endorsing the person for public office.	Michael Jordan for mayor of your town
Bring a historical figure into the modern day world.	Queen Isabella visiting NASA and learning about space exploration
Write a diary entry from a crucial day in the person's life.	Amelia Earhart's diary from the day her plane was lost over the Pacific Ocean
Rewrite an incident from the subject's life, changing one part slightly.	Abraham Lincoln not going to the theater where he was assassinated
Enact an on-the-spot news story with your subject.	A news interview with Clara Barton immediately after a Civil War battle

Journal Writing

In your journal, respond to a biography you have read or seen. Use one of the ideas from the chart on this page.

Teach

Using the Model

Ask students to discuss the opening sentence in the model on page 32. How does it set up what will follow? Later in the paragraph, Shella Calamba uses phrases that signal that she is drawing comparisons between herself and Earhart. Have students identify these phrases and discuss how they set up comparisons. **L2**

Creating a Biography Listing

Have students work together to create an annotated bibliography of biographies that they have read. The annotation should contain a short summary statement and a sentence describing the impact the book had on the reader. For example, a biography about a person who overcame great odds might teach students that their own problems are not insurmountable. Students might also list biographies they'd like to read and what they might learn from reading them. **L3**

Two-Minute Skill Drill

Tell students to list three formats for responding to biography with examples.

See also *Two-Minute Skill Drill Transparency 1.7*

Journal Writing Tip

Creative Thinking Before students begin creating their own charts, tell them that having a particular person in mind might help when they create a new format. Then they can try to figure out what would be the best way to explore their response to the person.

Teach

Cooperative Learning

Prepare for an imaginary interview activity by dividing the class into small groups. Pair the students within each group, and ask them to role-play a television talk show featuring a famous person they have enjoyed reading about. Students should take turns acting as the interviewer and the guest. After the partners have finished their interviews, students can regroup to share the information they learned. **L2**

Classifying Characters

Students may have difficulty choosing a format for relating to biography. Invite these students to imagine that they are casting a movie version of a biography they have read. In order to match the right actor with each character in the biography, they must first consider both the character's and the actor's physical attributes and personality. Encourage students to cast public figures, professional actors, and even classmates in the roles. **L1**

Additional Resources

For further stimuli for personal writing, see *Fine Art Transparencies* 1–6.

Writing Process Transparencies 1

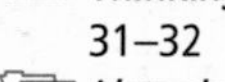

Cooperative Learning Activities

Thinking and Study Skills, pp. 11, 24, 31–32

Listening and Speaking Activities, pp. 9, 19, 20

Composition Practice, p. 7

Interview Your Subject

One way to get to know the subject of a biography is through an imaginary interview. To develop such an interview, work with a classmate and role-play. One of you should take the role of the interviewer and the other should portray the subject of the biography. Ask questions that get at the whys and hows of the person's life. Tailor your questions to your particular subject. Base the subject's responses on what you know from your reading.

Feel free to be creative and have fun with the interview. For example, you might choose the form of a late-night talk show discussion, such as Jay Leno interviewing Leonardo da Vinci. You might pretend that a historical character is visiting the present-day world, as Elizabeth Chen did an imaginary interview with Dr. Martin Luther King Jr. for a fictional newspaper, the *Chronicle.*

Sample Interview Questions

- What was the accomplishment you were most proud of?
- What was your greatest challenge?
- What surprises you most about today's world?
- If you could tell the people of today one thing, what would it be?

Student Model

Chronicle: Dr. King, what you did for the civil rights movement in the 1950s and 1960s obviously had an enormous impact then, but do you think it affects society today?

MLK: What the people did then, promoting the cause of civil rights through peaceful means, has led the way toward a day of equal rights for all people.

Chronicle: Do you think there is equality now?

MLK: Under the law, yes, but in the hearts and minds of some Americans, no. I cannot say there is equality when I hear of racial violence every day. There will not be equality until everyone is treated the same in practice as well as under the law.

Chronicle: But how can we change that?

MLK: Through education. Through the help of all people—black, white, red, and yellow—to show that the only difference between us is skin color. By showing that all people can achieve the same success if given an equal opportunity.

Elizabeth Chen,
Downers Grove North High School, Downers Grove, Illinois

English Language Learners

Choosing Words

Students who are learning English might find it helpful to ask a fluent English speaker to edit their work. Have each pair study the marginal boxes in the student model on page 32 before writing begins. Explain that these points will also be used by the peer editor in evaluating the personal response. The peer editor should also check that the writer has discussed the biography's relevance to others. Emphasize that the peer editor is there to help his or her partner, rather than to be a critic. The pair should work together to solve problems.

1.7 Writing Activities

Write a Response to a Biography

Choose a major event or decision in the life of a person whose biography you have read. Write a response to share with your classmates. You can use one of the formats suggested in the chart on page 33, you can write an imaginary interview, or you can write a more personal response.

PURPOSE To explore a section of a biography
AUDIENCE Your classmates
LENGTH 2–4 paragraphs

WRITING RUBRICS To write an effective response to a biography, you should

- show that you understand your subject
- make your response interesting to your audience
- write in clear, complete sentences

Listening and Speaking

RESEARCH AND REPORT In a small group, select a famous scientist, artist, or author whose work is familiar to everyone in the group. Divide up the task of researching the person's life, one member of the group taking the person's childhood, another the person's early career, and so on. Prepare a brief oral report on the area you researched; then combine the reports and give a group presentation for the class.

Spelling

COOPERATIVE LEARNING Exchange your response to a biography with a partner. Work together to identify spelling problems and develop a strategy for resolving them.

GrammarLink

When the subject of a sentence is a compound joined by *and* that refers to two or more different things, the verb that agrees with it must be plural.

Notice subject and verb in this sentence:
Her courage, determination, ***and*** *persistence* ***set*** *an inspiring example. . . .*

Add the correct verb form.

1. Washington and Adams ______ the first two presidents of the United States.
2. John Adams and his son, John Quincy Adams, ______ both presidents.
3. Both the House of Representatives and the Senate ______ in the Capitol.
4. The Declaration of Independence, the Constitution, and the Emancipation Proclamation ______ kept in the U.S. Archives.
5. The secretary of state and the attorney general ______ members of the president's cabinet.
6. Ulysses Grant and Dwight Eisenhower ______ generals.
7. John Quincy Adams and Andrew Jackson ______ born in 1767.
8. Kennedy, F. D. Roosevelt, and Wilson ______ students at Harvard.
9. Dwight Eisenhower and Lyndon Johnson ______ born in Texas.
10. Gerald Ford and Richard Nixon ______ born in 1913.

See Lesson 16.5, pages 616–617.

Personal Writing

Assess

Evaluation Rubrics

Write a Response to a Biography

Use these criteria when evaluating your students' writing:

- Is the rewritten event consistent with the biographical subject's views and life?
- Has the student responded personally to the subject's world?

See also *Writing Assessment & Evaluation Rubrics*

Listening and Speaking

Evaluate each student's paragraph plus first and last paragraphs on the following: how well the paragraph explains a period in the subject's life and how well the first and last paragraphs unify the essay.

Reteaching

Composition Reteaching, p.7

Enrichment

Composition Enrichment, p. 7

Fine Art Transparencies 1–6

Close

Ask students to suggest someone whose life story would make an interesting biography. This person may be a family member, a friend, or someone they have heard about. Ask students: *Why do you think people will be able to relate personally to this person? What do you think they will learn by reading this person's biography?*

GrammarLink

Answers

1. were
2. were
3. are
4. are
5. are
6. were
7. were
8. were
9. were
10. were

Quotation Marks After students have written their personal responses, tell them to check to see if they have properly used quotation marks in all direct quotations. Write examples of sentences containing direct quotations, and ask volunteers to insert quotation marks and any other necessary punctuation.

Focus

Lesson Overview

Objective

- To compose an account about an important personal incident or interaction

Skills

- using the five stages of the writing process: prewriting, drafting, revising, editing, and presenting

Critical Thinking

- recalling and evaluating; defining and clarifying

Listening and Speaking

- discussing; evaluating; questioning; presenting

Bellringer

Daily Language Activity

When students enter the classroom, have this assignment on the board: *List people and incidents that have made a difference in your life (such as a favorite relative, moving to a new town, winning an award).*

Grammar Link to the Bellringer

Have students review the lists they made for the Bellringer activity and choose two or three of the words to use in a complete sentence. Review students' sentences aloud, discussing any pronouns they use and whether the pronoun referents would be clear to a reader or listener.

See also *Daily Language Practice*

Motivating Activity

Explain that in this lesson students will write an autobiographical sketch about a person or incident that made an important difference in their lives. Discuss stories students might tell, or share your own story.

UNIT 1

Writing Process in Action

Personal Writing

Personal Writing

In preceding lessons you've learned about using personal writing for a variety of purposes. Now it's time to make use of what you learned. In this lesson you're invited to write an autobiographical sketch about an incident or a personal interaction that made a positive difference in your life—an event or a relationship that provided a good "lesson in living."

Assignment

Context

Everyday People magazine plans a special issue featuring autobiographical sketches by students. You are invited to write an uplifting story about a person or an incident that made a real difference in your life. Focus on your personal feelings and on why the event or person was so important to you.

Purpose

To write a vivid personal account that will allow readers to understand the impact of this event

Audience

"Everyday" people—students, parents, teachers, other townspeople

Length

1–2 pages

Planning to Write

The following pages can help you plan and write your autobiographical sketch. Read through them and then refer to them as you need to, but don't feel limited by them. You are in charge of your own writing process. As always, be sure to set a time frame for completion so that you allocate your time appropriately. Keep in mind the controlling idea as you write: writing an autobiographical sketch about an incident or personal interaction that has made a positive difference in your life.

LOG ON Writing Online

For prewriting, drafting, revising, editing and publishing tools, go to **glencoe.com** and enter QuickPass code WC97727p1.

Resource Manager

Planning Resources
- *Lesson Plans*

Transparencies
- *Bellringer*
- *Daily Language Practice*
- *Writing Process* 1

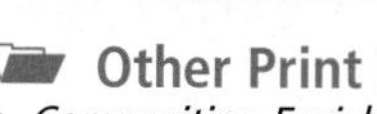

Other Print Resources
- *Composition Enrichment,* p. 8

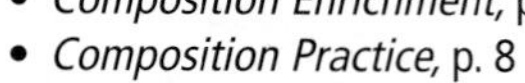

- *Composition Practice,* p. 8
- *Composition Reteaching,* p. 8

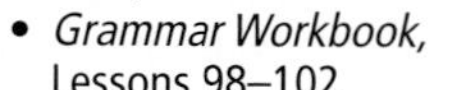

- *Grammar Workbook,* Lessons 98–102
- *Thinking and Study Skills,* pp. 1, 5

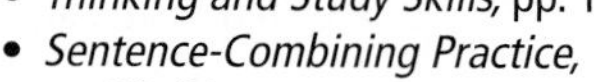

- *Sentence-Combining Practice,* pp. 30–31

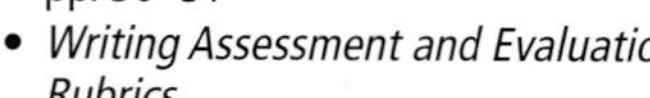

- *Writing Assessment and Evaluation Rubrics*

Web Site
- *glencoe.com*

Writing Process in Action

Prewriting

Begin by choosing an incident to write about. It might be from any period in your life. It might have taken place over several weeks or months, or it may have happened quickly. It may have been dramatic or quiet, serious or humorous. If you can't think of an incident, use some of the prewriting options listed here to help you get started. Once you have an idea in mind, try to recall what happened as fully as possible. You might begin by writing your answers to *who, what, when, where,* and *why* questions.

Part of your goal is to explain the significance of the event. One way to do this:

- List things that describe yourself, your attitudes, and your circumstances *before* the event or interaction took place.
- Then note the ways in which things were different afterward. Write a statement that summarizes what the experience meant to you, how it changed you, or what you learned from it.

Notice how these lines from Kareem Abdul-Jabbar's autobiography vividly describe the life-changing effect of his seeing a particular basketball game when he was young.

Prewriting Options

- Read over your journal entries.
- Make a list of important people in your life.
- Look through scrapbooks and photographs at home.
- Search your mental files for possible topics.
- Freewrite to discover your thoughts.

Literature Model

I was awestruck. I had never seen people dunk and soar and change direction in midstride the way these guys did. . . . The warmup was awe-inspiring, and I feel that evening in Brooklyn changed my concept forever of what is possible on the court. Baseball would remain close to my heart, but here was a game that was best played by individuals with *my* physical attributes. The possibilities seemed endless.

Kareem Abdul-Jabbar with Mignon McCarthy, *Kareem*

Teach

Prewriting

Developing Ideas for Autobiographical Writing

Suggest freewriting as a good way to identify a topic and its supporting details. Tell students to begin by freewriting possible ideas for their autobiographical sketch. They can choose one central idea. Then students should continue writing whatever comes to mind relative to their central idea. In the process they may uncover other possible ideas. **L2**

Teach

Drafting

Using the Model

Point out to students that one way to grab their audience's attention is to use vivid language. For example, in the model on p. 37 Kareem Abdul-Jabbar creates a sense of immediacy by using action verbs. These verbs help the reader experience the moment when players "dunk and soar and change direction in midstride." **L2**

Revising

Peer Editing

Students can work in writing conferences with peer editors before they revise their work. You may want to duplicate the Peer Response forms in *Writing Assessment & Evaluation Rubrics.* Suggest that peer editors respond to the question, *What are the main ideas and three supporting details?* **L2**

Cooperative Learning

Have students work in small groups. One student can read a draft aloud while others in the group listen to see whether ideas flow logically. **L2**

Editing/Proofreading

Peer Editing

After students have edited and proofread their work, have them review another student's writing. Discuss how to prepare students' papers for publication. Remind students to refer to the Editing Checklist on p. 39. **L2**

Drafting Tip

For more information about enlivening your personal writing, see Lesson 1.3, page 18.

Revising Tip

For help with adding significant details and finding a suitable structure for your sketch, see Lesson 1.4, pp. 20–23.

TIME

For more about drafting and revising, see **TIME Facing the Blank Page**, pp. 126-129.

Drafting

Start with your summary statement about the significance of the event. This will help you focus your thoughts as you write. It will also prepare your readers for what follows. Then add sentences and paragraphs to tell your story. Write freely, referring to your prewriting notes, but try to organize your thoughts in some logical way. If your experience involves a clear sequence of events, you might present the details in straight chronological order—the order in which they occurred.

As you write, look for ways to make your sketch come to life. What anecdotes, descriptions, comparisons, or other details can make your story vivid? Consider using dialogue to help bring your characters to life. To be sure the dialogue sounds natural, read your draft aloud.

Revising

To begin revising, look back at the assignment; then read your draft to see if you have met the goals. Next, have a **writing conference.** Read your draft to a partner or small group. Use your audience's reactions to help you evaluate your work so far. The following questions can help you and your listeners:

- Does my writing qualify as an autobiographical sketch?
- Is my sketch easy to follow?
- Is my sketch vivid and accurate?
- Is my tone natural? Does it sound like me talking?
- Does my writing show how this incident or interaction changed my life for the better?
- Is my writing appropriate for my audience?

Enrichment and Extension

Follow-up Ideas

- Set aside time to celebrate the conclusion of the writing projects.
- Encourage students to share their finished works with the class or small groups.
- Place the magazine *Everyday People* in a classroom library for all to read.

Extending Autobiography

- Suggest that students write a short story based on their autobiographical sketches.
- Brainstorm with students ways they can use personal writing in other subject areas.

Editing/Proofreading

Once you are happy with the basic content and setup of your autobiographical sketch, **proofread** it carefully for errors in grammar, usage, mechanics, and spelling. Use the questions at the right as a guide.

In addition to proofreading, use the self-evaluation list below to make sure your autobiographical sketch does everything you want it to do. When you're satisfied, make a clean copy of your sketch, and proofread it one more time.

Editing Checklist

- Have I avoided sentence fragments?
- Are all my verb forms and tenses correct?
- Have I used I and me correctly in compounds?
- Are my pronoun references clear?
- Have I checked spellings of any words I'm unsure of?

Self-Evaluation

Make sure your autobiographical sketch—

- ✔ Focuses on an incident or interaction that improved your life
- ✔ Conveys the significance of this incident or interaction
- ✔ Answers the *who, what, where, when, why,* and *how* questions
- ✔ Reflects your spoken rhythms and phrases
- ✔ Follows correct grammar, usage, and mechanics

Publishing/Presenting

You can use the autobiographical sketches you and your classmates have written to produce an issue of *Everyday People.* Create a cover and a table of contents. Add illustrations if you wish. Make it available for others to read. If you feel your sketch is too personal to share publicly, keep it with your journal so that you can refer to it later.

Proofreading Tip

For proofreading symbols, see pages 98 and 411.

Journal Writing: Write to Learn

Reflect on your writing process experience. Answer these questions in your journal: What do you like best about your personal writing? What was the hardest part of writing it? What did you learn in your writing conference? What new things have you learned as a writer?

Publishing/Presenting

Before students prepare their autobiographical writing for inclusion in *Everyday People,* discuss the importance of the final draft and remind students that it must be neatly done.

Additional Resources

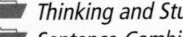

 *Writing Process Transparency* 1

 *Thinking and Study Skills,* pp. 1, 5

*Sentence-Combining Practice,*pp. 30–31

Composition Practice, p. 8

Grammar Workbook, Lessons 98–102

Assess

Evaluation Rubric

Use the following criteria to evaluate the students' finished writing:

- Does it clearly communicate why the person or event is important?
- Does the sketch show how the person or incident changed the writer's life?

See also *Writing Assessment & Evaluation Rubrics*

Reteaching

 *Composition Reteaching,* p. 8

Enrichment

Composition Enrichment, p. 8

Journal Writing Tip

Reflecting Students should think about how they overcame difficulties when they wrote and what procedures worked especially well.

Listening and Speaking

Listening to Autobiographies

Invite students to read aloud their finished autobiographical sketches. Audience members should tell what is most memorable about each sketch, including characters, images, dialogue, and description. What would they like to hear more about if the sketch were to continue? What are the strong points of the sketch?

Close

Invite students to discuss how the writing process can help them in any pieces they write in the future.

Literature Model

About the Author

Born Marguerite Johnson, Maya Angelou (b. 1928) and her brother Bailey were raised in Stamps, Arkansas, by their grandmother, whom they called Momma. Bailey nicknamed his sister Maya, meaning "mine." The literature passage takes place when the author was about ten years old.

Focus

Lesson Overview

Objectives

- To analyze a literature passage that illustrates effective autobiographical writing
- To write a friendly letter comparing and contrasting experiences

Skills

- monitoring comprehension; questioning; connecting

Critical Thinking

- evaluating; inferring; interpreting

Speaking and Listening

- discussing; oral reading; questioning

Bellringer

Daily Language Activity

When students enter the classroom, have this assignment on the board: *Write down the kinds of things you like to find out when you read autobiographical or real-life stories.*

See also  *Daily Language Practice*

Motivating Activity

Discuss students' responses to the Bellringer activity. Then ask students to work with a partner and tell each other about an interesting person or event from their own lives.

Personal Writing

UNIT 1

Literature Model

from

I Know Why the Caged Bird Sings

by Maya Angelou

Maya Angelou, best known for her autobiographies I Know Why the Caged Bird Sings *and* Gather Together in My Name, *has also been a poet laureate, playwright, movie and television writer, journalist, dancer, actress, director, composer, and civil rights worker. As you read this autobiographical sketch, see if the turning point she describes reminds you of any significant event in your own life. Then try the activities in Linking Writing and Literature on page 50.*

Resource Manager

Planning Resources

- *Lesson Plans*

Transparencies

- *Bellringer*
- *Daily Language Practice*
- *Fine Art* 1–6

Other Print Resources

- *Listening and Speaking Activities,* pp. 9, 19, 20
- *Thinking and Study Skills,* pp. 5, 19, 24
- *Writing Assessment and Evaluation Rubrics*

Web Sites

- *writerschoice.glencoe.com*
- *lit.glencoe.com*

Literature Model

For nearly a year, I sopped around the house, the Store, the school and the church, like an old biscuit, dirty and inedible. Then I met, or rather got to know, the lady who threw me my first life line.

Mrs. Bertha Flowers was the aristocrat of Black Stamps. She had the grace of control to appear warm in the coldest weather, and on the Arkansas summer days it seemed she had a private breeze which swirled around, cooling her. She was thin without the taut look of wiry people, and her printed voile[1] dresses and flowered hats were as right for her as denim overalls for a farmer. She was our side's answer to the richest white woman in town.

Her skin was a rich black that would have peeled like a plum if snagged, but then no one would have thought of getting close enough to Mrs. Flowers to ruffle her dress, let alone snag her skin. She didn't encourage familiarity. She wore gloves too.

I don't think I ever saw Mrs. Flowers laugh, but she smiled often. A slow widening of her thin black lips to show even, small white teeth, then the slow effortless closing. When she chose to smile on me, I

1 **voile** (voil) a thin, sheer fabric; often made of cotton

Harriet Powers, *Pictorial Quilt,* c. 1895–1898

Teach

Active Reading Strategies

Connect Ask students what Angelou means when she says she met "the lady who threw me my first life line." Then encourage students to think about people, places, or activities that have helped them get over bad times in their own lives.

Critical Thinking

Evaluate Ask students: "Do you think Angelou has done a good job of describing Mrs. Flowers? Does she seem believable?" Have students defend their judgments by explaining why or why not. *(Sample response: The description is effective because it helps the reader visualize Mrs. Flowers and get a feel for her personality. It's believable because her appearance and her personality seem to match.)*

Viewing the Art

Harriet Powers, *Pictorial Quilt,* c. 1895–1898

This appliqué quilt by Harriet Powers (1837–1911) reflects the artist's deep religious beliefs as well as her African American heritage. Ten of the panels represent biblical scenes; the other five illustrate events of local history. The appliqué techniques used by the artist, however, correspond closely to those practiced in West Africa. African traditions for appliqué textiles were probably passed down in her family from one generation to the next.

Teach

Active Reading Strategies

Monitor Comprehension Have students ask themselves whether they understand why Marguerite is embarrassed by the way her grandmother greets Mrs. Flowers. If the students are not clear, give them time to review the text to find the answer. Then ask a volunteer to explain Marguerite's embarrassment. *(Marguerite thinks her grandmother showed her ignorance and that Mrs. Flowers deserved a proper greeting.)*

Critical Thinking

Infer Ask students what they can infer—or guess—about Marguerite based on her reaction to her grandmother's grammatically incorrect speech. What specific information from the text can they cite to support their inference? *(Marguerite is sensitive about what others think of her and her family. When she mentally corrects her grandmother's speech, she shows that she knows the rules of grammar and that she doesn't want Mrs. Flowers to think that she and her family are uneducated.)*

always wanted to thank her. The action was so graceful and inclusively benign.[2]

She was one of the few gentlewomen I have ever known, and has remained throughout my life the measure of what a human being can be.

Momma had a strange relationship with her. Most often when she passed on the road in front of the Store, she spoke to Momma in that soft yet carrying voice, "Good day, Mrs. Henderson." Momma responded with "How you, Sister Flowers?"

Mrs. Flowers didn't belong to our church, nor was she Momma's familiar. Why on earth did she insist on calling her Sister Flowers? Shame made me want to hide my face. Mrs. Flowers deserved better than to be called Sister. Then, Momma left out the verb. Why not ask, "How *are* you, *Mrs.* Flowers?" With the unbalanced passion of the young, I hated her for showing her ignorance to Mrs. Flowers. It didn't occur to me for many years that they were as alike as sisters, separated only by formal education.

Although I was upset, neither of the women was in the least shaken by what I thought an unceremonious[3] greeting. Mrs. Flowers would continue her easy gait up the hill to her little bungalow,[4] and Momma kept on shelling peas or doing whatever had brought her to the front porch.

Occasionally, though, Mrs. Flowers would drift off the road and down to the Store and Momma would say to me, "Sister, you go on and play." As I left I would hear the beginning of an intimate conversation. Momma persistently using the wrong verb, or none at all.

"Brother and Sister Wilcox is sho'ly the meanest—" "Is," Momma? "Is"? Oh, please, not "is," Momma, for two or more. But they talked, and from the side of the building where I waited for the ground to open up and swallow me, I heard the soft-voiced Mrs. Flowers and the textured voice of my grandmother merging and melting. They were interrupted from time to time by giggles that must have come from Mrs. Flowers (Momma never giggled in her life). Then she was gone.

They were interrupted from time to time by giggles that must have come from Mrs. Flowers . . .

She appealed to me because she was like people I had never met personally. Like women in English novels who walked the moors (whatever they were) with their loyal dogs racing at a respectful distance. Like the women who sat in front of roaring fireplaces, drinking tea incessantly from silver trays full of scones and crumpets. Women who walked over the "heath"[5] and read morocco-bound[6] books and had two last names divided by a hyphen. It would be safe to say that she

---

2 **benign** (bi nīn′) good-natured
3 **unceremonious** (un′ ser ə mō′ nē əs) impolite
4 **bungalow** (bung′ gə lō′) a small house, usually one story high plus an attic
5 **heath** (hēth) an expanse of wasteland, especially in Britain, covered with heather and shrubs
6 **morocco-bound** (mə rok′ ō) having a leather cover

Critical Thinking

Interpret

Tell students that when they *interpret* something, they use their own understanding of the world to decide what the events or ideas in a selection mean. To model for students the kind of thinking interpreting requires say: "The events in this selection occurred in Arkansas in the 1930s, when African Americans were severely discriminated against. By telling how she felt as a child, Angelou might be saying something about combating the effects of racism."

Practice In the last sentence that begins on page 42, Angelou states that Mrs. Flowers "made me proud to be Negro, just by being herself." Ask students what Angelou might mean by this statement. Then ask them to explain their interpretation to the class or in a small group. *(Sample response: At a time when opportunities were limited for African Americans, Mrs. Flowers was as distinguished as any other woman Marguerite had ever met or read about.)*

Beverly Buchanan, *Bogart, Georgia,* 1989

made me proud to be Negro, just by being herself.

She acted just as refined as whitefolks in the movies and books and she was more beautiful, for none of them could have come near that warm color without looking gray by comparison.

It was fortunate that I never saw her in the company of powhitefolks. For since they tend to think of their whiteness as an evenizer, I'm certain that I would have had to hear her spoken to commonly as Bertha, and my image of her would have been shattered like the unmendable Humpty-Dumpty.

One summer afternoon, sweet-milk fresh in my memory, she stopped at the Store to buy provisions. Another Negro woman of her health and age would have been expected to carry the paper sacks home in one hand, but Momma said, "Sister Flowers, I'll send Bailey up to your house with these things."

She smiled that slow dragging smile, "Thank you, Mrs. Henderson. I'd prefer Marguerite, though." My name was

6+1 Trait® Writing

Word Choice Angelou uses vivid sensory language to help her readers see, hear, and feel what she experienced as a child. For example, she describes Mrs. Flowers's "slow dragging smile." Ask students to find other words and phrases on pages 42 and 43 that appeal to the senses. *(Sample response: "soft yet carrying voice," "easy gait," "textured voice," "merging and melting," "roaring fireplaces," "whiteness")*

Viewing the Art

Beverly Buchanan, *Bogart, Georgia,* 1989

In a number of her paintings, African American artist Beverly Buchanan depicts the tiny shacks common to many rural areas of the South, where both Angelou and Buchanan grew up. The dollhouse smallness and simplicity of these structures reflect Buchanan's recollection of them as a child. The oil pastel painting is 38 by 49¼ inches and is on display in the Bernice Steinbaum Gallery in New York City.

Teach

Critical Thinking

Infer Angelou doesn't reveal exactly why she was so embarrassed when her grandmother told her to take off the dress. Ask students what they can infer from the text about the reason Marguerite feels humiliated. *(Sample response: Her grandmother treats her like an object. Marguerite wants people, especially Mrs. Flowers, to see her as an individual.)*

Critical Thinking

Infer Ask: "Why does Mrs. Flowers respond the way she does to Marguerite and to Mrs. Henderson?" *(Sample response: Mrs. Flowers recognizes Marguerite as a sensitive individual, so she knows the girl will be embarrassed. However, Mrs. Flowers doesn't want to offend Mrs. Henderson by speaking out against her treatment of Marguerite.)*

beautiful when she said it. "I've been meaning to talk to her, anyway." They gave each other age-group looks.

Momma said, "Well, that's all right then. Sister, go and change your dress. You going to Sister Flowers's."

The chifforobe[7] was a maze. What on earth did one put on to go to Mrs. Flowers' house? I knew I shouldn't put on a Sunday dress. It might be sacrilegious.[8] Certainly not a house dress, since I was already wearing a fresh one. I chose a school dress, naturally. It was formal without suggesting that going to Mrs. Flowers' house was equivalent to attending church.

I trusted myself back into the Store.

"Now, don't you look nice." I had chosen the right thing, for once.

"Mrs. Henderson, you make most of the children's clothes, don't you?"

"Yes, ma'am. Sure do. Store-bought clothes ain't hardly worth the thread it take to stitch them."

"I'll say you do a lovely job, though, so neat. That dress looks professional."

Momma was enjoying the seldom-received compliments. Since everyone we knew (except Mrs. Flowers, of course) could sew competently, praise was rarely handed out for the commonly practiced craft.

"I try, with the help of the Lord, Sister Flowers, to finish the inside just like I does the outside. Come here, Sister."

I had buttoned up the collar and tied the belt, apronlike, in back. Momma told me to turn around. With one hand she pulled the strings and the belt fell free at both sides of my waist. Then her large hands were at my neck, opening the button loops. I was terrified. What was happening?

"Take it off, Sister." She had her hands on the hem of the dress.

"I don't need to see the inside, Mrs. Henderson, I can tell . . ." But the dress was over my head and my arms were stuck in the sleeves. Momma said, "That'll do. See here, Sister Flowers, I French-seams around the armholes." Through the cloth film, I saw the shadow approach. "That makes it last longer. Children these days would bust out of sheet-metal clothes. They so rough."

I had buttoned up the collar and tied the belt, apron-like, in back. Momma told me to turn around.

"That is a very good job, Mrs. Henderson. You should be proud. You can put your dress back on, Marguerite."

"No ma'am. Pride is a sin. And 'cording to the Good Book, it goeth before a fall."

"That's right. So the Bible says. It's a good thing to keep in mind."

I wouldn't look at either of them. Momma hadn't thought that taking off my dress in front of Mrs. Flowers would kill me stone dead. If I had refused, she would have thought I was trying to be "womanish" and might have remembered St. Louis. Mrs. Flowers had known that I would be embarrassed and that was even worse. I picked up the groceries and went out to wait in the

---

7 **chifforobe** (shif' ə rōb') a combination of wardrobe and chest of drawers

8 **sacrilegious** (sak' rə lij' əs) involving the violation of something holy

Active Reading Strategies

Monitor Comprehension

Explain to students that when they read, they should pause occasionally to think about whether they understand the selection. Give students the following tips to help them monitor their comprehension.

- Keep asking yourself questions about main ideas, characters, and events.
- When you can't answer a question, pause. Try to find the answer by reviewing, reading more slowly, or reading ahead. If all else fails, ask someone to help you.

Practice After students read this page, ask them to write two questions about main ideas, characters, and events in the passage. Then have students exchange questions with a partner. If they can't answer the questions they receive, tell them to reread the text or ask someone for help.

Charles Alston, *Girl in a Red Dress,* 1934

Critical Thinking

Interpret Ask students: "What do you think Angelou is suggesting about the relationship between children and adults by including the scene about Marguerite's grandmother showing the dress to Mrs. Flowers?" *(Sample response: Marguerite's grandmother seems to judge Marguerite harshly and disregard her feelings. By writing about her humiliation, Angelou is suggesting that this approach toward children can damage their self-esteem.)*

Viewing the Art

Charles Alston, *Girl in a Red Dress,* 1934

In the mid-1930s, Charles Alston (1907–1977) headed the Harlem Art Workshop, which was instrumental in producing many successful African American artists. Alston often combined realism with abstract techniques. In *Girl in a Red Dress,* these techniques allow the artist to accentuate the subject's features and celebrate them as a standard of beauty. The 28-by-22-inch oil painting is in the Evans-Tibbs Collection in Washington, D.C.

Teach

Active Reading Strategies

Monitor Comprehension Ask students why Mrs. Flowers is the only one speaking on this walk. What is she trying to accomplish? How? *(Marguerite hasn't been talking in school. Mrs. Flowers is trying to get Marguerite to start talking again by using her influence and Marguerite's love of reading.)* After volunteers respond, ask them to share with the class how they figured out answers to the questions.

hot sunshine. It would be fitting if I got a sunstroke and died before they came outside. Just dropped dead on the slanting porch.

There was a little path beside the rocky road, and Mrs. Flowers walked in front swinging her arms and picking her way over the stones.

She said, without turning her head, to me, "I hear you're doing very good school work, Marguerite, but that it's all written. The teachers report that they have trouble getting you to talk in class." We passed the triangular farm on our left and the path widened to allow us to walk together. I hung back in the separate unasked and unanswerable questions.

"Come and walk along with me, Marguerite." I couldn't have refused even if I wanted to. She pronounced my name so nicely. Or more correctly, she spoke each word with such clarity that I was certain a foreigner who didn't understand English could have understood her.

"Now no one is going to make you talk—possibly no one can. But bear in mind, language is man's way of communicating with his fellow man and it is language alone which separates him from the lower animals." That was a totally new idea to me, and I would need time to think about it.

"Your grandmother says you read a lot. Every chance you get. That's good, but not good enough. Words mean more than what is set down on paper. It takes the human voice to infuse them with the shades of deeper meaning."

I memorized the part about the human voice infusing words. It seemed so valid and poetic.

She said she was going to give me some books and that I not only must read them, I must read them aloud. She suggested that I try to make a sentence sound in as many different ways as possible.

"I'll accept no excuse if you return a book to me that has been badly handled." My imagination boggled at the punishment I would deserve if in fact I did abuse a book of Mrs. Flowers's. Death would be too kind and brief.

She said she was going to give me some books and that I not only must read them, I must read them aloud.

The odors in the house surprised me. Somehow I had never connected Mrs. Flowers with food or eating or any other common experience of common people. There must have been an outhouse, too, but my mind never recorded it.

The sweet scent of vanilla had met us as she opened the door.

"I made tea cookies this morning. You see, I had planned to invite you for cookies and lemonade so we could have this little chat. The lemonade is in the icebox."

It followed that Mrs. Flowers would have ice on an ordinary day, when most families in our town bought ice late on Saturdays only a few times during the summer to be used in the wooden ice-cream freezers.

She took the bags from me and disappeared through the kitchen door. I looked around the room that I had never in my wildest fantasies imagined I would see.

6+1 Trait® Writing

Word Choice

Tell students that good writers use vivid, precise language to convey exact meaning and create interest. To choose the best words to describe a particular thought or idea, writers must consider the literal meaning of a word—its **denotation**—as well as the unspoken or unwritten meaning associated with it—its **connotation.** For example, the adjectives *candid* and *blunt* both mean *openly truthful.* However, *candid* has a positive connotation. It describes someone who is honest and doesn't hide important information. *Blunt* has a negative connotation. It describes someone who is blatantly honest and makes no effort to avoid hurting others' feelings.

Practice Write this sentence from the selection on the board: "The odors in the house surprised me." Have students work with a partner to rewrite the sentence in several ways using words with similar denotations but different connotations. *(The stench in the house shocked me. The aromas in the house overwhelmed me.)* For more information about the 6+1 Trait® model, see **Writing and Research Handbook** pages 947–949.

Wilmer Angier Jennings, *Landscape,* 1945

Browned photographs leered or threatened from the walls and the white, freshly done curtains pushed against themselves and against the wind. I wanted to gobble up the room entire and take it to Bailey, who would help me analyze and enjoy it.

"Have a seat, Marguerite. Over there by the table." She carried a platter covered with a tea towel. Although she warned that she hadn't tried her hand at baking sweets for some time, I was certain that like everything else about her the cookies would be perfect.

Critical Thinking

Infer Ask students how Marguerite feels about being in Mrs. Flowers's house. What details from the passage reveal her feelings about being there? *(Marguerite is happy to be there, but she feels a bit nervous. Her nervousness is revealed by descriptions such as, "Browned photographs leered or threatened from the walls.")*

Viewing the Art

Wilmer Angier Jennings, *Landscape,* 1945

Wilmer Angier Jennings's *Landscape* could almost serve as an illustration of the hill and road that Marguerite ran down after her visit with Mrs. Flowers (page 49). The oil painting measures 20⅛ inches by 14 inches and is in the collection of B. R. Brazeal in Atlanta, Georgia.

Teach

Critical Thinking

Interpret Ask students: "What is Mrs. Flowers saying about the relationship between intelligence and formal education?" *(Sample answer: Mrs. Flowers is saying that having intelligence and having a formal education are two different things. A person who is uneducated can be intelligent, and a person who is educated can be ignorant.)*

Active Reading Strategies

Question Ask students: "What does Angelou mean when she says she knew from listening to preachers that Mrs. Flowers was coming to the end of her reading, even though Angelou had not been listening to the words?" If students aren't sure, have them reread the text slowly. Then ask volunteers to explain the comment to the class. *(Even though she hasn't been listening to the words, Angelou knows that Mrs. Flowers is coming to the end of the passage because her voice is slowing down and giving greater emphasis to the words, just like the preachers' voices do near the end of a sermon.)*

They were flat round wafers, slightly browned on the edges and butter-yellow in the center. With the cold lemonade they were sufficient for childhood's lifelong diet. Remembering my manners, I took nice little lady-like bites off the edges. She said she had made them expressly for me and that she had a few in the kitchen that I could take home to my brother. So I jammed one whole cake in my mouth and the rough crumbs scratched the inside of my jaws, and if I hadn't had to swallow, it would have been a dream come true.

As I ate she began the first of what we later called "my lessons in living." She said that I must always be intolerant of ignorance but understanding of illiteracy. That some people, unable to go to school, were more educated and even more intelligent than college professors. She encouraged me to listen carefully to what country people called mother wit. That in those homely sayings was couched the collective wisdom of generations.

"There's one more thing. Take this book of poems and memorize one for me. Next time you pay me a visit, I want you to recite."

When I finished the cookies she brushed off the table and brought a thick, small book from the bookcase. I had read *A Tale of Two Cities* and found it up to my standards as a romantic novel. She opened the first page and I heard poetry for the first time in my life.

"It was the best of times and the worst of times . . ." Her voice slid in and curved down through and over the words. She was nearly singing. I wanted to look at the pages. Were they the same that I had read? Or were there notes, music, lined on the pages, as in a hymn book? Her sounds began cascading gently. I knew from listening to a thousand preachers that she was nearing the end of her reading, and I hadn't really heard, heard to understand, a single word.

"How do you like that?"

It occurred to me that she expected a response. The sweet vanilla flavor was still on my tongue and her reading was a wonder in my ears. I had to speak.

I said, "Yes, ma'am." It was the least I could do, but it was the most also.

"There's one more thing. Take this book of poems and memorize one for me. Next time you pay me a visit, I want you to recite."

I have tried often to search behind the sophistication of years for the enchantment I so easily found in those gifts. The essence[9] escapes but its aura[10] remains. To be allowed, no, invited, into the private lives of strangers, and to share their joys and fears, was a chance to exchange the Southern bitter wormwood[11] for a cup of mead[12] with Beowulf or a hot cup of tea and milk with Oliver Twist. When I said aloud, "It is a far,

9 **essence** (es′ əns) the basic nature or most important quality

10 **aura** (ôr′ ə) the atmosphere or feeling that seems to surround a certain person or thing

11 **wormwood** (wurm′ wood′) a bitter oil

12 **mead** (mēd) a drink made of honey and water

Writing in the Real World

Writers and Writing

Listening to Literature Provide some background information on Charles Dickens's *A Tale of Two Cities.* (The book is set in London and Paris and chronicles the life of a fictional character, Sidney Carton, during the French Revolution.) Then read the first page of the novel aloud to the class. Ask students if they, like Marguerite, hear poetry in the lines. Then ask them if a literary work—that they have either read or heard recited—has ever had such an effect on them.

far better thing that I do, than I have ever done . . ." tears of love filled my eyes at my selflessness.

On that first day, I ran down the hill and into the road (few cars ever came along it) and had the good sense to stop running before I reached the Store.

I was liked, and what a difference it made. I was respected not as Mrs. Henderson's grandchild or Bailey's sister but for just being Marguerite Johnson.

Childhood's logic never asks to be proved (all conclusions are absolute). I didn't question why Mrs. Flowers had singled me out for attention, nor did it occur to me that Momma might have asked her to give me a little talking to. All I cared about was that she had made tea cookies for *me* and read to *me* from her favorite book. It was enough to prove that she liked me.

Literary Element

Autobiography Tell students that writers of autobiographies often look back at their lives and discover meaning in events that they had previously overlooked. Then ask students: "Based on the last three paragraphs of the selection, do you think as a child Angelou found meaning in her visit with Mrs. Flowers? Or do you think Angelou discovered meaning in the event later in life?" Then ask them to support their opinions with evidence from the text. *(Sample response: Angelou probably found some meaning in the visit as a child because she was immediately happy that Mrs. Flowers liked her. However, she probably found more meaning in the visit over the years as she realized that Mrs. Flowers changed her life by sharing her wisdom and courage.)*

Active Reading Strategies

Connect Ask students to think about memorable events in their own lives. Then ask: Does the turning point Angelou describes remind you of a significant event in your own life?

Additional Resources

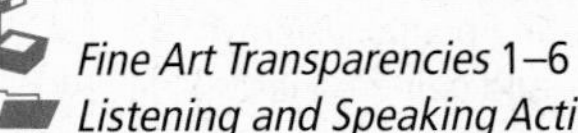

Fine Art Transparencies 1–6

Listening and Speaking Activities, pp. 9, 19, 20

Thinking and Study Skills, pp. 5, 19, 24

Compare and Contrast

Personal Comparison

Tell students that comparing and contrasting a selection to their own lives can help them deepen their understanding of both the literature and themselves. Then instruct students to think about Angelou's thoughts, feelings, and reactions to events in this autobiographical excerpt.

Practice Ask students to write a paragraph or two comparing and contrasting the way they might have reacted to the events in this selection to the way Marguerite reacted. Suggest that students record some similarities and differences in lists or in a Venn diagram before they start writing.

Linking Writing and Literature

Assess

Evaluation Rubrics

Talk About Reading

Possible responses to the questions:

1. Students may relate to Marguerite's embarrassment over her grandmother and her admiration for an adult who seems perfect. They may not have known that in the first half of the twentieth-century many people grew up wearing handmade clothes and living without refrigerators.
2. Students may admire Mrs. Flowers for her ability to relate to Marguerite in a noncondescending way.
3. Vivid images include the photographs that "leered or threatened" from the walls of Mrs. Flowers's house; the "rough crumbs" that scratched inside Marguerite's mouth when she bit into the butter cookie; and the way Mrs. Flowers's voice "slid in and curved down through and over the words" of Dickens.
4. Students' criteria might include telling about turning points, using vivid language, and being honest.

Write About Reading

The letter should do the following:

- identify a childhood experience
- tell how it is similar to and different from the experience described in the selection
- suggest a reason for the differences
- contain vivid, interesting language

Close

Divide the class into groups, and let each group enact one scene from the passage.

Personal Writing

Linking Writing and Literature

Learning to Learn

Use what you have read to jot down a sentence or two that describes Maya Angelou's childhood. Then think about ways her childhood was similar to and different from your own childhood and the childhoods of people you know or have read about. How do you think those similarities and differences affect the way you responded to this excerpt?

Talk About Reading

Talk with other students about the excerpt from *I Know Why the Caged Bird Sings.* Assign a group leader to keep everyone focused and a group secretary to take notes. Then use the questions below to guide your discussion.

1. **Connect to Your Life** How does Angelou's description of a special childhood relationship connect to your own life? What parts of her description do you relate to? Why? What parts of her description help you understand something new?
2. **Critical Thinking: Evaluate** In what ways do you share Marguerite's admiration for Mrs. Flowers?
3. **6+1 Trait®: Word Choice** How does Angelou use words to create images—or pictures—in your mind? Name some specific images that you found memorable.
4. **Connect to Your Writing** After reading this selection, what qualities do you think a memoir should have? Make a list of criteria for a good memoir.

Write About Reading

Friendly Letter Write a friendly letter to Angelou, telling her what her autobiography made you think about in regards to your own childhood. Compare and contrast Angelou's childhood experience with your own and try to identify reasons for any differences you notice. See the personal letter on page 416 for help with formatting your letter.

Focus on Word Choice Your letter will be more fun for Angelou to read if you use vivid language to create images of your own childhood. Review your letter, looking for places where you can replace general and abstract words with specific descriptive words.

For more information on word choice and the 6+1 Trait® model of writing, see **Writing and Research Handbook,** pages 947–949.

6+1 Trait® is a registered trademark of Northwest Regional Educational Laboratory, which does not endorse this product.

UNIT 1 Review

Reflecting on the Unit: Summarize What You Learned

Focus on the following questions to help summarize what you learned in this unit.

1. In what ways can personal writing help you make discoveries about yourself?
2. What can you keep in a personal journal and how can it serve as a valuable source of writing ideas?
3. What strategies can you use to explore ideas for personal essays?
4. What are some of the different methods you can use to present autobiographical materials?
5. What are some devices poets use to create memorable word pictures?
6. What is the purpose of a reader-response journal and how can it help you learn?

Adding to Your Portfolio

CHOOSE A SELECTION FOR YOUR PORTFOLIO Look over the personal writing you have done during this unit. Select a piece of writing to put into your portfolio. The piece should demonstrate that you have worked with one or more of the concepts listed above. In other words, look for a piece of writing that shows some or all of the following:

- a valuable self-discovery, or something special that makes you *you*
- an idea source for a future personal essay
- ideas generated by freewriting, clustering, or creating an idea map
- your own personal thoughts and feelings in poetic form

REFLECT ON YOUR CHOICE Attach a note to the piece you chose, explaining briefly why you chose it and what you learned from writing it.

SET GOALS How can you improve your writing? What skill will you focus on the next time you write?

Writing Across the Curriculum

MAKE A CIVICS CONNECTION Think about an experience you had with someone quite different from yourself—in age, culture, or economic status. Make brief notes about how the person was different from you and what you learned from the encounter. Then, using those notes, write a paragraph demonstrating how encountering this new person affected your life or beliefs.

Review

Reflecting on the Unit

You may have students respond to Reflecting on the Unit by writing a summary of what they've learned or through discussion.

Adding to Your Portfolio

Suggest that when students choose samples for their portfolio they look for material that resulted in true self-discovery. This material may be in a poem, a journal entry, or even a response to a piece of literature. Remind students, too, to keep an eye out for what Sandra Cisneros calls "nuggets"—a writing idea, an anecdote, a promising sentence.

Portfolio Evaluation

If you grade the portfolio selections, you may want to award two marks—one each for content and form. Explain your assessment criteria before students make their selections.

Commend

- experimentation with creative prewriting techniques
- clear, concise writing in which the main idea, audience, and purpose are evident
- successful revisions
- work that shows a flair for language

Writing Across the Curriculum

Before they begin writing, remind students that their paragraphs are like personal essays. They should contain a thesis statement that clearly conveys what they learned from the encounter. Encourage students to describe their feelings about the other person.

ASSESSMENT OPTIONS

Tests With Answer Key & Rubrics
Unit 1 Choice A Test, p. 1
Unit 1 Choice B Test, p. 2
Unit 1 Composition Objective Test, pp. 3–4

Testmaker
Unit 1 Choice A Test
Unit 1 Choice B Test
Unit 1 Composition Objective Test

You may wish to administer one of these tests as a mastery test.

MindJogger Videoquizzes

UNIT 2

Viewing the Art

In this photograph, honeysuckle grows against a blue and white house. The bright yellow flowers, unopened pink buds, and dark green leaves convey a sense of promise about what is to come, although the outcome is by no means certain. Plants need both water and sunlight if they are to flourish. Likewise, if students are to flourish as writers, they need both example and instruction.

Interpret and Analyze Use the following questions for discussion:

- How would you describe the mood of this photograph? What effect does the light have on the mood?
- Imagine that you have been hiking through a dark forest and suddenly emerge into a clearing flooded with light. How might this change affect your feelings and emotions?

Discussing the Quotation

This quotation is from *The Story of My Life,* the autobiography of Helen Keller (1880–1968). Helen Keller was afflicted with a serious illness when she was only nineteen months old, leaving her both deaf and blind. In the excerpt, Keller reflects on how uncertain she felt when she learned that she was to become formally educated. Discuss the quotation with the class, and ask students how they would interpret the author's meaning.

Writing Prompt Write a brief explanation of how Keller's words, coupled with the image of the honeysuckle, can be seen to connect to the writing process.

"The afternoon sun penetrated the mass of honeysuckle that covered the porch, and fell on my upturned face."

—Helen Keller,
The Story of My Life

52

Resource Manager

Planning Resources
- *Lesson Plans*
- *Block Scheduling*

Transparencies
- *Bellringer*
- *Daily Language Practice*
- *Fine Art*
- *Two-Minute Skill Drill*
- *Writing Process*

Other Print Resources
- *Composition Enrichment*
- *Composition Practice*
- *Composition Reteaching*
- *Cooperative Learning Activities*
- *Glencoe Literature Library*
- *Grammar and Composition Handbook*
- *Grammar Workbook*
- *Listening and Speaking Activities*
- *Spelling Power*
- *Tests with Answer Key and Rubrics*
- *Thinking and Study Skills*
- *Vocabulary and Spelling Strategies and Practice*
- *Writing Across the Curriculum*
- *Writing Assessment and Evaluation Rubrics*
- *Writing in the Real World*

UNIT 2
The Writing Process

53

Objectives

- To develop an understanding of the writing process through example and instruction
- To learn the five main stages associated with the writing process
- To write a family story

ASSESSMENT OPTIONS

Tests With Answer Key & Rubrics
Unit 2 Choice A Test, p. 5
Unit 2 Choice B Test, p. 6
Unit 2 Composition Objective Test, pp. 7–8

Testmaker
Unit 2 Choice A Test
Unit 2 Choice B Test
Unit 2 Composition Objective Test

You may wish to administer either the Unit 2 Choice A Test or the Unit 2 Choice B Test as a pretest.

Key to Ability Levels

L1 Level 1 activities are within the basic ability range of students.

L2 Level 2 activities are within the ability range of average students.

L3 Level 3 activities are more challenging activities.

Video
- *MindJogger Videoquizzes*

Web Site
- *glencoe.com*

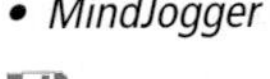

Software
- *Presentation Plus!*
- *Revising with Style*
- *Testmaker*

Focus

Lesson Overview

Objectives

- To define and clarify the topic for a feature article or story
- To identify the intended audience for a feature article or story

Skills

- discussing; analyzing; gathering information; writing a feature article

Critical Thinking

- identifying a main topic; defining and clarifying; analyzing information; summarizing

Listening and Speaking

- interviewing; note taking; discussing; evaluating; questioning; explaining

Bellringer

Daily Language Activity

When students enter the classroom, have this assignment on the board: *Suppose you wanted to write about a family tree. What are some of the first steps you would take to gather information?*

Grammar Link to the Bellringer

Have students read what they have just written for the Bellringer activity. Then have them rewrite what they wrote, combining sentences to make the writing more engaging to read.

See also *Daily Language Practice*

Motivating Activity

Discuss students' responses to the Bellringer activity. Initiate a discussion about the process of researching a family tree. How would students begin—by interviewing relatives and family members, conducting library research, asking questions, or searching on the Internet? Point out that whatever method they choose would be part of the prewriting stage of the writing process.

Writing in the Real World

As both a freelance writer and writing teacher, Lorenzo Chavez has lots of experience with the writing process. Chavez writes feature stories, or "human interest" stories, that cover a large range of topics. Below is an excerpt from a feature he wrote for *Vista,* a magazine for Hispanic readers inserted in about twenty Sunday newspapers nationwide.

The Writing Process

The Quest for Hispanic Roots

by Lorenzo Chavez

For 15 years, Mickey Garcia has searched quietly for clues to a lost treasure buried in history books, church records and dusty family albums. The Texan's "treasure" is her family history: a unique link with the past that may help her gain a better understanding of her Latin roots.

"Some of my Mexican cousins think I'm crazy," she says from her suburban Houston home. "They think: 'What in the world does she want with all these dead people?'"

Whether out of cultural pride, simple curiosity or legal necessity, Latinos like Garcia are actively tracing their ancestral roots for clues to their Hispanic identity.

Garcia's success challenges the notion that genealogy is reserved for university academicians and librarians . . . "It's my hobby and I enjoy it," says the working mother of three. "You don't have to have a college degree. I've always been interested in history."

Since the 1977 telecast of Alex Haley's *Roots* sparked interest in family history, Hispanics have enthusiastically joined other Americans in the rush to the libraries.

Mexican Americans in particular, especially in the Southwest, are tracing generations of family roots. The historical records of immigrants from Cuba, Puerto Rico and South America—more recent, by comparison—are still evolving.

Genealogical societies, libraries and universities in southern Texas eagerly compile church and civil records relating to pioneers who explored and settled the border between the United States and Mexico.

The sense of *familia* is a powerful unifying force. On July 7, 1984, approximately 1,500 Vela family members descended on Reynaldo Vela's ranch in McAllen, Texas, in what may have been the largest and most successful Hispanic family reunion ever held in the United States.

Through that warm summer weekend, they gathered at the 5,000-acre Laguna Seca ranch to celebrate their surname and to honor Salvador Vela and Leonor Zamora, who carried their children across the Rio Grande from Reynosa, Mexico, to McAllen in the late 1800s.

A book published last December, "Four Generations of Velas," was the result of ten years of research by those immigrants' descendants. . . .

Spanish surnames are more accessible than non-Spanish surnames, [George Ryskamp, a California genealogist] explains, thanks to the extensive records kept by the Spanish monarchy. The Archives of the Indies, a repository in Seville, houses more than 40 million documents dealing with Spain's conquest of the New

Resource Manager

Planning Resources

- *Lesson Plans*

Transparencies

- *Bellringer*
- *Daily Language Practice*
- *Writing Process* 2–8

Other Print Resources

- *Cooperative Learning Activities,* pp. 9–12
- *Thinking and Study Skills,* pp. 1–2
- *Vocabulary and Spelling Strategies and Practice,* p. 2
- *Writing Assessment and Evaluation Rubrics*
- *Writing in the Real World,* pp. 5–8

World from the 15th to the 19th centuries.

Amateur and professional researchers should be grateful for that bureaucratic system, which required three copies of every document. . . . The copies were kept by the local officials, the regional governor and the Crown. Catholic church records also helped unify the Hispanic world, says Ryskamp.

"Most people who get interested in genealogy are two or three generations removed from their mother country," Ryskamp notes. "Economically, they are middle-class or above. I expect the interest to grow in the next 10 to 20 years as the Hispanic population makes greater economic gains. . . ."

Meanwhile, Mickey Garcia continues searching for names and dates. She has traced her mother's family to the early 1700's, but remains "stuck" in the 1880's with the paternal branch of the tree.

"You have to be interested," Garcia explains. "One of my ancestors was married three times and ended up with 21 children. And in 1833 a lot of my relatives died of cholera. That makes for a lot of added research."

"To be a good genealogist you have to be a good detective," sums up Ryskamp, the California lawyer. "You never know what you are going to find."

A Writer's Process

Prewriting

Collecting the Facts

Chavez will tell you that ideas for feature stories are everywhere, in fact, there are "just too many," laughed Chavez. And, of course, you have to be alert and open to ideas. The idea for Chavez's story on family histories, "The Quest for Hispanic Roots," came from *Vista* readers. Over the years, hundreds of *Vista* readers had written in to "Rootsearch," a popular genealogy column devoted to tracing family histories. With so many readers writing in to the column, the *Vista* staff decided to run an article that could help people do family research on their own. They commissioned Chavez to write the article.

Before Chavez could start researching the article, he had to narrow the original idea to a few key points—no more than he could cover in the allotted space of 1,500 words, or about six pages in *Vista* magazine. Chavez then gathered the facts by looking for answers to these questions: Why do people search for their pasts? What libraries or associations can help?

It took Chavez about a week to get the answers. Some information came from newspaper clippings, but most of it came through the thirty or forty phone calls he made to libraries and researchers.

Vela family reunion

Teach

Reading Media

Have students preview the title and focus of the Media Connection on page 54. Tell students that feature articles, or "human-interest" stories, try to draw readers in by focusing on people and what they do or think. Remind students that they use human-interest stories every day, such as when they are summarizing a favorite sporting event, discussing news in the community, or learning about recent scientific breakthroughs. Have students read the article.

Discussion Prompts

- What approach will you take to collect facts or information for a feature article or human-interest story? For example, will you need to conduct interviews, use print or electronic media, or focus primarily on library research? How can you figure out the best approach to take in order to gather all the information you need?
- How would the focus of your story change if your audience consisted primarily of teenagers? Of adults in their thirties or forties? Of senior citizens? What might be different about your approach in each circumstance?
- Do you think it would be easier to find a focus for your article before or after you have gathered all your information? Why? (Most people find a focus after they have gathered all the information they can find.)

Cultural Connections

Tracing Family Names

A major part of genealogical research is tracing family names. For some cultures, researchers must be aware of differences in how names are passed on. Russian children, for example, bear a version of their father's first name as a second name. Spanish children add their mother's surname to their father's surname. That mother's name is dropped when a woman marries, but her children retain her father's surname.

Teach

Discussion Prompts

- What things did Chavez do to make his readers want to finish the article? Did he put all the information in the beginning or at the end, or did he spread it out?
- How are the writing process steps used for feature writing the same as the writing process steps students have used for other kinds of writing? How do they differ?
- Were students surprised by the importance of feature writing for a journalist? Why or why not?
- Now that students have seen this real-world application of feature writing, what other applications can they think of that they might find in their school and community? **L2**

Additional Resources

 *Writing Process Transparencies* 2–8
 *Writing in the Real World,* pp. 5–8
 *Cooperative Learning Activities*
Thinking and Study Skills, pp. 1–2
Vocabulary and Spelling Strategies and Practice, p. 2

Assess

Analyzing the Media Connection

1. "Middle-aged to older" Hispanic readers with an interest in history and politics.
2. Chavez uses anecdotes, quotes, and descriptions to spark interest, while also including enough information about genealogy to get people started researching their family history.

Drafting
Telling the Story

After his interviews, Chavez had twenty pages of notes, several taped conversations, a few newspaper clips, and a head full of ideas. Before sitting down at the computer, Chavez reminded himself of the people he was writing for. His audience was a "middle-aged to older generation, people of Mexican descent, mostly retirees, who have spare time and an interest in history and politics." To engage his readers, Chavez had to put himself in their shoes and anticipate questions they might ask.

Now Chavez was ready to write. To grab the reader, he used an anecdote about Mickey Garcia, a Texas genealogist who researches family histories. He portrayed Garcia as a treasure hunter. "She's searching for a valuable thing—not gold, but a family history," Chavez said. "I used that [approach] because I didn't want to frighten the reader by saying this was a long, time-consuming, arduous task."

From there Chavez stitched the story together using quotes, descriptions, and explanations about what sparked people's interest in genealogy. He introduced top researchers, described huge family reunions, and explained how to find family records.

Revising
Making Necessary Changes

Chavez wrote a rough draft in three days. "It was messy, but I knew I had everything I wanted there," he said. Now he was ready to revise.

At this stage, Chavez began working on a printout of his story instead of working at the computer. On hard copy, he could spot problems more clearly. "If the lead is too long, you can see it—the paragraph is all gray. No one is going to get through that first paragraph," he explains.

Editing
Bringing in Style

Chavez began editing his story by checking his facts, spelling, and grammar. "If you have poor spelling and grammar or the facts are wrong, the reader will ask, 'Why should I read this guy? He doesn't know what he's talking about.'"

After that, Chavez worked to improve his style. He rewrote dull sentences to make them bold and active. He varied sentence lengths to create rhythm, so the story sounded interesting, not monotonous. Finally, he checked to be sure the story had some mystery. "You can't put all the information at the top or the reader doesn't have anything to look forward to," Lorenzo said. "You have to have some suspense, something pushing the reader forward."

Finally, Chavez turned his copy over to staff editors who reviewed his work before publication. His editors, he said, catch mistakes and other problems because they have a fresh point of view.

Civic Literacy

Using Community Resources

If possible, invite a features editor from a local publication to visit the class and talk about his or her goals and standards when assigning and reviewing feature articles. Alternatively, ask students to contact features editors at local publications and inquire about their goals and standards. Ask students what they can conclude about their own feature writing as a result of this information.

Examining Writing in the Real World

Analyzing the Media Connection

Discuss the following questions about the article on pages 54–55.

1. For what audience did Chavez write his feature story?
2. In what ways does Chavez direct the article to the interests of his readers?
3. Chavez describes the Vela family reunion that 1,500 family members attended. How effective was this anecdote?
4. Why do you think Chavez opens the story by focusing on the family search of one woman, Mickey Garcia? Why does he return to Garcia at the closing?
5. Chavez includes some history about Spanish and Mexican migration. What do you think his reason is for including this information?

Analyzing A Writer's Process

Discuss these questions about Lorenzo Chavez's writing process.

1. How was the topic for Chavez's article selected?
2. What sources of facts did Chavez use for his story? What are some other possible sources he might have used?
3. Before he started to draft his story, what did Chavez need to know about his audience?
4. Why did Chavez revise on a printout rather than on the computer?
5. Why does Chavez take extra care to check his spelling and grammar?

Grammar*Link*

Vary sentence lengths.

Lorenzo Chavez writes that he varied sentence lengths to create rhythm, so the story sounded interesting, not monotonous. You can vary sentence lengths by using a variety of sentence patterns: simple, compound, complex, and compound-complex.

Revise each item below by combining each pair of simple sentences in two different ways. Add or change words or phrases as needed.

1. Feature story ideas are everywhere. Ideas often come from news articles.
2. Chavez writes for *Vista* magazine. *Vista* is targeted to Hispanic readers.
3. Chavez interviewed genealogists. He collected taped conversations.
4. Chavez improved his draft. He changed words and sentences.
5. Genealogists share their research findings. There are many genealogical societies.

See Lessons 13.3 and 13.4, pages 541–544.

3. Most students will agree that the Vela anecdote is powerful.
4. Garcia is portrayed as a "treasure hunter" to grab readers' interest as the story opens. Chavez returns to Garcia at the closing to show how important it is for good genealogists to be "good detectives."
5. Chavez probably includes this information to demonstrate how records can be found in different locations.

Analyzing A Writer's Process

1. Readers of *Vista* suggested the topic.
2. He used newspaper clippings and librarians and researchers. He might also have used genealogy societies and primary sources.
3. He needed to know their ages, interests, and cultural backgrounds.
4. He could fix problems more easily on a hard copy.
5. If readers see many spelling or grammatical errors, then they may question the accuracy of his writing or stop reading him.

Reteaching

Have students verify the clarity of their ideas, the flow of their sentences, and the grammatical correctness of their writing by reading their work aloud.

Enrichment

Challenge students to write an expository paragraph about a topic of concern in their community or school.

Close

Have students discuss how to use the process described in the Media Connection to write a feature story for the school newspaper.

Grammar*Link*

Answers

Answers will vary, but some suggestions are given below.

1. Feature story ideas are everywhere; they often come from news articles.
2. Chavez writes for *Vista* magazine, which is targeted to Hispanic readers.
3. Chavez interviewed genealogists, whose conversations he taped.
4. Chavez improved his draft by changing words and sentences.
5. There are many genealogical societies, and genealogists in these societies share their research findings with each other.

Focus

Lesson Overview

Objectives

- To identify and classify the five stages of the writing process
- To apply the five stages of the writing process to original writing

Skills

- prewriting; drafting; revising; editing/proofreading; publishing; presenting

Critical Thinking

- analyzing; synthesizing; summarizing; evaluating; main idea

Listening and Speaking

- discussing; evaluating; questioning; explaining; listening to a persuasive speech

Bellringer

Daily Language Activity

When students enter the classroom, have this assignment on the board: *Write two sentences to describe something you designed and made yourself from scratch—such as a special food or a model airplane. Include the steps needed to make the object.*

Grammar Link to the Bellringer

Have students read their two sentences. Ask students to make sure they have used commas correctly.

See also  *Daily Language Practice*

Motivating Activity

Have students compare the steps they listed for the Bellringer activity. Point out that the planning and construction stages they went through are like the first two stages of writing: prewriting and drafting.

LESSON 2.1

Overview of the Writing Process

Writing is a way for you to explore your thoughts and mental images. It is also a way to discover more about yourself and the people and experiences that helped make you who you are.

Michelangelo, detail of the Sistine Chapel ceiling, 1508–1512

Discover the Stages in the Process

After Michelangelo had begun painting the Sistine Chapel in Rome in the sixteenth century, he thought of new ideas and decided to resketch and repaint based on those new ideas. His finished painting is thus a product of many false starts and stops—a composite of all the different ideas that occurred to Michelangelo during the painting process.

A writer works in much the same way, exploring ideas in a rough draft, refining the draft, or even discarding it and starting again. Although no two writers approach the writing process in exactly the same way, most writers go through five stages: prewriting, drafting, revising, editing/proofreading, and publishing/presenting.

Prewriting During prewriting, you decide what you want to write about by exploring ideas, feelings, and memories. You also begin to think about your audience and your purpose. Your audience is the people who will read your work. Your purpose is what you hope to accomplish through your writing.

Drafting Writing a draft, or turning your ideas into paragraphs, is a stage in the writing process and a tool in itself. As you compose your draft, you explore and develop your ideas.

Resource Manager

Planning Resources

- *Lesson Plans*

Transparencies

- *Bellringer*
- *Daily Language Practice*
- *Fine Art* 7–12
- *Two-Minute Skill Drill*
- *Writing Process* 2–8

Other Print Resources

- *Composition Enrichment,* p. 9
- *Composition Practice,* p. 9
- *Composition Reteaching,* p. 9
- *Cooperative Learning Activities,* pp. 9–12
- *Listening and Speaking Activities,* p. 6–8
- *Thinking and Study Skills,* p. 13
- *Writing Assessment and Evaluation Rubrics*

Revising The purposes of revising are to make sure that your writing is clear and well organized, that it accomplishes your objectives, and that it reaches your audience. To achieve these goals, you may need to cut or add to your writing. Mark these changes right on your draft and then incorporate them. Compare the writer's revised draft with her earlier draft to see what changes she incorporated during revising.

Editing/Proofreading The purposes of editing are to make sure that you've chosen the best possible words to communicate your ideas and that your sentences are grammatically correct. Finally, you proofread your writing and correct mistakes in capitalization, punctuation, and spelling. Note the editorial changes this writer has marked on her revised copy.

Publishing/Presenting This is the stage at which you share your work with others. You might read what you've written aloud in class, submit it to the school newspaper, or give it to a friend to read. There are many avenues for presenting your work.

Prewriting

I remember when my dad finally took me fishing that summer. I was so afraid I would do something wrong. But even though it didn't turn out the way I hoped, it was great to ... boat, t... sides, ... back, ... and ... any...

Drafting

It was the summer I turned twelve. My father loved fishing and for months I had begged him to take me with him fishing. I wanted to be a part of his world. Mostly I wanted his praise. We took a boat out on a ...

Revising and Editing

It was the summer I turned twelve. For months I had begged my father to take me with him fishing. He loved fishing, and I hoped that by joining him I would win his af^f^ection. Finally he agreed, and we took a boat out on a lake near our house. I baited the hook ^myself^ and held it up for my father's approval. The worm w^r^iggled on the barbed tip, and I shut my eyes as I lowered ~~the hook~~ ^it^ into the water. As we sat there in silence, waiting, ^#^ the sunlight beat down on my back; ~~and~~ I felt happy and sleepy. Then I felt a tug on my line - - I had caught a fish.

Journal Writing: Write to Learn

In your journal, explain the stages you went through on a recent writing assignment. How do they compare with the five stages described above?

Teach

Discovering the Stages in the Process

Designing a school election poster, planning a graduation dance, and creating a garden all involve versions of the five creative stages described in the lesson. Each activity requires generating goals, drafting a plan, revising, correcting minor errors, and presenting the product to an audience. Help students see this similarity by asking them to name creative activities in their lives that involve distinct stages. **L2**

Cooperative Learning

To provide a demonstration of the five-stage writing process, have students form small groups. Each group should write a short poem about a noun or verb, in which the first letters of the lines spell out the word (for example, "CAT": Cunning eyes / Arched back / Taloned paws). Direct the groups through the writing process: For prewriting, help students make a list of suggestions for a noun or verb, choose the word, and divide the letters of the word among the group members. For drafting, each member writes a poem line starting with the assigned letter. For revising, group members read their lines in order and change words to make the poem sound more unified. For editing, the group makes a single copy of the poem, correcting misspellings and grammar errors. For presenting, one member reads the poem aloud. **L2**

Journal Writing Tip

Identifying Stages Students may be surprised to identify the five stages in their own writing process. On the other hand, they may discover they are skipping stages. Tell them to include such reactions in their journal entries.

Teach

Using the Model

Discoveries and learning occur as a writer works through the five stages. Ask students to list some clues in the model that indicate how Walker discovered through her writing that she had absorbed her mother's stories and manner of presentation and that she wanted to record these stories. **L2**

Classifying Writing Stages

To better understand the writing process, have students examine the samples on page 59 that show three stages of work on one paragraph. Ask students to write down any changes in the three stages and to suggest reasons why the writer may have made these changes. **L1**

Two-Minute Skill Drill

Ask students to insert commas correctly in the following sentences.

Susan rides a bicycle to school but her brother rides a motorbike.

Her brother locks up his motorbike but Susan leaves her bicycle unlocked.

See also *Two-Minute Skill Drill Transparency 2.1*

Additional Resources

For further stimuli for writing, see *Fine Art Transparencies* 7–12

Writing Process Transparencies 2–8

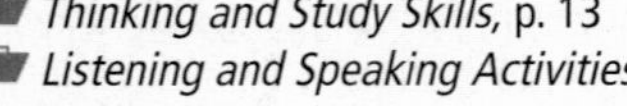

Cooperative Learning Activities

Thinking and Study Skills, p. 13

Listening and Speaking Activities, pp. 6–8

Composition Practice, p. 9

The Writing Process

Follow the Process

At any point in the writing process, you may return to any of the preceding stages. For example, if you're having trouble drafting a paragraph, you may go back to the prewriting stage and outline it first. If you get stuck as you revise, you may redraft some of your writing. You may even need to gather more information or reevaluate your purpose.

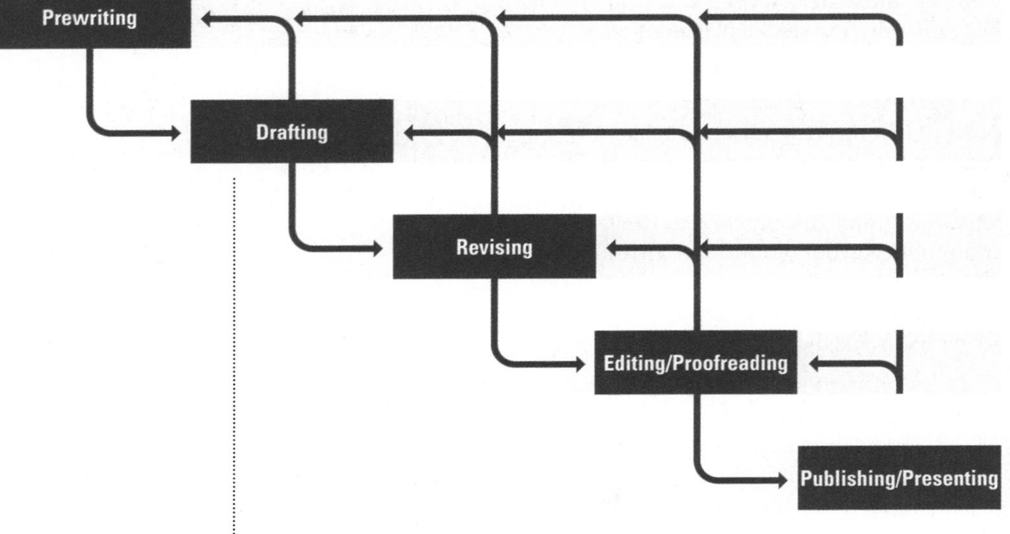

Remember, too, that because writing is a process of discovery, you may be surprised by what you find when you write. Like Alice Walker in the model below, you may discover something new about yourself, your world, and the forces that have shaped your life.

Literature Model

So many of the stories that I write . . . are my mother's stories. Only recently did I fully realize this: that through years of listening to my mother's stories of her life, I have absorbed not only the stories themselves, but something of the manner in which she spoke, something of the urgency that involves the knowledge that her stories—like her life—must be recorded.

Alice Walker, *In Search of Our Mothers' Gardens*

Through her writing, what did Walker discover about her mother?

After years of listening to her mother's stories, Walker decides she wants to write about them.

Meeting Individual Needs: English Language Learners

Brainstorming Ideas

To develop a free flow of ideas in prewriting, students with greater fluency in another language may want to brainstorm aloud with a peer in their primary language. Suggest that they note their ideas in their primary language and translate these notes into English during the drafting stage.

2.1 Writing Activities

Write a Comparison

Writer Lawrence Osgood noted that "writing is like exploring. . . . As an explorer makes maps of the country he has explored, so a writer's works are maps of the country he has explored." Use Osgood's analogy to suggest how writing is like another process, such as producing a school play, making a dress, or constructing a birdhouse.

PURPOSE To compare two processes
AUDIENCE Your classmates
LENGTH 1–2 paragraphs

WRITING RUBRICS To write a comparison of two processes, you should

- explain the actions that should occur at each stage of each process
- point out similarities and differences in the two processes
- give at least three reasons one might repeat one or more of the steps in either process

Using Computers

A diagram can often help you compare two things or two processes. Create a table using a word processing program. (Often "Table" is listed in the menu bar.) Use the table you construct to list the steps of the two processes you described in the writing activity. Compare the steps for each process and analyze which steps are repeated and why.

GrammarLink

Add commas to avoid run-on sentences.

The worm wriggled on the barbed tip, and I shut my eyes . . .

Revise the sentences below, correcting the run-on sentences by adding commas where needed.

1. It was the summer I turned thirteen and I longed to be independent.
2. My parents said the highway was too dangerous so they wouldn't let me ride my bike to the mall.
3. One day temptation grew too strong and the lure of my bike became irresistible.
4. Gasoline fumes made me feel queasy and the noise gave me a headache.
5. I got really tired and I thought I would never get there!

See Lesson 13.10, pages 555–557.

Viewing and Representing

CREATE A MEDIA PRODUCT With a partner, create a video demonstrating the two processes you compared for the writing activity. To illustrate the writing process, use the materials from a recent writing assignment, including drafts and revisions. As you demonstrate each stage of the writing process, orally describe your objectives and actions. Follow this procedure for the other process you have chosen as well. Then tell how the processes are similar and different.

LOG ON **Writing** Online | For more writing and grammar practice, go to **glencoe.com** and enter QuickPass code WC97727p1.

Assess

Evaluation Rubrics

Write a Comparison

In the comparison, use these criteria when evaluating your students' writing. The paragraph(s) should

- compare writing and exploring as processes
- cover all five stages of the process
- develop one analogy about writing
- compare all five stages of the writing process to stages of another process
- show a logical flow of ideas
- list changes and additional research
- show improvement in revision

See also *Writing Assessment & Evaluation Rubrics*

Using Computers

Consider the following in evaluating a student's diagram or chart:

- appropriate topic
- logical sequencing
- suitable labelling
- well-drawn comparisons

Reteaching

Composition Reteaching, p. 9

Enrichment

Composition Enrichment, p. 9

Fine Art Transparencies 7–12

Close

Have students outline a short story using the five-stage writing process taught in this lesson.

GrammarLink

Answers

1. turned thirteen, and
2. dangerous, so
3. strong, and
4. queasy, and
5. tired, and

Focus

Lesson Overview

Objectives
- To generate writing ideas through freewriting and collecting
- To explore writing ideas by making lists and asking questions
- To narrow a writing topic by using a network tree

Skills
- asking questions; making graphic organizers

Critical Thinking
- categorizing ideas; evaluating thoughts; defining and clarifying ideas

Listening and Speaking
- discussing; questioning

Bellringer
Daily Language Activity
When students enter the classroom, have this assignment on the board: *List all writing ideas you can think of for this topic:*

My earliest memories

Grammar Link to the Bellringer
Have students look at the phrases and sentences they wrote in the Bellringer activity. Have students think of collective nouns to refer to the singular nouns they have used (for example, *my family* for *I*; a *group of friends* for *me and my friends*)

See also *Daily Language Practice*

Motivating Activity
Discuss student ideas from the Bellringer activity. Then have the class discuss where they get their writing ideas. Explain that Leonard Bernstein got the idea for *West Side Story* from Shakespeare's play *Romeo and Juliet.* Ask students to imagine what their favorite TV show, movie, or book could inspire them to write. Explain that in this lesson they will learn how to generate and organize their writing ideas.

LESSON 2.2

Prewriting: Getting Started

Ideas for writing are everywhere. In prewriting you can use a variety of techniques to find and focus on a writing topic.

Prewriting is the stage during which you generate ideas. During prewriting you unleash your imagination to allow promising writing topics to emerge. Among the techniques that writers find useful for generating writing ideas are freewriting and collecting.

Begin with Ideas

Freewriting To freewrite, choose a topic and a time limit and then just start writing your ideas as they come to you. Don't worry about grammar, spelling, punctuation, or logic. If you run out of ideas, repeat the same word over and over until a new idea occurs to you. When the time is up, review what you've written. The ideas that most interest you are likely to be the ones that will be most worth writing about.

Take a look at the freewriting model generated by one writer. Note how many ideas she came up with in just a few minutes.

Model

I love spending time with my uncle Edward. He always has stories to tell—like how he used to roller-skate to work when he first got out of college. And stories about my father—his little brother—that make me laugh but that seem like they're about somebody else because I can't imagine my dad as a kid but I can imagine Uncle Edward as a kid, even though he's a lot older than my dad. Probably because he's so easy to talk to—he's more like my friend than my uncle. I told him that I wanted to be a writer someday, but he didn't laugh—he said I should start now. I wonder if I could write a story about Uncle Edward on skates.

Is the writer more interested in the quick flow of ideas or in following grammar or punctuation rules? How do you know?

The writer has discovered an idea for a possible writing project: her uncle's early experiences.

Resource Manager

Planning Resources
- *Lesson Plans*

Transparencies
- *Bellringer*
- *Daily Language Practice*
- *Fine Art* 7–12
- *Two-Minute Skill Drill*
- *Writing Process* 2–8

Other Print Resources
- *Composition Enrichment,* p. 10
- *Composition Practice,* p. 10
- *Composition Reteaching,* p. 10
- *Cooperative Learning Activities,* pp. 9–12
- *Listening and Speaking Activities,* p. 6–8
- *Thinking and Study Skills,* pp. 4, 11–12, 21, 24
- *Writing Across the Curriculum*
- *Writing Assessment and Evaluation Rubrics*

Collecting Books, magazines, newspapers, movies, and even conversations with other people are valuable sources of ideas and information. A good source of raw material is your journal. Based on a journal entry, Moses Thomas Greene II wrote the following reaction to a TV show.

Student Model

As a young person in America, I think of death as something that will occur when I am in my eighties or older. However, an episode of a TV show made me realize that I can't take this longevity for granted anymore.

In this episode, a group of college students in a public speaking class were given a unique assignment: they were asked to deliver their own eulogy. Although most of the students gave humorous speeches, one student took the assignment more seriously because she had Acquired Immune Deficiency Syndrome, or AIDS. Up until then, the student had kept her condition a secret, but she decided to tell her classmates the truth when she delivered her eulogy. As a result, the rest of the students began avoiding the young woman and didn't want to hear about how she was dealing with her condition.

What I liked best about the episode was that it handled the issue realistically. The students' reactions reflected the attitude of many "real" people toward the disease—ignore it and it will go away. However, the episode made me see that AIDS is a problem that needs to be dealt with and that can't be ignored.

Moses Thomas Greene II
Brentwood High School, Brentwood, New York

How does Moses "hook" you in the first paragraph of his essay?

Writing about this difficult subject helped Moses sort out his feelings about it.

Journal Writing

Pick one idea you find interesting from your own collection of raw material and freewrite about it for five minutes. What new ideas did your freewriting generate? Note these in your journal.

The Writing Process

Teach

Using the Model

Students may note that Moses hooks readers in his first paragraph by bringing up a question that interests many people: How long can we expect to live? Let students suggest other common questions or concerns that could serve as prewriting ideas. **L2**

Beginning to Freewrite

Students may feel pressured by freewriting. These students may find a group effort more accessible. Have students freewrite until they reach a dead end. As this happens, they can raise their hands and exchange notebooks with another student who has his or her hand raised. The students then freewrite about the idea in the other notebook. **L1**

Two-Minute Skill Drill

Choose one of these topics and write five words that you associate with it.

the ocean   *summer*
baseball   *winter*
gardening

See also *Two-Minute Skill Drill Transparency 2.2*

Journal Writing Tip

Drawing Conclusions Suggest that students imagine themselves to be magazine editors who are reading their freewriting for the first time. What conclusions would they draw as editors about the potential of the writing ideas they find in the freewriting?

Teach

Cooperative Learning

Organize students for a "Think-Pair-Share" activity that will help them generate lists of writing ideas. Propose topics such as "Advice for Teens," "Funny Family Stories," or "Ideal Vacations." Ask students to write individual lists, then work with a partner to discuss more ideas for their lists. Ask each pair to choose its best writing ideas to present to the class for additional comments and suggestions. **L2**

Classifying

List making involves a search for elements that share common characteristics. Initially in prewriting, students should define the classification broadly in order to generate a long list of ideas for writing. As the topic gets focused, the classification should get narrower, eliminating items from the list. For example, the students may begin by listing all embarrassing experiences and narrow the list to cases of mistaken identity. **L2**

Explore Your Ideas

Explore your ideas to clarify your thinking and find a focus for your writing. Two useful techniques for exploring ideas are making lists and asking questions.

Making Lists Start with a key word or idea and list other ideas as they occur to you. Don't worry about the order; just let your ideas flow freely from one to the next. This kind of free-association activity is also often referred to as brainstorming.

One writer used the technique of list making to generate the ideas shown below. What other ideas come to mind as you read through each list?

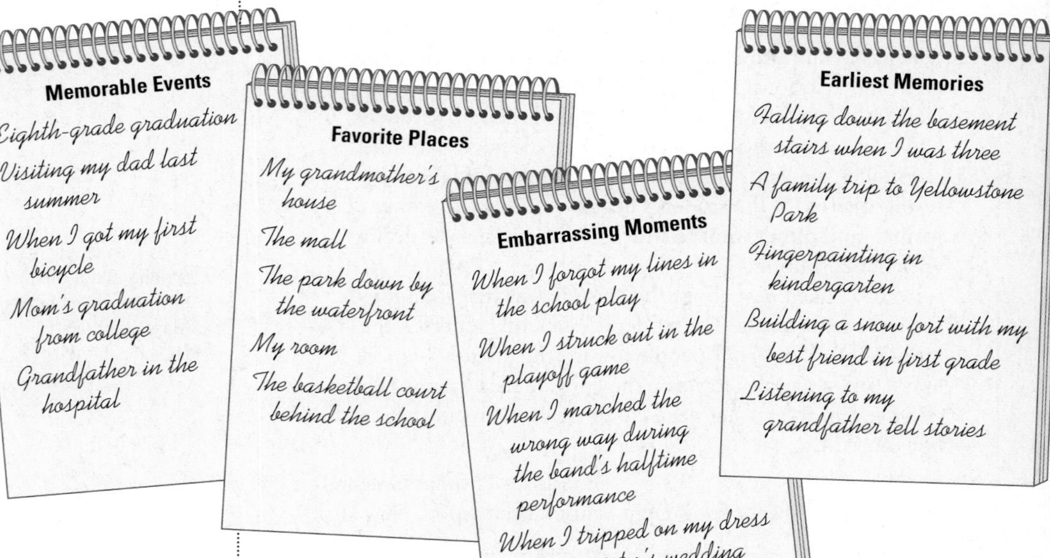

Memorable Events
Eighth-grade graduation
Visiting my dad last summer
When I got my first bicycle
Mom's graduation from college
Grandfather in the hospital
Favorite Places
My grandmother's house
The mall
The park down by the waterfront
My room
The basketball court behind the school
Embarrassing Moments
When I forgot my lines in the school play
When I struck out in the playoff game
When I marched the wrong way during the band's halftime performance
When I tripped on my dress at my sister's wedding
Earliest Memories
Falling down the basement stairs when I was three
A family trip to Yellowstone Park
Fingerpainting in kindergarten
Building a snow fort with my best friend in first grade
Listening to my grandfather tell stories

Once you've finished your lists, look them over and underline the ideas that seem most interesting to you. Draw lines between related ideas. Did any unexpected ideas appear? Did you recall events you had not thought about for a long time? Did you learn something new about yourself? These ideas may be worthwhile writing topics.

Viewing and Representing

Visual Lists

Students may find it easier to record ideas through visual means than through words. For example, students might clip advertisements, cartoons, or photographs from magazines. Alternatively, students might use objects they collect on a walk to create an idea collage. These visual "lists" can be explored and focused using the same processes described in the lesson.

Asking Questions To explore a topic by asking and answering questions about it, begin with six basic questions: *who? what? where? when? why?* and *how?* In the chart below, the writer explored an idea generated through list making by asking and answering questions based on these six questions.

Questions to Explore Ideas

Who	**Q.** Who or what do I want to write about? **A.** My 73-year-old grandfather, who grew up in Vietnam and came to the United States after the Vietnam War.
What	**Q.** What happened to my subject? **A.** During the war he was separated from his family. He finally escaped from Vietnam. He spent a long time in a refugee camp, until family members in the United States could arrange for him to come here.
Where	**Q.** Where did this happen? **A.** In a small village in Vietnam and later in a refugee camp just across the border of Thailand.
When	**Q.** When did this happen? **A.** He escaped in 1973 and lived in a makeshift tent in Thailand until 1978.
Why	**Q.** Why did this happen? **A.** He escaped from Vietnam because of the war. Many people left Vietnam because they were afraid of the new Communist leaders. They fled to nearby Thailand because it wasn't under Communist rule.
How	**Q.** How did this happen? **A.** He was able to escape from Vietnam and start a new life in the United States partly because of his determination to see his family again and partly because of luck.

Journal Writing

Choose a family member you might like to write about. In your journal, pose *who, what, where, when, why,* and *how* questions to explore your subject. Think of possible answers and record them in your journal.

Asking Oral Questions

Many students find writing of any kind difficult, even listing or freewriting. For these students, recording their ideas on a tape recorder allows them to focus on what they have to say rather than on the writing itself. If students do not have access to tape recorders, this activity can be performed by pairs of students, with one person taking notes to record the ideas of the other. **L1**

Meeting Individual Needs: Less Proficient Readers

Answering Questions

Some students may find that they organize their ideas best if they use diagrams or rough sketches. Have these students answer the questions *who? what? where? when? why?* and *how?* by drawing a simple pencil sketch or diagram. **L1**

Teach

Elaborating

Provide students with a few quotations from which to choose for the starting point of a network tree of writing ideas. Possible quotes include the following: "Instead of loving your enemies, treat your friends a little better"—E. W. Howe, journalist. "Big sisters are the crabgrass on the lawn of life"—Charles Schulz, cartoonist. Students may begin by putting the idea into their own words, and then listing examples to develop the idea beyond a simple statement. **L2**

Making Network Trees

Give students, or allow them to choose, a general topic to begin their trees. Remind them to narrow the focus further each time they move to a new level. Once the trees are complete, students can fill in sentences explaining the connections between adjacent entries. In other words, what made the writer leap from one thought to the next? **L3**

Additional Resources

For further stimuli for the writing process, see *Fine Art Transparencies* 7–12.

Writing Process Transparencies 2–8
Writing Across the Curriculum
Cooperative Learning Activities
Thinking and Study Skills, pp. 4, 11–12, 21, 24
Listening and Speaking Activities, pp. 6–8
Composition Practice, p. 10

Narrow Your Topic

Once you've chosen a general topic to write about, you need to narrow its scope. You can use a network tree to help you narrow your writing topic. Start by listing your general topic at the top of the tree. Then use the same free-association technique that you used in list making to generate ideas to fill out the tree. Notice in the network tree below how many ideas the writer identified by using the questions on page 65 to explore an idea generated during list making.

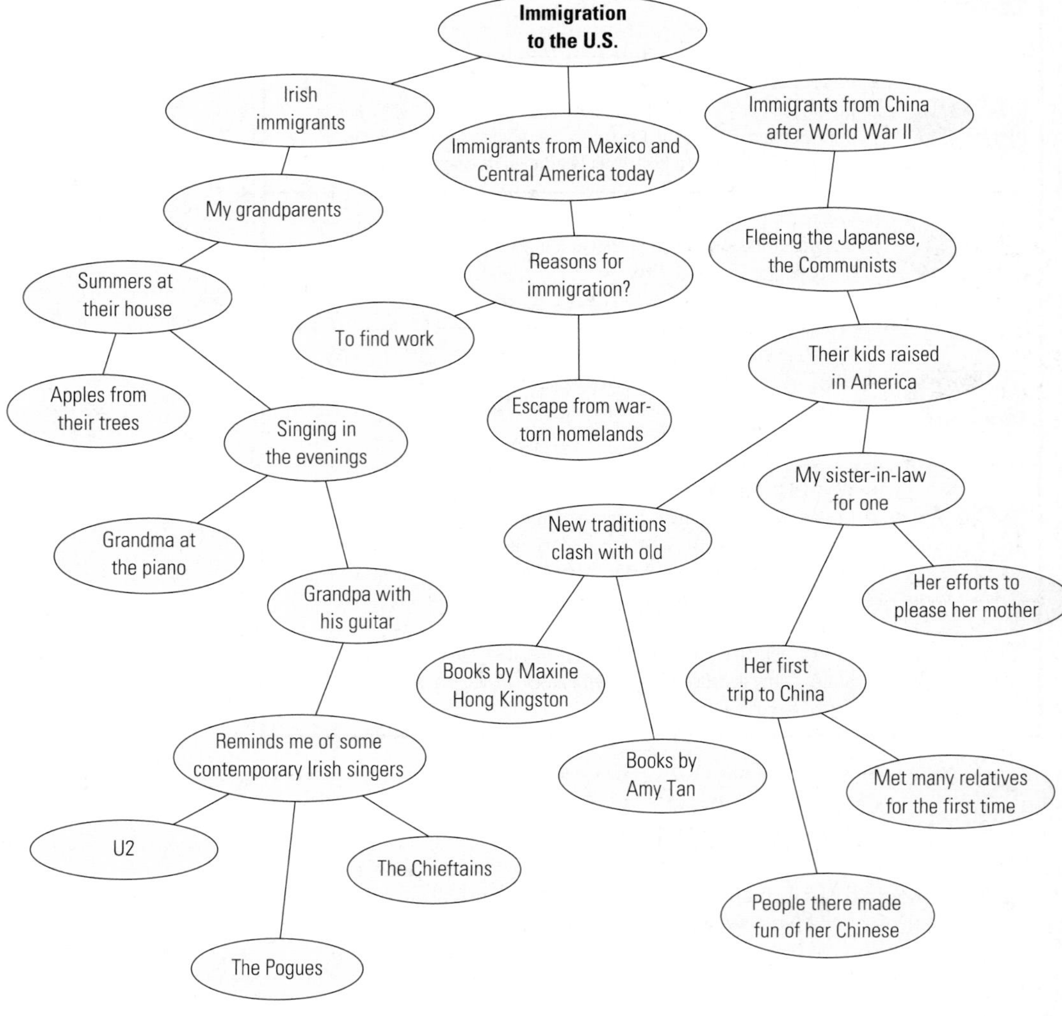

Meeting Individual Needs: English Language Learners

Explaining Ideas

Some students may have difficulty using English to express the connections between different levels. Have these students work in groups to practice explaining their ideas. They may want to use sketches or props to help explain the connections between ideas.

2.2 Writing Activities

Generate Story Ideas

In this unit you will be writing a human-interest feature story. Use the prewriting methods discussed in this lesson to choose three possible topics for your story.

PURPOSE To explore story ideas
AUDIENCE Yourself
LENGTH 1–2 pages

WRITING RUBRICS To effectively prewrite, you should

- freewrite or collect ideas from other sources
- list ideas and see how they relate to each other
- ask questions to explore and clarify ideas
- create a network tree to narrow a topic

Using Computers

Explore human-interest stories by checking the Web pages of newsmagazines on the Internet. Read the topics highlighted in the tables of contents of the issues. Use these topic ideas to help generate your own topic ideas for a human-interest feature story.

Listening and Speaking

COOPERATIVE LEARNING In a small group, study and discuss a painting in this book that features a person. What do the details in the painting reveal about the life of this person? Then brainstorm to develop a list of possible topics for human-interest stories suggested by the painting. Choose a group member to record the topics so that they can be shared with the entire class.

Grammar*Link*

Make collective nouns and verbs agree.

A *collective noun* takes a plural verb when it refers to individual members of a group and a singular verb when it refers to the group as a whole. In the second paragraph of the student model on page 63, Moses uses a plural verb, *were given,* with the collective noun, *group.*

Find the subject in each sentence and write it on your paper. Then write the verb in parentheses that agrees with the subject.

1. A group in English class (is/are) interested in brainstorming to gather ideas related to writing a family history.
2. The committee (is/are) quick to agree among themselves on several topics.
3. The class (agree/agrees) to pursue two or three of the suggested ideas.
4. The majority (enjoy/enjoys) writing stories about their families.
5. A panel (is chosen/are chosen) to evaluate the essays.

See Lesson 16.4, page 614.

LOG ON **Writing Online** For more writing and grammar practice, go to **glencoe.com** and enter QuickPass code WC97727p1.

Assess

Evaluation Rubrics

Generate Story Ideas

Ideas will vary. Ideas should relate to one another. A network tree should effectively narrow the topic.

See also *Writing Assessment & Evaluation Rubrics*

Listening and Speaking

Answers will vary. Students might notice the mood of a painting, the facial expressions of a figure, or the objects represented. Topics for a human-interest story could include growing up, receiving bad news, growing old, and so on.

Reteaching

Composition Reteaching, p. 10.

Enrichment

Composition Enrichment, p. 10.

Fine Art Transparencies 7–12

Close

Read aloud to students the first paragraph from a recent newspaper human-interest story. Have students freewrite to list ideas the author could have covered in the article.

Grammar*Link*

Answers

1. group is
2. committee are
3. class agrees
4. majority enjoy
5. panel is chosen

Focus

Lesson Overview

Objectives

- To determine the primary purpose for a piece of writing
- To communicate with an audience by finding the right level and language for a piece of writing

Skills

- determining purpose; addressing an audience

Critical Thinking

- analyzing; establishing and applying criteria; building background

Listening and Speaking

- oral reporting; discussing

Bellringer

Daily Language Activity

When students enter the classroom, have this activity on the board: *Choose a topic that you think would make a good magazine article. Explain why you would want the article published.*

Grammar Link to the Bellringer

Consider the different purposes people have for writing. For example, read the following sentences: *Fun, food, and friends are awaiting everyone who volunteers for the recycling jamboree. Sign-up sheets are in the gym.* What's the purpose of these sentences? How would you rewrite them to inform the reader about the recycling program?

See also *Daily Language Practice*

Motivating Activity

Discuss students' ideas from the Bellringer activity. On the board, list possible purposes for writing. How would the writing process differ in each case? Explain that in this lesson they will learn to identify the purpose for their writing and determine their audience.

LESSON 2.3

Prewriting: Identifying Purpose and Audience

You can focus your ideas by defining the reason for your writing (your purpose) and determining the people for whom you are writing (your audience).

The earlier you determine the audience and purpose for your writing, the more focused your final product will be. Here is how one writer narrowed her topic to establish a purpose. How will her choice of audience focus her topic still further?

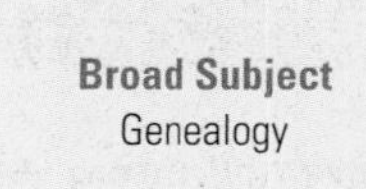
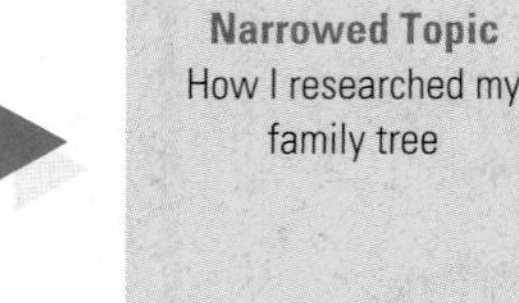

Broad Subject		Narrowed Topic		Purpose
Genealogy	▶	How I researched my family tree	▶	To explain to readers how they can research their own family histories

Determine a Purpose

Consider the primary purpose for your writing: to inform or explain, to persuade, to amuse or entertain, to narrate, or to describe. Sometimes, however, you may write to accomplish more than one purpose. For instance, if you write a letter to the editor of your school newspaper praising a campaign to raise money for a shelter for the homeless, your primary purpose might be to inform your fellow students about the campaign and the shelter. Your secondary purpose might be to persuade students to help with the campaign. To determine the primary purpose of your writing, answer the questions on page 69.

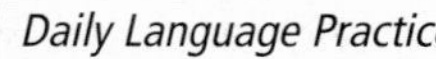

Resource Manager

Planning Resources

- *Lesson Plans*

Transparencies

- *Bellringer*
- *Daily Language Practice*
- *Fine Art* 7–12
- *Two-Minute Skill Drill*
- *Writing Process* 2–8

Other Print Resources

- *Composition Enrichment*, p. 11
- *Composition Practice*, p. 11
- *Composition Reteaching*, p. 11
- *Cooperative Learning Activities*, pp. 9–12
- *Listening and Speaking Activities*, pp. 6–8
- *Thinking and Study Skills*, pp. 2, 29–30
- *Writing Across the Curriculum*
- *Writing Assessment and Evaluation Rubrics*

Questions for Determining Your Purpose
1. Do I want to narrate, or tell, a story?
2. Do I want to describe someone or something?
3. Do I want to inform my readers about the topic or to explain something about it?
4. Do I want to persuade my readers to change their minds about something or take some action?

In the following paragraphs, writer Yoshiko Uchida explains her purpose in writing about the lives of Japanese Americans during World War II. At that time, the United States was at war with Japan. Many Japanese American families were forced to leave their homes and live in camps run by the U.S. government. Uchida often speaks to schoolchildren about her own experiences in one of the camps.

Literature Model

I always ask the children why they think I wrote *Journey to Topaz* and *Journey Home,* in which I tell of the wartime experiences of the Japanese Americans. "To tell about the camps?" they ask. "To tell how you felt? To tell what happened to the Japanese people?"

"Yes," I answer, but I continue the discussion until finally one of them will say, "You wrote those books so it won't ever happen again."

And that is why I wrote [*Desert Exile*]. I wrote it for the young Japanese Americans who seek a sense of continuity with their past. But I wrote it as well for all Americans, with the hope that through knowledge of the past, they will never allow another group of people in America to be sent into a desert exile ever again.

Yoshiko Uchida, *Desert Exile*

What is Uchida's primary purpose? Do you think Uchida believes that "the pen is mightier than the sword"?

Uchida considers the needs of her two audiences: Japanese Americans and all other Americans.

Journal Writing

Choose a topic that appeals to you. How might you approach that topic if your purpose were to inform? To persuade? To entertain? To narrate? To describe? In your journal, jot down ideas about different ways to approach the same topic.

Teach

Using the Model

Uchida's primary purpose is to be sure that this kind of mistreatment and persecution never happens again; thus she may well believe that "the pen is mightier than the sword." **L2**

Two-Minute Skill Drill

Have students write a purpose they might have in addressing the following audiences on the topic *A Fund Drive to Buy Band Uniforms.*

parents	*merchants*
students	*Student Council*

See also *Two-Minute Skill Drill Transparency 2.3*

Journal Writing Tip

Setting Goals You might remind students that communication often combines more than one purpose. For example, persuasive writing can also be entertaining.

Teach

Understanding Audience

Students who have difficulty grasping the idea of tone may find it helpful to role-play conversations with a partner. First suggest topics for students to role-play, such as explaining to the teacher why they were late to school or telling a teacher their plans for the weekend. Then ask them to assume different roles (for example, a student explaining plans for the weekend to a friend or to the parents of the friend). Discuss how the tones of the two conversations differ. **L1**

Understanding Tone

One skill advanced writers must learn is how to adapt their tone to the intended purpose and audience. To help students master this skill, have them practice revising passages for different purposes and different audiences. For example, ask them to take a passage explaining how a camera works and rewrite it to introduce the camera to a group of fourth graders. **L3**

Additional Resources

For further stimuli for writing, see *Fine Art Transparencies* 7–12.

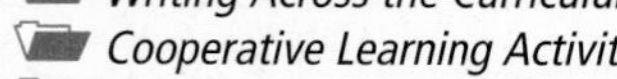

Writing Process Transparencies 2–8

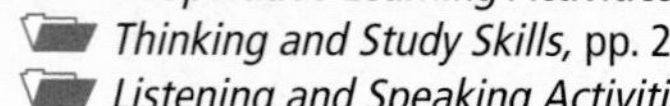

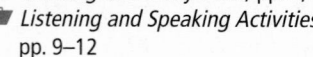

Writing Across the Curriculum

Cooperative Learning Activities

Thinking and Study Skills, pp. 2, 29–30

Listening and Speaking Activities, pp. 9–12

Composition Practice, p. 11

Address Your Audience

To best communicate with your audience, put yourself in their place. Think about what your readers need or want to know about the subject. Consider also the language that would best communicate your ideas to them.

Find the Right Level Identify the various aspects of the subject that will most interest your readers. For example, an audience of tennis enthusiasts may enjoy reading about the specific shots a player used to win a game. However, an audience that is less familiar with the sport may be more interested in reading about the player's personality.

Then consider how much your audience already knows about the topic you've chosen. This will help you avoid explaining something most of your readers already know or writing about something they don't understand.

Find the Right Language Choose words that are appropriate to your audience and purpose. For a research paper or a letter to the principal, you would use formal English, paying attention to rules of standard grammar and usage. For a letter to a friend, conversational English would be more appropriate.

To make sure that your writing will reach its intended audience, you can ask yourself several questions. The questions below helped one writer determine how to address his audience. The writer chose to write on the following topic: "How My Sister Ann Drives Me Crazy." His basic purpose was to entertain.

Questions to Help You Address Your Audience	
1. Whom am I writing for?	My English class, other ninth graders
2. How much do they know about Ann?	Not much. I'll have to present a vivid description and character sketch of my sister.
3. What writing style should I use?	I'll use a humorous, informal, conversational style to help keep them interested in what I'm saying.
4. What vocabulary is appropriate?	Words they understand, especially some contractions and slang to get across the way my sister talks.

Listening and Speaking

Understanding Purpose and Audience

To help students recognize how they change their speaking to suit their purpose and audience, draw a two-column chart on the board. Under *Purpose* list *inform, persuade, entertain, narrate a story, describe.* Under *Audience* list *classmates, teachers, friends, family, people in authority.* Draw a line to connect a purpose and an audience. Ask questions such as *How is the way you persuade a teacher to believe you the same or different from the way you persuade your friends?*

2.3 Writing Activities

Identify Purpose and Audience

For each of the possible topics you listed in the Generate Story Ideas activity, page 67 of Lesson 2.2, ask yourself the questions on page 69 to define your purpose for writing. Likewise, use the questions on page 70 to identify your audience and determine how to address that audience. Then select a final topic for your human-interest story.

PURPOSE To choose a final topic
AUDIENCE Yourself
LENGTH 1–2 pages

WRITING RUBRICS To choose a final topic, you should

- determine if your purpose is to inform, persuade, entertain, or describe
- consider the aspects of a topic suitable for your audience

Using Computers

Write e-mails to three friends, describing your final topic. Ask each to comment on your topic, to share ideas on how he or she would make the topic more specific or interesting, and to offer suggestions for developing the topic into a story. Make a list or printout of their suggestions and keep it handy as you work on the story.

Listening and Speaking

COOPERATIVE LEARNING In a small group, prepare and give a short presentation describing an event from your history textbook. Each group member should choose a different purpose and audience for his or her presentation. For example, one student might describe the event as if he or she were talking to a kindergarten class, with the purpose of illustrating courageous behavior. Another student might describe the event as if talking to a history class, with the purpose of analyzing the factors that led up to the event. After the presentations, discuss how vocabulary, sentence structure, content, and other elements vary with differences in purpose and audience.

GrammarLink

Revise sentences to suit an audience.

Revise each complex sentence into two simple sentences to make it more suitable for a young audience.

1. When our big family reunion took place last August, we all looked forward to a good time.
2. Because we had planned so many special events, there was scarcely time to visit with everybody.
3. Despite the fact that some of the younger cousins ate too much, no one became ill.
4. We tried to include a picture of everyone in the big photo album that we made to record the event.

See Lesson 13.3, pages 541–542.

LOG ON **Writing** Online | For more writing and grammar practice, go to **glencoe.com** and enter QuickPass code WC97727p1.

Assess

Evaluation Rubrics

Identify Purpose and Audience

Use these criteria when evaluating your students' writing.

- Is the purpose clear?
- Are the style and vocabulary appropriate to the audience?
- Does the topic address the needs and backgrounds of the audience?

See also *Writing Assessment & Evaluation Rubrics*

Listening and Speaking

Use the following criteria to evaluate student groups.

- Does the group give everyone the opportunity to participate?
- Do group members work together to help create each member's presentation?
- Do presentations clearly vary in terms of audience and purpose?

Reteaching

Composition Reteaching, p. 11

Enrichment

Composition Enrichment, p. 11

Fine Art Transparencies 7–12

Close

Ask students to bring in articles from newspapers and magazines to read aloud to the class. Then have students discuss the intended purpose and audience for each piece.

GrammarLink

Answers

Answers will vary, but some suggestions are given below.

1. Our big August . . . We . . . time.
2. We had planned . . . events. There . . . everybody.
3. Some . . . ate too much. No . . . ill.
4. We . . . album. We made it to record the event.

Focus

Lesson Overview

Objectives

- To use library resources to obtain information for a writing project
- To learn how to use informational interviews and oral histories as resources for a writing project

Skills

- using the library; conducting interviews; taking notes

Critical Thinking

- synthesizing; categorizing; classifying; recalling; relating; evaluating; summarizing

Listening and Speaking

- interviewing; note taking; questioning

Bellringer

Daily Language Activity

When students enter the classroom, have this assignment on the board: *Describe the last interview you saw, conducted, or granted. Who were the participants? What was the subject? How might the information obtained through an interview differ from information gathered at a library?*

Grammar Link to the Bellringer

Ask students how the spoken word is indicated in writing. (quotation marks) Point out that quotation marks are used not only to indicate what a person actually said but also to identify material quoted from other authors.

See also  *Daily Language Practice*

Motivating Activity

Invite volunteers to share what they wrote for the Bellringer activity. Lead a discussion of students' experiences with interviews and library research.

LESSON 2.4

Prewriting: Gathering Information

Whatever your writing project is, you will need some type of information. Using the library and interviewing people can usually provide you with the information you need.

Use the Library

If your writing project requires information that you do not already have, your school or public library is the best place to find the information you need. Use these tips to make your research more efficient.

- Search for books by title, subject, or author, using either the card catalog or the online computer system.
- Use the subject headings for each listing as cross-references to related material.
- Browse among other books in the section in which you locate a useful book.
- Jot down the author, title, and call number of each book you think you will use.
- Record books that *don't* provide help (so you won't search for them again).
- Examine each book's bibliography for related titles.
- Try to be an independent researcher, but ask a librarian for help if you cannot locate much information on your topic.

See Unit 23, pages 798–810, for more information on using library resources.

Resource Manager

Planning Resources

- *Lesson Plans*

Transparencies

- *Bellringer*
- *Daily Language Practice*
- *Fine Art* 7–12
- *Two-Minute Skill Drill*
- *Writing Process* 2–8

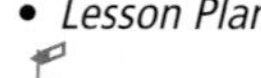

Other Print Resources

- *Composition Enrichment,* p. 12
- *Composition Practice,* p. 12
- *Composition Reteaching,* p. 12
- *Cooperative Learning Activities,* pp. 9–12
- *Listening and Speaking Activities,* pp. 6–8
- *Thinking and Study Skills,* pp. 4, 6–7
- *Writing Across the Curriculum*
- *Writing Assessment and Evaluation Rubrics*

Conduct Interviews

Some of your best sources for information may be people. Use interviews to find out about a person's ideas, feelings, and experiences.

Informational Interviews In an informational interview, you ask a person to speak about a subject he or she knows well. The interview may be informal (that is, a casual conversation) or formal (that is, one for which you need to make an appointment).

Whether your interview will be formal or informal, prepare for it carefully. Learn as much as you can about your subject and about the person you are going to interview. Think about what your readers will want to know. Then write down at least four or five major questions that will help you get at this material. Use *who, what, where, when, why,* and *how* questions so that you get answers that provide information, not just a yes or no response.

During the interview, listen carefully so that you can ask intelligent follow-up questions. Often the most interesting information emerges in response to a question you had not planned to ask. Take notes or tape-record the interview.

As soon as possible after the interview, write up a full account of it, based on your notes or your tapes. Write down everything you remember. If necessary, contact the person you interviewed to clarify any confusing ideas or questionable facts.

Before the Interview
- Make the appointment.
- Research your topic and find out about your source.
- Write out four or five basic questions.

During the Interview
- Ask informational questions (*who, what, where, when, why,* and *how*).
- Listen carefully.
- Ask follow-up questions.
- Take accurate notes (or tape-record).

After the Interview
- Write a more detailed account of the interview.
- Contact source for any needed clarification or to double-check facts.

Journal Writing

You are researching services for senior citizens in your community for a class assignment. In your journal, write down four or five informational questions you might ask a senior citizens' program director during an interview.

Teach

Taking Notes

Let students who might have difficulty taking complete notes practice interviewing in groups of three. Have group members alternate acting as interviewer, note taker, and respondent. For each interview, have the interviewer and note taker formulate questions. When the interviews are concluded, have the groups discuss any problems they encountered and share any suggestions. **L2**

Preparing for Library Research

Remind students that it is important to have a goal before going to the library. Choose a topic—pet care, a sport, a popular computer game, or a current event, for example—and write it on the board. Tell students to imagine that you plan to research the topic at a library. Beneath the topic, write a question you might answer through library research. Then ask students to suggest some more questions. Next, have students work in pairs to identify a topic they will, or might, research together at a library. Finally, have them record their topic and list their questions below it. **L1**

Journal Writing Tip

Formulating Questions Emphasize to students the importance of determining the purpose and audience for their writing before they formulate interview questions. In this way, the questions will be more likely to yield relevant information.

Teach

Setting Interview Guidelines

Have students list responsibilities they have toward the people they interview. Let students share their lists. If necessary, point out the following:

- Come to the interview with an open mind about the subject.
- Edit and use the information honestly, in a way that communicates the important facts as well as the flavor of the respondent's words.
- Respect the subject's wishes regarding comments that should remain "off the record." **L3**

Two-Minute Skill Drill

Write the questions below on the board. Have students record their answers in their notebooks.

Under what three categories is a book listed in an online or a card catalog? (title, subject, author)
What types of informational questions should be asked in interviews? (who, what, where, when, why, and how)

See also *Two-Minute Skill Drill Transparency 2.4*

Additional Resources

For further stimuli for writing, see *Fine Art Transparencies* 7–12.

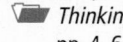

Writing Process Transparencies 2–8
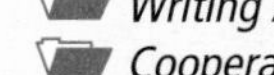
Writing Across the Curriculum
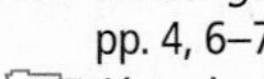
Cooperative Learning Activities
Thinking and Study Skills, pp. 4, 6–7
Listening and Speaking Activities, pp. 6–8
Composition Practice, p. 12

Oral Histories To obtain information about an event in recent history, you might interview someone who lived through the event. For example, if you want information about your family history, interview a relative who can tell you about the lives of other family members. Such "spoken memories" are called oral history.

Family stories can tell you a great deal about both the storyteller and life in the past. The excerpt below is from the oral history *Hannah's Daughters,* which was compiled by Dorothy Gallagher. In this excerpt, Hannah Lambertson Nesbitt, who lived from 1876 to 1974, describes life on her grandfather's farm.

Literature Model

In my grandaddy's time it was different than it is now. It was all hand labor, and men could support their families. . . . We had poorhouses, yes. A lot of men lived on a poor farm. I used to know a portion of a song about a son who persuaded his parents to deed him their farm. Well, they yielded to him and he turned them out. They had to go "over the hills to the poorhouse." That's what the song was called. There's many children did that to their folks. But I'm talking about what *my* folks done. They looked after those that needed help. If a man took sick or died, they looked after his family. Grandaddy sent Grandma to different places; she had several families she used to keep. She'd clothe them and everything else. She'd just go to visit and see what they had to have. . . . And if they needed a barrel of flour, they got it. . . . The farmers just did it. They helped those that needed it. Not like it is today.

Dorothy Gallagher, *Hannah's Daughters*

Observation

One tool that newswriters use is observation—witnessing an event and recording it. Trials, ball games, and congressional debates are examples of events that are described for millions by people observing the events. Careful observation requires the use of the observer's five senses to gather information. The observer takes notes, writing down the important points so that nothing is forgotten or overlooked. The notes then are the basis for the written report of the event—perhaps in a newspaper or magazine article.

English Language Learners

Finding a Focus

Students who have difficulty gathering information in English might find it helpful to first brainstorm with a fluent English speaker to develop a list of ideas and organizational tasks. Have a third student list the ideas—topics, people to interview, preparations, and even specific interview questions. This method allows all three students to clarify in English an overall direction for the research before being required to do any interviewing, reading, or writing.

2.4 Writing Activities

Gather Information About Your Topic

Think carefully about your topic. What kind of information do you need? What is the most effective method of gathering that information? Using the method you have chosen, start making informational notes that you might include in your paper.

PURPOSE To gather information
AUDIENCE Yourself
LENGTH Varies

WRITING RUBRICS To gather information for your topic, you should

- locate the best sources of information
- make arrangements to interview sources
- prepare a list of questions you will ask in an interview
- include enough information in your notes

Using Computers

Your computer can be an excellent tool to save valuable information for research projects. You can use it when compiling a family history or any research project for which you will gather information over a long period of time. Establish a classification system, and use it to list the information you've obtained, the source, and the date. As you gather additional data, create subheads to classify, store, change, and retrieve information as needed.

Grammar*Link*

Use quotation marks to indicate speech.

Rewrite each of the sentences below, adding quotation marks wherever they are necessary.

1. When I first began teaching, said my former teacher Mrs. Moody, things were very different.
2. Can you tell me about some of those differences? I asked.
3. Well, she said, for one thing, many classes were bigger.
4. We really didn't do much group work, she added.
5. I also remember, she continued, that there was time for physical education as well as art and music.

See Lesson 21.9, pages 752–756.

Listening and Speaking

PREPARING TO INTERVIEW In a small group, plan questions you might ask a subject in order to explore your topic. Write your questions legibly on note cards or notebook paper. Then role-play an interview with one member of the group. Invite other group members to share suggestions for improving your interview. Repeat the process so that all group members participate.

LOG ON **Writing** Online | For more writing and grammar practice, go to glencoe.com and enter QuickPass code WC97727p1.

Assess

Evaluation Rubrics

Gather Information About Your Topic

Use these criteria when evaluating your students' notes:

- Has the student located the best sources of information?
- Has the student made arrangements to interview sources?
- Has the student prepared questions to ask in an interview?
- Has the student included enough information in his or her notes?

See also *Writing Assessment & Evaluation Rubrics*

Using Computers

Ask students to provide a diskette or a paper printout of their work. Check that students' classification systems include

- a list of information gathered at a library or through an interview
- a record of sources
- the date when the information was gathered

Reteaching

Composition Reteaching, p. 12.

Enrichment

Composition Enrichment, p. 12.

Close

Conclude the lesson with a discussion of tips on using the library to gather information and on conducting a successful interview. Ask students to share their experiences. What was most difficult? Easiest? What would they change to improve how they conduct library research and interviews?

Grammar*Link*

Answers

1. "When . . . teaching," said . . . Mrs. Moody, "things . . . different."
2. "Can . . . differences?" I asked.
3. "Well," she said, "for . . . bigger."
4. "We . . . work," she added.
5. "I also remember," she continued, "that . . . music."

Focus

Lesson Overview

Objectives

- To organize writing ideas by sorting prewriting notes into categories
- To generate a paragraph that is organized around a main idea or topic sentence

Skills

- ordering ideas; writing paragraphs

Critical Thinking

- developing a main idea; defining and clarifying ideas

Listening and Speaking

- explaining; oral reporting; discussing

Bellringer

Daily Language Activity

When students enter the classroom, have this assignment on the board: *Suppose you want to convince your parents to let you travel to a concert performed by your favorite group. Develop a good argument to convince them.*

Grammar Link to the Bellringer

Have students share ideas. Encourage them to notice all possessive pronouns.

See also *Daily Language Practice*

Motivating Activity

Discuss student responses to the Bellringer activity. Explain that when students write, they must organize their thoughts in a logical and coherent manner in order to convince readers of the validity of their points. In this lesson, students will learn to develop a paragraph with supporting details.

LESSON 2.5

Drafting: Turning Notes into Paragraphs

When you draft, you use your prewriting notes to create a piece of writing.

Family ties, sometimes I feel like I've got so many responsibilities to my family I don't have a life of my own. Babysitting my brothers. If I have to do that again next weekend I'll just scream. And when they do something wrong, I get the blame. Can't Mom see I need to have some time to myself? Wasn't she ever my age? Life must have been so different when she was growing up.

Prewriting Notes

Swimming

First experience—nearly drowned when I fell into a pond when I was four years old

Learning to swim was a nightmare for me

If we were meant to swim, we'd have gills and fins

The time my uncle taught me how to tread water—he was so patient, didn't laugh at me

Overcame fears

Wonder what a wave-action pool is like . . .

Prewriting Notes

Your first draft will not be perfect. It's your first try at presenting your ideas in an order that makes sense and shaping them into paragraphs.

Put Your Ideas in Order

One way to put your ideas in order is to sort them into categories. If an idea doesn't seem to fit anywhere, leave it out. If a new idea occurs to you while you are sorting, include the idea if it fits. Look at the way one writer organized her ideas on the topic "I always liked my aunt Alicia best."

Resource Manager

Planning Resources

- *Lesson Plans*

Transparencies

- *Bellringer*
- *Daily Language Practice*
- *Fine Art* 7–12
- *Two-Minute Skill Drill*
- *Writing Process* 2–8

Other Print Resources

- *Composition Enrichment,* p. 13
- *Composition Practice,* p. 13
- *Composition Reteaching,* p. 13
- *Cooperative Learning Activities,* pp. 9–12
- *Listening and Speaking Activities,* pp. 6–8
- *Thinking and Study Skills,* pp. 2, 17, 23
- *Writing Assessment and Evaluation Rubrics*

Organizing Ideas

- My aunt Alicia
- Her mysterious apartment in the city
- Apartment filled with books and the little clay animals she found in Mexico
- I got lost once on my way there
- Her embroidered jeans jacket
- Her flashy jewelry
- Long dark hair, held up with a comb
- Treated me like a person, not just her niece
- Listening to her old rock-and-roll records

Introductory Material
- My aunt Alicia
- Her flashy jewelry
- Her embroidered jeans jacket
- Long dark hair, held up with a comb

Body
- Her mysterious apartment in the city
- Listening to her old rock-and-roll records
- Apartment filled with books and the little clay animals she found in Mexico

Concluding Material
- Treated me like a person, not just her niece
- One place in the world I felt at home

Write Paragraphs

Each paragraph in your draft should be organized around one main, controlling idea. Often the main idea is stated in a topic sentence. The supporting details develop the main idea by proving, clarifying, or expanding upon it. Like building blocks, the supporting ideas provide the foundation on which the main idea rests.

There is no magic formula for writing a paragraph. One approach is to write supporting sentences first to help determine a main idea and then write a topic sentence to express that idea. An alternative approach is to write the topic sentence first. Keep in mind that you can revise any part of your paragraph at any point in the writing process.

Journal Writing

Look through your journal for possible main ideas for paragraphs. Pick one idea and list supporting details that you might use to develop that idea in a paragraph.

The Writing Process

Teach

Ordering Ideas

Ask students to think of times they have prepared for a conversation, such as when breaking bad news to their parents or asking someone out on a date. You might compare this to the drafting stage of a writing project. In preparing for the conversation, they probably thought about their audience and their objective, and then tried out a few opening lines. When beginning a draft, students should remember not to try to put each sentence down in its final form. **L2**

Visualizing a Paragraph

Students may have difficulty creating a paragraph from a set of related ideas. A visual exercise may help. Have students write each of their ideas on separate papers which they move around until a logical structure emerges. Note that a main idea is like a title; the details support it. **L1**

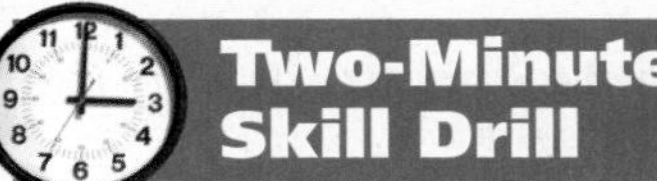

Two-Minute Skill Drill

Write five supporting details for one of the following topics:

my best friend *my mother or father*
my hobby *last summer*
ice cream

See also *Two-Minute Skill Drill Transparency 2.5*

Journal Writing Tip

Identifying Main Ideas Mention that instead of identifying main ideas, students may be drawn to a group of details in their journal that can be turned into a paragraph with the addition of a main-idea sentence.

Teach

Using the Model

The topic sentence introduces the comparison in an intriguing manner, while the concluding sentence restates the comparison and adds a new dimension—grandfather's respect for Mary and for no one else in the family. **L2**

Analyzing Topic Sentences

As students begin to develop their own style, they may experiment with the structure of their paragraphs. Discuss other goals for the topic sentence in addition to expressing the main idea. These may include arousing interest, curiosity, suspense, or concern; and conveying a tone, such as shock or surprise. Allow students to experiment by writing different topic sentences for the same topic to achieve these or other effects. **L3**

Additional Resources

For further stimuli for writing, see *Fine Art Transparencies* 7–12.

Writing Process Transparencies 2–8
Cooperative Learning Activities
Thinking and Study Skills
Listening and Speaking Activities, pp. 6–8
Composition Practice, p. 13

A topic sentence may be a statement or a question. Whatever its form, a good topic sentence expresses the main idea clearly and makes the reader want to keep reading. Your choice of topic sentence also helps determine how you will develop the paragraph.

Eastman Johnson, *The Hatch Family,* 1871

Try out several possible topic sentences before choosing the one that best expresses your main idea. Each of the following topic sentences is based on the painting shown here. Note how each would take a paragraph in a different direction.

- Just a century ago, several generations of a family often lived together under one roof.
- Although a frail man, my grandfather still ruled the family.
- The dark wood paneling glowed in the firelight.

Notice how the writer in the model below relates every detail to the idea stated in the topic sentence.

Literature Model

No one was particularly glad that Mary Fortune looked like her grandfather except the old man himself. He thought it added greatly to her attractiveness. He thought she was the smartest and the prettiest child he had ever seen and he let the rest of them know that if—IF that was—he left anything to anybody, it would be Mary Fortune he left it to. She was now nine, short and broad like himself, with his very light blue eyes, his wide prominent forehead, his steady penetrating scowl and his rich florid complexion; but she was like him on the inside too. She had, to a singular degree, his intelligence, his strong will, and his push and drive. Though there was seventy years' difference in their ages, the spiritual distance between them was slight. She was the only member of the family he had any respect for.

Flannery O'Connor, "A View of the Woods"

Why do you suppose O'Connor puts a topic sentence up front and reinforces it at the paragraph's conclusion?

Details reveal physical resemblance and point out similarities in personality traits.

MEETING INDIVIDUAL NEEDS

English Language Learners

Choosing a Topic

To help students find a topic for which they have sufficient English vocabulary, provide a list of topic sentences with blanks, such as the following: "One habit I'd like to break/learn is ______"; and "My mother scolds me for being ______, but I think I'm ______." Be sure the sentences are on subjects familiar to students. Once students have chosen a topic sentence, ask them to provide supporting details and create an effective paragraph.

2.5 Writing Activities

Write a First Draft

Use your prewriting notes to get your ideas down on paper. Do not worry about spelling, grammar, or correct usage at this point.

PURPOSE To write a first draft
AUDIENCE Yourself
LENGTH 1–2 pages

WRITING RUBRICS To write an effective first draft, you should

- arrange your ideas in an order that makes sense
- organize your draft into paragraphs
- make sure that each paragraph is organized around one main idea

Listening and Speaking

COLLABORATIVE WRITING In a small group, discuss the collage shown below. Then individually write a topic sentence focusing on some aspect of the picture. List details to support the topic sentence. Draft a paragraph, using the topic sentence and details.

Romare Bearden, *Blue Interior, Morning,* 1968

GrammarLink

Use apostrophes with possessive indefinite pronouns.

Indefinite pronouns, such as *everyone* and *no one,* use apostrophes to form the possessive. *Personal pronouns,* such as *his* and *hers,* do not.

Rewrite the following sentences, underlining each personal and indefinite pronoun. Add apostrophes where they are needed.

1. Someones idea was to make a list of everybodys names and special skills for a school directory.
2. You and your classmates think about each others unique talents and strengths.
3. While you compile your list, others are working on theirs.
4. Your friend Carol says that no ones list is exactly like hers.

See Lesson 17.1, page 633, and Lesson 21.11, page 759.

Using Computers

In the draft you write for the Listening and Speaking activity, boldface the topic sentence of each paragraph. Underline the supporting sentences. Then check your draft's content and organization. Evaluate your topic sentences. Check that your main ideas are well supported.

The Writing Process

LOG ON **Writing** Online | For more writing and grammar practice, go to glencoe.com and enter QuickPass code WC97727p1.

Assess

Evaluation Rubrics

Write a First Draft

Use these criteria when evaluating your students' writing.

- Are ideas in a logical order?
- Is the draft in paragraph form?
- Does each paragraph contain one main idea?

See also *Writing Assessment & Evaluation Rubrics*

Listening and Speaking

Evaluate the paragraphs on the following: each contains a clear topic sentence; each paragraph contains several supporting details; and details are presented in a logical order.

Reteaching

Composition Reteaching, p. 13

Enrichment

Composition Enrichment, p. 13

Fine Art Transparencies 7–12

Close

Have students find a paragraph in a science or history textbook and then explain its use of a topic sentence and supporting details.

GrammarLink

Answers

1. Someone's idea . . . list everybody's names and special skills . . .
2. each other's unique talents and strengths
3. correct
4. . . . no one's list is exactly like hers.

Viewing the Art

Romare Bearden, *Blue Interior, Morning,* 1968

Bearden's depiction of life in this 44-by-56-inch collage uses exaggerated images to express emotional intensity in an otherwise typical scene. This work is in the Chase Manhattan Bank collection in New York City.

Focus

Lesson Overview

Objectives

- To express the main idea of a paragraph through a topic sentence
- To construct a unified paragraph by using supporting ideas such as sensory details, examples or incidents, facts and statistics, or reasons

Skills

- developing main ideas; including supporting details; writing unified paragraphs

Critical Thinking

- synthesizing ideas; categorizing ideas; summarizing ideas; developing a main idea

Listening and Speaking

- discussing; questioning; explaining

Bellringer

Daily Language Activity

When students enter the classroom, have this assignment on the board: *What does the following paragraph describe?*

> *It is blue. Its waves crest and gently break. On windy days a small group of surfers rides its tumultuous waters.*

Grammar Link to the Bellringer

Have students analyze the verb used in the last sentence in the Bellringer activity. How would it change if *surfers* were used instead of a *small group of surfers*?

See also *Daily Language Practice*

Motivating Activity

Discuss student responses to the Bellringer activity. Remind students that implied main ideas are often found in descriptive and narrative writing. Ask why this would be so. (Showing is livelier than telling as a way of narrating a story or describing a scene.)

LESSON 2.6

The Writing Process

Drafting: Writing Unified Paragraphs

While every paragraph in your draft should be about one main idea, not every paragraph needs a topic sentence. What is the main idea of each paragraph in the model below?

Literature Model

My great-grandmother. I would've liked to have known her, a wild horse of a woman, so wild she wouldn't marry until my great-grandfather threw a sack over her head and carried her off. Just like that, as if she were a fancy chandelier. That's the way he did it.

And the story goes she never forgave him. She looked out the window all her life, the way so many women sit their sadness on an elbow. I wonder if she made the best with what she got or was she sorry because she couldn't be all the things she wanted to be. Esperanza. I have inherited her name, but I don't want to inherit her place by the window.

Sandra Cisneros, *The House on Mango Street*

The narrator, Esperanza, uses details from her great-grandmother's life to support the selection's main idea.

Do you like the way Cisneros has delayed stating the main idea until the last sentence? Why or why not?

Keep to the Main Idea

You can express a paragraph's main idea in a direct statement—that is, in a topic sentence. Or you can imply the main idea by suggesting it indirectly through your choice of supporting details.

Main Idea Stated in a Topic Sentence There are several advantages to stating your main idea in a topic sentence. First, providing a clear statement of what the paragraph is about helps give your writing direction. Second, the sentence tells the reader what to focus on.

A topic sentence may appear anywhere in the paragraph. A topic sentence that appears at the beginning of a paragraph lets the reader know what's to come. A topic sentence that appears at the end summarizes the preceding supporting details and ensures that the reader has understood the main idea.

Resource Manager

Planning Resources

- *Lesson Plans*

Transparencies

- *Bellringer*
- *Daily Language Practice*
- *Fine Art* 7–12
- *Two-Minute Skill Drill*
- *Writing Process* 2–8

Other Print Resources

- *Composition Enrichment,* p. 14
- *Composition Practice,* p. 14
- *Composition Reteaching,* p. 14
- *Cooperative Learning Activities,* pp. 9–12
- *Listening and Speaking Activities,* pp. 6–8
- *Thinking and Study Skills,* pp. 3, 13
- *Writing Across the Curriculum*
- *Writing Assessment and Evaluation Rubrics*

Implied Main Idea In some paragraphs, particularly descriptive or narrative paragraphs, the main idea is implied, or stated indirectly. In these types of writing, the supporting details are so strongly linked by a main idea that this main idea shines through without having to be stated directly. Instead of saying "I was happy to be home," a narrative writer might use details to *show* he or she was happy.

Include Supporting Details

In a unified paragraph, each sentence provides one or more details that support the main idea. The supporting details can be sensory details, examples or incidents, facts, statistics, and reasons. Your purpose in writing will help you determine which kinds of supporting details to use.

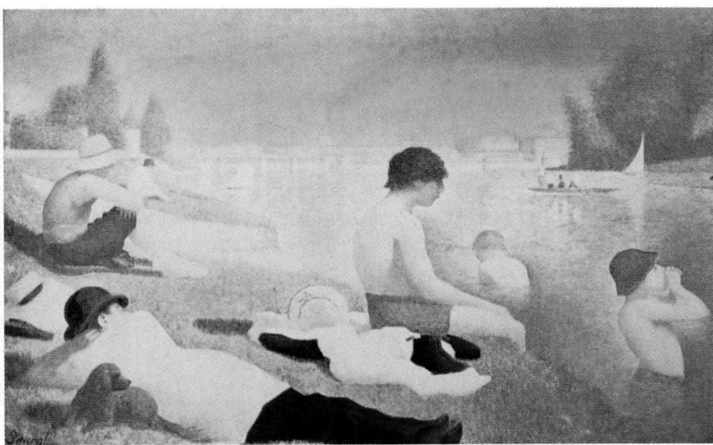

Georges Seurat, *Bathers at Asnières,* 1883–1884

Sensory Details Vivid sensory words describe how things look, sound, smell, feel, or taste. They draw your readers in and help them experience the scene or subject. To develop sensory details, try to visualize the scene you are describing and think about each of the senses in turn. For example, how would you use sensory details to describe the scene in the painting above? First, think about what you would see, hear, smell, feel, and taste if you could step inside it. Then decide what words you would use to make the scene come alive for your readers.

Journal Writing

Pick a place that's important to you or your family. Close your eyes and try to "see" it. Now listen for the sounds you hear there. Work your way through each of the other senses. In your journal, jot down the sensory details that come to mind.

Teach

Using the Model

In discussing students' reactions to placing the main idea last, note that the writer will usually have a good reason for doing so (such as letting the reader form an opinion first). To illustrate the selection's unity, ask students to go over each sentence and fragment to explain how it is related to the topic sentence.

Sandra Cisneros creates intimacy between reader and narrator by writing the passage as Esperanza might speak it. The use of sentence fragments reinforces this effect. Also, the opening fragment, "My great-grandmother," contains two important pieces of information: *My* refers to the narrator, and *great-grandmother* to the subject. Using that fragment allows the author to isolate the main issue. **L2**

Understanding Implied Main Idea

You can make the concept of an implied main idea more concrete by using tangible supporting details. Gather several objects that could serve as supporting details for a statement about the weather, such as a window scraper or earmuffs to imply cold and ice. Ask students to suggest a main idea that the objects would imply. (For example, *today the weather is cold and snowy.*) **L2**

Journal Writing Tip

Observing Before students make journal entries, remind them that sensory details needn't be noted in complete sentences. In fact, students may gather more vibrant information when they feel free of grammatical constraints.

2.6

Teach

Promoting Discussion

Discuss ways that advertisers use types of supporting details. Ask students to give examples of ads that use sensory details, examples, incidents, facts, statistics, or reasons. (For example, students might mention a TV ad that shows a sunny beach full of attractive young people quenching their thirst with a certain soft drink.) **L2**

Advanced Learners

Students can stretch their skills by completing a paragraph that has a stated main idea and then rewriting the same paragraph so that its main idea is implied. Ask students to comment on whether certain topics or purposes lend themselves to one approach or the other. **L3**

Two-Minute Skill Drill

Write a brief paragraph describing your day so far. Use the following organizing words:

First *Next*
Then *Finally*
Last

See also *Two-Minute Skill Drill Transparency 2.6*

Additional Resources

For further stimuli for writing, see *Fine Art Transparencies* 7–12.

Writing Process Transparencies 2–8
Writing Across the Curriculum
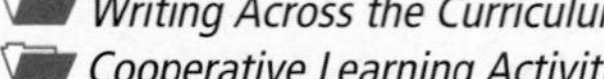
Cooperative Learning Activities
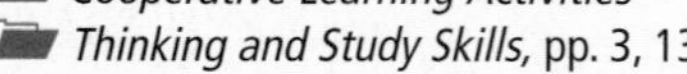
Thinking and Study Skills, pp. 3, 13
Listening and Speaking Activities, pp. 6–8
Composition Practice, p. 14

The Writing Process

Examples or Incidents Sometimes the best way to develop a main idea is through describing examples or incidents. For example, to develop the main idea that "starting high school was one of the hardest things I've ever done," you might tell about something that happened when you started high school. Then, to explore a specific incident, ask yourself *who, what, where, when, why,* and *how* questions.

Facts and Statistics Another way to support a main idea is to use facts and statistics. A fact is a statement that has been proved by observation, experience, or study—for example, "Washington, D.C., is the capital of the United States." Statistics are facts that involve numbers—for example, "The average person sees three hundred ads a day."

Suppose you wanted to write a paragraph with the following topic sentence: "There's not enough free time in the average high school student's life." Here's how one student used a time line to organize facts and statistics that could help support this topic sentence.

Facts and Statistics Organized on a Time Line

	1 P.M.	2 P.M.	3 P.M.	4 P.M.	5 P.M.	6 P.M.	7 P.M.	8 P.M.	9 P.M.
Above	Algebra: 25 word problems due tomorrow.		Track practice: 1 hour.		Eat dinner: 30 minutes. Then spend 30 minutes cleaning up, taking out the garbage.			Begin practicing lines for drama club play.	
Below		English: essay assigned. Get 85% on quiz.		Go home. Take care of brother until Mom gets home in 1.5 hours.		Start homework.			

Reasons If your topic sentence expresses an opinion or gives an explanation, you can back it up with reasons. For example, if the topic sentence of your paragraph is "Husbands and wives should undertake an equal share of the housework and child care," you might use a graphic organizer like the one below to help you develop and outline reasons that document your topic sentence.

Why should husbands and wives undertake an equal share of the housework and child care?

- The notion that taking care of the home and children is "women's work" is sexist.
- An equal relationship between parents presents a good model for their children.
- Spending more time together benefits both fathers and their children.
- It is unfair to expect women employed outside the home to shoulder all of the domestic responsibilities as well.

Less Proficient Readers

Using Statistics

Using statistics to support a main idea may be especially difficult for some students. They may have trouble understanding units of measure used in a statistic, particularly if those units are not internationally used (feet versus meters, for example). Write on the board a list of common units of measure, along with any abbreviations for the terms. Ask students to define the terms and describe a typical use. Correct any misunderstandings.

Check Your Paragraphs

Look over your draft to make sure that your paragraphs are unified.

PURPOSE To check paragraphs for unity
AUDIENCE Yourself
LENGTH 1–2 pages

WRITING RUBRICS To check paragraphs for unity, ask yourself whether

- every paragraph has an implied or a stated topic sentence
- you have used sensory details
- examples or incidents help make your point
- facts help support your main idea

Cross-Curricular Activity

SCIENCE Perform this simple experiment:

1. Fill two identical glasses nearly to the top with water.
2. Guess how many paper clips you will have to drop into each glass before the water overflows if you drop the paper clips one at a time into one glass and ten at a time into the other.
3. Explain whether you think there will be a difference and why.
4. Now drop one paper clip at a time into one glass and ten paper clips at a time into the other glass. Take notes as you observe what happens.
5. Was your guess correct?

Draft a paragraph, using your guess or theory as your topic sentence. Use your observations to support or refute your topic sentence. Include any reasons you can provide for your results.

Grammar*Link*

Make sure subjects agree with verbs.

Rewrite the following paragraph. Choose the form of the verb in parentheses that agrees with each statistical subject.

[1]When 100 percent of the world's population (is/are) considered, more than 56 percent of the people (live/lives) in rural areas. [2]In the United States, however, the opposite is true; nearly 80 percent (live/lives) in metropolitan areas. [3]More than 971,000 people now (live/lives) in Las Vegas, Nevada, making it the fastest-growing area in the country. [4]In actual numbers, more than 500,000 people (was added/were added) to the population of Los Angeles from 1990 to 1992; 231,000 (was/were) the increase in Houston. [5]Only 20 of the 268 metropolitan areas in the United States (has/have) lost population since 1990.

See Lesson 16.4, page 614.

Viewing and Representing

ANALYZING DESIGN With a partner, select a painting from this book. View the painting in terms of its elements of design: check the use of shape, color, and texture in the painting. Keep a list of your impressions. Then use your list and refer to the painting. Do all the elements of design work together to achieve one effect or to give one message to the viewer?

Writing Online — For more writing and grammar practice, go to **glencoe.com** and enter QuickPass code WC97727p1.

Assess

Evaluation Rubrics

Check Your Paragraphs

Use these criteria when evaluating your students' writing.

- Is there a topic sentence?
- Do supporting details enhance the main idea?
- Are all opinions supported by details?
- Are sensory details used effectively?

See also *Writing Assessment & Evaluation Rubrics*

Cross-Curricular Activity

Evaluate the paragraph on the following:

- a clear topic sentence
- observations that refute or support the topic sentence
- reasons for the results

Reteaching

Composition Reteaching, p. 14

Enrichment

Composition Enrichment, p. 14

Fine Art Transparencies 7–12

Close

Invite students to explain how the methods of organizing information can help them in other classes, especially science or history classes.

Grammar*Link*

Answers

1. is; live
2. live
3. live
4. were added; was
5. have

Focus

Lesson Overview

Objectives

- To identify four different methods for organizing supporting ideas in a paragraph
- To arrange supporting details in a paragraph appropriately, depending on purpose

Skills

- organizing details in logical order; using chronological order, spatial order, cause-and-effect order, and order of importance

Critical Thinking

- using patterns of organization; identifying attributes and components

Listening and Speaking

- discussing

Bellringer

Daily Language Activity

When students enter the classroom, have this assignment on the board: *Think of four items you would include if you were writing a description of this classroom. Write a sentence identifying those items in the order in which you would describe them.*

Grammar Link to the Bellringer

Have one or two students write their sentences on the board. Point out that the descriptive items in the sentences should be separated by commas.

See also  *Daily Language Practice*

Motivating Activity

Call on volunteers to share the items they would choose to describe and the order in which they would present those items. After a few students have spoken, ask the class whether they can see any similarities among the organizational patterns.

LESSON 2.7

Drafting: Ordering the Details

The way you organize details will depend on your purpose—whether you are narrating, explaining, persuading, or describing.

The computer screen below lists various methods of organizing supporting details and the most common purposes for which these methods are used. However, do not feel that you have to limit the organization of your writing to just what is shown here.

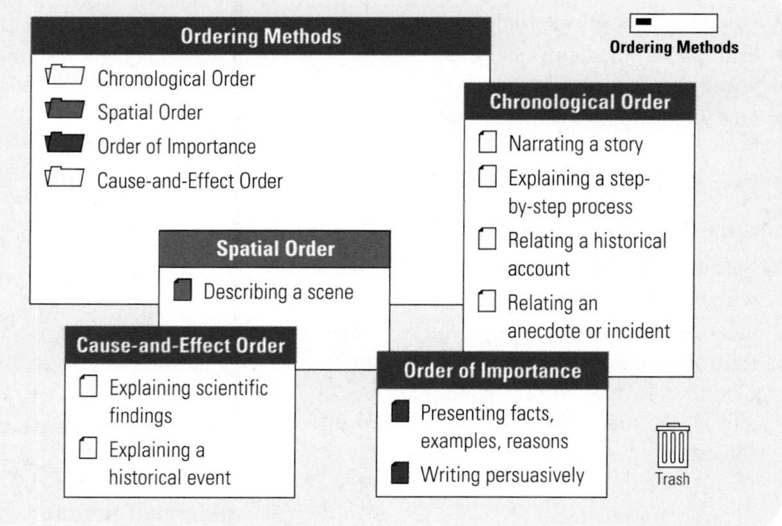

Chronological Order

Chronological order—presenting events in the order in which they happened—is often used to organize narrative writing. Study the model on page 85. Notice how writer Jim Barnes uses chronological order to narrate the details of a frightening incident.

Resource Manager

Planning Resources

- *Lesson Plans*

Transparencies

- *Bellringer*
- *Daily Language Practice*
- *Fine Art* 7–12
- *Two-Minute Skill Drill*
- *Writing Process* 2–8

Other Print Resources

- *Composition Enrichment,* p. 15
- *Composition Practice,* p. 15
- *Composition Reteaching,* p. 15
- *Cooperative Learning Activities,* pp. 9–12
- *Listening and Speaking Activities,* pp. 6–8
- *Thinking and Study Skills,* pp. 13–15
- *Writing Assessment and Evaluation Rubrics*

Literature Model

A deep, low moan—ghostly but unmistakably human—rolled up from the bowels of the black earth. There was for a moment, my brother recalls, a stillness like doom upon all of them. Then everybody was running, running. . . . A great shadow passed beside my brother. It was a horse. The moan persisted, even over the sound of thumping boots and racing hoofs. Now my brother passed the horse, and burst through the barbed wire fence at the edge of the field with one wild bound. He flung himself down the lane and plunged through the doorway of our house and hugged himself close to the dying coals in the fireplace. An hour passed before he began to cry.

Jim Barnes, "On Native Ground"

How many major events are signaled by transitions like "then," "now," and "an hour passed"?

Because Barnes describes the action almost minute by minute, the reader feels drawn into the events.

Spatial Order

Spatial order—the order in which objects appear in a physical place—is often used to organize descriptive writing. To use spatial order, describe items as they appear from left to right, from top to bottom, from back to front, or in any other logical combination. Use words like *above, below, behind,* and *next to* to help readers "see" the scene you are describing.

For example, to describe the scene shown, you might begin by identifying the checkerboard in the middle of the room. From that starting point, you might go on to describe the two men on either side of the checkerboard. Then you might move behind the men to the fireplace against the wall. Finally, you could describe the women.

Henri Matisse, *The Painter's Family*, 1911

Journal Writing

Use spatial order to describe your favorite room. Identify a starting point in the room and use words like *next to* and *above* to indicate clearly the placement of each object in the room.

The Writing Process

Teach

Using the Model

The author signals three major events by the transitions listed in the box in the margin. Ask what transitions students could use to replace these transitions (for example, *Then* might be replaced by *Suddenly*). **L2**

Cooperative Learning

Have pairs use spatial order to describe some relatively simple place or object, such as the entrance to the school or a wall of the classroom. Tell them to describe the place from left to right. They should begin by observing the place and working together to choose the details they want to include. Then one student in the pair should list those details in order from left to right; the second student should check to make sure they are in correct order. After the students have agreed on the order, each can write his or her own description. **L1**

Journal Writing Tip

Ordering Suggest that before students begin writing, they think about the room and decide on a direction to order their description—for example, clockwise or left to right.

Viewing the Art

Henri Matisse, *The Painter's Family,* 1911
Henri Matisse (1869–1954), an influential French painter, was known for his use of bright colors and bold shapes. Matisse uses color and lines to guide the viewer across his paintings. *The Painter's Family* is at the Hermitage in St. Petersburg, Russia.

2.7

Teach

Using the Visual

Call students' attention to the graphic of the dominoes. To show what this graphic illustrates, stand four dominoes in a row, push the first one over, and then ask students what made the other dominoes fall. Help them see that the fall of the last domino is the culminating event in a series of cause-and-effect relationships. Then go over the events shown in the graphic, explaining how each event caused the following event. **L1**

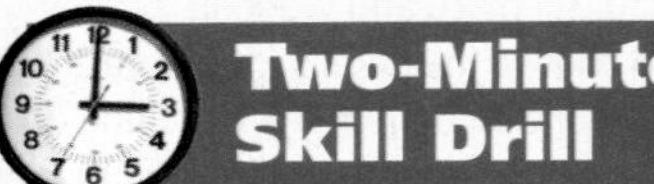

Two-Minute Skill Drill

Have students list three reasons they like (or dislike) watching television and then rank those reasons in order of importance, beginning with the least important.

See also *Two-Minute Skill Drill Transparency 2.7*

Additional Resources

For further stimuli for writing, see *Fine Art Transparencies* 7–12.

Writing Process Transparencies 2–8

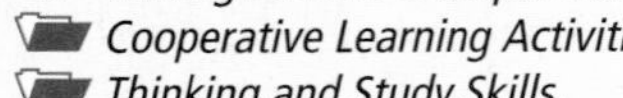

Cooperative Learning Activities

Thinking and Study Skills, pp. 13–15

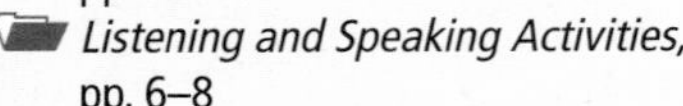

Listening and Speaking Activities, pp. 6–8

Composition Practice, p. 15

Order of Importance

Order of importance is an appropriate method to use when your supporting details are facts, statistics, incidents, or examples. For example, if you want to make an immediate impact on your reader, start with your most important detail. If you want to leave your reader thinking about your strongest point, build up to the most important detail.

Cause-and-Effect Order

When you want to show that one event took place because of another, you can use cause-and-effect order. In a cause-and-effect paragraph, the topic sentence may state the cause and the supporting details identify the effects. Conversely, the topic sentence may state the effect and the supporting details present the causes. This method works well when you write about science, history, or even about yourself. In the paragraph below, Ginger Lumpkin uses cause-and-effect order.

The topic sentence prepares the reader for a cause-and-effect ordering of the supporting details.

How do these details support the topic sentence?

Student Model

A teacher who once doubted me ironically became a source of inspiration. In the seventh grade, I wrote a poem entitled "Lost on a Desert." After my teacher read my poem, she asked me who I had copied it from—she didn't believe that I had written it. Her remarks hurt me, but the experience made me feel determined to prove my creative writing abilities. As a result, I began to write a variety of poems, short stories, and plays, all of which my teacher praised. In the end, I not only showed my teacher that I could write well, but through my writing, I also gained a better understanding of myself.

Ginger Lumpkin, Hyde Park Career Academy, Chicago, Illinois

The graphic below shows the cause-and-effect relationships presented in the paragraph. Note that most of the effects in turn act as causes.

Listening and Speaking

Using Cause-and-Effect Words

Explain that certain words and phrases may be clues that indicate causes and effects. As an example, point out the phrase *As a result* in the student model, and demonstrate how it indicates an effect. Write the head *Cause Words* on the board, and under that write the words *because* and *since.* Under the head *Effect Words,* write *therefore* and *consequently.* Work with students to use each of these words correctly to indicate cause-and-effect relationships.

2.7 Writing Activities

Check Organization

Read over your draft to make sure that the details in your paragraph are ordered. Remember that not all your paragraphs will be organized in the same way.

PURPOSE To check order of details
AUDIENCE Yourself
LENGTH 1–2 pages

WRITING RUBRICS To evaluate the order of details in your paragraphs, you should

- describe the type of order you have used
- decide how to organize supporting details
- decide whether to change your order

GrammarLink

Use commas to separate three or more words, phrases, or clauses in a series.

Answer each question in one complete sentence. Remember to write commas where they are needed.

1. What three pizza toppings do you like?
2. Who are your four favorite singers?
3. What four TV programs do you watch?

See Lesson 21.6, page 739.

Iranian glazed ceramic bowl, c. 1200

Writing Online | For more writing and grammar practice, go to **glencoe.com** and enter QuickPass code WC97727p1.

Assess

Evaluation Rubrics

Check Organization

Use these criteria when evaluating your students' writing.

- Is the use of a specific ordering pattern appropriate and consistent?
- Is the method of matching the purpose and subject matter thoughtful?

See also *Writing Assessment & Evaluation Rubrics*

Cross-Curricular Activity

Students' analysis of the visual details on the ceramic bowl should demonstrate the following: an accurate perception of the visual details; sensitivity to the subject and mood of the art; and creativity in interpretation.

Reteaching

Composition Reteaching, p. 15

Enrichment

Composition Enrichment, p. 15

Fine Art Transparencies 7–12

Close

The class can list possible topics for paragraphs. Write these ideas on the board. Then have each student choose one of these ideas, decide which organizational pattern would probably be best for that topic, and write a brief explanation of why this organizational pattern is appropriate.

GrammarLink

Answers

Answers will vary; samples follow.

1. I like mushrooms, olives, and pepperoni.
2. My favorite singers are Whitney Houston, Bruce Springsteen, Celine Dion, and Eddie Vedder.
3. I watch the news, *Seinfeld, Mystery,* and *Today.*

Viewing the Art

Iranian glazed ceramic bowl, c. 1200

This bowl depicts a narrative scene often shown in illuminated manuscripts of the period. The bowl, 3⅜ inches deep and 8½ inches in diameter, can be seen in the Brooklyn Museum in New York City.

Focus

Lesson Overview

Objectives

- To write a coherent paragraph in which all the sentences are clearly and logically connected

Skills

- using transition words and phrases; using repetitions, synonyms, and pronouns

Critical Thinking

- identifying logical relationships; identifying patterns; sequencing information

Listening and Speaking

- listening accurately; listening critically

Bellringer

Daily Language Activity

When students enter the classroom, have this assignment on the board: *What do these words have in common? Use each one in a sentence.*

when	*then*	*next*
meanwhile	*finally*	*before*

Grammar Link to the Bellringer

Challenge students to combine pairs of Bellringer sentences. In a follow-up discussion, list the ways students combined the sentences coherently.

See also *Daily Language Practice*

Motivating Activity

Ask students to think of ways filmmakers provide transitions from one scene or time to another. (Students might mention the picture getting blurry to indicate that the character is remembering a scene, subtitles like "three months later," or changes of seasons.) Ask students to compare these transitions with those used to connect the parts of a piece of writing.

The Writing Process

LESSON 2.8

Drafting: Writing Coherent Paragraphs

In a coherent paragraph, all the sentences are clearly and logically connected to one another. Transition words and phrases, repeated words, synonyms, and pronouns are the "glue" or "mortar" you can use to link together sentences and build a better paragraph.

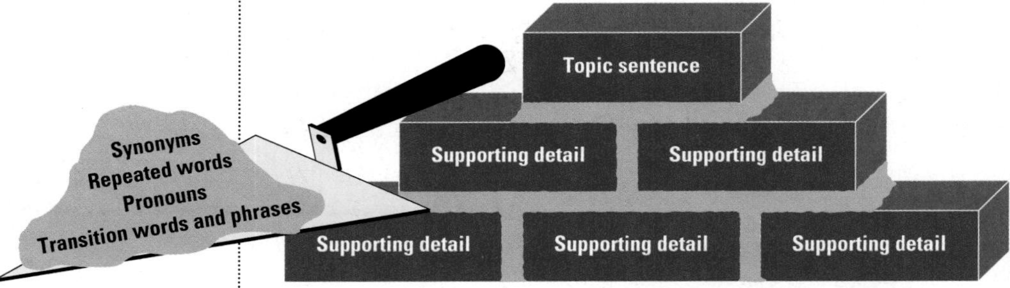

Build a Coherent Paragraph

Use the following checklist to help make sure your paragraphs are coherent.

Checklist for Writing Coherently

1. Are all the sentences linked clearly and logically to one another?
2. Can I repeat any words to help show the connections between ideas?
3. Have I used synonyms that my readers will be able to understand?
4. Does each pronoun have an antecedent?
5. Are there any transitions I can use to link the sentences?

Resource Manager

Planning Resources

- *Lesson Plans*

Transparencies

- *Bellringer*
- *Daily Language Practice*
- *Fine Art* 7–12
- *Two-Minute Skill Drill*
- *Writing Process* 2–8

Other Print Resources

- *Composition Enrichment*, p. 16
- *Composition Practice*, p. 16
- *Composition Reteaching*, p. 16
- *Cooperative Learning Activities*, pp. 9–12
- *Listening and Speaking Activities*, pp. 6–8
- *Thinking and Study Skills*, pp. 13–15
- *Writing Across the Curriculum*
- *Writing Assessment and Evaluation Rubrics*

Use Transition Words and Phrases

Use transitions—words or phrases that show relationships between ideas—to help you write coherent paragraphs. Transitions create logical links between sentences in a paragraph and help the reader follow your train of thought. The chart below shows some common transitions.

Transitions				
Kinds	**Examples**			
Time	after first	before meanwhile	finally then	next when
Place	above below	beside here	next to near	there opposite
Importance	first primary	second mainly	more important last	most important least important
Cause and effect	as a result so	consequently therefore	for that reason on account	because due to
Comparison and contrast	although similarly	in contrast however	on the other hand like	in the same way unlike
Example	for example together with	for instance along with	namely likewise	that is such as

You can also use transitions to link paragraphs in a longer piece of writing. Transitions such as *first*, *second*, and *most important* can help readers understand the relative importance of each paragraph. Other transitions can help the reader understand relationships between paragraphs. Transitions such as *finally* and *therefore* often create a successful link to the concluding paragraph.

Journal Writing

Look through your journal, and select a paragraph. Then use the list of questions on page 88 to make sure the paragraph is coherent. Insert transitions listed in the chart above to create links between your sentences.

Teach

Promoting Discussion

Provide students with two simple statements of fact that have a possible connection. *(Uncle Stan bought a car. Our family bought a new van.)* Then ask students to see how many transition words from the chart can be used to link the two statements. Discuss how the message changes with different transitions. **L2**

Two-Minute Skill Drill

Have students think of a place they know well and have them describe it using four of these words:

near	*opposite*
above	*below*
beside	*there*

See also *Two-Minute Skill Drill Transparency 2.8*

Journal Writing Tip

Identifying Relationships Encourage students to select a paragraph that can be improved by the addition of a transition word; for example, one that shows cause and effect, sequence, or comparison or contrast.

2.8

Teach

Using the Model

Point out that the use of synonyms, as in "the old people" and "aged visitors," helps tie the sentences together in a more colorful way than a pronoun would. Ask what other reasons Momaday might have had to use synonyms. (Momaday may have wanted to emphasize this detail.) **L2**

Choosing Synonyms

Discuss the need to carefully consider what synonym to use. Good writers choose synonyms not only to achieve variety but also to express precise meaning. Most synonyms have slightly different shades of meaning or association, and the wrong synonym can distort the message. Point out some examples of synonyms with slightly different shades of meaning (e.g., old man, senior citizen; knowledgeable, intellectual), and ask students to explain the differences. Invite students to suggest other examples. **L3**

Understanding Parallelism

Tell students that using parallel sentence structure improves the clarity and coherence of a piece of writing. Challenge students to find another example of parallelism in the model. Then as a class, determine the word pattern that is repeated and discuss the effect that the parallelism has on the writing. (In the phrase, "a fine sense of pageantry and a wonderful notion of decorum," the word pattern *a* + *(adjective)* + *(noun)* + *of* + *(noun)* is repeated. The parallelism creates a consistent rhythm and helps the reader connect the ideas.) **L3**

Additional Resources

- For further stimuli for writing coherent paragraphs, see *Fine Art Transparencies* 7–12.
- *Writing Process Transparencies* 2–8
- *Writing Across the Curriculum*
- *Cooperative Learning Activities*
- *Thinking and Study Skills*, pp. 13–15
- *Listening and Speaking Activities*, pp. 6–8
- *Composition Practice*, p. 16

Use Repetition and Synonyms

Another way to link sentences is to repeat the same word from sentence to sentence. But be careful: too much repetition will bore your readers. One way to avoid too much repetition is to read your work aloud. If you hear the same word too often, it's probably time to use synonyms—words that have similar meanings. Keep your audience in mind, however. Unfamiliar synonyms may make your ideas more difficult to follow.

In the paragraph below, N. Scott Momaday repeats words and phrases and uses synonyms to link his sentences.

Literature Model

My grandmother lived in a house near the place where Rainy Mountain Creek runs into the Washita River. Once there was a lot of sound in the house, a lot of coming and going, feasting and talk. The summers there were full of excitement and reunion. The Kiowas are a summer people; they abide the cold and keep to themselves, but when the season turns and the land becomes warm and vital they cannot hold still; an old love of going returns upon them. The old people have a fine sense of pageantry and a wonderful notion of decorum. The aged visitors who came to my grandmother's house when I was a child were men of immense character, full of wisdom and disdain. They dealt in a kind of infallible quiet and gave but one face away; it was enough. They were made of lean and leather, and they bore themselves upright. They wore great black hats and bright ample shirts that shook in the wind. They rubbed fat upon their hair and wound their braids with strips of colored cloth. Some of them painted their faces and carried the scars of old and cherished enmities. They were an old council of war lords, come to remind and be reminded of who they were.

N. Scott Momaday, *House Made of Dawn*

Repetition of words such as "they" and "there" helps link sentences.

What effect does the use of synonyms have?

Momaday repeats the word pattern *they* + *(past tense verb)*. The parallelism links the sentences and emphasizes the descriptive details.

Use Pronouns

To avoid the boring repetition of specific nouns, substitute pronouns for a word, a group of words, or an idea that appears in a preceding sentence. Note the use of pronouns in the literature model above. As an experiment, mentally substitute nouns for the pronouns. How does the selection read?

English Language Learners

Identifying Transitions

Students learning English may have difficulty identifying transitions in their reading. However, they may be more likely to recognize them with the help of a graphic. Read aloud a passage, putting emphasis on transition words.

Help students jot down these transition words in order as you read. Then use a graphic organizer such as a sequence chart or a cause-and-effect diagram to help students visualize the relationships.

2.8 Writing Activities

Check Your Paragraphs for Coherence

Make any changes to your paragraphs that will make them more coherent.

PURPOSE To make paragraphs coherent
AUDIENCE Yourself
LENGTH 1–2 pages

WRITING RUBRICS To make paragraphs coherent, you should

- use transition words and phrases
- use repeated words, parallel structures, or synonyms to link sentences and paragraphs
- use pronouns to avoid unnecessary repetition

Viewing and Representing

DESIGN What might artist Aaron Douglas be saying about the creation of historically significant structures? How does the design help communicate this message? Write a paragraph about the theme and style of the painting and the use of color and shape to express the theme.

Aaron Douglas, *Building More Stately Mansions*, 1944

GrammarLink

Use conjunctive adverbs to show relationships.

The following words are conjunctive adverbs: *so, consequently, therefore, similarly, however,* and *likewise*. They are preceded by semicolons and followed by commas.

Use a conjunctive adverb to join each pair of sentences below into one.

1. When she grew older, Amy Tan decided to become a writer. Her parents did not encourage her in this pursuit.
2. As time passed, she sold several stories she had written. She decided to become a full-time writer.
3. Today Amy Tan is the author of two best-selling novels. She is researching a third book.

See Lesson 10.7, page 479.

Cross-Curricular Activity

ART Investigate historical murals created for the WPA (Works Progress Administration) during the 1930s. What themes are presented? How does each artist achieve unity in presenting his or her message? Share your findings with the class.

LOG ON **Writing Online** For more writing and grammar practice, go to **glencoe.com** and enter QuickPass code WC97727p1.

Assess

Evaluation Rubrics

Check Your Paragraphs for Coherence

Use these criteria when evaluating your students' writing.

- Are transition words and phrases used appropriately?
- Is the paragraph coherent?
- Is there a logical sentence sequence?
- Are synonyms used appropriately and clearly?

See also *Writing Assessment & Evaluation Rubrics*

Cross-Curricular Activity

Suggest that students look for specific details in the painting to explain its meaning and title, and link their sentences by using appropriate techniques of coherence, especially repetition and synonyms.

Reteaching

Composition Reteaching, p. 16

Enrichment

Composition Enrichment, p. 16

Fine Art Transparencies 7–12

Close

Encourage students to share their cross-curricular paragraphs with the class. In a follow-up discussion, identify ways students linked the sentences in each paragraph.

GrammarLink

Answers

Answers may vary, but some suggestions are given below.

1. ; however,
2. ; as a result,
3. ; meanwhile,

Viewing the Art

Aaron Douglas, *Building More Stately Mansions,* 1944

Douglas was part of the Harlem Renaissance, a group of artists and writers whose portrayal of the African American experience influenced modern art and literature. This 58-by-42-inch oil painting is at the Fisk University Museum of Art in Nashville, Tennessee.

Focus

Lesson Overview

Objective

- To identify and solve writing problems relating to clarity, unity, and coherence

Skills

- checking for meaning, unity, and coherence

Critical Thinking

- analyzing word choice; defining and clarifying meaning; identifying problems

Listening and Speaking

- discussing; evaluating; questioning

Bellringer

Daily Language Activity

When students enter the classroom, have this assignment on the board: *You have written an assignment that didn't flow smoothly or make complete sense. What could you have done to improve the writing?*

Grammar Link to the Bellringer

Supply students with some verbs, such as *make, teach,* and *inform.* Ask students to tell you what each would be in the passive voice (*is made, is taught, is informed*).

See also *Daily Language Practice*

Motivating Activity

Discuss students' responses to the Bellringer activity. Then explain that Ernest Hemingway rewrote the ending to *A Farewell to Arms* thirty-nine times until he got the words right. Ask students to name activities other than writing that they've done over and over until they got them right. (To spark ideas, suggest they think of activities in cooking, sports, music, and computers.) Discuss the pluses and minuses of doing something over and over until it is exactly right.

LESSON 2.9

Revising: Improving Paragraphs

Revising is the stage of the writing process in which you step back and take a new look at your work. You evaluate it, get the reaction of others, and then rewrite your draft to solve any problems.

As you revise, you may learn something new about your piece of writing. You may clarify its meaning, find a way to say it more effectively, or even discover entirely new ideas. Sometimes you don't get the words quite right the first time. For instance, Abraham Lincoln, universally considered the greatest writer among our nation's presidents, may have written many drafts before he approved The Gettysburg Address for delivery on November 19, 1863.

It is entirely possible that he had originally planned to begin the speech by recalling the country's beginnings in 1776 by opening with the words: *"Eighty-seven years ago."*

Instead, perhaps dissatisfied with the sound or pacing, he may have revised it, choosing the final words: *"Four score and seven."*

After all, a score is twenty years, so four score would be eighty. Adding seven would result in 87.

Of course, the result is the same numerically, but the effect is wholly different. By selecting those opening four words, Lincoln achieved a more rhythmic, cadenced effect that set the tone for the solemn occasion and that has endured for more than 200 years as a model of poetic oratory.

Revise in Stages

One useful strategy for revising is to break the process down into three parts. First, put yourself in the place of your readers and go through the draft quickly, checking to make sure that your meaning is clear. Make any necessary changes.

Next, read your draft aloud to a partner or small group. Often ideas that seem clear to you will need to be rephrased for an audience. Take notes on the questions your peer reviewers ask and on their suggestions.

Finally, go back to your draft and read it carefully one final time. Look at the notes from your writing conference. Now is the time to decide what changes you want to make.

Resource Manager

Planning Resources

- *Lesson Plans*

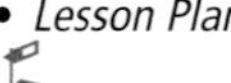

Transparencies

- *Bellringer*
- *Daily Language Practice*
- *Fine Art* 7–12
- *Two-Minute Skill Drill*
- *Writing Process* 2–8

Other Print Resources

- *Composition Enrichment,* p. 17
- *Composition Practice,* p. 17
- *Composition Reteaching,* p. 17
- *Cooperative Learning Activities,* pp. 9–12
- *Listening and Speaking Activities,* pp. 6–8
- *Thinking and Study Skills,* pp. 5, 27–28
- *Writing Across the Curriculum*
- *Writing Assessment and Evaluation Rubrics*

Check for Meaning

After you finish your first draft, set it aside for a while. Then when you pick it up to revise it, you'll see it with fresh eyes.

Read it through once quickly and jot down notes or ideas in the margins. Don't worry about word choices, grammar, spelling, or punctuation. Use the checklist below to help you focus on the big picture—the meaning.

Meaning Checklist

1. Have I presented the main idea clearly? What is the main idea? (Hint: If you cannot easily answer this question after reading your writing, chances are you have not presented the main idea clearly.)
2. Have I achieved my purpose through my writing?
3. Who is my audience? Have I written this piece with their needs in mind?
4. Do I need to give my readers more information?

If you have trouble answering any of these questions, you may need to return to the prewriting or drafting stages to rework your ideas. Don't be discouraged. Going back and forth between the stages is part of the writing process. Even writers like Joan Didion rework their ideas: "My writing is a process of rewriting, of going back and changing and filling in. In the rewriting process you discover what's going on."

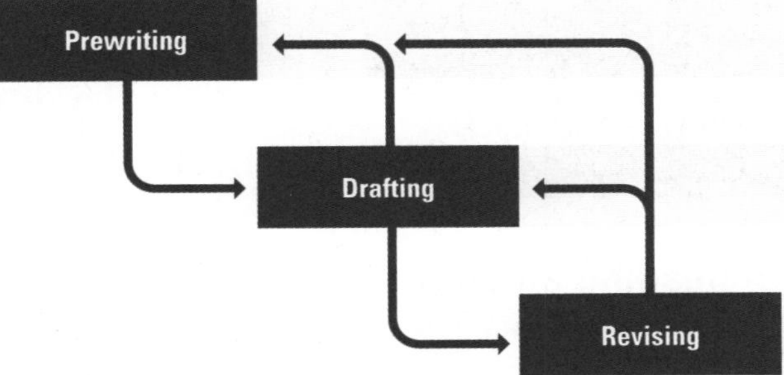

Journal Writing

Review an entry in your journal that you have not looked at recently. Using the checklist above, write any suggestions you now have for clarifying the main idea in the space below your entry.

Teach

Using the Checklist

Provide students with simple paragraphs that contain obvious problems in meaning. First, find a clear, unified paragraph and change it to remove the main idea and supporting details. Give students copies of the altered paragraph and lead them in identifying and correcting the lack of a main idea and other missing information. **L2**

Critiquing a Lesson

To underscore the questions in the Meaning Checklist on this page, suggest that students use them to critique the opening of this lesson. First, ask them to state the purpose and main idea of the opening in complete sentences. Then point out that, because they are students, they can answer questions 3 and 4 with special insight. If anyone needs more information, point out that the purpose of the passage is to introduce a lesson that will provide just that—an explanation of the revising process. **L3**

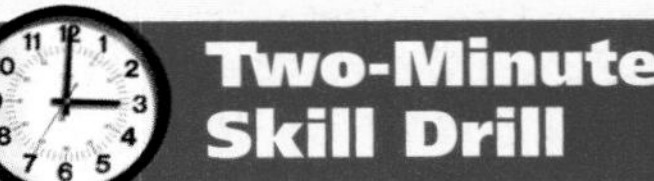

Look at these words in the passive voice. Change them to the active voice.

was told — *was helped*
was given — *was taken*
was questioned

See also *Two-Minute Skill Drill Transparency 2.9*

Journal Writing Tip

Clarifying Meaning Remind students to use the questions in the Meaning Checklist to help them identify missing ideas or details.

Teach

Cooperative Learning

Have partners conduct a three-step interview as they edit each other's writing. Each writer selects a piece that he or she did for an earlier lesson. Each editing partner reads the piece and makes comments based on the three checklists on pages 93 and 94. (Encourage constructive comments and respect for a writer's privilege to disagree.) Writers prepare a revision based on the comments. Afterward, in a class discussion, volunteers can read their revised pieces aloud, identifying one change they made for meaning, unity, or coherence. **L2**

When Revising Can Help

You might ask how the ability to revise for meaning, unity, and coherence can help students throughout their lives. Discuss ways in which these writing qualities might help students achieve their goals in specific situations: a biology essay exam, a letter to a friend with whom the student had an argument, a cover letter for a job application, an autobiographical essay for a college application. **L3**

Additional Resources

For further stimuli for writing, see *Fine Art Transparencies* 7–12.

Writing Process Transparencies 2–8
Writing Across the Curriculum
Cooperative Learning Activities
Thinking and Study Skills, pp. 5, 27–28
Listening and Speaking Activities, pp. 6–8
Composition Practice, p. 17

Revising Tip

For more information about revising, see **Writing and Research Handbook,** pages 940–949.

Have a Writing Conference

Read your draft to a peer reviewer or reviewers. Ask them to read the checklist below and keep it in mind as they listen.

Unity Checklist

1. Does every detail I have selected support the main idea?
2. Have I organized the supporting details in the most logical way?
3. Have I included any sentences that are unnecessary because they simply restate the main point without adding any new information or meaning?
4. Have I made the relationships among my ideas clear?

After you have read your draft aloud, ask your listeners these questions:

- What was the strongest part of my writing?
- What, if anything, was not clear?

Then go over the questions in the checklist with your listeners. They may ask you to read your draft again as they listen carefully.

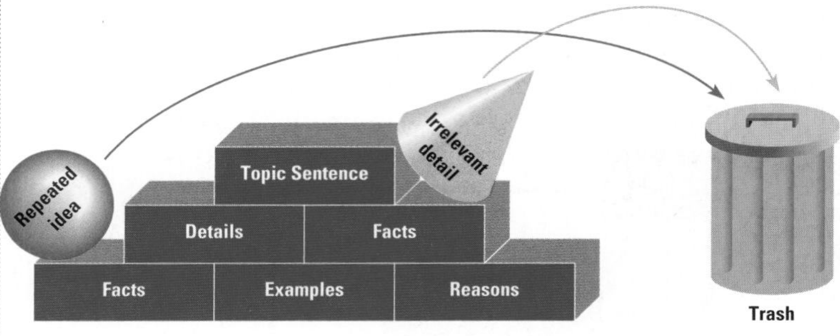

Revising Tip

Parallelism To help keep the relationships among your ideas clear, use phrases and sentences that have similar grammatical form.

Do a Final Reading and Revise

Use the checklist below for your final reading. Make your revisions, using your notes from the writing conference and from your own checking of your draft.

Coherence Checklist

1. Have I written sentences that flow logically and clearly?
2. Would pronouns, synonyms, repeated words, parallel structures, or transitions improve the flow of my writing?
3. Have I made appropriate word choices?
4. Have I used specific nouns and active verbs?
5. Have I deleted all unnecessary words?

Viewing and Representing

Understanding the Graphic

Ask students to explain in their own words the message of the graphic on this page (to achieve unity, get rid of sentences with unneeded or repeated ideas). Ask whether students think the graphic is clear or useful to them. Some students may want to design another graphic with the same message.

2.9 Writing Activities

Revise Your Draft

To revise, use circles and arrows, taped-on additions, or cross-outs to mark your changes.

PURPOSE To revise your draft
AUDIENCE Yourself, peer reviewers
LENGTH 1–2 pages

WRITING RUBRICS To revise your draft, you should

- read your draft over once for meaning
- have a writing conference and take notes
- do a final reading and make changes

Cross-Curricular Activity

SOCIAL STUDIES Revise the following paragraph about families in western Sumatra in Indonesia. Use the checklists presented in this lesson to help you.

The society is matrilineal. All inherited property and family names are handed down from mother to daughter. Most of the people are rice farmers. The grandmother is the most powerful member of the family. Children are given the name of their mother's family. All the descendants of one grandmother live together in one big house. Up to thirty family members live in one house. A woman marries and the husband moves in with his wife's family.

Listening and Speaking

PEER REVIEW Follow the writing process to revise your draft. Read the draft quickly to yourself for meaning. Then have a writing conference, and read your draft aloud to a partner. Take notes on your reviewer's comments in the margins of your draft. Look over the comments and make any changes you find valid.

GrammarLink

Use active and passive voice.

Rewrite each sentence below that you think should be in the active voice. If you think a sentence belongs in the passive voice, write *passive.*

1. Great tennis talent is being developed by a young Californian named Venus Ebonistarr Williams, trained by her father to become a tennis star.
2. At the age of ten, Venus was ranked by some tennis experts as number one in southern California in the girls' twelve-and-under division.
3. This ranking was attained only after a great deal of hard work.
4. As part of her routine, she is coached by her father at the tennis courts every day.
5. Great discipline is required to practice tennis skills on a daily basis.
6. Net shots, as well as forehand and backhand drills, are some of the skills practiced by this rising star.
7. Tennis is played by Venus's entire family.
8. In the family's life, an important role is played by tennis.
9. A journal has been kept by Venus's father of the important events in her life.
10. A winning future is predicted by coaches and pros for this young player.

See Lesson 15.7, page 596.

LOG ON **Writing** Online | For more writing and grammar practice, go to **glencoe.com** and enter QuickPass code WC97727p1.

Assess

Evaluation Rubrics

Revise Your Draft

Use these criteria when evaluating your students' writing.

- Is the meaning clear?
- Are the paragraphs unified?
- Are the paragraphs coherent?

See also *Writing Assessment & Evaluation Rubrics*

Cross-Curricular Activity

Answers will vary, but check to see that the paragraph as revised is coherent and unified with a clear main idea.

Reteaching

Composition Reteaching, p. 17

Enrichment

Composition Enrichment, p. 17

Fine Art Transparencies 7–12

Close

Have students choose a paragraph from a magazine. Let them alter it so that it is no longer unified or coherent. Have them remove the main idea. Let students exchange their paragraphs with a partner and rewrite them to improve the meaning.

GrammarLink

Answers

1. A young Californian named Venus Ebonistarr Williams is developing great tennis talent. Her father is training her to become a tennis star.
2. When Venus was ten, some tennis experts ranked her . . .
3. Venus attained this ranking only after a great deal of hard work.
4. As part of her routine, her father coaches her at the tennis courts . . .
5. passive
6. This rising star practices net shots as well as forehand and backhand drills.
7. Venus's entire family plays tennis.
8. Tennis plays an important role . . .
9. Venus's father has been keeping a journal of the important events . . .

Focus

Lesson Overview

Objectives
- To learn how to edit writing for sense
- To use proofreading symbols to edit and proofread writing

Skills
- editing for sense; proofreading

Critical Thinking
- evaluating writing; establishing criteria

Listening and Speaking
- discussing errors; evaluating writing

Bellringer

Daily Language Activity

When students enter the classroom, have this assignment on the board: *Correct the following sentence:*

When I was at camp I place a telephone call to my mother everyday last month.

Grammar Link to the Bellringer

Have students correct this sentence so that it makes sense:

I called my mother using a quarter.

See also  *Daily Language Practice*

Motivating Activity

Discuss students' answers to the activities above. Explain that in this lesson, they will learn to edit and proofread their work so that it makes sense. Discuss why the mistakes, or "bloopers," that open this chapter are confusing and what each writer meant to say. Ask students to suggest ways of rewording these sentences and headlines. Ask them to share any bloopers they've made in their own writing. Mention that many bookstores have entire books of bloopers. If students have such books, they might want to bring them in to share with the class.

The Writing Process

LESSON 2.10

Editing/Proofreading: Final Checking

During the editing stage, you make sure that you've used words correctly. Check your writing for errors in grammar, word usage, punctuation, capitalization, and spelling. The goal of editing, as in the other stages in the writing process, is to communicate your ideas clearly to your readers.

COMPLAINTS ABOUT NBA REFEREES GROWING UGLY

It is bad manners to break your bread and roll in your soup.

Plunging 1,000 feet into the gorge, we saw Yosemite Falls.

TUNA BITING OFF WASHINGTON COAST

GRANDMOTHER OF EIGHT MAKES HOLE IN ONE

No bear feet allowed.

Edit Your Draft for Sense

To edit for sense, make sure that your words and sentences say what you want them to say. For example, check for and correct any unclear or misplaced modifiers like those shown in the examples above. Use the checklist on page 97 to help identify and correct errors in your writing.

Resource Manager

Planning Resources
- *Lesson Plans*

Transparencies
- *Bellringer*
- *Daily Language Practice*
- *Fine Art* 7–12
- *Two-Minute Skill Drill*
- *Writing Process* 2–8

Other Print Resources
- *Composition Enrichment,* p. 18
- *Composition Practice,* p. 18
- *Composition Reteaching,* p. 18
- *Cooperative Learning Activities,* pp. 9–12
- *Listening and Speaking Activities,* pp. 6–8
- *Thinking and Study Skills,* pp. 13, 18, 25, 27–28
- *Writing Assessment and Evaluation Rubrics*

Question	Example
1. Are all words used correctly?	She could ~~of~~ have waited.
2. Do subjects and verbs agree?	Each of my brothers drive^s a truck.
3. Are verb tenses correct?	If you wanted it, you should ~~say~~ have said so.
4. Are pronoun references clear and correct?	~~Ann~~ she called her mother every day~~,~~. When ~~she~~ Ann was away at camp~~.~~
5. Have I corrected all run-ons and fragments?	She turned on the radio, but she heard only static~~,~~. ~~W~~hich was annoying.

Self-Editing To edit your own writing, you need to approach your work objectively and critically. Reading your work aloud is crucial. Note the changes Rachelle Netkow chose to make in the model below.

Student Model

My family is a typical ~~of a~~ family ~~in~~ of the times. Both of my parents work, which means many of the household responsibilities are left to my brother and ~~I~~ me. We do them, of course, even though we don't like ~~it~~ the extra work. Since everyone in my family is busy with various activities, it is unusual for all of us to be home at the same time. ~~But~~ Occasionally, though, we try to do special things together. My family is very close even if we don't see each other ~~all that~~ very often.

Rachelle Netkow, Centennial High School, Pueblo, Colorado

Change makes pronoun reference grammatically correct.

Why did Rachelle add "everyone in" here?

Journal Writing

How can you make sure that your changes in one sentence do not alter the meaning of the following sentence? Write down a few general tips that will help you edit any writing project.

Teach

Using the Model

Rachelle added *everyone in* and *various* to clarify that family members do not all do the same activities. Point out each editorial change Rachelle made, and ask students how it improves the paragraph. **L2**

Types of Editing

In publishing companies, professional editors read and edit a writer's product. In class, students edit their own work, or they have peer editors or teachers edit their writing. Discuss whether it is easier to edit one's own work or someone else's. Ask what makes the one easier and the other more difficult. (Elicit that an outsider may be able to evaluate the writing objectively. Still, learning the writing process includes developing an inner ear that enables writers to tell how their writing will sound to readers.) **L2**

Two-Minute Skill Drill

Ask students to correct the following:

thier   *could of eatten*

each others   *each work hard*

Every day I am going to school.

See also *Two-Minute Skill Drill Transparency 2.10*

Journal Writing Tip

Establishing and Assessing Criteria Students should realize that certain changes have ramifications for the rest of the piece, so they should read on to make sure they haven't created new problems. The purpose of the checklist is to help them make the most important changes.

Teach

Using Proofreading Marks

Many students may find the standard proofreading symbols difficult to remember. Some memory tricks can help solve this problem. For example, point out that the squiggle indicating a deletion looks like the gesture of throwing something off to the side. Ask students if they can devise any other tricks for remembering the symbols in the chart. **L2**

Editing and Proofreading

Challenge students to edit and proofread articles in local newspapers. Have them bring in errors they find or articles that could be improved with editing. Ask why they think newspaper articles are not always perfectly edited or proofread. (Deadlines for a daily or weekly newspaper create serious time constraints. Writers must work fast with little time for self-editing, and editors and proofreaders often have no time to take a second look.) **L3**

Additional Resources

For further stimuli for writing, see *Fine Art Transparencies* 7–12.

Writing Process Transparencies 2–8
Cooperative Learning Activities
Thinking and Study Skills, pp. 13, 18, 25, 27–28
Listening and Speaking Activities, pp. 6–8
Composition Practice, p. 18

Peer Editing To edit another's writing, focus on the ideas and organization of a piece of writing rather than on its grammar and mechanics. Be honest, but respect the writer's feelings. Identify strengths as well as weaknesses. Offer suggestions for improvement, not just criticisms. Note the peer editor's comments on the paragraph below.

Avoid repetition of pronouns.
Good transition!
Expand—tell us what she talked about.
Rearrange sentences.

Last fall, my family drove my older sister Shana to college. It was her freshman year, and even though she didn't say so, I could tell ~~she~~ *Shana* was scared and sad to leave home. For one thing, she talked more during the drive than she has for the past three years. She didn't even yell at me when I helped carry her stereo equipment to her room. Normally, ~~She~~ *Shana* has a fit if I so much as touch one of her things. It really was a day full of surprises. When it was time to go, she even hugged me.

Proofread and Mark Your Draft

Proofreading is reading closely to find errors in spelling, punctuation, and capitalization. For marking corrections, use a set of basic proofreading symbols. The chart below shows a few.

Proofreading Marks

Mark	Meaning	Example
∧	Insert	My granmother is eighty-six years old.
℘	Delete	She grew up on a dairry farm.
# ∧	Insert space	She milkedcows every morning.
⁀‿	Close up space	She fed the chickens in the barn yard.
≡	Capitalize	times have changed.
/	Make lowercase	Machines now do the Milking.
⬭ sp	Check spelling	Chickens are fed automatically.
⌐∼	Switch order	Modern farms are like more factories.
¶	New paragraph	Last year I returned to the farm.

MEETING INDIVIDUAL NEEDS

English Language Learners

Editing Work

Students who have difficulty writing English can divide the editing/proofreading phase of the writing process. Review each student's writing and suggest that the student focus on one or two questions from the editing checklist. Peer editors can be helpful, especially if they are aware of the need to give writers positive responses along with suggestions for improvement.

2.10 Writing Activities

Edit Your Human-Interest Story

After you have prewritten, drafted, and revised your story, you must edit it. Check to make sure your story makes sense (see the checklist on page 97). Then proofread your draft for spelling, grammar, and usage errors. Use proofreading symbols (see the chart on page 98).

PURPOSE To polish your paper
AUDIENCE Yourself
LENGTH 1–2 pages

WRITING RUBRICS To polish your paper, you should

- edit your sentences so they make sense
- be objective when editing your own work
- proofread closely to find errors

Using Computers

A useful proofreading tool is the spelling checker in your word processing program. The spelling checker will probably identify your name as a spelling error until you enter your first and last names into the computer's spelling dictionary.

Remember that the spelling checker feature on your personal computer cannot be relied on as the only method of proofreading your work. For example, the computer will not tell you when you typed *form* but meant *from*.

Grammar*Link*

Correct dangling and misplaced modifiers.

Dangling modifiers modify no word at all; misplaced modifiers modify the wrong word.

Rewrite the following sentences, correcting the misplaced or dangling modifiers in each.

1. The large mural attracts the visitor's eye on the wall.
2. Working out too long, the volleyball practice session made me feel stiff and sore.
3. We bought souvenirs at the main lodge that only cost $5.50.
4. Tacos and enchiladas were served at the buffet covered with salsa.
5. The air was released from the balloon with a hissing sound.

See Lesson 18.7, pages 670–675.

Viewing and Representing

COOPERATIVE LEARNING Evaluate the presentation of one human-interest story that has been covered in the daily newspaper, in a newsmagazine, and on the television news (recorded on a video recording). How are the media presentations alike and different? What techniques are particularly effective for each type of media? Display the media coverages you have gathered, and share your conclusions with the class.

LOG ON **Writing** Online | For more writing and grammar practice, go to **glencoe.com** and enter QuickPass code WC97727p1.

Assess

Evaluation Rubrics

Edit Your Human-Interest Story

Use these criteria when evaluating your students' writing.

- Do the sentences make sense?
- Is the work free from spelling, grammar, or usage errors?

See also *Writing Assessment & Evaluation Rubrics*

Using Computers

Spelling checkers cannot find usage and grammar errors. A word, if it is confused with its homophone, may be misspelled even if the spelling checker doesn't identify it as such. Students will have to review their work to find these kinds of mistakes.

Reteaching

Composition Reteaching, p. 18

Enrichment

Composition Enrichment, p. 18

Fine Art Transparencies 7–12

Close

Have students choose a paragraph they have written for another class. Let them edit it for errors in grammar, usage, and spelling.

Grammar*Link*

Answers

Answers will vary, but some samples are given below.

1. The large mural on the wall . . .
2. Working out too long, I felt . . . after . . . session.
3. We bought souvenirs that . . . $5.50 at the main lodge.
4. Tacos and enchiladas covered with salsa were . . .
5. With a hissing sound, the air . . .

Focus

Lesson Overview

Objectives

- To identify different forums for presenting work
- To decide on the best forum for a specific writing project

Skills

- choosing the appropriate forum for sharing a written piece

Critical Thinking

- establishing and evaluating criteria; decision-making

Listening and Speaking

- evaluating; discussing; questioning

Bellringer

Daily Language Activity

When students enter the classroom, have this assignment on the board: *If you were to write an article, story, or poem, what would you title it, and where would you like to see it published?*

Grammar Link to the Bellringer

Have students share the titles they listed in the Bellringer activity. Make sure they understand that the titles of magazines, newspapers, books, and long poems should be italicized.

See also  *Daily Language Practice*

Motivating Activity

Ask students whether they've ever had any writing published. If so, ask how the experience made them feel. If not, ask whether there's a magazine or newspaper in which they'd like to see their work. Ask how your students have been affected by other students' published writings. Would they respond to a student's published work differently than they would to the work of a professional writer? If so, why?

LESSON 2.11

The Writing Process

Publishing/Presenting: Sharing Writing

The last stage in the writing process is sharing or presenting your work. A school newspaper, such as that shown below, is just one of the many places, or forums, in which you can present your writing.

10 SPORTS The Peninsula Outlook November 20, 1990

Forever a Seahawk: Erstwhile PHS football great shines with Seattle Seahawks

by Cain Claxton

Twelve years have passed since Paul Skansi played split end for Peninsula High School.

Since Skansi played football in high school, he has gone on to play the sport for the University of Washington Huskies, the Pittsburgh Steelers, and the Seattle Seahawks. Along the way he impressed many people: his coaches, his friends and relatives, and even people who have never met him.

"In the sixth grade you could see that he was a blue chipper," Key Peninsula Middle School teacher John Leverett said. Leverett, who taught Skansi in the sixth grade at Goodman Middle School, threw passes to him before any professional quarterbacks did.

"That was one of the funnest years I've had growing up," Skansi said, adding that Leverett "was a teacher that I'll never forget. We did a lot of math, a lot of social studies, and played a lot of football."

Skansi's small size worried his parents, Nick and Patti Skansi. They were concerned that he might get injured playing against larger players. They didn't let Skansi play his freshman and sophomore years, and were reluctant to let him play his junior year.

"He was engaged in all the other athletic events that were offered," Skansi's father said. "I just thought that was enough."

When Skansi finally got a chance to play his junior year, 1977, former Head Football Coach Larry Lunke, now coaching Anacortes High School, already had Mike Bos, a star receiver in his senior year. Lunke needed Skansi to play in other areas and placed him at

Photos courtesy of Corry Trewin (Seattle Seahawks)

CATCH AND CELEBRATION—Seattle Seahawk Paul Skansi (#82) in the end zone after catching the game-tying touchdown pass from teammate Dave Krieg between Kansas City Chief players Pearson (#24) and Martin (#57). Seahawk John L. Williams (#32) looks on. After Seahawk kicker Norm Johnson lifted Seattle over the Chiefs, 17-16, Skansi and Krieg (#17) revel over the come-from-behind win.

Skansi's Collegiate Records

Paul Skansi

Resource Manager

Planning Resources

- *Lesson Plans*

Transparencies

- *Bellringer*
- *Daily Language Practice*
- *Fine Art* 7–12
- *Two-Minute Skill Drill*
- *Writing Process* 2–8

Other Print Resources

- *Composition Enrichment*, p. 19
- *Composition Practice*, p. 19
- *Composition Reteaching*, p. 19
- *Cooperative Learning Activities*, pp. 9–12
- *Listening and Speaking Activities*, pp. 6–8
- *Thinking and Study Skills*, pp. 11, 13, 23, 29–30
- *Writing Across the Curriculum*
- *Writing Assessment and Evaluation Rubrics*

Publish or Present Your Writing

Because presentation often depends on your particular audience, you should begin thinking during the prewriting stage about where and how you'd like your writing to appear. You have many options for presenting your work to others: at school, in your community, and in the wider world.

School Forums The diagram below shows some of the presenting options that may be available at your school. Consider the nature of your writing project to help you determine its forum. For example, a short story or poem might be ideal for a class anthology. A movie review might appear in a school newspaper.

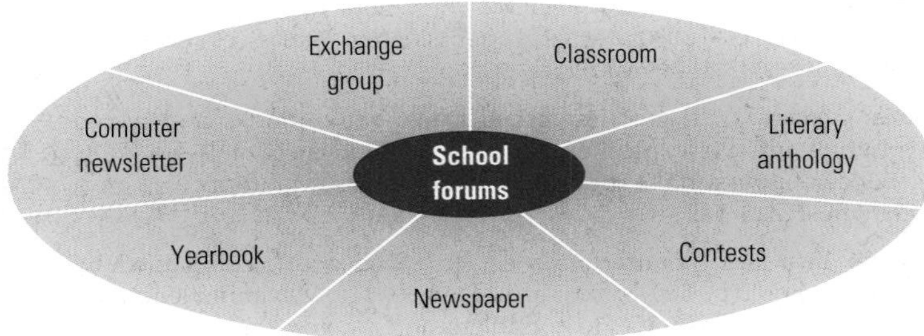

Community Forums If you'd like to reach a wider audience, find out what's being published in your community. Community newspapers may print feature stories about local people and events. Community groups, too, may publish newsletters that accept student work.

Contests Magazines, such as *Redbook*, *Seventeen*, and *Merlyn's Pen*, and organizations, such as the National Council of Teachers of English (NCTE), often sponsor writing contests. The winners may receive prizes and have their work published.

Journal Writing

In your journal, create a diagram like the one shown above. Add other forums that are not shown. Put a check mark next to each of the school forums in which you currently present your work. Circle those to which you would like to submit your work. Find out more about each new forum you have circled.

Teach

Cooperative Learning

Have students use a cooperative approach to create guidelines for submitting writing to various publications. Divide the class into small groups, and assign each group a publication. Ask each group to list general guidelines for their publication on the board, such as average length of articles, what typical readers are like, topics (such as health and beauty, fiction, sports). Then have students examine the actual magazine. The class then reconvenes to share and discuss their findings. **L2**

Writing Cover Letters

At small publications with more personalized submission procedures, a convincing cover letter can gain an editor's attention. Explain to students that in a cover letter, a writer can highlight the reasons his or her piece is appropriate for the forum selected. Ask students to choose a specific piece of writing and draft a letter to an appropriate forum. Read selected letters aloud and invite students to comment about their effectiveness. **L3**

Journal Writing Tip

Gathering Information As students look for a forum for their writing, encourage them to consider both the genre (such as poetry or nonfiction articles) and the subject matter (such as cooking or sports). For example, a poem about sports might be considered by a sports magazine or a poetry magazine.

Teach

Creating a Class Booklet

Remind students that there are probably publishing opportunities in their school. Explain that class booklets are rewarding projects for writers, computer buffs, artists, and others. Ask students what kind of class booklet they might like to create. Explain that a class booklet can be limited to a specific kind of writing, such as poetry, or booklets can be general, featuring the favorite works of all class members. After students choose the type of class booklet they would like to publish, help them organize the presentation. **L2**

Two-Minute Skill Drill

Ask students to list two places they could give an oral presentation. Then have them write a specific example of each of the following forums for written presentations: school, community, and open-market forums.

See also  *Two-Minute Skill Drill Transparency 2.11*

Additional Resources

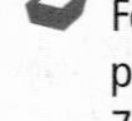 For further stimuli for specific writing projects, see *Fine Art Transparencies* 7–12.

 *Writing Process Transparencies* 2–8
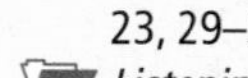 *Writing Across the Curriculum*
Cooperative Learning Activities
Thinking and Study Skills, pp. 11, 13, 23, 29–30
Listening and Speaking Activities, pp. 6–8
Composition Practice, p. 19

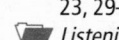

Open-Market Forums If you're interested in writing for periodicals, you might target magazines aimed at teenagers, such as *Seventeen*, *Sassy*, or *'Teen*. You also might choose special-interest magazines, such as *Bicycling* or *American Photo*.

Start with something you've already written and try to find a market for it. Or do the reverse: find a magazine first and then write a piece for that publication. *Writer's Market* and the *Market Guide for Young Writers* list publications that accept material from young writers, describe the type of material each publication accepts, explain how to prepare a manuscript for submission, and often tell about writing contests.

The first paragraph lists the name of the publication, the publisher's name and address, and a description of the publication and its audience

* **PURPLE COW,** Signa Publications, 3423 Piedmont Road N.E., Ivy Place Suite 320, Atlanta, GA 30305. Monthly tabloid (ten issues) covering any subject of interest to 13 to 18 year olds.

Publishes: General articles of interest to teens; book, movie, and record reviews; humor; interview/profile; sports (general and anecdotal—no "How to Play Soccer"); personal experience: coping with problems . . . ; and seasonal interest material.

Submission Info: All manuscripts must be typed and accompanied by SASE. Articles should be 500–3,000 words. Pays $5–$40. Maximum length for fillers is 150 words. Pays $5–$10 for fillers and photos. Send complete manuscript or query with published clips of published work.

The second paragraph describes the type of material published.

The third paragraph explains how to submit material. Note that "SASE" stands for "self-addressed, stamped envelope."

Give Oral Presentations

The most common forum for oral presentation is the classroom, where you may give an oral report or your teacher may read your writing aloud. Other opportunities in your school may include

- a drama club (for presenting your original play)
- a competitive tournament (for presenting a speech)
- a school radio station

Meeting Individual Needs: English Language Learners

Understanding Terminology

Students who have difficulty reading English may have trouble using reference sources such as the *Market Guide for Young Writers.* With students, review the special terminology and abbreviations used. For example, write the word *tabloid* on the board. Ask students to try to explain what the word means. Then tell them that a tabloid is a small newspaper that contains news that is often sensational in nature. Students should also understand abbreviations such as *SASE*—self-addressed, stamped envelope.

2.11 Writing Activities

Present Your Human-Interest Story

You have followed all the steps in the first four stages of the writing process: prewriting, drafting, revising, and editing. You are through with the actual writing of your piece. Now you must decide how to present your story. You might submit it to a newspaper or magazine, or decide to present it orally to a group. If you have made any of these decisions, then the paper must be prepared in a way that best fits the requirements of the presentation.

PURPOSE To make a final version of a human-interest story for presentation
AUDIENCE Varies with the type of presentation
LENGTH 1–2 pages

WRITING RUBRICS To prepare for presentation, you should

- decide the best way to share your writing, considering all the options, written and oral
- prepare a final, legible version suited to your audience, which might be a school, community, open-market, forum, or contest
- check that your draft meets the requirements of the presentation

Using Computers

When appropriate, use your computer program function to italicize, underline, or boldface words, phrases, and sentences. For example, italicize stage directions to distinguish them from dialogue in a script. To emphasize words or phrases in a speech, use bold-faced type.

Grammar*Link*

Italicize or underline titles.

Titles of books, newspapers, magazines, lengthy poems, plays, and films should always be italicized. If you are typing or handwriting a paper, indicate italics by underlining.

Rewrite the sentences below, underlining the parts that should be italicized.

1. I have submitted my story to Reader's Digest.
2. Who is the book editor of the Boston Globe?
3. I have just finished reading Palace Walk by Naguib Mahfouz.
4. Her poems have been published in The Norton Anthology of American Literature.
5. That was a very interesting Time magazine article.

See Lesson 21.10, pages 757–758.

Viewing and Representing

WEB SITE As a class project, create your own school electronic literary magazine and publish your human-interest stories on the World Wide Web. Check several electronic magazines to get a sense of what they contain. Assign appropriate tasks (design, editing, inputting) to class members and publish your stories. Be sure to consult your school's Internet policy to ensure your magazine conforms to school requirements.

Writing Online — For more writing and grammar practice, go to **glencoe.com** and enter QuickPass code WC97727p1.

Assess

Evaluation Rubrics

Present Your Human-Interest Story

Use these criteria when evaluating your students' writing.

- Is the forum likely to accept the student's piece?
- Is the presentation appropriate to the forum?
- Does the style, vocabulary, and content match the audience?

See also *Writing Assessment & Evaluation Rubrics*

Using Computers

Using a computer can be a great advantage in getting works published. Many publications ask writers to submit both disks and printed copy. Some writers even transmit their work to the editor via modem.

Reteaching

Composition Reteaching, p. 19

Enrichment

Composition Enrichment, p. 19

Fine Art Transparencies 7–12

Close

Have students discuss the most appropriate forums for different types of student work. Then review the requirements for their presentations.

Grammar*Link*

Answers

1. I have . . . *Reader's Digest.*
2. Who is . . . the *Boston Globe?*
3. I have . . . *Palace Walk* . . . Mahfouz.
4. Her . . . in *The Norton Anthology of American Literature.*
5. That . . . *Time* . . . article.

Focus

Lesson Overview

Objectives

- To discover themes in a piece of literature
- To analyze literary themes

Skills

- assessing the literature; identifying the theme; using the theme in writing

Critical Thinking

- analyzing; relating ideas; establishing and evaluating criteria; identifying; building background

Listening and Speaking

- note taking; discussing; listening; evaluating; questioning; explaining a process

Bellringer

Daily Language Activity

When students enter the classroom, have this assignment on the board: *Every person has a story to tell. Write down the title of a story you could tell.*

Grammar Link to the Bellringer

Have students read aloud their story titles. Ask them if they think their story titles will provide the reader with the themes. *(Not necessarily, because the theme is more often the underlying meaning of a story.)*

See also *Daily Language Practice*

Motivating Activity

Ask students if any piece of literature ever influenced them so much that it changed their attitudes, their beliefs, or even their behavior. (Explanations may focus on various elements, such as the characters, the story line, or the author's message about life or the world.)

LESSON 2.12

The Writing Process

WRITING ABOUT LITERATURE

Explaining Theme

To analyze a piece of literature, you must first identify a theme, or underlying meaning, in the work. In the model below, Tad Burton identifies a theme in Louise Erdrich's poem "Indian Boarding School"—the meaning of freedom—and uses that theme to analyze the piece.

Student Model

In Louise Erdrich's poem "Indian Boarding School," the poet suggests that freedom is a state of mind. Although the Native American girls who live in the boarding school are subjected to physical abuse and are forced to deny their heritage, their will is not crushed. The girls imagine what a real home would be like and visit it in their dreams. In addition, even though they really have no chance to escape from their captors, some of the boarding school's inmates feel free when they hide out for a brief time in the enclosed boxcar of a train.

The idea that freedom is in one's mind is also extended to encompass a broader scope. In the last line of the poem, speaking about "the old injuries of the past," Erdrich compares the girls' situation with the experience of the Native American people at the hands of the early settlers. Like the girls in the school, the Native Americans underwent much suffering. They were taken away from their homes and placed on reservations. Nonetheless, the poet believes that the Native American people ultimately remained free because no one could manipulate their thoughts.

Tad Burton, Rangeview High School, Aurora, Colorado

Tad states Erdrich's theme in his topic sentence: freedom does not depend upon physical restrictions for it is a state of mind.

Tad uses specific details as well as lines from the poem to support his main idea.

How does Tad broaden his theme? How does he link this theme to his original one?

Resource Manager

Planning Resources

- *Lesson Plans*

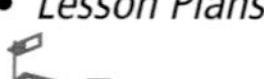

Transparencies

- *Bellringer*
- *Daily Language Practice*
- *Fine Art* 7–12
- *Two-Minute Skill Drill*
- *Writing Process* 2–8

Other Print Resources

- *Composition Enrichment,* p. 20
- *Composition Practice,* p. 20
- *Composition Reteaching,* p. 20
- *Cooperative Learning Activities,* pp. 9–12
- *Listening and Speaking Activities,* pp. 6–8
- *Thinking and Study Skills,* pp. 5, 13, 19, 24–25
- *Writing Across the Curriculum*
- *Writing Assessment and Evaluation Rubrics*

Identify a Theme

A theme is a generalization about life or human nature that the writer communicates through the piece of literature. For example, one theme in Shakespeare's play *Romeo and Juliet* is that love can triumph over hate.

To discover themes in a piece of literature, you need to see what messages the writer is trying to communicate. One way to discover a theme is to use prewriting techniques such as freewriting. For example, begin with the line "What [title of work] tells me" and freewrite for five minutes. Another way to close in on a theme is to brainstorm. For example, in a small group, take turns completing the following: "I think one of the author's messages is . . . " Discuss each group member's answer.

Freewriting

What Romeo and Juliet tells me is that love can spring up in the most unlikely circumstances, that love can triumph over hate, that love and hate are closely related, that strong emotions can lead to violent ends.

Brainstorming

Maria: I think one of Shakespeare's messages is that hatred can destroy lives.

Jamal: I think one of Shakespeare's messages is that even though hatred can destroy lives, love can triumph over hatred.

Journal Writing

What other strategies—besides the freewriting and brainstorming techniques described above—might you use for discovering the themes in a piece of literature? Write your ideas in your journal.

Teach

Using the Model

Discuss the Student Model on page 104. Point out that Tad broadens his theme from the internal freedom of the girls in the boarding school to a concept of freedom applicable to all Native Americans. Guide students to see that the writer links the two themes by citing Erdrich's reference to Native Americans in the time of the early settlers. **L2**

Explaining Theme

Ask questions to help students understand the idea of theme: Why is it important to think about the theme of a work? What might you miss if you just enjoyed the story and never went deeper? (*The theme is what the writer wants to say, and understanding a theme can enrich our lives.*) Does a piece of literature have just one theme, or can it have several? (*A piece can have more than one theme, although one is usually primary.*) Have students explain their answers and give examples from their reading. **L1**

Two-Minute Skill Drill

Have students write other strategies—besides freewriting and brainstorming techniques—that they might use for discovering the theme in a piece of literature.

See also *Two-Minute Skill Drill Transparency 2.12*

Journal Writing Tip

Inferring Help students find methods of inferring the theme by providing the analogy of detective work. This analogy suggests useful strategies such as asking questions, finding clues, and analyzing the evidence.

Teach

Analyzing the Theme

Some students may find the process of selecting supporting details confusing, especially if they think they have to account for all the story elements—characters, setting, and plot—and relate them to the theme. Assure students that their analysis of theme can focus on the element most important to the story's meaning. Often that element will be plot, which begins with the main character confronting a problem. Suggest that a good way to get at a story's theme is to focus on the main character's problem and the solution. **L1**

Evaluating the Theme

Help students understand that just as life can be complex, so can literature, which includes many works that have multiple, interwoven themes. Like other writers, Shakespeare created characters and events that supported his themes. Refer to a Shakespeare play that the students have read and review its major themes with them. **L3**

Additional Resources

For further stimuli for theme writing, see *Fine Art Transparencies* 7–12.

- *Writing Process Transparencies* 2–8
- *Writing Across the Curriculum*
- *Cooperative Learning Activities*
- *Thinking and Study Skills,* pp. 5, 13, 19, 24–25
- *Listening and Speaking Activities,* pp. 6–8
- *Composition Practice,* p. 20

Support the Theme with Evidence

Once you have identified a theme, look to the piece of literature for details that reflect or support that theme. You need to provide evidence to convince your readers that the message you have discovered is indeed one that the author was trying to convey.

The basic elements of any piece of narrative literature are character, setting, and plot. Use prewriting techniques to examine each of these elements as you seek details to support the theme you have found. Your evidence may include quotations, descriptions, summaries of key events, and explanations of passages in the text.

A scene from the movie *Romeo and Juliet*

Characters To support your analysis of a theme, study the characters' physical descriptions, thoughts, actions, words, and relationships with other characters. For example, to show that one of Shakespeare's themes in *Romeo and Juliet* is that love can triumph over hate, you might describe Romeo's impulsive behavior at the masked ball.

Setting The setting—time of day, place, mood, and other details—can also help develop a theme. Try to determine what message the author is conveying through the choice of setting. For example, Romeo and Juliet first meet at a masked ball. Perhaps, in choosing this setting, Shakespeare is saying something about the senselessness of a feud based only on appearances and one's last name.

Plot The plot—the sequence of events in the story being told—can also reveal the theme. Generally, the plot begins with a central conflict and develops to its climax and resolution. Romeo and Juliet's meeting at the ball triggers the central conflict—that is, the conflict between their love and the hatred between their families.

Write About the Theme

Once you have identified a theme and have gathered the details to support it, you're ready to draft your paragraph. Like any other paragraph you write, your analysis should be unified and coherent. Generally, you will want to state the theme in your topic sentence and then present the supporting details in a logical order—perhaps in order of importance. As you revise your work, be sure to use transitions to help the reader understand relationships between ideas.

Less Proficient Readers

Targeting the Theme

To help students understand the concept of theme, draw a cluster diagram on the board. In the outlying circles, have students relate the most important problems of the main characters in a book or in a movie. Have students notice that these problems are all linked to the one central idea. Have students list concept words such as *love, honor,* and *freedom* and use these to help write a theme for the main circle. One way to find the theme is to ask, "What is this (*movie, book*) all about?" **L1**

2.12 Writing Activities

Write an Analysis

Choose a piece of literature with which you are familiar. Freewrite for five minutes to try to discover a theme that you can then write about. Use quotations, descriptions, and summaries of events in the story to support your analysis. Use the five stages of the writing process to write a paragraph based on the theme. For information about what makes a good paragraph, see **Writing and Research Handbook,** pages 943–945.

PURPOSE To analyze literature
AUDIENCE Your teacher
LENGTH 1 paragraph

WRITING RUBRICS To write an analysis of literature, you should

- look for a generalization about life or human nature
- support the theme with details of character, setting, and plot
- check that your paragraph is unified and coherent

Viewing and Representing

ILLUSTRATING THEME Create a book jacket that expresses the theme of the story you have recalled for the writing activity. Select an image that visually expresses a generalization about life or human nature that the story communicates. Draw your book jacket on poster board or create it on the computer using drawing software.

GrammarLink

Capitalize proper nouns.

Rewrite the following paragraph, correcting errors in capitalization.

[1]In william shakespeare's play *macbeth*, the writer suggests that the lust for power corrupts people. [2]Witches tell macbeth that he will eventually become king of scotland. [3]Convinced that the witches have told the truth, he and his wife, lady macbeth, murder king duncan. [4]Macbeth then becomes involved in other murders, including those of the wife and son of macduff. [5]By the time macbeth is killed by the scots, the desire for power has corrupted him completely.

See Lesson 20.2, pages 713–719.

Cross-Curricular Activity

ART Identify features of a painting from this book that attract your interest or attention or that evoke memories or mental images. Freewrite for five minutes or use a cluster map to define the painting's theme. To find details that support the theme, look for elements of character, setting, and plot. Use the theme and details to write one or two paragraphs analyzing the painting.

LOG ON **Writing** Online | For more writing and grammar practice, go to **glencoe.com** and enter QuickPass code WC97727p1.

Assess

Evaluation Rubrics

Write a Literature Analysis

Use these criteria when evaluating your students' writing:

- Is there a strong topic sentence?
- Is there evidence that the student considered various ideas?
- Is the theme precise, not vague?
- Is the theme supported with specific details?

See also *Writing Assessment & Evaluation Rubrics*

Cross-Curricular Activity

Have students form pairs and exchange their analyses of the art they've examined. Have them read aloud their paragraphs and compare their impressions of the art. Students should also examine each other's paragraphs, looking for statements of theme and supporting details.

Reteaching

Composition Reteaching, p. 20

Enrichment

Composition Enrichment, p. 20

Fine Arts Transparencies 7–12

Close

Tell students that they can find themes in conversations, commercials, and songs. Have them write one or two paragraphs on the theme of a favorite song, movie, or TV episode.

GrammarLink

Answers

1. William Shakespeare's; *Macbeth*
2. Macbeth; King of Scotland
3. Lady Macbeth; King Duncan
4. Macduff
5. Macbeth; Scots

Focus

Lesson Overview

Objective

- To write a story derived from family history, using the five-stage writing process

Skills

- using the five stages of the writing process: prewriting, drafting, revising, editing, and presenting

Critical Thinking

- analyzing and synthesizing information; evaluating ideas; defining and clarifying ideas

Listening and Speaking

- discussing; interviewing; note taking; informal speaking; evaluating; questioning

Bellringer

Daily Language Activity

When students enter the classroom, have this assignment on the board: *What makes certain friends or family members good story tellers? Write briefly about these people.*

Grammar Link to the Bellringer

Have students review their Bellringer sentences. Let them check names and foreign words or spelling and capitalization. Did they avoid run-ons?

See also *Daily Language Practice*

Motivating Activity

Discuss students' responses to the Bellringer activity. Then discuss the appeal of family sagas. Ask why such stories are popular. Point out that similar stories can be told in an endless number of ways. Students should consider what they like about stories (humor? realism? dialogue?) and try to use the same techniques in their writing.

UNIT 2

Writing Process in Action

The Writing Process

The Writing Process

In the preceding lessons, you've learned about the stages of the writing process. Now it's time to make use of what you learned. In this lesson, you are invited to retell a story a family member has told you—whether the story has been in your family for generations or is a new addition to your family's collection of favorites.

Assignment

Context

Your cousin has decided to create a written collection of memorable family stories so that future generations will be able to know about their ancestors and their past. You have been asked to contribute your favorite family tale to the collection.

Purpose

To write a story that captures something of your family members and their experiences.

Audience

Family members, friends, and future generations

Length

1–2 pages

LOG ON Writing Online

For prewriting, drafting, revising, editing and publishing tools, go to **glencoe.com** and enter QuickPass code WC97727p1.

TIME

For more about the writing process, see **TIME Facing the Blank Page**, 121-131.

Planning to Write

The following pages can help you plan and write your family story. Read through them and then refer to them as you need to. But don't be tied down by them. You're in charge of your own writing process. Be sure to set a time frame for completion and to keep the controlling idea in mind as you write.

Resource Manager

Planning Resources

- *Lesson Plans*

Transparencies

- *Bellringer*
- *Daily Language Practice*
- *Writing Process* 2–8

Other Print Resources

- *Composition Enrichment*, pp. 9–20
- *Composition Reteaching*, pp. 9–20
- *Grammar Workbook*, Lessons 98–102
- *Thinking and Study Skills*, pp. 5, 13, 23
- *Writing Assessment and Evaluation Rubrics*

Web Site

- *glencoe.com*

Literature Model

The aged visitors who came to my grandmother's house when I was a child were men of immense character, full of wisdom and disdain. . . . They were made of lean and leather, and they bore themselves upright. They wore great black hats and bright ample shirts that shook in the wind. They rubbed fat upon their hair and wound their braids with strips of colored cloth. . . . They were an old council of war lords, come to remind and be reminded of who they were.

N. Scott Momaday, *House Made of Dawn*

Prewriting

Where will you get your story idea? Talk with your family, look through old pictures, and think about your own memories. Once you've identified a story, use freewriting, list making, or questioning to brainstorm for details.

To bring your story into sharper focus, think about your purpose and audience and keep them in mind as you gather details to provide a full and accurate account. In the literature model below, notice how the author uses story details to reinforce the theme of the writing.

Now that you have a story in mind, think about your purpose. You want to tell a memorable story, but is there anything else you want to accomplish? Do you want to make your readers laugh? Persuade them to be proud of their roots? If you do have a secondary purpose, identify it so that you can keep it in mind as you draft.

Next, consider your audience. Friends and future generations might lack your and your family's current familiarity with your subject. So you might add to your prewriting notes any information these readers would need to understand your story.

Finally, gather any remaining details you may need to tell your story effectively. You want to provide a full and accurate account of your chosen tale.

Prewriting Options

- Check your journal. What have you already written about family members or personal experiences?
- Talk with your family. What family stories have they especially enjoyed?
- Look at family albums. What clues do faces and places provide?

Teach

Prewriting

Developing Ideas for Writing a Family Story

Have students talk to family members about events or celebrations in the past. Encourage them to freewrite or draw a network tree. **L2**

Drafting

Organizing Ideas

Students can use a story map to record the family story. The map can be organized using boxes labeled beginning, middle, and end or by numbering the events in sequence. **L2**

Ordering Ideas

Students can select several family photographs that capture the essence of a person or experience, arrange them in a chronological sequence, and draft a paragraph about each. **L1**

Cooperative Learning

Students who don't have access to their own family history can contact organizations such as Big Brothers/Big Sisters of America or look at books of traditional folk tales to find stories. Groups might visit a family shelter or a children's home and tell or read stories, selecting those that reflect their cultural background. **L2**

Teach

Revising

Peer Editing

Students can work in writing conferences with peer editors before they revise their work. You may want to duplicate the Peer Response forms in the *Writing Assessment and Evaluation Rubrics.* Suggest that peer editors respond to the following:

- Does the story answer who? what? where? when? why?
- Is the story chronological or cause-effect? Is the organization clear?
- Is the main idea clear? Are there supporting details? **L2**

Editing/Proofreading

Peer Editing

After students have edited their own work, have them edit and proofread another student's writing. Remind them to refer to the Editing/Proofreading Questions on student page 111. **L2**

Publishing/Presenting

Before students present their family stories, discuss how to prepare papers to send to family members. Emphasize the importance of the final draft and the necessity of neatness.

Additional Resources

Writing Process Transparencies 2–8

Thinking and Study Skills, pp. 5, 13, 23

Grammar Workbook, Lessons 98–102

Drafting

A good way to start drafting is to just jump in. Let the story tell itself, flowing naturally from beginning to end. As you draft, refer to your prewriting notes for details that will make your story stick in the reader's mind.

If you have trouble starting your story, think about the main idea you're trying to communicate and write it as a topic sentence. Then try to develop your idea by describing incidents that support it. Ask yourself *who, what, where, when, why,* and *how* questions to help you think of details about the event.

If you're telling the story in chronological order, consider ordering the details in the same way. Sometimes, however, using cause-and-effect order works well too. Do not be too concerned with spelling and grammar at this point. Your goal at this stage is to get the story and supporting details down on paper.

Once you've finished your draft, put it away for a while. You will return to it later with a fresh perspective.

Drafting Tip

For help writing coherent paragraphs, see Lesson 2.8, pages 88–91.

Revising

To begin revising, read over your draft to make sure that what you have written fits your purpose and your audience. Then have a **writing conference.** Read your draft to a partner or small group. You might also ask a family member who is familiar with the story to read your draft to help you identify whether any important details are missing or whether you have told anything incorrectly. Then revise the story to strengthen it. You can use the questions on this checklist to help you.

Revising Tip

To check the paragraphs in your story for unity and coherence, use the checklists in Lesson 2.9, page 94.

Revising Checklist

- Does this story match the one in my head?
- Does the story have a clear beginning and end?
- Does the story capture something of the essence of the people in my family and our experiences?
- Does the "flavor" of the people and their experiences come through?

Listening and Speaking

Listening to Stories

Invite students to read their stories aloud to the class. Have class members discuss what works especially well in the stories. What images do they remember, and how would they characterize the people in the stories? Is the story chronological or cause-effect? What happens in the beginning, the middle, and the end? What suggestions do they have for improving the story even further?

Editing/Proofreading

After you're satisfied with the basic content and flow of your story, **proofread** it carefully to correct errors in grammar, usage, mechanics, and spelling. Use the Editing/Proofreading Questions as a guide. You'll also need to consider the following special questions:

- If you used any foreign words or names, did you spell and capitalize them correctly?
- If you used any family expressions, dialect, or slang, did you include enough explanation so that readers will be able to understand them?

Editing/Proofreading Questions

- Have I used commas to avoid run-ons with "and"?
- Have I used quotation marks to enclose all direct quotes in the dialogue?
- Have I punctuated possessive pronouns correctly?
- Have I capitalized names, groups, and places correctly?
- Have I used my spelling checker or checked the spelling of any unfamiliar words?

Self-Evaluation

Make sure your family story—

✔ focuses on a tale about a family member or experience
✔ hooks interest early on by establishing relevance to the reader
✔ uses vivid sensory details and realistic dialogue
✔ provides any needed explanations
✔ follows correct grammar, usage, mechanics, and spelling

Proofreading Tip

For proofreading symbols, see page 411.

Publishing/Presenting

You can use your story to start your own family collection. Send your story along with a request to members of your family, asking them to send you *their* favorite family tales in return. You can also tell your story at your next family gathering.

Journal Writing

In your journal, write down the names of three or four characters from your story. Under each name, list as many words and phrases as you can that describe that character.

Assess

Evaluation Rubric

Use the following questions to evaluate student's finished writing.

- Does it fulfill a clear purpose, centering around a specific family member or experience?
- Does it hook the reader?
- Does it use vivid imagery, figurative language, and realistic dialogue?
- Does it strike a balance between too much explanation and too little?
- Does it capture the flavor of the people and their experiences?
- Does it follow correct grammar and usage?
- Does it follow correct mechanics, with special attention to the spelling of foreign words and proper names?

See also *Writing Assessment & Evaluation Rubrics* for further help with evaluating student writing.

Reteaching

Composition Reteaching, pp. 9–20

Enrichment

Composition Enrichment, pp. 9–20

Close

Initiate a discussion in which students talk about what they learned about their writing habits and writing process. What methods worked best for them? What didn't seem to work well, and why? If they were to write this assignment over, what would they do differently? What would they do the same?

Journal Writing Tip

The Senses If students are having trouble describing their characters, ask them to use their senses to help them write. What do they see, feel, or hear when they think of each character?

Enrichment and Extension

Follow-up Ideas

- Set aside time for students to celebrate the conclusion of their writing projects. Encourage them to share their finished pieces with the whole class or in small groups.
- If students send their work to family members, keep photocopies.

Extending Family Stories

- Brainstorm with students about times they can use their expertise in telling family stories, such as when they are taking care of younger children.
- Explore opportunities for submitting stories to a local newspaper or reading them aloud at a local library.

About the Author

Amy Tan writes about the world in which she was raised: California's immigrant Chinese community. Her parents came to Oakland, California, around 1950, just two years before Amy was born. Tan's writing explores her Chinese heritage. When she visited China, she experienced that heritage. She says, "As soon as my feet touched China, I became Chinese."

Focus

Lesson Overview

Objectives

- To discover how a writer uses vivid description to tell a story and convey an aspect of a culture
- To compare and contrast two selections
- To write an evaluative essay

Skills

- clarifying; summarizing

Critical Thinking

- analyzing; inferring; interpreting; drawing conclusions

Listening and Speaking

- discussing; making personal connections

Bellringer

Daily Language Activity

When students enter the classroom, have this assignment on the board: *Think of an unusual or special gift you have received or given. Write a brief but specific description of that gift.*

See also  *Daily Language Practice*

Motivating Activity

Call on one or two volunteers to read aloud their response to the Bellringer activity. Ask those students to identify what made the gift unusual or special.

UNIT 2

Literature Model

from

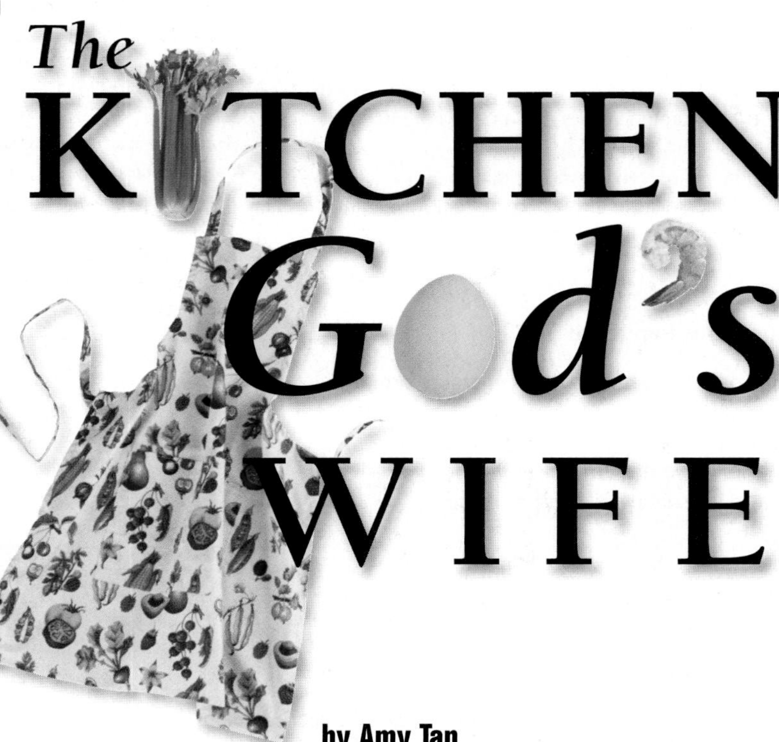

The Kitchen God's Wife

by Amy Tan

Amy Tan, who was born of Chinese parents in the United States, uses incidents from her own family history as the raw material of her writing process. In this excerpt, Tan depicts the differences between the narrator, Pearl, and Pearl's mother, while at the same time emphasizing the ties that bind them together. Pay special attention to how the author uses detail in the dialogue to bring the characters to life. When you finish the excerpt, try the activities in Linking Writing and Literature on page 119.

Resource Manager

Planning Resources

- *Lesson Plans*

Transparencies

- *Bellringer*
- *Daily Language Practice*
- *Fine Art* 7–12

Other Print Resources

- *Listening and Speaking Activities,* pp. 6–8
- *Thinking and Study Skills,* pp. 5, 13, 23
- *Writing Assessment and Evaluation Rubrics*

Web Sites

- *writerschoice.glencoe.com*
- *lit.glencoe.com*

My mother is standing outside the house when we return. "I tried to chase you, but you were too fast," she says as soon as I get out of the car. "And then I knew you would remember and come back." Tessa and Cleo are already racing up the stairs.

"Remember what?"

"Grand Auntie's farewell gift. Remember? Two, three days ago I told you not to forget. Yesterday I said, Don't forget. You forgot?"

"No, no," I say. "Where is it?"

"In back, in the laundry room," she says. "Very heavy, though. Better ask your husband to carry it." I can just imagine what it must be: the old vinyl ottoman Grand Auntie used to rest her feet on, or perhaps the set of chip-proof Melmac dishes. As we wait for Phil to come back with the girls, my mother hands me a cup of tea, waving off my protests. "Already made. If you can't drink it, I only have to throw it away."

> *"She told me, 'If I buy myself the cheap tea, then I am saying my whole life has not been worth something better.' So she decided to buy herself the best tea, so she could drink it and feel like a rich person inside."*

I take a few quick sips. "This is really good." And I mean it. I have never tasted tea like this. It is smooth, pungent, and instantly addicting.

"This is from Grand Auntie," my mother explains. "A few years ago she bought it for herself. One hundred dollars a pound."

"You're kidding." I take another sip. It tastes even better.

"She told me, 'If I buy myself the cheap tea, then I am saying my whole life has not been worth something better.' So she decided to buy herself the best tea, so she could drink it and feel like a rich person inside."

I laugh.

My mother looks encouraged by my laughter. "But then she thought, If I buy just a little, then I am saying my lifetime is almost over. So she bought enough tea for another lifetime. Three pounds! Can you imagine?"

"That's three hundred dollars!" I exclaim. Grand Auntie was the most frugal[1] person I knew. "Remember how she used to keep all the boxes of See's candies we gave her for Christmas, telling us they were too good to eat? And then one year, she gave a box back to us for Thanksgiving or something. Only it was so old—"

My mother was nodding, already laughing.

"—all the candies were white with mold!"

"Bugs, too!" my mother adds.

"So she left you the tea in her will?" I say.

"Already gave it to me a few months ago. She was thinking she was going to die soon. She didn't say, but she started to give things away, good things, not just junk. And one time we were visiting, drinking tea. I said, 'Ah, good tea!' same as always. This time, Grand Auntie went to her kitchen, brought back the tea. She told me, '*Syau ning,* you take this tea now.' That's what she called me, *syau ning,* 'little person,' from the old days when we first knew each other.

1 **frugal** (froo′ gəl) thrifty

The Writing Process

Teach

Active Reading Strategies

Clarify The first few paragraphs of this novel excerpt might be confusing to students. Have students ask questions about them. *(Sample answer: What is happening? Where are the characters? Who are Tessa and Cleo?)* Remind students that a good strategy for answering these questions is to reread a confusing section or read on for further information.

Critical Thinking

Draw Conclusions Ask students: "How do Pearl and her mother treat each other?" *(Sample answer: The mother treats Pearl with concern; she gives her things and laughs with her. She is also a little overbearing. Pearl does what her mother asks and, in conversation, accepts what her mother says, but she also has her own thoughts.)*

Active Reading Strategies

Clarify

Explain to students that to *clarify* is to look at difficult sections of the text in order to clear up what is confusing. Present these tips for clarifying.

- Go back and reread confusing sections more slowly.
- Ask yourself questions about what you don't understand.
- Remember that sometimes you have to read on before everything becomes clear.

Practice After students read this page, have them ask one or more questions about Grand Auntie, her farewell gift, Pearl, or Pearl's mother. Students can then reread to find the answers or decide to read on to learn more.

Teach

Literary Element

Character Explain that characters are often revealed by what others say about them. What do students find out about Grand Auntie through Pearl's mother's words? *(She was frugal and hoarded gifts. But late in life, she indulged herself in a very special tea, so she could "feel like a rich person inside." She then gave the tea to Pearl's mother, showing how much she valued her.)*

Critical Thinking

Infer Ask students why the narrator is sorry to have to leave when her husband and children return. *(She is enjoying her conversation with her mother about Grand Auntie and doesn't want it to end.)* Point out to students that Pearl's exact words are, "I am actually sorry we have to leave." Ask students what Pearl's use of the word *actually* implies about how Pearl usually feels about visiting with her mother. *(Pearl is often glad to leave her mother, even if she tells her mother otherwise.)*

Tomie Arai, *Laundryman's Daughter,* 1988

"I said, 'No, no! I wasn't saying this to hint.' And she said, '*Syau ning,* you take this now so I can see how happy you are to receive it while I am still alive. Some things can't wait until I'm dead.' How could I refuse? Of course, every time I came to visit, I brought back her tea."

Phil returns with Cleo, Tessa is right behind. And now I am actually sorry we have to leave.

"We better hit the road," says Phil. I put the teacup down.

"Don't forget," my mother says to Phil. "Grand Auntie's present in the laundry room."

"A present?" Cleo says. "Do I have a present too?"

Phil throws me a look of surprise.

"Remember?" I lie. "I told you—what Grand Auntie left us in her will."

He shrugs, and we all follow my mother to the back.

Viewing the Art

Tomie Arai, *Laundryman's Daughter,* 1988

Tomie Arai's silkscreen *Laundryman's Daughter* (22 by 30 inches) is based on interviews with Chinese women in New York. Arai is American-born, but she says she is "still defined by the immigrant experience." She depicts two women with images of their lives and cultures floating in space, because "the sojourner . . . uprooted . . . is a central character in Asian American art." The piece was included in a 1989 show at New York's Chinatown History Project.

"Of course it's just old things," says my mother. She turns on the light, and then I see it, sitting on the clothes dryer. It is the altar for Grand Auntie's good-luck god, the Chinese crèche.[2]

"Wow!" Tessa exclaims. "A Chinese dollhouse."

"I can't see! I can't see!" Cleo says, and Phil lifts the altar off the dryer and carries it into the kitchen.

The altar is about the size of a small upturned drawer, painted in red lacquer. In a way, it resembles a miniature stage for a Chinese play. There are two ornate[3] columns in front, as well as two ceremonial electric candles made out of gold and red plastic and topped by red Christmas tree bulbs for flames. Running down the sides are wooden panels decorated with gold Chinese characters.

"What does that say?" I ask my mother.

She traces her finger down one, then the other. "*Jye shiang ru yi.* This first word is 'luck,' this other is another kind of luck, and these two mean 'all that you wish.' All kinds of luck, all that you wish."

"And who is this on the inside, this man in the picture frame?" The picture is almost cartoonlike. The man is rather large and is seated in regal splendor, holding a quill[4] in one hand, a tablet in the other. He has two long whiskers, shaped like smooth, tapered black whips.

"Oh, this we call Kitchen God. To my way of thinking, he was not too important. Not like Buddha, not like Kwan Yin, goddess of mercy—not that high level, not even the same level as the Money God. Maybe he was like a store manager, important, but still many, many bosses above him."

Phil chuckles at my mother's Americanized explanation of the hierarchy of Chinese deities.[5] I wonder if that's how she really thinks of them, or if she's used this metaphor[6] for our benefit.

"What's a kitchen god?" says Tessa. "Can I have one?"

"He is only a story," answers my mother.

"A story!" exclaims Cleo. "I want one."

My mother's face brightens. She pats Cleo's head. "You want another story from Ha-bu? Last night, you did not get enough stories?"

The altar is about the size of a small upturned drawer, painted in red lacquer. In a way, it resembles a miniature stage for a Chinese play.

"When we get home," Phil says to Cleo. "Ha-bu is too tired to tell you a story now."

But my mother acts as if she has not heard Phil's excuses. "It is a very simple story," she says to Cleo in a soothing voice, "how he became Kitchen God. It is this way."

---

2 **crèche** (kresh) a display representing the birth of Jesus

3 **ornate** (ôr nāt′) heavily decorated and ornamented

4 **quill** (kwil) a pen made from the stem of a feather

5 **the hierarchy of Chinese deities** (hī′ ə rär′ kē) (dē′ ə tēz) the order of importance of all the Chinese gods

6 **metaphor** (met′ ə fôr′) a comparison of two unlike things used to clarify the meaning of the less familiar one

Critical Thinking

Draw Conclusions Ask students: "How does Pearl feel about Grand Auntie's beliefs in the altar and the Kitchen God? Do you think she shares Grand Auntie's beliefs?" *(Sample answer: She is curious about these traditional Chinese beliefs, but she doesn't know much about them, which shows she cannot share them.)*

Literary Element

Dialogue Ask students how the author explains Grand Auntie's rituals and beliefs to the reader. *(She uses Pearl's dialogue with her husband and mother to explain them. She also has the mother tell the story of the Kitchen God and explain what it meant to Grand Auntie.)*

Critical Thinking

Analyze

Tell students that to *analyze* a selection means to look at its separate parts in order to arrive at a general understanding. For example, by examining Pearl's view of Grand Auntie, a reader can learn about Pearl's relationship to Chinese culture. Say: "At first, Pearl seems to view Grand Auntie as a comical and slightly annoying figure. She doesn't expect Grand Auntie's farewell gift to be good, and she makes jokes about her. But when Pearl learns that Grand Auntie bought expensive tea and later gave it away as a gift, she seems to gain a new interest in Grand Auntie—and in traditional Chinese culture in general.

Practice Ask students to analyze the scene in which Pearl and her family respond to Grand Auntie's altar. Then ask students to make a general statement about the cultural differences in her family. *(Pearl knows very little about the Chinese culture that her mother comes from, but she and her children are interested in learning. Pearl's husband is impatient.)*

Teach

Active Reading Strategies

Summarize Have students briefly retell the story of the Kitchen God. *(Zhang had a good life with Guo, but he took up with another woman. The woman chased Guo out of her own home and then left Zhang, who became a beggar. One day, when Zhang was near death, he woke up in Guo's house and was so embarrassed about it that he leapt into the fire. He burned with shame and was turned into the Kitchen God.)*

Critical Thinking

Analyze Ask students: "Why does the author include this entire story? How does it fit in with the author's purpose for writing?" *(It helps to show how connected the mother is to traditional beliefs of her Chinese culture. The story also helps to show the distance between the daughter's modern life in America and her mother's past.)*

Literature Model

And as my mother begins, I am struck by a familiar feeling, as if I am Cleo, again three years old, still eager to believe everything my mother has to say.

"In China long time ago," I hear my mother say, "there was a rich farmer named Zhang, such a lucky man. Fish jumped in his river, pigs grazed his land, ducks flew around his yard as thick as clouds. And that was because he was blessed with a hard-working wife named Guo. She caught his fish and herded his pigs. She fattened his ducks, doubled all his riches, year after year. Zhang had everything he could ask for—from the water, the earth, and the heavens above.

"But Zhang was not satisfied. He wanted to play with a pretty, carefree woman named Lady Li. One day he brought this pretty woman home to his house, made his good wife cook for her. When Lady Li later chased his wife out of the house, Zhang did not run out and call to her, 'Come back, my good wife, come back.'

"Now he and Lady Li were free to swim in each other's arms. They threw money away like dirty water. They slaughtered ducks just to eat a plate of their tongues. And in two years' time, all of Zhang's land was empty, and so was his heart. His money was gone, and so was pretty Lady Li, run off with another man.

"Zhang became a beggar, so poor he wore more patches than whole cloth on his pants. He crawled from the gate of one household to another, crying, 'Give me your moldy grain!'

"One day, he fell over and faced the sky, ready to die. He fainted, dreaming of eating the winter clouds blowing above him. When he opened his eyes again, he found the clouds had turned to smoke. At first he was afraid he had fallen down into a place far below the earth. But when he sat up, he saw he was in a kitchen, near a warm fireplace. The girl tending the fire explained that the lady of the house had taken pity on him—she always did this, with all kinds of people, poor or old, sick or in trouble.

"'What a good lady!' cried Zhang. 'Where is she, so I can thank her?' The girl pointed to the window, and the man saw a woman walking up the path. Ai-ya! That lady was none other than his good wife Guo!

"Zhang began leaping about the kitchen looking for some place to hide, then jumped into the kitchen fireplace just as his wife walked into the room.

"Good Wife Guo poured out many tears to try to put the fire out. No use! Zhang was burning with shame and, of course, because of the hot roaring fire below. She watched her husband's ashes fly up to heaven in three puffs of smoke. Wah!

"In heaven, the Jade Emperor heard the whole story from his new arrival. 'For having the courage to admit you were wrong,' the Emperor declared, 'I make you Kitchen God, watching over everyone's behavior. Every year, you let me know who deserves good luck, who deserves bad.'

> *"And once a year, seven days before the new year, Kitchen God flew back up the fireplace to report whose fate deserved to be changed, better for worse, or worse for better."*

6+1 Trait® Writing

Ideas

Explain to students that **ideas** are used to elaborate upon a message or theme. Characters, settings, and other elements are presented because the writer has a **theme,** or something to say. Rich, strong **details** help the writer express the theme. In this selection, details about Pearl's mother show how much closer she is to her Chinese heritage than her daughter Pearl. For example, Pearl's mother frequently uses her Chinese language when speaking. At times, she translates Chinese phrases for Pearl, which indicates that Pearl may not comprehend them.

Practice Have students find other details that show how Pearl and her mother have a different relationship to Chinese culture. *(Details show that the mother can read Chinese, but the daughter cannot; the mother knows the story of the Kitchen God, but the daughter does not; the mother clearly attaches significance to the story, but the daughter senses only that it may matter.)*

For more information on ideas and the 6+1 Trait® model, see **Writing and Research Handbook,** pages 947–949.

Ch'ing dynasty, porcelain teapot and beaker, c. 1700

"From then on, people in China knew Kitchen God was watching them. From his corner in every house and every shop, he saw all kinds of good and bad habits spill out: generosity or greediness, a harmonious nature or a complaining one. And once a year, seven days before the new year, Kitchen God flew back up the fireplace to report whose fate deserved to be changed, better for worse, or worse for better."

"The end!" shouts Cleo, completely satisfied.

"Sounds like Santa Claus," says Phil cheerfully.

"Hnh!" my mother huffs in a tone that implies Phil is stupid beyond words. "He is not Santa Claus. More like a spy—FBI agent, CIA, Mafia, worse than IRS, that kind of person! And he does not give *you* gifts, you must give *him* things. All year long you have to show him respect—give him tea and oranges. When Chinese New Year's time comes, you must give him even better things—maybe whiskey to drink, cigarettes to smoke, candy to eat, that kind of thing. You are hoping all the time his tongue will be sweet, his head a little drunk, so when he has his meeting with the big boss, maybe he reports good things about you. This family has been good, you hope he says. Please give them good luck next year."

"Well, that's a pretty inexpensive way to get some luck," I say. "Cheaper than the lottery."

"No!" my mother exclaims, and startles us all. "You never know. Sometimes he is in a bad mood. Sometimes he says, I don't like this family, give them bad luck. Then you're in trouble, nothing you can do about it. Why should I want that kind of person to judge me, a man who cheated his wife? His wife was the good one, not him."

Critical Thinking

Infer Have students infer how Pearl's mother feels about the Kitchen God. *(She doesn't really respect his character or think he's hugely important, but she does believe he can determine whether a family has good luck.)*

Viewing the Art

Ch'ing dynasty, porcelain teapot and beaker, c. 1700

This Blanc de Chine porcelain teapot and beaker are from the Ch'ing Dynasty (1644–1912) in the K'ang Hsi period (1662–1722). The pieces are decorated with raised flowers, which are also porcelain. The Chinese developed porcelain by mixing two substances: kaolin, a white, heat-resistant clay, and petuntse, a substance that is ground to a powder and melted at high temperatures to form glass.

Teach

Critical Thinking

Interpret Ask students: "Why is Pearl's mother unhappy when Phil suggests that the altar might be a curse?" *(She's unhappy because she knows that Grand Auntie believed the altar was a good gift, but she also knows the Kitchen God is a problematic figure.)*

6+1 Trait® Writing

Ideas Ask students to explain which details on this page help show the difference between Pearl's view of the altar and her mother's view of the altar. *(The altar has so little meaning for Pearl that she suggests her children use it as a toy. However, it has enormous significance for Pearl's mother: it is a gift from Grand Auntie; it is a piece of her family's past; it is part of her culture and belief system. Yet it also has troubling implications.)*

Additional Resources

For further stimuli for writing, see *Fine Art Transparencies* 7–12.

Listening and Speaking Activities, pp. 6–8

Thinking and Study Skills, pp. 5, 13, 23

6+1 Trait® is a registered trademark of Northwest Regional Educational Laboratory, which does not endorse this product.

"Then why did Grand Auntie keep him?" I ask.

My mother frowns, considering this. "It is this way, I think. Once you get started, you are afraid to stop. Grand Auntie worshiped him since she was a little girl. Her family started it many generations before, in China."

"Great!" says Phil. "So now she passes along this curse to us. Thanks, Grand Auntie, but no thanks." He looks at his watch and I can tell he's impatient to go.

"It was Grand Auntie's gift to you," my mother says to me in a mournful voice. "How could she know this was not so good? She only wanted to leave you something good, her best things."

> *"It was Grand Auntie's gift to you," my mother says to me in a mournful voice. "How could she know this was not so good?"*

"Maybe the girls can use the altar as a dollhouse," I suggest. Tessa nods, Cleo follows suit. My mother stares at the altar, not saying anything.

"I'm thinking about it this way," she finally announces, her mouth set in an expression of thoughtfulness. "You take this altar. I can find you another kind of lucky god to put inside, not this one." She removes the picture of the Kitchen God. "This one, I take it. Grand Auntie will understand. This kind of luck, you don't want. Then you don't have to worry."

"Deal!" Phil says right away. "Let's pack 'er up."

But now I'm worried. "Are you sure?" I ask my mother. She's already stuffing the plastic candlesticks into a used paper bag. I'm not exactly superstitious. I've always been the kind who hates getting chain letters—Mary used to send them to me all the time. And while I never sent the duplicate letters out as instructed, I never threw the originals away either.

Phil is carrying the altar. Tessa has the bag of candlesticks. My mother has taken Cleo upstairs to find a plastic neon bracelet she left in the bathroom. And now my mother comes back with Cleo and hands me a heavy grocery sack, the usual care package, what feels like oranges and Chinese candy, that sort of thing.

"Grand Auntie's tea, I gave you some," my mother says. "Don't need to use too much. Just keep adding water. The flavor always comes back."

Compare and Contrast

Comparing Selections

Tell students that comparing and contrasting one selection with another can help them deepen their understanding of both works. It can also help them understand how certain types of characters, settings, and themes reappear in literature. Ask students to discuss the relationship between the mother and daughter in this excerpt and the relationship between the grandmother and daughter in the excerpt from *I Know Why the Caged Bird Sings* (pp. 40–49).

Practice Ask students to write two or more paragraphs comparing and contrasting the two relationships. Encourage students to use a prewriting organizer, such as a two-column chart, to name and develop points of comparison before they write.

Linking Writing and Literature

Learning to Learn

Think about the relationship between Pearl and her mother. How are the two women alike? How are they different? Jot down a few sentences explaining what separates them and what brings them together.

Talk About Reading

Talk with other students about this excerpt from *The Kitchen God's Wife.* Choose one person to lead your group and another to take notes. Then use the questions below to guide your discussion.

1. **Connect to Your Life** What differences between generations do you see in your own life? Do you relate to a parent or grandparent the way Pearl relates to her mother? Explain.
2. **Critical Thinking: Analyze** How do details in the dialogue point out differences between the mother's and daughter's generations?
3. **6+1 Trait®: Ideas** How does Amy Tan explore the idea of cultural differences? Identify some important details within the selection that highlight this idea.
4. **Write to Learn** What do you think the author did well in this selection? Consider characters; dialogue; details that were funny, interesting, or believable; plot; and theme. Which of Tan's strengths as a writer can you try to apply to the writing you do for school?

Write About Reading

An Evaluation In this excerpt from *The Kitchen God's Wife,* Tan explores differences that exist between two generations. She uses her characters, dialogue, and a story about a minor Chinese god to help show how elements of culture can separate and unite a mother and daughter. Do you think Tan does a good job? Write an essay evaluating the author's approach to her theme.

Focus on Ideas Remember to use details to make your ideas strong and clear. As you write and revise, look for places where well-chosen, informative details from the story help you make your point.

For more information on ideas and the 6+1 Trait® model, see **Writing and Research Handbook,** pages 947–948.

Linking Writing and Literature

Assess

Evaluation Rubrics

Talk About Reading

Possible responses to the questions:

1. Students may know parents or grandparents who hang on to unlikely stories or superstitions from their past. They may also belong to or know of families where one generation is fluent in a language that the next generation does not know as well.
2. Chinese words in the dialogue show that the mother can read and speak Chinese and the daughter cannot. Dialogue about the Kitchen God shows the mother's knowledge of and belief in stories from her past and the daughter's distance from them.
3. Phil, who represents modern America, is impatient with his mother-in-law's stories and compares the Kitchen God to Santa Claus. Pearl considers using the altar as a dollhouse for her children. Pearl's mother removes the picture of the Kitchen God in order to protect her daughter's family from bad luck.
4. Students may have enjoyed the story of Grand Auntie hoarding chocolates and then giving them away after they were white with mold; they may have been surprised by the one-hundred dollar per pound tea; they may have found the Kitchen God plot within a plot entertaining.

Write About Reading

The evaluation should do the following:

- contain a thesis statement that tells whether Tan does a good job presenting her theme
- use details from the story to support the thesis
- quote or paraphrase the selection accurately

Close

Have volunteers share their responses to the discussion questions.

Reflecting on the Unit

You may have students respond to Reflecting on the Unit by writing a summary of what they've learned or through discussion.

Adding to Your Portfolio

Remind students that a portfolio is usually assembled to display positive examples of an artist's or a writer's work. Suggest that students select pieces for which they have a good "how-I-wrote-this" story that explains why they selected this piece for their portfolio.

Portfolio Evaluation

If you grade the portfolio selections, you may want to award two marks—one each for content and form. Explain your assessment criteria before students make their selections.

Commend

- experimentation with creative prewriting techniques
- clear, concise writing in which the main idea, audience, and purpose are evident
- successful revisions
- work that shows a flair for language

Writing Across the Curriculum

Before students begin writing, suggest that they brainstorm to develop a list of all the things they know or would like to know about daily life in the early twentieth century. This could be a good starting point for sifting out the one or two important aspects of daily life that they will compare in their paragraphs.

ASSESSMENT OPTIONS

Tests With Answer Key & Rubrics
Unit 2 Choice A Test, p. 5
Unit 2 Choice B Test, p. 6
Unit 2 Composition Objective Test, pp. 7–8

Testmaker
Unit 2 Choice A Test
Unit 2 Choice B Test
Unit 2 Composition Objective Test

You may wish to administer one of these tests as a mastery test.

MindJogger Videoquizzes

UNIT 2 Review

Reflecting on the Unit: Summarize What You Learned

Focus on the following questions to help summarize what you learned in this unit.

1. What are the five stages of the writing process?
2. What are the important elements of each stage of the process?
3. What strategies and techniques can help you at each stage of the writing process?
4. What are some ways to analyze theme in a piece of literature?

Adding to Your Portfolio

CHOOSE A SELECTION FOR YOUR PORTFOLIO Look over the writing you did for this unit. Select a completed piece for your portfolio. The writing you choose should show some or all of the following:

- ideas generated by using such techniques as freewriting or listing
- words and ideas chosen with a particular audience in mind
- a clear topic sentence that controls appropriate supporting details
- careful revising and editing
- development through all five stages of the writing process, including presenting

REFLECT ON YOUR CHOICE Attach a note to the piece you chose, explaining briefly why you chose it and what you learned from writing it.

SET GOALS How can you improve your writing? What skill will you focus on the next time you write?

Writing Across the Curriculum

MAKE A SOCIAL STUDIES CONNECTION Choose a family member who lived either in another country or in the United States during the early twentieth century. Write a paragraph comparing one or two important aspects of this person's daily life with your daily life today.

TIME

Facing the Blank Page

Inside the writing process with TIME writers and editors

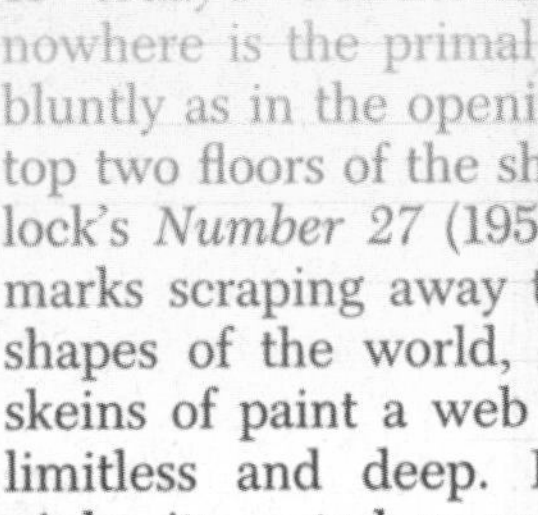

OCTOBER 25, 1999 $3.50 www.time.com

SPECIAL ★ REPORT

121

TIME
Facing the Blank Page

Focus

Lesson Overview

Objectives

- To apply the strategies of professional writers to all stages of the writing process
- To develop visual aids to enhance written and oral presentations
- To use print and electronic resources to research writing topics
- To generate ideas for writing by using prewriting strategies
- To develop ideas through the use of the drafting process
- To revise writing based on peer and self-directed evaluation
- To edit writing for specific purposes and for clarity and conciseness
- To use available technology to support aspects of creating, revising, editing, and publishing texts

Bellringer
Daily Language Activity

When students come into the classroom, have this assignment on the board: *You have been asked to write an article for a new magazine for high school students. What steps will you need to take to complete the assignment?*

Motivating Activity

As students answer the Bellringer question, list their responses on the board, in the order in which students give them. Do not sequence or edit the steps. Have students form small groups, and direct groups to develop and organize the steps on the board into a coherent process. (Define *process* as a sequence of interconnected steps that lead to a desired goal.) Tell groups that they may reword, add, combine, or omit steps from the list.

Resource Manager

Planning Resources

- *Lesson Plans*

Transparencies
- *Writing Process*

Other Print Resources

- *Composition Enrichment*
- *Composition Practice*
- *Composition Reteaching*
- *Grammar and Composition Handbook*
- *Guide to Using the Internet and Other Electronic Resources*
- *Writing Assessment and Evaluation Rubrics*

Video
- *Facing the Blank Page*

Software
- *Presentation Plus!*
- *Revising with Style*

Web Sites
- *writerschoice.glencoe.com*
- *lit.glencoe.com*

Teach

Discussion Prompt

The professionals at TIME say that collaboration helps them learn from one another. What did you learn by collaborating in groups? Did working together make it easier to think of all the steps that might be involved in writing an article? To identify omissions or ineffective repetition? To express ideas and organize them?

Think about the writing process—prewriting, drafting, revising, editing and proofreading, publishing and presenting. Which steps in the writing process lend themselves to collaboration? (Most of the steps can benefit from collaboration such as brainstorming or peer editing.) How might collaboration be helpful when writing? (Answers might include the following: Collaboration can help a writer generate ideas, refine thoughts, or catch errors.)

Viewing the Chart

Have students read the chart and summarize what each member of the TIME writing team contributes to the process. (*Writer:* helps come up with a story idea; reads, selects, and organizes information; drafts story; revises story. *Correspondent:* helps come up with a story idea, investigates and interviews, reviews writer's draft and makes suggestions. *Researcher:* gathers material from reliable sources, compiles and submits research files, checks accuracy of draft. *Editor:* helps come up with a story idea; reviews draft; suggests revisions; reviews revisions; "greens"; chooses to print, hold, or "kill" story. *Copyeditor:* checks style, grammar, mechanics, and spelling.) Ask students to compare and contrast their writing processes with the process that the professionals at TIME follow. What steps, if any, would students like to add to their processes? Why?

Writing for TIME

Every story published in TIME is the work of experienced professionals. The writing is strong; the facts are accurate; the grammar, spelling, and punctuation are error-free (or close!). Behind the scenes, however, there is another story to be told. As these pages reveal, TIME staffers struggle with many of the same challenges that students face in the messy, trial-and-error process that is writing: selecting among topics; finding information; getting organized; starting to draft; and then revising, revising, and revising some more.

What is the secret to the quality of writing in TIME? Beyond experience and hard work, the key lies in collaboration. As the chart on these pages illustrates, TIME stories are created through a form of "group journalism" that has become the magazine's hallmark. The writers and editors teach and learn from one another at every step in the writing process; student writers can do the same. Try out and adapt the writing and collaboration strategies presented in "Facing the Blank Page" to discover what works for you.

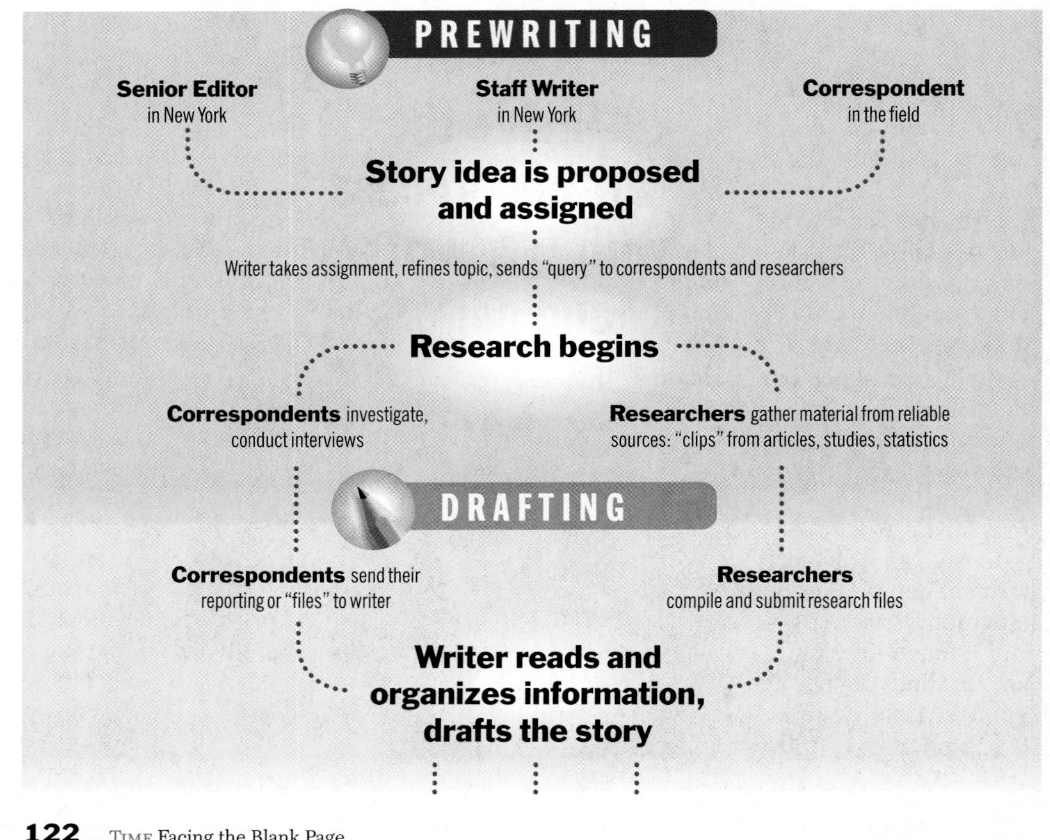
PREWRITING
Senior Editor
in New York
Staff Writer
in New York
Correspondent
in the field
Story idea is proposed and assigned
Writer takes assignment, refines topic, sends "query" to correspondents and researchers
Research begins
Correspondents investigate, conduct interviews
Researchers gather material from reliable sources: "clips" from articles, studies, statistics
DRAFTING
Correspondents send their reporting or "files" to writer
Researchers
compile and submit research files
Writer reads and organizes information, drafts the story

Viewing and Representing

Learning from Charts

As a class, discuss the advantages to writers of presenting information in chart form. (Charting can help writers logically organize information and succinctly express ideas.) How do charts benefit readers? (Charts present information in a brief, organized, easy-to-follow format.) Encourage students to review recent pieces of their own writing to identify how they might be improved through the addition of charts or other visual aids.

REVISING

Editor reads draft, asks for revisions

Correspondents check interpretation, make suggestions ⟷ **Writer revises, resubmits for comments** ⟷ **Researchers** check accuracy, details

Writer and editor revise again, "green" (edit for length)

EDITING AND PROOFREADING

Checks for conformity to TIME style and conventions ⟷ **Copy Desk** ⟷ Checks and corrects grammar, mechanics, spelling

PUBLISHING AND PRESENTING

Managing Editor chooses to print, hold, or "kill" (omit) story

Circulation of TIME rises or falls ⟷ **Readers respond to published story** ⟷ E-mail and letters to the editor

Teach

Analyzing Process

Stages and Steps

Point out that the capitalized headings of the TIME chart describe stages in the writing process, while the brief descriptions below the headings describe steps. Ask students to define the difference between stages and steps. (Stages are general phases of a process; steps are specific tasks performed during each stage.) As a class, generate a list of steps one must follow to complete a simple process, such as baking a cake. Then challenge students to group the steps into stages and to label each stage. (The cake-baking process might include these stages: gathering ingredients and utensils, preparing the batter, baking, cooling, decorating.)

Connections Across the Curriculum

Processes

Ask students to jot down the steps in a process that they have studied in another class, such as algebra, biology, physical education, or home economics. Have students group the steps in their processes and write headings that describe the stages. Then ask students to create charts based on their notes.

Listening and Speaking

Delivering an Oral Report

Have students use their process-analysis charts as the basis for brief "how-to" oral reports. To help students build skills in using visual aids, encourage presenters to display and refer to their charts during their reports.

Teach

Using the Strategies

Review with your class the prewriting strategies discussed in Lesson 2.2 (freewriting, making lists, and creating network trees). Point out that the strategies may also be used during other stages of the writing process. For example, freewriting can help students overcome writer's block while drafting.

interNET CONNECTION

The home pages of many Internet access providers include a menu of general subject headings, such as *arts, education, sports,* and *home and family.* Point out that skimming menu options and connecting to links can spark ideas for research and writing.

Assess

Evaluation Rubrics

Discussion

Through discussion, students should come to understand that a subject is a general idea and that a story makes a point or points about a specific aspect of the subject. After students generate a list of subjects and story ideas, help them develop a sense of audience by asking which story ideas they would include in a magazine for high school students and why.

Try It Out

Students' stories should

- cover a school event or everyday ritual
- describe the event through the use of eyewitness detail

During discussion of each other's stories, students should

- demonstrate that they understand the difference between a subject and an angle
- describe how and why individuals' perceptions of an event may vary

Prewriting

Finding an Angle

At TIME, story ideas can be proposed by any member of the editorial staff. But once a story is assigned, it is the staff writer's job to develop the idea and find the most compelling way to approach and tell it.

Senior Editor Janice Simpson:

"In magazine or feature writing, you need to determine what we call the angle on a subject. Imagine asking a random group of people, 'What was the best thing about the movie *Titanic*?' Some people might say Leo DiCaprio right off the bat. Leo DiCaprio is a story. We can do a feature story on this young actor. Someone else might say, 'The special effects. The way they made that ship crack in half and go down.' We could do a story on the special effects in the movie. That's the difference between a subject and a story. The *subject* is the movie *Titanic*. The *story* is either the career of Leonardo DiCaprio or the amazing special effects. Those are stories, something I can tell you about what happened. We take a subject—a movie, a presidential campaign—and we look for the stories within it.

One of the best exercises for people learning to be journalists is to send a whole bunch of people to the same event, and have them come back and write about it. You'll get as many different stories or angles as there are writers!"

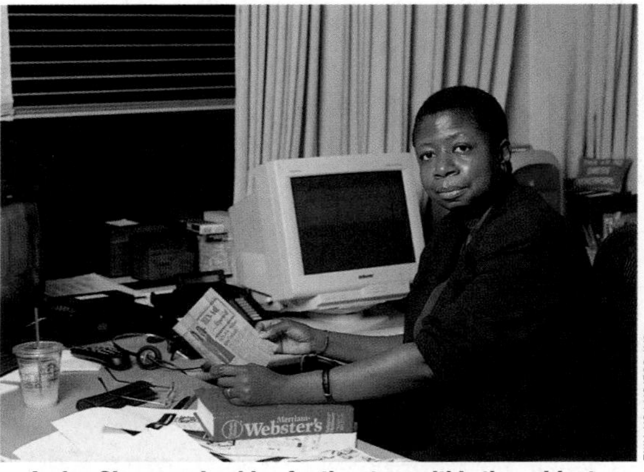
JAY COLTON FOR TIME

Janice Simpson: Looking for the story within the subject.

LEARNING FROM THE EDITOR

DISCUSSION
In your own words, explain the distinction that Janice Simpson makes between a subject and a story. Brainstorm a list of several subjects as a class. Then, working in smaller groups, come up with several different story ideas for each subject.

TRY IT OUT
Try the exercise Simpson recommends. In pairs or groups, "cover" an event at school: an assembly, a sports or arts event, a daily ritual such as eating in the cafeteria. Write a page or two about what you witness, and then switch papers or read them aloud. What do you hear?

HOW I WRITE
Look through your writing portfolio. For each piece, identify the subject and the story. Then look through your journal or learning log and make a list of possible subjects and stories that could be developed from these entries you have written. See Lesson 2.2, "Explore Your Ideas."

Critical Thinking

What's the Angle?

Challenge students to analyze how different news media cover the same stories. Assign students to watch the lead stories of an evening newscast. The following day, bring a newspaper to class and ask students to compare and contrast the lead stories on the TV news program with those on the front page of the newspaper. Help students to deconstruct each story to discover its main idea. Are the subjects and angles the same? In what ways does the coverage differ? How might students account for the similarities and differences?

Refining a Topic: "Simplicity in Conception"

Assistant Managing Editor Howard Chua-Eoan:

"When we sit down and talk about story ideas, we'll say, 'This is an important subject.' But it can't be just a subject without anything to hold onto. There has to be something controversial or a pressing question. Then we try to investigate that, to provide an answer. You want to be sure you focus on the part that will make people say, 'Yes, that's an important subject for me, and that's an important point. I want to find out more about it.' Don't make the subject too broad: you'll start in one place but lose sight of where you are going. Simplicity in conception is the best starting point, and then you can elaborate as you go on, piling on the detail until you have a really ornate and detailed story."

LEARNING FROM THE EDITOR

Read this excerpt from one of Howard Chua-Eoan's stories in TIME:

Her Serena Highness

What am I doing here? Serena Williams asked herself in the middle of the championship tie breaker that would help her make history, allow her to fulfill her father's predictions and alter her relationship with her older sister. It was a moment of doubt. But being 17, she dismissed it quickly—just as swiftly as she recovered from the nervousness that tripped up two earlier chances to win the title outright in her match against Martina Hingis. Serena's prevailing ethos reasserted itself: she doesn't lose tie breakers. She hasn't lost one all year. The rule held. She won.

And so Serena Williams was transformed. On Saturday evening in New York City, she became the first African American to win a tennis Grand Slam singles title since Arthur Ashe won Wimbledon in 1975, and the first African-American woman to win the U.S. Open since Althea Gibson in 1958. As a historymaker, Serena transfigured her family as well. She, her sister Venus and their father Richard were no longer the loudest mouths on the tennis circuit. She had shown the world that her father was not just some voice crying in the wilderness but a true prophet. He had long predicted his daughters would dominate the world of women's tennis. Daddy did know best.

—Howard Chua-Eoan

DISCUSSION

1. What does Chua-Eoan mean by the phrase "simplicity in conception"? Do you agree that this is a helpful idea to use when drafting?

2. Read the excerpt above from one of Chua-Eoan's own pieces. What is the focus of his article on tennis champion Serena Williams? Does he follow his own advice: start out simply and then elaborate? Refer to specific lines in his text.

TRY IT OUT

Write a feature story. Begin by reading the tips and strategies presented in Lesson 5.8, "Writing a Feature Article." Then choose and refine your own subject and story. What is the concept you will begin with? What story will you tell? How do you plan to "pile on the detail"?

Teach

Refining a Topic

To help students practice refining, or focusing, a topic, propose a general subject such as *computers*, and ask the following questions: Who is your audience? (other high school students) What does your audience need or want to know about computers? (Answers might include saving money when buying a computer, selecting good computer games, finding reference tools on the Internet.) Why will these topics be of special interest to your audience? (Most teenagers cannot afford to spend a lot of money on computers; many teenagers enjoy video games; most students need help doing research.)

Assess

Evaluation Rubrics

Discussion

1. In their discussion, students should explain what the phrase "simplicity in conception" means ("start out simply"), voice their opinions about this advice, and support their opinions with persuasive reasons.
2. Chua-Eoan's article focuses on how Serena Williams overcame self-doubts to make sports history. Chua-Eoan follows his own advice. For example, the first line of the story is a short, simply worded question.

Try It Out

Students' story plans should
- state the opening concept, or lead
- describe the story that they would like to tell
- include details that they might use to develop the story

Exploring Language

Evaluating Titles

Ask students whether they think the pun in the title "Her Serena Highness" is effective and why authors often include word play in titles (to capture readers' attention, to be entertaining as well as informative). Challenge students to evaluate the titles of pieces of their own writing. Which titles, if any, might be made more interesting and informative?

Teach

Technology Tip

Encourage students to word process their first drafts. Copy, paste, and delete functions free writers to try a variety of leads and retain the best one.

Evaluating Introductions

The professionals at TIME offer a variety of tips for writing effective introductions. Challenge students to use the professionals' advice to create a set of evaluation criteria. (Introductions should include an attention-getting device, motivate readers to continue reading, and state or imply the main idea of the story.) Have each student select a recent piece of writing from his or her portfolio and use the criteria to evaluate the introduction. What revisions, if any, would students like to make?

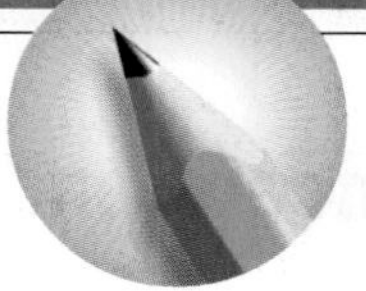

Drafting

Starting Strong: Leads and Billboards

You don't have to write the opening paragraph of a story or article first, but at some point in the writing process you must decide how your piece will begin. At TIME, writers call the opening paragraphs of a piece *leads* and *billboards*.

From *Writing for TIME*, a stylebook distributed to staff.

L

Lead: It hardly needs saying that the lead is the toughest part of a story to get right. It is an invitation into the piece, so it must tantalize. It states the theme, so it must touch on the essentials of the story. It is a road map for the journey ahead, so it must provide a guide that will steer the reader through to the end.

A group of TIME writers discusses the importance of strong leads and billboards.

Senior Editor Nancy Gibbs:
"The hardest part, the most fun part, and the most important part is the first paragraph. I think that's true of every kind of writing. No matter how brilliant your information or elegant your argument, if you lose the reader at the beginning of a piece, then you've lost the reader forever. It doesn't matter what comes next. It's really a free ride for the writer: you have permission to do almost anything that's going to provoke or intrigue your reader. It doesn't necessarily have to include any information. It can just be a bewitching little sentence that says, 'This is why you're going to read this story.' It can be some fantastic illustration of an issue you're going to raise three pages later. It can be a quote that's like an explosive. It can be anything captivating."

Senior Reporter Andrea Sachs:
"A good lead draws the reader in quickly. You lose people really fast. People glance at a story and decide in a few seconds whether it's worth reading. So you've got to find something catchy to draw them in. The common wisdom is that anecdotal leads do very well. If you break it down to the level of one person, it's easier to understand. I think that's true. That's what I like when I'm reading."

What needs to follow an attention-grabbing lead?

Senior Editor Janice Simpson:
"After your lead, you need to reach out and pull the readers in, and you need to tell them why they're there. We call that the *billboard*. It's the place where you very briefly let the reader know what the rest of

Cooperative Learning

Peer Editing

Pair students and ask them to exchange pieces of their writing. Encourage students to evaluate the introduction to their partner's paper and offer specific suggestions for revising. Give students time to revise in class.

your story is going to say. Then you go through the story, developing your arguments, giving examples, using quotes to bolster and support the argument or information you're trying to impart."

Writing a good billboard paragraph can help focus and structure the rest of the draft.

JAY COLTON FOR TIME (2)

Assistant Managing Editor Howard Chua-Eoan:
"Sometimes the best way to start is by writing the billboard paragraph, so you know exactly what the story is about. It's the flag you're waving, the advertisement for more that comes toward the middle and end of the story."

Nancy Gibbs:
"The billboard is hard to do well, because those few paragraphs have to do a lot of heavy lifting. Ideally, it has to touch on the important points that the story is going to raise. It has to signal why the story is important. Why are you writing about this in the first place? It has to foreshadow where you're going to go.

Ideally, a billboard ought to answer these questions in a way that is rather seamless, so that it isn't saying: 'The first point I'm going to make is X, and then I'm going to argue Y, and then I'm going to argue Z.' You want it to be a little more organic than that, to serve almost as a table of contents to your story. After that, the story starts to unfold itself."

LEARNING FROM THE WRITERS

DISCUSSION

1. What is a *billboard* as defined by TIME writers? What is a *lead*? Why do you think they use these names? Note how similarly each writer defines and describes the process of writing leads and billboards. What do you think accounts for this similarity?

2. There are conventional ways to open the pieces of expository writing you do in school (reports, essays, and research papers, for example). Read Lesson 2.5 on topic sentences and Lesson 7.2 on developing a thesis statement for a research paper. How is a journalistic lead similar to a topic sentence? How is a billboard like a thesis statement?

3. What genres of writing (short stories, novels, poetry, autobiographies, journals, memoirs) lend themselves to the kind of lead and billboard strategies used by TIME writers? How can the advice from these writers help make the opening paragraphs of school papers more interesting?

TRY IT OUT

What is an anecdote? What do you think Andrea Sachs means by an "anecdotal lead"? Find one in a current newspaper or magazine article, or in one of the Literature Models in this textbook. Do you think anecdotal leads are effective? Why or why not? Try using one for your next writing assignment.

HOW I WRITE

At what point in your writing do you usually write your lead paragraph? Do you tend to write the lead first, last, or at some other point in the drafting process? Next time you're writing a paper, try the opposite approach. Is the new method better?

Teach

The Writing-Reading Connection

Nancy Gibbs suggests that the "billboard," or opening paragraphs of a story, should serve as a table of contents. Ask how a general knowledge of the purpose and structure of introductions might help students become more effective readers. (An understanding of the purpose and structure of introductions can help students make accurate predictions about content, differentiate between main ideas and supporting details as they read, and monitor their own comprehension.)

Assess

Evaluation Rubrics

Discussion

1. Through discussion, students should come to an understanding of the terms *billboard* (the introductory paragraphs of a story) and *lead* (the opening attention-getting device.) Encourage students to identify similarities in the writers' definitions of these terms and to explain why the definitions are similar. (*Sample answer:* Professionals know and apply generally accepted principles of writing.)
2. Students should understand that both the lead and the topic sentence draw readers into a topic. A billboard is similar to a thesis statement in that it states or implies the points that a writer intends to make.
3. Students' responses will vary but should show an understanding of the purpose and structure of various genres of writing. Encourage students to describe specific ways that they might apply the professionals' advice to their own writing.

Try It Out

Students should be able to
- define *anecdote* and identify an anecdote in a piece of writing
- state whether they think the anecdote is an effective introductory device and why

Listening and Speaking

Speech Writing

Point out that the guidelines for writing introductions to articles, essays, and reports also apply to speech writing. Challenge each student to present a two- or three-minute speech based on a recent piece of writing. Ask students to use the criteria that they created to evaluate the introduction to each speech given.

Teach

interNET CONNECTION

The Internet has many good quotation sites. Encourage students to use search engines to find quotable statements about a subject.

Revising *vs.* Proofreading

Many students erroneously believe that revising and proofreading are synonymous. Ask students to differentiate between these two stages of the writing process. (Revising is reviewing a piece of writing from the reader's point of view; considering how the organization, development, and diction of the piece might be improved to meet the reader's needs and interests; and recasting elements that need improvement. Proofreading is reviewing a piece for errors in spelling, grammar, sentence structure, mechanics, and usage and then correcting the errors.)

Cross-Referencing: Revising

To provide students with instruction and practice in revising, refer them to Lesson 2.9.

Discussion Prompt

The professionals at TIME suggest that quotations impart a sense of immediacy and make stories more interesting. What other reasons might writers have for quoting someone? For example, how might quoting an expert on a subject enhance a report? (Students should see that quotations from experts can enhance the credibility of a report.)

Revising

Incorporating Quotes

Howard Chua-Eoan: Get close to the subject.

Revising (literally, "looking again") is an essential part of the writing process. First drafts can always be improved, and one way of strengthening a piece of writing is to incorporate direct quotations. These may be written quotes from a book or another source of information, or spoken quotes from an interview or conversation. They are always set off with quotation marks. TIME writers share their thoughts on the importance of using direct quotations, and the process of refining and editing them.

Assistant Managing Editor Howard Chua-Eoan explains why well-selected quotations add value to a story:

"Using quotations is always important. It gives a sense that your reporters have talked to the people involved. Quotations give a sense that the writer—and the reader—are as close to the subject as they can get. Quotes impart a sense of immediacy to the story. Unlike television, where quotes are basically sound bites, in a newsmagazine you can stop and analyze the quote, and you can give it background. You can say what the speaker looked like, that he paused, that he was uncomfortable when he said something."

Senior Reporter Andrea Sachs knows an effective quote when she "hears" it on the page:

"Some quotes sing, and some people are naturally articulate. Using quotes can be a way of compressing the central idea. It could be a way of illustrating something about the personality of the speaker. It juices up the story.

You rarely get anything surprising from well-known people because what they say tends to be rehearsed. They've been through it before. It's people who are new to the process who sometimes say things that make you gasp, because they don't know they're not supposed to."

Do writers go back to their interview subjects to verify quotes? Andrea Sachs:

JAY COLTON FOR TIME (2)

Andrea Sachs: Some quotes sing.

"At TIME, we never read quotes back to people. Some magazines do. Certainly you want to get it right the first time, but if you read quotes back, people start changing what they've said: 'Did I say that? I can't say that!' Sometimes people beg you to read them their quotes, but we don't do it. It's the policy here not to. Get it right the first time."

Real-World Connection

The Use of Quotations

Challenge students to skim current newspapers and news magazines to find stories that incorporate direct quotations, including pull-out quotations. Have students bring copies of the stories to class and discuss how the quotations enhance the stories.

Can writers and editors change and polish quotes for readability?

Judy Paul, Deputy Copy Chief at TIME, explains the policy that her department follows:

“We try to clean up people’s quotes. If someone speaks ungrammatically, we’ll fix it (unless the writer is trying to show that this is how the speaker really talks). Of course, you can’t change written quotes, but with spoken quotes, we generally delete words such as *um* and *like,* which occur frequently in speech but are distracting in print.”

LEARNING FROM THE WRITER

Read this excerpt from a cover story based on an interview conducted by Andrea Sachs:

Author Tom Wolfe Writes Again

The megayield critical and commercial success of *The Bonfire of the Vanities* in 1987 made Tom Wolfe a rich and very gratified author indeed. After *Bonfire,* though, came the inevitable question. What next? Topping his first novel would be hard, the risk of failure and I-told-you-so reviews high. But Wolfe found the challenge irresistible. “I was 57,” he says, “and I thought the eight or nine years I’d spent on *Bonfire* had taught me what not to do the second time. So, I proceeded to make every blunder a beginning writer could stumble into.”

As he lists them, it becomes clear why readers have had to wait 11 years for *A Man in Full.* “First, I tried to take the easy way out by setting most of the new novel in Manhattan, the same locale I’d used in *Bonfire.* I didn’t realize until 1995 that this approach wasn’t working and that I was repeating myself. Second, I always recommend to people that they start with an outline. Naturally, I didn’t take my own advice and do an outline until I was years into this project.

“A third mistake,” he adds, “was feeling that the new book had to raise the stakes and include more than *Bonfire,* that I was obligated to write the biggest book in the world. I have bales of discarded manuscripts.”

—**Paul Gray**

DISCUSSION

1. According to these TIME writers, what do direct quotations add to a story?

2. Why did Paul Gray use so many direct quotes in the excerpt above?

3. Do you agree with TIME’s policy not to read quotes back to people who have been interviewed? Have you ever had the experience of being interviewed and then quoted—or misquoted? How did you feel? What policy for quotes do you think student publications should set?

TRY IT OUT

1. Interview a friend or family member about a topic of your choice and take notes as you do so, using the tips in Lesson 2.4. Then write a paragraph incorporating your interview subject’s words as direct quotes. Units 5, 20, and 21 explain more about using and punctuating quotations.

2. Quoting accurately. Did you find you needed to edit the quotes? Show your revised quotes to your interview subject. Does he or she feel the quotes are accurate?

Assess

Evaluation Rubrics

Discussion

1. According to the writers, direct quotations bring writers and readers closer to subjects, can help illustrate a speaker’s personality, are effective ways to sum up central ideas, and can make a story more interesting.
2. Gray probably used direct quotations to help illustrate Wolf’s personality.
3. Encourage students to voice and support their opinions and to generate a list of specific guidelines that they can use when quoting sources. To extend the discussion, encourage students to interview members of the school newspaper staff or yearbook staff to see what guidelines student publications have established.

Try It Out

1. Students’ paragraphs should
   - include pertinent direct quotations from a friend or family member
   - exhibit an understanding of how to punctuate direct quotations
2. Students should
   - apply criteria to decide whether to edit the quotations
   - have the interview subject review edits to ensure that the quotations are accurate

Enrichment and Extension

Collecting Quotations

Ask students to use print or electronic sources to find quotations about a general subject. Skim the index to a collection of quotations, and assign each student a different subject to research. Have students bring their favorite quotations to class, and ask a volunteer to compile a master print or electronic list that students might use as a reference.

Assess

Evaluation Rubrics

Discussion

1. Students should check to see whether the subject of a sentence does the action (active) or receives the action (passive). Writers generally prefer the active voice because it is clear and direct. The active voice clarifies who or what performed an action. Writers generally use the passive voice when they want to conceal who performed an action, as in the sentence "A decision was made to fire him"; when who performed an action is unclear or irrelevant, as in the sentence "The legend was handed down from generation to generation"; or when they want to avoid creating an accusatory tone, as in the sentence "The check was not included with the invoice."
2. Encourage students to revise several sentences and contrast the revision with the original.
3. The memo suggests that clarity, vitality, surprise, and viewpoint are hallmarks of good writing and that reviewing other writers' work can help a writer determine what style and tone to adopt. Students will probably agree that any writer can benefit from following these guidelines.

Try It Out

1. Through revision and discussion, students should
   - demonstrate an understanding of the difference between active and passive voice
   - compare and contrast various revisions and the overall effects of the revisions
2. Students should
   - identify the passive voice in the first or second to the last sentence of the memo
   - explain why the writer might have chosen to use the passive voice

Editing and Proofreading

Refining Style: The Voice of Verbs

The following memo, drafted for the benefit of TIME correspondents and writers, offers general advice on matters of style and usage.

Deputy Copy Chief Judy Paul is always on the lookout for sentences written in the passive voice. In most instances, Paul and her colleagues will change this construction before the story runs in the magazine.

Memo to Correspondents:

Though much of the ornamentation that marked the old TIME style has been abandoned, the essentials remain the same: we still prize, among other things, clarity, vitality, surprise and viewpoint. Sure, we do keep a few conventions and frequently used devices. Yet nowadays a hundred stylistic flowers bloom in our pages. Read the magazine closely; you'll be able to figure out what style and tone are appropriate for a particular story. Moreover, as you have no doubt found, different senior editors have different tastes. A particular rhetorical flourish of yours may be praised one week and edited out of your copy the next. Do not despair...

Judy Paul:

"We always try to shoot for the active voice. We're trying to make writing punchy and clear, and the passive voice just stops that."

WRITING TIP

Verbs: an active verb gives vitality to a sentence; a passive verb puts a sentence to sleep.

—from *Writing for TIME*, a style handbook for TIME staff

LEARNING FROM THE EDITOR

DISCUSSION

1. Review Lesson 15.7, "Voice of Verbs." How can you tell if a verb is active or passive? Why do writers generally prefer to write in the active voice? How does the active voice make writing "punchy and clear"? Under what circumstances might you choose to use the passive voice?

2. Choose one of the Literature Models in *Writer's Choice* and read a page, noting which verb forms are active and which are passive. What overall effect does the writer's decision to use active or passive voice have on the story?

3. Read the "Memo to Correspondents" above. What message is conveyed to TIME writers? Is there good advice here for student writers, as well? Which points?

TRY IT OUT

1. Using passive verbs, rewrite the *Writing for TIME* entry on verbs. Compare your entry with those of your classmates.

2. Identify a passive verb used in the "Memo to Correspondents," above. Why do you think the writer composed the sentence in this way, ignoring the advice in the TIME style handbook?

Writing in the Real World

Avoiding the Passive Voice

Some word-processing programs include editing functions that alert the writer when he or she uses the passive voice. Encourage students to make use of these online editorial aids, but warn students that even the best aids do not find all structural problems. Students will still need to make decisions about whether to revise.

Publishing and Presenting

A Measure of Success

The final phase of the writing process is publishing and presenting your work—sharing your writing with friends, family, school, or community. How do you measure success? First, you must be clear about what your purpose is. What are you trying to communicate? What do you hope your readers will learn? Then listen to your readers' responses.

Senior Editor Bruce Nelan explains his criteria for successful news writing:

"Objective standards of writing don't have much to do with style. They have to do with how well the writer achieves what he or she sets out to do. If it's a news story, it should be accurate, it should be clear, and it should be relatively concise. It should include interesting and important material.

News writing is a craft. It's not short story or poetry writing. It's using the writer's tools for another purpose: to deliver information. If there's a little style in there, so much the better. But the central purpose of news writing is to get people to understand what happened and why.

Henry Luce, the founder of TIME, said that what mattered was not what you got on to the printed page. What mattered was what you got *off* the printed page and into the minds of the people who were reading the magazine. I think that's right. I think that what really matters is what people get out of it, and how well you deliver it to them."

When he can give his readers the information they need, Nelan derives real satisfaction from the hard work of writing:

"I do view writing in the same way I suspect that people who have the calling to teach feel about teaching. To me, what I do is a form of education, in the sense that we are explaining things, teaching people. I like that feeling. I find it very rewarding. If I've done a good job on a story and someone says, 'That really told me something,' then that's my reward."

LEARNING FROM THE WRITER

DISCUSSION

1. What is Bruce Nelan's definition of good news writing? How do you define success for the genre of writing you like best?

2. Do you agree with Henry Luce that what matters is not what writers put on to the printed page, but what readers get off it? Nelan makes a distinction between the purpose of news writing and imaginative genres such as short story and poetry writing. Does Luce's notion apply to these genres, as well?

3. Have you ever had a writing experience that brought you satisfaction? What made it rewarding? Did your readers respond favorably to your writing? What did they say?

TRY IT OUT

Defining success. Look at a piece of your writing in progress. What is the purpose of this piece? How will you know if this is a successful work of writing? Remind yourself of the composition's purpose as you continue to develop the piece.

Assess

Evaluation Rubrics

Discussion

1. For Bruce Nelan, good news writing is accurate, clear, concise, and interesting. It delivers important information that lingers in readers' minds. Through discussion, students should define their own standards of good writing.
2. Encourage students to voice their opinions about Henry Luce's advice and to explain whether they think the advice applies equally well to all genres of writing.
3. Encourage students to discuss how they feel about their writing and whether they find it difficult to take criticism in stride. Together as a class, discuss how to give criticism in a manner that is helpful rather than hurtful.

Try It Out

Students should

- identify the purpose of a piece of their own writing in progress
- apply criteria to evaluate and meet the stated purpose of the piece

Close

Invite a professional writer to class to discuss the writing process with students. Candidates include authors living in your community, reporters for a community newspaper, and parents who write frequently on the job. Have students prepare interview questions in advance.

interNET CONNECTION

Publishing Online

Encourage students to submit their writing to online magazines and other sites for young writers. Some sites that accept young writers' work are: Global Wave (http://www.cs.bilkent.edu.tr/~david/derya/gw/gw12-1.htm), Young People's Press Online (http://www.ypp.net/), The Young Writer's Club (http://www.cs.bilkent.edu.tr/~david/derya/ywc.html), and Writer's Gallery (http://www.onestep.com:80/writers/). You should review these sites to be sure their content is appropriate for your class.

UNIT 3

Viewing the Art

This photograph of a field of dried sunflowers, their heads bent as if weeping, portrays a landscape during harvest season. The dark, rolling clouds in the distance suggest an oncoming storm. Together, the details of the photograph suggest the mood of this place in much the same way that descriptive techniques in writing create pictures with words.

Interpret and Analyze Use the following questions for discussion:

- What details in the photograph help you describe the mood of this scene?
- How do the brown colors of the landscape and gray of the horizon affect the emotions of an observer?
- Imagine that this same field was photographed again on a warm July afternoon. How might this change in scenery affect the emotions felt by an observer?

Discussing the Quotation

This quotation is from a contemporary essay by Linda Hogan (b. 1947). The essay, "Walking," was inspired by several walks that the author took along a country road. Discuss the quotation with the class, and ask students how they would interpret the author's meaning. What details in the quotation suggest how the author feels about this field of sunflowers?

Writing Prompt Write a brief explanation of how Hogan's words, coupled with the image of the sunflowers, can be seen to connect to the process of descriptive writing.

"On this day the faded dry petals of the sunflower were swept across the land."

—Linda Hogan, "Walking"

Resource Manager

Planning Resources

- *Lesson Plans*
- *Block Scheduling*

Transparencies

- *Bellringer*
- *Daily Language Practice*
- *Fine Art*
- *Two-Minute Skill Drill*
- *Writing Process*

Other Print Resources

- *Composition Enrichment*
- *Composition Practice*
- *Composition Reteaching*
- *Cooperative Learning Activities*
- *Glencoe Literature Library*
- *Grammar and Composition Handbook*
- *Grammar Workbook*
- *Listening and Speaking Activities*
- *Sentence-Combining Practice*
- *Tests with Answer Key and Rubrics*
- *Thinking and Study Skills*
- *Writing Across the Curriculum*
- *Writing Assessment and Evaluation Rubrics*
- *Writing in the Real World*

UNIT
3

Descriptive Writing

133

 Video
- *MindJogger Videoquizzes*

 Software
- *Presentation Plus!*
- *Revising with Style*
- *Testmaker*

 Web Site
- *glencoe.com*

Objectives

- To develop an understanding of descriptive writing
- To learn how to select and organize details and use precise language in order to create a mood or an image of a place or person
- To analyze and draw conclusions about literary characters based on the descriptive details provided in a piece of writing
- To write a description of an imaginary place

ASSESSMENT OPTIONS

Tests with Answer Key & Rubrics
Unit 3 Choice A Test, p. 9
Unit 3 Choice B Test, p. 10
Unit 3 Composition Objective Test, pp. 11–12

Testmaker
Unit 3 Choice A Test
Unit 3 Choice B Test
Unit 3 Composition Objective Test

You may wish to administer either the Unit 3 Choice A Test or the Unit 3 Choice B Test as a pretest.

Key to Ability Levels

L1 Level 1 activities are within the basic ability range of students.

L2 Level 2 activities are within the ability range of average students.

L3 Level 3 activities are more challenging activities.

Focus

Lesson Overview

Objective

- To elaborate details that convey a specific mood in a piece of descriptive writing

Skills

- analyzing; writing descriptive details

Critical Thinking

- defining and clarifying; visualizing; setting goals

Listening and Speaking

- discussing; questioning; sharing ideas

Bellringer

Daily Language Activity

When students enter the classroom, have this assignment on the board: *Describe a scene from a favorite science fiction or fantasy story.*

Grammar Link to the Bellringer

Combine these two short sentences into a longer sentence, changing the verb in the second sentence to an *-ing* form:

Two boys stand alone on the grass.

They shag flies in the fading light.

See also *Daily Language Practice*

Motivating Activity

Discuss students' responses to the Bellringer activity. Then ask students to consider how, if they were screenwriters, they would bring the scene to life in a movie. What details would they emphasize? What mood would they convey? Explain that in this case study, they will learn how one screenwriter uses description to bring his world to his viewers.

Writing in the Real World

Writing a screenplay, or movie script, involves more than creating dialogue and a plot. Description is important too. Actors and directors need a script that conveys a real sense of mood so that they can visualize the movie they are about to make. The following excerpts are from Gary Ross's screenplay *Big,* which he wrote with his friend Anne Spielberg. The story tells of a boy who wishes he were bigger and suddenly gets his wish.

from *Big* by Gary Ross and Anne Spielberg

```
JOSH AND SUSAN
They look at it awkwardly for a moment, then glance at
each other. It seems like each of them is about to say
something, but neither one does. They stay like that for
a second, when Susan cocks her head to the side.
                    SUSAN
              You hear that?
                    JOSH
                    What?
                    SUSAN
                    Music.
EXT. BOARDWALK
The sounds of Big Band Music drift out of the old dance
Pavilion. Built near the turn of the century, it is part
Mosque, part Opera Hall, part Seaside Pleasure Palace.
All the obelisks have flagpoles for the banners that have
long since gone away. The sound of Moonlight Serenade
echoes up the boardwalk as the ocean pounds in the dis-
tance.
EXT. ARCADE
Josh and Susan walk out of the arcade onto the nearly
deserted boardwalk. Towering above them ...
hulk of a roller coaster ...
on is the lat...
```

```
EXT. BASEBALL FIELD
It's late afternoon as the sun turns the field a light
gold. Two boys stand alone on the grass, shagging
flies in the faded light. There is silence, then the
crack of a bat, then the distant pop of a ball hitting
leather. Josh watches silently from the side of the
field leaning back in his business suit. There is no
conversation as the ritual continues between them—just
the swing of the bat and the long lazy arc of a fly
ball as it goes from one boy to another. Josh loosens
the knot of his tie as he stares at the boys in front
of him. A light breeze ruffles his hair.
```

Screenwriter Gary Ross

Resource Manager

Planning Resources
- *Lesson Plans*

Transparencies
- *Bellringer*
- *Daily Language Practice*
- *Writing Process* 9, 13–17

Other Print Resources
- *Cooperative Learning Activities,* pp. 13–16
- *Thinking and Study Skills,* pp. 3, 5, 21
- *Writing Assessment and Evaluation Rubrics*
- *Writing in the Real World,* pp. 9–12

A Writer's Process

Prewriting

Getting Ideas and Getting Started

When Gary Ross is asked how he came to write *Big*, he replies, "Every child says, 'I wish I were a grown-up.' The screenplay for *Big* came out of wondering what would happen if that wish were ultimately fulfilled."

The inspiration for different scenes came in various ways. One of Ross's favorite scenes takes place at a seaside carnival (see excerpt on page 134). Josh has been transformed to an adult at this stage. As he and his girlfriend stand on the boardwalk, they hear music coming from an old dance pavilion. Ross says, "I was inspired by something I'd read in an F. Scott Fitzgerald book, about life on the French Riviera. We wanted to evoke the same romance and magic but also the decline and the sadness that's coming."

Ross worked on the *Big* script with fellow screenwriter Anne Spielberg. Describing their process, he says, "First, we outlined the whole movie. We planned out every scene in detail, and we each wrote our own scenes. Then we'd rewrite each other's scenes until the script was unified into one voice."

Even in the early stage of outlining the movie, Ross and Spielberg were aware of the mood they wanted the finished film to evoke. This awareness helped them select dramatic details and develop them into descriptive paragraphs in the script.

Drafting

Writing the Scenes

Descriptive details are especially important in describing a setting. As Ross and Spielberg draft scenes, they look for just the right setting to underscore the character's experience and feelings. The baseball scene in *Big* needed to be nostalgic. Ross says, "We knew if we wrote this scene poetically, the director would end up putting the poetry into the film. Usually you have to write lean for the screen, but this time we really pulled out all the stops and went for it. We even used

Teach

Reading Media

Have students preview the title and focus of the Media Connection on page 134. Remind students that they use description every day in speaking and in writing. Invite students to provide examples of different ways they might communicate to a friend how something looks, smells, tastes, or feels. Then discuss the purpose and audience for a screenplay, pointing out that screenwriters use descriptive writing to provide actors with clues about how to interpret their characters and to give directors guidance about what tone the movie should set. Have students read the article.

Discussion Prompts

- How and why does it help to know the mood you want to create before you begin writing? If you were writing this screenplay, what mood would you try to evoke? Why?
- What images would you use in a screenplay to help the actors interpret their characters? To help the director visualize the tone and mood that the finished movie should convey to audiences?
- Why might it help a writer to have a real place in mind when writing a description?
- What details did Ross and Spielberg add to the description of the pavilion scene in order to create the mood they wanted?

Real World Connection

The Worlds of Adult and Child

Gary Ross used a fantastic premise to write about growing up. Although the film's main character Josh becomes "big" overnight, he remains a child inside. Thrust into the adult world, Josh interprets what happens to him from a child's point of view. As a result, the audience is encouraged to acknowledge the child within themselves and examine their experiences from this perspective. Ross may wish to show that the two worlds have more in common than many people believe.

Teach

Discussion Prompts

Invite students to talk about

- how the writing process for descriptive writing is the same or different from the writing process they have used for other modes of writing
- whether or not they were surprised by the importance of descriptive writing for a screenwriter
- what other applications of descriptive writing in the real world they can envision now that they have seen this application **L2**

Additional Resources

 *Writing Process Transparencies* 9, 13–17

 *Cooperative Learning Activities*

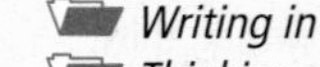 *Writing in the Real World,* pp. 9–12

Thinking and Study Skills, pp. 3, 5, 21

Assess

Analyzing the Media Connection

1. Possible answers: The mood is dreamy. The alliteration in "long, lazy arc" makes the scene appear poetic and dreamlike.
2. Twilight captures the "mystical, magical, temporal instance between day and night." Other times would not have that "fleeting quality."
3. Possible answers: "sun turns the field a light gold"; "shagging flies in the fading light"
4. From the perspective of an outside observer; from Josh's perspective; emphasizes that Josh has lost the beauty of the childlike scene
5. The mood is nostalgic and quiet. Answers will vary. Possible answers: "sounds . . . drift"; empty flagpoles for "banners that have long since gone away"

a poetic device, alliteration, to describe the 'long, lazy arc' of the fly ball."

The baseball field scene takes place in what Ross calls "that mystical, magical, temporal instance between night and day. The sun turns the field gold for only a few minutes a day, so there's a fragile, fleeting quality of something that's there for only an instant and then is lost." Ross continues, "The fact that the two boys stand alone gives the scene a beautiful, isolated quality. There's nothing in the world except them."

Ross and Spielberg empower their descriptions with language that appeals to the senses. They enhance the "fragile, fleeting quality" of the baseball scene by emphasizing how quiet the world seems at this moment. They use sensory language that appeals to the senses of sight, touch, and—especially—sound.

A scene from the movie *Big*

Revising/Editing

Choosing the Right Details

As Ross and Spielberg revise and edit, they focus on getting the right details. Small, well-chosen details can create a powerful impact. In the baseball scene, Josh watches kids playing ball. Ross says, "Josh is privy to this scene, but he's lost the beauty of it because of his wish to be big. Showing Josh in a business suit emphasizes that he's constrained by being an adult. And when he loosens his tie, he shows that being big is constricting him. That's what I mean by writing description that bolsters a point. When the light breeze ruffles his hair, it harkens back to the magical wind that blew when he first wished to be big. This time the wind shows he's drawn back to the world of childhood."

Crafting a revised script requires close attention to these sorts of details. A loosened tie and a slight breeze are small elements that contribute hugely to both an understanding of the main character and the development of the story.

Presenting

Turning the Screenplay into a Film

Once Ross and Spielberg are satisfied with their last draft, they make copies for the director, producers, and others involved in turning the screenplay into a film. As the movie is shot, the writers are often asked to make further changes. At this point in the process, the collaboration widens.

Civic Literacy

Using Community Resources

Many screenwriters adapt stories from books or stage plays. Invite students to work in a group to choose a book and then think about how they might turn some scenes or passages into a movie scene without losing the original writer's essential vision. Students can outline their scene, write the dialogue, and include suggestions to the director for location shots and musical score. Encourage students to present their scene to the class.

Examining Writing in the Real World

Analyzing the Media Connection

Discuss these questions about the excerpts from the screenplay on page 134.

1. What is the mood of the baseball scene? How does the use of alliteration contribute to that mood?
2. How does the time of day contribute to the mood of the baseball scene? How might the mood shift if the action were to take place earlier in the day or later in the evening?
3. What sensory details enhance the mood of the baseball scene?
4. From whose perspective is the baseball scene described in the first three sentences? In the last four sentences? What is the effect of that shift in perspective?
5. What is the mood of the old dance pavilion scene? Which words and phrases contribute to this mood?

Analyzing a Writer's Process

Discuss these questions about Ross and Spielberg's writing process.

1. How is writing a screenplay similar to writing a feature story? How do the two processes differ?
2. Who is the audience for the screenplay? How does that audience differ from the audience for a feature story?
3. What difficulties might you expect when two or more writers collaborate on a screenplay or story? How did Ross and Spielberg collaborate?
4. How closely do you think a finished movie resembles the screenplay from which it was made? Explain.
5. To what extent does Ross imagine specific locations in creating settings and characters for his work? How might thinking about real places and people influence the writing process?

GrammarLink

A **participle** is a verb form used as an adjective. A **participial phrase** is a participle with its complements and modifiers.

Standing *on the platform,* the mayor waved to the crowd.

Use each participial phrase below in a sentence. Start by thinking of a noun or pronoun for each phrase to modify.

1. wandering in the neighborhood
2. blowing wildly through the bare-limbed trees
3. nervously clutching her purse
4. scratching against the darkened window
5. whispering fearfully behind the broken gate

See Lesson 12.3, page 523.

Descriptive Writing

Analyzing a Writer's Process

1. Both processes require finding a good idea, outlining, writing a draft, revising, and editing. A feature writer may have to do more research.
2. The audience for a screenplay is producers, directors, and actors; a feature story's audience may be editors or readers.
3. Students may suggest that collaborators will sometimes disagree about scenes. Ross and Spielberg wrote different scenes then rewrote each other's scenes until the script was "unified into one voice."
4. Possible answers: The finished version may vary from the screenplay due to changes made by actors, directors, and producers.
5. Ross had a real-life amusement park in mind for the pavilion scene. Thinking about real places and people can help give the writing more detail.

Reteaching

Have students supply adjectives or adverbs that relate to each of the five senses. The lists can help them write future descriptions.

Enrichment

Challenge students to write a paragraph that evokes a lighthearted mood.

Close

Have students discuss how to use the process described in the Media Connection to adapt a scene from a favorite book into a screenplay.

GrammarLink

Answers

Answers will vary.

1. I paused, wandering in . . . .
2. The wind, blowing wildly . . . .
3. The . . . woman, nervously clutching . . . .
4. Birch branches, scratching against . . . .
5. They huddled, whispering . . . .

Focus

Lesson Overview

Objectives

- To learn how to enhance a description by using mood
- To create topic sentences that give an overview of a scene and summarize the contents of a paragraph
- To learn how to orient a reader by providing a sense of direction and order in a descriptive paragraph

Skills

- choosing connotations; using precise nouns; selecting vivid adjectives and adverbs; using prepositional phrases to convey spatial relationships

Critical Thinking

- analyzing; synthesizing; categorizing; classifying

Listening and Speaking

- discussing; questioning; sharing ideas

Bellringer

Daily Language Activity

When students enter the classroom, have this assignment on the board: *What words and phrases might you use to describe a volcano erupting?*

Grammar Link to the Bellringer

Have students incorporate the following prepositions into their descriptions from the Bellringer activity: *below, above, beside.*

See also *Daily Language Practice*

Motivating Activity

Discuss students' responses to the Bellringer activity. Explain that in this lesson, students will learn to write effective description, and they will learn how writers can express reality in their work.

LESSON 3.1

Descriptive Writing

Writing a Descriptive Paragraph

In the model below author J. R. R. Tolkien uses his descriptive skills to transport you to an eerie scene. Notice how Tolkien creates a mood in his topic sentence and then uses well-ordered details to paint a vivid picture that reinforces the mood.

Literature Model

Hard and cruel and bitter was the land that met his gaze. Before his feet the highest ridge of Ephel Dúath fell steeply in great cliffs down into a dark trough, on the further side of which there rose another ridge, much lower, its edge notched and jagged with crags like fangs that stood out black against the red light behind them: it was the grim Morgai, the inner ring of the fences of the land. Far beyond it, but almost straight ahead, across a wide lake of darkness dotted with tiny fires, there was a great burning glow, and from it rose in huge columns a swirling smoke, dusky red at the roots, black above where it merged into the billowing canopy that roofed in all the accursed land.

Tolkien's first sentence conveys the overall impression of the scene.

What is Tolkien's writing strategy, as indicated by words like "before his feet," "on the further side," and "far beyond it"?

Resource Manager

Planning Resources

- *Lesson Plans*

Transparencies

- *Bellringer*
- *Daily Language Practice*
- *Fine Art* 13–18
- *Two-Minute Skill Drill*
- *Writing Process* 9, 13–17

Other Print Resources

- *Composition Enrichment,* p. 21
- *Composition Practice,* p. 21
- *Composition Reteaching,* p. 21
- *Cooperative Learning Activities,* pp. 13–16
- *Listening and Speaking Activities,* pp. 1, 2, 19, 21
- *Sentence-Combining Practice,* pp. 28–29
- *Thinking and Study Skills,* pp. 14, 15, 17
- *Writing Across the Curriculum*
- *Writing Assessment and Evaluation Rubrics*

> Sam was looking at Orodruin, the Mountain of Fire. Ever and anon the furnaces far below its ashen cone would grow hot and with a great surging and throbbing pour forth rivers of molten rock from chasms in its sides. Some would flow blazing toward Barad-dûr down great channels; some would wind their way into the stone plain, until they cooled and lay like twisted dragon-shapes vomited from the tormented earth. In such an hour of labor Sam beheld Mount Doom, and the light of it, cut off by the high screen of the Ephel Dúath from those who climbed up the path from the West, now glared against the stark rock faces, so that they seemed to be drenched with blood.
>
> J. R. R. Tolkien, *The Return of the King*

Create an Overall Impression

There are many ways to begin putting together a description. One way is to think of the overall impression, or mood, you want to communicate. Then, in your topic sentence, use words and phrases that will help convey this mood to your reader.

Mood Your descriptive paragraph will have greater impact if it evokes a particular mood rather than just presenting details that aren't unified. Perhaps you want to express horror or inspire fear, as Tolkien does. Maybe you intend to communicate a happy, light-hearted feeling or a sad, nostalgic one. Whatever impression you choose, carefully write your paragraph to present that impression clearly.

Concentrate on conveying a single, effective picture to the reader. In the Tolkien model, for example, the author creates a picture of a forbidding, polluted, "accursed land." He appeals to the reader's senses with images of dull fires, smoke, jagged rocks like fangs, and a "lake of darkness." The overall impression in the reader's mind is of a grim, tormented, and frightening landscape.

Grammar Tip

When you revise your writing, you can add vivid adjectives to help create a mood and draw a picture. Refer to Lesson 10.4, page 461.

Journal Writing

Think of a powerful scene in a book or movie—one that was incredibly beautiful, scary, or hilarious. In your journal jot down the overall impression, or mood, the scene conveyed. Make a list of the details in the scene that supported the overall impression.

Descriptive Writing

3.1

Teach

Using the Model

Tolkien's strategy is to describe the scene from near to far, as the character sees it. Discuss why Tolkien might have chosen this strategy. (It allows the reader to see the scene from the character's perspective.) **L2**

Understanding Connotation

Let students experiment with rewriting the first two sentences of the Tolkien model to express a distinctly different mood (such as hopeful, excited at facing a new challenge, or peaceful). Then ask students to read their sentences aloud to the class or exchange papers with a partner to see if others sense the mood they intended in their rewritten sentences. **L3**

Two-Minute Skill Drill

Have students use each of the following prepositions in sentences:

beneath *over* *near*
beside *inside*

See also *Two-Minute Skill Drill Transparency 3.1*

Journal Writing Tip

Supporting Details Encourage students to trust their first reaction to the scene, which is usually a good indicator of the writer's intent. Then, as they list details, students may refine their idea of the overall impression.

Teach

Understanding a Graphic

The graphic shows that each detail (outer circle) of a paragraph supports the topic sentence (inner circle). Let students identify the key word that suggests the mood in this topic sentence (*wildest*). Then ask which words in the details support the mood of wildness (*music nonstop and fast-paced, multicolored jumpsuits, strobe lights flashing*).

Students might draw a similar diagram to ensure that their details support their topic sentence. **L2**

Using the Model

The writer's description begins with details at the far left and moves across the room, following sights and sounds. Ask students to identify how the sound details support the main idea expressed in the topic sentence. (Details like *guided wordlessly, whirring sound,* and *All rise* confirm that these aliens are highly disciplined.) **L2**

Vocabulary Tip

In the revising stage of your work, check to make sure the details you have used actually support your topic sentence.

Topic Sentence In a descriptive paragraph, the topic sentence should "overview" the scene and summarize the content of the paragraph. In doing so, it can also help establish the paragraph's mood. The rest of the paragraph should contain details that support the topic sentence. You might want to envision the parts of your paragraph like this.

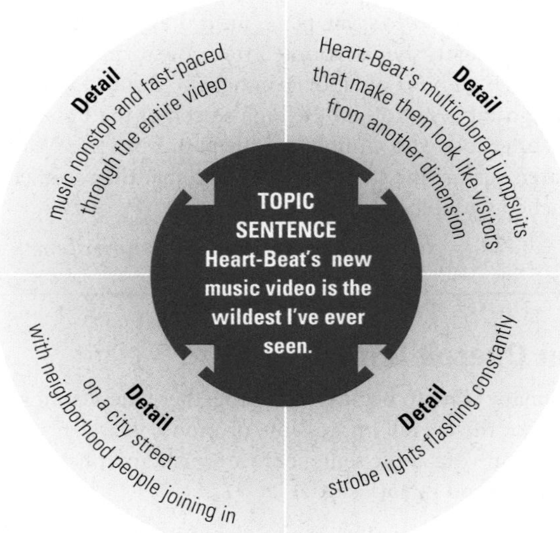

Notice that the topic sentence of the literature model on page 138 is at the very beginning of the paragraph. A topic sentence at or near the beginning of the paragraph lets the reader know what's coming. On the other hand, a topic sentence at or near the end of a paragraph, as in the model below, can summarize what you have just described.

Model

Ambassador Aleesa Aguilar entered the control room of the Galavian spacecraft, guided wordlessly by two of the craft's security officers. As the first earthling to meet the Galavians and to see a Galavian craft, she instinctively did a quick scan of her surroundings. A whirring sound directed her eyes to the far left of the brightly lit, cavernous white room. There she saw the "pilots," actually two androids—robots—who monitored the ship's course. Her experienced eyes next followed a series of about fifteen "space windows," computer screens that simulated the view off into space in fifteen directions. At five of these "windows" sat groups of

MEETING INDIVIDUAL NEEDS

English Language Learners

Brainstorming for Effective Description

Students who have difficulty writing in English may prefer to list sensory observations before determining a mood and using descriptive language in their writing. Suggest that students look at a photograph or painting of a place and list details about the place for each of the five senses. Then students can experiment with different adjectives for each detail until they can identify a coherent mood for their description.

Galavians, as expressionless as the androids, rapidly making calculations and plotting courses. Then a sharp voice to her right blared "All rise," as the craft's commander entered. In these few seconds, the savvy Ambassador Aguilar learned much about these hard-working, severe, highly regimented aliens.

The topic sentence at the end summarizes the importance of this brief description.

Orient the Reader

In writing a descriptive paragraph, your goal is to transport the reader to the scene. Yet you must also help to orient the reader by providing a sense of direction and of where things are. Describing items in spatial order is one way to help orient the reader.

Spatial Order There are many kinds of spatial orders. For example, the Tolkien model on pages 138–139 uses near-to-far spatial order. The author begins by describing what lies nearest the character and proceeds to describe things farther and farther away. In fact, he follows the order your own eyes might follow if you were looking at the scene. Other ways your eyes might move include left to right (or right to left), as in the model on pages 140–141, and top to bottom (or bottom to top).

Prewriting Tip

Before you begin drafting, decide how you want to arrange the details in your description.

Near to far

Left to right

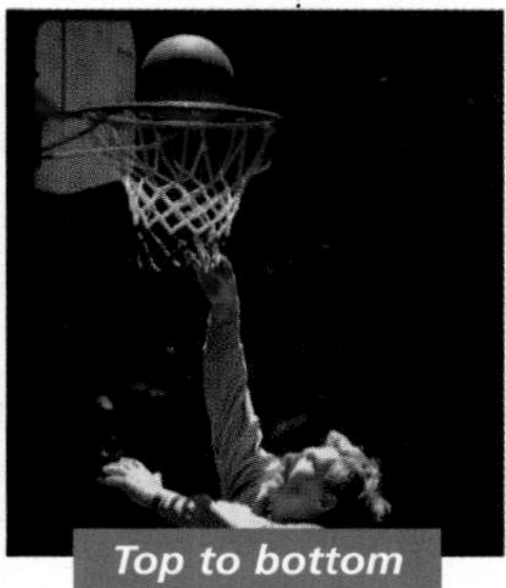
Top to bottom

Journal Writing

What are some other ways to look at and describe a scene? In your journal suggest two alternatives to spatial order. Then write a brief description of your room, the street you live on, or your school, using spatial order or one of your alternative suggestions.

Descriptive Writing

Cooperative Learning

In small groups students can play a Roundtable game in which one person writes a topic sentence for a place description, and the others in turn write supporting details. (Sample topic sentence: *Stacy marveled at the panorama from the snowy peak of Sulphur Mountain.* Possible details: *snow-dusted evergreens; skiers tracing paths through glistening snow; pure white clouds*) After everyone has contributed, each group should evaluate and revise their descriptions: Does the topic sentence provide an overview and mood? Do all the details support the topic sentence? **L2**

Organizing Details

Students who have difficulty organizing descriptive details in their writing may benefit from the following activity. Suggest that students look closely at a real scene or photograph and write each detail they notice on an index card. Then they can experiment with arranging the cards in different kinds of spatial order. The arrangement of cards can serve as a guide for writing a paragraph that describes the scene. **L1**

Journal Writing Tip

Identifying Relationships and Patterns Suggest that students think about the purpose for a description, and the overall impression they want to create, before choosing the ordering method. Perhaps describing the most important or noticeable details first would bring the scene more vividly to the reader. A writer's purpose might also lead to grouping details according to some nonspatial criteria, such as natural and artificial elements.

Viewing and Representing

Creating Descriptive Details

Interpreting Visuals Have students who have difficulty generating specific descriptive details from a mental image work with a partner. Supply each student with a picture or suggest that students bring in a picture of a place they've lived or would like to visit, whether across town or around the world. Have students study each picture and decide on how to express its mood in a topic sentence, what supporting details to include, and how to order these details in a descriptive paragraph. Let students take turns recording their ideas for each picture. **L1**

Teach

Using the Model

Have students discuss how spatial-order details are used. What would the effect be of using a different type of spatial order? Can students think of other ways to organize this paragraph? How? **L2**

Peer Editing

When students exchange descriptive paragraphs, suggest that editors read the paragraph once to gain an overall impression, and a second time to evaluate the effectiveness of the topic sentence, supporting details, and transitions. Editors should point out any elements that confuse or weaken the overall impression. **L2**

Additional Resources

For further stimuli for descriptive writing, see *Fine Art Transparencies* 13–18.

Writing Process Transparencies 9, 13–17
Writing Across the Curriculum
Cooperative Learning Activities
Thinking and Study Skills, pp. 14, 15, 17
Sentence-Combining Practice, pp. 28–29
Listening and Speaking Activities, pp. 1, 2, 19, 21
Composition Practice, p. 21

Descriptive Writing

Grammar Tip

Many transitions begin with prepositions. To write more precisely as you draft, refer to the list of common prepositions in Lesson 10.6, page 473.

Transitions Transitions are words that connect one sentence or idea to the next and help show the relationship between the two—words like *before, then, next, under, in front of, to the right of,* and *inside.* In descriptive writing, transitions can help the reader keep track of where things are. What transitions might you use in describing the scene pictured below?

Nancy Thill

The model below, by Mary Stewart, is from a story about Merlin, teacher and friend of the legendary King Arthur. Notice how the author ties together her description with spatial-order transitions.

Stewart uses the following spatial-order transitions: "behind," "against," "over," "around," "in front," "a few paces away," "between," "above," "beyond," "to the peak," "at," "where we had seen."

Literature Model

At first, after the blaze of the guard-room, I could see nothing. I shut the door behind me and leaned back against the damp wall, while the night air poured over me like a river. Then things took shape around me. In front and a few paces away was a battlemented wall, waist high, the outer wall of the castle. Between this wall and where I stood was a level platform, and above me a wall rising again to a battlement, and beyond this the soaring cliff and the walls climbing it, and the shape of the fortress rising above me step by step to the peak of the promontory. At the very head of the rise, where we had seen the lighted window, the tower now showed black and lightless against the sky.

Mary Stewart, *The Crystal Cave*

Viewing the Art

Nancy Thill, computer-generated art

Nancy Thill (pronounced "Till") used a computer to generate the illustration on this page, which is a composite of several photographic images. Ask students to suggest sentences that include transitions to describe details in the illustration. This work measures 20-by-24 inches, and belongs to the School of the Art Institute in Chicago.

3.1 Writing Activities

Write a Descriptive Paragraph

Imagine your school gymnasium or some other sports arena at night, after a game is over and the crowd has left. Write a one-paragraph description that gives the reader a clear visual picture of the place.

PURPOSE To describe a place and evoke a mood
AUDIENCE Other students
LENGTH 1 paragraph

WRITING RUBRICS To write a descriptive paragraph, you should

- decide what mood you want to create in the paragraph
- write a strong topic sentence
- orient the reader by presenting details in a logical order
- select precise transition words

Cross-Curricular Activity

ART Look closely at a painting in this textbook. How do the colors and form of the landscape or figures contribute to the painting's mood? Identify specific details in the painting, and write a paragraph that vividly describes the scene.

GrammarLink

Use prepositional phrases to show spatial relationships.

A **prepositional phrase** is made up of a preposition such as *under, over,* and *above* plus an object.

Revise the following sentences by adding at least one prepositional phrase to each sentence to clarify a spatial relationship.

1. The vase fell.
2. A flock of Canada geese flew.
3. There was a bright flash of lightning.
4. The artist painted.
5. The sun set and the moon rose.

See Lesson 12.1, page 519.

Viewing and Representing

COLLABORATIVE WRITING Complete the assignment outlined in the Cross-Curricular Activity. Then exchange papers within a small group. Try to sketch the painting a classmate has written about. How difficult is it to figure out exactly how the scene should look? What words or phrases help you? Next, look at the painting in the textbook together. What words or phrases would you now add to the description?

Writing Online | For more writing and grammar practice, go to **glencoe.com** and enter QuickPass code WC97727p1.

Assess

Evaluation Rubrics

Write a Descriptive Paragraph

Use these criteria when evaluating your students' writing:

- Does the paragraph include a strong topic sentence?
- Does the paragraph convey a mood that is supported by all of the details?
- Does the paragraph present details in a logical order?
- Does the paragraph include precise transition words?

See also *Writing Assessment & Evaluation Rubrics*

Cross-Curricular Activity

Evaluate the paragraph on the following points: how well it conveys the mood of the painting; how vividly it describes specific details in the painting that contribute to the mood.

Reteaching

Composition Reteaching, p. 21

Enrichment

Composition Enrichment, p. 21

Fine Art Transparencies 13–18

Close

Have students choose a paragraph from *The Crystal Cave* (pp. 164–171) and discuss why this paragraph is or is not a good example of descriptive writing.

GrammarLink

Answers

Answers will vary, but some suggestions are given below.

1. The vase fell off the table.
2. A flock . . . flew overhead.
3. There was . . . beside the oak tree.
4. The artist painted next to the tree.
5. The . . . rose above the clouds.

Focus

Lesson Overview

Objectives

- To write a descriptive paragraph by using precise nouns
- To bring descriptions to life by using vivid modifiers

Skills

- choosing connotations; using precise nouns; selecting vivid adjectives and adverbs

Critical Thinking

- categorizing; comparing; establishing criteria for choosing effective, descriptive words

Listening and Speaking

- discussing; questioning

Bellringer

Daily Language Activity

When students enter the classroom have this assignment on the board: *Write this simple sentence: She ran past the house. Underline the noun and the verb. Beneath each, list words that can be used to modify that word.*

Grammar Link to the Bellringer

Have students share lists. Make sure they understand that words used to modify verbs and nouns help bring writing to life.

See also  *Daily Language Practice*

Motivating Activity

Discuss students' responses to the Bellringer activity. Ask students why descriptive words make writing livelier. Invite students to select a scene and then to form a mental picture of the scene. Ask volunteers for words that will describe the scene vividly. Then explain that in this lesson students will learn how to form mental pictures as they read and how to write descriptive details.

LESSON 3.2

Using Descriptive Language

In the model below, Madeleine L'Engle seems to choose just the right words to convey a feeling or a vision. Notice how she uses precise nouns and vivid modifiers to capture your attention and help you picture the experience she is describing.

Literature Model

She looked around rather wildly. They were standing in a sunlit field, and the air about them was moving with the delicious fragrance that comes only on the rarest of spring days when the sun's touch is gentle and the apple blossoms are beginning to unfold. She pushed her glasses up on her nose to reassure herself that what she was seeing was real.

They had left the silver glint of a biting autumn evening; and now around them everything was golden with light. The grasses of the field were a tender new green, and scattered about were tiny, multicolored flowers. Meg turned slowly to face a mountain reaching so high into the sky that its peak was lost in a crown of puffy white clouds. From the trees at the base of the mountain came a sudden singing of birds. There was an air of such ineffable peace and joy all around her that her heart's wild thumping slowed.

Madeleine L'Engle, *A Wrinkle in Time*

What is the combined effect of such phrases as "delicious fragrance," "when the sun's touch is gentle," and "golden with light"?

With the words "tender," "new," and "tiny," L'Engle suggests that the world she describes is innocent, unsullied, and young.

Claude Monet (1840–1926), *Arbres En Fleurs*

Resource Manager

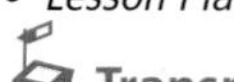

Planning Resources

- *Lesson Plans*

Transparencies

- *Bellringer*
- *Daily Language Practice*
- *Fine Art* 13–18
- *Two-Minute Skill Drill*
- *Writing Process* 9, 13–17

Other Print Resources

- *Composition Enrichment,* p. 22
- *Composition Practice,* p. 22
- *Composition Reteaching,* p. 22
- *Cooperative Learning Activities,* pp. 13–16
- *Listening and Speaking Activities,* pp. 1, 2, 19, 21
- *Sentence-Combining Practice,* pp. 28–29
- *Thinking and Study Skills,* p. 25
- *Writing Across the Curriculum*
- *Writing Assessment and Evaluation Rubrics*

Choose Words for Their Connotations

Connotations are the feelings and the values readers usually associate with any given words—associations that go beyond the *denotations,* or the simple dictionary definitions of the words. In her first paragraph, L'Engle writes of a "delicious fragrance." Why didn't she use the word *odor,* since *odor* and *fragrance* have the same basic meaning—smell? The answer is simple: most readers associate *odor* with an unpleasant smell and *fragrance* with an appealing one.

In choosing words for your descriptive writing, remember that many words come loaded with such connotations. Just as L'Engle chose "delicious fragrance," you should choose the best words you can find to re-create your vision.

Use Precise Nouns

Precise, vivid nouns are an important tool for re-creating your vision and making your writing more lively. By choosing nouns that are specific (*cloak,* for example) instead of general (*clothes*), you convey a clearer, more complete picture to your reader. The chart below shows some examples of nouns going from general to specific.

Nouns		
General	**Specific**	**More Specific**
monster	vampire	Count Dracula
animal	amphibian	bullfrog
rain	storm	hurricane

Grammar Tip

When drafting a description, you can refer to the material about concrete nouns in Lesson 10.1, page 439.

Journal Writing

How specific can you get? In your journal write the words *plant, machine, person, music, art, sport,* and *game* down the left side of one page. Next to each word, write as many nouns as you can think of that are increasingly specific examples of the general word.

Descriptive Writing

3.2

Teach

Using the Model

Ask students to close their eyes and form a mental picture of the scene as you read the literature model. Pause after reading each descriptive detail to let students process the image. Ask students to list the words and phrases in the model that appeal to each of the following senses: sight, hearing, smell, and touch. **L2**

Understanding Connotation

Write a sentence like the following on the chalkboard. *Despite his rough appearance, the unexpected visitor proved quite harmless.* Discuss how the meaning of the sentence changes with substitution of words that have similar denotations but different connotations. (*Rough* may be replaced by *craggy, harsh,* or *coarse; visitor* by *guest* or *caller.*) **L3**

Two-Minute Skill Drill

List these general nouns on the board and have students write a specific noun for each.

shoes	*hat*
pet	*holiday*
car	*plant*

See also *Two-Minute Skill Drill Transparency 3.2*

Journal Writing Tip

Precise Nouns To decide whether a noun can be classified as more specific than previously listed words, students can try to form a mental picture of exactly what the noun represents. Generally, the clearer the image, the more specific it is.

3.2

Teach

Using the Model

Massive claws creates a threatening image, intensifying the humorous contrast of the ending. Suggest that students review the model and pick out the words and phrases that add to the overall impression of danger (*beating wildly; horrible, nightmarish creature;* and *looming shadow*). **L2**

Using a Thesaurus

Suggest that students who have difficulty thinking of precise nouns and vivid modifiers use a thesaurus. Have students look up alternatives for words they wrote and list them in pairs. (*pleasant/lively*) Have students rewrite their sentences with more descriptive language. **L1**

Using Descriptive Techniques to Communicate

Ask students for examples of "communication breakdown" between themselves and others. Could the misunderstandings have been resolved if more precise words had been used? Ask students how they think the descriptive techniques in the lesson might be used to help people communicate better. **L3**

Additional Resources

For further stimuli for descriptive writing, see *Fine Art Transparencies* 13–18.

Writing Process Transparencies 9, 13–17
Writing Across the Curriculum
Cooperative Learning Activities
Thinking and Study Skills, p. 25
Listening and Speaking Activities, pp. 1, 2, 19, 21
Composition Practice, p. 22

Descriptive Writing

Vocabulary Tip

When revising your writing, you can use a thesaurus to help you find more colorful and appropriate modifiers. A thesaurus lists words with their synonyms and antonyms.

Select Vivid Adjectives and Adverbs

Vivid modifiers—that is, adjectives and adverbs—can bring your descriptions to life. Make sure each word's connotation fits the impression you want to create. For example, a *shining* sword gives a different impression from a *blazing* one.

Don't settle for dull, overused modifiers, like *good* or *bad*. Select more colorful and original modifiers, such as *honorable* and *wicked*. Sometimes you may even want to use exaggeration to make your description more colorful. You might say, for example, "My date last night was horrendous—everything went wrong." For help finding more colorful and appropriate words, you can check the listings in a thesaurus.

Making Your Modifiers More Lively

funny	amusing	hilarious
heavy	weighty	ponderous
well	adequately	expertly

Here's how one student used precise nouns and lively modifiers in her writing. Notice how the carefully chosen words re-create an eerie scene from her imagination.

Notice the dramatic effect created by "nightmarish," "looming shadow," and the narrator "flattened . . . against the far wall."

What is the effect of the words "massive claws"? What impact does this effect have on the ending?

Student Model

It was after me again. I kept on running, my heart beating wildly. But it kept on coming, more determined than ever to catch me. I ran into a small hut near the end of the village, hoping I could find protection there; but the hut was empty and that horrible, nightmarish creature grew closer with every step. When I saw its looming shadow in the doorway, I flattened myself against the far wall. It came toward me, my screams for help growing louder with every step it took. Finally, it was but mere inches from my face. I closed my eyes and prayed for a quick demise. It reached slowly with its massive claws toward me and said, "You're it!"

Nikki Phipps,
Hamilton Heights High School, Arcadia, Indiana

MEETING INDIVIDUAL NEEDS

English Language Learners

Using a Thesaurus

Students who are learning English may need extra assistance in choosing precise, vivid, descriptive words. You might, at this point, teach them to use a thesaurus. Provide some modifiers like those on the left of the chart. Ask students to come up with livelier substitutes for each. Then have them look up each word in a thesaurus to see what additional substitute words they can find. Remind them to use a dictionary to check the exact definition of any words they find in a thesaurus.

Write a Vivid Paragraph

Imagine you will write a story in which you wake up one day in an imaginary world. Write a paragraph describing the place. Perhaps you are inside a television or in your own house but you are only one inch tall.

PURPOSE To write a vivid description of a fantasy world
AUDIENCE Readers of a journal
LENGTH 1 paragraph

WRITING RUBRICS To write a vivid paragraph, you should

- use precise nouns
- select vivid modifiers
- choose words with accurate denotations and precise connotations
- proofread for spelling, punctuation, and grammar

Using Computers

Use a word processing program to compose your descriptive paragraphs. Use its thesaurus feature to add lively modifiers as you revise your work.

Viewing and Representing

COLLABORATIVE WRITING In a small group, discuss the painting at the right. Identify specific details, such as the heart in the man's palm. Work together to come up with vivid and specific nouns and modifiers to describe these details. Then write individual paragraph descriptions of the scene. As a group, decide how best to present the paragraphs to the class.

Grammar*Link*

Use specific language to write effective descriptions.

Revise this descriptive paragraph, using precise nouns and adding vivid modifiers.

[1]They entered the woods at night. [2]Trees stood all around and blocked out the sky. [3]The air smelled. [4]As they walked farther, they could hear noises behind and beside them. [5]The ground under their feet felt soft. [6]Lights flickered ahead of them, then died. [7]Something flew into one girl's face. [8]Then they heard another sound and tried to run out of the woods.

See Lesson 10.1, page 439, Lesson 10.4, page 461, and Lesson 10.5, page 467.

Marc Chagall, *Paris Through the Window,* 1913

Descriptive Writing

Writing Online For more writing and grammar practice, go to glencoe.com and enter QuickPass code WC97727p1.

Assess

Evaluation Rubrics

Write a Vivid Paragraph

Use these criteria when evaluating your students' writing:

- Are precise nouns and vivid modifiers used?
- Have the correct connotations of words been selected?

See also *Writing Assessment & Evaluation Rubrics*

Viewing and Representing

The paragraph should include nouns and modifiers precisely describing images from the painting and convey an overall impression of the painting.

Reteaching

Composition Reteaching, p. 22

Enrichment

Composition Enrichment, p. 22

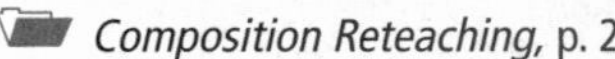

Fine Art Transparencies 13–18

Close

Have students discuss the techniques they have learned to write descriptive paragraphs. Ask them to find a paragraph in the text and to discuss whether the author uses precise nouns and vivid modifiers in his or her writing.

Grammar*Link*

Answers

Answers will vary.

1. hesitantly entered; dark woods at midnight
2. enormous oak trees; moonlit sky
3. night air smelled dank
4. small squeaking noises
5. leaf-covered ground
6. Strange lights; mysteriously died
7. Suddenly, something warm and furry flew
8. squeaking sound

Viewing the Art

Marc Chagall, *Paris Through the Window,* 1913

Marc Chagall (1887–1985) shows the influence of Impressionists, Post-impressionists, and Fauvists in this whimsical, dreamlike painting. The 55-by-52-inch work hangs in New York City's Guggenheim Museum.

Focus

Lesson Overview

Objectives
- To identify appropriate details that will convey the mood of an imaginary place
- To learn how to organize details in order to convey a description to a reader

Skills
- identifying details; conveying a mood; writing descriptive details; organizing details; determining a mood

Critical Thinking
- analyzing details; synthesizing information; comparing to known elements; visualizing details

Listening and Speaking
- discussing ideas; evaluating; questioning; peer editing

Bellringer
Daily Language Activity
When students enter the classroom, have this assignment on the board: *Think about a place you know. Write five descriptive details about the place.*

Grammar Link to the Bellringer
Have students write an appositive for each noun below, for example, *my brother—my brother, Fred.*

my sister	*the dog*
the book	*the movie*

See also *Daily Language Practice*

Motivating Activity
Discuss students' responses to the Bellringer activity. Then have students describe a memorable imaginary place from a book or film. Ask them whether the place was otherworldly or simply unfamiliar. Point out that many writers create imaginary places by building on familiar elements, such as projecting a city of today into a future of flying cars and increased pollution.

Descriptive Writing

LESSON 3.3

Describing an Imaginary Place

In the model below Ray Bradbury orders details to create a mood and allow the reader to picture an imaginary place.

"Fossil sea," "motionless," "stiff," "bone town"—what is the overall feeling created by this description?

How does the order in which various activities are described contribute to the overall effect of the description?

Literature Model

They had a house of crystal pillars on the planet Mars by the edge of an empty sea, and every morning you could see Mrs. K eating the golden fruits that grew from the crystal walls, or cleaning the house with handfuls of magnetic dust which, taking all the dirt with it, blew away on the hot wind. Afternoons, when the fossil sea was warm and motionless, and the wine trees stood stiff in the yard, and the little distant Martian bone town was all enclosed, and no one drifted out of their doors, you could see Mr. K himself in his room, reading from a metal book with raised hieroglyphs over which he brushed his hand, as one might play a harp. And from the book, as his fingers stroked, a voice sang, a soft ancient voice, which told tales of when the sea was red steam on the shore and ancient men had carried clouds of metal insects and electrical spiders into battle.

Mr. and Mrs. K had lived by the dead sea for twenty years, and their ancestors had lived in the same house, which turned and followed the sun, flower-like, for ten centuries.

Mr. and Mrs. K were not old. They had the fair, brownish skin of the true Martian, the yellow coin eyes, the soft musical voices. Once they had liked painting pictures with chemical fire, swimming in the canals in the seasons when the wine trees filled them with green liquors, and talking into the dawn together by the blue phosphorus portraits in the speaking room.

Ray Bradbury, *The Martian Chronicles*

Resource Manager

Planning Resources
- *Lesson Plans*

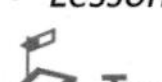

Transparencies
- *Bellringer*
- *Daily Language Practice*
- *Fine Art* 13–18
- *Two-Minute Skill Drill*
- *Writing Process* 9, 13–17

Other Print Resources
- *Composition Enrichment*, p. 23
- *Composition Practice*, p. 23
- *Composition Reteaching*, p. 23
- *Cooperative Learning Activities*, pp. 13–16
- *Listening and Speaking Activities*, pp. 1, 2, 19, 21
- *Sentence-Combining Practice*, pp. 28–29
- *Thinking and Study Skills*, pp. 4, 13
- *Writing Across the Curriculum*
- *Writing Assessment and Evaluation Rubrics*

Create Your Own Imaginary Place

You might already have an idea for an imaginary place. If not, try brainstorming, freewriting, or clustering to come up with an idea. A few words that might help you focus on imaginary places include *beneath, beyond, inside, before,* and *after*. Let your mind wander or simply let yourself wonder, "What would it be like there?" Look at something familiar, like your school, from a different point of view—such as through the eyes of a bug. Maybe one of the following topics will start you on the way to your own imaginary place:

fantasy lands	future societies	glacial caves
under the sea	behind the wall	a laboratory
an ancient castle	inside a chrysanthemum	alien planets

Explore Your Imaginary Place

Mentally exploring your imaginary place will help you see it in greater detail, and these details will enable you to describe the place to your reader. One good way to explore a place in detail is by asking and answering questions about it. What are its inhabitants like, if there are any? What can I see, hear, smell, feel, and taste here? What, if anything, does this place resemble? Don't be afraid to ask creative questions, such as the ones below.

Creative Questions and Answers

Q: What colors do I see here?
A: Neon-green atmosphere, acid-yellow swampland, and orange vines

Q: What do the inhabitants do for fun?
A: March stiffly in long lines around the main swamp

Q: What presents the greatest danger here?
A: Deadly purple vapors from the swamp

Q: What do the inhabitants eat?
A: Yellow vapors that spray from the swamp vines

Journal Writing

In your journal, list questions you could use to explore any imaginary place. Try to come up with questions about specific, even unusual, details of the place. Keep the list. You can use it when you begin planning and creating your own imaginary world or place.

Grammar Tip

To explore the details of your imaginary place, think about vivid adjectives and adverbs that help evoke clear images. See Lessons 10.4 and 10.5, pages 461–472.

Descriptive Writing

Teach

Using the Model

Terms like *fossil sea* and *motionless* help to create a feeling of long-lasting desolation. In the first paragraph of the model on page 148, Bradbury moves from descriptions of activities involving a considerable amount of motion to one involving almost no motion at all, reinforcing the impression that Martian civilization is winding down and dying. **L2**

Charting Details

Students who have difficulty with abstractions may prefer to create an imaginary place by comparing it to a familiar one. Show students how to make a chart by dividing a sheet of paper into five horizontal rows for the five senses and into two vertical columns labeled *Alike* and *Different*. For each familiar sensory detail, they can record how their imaginary place is similar or different. The complete chart can help them write about this place. **L1**

Two-Minute Skill Drill

Write sentences using each of these words as well as an appositive describing each word:

hat *car* *toy*
uncle *CD*

See also *Two-Minute Skill Drill Transparency 3.3*

Journal Writing Tip

Formulating Questions Encourage students to ask questions not only about the appearance of a place, but also about its past and future, the characteristics of its inhabitants, and its surroundings.

Teach

Cooperative Learning

Set up small groups in a Simultaneous Roundtable activity to invent an imaginary place. Each group decides on the type of place (underwater city, outer-space colony, and so on) and the mood. Then each member writes at the top of a sheet of paper a general question about the place. (*What does it look like? What is the weather?*)

Each group member reads the paper and answers the question by making up a descriptive detail about the place. The details should be consistent with the mood. Together, group members can revise details to remove inconsistencies. **L2**

Listing Details

By watching science fiction films on videotape, students may get creative inspiration for their own imaginary settings. Suggest that students watch enough of a film to become familiar with the world it portrays. They can list specific descriptive details and later evaluate how each contributes to the mood of the film. **L2**

Additional Resources

For further stimuli for descriptive writing, see *Fine Art Transparencies* 13–18.

Writing Process Transparencies, 9, 13–17

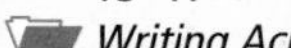
Writing Across the Curriculum
Cooperative Learning Activities
Thinking and Study Skills, pp. 4, 13
Sentence-Combining Practice, pp. 28–29
Listening and Speaking Activities, pp. 1, 2, 19, 21
Composition Practice, p. 23

Vocabulary Tip

As you revise, eliminate details that detract from the mood of your description. Do the sounds of your words help create the feeling you want? To review how to create mood, see Lesson 3.1, page 138.

Determine the Mood of Your Place

The description you write of your imaginary place will be more effective if it conveys a strong mood. Create a chart like the one below to help you come up with sensory details that will help you create a mood. Some of the most effective details are those that appeal to a reader's senses. What details can you add to the ones below?

Using Details to Create a Mood

FEELING	SAMPLE DETAILS
loneliness	utter silence, dusty furniture, ticking clock, dead air, musty odors
mystery, horror	secret passages, distant moaning, creaking floors
excitement	fast pace, lively music, bright colors, laughter
warmth, safety	glowing lights, crackling fire, steaming tea kettle, soft cushions

Organize the Details of Your Place

After you've decided on what details you want to use to create a mood, the next step is to choose the method of organization that will best convey your description to the reader. What is the most important feature of the scene—a castle, a tree, clouds of purple mist? How does that feature relate to other details?

As you draft your description, follow the spatial order that works best for your scene. If, for example, a tree or tall building dominates the picture, top-to-bottom spatial order might work best. What kind of organization would you choose to describe the place pictured below?

MEETING INDIVIDUAL NEEDS

English Language Learners

Visual Prewriting

Imaginary places begin as pictures in the mind's eye. Students who are uncomfortable prewriting in English may want to convey these pictures by sketching them or assembling a photo collage. Students can use their nonverbal images as a basis for written descriptions.

Viewing the Art

Masahiro Sano, computer-generated art, 1989

Masahiro Sano is a high-tech artist who creates artwork on a computer. This piece is a montage of images—some photos and some drawings. Ask students, *What mood is conveyed? How do specific details show the mood?*

3.3 Writing Activities

Describe a Scene

Write a paragraph describing a backyard barbecue from the point of view of a fly. In your description, include details that appeal to each of the five senses—sight, hearing, touch, taste, and smell. Taken together, the details should convey a single, specific mood or idea.

PURPOSE To write a description of a place from an unusual perspective
AUDIENCE Your classmates
LENGTH 1–2 paragraphs

WRITING RUBRICS To describe a scene, you should

- decide on the mood you wish to evoke
- select sensory details to convey the information
- use appropriate spatial order

Cross-Curricular Activity

MUSIC Music can evoke a scene or setting in one's imagination. Listen to a piece of classical or other instrumental music with your eyes closed. Then write a paragraph describing the setting the music evokes for you. Use specific sensory details in your description. You may wish to exchange papers with a classmate for peer review.

Listening and Speaking

COOPERATIVE LEARNING Working with a partner, choose a setting from real life or a book, movie, or TV show. Describe the scene to classmates. Then play a piece of music appropriate to the mood of the scene. Ask your classmates to identify the mood you tried to evoke. Discuss how important rhythm and repetition were to establishing the mood. What other elements do composers use to convey a mood?

Grammar*Link*

Use appositives to clarify.

An **appositive** is a noun or pronoun that follows another noun or pronoun to identify or give additional information:

a house of crystal pillars on the planet ***Mars***

Expand each of the following sentences. Add an appositive or an appositive phrase—an appositive plus a modifier or modifiers—to follow each italicized term. Remember to add commas where necessary—when the appositive is not essential to the meaning.

1. An excerpt from Ray Bradbury's *book* can be found on page 148.
2. Although the description is imagined, the reader can almost see the *place*.
3. The description of the place includes a description of some of its *inhabitants*.
4. The way the *author* arranges details that appeal to the senses helps evoke a mood.
5. One *character* liked to read.
6. His *wife* cleaned house with magnetic dust.
7. The inhabitants had lived by the dead sea a *long time*.
8. They used to have a *shared interest*.
9. The *book* is science fiction.
10. *Ray Bradbury* has a rich imagination.

See Lesson 12.2, page 521.

Writing Online For more writing and grammar practice, go to **glencoe.com** and enter QuickPass code WC97727p1.

Assess

Evaluation Rubrics

Describe a Scene

Use these criteria when evaluating your students' writing:

- Did the student use details that appeal to the five senses?
- Did the student write from the point of view of a fly?
- Did the student use details to convey a specific mood?
- Did the student use appropriate spatial order?

See also *Writing Assessment & Evaluation Rubrics*

Cross-Curricular Activity

Use the following questions to evaluate the paragraph:

- Did the student create a detailed description of the setting?
- Did the student use sensory images?
- Did the student create a specific mood?

Reteaching

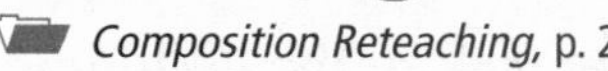

Composition Reteaching, p. 23

Enrichment

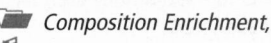

Composition Enrichment, p. 23

Fine Art Transparencies 13–18

Close

Have students consider how they might use description to tell about an imaginary city of the future that is too polluted for humans to live in.

Grammar*Link*

Answers

Answers will vary, but some suggestions are given below.

1. book, *The Martian Chronicles,*
2. place, a world of the future.
3. inhabitants, Mr. and Mrs. K.
4. the author, Ray Bradbury,
5. One character, Mr. K,
6. wife, Mrs. K,
7. a long time, twenty years.
8. a shared interest, painting pictures.
9. the book, *The Martian Chronicles,*
10. Ray Bradbury, my favorite author,

Focus

Lesson Overview

Objective
- To identify the correlation between a character's personality and appearance

Skills
- visualizing a character; describing a character

Critical Thinking
- analyzing details; synthesizing ideas; visualizing; identifying unique characteristics

Listening and Speaking
- discussing ideas; evaluating ideas; questioning

Bellringer
Daily Language Activity

When students enter the classroom, have this assignment on the board: *Name and describe a memorable character from literature, movies, or television.*

Grammar Link to the Bellringer
Have students check what they wrote in the Bellringer activity to see that they used the correct form of every verb.

See also  *Daily Language Practice*

Motivating Activity
Discuss students' responses to the Bellringer activity. For each character, ask what one factor makes the character stand out from others the student has encountered. As students suggest outstanding traits for the characters, list them on the board. Suggest that students keep these traits in mind and try to create equally memorable characters in their own writing. This lesson will help them explore how to create memorable characters.

Descriptive Writing

LESSON 3.4

Describing an Imaginary Person

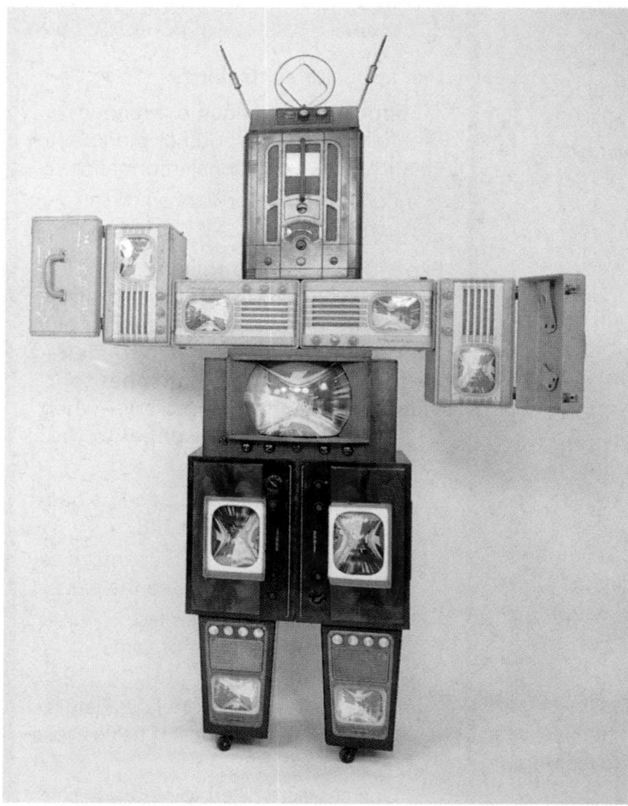

Nam June Paik, *Family of Robot: Grandfather,* 1986

To describe a fictional character, first imagine the character. Then think up details of appearance, movement, or personality that will help bring that character to life.

Imagine a Character

To create an imaginary character, begin by deciding on the type of character you want to create. Your own imaginary character can be based on just about anything—from your wildest fantasy to someone you observe on the bus. Then ask yourself some creative questions to help develop details about your character. Questions like those in the chart below might help.

Questions for Developing Character Details

1. What are my character's most prominent features?
2. How does my character move and communicate?
3. What trait or traits set my character apart from others?
4. Does my character's appearance fit his, her, or its personality?

Resource Manager

Planning Resources
- *Lesson Plans*

Transparencies
- *Bellringer*
- *Daily Language Practice*
- *Fine Art* 13–18
- *Two-Minute Skill Drill*
- *Writing Process* 9, 13–17

Other Print Resources
- *Composition Enrichment,* p. 24
- *Composition Practice,* p. 24
- *Composition Reteaching,* p. 24
- *Cooperative Learning Activities,* pp. 13–16
- *Listening and Speaking Activities,* pp. 1, 2, 19, 21
- *Sentence-Combining Practice,* pp. 28–29
- *Thinking and Study Skills,* pp. 4, 10, 21, 31–32
- *Writing Across the Curriculum*
- *Writing Assessment and Evaluation Rubrics*

In the model below an aged woman from the imaginary town of Gont is trying to help a child. The observer, Tenar, has doubts about this woman.

Literature Model

Tenar was not at all sure what she wanted Aunty Moss to be, finding her unpredictable, unreliable, incomprehensible, passionate, ignorant, sly, and dirty. But Moss got on with the burned child. Perhaps it was Moss who was working this change, this slight easing, in Therru. With her, Therru behaved as with everyone—blank, unanswering, docile, in the way an inanimate thing, a stone, is docile. But the old woman had kept at her, offering her little sweets and treasures, bribing, coaxing, wheedling. "Come with Aunty Moss now, dearie! Come along and Aunty Moss'll show you the prettiest sight you ever saw. . . ."

Moss's nose leaned out over her toothless jaws and thin lips; there was a wart on her cheek the size of a cherry pit; her hair was a gray-black tangle of charm-knots and wisps; and she had a smell as strong and broad and deep and complicated as the smell of a fox's den. "Come into the forest with me, dearie!" said the old witches in the tales told to the children of Gont. "Come with me and I'll show you such a pretty sight!" And then the witch shut the child in her oven and baked it brown and ate it, or dropped it into her well, where it hopped and croaked dismally forever, or put it to sleep for a hundred years inside a great stone, till the King's son should come, the Mage Prince, to shatter the stone with a word, wake the maiden with a kiss, and slay the wicked witch. . . .

"Come with me, dearie!" And she took the child into the fields and showed her a lark's nest in the green hay, or into the marshes to gather white hallows, wild mint, and blueberries.

Ursula K. LeGuin, *Tehanu: The Last Book of Earthsea*

LeGuin contrasts unpleasant aspects of Moss's appearance with her good side, both here and later in the selection.

What is the picture of Aunty Moss created by such details as "toothless jaws," "thin lips," and "gray-black tangle"?

By contrasting Moss's behavior with that typically attributed to witches, LeGuin helps us to see her more as an individual than as a stereotype.

Journal Writing

In your journal describe a fantasy or science-fiction character with whom you are familiar. Explain how the character's personality does or does not fit his or her appearance.

Teach

Using the Model

The details create a picture of a physically unattractive person. Ask students to find three details of Aunty Moss's *behavior* that contradict this picture. Stereotyped characters frequently appear in films and TV shows. What stereotypes can students think of, and what problems can these stereotypes cause? What stereotypes would students like to refute? **L2**

Describing Characters

One way to describe a character is to show him or her through the eyes of another character. Details should reflect a consistent attitude on the part of the observer (such as jealousy, adoration, or fear), and should be limited to information the observer could know. Have students practice this technique by writing a description of Aunty Moss from Therru's viewpoint. **L3**

Two-Minute Skill Drill

Rewrite each of the following verbs in the past tense. Then write them in another tense.

fly *run* *drive*
grunt *howl*

See also *Two-Minute Skill Drill Transparency 3.4*

Journal Writing Tip

Comparing To help students distinguish between personality and appearance, you might have them create a chart for their character with appearance details in one column and personality details in another.

Viewing the Art

Nam June Paik, *Family of Robot: Grandfather,* 1986
Nam June Paik, born in Korea, now lives in New York City. His interest in composing avant-garde music led him to creating video art. This 8½-foot sculpture is made of radio and television cabinets and television sets.

Teach

Using the Model

The sensory details give the overall impression of a powerful, dangerous, experienced fighter. Ask students to list all the sensory details that help convey this impression. How does the last sentence change this impression? (Instead of a dangerous prisoner, the character turns out to be the warden.) **L2**

Describing Characters

Some students find character description more accessible if they can interact with the character in some way. Tell students to imagine that a superhero or recognizable media figure comes to dinner at their home or becomes a classmate in school. Ask them to write a description of that character in such a setting. Remind students to think carefully about what inconsistencies the character might display in the setting. **L2**

Additional Resources

- For further stimuli for descriptive writing, see *Fine Art Transparencies* 13–18.
- *Writing Process Transparencies* 9, 13–17
- *Writing Across the Curriculum*
- *Cooperative Learning Activities*
- *Thinking and Study Skills,* pp. 4, 10, 21, 31–32
- *Sentence-Combining Practice,* pp. 28–29
- *Listening and Speaking Activities,* pp. 1, 2, 19, 21
- *Composition Practice,* p. 24

Grammar Tip

When editing a character sketch, make sure you have used pronouns correctly. See Lessons 17.5 and 17.6, pages 640–647.

Make a Character Come to Life

If you were to describe your best friend, you would probably mention your friend's looks and personality. You might also note some of your friend's unique quirks, strengths, or habits. Such details would help other people to see your friend as you do.

When describing an imaginary character, use these same kinds of details to make your character come to life. The details that are most unusual or most inconsistent with the rest of the description will do the most to make your character real. Such details will help give your character a three-dimensional quality. In addition, inconsistencies will tend to arouse your reader's curiosity. Aunty Moss, in the model on page 153, is interesting because she seems to look like a witch, but she does not behave as we might expect a witch to behave.

Here's a character description from the imagination of student Todd Crusey. How does he bring life to his character? Think about what inconsistencies you might add to make the character more interesting, yet still believable.

How would you describe the overall impression created by sensory details such as sweat rolling down his forehead "like an avalanche" and "the carved stones he called hands"?

Crusey holds our interest by describing the character but waiting until the very end to reveal his identity.

Student Model

Sweat rolled like an avalanche down his broad, sloping forehead. It collected on the ledge of his square jutting brow and was then absorbed by the dense brown forest of his eyebrows. Slowly the perspiration dripped down into the large sockets that housed his squinting onyx eyes. From his hollow temples ran a flood of exhaustion that made his whole face glisten in the dark amber light of the prison wall. His nose was a wide, flat wedge, beaten down by the fists of over a hundred men. From his broad shoulders to the carved stones he called hands, he was a warrior. He had done battle in countless brawls and riots and had the scars to show for it. His only reward was his heartbeat; he had survived. This mean and relentless beast of a man always prevailed and was feared by all sane men. That's why they brought him here. Within these prison walls he reigned. He was truly a giant; he made the rules and he had the power to enforce them. That's why they called him warden.

Todd Crusey, Jefferson Davis High School,
Montgomery, Alabama

Less Proficient Readers

Role Playing

For students having difficulty identifying character descriptions, write on the board a simple sentence that can be interpreted in various ways. Prepare in advance flash cards with prompts for different personality traits, such as *anger, cheerfulness, hostility, aggression, timidity,* or *depression.* Invite volunteers to select a flash card and read the sentence according to the prompt. Then ask students to describe the characters based on the role plays. Encourage students to see how changes in detail cause the same character to appear different. **L1**

3.4 Writing Activities

Write About an Imaginary Person

Observe someone while you are riding on a bus, looking out your window, or from another location of your choice. Take notes on the person's appearance, and use your notes to create a description of an imaginary person you could later include in a short story.

PURPOSE To create an imaginary person based on a real one
AUDIENCE Your teacher and classmates
LENGTH 1–2 paragraphs

WRITING RUBRICS To describe an imaginary person, you should

- list unique physical traits
- create possible personality quirks
- describe inconsistencies between appearance and personality

Cross-Curricular Activity

HISTORY Choose a historical work of art from your history book. In a group, brainstorm to come up with details that describe the character in the painting. What does the environment add to your perceptions of the character? After each person writes a one-paragraph description, combine the paragraphs into a group description.

GrammarLink

Use correct forms of verbs.

Write the correct form of the verb in parentheses to complete each sentence.

1. When you edit your character sketch, make sure that you have (do) all you can to bring the character to life.
2. The details Ursula K. LeGuin used in writing about Aunty Moss (bring) the character to life.
3. I have (feel) that I've known many of the characters I've read about.
4. I also have (write) about characters I have created myself.
5. Some of these imaginary characters (begin) to seem like friends as I wrote about them.

See Lesson 15.2, page 582.

Listening and Speaking

SPELLING Homophones are words that sound the same but have different meanings and usually different spellings. The spelling checker feature on your computer will not detect a wrong word choice. Common homophones include *allowed* and *aloud, band* and *banned, cent* and *scent, council* and *counsel.* Create a strategy for checking to be sure that you have used the correct homophone. One idea is to exchange papers with a peer and have your writings read aloud. The reader is likely to notice the difference between what is written and what is meant.

For more writing and grammar practice, go to glencoe.com and enter QuickPass code WC97727p1.

Assess

Evaluation Rubrics

Write About an Imaginary Person

Use these criteria when evaluating your students' writing:

- Does the description include unique physical traits?
- Does it include descriptions of interesting personality quirks?
- Does it include inconsistencies between appearance and personality?

See also *Writing Assessment & Evaluation Rubrics*

Cross-Curricular Activity

Evaluate the group description on the following: use of sensory detail; imagination; use of physical detail and personality quirks.

Reteaching

Composition Reteaching, p. 24

Enrichment

Composition Enrichment, p. 24

Fine Art Transparencies 13–18

Close

Have the class brainstorm to list physical traits, personality quirks, and inconsistencies between the two for a character in a story everyone in the class is familiar with. List ideas on the board.

GrammarLink

Answers

1. done
2. brought
3. felt
4. written
5. began

Focus

Lesson Overview

Objectives

- To analyze literary characters based on their physical appearances, thoughts, words, and actions
- To draw conclusions about literary characters by considering how other people in a story react to them

Skills

- describing a character's appearance; drawing conclusions about a character's thoughts, words, and actions; inferring from the reactions of other characters

Critical Thinking

- analyzing a character; making inferences about a character; evaluating a character

Listening and Speaking

- discussing; evaluating ideas; questioning; sharing ideas

Bellringer

Daily Language Activity

When students enter the classroom, have this assignment on the board: *What character from a book or a movie have you, at some point in your life, wanted to be like? Describe the character.*

Grammar Link to the Bellringer

Have students rewrite the following sentences in a way that makes sense:

She said that she called her a helper.

He wants me to put his things away.

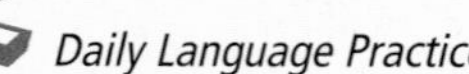

See also *Daily Language Practice*

Motivating Activity

Discuss students' responses to the Bellringer activity. Ask them what they admire about the character. Point out that by looking closely at the way characters are described, students can gain a deeper appreciation of these characters. This lesson teaches more about describing character traits and actions.

LESSON 3.5

Descriptive Writing

WRITING ABOUT LITERATURE

Analyzing Character Descriptions

When you write to analyze a character in literature, pay attention to what you can learn from the character's physical appearance, thoughts, words, and actions.

One student writer chose a dragon to describe. The dragon is a character from "The Rule of Names" by science-fiction writer Ursula K. LeGuin. As you read the model below, notice the aspects of the dragon that Arthur Housinger focuses on.

Student Model

One common desire links one living being to another, to be happy. Some find happiness with friends and money. In this respect, the dragon in "The Rule of Names," Yevaud, was no different from a man. He was a slightly egocentric being who just wanted some friends and some treasure.

Yevaud showed his egocentricity several times. As Blackbeard told Birt, Yevaud attacked the island of Pendor and killed many men just so he could have a treasure all for himself. After one hundred years, he ran away from the island with the treasure. He locked it in his inner chamber at Sattins Island.

Yevaud knew that this would not be enough to ensure happiness, but he had a few more tricks up his sleeve. First, he changed his appearance. Yevaud knew the unfortunate truth that people often judge a book by its cover; therefore, he changed his cover to a "little fat man of fifty who waddled along with his toes turned in." By changing his appearance, Yevaud, also known as Mr. Underhill, not only made a few friends, but he covered his tracks as the thief of the treasure.

Housinger notes the importance of this character's change in appearance.

Resource Manager

Planning Resources

- *Lesson Plans*

Transparencies

- *Bellringer*
- *Daily Language Practice*
- *Fine Art* 13–18
- *Two-Minute Skill Drill*
- *Writing Process* 9, 13–17

Other Print Resources

- *Composition Enrichment,* p. 25
- *Composition Practice,* p. 25
- *Composition Reteaching,* p. 25
- *Cooperative Learning Activities,* pp. 13–16
- *Listening and Speaking Activities,* pp. 1, 2, 19, 21
- *Sentence-Combining Practice,* pp. 28–29
- *Thinking and Study Skills,* pp. 14–16, 24
- *Writing Across the Curriculum*
- *Writing Assessment and Evaluation Rubrics*

Blackbeard accurately called him a "wise, cunning monster, full of strength and subtlety."

Yevaud's tricks lacked perfection, though, just as many of his elixirs did. Since Yevaud was constantly showing a false front, a barrier came between him and the villagers. His smiles were even false and made the village girls feel nervous. Yet since he was such a bumbling wizard, the townspeople simply treated Mr. Underhill as a fellow villager. This too was a falsehood, as was shown when Yevaud used his great powers to fight Blackbeard.

Yevaud tried to be something he wasn't, a friendly, inept wizard called Mr. Underhill. Once this barrier of deceit disappeared, Yevaud's true self, along with his true name, could spread its wings. Although Blackbeard's description of Yevaud was accurate, it was not complete. Yevaud was also a friendly being who found a home where he felt comfortable, one who wanted friends and treasure.

Arthur Housinger, Rich East High School,
Park Forest, Illinois

Here Housinger shows the villagers' reactions to Yevaud/Underhill.

Housinger next analyzes Yevaud/Underhill's actions and how these actions affected other characters.

Descriptive Writing

Consider a Character's Appearance

A character's physical appearance can suggest a great deal about the nature and background of the person. In "The Rule of Names," for example, the details of the main character's appearance are especially significant, because they hint at his true nature and background.

The order and way in which these physical details are presented may also be important. An author may put the most important facts about a character first, or describe them in the greatest detail so as to impress them upon you. In *Robin Hood: Prince of Thieves,* for example, novelist Simon Green first describes Robin Hood's friend Azeem as follows: "Tall and heavily muscled, he had dark skin covered with intricate tattoos. Even his shaved head was ornamented with them." Thus, Green emphasizes Azeem's strength and his exotic quality, suggesting that these are important features. As the story unfolds, readers learn that these are, in fact, among the most important things to know and remember about Azeem.

Presenting Tip

When you present your description orally, you can create or emphasize a mood with vocal techniques such as lowering your voice, or drawing out a phrase or word.

Journal Writing

In your journal jot phrases to describe someone you know. Circle the most significant details.

Teach

Using the Model

Discuss whether the saying "Appearances can be deceiving" applies to literary characters. Would readers admire a physically attractive character, regardless of negative personality traits? What physical characteristics are most likely to trigger assumptions about a character? In literature, as in real life, students should consider the available information before forming an opinion. **L2**

Comparing Characters

Ask students to compare other familiar literary characters to the dragon Yevaud as Housinger describes him. By what means do other characters seek happiness? Do any other characters try to change their personalities or fool people? What strategies were employed by characters who were more successful than Yevaud in the search for happiness? Point out that such comparisons can be helpful in analyzing literary characters. **L3**

Two-Minute Skill Drill

Write three sentences. Use two of the following pronouns in each sentence. Be sure pronoun references are clear.

he	*him*	*they*
her	*their*	*our*
them	*she*	*we*

See also *Two-Minute Skill Drill Transparency 3.5*

Journal Writing Tip

Identifying Relationships and Patterns Encourage students to give careful consideration to details that reveal the most information about the person.

Teach

Role-playing Characters

Students may find role-playing a useful way to understand characters in a story. For example, after role-playing Robin Hood and Azeem, students could answer questions such as *Azeem, how do you feel about Friar Tuck's distrust of you?* or *Robin, what makes you determined to win against the Sheriff of Nottingham?* **L2**

Note Taking

Instruct students to draw a blank chart like the one on this page, in which they can record important thoughts, words, and actions of a character. Students can look for key words that appear on the chart and use these to make general statements about the character. **L1**

Additional Resources

- For further stimuli for descriptive writing, see *Fine Art Transparencies* 13–18.
- *Writing Process Transparencies* 9, 13–17
- *Writing Across the Curriculum*
- *Cooperative Learning Activities*
- *Thinking and Study Skills,* pp. 14–16, 24
- *Sentence-Combining Practice,* pp. 28–29
- *Listening and Speaking Activities,* pp. 1, 2, 19, 21
- *Composition Practice,* p. 25

Note Thoughts, Words, and Actions

Because a character's thoughts, words, and actions might not always be consistent with his or her appearance, you should consider all information you have about the character. For example, although Azeem looks like a powerful and exotic person, his thoughts, words, and actions reveal him also to be a loyal, honorable, and loving friend.

Thoughts		Words		Actions		Conclusion
"Not for the first time, Azeem realized he was a long way from home, and those he had loved."	+	"It is because I love them so dearly that I cannot dishonor them by breaking my vow."	+	"Azeem examined Fanny's swollen belly... and then looked at her compassionately." He then delivered Fanny's baby.	=	These thoughts, words, and actions indicate that Azeem is a loving, loyal, and compassionate man.

Revising Tip

When you revise, look for places where you might strengthen your draft by adding details about a character's appearance, thoughts, words, and/or actions. Use quotations from the literature to support your ideas.

When you analyze a character's thoughts, words, and actions, you may want to ask yourself how you feel about what the character says and does. You might also ask such questions as these: How would I feel around this person? What qualities does this character have that I admire or dislike? Asking and answering such questions will help you get to "know" the character personally and will help make your writing about the character fresh and stimulating.

Think About Reactions of Other Characters

An author can also reveal much about a character by showing how other people react to that character. Be aware of these reactions as you analyze a character, but be sure to consider the nature of each person who is doing the reacting too. For example, the character's enemies would naturally dislike him or her, while the character's friends would be biased in his or her favor. The reactions of either group should be analyzed. The chart below shows two reactions to Azeem. Which do you think shows the truer picture?

Reaction A
Robin Hood tells his men his opinion of Azeem: "I trust him."

Reactions to Azeem

Reaction B
Friar Tuck and the others distrust Azeem because his ways are so different from their own.

3.5 Writing Activities

Write a Character Analysis

Select a character from one of the books or stories mentioned in this unit, or from another work you know and like. Imagine that the character was a dinner guest in your home last night. Write in your journal about your family's reactions to the character as well as any discussions or activities that may have happened during the evening.

PURPOSE To analyze a character from literature who has been put in another setting
AUDIENCE Yourself
LENGTH 3–4 paragraphs

WRITING RUBRICS To write a character analysis, you should

- describe the character's appearance
- analyze his or her words and actions
- describe the reactions of others to the character

Using Computers

You can help organize the details for your character analysis with the help of your word processor. Type in each significant detail you discover about the character. Hit the return key after each note you type. Then you can later rearrange your details without having to retype the pieces of information into your file. You can use each detail wherever you want as you develop your writing structure.

Grammar*Link*

Make pronoun references clear.

When you write to analyze a character, use clear, consistent, and unambiguous pronoun references.

Rewrite the sentences below to correct each unclear pronoun reference.

1. Arthur writes about Yevaud and Blackbeard, and he says that he called him a "wise, cunning monster."
2. Yevaud and Mr. Underhill are really the same character, because he turns himself into him.
3. When writers describe characters, they should make them come alive.
4. Azeem, who was a friend of Robin Hood, had an exotic appearance, and he told his men his opinion of him.
5. It is important to write clearly when you analyze a character one has read about.

See Lesson 17.6, page 645.

Viewing and Representing

EVALUATING A CHARACTER Create a poster of a favorite character who undergoes a physical transformation. Create a before-and-after illustration. For both pictures, identify distinctive physical features of the character. Write two or three sentences that describe the character's thoughts and actions and note any changes that they undergo. Compare your illustration with an illustration of the character in a book or on a Web site.

LOG ON Writing Online For more writing and grammar practice, go to glencoe.com and enter QuickPass code WC97727p1.

Assess

Evaluation Rubrics

Write a Character Analysis

Use these criteria when evaluating your students' writing:

- Did the student describe the character's appearance?
- Did the student analyze the character's words and actions?
- Did the student describe reactions of family members?

See also *Writing Assessment & Evaluation Rubrics*

Using Computers

Check to see that details are listed (in any order), each on a separate line, and that the best observations have been incorporated into the character analysis.

Reteaching

Composition Reteaching, p. 25

Enrichment

Composition Enrichment, p. 25

Close

Discuss how the skills students use to analyze literary characters are also helpful in real life. For example, under what circumstances would students need to watch for and interpret clues that reveal the motivation, feelings, or character of an acquaintance? How would this kind of analysis help them in their future careers, and in their future roles as parents and voters?

Grammar*Link*

Answers

Answers will vary, but suggestions are given below.

1. . . . and Arthur says that Blackbeard called Yevaud a "wise, cunning monster."
2. . . . because Yevaud turns himself into Mr. Underhill.
3. . . . they should make the characters come alive.
4. . . . Robin Hood gave his opinion of Azeem to his men.
5. . . . when you analyze a character you have read about.

Focus

Lesson Overview

Objective
- To describe an imagined place so vividly that the reader feels transported there

Skills
- using the five stages of the writing process: prewriting, drafting, revising, editing, and presenting; focusing writing; presenting details in order; using sensory details and figurative language; using first-person point of view; using correct grammar

Critical Thinking
- visualizing a place; relating details; defining and clarifying

Listening and Speaking
- discussing; peer editing; evaluating; questioning; listening to others' ideas

Bellringer
Daily Language Activity

When students enter the classroom, have this assignment on the board: *Imagine a place you have never seen but would like to visit. List some vivid descriptive details you could use to create an impression of the place.*

Grammar Link to the Bellringer

Have students categorize their details according to the senses: sight, touch, sound, taste, and smell. If the detail words are very general, ask students to make them more precise.

See also 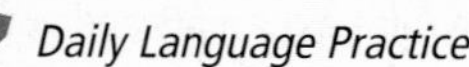 *Daily Language Practice*

Motivating Activity

Discuss students' responses to the Bellringer activity. Tell students that this lesson will teach them to create descriptions that should make readers feel transported to the imagined place.

UNIT 3

Writing Process in Action

Descriptive Writing

Descriptive Writing

In preceding lessons you've learned about describing imaginary places and characters and about the kinds of words and details that can make descriptions effective. You've also had a chance to write your own descriptive paragraphs. Now it's time to make use of what you have learned. In this lesson you're invited to create a place in your imagination and then describe it. This place may be one that could actually exist in this world or it may be an entirely fantastical place—one that's out of this world.

Assignment

Context

You are a staff writer for *Vicarious Voyager,* a magazine filled with descriptive writing that lets "even dedicated couch potatoes expand their horizons." You have been asked to write an article describing an imagined place. Focus on describing personal impressions and sensations.

Purpose

To write a description of a place you've imagined that is so vivid that it helps readers feel transported there

Audience

Teenagers who want the experience of visiting new places

Length

1–2 pages

Planning to Write

The following pages can help you plan and write your description. Read through them and then refer to them as you need to—but don't be tied down by them. You're in charge of your own writing process. Before you begin, set a time frame for completing the assignment. By doing so, you can properly allocate your time to the process. Always keep in mind the controlling idea: to write a vivid description of an imaginary place so that your reader can actually experience it.

LOG ON Writing Online

For prewriting, drafting, revising, editing and publishing tools, go to **glencoe.com** and enter QuickPass code WC97727p1.

Resource Manager

Planning Resources

- *Lesson Plans*

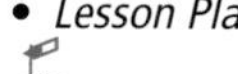

Transparencies
- *Bellringer*
- *Daily Language Practice*
- *Writing Process* 9, 13–17

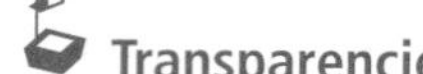

Other Print Resources
- *Composition Enrichment,* p. 26
- *Composition Practice,* p. 26

- *Composition Reteaching,* p. 26
- *Grammar Workbook,* Lessons 98–102
- *Sentence-Combining Practice,* pp. 28–29
- *Thinking and Study Skills,* pp. 13, 21
- *Writing Assessment and Evaluation Rubrics*

Web Site
- *glencoe.com*

Writing Process in Action

Prewriting

What kind of place will you be describing—an exotic country, an alien wilderness, a landscape that might exist on the head of a pin? Use a place that you think up yourself, or review the literature models in this unit for possible ideas. Then start exploring your place by mentally wandering through it. The prewriting questions shown here may help you get started.

As you wander, write down your impressions, using as many sensory details as you can. Think, too, about the mood you want to create and what details you could accentuate to convey this mood. In the model below, T. H. White creates a sense of nostalgia in his description of an imaginary castle by using details that describe not only the ruins, but also the living things that still inhabit them.

Prewriting Questions

- What type of place is it?
- Who or what lives here, if anything?
- What do the inhabitants do?
- Do natural laws as we know them hold here?
- What is the overall mood of the place?

Literature Model

The castle of the Forest Sauvage is still standing, and you can see its lovely ruined walls with ivy on them, standing broached to the sun and wind. Some lizards live there now, and the starving sparrows keep warm on summer nights in the ivy, and a barn owl drives it methodically, hovering outside the frightened congregations and beating the ivy with its wings, to make them fly out. Most of the curtain wall is down, though you can trace the foundations of the twelve round towers which guarded it. . . .

T. H. White, *The Once and Future King*

TIME

For more about the writing process, see **TIME Facing the Blank Page**, pp. 121–131.

Drafting

To begin drafting, think of a likely place of entry to your scene. One approach is to choose a spot from which you could easily orient your readers to the surroundings. For example, you could be crouched behind a door, or you might be up on a hill, with an overview of a whole scene below.

Teach

Prewriting

Developing Ideas for Descriptive Writing

Encourage students who have trouble coming up with ideas for their descriptive writing to examine a familiar place from a different perspective. For example, students might try to imagine how their room would appear if they were transformed into flies, or they might try to imagine their impressions if their school were under water. Suggest that students freewrite to discover their personal impressions and sensations of a familiar place seen from a different perspective. **L2**

Drafting

Beginning a Draft

At this point, encourage students to set all of their ideas down on paper. They can find better word choices, transitions, and methods of organization later in the revising stage. Right now, the most important goal is to begin drafting. **L2**

Teach

Revising

Peer Editing

Students can work in conferences with peer editors before they revise their writing. You may want to duplicate the Peer Response forms in *Writing Assessment and Evaluation Rubrics*. Suggest that peer editors respond to the following questions:

- Is the place interesting? Would you like to go there?
- Does the place suggest a particular mood? Do the details consistently support this mood?
- If the details are organized spatially, could you find your way around the imagined place?
- Are the details about the place so precise that you can picture it? **L2**

Editing/Proofreading

Peer Editing

After students have edited their own work, have them edit another student's writing. Remind them to refer to the Editing/Proofreading Checklist on page 163. **L2**

Publishing/ Presenting

Before students present their descriptive writing, discuss how to prepare their papers for publication in the class magazine. Emphasize the importance of the final draft, and remind students to write it neatly.

Additional Resources

 *Writing Process Transparencies* 9, 13–17

 *Thinking and Study Skills*, pp. 13, 21

Sentence-Combining Practice, pp. 28–29

Composition Practice, p. 26

 *Grammar Workbook*, Lessons 98–102

Drafting Tip

For more information about using spatial order, see Lesson 3.1, page 138.

Now visualize your place from your chosen point of entry and, using your prewriting notes, begin drafting. Don't stop writing just to find the absolutely "right word." For now, just keep your ideas flowing.

As you may have done in prewriting, you can let your "journey" be guided by your reaction to various sensations, or you can use one of these methods of organization:

- **Spatial order** To organize details spatially, describe all of the elements in a place by their location as you perceive them—top to bottom, left to right, or front to back.
- **Order of importance** Start by describing key details and then move on to less important ones. This method works well if your readers need to grasp certain basic elements of your world first.

Once you have everything down on paper, even if you're not totally happy with how you said it, put your draft aside. A few hours' or even a day's time away from it can help you see its strengths and weaknesses more clearly.

Revising

To begin revising, read over your draft to make sure that what you've written fits your purpose and audience. Then have a **writing conference.** Read your draft to a partner or small group. Use your audience's reactions to help you evaluate your work.

Revising Tip

For help with transitions and word choice, see Lesson 3.1 and Lesson 3.2, pages 138–147.

Revising Checklist

- Have I used details consistently to establish and maintain a believable reality and mood?
- Do I keep to the same kind of order throughout the description?
- Would adding transitional words and phrases help orient my readers?
- Are my nouns and modifiers carefully and precisely chosen?

Enrichment and Extension

Follow-up Idea

Set aside time for students to celebrate the publication of their magazine. Encourage them to share their finished pieces with another class.

Extending Description

Brainstorm with students ways they can use their expertise in descriptive writing in other subject areas. Some possibilities include: describing historical events or places, describing scientific phenomena, and describing other countries and places.

Editing/Proofreading

Once you are happy with the basic content and set-up of your description, **proofread** it carefully for errors in grammar, usage, mechanics, and spelling. Use the questions at the right as a guide.

In addition to proofreading, use the self-evaluation list below to make sure your description does all the things you want it to do. When you're satisfied, make a clean copy of your description and proofread it one more time.

Editing/Proofreading Checklist

- Have I used appositives and phrases correctly?
- Have I used precise nouns and modifiers?
- Are my pronoun references clear?
- Are all my verb forms and tenses correct?
- Have I checked spellings of any words I'm unsure of?

Self-Evaluation

Make sure your description—

- ✔ focuses on an imagined place
- ✔ orients readers by presenting details in logical order
- ✔ uses vivid sensory details and appropriate figurative language
- ✔ uses first-person point of view consistently
- ✔ follows correct grammar, usage, mechanics, and spelling

Publishing/Presenting

You can use the descriptions that you and your classmates have written to create your own magazine of travel writing. Form an editorial board to select the best descriptions based on the criteria in the text; then create a cover, a table of contents, and an introduction for your collection, and make it available for others to read.

Proofreading Tip

For proofreading symbols, see pages 98 and 411. Use the spelling checker and grammar checker features on the computer to catch and correct errors.

Journal Writing: Write to Learn

Reflect on your writing process experience. Answer these questions in your journal: What do you like best about your description? What was the hardest part of writing it? What did you learn in your writing conference? What new things have you learned as a writer?

Descriptive Writing

Assess

Evaluation Rubric

Use the following questions to evaluate your students' finished writing.

- Does the writing suggest a mood?
- Can a reader picture the place?
- Is the writing focused in one place?

See also *Writing Assessment & Evaluation Rubrics* for further help with evaluating student writing.

Journal Writing Tip

Reflecting Explain that by answering these questions thoughtfully, students can improve their writing.

Reteaching

Composition Reteaching, p. 26

Enrichment

Composition Enrichment, p. 26

Close

List these words on the board: *plant, game, machine, person, music, art, sport.* Have students think of as many nouns as they can that are specific examples of these words.

Listening and Speaking

Listening to Descriptions

Have students read or reread their favorite works to find descriptions they especially appreciate. Then set aside time in class for students to read a paragraph or two aloud. Encourage readers to try to use their voices effectively to create the mood. Have listeners visualize the place and think about the mood and how the details support the mood. Can they tell how the details are organized (for example, spatially, chronologically)? Can they picture and describe the place in their own words?

About the Author

Mary Stewart was born in Sunderland, England. During her childhood, she traveled widely with her father, a clergyman. Before beginning her professional writing career, she taught at Durham University in England. Stewart has written almost 20 novels. In *The Crystal Cave, The Hollow Hills,* and *The Last Enchantment,* Stewart tells stories about Arthur and Merlin.

Focus

Lesson Overview

Objective

- To examine how a professional writer uses descriptive language and conventions of writing to create a vivid scene

Skills

- predicting; connecting; summarizing; visualizing

Critical Thinking

- evaluating; interpreting; predicting; drawing conclusions

Listening and Speaking

- discussing; evaluating; questioning; making personal connections

Bellringer

Daily Language Activity

When students enter the classroom, have this assignment on the board: *List any details you know about Merlin or other magicians from books or films.*

See also  *Daily Language Practice*

Motivating Activity

Discuss students' responses to the Bellringer activity. Tell students that the passage they will be reading tells about the magician Merlin when he was a young boy. Ask students to form impressions of Merlin as they read.

Literature Model

from

by Mary Stewart

In The Crystal Cave, *Mary Stewart vividly describes the world of King Arthur's sixth-century England through the eyes of the magician Merlin. She calls these imaginative stories "somewhere between legend and truth and fairy tale and known history." As you read, pay special attention to Stewart's effective use of descriptive language. Then try the activities in Linking Writing and Literature on page 172.*

Resource Manager

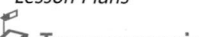

Planning Resources

- *Lesson Plans*

Transparencies

- *Bellringer*
- *Daily Language Practice*
- *Fine Art* 13–18

Other Print Resources

- *Listening and Speaking Activities,* pp. 1, 2, 19, 21
- *Thinking and Study Skills,* pp. 3, 10, 19
- *Writing Assessment and Evaluation Rubrics*

Web Sites

- *writerschoice.glencoe.com*
- *lit.glencoe.com*

Literature Model

This was bigger than had appeared from outside. Only a couple of paces inside the archway—and my paces were very short—the cave opened out into a seemingly vast chamber whose top was lost in shadow. It was dark, but—though at first I neither noticed this nor looked for its cause—with some source of extra light that gave a vague illumination, showing the floor smooth and clear of obstacles. I made my way slowly forward, straining my eyes, with deep inside me the beginning of that surge of excitement that caves have always started in me. Some men experience this with water; some, I know, on high places; some create fire for the same pleasure: with me it has always been the depths of the forest, or the depths of the earth. Now, I know why; but then, I only knew that I was a boy who had found somewhere new, something he could perhaps make his own in a world where he owned nothing.

Next moment I stopped short, brought up by a shock which spilled the excitement through my bowels like water. Something had moved in the murk, just to my right.

I froze still, straining my eyes to see. There was no movement. I held my breath, listening. There was no sound. I flared my nostrils, testing the air cautiously round me. There was no smell, animal or human; the cave smelt, I thought, of smoke and damp rock and the earth itself, and of a queer musty scent I couldn't identify. I knew, without putting it into words, that had there been any other creature near me the air would have felt different, less empty. There was no one there.

I tried a word, softly, in Welsh. "Greetings." The whisper came straight back at me in an echo so quick that I knew I was very near the wall of the cave, then it lost itself, hissing, in the roof.

There was movement there—at first, I thought, only an intensifying of the echoed whisper, then the rustling grew and grew like the rustling of a woman's dress, or a curtain stirring in the draft. Something went past my cheek, with a shrill, bloodless cry just on the edge of sound. Another followed, and after them flake after flake of shrill shadow, pouring down from the roof like leaves down a stream of wind, or fish down a fall. It was the bats, disturbed from their lodging in the top of the cave, streaming out now into the daylight valley. They would be pouring out of the low archway like a plume of smoke.

Something went past my cheek, with a shrill, bloodless cry just on the edge of sound.

I stood quite still, wondering if it was these that had made the curious musty smell. I thought I could smell them as they passed, but it wasn't the same. I had no fear that they would touch me; in darkness or light, whatever their speed, bats will touch nothing. They are so much creatures of the air, I believe, that as the air parts in front of an obstacle the bat is swept aside with it, like a petal carried downstream. They poured past, a shrill tide of them between me and the wall. Childlike, to see what the stream would do—how it would divert itself—I took a step nearer to the wall. Nothing touched me. The stream divided

Teach

Literary Element

Narrator After they read the first few paragraphs, ask students what they have learned so far about the narrator. *(The narrator is the main character. He has a deep love of the forest and of caves. He is looking back on a time when he was younger. He is remembering the time when he was feeling his way through a cave that had many bats in it.)*

Critical Thinking

Evaluate Ask students: "Do you think Stewart has done a good job so far of describing the cave? Why or why not?" *(Sample response: The description is effective because it is full of images that appeal to the senses, such as the smell of smoke and damp rock, the rustling sound, and the touch of a hand on metal.)*

Active Reading Strategies

Predict

Explain to students that to *predict* means to make an educated guess about what will happen next in a story. Offer these tips for predicting.

- Use the details in a selection as well as your own knowledge and experience to make predictions.
- Revise your predictions as you read.
- Check your predictions, but don't worry if you're not always right. Part of the fun of reading is being surprised.

Practice After students read this page, have them make a prediction about what will happen to the narrator. They might predict whom or what the narrator will meet up with in the cave. They might also predict if or how he will get out. Encourage students to revise or confirm their predictions as they read on.

Teach

Active Reading Strategies

Connect Ask students: "How would you feel if you were in this cave?" Then ask students whether they think their own experiences, gender, or age influence how well they can identify with this situation or this setting.

Literary Elements

Mood Tell students that *mood* is the feeling or atmosphere an author creates. Ask: "What mood does Mary Stewart create in this selection?" *(The author creates a quiet and suspenseful mood. The reader expects that something will happen, and it could be sinister.)* Then ask: "What details contribute to this mood?" *(Sample response: the murky light, the echo, the rustling that grows louder, the "bloodless cry" of the bats, and the "musty smell.")*

and poured on, the shrill air brushing both my cheeks. It was as if I did not exist. But at the same moment when I moved, the creature that I had seen moved, too. Then my outstretched hand met, not rock, but metal, and I knew what the creature was. It was my own reflection.

Hanging against the wall was a sheet of metal, burnished[1] to a dull sheen. This, then, was the source of the diffused[2] light within the cave; the mirror's silky surface caught, obliquely,[3] the light from the cave's mouth, and sent it on into the darkness. I could see myself moving in it like a ghost, as I recoiled[4] and let fall the hand which had leapt to the knife at my hip.

I grinned, and the mirror flashed a sudden smile that changed the picture completely and at once . . .

Behind me the flow of bats had ceased, and the cave was still. Reassured, I stayed where I was, studying myself with interest in the mirror. My mother had had one once, an antique from Egypt, but then, deeming such things to be vanity, she had locked it away. Of course I had often seen my face reflected in water, but never my body mirrored, till now. I saw a dark boy, wary, all eyes with curiosity, nerves, and excitement. In that light my eyes looked quite black; my hair was black, too, thick and clean, but worse cut and groomed than my pony's; my tunic and sandals were a disgrace. I grinned, and the mirror flashed a sudden smile that changed the picture completely and at once, from a sullen young animal poised to run or fight, to something quick and gentle and approachable; something, I knew even then, that few people had ever seen.

Then it vanished, and the wary animal was back, as I leaned forward to run a hand over the metal. It was cold and smooth and freshly burnished. Whoever had hung it—and he must be the same person who used the cup of horn[5] outside—had either been here very recently, or he still lived here, and might come back at any moment to find me.

I was not particularly frightened. I had pricked to caution when I saw the cup, but one learns very young to take care of oneself, and the times I had been brought up in were peaceful enough, at any rate in our valley; but there are always wild men and rough men and the lawless and vagabonds to be reckoned with, and any boy who likes his own company, as I did, must be prepared to defend his skin. I was wiry, and strong for my age, and I had my dagger. That I was barely seven years old never entered my head; I was Merlin, and, bastard or not, the King's grandson. I went on exploring.

The next thing I found, a pace along the wall, was a box, and on top of it shapes which my hands identified immediately as flint and iron and tinderbox,[6] and a big, roughly made candle of what smelled like

1 **burnished** (bur′ nisht) polished
2 **diffused** (di fūsd′) spread out in every direction
3 **obliquely** (ə blēk′ lē) indirectly
4 **recoiled** (ri koild′) fell back
5 **cup of horn** a cup made from an animal's horn
6 **tinderbox** (tin′ dər boks′) a metal box holding the materials to make a fire

Writing in the Real World

Genre and Style

The Crystal Cave is a historical novel; that is, it combines historical fact with narrative fiction. The novel is the first part of a trilogy based on the legend of King Arthur. Narrated from Merlin's first-person point of view, the story reveals the character's thoughts, emotions, and actions as a young boy. Highly descriptive passages help the reader see the actions through Merlin's eyes. Drawn into the story, the reader vicariously participates in Merlin's experiences.

sheep's tallow.[7] Beside these objects lay a shape which—incredulously and inch by inch—I identified as the skull of a horned sheep. There were nails driven into the top of the box here and there, apparently holding down fragments of leather. But when I felt these, carefully, I found in the withered leather frameworks of delicate bone; they were dead bats, stretched and nailed on the wood.

This was a treasure cave indeed. No find of gold or weapons could have excited me more. Full of curiosity, I reached for the tinderbox.

Then I heard him coming back.

My first thought was that he must have seen my pony, then I realized he was coming from further up the hill. I could hear the rattling and scaling of small stones as he came down the scree[8] above the cave. One of them splashed into the spring outside, and then it was too late. I heard him jump down on the flat grass beside the water.

It was time for the ring-dove again; the falcon was forgotten.[9] I ran deeper into the cave. As he swept aside the boughs[10] that

---

7 **tallow** (tal' ō) animal fat used to make candles

8 **scree** (skrē) a slope covered with rock fragments

9 **It was time for the ring-dove again; the falcon was forgotten.** Unlike the ferocious falcon, the ring-dove was a bird that kept quiet and knew when to run away. While Young Merlin was often called "falcon," one character had told him that he was still a ring-dove.

10 **boughs** (bouz) tree branches

John James Audubon (1785–1851), *Labrador Falcon*

6+1 Trait® Writing

Conventions Point out to students the following sentence from the last paragraph on this page: "It was time for the ring-dove again; the falcon was forgotten." Ask students to identify the form of punctuation used in the middle of this sentence and to explain its purpose. *(This sentence contains a semicolon. Its purpose is to join two related sentences together to create one compound sentence.)*

Critical Thinking

Predict At the end of this page, ask students whether their initial predications have proved accurate. Then have students predict what will happen next. *(Sample response: The man will soon encounter Merlin and question him about his presence in the cave.)* Encourage students to revise or confirm their predictions as they read on.

Viewing the Art

John James Audubon (1785–1851),
Labrador Falcon

Tell students that *Labrador Falcon* is one of the many hundreds of bird illustrations completed by self-taught artist and naturalist John James Audubon. Born in the West Indies and raised in France, Audubon came to the United States when he was eighteen years old. He pursued his interest in ornithology, the study of birds, and began making detailed illustrations of the birds he observed in the North American wilderness. When a British engraver helped him publish his illustrations in a series of volumes called *The Birds of America,* Audubon's work became famous. Although the illustrations are sometimes criticized for being scientifically inaccurate, they are regarded as excellent works of art.

Teach

Active Reading Strategies

Summarize Have students briefly retell the story so far. *(Seven-year-old Merlin has entered a deep, dark cave alone. He has startled the bats and has discovered a mirror, a tinderbox, and other objects that show that the cave is inhabited. He has also heard a man approaching and then entering the cave. Merlin has slithered into a tiny hiding place. It appears that the man is on the verge of discovering him.)*

Active Reading Strategies

Visualize Ask students to describe the scene on this page. Where is the narrator? What does the cave look like? What does he see? *(The narrator is lying on a ledge in a small, rounded cave with jagged walls. Through the small opening that leads to the larger cave, he sees a blindingly bright, red and gold flashing light.)*

darkened the entrance, the light grew momentarily, enough to show me my way. At the back of the cave was a slope and jut of rock, and, at twice my height, a widish ledge. A quick flash of sunlight from the mirror caught a wedge of shadow in the rock above the ledge, big enough to hide me. Soundless in my scuffed sandals, I swarmed on to the ledge, and crammed my body into that wedge of shadow, to find it was in fact a gap in the rock, giving apparently on to another, smaller cave. I slithered in through the gap like an otter into the river-bank.

It seemed that he had heard nothing. The light was cut off again as the boughs sprang back into place behind him, and he came into the cave. It was a man's tread, measured and slow.

If I had thought about it at all, I suppose I would have assumed that the cave would be uninhabited at least until sunset, that whoever owned the place would be away hunting, or about his other business, and would return only at nightfall. There was no point in wasting candles when the sun was blazing outside. Perhaps he was here now only to bring home his kill, and he would go again and leave me the chance to get out. I hoped he would not see my pony tethered[11] in the hawthorn brake.[12]

Then I heard him moving, with the sure tread of someone who knows his way blindfold, towards the candle and the tinderbox.

Even now I had no room for apprehension,[13] no room, indeed, for any but the one thought or sensation—the extreme discomfort of the cave into which I had crawled. It was apparently small, not much bigger than the large round vats they use for dyeing, and much the same shape. Floor, wall and ceiling hugged me round in a continuous curve. It was like being inside a large globe; moreover, a globe studded with nails, or with its inner surface stuck all over with small pieces of jagged stone. There seemed no inch of surface not bristling like a bed of strewn flints, and it was only my light weight, I think, that saved me from being cut, as I quested about blindly to find some clear space to lie on. I found a place smoother than the rest and curled there, as small as I could, watching the faintly defined opening, and inching my dagger silently from its sheath into my hand.

Light poured and flashed, crimson, golden, white, red, intolerable into my cave.

I heard the quick hiss and chime of flint and iron, and then the flare of light, intense in the darkness, as the tinder caught hold. Then the steady, waxing[14] glow as he lit the candle.

Or rather, it should have been the slow-growing beam of a candle flame that I saw, but instead there was a flash, a sparkle, a conflagration[15] as if a whole pitch-soaked beacon was roaring up in flames. Light poured and flashed, crimson, golden, white, red, intolerable into my cave. I winced back from it, frightened now, heedless of pain and cut flesh as I shrank against the sharp

11 **tethered** (teth′ ərd) tied with a rope or chain
12 **brake** (brāk) a thicket
13 **apprehension** (ap′ ri hen′ shən) dread
14 **waxing** (waks′ ing) slowly growing larger
15 **conflagration** (kon′ flə grā′ shən) an enormous fire

Critical Thinking

Evaluate

Tell students that to *evaluate* means to make a judgment or form an opinion about something they have read. Sometimes readers might evaluate a character or a theme. Other times readers might evaluate the author's craft. Model evaluating by saying: "Stewart does a great job of describing the boy, his actions, and the setting. When she writes 'I slithered in through the gap like an otter into the river-bank,' the simile really helps me understand what it must have been like to slip through that opening."

Practice Ask students to evaluate the descriptive writing in the paragraph in the second column that begins with the words "I heard the quick hiss." *(Sample response: Although the paragraph is short, it is highly descriptive and well written. There are images that appeal to both the sense of sound and the sense of sight.)*

walls. The whole globe where I lay seemed to be full of flame.

It was indeed a globe, a round chamber floored, roofed, lined with crystals. They were fine as glass, and smooth as glass, but clearer than any glass I had ever seen, brilliant as diamonds. This, in fact, to my childish mind, was what they first seemed to be. I was in a globe lined with diamonds, a million burning diamonds, each face of each gem wincing with the light, shooting it to and fro, diamond to diamond and back again, with rainbows and rivers and bursting stars and a shape like a crimson dragon clawing up the wall, while below it a girl's face swam faintly with closed eyes, and the light drove right into my body as if it would break me open.

I shut my eyes. When I opened them again I saw that the golden light had shrunk and was concentrated on one part of the wall no bigger than my head, and from this, empty of visions, rayed the broken, brilliant beams.

There was silence from the cave below. He had not stirred. I had not even heard the rustle of his clothes.

Then the light moved. The flashing disc began to slide, slowly, across the crystal wall. I was shaking. I huddled closer to the sharp stones, trying to escape it. There was nowhere to go. It advanced slowly round the curve. It touched my shoulder, my head, and I ducked, cringing. The shadow of my movement rushed across the globe, like a wind-eddy[16] over a pool.

The light stopped, retreated, fixed glittering in its place. Then it went out. But the glow of the candle, strangely, remained; an ordinary steady yellow glow beyond the gap in the wall of my refuge.

"Come out." The man's voice, not loud, not raised with shouted orders like my grandfather's, was clear and brief with all the mystery of command. It never occurred to me to disobey. I crept forward over the sharp crystals, and through the gap. Then I slowly pulled myself upright on the ledge, my back against the wall of the outer cave, the dagger ready in my right hand, and looked down.

The light stopped, retreated, fixed glittering in its place. Then it went out.

He stood between me and the candle, a hugely tall figure (or so it seemed to me) in a long robe of some brown homespun stuff. The candle made a nimbus[17] of his hair, which seemed to be grey, and he was bearded. I could not see his expression, and his right hand was hidden in the folds of his robe.

I waited, poised warily.

He spoke again, in the same tone. "Put up your dagger and come down."

"When I see your right hand," I said.

He showed it, palm up. It was empty. He said gravely: "I am unarmed."

"Then stand out of my way," I said, and jumped. The cave was wide, and he was standing to one side of it. My leap carried me three or four paces down the cave, and I was past him and near the entrance before he could have moved more than a step. But in fact he never moved at all. As I reached

16 **wind-eddy** (wind ed' ē) a current of wind
17 **nimbus** (nim' bəs) a bright cloud or aura surrounding a person or object

Descriptive Writing

Critical Thinking

Interpret Ask students how they interpret the vision that Merlin has once the light flashes into the crystal globe where he's hiding. What do they think the dragon might represent? What might the girl's face represent? *(Students may say that the vision foreshadows the magical powers Merlin will harness in the future. They may interpret the dragon as a symbol of mystical power and the girl as a figure who will be important to him at some point in his life.)*

Critical Thinking

Draw Conclusions Ask students to tell what they have learned about Merlin from the story up to this page. Have them use that information to draw a conclusion about him. *(Students may select details such as what Merlin says and does upon meeting the man to draw the conclusion that Merlin is exceptionally brave and confident for a seven-year-old boy.)*

6+1 Trait® Writing

Conventions

Remind students that writers follow special rules or **conventions** of writing that apply to grammar, usage, spelling, and also punctuation. For example, a pair of quotation marks should appear at the beginning and end of a sentence or set of sentences to let a reader know when a character begins speaking and when a character stops speaking. Point out that the usual closing punctuation mark, such as a period or exclamation point, should be placed on the inside of the last set of quotation marks.

Practice Have students locate dialogue within the text that follow this rule. Then tell them to think of a couple characters—people who exist in real life or only in their imagination—and to write three or four sentences of dialogue between them. Remind students to correctly use quotation marks.

For more information about the 6+1 Trait® model, see the **Writing and Research Handbook,** pages 947–949.

Teach

Critical Thinking

Interpret Ask students: "What does the man's laughter seem to say about him and his intentions?" *(Sample response: The man's laughter indicates that he intends no harm and is amused by Merlin.)*

Peter Paul Rubens (1577–1640), *Portrait of an Old Man*

the mouth of the cave and swept aside the hanging branches I heard him laughing.

The sound brought me up short. I turned.

From here, in the light which now filled the cave, I saw him clearly. He was old, with grey hair thinning on top and hanging lank over his ears, and a straight growth of grey beard, roughly trimmed. His hands were calloused and grained with dirt, but had been fine, with long fingers. Now the

Viewing the Art

Peter Paul Rubens (1577–1640),
Portrait of an Old Man

Tell students that Flemish painter Peter Paul Rubens was a leading artist of the European Renaissance. He was celebrated for his work and accepted into the highest intellectual and social circles of his day. Known for his productivity and versatility, his masterpieces include portraits, landscapes, and religious and mythological paintings. Ask students for their reaction to "Portrait of an Old Man." Encourage them to discuss how the shape, lines, color, and texture of the painting contributes to their understanding and appreciation of it.

old man's veins crawled and knotted on them, distended[18] like worms. But it was his face which held me; it was thin, cavernous almost as a skull, with a high domed forehead and bushy grey brows which came down jutting over eyes where I could see no trace of age at all. These were closely set, large, and of a curiously clear and swimming grey. His nose was a thin beak; his mouth, lipless now, stretched wide with his laughter over astonishingly good teeth.

"Come back. There's no need to be afraid."

"I'm not afraid." I dropped the boughs back into place, and not without bravado[19] walked towards him. I stopped a few paces away. "Why should I be afraid of you? Do you know who I am?"

"Come back. There's no need to be afraid."

He regarded me for a moment, seeming to muse. "Let me see you. Dark hair, dark eyes, the body of a dancer and the manners of a young wolf . . . or should I say a young falcon?"

My dagger sank to my side. "Then you do know me?"

"Shall I say I knew you would come some day, and today I knew there was someone here. What do you think brought me back so early?"

---

18 **distended** (dis tend' əd) swollen
19 **bravado** (brə vä' dō) pretended confidence or courage

Critical Thinking

Predict Ask students: "Who might this old man be, and what do you think will happen next?" *(This old man is someone connected with Merlin's destiny. He may help in some way to guide Merlin, to teach him skills, or to send him along a certain path.)*

Additional Resources

- *Fine Art Transparencies* 13–18
- *Listening and Speaking Activities,* pp. 1, 2, 19, 21
- *Thinking and Study Skills,* pp. 3, 10, 19

Compare and Contrast

Comparing and Contrasting Styles

Tell students that comparing and contrasting an author's style can help them understand their own preferences in literature. Remind students that many things contribute to an author's style. Word choice, sentence structure, and voice are all parts of an author's style. The way an author reveals character and uses dialogue and description can be part of his or her style, as well as the pace at which the author moves the action forward. Ask students to compare Amy Tan's style in the excerpt from *The Kitchen God's Wife* (pp. 112–118) with Mary Stewart's style in this excerpt.

Practice Have students write two or more paragraphs comparing and contrasting the writers' styles. Suggest that students choose two or three elements of style to compare. For example, they might compare the kinds of descriptive details or the level of language the authors use. Suggest that students list and organize their ideas before they begin to draft their essay.

Linking Writing and Literature

Assess

Evaluation Rubrics

Talk About Reading

Possible responses to the questions:

1. Students may have had an experience in which they waited in the darkness for someone to arrive, and every sound of a leaf or footstep spooked them.
2. Stewart brings the setting to life very well by using sensory images such as those that describe the small space into which Merlin crawled: "It was like being inside a large globe; moreover, a globe studded with nails, or with its inner surface stuck all over with small pieces of jagged stone."
3. The reader should be aware that the author will briefly introduce an additional thought. The reader should pause when he or she sees a dash and then continue reading.
4. Students may say they wish to create suspense, add mystery, or use sensory details.

Write About Reading

The narrative essay should do the following:

- create a clear, effective picture of the setting
- use sensory details
- use first-person point of view
- lead up to an event

Close

Divide the class into groups of three. Ask students within each group to discuss the end of the selection and describe how they think the rest of the scene in the cave might be played out. Groups can share their ideas with the rest of the class.

Linking Writing and Literature

Learning to Learn

What aspect of this selection made the greatest impression on you? The characters? The setting? The plot? Something else? Write a few notes about why this part of the selection stands out in your mind.

Talk About Reading

Form a reading circle to discuss this excerpt from *The Crystal Cave.* Assign someone to lead the discussion of each question below. Assign someone else to take notes.

1. **Connect to Your Life** Even if you haven't pulled a dagger in a dark cave, you have probably built up fear or worry about an upcoming meeting or event. Discuss experiences from your life that help you relate to Merlin's feelings in the cave.
2. **Critical Thinking: Evaluate** How well do you think the author brings the characters and setting to life? Give details from the story to support your judgment.
3. **6+1 Trait®: Conventions** On page 165 the author uses dashes within sentences to emphasize a thought. What should readers do when they encounter this form of punctuation? How do the dashes affect the way you read this sentence?
4. **Connect to Your Writing** What would you like to be able to do in your own writing that Mary Stewart does in hers?

Write About Reading

Narrative Essay Write like Mary Stewart. Choose a narrator and place him or her in a setting. Describe the setting by creating one overwhelming impression of it, such as dark and fearful, magical and bright, small and cramped, or warm and inviting. Use your details to lead up to one key event. To help you get started, you might want to think about your narrator and your setting and jot down lists of adjectives that apply to each.

Focus on Conventions As you write, pay special attention to the rules of usage, grammar, spelling, and mechanics. Try to write at least one sentence that includes dashes to emphasize a thought and one sentence that uses a semicolon to connect two closely related ideas.

For more information on conventions and the 6+1 Trait® model, see **Writing and Research Handbook,** pages 947–948.

UNIT 3 Review

Reflecting on the Unit: Summarize What You Learned

Focus on the following questions to help summarize what you learned in this unit.

1. What are the important elements of a well-written descriptive paragraph?
2. In what ways does word choice affect the quality of descriptive writing?
3. What are the important aspects of describing an imaginary place? Of creating a convincing character?
4. What are some things to keep in mind when you analyze a fictional character?

Adding to Your Portfolio

Follow this procedure to choose selections for your portfolio. Look over the descriptive writing you have done during this unit. Select a completed piece of writing to put into your portfolio. The writing you choose should show some or all of the following:

- descriptive details that contain a strong overall impression
- precise, vivid language that has the appropriate connotations
- a well-defined mood
- attributes that convey a character's uniqueness

REFLECT ON YOUR CHOICE Attach a note to the piece you chose, explaining briefly why you chose it and what you learned from it.

SET GOALS How can you improve your writing? What skill will you focus on the next time you write?

Writing Across the Curriculum

MAKE A GEOGRAPHY CONNECTION Decide on a real country in which you'd like to situate the imaginary place you just wrote about. Choose the country because of such things as its climate and terrain, its political system, or any other factors you think are relevant. Then write a paragraph explaining some of the attributes of the country that made you think your imaginary place belongs there.

Reflecting on the Unit

You may have students respond to Reflecting on the Unit by writing a summary of what they've learned or through discussion.

Adding to Your Portfolio

Suggest that students begin the selection process by choosing a few of their favorite pieces of descriptive writing. These samples should communicate a specific mood, use descriptive details, and contain precise, vivid language. To help them narrow down possible portfolio selections, suggest that students exchange papers and use peer responses as an additional guide.

Portfolio Evaluation

If you grade the portfolio selections, you may want to award two marks—one each for content and form. Explain your assessment criteria before students make their selections.

Commend

- inventive prewriting techniques
- clear, concise writing in which the main idea, audience, and purpose are evident
- successful revisions
- work that shows a flair for language

Writing Across the Curriculum

Before students begin writing, suggest that they do some research on the geography of the country that they have chosen. Encourage students to identify a particular section of the country that will help them set the mood or create an overall impression.

ASSESSMENT OPTIONS

Tests With Answer Key & Rubrics
Unit 3 Choice A Test, p. 9
Unit 3 Choice B Test, p. 10
Unit 3 Composition Objective Test, pp. 11–12

Testmaker
Unit 3 Choice A Test
Unit 3 Choice B Test
Unit 3 Composition Objective Test

You may wish to administer one of these tests as a mastery test.

MindJogger Videoquizzes

UNIT 4

Viewing the Art

The details in the photograph help to tell a story in much the same way that narrative writers use details to relate events.

Interpret and Analyze Use the following questions for discussion:

- As you look at this photograph, what can you imagine about the people who might live behind the window?
- Imagine that you are sitting inside, looking out the window. What events might you see unfold?

Discussing the Quotation

This quotation is from "Kipling and I," an essay found in *A Puerto Rican in New York and Other Sketches* by Jesus Colon (1901–1974). In his book, Colon describes the poverty he faced as an immigrant to the United States in 1918, where he lived in a crowded tenement building without the benefit of running water or electricity and also struggled to find suitable work. Discuss the quotation with the class, and ask students why Colon might have said this.

Writing Prompt Write a brief explanation of how Colon's words, coupled with the image, can be seen to connect to the process of narrative writing.

"On hot summer nights I would sit at the window reading by the electric light from the street lamp..."

—Jesus Colon, "Kipling and I"

174

Resource Manager

Planning Resources
- *Lesson Plans*
- *Block Scheduling*

Transparencies
- *Bellringer*
- *Daily Language Practice*
- *Fine Art*
- *Two-Minute Skill Drill*
- *Writing Process*

Other Print Resources
- *Composition Enrichment*
- *Composition Practice*
- *Composition Reteaching*
- *Cooperative Learning Activities*
- *Glencoe Literature Library*
- *Grammar and Composition Handbook*
- *Grammar Workbook*
- *Listening and Speaking Activities*
- *Research Paper and Report Writing*
- *Sentence-Combining Practice*
- *Tests with Answer Key and Rubrics*
- *Thinking and Study Skills*
- *Writing Across the Curriculum*
- *Writing Assessment and Evaluation Rubrics*
- *Writing in the Real World*

UNIT 4

Narrative Writing

175

Objectives

- To develop an understanding of the elements and style of narrative writing
- To learn narrative techniques for developing conflict, creating dialogue, and revealing characters
- To write a narrative about family life

ASSESSMENT OPTIONS

Tests With Answer Key & Rubrics
Unit 4 Choice A Test, p. 13
Unit 4 Choice B Test, p. 14
Unit 4 Composition Objective Test, pp. 15–16

Testmaker
Unit 4 Choice A Test
Unit 4 Choice B Test
Unit 4 Composition Objective Test

You may wish to administer either the Unit 4 Choice A Test or the Unit 4 Choice B Test as a pretest.

Key to Ability Levels

L1 Level 1 activities are within the basic ability range of students.

L2 Level 2 activities are within the ability range of average students.

L3 Level 3 activities are more challenging activities.

 Video
- *MindJogger Videoquizzes*

 Software
- *Presentation Plus!*
- *Revising with Style*
- *Testmaker*

 Web Site
- *glencoe.com*

Focus

Lesson Overview

Objective

- To restructure information about a sports event in the form of a narrative

Skills

- researching the narrative; writing a sports narrative

Critical Thinking

- analyzing and synthesizing information; summarizing; finding a main idea

Listening and Speaking

- discussing; questioning; evaluating; presenting

Bellringer
Daily Language Activity

When students enter the classroom, have this assignment on the board: *Use sentences to answer the following questions:*

Which sports do you watch or play?

Which teams or players are your favorites?

Grammar Link to the Bellringer

Have students discuss their Bellringer sentences and then check each one for capitalization of proper nouns.

See also *Daily Language Practice*

Motivating Activity

Discuss students' responses to the Bellringer activity. Then pose these questions:

- Have you ever witnessed an athlete overcome great odds to win an event?
- Have you ever cheered as a seemingly defeated team achieved a dramatic come-from-behind victory?
- What would you emphasize about such an event in a sports story for a newspaper or a magazine?

Writing in the Real World

The mass media, such as newspapers and magazines, and the Internet, are terrific sources for narrative writing. Most sports stories focus on character and conflict—conflict between players or between teams, or an individual's struggle to overcome physical limitations. The following is an excerpt from a narrative article about triathlete Jim MacLaren. It was written by Lisa Twyman Bessone, a writer for *Sports Illustrated.*

Salute to an Amazing Ironman

By Lisa Twyman Bessone

In the marathon leg of the . . . Ironman Triathlon in Hawaii, Jim MacLaren, a 27-year-old professional triathlete and a former linebacker for Yale, fell in step with 41-year-old Ken Mitchell, who played the same position for the Atlanta Falcons from 1972 to '75. Given the demands of the race (a 2.4-mile swim, a marathon run and a 112-mile bike ride), conversation had to be minimal, but the two did talk a bit about Mitchell's 11 knee operations, the result of his football career. After about a mile MacLaren decided to pull ahead. "I'm saying a little prayer for you, Jimmy," Mitchell called out as he dropped farther and farther behind. MacLaren, you see, was running with a prosthesis on his left leg.

. . . The challenges in that [Ironman] event are "enormous," MacLaren says. "To do well, you need some sense of humor and some sense of your own mortality." MacLaren qualifies on both counts—especially the latter. MacLaren, who is also an actor, lost his leg in a traffic accident on Oct. 20, 1985. He was riding his motorcycle down Fifth Avenue in New York City. . . . A westbound city bus weighing 40,000 pounds roared into the intersection and hit MacLaren. According to the police report, the bus threw MacLaren, who was still at his football weight of 290 pounds, 89 feet.

The force of the impact sent MacLaren's helmet flying. His unprotected head hit the pavement first, and his skull split open across the forehead. A lung was punctured, his spleen was ruptured, his kidneys were lacerated, and all his ribs were broken. He was bleeding profusely, both externally and internally. His left leg, which the bus had mashed into the engine of his bike, was burned and crushed.

MacLaren was pronounced dead on arrival at Bellevue Hospital, but doctors were able to restart his heart—twice. They then had to restrain him when he tried to get off the operating table. . . .

MacLaren awoke from a coma six days later to the sound

Resource Manager

Planning Resources

- *Lesson Plans*

Transparencies

- *Bellringer*
- *Daily Language Practice*
- *Writing Process* 10, 18–22

Other Print Resources

- *Cooperative Learning Activities,* pp. 17–20
- *Thinking and Study Skills,* pp. 6–8, 23
- *Writing Assessment and Evaluation Rubrics*
- *Writing in the Real World,* pp. 13–16

of a respirator pumping air into his lungs. His left leg had been amputated just below the knee. . . . "My leg was gone," he says, "but I felt extremely lucky to be around." . . .

About the only person who isn't especially impressed with MacLaren is MacLaren himself. But even he admits that the '89 Ironman was a high note in his career.

"You know, we all have our own dramas in life," MacLaren adds. "Not everyone has to do a triathlon to push themselves. Maybe your challenge is simply getting along with your father. Everything is relative. I don't want to sound like I have all the answers; I just believe that there are no limits on any of us."

A Writer's Process

Prewriting

Finding and Researching the Narrative

While watching a triathlon, Lisa Bessone knew she'd found a great story. She recalls, "A couple of my friends were running. Along comes this guy running with a prosthesis [artificial leg] and doing incredibly well. We all remarked on how amazing it was. A small feature appeared in the paper the next day about this football player, Jim MacLaren, who had lost his leg in a motorcycle accident and was now running triathlons in excellent times." So Bessone's idea for the nonfiction narrative came from her observation of MacLaren running in the triathlon and from reading the newspaper feature story about him later.

Once she got the idea for the narrative, Bessone was ready to do the research. Armed with a tape recorder, she flew to New England to interview Jim MacLaren. Before an interview Bessone always writes down questions. She calls her notes "touchstones to remind myself of the direction I want to go. Usually one question will spark a half-hour discussion."

At first, MacLaren didn't want to talk about the injury that destroyed his leg and nearly took his life. Bessone was willing to wait. "As a sportswriter, you learn the art of hanging out. The more people know you, the more they trust you. After a while Jim told me about the accident. . . . It was obviously traumatic that he'd lost his leg, but most of the other aspects of his story were really upbeat."

In addition to interviewing MacLaren, his mother, and several of his friends, Bessone sought statistics from the Triathlon Federation: "You need that kind of stuff to give your story a factual basis." Even as she was collecting information, Bessone considered how best to arrange those crucial elements of character and conflict into a compelling narrative.

Teach

Reading Media

Have students preview the title and focus of the Media Connection on page 176. Discuss the purpose of a sports narrative, pointing out that every narrative tries to communicate to an audience how an athlete felt, acted, or looked during a particular game or event. The perspective of a sports narrative may focus on the special abilities of the athlete; the relationship of the athlete with his or her team members, or with opponents; or the performance of the athlete during a specific moment of a contest. Have students read the article.

Discussion Prompts

- In what ways can people get ideas for sports stories?
- What kind of elements do sports writers use to write a profile of an athlete? How might sports writers use plot, character, conflict, and setting to make an athlete's story come alive?
- If you were interviewing an athlete, what kinds of questions would you ask? What would you do if the athlete gave an unexpected response?
- What are some techniques you can use to organize a narrative chronologically? What other methods of organization might a writer use?

Cultural Connections

Sports Around the World

Among many families and within many communities, sports are a major interest. Ask students if sports are a part of their lives. Do they often participate in or watch sporting events? According to Bessone, "Sports are about games, but they can be a metaphor for so much more." Is this statement true in students' homes or communities? Why are certain sports more popular in some countries than others?

Teach

Discussion Prompts

- Do you think action photos should be included to help convey the excitement of a sporting event? Or do you like more personal photos? Why?
- If you were writing or editing this story, what photographs or other visuals would you use to communicate important elements of the story? What headings and subheadings would you use? What captions for photos and graphics would you write? L2

Additional Resources

 *Writing Process Transparencies* 10, 18–22

 *Writing in the Real World,* pp. 13–16

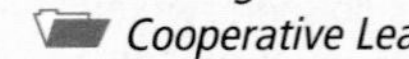 *Cooperative Learning Activities*

Thinking and Study Skills, pp. 6–8, 23

Drafting

Getting the Story Down

To select the information for her draft, Lisa Bessone listened to her tapes. She noted all the things she wanted to include in the narrative.

The next step was organizing the material. Bessone notes that a sportswriter usually has some idea of the organization she's going to use. "That's like a road map you're following the whole time," she says. Bessone's "road map" for this narrative was MacLaren's progression from his accident and rehabilitation to competing in races.

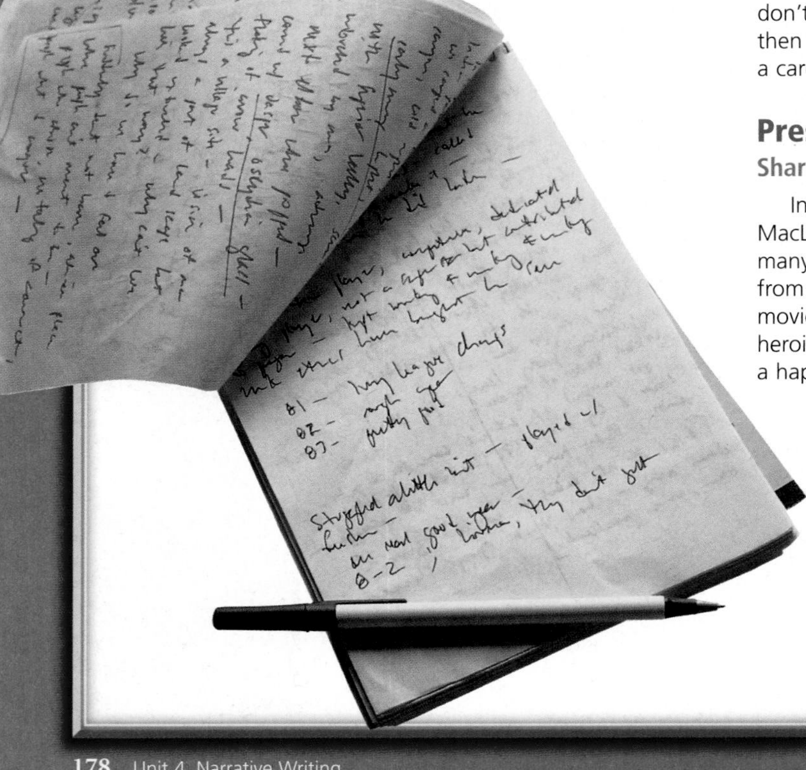

Revising/Editing

Making Necessary Changes

After Bessone had completed her draft, MacLaren ran the Ironman Triathlon. At this triathlon, held annually in Hawaii, MacLaren bested the previous amputee record by almost two hours. Bessone decided to revise her original draft to include the event.

When MacLaren told her about an incident that occurred during the marathon leg of the triathlon, Bessone decided to use his anecdote in her opening paragraph. This new lead sets a scene that arouses curiosity, creates drama, and then reels the reader in with the last sentence. Bessone comments, "At first you don't know why you're reading; then you find out. It's like holding a card back."

Presenting

Sharing with the World

In response to her article about MacLaren, Bessone says she got many telephone calls, including one from someone who wanted to do a movie about Jim MacLaren. "He's a heroic figure," says Bessone. "It was a happy story."

Civic Literacy

Using Community Resources

Many writers use query letters to interest editors in their ideas. In the query letter, the writer not only outlines his or her idea for a story, but also uses persuasive techniques to convince the editor that the finished story will be worth publishing. Some students may want to send a query letter to a local magazine editor after they come up with an idea for a sports story.

Examining Writing in the Real World

Analyzing the Media Connection

Discuss these questions about the article on pages 176–177.

1. What does Lisa Bessone reveal about Jim MacLaren in the excerpt?
2. What is the conflict in the story?
3. How does Bessone use concrete details to establish the enormity of MacLaren's accident?
4. Why do you think Bessone began her article with a conversation between MacLaren and Ken Mitchell? What does the anecdote reveal about MacLaren as a character? About the conflict?
5. How does Bessone reel the reader in with the last sentence in her opening paragraph?

Analyzing a Writer's Process

Discuss these questions about Lisa Bessone's writing process.

1. What prompted Lisa Bessone to write a story about Jim MacLaren?
2. How did Bessone research her article?
3. What did Bessone use as her "road map" for the story?
4. What influenced Bessone to revise her article?
5. How did Bessone arrange her character and conflict to create a compelling narrative?

GrammarLink

Capitalize proper nouns.

In her writing, Lisa Bessone uses many proper nouns naming athletes, places, and teams. Correct the following sentences, capitalizing proper nouns as necessary.

1. The ironman triathlon, the grandfather of all triathlons, is held annually in hawaii.
2. The contestants run more than twenty-six miles after bicycling on hot lava flats and swimming miles in the pacific.
3. Famous marathons are held each year in new york city and boston, massachusetts.
4. The marine corps marathon in washington, d.c., passes the lincoln memorial and the capitol.
5. Patrick Ewing of the new york knicks helped the United States win the Olympic basketball gold medal in 1992.

See Lesson 20.2, pages 713–719.

Narrative Writing

Assess

Analyzing the Media Connection

1. MacLaren is a professional triathlete; runs with a prosthesis due to a motorcycle accident; works as an actor; and possesses a courageous, positive spirit.
2. competing in a rigorous triathlon with a serious disability
3. Bessone gives the exact date and location of the accident, the weight of the bus, MacLaren's weight, and the nature and location of his injuries.
4. Bessone wanted to present MacLaren first as a strong, competitive athlete; the fact that he runs with a prosthesis comes as a surprise. He doesn't consider himself a victim—he is a serious competitor despite his disability.
5. After describing MacLaren's sympathy for another athlete's knee operations, Bessone surprises the reader with MacLaren's handicap.

Analyzing a Writer's Process

1. Bessone saw MacLaren running in a triathlon and later read a newspaper feature story about him.
2. Bessone interviewed MacLaren, his mother, and several of his friends; she also got statistics from the Triathlon Federation.
3. MacLaren's progression from his accident and rehabilitation to competing in races
4. She wanted to include incidents from the Ironman Triathlon that MacLaren competed in after Bessone wrote her first draft.
5. Bessone first presents the character's strength and compassion; then she lets the reader know about his handicap.

Reteaching

Have students watch a sporting event and identify the characters and conflict for a possible sports narrative.

GrammarLink

Answers

1. Ironman Triathlon; Hawaii
2. Pacific
3. New York City; Boston, Massachusetts
4. Marine Corps Marathon; Washington, D.C.; Lincoln Memorial; Capitol
5. New York Knicks

Close

Have students discuss how to use the Media Connection to help write a narrative about a local athlete.

Closing Note

For models of good sports writing, refer students to *Best Sports Stories* (published annually by The Sporting News Publishing Co.) and *Press Box: Red Smith's Favorite Sports Stories* (1976, Norton).

Focus

Lesson Overview

Objectives

- To identify three basic elements of a good narrative
- To understand how successful narratives involve realistic characters and situations brought to life with specific details
- To learn how to plot the events in a narrative in chronological order

Skills

- developing characters, setting, and plot; establishing a sequence of events; generating ideas

Critical Thinking

- patterning; identifying; generating ideas

Listening and Speaking

- note taking; discussing; questioning

Bellringer

Daily Language Activity

When students enter the classroom, have this assignment on the board: *Recall a time in your life when you faced a challenge, overcame an obstacle, or confronted a fear. Write a brief summary of your story.*

Grammar Link to the Bellringer

Ask students to identify any adverbs they used or those they might use if they developed their story further. Ask how adverbs might help make their writing more precise or help define the story's mood.

See also  *Daily Language Practice*

Motivating Activity

Discuss students' responses to the Bellringer activity. Ask students what elements the stories have in common. Help students see that every story has characters, setting, and plot—the basic elements of all stories, or narratives.

LESSON 4.1

Writing Simple Narratives

Narrative Writing

A narrative is a story that relates a sequence of events. The story may be true (nonfiction) or imagined (fiction). A successful narrative involves realistic characters and situations brought to life with specific details. In the following narrative, Jamaica Kincaid tells the true story of how her mother came to live on the island of Antigua.

Literature Model

When my mother, at sixteen, after quarreling with her father, left his house on Dominica and came to Antigua, she packed all her things in an enormous wooden trunk that she had bought in Roseau for almost six shillings. She painted the trunk yellow and green outside, and she lined the inside with wallpaper that had a cream background with pink roses printed all over it. Two days after she left her father's house, she boarded a boat and sailed for Antigua. It was a small boat, and the trip would have taken a day and a half ordinarily, but a hurricane blew up and the boat was lost at sea for almost five days. By the time it got to Antigua, the boat was practically in splinters, and though two or three of the passengers were lost overboard, along with some of the cargo, my mother and her trunk were safe.

Jamaica Kincaid, "The Circling Hand"

Notice that the story has a beginning—the departure from Dominica; a middle—the journey; and an end—the safe arrival in Antigua.

What vivid images help you "see" Kincaid's story?

Understand the Basics of Narrative

All narratives contain characters, setting, and plot. Characters are the individuals in a story. In the narrative above, the characters include Kincaid's mother and grandfather. Setting establishes a story's time and place, such as the boat bound for Antigua. Finally, the events that occur in a story make up its plot.

Narratives may contain a conflict, or a struggle that triggers the action. The conflict in Kincaid's story relates to the mother and the hurricane.

Resource Manager

Planning Resources

- *Lesson Plans*

Transparencies

- *Bellringer*
- *Daily Language Practice*
- *Fine Art* 19–24
- *Two-Minute Skill Drill*
- *Writing Process* 10, 18–22

Other Print Resources

- *Composition Enrichment*, p. 27
- *Composition Practice*, p. 27
- *Composition Reteaching*, p. 27
- *Cooperative Learning Activities*, pp. 17–20
- *Listening and Speaking Activities*, pp. 13, 18, 20, 21
- *Sentence-Combining Practice*, pp. 30–31
- *Thinking and Study Skills*, pp. 13, 21
- *Writing Across the Curriculum*
- *Writing Assessment and Evaluation Rubrics*

Generate Ideas for Writing

The best narratives contain believable characters and situations. Therefore, it's a good rule of thumb to base the narratives you write on what you know, drawing on the ordinary and not-so-ordinary experiences that shape your life. A family trip, for example, probably contains all the basic elements of a narrative. Here are some ways to get started.

Talking Talking about what you've done and where you've been can help you discover what you want to say in writing. In addition, reaction to your stories can help you gauge their audience appeal. Listening to other people's stories might also trigger writing ideas.

Freewriting You can also freewrite as a way to generate a topic for a story. Then, when you come up with an idea that interests you, use freewriting again to explore it. Write down whatever comes into your mind about your topic for about five minutes. In the following model of freewriting, a writer decided to explore an everyday experience: a routine trip to the dentist.

Grammar Tip

Use personal pronouns correctly when you write a personal narrative. See Lesson 17.1, page 633.

Model

Terror. Anticipation. What else do I feel when I go to the dentist? Sitting in that waiting room, trying to read a magazine. Wondering whether I'll need a filling. I wish my tooth didn't hurt. I wish my gums didn't bleed. If only I'd flossed regularly, not just two or three days before this appointment. That doesn't fool anybody. Certainly not my dentist. Does he enjoy poking around in my mouth, making me squirm? I picture him putting on his gloves, snapping the elastic loudly and watching me jump. Then, he'll grin like the dentist in *Little Shop of Horrors.* He'll say the words that frighten me most: "Open wide."

This example of freewriting contains some narrative elements. Can you identify them?

Journal Writing

Look through your journal to find story ideas. Underline any incidents that seem significant or interesting to you. Freewrite about each incident for five minutes to generate more story ideas.

Teach

Using the Model

Reinforce students' knowledge of the basic narrative elements by asking students to summarize the plot of Kincaid's paragraph on page 180. If necessary, remind students to note the story's characters, setting, and conflict. Invite students to point out some of the vivid images that bring the story to life. (examples: "an enormous wooden trunk," "the boat was practically in splinters") **L2**

Using the Model

Ask students to identify any basic narrative elements in the freewriting from the model on this page. If necessary, guide students to identify the characters, setting, plot, and conflict. **L2**

Two-Minute Skill Drill

List three things that you saw or did today that could be elaborated on and turned into a funny or an interesting narrative.

See also *Two-Minute Skill Drill Transparency 4.1*

Journal Writing Tip

Elaborate on Ideas Point out that freewriting about one incident may reveal several directions a story could take. Freewriting may also help students recall related incidents, thereby generating even more story ideas.

4.1

Teach

Using Chronological Order

Ask students to list some events that are organized by chronological order. (examples: a calendar, a weekly guide to television programming, or a daily school schedule) Suggest that students clarify the chronological order of events in their narratives by writing each event on a separate index card and then ordering the cards. **L2**

Using Technology

Encourage students to use visuals, such as family photographs, to help them recall details of events they want to relate in narratives. If handwriting hinders students' freewriting, suggest that they use tape recorders, word processors, or a word processing program on a computer to help them with their prewriting activities. **L1**

Additional Resources

 For further stimuli for narrative writing, see *Fine Art Transparencies* 19–24.

 *Writing Process Transparencies* 10, 18–22

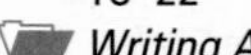
Writing Across the Curriculum
Cooperative Learning Activities
Listening and Speaking Activities, pp. 13, 18, 20, 21
Composition Practice, p. 27
Thinking and Study Skills, pp. 13, 21
Sentence-Combining Practice, pp. 30, 31

Prewriting Tip

Jot down ideas for possible narratives in your journal. Anything can serve as inspiration: talking to people, reading, or even watching television.

Build on Your Ideas

You can build on your ideas by answering questions about your story's basic elements and by constructing a framework of your story's events. Remember, however, that you may not even discover your story until you begin writing it. As writer Flannery O'Connor once said, "I write because I don't know what I think until I read what I say."

Answering Questions If you want to flesh out the basic elements in your narrative before you begin drafting, try answering the questions in the chart below. If you would prefer to just begin drafting, you may want to refer to these questions as you write your draft.

Questions to Flesh Out the Basic Narrative Elements
1. Who are my characters? About whom do I want to write?
2. What conflict(s) will my characters be involved in?
3. When does my story take place?
4. Where does my story take place?
5. Why do my characters get involved in their conflict(s)?
6. How does the setting affect my characters? How do they overcome their conflict(s)?
7. Do my characters change in any way during the course of the story? If so, in what ways and why?

Constructing a Framework Most narratives are organized in chronological order, the order in which the events happened. Try plotting the events in your narrative in chronological order along a time line. Keep asking yourself the question, *What happened next?* This will help you keep track of the events and write them down in order.

1:30 P.M.
First Event

Paul and Carlos set off to ride their mountain bikes through the woods near their home.

4:45 P.M.
Second Event

They become confused by the many trails and take a wrong turn. As night falls, they are hopelessly lost.

9:00 P.M.
Third Event

They try to keep warm and build a shelter with branches. They spend a miserable night in the woods.

7:00 A.M.
Fourth Event

The next day, they continue to try to find their way back home. They came upon old railroad tracks.

8:00 A.M.
Final Event

By following the tracks, they reach town and safety.

MEETING INDIVIDUAL NEEDS

English Language Learners

Using Transitions

Have students make brief sketches that show the series of events in the narrative that they plan to write. Have students cut out the sketches and lay them in chronological order. Then pair students learning English with native speakers of English. Let pairs work together to list transitional words that could lead a reader from one scene to the next. Encourage students learning English to work with their partners to develop sentence-to-sentence transitions for a paragraph.

4.1 Writing Activities

Write a Personal Narrative

You've decided to enter a writing contest sponsored by a national teen magazine. The contest rules state that you must write a one-page narrative about an experience that did not turn out as you expected. Use the prewriting techniques described in this lesson to help you explore your topic and build on your narrative's basic elements. Refer to your prewriting samples as you draft your narrative, but don't feel limited by the ideas you came up with at that stage in the writing process.

PURPOSE To write a personal narrative for a contest
AUDIENCE Editors of a teen magazine
LENGTH 2–4 paragraphs

WRITING RUBRICS To write an effective personal narrative, you should

- test your ideas by talking them through or by freewriting
- ask yourself questions to fill out details of the narrative
- construct a time line or other graphic organizer for your narrative
- include believable characters, setting, and plot

Listening and Speaking

COOPERATIVE LEARNING Interview a classmate about an important experience in his or her life. Formulate questions beforehand that will elicit details of the setting, people, and events involved. Record the interview on audiotape or videotape; then review it. Take notes on the details you will include in your narrative. Use the steps in the writing process to create a narrative about your classmate's experience.

Using Computers

If your word processor has an outlining feature, you can use it to outline your personal narrative. As you create your outline, this feature simultaneously creates a skeleton draft of your writing. In addition, as you come up with new ideas and enter the changes on your outline, the draft also changes. After you have completed your outline, "flesh out" your skeleton draft. Then use the cut-and-paste feature on your computer to help you revise and edit the draft.

GrammarLink

Use strong adverbs to make writing more precise.

Note how the writer on page 181 pictures the dentist "putting on his gloves, snapping the elastic loudly."

Revise the following sentences by adding at least one strong adverb to each.

1. I wish I had flossed my teeth.
2. I imagine that the dentist has told someone to "open wide."
3. My own teeth begin to vibrate as the buzz of the drill reaches my ears.
4. I can feel the pull and push of an instrument in my mouth.
5. I remember that I'm waiting for my brother to have his teeth checked.

See Lesson 10.5, page 467.

Assess

Evaluation Rubrics

Write a Personal Narrative

Use these criteria when evaluating your students' writing:

- Student used freewriting or other techniques to generate ideas.
- Events are organized chronologically.
- The story contains characters, setting, and plot.
- All basic elements are included.
- The main focus is a personal experience that turned out unexpectedly.
- The story builds on ideas listed in the prewriting.
- The resolution is consistent with the characters' personalities.

See also *Writing Assessment & Evaluation Rubrics*

Using Computers

If students are using a school computer, you may need to show them how this feature works. After they have used this feature for a while, have students compare an early outline with a later outline.

Reteaching

Composition Reteaching, p. 27

Enrichment

Composition Enrichment, p. 27

Close

Have students write a summary of what they learned about the elements of preparing a narrative. What approach do they find works best for them?

GrammarLink

Answers

Answers will vary. Suggestions:

1. I sincerely wish that I had flossed my teeth carefully.
2. I fretfully imagine that the dentist has told someone to "open wide."
3. My own teeth begin to vibrate sympathetically as the buzz of the drill reaches my ears.
4. I can almost feel the pull and push of a sharp instrument in my mouth.
5. I thankfully remember that I'm waiting for my brother to have his braces checked.

Focus

Lesson Overview

Objectives

- To identify four types of conflict
- To choose the type of conflict that works best for a particular piece of narrative writing

Skills

- understanding the types of conflict and ways to develop conflict

Critical Thinking

- analyzing conflict; evaluating conflict; establishing and evaluating criteria

Listening and Speaking

- discussing; evaluating; questioning

Bellringer

Daily Language Activity

When students enter the classroom, have this assignment on the board: *Briefly jot down notes about the plot of a television program or movie you have seen recently.*

Grammar Link to the Bellringer

Have students read their Bellringer notes, and then ask them to rewrite any sentence fragments as sentences. Next, ask them to rewrite these fragments as complete sentences.

See also *Daily Language Practice*

Motivating Activity

Discuss students' responses to the Bellringer activity. Help them identify the conflict(s) at the heart of each plot. One approach is to use the words *struggles to save* with the name of one or more characters. (The doctor struggles to save the accident victim.) Then discuss the ways in which each conflict helped move the plot along.

LESSON 4.2

Developing Conflict in Narrative

In a narrative, as in a movie, it is often the conflict, or struggle, that keeps the audience interested. There are several types of conflict. Choose the one that works best with your characters and situations.

Use Events to Develop Conflict

The conflict, or struggle, in a story is what sets events in motion and makes the audience want to find out what happens. In the movie *Jaws*, for example, the uncertain outcome in the struggle between people and shark creates a gripping story.

Conflict plays the same role in a narrative that a main idea plays in other types of writing. Just as all supporting details help develop a main idea, all events in a narrative help develop its conflict.

As a character grapples with the conflict, the plot builds to a climax, the high point of the story. The resolution, in which the aftermath of the climax is revealed, brings the narrative to an end. The graph on page 185 shows how the development and eventual resolution of a conflict form the basis for the plot.

Resource Manager

Planning Resources

- *Lesson Plans*

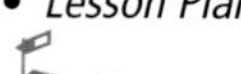

Transparencies

- *Bellringer*
- *Daily Language Practice*
- *Fine Art* 19–24
- *Two-Minute Skill Drill*
- *Writing Process* 10, 18–22

Other Print Resources

- *Composition Enrichment,* p. 28
- *Composition Practice,* p. 28
- *Composition Reteaching,* p. 28
- *Cooperative Learning Activities,* pp. 17–20
- *Listening and Speaking Activities,* pp. 13, 18, 20, 21
- *Sentence-Combining Practice,* pp. 30–31
- *Thinking and Study Skills,* pp. 10, 13
- *Writing Across the Curriculum*
- *Writing Assessment and Evaluation Rubrics*

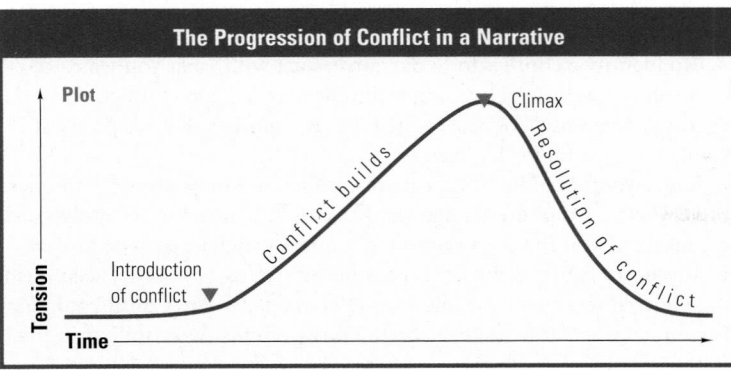

The Progression of Conflict in a Narrative

Plot — Introduction of conflict — Conflict builds — Climax — Resolution of conflict — Tension — Time

Learn the Types of Conflict

Conflicts can be internal or external. External conflicts involve one or more characters and an outside force. Internal conflicts occur within a character. The chart below lists four types of conflicts—three external and one internal.

Drafting Tip

As you draft the conflict in your narrative, remember that a conflict with a less predictable climax and resolution is more likely to involve your readers.

Four Types of Conflict

CONFLICT	EXAMPLES
Person Against Person The narrative pits one character against another.	One character exposes a flaw in another. One character attempts to harm another. One character opposes the beliefs of another.
Person Against Nature A character struggles against a dangerous animal, place, or condition.	A character is attacked by a rampaging elephant. A character tries to scale a dangerous peak. A character is threatened by a hurricane.
Person Against Society Society or tradition stands in the way of a character's desires.	Society prevents a character from doing something. A group tries to impose its beliefs and ideas on a character.
Person Against Self The conflict is within the character's mind.	A character struggles with a lack of ambition. A character seeks to achieve an unrealistic goal. A character tries to overcome a fear of flying.

Journal Writing

Think about a narrative you've read in which a character (or characters) faces a particular conflict. How is the conflict resolved? Write your answer in your journal.

Teach

Cooperative Learning

Initiate a Think-Pair-Share activity. First, ask students to think of a story idea. Encourage them to identify characters, setting, and a general plot. Then ask each student to discuss and develop a conflict for a possible narrative. Finally, invite students to share their stories with the class. This activity can help students generate details and dialogue for their narratives. **L2**

Understanding Conflict

Students may benefit from identifying familiar examples of the four types of conflict. Copy the chart headings on the board and invite students to summarize the conflicts in books, television programs, and films. Help students decide in which category each example belongs, and then write a capsule description of the conflict under the appropriate heading. **L3**

Two-Minute Skill Drill

Which of the following are sentence fragments, and which are complete sentences?

I looked.
Although I looked.
together with friends.
My friends and I.
Look!

See also *Two-Minute Skill Drill Transparency 4.2*

Journal Writing Tip

Comparing Ask students to consider the following questions: Was the character's personality similar to your own? Was the conflict similar to something you have experienced?

Teach

Using the Model

You might want to read the model aloud, to emphasize the central role played by dialogue. You might also want to have students graph the introduction, climax, and resolution of the conflict in the model. Students should note that the climax of both conflicts occurs when Baker jumps into the pool. The conflict between Baker and the Navy instructor is resolved when Baker finally follows the instructor's order. The conflict between Baker and his own fear is resolved when Baker finds that he won't drown after all. **L2**

Organizing Causes and Effects

As students develop conflict in their narratives, suggest that they not only ask themselves "What happens next?" but also try to figure out why the events occur. Students might use a cause-and-effect graphic organizer to organize their thoughts about the events and their characters' motivations. Tell students to make sure that each effect is the direct result of the preceding cause. **L3**

Additional Resources

For further stimuli for narrative writing, see *Fine Art Transparencies* 19–24.

Writing Process Transparencies 10, 18–22

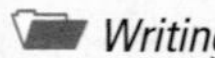

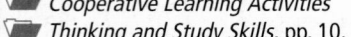

Writing Across the Curriculum

Cooperative Learning Activities

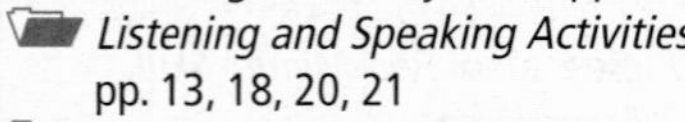

Thinking and Study Skills, pp. 10, 13

Listening and Speaking Activities, pp. 13, 18, 20, 21

Composition Practice, p. 28

Sentence-Combining Practice, pp. 30–31

Develop Conflict

To identify a conflict for a narrative, start with what you want to write about and use prewriting techniques to develop conflict. For example, freewrite to discover the types of conflicts that would most challenge your main characters.

Once you have identified a main conflict, use prewriting techniques to generate a list of events that might be used to develop or resolve such a conflict. If you think an event might affect the characters or forces involved, try listing some of its possible effects. As you write, keep pushing yourself to answer the question *What happens next?* until your story is complete. See how writer Russell Baker presents two conflicts in the following model.

Literature Model

On the first day in the pool a [Navy] instructor with a voice like a bullhorn ordered fifty of us to climb a high board and jump in feet first. . . . A line was formed to mount the ladder and jump. I drifted to the end of the line, then stepped out when the splashing started and introduced myself to the instructor.

Baker sets up two types of conflict: Baker versus his own fear of deep water, and Baker versus the Navy instructor.

"I'm a nonswimmer," I said. "You want me to go to the shallow end of the pool?" At City College I'd spent four years in the shallow end of the pool.

"This pool doesn't have a shallow end," the instructor said.

"Well, what am I going to do?"

"Get up on that platform and jump," he said.

The pool depth was marked as fifteen feet at that point.

"I'm not kidding. I can't swim a stroke."

Baker uses dialogue to develop the conflict between himself and the Navy instructor.

"Up! Up!" he shouted.

"But I'll drown."

"This pool's got the best lifesaving equipment in the Navy," he said. "Don't worry about it."

"Come on."

"I'm giving you an order, mister. Up!" . . .

I stepped to the edge, closed my eyes, and walked into space. The impact of the water was like being smacked on the bottom by a two-by-four, then I was sinking, then—my God! —I was rising irresistibly to the surface. My head broke water. The water was actually supporting me, just as everybody had always said it would.

What is the climax of each conflict? How are the conflicts resolved?

Russell Baker, *Growing Up*

Viewing and Representing

Interpreting Visuals

Draw a conflict diagram on the board, and discuss the meanings of words such as *tension, plot, climax,* and *resolution.* Pick a story, movie, or scene from a play that students are familiar with, and help students identify both the elements of the plot and the main conflict. Then draw a second conflict diagram on the board, and ask students to write a short narrative that reflects all of the elements present in the diagram.

4.2 Writing Activities

Write a Narrative About a Conflict

You've decided to contribute a one-page narrative to a booklet prepared by and designed for students at your school.

Choose one of these topics if you wish: a student is afraid to speak out when her friend is jeered at by classmates; a shy student wants to try out for a part in the school play; a student feels pressured by her friends to stay at a party after her curfew.

PURPOSE To write a narrative
AUDIENCE Students at your school
LENGTH 3–4 paragraphs

WRITING RUBRICS To write an effective narrative, you should

- include events that develop the conflict
- build your plot to a climax
- create a resolution to the conflict

Viewing and Representing

CREATING A POSTER Use one of your favorite narratives—fiction or nonfiction—to create a poster mapping the central conflict in the story. Show how the conflict builds, what occurs at the climax, and how the conflict is resolved. Include an illustration of the climax.

César A. Martinez, *Mestizo*, 1987

Grammar*Link*

Avoid sentence fragments.

Each item below contains a *sentence fragment,* or incomplete sentence. Rewrite the item to eliminate the fragment. Change words as necessary.

1. The conflict in a narrative engages a reader's interest. Because a reader wants to find out how the conflict will be resolved.
2. The plot is set in motion by the conflict. Which can be an internal conflict or an external one.
3. The plot building to a climax, the high point of the story. After the climax, the resolution ends the narrative.
4. A conflict within the character's mind. Internal conflict pits the character against himself or herself.
5. Much of the conflict in young adult literature is internal. Adolescents experiencing the pains of growing up.

See Lesson 13.9, pages 553–554.

Cross-Curricular Activity

FINE ART The drawing at left is a self-portrait by César A. Martinez. Entitled *Mestizo*, it shows the artist flanked by a jaguar, native to the Americas, and a Spanish bull, which represents Europe. The drawing reflects Martinez's struggle to come to terms with his own cultural identity, rooted in both North America and Spain. Generate a list of events that might be used to develop and eventually resolve the conflict. Then write a brief narrative based on the drawing.

Writing Online — For more writing and grammar practice, go to glencoe.com and enter QuickPass code WC97727p1.

Assess

Evaluation Rubrics

Write a Narrative About a Conflict

Use these criteria when evaluating your students' writing:

- Does the narrative reveal characters' feelings, enabling you to identify with the conflict?
- Do all of the events in the narrative help develop its conflict?
- Does the plot build to a believable climax?
- Does the conflict have a suitable resolution?

See also *Writing Assessment & Evaluation Rubrics*

Cross-Curricular Activity

Evaluate the narrative on how well it fleshes out the artist's internal struggle and how well it describes a series of events that develop and resolve the conflict.

Reteaching

Composition Reteaching, p. 28

Enrichment

Composition Enrichment, p. 28

Fine Art Transparencies 19–24

Close

Discuss how writers try to engage the reader by introducing the conflict at the beginning of the story. What do students think are the advantages of presenting the conflict at the beginning? (Presenting the conflict at the beginning hooks the reader, and the writer has a better chance of maintaining the reader's interest.)

Grammar*Link*

Answers

1. The conflict . . . because a reader wants to find out how the conflict . . .
2. The plot is set in motion by the conflict, which can be an internal . . .
3. The plot builds to a climax, the high point of the story. . . .
4. Internal conflict, a conflict within the character's mind, pits . . .

Viewing the Art

César A. Martinez, *Mestizo,* 1987

Point out that Martinez's *Mestizo* illustrates the two ethnic loyalties (North American and Spanish) that pull the artist in different directions. The 29-by-41-inch charcoal and pastel drawing is in a private collection.

Focus

Lesson Overview

Objectives

- To discover three uses of dialogue
- To create dialogue that reflects characters' personalities and that advances a plot

Skills

- thinking about real people to develop dialogue; developing a story with dialogue

Critical Thinking

- analyzing; recalling; comparing; building background; defining and clarifying; visualizing; identifying

Listening and Speaking

- informal speaking; discussing

Bellringer

Daily Language Activity

When students enter the classroom, have this assignment on the board: *Draw a cartoon sketch of the last conversation you had before entering the classroom. Fill the speech balloons with dialogue.*

Grammar Link to the Bellringer

Ask students to add quotation marks to the dialogue they wrote.

See also  *Daily Language Practice*

Motivating Activity

Discuss students' responses to the Bellringer activity. Then ask students to look at the cartoon on page 188 without turning the page upside down to read the dialogue. Suggest that students create dialogue to fill in the speech balloons. Invite volunteers to share their versions. Remind students that their dialogue should fit both the situation shown and the ages of the characters. Then read the actual dialogue aloud.

LESSON 4.3

Narrative Writing

Writing Dialogue

Dialogue, or conversation between characters, brings the characters in a story to life. Like the cartoon below, a story would be hard to follow without the dialogue.

"Mom, can I drive on the way back?"
"Of course not, Calvin."

"Can I just steer then? I promise I won't crash."
"No, Calvin."

"Can I work the gas and brakes while you steer?"
"No, Calvin."

"You never let me do anything."

Discover the Uses of Dialogue

You can use dialogue to help advance a narrative's plot. For example, if the plot involves an argument between two characters, you can let the characters speak for themselves rather than summarizing their dispute.

You can also use dialogue to reveal your characters' personality traits or to show relationships between characters. For instance, instead of telling the reader, "Robert was shy," use Robert's actions and words to reveal his shyness: "Robert shuffled uneasily, looked at his feet, and mumbled, 'Nice to meet you.' "

Additionally, you can use dialogue to make the reader feel closer to the action, to help the reader "see" the story as it unfolds rather than to hear about it from a narrator. Dialogue can also help establish character and conflict, and it can make a conflict more powerful and real to the reader.

Think About Real People to Develop Dialogue

When you're writing dialogue for a story about something that really happened, try to remember as closely as possible what each person said. If your story is fictional, you'll need to invent dialogue. To do

Resource Manager

Planning Resources

- *Lesson Plans*

Transparencies

- *Bellringer*
- *Daily Language Practice*
- *Fine Art* 19–24
- *Two-Minute Skill Drill*
- *Writing Process* 10, 18–22

Other Print Resources

- *Composition Enrichment,* p. 29
- *Composition Practice,* p. 29
- *Composition Reteaching,* p. 29
- *Cooperative Learning Activities,* pp. 17–20
- *Listening and Speaking Activities,* pp. 13, 18, 20, 21
- *Sentence-Combining Practice,* pp. 30–31
- *Thinking and Study Skills,* pp. 21, 25
- *Writing Across the Curriculum*
- *Writing Assessment and Evaluation Rubrics*

so, you might try to imagine that you are one of the characters and freewrite about the conflict from that character's point of view. Keep in mind the character's age, background, and personality and how those qualities may be reflected in speech.

Sometimes my mother makes me want to scream. Why won't she let me get an after-school job? All my friends are working and making their own money. Why does Mom still treat me like a kid?

If the conflict involves two characters, you might try freewriting a letter from one character to the other. Each letter should reflect the letter writer's point of view and feelings about the conflict.

Dear Angela,
I know you're angry with me because I won't let you work after school. But I'm afraid a job would interfere with your studies. You know you won't get into a good college if your grades are poor. Besides, I'd worry when you'd be coming home after dark.

Dear Mom,
I promise you a job won't hurt my grades. I'll be home every day by 7:00, which gives me tons of time to do my homework. And Carla's already said she can give me a lift home after work. Best of all, I'll be able to buy that winter jacket I saw at the mall with my own money.

Dialogue should sound like real speech. In real speech, people often interrupt each other, ignore each other's comments, speak in fragments, and break the rules of grammar. To test whether your dialogue sounds natural, read it aloud.

Grammar Tip

When you edit your dialogue, be sure to use quotation marks to enclose direct quotations. For help see Lesson 21.9, pages 752–756.

Journal Writing

In your journal write down three pieces of dialogue that you have overheard and that struck you as interesting. Why do you think you remembered these particular conversations? What made them interesting? Write your ideas in your journal.

Teach

Cooperative Learning

Divide the class into groups. Provide each group with an idea for a scene in a mini-play (e.g., a family at the dinner table debating the advantages and disadvantages of moving; a bunch of friends hanging out at the mall discussing their plans for the summer). Ask students to develop dialogue for their scene, giving each group member a role. When ready, have each group share their play with the rest of the class. **L2**

Recalling Dialogue

Some students may have trouble imagining fictional characters. Have these students recreate a family conversation or an important event in their lives that included dialogue. Have them record this dialogue in the form of a short scene. **L1**

Two-Minute Skill Drill

Write the following sentences on the board. Then have students add quotation marks where appropriate.

I'll see you next week, he shouted.

Tonya whispered Have you heard the news?

See also *Two-Minute Skill Drill Transparency 4.3*

Journal Writing Tip

Choosing Words Before students begin their journal activity, ask them to try remembering which adjectives and specific nouns the speakers used.

Teach

Using the Model

Ask students to identify elements that make the dialogue sound natural. (sentence fragments, shortened forms of words, slang) Students should note that Hank's short, angry bursts of dialogue and the questions he fires at Chucky help convey Hank's anger and confusion. **L2**

Writing a Dramatic Scene

Challenge students to write an emotional scene in which the characters communicate their feelings solely through dialogue and limited action. Remind students that the dialogue should sound true to life, the way people actually talk when they're experiencing a particular emotion. **L3**

Additional Resources

For further stimuli for writing dialogue, see *Fine Art Transparencies* 19–24.

Writing Process Transparencies 10, 18–22

Writing Across the Curriculum
Cooperative Learning Activities
Listening and Speaking Activities, pp. 13, 18, 20, 21
Thinking and Study Skills, pp. 21, 25
Composition Practice, p. 29
Sentence-Combining Practice, pp. 30, 31

Prewriting Tip

To develop your ability to write realistic dialogue, watch a favorite television show. Note how the dialogue reflects the ages, backgrounds, and personalities of the characters.

Develop Your Story with Dialogue

Dialogue can bring your writing to life. In Matthew Cheney's short story "The Nauga Hunters," Hank invites his younger brother Chucky to hunt for a nauga, an imaginary beast. Note how Cheney uses dialogue to develop his characters and advance the story.

Student Model

Chucky stood next to his brother without saying anything. Then he asked quietly, "Is it about Mom and Dad?"

"Jus' beat it!"

"What's gonna happen? Is Dad gonna leave?"

"You wanna know? You really wanna know, you little jerk? Las' night I heard Mom and Dad talkin'."

"Fightin'?"

"Nope, jus' talkin'. Dad said he's gonna leave and go ta New York and take me, and Mom can have you. So I brought you out here jus' ta be nice 'cause I may never really be able ta do anythin' like this again. Okay? Satisfied?"

"You sure yer tellin' the truth?"

Hank stood up and jumped on his brother; they fell to the damp ground. His eyes were sparkling and his lips were unfirm. "Would I lie about that, you little . . . " His voice faded as he pulled his arm up to punch Chucky. Chucky was crying now. Hank stood up. "Forget it," he said. "Supper'll be almost ready." Chucky was still on the ground. "You comin'?"

Chucky pulled himself up and brushed off his rear end. His face was streaked with tears. "Yup," he said softly.

Matthew Cheney, New Hampton School, New Hampton, New Hampshire. First appeared in *Merlyn's Pen: The National Magazine of Student Writing*

Dialogue effectively reveals the story's central conflict and its climax: the boys' parents are getting a divorce.

How does Cheney use dialogue to convey Hank's anger and confusion?

Try to make your dialogue as realistic as possible. As you write it, keep the following guidelines in mind.

Dialogue Guidelines

- Use language that reflects the age, background, and personality of each character.
- Make sure your dialogue has a purpose—to advance the action, to reveal a character's personality or relationships between characters, or to show the conflict.
- Begin a direct quotation with a capital letter, and enclose it in quotation marks.
- Begin a new paragraph each time the speaker changes.

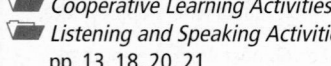

Meeting Individual Needs: English Language Learners

Creating Dialogue

Many students learning English will have stronger speaking skills than writing skills in the English language. Encourage these students to work in pairs with native English speakers, speaking their dialogue while their partners take notes. The students taking notes could then suggest improvements to the dialogue.

4.3 Writing Activities

Write a Dialogue

You've been chosen to write the dialogue for a skit for your school's theater group. Use the information below to develop the dialogue.

> Chen and Kirby are best friends, but their personalities are very different. Chen is an optimist, always able to see the bright side. Kirby is a pessimist, always assuming the worst. Both are on the track team. For the first time in years, the team has a chance to win the state title. As they warm up before the final relay, Kirby admits to Chen that he wants to withdraw. He's afraid he'll cause the team to lose. Chen inspires Kirby with his own enthusiasm. By the time the starting signal sounds, both friends are ready to give their personal best.

As you develop your dialogue, read it aloud to find out how it sounds. Try to imagine yourself in each character's place.

PURPOSE To write dialogue for a skit to be performed by your school's theater group
AUDIENCE Your school's student body
LENGTH 1 page

WRITING RUBRICS To write effective dialogue, you should

- let the characters speak for themselves
- use dialogue for a purpose
- use language that sounds real and appropriate to the characters
- use quotation marks appropriately

Viewing and Representing

DRAW A CARTOON Using a favorite comic strip as a guide, draw a four-panel cartoon. Leave enough space for dialogue balloons. Be sure your dialogue is appropriate to your characters and advances the plot.

GrammarLink

Know when and how to use quotation marks.

Dialogue, the exact words of a speaker, is written with quotation marks.

Rewrite the sentences below, using quotation marks to enclose every direct quotation. Make other changes in capitalization and punctuation as necessary.

1. My little sister stamped her right foot and exclaimed I'm so mad.
2. Nibbling at the cuticle of her right thumb, my older sister whispered why is Alicia so mad?
3. Don't ask me I answered, lowering my voice.
4. People who have something to say my angry sister hissed should have the courage to say it so that other people can hear.
5. This is a new idea I murmured in return.

See Lesson 21.9, pages 752–756.

Cross-Curricular Activity

AMERICAN HISTORY In a small group, choose a scene from American history to dramatize. First discuss the personalities and backgrounds of the characters. Then meet with your group to write dialogue that develops the action and accurately reflects each character's personality and background. After all the dialogue has been written, present your group scene to the rest of the class.

LOG ON **Writing** Online | For more writing and grammar practice, go to **glencoe.com** and enter QuickPass code WC97727p1.

Assess

Evaluation Rubrics

Write a Dialogue

Use these criteria when evaluating your students' writing:

- Do the details reflect the age, personality, and background of each character?
- Does the dialogue reflect Chen's optimism and Kirby's pessimism?
- Did the dialogue make use of prewriting notes?
- How effectively does the dialogue advance the action?

See also *Writing Assessment & Evaluation Rubrics*

Cross-Curricular Activity

When evaluating your students' writing, use these criteria as well as the criteria listed above:

- Did the presentation bring the historical event to life?
- If so, what details in the dialogue were most effective?
- If not, how could the group improve its dialogue?

Reteaching

Composition Reteaching, p. 29

Enrichment

Composition Enrichment, p. 29

Close

Hold a discussion of the ways people speak on television. Ask students if they know of any television characters who have distinctive ways of speaking. How does this distinctive speech make the character interesting or memorable?

GrammarLink

Answers

1. My little sister stamped her right foot and exclaimed, "I'm so mad."
2. Nibbling at the cuticle of her right thumb, my older sister whispered, "Why is Alicia so mad?"
3. "Don't ask me," I answered, lowering my voice.
4. "People who have something to say," my angry sister hissed, "should have the courage to say it so that other people can hear."
5. "This is a new idea," I murmured in return.

Focus

Lesson Overview

Objectives

- To understand the purpose of anecdotes
- To generate true-life anecdotes and invented anecdotes
- To determine whether a specific anecdote enhances or detracts from a piece of writing

Skills

- using anecdotes; drafting; using dialogue

Critical Thinking

- classifying; contrasting; evaluating; making inferences; identifying

Listening and Speaking

- discussing; evaluating; explaining a process

Bellringer

Daily Language Activity

When students enter the classroom, have this assignment on the board: *Write an adjective that describes one of your personality traits or one that others have used to describe you.*

Grammar Link to the Bellringer

Let students use the adjective they chose for the Bellringer activity. Have them write a sentence using the adjective's comparative and superlative forms.

See also  *Daily Language Practice*

Motivating Activity

Discuss students' responses to the Bellringer activity. Ask students to think of an incident in their lives that illustrates the trait they described. (For example, chasing a purse snatcher might illustrate a student's *bravery*.) Invite volunteers to share their stories. Explain that these types of stories are called anecdotes and can be useful in longer narratives.

Narrative Writing

LESSON 4.4

Using Anecdotes

An anecdote is a short narrative used to illustrate a point or reveal character. In the model below the writer uses an anecdote to demonstrate poet Langston Hughes's scorn for the so-called "Jim Crow" laws.

Most anecdotes instruct or entertain, and they often contain dialogue. Although anecdotes can stand on their own, they are frequently used as supporting details in longer pieces of writing.

This anecdote contains a plot—Hughes is trying to get served dinner; characters—Hughes, the steward, the naval officer; and a setting—a train's dining car.

How is dialogue used to reveal Hughes's attitude toward the Jim Crow laws?

Literature Model

By this time he unquestionably had become bolder in confronting Jim Crow. Always now he entered the dining car at the first call, instead of shrinking back and waiting for the last as blacks were supposed to do.

Picking a center table, he usually tried to brazen it out before incredulous but discreetly supportive black waiters and often indignant, but often yielding, white stewards. "Are you a Puerto Rican?" a steward demanded in Alabama. "No, hungry!" The man handed over a menu. "Are you Cuban?" a curious white Navy officer then asked. "No, American," Langston coolly replied. "Are you Cuban?"

Arnold Rampersad, *The Life of Langston Hughes, Volume II: 1941–1967*

Generate Anecdotes

You can generate anecdotes by drawing on real-life experiences or by using prewriting techniques to invent them. Keep in mind that you will use the anecdote to illustrate a point in a longer piece of writing.

Resource Manager

Planning Resources

- *Lesson Plans*

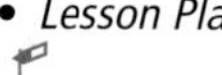

Transparencies

- *Bellringer*
- *Daily Language Practice*
- *Fine Art* 19–24
- *Two-Minute Skill Drill*
- *Writing Process* 10, 18–22

Other Print Resources

- *Composition Enrichment*, p. 30
- *Composition Practice*, p. 30
- *Composition Reteaching*, p. 30
- *Cooperative Learning Activities*, pp. 17–20
- *Listening and Speaking Activities*, pp. 13, 18, 20, 21
- *Sentence-Combining Practice*, pp. 30–31
- *Thinking and Study Skills*, pp. 6–8, 11, 25
- *Writing Across the Curriculum*
- *Writing Assessment and Evaluation Rubrics*

Anecdotes Based on Fact Some anecdotes are based on incidents that actually happened. To generate true-life anecdotes, think about significant or entertaining incidents from your own life. You might want to look through your journal for ideas. Then think about the point each anecdote could make in a longer piece of writing.

Factual Anecdotes	
ANECDOTE	**POINT**
The time I stood up for myself even though my friends disagreed	To show that you should voice your opinions, even if they are unpopular
The time my brother first went away to college	To show that life is a process of change
The time I struck out and my team lost the game	To show that true friends stand by you when you fail

Invented Anecdotes When you're writing a fictional narrative, you can invent anecdotes. First decide on the point you want to make. Then freewrite to come up with an anecdote that could illustrate that point.

Invented Anecdotes	
ANECDOTE	**POINT**
A character thinks only of himself or herself at the expense of others	To show a character's selfishness
An argument between two characters	To show that two characters have different values
A character confronts his or her fear of heights by climbing a mountain	To show that you have to confront a fear to overcome it

Journal Writing

Look through your journal for incidents that could be written up as possible anecdotes. Then list the incidents, and identify the point each could make in a longer piece of writing.

Vocabulary Tip

When you draft your anecdote, be sure to present the events of the story in chronological order. Helpful transition words include *after, before, as soon as, first, next, now, soon, finally, meanwhile,* and *then.*

Presenting Tip

One effective method to present an anecdote is to read it aloud.

Teach

Using the Model

Ask students to identify the types of conflict present in the model on page 192. (person against society: Hughes vs. the "Jim Crow" laws; person against person: Hughes vs. the steward) Students should note that Hughes's replies to the steward and the officer show that he expects equal treatment and will not back down. **L2**

Drafting Anecdotes

Work through at least one example of writing an anecdote so that students can see the process broken down into smaller steps. Start with one of the suggested points and anecdotes shown in the charts. Then take students through the process of identifying specific characters, plot, and setting for a proposed anecdote. Finally, with students' suggestions, draft a one-paragraph anecdote. **L1**

Two-Minute Skill Drill

Ask students to write an invented anecdote to illustrate one of the following points:

- a pet's devotion
- Honesty is the best policy.
- Good friends are worth more than gold.

See also *Two-Minute Skill Drill Transparency 4.4*

Journal Writing Tip

Classifying Explain to students that the points in the two charts can be classified as narrative themes. Tell students that the points they develop should also have a universal application.

Teach

Using the Model

Ask students to compare this anecdote with the one by Arnold Rampersad on page 192 and to note how both writers use dialogue to bring their short scenes to life. Also point out the economy with which both writers establish setting and characters. In her first sentence, Jennifer Tuck introduces both characters and setting. Emphasize that anecdotes are intended to be brief, focusing on only a few important details. Students should also note that the anecdote reveals the narrator's grandmother as a compassionate, understanding person. **L2**

Classifying Information

Encourage students to collect from newspaper or magazine articles anecdotes about people or issues that interest them. Short anecdotes within a longer piece can be highlighted in color and possibly annotated by the students. They can then use the anecdotes as models to help them with their own writing. **L1**

Additional Resources

For further stimuli for narrative writing, see *Fine Art Transparencies* 19–24.

Writing Process Transparencies 10, 18–22

Writing Across the Curriculum

Cooperative Learning Activities

Thinking and Study Skills, pp. 6–8, 11, 25

Sentence-Combining Practice, pp. 13, 18, 20, 21

Listening and Speaking Activities, pp. 13, 18, 20, 21

Composition Practice, p. 30

Prewriting Tip

If you are writing about yourself, you might ask family members to discuss their early memories of you. Their stories could supply you with useful anecdotes.

Decide Where and How to Use Anecdotes

Once you have an anecdote, you need to consider whether or not to use it to make a specific point in a longer piece of writing. To help you decide, ask yourself the questions in the chart below.

Questions to Determine the Usefulness of an Anecdote

1. Does this anecdote make the point I want to make?
2. Does the anecdote advance the narrative?
3. Is the anecdote brief, yet meaningful?
4. Does the anecdote instruct or entertain?

In Jennifer Tuck's short story "My Grandmother's House," the narrator dreads returning to her grandmother's house after her grandmother dies. As a little girl, she had been afraid of the house because it was so large and dark. As this anecdote reveals, however, on one particular occasion her grandmother helped her overcome her fears.

Student Model

I had been sitting on the porch for nearly an hour when my grandmother came out, quietly letting the screen door creak on its old rusty hinges and then sigh as it came to rest against the crooked door frame Grandpa was always saying he would fix.

"Why don't you come inside?" she said. "We are going to eat dinner soon and I would hate to think of sitting at the table without you."

"I'm afraid." I barely whispered this shameful feeling, and stared straight down at my untied shoes.

"That's OK. I was afraid when we first moved here, too. You just have to remember that this house is a lot like your house, only there's love from many families here instead of just our own. Did you ever stop to wonder who could have lived here before? There must be so many memories within these walls!"

We talked on and on and gradually my fear began to fade. When my mother called us inside, I didn't hesitate for an instant before following my grandmother inside.

Jennifer Tuck, Central High School,
Manchester, New Hampshire
First appeared in *Merlyn's Pen: The National Magazine of Student Writing*

What does the anecdote reveal about the narrator's grandmother?

Notice that the anecdote could stand on its own as a brief narrative, complete with plot, setting, and characters.

MEETING INDIVIDUAL NEEDS

English Language Learners

Choosing Anecdotes

Encourage students who are less proficient in English to talk to family members about personal incidents that could be turned into anecdotes. Suggest that students tape record these stories. To help write the anecdotes, students can use the recorder's stop and rewind features to create the English dialogue. Then have students share their anecdotes with partners who can help clarify the writing.

4.4 Writing Activities

Write an Anecdote

Your English class is collecting an anecdote from each class member for a get-to-know-your-classmates project. The collection will be distributed to all of the students in the class. Write an anecdote that reveals something about your personality. You may choose to write about a time when you made a fool of yourself in front of someone you wanted to impress, or a time when your sense of humor helped relieve an unpleasant situation. You might choose to reveal another aspect of your personality.

PURPOSE To write an anecdote that reveals something about yourself.
AUDIENCE The members of your class
LENGTH 3–4 paragraphs

WRITING RUBRICS To write an effective anecdote, you should

- be sure your anecdote supports your point
- include significant details regarding character, setting, and plot

Cross-Curricular Activity

Joan Brown, *After the Alcatraz Swim #3*, 1976

FINE ART Look at the painting. What ideas for anecdotes does it suggest? Freewrite or list to generate ideas for anecdotes and for the points they could illustrate.

GrammarLink

Use comparative and superlative forms of adjectives and adverbs correctly.

Comparative adjectives and adverbs compare two things—for example, Langston Hughes's becoming "bolder" in confronting Jim Crow. *Superlative forms* of adjectives and adverbs compare more than two things.

Complete each sentence below with the correct form of the word in parentheses.

1. After some time, Langston Hughes entered the dining car ________ than he first had. (courageously)
2. Who were ________ (amazed): the white stewards or the black waiters?
3. Perhaps ________ of all were the fellow passengers Hughes encountered in the dining cars. (surprised)
4. Some passengers moved to the ________ corner of the dining car when they saw the poet approach. (far)
5. They showed ________ what they thought than did those passengers who just ignored Hughes. (clearly)

See Lessons 18.1–18.3, pages 659–664.

Listening and Speaking

COOPERATIVE LEARNING With a classmate, create a dialogue based on your responses to the painting to the left and present it to the class as a dramatic reading.

LOG ON **Writing Online** For more writing and grammar practice, go to glencoe.com and enter QuickPass code WC97727p1.

Assess

Evaluation Rubrics

Write an Anecdote

Use the following criteria when evaluating your students' writing. The anecdotes should

- include significant details
- reveal the writer's intent
- use dialogue to enliven the piece
- disclose aspects of character
- contain basic narrative elements
- succeed in making its point

See also *Writing Assessment & Evaluation Rubrics*

Cross-Curricular Activity

Have students take turns reciting their completed anecdotes. Invite listeners to point out effective dialogue in each piece as it is read to the class.

Reteaching

Composition Reteaching, p. 30

Enrichment

Composition Enrichment, p. 30

Fine Art Transparencies 10, 18–22

Close

Tell students to write about returning to a familiar place, as Jennifer Tuck does in the passage from her short story "My Grandmother's House." Ask them to use anecdotes to make their point and advance their narratives.

GrammarLink

Answers

1. more courageously
2. more amazed
3. most surprised
4. farthest

Viewing the Art

Joan Brown, *After the Alcatraz Swim #3*, 1976
This enamel painting shows Joan Brown seated at a table. She competed in a swim meet near Alcatraz, the infamous island prison. The scene behind Brown depicts her rescue after she nearly drowned in the wake of a passing ship.

Focus

Lesson Overview

Objectives

- To identify four elements of a good sports narrative
- To develop a narrative about a sporting event that includes a starting point, conflict, climax, and resolution

Skills

- choosing vivid images; using action verbs; stating facts clearly; drafting a narrative

Critical Thinking

- identifying; classifying; reporting

Listening and Speaking

- discussing; reading aloud; listening to a narrative

Bellringer

Daily Language Activity

When students enter the classroom, have this assignment on the board: *How does the writing in the sports section of your newspaper differ from the writing in the news sections? List your ideas.*

Grammar Link to the Bellringer

Read aloud a sports article from a newspaper or magazine. Suggest that students raise their hands every time they hear a vivid verb. Point out that sports writing emphasizes the use of action verbs.

See also *Daily Language Practice*

Motivating Activity

Initiate a discussion about exciting sports events that students have either watched or participated in. Ask students what made the events exciting. Point out that sports events lend themselves to narrative writing because all of the basic elements—setting, characters, plot, and conflict—are present.

LESSON 4.5

Narrative Writing

Writing a Sports Narrative

A good sports narrative, such as the model below, contains all the elements of any good narrative: character, setting, and conflict that builds to a climax and resolution.

The conflict in a sports narrative is often person against person, as each athlete struggles to win the sports event.

What is the climax in this sports narrative? How is it resolved?

Student Model

The pop of the gun sets the swimmers' legs in motion and arms flawlessly scooping pockets of water. Their heads bob rhythmically, each straining to reach the end of the pool. At the end of each lane, fellow swimmers stand and cheer their teammates, with a single exception. One blond-haired swimmer receives cries from teammates who lean close to the water, straining to show the swimmer their enthusiasm and their lips. The swimmer is deaf, and the encouraging motions of her friends urge her to go faster.

The race is close. The blond head edges out in front, neck and neck, with another swimmer beside her. However, with a last, powerful stroke, the blond swimmer breaks the tie and hits the timer seconds before her competitor. As she rests against the wall of the pool, accepting the congratulations of her teammates, an ear-to-ear grin appears across her face.

Charissa Adelman, Quartz Hill High School,
Quartz Hill, California

Resource Manager

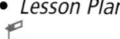

Planning Resources

- *Lesson Plans*

Transparencies

- *Bellringer*
- *Daily Language Practice*
- *Fine Art* 19–24
- *Two-Minute Skill Drill*
- *Writing Process* 10, 18–22

Other Print Resources

- *Composition Enrichment,* p. 31
- *Composition Practice,* p. 31
- *Composition Reteaching,* p. 31
- *Cooperative Learning Activities,* pp. 17–20
- *Listening and Speaking Activities,* pp. 13, 18, 20, 21
- *Sentence-Combining Practice,* pp. 30–31
- *Thinking and Study Skills,* pp. 3, 13
- *Writing Across the Curriculum*
- *Writing Assessment and Evaluation Rubrics*

Begin with Intensifying Action

You'll want to begin your sports narrative at the point in the event when conflict starts to build. Usually this is the moment when the action intensifies. For example, to tell the story of a team's dramatic, come-from-behind victory, you might begin at the point in the game in which the team seized control and began its push for victory.

Include Supporting Details

Like other narratives, most sports narratives develop a conflict to its climax and resolution. You may want to chart the action that develops the conflict. This technique can help you identify the important events —the supporting details—that you'll want to include.

Development of Conflict in a Sports Narrative

Starting Point:
A baseball game is tied in the bottom of the ninth inning, with two outs. A runner on third represents the winning run.

Conflict:
The pitcher stares at third base. The base runner, determined to break the record for stolen bases, boldly stares back.

Climax:
As the pitcher fires the ball, the base runner makes a dash for home and plows into the catcher.

Resolution:
When the dust clears, the umpire waves his arms and yells, "Safe!" The crowd roars with delight.

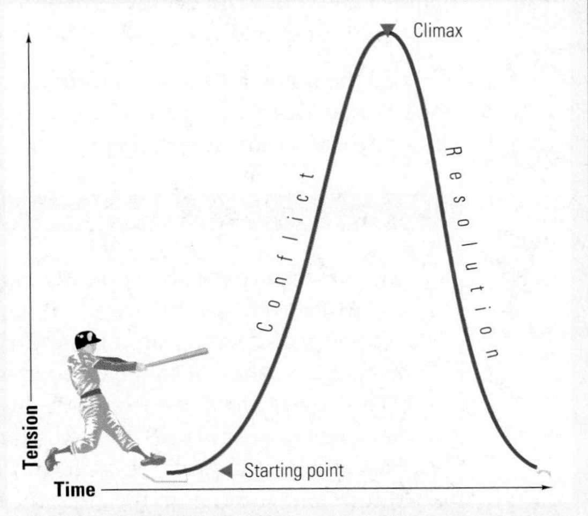

Journal Writing

Watch a sports event at school or on television. Use it as the basis for preparing a sports narrative. Choose a starting point, graph the development of the conflict to its climax and resolution, and then write a brief summary of each point in the plot.

Teach

Using the Model

Ask students to identify images that are particularly vivid in the model on page 196. (arms scooping water, heads bobbing rhythmically, cheering teammates leaning close to the water, the blond head moving through the water, the ear-to-ear grin) Then ask students to point out verbs that are active and precise. (scooping, bobbing, straining) Remind students that a good sports narrative—like other narratives—has a climax and a resolution. Students should identify the point at which the swimmers are neck and neck as the climax. The conflict is resolved when the deaf swimmer wins the race. **L2**

Two-Minute Skill Drill

List the four literary elemen[illegible] on the board, and have students use them to describe the events in a sporting event they have seen or participated in. Have students write one sentence for each element.

See also *Two-Minute Skill Drill Transparency 4.5*

Journal Writing Tip

Using Body Language As action in a sporting event intensifies, spectators often find themselves literally on the edge of their seats. When the conflict is resolved and the tension eases, spectators relax. Suggest that students observe their own body language to help them identify the starting point, climax, and resolution of the conflict in their narratives.

Teach

Using the Model

Encourage students to discuss how Angell makes this portion of the baseball game interesting. Some of the auditory details students should point out include the muttering of somebody in the press box, the "spatters of applause," a "thin, a-cappella rendering of 'Happy Birthday,'" and "the hum of voices, the undercurrent of talk and cheers and laughter and vender cries." **L2**

Graphing a Story

Graphing a story's development may help students who have difficulty understanding the more abstract concepts of conflict, climax, and resolution. Choose another example from a sports story suggested by a student. Let the student tell or read the story, and then graph it on the board. This will reinforce how the concepts apply in a specific narrative. **L1**

Additional Resources

- For further stimuli for narrative writing, see *Fine Art Transparencies* 19–24.
- *Writing Process Transparencies* 10, 18–22
- *Writing Across the Curriculum*
- *Cooperative Learning Activities*
- *Thinking and Study Skills,* pp. 3, 13
- *Sentence-Combining Practice,* pp. 30–31
- *Listening and Speaking Activities,* pp. 13–18
- *Composition Practice,* p. 31

Prewriting Tip

When prewriting about a sports event, try list-making to generate details. Use the significant details to develop your narrative.

Vocabulary Tip

When revising your writing, use a thesaurus to help you find more precise, vivid verbs. A thesaurus lists words with their synonyms and, if applicable, their antonyms.

What verbs does Angell use to help the reader "see" the action in the ballpark?

Build a Memorable Story

After you've chosen a sports event, determined your starting point, and charted the action, you're ready to draft your sports narrative. Begin by considering your lead. A **lead** is a strong opening sentence that grabs the reader's attention and gets the story moving. Examine your story's starting point. Is there anything dramatic, amusing, or surprising about it? If so, you might use that for your lead. Remember, however, that a narration of the event will only make up part of your article. (For tips on how to write a sports feature, see the Unit 4 Media Connection on pages 176–178.)

State the Facts Clearly Be sure that you have presented the sequence of events and all the facts clearly. Double-check quotations for accuracy, and make sure each source is identified.

Use Vivid Language Wherever possible, show the action rather than tell about it. Vivid action verbs and sensory details can bring your story to life and hold your readers' interest.

Read the following selection from baseball writer Roger Angell's book *Season Ticket.* Notice how Angell makes even a seemingly actionless stretch of a game interesting.

Literature Model

A base runner leads cautiously away from first, then trots back as the pitcher steps off the rubber. The third-base ump walks seven steps out toward left field, turns, and strolls back again. Another foul ball, bounced softly past first base. "Throw it *straight,*" somebody in the press box mutters. There are spatters of applause in the stands, but they die away for lack of hope. . . . I can see some fans getting up, in twos and threes, and heading up the aisles for home and dinner. The park is half empty by now. Out in the sloping right-field sector of the seats, there is a thin, a-cappella rendering of "Happy Birthday," for somebody—her name is Ella, it turns out—and other fans around the park join in on the last "happy birthday to you-ooo!" and Ella gets a little round of applause, too. But that ends as well (a coach is out talking to the pitcher now), and even the everyday noises of the baseball park—the hum of voices, the undercurrent of talk and cheers and laughter and vender cries—drop and fade, and Fenway Park is almost silent, just for a minute.

Roger Angell, *Season Ticket*

Cooperative Learning

Understanding Sports Terms

Some students may be unfamiliar with the specialized terminology used in sports and sports writing. Before these students choose a topic for a sports narrative, you may want to ask a small group of students to list appropriate sports terms and explain or act out their definitions.

4.5 Writing Activities

Write a Sports Narrative

The editor of your school newspaper has asked you to write a sports narrative based on an important basketball game. Use the following information to write the narrative.

> West High and East High, long-standing rivals, meet in the state basketball finals. The game is close until the fourth quarter, when East High pulls ahead, 78–70. Finally, West High rallies to win the game 82–80, on a last-second basket.

PURPOSE To narrate an exciting sports event for a school newspaper
AUDIENCE Student and teacher sports fans
LENGTH 3–6 paragraphs

WRITING RUBRICS To write an effective sports narrative, you should

- provide essential background information
- bring your conflict to a climax and provide a resolution
- state the facts clearly in vivid language

Listening and Speaking

COOPERATIVE LEARNING Work in small groups to brainstorm ideas for a sports narrative. Chart the action. Then have one group member begin the story, someone else write the next section, and so on until everyone has written a section and the story is brought to a conclusion.

GrammarLink

Use vivid verbs in your narratives.

Effective sports stories contain verbs that let the reader "see" what is happening. Rewrite the sentences below, replacing all bold-faced words with more vivid action verbs.

1. The Phoenix Suns **went** out onto the basketball court as the overflow hometown crowd **clapped.**
2. The power forward **got** the tip and immediately **ran** to the basket.
3. The crowd **applauded** as he moved around the opposing center to score.
4. When the point guard **made** 6 of 13 three-point shots, the arena **shook.**
5. After the center **took** the ball from an opposing player and scored to win the game for Phoenix, the Phoenix coach **got up** from the bench.

See Lesson 10.3, page 452.

Cross-Curricular Activity

BROADCAST JOURNALISM With a partner, write a script describing a crucial moment in an actual sports event, such as a football game or a soccer match. Using television or radio sportscasts as your guide, create a narrative of the moment that builds to a dramatic climax, sets the scene, and provides a detailed, colorful analysis of the contest and the players. Record your script on audiotape, being sure to perform your parts with the proper enthusiasm.

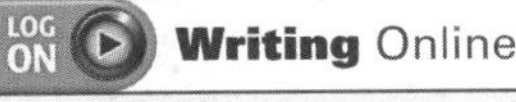
Writing Online — For more writing and grammar practice, go to glencoe.com and enter QuickPass code WC97727p1.

Assess

Evaluation Rubrics

Write a Sports Narrative

Use these criteria when evaluating your students' writing:

- Does the narrative include essential background information?
- Is the conflict brought to a climax and resolved?
- Does the narrative contain action verbs and sensory details?

See also *Writing Assessment & Evaluation Rubrics*

Listening and Speaking

Evaluate the narrative on the following: sequencing of events; use of detail in describing setting and characters; use of a conflict that leads to a climax and ultimate resolution.

Reteaching

Composition Reteaching, p. 31

Enrichment

Composition Enrichment, p. 31

Fine Art Transparencies 19–24

Close

Ask students how they would cover a sports event for their school or for a community newspaper. Students might be attending the event, watching it on television, or listening to it on the radio. What kinds of details would they include? What background would they provide?

GrammarLink

Answers

Answers will vary, but some suggestions are given below.

1. trotted; roared
2. snagged; raced
3. thundered
4. sank; exploded
5. stole; jumped up

Focus

Lesson Overview

Objectives
- To identify two common ways to create suspense in a narrative
- To analyze the elements that create suspense in literature

Skills
- recognizing foreshadowing; recognizing when information is being withheld from the reader or from a character

Critical Thinking
- analyzing; evaluating; synthesizing; making inferences

Listening and Speaking
- discussing

Bellringer
Daily Language Activity

When students enter the classroom, have this assignment on the board: *Write the name of a character from a suspenseful book or movie. Then write one or two sentences describing the problem or conflict the character faces.*

Grammar Link to the Bellringer

Call on volunteers to write their Bellringer sentences on the board. Identify any possessive nouns and check their punctuation.

See also  *Daily Language Practice*

Motivating Activity

Discuss students' responses to the Bellringer activity. Ask students what makes books and movies suspenseful. Write their ideas on the board. When they have finished this lesson, they may want to add more ideas to the list.

Narrative Writing

LESSON 4.6

WRITING ABOUT LITERATURE

Writing About Suspense

Two of the most common ways to build suspense in a narrative are to use foreshadowing and to withhold information from the reader. In this painting the artist effectively creates suspense, or anxiety about what will happen next.

Grant Wood, *Death on the Ridge Road,* 1935

Ways to Create Suspense

- **Foreshadowing** Foreshadowing gives clues about what is going to happen later in the story. Writers often use this technique to prepare the reader for an ominous turn of events. The clues may include details of setting, characters, or plot. In the example on page 201, note how writer Mario Vargas Llosa uses a character's fearful imaginings to foreshadow events to come.
- **Withholding Information** In withholding information from the reader, a writer creates a puzzle with a few pieces missing and leaves a mystery to be solved. Curious to find out what will happen, the reader reads on. Mystery writers often withhold some key piece of information until the final scene when the mystery is solved.

Resource Manager

Planning Resources
- *Lesson Plans*

Transparencies
- *Bellringer*
- *Daily Language Practice*
- *Fine Art* 19–24
- *Two-Minute Skill Drill*
- *Writing Process* 10, 18–22

Other Print Resources
- *Composition Enrichment,* p. 32
- *Composition Practice,* p. 32
- *Composition Reteaching,* p. 32
- *Cooperative Learning Activities,* pp. 17–20
- *Listening and Speaking Activities,* pp. 13, 18, 20, 21
- *Sentence-Combining Practice,* pp. 30–31
- *Thinking and Study Skills,* pp. 5, 13
- *Writing Across the Curriculum*
- *Writing Assessment and Evaluation Rubrics*

Literature Model

After swimming for a few minutes Miguel felt the cold that had momentarily vanished coming over him again, and he speeded up his strokes because it was in his legs, especially in his calves, that the water had a greater effect, first making them insensitive, then stiffening them. He was swimming with his face in the water, and each time his right arm rose out of it, he turned his head to expel air and breathe in another supply, at which he submerged his face and chin once more, just barely, so as not to hinder his own progress but, on the contrary, to split the water like a prow and make his forward movement easier. With each stroke he glanced at Rubén swimming smoothly, effortlessly on the surface, not splashing now, with the delicacy and ease of a seagull gliding. Miguel tried to forget Rubén and the sea and the breakers, which must still be far off, for the water was clear and calm, and they were swimming only through newly risen surf. He wanted to remember nothing but Flora's face and the down on her arms that sparkled on sunny days like a little forest of golden threads. But he could not prevent another image from succeeding to that of the girl—the image of a mountain of raging water . . . in a real ocean stirred by inner cataclysms in which were thrown up unusual waves that could have swamped an entire ship and upset it with astonishing rapidity, hurling passengers, lifeboats, masts, sails, sailors, porthole covers, and flags into the air.

Mario Vargas Llosa, "Sunday"

The writer builds suspense by describing Miguel's progress, stroke by stroke. As a result, the reader feels the character's weariness and fear.

What image does the author use to foreshadow the possible dangers ahead for Miguel?

Narrative Writing

Journal Writing

Sometimes a writer withholds information from the character(s) in a story but reveals it to the readers. What effect does this have on the reader? How does it create suspense? Write your ideas about this technique in your journal.

Teach

Using the Model

Point out how Mario Vargas Llosa contrasts pleasant images (Rubén swimming smoothly, the clear and calm water, Flora's face) with disturbing ones (a mountain of raging water, the image of a ship overturned by waves) in the model. Students should respond that Llosa uses an image of tidal waves to foreshadow dangers that may lie ahead for Miguel. Tell students that suspense can also be created by setting up a contrast between images. Grant Wood does this in his painting through the contrast between light and dark. **L2**

Analyzing Suspense

Mystery writer Leonard Tourney claims that "Suspense is possible in fiction because of two human traits: the first is curiosity; the second is the capacity we all share of being able to experience vicariously the predicaments and states of mind of imaginary persons." Ask students whether or not they agree with Tourney, or if there are other suspense-inducing traits they would identify. Have them choose a work of suspense and write a brief analysis of it in reference to Tourney's statement. **L3**

Journal Writing Tip

Activating Prior Knowledge
Suggest that students try to recall a particular situation in a suspenseful movie or story when they knew what was about to happen but the character did not. What was their reaction?

Viewing the Art

Grant Wood, *Death on the Ridge Road,* 1935
Grant Wood painted *Death on the Ridge Road* (page 200) after a friend was hurt in a car crash. Wood, who painted primarily Midwestern farm scenes, belonged to the Regionalism art movement.

Teach

Using the Model

Students should respond that Elizabeth Chen withholds information by not telling what "the biggest game" is, alluding only to the "diabolical" nature of the answer. **L2**

Choosing a Story

Some suspense stories that students might read and analyze include "The Tell-Tale Heart," by Edgar Allan Poe; "Through the Tunnel," by Doris Lessing; "Witness for the Prosecution," by Agatha Christie; and "The Sniper," by Liam O'Flaherty. Suggest that when they write about their chosen stories, students might want to focus on one or two suspense-building techniques. **L2**

Two-Minute Skill Drill

Have students choose either a suspenseful film or written work and write down two things that contribute to the suspense.

See also *Two-Minute Skill Drill Transparency 4.6*

Additional Resources

For further stimuli for analyzing suspense, see *Fine Art Transparencies* 19–24.

Writing Process Transparencies 10, 18–22

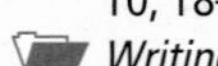

Writing Across the Curriculum

Cooperative Learning Activities
Thinking and Study Skills, pp. 5, 13
Sentence-Combining Practice, pp. 30–31
Listening and Speaking Activities, pp. 13, 18, 20, 21
Composition Practice, p. 32

Narrative Writing

Drafting Tip

Sensory details can add immediacy to your suspense writing and draw the reader into your story. See Lesson 2.6 on page 81 to help you develop these details.

Grammar Tip

When you edit your writing, check to see that you have formed all possessive nouns, such as *General Zaroff's* island, correctly. You may want to refer to Lesson 9.10, pages 406–407, and Lesson 21.11, pages 759–761, for help.

Write About a Suspenseful Story

When you analyze a suspenseful story, focus on the ways in which the writer creates suspense. Provide examples from the text to support your ideas. As you read, ask yourself the questions in the chart below.

Questions to Determine How a Writer Creates Suspense

1. What details in the descriptions of the characters help build suspense?
2. Which events in the plot help build suspense?
3. What aspects of the setting build suspense?
4. What are the characters' reactions as suspense builds?
5. What atmosphere or mood does the writer create? How does the mood change?
6. In what ways does the writer foreshadow events to come?
7. What information does the writer withhold from the characters?

By exploring your answers to these questions through freewriting or brainstorming, you can develop a focus for an analysis of a suspense story. In the model below, Elizabeth Chen analyzes some of the techniques writer Richard Connell uses to build suspense in his short story "The Most Dangerous Game."

Student Model

Richard Connell uses foreshadowing to heighten suspense in "The Most Dangerous Game." When Rainsford falls off his yacht and swims to General Zaroff's island, he is relieved to reach its "dense jungle." However, the narrator states, "What perils that tangle of trees and underbrush might hold for him did not concern Rainsford just then." This statement suggests that the character will soon be in danger. By foreshadowing this future event, the author creates a sense of anticipation in the reader and compels him to read on.

Connell also draws the reader into the story by withholding information. When Zaroff asserts that he hunts "the biggest" game on his island, he does not at first reveal what that game might be. As a result, Rainsford and the reader are forced to guess. The diabolical answer, which directs the course of the rest of the story, becomes clear to both at about the same time.

Elizabeth Chen, Downers Grove North High School, Downers Grove, Illinois

Chen uses specific examples from the story to develop the focus of her essay.

At the end of her essay, how does Chen herself withhold information in order to pique the reader's interest in the story?

Critical Thinking

Focusing the Analysis

When students read suspense stories, have them focus on questions 1–3 in the guidelines at the top of this page. These three questions ask for more concrete kinds of analysis than do questions 4–7. As students notice the details in the descriptions of characters and setting, have them write any unfamiliar words and then look these words up in a dictionary or ask another student to explain their meanings.

4.6 Writing Activities

Write to Analyze Setting

Read the following excerpt from Edgar Allan Poe's short story "The Pit and the Pendulum." Then use the questions from page 202 to help you write an analysis.

> So far, I had not opened my eyes. I felt that I lay upon my back, unbound. I reached out my hand, and it fell heavily upon something damp and hard. There I suffered it to remain for many minutes, while I strove to imagine where and *what* I could be. I longed, yet dared not to employ my vision. I dreaded the first glance at objects around me. It was not that I feared to look upon things horrible, but that I grew aghast lest there should be *nothing* to see.

PURPOSE To identify the details in a story's setting that help create suspense
AUDIENCE Your classmates
LENGTH 1–2 paragraphs

WRITING RUBRICS To write an effective analysis of a setting, you should
- identify the mood of the passage
- identify the physical details that contribute to the mood of the passage
- explain how the passage foreshadows events or creates mystery or suspense

Cross-Curricular Activity

MEDIA STUDIES In two or three paragraphs, analyze how your favorite suspenseful movie uses foreshadowing, withholds information, and creates mood through lighting, camera angles, music, and sound.

Grammar*Link*

Use possessive nouns correctly.

Words like *Flora's* and *General Zaroff's* are *possessive nouns.*

Possessive nouns can be singular or plural. Revise the following sentences about the student model on page 202 by creating possessives using the words in boldface.

1. **The story of Richard Connell** uses foreshadowing to heighten suspense.
2. **The conflict of Rainsford and General Zaroff** is a serious one.
3. Only one man can win **the contest of the two men.**
4. The suspense of the situation grabs **the interest of the readers.**
5. **The analysis of Elizabeth Chen** does not reveal the outcome of the contest.

See Lesson 21.11, pages 759–761.

Listening and Speaking

CREATING A STORY Introduce a story by describing a scene in a way that creates mystery. Then turn to a classmate and ask him or her to continue the story. When he or she reaches a turning point, ask another classmate to pick up the story. Continue in this manner until the story reaches a satisfying close.

LOG ON **Writing** Online | For more writing and grammar practice, go to glencoe.com and enter QuickPass code WC97727p1.

Assess

Evaluation Rubrics

Write to Analyze Setting

Use these criteria to evaluate your students' writing:
- Does the analysis deal with the points in the questions on page 202?
- Are ideas logical and explained clearly?
- Are ideas supported with specific examples from the story?

See also *Writing Assessment & Evaluation Rubrics*

Cross-Curricular Activity

Use these criteria to evaluate your students' analyses:
- Does the analysis deal with the points in the questions on page 202?
- Are ideas logical and explained clearly?
- Are ideas supported with specific examples from the movie?

Reteaching

Composition Reteaching, p. 32

Enrichment

Composition Enrichment, p. 32

Fine Art Transparencies 19–24

Close

Have students write a concluding sentence for a suspense story. Students may work alone or in groups to generate story ideas.

Grammar*Link*

Answers

1. Richard Connell's story . . .
2. Rainsford's and General Zaroff's conflict . . .
3. . . . the two men's contest.
4. . . . readers' interest.
5. Elizabeth Chen's analysis . . .

Focus

Lesson Overview

Objectives
- To identify three points of view available to a writer
- To write an analysis of a narrator's point of view

Skills
- identifying first-person and third-person points of view; analyzing the effects of point of view

Critical Thinking
- drawing conclusions

Listening and Speaking
- discussing

Bellringer
Daily Language Activity

When students enter the classroom, have this assignment on the board: *If you were writing in a diary, from whose point of view would you write? Write a sample sentence for a diary.*

Grammar Link to the Bellringer

Correct the following sentence to avoid shifting from one pronoun to another:

He had no trouble finding their way back.

See also *Daily Language Practice*

Motivating Activity

Discuss students' responses to the Bellringer activity. Explain that in a diary the point of view is usually first person, so the narrator would use pronouns such as *I, we,* and *us.*

Narrative Writing

LESSON 4.7

WRITING ABOUT LITERATURE

Analyzing Point of View in a Narrative

Just as a performer on the stage and a person in the audience would describe a rock concert differently, so would different narrators tell a story differently. The author's choice of narrator determines how a particular story is told and how, in turn, a reader understands the story.

Identify the Point of View

The writer of a narrative selects a point of view, or a perspective, from which to tell the story. The author usually chooses from among three basic points of view.

In a story told from a first-person point of view, the narrator is a character in the story. This type of narrator uses first-person pronouns, such as *I* and *we,* in telling the story. A first-person narrator knows only what he or she is thinking and describes only the events he or she witnesses.

In a story told from a third-person limited point of view, the narrator stands outside the story. This type of narrator uses third-person pronouns such as *he, she, it,* and *they.* The third-person limited narrator describes the actions and words of all the characters but the thoughts and feelings of only one character.

In a story told from a third-person omniscient point of view, the narrator stands outside the action but knows all and sees all. A third-person omniscient narrator can relate everything that happens in the story, including the thoughts and feelings of all the characters.

Resource Manager

Planning Resources
- *Lesson Plans*

Transparencies
- *Bellringer*
- *Daily Language Practice*
- *Fine Art* 19–24
- *Two-Minute Skill Drill*
- *Writing Process* 10, 18–22

Other Print Resources
- *Composition Enrichment,* p. 33
- *Composition Practice,* p. 33
- *Composition Reteaching,* p. 33
- *Cooperative Learning Activities,* pp. 17–20
- *Listening and Speaking Activities,* pp. 13, 18, 20, 21
- *Research Paper and Report Writing,* p. 49
- *Sentence-Combining Practice,* pp. 30–31
- *Thinking and Study Skills,* p. 24
- *Writing Across the Curriculum*
- *Writing Assessment and Evaluation Rubrics*

Examine the Effect of Point of View

After identifying the point of view of a narrative, notice what effect the choice of point of view has on the presentation of the story. Then use examples from the text to support your opinion.

- **First-Person Narrator** Stories told by a first-person narrator tend to draw the reader into the action because the reader identifies with the "I" who is telling the story. As you evaluate the effect of point of view of a narrative, remember that the first-person narrator may be a biased or unreliable witness. In the following selection from Eugenia Collier's short story "Marigolds," the first-person narrator recalls how she felt after hearing her father cry for the first time.

Literature Model

> The world had lost its boundary lines. My mother, who was small and soft, was now the strength of the family; my father, who was the rock on which the family had been built, was sobbing like the tiniest child. Everything was suddenly out of tune, like a broken accordion. Where did I fit into this crazy picture? I do not now remember my thoughts, only a feeling of great bewilderment and fear.
>
> Eugenia Collier, "Marigolds"

Notice that the first-person narrator only reports her own pain and confusion. She does not consider how her father must be feeling.

Do you identify with the child telling the story? Why?

- **Third-Person Limited Narrator** A third-person limited narrator stands outside the story but relates events as if he or she were looking over the shoulder of one of the characters. Because the narrator is so close to this one character, the reader tends to identify with and sympathize with the character. Be aware, however, that this narrator may withhold information or tell more than the character would tell.

Grammar Tip

When writing about point of view, be sure to refer to the narrator rather than the author of the narrative. As you edit your writing, check that all pronoun references are clear. See Lessons 9.5–9.6, pages 398–400.

Journal Writing

Choose a piece of narrative writing told by a third-person limited narrator. Now imagine the same piece told by a first-person narrator. What effect might the change in point of view have on the story? Write down your ideas in your journal.

Narrative Writing

Teach

Using the Model

Tell students that the narrator's descriptions of her mother and father reflect a child's view of parents—larger than life—and a child's fear in seeing a seemingly powerful parent displaying childlike behavior. Students may identify with the narrator's fear if they have had a similar experience. Students may also identify with the child because of the use of *I*. **L2**

Identifying Point of View Through Photography

Suggest that students study the photograph on page 204 and consider the following question: How is the viewer's impression of the subjects in the photograph affected by how the photographer chose to capture them? Ask whether the viewer sees the musicians as if he or she were one of them. Does the viewer see the musicians as if he or she is a member of the audience? How is a photographer like a writer in choosing point of view? **L1**

Two-Minute Skill Drill

Have students quickly list five subject-verb expressions that reflect point of view. Use the following as prompts:

I was . . .

She thought . . .

See also *Two-Minute Skill Drill Transparency 4.7*

Journal Writing Tip

Drawing Conclusions Suggest that students try to imagine themselves as the first-person narrator to help them draw conclusions about the effect on the story.

4.7

Teach

Using the Models

Point out that Mathew Isaac begins by identifying the point of view and then identifies the effect of point of view on the story. (The writer supports his opinions with a quotation from the text, a reference to a comparison made by the story's narrator, and a discussion of the story's ending.)

In the John Updike selection, students may comment that the reader feels some anxiety because the narrator doesn't tell what happened to the skier. (The use of the phrases *as if she might know* and *her tone suggested* indicate that the narrator may not be telling the reader everything about the characters' thoughts.) **L2**

Cooperative Learning

Read the first model aloud. Then pose the callout question. Give students time to think about their responses, then have them discuss their ideas with a partner. Finally, invite several pairs to share their thoughts with the class. **L2**

Additional Resources

For further stimuli for narrative writing, see *Fine Art Transparencies* 19–24.

Writing Process Transparencies 10, 18–22

Thinking and Study Skills, p. 24

Writing Across the Curriculum

Research Paper and Report Writing, p. 49

Cooperative Learning Activities

Sentence-Combining Practice, pp. 30–31

Listening and Speaking Activities, pp. 13, 18, 20, 21

Composition Practice, p. 33

Narrative Writing

In the following example, Mathew Isaac analyzes the effect of a third-person limited narrator in O. Henry's "The Gift of the Magi."

Student Model

Isaac maintains that O. Henry uses a third-person limited narrator to make the story's ironic ending more effective.

What specific examples and quotations from the story does Isaac use to support his opinion?

In O. Henry's "The Gift of the Magi," a third-person limited narrator primarily relates the actions, thoughts, and feelings of the character Della. The narrator withholds information from the reader about her husband, Jim, and thereby sets up the story's final, ironic twist.

The story's narrator is also used to comment ironically on the characters themselves. For example, when Della cries because she doesn't have enough money to buy Jim a present, the narrator remarks that "life is made up of sobs, sniffles, and smiles, with sniffles predominating." . . .

Although we are encouraged to laugh at Della and Jim, at the story's end, the reader is the object of the narrator's irony. There it is implied that the reader who only laughs at the pair, without recognizing their deep love, is the real fool.

Mathew Isaac, Rich East High School, Park Forest, Illinois

- **Third-Person Omniscient Narrator** The third-person omniscient narrator stands outside the action of the story but relates the thoughts, feelings, words, and actions of all the characters. Although this narrator seems objective, keep in mind that he or she still tells only as much or as little as the author wants to reveal.

In the selection below, Ethan and his daughter Becky ride a ski lift. Consider what the narrator tells about the story's events and characters.

Literature Model

The narrator doesn't reveal what happens to the out-of-control skier. What effect does this have on the reader?

What words and phrases suggest that the narrator may not be telling the reader everything about the characters' thoughts?

A dark figure with spreading legs veered out of control beneath them, fell forward, and vanished. Ethan cried out, astonished, scandalized; he imagined the man had buried himself alive. Becky was barely amused, and looked away before the dark spots struggling in the drift were lost from sight. As if she might know, Ethan asked, "Who was that?"

"Some kid." Kids, her tone suggested, were in plentiful supply; one could be spared.

John Updike, "Man and Daughter in the Cold"

English Language Learners

Analyzing Literature

Limited English vocabulary may make it difficult for some students to analyze a piece of literature. Let these students work with partners who can help explain difficult passages and define words, including their connotations.

Evaluate students' work by assessing how well ideas are communicated and what improvement is shown as they work through subsequent drafts.

Write to Analyze Point of View in a Story

Write a letter to a friend in which you discuss a short story you have read recently. Give the story's title and author, and tell about the story by analyzing its point of view. What effect does the story's viewpoint have on the conflict? What effect does its point of view have on the resolution? How would the story be different if it had been written from another point of view? Close your letter by telling whether or not you recommend the story.

PURPOSE To analyze the effect of point of view on a short story
AUDIENCE Your friend
LENGTH 1–2 paragraphs

WRITING RUBRICS To write an effective analysis of point of view, you should

- clearly identify the point of view as first person, third-person limited, or third-person omniscient
- use examples from the text to discuss the effect of the point of view

When you're ready to edit your analysis, use the spelling checker on your computer to help you proofread your work. Remember that the checker can't catch correctly spelled words that are used incorrectly. If you write *their* when you mean to say *there,* for example, the checker won't recognize the error. Therefore, it's a good idea to proofread your work yourself line by line to find the less obvious mistakes.

GrammarLink

Avoid incorrect pronoun shift.

When you write, avoid shifting pronouns from one person to another.

Incorrect: If one works hard,
you can succeed.

Revise the sentences below to avoid incorrect pronoun shifts.

1. One's point of view is reflected in your understanding of an event.
2. They enjoy first-person narration because you feel close to the action.
3. I use a third-person omniscient narrator so you can relate everything that happens in a story.
4. An author entertains me best by capturing your interest.
5. One's interest will most likely be captured if their curiosity is aroused.

See Lesson 17.5, page 640.

Viewing and Representing

COOPERATIVE LEARNING In groups of three or four, use your school's video equipment to make a brief video of a journey from your classroom to the school office. Review the video and have each group member write a narration from the first-person point of view describing the journey. Use elements of setting, character, and plot to shape the narrative. Then present your video to the class and share the various narratives to demonstrate how the same event might elicit different responses and descriptions.

Assess

Evaluation Rubrics

Write to Analyze Point of View in a Story

Use these criteria when evaluating your students' writing:

- Is the narrator's point of view clearly identified?
- Is the effect of point of view on the story discussed?
- Are specific examples from the story used to support the analysis?

See also *Writing Assessment & Evaluation Rubrics*

Using Computers

Students should use the spelling checker to correct any misspelled words. Check students' writing for correct spelling.

Reteaching

Composition Reteaching, p. 33

Enrichment

Composition Enrichment, p. 33

Close

Ask students to imagine writing a story about a sports event. Ask them from whose point of view the story might be told. (coach, athlete, fan, cheerleader, professional scout) Then ask students to discuss whether the narrator should tell the story in the first-person, third-person limited, or third-person omniscient. Have students review the advantages and disadvantages of telling a story from each point of view.

GrammarLink

Answers

1. Your point of view is reflected in your . . .
2. They enjoy first-person narration because they feel close to the action.
3. I use a third-person omniscient narrator so I can relate . . .
4. An author entertains me best by capturing my interest.
5. One's interest will most likely be captured if one's curiosity is aroused.

Focus

Lesson Overview

Objective
- To develop a narrative based on a real or imagined conflict

Skills
- writing a coherent narrative using the five stages of the writing process: prewriting, drafting, revising, editing/proofreading, publishing/presenting

Critical Thinking
- synthesizing information from real life; questioning; evaluating

Listening and Speaking
- discussing; presenting information

Bellringer
Daily Language Activity

When students enter the classroom, have this assignment on the board: *Write about a conflict you have seen or experienced. It may be one you have read about or seen in a movie or television program. How was it resolved?*

Grammar Link to the Bellringer
Have students check their answers and make sure all proper nouns are capitalized.

See also *Daily Language Practice*

Motivating Activity
Discuss students' responses to the Bellringer activity. Explain that in this lesson students will write a narrative based on a conflict. Suggest that students use conflict in a narrative much the same way Julia Alvarez does. Have students consider how to use characters, plot, and setting in their stories. Remind students that they may write about an imaginary conflict.

UNIT 4
Writing Process in Action

Narrative Writing

Narrative Writing

In preceding lessons you've learned the basics of narrative—characters, setting, plot, and conflict. You've also had the chance to analyze anecdotes and elements of suspense and to create dialogue. Now it's time to put into practice what you've learned. You're invited to write a narrative that is based on a central conflict and its resolution.

Assignment

Context

You have been asked to contribute to an anthology of student writing called *Resolutions,* a book of stories about various kinds of conflicts. Your story, which can be happy or serious, may be based on a real incident or may be wholly imaginary. It may be told in the first or the third person.

Purpose

To write a true or fictionalized narrative about a conflict.

Audience

High school students and teachers throughout the nation

Length

1–2 pages.

Planning to Write

You will find the next few pages helpful for planning and writing your narrative. Begin by reading through the pages, but don't feel you have to remember everything on them. You can refer to the pages when you need to. Use the suggestions, but don't feel limited by them. Remember, you're in charge of your own writing process. Before you begin, set a time frame for completing this assignment. Doing so will help you pace yourself throughout the writing process. Make sure to keep in mind the controlling idea: to write a true or fictionalized narrative about a conflict.

For prewriting, drafting, revising, editing and publishing tools, go to **glencoe.com** and enter QuickPass code WC97727p1.

Resource Manager

Planning Resources
- *Lesson Plans*

Transparencies
- *Bellringer*
- *Daily Language Practice*
- *Writing Process* 10, 18–22

Other Print Resources
- *Composition Enrichment,* p. 34
- *Composition Practice,* p. 34
- *Composition Reteaching,* p. 34
- *Grammar Workbook,* Lessons 98–102
- *Sentence-Combining Practice,* pp. 30–31
- *Thinking and Study Skills,* pp. 23, 31–32
- *Writing Assessment and Evaluation Rubrics*

Web Site
- *glencoe.com*

Prewriting

What to write about—something imaginary or something that has actually happened to you or someone you know? Something amusing, suspenseful, or unusual? Your first task is choosing a problem or incident in which a character faces a conflict that needs to be resolved. The prewriting options may help you think of a conflict you can use.

Once you have selected an incident, map out the sequence of events involved in it. Next, arrange these details on a time line, even though you don't have to tell your story in strictly chronological order. Finally, decide what point of view you will use: first-person, third-person limited, or third-person omniscient narrator.

Prewriting Options

- List events that you remember.
- Skim your journal for ideas.
- Brainstorm imaginary conflict situations.
- Freewrite about an issue or topic you feel strongly about.
- Narrow your choices to conflicts your characters can resolve.

Drafting

To begin drafting, envision the scene in which the conflict of your story reaches its crisis point. If you've chosen to write from a particular character's point of view, get inside that character's head. Then begin writing about that crisis moment. Use vivid action verbs and strong sensory details to describe what is going on. Notice the language Julia Alvarez uses to convey how a crisis erupts in the model below.

Prewriting Tip

If you want to review information about third-person narration, see Lesson 4.7, pages 204–207.

Literature Model

The expression on his face shocked both mother and daughter. Carlos's toothless mouth had collapsed into a dark zero. His eyes bored into Yoyo, then shifted to Laura. In barely audible Spanish, as if secret microphones or informers were all about, he whispered to his wife, "You will permit her to read *that*?"

Julia Alvarez, *How the García Girls Lost Their Accents*

Drafting Tip

To find out more about developing conflict in a narrative, see Lesson 4.2, pages 184–187.

Teach

Prewriting

Developing Ideas for Narrative Writing

Remind students not to worry about errors in grammar, spelling, or punctuation during prewriting. Encourage them to return to the prewriting stage as often as necessary to help them develop characters, write dialogue, or come up with an idea for an anecdote.

Suggest that in prewriting students tell their story as if they were writing it in a letter to a best friend. This can get their ideas flowing freely and release them from the self-consciousness and anxieties that may accompany writing for an assignment. **L2**

Additional Resources

Listening and Speaking Activities, pp. 13, 18, 20, 21

Drafting

Cooperative Learning

To help students draft their stories, divide the class into small groups for a round-robin activity. Ask students to take turns telling their stories aloud to the group. Following each presentation, each group member in turn should offer at least one comment about the story. Group responses may help students identify both weak and strong points in their narratives. **L2**

Using the Model

Have students identify the conflict in this passage. Does the writer give any details about cultural background? Remind students that including cultural details in their stories can help them create realistic characters like the Garcías. **L2**

Teach

Revising

Peer Editing

Students can work in writing conferences with peer editors before they revise their work. You may want to duplicate the Peer Response form in *Writing Assessment & Evaluation Rubrics.* Suggest that peer editors respond to the following questions:

- How would you sum up the main conflict of the story in one or two sentences?
- What are the most memorable anecdotes in the story? Why?
- What did you find confusing about the story? Why? L2

Cooperative Learning

Have small groups of students listen to what each group member has written. Listeners should note the narrative's flow and rhythm, whether transitions are effective, and passages that seem confusing or jarring. Readers should try to convey the emotion of their narrative with their voices. L2

Journal Writing Tip

Encourage students to think about how they can apply what they have learned about themselves to other writing projects.

Additional Resources

 *Writing Process Transparencies* 10, 18–22

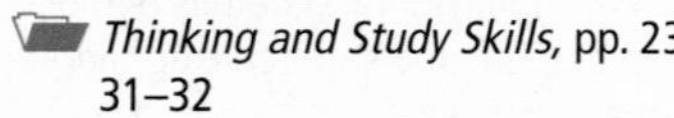 *Thinking and Study Skills,* pp. 23, 31–32

Sentence-Combining Practice, pp. 30–31

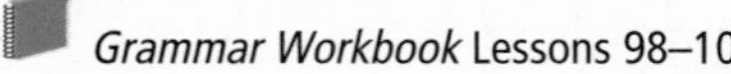 *Composition Practice,* p. 34

Grammar Workbook Lessons 98–102

Drafting Tip

To help you identify where to add dialogue and anecdotes, see Lessons 4.3 and 4.4, pages 188–195.

Next, work backward from your central paragraph. Try to fill in the information about characters, setting, and events the reader needs to know to understand what leads up to this scene.

- Who appears in the scene?
- Why are these characters there?
- How did these characters get there?
- Where does this scene take place?
- Why does it take place in this particular setting?

Then work forward from your central scene. Write about the events that resolve the complication. If you get stuck, focus on answering "What happens next?" Once you have drafted the pieces of your story, refer to your time line to arrange them. Finally, look for good places to add dialogue or anecdotes.

Revising

To begin revising, read over your draft to make sure that what you've written fits your purpose and audience. Then have a **writing conference.** Read your draft to a partner or small group. Use your audience's reactions to help you evaluate your work.

Revising Tip

To review ideas that can help you create suspense, see Lesson 4.6, pages 200–203.

TIME

For more about revising, see **TIME Facing the Blank Page**, pp. 128–129.

Revising Checklist

- Did I select and develop a conflict that can hold my readers' attention?
- Did I present background events and details that explain the basis of the conflict?
- Do my characters believably resolve the conflict?
- Does my narration present a clear and consistent point of view?
- Does the order in which I presented the events in the narrative make sense?
- Did I use dialogue and anecdotes correctly?

Enrichment and Extension

Follow-up Ideas

- Set aside time for students to celebrate the conclusion of their writing projects.
- Encourage students to share their finished pieces with the whole class or in small groups.

Extending Narrative Writing

- Brainstorm with students ways they can use their expertise in narrative writing in other subject areas, such as writing for a local magazine or a school publication.

Editing

When you are satisfied with your narrative, **proofread** it carefully for errors in grammar, usage, mechanics, and spelling. Use the questions in the Editing Checklist as a guide.

In addition to proofreading, use the self-evaluation list below to make sure your narrative does all the things you want it to do. When you feel that it does, make a clean copy of your story and proofread it one more time.

Editing Checklist

- Have I capitalized all proper nouns?
- Have I avoided sentence fragments?
- Have I correctly punctuated direct quotations?
- Have I avoided pronoun shifts?
- Have I used vivid verbs and strong adverbs?
- Have I checked spellings of any words I'm unsure of?

Self-Evaluation

Make sure your conflict narrative—

- ✔ focuses on an interesting conflict
- ✔ hooks interest by establishing setting, characters, and conflict early
- ✔ uses dialogue, anecdotes, and figurative language effectively
- ✔ uses point of view consistently
- ✔ follows correct grammar, usage, mechanics, and spelling

Presenting

Although for this assignment you have written a narrative for a fictitious anthology, there's no reason you can't submit it to a real anthology. You might have your story published in your school literary magazine. If you want to submit it for publication for a wider audience, ask your teacher or librarian to suggest suitable journals.

Proofreading Tip

For proofreading symbols, see pages 98 and 411.

Journal Writing: Write to Learn

Reflect on your writing process experience. Answer these questions in your journal: What do you like best about your narrative? What was the hardest part about writing it? What did you learn in your writing conference? What new things have you learned as a writer?

Editing/Proofreading

Peer Editing

After students have edited their own work, have them edit another student's writing. Remind them to refer to the Editing Checklist on page 211. **L2**

Publishing/Presenting

Before students present their narrative writing, discuss how to prepare their papers for publication. Emphasize the importance of the final draft and that it must be neatly done. **L2**

Assess

Evaluation Rubric

Use the following criteria to evaluate students' finished writing:

- Does the narrative contain fresh and effective use of figurative language and anecdotes?
- Does the narrative contain correct grammar, usage, and mechanics?
- Is the conflict clear?
- Are the climax and resolution predictable or fresh?
- Is the dialogue realistic?

Reteaching

Composition Reteaching, p. 34

Enrichment

Composition Enrichment, p. 34

Close

Discuss with students other opportunities to use the five stages of the writing process.

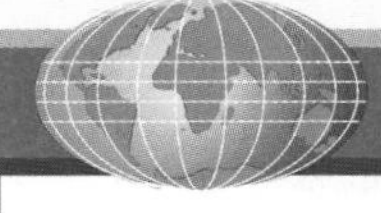

Cultural Connections

Cultural Information

Students writing about their families may need to provide cultural background on their characters and setting. Backround information can be woven into narrative action, conveyed through dialogue, or shown in a flashback or anecdote.

Literature Model

About the Author

In her book *How the García Girls Lost Their Accents,* Julia Alvarez chronicles the lives of a wealthy family from the Dominican Republic living in exile in New York City. The novel unfolds in a series of short stories, each focusing on one or more of the four García sisters. Like the García sisters, Alvarez was born in the Dominican Republic, but has spent most of her life in the United States. A poet and teacher, she published her first collection of poems, *Homecoming,* in 1986.

Focus

Lesson Overview

Objectives

- To examine how a professional writer organizes a compelling story
- To write a friendly letter

Skills

- monitoring comprehension; predicting; summarizing; connecting

Critical Thinking

- inferring; drawing conclusions; analyzing; evaluating

Listening and Speaking

- discussing

Bellringer
Daily Language Activity

When students enter the classroom, have this assignment on the board: *Write about a time you struggled with something you had to write.*

See also  *Daily Language Practice*

Motivating Activity

Discuss students' responses to the Bellringer activity. Did someone or something finally trigger inspiration?

UNIT 4

Literature Model

Narrative Writing

from

How the García Girls Lost Their Accents

by Julia Alvarez

Born in the Dominican Republic, Julia Alvarez came to the United States with her family when she was ten years old. In this selection from "Daughter of Invention," one of the short stories in Alvarez's first book of fiction, How the García Girls Lost Their Accents, *the author presents a simply structured narrative about her family. As you read, focus on characters and conflict. Then respond in the activities in Linking Writing and Literature on page 220.*

Resource Manager

Planning Resources

- *Lesson Plans*

Transparencies

- *Bellringer*
- *Daily Language Practice*
- *Fine Art* 19–24

Other Print Resources

- *Listening and Speaking Activities,* pp. 13, 18, 20, 21
- *Thinking and Study Skills,* pp. 10, 13
- *Writing Assessment and Evaluation Rubrics*

Web Sites

- *writerschoice.glencoe.com*
- *lit.glencoe.com*

Literature Model

The weekend before the assembly Monday morning Yoyo went into a panic. Her mother would just have to call in tomorrow and say Yoyo was in the hospital, in a coma.

Laura tried to calm her down. "Just remember how Mister Lincoln couldn't think of anything to say at the Gettysburg, but then, bang! *Four score and once upon a time ago,*" she began reciting. "Something is going to come if you just relax. You'll see, like the Americans say, *Necessity is the daughter of invention.* I'll help you."

That weekend, her mother turned all her energy towards helping Yoyo write her speech. "Please, Mami, just leave me alone, please," Yoyo pleaded with her. But Yoyo would get rid of the goose only to have to contend with the gander. Her father kept poking his head in the door just to see if Yoyo had "fulfilled your obligations," a phrase he had used when the girls were younger and he'd check to see whether they had gone to the bathroom before a car trip. Several times that weekend around the supper table, he recited his own high school valedictorian speech. He gave Yoyo pointers on delivery, notes on the great orators and their tricks. (Humbleness and praise and falling silent with great emotion were his favorites.)

Laura sat across the table, the only one who seemed to be listening to him. Yoyo and her sisters were forgetting a lot of their Spanish, and their father's formal, florid diction was hard to understand. But Laura smiled softly to herself, and turned the lazy Susan at the center of the table around and around as if it were the prime mover, the first gear of her attention.

That Sunday evening, Yoyo was reading some poetry to get herself inspired: Whitman's poems in an old book with an engraved cover her father had picked up in a thrift shop next to his office. *I celebrate myself and sing myself. . . . He most honors my style who learns under it to destroy the teacher.* The poet's words shocked and thrilled her. She had gotten used to the nuns, a literature of appropriate sentiments, poems with a message, expurgated[1] texts. But here was a flesh and blood man, belching and laughing and sweating in poems. *Who touches this book touches a man.*

That night, at last, she started to write, recklessly, three, five pages, looking up once only to see her father passing by the hall on tiptoe. When Yoyo was done, she read over her words, and her eyes filled. She finally sounded like herself in English!

The poet's words shocked and thrilled her. She had gotten used to the nuns . . . But here was a flesh and blood man . . .

As soon as she had finished that first draft, she called her mother to her room. Laura listened attentively while Yoyo read the speech out loud, and in the end, her eyes were glistening too. Her face was soft and warm and proud. "*Ay,* Yoyo, you are going to be the one to bring our name to the headlights in this country! That is a beautiful, beautiful speech. I want

1 **expurgated** (eks′ pər gāt′ əd) with objectionable passages removed

Teach

Active Reading Strategy

Monitor Comprehension Ask students if they know who Laura is and why she is so concerned about what Yoyo is doing. If students don't know, suggest that they reread to find the answer. *(Laura is Yoyo's mother. Yoyo is in a panic about a speech she has to give Monday morning.)*

Active Reading Strategies

Predict Ask students: "What effect do you think reading Whitman might have on the content of Yoyo's speech?" *(She might use some of his ideas about celebrating one's self. She might say something a little unusual.*

Critical Thinking

Infer

Tell students that to *infer* is to use reason, experience, and clues from the text to guess at what an author does not come right out and say. You might model inferring in this way: "Yoyo's mother wants to help her daughter, so I can infer that she is pretty supportive and positive about Yoyo's effort. I can also infer from Laura's response to the speech that she is very accepting of her daughter's ideas and enthusiastic about her accomplishments."

Practice Ask students what they can infer about Yoyo's father. *(He is also interested in the speech, but he is more distant from and out of touch with his daughter than Laura is.)* Have students give examples from the story to support their inference. *(His asking about fulfilling "obligations" makes him sound a bit formal and out of touch; his advice makes him sound as if he lives in a different world than Yoyo and her mother.)*

Teach

Critical Thinking

Draw Conclusions The author supplies many details about Yoyo's father. Ask students what conclusion they can draw from these details. *(Although Yoyo's father lives in the United States, much of what he values and is concerned about has been shaped by the troubles and dangers of his former life in the Dominican Republic. He is also somewhat of a stereotypical father, who sits reading the newspaper while his wife and daughter deal with the events of daily life.)*

Critical Thinking

Infer Ask students to infer how Yoyo feels about her speech. *(She is extremely proud of it.)* Have students name some details that support their inference. *(Yoyo doesn't need encouragement to read; she reads without looking up; she turns to her father to "share her pride.")*

for your father to hear it before he goes to sleep. Then I will type it for you, all right?"

Down the hall they went, mother and daughter, faces flushed with accomplishment. Into the master bedroom where Carlos was propped up on his pillows, still awake, reading the Dominican papers, already days old. Now that the dictatorship had been toppled, he had become interested in his country's fate again. The interim government was going to hold the first free elections in thirty years. History was in the making, freedom and hope were in the air again! There was still some question in his mind whether or not he might move his family back. But Laura had gotten used to the life here. She did not want to go back to the old country where, de la Torre or not, she was only a wife and a mother (and a failed one at that, since she had never provided the required son). Better an independent nobody than a high-class houseslave. She did not come straight out and disagree with her husband's plans. Instead, she fussed with him about reading the papers in bed, soiling their sheets with those poorly printed, foreign tabloids. "*The Times* is not that bad!" she'd claim if her husband tried to humor her by saying they shared the same dirty habit.

The minute Carlos saw his wife and daughter filing in, he put his paper down, and his face brightened as if at long last his wife had delivered the son, and that was the news she was bringing him. His teeth were already grinning from the glass of water next to his bedside lamp, so he lisped when he said, "Eh-speech, eh-speech!"

"It is so beautiful, Cuco," Laura coached him, turning the sound on his TV off. She sat down at the foot of the bed. Yoyo stood before both of them, blocking their view of the soldiers in helicopters landing amid silenced gun reports and explosions. A few weeks ago it had been the shores of the Dominican Republic. Now it was the jungles of Southeast Asia they were saving. Her mother gave her the nod to begin reading.

In the old country, any whisper of a challenge to authority could bring the secret police in their black V.W.'s. But this was America.

Yoyo didn't need much encouragement. She put her nose to the fire, as her mother would have said, and read from start to finish without looking up. When she concluded, she was a little embarrassed at the pride she took in her own words. She pretended to quibble with a phrase or two, then looked questioningly to her mother. Laura's face was radiant. Yoyo turned to share her pride with her father.

The expression on his face shocked both mother and daughter. Carlos's toothless mouth had collapsed into a dark zero. His eyes bored into Yoyo, then shifted to Laura. In barely audible Spanish, as if secret microphones or informers were all about, he whispered to his wife, "You will permit her to read *that?*"

Laura's eyebrows shot up, her mouth fell open. In the old country, any whisper of a challenge to authority could bring the secret police in their black V.W.'s. But this was America. People could say what they

6+1 Trait® Writing

Organization

Explain that most stories are told in *chronological order* (or time order), which helps readers follow the sequence of events. Organization isn't just order, however. It's also *pacing*—telling the story in a controlled way. In a well-paced story, the writer knows when to keep the pace moving and when to slow it down and elaborate on important details. You might, for example, reflect with students on how Alvarez opens the story by elaborating on the characters and presenting the initial problem—Yoyo's anxiety over the speech.

Practice Note that Alvarez slows down the action in column one of this page to elaborate on the differences between Yoyo's mother and father. Have students identify that part of the text and summarize the differences the passage points out. *(The father is interested in his Dominican homeland now that the dictator has been overthrown. He reads papers from there and hopes to move back. But the mother prefers her life and role in the United States.)*

For more information on organization and the 6+1 Trait® model, see **Writing and Research Handbook**, pp. 947–949.

Diego Rivera, *Tina Modotti,* 1927

thought. "What is wrong with her speech?" Laura questioned him.

"What ees wrrrong with her eh-speech?" Carlos wagged his head at her. His anger was always more frightening in his broken English. As if he had mutilated the language in his fury—and now there was nothing to stand between them and his raw, dumb anger. "What is wrong? I will tell you what is wrong. It show no gratitude. It is boastful. *I celebrate myself*? *The best student learns to destroy the teacher*?" He mocked Yoyo's pla-

Critical Thinking

Draw Conclusions Call students' attention to the sentences *"I celebrate myself? The best student learns to destroy the teacher?"* Ask students why are they printed in italics. *(These lines, taken from Whitman, come from Yoyo's speech. Yoyo's father speaks these lines with special emphasis—and as questions—because he finds them upsetting and inappropriate.)*

Critical Thinking

Infer Ask students to infer why Yoyo's father is so opposed to Yoyo's speech. *(He thinks it is disrespectful.)* Have students explain their answer. *(Yoyo's father has different values than Yoyo and her mother. His values developed in a society where "any whisper of a challenge to authority could bring the secret police." In his opinion, Yoyo's speech is inappropriate for the occasion and an audience of teachers.)*

Viewing the Art

Diego Rivera, *Tina Modotti,* 1927

Mexican artist Diego Rivera (1886–1957) was best known for his murals of Mexican life and history. Many of his works reflect his radical politics and include elements of social criticism aimed at the Mexican government, church, and upper classes. This picture of Tina Modotti, a model and a student, is a study for a mural in the former chapel of Chapingo in Mexico. The charcoal-on-paper drawing measures 24 by 18½ inches and is in the Galería Arvil in Mexico.

Teach

Active Reading Strategies

Summarize Have students briefly retell the story so far. *(Yoyo is writing a speech for an assembly on Monday. She uses an idea from Walt Whitman as a starting point for writing a speech that fills her with pride. Her mother congratulates her on it, but her father is outraged. He tears the speech into shreds, and Yoyo weeps.)*

6+1 Trait® Writing

Organization Note that Alvarez shifts back to Carlos's past in order to help the reader understand Yoyo's father and his actions. Ask students why this elaboration occurs here and not earlier. *(At this point, after Yoyo's father has acted so unkindly, the reader needs to know why. Yoyo has more than one reason to forgive her father; these details help make one of those reasons clear.)*

giarized words. "That is insubordinate.[2] It is improper. It is disrespecting of her teachers—" In his anger he had forgotten his fear of lurking spies: each wrong he voiced was a decibel[3] higher than the last outrage. Finally, he shouted at Yoyo, "As your father, I forbid you to make that eh-speech!"

Laura leapt to her feet, a sign that *she* was about to deliver her own speech. She was a small woman, and she spoke all her pronouncements standing up, either for more projection or as a carry-over from her girlhood in convent schools where one asked for, and literally, took the floor in order to speak. She stood by Yoyo's side, shoulder to shoulder. They looked down at Carlos. "That is no tone of voice—" she began.

But now, Carlos was truly furious. It was bad enough that his daughter was rebelling, but here was his own wife joining forces with her. Soon he would be surrounded by a houseful of independent American women. He too leapt from the bed, throwing off his covers. The Spanish newspapers flew across the room. He snatched the speech out of Yoyo's hands, held it before the girl's wide eyes, a vengeful, mad look in his own, and then once, twice, three, four, countless times, he tore the speech into shreds.

"Are you crazy?" Laura lunged at him. "Have you gone mad? That is her speech for tomorrow you have torn up!"

"Have *you* gone mad?" He shook her away. "You were going to let her read that . . . that insult to her teachers?"

"Insult to her teachers!" Laura's face had crumpled up like a piece of paper. On it was written a love note to her husband, an unhappy, haunted man. "This is America, Papi, America! You are not in a savage country anymore!"

Meanwhile, Yoyo was on her knees, weeping wildly, collecting all the little pieces of her speech, hoping that she could put it back together before the assembly tomorrow morning. But not even a sibyl[4] could have made sense of those tiny scraps of paper. All hope was lost. "He broke it, he broke it," Yoyo moaned as she picked up a handful of pieces.

Yoyo was on her knees, weeping wildly, collecting all the little pieces of her speech . . .

Probably, if she had thought a moment about it, she would not have done what she did next. She would have realized her father had lost brothers and friends to the dictator Trujillo. For the rest of his life, he would be haunted by blood in the streets and late night disappearances. Even after all these years, he cringed if a black Volkswagen passed him on the street. He feared anyone in uniform: the meter maid giving out parking tickets, a museum guard approaching to tell him not to get too close to his favorite Goya.

2 **insubordinate** (in′ sə bôrd′ ən it) disobedient
3 **decibel** (des′ ə bel′) a numerical measure of the loudness of sound
4 **sibyl** (sib′ əl) a fortune teller

Writing in the Real World

Writers and Writing

Using Familiar Details Alvarez chose to write about a world she knew intimately—a Dominican-American family living in the United States. Although she writes in English, many of the characters' nicknames, such as *Cuquita, Mami,* and *Papi,* are Hispanic. Details in the story also reflect Alvarez's intimacy with the culture she's describing. For example, the writer may have gathered details about Trujillo and the black Volkswagens driven by the secret police from personal knowledge or by listening to her own parents.

On her knees, Yoyo thought of the worst thing she could say to her father. She gathered a handful of scraps, stood up, and hurled them in his face. In a low, ugly whisper, she pronounced Trujillo's hated nickname: "Chapita! You're just another Chapita!"

It took Yoyo's father only a moment to register the loathsome nickname before he came after her. Down the halls they raced, but Yoyo was quicker than he and made it into her room just in time to lock the door as her father threw his weight against it. He called down curses on her head, ordered her on his authority as her father to open that door! He throttled that doorknob, but all to no avail. Her mother's love of gadgets saved Yoyo's hide that night. Laura had hired a locksmith to install good locks on all the bedroom doors after the house had been broken into once while they were away. Now if burglars broke in again, and the family were at home, there would be a second round of locks for the thieves to contend with.

Down the halls they raced, but Yoyo was quicker than he and made it into her room just in time to lock the door as her father threw his weight against it.

"Lolo," she said, trying to calm him down. "Don't you ruin my new locks."

Finally he did calm down, his anger spent. Yoyo heard their footsteps retreating down the hall. Their door clicked shut. Then, muffled voices, her mother's rising in anger, in persuasion, her father's deeper murmurs of explanation and self-defense. The house fell silent a moment, before Yoyo heard, far off, the gun blasts and explosions, the serious, self-important voices of newscasters reporting their TV war.

A little while later, there was a quiet knock at Yoyo's door, followed by a tentative attempt at the doorknob. "Cuquita?" her mother whispered. "Open up, Cuquita."

"Go away," Yoyo wailed, but they both knew she was glad her mother was there, and needed only a moment's protest to save face.

Together they concocted a speech: two brief pages of stale compliments and the polite commonplaces on teachers, a speech wrought by necessity and without much invention by mother and daughter late into the night on one of the pads of paper Laura had once used for her own inventions. After it was drafted, Laura typed it up while Yoyo stood by, correcting her mother's misnomers[5] and mis-sayings.

Yoyo came home the next day with the success story of the assembly. The nuns had been flattered, the audience had stood up and given "our devoted teachers a standing ovation," what Laura had suggested they do at the end of the speech.

She clapped her hands together as Yoyo recreated the moment. "I stole that from your father's speech, remember? Remember how he put that in at the end?" She quoted him in Spanish, then translated for Yoyo into English.

That night, Yoyo watched him from the upstairs hall window, where she'd retreated

5 **misnomers** (mis nō′ mərz) errors in naming persons or places

Critical Thinking

Evaluate Ask students whether they think that Yoyo's father is right. Should Yoyo have redone and presented her original speech anyway, or should she have bowed, as she does, to her father's wishes? Encourage students to give reasons for their judgment.

Active Reading Strategies

Connect

Explain that to *connect* with a piece of writing is to link its ideas or events to your own life or to other selections you've read. To connect with a work of literature, suggest that students ask themselves questions like these:

- Do I know someone like this person?
- Have I ever felt this way?
- What would *I* do in this kind of situation?
- What else have I read that is like this selection?

Practice After students read this page, ask them to think about occasions when arguments at home might have led to behaviors that no one was proud of later. Instead of sharing such experiences, students might reflect on ways that Yoyo and her father could have dealt more maturely with the situation. Alternatively, students might compare and contrast other works in this book (the excerpts from *I Know Why the Caged Bird Sings* and *The Kitchen God's Wife)* that reveal conflicts between generations and/or highlight cultural differences between characters.

Teach

Literary Element

Plot Ask: "What is the point of highest tension, or climax, of this story?" *(when Laura calls her father Chapita)* "How is the conflict resolved?" *(Laura accepts the new typewriter her father offers as a token of apology.)*

Critical Thinking

Analyze Ask students how Alvarez might be using the new typewriter as a symbol. *(The new typewriter may represent Carlos's willingness to let Yoyo embrace modern American ways and values. It may show that he will now let her write what she thinks.)*

the minute she heard his car pull up in front of the house. Slowly, her father came up the driveway, a grim expression on his face as he grappled with a large, heavy cardboard box. At the front door, he set the package down carefully and patted all his pockets for his house keys. (If only he'd had Laura's ticking key chain!) Yoyo heard the snapping open of locks downstairs. She listened as he struggled to maneuver the box through the narrow doorway. He called her name several times, but she did not answer him.

"My daughter, your father, he love you very much," he explained from the bottom

Adrián Luis González, Painted pottery typewriter, c. 1980

Viewing the Art

Adrián Luis González, *Painted pottery typewriter,* c. 1980
Mexican artist Adrían Luis González made this painted, miniature clay typewriter (only 4⅜ inches wide) as a plaything for his daughter. The toy is a model of a manual typewriter, the kind Laura probably used to type the speech.

of the stairs. "He just want to protect you." Finally, her mother came up and pleaded with Yoyo to go down and reconcile[6] with him. "Your father did not mean to harm. You must pardon him. Always it is better to let bygones be forgotten, no?"

Downstairs, Yoyo found her father setting up a brand new electric typewriter on the kitchen table. It was even better than her mother's. He had outdone himself with all the extra features: a plastic carrying case with Yoyo's initials decaled below the handle, a brace to lift the paper upright while she typed, an erase cartridge, an automatic margin tab, a plastic hood like a toaster cover to keep the dust away. Not even her mother could have invented such a machine!

But Laura's inventing days were over just as Yoyo's were starting up with her school-wide success. . . . Yoyo thinks of the speech her mother wrote as her last invention.

But Laura's inventing days were over just as Yoyo's were starting up with her school-wide success. Rather than the rolling suitcase everyone else in the family remembers, Yoyo thinks of the speech her mother wrote as her last invention. It was as if, after that, her mother had passed on to Yoyo her pencil and pad and said, "Okay, Cuquita, here's the buck. You give it a shot."

6 **reconcile** (rek′ ən sīl′) to make up; to settle a disagreement

Critical Thinking

Analyze Ask: "What do you think the title of the novel means?" *(Sample response: It refers to the process by which the García girls became Americanized.)*

Additional Resources

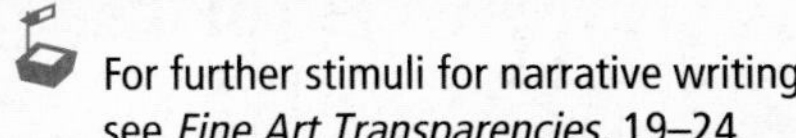

For further stimuli for narrative writing, see *Fine Art Transparencies,* 19–24

Listening and Speaking Activities, pp. 13, 18, 20, 21

Thinking and Study Skills, pp. 10, 13

Compare and Contrast

Compare Organizational Structure

Tell students that comparing and contrasting the way authors organize their writing can help students deepen their understanding of style and craft. Then ask students to think about the internal structures of this story and the excerpt from *The Kitchen God's Wife* (pp. 112–118). Help students see that this story relies mainly on chronological order, whereas Tan's excerpt includes a story within a story.

Practice Ask students to write two or more paragraphs comparing and contrasting the organizational structure each writer uses. Students should explain how the writers' choices help develop the characters and theme. Suggest that students use a Venn diagram or other organizer to explore ideas before writing.

Linking Writing and Literature

Assess

Evaluation Rubrics

Talk About Reading

Sample responses to the questions:

1. Students may be able to describe a scene in which parents or children lose control and say or do things they regret later. They may describe yelling, crying, and locking oneself in one's room. They may also describe how anger cools, gives way to regret, and, often, is followed by reconciliation. Students may say that these are events and issues that many teens face.
2. Yoyo's family may be less traditional since they moved to the United States. The children may show less respect to the parents than they used to. For example, when Carlos is speaking in Spanish at the dinner table, Yoyo and her sisters don't pay attention.
3. Alvarez begins the story by telling of the speech Yoyo will have to present. She also presents details that suggest Yoyo has a good relationship with her mother. Then, at a measured rate, Alvarez weaves the conflict with Yoyo's father into the story. She does not deliver all the details about the father at once but, instead, saves some of the most significant ones for appropriate moments. Students might say that these organizational decisions make the story more gripping.
4. Criteria include good organization, careful characterization, a conflict with a good resolution, and controlled pacing.

Write About Reading

The friendly letter should do the following:

- reflect on events in the story
- use an effective order for presenting events and ideas
- be written from an older Yoyo's point of view

Linking Writing and Literature

Learning to Learn

Think about how Yoyo and her father feel about each other by the end of this excerpt. Reflect on the progress they have made and on the possibility of progress yet to come. Record your ideas in your journal.

Talk About Reading

In a small group, discuss this excerpt from *How the García Girls Lost Their Accents.* Use the questions that follow to guide your discussion.

1. **Connect to Your Life** Do you think that many people your age have had experiences similar to those in the story? Explain your answer, using details from the selection.
2. **Critical Thinking: Infer** How do you think the relationships of Yoyo's family have changed since moving to the United States? Support your answer with details from the selection.
3. **6+1 Trait®: Organization** Describe some specific decisions Alvarez made about *what* to tell readers and *when* to tell them. How did her organizational decisions affect your enjoyment of the story?
4. **Write to Learn** After reading this story, what qualities do you think a good story should have? Make a list of these qualities.

Write About Reading

Friendly Letter Imagine that you are Yoyo and that fifteen years have passed since the events in this excerpt. Write a letter to your father in which you look back on the conflict over your speech. Tell what the incident means to you now.

Focus on Organization As you write, think about the most logical and effective order for your information. Lead up, in a controlled way, to your most important points.

For more information on organization and the 6+1 Trait® model, see **Writing and Research Handbook,** pages 947–949.

Close

Discuss the characters in the selection. Have students retell the story from the point of view of each of these characters. Ask: *How can retelling the story from a character's point of view help you understand the characters?*

UNIT 4 Review

Reflecting on the Unit: Summarize What You Learned

Focus on the following questions to help summarize what you learned in this unit.

1. What are the basic elements of narrative writing?
2. What is the role of conflict in a plot?
3. What purposes do dialogue and anecdotes serve in a narrative?
4. What are the three narrative points of view and the characteristics of each?
5. What are some important elements and techniques in writing a sports narrative? In writing about suspense?

Adding to Your Portfolio

CHOOSE A SELECTION FOR YOUR PORTFOLIO Look over the narrative writing you have done during this unit. Select a completed piece of writing to put into your portfolio. The piece that you choose should show some or all of the following:

- believable situations and characters
- clear, realistic dialogue
- a clear sequence of events

REFLECT ON YOUR CHOICE Attach a note to the piece you chose, explaining briefly why you chose it and what you learned from writing it.

SET GOALS How can you improve your writing? What skill will you focus on the next time you write?

Writing Across the Curriculum

MAKE A LITERATURE CONNECTION Think about Julia Alvarez's story from *How the García Girls Lost Their Accents.* What other short stories have you recently read and enjoyed that involved conflict? Choose one of these stories and write a paragraph or two about it, narrating the basic conflict and explaining how the conflict was resolved.

You may wish to share your completed piece with a small group or with the whole class. Consider setting up a book and story display so that students can read each other's recommended stories.

Reflecting on the Unit

You may have students respond to Reflecting on the Unit by writing about what they've learned or through discussion.

Adding to Your Portfolio

Suggest that students read their work first as a reader and then as a writer. As readers, they should ask themselves such questions as: *Did the story hold my interest and make me care about the characters?* As writers, they should ask such questions as: *Was the dialogue realistic? Were the details and anecdotes effective?*

Portfolio Evaluation

If you grade the portfolio selections, you may want to award two marks—one each for content and form. Explain your assessment criteria before students make their selections.

Commend

- experimentation with creative prewriting techniques
- clear, concise writing in which the main idea, audience, and purpose are evident
- successful revisions
- work that shows a flair for language

Writing Across the Curriculum

Before students begin writing, they should decide whether they are going to set up a book display so that they can read each other's recommended stories. Remind them that if they decide to do the display, an explanation of how the conflict in the story is resolved would make the reading of the story anticlimactic.

ASSESSMENT OPTIONS

Tests With Answer Key & Rubrics
Unit 4 Choice A Test, p. 13
Unit 4 Choice B Test, p. 14
Unit 4 Composition Objective Test, pp. 15–16

Testmaker
Unit 4 Choice A Test
Unit 4 Choice B Test
Unit 4 Composition Objective Test

You may wish to administer one of these tests as a mastery test.

MindJogger Videoquizzes

UNIT 5

Viewing the Art

This photograph of a pitcher reading the signal from the catcher during a baseball game is dramatic and forceful. Although no words are exchanged, the pitcher knows exactly what type of pitch to throw. In place of signals, expository writers communicate with an audience by using words to inform and explain, while keeping in mind what the audience needs to know.

Interpret and Analyze Use the following questions for discussion:

- What type of pitch do you think the pitcher is about to throw to the batter? What qualities, knowledge, and skills does the pitcher need to have to correctly interpret the signal?
- What other signals might be used during a professional sporting activity in order to communicate a ruling or a decision?

Discussing the Quotation

This quotation is from an article called "Sign Language: The Game Within the Game of Baseball," which was written by Tim Kurkjian and published in *Sports Illustrated* on July 28, 1997. Discuss the quotation with the class, and ask students how they interpret the author's meaning. How might signals get "lost in the translation"?

Writing Prompt Write a brief explanation of how Kurkjian's words, coupled with the image of the umpire, can be seen to connect to the process of expository writing.

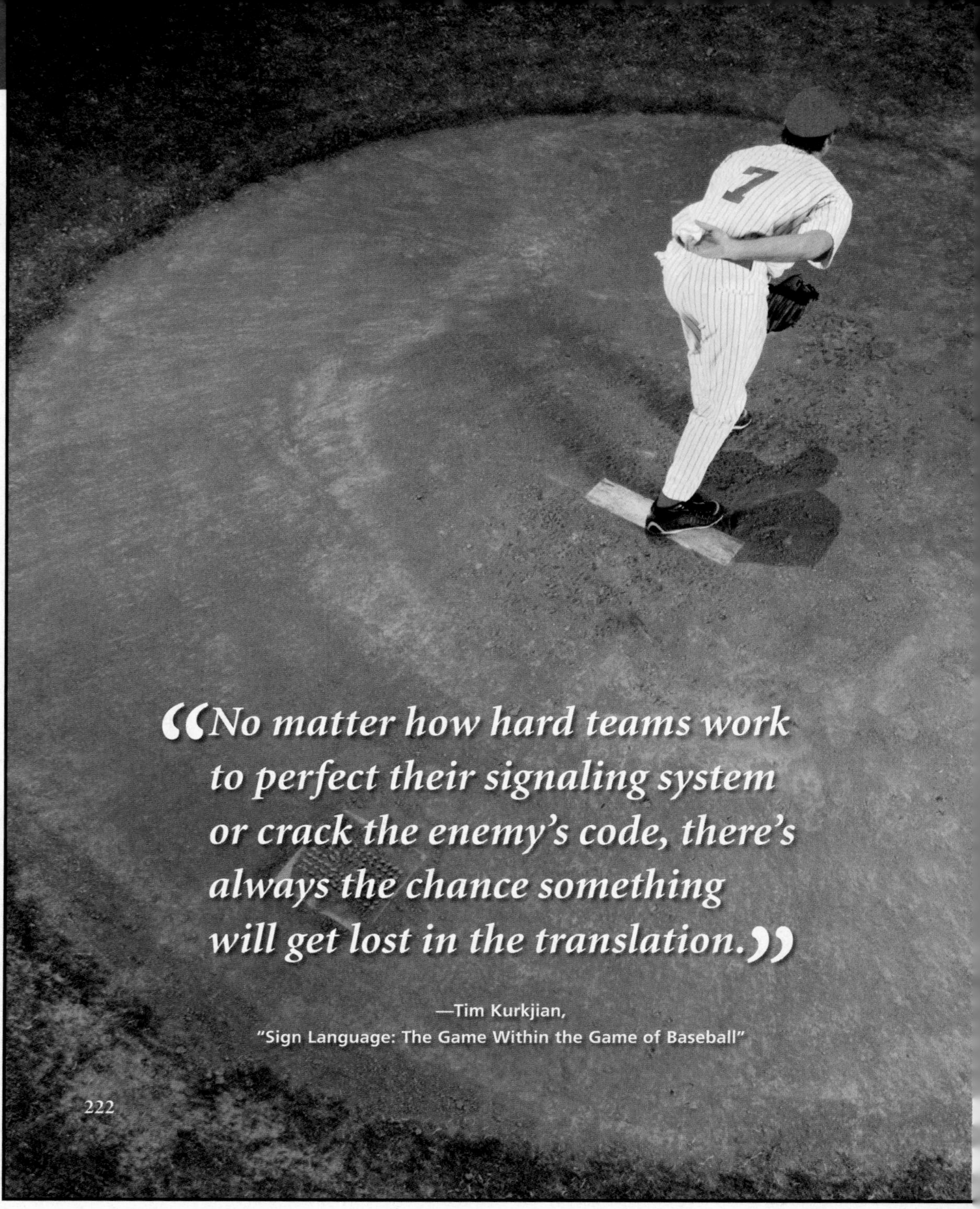

"No matter how hard teams work to perfect their signaling system or crack the enemy's code, there's always the chance something will get lost in the translation."

—Tim Kurkjian,
"Sign Language: The Game Within the Game of Baseball"

222

Resource Manager

Planning Resources
- *Lesson Plans*
- *Block Scheduling*

Transparencies
- *Bellringer*
- *Daily Language Practice*
- *Fine Art*
- *Two-Minute Skill Drill*
- *Writing Process*

Other Print Resources
- *Composition Enrichment*
- *Composition Practice*
- *Composition Reteaching*
- *Cooperative Learning Activities*
- *Glencoe Literature Library*
- *Grammar and Composition Handbook*
- *Grammar Workbook*
- *Listening and Speaking Activities*
- *Research Paper and Report Writing*
- *Sentence-Combining Practice*
- *Tests with Answer Key and Rubrics*

Expository Writing

- To develop, through example and instruction, an understanding of expository writing
- To learn written and graphic techniques that will help an expository writer explain processes, causes and effects, categories, and similarities and differences
- To apply the techniques learned to writing an informative article

ASSESSMENT OPTIONS

Tests with Answer Key & Rubrics
Unit 5 Choice A Test, p. 17
Unit 5 Choice B Test, p. 18
Unit 5 Composition Objective Test, pp. 19–20

Testmaker
Unit 5 Choice A Test
Unit 5 Choice B Test
Unit 5 Composition Objective Test

You may wish to administer either the Unit 5 Choice A Test or the Unit 5 Choice B Test as a pretest.

Key to Ability Levels

L1 Level 1 activities are within the basic ability range of students.

L2 Level 2 activities are within the ability range of average students.

L3 Level 3 activities are more challenging activities.

- *Thinking and Study Skills*
- *Writing Across the Curriculum*
- *Writing Assessment and Evaluation Rubrics*
- *Writing in the Real World*

Video
- *MindJogger Videoquizzes*

Software
- *Presentation Plus!*
- *Revising with Style*
- *Testmaker*

Web Site
- *glencoe.com*

Focus

Lesson Overview

Objective

- To explore how expository writing and the writing process are used in a real-life application

Skills

- analyzing; researching and reordering information

Critical Thinking

- defining and clarifying ideas; analyzing information; categorizing, contrasting, and comparing details

Listening and Speaking

- tape recording observations; discussing; evaluating; questioning

Bellringer

Daily Language Activity

When students enter the classroom, have this assignment on the board: *List objects from nature that you have collected or watched, such as leaves, insects, or birds. Describe the objects.*

Grammar Link to the Bellringer

Read the following sentences and choose the verb that is best in each:

(Is, Are) the flowers common?

How (do, does) Winckler help?

On a cactus (sit, sits) an owl.

See also  *Daily Language Practice*

Motivating Activity

Discuss students' responses to the Bellringer activity. Ask students how observing and writing about nature might help writers sharpen their skills, explore their thoughts and ideas, and learn about the world.

Expository Writing

Writing in the Real World

Suzanne Winckler wrote the following expository article about the first big day in cactus hunting. Big day? Winckler got this idea from a tradition in the bird world. In bird watching, a "big day" means spotting as many birds as possible in twenty-four hours. In her article, which appeared in *Audubon* magazine, Winckler conveys technical information about cacti, yet she makes the subject lively through her first-person point of view and informal style.

Counting Cacti

By Suzanne Winckler

Whenever I look back on the world's first cactus big day I will remember the Cassin's kingbirds. They started yapping in the trees over my tent at 4:30 in the morning. I lay there thinking how they sounded like a pack of overindulged miniature poodles, an analogy that distressed me, since as a birdwatcher I don't really like to disparage the objects of my esteem. They also seemed to be taunting me, as kingbirds have a way of doing, reminding me that I know more about birds than cacti, but it was too late now.

Five of us had converged the night before in the Davis Mountains, a little chip off the Rockies in far west Texas, having agreed some weeks earlier that it was time to expand the parameters of the big day . . . . We were going to crisscross west Texas in search of opuntias, chollas, hedgehogs, horse cripplers, barrel cacti, and even give a stab at finding *Coryphantha minima,* which is the smallest cactus in the world.

Large expanses of west Texas are flat and empty, and as scenery an acquired taste. The awesome monotony is broken in places by island ranges like the Davis and Chisos mountains, which by contrast are gorgeous each in its own way. . . . We were going to be operating on several hundred miles of road in and between these two mountain ranges.

There are about sixty species of cactus in west Texas out of a family total of two or three thousand. Some of them, like the chollas, which grow out on the desert like enormous candelabras, are quite common and widespread, while other species exhibit a fierce partiality to small and scattered plots of certain soils. Needless to say these finicky ones are, first, rare and, second, highly prized by cactus fanciers . . .

One complaint I have about birds is that too few of them are pink. This is not the situation with cactus flowers. They occur in many lurid and neon shades of that color, and although I could have faked a loftier purpose, it was the possibility of encountering a lot of tawdry pink flowers glowing in the desert that motivated me to participate in the cactus big day . . . .

When I found *Echinomastus intertextus* my heart leapt. I'm certain I had the look on my face that my dog does when she brings back her stick. (It is a gaze of contentment and pride in excess

Resource Manager

Planning Resources

- *Lesson Plans*

Transparencies

- *Bellringer*
- *Daily Language Practice*
- *Writing Process* 11, 23–27

Other Print Resources

- *Cooperative Learning Activities,* pp. 21–24
- *Thinking and Study Skills,* p. 1
- *Writing Assessment and Evaluation Rubrics*
- *Writing in the Real World,* pp. 17–20

of the accomplishment.) The time was 9:15 A.M., and we were milling about in a grassy mountain pasture just south of the town of Fort Davis. We had already driven something like sixty miles to find an odd little lime-green prickly-pear (Opuntia polyacantha var. rufispina), but for two hours' effort the list was small—only four species. I had to remind myself that while the early morning hours are best for birds, cacti do not fly away when it gets hot. E. intertextus was number five. I didn't know what it was, of course. I had simply stumbled upon a cactus that fit Allan [Zimmerman's] description: "Look for something that resembles a brown tennis ball."

A Writer's Process

Prewriting

Getting the Idea

Suzanne Winckler, a freelance writer and passionate bird watcher, had participated in several big days while birding. She wanted to take the big day tradition—finding as many species as possible in twenty-four hours—and apply it to another organism, in this case cactus.

Winckler's first step was to contact Dr. Allan Zimmerman, an expert taxonomist, to see if he would participate. She then got the go-ahead from an editor at *Audubon,* who gave her a two-thousand-word limit and a deadline. Winckler then readied herself for the field.

While the research for some expository writing is done by reading texts, it sometimes requires field research. In this case, Winckler went to Big Bend, a vast desert area in southwest Texas, to conduct her big day of cacti hunting. Her team, which included Zimmerman and three other biologists, started before daylight and worked intensely until after dark.

For Winckler, the day was a juggling act—stalking rare cacti with the team, then stepping back to record the experience as a writer. She jotted information in a hard-bound record book. She also sketched all the cacti and asked Zimmerman to tell her their scientific names.

At home, she interviewed several more cactus experts by phone. She then organized her notes, transcribed tapes that were made during the hunt, and mapped out a rough structure for the piece.

Suzanne Winckler, Freelance writer

Teach

Reading Media

Have students preview the title and focus of the Media Connection on page 224. Discuss the purpose and audience of an expository article, pointing out that every expository writer must not only explain as well as inform, but also decide what specific information the audience needs to know. Have students read the article.

Discussion Prompts

- What types of research might be required for expository writing? (reading texts, interviewing experts, conducting field research)
- What ways might you use to record information when you are in the field? (writing in journals, using tape recorders, drawing sketches, taking photographs)
- How can you organize information if it comes from many different sources? (Students might suggest compiling ideas from all sources and then ordering them chronologically, by order of importance, or by some other method.)

Cultural Connections

Environmentalists Worldwide

Suzanne Winckler's interest in nature and its vulnerability is part of an expanding awareness of the environment. The conservation movement in the United States has its roots in the writing and paintings of naturalists from the mid-1800s. Because of their work, the first national park (Yosemite National Park in California) was created. By the 1920s every continent in the world had set aside land for national parks. Encourage students to research the origins of the conservation movement and to summarize what they have learned in a poster or collage.

Teach

Discussion Prompts

- Have you ever read informative articles that prompted you to change your behavior? What was it about the article that made you change? What details does Winckler include that would be especially effective at prompting action?
- Winckler says that the world needs more editors. How can other people help your writing? What kinds of information from peer editors do you find most helpful when revising and editing?
- How are the writing process stages for expository writing the same or different from the ones you have used for other modes of writing?
- Were you surprised by the importance of expository writing for a naturalist?
- What other applications for writing about the natural world can you envision? **L2**

Additional Resources

Writing Process Transparencies 11, 23–27

Writing in the Real World, pp. 17–20

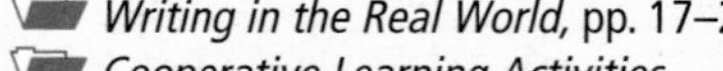
Cooperative Learning Activities

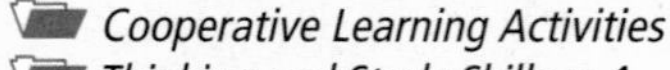
Thinking and Study Skills, p. 1

Expository Writing

Drafting

Crafting the Story

With her plan in mind, it took Winckler about five mornings at the computer to craft the story.

She began with noisy kingbirds. "I wanted to emphasize that what I was picking up on in the landscape was birds—not cacti—and the sense that it was an incredible experience in the tent." From there, Winckler tried to teach readers about Big Bend and rare cacti, and leave them caring about the place and its garden of obscure plants.

Winckler kept her audience in mind as she wrote. She knew that most readers would be unfamiliar with cacti, so she compared these plants to everyday things. She wrote that one cactus smelled like "floor polish" while another looked like a "candelabra."

With all her descriptions, Winckler resisted the urge to "be too flowery." As a nature writer, she stressed the importance of grounding the article with solid and interesting facts. "You can use description to get readers involved in an expository article. But you can't just ride on that. You have to introduce the science of nature so people will understand how things function."

Revising/Editing

Playing With Sentences

Once Winckler finished her first draft, she began to revise—adding some details, deleting other information. She also worked on her sentence structure. "I spend a lot of time writing a sentence and then turning it on its head, putting something in the middle. I play at it a lot."

Once Winckler's editor read the story, she had relatively few changes to suggest. Most of Winckler's larger pieces do take more editing—something she appreciates. "I wish I were edited more heavily," Winckler observed. "The world needs more editors. I'm aware of how much other people can help your writing."

An elf owlet sits on a saguaro cactus.

Writing in the Real World

Writers and Writing

Recording and Writing Details Suzanne Winckler used a notebook to bridge the gap between her two roles: naturalist and nature writer. By writing down and sketching her many observations, she was able to capture her experiences in nature for later description. After roughly mapping out the article, she "sat down, took a deep breath, and started writing."

Examining Writing in the Real World

Analyzing the Media Connection

Discuss these questions about the article on pages 224–225.

1. Suzanne Winckler wrote her article in the first-person point of view. If written in the third person, how would the article have been different?
2. How does Winckler use comparison and contrast in the excerpt of her article?
3. What is the effect of Winckler's use of informal speech?
4. How does Winckler employ both vivid description and factual information when she tells about different types of cacti?
5. What effect is Winckler trying to achieve with the opening sentences of her paragraphs?

Analyzing a Writer's Process

Discuss these questions about Suzanne Winckler's writing process.

1. How did Winckler gather information for her expository article about hunting cacti?
2. What were Winckler's purposes in writing the article?
3. How did Winckler help her readers over the hurdle of understanding an unfamiliar subject?
4. As she drafted her article, how did Winckler strike a balance between description and technical information?
5. How does Winckler value collaboration in the writing process?

GrammarLink

Make subject and verb agree in an inverted sentence.

In inverted sentences, the subject follows the verb:

*There **are** about sixty **species** of cactus in west Texas. . . .*

An inverted sentence may also begin with a prepositional phrase:

*On a saguaro cactus **sits** an **elf owlet.***

Find the simple subject in each sentence below. Then write the verb that agrees with the subject.

1. Outside Winckler's tent (scream, screams) the annoying kingbirds.
2. Here (come, comes) Zimmerman.
3. In southwestern Texas (grow, grows) many kinds of cacti.
4. There (was, were) cactuses Zimmerman had never heard of before.
5. There (is, are) similarities between bird watching and cactus watching.

See Lesson 16.3, pages 612–613.

GrammarLink

Answers

1. scream
2. comes
3. grow
4. were
5. are

Assess

Analyzing the Media Connection

1. The article may have been more impersonal and formal.
2. Winckler compares kingbirds to "overindulged miniature poodles" and a species of cacti to "candelabras."
3. Informal speech helps make an academic subject more readable and entertaining.
4. Answers will vary. Possible answer: Winckler vividly describes the colors of cacti and their appearance while giving facts about the cacti, such as their numbers, location, and Latin classifications.
5. to grab the reader's attention with surprising or unusual ideas and images

Analyzing a Writer's Process

1. by doing field research through participating in a cacti hunt with scientific experts
2. "to teach readers about Big Bend and rare cacti, and leave them caring about the place and its garden of obscure plants"
3. Winckler compared the cacti to everyday things.
4. Winckler used description to get readers involved, and she grounded the article with solid and interesting facts.
5. Winckler highly values the role of editors as collaborators because "other people can help your writing."

Reteaching

Have students check their research reports to see that they put their subject in a scientific context.

Enrichment

Challenge students to use humor to draw attention to a serious subject.

Close

Have students discuss how to use the process described in the Media Connection to write an expository paper about local birds or plants.

Focus

Lesson Overview

Objectives

- To study two models of expository writing
- To analyze and classify five kinds of expository writing
- To learn how to explain and provide information about a topic in a clear and concise manner

Skills

- defining; explaining; informing; analyzing cause and effect

Critical Thinking

- comparing; evaluating; relating cause and effect; processing; identifying

Listening and Speaking

- defining; discussing; explaining; informing

Bellringer

Daily Language Activity

When students enter the classroom, have this assignment on the board: *Write a brief summary of an activity you enjoyed recently, explaining how to do it and why you enjoy it.*

Grammar Link to the Bellringer

Have students examine their Bellringer summaries and replace bland verbs with more precise and lively ones. (For example: I *ran* to the base/I *sprinted* to the base.)

See also  *Daily Language Practice*

Motivating Activity

To make the concept of expository writing more concrete for students, ask them to imagine that the class is creating a new magazine with "How to" and "Why" articles on topics of interest to teens. What topics might students suggest? (Possible suggestions include "Why Play Sports" or "How to Master In-Line Skating.")

LESSON 5.1

Expository Writing

Explaining and Informing

Expository writing is writing that explains and informs. In the model below, a science writer explains what really happens when a person gets out of bed.

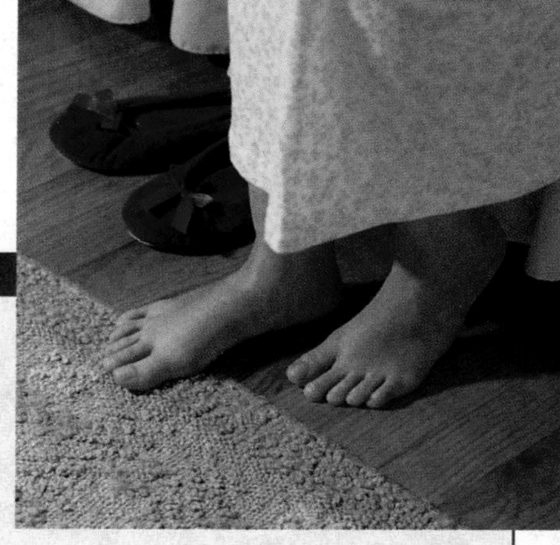

Literature Model

Whack thump bam! The man's foot extends out of bed and lands on the floor. The floorboards jam down and their vibrations travel sideways like pond waves to the wall. The whole house compresses in the new loading—bricks where the floor fits into the wall shrinking smaller by 1/100,000 inch from the weight.

Any impact that doesn't get lost in the walls stays quivering in the floor. The chest of drawers starts lifting up and down, as does the bed, the chair, the table with its plant on top, the stack of magazines and Sunday papers in the corner, and even the old coffee cup left down on the floor. All lift up and bounce down, rebound up and crash down again as the floor reverberates to get rid of its buzzing energy. In a particularly energetic leap out of bed this bouncing of furniture can be seen (lampshades especially are prone to being knocked over in such moments), but even with a softer landing the furniture shaking takes place.

Then the second foot touches down, the waker stands up, and he steps to the double-glazed window to see what is happening outside.

David Bodanis, *The Secret House*

Bodanis introduces the cause of the surprising chain of tiny, imperceptible events that follows the simple act of getting out of bed.

The writer uses examples to make his point memorable.

Resource Manager

Planning Resources

- *Lesson Plans*

Transparencies

- *Bellringer*
- *Daily Language Practice*
- *Fine Art* 25–28
- *Two-Minute Skill Drill*
- *Writing Process* 11, 23–27

Other Print Resources

- *Composition Enrichment,* p. 35
- *Composition Practice,* p. 35
- *Composition Reteaching,* p. 35
- *Cooperative Learning Activities,* pp. 21–24
- *Listening and Speaking Activities,* pp. 15–16
- *Research Paper and Report Writing,* pp. 43–48
- *Sentence-Combining Practice,* pp. 32–33
- *Thinking and Study Skills,* pp. 5–7, 11, 14
- *Writing Across the Curriculum*
- *Writing Assessment and Evaluation Rubrics*

The Nature of Expository Writing

Bodanis's explanation of the strange and jarring events caused by stepping out of bed is an example of expository writing. The student model below shows another type of expository writing. It describes the step-by-step process of a flower sprouting, growing, and blooming. Although there are different kinds of expository writing, all writers of exposition share one goal: to present a clear, concise explanation that readers will find interesting and informative.

Student Model

The flower, one of nature's many miracles, is created through a series of complex steps. With an embryo, a supply of stored food, and a protective covering, the seed begins the process. Most seeds remain dormant at first, usually because conditions are not favorable for growth. Seeds have been known to stay dormant from one week to fifty years and still germinate properly. Germination occurs when there is an abundant supply of water, an adequate amount of oxygen, and the proper temperatures. Crucial to the plant's life, water begins the next step in the process. The seed absorbs large amounts of water, causing the protective coating to soften. The internal tissues then swell and break through the coating. This new life, this plant, immediately begins to burn food, and it produces the energy necessary for growth. The vulnerable plant now becomes susceptible to sunlight. Too much or too little can harm it. However, the sun helps make the food for the plant to burn and receive energy. This process continues even after the first leaves develop. The plant grows stronger and more mature each day. Finally, the full-grown plant is ready to receive its crowning glory—the flower.

Billy McKnight,
Jefferson Davis High School, Montgomery, Alabama

McKnight introduces this paragraph with a clear statement of what he will explain.

McKnight ties his process explanation together with transitions that show chronological order. What are some transitions that he uses?

Vocabulary Tip

As you revise, make your explanations livelier and more informative by replacing general verbs with more precise action verbs. Bodanis, for example, uses *bounce, rebound,* and *reverberates,* in his explanation. See Lesson 10.3, pages 452–460.

Journal Writing

Look through some books and magazines for three expository paragraphs on different topics—for example, the development of a frog or the construction of a house. In your journal, briefly explain why each is an expository paragraph.

Expository Writing

Teach

Identifying Cause and Effect

Ask students to visualize and describe the main cause and resulting effects in the model on page 228. (The main cause includes the foot landing as the man gets out of bed. The resulting effects include the house compressing; the floor vibrating; and the bouncing of furniture, magazines, papers, and the coffee cup.) Point out that words and phrases such as "jam down," "vibrations," and "quivering" express how objects cause movement when they touch other objects. **L2**

Using the Model

Explain to students that in the model on page 229, McKnight first suggests chronological structure with the words "series of complex steps." He then uses transitions such as "begins," "at first," "next step," "immediately," and "now" to lead the reader through the sequence of events. **L1**

Explaining and Informing

Encourage students to give examples of expository writing they use often, such as computer manuals, recipes, repair or assembly instructions, or catalog information. Discuss what can make such writing confusing to a reader. (unfamiliar terms not defined, important facts or steps left out, and steps out of order) **L3**

Journal Writing Tip

Identifying Remind students that expository writing is writing that informs or explains. Suggest that they determine whether a paragraph is expository by asking themselves, "Does this paragraph explain or help me understand a topic?"

Teach

Defining Kinds of Expository Writing

To help students distinguish different kinds of expository writing, propose a general subject, such as "Mountains," and have students name a subtopic for each kind of expository writing. For example, "What Is a Mountain?" (definition); "How to Scale a Mountain" (process); "A Mountain Is Formed" (cause and effect); "Kinds of Mountains" (classification); and "Everest and Kilimanjaro" (Comparison-Contrast). **L2**

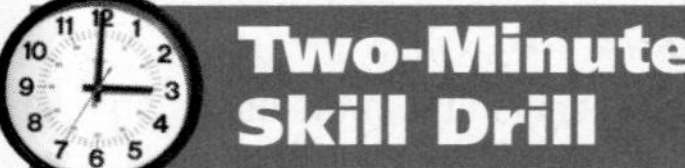

Two-Minute Skill Drill

Have students outline a topic of their own choice—using the step-by-step process for organizing ideas illustrated on page 77.

See also *Two-Minute Skill Drill Transparency 5.1*

Additional Resources

For further stimuli for expository writing, see *Fine Art Transparencies* 25–28.

Writing Process Transparencies 11, 23–27

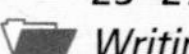
Writing Across the Curriculum

Cooperative Learning Activities

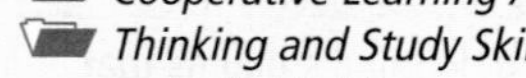
Thinking and Study Skills, pp. 5–7, 11, 14

Listening and Speaking Activities, pp. 15–16

Sentence-Combining Practice, pp. 32–33

Research Paper and Report Writing, pp. 43–48

Composition Practice, p. 35

Expository Writing

The Varieties of Expository Writing

The essay is one of the most common forms of expository writing. Usually, it consists of an introduction, body, and conclusion. The **introduction** includes a thesis statement—a one-sentence summary of your purpose for writing. The **body** consists of one or more paragraphs of details that support the thesis. The **conclusion** summarizes or gives the implications of what you've said in your essay.

You probably use other forms of expository writing quite often without even realizing it. You are using expository writing if you write out instructions for a neighbor on taking care of your cat while you are on vacation, or if you jot down directions for a friend.

The chart below presents the various kinds of expository writing, the basic purpose of each kind, and an example of each. While each variety has a distinct purpose, you can use two or more varieties in combination to explain and inform.

Kinds of Expository Writing

Kind	Basic Purpose	Example
Definition	To define a term or give the basic tenets of a theory	A supernova is a star that explodes, becoming extremely bright before fading and leaving a huge cloud of dust and gas.
Process	To give the steps in a process or explain a sequence of events	To locate their prey, bats use a process called echolocation, in which they send out high-pitched sound waves. These waves bounce off insects and echo back to the bat.
Cause and Effect	To explain how or why one or more events or actions cause other things to happen	The rubbing and grinding of the Earth's crustal plates against one another causes earthquakes.
Classification	To break down a broad topic into narrower categories	There are two main types of whales: toothed whales and baleen whales.
Comparison-Contrast	To discuss similarities in and differences between two related phenomena or events	Venus's-flytraps and pitcher plants are both meat-eating plants. Venus's-flytraps trap insects in their leaves. Pitcher plants capture insects that drown in their jug-shaped leaves.

Less Proficient Readers

Outlining a Process

Some students may have difficulty explaining the time relationships in a process such as the blooming of a flower. Documenting the process visually may help students organize their thoughts for writing. Suggest that they sketch each step of a process and write a caption for each image. By placing these images in order, students will have an outline for a process explanation.

5.1 Writing Activities

Write an Expository Paragraph

Pick a simple process or event to explain or define. Be sure that you are familiar enough with the parts of it to explain it clearly. Write a paragraph or two about it. For help with writing unified and coherent paragraphs, see **Writing and Research Handbook,** pages 943–945.

PURPOSE To explain the details of a process or event
AUDIENCE Your teacher and classmates
LENGTH 1–2 paragraphs

WRITING RUBRICS To write an effective expository paragraph, you should
- give a clear, concise explanation
- include a clear opening and conclusion
- use details to support your thesis in the body

Cross-Curricular Activity

ART Find a painting or a photograph that conveys a message or illustrates a process in a visual way. Then write a short paper explaining the message or process. Let other students read your paper before you show them the picture, to see whether your explanation is clear. Organize your explanation so readers can see the connections to specific parts of the picture.

Viewing and Representing

GIVING DIRECTIONS You have been asked to share with your classmates a special place that you've visited that was difficult to find. Write directions to this place. Use your school as a starting point. Be sure to use cardinal and ordinal directions and landmarks. Draw a map to go with these directions and present them to your class orally.

GrammarLink

Use precise verbs.

In both models the writers use precise action verbs to make their explanations vivid as well as informative. Use precise verbs to revise the sentences below.

1. The Aries spacecraft is off the Cape Canaveral launch pad.
2. Crowds look at the craft atop its pillar of flame.
3. In the third booster stage, the capsule leaves Earth's orbit.
4. Through their porthole, the astronauts see the red planet Mars.
5. Endless plains and jagged chasms are on Mars.

See Lesson 10.3, pages 452–460.

Using Computers

Use a search engine to find an expository article in an online magazine. In one or two paragraphs, identify the thesis statement and summarize the article. Explain which of the five types of expository writing listed in the chart on page 230 are used in the article, and how they are appropriate to the purpose of the article. Be as critical as any good magazine editor would be!

Writing Online | For more writing and grammar practice, go to glencoe.com and enter QuickPass code WC97727p1.

Assess

Evaluation Rubrics

Write an Expository Paragraph

Use these criteria when evaluating your students' writing:
- Does the paragraph use concrete words and simple explanations?
- Does the paragraph include a clear introduction and conclusion?
- Is there evidence of the accurate use of available facts and details?

See also *Writing Assessment & Evaluation Rubrics*

Cross-Curricular Activity

Evaluate students' papers on these points:
- The information is organized and presented in a reasonable order.
- There is a clear explanation of the process or message.

Viewing and Representing

Evaluate student presentations on these points:
- The directions are clear, concise and logical.
- The map is legible and accurate.

Reteaching

Composition Reteaching, p. 35

Enrichment

Composition Enrichment, p. 35

Fine Art Transparencies 25–28

Close

Tell students to imagine that they are writing a column for the school newspaper. Suggest that they answer perplexing questions on a topic of their choice.

GrammarLink

Answers

Answers will vary, but some suggestions are given below.

1. bursts
2. stare
3. departs
4. admire
5. enhance

Focus

Lesson Overview

Objectives

- To identify five different types of supporting details
- To analyze key factors in selecting appropriate supporting details
- To organize relevant supporting details regarding a topic

Skills

- selecting the type of supporting detail that best suits a main idea; deciding the order in which supporting details should be organized

Critical Thinking

- identifying main ideas; analyzing information; analyzing the audience; sequencing information; identifying supporting details

Listening and Speaking

- listening for supporting details; distinguishing fact from opinion

Bellringer

Daily Language Activity

When students enter the classroom, have this assignment on the board: *Write a note to a friend in which you explain your enthusiasm for a favorite interest, such as music or a sport.*

Grammar Link to the Bellringer

Have students identify the types of punctuation they used in their note. Why did they use each type?

See also *Daily Language Practice*

Motivating Activity

Point out to students that supporting details enliven expository writing as much as they bring fictional characters or scenes to life. Ask students what subjects or activities particularly interest them and why. If they were explaining an interest to a friend, what kinds of details would they use to show their excitement about the subject?

Expository Writing

LESSON 5.2

Going into Detail

Supporting details are essential elements in expository writing. Note how a science writer uses statistics and specific examples to explain the relationship between scents and human behavior.

Literature Model

We have already developed a system to control the environment by fragrance," says Junichi Yagi, vice president of S. Technology Center-America, a subsidiary of Shimizu, Japan's largest architectural, engineering, and construction firm. . . . Experiments in Japan with thirteen keypunch operators, monitored eight hours a day for thirty days, showed that the average number of errors per hour dropped by 21 percent when office air was scented with lavender (it reduces stress) and by 33 percent when laced with jasmine (it induces relaxation); a stimulating lemon scent reduced errors by 54 percent. . . .

Shimizu researchers also find that orange, peppermint, eucalyptus, chamomile, and Japanese cypress are soothing, while scarlet sage and rosemary are stimulating. (I would add Play-Doh and Rockin' Roger's Bar-B-Q Sauce to the stimulating list.)

Judith Stone, *Light Elements*

Here Judith Stone provides statistics to illustrate her point.

Stone adds two scents to the list. Which smells might you add?

Resource Manager

Planning Resources

- *Lesson Plans*

Transparencies

- *Bellringer*
- *Daily Language Practice*
- *Fine Art* 25–28
- *Two-Minute Skill Drill*
- *Writing Process* 11, 23–27

Other Print Resources

- *Composition Enrichment,* p. 37
- *Composition Practice,* p. 37
- *Composition Reteaching,* p. 37
- *Cooperative Learning Activities,* pp. 21–24
- *Listening and Speaking Activities,* pp. 15–16
- *Research Paper and Report Writing,* pp. 43–48
- *Sentence-Combining Practice,* pp. 32–33
- *Thinking and Study Skills,* pp. 5, 25
- *Writing Across the Curriculum*
- *Writing Assessment and Evaluation Rubrics*

Kinds of Supporting Details

Supporting details give expository writing its strength. Note the types of supporting details listed in the chart below.

Supporting Details for Expository Writing	
Kinds	**Example of Use in Exposition**
Facts	Alligators live largely in freshwater, while crocodiles live mostly in saltwater or in at least slightly salty water.
Statistics	The world's largest tree is a giant sequoia called the General Sherman tree. It measures 101.5 feet at the base, is 272.4 feet tall, and weighs about 12,334,000 pounds.
Examples/ Incidents	The chimpanzee is an example of an animal that makes and uses tools. Chimpanzees cut pieces of grass to specific lengths for fishing termites out of termite mounds.
Sensory details	The aurora borealis appears as a glimmering curtain of light flashing in the night sky.
Reasons	One reason some people think penguins are mammals rather than birds is that their feathers are short and fluffy and, from a distance, resemble hair.

How to Select Supporting Details

Common sense will help you select supporting details. For example, if you are explaining a process, you will want to present all the steps. The following factors are the most important for selecting types of supporting details for a particular exposition:

- the type of exposition you are writing
- your purpose for writing, especially your secondary purpose (see examples of secondary purpose in the chart on page 234)
- the level of knowledge or expertise of your audience

Journal Writing

Read a magazine or newspaper article. Next, without reviewing the article, list in your journal the supporting details you recall. What makes these details memorable? Write your ideas.

Prewriting Tip

To help come up with supporting details, you can brainstorm with other students. To learn more about brainstorming, see Lesson 2.2, p. 62.

Teach

Using the Model

Ask students what information they would need to evaluate the reliability and meaning of the statistics presented in the model on page 232. (Students might question how long effects lasted and whether they could be replicated in further tests.)

Students might add smells such as chicken soup to the soothing list, and include a cut lawn in the list of stimulating scents. **L2**

Visual Thinking

Point out that the chart on page 234 shows two ways a writer might handle a topic, based on a list of important factors. Have students make similar charts during prewriting if they want to consider several topics before choosing one. Suggest that under each situation heading they list supporting details specific to their own work. **L2**

List kinds of supporting details on the board and have students write a sentence illustrating each type.

See also *Two-Minute Skill Drill Transparency 5.2*

Journal Writing Tip

Activating Prior Knowledge Suggest that students use freewriting techniques to recall supporting details mentioned in the article. Encourage students to separate actual details from associations brought out by those details.

Teach

Promoting Discussion

Point out that because writers include or omit details according to their purpose, expository writing may be misleading even when all the details are true. For example, ask what kinds of factual details an advertiser might omit in a press release promoting a new product. **L2**

Using the Model

This writer lists the supporting details in order of increasing importance—price, a desire for healthful and pesticide-free vegetables, and better taste. **L2**

Distinguishing Fact from Opinion

Remind students that a fact can be proved or disproved. For example, it is a fact that clothing styles change. It is an opinion that styles reflect optimism or pessimism in society. **L1**

Additional Resources

- For further stimuli for expository writing, see *Fine Art Transparencies* 25–28.
- *Writing Process Transparencies* 11, 23–27
- *Cooperative Learning Activities*
- *Writing Across the Curriculum*
- *Thinking and Study Skills,* pp. 5, 25
- *Sentence-Combining Practice,* pp. 32–33
- *Listening and Speaking Activities,* pp. 15–16
- *Research Paper and Report Writing,* pp. 43–48
- *Composition Practice,* p. 36

Expository Writing

The chart below shows how to analyze key factors in selecting appropriate supporting details for two kinds of exposition.

Using Supporting Details

Factor	Situation #1	Situation #2
Main purpose and type of your exposition	To explain the cause and effects of a natural phenomenon	To compare two theories about a natural phenomenon
Your secondary purpose	To interest your audience in the topic	To show your knowledge of different scientific theories
Level of knowledge of your audience	Audience unfamiliar with the topic	Specialized audience (scientists) familiar with the topic
Kinds of supporting details you might rely on most heavily	Incidents and interesting sensory details	Facts and statistics that provide convincing support

How to Organize Supporting Details

How you organize your supporting details depends in part on the type of exposition you are writing. For example, if you are writing about a cause and its effects, you might present the least important effect first and the most important effect last, as illustrated in the model below.

Model

Urban gardens—plots overflowing with juicy red tomatoes, shiny green cukes, crisp beans, and myriad flowers—have been popping up in greater numbers all over our neighborhood since spring. You've probably seen them in backyards, empty lots, even on rooftops. Rising vegetable prices, up 35 percent from last year, are surely one reason behind the spread of these garden plots. Even more important reasons include the desire for healthful, pesticide-free vegetables and for the better taste of the home-grown vegetables. Delia Jackson exemplifies this trend. She even took a course called City Gardens at the local community center. Soon after the class ended, she began a roof garden atop the high-rise where she lives. "My friends joked about it at first," she says, "but now the same ones are coming over for my vine-ripened tomatoes."

In what order does the writer list supporting details?

The writer concludes with a prime example of one urban gardener.

MEETING INDIVIDUAL NEEDS

English Language Learners

Generating Details

Some students may have difficulty listing sensory details in English. As part of a small group activity, ask students to choose a topic, such as trees, to write about. Tell each student to write a paragraph on the topic, using as many sensory details as possible, and to note the places where they cannot think of the English words they want. After students share their paragraphs, group members can discuss strategies for solving word-choice problems such as using a thesaurus, asking a person fluent in English, and so on.

5.2 Writing Activities

Write a Background Information Article

Use the following details to write an explanation of the term *hurricane.* Your writing will be a background information piece for your community newspaper.

1. In 1992 one hurricane caused $20 billion in damage and killed at least 38 people.
2. Hurricanes develop over warm tropical ocean waters.
3. The winds and rain produce massive waves, called a storm surge, which bring floods.
4. A hurricane is a powerful, swirling storm with winds over 75 miles per hour.
5. The most destructive part of the hurricane (where winds may reach 150 miles per hour) is the area of wall clouds surrounding the eye, an area of calm about 20 miles in diameter.
6. A hurricane may cover an area of 200 to 300 miles in diameter.

PURPOSE To explain what a hurricane is and to describe its destructive power
AUDIENCE Newspaper readers
LENGTH 2–3 paragraphs

WRITING RUBRICS To write an effective background information article, you should

- choose memorable statistics and sensory details to get your readers' attention
- define new terms for a general audience
- order your details for their best effect

Viewing and Representing

Use an article from a print or an electronic source to create a poster illustrating the use of effective detail. Label the details that support the main and secondary purposes of the article and those that most forcefully or vividly convey the message.

Cross-Curricular Activity

SCIENCE Explain a natural process, such as soil erosion, for a science room reference notebook. In a small group, make a list of the supporting details that you will use to explain the process, and then write a draft of your explanation. Your audience will be students who need help to understand a process.

Grammar*Link*

Use commas correctly in a series.

Rewrite the following sentences, adding commas to separate three or more words or phrases.

1. Peppermint orange jasmine and chamomile are scents commonly used in teas.
2. Popular dessert coffees include those flavored with hazelnut Dutch chocolate or Swiss mocha.
3. She ground the coffee beans scooped them into the filter added four cups of water and turned on the coffeemaker.
4. Coffee is a tree or shrub native to tropical Africa Asia and Central and South America.
5. Coffee trees grow about fifteen feet tall have long leaves and produce white or cream flowers.

See Lesson 21.6, page 738.

Writing Online — For more writing and grammar practice, go to **glencoe.com** and enter QuickPass code WC97727p1.

Expository Writing

Assess

Evaluation Rubrics

Write a Background Information Article

Use these criteria when evaluating your students' writing. The article should

- include a variety of supporting details, such as facts, reasons, statistics, examples, and sensory details
- be understandable by nonexperts
- present details in logical order

Viewing and Representing

The finished poster should clearly organize and present supporting ideas for both the purposes and the message of the article selected.

Cross-Curricular Activity

The explanation should list all relevant supporting details, be aimed at a general audience, and include appropriate definitions.

See also *Writing Assessment & Evaluation Rubrics*

Reteaching

Composition Reteaching, p. 37

Enrichment

Composition Enrichment, p. 37

Close

Have students explain how some politicians might use a poll to show that most people agree with them, while others might use the same poll to show that they are gaining support. Discuss what other information each of the politicians might use and how each would organize it to support a position. Students may want to refer to the charts on pages 233 and 234.

Grammar*Link*

Answers

1. Peppermint, orange, jasmine, and . . .
2. . . . hazelnut, Dutch chocolate, or . . .
3. . . . coffee beans, scooped . . . filter, added . . . water, and turned on . . .
4. . . . Africa, Asia, and Central and South America.
5. . . . tall, have long leaves, and produce white or cream flowers.

Focus

Lesson Overview

Objectives

- To define the purpose of a "how to" paper
- To select a process topic and then summarize all steps in that process in chart form
- To use the completed chart to write a paper that explains all the steps in the process in a clear and organized manner

Skills

- using sequential order; transition words; understanding audience

Critical Thinking

- categorizing; evaluating; visualizing; generating new information

Listening and Speaking

- discussing; explaining a process

Bellringer

Daily Language Activity

When students enter the classroom have this assignment on the board: *What might happen if you tried to build a model spaceship without reading the directions first?*

Grammar Link to the Bellringer

Have students correct the verb tenses in the following sentences so they make sense: *First, check that you have all the pieces. Then, got the proper tools. Finally, puts it together.*

See also *Daily Language Practice*

Motivating Activity

Discuss students' responses to the Bellringer activity. Ask students why it is important to follow directions in sequence. Invite students to describe any of their own problems with following instructions. (Students might describe learning how to play a game or fixing something that has broken.) Explain that in this lesson they will learn how to write instructions.

LESSON 5.3

Explaining How To . . .

A "how to" paper, a common form of expository writing, is used to teach a skill or just to share knowledge. Usually the writer presents the instructions as a series of steps. What process is Patrick McManus explaining in the model below?

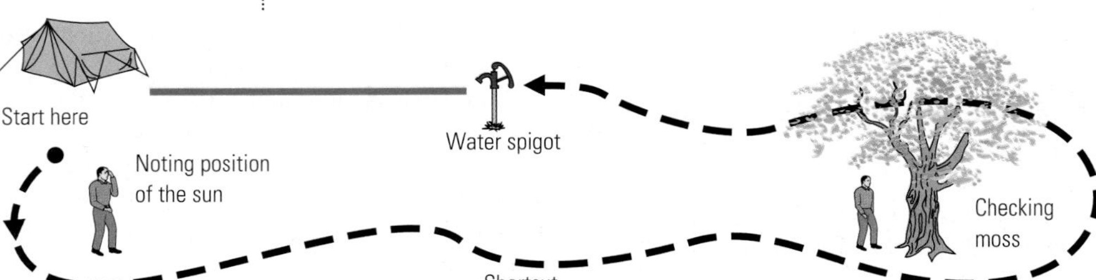

In his introductory sentence, McManus identifies the process he will be explaining.

McManus gives tips to help a camper get lost. Have you gotten lost anywhere besides in the woods? What tips would you give to get lost where you did?

Literature Model

Now how should you go about getting lost? . . . If you are camped in a public campground, simply say that you are going to take a shortcut to the communal spigot [water faucet] to fill the water bucket. . . . Shortcuts rank number one among ways to get lost quickly and thoroughly. . . . Before starting your shortcut, take careful note of the position of the sun. This will give the impression that you know what you're doing. . . . [Also,] always study on which side of the trees the moss is growing. Guides and other experienced woodsmen are fond of giving this advice, because looking at moss helps even them to get lost.

Patrick McManus, *Rubber Legs and White Tail-Hairs*

How do you steer a canoe? How do bees make honey? Any process can be explained clearly, step by step.

Resource Manager

Planning Resources

- *Lesson Plans*

Transparencies

- *Bellringer*
- *Daily Language Practice*
- *Fine Art* 25–28
- *Two-Minute Skill Drill*
- *Writing Process* 11, 23–27

Other Print Resources

- *Composition Enrichment,* p. 37
- *Composition Practice,* p. 37
- *Composition Reteaching,* p. 37
- *Cooperative Learning Activities,* pp. 21–24
- *Listening and Speaking Activities,* pp. 15–16
- *Research Paper and Report Writing,* pp. 43–48
- *Sentence-Combining Practice,* pp. 32–34
- *Thinking and Study Skills,* pp. 13, 17, 23
- *Writing Across the Curriculum*
- *Writing Assessment and Evaluation Rubrics*

Think About Your Purpose

Sometimes you explain a process in order to teach a skill, such as how to feed a pet snake.

Sometimes you may explain a process just to share knowledge, such as how fireflies make their flashing lights.

Suppose you wanted to explain how to bathe a dog. During prewriting, list all the steps in a chart similar to the one below.

Planning a "How To" Paper

1. Choose topic: how to bathe a dog.
2. Define audience: first-time dog owners.
3. Gather information: read manuals, interview, observe.
4. List steps of the process in chronological order.
   a. Set up safe bathing area—rubber mat in the tub, nonskid rug on floor.
   b. Gather shampoo, sponge, bucket or shower head, towels, comb or brush, and other equipment you need.
   c. If you don't have a hand-held shower head, fill tub half-full with lukewarm water.
   d. Plug dog's ears with cotton to prevent water from entering. (Remember to take cotton out after bath.)
   e. Wet dog all over with lukewarm water.
   f. Shampoo dog, using your fingers to scrub.
   g. Rinse dog with water, using bucket or shower head.
   h. Wash dog's face with sponge dipped in clear water.
   i. Let dog shake off excess water.
   j. Rub dog dry with towels, or use hair dryer.
   k. Comb dog when coat is dry.
5. Note any special instructions.
6. Tell result of process: clean, happy dog.

Grammar Tip

Some transitions useful in process writing are *after, always, as soon as, before, first, following, in order to, now, soon, so that, then, until.* To learn when to punctuate these transitions, see Lessons 21.5, page 735, and 21.6, page 738.

Journal Writing

In your journal, list five possible topics for a process explanation. Then write a brief statement explaining whether the purpose of each would be to teach a skill or simply to share knowledge.

Expository Writing

Teach

Using the Model

Students might discuss getting lost in malls, subdivisions, or downtown areas. Their tips for getting lost might include reading twisted street signs, ignoring landmarks, or using several doorways. **L2**

Understanding Connotation

Students might enjoy experimenting with stylistic changes such as obvious exaggerations and anecdotes to add humor or irony to an explanation. Direct students to study the planning chart, and then ask them to outline a set of instructions for a common task, such as making a bed. Challenge students to include humor to enliven and illustrate the process. Remind students that even humorous instructions must be clear. **L3**

Two-Minute Skill Drill

Put the following words in the order you might use them when explaining how to do something:

Then	Third
First	Second
Last	

See also *Two-Minute Skill Drill Transparency 5.3*

Journal Writing Tip

Identifying Main Ideas Suggest to students that they think of topics such as how to find materials in the library, how to use a computer catalog, or how to change a bicycle tire. They might also be interested in tracing a family tree or explaining a sport.

Teach

Writing Explanations

To help students understand explanations better, invite them to describe their own problems with following instructions. (Students might describe programming a VCR or assembling a child's toy.) Discuss why instructions might be challenging to write. Encourage students to recognize that instructions must include definitions of unfamiliar terms and simple, step-by-step directions that audiences can understand. **L2**

Using Transitions

Students may need help to use transitions effectively. Ask them to outline the steps in a familiar process (such as making a grilled cheese sandwich or programming a CD player) using a flow chart like the one on this page. Students should use a transition word or phrase that relates each step to the one before it. After they finish their flow charts, students can exchange papers. Partners can check for missing steps or unclear transitions. **L1**

Additional Resources

For further stimuli for expository writing, see *Fine Art Transparencies* 25–28.

Writing Process Transparencies 11, 23–27

Writing Across the Curriculum

Cooperative Learning Activities

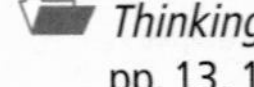
Thinking and Study Skills pp. 13, 17, 23

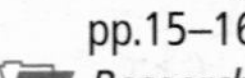
Listening and Speaking Activities, pp.15–16

Research Paper and Report Writing, pp. 43–48

Composition Practice, p. 37

Write About a Process

You can use the chart you made during the prewriting stage to help you write the first draft of your explanation. First, make sure the steps in the process are clear. You may need to combine steps for simplicity, as illustrated in the diagram below. Next, show the relationships between these steps with appropriate transitional words and phrases. The diagram indicates some transitions you might use to create a smooth chronological flow.

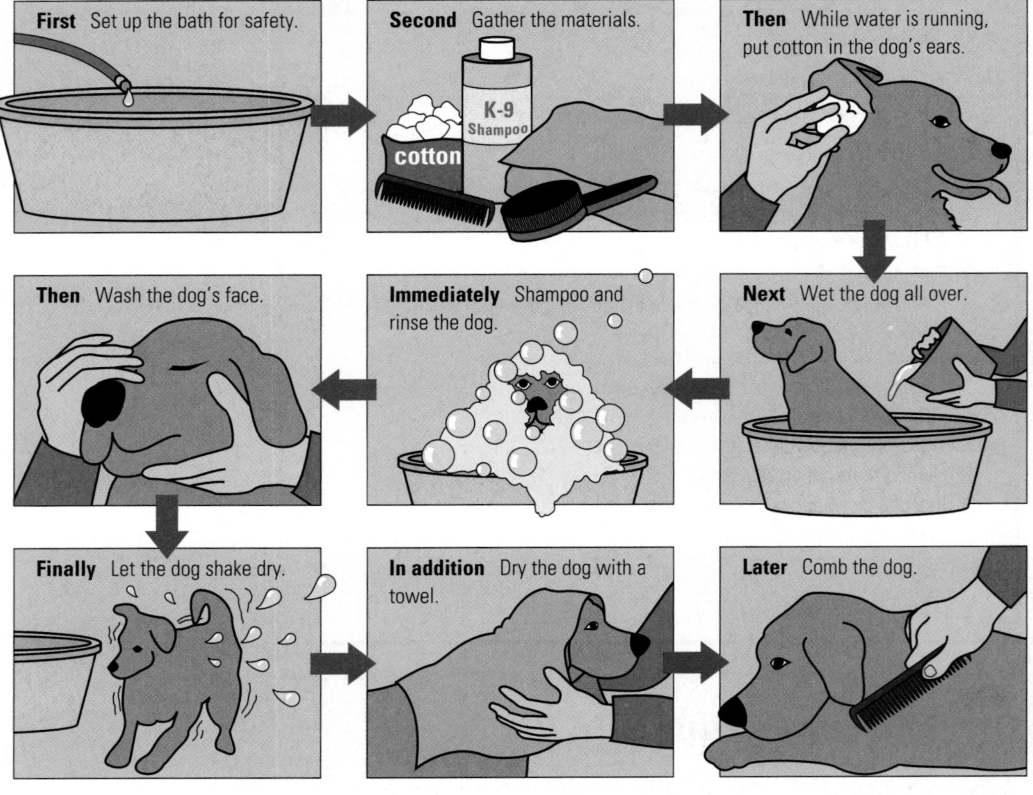

In your **introduction** state the process you are explaining and the relevance of the process. This will help capture your reader's interest. Also, you can often use humor to engage your readers. In your **conclusion** emphasize the importance of the process you have explained, identifying its benefits to your audience. This will help leave your reader with a strong impression.

MEETING INDIVIDUAL NEEDS

English Language Learners

Understanding Vocabulary

Some students who are learning English may lack familiarity with English vocabulary for units of measure. To give these students practice with using this vocabulary, ask them to identify a cooking process with which they are familiar. They should break down this process into a series of brief steps. Ask them to organize their steps into a chart similar to the one on page 237. Suggest that they label the chart in their primary language as well as in English.

5.3 Writing Activities

Write a "How To" Paper

Think of something you know how to make or do that you could demonstrate to the class. Write a short paper about the process. Be prepared to give the demonstration in class.

PURPOSE To explain a process that involves a demonstration
AUDIENCE Your teacher and classmates
LENGTH 1–2 paragraphs

WRITING RUBRICS To write an effective "how to" paper, you should

- list all the materials you'll need
- list all the steps in order
- include an introduction and a conclusion
- use transitional words and phrases

Cross-Curricular Activity

HEALTH Think of a process you have learned about in your health class. Write an explanation of the process as you would for an essay test. Use transitions to show your teacher that you understand the steps in the process and the order in which they occur. If you wish, include a diagram or other illustration to help explain the process. Proofread carefully.

Listening and Speaking

Ask an adult who is an expert at something to explain a process to you. You might ask an electrician how to install a light switch or a librarian how to catalogue a book. Make notes of the steps in the process; then repeat the explanation back to your expert. Discuss how a speaker's knowledge of a procedure might affect an explanation: Can too much knowledge make the explanation too technical? Can too little make it too vague?

Grammar*Link*

Do not shift verb tenses unnecessarily.

Rewrite the following steps, using consistent verb tenses throughout the instructions.

How to Start Up the Computer

1. Found the ON and OFF power switch. This switch was somewhere on the monitor—at the bottom front, on one side, or in the back.
2. Move the power switch to the ON position.
3. After a few seconds the monitor screen will brighten.
4. Adjust the brightness control, usually located at the side or the bottom of the monitor, if it was not set at a level you preferred.
5. From the main menu or desktop, select the software program in which you wished to work.
6. If you are inserting a diskette, make sure that you inserted the diskette with the metal end first and the side with the arrow facing up.
7. If you experienced problems starting up, ask yourself the following questions:
8. Was the computer plugged into an electrical outlet?
9. Is the ON/OFF power switch turned to the ON position?
10. Had the brightness control been properly adjusted?

See Lesson 15.6, page 594.

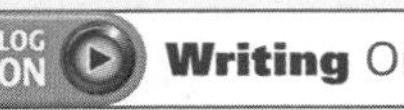

Writing Online | For more writing and grammar practice, go to **glencoe.com** and enter QuickPass code **WC97727p1**.

Assess

Evaluation Rubrics

Write a "How to" Paper

Use these criteria when evaluating your students' writing:

- Are all materials included?
- Are the steps in the right order?
- Does the report begin with an introduction and end with a conclusion?
- Are transitional words used to guide the reader from step to step?

See also *Writing Assessment & Evaluation Rubrics*

Cross-Curricular Activity

Evaluate students' work using the following criteria:

- Unfamiliar terms are defined.
- Vocabulary and sentence length are appropriate for the audience.
- Transitions have been made so that each step is clear.
- Any diagrams or illustrations supporting the process are explained.
- The presentation follows a step-by-step order.

Reteaching

Composition Reteaching, p. 37

Enrichment

Composition Enrichment, p. 37

Close

Have students discuss the process involved in writing an explanation. Ask them to compare an explanation that shares knowledge to one that teaches a skill. Ask students to give examples of each kind of explanation.

Grammar*Link*

Answers

Answers will vary, but some suggestions are given below.

1. Find the . . . switch. This switch is somewhere . . .
2. (correct)
3. (correct)
4. Adjust the brightness control . . . if it is not set . . . you prefer.
5. From the main menu . . . in which you wish to work.
6. If you are inserting . . . you insert . . .
7. If you experience . . .
8. Is the computer . . .
9. (correct)
10. Has the brightness control . . .

Focus

Lesson Overview

Objectives
- To identify valid cause-and-effect relationships
- To select a clear thesis statement and organize a draft following either a cause-to-effect pattern or an effect-to-cause pattern
- To compose a cause-and-effect paragraph with an appropriate introduction and a conclusion

Skills
- identifying cause and effect; organizing causes and effects

Critical Thinking
- analyzing; categorizing; clarifying

Listening and Speaking
- note taking; evaluating; questioning

Bellringer
Daily Language Activity

When students enter the classroom, have this assignment on the board: *Think of a simple action you might perform, such as shooting a basketball at a hoop. Write a list of both immediate and far-reaching effects of the action.*

Grammar Link to the Bellringer

Ask volunteers to record their lists on the chalkboard. Underline the verbs and ask students to identify the subjects in each suggested effect. Emphasize to students the importance of subject-verb agreement.

See also *Daily Language Practice*

Motivating Activity

Identify students' suggestions in the Bellringer activity as either causes or effects. Ask students to describe other cause-and-effect relationships they encounter daily.

LESSON 5.4

Expository Writing

Explaining Cause and Effect

Cause-and-effect writing helps a reader understand the relationships between events or facts. In the model below, two science writers explain the surprising effects of gravity.

Sagan and Druyan describe a general effect and explain its cause in the first sentence.

Sagan and Druyan use this simple comparison to help make their point.

Do you think Sagan and Druyan's hypothetical example of Mount Everest is effective? Explain why or why not.

Literature Model

The Earth and the other planets tend to be almost perfect spheres because, as Newton showed, gravity is a central force—it pulls everything equally toward the center of the world, itself held together by the force of gravity. The mountains sticking up above the spherical surface of the Earth represent less of a deviation from a perfect sphere than does the layer of paint or enamel on the surface of a typical globe that represents the Earth. If you were able to pile a sizable mountain on top of Mount Everest, it would not just sit there, poking in solitary magnificence into the stratosphere. The additional weight you had added would crush the base of Everest, and the new composite mountain would collapse until it was no larger than Everest is today. The Earth's gravity severely limits how much deviation from a perfect sphere our planet is permitted.

Carl Sagan and Ann Druyan, *Comet*

The explanation in the model focuses mainly on effects. As the chart on the next page shows, cause-and-effect writing may also focus on the causes.

Resource Manager

Planning Resources
- *Lesson Plans*

Transparencies
- *Bellringer*
- *Daily Language Practice*
- *Fine Art* 25–28
- *Two-Minute Skill Drill*
- *Writing Process* 11, 23–27

Other Print Resources
- *Composition Enrichment,* p. 38
- *Composition Practice,* p. 38
- *Composition Reteaching,* p. 38
- *Cooperative Learning Activities,* pp. 21–24
- *Listening and Speaking Activities,* pp. 15–16
- *Research Paper and Report Writing,* pp. 43–48
- *Sentence-Combining Practice,* pp. 32–33
- *Thinking and Study Skills,* pp. 14, 18
- *Writing Across the Curriculum*
- *Writing Assessment and Evaluation Rubrics*

Earthquake: Cause and Effects
Cause Massive plates that make up the earth's surface move, putting great pressure on the rocks at the plates' edges. Sometimes the pressure becomes too great for the rocks to bear.
Effects Rocks along the edges break and shift when pressure becomes too great, creating an earthquake.
▼
The earthquake releases energy in the form of waves, or vibrations.
▼
The waves shake the earth's surface, buildings, and bridges, sometimes causing great damage.

Link Cause and Effect

Cause-and-effect writing explains how one event causes another. Note how each effect listed in the chart above serves as the cause for the next effect. While some cause-and-effect writing is based on a complex series of causes and effects, some deals with only one cause and only one effect, giving a clear, detailed explanation of the relationship.

Beware of false cause-and-effect relationships. If one event follows another, the second wasn't necessarily caused by the first. Consider the sentence "The moon eclipsed the sun; then clouds covered the sky." This sentence does not show cause and effect, only sequential events. The eclipse did not cause the clouds to cover the sky.

An important way to make a true cause-and-effect relationship clear is with a thesis statement—a clear statement of your main idea—presented in a topic sentence. A thesis statement for an essay on earthquakes might be the following: "Great pressure along the edges of the earth's moving plates causes rocks to break and shift, creating an earthquake that can bring its destructive shock waves to the earth's surface."

Grammar Tip

When writing a cause-and-effect explanation of a recurring event or a natural phenomenon such as an earthquake, use the present tense. For information on other times present tense should be used, see Lesson 15.3, page 586.

Journal Writing

If you can use the word *because* to show the relationship between events or facts, the relation is causal, not just sequential. In your journal, write possible causal relationships, such as effects caused by watching television or causes for earning good grades, and try the "*because* test" on them.

Expository Writing

Teach

Using the Model

Ask a volunteer to describe the cause and effect in Sagan and Druyan's hypothetical example of Mount Everest. If necessary, point out that the effect is the collapse of Mount Everest and the hypothetical mountain; the cause is the earth's gravity. Explain to students that the example is effective because it presents a single cause and its effect in a concrete manner. **L2**

Two-Minute Skill Drill

Have students identify the cause and effect in each of the following sentences.

It rained, so the picnic was cancelled.
Because the show was expensive, we rented a video.

See also *Two-Minute Skill Drill Transparency 5.4*

Teach

Organizing Cause-Effect Writing

On the board write *Someone dropped a plate. Broken pieces of china lay on the floor.* Ask students to use transitions from the chart on this page to combine the phrases into as many different cause-and-effect sentences as they can. (For example, *Broken pieces of china lay on the floor, so someone probably dropped a plate.* The word *probably* indicates that the writer did not directly observe the cause.) **L2**

Using the Model

Ask students to list the words Eric Koszyk uses to stress the uncertainty of the cause-and-effect relationship he describes. (usually, likely, would, could) Point out that the phrase *Some scientists disagree* also indicates uncertainty. Have students discuss the type of writing in which such words and phrases can be of great importance. (Example: Medical articles and advertisements, especially those written about or for procedures and products that can affect the health and safety of the public) **L2**

Additional Resources

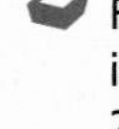 For further stimuli for expository writing, see *Fine Art Transparencies* 25–28.

 *Writing Process Transparencies* 11, 23–27

- *Cooperative Learning Activities*
- *Writing Across the Curriculum*
- *Thinking and Study Skills*, pp. 1, 14, 18
- *Listening and Speaking Activities*, pp. 15–16
- *Sentence-Combining Practice*, pp. 32–33
- *Composition Practice*, p. 38

Revising Tip

As you revise your cause-and-effect piece, decide whether you are placing proper emphasis on the causes, the effects, or both to achieve your purpose.

Organize Causes and Effects

Once you have a thesis statement, you can begin organizing your draft. You can follow either a cause-to-effect pattern or an effect-to-cause pattern. For example, you might organize a piece about the greenhouse effect by listing and explaining the many causes and concluding with the possible effects. A piece on the tides might first describe tides and the changes they bring to coastlines and then discuss their cause.

Whichever form of organization you use, you will need to connect your events, facts, and ideas with effective **transitions.** The chart below shows two types of transitions you may need to use.

Some Transitions for Cause-and-Effect Writing

CAUSE AND EFFECT	as a result because consequently	due to if, then since	so therefore thus
DEGREES OF CERTAINTY	certainly likely maybe	necessarily possibly probably	undoubtedly unquestionably of course

Your cause-and-effect piece will also need an **introduction** and a **conclusion**. In your introduction you should catch the reader's attention and give your purpose. Your thesis statement can serve as the introduction. Then you can conclude by summarizing the cause-and-effect relationship or extending the information you have presented. Note the introduction, transitions, and conclusion in the selection below by Eric Koszyk.

Eric begins with a topic sentence that clearly states the causal relationship he plans to explain.

What are some words in addition to "believe" that Eric uses to stress the uncertainty of the theory?

In his conclusion, Eric restates his cause-and-effect relationship but again stresses its uncertainty.

Student Model

An ice age usually occurs every couple of million years or so, but some scientists now believe that the current warming of the earth is likely to speed up this process. They believe that the warming of the planet will melt the polar ice caps. This, then, will change the level of water in the planet's oceans, which, therefore, will change the salt composition of the oceans. This altered salt composition would bring about a change in the jet stream winds that circle the earth. And this change in the jet stream would bring about the cooling trend that could well speed up the coming of the next ice age. Some scientists disagree, but a large number of other scientists and environmentalists believe in this theory.

Eric Koszyk
Quartz Hill High School, Quartz Hill, California

Listening and Speaking

Identifying Cause-and-Effect Relationships

Provide concrete, familiar examples of cause-and-effect relationships. Suggest a familiar model—a student arrives late for school. On the board, write *Causes* and *Effects* and have students suggest some causes and effects of lateness; be sure to identify each suggestion. Then discuss instances in which an effect becomes a cause of another problem. (For example, one effect of lateness might be missing an exam, which could, in turn, cause the student's grade to be lowered.)

5.4 Writing Activities

Write a Cause-and-Effect Paragraph

Plan and write a cause-and-effect paragraph on the relationship between hours of study and good grades, or on another cause-and-effect topic of your choice. For help with using transitions, see **Writing and Research Handbook,** page 945.

PURPOSE To explain a cause-and-effect relationship
AUDIENCE Your teacher and classmates
LENGTH 1 paragraph

WRITING RUBRICS To write an effective cause-and-effect paragraph, you should

- decide whether to focus on causes or effects
- write a clear thesis statement
- include an introduction and a conclusion
- use appropriate transitions

Viewing and Representing

COLLABORATIVE WRITING Working in groups of three or four, find a painting or photograph in which an event has occurred (a triumphant athlete or the aftermath of a storm, for example). Write a brief cause-and-effect paragraph explaining what has occurred in the scene, presenting at least two causes and two effects. Take turns presenting your paragraphs orally to your group, to compare and contrast your interpretations of the event.

GrammarLink

Make subjects and verbs agree.

Subjects must agree with verbs no matter how many words come between them.

Rewrite the sentences below to make subjects and verbs agree.

1. According to environmentalists, current temperature changes of the earth signals the coming of the next ice age.
2. Thousands of years ago, many parts of the earth's surface was covered by ice sheets.
3. The movement of glaciers cause erosion.
4. Rocks buried in the ice scrapes and digs at the land.
5. Scientists at the local university is preparing reports on climate changes.

See Lesson 16.1, pages 609–610.

Cross-Curricular Activity

SPELLING Check the spelling in your paragraph by exchanging papers with a partner. Discuss the errors you found on one another's papers. What words are you misspelling? What do they have in common? Develop a strategy for learning to spell these words. Share it with your partner.

LOG ON **Writing Online** For more writing and grammar practice, go to glencoe.com and enter QuickPass code WC97727p1.

Assess

Evaluation Rubrics

Write a Cause-and-Effect Paragraph

Use the following criteria when evaluating your students' writing. Each paragraph should

- focus on causes or effects
- contain a clear thesis statement
- include an introduction and a conclusion
- clearly state a valid causal relationship between two items
- use appropriate transitions

See also *Writing Assessment & Evaluation Rubrics*

Viewing and Representing

Students' paragraphs should include at least two causes and two effects and contain transitions that qualify the degree of certainty.

Reteaching

Composition Reteaching, p. 38

Enrichment

Composition Enrichment, p. 38

Fine Art Transparencies 25–28

Close

Invite students to summarize cause-and-effect relationships from a favorite book or movie. Ask them to identify a cause and an effect, using appropriate transitions.

GrammarLink

Answers

1. . . . changes . . . signal . . .
2. . . . parts . . . were . . .
3. . . . movement . . . causes . . .
4. . . . Rocks . . . scrape and dig . . .
5. . . . Scientists . . . are . . .

Focus

Lesson Overview

Objectives

- To learn how to classify information according to common attributes, or qualities
- To use a classification scheme to construct a piece of expository writing

Skills

- planning for an audience; constructing an organized classification

Critical Thinking

- identifying features; classifying

Listening and Speaking

- speaking to inform; explaining a process; listening critically

Bellringer

Daily Language Activity

When students enter the classroom, have this assignment on the board: *List as many ways as you can think of to organize a tape or CD collection.*

Grammar Link to the Bellringer

Ask students to identify the parts of speech in their organizational plan categories. Encourage students to give examples of the more precise and concrete nouns in each category.

See also *Daily Language Practice*

Motivating Activity

Ask students how possessions are organized on shelves or in drawers in their rooms. Do they place certain items, such as socks, in one drawer, and other items, such as toiletries, on a shelf? Why is any method of organization preferable to placing items haphazardly? (It's easier to remember where items are stored when they're grouped together.) Point out that when students group similar things together, they are classifying. Explain that writers classify information to make it easier to understand.

Expository Writing

LESSON 5.5

Classifying a Subject

When you classify, you group items into categories based on common attributes, or qualities. Notice how loon calls are classified in the passage below.

Literature Model

In recent years, loon calls have been studied by researchers and it is now generally accepted that there are at least four basic calls in the loon's vocabulary, with gradations and combinations and shading to refine the meanings. Within a family, loons call to one another with a soft hoot. The wail, the cry with which the nightly chorus commences, is used when one loon is trying to establish contact with other loons. The tremolo calls that are supposed to sound like a madman's laughter are alarm calls. . . . The yodel is the song of the male loon, a complex series of rising notes followed by an undulation [pulsating tone]; it is gorgeous to human ears but a loon uses it to define and defend his territory. Very recently, researchers have discovered that male loons' yodels are distinctive, each from the other, and can be used as aural tags to study and follow individuals.

Sue Hubbell, "For the Love of Loons," *Smithsonian*

What does Hubbell tell the reader in her first sentence?

Hubbell describes the hoot, the wail, the tremolo, and the yodel as the four basic types of loon calls.

What do you learn from Hubbell's conclusion?

Why Do You Classify?

Classification is an effective way to organize ideas. In the diagram below, one writer has classified clouds according to their general shapes. She has done so to help organize her ideas about clouds. With that type of classification, she will be able to provide a clear overview of the topic, make information accessible, and better inform or instruct her audience.

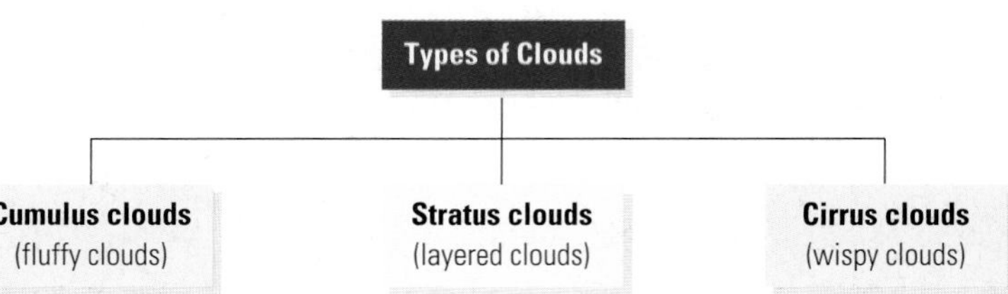

Resource Manager

Planning Resources

- *Lesson Plans*

Transparencies

- *Bellringer*
- *Daily Language Practice*
- *Fine Art* 25–28
- *Two-Minute Skill Drill*
- *Writing Process* 11, 23–27

Other Print Resources

- *Composition Enrichment,* p. 39
- *Composition Practice,* p. 39
- *Composition Reteaching,* p. 39
- *Cooperative Learning Activities, pp.* 21–24
- *Listening and Speaking Activities, pp.* 15–16
- *Research Paper and Report Writing,* pp. 43–48
- *Sentence-Combining Practice,* pp. 32–33
- *Thinking and Study Skills,* pp. 11, 13
- *Writing Across the Curriculum*
- *Writing Assessment and Evaluation Rubrics*

How Do You Plan a Classification?

Your most important task in planning a classification is to create meaningful categories appropriate for your purpose and audience. The chart below shows how different purposes and audiences may affect the way items are classified. Look at the common feature that ties together each category of trees in the chart.

Three Ways of Classifying Trees

AUDIENCE	CLASSIFICATION	COMMON FEATURE
SCIENTISTS	• Cone-bearing trees • Seed-bearing trees • Spore-bearing trees	Methods of reproduction
LANDSCAPE ARCHITECTS	• Shade trees • Trees for windbreaks • Ornamental trees	Usefulness
WILD-FOOD COLLECTORS	• Trees that bear edible nuts • Trees that bear edible fruits • Trees that have edible sap	Source of food

Journal Writing

Think of a subject for which you will plan a classification, such as types of writing in your journal or types of music. In your journal create a diagram like the one at the top of this page in which you classify your subject. Make sure your categories are mutually exclusive and based on a common feature.

How Do You Write a Classification?

As you draft your classification, follow the organization shown in the diagram on page 246. Study the organization of the student model that follows.

Vocabulary Tip

When drafting your classification, you may want to use some of the following terms: *categories, classes, groups, kinds, types, varieties, divisions, branches,* and *subclasses.*

Teach

Using the Model

In the model on page 244, Hubbell opens by telling readers what she will be classifying (loon calls), how many categories there are (four), and what feature she will be using to classify them (their sound). In her conclusion, she adds that in one category—male loons' yodels—significant new information has emerged. **L2**

Classifying

To give students a sense of the classifications they use daily, invite them to name items of clothing. List these items on the board. If offerings lag, prompt students with situations for which they need special clothing. (For example, ask what they would wear to help paint a room.)

Ask students to suggest terms that include a number of items on the list (such as sportswear, outerwear, or accessories). Can students think of ways in which they use classifications spontaneously each day? (For example, students must decide whether they want value, variety, or convenience when they shop; when they go out, they must determine what to wear, depending on the weather and their destination.) **L2**

Journal Writing Tip

Classifying Suggest that students use a simple test to determine whether their categories are mutually exclusive. If any of the items they are classifying can be placed in more than one category, the categories may need to be either narrowed or more fully defined.

5.5

Teach

Using the Model

Alli Arnold's categories are based on the location in which each group of flowers grows. She is then able to discuss how the features of each climate contribute to the beauty of its wildflowers.

In her conclusion, Arnold praises the "simple dignity and elegance" of wildflowers. This implies that her attraction to wildflowers comes from an appreciation of their beauty. **L2**

Two-Minute Skill Drill

Have students list specific, concrete nouns for the following words:

car dog tree
book flower

See also *Two-Minute Skill Drill Transparency 5.5*

Additional Resources

For further stimuli for expository writing, see *Fine Art Transparencies* 25–28.

- *Writing Process Transparencies* 1, 23–27
- *Writing Across the Curriculum*
- *Cooperative Learning Activities*
- *Thinking and Study Skills*, pp. 11, 13
- *Listening and Speaking Activities*, pp. 15–16
- *Composition Practice*, p. 39
- *Sentence-Combining Practice*, pp. 32–33

Expository Writing

Revising Tip

As you revise your classification, make sure your thesis statement is clear. For advice on writing thesis statements, see Lesson 7.2, pages 330–333.

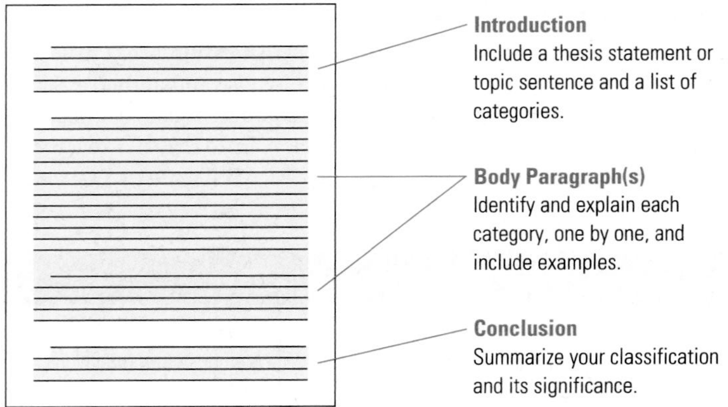

Introduction
Include a thesis statement or topic sentence and a list of categories.
Body Paragraph(s)
Identify and explain each category, one by one, and include examples.
Conclusion
Summarize your classification and its significance.

Student Model

Wildflowers, admired for their beauty and magnificence, include flowers from woodlands, mountains, prairies, deserts, and swamps.

Woodland flowers rely on humus, the product of decaying leaves and wood, for food. Unable to grow in bright sunlight, they favor early spring for growth. Typical woodland flowers include rhododendron and violets. Mountain flowers flourish on any high mountaintop, but grow only after the ice and snow melt. Examples are alpine roses and saxifrages. Prairie flowers are voluptuous and plentiful; their bright colors represent the stereotypical wildflower. Masses of globemallows, sunflowers, and beardtongues clothe the prairie. The beauty of desert flowers is only temporary, as they quickly grow and flower after infrequent rains, then wither in the blinding sun. They have thorny branches, no leaves or very few, and thick, fleshy, water-holding stems. Desert plants include octillos and cacti. Finally, swamp flowers, such as lizard's-tails and willows, love wet meadows and ponds. Others, including pitcher plants and spider lilies, thrive in marshes.

Their simple dignity and elegance make wildflowers an unequaled natural phenomenon and a worthy topic of study.

Alli Arnold,
Henry Clay High School, Lexington, Kentucky

On what feature does Arnold base the categories she introduces in her first sentence?

Body paragraph includes images such as "beardtongues clothe the prairie."

From reading her conclusion, how would you explain Arnold's own attraction to this topic?

Meeting Individual Needs: English Language Learners

Defining Categories

Students learning English may need a great deal of help with classification vocabulary. Encourage them to work with a partner who can help them define categories appropriately. You might ask students to work in pairs to categorize all the items in a photograph of a familiar place, such as a kitchen, living room, school, or bedroom.

5.5 Writing Activities

Write a Classification

Choose a group of items to classify. Select any group that interests you or one of the following topics: rocks and minerals; friends; movies; popular music groups; precipitation. Write a paragraph classifying the items.

PURPOSE To classify items
AUDIENCE Your classmates; an audience of your choice
LENGTH 1 paragraph

WRITING RUBRICS To develop an effective paragraph describing your classification scheme, you should

- classify the items in a way that fits your purpose and your audience
- include an introduction and a conclusion
- use complete sentences that state your classifications clearly

Viewing and Representing

COLLABORATIVE WRITING In a small group discuss the painting on this page. Have each group member then choose a different way to classify the items in the painting. Together, make a chart showing your classifications.

Using Computers

Using presentation software, create a presentation of your classification scheme. Devote one slide to an introduction, one slide to each of the classifications, and one to a conclusion. Write text for each slide that fits the purpose and audience. Present your project to the class.

Grammar*Link*

Use specific concrete nouns.

Alli Arnold uses precise concrete nouns such as "woodlands, mountains, prairies, deserts, and swamps" in her classification of wildflowers on page 246.

In the sentences below, replace the underlined words with specific concrete nouns.

1. As I hiked, I heard some strange sounds.
2. Beautiful flowers grew wild along the trail.
3. During the storm, a few pieces of camping gear were damaged.
4. Many things in my backpack were ruined.
5. Next year, I plan to visit tourist attractions in Washington, D.C.

See Lesson 10.1, page 439.

Pablita Velarde, *Old Father Storyteller*, 1960

Expository Writing

LOG ON **Writing Online** For more writing and grammar practice, go to glencoe.com and enter QuickPass code WC97727p1.

Assess

Evaluation Rubrics

Write a Classification

Use these criteria when evaluating your students' writing:

- Are the items classified in a way that suits the purpose and audience?
- Is there a clear introduction and conclusion?
- Do paragraphs use complete sentences that state classifications clearly?

See also *Writing Assessment & Evaluation Rubrics*

Viewing and Representing

Evaluate students' charts on the following: how effective the features chosen for use in classifying are; how broad or narrow the categories are; how clear the subject of classification is.

Using Computers

Evaluate projects based on the presence of a clear introduction and conclusion, as well as the appropriateness of the classification scheme chosen.

Reteaching

Composition Reteaching, p. 39

Enrichment

Composition Enrichment, p. 39

Fine Art Transparencies 25–28

Close

Have students discuss applications for expository writing. When do they think knowledge of classification will be useful in their other classes and in the real world? Write ideas on the board.

Grammar*Link*

Answers

Answers will vary. Some samples follow:

1. gurgles
2. Bluebells
3. our tent and several sleeping bags
4. Packages of oatmeal and peanuts
5. the Washington Monument and the Smithsonian Institution

Viewing the Art

Pablita Velarde, *Old Father Storyteller,* 1960
Velarde depicts her grandfather telling stories at her Santa Clara Pueblo in New Mexico. Old Father points to a constellation as he tells each story. This 19-by-24-inch watercolor is in the artist's collection.

Focus

Lesson Overview

Objectives

- To understand the difference between comparing and contrasting
- To explore similarities and differences between two or more related things by using techniques such as a Venn diagram or a chart
- To organize a comparison-contrast paper by subject and by feature

Skills

- making a Venn diagram; using transition words; comparing and contrasting using a chart; making compound subjects and verbs agree

Critical Thinking

- contrasting; comparing; classifying; analyzing

Listening and Speaking

- discussing; experimenting with sentences

Bellringer

Daily Language Activity

When students enter the classroom, have this assignment on the board: *List as many things as you can that are similar about dancing and jogging. Now list as many things as you can that are different about them.*

Grammar Link to the Bellringer

Ask students to write three sentences each about dancing and jogging. Then ask students to underline the verb in each sentence.

See also *Daily Language Practice*

Motivating Activity

Ask students how they select classes or extracurricular activities. Do they decide based upon their interests? School requirements? A friend's advice? A list of pros and cons? Invite students to describe any methods they use to help them decide. Point out that decision-making often involves comparison and contrast.

Expository Writing

LESSON **5.6**

Comparing and Contrasting

Comparing involves discussing similarities between two or more related things. Contrasting involves discussing differences between such items. In the model below, a nature writer uses comparison and contrast to present information about two extinct birds.

In the first sentence the writer introduces the main idea—that two related birds suffered a similar fate on Mauritius.

How were the birds alike? How were they different?

Literature Model

The Dodo was not the only pigeon to suffer extinction on Mauritius. There was also the striking crested Pigeon Hollandaise, which is commonly called the Mauritius Blue Pigeon (*Alectroenas nitidisima*). Like the Common Dodo, it was endemic [native only] to Mauritius. This exotic Blue Pigeon did not suffer from the Dodo's inability to fly, nor did it nest on the ground. It was a graceful forest bird that fed on fruit, berries and seeds. It lived in large flocks and nested communally in trees. Again, unlike the Dodo, this bird was delicious to eat. "Shooting parties" were often organized by the resident Europeans for sport and food.

David Day, *The Doomsday Book of Animals*

How might you compare and contrast two creatures with which you are familiar? How are a dog and a cat alike and different? What features do a goldfish and a shark have in common? How are they different?

Resource Manager

Planning Resources

- *Lesson Plans*

Transparencies

- *Bellringer*
- *Daily Language Practice*
- *Fine Art* 25–28
- *Two-Minute Skill Drill*
- *Writing Process* 11, 23–27

Other Print Resources

- *Composition Enrichment,* p. 40
- *Composition Practice,* p. 40
- *Composition Reteaching,* p. 40
- *Cooperative Learning Activities,* pp. 21–24
- *Listening and Speaking Activities,* pp. 15–16
- *Research Paper and Report Writing,* pp. 43–48
- *Sentence-Combining Practice,* pp. 32–33
- *Thinking and Study Skills,* pp. 10, 12
- *Writing Across the Curriculum*
- *Writing Assessment and Evaluation Rubrics*

Dodo Bird

- Flightless
- Nested on the ground
- Not good to eat

Similarities

- Members of the pigeon family
- Native only to Mauritius
- Suffered extinction

Mauritius Blue Pigeon

- Flying bird
- Nested in trees
- Good to eat

Think About Similarities and Differences

One technique you can use to explore similarities and differences between two subjects is a Venn diagram. The Venn diagram above shows the similarities and differences between the two extinct birds described in the model on page 248. To set up a Venn diagram, follow these steps:

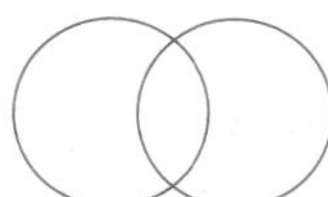

1. Draw two intersecting circles.

2. Title the circles with the subjects to be compared.

3. List unique features of each subject.

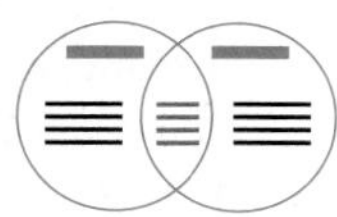

4. List the similarities of the two subjects in the space where the circles intersect.

Journal Writing

What are some other tools you could use to explore similarities and differences between two subjects, such as you and your best friend? In your journal, try creating a chart or other tool to help you compare two subjects of your choosing.

Vocabulary Tip

Transitions like the following help you organize a comparison-contrast paper: *but, however, in the same way, like, unlike, similarly.*

Teach

Using the Model

Write the following transition words on the board: *but, however, in the same way, like, unlike, similarly.* Transition words help clarify the relationship between two ideas. Ask students to read the Literature Model on page 248 and find the transition words. (*like, unlike*) Then ask volunteers to explain how the transition words are clues to the similarities or differences between the two birds. **L2**

Understanding Diagrams

Help students understand Venn diagrams by constructing one with them. First, have them choose two things to compare, such as an ocean and a lake. Then draw and label a diagram on the board, and ask students to list features that both things have (water, fish) and then features that one has but the other doesn't (salt water, marine organisms). **L1**

Two-Minute Skill Drill

List these compound subjects on the board; have students write a predicate for each:

Bill and Tim

Neither I nor my cats

Three birds and a duck

Either Mr. Smith or his twin

See also *Two-Minute Skill Drill Transparency 5.6*

Journal Writing Tip

Suggest that students choose *either* to compare general features of their subjects, *or* to focus on a narrower part, such as interests and hobbies.

Teach

Using the Model

Ask students whether the model compares the elephant and the hippo by subject or by feature. (by subject) Have students work in small groups to outline the model, organizing it feature by feature. Tell students to look at the By Feature section of the chart above the model to get an idea of how to organize the information. Then tell them that they should go through the model to find each piece of information they need. After the groups finish reorganizing and rewriting the information, have volunteers read aloud their new comparison-contrast papers. Encourage students to discuss which method of organization they think is most effective, and why. **L2**

Additional Resources

- For further stimuli for expository writing, see *Fine Art Transparencies* 25–28
- *Writing Process Transparencies* 11, 23–27
- *Cooperative Learning Activities*
- *Writing Across the Curriculum*
- *Thinking and Study Skills,* pp. 10, 12
- *Sentence-Combining Practice,* pp. 32–33
- *Listening and Speaking Activities,* pp. 15–16
- *Research Paper and Report Writing,* pp. 43–48
- *Composition Practice,* p. 40

Grammar Tip

When you edit your comparison-contrast paper, make sure that your comparisons are complete. See Lesson 18.4, page 665.

Organize a Comparison-Contrast Paper

Once you have explored similarities and differences between two subjects, you can organize your comparison-contrast paper. The chart below shows two methods of organization: (1) by subject and (2) by feature. Notice how the writer organized the essay in the model that follows.

Comparison-Contrast: Elephants and Hippos		
By Subject	**Subject 1: Elephants** Feature A: Habitat Feature B: Size Feature C: Anatomy Feature D: Endangered	**Subject 2: Hippos** Feature A: Habitat Feature B: Size Feature C: Anatomy Feature D: Endangered
By Feature	**Feature A: Habitat** Subject 1: Elephants Subject 2: Hippos **Feature B: Size** Subject 1: Elephants Subject 2: Hippos	**Feature C: Anatomy** Subject 1: Elephants Subject 2: Hippos **Feature D: Endangered** Subject 1: Elephants Subject 2: Hippos

Does the writer's use of organization by subject successfully create a vivid comparison between elephants and hippos? Explain.

Note the writer's use of visual details in this comparison-contrast.

Model

Two of the world's most wondrous and enormous animals, the elephant and the hippopotamus, may one day disappear. Just think of the majestic elephant, the largest land-dwelling animal. A typical African bull, or male, measures eleven feet tall at the shoulders and weighs about four tons. African cows, or females, and Asiatic elephants are only slightly smaller. And, as you picture an elephant, you probably think of its thick gray skin, long trunk, fan-shaped ears, and great ivory tusks. The valuable ivory of the tusks presents the greatest danger for elephants, as ivory-seeking hunters kill thousands each year.

Not quite as massive as the elephant, the hippo is the third largest land animal, just behind the rhino. But the hippo doesn't live only on land—it spends its days resting in or near lakes, rivers, or swamps. A typical hippo weighs about 2,500 to 3,000 pounds and is about five feet tall at the shoulders. Besides its huge body, among the hippo's most recognizable features are its bulging eyes and gigantic mouth. Farmers and hunters kill many hippos each year to protect farmlands and to sell the animals' meat, hide, and tusklike ivory canine teeth.

MEETING INDIVIDUAL NEEDS

English Language Learners

Choosing Words

Students learning English may have difficulty choosing or understanding words that describe visual details. Write the following adjectives from the model on page 250 on the board: *wondrous, majestic, great, massive, huge.* Have students work in pairs to think of synonyms for them. Encourage students to use a dictionary or a thesaurus when necessary. Next, have pairs of students think of five words that describe a dog or a cat. Encourage students to share lists.

5.6 Writing Activities

Write a Comparison-Contrast Paper

Choose a pair of places or items to compare, such as big cities and small towns, board games and video games, or another pair of your choice. Write a brief paper comparing and contrasting the items.

PURPOSE To compare and contrast two items
AUDIENCE Your teacher and classmates
LENGTH 2 paragraphs

WRITING RUBRICS To write an effective comparison-contrast paper, you should

- choose related items
- use a Venn diagram to clarify similarities and differences
- organize your paper by comparing subjects or by comparing features
- use appropriate transitions

Cross-Curricular Activity

ART AND SCIENCE Study the painting below and think about how an art critic and a scientist might respond to it. With a partner, draw a Venn diagram that compares and contrasts the ways in which two such viewers might describe the painting. Share your diagram with the class.

Katsushika Hokusai, *The Great Wave off Kanagawa*, c. 1830

Grammar*Link*

Make compound subjects and verbs agree.

When compound subjects are joined by *either . . . or* or *neither . . . nor,* the verb always agrees with the subject nearer the verb.

Rewrite each sentence below so that the compound subjects and verbs agree.

1. Neither the Dodo bird nor the Blue Pigeon were safe from European hunters.
2. Either Mauritius or other islands in the Indian Ocean was home to the Dodo.
3. Either farmers or hunters has killed the hippos for their hides and teeth.
4. Either the African bull or the Asiatic elephant weigh about four tons.
5. Neither Kenya nor other African nations protects these animals adequately.

See Lesson 16.5, page 616.

Listening and Speaking

Interview a number of people in your school about a topic that invites comparison (for example, the similarities and differences in skiing and snowboarding). Take notes on the similarities and differences each person mentions. Then give a brief talk on the topic, using the similarities and differences you recorded. Ask classmates to evaluate the clarity and completeness of your talk.

LOG ON **Writing** Online | For more writing and grammar practice, go to glencoe.com and enter QuickPass code WC97727p1.

Expository Writing

Assess

Evaluation Rubrics

Write a Comparison-Contrast Paper

Use these criteria when evaluating your students' writing:

- Are two items compared and contrasted?
- Did the students use a Venn diagram to organize ideas?
- Does the paper employ subject-by-subject or feature-by-feature analysis?
- Does the paper include enough specific details to see similarities and differences?

See also *Writing Assessment & Evaluation Rubrics*

Cross-Curricular Activity

Use these criteria when evaluating your students' Venn diagrams:

- Did the students use a Venn diagram correctly to organize ideas?
- Did the diagram compare and contrast the possible attitudes of both viewers?
- Were specific details from the painting included in the diagram?

Reteaching

Composition Reteaching, p. 40

Enrichment

Composition Enrichment, p. 40

Fine Art Transparencies 25–28

Close

Discuss the similarities and differences between going to school and working. Use a Venn diagram or a chart to organize students' ideas.

Grammar*Link*

Answers

1. was
2. were
3. have
4. weighs
5. protect

Using Verbs with Compound Subjects Ask students to write five sentences that begin with *Either* or *Neither.*

Viewing the Art

Katsushika Hokusai, *The Great Wave off Kanagawa,* c. 1830

Hokusai's woodblock print is a dramatic comparison-contrast. The wave, poised to strike the boats, appears capable of overpowering Mount Fuji in the background. This 10⅛-by-15-inch print is in the Museum of Fine Arts, Boston.

Focus

Lesson Overview

Objectives

- To understand the function of graphics in supporting expository writing
- To identify four main types of graphics
- To create graphics that support a piece of expository writing

Skills

- making charts and graphics; illustrating; analyzing

Critical Thinking

- analyzing; evaluating; categorizing; comparing; establishing criteria; determining relevance

Listening and Speaking

- discussing

Bellringer

Daily Language Activity

When students enter the classroom, have this assignment on the board: *Imagine friends from out of town just arrived at your local bus depot or airport. In three sentences, direct them to your home.*

Grammar Link to the Bellringer

Have students check their sentences for punctuation and clarity. If students used run-on sentences, suggest that they correct them.

See also  *Daily Language Practice*

Motivating Activity

Explain to students that they are already using some of the graphics they'll learn about in this lesson. Have students discuss whether they have ever been involved in a sport in which plays were diagramed for the team. Ask students to name graphics they use frequently. (diagrams of museums or team standings) Discuss why graphics are so helpful. (They present information in a condensed visual form.)

LESSON 5.7

Expository Writing

Writing with Graphics

Sometimes words alone can't convey enough information about a topic. Notice how the map and text work together in this magazine feature, a piece of exposition.

Literature Model

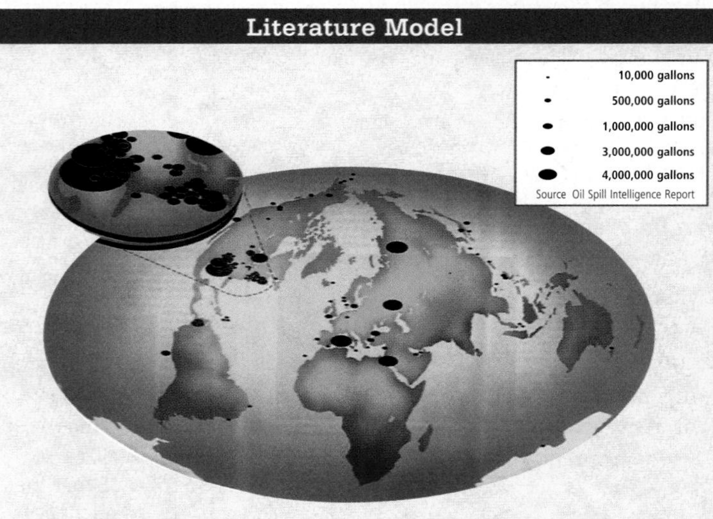

In March 1989 the world watched in horror as the *Exxon Valdez* disgorged 10.8 million gallons of North Slope crude [oil] into the pristine waters of Prince William Sound. It was the largest spill ever off the United States. But whatever lessons may have been learned about preventing spills were not effectively applied in 1990. Hardly a week passed without news of yet another disturbing spill. The first ten months of the year saw an estimated 28 million gallons of oil discharged around the world, which makes 1990 a typical year. . . . On our oil-soaked map you'll see the spills that reached at least 10,000 gallons, whether from tanker accidents caused by human error . . . or storage tanks struck by lightning.

"Another Crude Year," *Discover,* January 1991

Why do you think the writer uses the term "oil-soaked map"?

Here the writer explains to the reader what the map shows.

Resource Manager

Planning Resources

- *Lesson Plans*

Transparencies

- *Bellringer*
- *Daily Language Practice*
- *Fine Art* 25–28
- *Two-Minute Skill Drill*
- *Writing Process* 11, 23–27

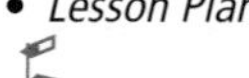

Other Print Resources

- *Composition Enrichment,* p. 41
- *Composition Practice,* p. 41
- *Composition Reteaching,* p. 41
- *Cooperative Learning Activities,* pp. 21–24
- *Listening and Speaking Activities,* pp. 15–16
- *Research Paper and Report Writing,* pp. 43–48
- *Sentence-Combining Practice,* pp. 32–33
- *Thinking and Study Skills,* p. 12
- *Writing Across the Curriculum*
- *Writing Assessment and Evaluation Rubrics*

Know Your Basic Options

Graphics come in four main forms: maps, diagrams, tables, and graphs. Each type can help illustrate your expository writing.

Maps A map is a graphic most commonly showing all or part of the earth's surface. Maps often show what might take many paragraphs to describe. Whenever you use a map, be sure to include its legend, which explains the map's symbols.

Diagrams Diagrams use pictures to clarify the relationship among parts of a whole or to show how something works. The diagram at the right shows how the water cycle works. Such a diagram can help your reader visualize a process.

Tables By examining the information in the rows and columns of a table, you can see how a subject changes under different conditions, such as time or location. The table on page 254, for example, compares temperature range and precipitation among four of the world's biological zones, or biomes (regions divided according to climate and soil conditions).

Graphs Often the best way to convey numerical information will be a graph. Graphs can reveal patterns of information, showing relationships among different facts or statistics. They can thus be a useful tool in comparison-contrast writing: a bar graph, for example, may compare the wealth of three nations. Graphs can also show how something develops over time. The line graph at the right shows the change in sunspot activity over 36 years.

Editing Tip

Make sure you label all parts of any graphic clearly and accurately. Labels help the reader recognize and understand information.

The Water Cycle

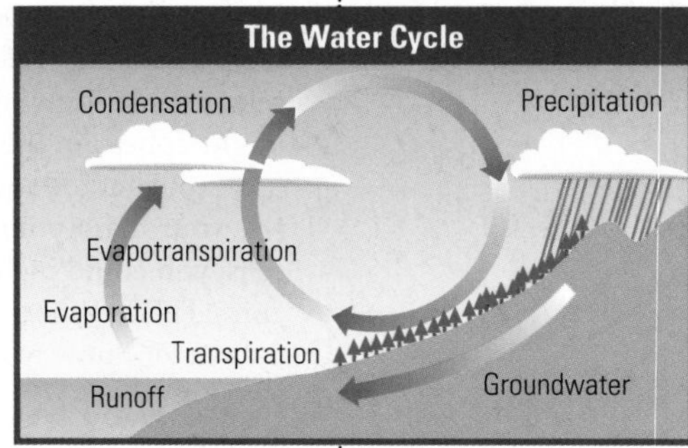

Sunspot Activity over 36 Years

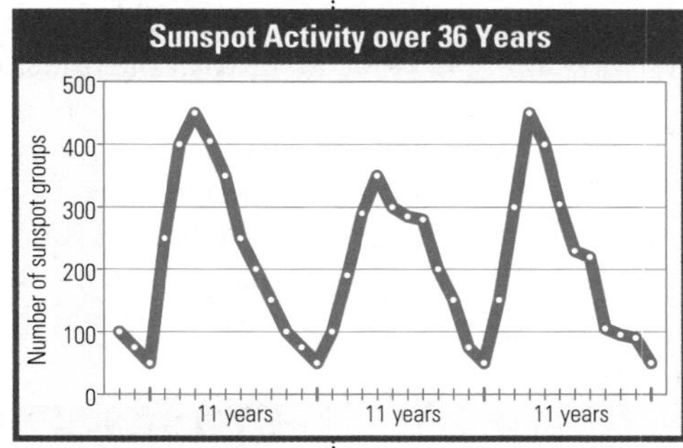

Journal Writing

Try using a graphic to explain something about yourself, for example, your study habits, eating habits, or how your tastes have changed. Place your graphic in your journal.

Teach

Using the Model

Tell students that the term *oil-soaked map* informs them that the splotches of color on the map show figuratively how large amounts of oil are spreading over waters of the world. **L2**

Reading Graphics

Point out that on page 252, the legend gives the reader instructions. What is the message of this map? (Oil spills are a widespread problem.) Explain that in the water-cycle diagram on page 253, each word describes one part of the cycle. What is the most obvious characteristic of the diagram? (It is circular; the cycle repeats.) On the sunspot graph, the thirty-six dots show that the pattern of sunspot activity is repeated every eleven years. **L2**

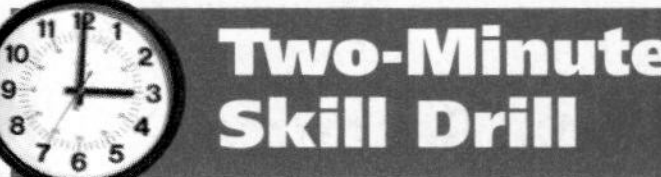

Two-Minute Skill Drill

Have students close their texts. On the board, have volunteers list the four graphic types described on this page. Ask students to write a sentence providing a short definition for each graphic type.

See also *Two-Minute Skill Drill Transparency 5.7*

Journal Writing Tip

Collecting and Gathering Information Suggest to students that using graphics is a useful way to outline writing. Encourage students to construct a diagram before they write.

Teach

Mapping Historical Events

Tell students that accurate maps have historically provided important economic advantages to merchants and investors. After Columbus sailed to the Americas, the Spanish government committed itself to mapping and charting the newly discovered trade routes. Have students make their own maps of a historical event of their choice. **L3**

Cooperative Learning

Form pairs for a partners activity in which students plan a graphic for a piece of writing. Ask each pair to create a graphic to illustrate a model in this unit. The partners should plan what type of graphic to use, what it will communicate to the reader, and where it will be positioned in the model. (For example, the student model on page 242 might conclude with a diagram summarizing the sequence of events.) **L1**

Additional Resources

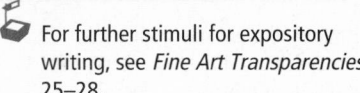

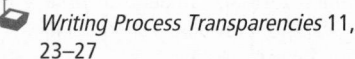

- For further stimuli for expository writing, see *Fine Art Transparencies* 25–28.
- *Writing Process Transparencies* 11, 23–27
- *Writing Across the Curriculum*
- *Cooperative Learning Activities*
- *Thinking and Study Skills,* p. 12
- *Sentence-Combining Practice,* pp. 32–33
- *Listening and Speaking Activities,* pp. 15–16
- *Composition Practice,* p. 41
- *Research Paper and Report Writing,* pp. 43–48

Revising Tip

As you read your first draft, check all references to graphics to be sure that they are helpful to the reader—that is, that they really add to the explanation.

Use Graphics for Greatest Impact

Whenever you use graphics in your writing, place them and refer to them so that they make the greatest impact on the reader.

Positioning Graphics Where you place a graphic depends on the function of the graphic and your purpose for using it. For example, to capture the reader's attention and establish a basic framework, you could put a graphic at the beginning of your piece. Imagine you're writing an explanation of cells. You might use a diagram of a basic cell, with all its parts labeled, as part of the opening paragraph.

In the middle of the essay, you might include graphics that convey a great amount of information in a concise way, reinforce information, or serve as a handy reference for the reader. In the example of an essay on cells, a table showing the variation in sizes of different types of cells might appear in the middle.

At the end of your explanation, you will probably want to summarize your main points. For example, in the conclusion of an essay on cells, you could include a table comparing and contrasting plant and animal cells. Wherever and however you use graphics, you need to let the reader know why they are there and when to look at them.

Referring to Graphics In referring to a graphic, you might simply tell the reader to look at it when the graphic helps illustrate a point you are making. For example, with a table of cell sizes, you might write, "Different kinds of cells vary in size, as shown in the table." You can also instruct the reader to use the information from a graphic in a specific way. If you were using the table below in a piece of exposition about biomes, you might tell the reader to use the table to compare the different levels of precipitation in *each biome.*

Whatever your purpose, title graphics clearly when you present more than one. In that way you will be sure that the reader is not confused and can refer to the appropriate graphic easily.

Four Biomes: Temperature and Precipitation

Biome	Avg. Yearly Temperature	Avg. Yearly Precipitation
Deciduous forest	6° C to 28° C	75 to 125 cm
Grassland	0° C to 25° C	25 to 75 cm
Desert	24° C to 34° C	less than 25 cm
Tropical rain forest	25° C to 27° C	200 to 400 cm

Real World Connection

Using Graphics

Encourage students to research books, magazines, newspaper articles, or the Internet to find one example of each of the four types of graphics discussed on page 253. Then have students write a one-page paper that summarizes how each of the four selections chosen would have been affected had graphics not been included. Have students present their papers to the class.

5.7 Writing Activities

Write a Paragraph with a Graphic

Think of something you have learned about recently. How could the information be shown in a graphic? Create a graphic to show the information.

PURPOSE To use a graphic to show a concept
AUDIENCE Your classmates
LENGTH 1 page

WRITING RUBRICS To write an effective paragraph with a graphic, you should

- make a map, diagram, table, or graph
- write a paragraph about your subject, and in your paragraph refer to your graphic
- make sure your paragraph makes clear references to the graphic

Using Computers

Some graphics can be created using your computer's word processing program. You might also be able to use illustration software to create graphics. Experiment with different arrangements and styles to see which pre-sents your information most clearly.

Viewing and Representing

Use a simple set of statistical data such as the number of male and female students in each grade in your school to create at least three different visual representations of the information. Your graphics could include a table, a graph, and a pie chart. Write a paragraph explaining which type of graphic best represents your data and why.

Grammar*Link*

Avoid using run-on sentences.

Run-on sentences occur when two or more complete sentences are written without proper punctuation between them.

Rewrite the run-on sentences below to make them grammatically correct.

1. Graphics come in four basic forms each type can enhance a piece of exposition.
2. Information in a table is organized in a concise, systematic way, it is presented in rows and columns.
3. Be sure to label all parts of your graphic clearly labels help the reader recognize and understand data.
4. Diagrams clarify relationships among parts of a whole and graphs reveal patterns of information.
5. There are many kinds of graphs, line, bar, and pictographs are among them.
6. A map needs a legend and it may need a scale, too.
7. Check all references to graphs in your writing they really add to the exposition.
8. The data in the table was easy to understand, the diagram was confusing.
9. He positioned the map in the middle of the essay and he used a table in his conclusion.
10. The water cycle is shown in the diagram you can find it on page 253.

See Lesson 13.10, pages 555–557.

Expository Writing

LOG ON **Writing** Online | For more writing and grammar practice, go to glencoe.com and enter QuickPass code WC97727p1.

Assess

Evaluation Rubrics

Write a Paragraph with a Graphic

Use these criteria when evaluating your students' writing. The paragraph should

- be appropriate for the intended audience and purpose
- explain the graphic and effectively support the general topic
- support a graphic that is appropriately titled and labeled
- effectively explain the chosen topic and include a reference to the graphic

See also *Writing Assessment & Evaluation Rubrics*

Viewing and Representing

Use these criteria when evaluating your students' graphics:

- Does the information presented support the general topic?
- Is the graphic appropriately titled and labeled?
- Is the design attractive and appealing to the reader?

Reteaching

Composition Reteaching, p. 41

Enrichment

Composition Enrichment, p. 41

Close

Have students choose a graphic from a recent newspaper or magazine and evaluate whether the graphic does or does not succeed in conveying the information on the legend.

Grammar*Link*

Answers

Answers may vary, but some suggestions are given below.

1. . . . forms. Each . . .
2. . . . way. It . . .
3. . . . clearly. Labels . . .
4. . . . whole, and . . .
5. . . . graphs. Line, . . .
6. . . . legend, and . . .
7. . . . writing. They . . .
8. . . . understand. The . . .

Focus

Lesson Overview

Objectives
- To understand the purpose of a feature article
- To learn how to plan a feature article by finding a suitable topic and gathering relevant information
- To construct a feature article that includes a compelling lead, lively details, and an effective ending

Skills
- researching a topic; planning an article; drafting an article

Critical Thinking
- generating new information; building background; synthesizing

Listening and Speaking
- discussing; interviewing; note taking; questioning

Bellringer
Daily Language Activity

When students enter the classroom, have this assignment on the board: *What kind of newspaper and magazine articles do you like to read? Why?*

Grammar Link to the Bellringer

Have students share their responses to the Bellringer activity. Identify any nonessential appositives or adjective clauses students may have used. Remind students that these clauses should be set off by commas.

See also *Daily Language Practice*

Motivating Activity

Discuss students' responses to the Bellringer activity. Point out that although news stories cover the most important facts, readers often turn to feature stories to learn more about some aspect of a news story. Have students identify recent headline events and then suggest feature stories they would like to read about any of the events identified.

LESSON 5.8

Writing a Feature Article

Expository Writing

A feature story in a newspaper or magazine often presents in-depth information on a topic related to a current issue or event. The feature story may include photographs, such as the ones below, that focus on the setting and the subject of the story.

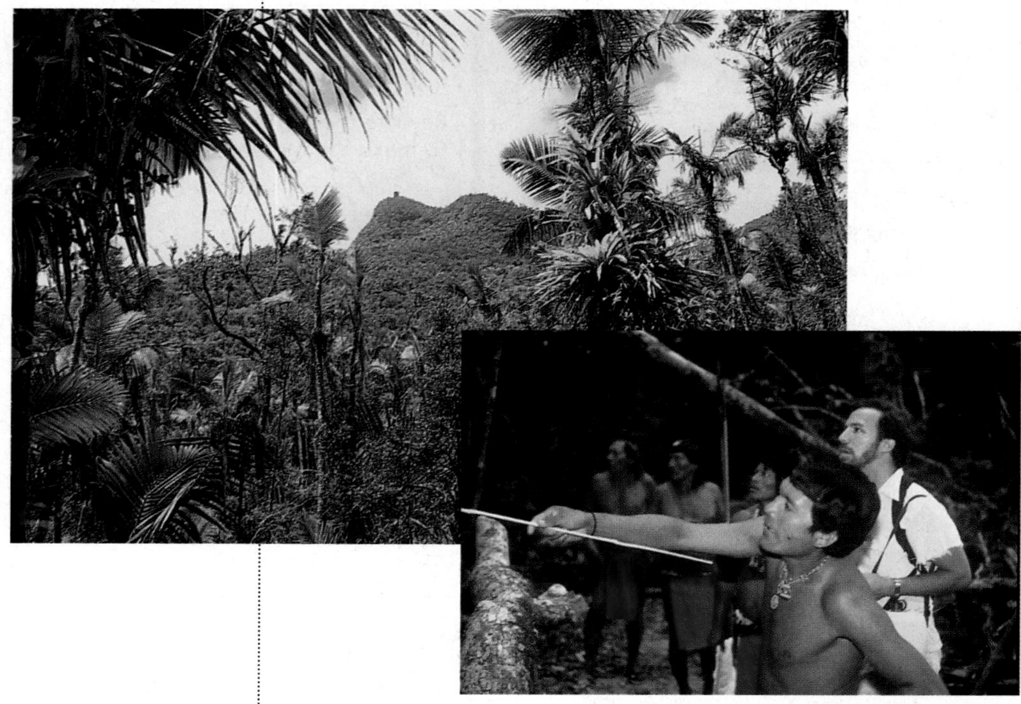

Usually longer than a news article, the feature story may try to capture a mood or a moment, or it may highlight a person, experience, or other topic of general human interest. Because feature writers use description, narration, and exposition, their stories tend to be both entertaining and informative. The literature models in this lesson are excerpts from a feature story, "Searching for Medicinal Wealth in Amazonia," published in *Smithsonian* magazine. Note how the writer, Donald Dale Jackson, opens his story with a detailed description of the rain forest and a scientist.

Resource Manager

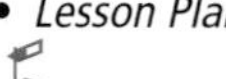

Planning Resources
- *Lesson Plans*

Transparencies
- *Bellringer*
- *Daily Language Practice*
- *Fine Art* 25–28
- *Two-Minute Skill Drill*
- *Writing Process* 11, 23–27

Other Print Resources
- *Composition Enrichment,* p. 42
- *Composition Practice,* p. 42
- *Composition Reteaching,* p. 42
- *Cooperative Learning Activities,* pp. 21–24
- *Listening and Speaking Activities,* pp. 15–16
- *Research Paper and Report Writing,* pp. 43–48
- *Sentence-Combining Practice,* pp. 32–33
- *Thinking and Study Skills,* pp. 8, 11, 21–23
- *Writing Across the Curriculum*
- *Writing Assessment and Evaluation Rubrics*

Literature Model

An hour and a half had passed since we had seen any human scratches on the great green kingdom below us, the rain forest of southern Suriname at the northern fringes of Amazonia. Since then our Cessna six-seater had droned over an unforgiving landscape of jungle dotted with cloud-shadow puddles and tree-choked arroyos [stream beds] streaked by brown rivers. Even at 4,000 feet I could feel the oppressive heat, and we were beginning to descend. The lumpy carpet of rain forest gradually metamorphosed into a canopy of high trees that hid the ground.

Mark Plotkin leaned forward and squinted. Three plumes of smoke stained the horizon ahead. A few seconds later a clearing suddenly materialized, dun-colored and impossibly puny amid the green sea. Now I saw a village of about 80 thatched huts clustered beside a chocolate river. . . . Plotkin grinned. "Welcome to Kwamalasamutu," he said. "The first time I came here I thought I'd found paradise. I still think it's as close as we're apt to get."

Plotkin—New Orleans born, Harvard trained and Washington based—was coming home, in a sense, to this tiny settlement in Amazonia. . . . Plotkin has assigned himself the task of collecting and documenting the plants the Tiriós [Amazonian Indians] use before the mixed blessings of creeping civilization supplant the tribal medicine men and their wisdom. . . .

As a field ethnobotanist . . . Plotkin is the most visible exponent of a discipline that has only recently come into its own. Where ethnobotany was once mainly concerned with plant identification, it is viewed today as a potential lifesaver. The chemical components of plants that medicine men use in healing rites could conceivably be building blocks for new drugs or even cures for such scourges as cancer and AIDS.

Donald Dale Jackson
"Searching for Medicinal Wealth in Amazonia"
Smithsonian magazine

What do you learn from the opening sentence of Jackson's feature article?

The writer's direct quotes and sensory details give the reader an intimate view of people and places.

How would you define "ethnobotany" and explain its importance, based on Jackson's fourth paragraph?

Journal Writing

Look through a newspaper for an interesting feature story. In your journal, note what types of writing are used.

Teach

Using the Model

Students should respond that Jackson's opening sentence identifies the story's setting (a rain forest in Suriname) and tells readers that the location is isolated from other human societies. Ask students to discuss why Jackson might have thought it important to open his article with this information. Have students suggest other opening sentences.

Students might define ethnobotany as the systematic study of the plant lore of a race or people. Ethnobotany is important because it encourages scientists to think of new ways of using chemical components found in plants. **L2**

Understanding the Timing of Feature Articles

Explain to students that news stories should be current and accurate, but feature writers can take time to examine implications of the news. Provide students with a section of a local newspaper, and direct them to locate a feature article. Ask students to determine when the originating events took place. How did the writer frame his or her topic so that it did not seem dated? **L3**

Journal Writing Tip

Summarizing Suggest to students that they reread the lead and final paragraphs of the article. These often provide the basis for a summary. If necessary, remind students of some different types of writing: personal, descriptive, narrative, or expository.

Teach

Learning Cooperatively

Form small groups for a cooperative activity. Direct the groups to choose a topic for a feature story on a person or place in the community. Ask students to brainstorm possible sources of information (such as the local historical museum, articles about the area, interviews, and meetings). Each student should then list questions to be answered by one of the sources. Invite each group to report to the class on which sources were most useful for its topic. **L2**

Restructuring Articles

Ask students to choose a feature story from a newspaper or magazine and to write an outline or other plan for changing the focus of the story. For example, if the story focuses on the history of an event, students might restructure it to focus on the people behind the event. The plan for the new version should focus on a particular audience and may use some of the information found in the existing feature, along with questions for further examination. **L3**

Two-Minute Skill Drill

Write these categories on the board. Have students write a specific topic for each category that would make an interesting feature article.

sports	local news
travel	entertainment
business	education

See also *Two-Minute Skill Drill Transparency 5.8*

Plan a Feature Article

Feature writers face two basic challenges. First, they must identify current topics that will interest their readers. Then they must gather the information and uncover the details to bring that topic to life and give readers important background to the news.

Find a Topic Feature articles can be on just about anything. Many, but not all, feature articles focus on current news stories, casting them in new light with important background or interesting approaches. Feature writers may also provide information not related to the news. For example, they might tell of intriguing people or share personal experiences.

Coming up with a good topic for your own feature article requires insight into your audience. You need to know their general age, their interests, what they might hope to learn, and what it might take to capture their imaginations.

The best way to find an interesting topic is to think about things in the news or in your own life that are of special interest to you. What are you curious about? If an idea seems intriguing to you, it may also fascinate your audience. The following tips may help you think of fresh feature ideas.

Prewriting Tip

When you interview, double-check the correct spelling of the person's name and his or her exact title or position. If you plan to use a statement from the interview or from printed material as a direct quotation, be sure you have permission. For more tips on interviewing, see Lessons 2.4, pages 72–75, and 29.4, page 892.

Some Ways to Get Ideas for Your Feature Story

- Take a different route to school. What new things do you see?
- Go someplace you don't usually go. Listen to conversations. Watch what people do. What questions do these people spark?
- Sit in a familiar spot and note anything that seems out of the ordinary about the people or the place. What did you see that you didn't expect to see?
- Put yourself in the place of someone in the news, a character in a book, a person you see on the street. What ideas do you get from looking at the world through his or her eyes?
- Leaf through a type of book or magazine you don't generally read. What new topics spark your interest?

Gather Information Once you have settled on an idea for a feature story, you need to gather information. Reading will give you background. Visiting places related to your topic may help you write descriptions with greater detail and authority and even re-create a mood. The first chart on the next page will provide the most valuable information for your feature story. It presents some questions a writer might ask when interviewing a scientist such as Mark Plotkin about the rain forest.

Meeting Individual Needs: English Language Learners

Choosing Topics

Many students learning English will find it easier to write when the assignment has personal significance. Focus students' attention on the list of ways to get ideas for feature stories. Encourage them to write a piece about someone or something familiar and to share their topic with a friend in order to get a different perspective.

Some Questions for a Rain Forest Scientist
• How did you first become interested in rain forests?
• How would you summarize the importance of your work in the rain forest?
• In what parts of the world do you think the rain forest is most likely to survive? Why?
• What is the most surprising thing you have seen on all your trips to the rain forest?

Draft a Feature Article

After you have gathered information for your feature, you can begin writing a draft of your article. Construct an outline to organize your ideas. Then use the following advice to create a lively article.

Begin with a Lead That Pulls Journalists use the term *lead* to refer to the opening of a story. An effective lead sets the story in motion and draws the reader into the writing. The chart below lists some ways to create a successful lead.

A Lead for Your Feature Story
• a surprising detail
• an anecdote that gets at the story's essence
• a revealing image that indicates the direction of the story
• a vivid description of the place
• a summary of the central conflict
• a portrait of one of the main people
• a lively quote
• an event that kicks off the story

Journal Writing

Look through newspapers and magazines for feature stories. Clip some leads that catch your attention. Tape these clippings into your journal.

Revising Tip

When you revise, have a friend look for places where your story lacks supporting details (see Lesson 5.2, pages 232–235) or doesn't flow smoothly.

Editing Tip

Make sure your quotes are accurate and you have been fair to everyone. You might phone the people involved in the story to read them the final version.

Presenting Tip

When your feature story is complete, present it in a form and a place that will reach the appropriate audience. Choose illustrations for the feature that will add useful information to the story as well as catch the attention of the intended audience.

Expository Writing

Writing Leads

Students with attention difficulties might focus better on the importance of lead paragraphs by playing a game. Clip several short feature articles with attention-getting leads. Remove the lead paragraphs from the features and distribute both parts randomly among the students. Ask each student who was given a lead paragraph to read it aloud. The student who thinks he or she has the rest of the story should read it to the class. Discuss which technique from the second chart on page 259 is used in each lead. **L1**

Journal Writing Tip

Elaborating Suggest that students share some of the feature stories that they found interesting enough to tape into their journal. Ask them to explain what they found interesting about each lead. Point out that this will help them write focused leads that are just as effective as the examples they collected.

Cultural Connections

Gathering Information

Feature stories about places and people are valuable sources of information about cultural diversity and students' own cultures. Many people are interested in reading these kinds of stories. Suggest that students work with a partner. Tell pairs to choose a topic about their culture that they would like to share as a feature article. Together, students can list the information to be included. Then each student can draft his or her article.

Teach

Using the Model

Ask students what Jackson's quotations reveal about Plotkin's relationship with the people in the article. (He has an ongoing friendship with them; they like him.) The quotations also imply that crying is acceptable in that culture. **L2**

Using the Model

Ask students to summarize Jackson's ending. Invite volunteers to read their summaries aloud. Ask students how the summaries and the actual ending were similar and how they differed. (Both tie the information in the story together; the summaries probably lack interesting details.) **L2**

Editing Feature Articles

Challenge students to edit a newspaper or magazine feature. Tell students to list things they like about the article and then list suggested additions or changes that would make the feature more appealing to an audience their age. **L3**

Additional Resources

- For further stimuli for expository writing, see *Fine Art Transparencies* 25–28.
- *Writing Process Transparencies* 11, 23–27
- *Writing Across the Curriculum*
- *Cooperative Learning Activities*
- *Thinking and Study Skills,* pp. 8, 11, 21–23
- *Sentence-Combining Practice,* pp. 32–33
- *Listening and Speaking Activities,* pp. 9, 15–16
- *Research Paper and Report Writing,* pp. 43–48
- *Composition Practice,* p. 42

Grammar Tip

When editing your article, make sure that your quotations are punctuated correctly. For tips on when and how to use quotation marks, see Lesson 21.9, pages 752–756.

Add Lively Details The details you include in your feature will make or break your story. Pick details that make your main points vivid and memorable. Include anecdotes that create empathy for your subject. Include quotes that let the reader hear your subject speaking in his or her own voice. Craft explanations that give your audience a clear understanding of the history, significance, or inner workings of a topic. Notice the details Jackson includes in this excerpt from his article.

Literature Model

The Indians mobbed him [Plotkin] as he climbed out of the plane. Boys tugged at his arms and grabbed his luggage. Speaking Sranan tongo, the trading language of Suriname, Plotkin had a smile or joke for each of them. "We thought you forgot us," one boy said—he hadn't been there for two years. "We were crying." Here in this exotic outpost light-years removed from his own culture, in a remote corner of a country that few Americans can identify or pronounce, the kid from New Orleans was among friends. "It feels terrific," he said.

Jackson uses sensory details to make this scene come to life.

What do you learn about the people in this article from the quotations Jackson presents?

Use an Effective Ending The ending of your feature should be as fresh and vigorous as the lead. It should tie the feature together and, if possible, leave the reader with a new thought to ponder.

Some of the best ways to begin a feature are also good ways to end it. Quotes, humorous anecdotes, close-up portraits, lively details, and vivid scenes work as well at the end of a story as at the beginning. Why do you suppose Jackson concludes his article with an image of the rain forest as seen from the airborne Cessna?

Literature Model

The Cessna finally appeared in the northeast sky and touched down five minutes later. Thirty tense minutes ensued before the pilot could get the engine started for the return trip. The plane's cabin felt like a broiler. . . .

A few minutes later we were airborne. The dust-brown clearing that was Kwamalasamutu became smaller and smaller until it was a tiny brown speck lost in the great green, and then it was gone and there was only the green, the endless, timeless, pitiless, life-giving, suffocating green of the rain forest.

Jackson uses strong sensory details to help bring his ending to life.

Note Jackson's use of adjectives to tell his story, especially the string of adjectives in the concluding sentence.

English Language Learners

Adding Details

Students whose first language is not English may need help in adding details to make their story more interesting or to create an effective ending. Pair students and have them take turns telling their stories to each other. As the story is being told, the partner can identify places in the story that might benefit from a direct quote, descriptive detail, an anecdote, and so forth. Students can then incorporate these changes when editing the drafts of their feature articles.

5.8 Writing Activities

Write a Feature Story

Choose a topic that interests you and write a feature story for publication in your school paper or a community newspaper. The chart on page 258 can help you select a topic. Use illustrations with your feature if you wish.

PURPOSE To create a feature story
AUDIENCE Students or adults
LENGTH 5–8 paragraphs

WRITING RUBRICS To write an effective feature story, you should

- create a strong lead
- use vivid details
- include at least one quotation
- proofread to insure accurate spelling and punctuation

Viewing and Representing

COLLABORATIVE WRITING In a small group, discuss your individual impressions of the 53-foot-high sculpture shown below. Generate ten quotations about the work. Then have each member write a feature story that uses a quotation about how viewers react to the sculpture, which stands in the Federal Center Plaza in Chicago, Illinois.

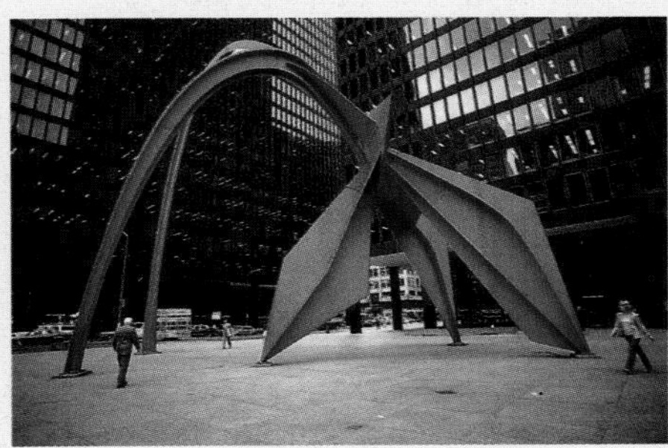

Alexander Calder, *Flamingo,* 1974

GrammarLink

Use commas to set off nonessential appositives and adjective clauses.

Feature writers often use appositives and adjective clauses to add informative details. Appositives and adjective clauses that are not essential to the meaning of the sentence should be set off by commas.

Rewrite the sentences below, adding commas where they are needed.

1. The Amazon Basin a region two-thirds the size of the United States is home to thousands of plant species.
2. Field ethnobotanist Mark Plotkin lives and works among the Tiriós.
3. Plotkin who is Harvard trained and Washington based is also a speaker about conservation.
4. Ethnobotany is a complex field that I do not understand.
5. Ethnobotany which was once mainly concerned with plant identification is today viewed as a potential lifesaver.

See Lesson 21.6, pages 738–748.

Using Computers

Add depth to your feature story by gathering related information from the Internet. Use government sites to add statistics to your story. Check newspaper and other media sites for anecdotes and other human interest features.

LOG ON **Writing Online** For more writing and grammar practice, go to **glencoe.com** and enter QuickPass code WC97727p1.

Assess

Evaluation Rubrics

Write a Feature Story

Use these criteria when evaluating your students' writing. Feature stories should

- begin with an interest-grabbing lead
- provide enough details for in-depth coverage of a topic
- include information from library research or interviews
- include at least one quotation
- close with an effective ending

See also *Writing Assessment & Evaluation Rubrics*

Viewing and Representing

Evaluate each group's feature story on the following: creativity in the creation and application of a quotation, focus on reactions to the sculpture, inclusion of details and facts.

Reteaching

Composition Reteaching, p. 42

Enrichment

Composition Enrichment, p. 42

Fine Art Transparencies 25–28

Close

Invite students to discuss writing a feature article entitled, "How to Write a Feature Article." Tell them that the audience for the article is high school students. What would be some compelling leads? What kind of information should be in the body of the feature? What would be an effective ending?

GrammarLink

Answers

1. The Amazon Basin, a region . . . States, is . . .
2. (correct)
3. Plotkin, who . . . based, is . . .
4. (correct)
5. Ethnobotany, which . . . identification, is . . .

Viewing the Art

Alexander Calder, *Flamingo,* 1974
The sculpture is made of painted steel plates, and it stands fifty-three feet high. Calder's stationary sculptures, like this one, are called *stabiles;* his movable sculptures are called *mobiles.* Sculptor Alexander Calder lived from 1898 to 1976.

Focus

Lesson Overview

Objectives

- To analyze the basic format of an essay answer
- To identify clue verbs and other key words within an essay question
- To learn how to organize an answer to an essay question by listing notes, developing a thesis statement, creating an outline, and drawing a conclusion

Skills

- looking for key words; focusing an answer; writing an answer

Critical Thinking

- analyzing; contrasting; comparing; evaluating; making inferences; establishing and evaluating criteria

Listening and Speaking

- discussing; evaluating; questioning

Bellringer

Daily Language Activity

When students enter the classroom, have this assignment on the board: *Work with a partner. Write a short essay question for your partner. Exchange papers and write a paragraph explaining how you would answer your partner's question.*

Grammar Link to the Bellringer

Have students find and list pronouns that they find in their partner's question, such as *each, many, both,* or *everything.*

See also *Daily Language Practice*

Motivating Activity

Ask students what they find the most difficult about answering essay questions. (time limits, remembering details, organization) Point out that an essay question is best answered through careful planning.

LESSON 5.9

Expository Writing

Answering an Essay Question

When you take an essay test, plan your time carefully, and write answers that demonstrate your knowledge. In the model below, columnist Cecil Adams's response to "Why Do Cats Purr?" gives you an idea of what it takes to answer an essay question successfully.

Literature Model

Cats don't purr just when they're feeling chipper—they also purr when they're frightened or badly hurt. Purring doesn't have any specific emotional connotation; rather it seems to be a kind of homing device. Cats learn the signal in the first few days of kittenhood, when they can't see, hear, or smell very well. The mother cat purrs to call the kittens to nurse—unable to hear the sound, the kitten can feel the vibrations.

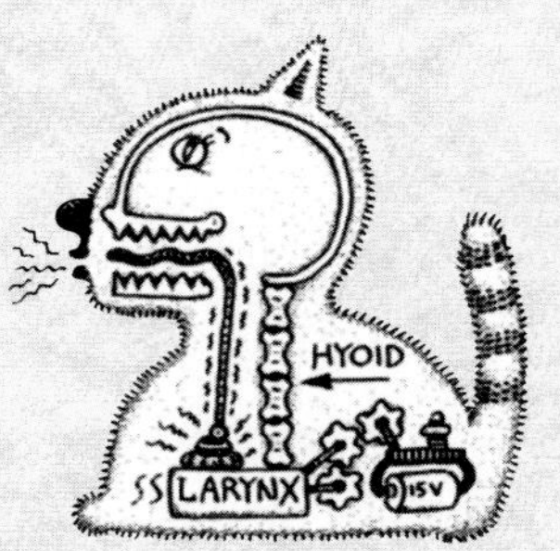

There are two schools of thought on exactly *how* a cat purrs. One theory traces the vibrations to a set of "false vocal chords," a bundle of membranes that lies above the genuine vocal chords and seems to have no other clear function. The other opinion locates the purr in the vibrations of the hyoid apparatus, a series of small bones connecting the skull and the larynx that nominally serves to support the tongue. Since it's very difficult to induce a cat to purr while you are examining his hyoid apparatus, the truth may never be known.

Cecil Adams, *The Straight Dope*

Adams begins his answer by explaining one thing he knows for sure about cats' purring: when they do it.

What does Adams mean when he says purring "seems to be a kind of homing device"? Does this hypothesis make sense to you?

Adams concludes with a theory that highlights what we don't know about cats' purring.

Resource Manager

Planning Resources

- *Lesson Plans*

Transparencies

- *Bellringer*
- *Daily Language Practice*
- *Fine Art* 25–28
- *Two-Minute Skill Drill*
- *Writing Process* 11, 23–27

Other Print Resources

- *Composition Enrichment,* p. 43
- *Composition Practice,* p. 43
- *Composition Reteaching,* p. 43
- *Cooperative Learning Activities,* pp. 21–24
- *Listening and Speaking Activities,* pp. 15–16
- *Research Paper and Report Writing,* pp. 43–48
- *Sentence-Combining Practice,* pp. 32–33
- *Thinking and Study Skills,* pp. 4–5, 8, 12, 23
- *Writing Across the Curriculum*
- *Writing Assessment and Evaluation Rubrics*

Look for Key Words in the Question

Answers to essay questions follow a basic format—the format of the essay. The **introduction** contains a **thesis statement,** a one-sentence summary of the thrust of your answer. The **body** of the answer supports the thesis statement with facts, examples, details, and reasons. The **conclusion** summarizes or gives the implications of your answer. The essay question itself often gives strong clues as to how the answer should be structured. The chart below can help you decipher the clues.

What Essay Questions Tell You

Clue Verb	Action to Take
Describe	Paint word pictures by providing precise details of an event, a process, or a person.
Explain	Tell why or how by using facts, examples, or reasons, and emphasize cause-and-effect relationships or step-by-step processes.
Compare	Show how two or more subjects are alike.
Contrast	Highlight the differences between two or more subjects.
Classify	Group and label the important features of a subject, and discuss the different categories into which you have grouped them.
Analyze	Break something down into the parts that compose it, show the relationship between the parts and the whole, and tell the function or significance of each of the parts.

Grammar Tip

Restate the essay question as the beginning of your thesis statement. "What were the causes of the Civil War?" becomes "The Civil War was caused by . . ." For information on using active and passive voices of verbs, see Lesson 15.7, page 596.

Journal Writing

For each clue verb in the chart above, identify one or more prewriting tools, such as a Venn diagram, that could help you answer that particular kind of essay question efficiently. List each tool in your journal next to the corresponding clue verb.

Teach

Using the Model

Point out that Adams's use of the term *homing device* (page 262) suggests that cats' purring originates as a sixth sense for kittens who need to find "home" by their mother's side. It is reasonable to guess that cats purr when they feel at home or when they are frightened and wish to be at home. Discuss whether Adams has answered the essay question successfully. **L2**

Writing an Essay Question

Students who tend to give too much information in their essay answers can work in pairs to select a brief passage from this unit. Each partner should write an essay question for which the passage would be an appropriate answer. Then the partners should compare their efforts and discuss how to answer the questions. **L3**

Journal Writing Tip

Prewriting Tools Remind students to consider prewriting tools such as freewriting, brainstorming, clustering, diagraming, and graphing when answering essay questions.

Teach

Organizing Information

Have students work in groups, with each group choosing one of the clue verbs listed in the chart on page 263. One person in the group should think of an essay question that includes the clue word that the group has chosen. Members of the group should indicate how they would answer the question by filling out a diagram like the one shown. **L2**

Writing a Paragraph

Students who have attention-related difficulties may find the time limits for answering essay questions quite unnerving. To provide practice overcoming this anxiety, give students ten minutes to answer a sample essay question based on general knowledge. (For example: *Describe how to make a peanut butter sandwich.*) Direct students to make a list of main steps, or points, and use each point as the topic sentence of a short paragraph. Suggest that they develop each paragraph with the time they have left. Explain to students that even if each paragraph is not fully developed, they have stated the main points they need to address in order to answer the question adequately. **L1**

Two-Minute Skill Drill

Complete each sentence with the correct personal pronoun that agrees with its indefinite pronoun antecedent.

Neither boy brought ___ book.

Many of the people carried ___ belongings.

See also *Two-Minute Skill Drill Transparency 5.9*

Expository Writing

Focus Your Answer

By taking time to identify and organize your information, you can avoid the common mistake of writing down everything you know about a subject in a haphazard, disjointed fashion.

Organize Your Information The following diagram details the process you might use to answer a "take home" essay question.

Answering an Essay Question

Question
Describe hail, and explain how and when hailstones form.

Underline clue verbs and other key words.
Describe hail, and explain how and when hailstones form.

List notes.

- Hail: form of precipitation made up of lumps of ice
- Begins as tiny ice crystal in thundercloud
- Strong winds in cloud toss crystal up and down; water condenses around crystal and freezes, forming layers of ice on the crystal, thus creating a hailstone and making it grow larger and heavier.
- Hailstone becomes too heavy to remain aloft, so falls to ground.
- Size of stone depends on strength of wind, length of time in cloud.
- Most hailstones smaller than one inch in diameter, but some larger than a baseball.
- Large hailstones smash windows, dent cars, destroy crops.
- Hailstorms usually occur in summer, when thunderstorms are more frequent, violent.

Develop thesis statement.
Hail is a form of precipitation made up of lumps of ice that form within thunderclouds.

Outline answer and develop conclusion.
Organize your answer into main points and supporting details. The conclusion might summarize the answer.

Meeting Individual Needs: Less Proficient Readers

Giving Definitions

Less proficient readers may have difficulty with some of the words that appear in the diagram "Answering an Essay Question." Have students write down (or illustrate) the definitions of the following words: *hail, precipitation, crystal, condense.* Then have students use these words in sentences of their own.

Hail: What is it and how and when does it form?

What?
- A form of precipitation made up of lumps of ice

How?
- Begins as crystal in thundercloud
- Strong winds toss it up and down
- Water condenses around crystal, freezing into layer of ice
- Layers of ice build up around crystal, creating a hailstone, which continues to get larger and heavier
- Hailstone becomes too heavy to stay aloft, so falls to ground

When?
- Usually forms in summer, when thunderstorms are more frequent and violent

Write Your Answer If you follow a process like the one just laid out, writing an answer to an essay question will become a much easier task. Your plan for your answer will help you focus your ideas, write quickly, and avoid including unnecessary information. Follow the steps below when writing your answer to an essay question.

Writing Your Essay Answer

1. Express your thesis in the opening sentence to show that you understand the question. Writing your thesis at the beginning will also help you focus your answer.
2. Use your notes, thesis statement, and organizational plan to develop your major points and supporting details. You can draw additional supporting details from your notes.
3. Include transitions between each major point.
4. Do not stray from your plan unless you realize some point is incorrect or unworkable. Do not add information that does not support your thesis.
5. Provide an ending that reflects the basic answer you have written.

Prewriting Tip

Before working on one question in a test, read the directions and all the questions to find out what the essay exam involves. Budget time by the number of points each question is worth.

Journal Writing: Write to Learn

In your journal, copy two essay questions from your science textbook, or make up two sample questions. For each question do some research to list enough notes to form an answer, and then write a thesis statement to help focus your answer.

Writing a First Sentence

Some students have trouble generating a first sentence when answering an essay question. Suggest that one way to overcome this hurdle is to write an opening sentence that not only rephrases the question, but also lists the basic points to be explained in the answer. (For example, in an essay question asking what a high-school freshman studies, the opening sentence might state, "A high-school freshman ordinarily takes classes in English, history, algebra, earth science or biology, physical education, and art or music.") Suggest that students lightly number the items in the sentence and then write a separate paragraph for each numbered item. **L2**

Gathering Information

Urge students not to try to answer the questions but to concentrate on planning their answers. Explain that answering essay questions is made easier by planning and prewriting. Suggest that it is reasonable to spend up to half the allotted time on such preparation. **L1**

Journal Writing Tip

Writing Thesis Statements Have students practice writing thesis statements by rewriting the questions as statements.

Civic Literacy

Ordering Details

Television talk shows such as *Firing Line* or *Crossfire* serve as an oral essay exam for politicians and other public figures. Speakers take turns answering questions from a panel of colleagues and political journalists. Each speaker must be prepared with specific examples and facts to answer controversial questions in a way that furthers his or her political agenda.

5.9

Teach

Using the Model

Jason Larmore demonstrates his understanding of the questions by restating them in his first paragraph, where he also lays out the classification structure for the remaining paragraphs. Larmore differentiates the classes by size, using comparisons to enliven his examples. He also points out the color of stars in each group. **L2**

Applying and Extending

The suggestions in this lesson provide a unique opportunity for direct application in other subject areas. Encourage students who have other classes together to use the techniques they have learned to help each other prepare for an essay test. Students could meet in small groups and devise essay questions on the material to be tested. Then members can exchange questions and answer them. Finally, students can share their answers. The group can correct inaccurate statements and add information if needed. **L3**

Additional Resources

For further stimuli for expository writing, see *Fine Art Transparencies* 25–28.

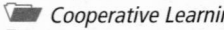

Writing Process Transparencies 11, 23–27

Cooperative Learning Activities

Writing Across the Curriculum

Thinking and Study Skills, pp. 4–5, 8, 12, 23

Sentence-Combining Practice, pp. 32–33

Listening and Speaking Activities, pp. 15–16

Research Paper and Report Writing, pp. 43–48

Composition Practice, p. 43

Expository Writing

Editing Tip

When you edit your essay answer, omit unnecessary details simply by crossing them out. Proofread to check your grammar and spelling. Make all corrections neatly, so that your answer is legible.

Revise and Edit Your Answer Leave time to read over your answer once you have finished. Make sure that your thesis statement is clear and that you have covered all important points. Correct any content errors first. Add details by inserting sentences where necessary. You can clarify a relationship between ideas by adding or changing a transitional word.

Now look at Jason Larmore's essay answer to the questions "Into what three general classes do astronomers group stars? What are the characteristics of each class of stars?"

Student Model

Astronomers group stars into three general classes: the main-sequence, the giant and supergiant, and the white dwarf. Each class has its own characteristics; size, brightness, and color all help determine a star's group. Of these three factors, size is the most important because size differences between classes are dramatically obvious.

Main-sequence stars are the most common. The yellowish main-sequences form an average between the white dwarves and the "red" giants, but because of the giant's immensity, everything seems microscopic in comparison.

The enormousness of the giant-class stars can be shown by comparing them to our own solar system. A single supergiant, placed where our sun is, would engulf all of the inner planets and some of the outer planets. Because the giant stars are so massive, they sometimes are unable to burn gases at a normal temperature. A decrease in this temperature causes them to have a reddish color, common to many giants. There are, however, exceptions to the "red" giant pattern. Deneb is a giant that shines with a blue light. This indicates an extremely high temperature. These exceptions comprise the brightest stars in the night sky.

The final class of stars is the white dwarf. These stars are the result of giant stars that collapsed because they couldn't maintain their mass. The white dwarves are very dense and shine white. These stars are much smaller than our sun, yet they outweigh it exponentially. The fact that white dwarves come from giant stars shows that even though stars are divided into classes, they are in some ways related.

Jason Larmore, Henry Clay High School, Lexington, Kentucky

How does Larmore's first paragraph demonstrate that he understands the question?

What supporting details does Larmore use to point out the characteristics of the stars in each of the three groups?

In his conclusion, Larmore stresses the relationship among the different classes of stars.

Cultural Connections

Jewish Religious Study

Answering essay questions is a common activity for Jewish students who attend schools called *yeshivas*. Typically, students work in pairs or small groups, studying Jewish religious law. Then the teacher delivers a lecture on the subject. To demonstrate their knowledge, students then ask and answer essay questions about the lecture and the text, sometimes quoting long passages from memory.

5.9 Writing Activities

Write an Essay Answer

Find an end-of-chapter question in your history or science book that could be answered in a short essay. Review the chapter and then write your essay.

PURPOSE To write an essay answering a history or science question
AUDIENCE Your teacher
LENGTH 1–2 paragraphs

WRITING RUBRICS To write an effective answer to an essay question, you should

- decide exactly what the question is asking
- recast the question as a thesis statement
- make notes and organize them
- revise and edit your answer

Cross Curricular Activity

SCIENCE Work together in a small group, and brainstorm your own list of "imponderables," questions about the natural world like those Cecil Adams might answer in his column. (See the model on page 262.) What parts of the natural world puzzle or mystify you? Here's your chance to have someone else find the answers for you. Exchange lists with another group. Select one question from their list for your group to research and answer. Each group member should research and write an answer individually, using print and electronic sources to gather information.

GrammarLink

Make pronouns and their antecedents agree.

In this passage from Jason Larmore's essay answer, note how the indefinite pronoun and the antecedent agree: "Astronomers group stars into three general classes . . . *each* . . . has *its* own characteristics."

Use each indefinite pronoun below and an antecedent in a sentence.

Sample Answer *several*
Several *of the astronomers explained* their *theories.*

1. everything	**6.** no one
2. everyone	**7.** many
3. both	**8.** one
4. few	**9.** either
5. each	**10.** neither

See Lesson 16.7, pages 619–621, and Lesson 17.5, pages 640–644.

Listening and Speaking

COOPERATIVE LEARNING After students have done their individual research and writing, the original groups should reassemble and blend their work into one coherent answer. Each group should then present its answer to the whole class, which may grade the group's effort based on how well it responded to the question.

LOG ON **Writing** Online | For more writing and grammar practice, go to glencoe.com and enter QuickPass code WC97727p1.

Assess

Evaluation Rubrics

Write an Essay Answer

Use these criteria when evaluating your students' writing:

- Does the essay answer include a thesis statement?
- Does it answer the question?
- Is the answer correctly organized, fully edited, and complete?

See also *Writing Assessment & Evaluation Rubrics*

Cross-Curricular Activity

Make sure that students' answers communicate specific information that addresses the question, reflects research, and includes group revisions.

Reteaching

Composition Reteaching, p. 43

Enrichment

Composition Enrichment, p. 43

Close

Have students write an answer to the essay question, "What are the best ways to answer essay questions?"

GrammarLink

Answers

Answers will vary. Be sure students' sentences illustrate the following agreement between pronoun and antecedent:

1. everything + (singular)
2. everyone + (singular)
3. both + (plural)
4. few + (plural)
5. each + (singular)
6. no one + (singular)
7. many + (plural)
8. one + (singular)
9. either + (or + singular)
10. neither + (nor + singular)

Focus

Lesson Overview

Objectives

- To define and explain the purpose of a myth
- To identify five common elements of literature
- To identify and explain similarities and differences between myths of different cultures

Skills

- comparing and contrasting literature; understanding the format and role of myths; identifying common literary elements

Critical Thinking

- summarizing; identifying; comparing; contrasting

Listening and Speaking

- discussing; informal speaking; narrating

Bellringer

Daily Language Activity

When students enter the classroom, have this assignment on the board: *Do you know any nonscientific explanations or stories about how natural phenomena such as thunder or rain came to be? In a few sentences, write the explanation.*

Grammar Link to the Bellringer

If students' explanations yield two different myths or explanations for the same phenomena, discuss any similarities and differences. Make sure students state comparisons clearly and completely.

See also *Daily Language Practice*

Motivating Activity

Point out that many of our myths are economic and social, as well as natural or supernatural. Encourage students to suggest examples of myths they know. For example, how did something in nature come to be? (thunder—angry gods)

LESSON **5.10**

WRITING ABOUT LITERATURE

Comparing and Contrasting Two Myths

A myth is an ancient story that offers an explanation about some aspect of the natural world. Notice the similarities in the Sioux and Zulu creation myths.

According to a myth of the Sioux, Native Americans of the Plains, the first man sprang from the soil of the Great Plains. As he emerged, he saw only the sun. After freeing himself from the clinging soil, he began to take halting steps. The sun shone on his body, toughening his skin and making him strong. The Sioux descended from this man.

A myth of the Zulu people of Africa describes how the sky god created the first people. After his marriage to the earth goddess, the sky god walked through a swamp. He broke off reeds of different colors and fashioned a man and a woman from each different colored reed. A different tribe descended from each pair of reed people.

Student Mathew Isaac read these ancient stories and pondered their similarities and differences. Here's what he came up with.

Student Model

The Sioux and Zulu myths attempt to explain the creation of mankind. The setting and the characters in the myths reveal a great deal about these groups. Both deeply revered their soil, for their pastoral life-styles revolved around it. This reverence may be inferred from the fertile land, the setting for both myths. The Sioux man emerged from the soil, while the Zulu were created from reeds in a swamp. The Zulu people recognized a god as their creator. The Sioux did not, at least according to this myth, although their myth notes the importance of the sun for continued life.

The beliefs and values of the Sioux and Zulu, some of which were shared, are visible in their creation myths.

Mathew Isaac, Rich East High School, Park Forest, Illinois

Isaac finds a central point of comparison between the two myths—the fertile soil.

What central difference does Isaac find between the two myths?

Resource Manager

Planning Resources

- *Lesson Plans*

Transparencies

- *Bellringer*
- *Daily Language Practice*
- *Fine Art* 25–28
- *Two-Minute Skill Drill*
- *Writing Process* 11, 23–27

Other Print Resources

- *Composition Enrichment,* p. 44
- *Composition Practice,* p. 44
- *Composition Reteaching,* p. 44
- *Cooperative Learning Activities,* pp. 21–24
- *Listening and Speaking Activities,* pp. 15–16
- *Research Paper and Report Writing,* pp. 43–48
- *Sentence-Combining Practice,* pp. 32–33
- *Thinking and Study Skills,* pp. 10, 12–13, 24
- *Writing Across the Curriculum*
- *Writing Assessment and Evaluation Rubrics*

Explain a Myth

Myths sometimes offer explanations for why things happen as they do. Science provides one kind of explanation, but myths offer alternative views. The ancient Romans explained the seeming movement of the sun across the sky as the work of a heavenly charioteer circling the earth daily. The ancient Japanese explained the creation of their islands with a myth about the spear of a god named Izanagi. In fact, there are probably as many distinctly different mythologies as there are different cultures.

Find Similarities and Differences

The chart below shows the common elements of literature, which all myths share. You can cite these elements to compare myths from different cultures.

Drafting Tip

In a comparison of two stories, use a feature-by-feature comparison. This form will help you weave together your points of comparison. See Lesson 5.6, page 248.

Common Elements of Literature

Element	Definition
Setting	The place and time in which the action of the story occurs The location can be real or imaginary. In a myth, the time is usually the past.
Characters	The people, animals, or gods that participate in the action of the story
Conflict	The struggle that is central to the story It can be a struggle between characters or forces.
Plot	The story's sequence of events A plot revolves around a conflict and builds to a climax that is later resolved.
Theme	The message or main idea of the story The theme may or may not be stated directly.

Journal Writing

Think about a myth with which you are familiar. In your journal, write a brief summary of the myth, and then, in a short list, identify each of the literary elements in that myth.

Teach

Using the Model

Lead students in a discussion of Mathew Isaac's conclusion that the central difference between the two myths is that "the Zulu people recognized a god as their creator," and that the Sioux did not. What support is there for Isaac's conclusion? Are there any other conclusions that could be drawn? (A creator could be implied in the Sioux myth.) Besides a reverence for the soil, ask students if there are any other central similarities between the two myths. (Both start with a male.) Have students discuss the importance of these similarities. **L2**

Defining Literary Elements

For students having difficulty identifying the literary elements in a myth, suggest that they think of themselves as newspaper reporters. Explain that the five common elements of literature answer the same questions that reporters ask. List the questions on the board. Ask students which question corresponds to each literary element. (who, characters; what, plot; when and where, setting; how, conflict; why, theme) Have students identify the literary elements of the Zulu and Sioux myths in the model on page 268. **L1**

Journal Writing Tip

Identifying Attributes and Components Remind students that some literary elements, such as character and setting, will probably be overtly present in an oral or written myth. An element such as theme may need to be inferred. To identify the plot and conflict, suggest that students summarize specific details about the action in the myth.

Teach

Cooperative Learning

To help students gain familiarity with the common elements of literature, direct them in a "Think-Pair-Share" activity. Ask students to recall a myth or fairy tale and take turns summarizing it for a partner while the partner jots down the elements of literature imbedded in the story. If any elements are missing from a student's account, the recorder should ask questions. The teller may improvise answers, if necessary. **L2**

Two-Minute Skill Drill

Have students set up a comparison frame chart. Then ask them to write a brief explanation of how they would use the chart to compare two myths.

See also *Two-Minute Skill Drill Transparency 5.10*

Additional Resources

For further stimuli for expository writing, see *Fine Art Transparencies* 25–28.

Writing Process Transparencies 11, 23–27

Writing Across the Curriculum

Cooperative Learning Activities

Thinking and Study Skills, pp. 10, 12–13, 24

Research Paper and Report Writing, p. 41

Sentence-Combining Practice, pp. 32–33

Listening and Speaking Activities, pp. 15–16

Composition Practice, p. 44

Grammar Tip

When explaining a myth or describing past events, be consistent in your choice of verb tense. For more information on consistent tenses, see Lesson 15.6, page 594.

Revising Tip

Notice that the two main paragraphs begin with parallel introductory phrases. When making a comparison, use parallelism to make clear transitions and to improve the coherence of your essay.

Use a Comparison Frame

How did the sun and the moon get into the sky? Here are two answers in the form of myths, one ancient Mexican and one ancient Nigerian.

According to the Mexican myth, the gods were arguing about who among them should light the earth by day and who by night. After four days of arguing, two gods volunteered. One was rich and strong, and the other was poor and feeble. The gods then built a huge bonfire, and the two volunteers stepped toward it. The rich god was afraid of the flames and drew back from the fire. The poor god jumped right into the fire and was catapulted high into the sky. He became the sun. The bonfire began to die. The rich god still wanted a share of the glory. He leaped into the embers, sailed into the sky, and became the moon.

According to the Nigerian myth, before there were people, the sun and the moon were married and lived on earth. The sun was good friends with the water and one day invited him to his village to meet his wife. The water flowed into the village, with the fish, the crabs, the whales, and all the other living things swimming in the seas. Soon the sun and the moon had to climb on top of the village huts because of all the water. But the water kept coming and began lapping the rooftops. The sun and the moon had to flee to safety. They each took a bounding leap into the sky, and there they remain.

The comparison frame below will help you compare and contrast the two myths.

Comparison of Two Myths

Element	Mexican Myth	Nigerian Myth
Setting	A long time ago on earth	A long time ago on earth
Characters	The Mexican gods	The sun and moon, a married couple, and the water
Conflict	Which of the gods will get to be the sun and which the moon?	Water threatens to drown the sun and moon during a visit.
Plot	The gods argue. Two gods volunteer, one rich and strong, the other poor and feeble. . . .	The sun invites water to his village. Water flows into the village, rising up to the rooftops. . . .
Theme	Bravery, not wealth, brings great glory.	Some guests can't be accommodated in one's home.

Meeting Individual Needs: English Language Learners

Identifying Similarities and Differences

Listening and speaking are useful alternatives for students who have difficulty reading and writing in English. Ask students to take turns reading aloud or simply narrating myths from their cultural heritage. Students may use their own journal entries as source material if they wish. Ask the class to identify the similarities and differences among the various myths presented.

Write a Comparison-Contrast Essay

Imagine that you are writing a paper entitled "Some Common Themes in World Mythology" for your literature class. Write a comparison-contrast of the two myths below.

Iroquois myth: Four animals, bound on leashes by a giant, are responsible for the winds. A strong, fierce bear brings on the north winds of winter. A gentle fawn brings on the south winds of summer. An angry panther brings on the west winds that accompany storms and whirlwinds. A moose brings on the east winds with their chilling mists. The giant unleashes these animals to match his moods, but he tries to unleash each wind in its proper season.

Italian myth: The north wind is a woman who had wanted to marry the south wind. But the south wind told the north wind he couldn't marry her without a dowry. The north wind blew for three days and nights, covering the land with silver snow. This she presented as her dowry. The south wind, not wanting to marry, blew for three days and nights and melted all the snow. The north wind decided that she no longer wanted to marry someone who had frittered away her entire dowry in only three days.

PURPOSE To compare two myths
AUDIENCE Your high school literature teacher
LENGTH 1–2 paragraphs

WRITING RUBRICS To write an effective comparison-contrast essay, you should

- compare and contrast the literary elements of the two myths
- use a feature-by-feature treatment to weave together your points of comparison

Make clear comparisons.

Rewrite each sentence below to correct the incomplete or unclear comparison.

1. There are more myths about creation than about any subject.
2. The Zulu myth is more religious in tone than the Sioux.
3. Did the ancient Greeks worship more gods than anyone?
4. The cleverness of the gods was always greater than the people.
5. Myths explaining the natural world are more ingenious than scientists.

See Lesson 18.4, page 665.

Listening and Speaking

COOPERATIVE LEARNING With a small group, find a brief myth. Produce a videotaped reading using sound effects and props. Practice your reading several times before taping it so that it is fluid and dramatic.

Use the copy feature of your word processing program to save the first draft of your comparison-contrast essay. Save your first draft, either as a new file or as a new page in the existing file. Continue to work on your essay, saving each successive draft to record your earlier ideas and the changes you've made.

Writing Online — For more writing and grammar practice, go to glencoe.com and enter QuickPass code WC97727p1.

Expository Writing

Assess

Evaluation Rubrics

Write a Comparison-Contrast Essay

Use these criteria when evaluating your students' writing:

- Does the essay identify the five literary elements in each myth?
- Does the essay draw valid conclusions about similarities and differences based on the literary elements?
- Does the essay emphasize common elements between the myths?

See also *Writing Assessment & Evaluation Rubrics*

Using Computers

Evaluate the essay on the improvement shown on each successive draft as well as the identification of passages that need revision.

Reteaching

Composition Reteaching, p. 44

Enrichment

Composition Enrichment, p. 44

Fine Art Transparencies 25–28

Close

Have students use the comparison frame shown on page 270 to draw conclusions about similarities and differences between the Mexican and Nigerian myths described. Ask students to write one comparison-contrast statement for each literary element.

GrammarLink

Answers

Answers will vary, but some suggestions are given below.

1. There are more myths about creation than there are about any other subject.
2. The Zulu myth is more religious in tone than the Sioux myth.
3. Did the ancient Greeks worship more gods than any other people?
4. The cleverness of the gods was always greater than that of the people.
5. Myths explaining the natural world are more ingenious than the theories that scientists put forward.

Focus

Lesson Overview

Objective
- To write an explanation that corrects misconceptions

Skills
- using the fives stages of the writing process: prewriting, drafting, revising, editing/proofreading, and publishing/presenting

Critical Thinking
- comparing and contrasting; identifying features

Listening and Speaking
- discussing; peer editing; questioning; evaluating; explaining

Bellringer
Daily Language Activity
When students enter the classroom, have this assignment on the board: *List attributes observers might include in an expository essay about human beings.*

Grammar Link to the Bellringer
Ask students to combine the following sentences:

People love animals.
They love dogs.
They love horses.

See also *Daily Language Practice*

Motivating Activity
Discuss students' responses to the Bellringer activity. Explain that in this lesson they will correct stereotypes or misunderstandings about a type of animal. Point out that students can use this type of expository writing to explore stereotypes, which are based on limited knowledge.

UNIT 5

Writing Process in Action

Expository Writing

Expository Writing

In preceding lessons you learned about the different types of expository writing, the purpose of each, and ways to make expository writing informative and appealing. You have written cause-and-effect explanations, comparison-contrasts, and essays. Now it is time to apply what you have learned. In this lesson you are invited to write about an insect or other animal that repels most people, presenting information in a way that will help your reader better understand and empathize with the creature.

Assignment

Context

A science teacher has a problem: this year most of his sixth-grade students seem to be afraid of or disgusted by the creatures about which he wants to teach them. He wants your class to write brief articles about the insects and other animals. The articles should help his students appreciate these creatures.

Purpose

To write a brief article about a creature people often label "bad" to help children experience and appreciate this animal in its own right

Audience

Sixth-grade science students

Length

1–2 pages

Planning to Write

The guidelines on the following pages can help you plan and write your article. Read through them, and then refer to them as you complete this assignment. Don't be tied down by the guidelines, however. Remember, you're in charge of your own writing process. Start by setting a time frame for completing this assignment. This will help you pace yourself as you write. Be sure to keep in mind the controlling idea for this assignment: to write about an insect or other animal that repels most people.

LOG ON Writing Online

For prewriting, drafting, revising, editing and publishing tools, go to **glencoe.com** and enter QuickPass code WC97727p1.

Resource Manager

Planning Resources
- *Lesson Plans*

Transparencies
- *Bellringer*
- *Daily Language Practice*
- *Writing Process* 11, 23–27

Other Print Resources
- *Composition Enrichment,* p. 44
- *Composition Practice,* p. 44
- *Composition Reteaching,* p. 44
- *Grammar Workbook,* Lessons 98–102
- *Sentence-Combining Practice,* pp. 32–33
- *Thinking and Study Skills,* pp. 10, 18
- *Writing Assessment and Evaluation Rubrics*

Web Site
- *glencoe.com*

Prewriting

What would you like to write about—wolves, sharks, spiders, bats? Any of these creatures are fair game, but see what other ideas you can come up with. Brainstorm with classmates to generate a list of "vicious," "disgusting," or just misunderstood creatures. From this list select a subject that both interests you and is likely to repel or intrigue your audience.

Once you have identified your subject, freewrite or brainstorm to create an inventory of what you already know about this creature. The Prewriting Questions will help you get started.

Prewriting Questions

- If you experienced the creature close up, what would you see, hear, smell, and feel?
- How does the animal perceive the world?
- How does it interact with others of its species?
- How does it find a mate?
- How does it obtain its food?

Next, do research to find the facts. Start by checking encyclopedias, magazines, and videotapes to determine the accuracy of each characteristic you listed in your initial inventory. Expand your inventory by interviewing authorities on this creature. These experts might include zookeepers, animal trainers and breeders, pet store owners, farmers, or rangers. Record your findings on note cards or in a journal.

Once you have gathered your data, look over your notes to determine how you can best organize your information. The notes themselves may suggest a particular kind of organization. However, if they don't, look for a main idea or focus, and consider weeding out all details not related to that focus. Select the most interesting details to use in your lead, or introduction, and then try to determine what would most logically flow from that.

TIME

For more information about the writing process, see **TIME Facing the Blank Page**, pp. 121-131.

Drafting

For this assignment, you need to grab and hold your readers' attention. You might want to start with a fact or myth that is likely to intrigue young readers.

As you write the body of your paper, be sure to support the points you want to make with specific details. Try also to bring your subject to life with facts, analogies, and other evidence. Read the passage on page 274 to see how natural history writer Barry Holstun Lopez brings to life the relationship between the wolf and his habitat.

Teach

Prewriting

Developing Ideas for Expository Writing

To initiate a discussion on social evaluations of animals, point out to students that the economic benefit or liability of an animal is related to its reputation. (Koalas attract tourists; sharks scare people off.) Ask students to name other ways in which society reflects individual or commercial responses to an animal. For example, which animals are kept as pets and which are kept in zoos? **L2**

Gathering Information

As students gather information about their animal, they will discover its relationship with its environment. To clarify this relationship, help students locate areas where their animal is concentrated. Suggest sources such as almanacs, encyclopedias, animal welfare organizations, and nonfiction studies. **L2**

Additional Resources

Thinking and Study Skills, pp. 10, 18

Drafting

Animals in Our Cultures

As Barry Holstun Lopez discovered when writing *Of Wolves and Men,* predator animals have different reputations and roles in various cultures. Early Native Americans saw the wolf as a symbol of group and individual strength; European settlers saw the animal as a ruthless killer. Ask students whether the animal they are writing about has any special meaning within their culture or other cultures. **L2**

Teach

Drafting

Writing a Lead

Remind students to draft an opening that sets the story in motion and draws the reader into the writing. Refer students to the chart on page 259 and ask them to experiment with different leads.

Using Computers

Students who have access to computers can experiment with margins, type styles, and spacing. **L2**

Revising

Peer Reviewing

Students can work in conferences with peer reviewers before they revise their work. You may want to duplicate the Peer Response forms in *Writing Assessment & Evaluation Rubrics.* Suggest that peer reviewers respond to the following questions:

- Does the lead get your attention?
- Is it age-level appropriate?
- Is it logical and coherent? **L2**

Cooperative Learning

Have groups work together to listen to each other's writing. Listeners should note abrupt transitions, unclear references, and faulty logic. Have groups consider how reading a work aloud helps in ways that reading silently does not. **L2**

Drafting Tip

For suggestions about how to find an effective lead for your story, see Lesson 5.8, page 259.

When you've accomplished the purpose of your feature, conclude your article. If you chose to present one animal's life from birth to death, your conclusion might focus on the death. If you wrote your feature as a flashback, your conclusion would bring readers back to the present. Your conclusion should give your feature a sense of closure or completeness.

Literature Model

The wolf is tied by subtle threads to the woods he moves through. His fur carries seeds that will fall off, effectively dispersed, along the trail some miles from where they first caught in his fur. And miles distant is a raven perched on the ribs of a caribou the wolf helped kill ten days ago, pecking like a chicken at the decaying scraps of meat. A smart snowshoe hare that eluded the wolf and left him exhausted when he was a pup has been dead a year now, food for an owl. The den in which he was born one April evening was home to porcupines last winter.

Barry Holstun Lopez, *Of Wolves and Men*

Revising Tip

For examples of vivid supporting details, see Lesson 5.2, pages 232–234, and Lesson 5.8, page 260.

Revising

To begin revising, read over your draft to make sure that what you've written fits your purpose and audience. Then have a **writing conference.** Read your draft to a partner or small group. Use your audience's reactions to help you evaluate your work.

Revising Checklist

- Does the reader gain an understanding of the creature and its habitat?
- Is the lead engaging, the conclusion effective?
- Is the information well organized?
- Do supporting details bring the subject to life?

Enrichment and Extension

Follow-up Idea

Set aside time for students to celebrate the conclusion of their writing projects. Encourage them to share their finished pieces with the whole class or in small groups.

Extending Expository Writing

Explore possibilities for extending expository writing beyond the classroom in ways such as writing an article for a nature magazine or explaining to others local regulations or voting procedures.

Editing/Proofreading

When you have revised your article for basic content and organization, **proofread** it carefully for errors in grammar, usage, mechanics, and spelling. Think again about your audience. You may find that you will need to simplify or shorten some of your sentences and make your tone more informal. Use the questions at the right as a guide.

Editing Questions

- Do my subjects and verbs agree?
- Are there any run-on sentences?
- Have I used commas where they are needed?
- Are my comparisons complete and clearly stated?
- Have I checked carefully for misspellings?

Self-Evaluation

Make sure your article—

- ✔ focuses on a creature likely to repel young students
- ✔ uses vocabulary and a writing style appropriate for your audience
- ✔ develops in a logical, natural way
- ✔ supports points with specific details
- ✔ follows correct grammar, usage, mechanics, and spelling

Proofreading Tip

For proofreading symbols, see page 411.

Publishing/Presenting

Think about how you can make your essay easy for sixth graders to read and understand. Would a map help you explain your animal's habitat? Would a graph help you present statistical information about your subject?

Presenting Tip

For information about how to enhance your paper with graphics, see Lesson 5.7, pages 252–254.

Journal Writing

Reflect on your writing process experience. Answer these questions in your journal: What do you like best about your article? What was the hardest part of writing it? What did you learn from talking to others about it? What new things have you learned as a writer?

Editing/Proofreading

Peer Editing

After students have edited their own work, have them edit another student's writing. They can look to see that it

- uses vocabulary and a writing style appropriate for sixth graders
- supports ideas with specific details
- uses correct grammar, spelling, and punctuation **L2**

Publishing/Presenting

Before students present their expository writing, discuss how to prepare their papers for their sixth-grade readers. Emphasize the importance of a neat final draft.

Additional Resources

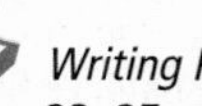

Writing Process Transparencies 11, 23–27

Thinking and Study Skills, p. 10, 18

Sentence-Combining Practice, pp. 32–33

Composition Practice, p. 44

Grammar Workbook, Lessons 98–102

Assess

Evaluation Rubric

Use the following criteria to evaluate your students' finished writing:

- Are comparisons complete and clearly stated?
- Does it follow correct grammar, usage, and mechanics?
- If graphics are used, do they help explain the writer's ideas? Are they understandable and clear?
- Does the article grab and hold a reader's attention?

See also *Writing Assessment & Evaluation Rubrics*

Close

Initiate a discussion about the value of this lesson by asking students to name professional uses for expository writing. (reporting, scientific classification, software directions) Invite students to discuss which skills from the lesson will be most useful to them.

Journal Writing Tip

Writing for an Audience Have students consider the role their audiences played in their writing. What assumptions did they make about their audiences? How did these assumptions affect their writing?

Literature Model

About the Author

Barry Holstun Lopez grew up in rural Southern California and in New York. His love of nature was forged during childhood, when animals were part of his life. After studying folklore in graduate school, he began his writing career by retelling Native American stories about a coyote. His recent writing also focuses on animals and our relationship to them.

Focus

Lesson Overview

Objectives

- To observe how a writer uses vivid, compelling scientific details and sentence fluency to draw readers into an expository piece
- To write informational text

Skills

- monitoring comprehension; summarizing; questioning

Critical Thinking

- analyzing; drawing conclusions

Listening and Speaking

- discussing; questioning

Bellringer

Daily Language Activity

When students enter the classroom, have this assignment on the board: *List all the traits you can think of that people associate with wolves.*

Motivating Activity

Discuss students' responses to the Bellringer activity. Initiate a discussion about how literature tends to associate certain animals with particular personality traits, strengths, and weaknesses. Discuss possible consequences of knowing only what we have read about an animal.

UNIT 5

Literature Model

Expository Writing

from

Of Wolves and Men

by Barry Holstun Lopez

Barry Holstun Lopez writes about natural history and the environment in short fiction, articles, essays, and books. Among his many books is Of Wolves and Men, *which grew out of a 1974 article he wrote for* Smithsonian *magazine. As you read, notice how Lopez's explanations help his reader "see" the wolf in its own right and its own world. Then try the activities in Linking Writing and Literature on page 280.*

Imagine a wolf moving through the northern woods. The movement, over a trail he has traversed many times before, is distinctive, unlike that of a cougar or a bear, yet he appears, if you are watching, sometimes catlike or bearlike. It is purposeful, deliberate movement. Occasionally the rhythm is broken by the wolf's pause to inspect a scent mark, or a move off the trail to paw among stones where a year before he had cached[1] meat.

The movement down the trail would seem relentless if it did not appear so effortless. The wolf's body, from neck to hips, appears to float over the long, almost

1 **cached** (kashd) stored up

Resource Manager

Planning Resources

- *Lesson Plans*

Transparencies

- *Bellringer*
- *Daily Language Practice*
- *Fine Art* 25–28

Other Print Resources

- *Listening and Speaking Activities,* pp. 15–16
- *Writing Assessment and Evaluation Rubrics*

Web Sites

- *writerschoice.glencoe.com*
- *lit.glencoe.com*

spindly legs and the flicker of wrists, a bicycling drift through the trees, reminiscent of the movement of water or of shadows.

The wolf is three years old. A male. He is of the subspecies *occidentalis,* and the trees he is moving among are spruce and subalpine fir on the eastern slope of the Rockies in northern Canada. He is light gray; that is, there are more blond and white hairs mixed with gray in the saddle of fur that covers his shoulders and extends down his spine than there are black and brown. But there are silver and even red hairs mixed in, too.

Nancy Schutt, *Encroachment,* 1987

It is early September, an easy time of year, and he has not seen the other wolves in his pack for three or four days. He has heard no howls, but he knows the others are about, in ones and twos like himself. It is not a time of year for much howling. It is an easy time. The weather is pleasant. Moose are fat. Suddenly the wolf stops in midstride. A moment, then his feet slowly come alongside each other. He is staring into the grass. His ears are rammed forward, stiff. His back arches and he rears up and pounces like a cat. A deer mouse is pinned between his forepaws. Eaten. The wolf drifts on. He approaches a trail crossing, an undistinguished crossroads. His movement is now slower and he sniffs the air as though aware of a possibility for scents. He sniffs a scent post, a scrawny blueberry bush in use for years, and goes on.

The wolf weighs ninety-four pounds and stands thirty inches at the shoulder. His feet are enormous, leaving prints in the mud along a creek (where he pauses to hunt crayfish but not with much interest) more than five inches long by just over four wide. He has two fractured ribs, broken by a moose a year before. They are healed now, but a sharp eye would notice the irregularity. The skin on his right hip is scarred, from a fight with another wolf in a neighboring pack when he was a yearling. He has not had anything but a few mice and a piece of arctic char[2] in three days, but he is not

2 **char** (chär) a kind of trout

Teach

Critical Thinking

Analyze Ask students how Barry Holstun Lopez draws the reader into the subject; that is, how he makes the wolf understandable and interesting. *(Lopez turns the ordinary activities of the wolf into a drama that the reader can experience along with the wolf.)*

Active Reading Strategies

Monitor Comprehension Ask students: "What is the time and place?" *(It is early September in a forest on the east side of the Rockies in northern Canada.)* If students cannot answer, suggest they reread to find the information. Also remind them that they may have to adjust their reading rate at the beginning of the piece or throughout to be sure they process all the details.

Viewing the Art

Nancy Schutt, *Encroachment,* 1987
Encroachment (40 by 54 inches) questions "Who is moving in on whom?" The oil painting was inspired in part by four years Schutt spent in an isolated mountain cabin. Schutt's work often explores the theme of interactions between human beings and animals.

6+1 Trait® Writing

Sentence Fluency

Explain to students that writing that "flows" is often created through careful attention to sentences. To create fluency, writers use **variation** in both sentence length and sentence structure. As a result, ideas flow both smoothly and rhythmically. For example, read aloud the first full paragraph on this page. Have students notice that sentences vary in length from two words to thirty-six words. There is a fragment, a simple sentence, a compound sentence, and a compound-complex sentence.

Practice Have students note variations in length and structure in the second full paragraph. *(Sentences range in length from one word to twenty-five words. The many short sentences emphasize the sudden movement of the wolf. There are also compound sentences.)* Then discuss how the author creates interest and drama by means of sentence variation.

For more information on sentence fluency and the 6+1 Trait® model, see **Writing and Research Handbook**, pp. 947–949.

Teach

Literary Element

Personification Ask students what human characteristics the writer attributes to the wolf. *(The wolf is playful in the scene with the pinecone. He seems like a team player when he helps to kill animals. His position on the ground seems endearing when he is having his afternoon nap.)*

Active Reading Strategies

Summarize Ask students to summarize what they have learned so far. *(A three-year-old male wolf is traveling alone in September. It is an easy time of year now, but the wolf has seen hard times in other seasons. The wolf takes an afternoon nap and wakes up in a playful mood. He uses his senses to understand the world around him.)*

hungry. He is traveling. The char was a day old, left on rocks along the river by bears.

The wolf is tied by subtle threads to the woods he moves through. His fur carries seeds that will fall off, effectively dispersed, along the trail some miles from where they first caught in his fur. And miles distant is a raven perched on the ribs of a caribou the wolf helped kill ten days ago, pecking like a chicken at the decaying scraps of meat. A smart snowshoe hare that eluded the wolf and left him exhausted when he was a pup has been dead a year now, food for an owl. The den in which he was born one April evening was home to porcupines last winter.

It is now late in the afternoon. The wolf has stopped traveling, has lain down to sleep on cool earth beneath a rock outcropping. Mosquitoes rest on his ears. His ears flicker. He begins to waken. He rolls on his back and lies motionless with his front legs pointed toward the sky but folded like wilted flowers, his back legs splayed,[3] and his nose and tail curved toward each other on one side of his body. After a few moments he flops on his side, rises, stretches, and moves a few feet to inspect—minutely, delicately—a crevice in the rock outcropping and finds or doesn't find what draws him there. And then he ascends the rock face, bounding and balancing momentarily before bounding again, appearing slightly unsure of the process—but committed. A few minutes later he bolts suddenly into the woods, achieving full speed, almost forty miles per hour, for forty or fifty yards before he begins to skid, to lunge at a lodgepole pine cone. He trots away with it, his head erect, tail erect, his hips slightly to one side and out of line with his shoulders, as though hindquarters were impatient with forequarters, the cone inert in his mouth. He carries it for a hundred feet before dropping it by the trail. He sniffs it. He goes on.

The underfur next to his skin has begun to thicken with the coming of fall. In the months to follow it will become so dense between his shoulders it will be almost impossible to work a finger down to his skin. In seven months he will weigh less: eighty-nine pounds. He will have tried unsuccessfully to mate with another wolf in the pack. He will have helped kill four moose and thirteen caribou. He will have fallen through ice into a creek at twenty-two below zero but not frozen. He will have fought with other wolves.

He moves along now at the edge of a clearing. The wind coming down-valley surrounds him with a river of odors, as if he were a migrating salmon. He can smell ptarmigan[4] and deer droppings. He can smell willow and spruce and the fading sweetness of fireweed. Above, he sees a hawk circling, and farther south, lower on the horizon, a flock of sharp-tailed sparrows going east. He senses through his pads with each step the dryness of the moss beneath his feet, and the ridges of old tracks, some his own. He hears the sound his feet make. He hears the occasional movement of deer mice and voles.[5] Summer food.

---

3 **splayed** (splād) spread out
4 **ptarmigan** (tär′ mi gən) a kind of northern or alpine bird
5 **voles** (vōlz) field mice

Critical Thinking

Draw Conclusions

Tell students that to *draw conclusions* is to use several pieces of information in order to make a general statement. You might model drawing conclusions this way: "This is a very detailed account of a wolf. Yet, it's not just boring facts. There's beauty in the sentences, and the account also uses the second person in the first paragraph. I'm going to draw the conclusion that Lopez wants to draw his readers into his description."

Practice Ask students what other conclusions they might draw about Lopez's purposes or attitudes. *(Lopez admires wolves. He wants his readers to understand why.)* Have students identify pieces of information they used to draw their conclusion. *(Lopez personifies the wolf. He makes the wolf seem necessary when he describes its connection to nature, agile when he describes the wolf bolting, and like a strong survivor when he describes his healed wounds and near-death encounters.)*

Makah wolf mask, late nineteenth century

Toward dusk he is standing by a creek, lapping the cool water, when a wolf howls—a long wail that quickly reaches pitch and then tapers, with several harmonics,[6] long moments to a tremolo.[7] He recognizes his sister. He waits a few moments, then, throwing his head back and closing his eyes, he howls. The howl is shorter and it changes pitch twice in the beginning, very quickly. There is no answer.

The female is a mile away and she trots off obliquely through the trees. The other wolf stands listening, laps water again, then he too departs, moving quickly, quietly through the trees, away from the trail he had been on. In a few minutes the two wolves meet. They approach each other briskly, almost formally, tails erect and moving somewhat as deer move. When they come together they make high squeaking noises and encircle each other, rubbing and pushing, poking their noses into each other's neck fur, backing away to stretch, chasing each other for a few steps, then standing quietly together, one putting a head over the other's back. And then they are gone, down a vague trail, the female first. After a few hundred yards they begin, simultaneously, to wag their tails.

In the days to follow, they will meet another wolf from the pack, a second female, younger by a year, and the three of them will kill a caribou. They will travel together ten or twenty miles a day, through the country where they live, eating and sleeping, birthing, playing with sticks, chasing ravens, growing old, barking at bears, scent-marking trails, killing moose, and staring at the way water in a creek breaks around their legs and flows on.

6 **harmonics** (här mon′ iks) overtones
7 **tremolo** (trem′ ə lō′) a pulsating tone

Critical Thinking

Draw Conclusions Ask students how personifying the wolf helps Lopez achieve his purpose. *(Personifying the wolf helps create sympathy on the part of the reader. The wolf seems less distant from and less an enemy of our human world.)*

6+1 Trait® Writing

Sentence Fluency Have students read aloud the final sentence of this selection. Note that it is a long sentence, but it flows smoothly and is easy to follow. Ask students how they think Lopez accomplishes this. *(Students may suggest that the list of activities is made up of a number of clear, short phrases that create vivid images of the animals' activities.)*

Active Reading Strategies

Question Invite students to ask a question about the conclusion of this selection. *(Why does the selection end here? What feelings is the reader left with? What might be ahead for the wolf?)* Have students work in pairs to answer the questions.

Additional Resources

Fine Art Transparencies 25–28
Listening and Speaking Activities, pp. 15–16

Viewing the Art

Makah wolf mask, late nineteenth century
Carved wolf masks such as this one from the Makah (7 by 18½ inches) were used as displays of personal privilege. This mask is in the Burke Museum at the University of Washington, Seattle.

Active Reading Strategies

Summarize

Explain that to *summarize* is to state the main ideas of a selection briefly, in one's own words, and in a logical sequence. When summarizing, students might do the following:

- Ask: What is the selection about?
- Answer *who, what, where, when, why*, and *how?* and put that information in a logical sequence.

Practice After students read this page, ask them to write a brief summary of this excerpt. Students can then write three criteria for self-evaluating their summaries and apply them to what they have written.

Linking Writing and Literature

Assess

Evaluation Rubrics

Talk About Reading

Sample responses to the questions:

1. Students may have a more positive view of wolves.
2. Conclusion: Wolves are quite smart and resourceful. Support: The wolf recognizes scent marks and places he has stored meat, knows that others of his pack are wandering in ones and twos, easily catches and eats a deer mouse, survives falling through the ice, recognizes his sister's howl and finds her, and recognizes other wolves of his pack.
3. Lopez uses sentences that draw the reader effortlessly through the piece, creating a rhythm as natural as the movements of the wolf. He varies his sentences to reflect the grace, beauty, and wonder he observes.
4. Lopez would not have personified the wolf. He would have concentrated more on facts. He would have been less concerned with drama and more concerned with information.

Write About Reading

The encyclopedia entry should do the following:

- inform the reader
- accurately reflect facts from the selection
- contain sentences that flow smoothly and that vary in length and structure

Close

Ask students to write a song or verse, with or without rhymes, to reflect an experience they've had that relates to nature. Students can write about an everyday experience in a park or yard, or they can write about a camping trip or other outing. If any students play musical instruments, have them perform some of the songs for the class.

Literature Model

Linking Writing and Literature

Learning to Learn

Think about all you have learned about wolves. Consider what you now know about where they live, what they eat, and what threatens them. Jot down these facts and others you recall.

Talk About Reading

Form a discussion group to talk about this excerpt from *Of Wolves and Men.* Assign one group member to guide the conversation and another to take notes. Use the questions below to focus your discussion.

1. **Connect to Your Life** How has your view of wolves changed from reading this excerpt?
2. **Critical Thinking: Draw Conclusions** What is one conclusion you might draw about wolves from this selection? Give details to support your answer.
3. **6+1 Trait®: Sentence Fluency** How does Barry Lopez use the flow of sentences to help create an interesting and positive portrayal of the wolf?
4. **Connect to Writing** Barry Lopez informs the reader about wolves, but he also conveys an attitude toward them. If Lopez had *only* been interested in providing information, what would he have done differently in this selection?

Write About Reading

Write an Encyclopedia Entry Rewrite part of this selection by turning it into two or three paragraphs of an encyclopedia entry on wolves. (Focus on male wolves about three years of age.) Use an entry word and other heads and subheads to break up your text. In a side note, describe the illustration that should accompany your entry.

Focus on Sentence Fluency As you write, you need not create drama as Lopez did. Nevertheless, your sentences should flow smoothly and evenly, so aim for variation in sentence structure.

For more information on sentence fluency and the 6+1 Trait® model, see **Writing and Research Handbook,** pages 947–949.

Enrichment and Extension

Science

Lopez describes the wolf's howl as a form of conversation with its sister. Wolf communication falls into three categories: vocalization, postural signaling, and scent marking. According to Lopez, wolves howl to assemble the pack, to pass on an alarm, to locate each other in a storm or unfamiliar territory, and to talk across great distances.

UNIT 5 Review

Reflecting on the Unit: Summarize What You Learned

Focus on the following questions to help summarize what you learned in this unit.

1. What are the important characteristics of effective expository writing?
2. What are the purposes of these types of expository writing: process explanation; cause-and-effect; classification; comparison-contrast? How does the writer organize each type?
3. How do graphics enhance expository writing?
4. What are the important steps in preparing a feature article?
5. What strategies are helpful for answering an essay question?

Adding to Your Portfolio

CHOOSE A SELECTION FOR YOUR PORTFOLIO Look over the expository writing you have done in this unit. Select a favorite piece to put into your portfolio. The piece you choose should show some or all of the following:

- a clear expository purpose
- a well-formulated thesis statement
- supporting details appropriate for its purpose and audience
- in-depth information presented appealingly
- an interesting introduction and a conclusion that gives a sense of closure.

REFLECT ON YOUR CHOICE Attach a note to the piece you chose, explaining briefly why you chose it and what you learned from writing it.

SET GOALS How can you improve your writing? What skill will you focus on the next time you write?

Writing Across the Curriculum

MAKE A SOCIAL STUDIES CONNECTION Choose a recent event that has affected the environment in some way. The event can be a natural disaster, an accident such as an oil spill, or the passage of an environmental protection law. Then write a cause-and-effect paragraph explaining the event. Try to identify at least two causes of the event and two possible consequences. Include a suggestion for one or more graphics that will strengthen your writing. Don't forget to use vivid details.

Review

Reflecting on the Unit

You may have students respond to Reflecting on the Unit by writing a summary of what they've learned or through discussion.

Adding to Your Portfolio

Suggest that students keep the list of criteria from this page at hand while reviewing their expository writing. They should use the criteria to select their most successful pieces.

Portfolio Evaluation

If you grade the portfolio selections, you may want to award two marks—one each for content and form. Explain your assessment criteria before students make their selections.

Commend

- experimentation with creative prewriting techniques
- clear, concise writing in which the main idea, audience, and purpose are evident
- successful revisions
- work that shows a flair for language

Writing Across the Curriculum

Before students begin writing, remind them that their paragraphs should begin with a topic sentence and end with a conclusion that summarizes the cause-and-effect relationship introduced in the topic sentence. Students should be careful not to overstate the degree of certainty in a cause-and-effect relationship.

ASSESSMENT OPTIONS

Tests With Answer Key & Rubrics
Unit 5 Choice A Test, p. 17
Unit 5 Choice B Test, p. 18
Unit 5 Composition Objective Test, pp. 19–20

Testmaker
Unit 5 Choice A Test
Unit 5 Choice B Test
Unit 5 Composition Objective Test

You may wish to administer one of these tests as a mastery test.

MindJogger Videoquizzes

UNIT 6

Viewing the Art

This photo of a voter in an election booth reinforces the importance of voting as an American's civic duty as suggested by the quotation. The subtle message associated with the image attempts to persuade the viewer to action in much the same way that persuasive writers aim at influencing the decisions of others.

Interpret and Analyze Use the following questions for discussion:

- How does the image of a voter at a voting booth convey the significance of the right to vote embodied in the quotation?
- Why might the author of the quotation believe that time is so critical to her position?

Discussing the Quotation

This quotation is excerpted from an article about Susan B. Anthony and her struggle to help women achieve many of the same rights as men, including the right to vote. Discuss the quotation with the class, and ask students how they would interpret the author's meaning.

Writing Prompt Write a brief explanation of how this quotation, coupled with the image of the voter at the voting booth, can be seen to connect to the process of persuasive writing.

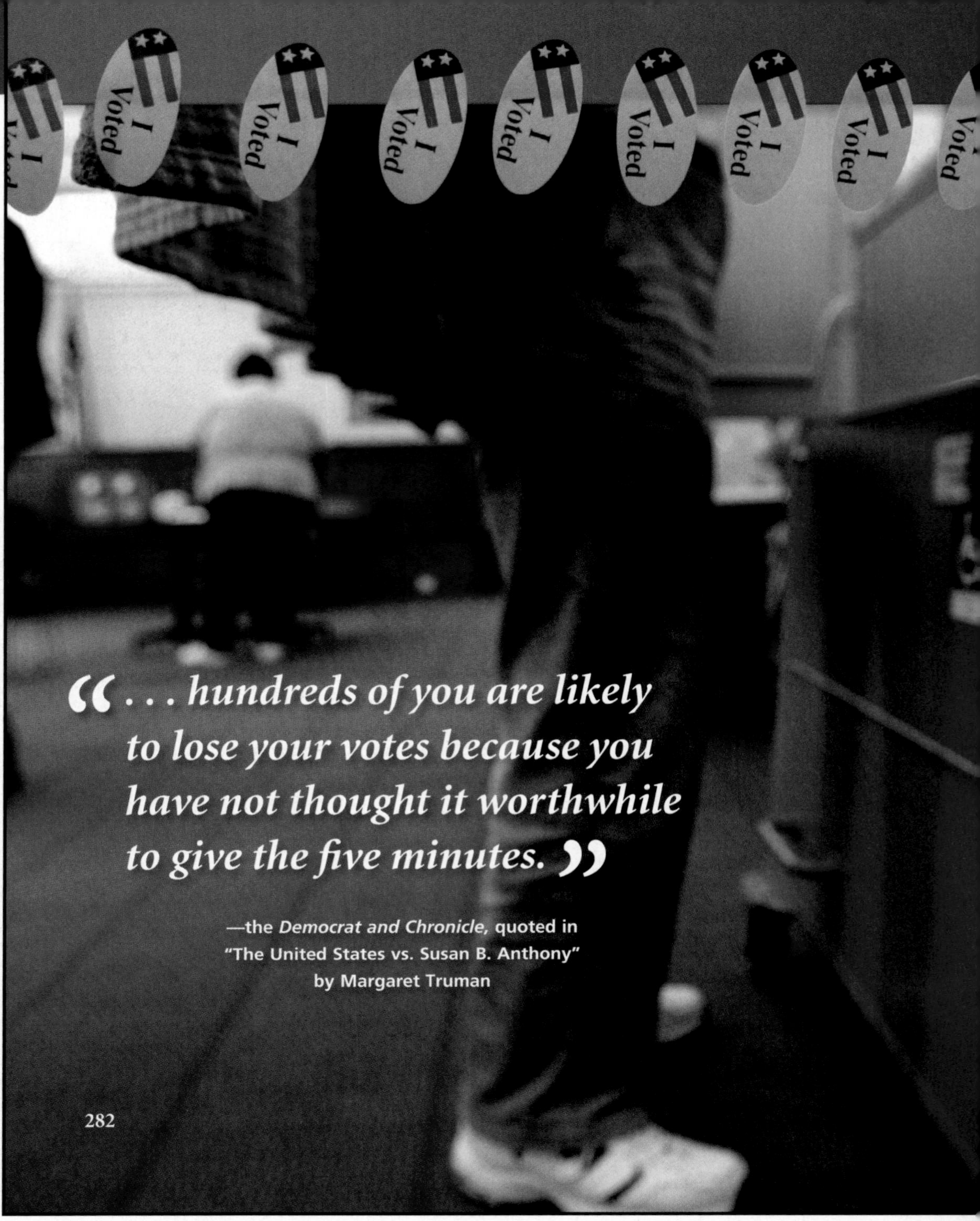

I Voted I Voted I Voted I Voted I Voted I Voted I Voted I Voted I Voted

“. . . hundreds of you are likely to lose your votes because you have not thought it worthwhile to give the five minutes.”

—the *Democrat and Chronicle,* quoted in "The United States vs. Susan B. Anthony" by Margaret Truman

282

Resource Manager

Planning Resources
- *Block Scheduling*

Transparencies
- *Bellringer*
- *Daily Language Practice*
- *Fine Art*
- *Two-Minute Skill Drill*
- *Writing Process*

Other Print Resources
- *Composition Enrichment*
- *Composition Practice*
- *Composition Reteaching*
- *Cooperative Learning Activities*
- *Glencoe Literature Library*
- *Grammar and Composition Handbook*
- *Grammar Workbook*
- *Listening and Speaking Activities*
- *Research Paper and Report Writing*
- *Sentence-Combining Practice*
- *Tests with Answer Key and Rubrics*
- *Thinking and Study Skills*
- *Writing Across the Curriculum*
- *Writing Assessment and Evaluation Rubrics*

6

Persuasive Writing

Objectives

- To develop, through example and instruction, an understanding of persuasive writing
- To examine the components of persuasive writing, including logical arguments, substantiated evidence, error-free reasoning, and effective word choice.
- To apply the techniques learned to write an editorial

ASSESSMENT OPTIONS

Tests with Answer Key & Rubric
Unit 6 Choice A Test, p. 21
Unit 6 Choice B Test, p. 22
Unit 6 Composition Objective Test, pp. 23-24

Testmaker
Unit 6 Choice A Test
Unit 6 Choice B Test
Unit 6 Composition Objective Test

You may wish to administer either the Unit 6 Choice A Test or the Unit 6 Choice B Test as a pretest.

Key to Ability Levels

L1 Level 1 activities are within the basic ability range of students.

L2 Level 2 activities are within the ability range of average students.

L3 Level 3 activities are more challenging activities.

- *Writing in the Real World*

Video
- *MindJogger Videoquizzes*

Software
- *Presentation Plus!*
- *Revising with Style*
- *Testmaker*

Web Site
- *glencoe.com*

Writing in the Real World

Focus

Lesson Overview

Objectives

- To assess the judgment criteria used by one movie reviewer in her work
- To identify the writing process used by one movie reviewer in her work

Skills

- writing persuasively; understanding how writers use the stages of the writing process to write persuasively

Critical Thinking

- analyzing; synthesizing; evaluating information; identifying a main idea

Listening and Speaking

- discussing; questioning; evaluating ideas

Bellringer

Daily Language Activity

When students enter the classroom, have this assignment on the board: *What movie have you seen that you enjoyed? List five reasons you would recommend the movie to a friend.*

Grammar Link to the Bellringer

Have students use the following words in sentences about the movie they discussed in the Bellringer:

your	you're
to	too
its	it's

See also  *Daily Language Practice*

Motivating Activity

Discuss students' responses to the Bellringer activity. What makes a movie interesting? If they were writing a review of a movie, what interesting details would they include to make a reader want to see the movie?

Writing in the Real World

Persuasive Writing

Persuasive writing relies on facts, examples, logic, and strong feelings to sway a reader's opinion. Below is a persuasive article written by Melanie McFarland when she was a high school senior at Morgan Park Academy in Chicago, Illinois. Her movie reviews appeared in a monthly teen newspaper called *New Expression.* Today McFarland reviews movies for the *Seattle Times.*

Petrie's "Toy Soldiers" Has Glitches

by Melanie McFarland

People probably don't know Daniel Petrie, Jr. by name, but they probably know the screenplays he has written or co-written. . . . I had high expectations for his newest film, which was his directing debut: "Toy Soldiers."

It wasn't exactly what I expected.

"Toy Soldiers" is a film about a prep school called the Regis School (aka The Rejects School). Many students are discipline cases who were kicked out of other schools, and are also the sons of powerful families.

So it's not exactly surprising that one day, a group of Colombian terrorists led by Luis Cali, the son of the powerful drug lord Enrique Cali, take over the school. Luis Cali demands his father's release, or else he will kill off one hostage per day. Sounds grim, huh? Not exactly. Class prankster Billy Tepper and his entourage decide they are going to fight back and free their school.

Daniel Petrie, Jr. has great potential as a director. The cinematography was excellent, and the casting was right on. The executions of the scenes were great.

Sean Astin is excellent as Billy Tepper. The part seemed to come very naturally to him.

Wil Wheaton, however, really surprised me. Best known as the ingenious Wesley Crusher in "Star Trek: The Next Generation," he is usually cast as the shy youth. In "Toy Soldiers" he plays Joey Trotta, the son of a powerful mafia figure, who is tough as nails and full of rage. He certainly broke his mold.

In fact, all of the actors were wonderful. But their acting does not save them from a lackluster script. Billy Tepper, though he does have his share of pranks, does nothing spectacular. Other characters could have been more developed as well, such as Joey Trotta. The only thing we know about Joey is that he hates his mafia father.

The dialogue also lacked Petrie's usual spark. The villain, Luis Cali (Andrew Divoff) looked like a cartoon character, thanks to the script. . . .

Resource Manager

Planning Resources

- *Lesson Plans*

 Transparencies

- *Bellringer*
- *Daily Language Practice*
- *Writing Process* 12, 28–32

 Other Print Resources

- *Cooperative Learning Activities,* pp. 25–28
- *Research Paper and Report Writing,* p. 42
- *Thinking and Study Skills,* pp. 13, 25
- *Writing Across the Curriculum*
- *Writing Assessment and Evaluation Rubrics*
- *Writing in the Real World,* pp. 21–24

What's really exciting about a villain in an action film is that he or she seems invincible, but the audience and the hero have to find the villain's Achilles' heel. Cali and his boys weren't ruthless or cunning enough, but I guess that's why a bunch of teenaged mouth-wash swigging boys were able to overpower them.

Finally, the score did not fit. The music was the critical, yet playful kind used in films like "Bambi."

The bottom line is this: the actors deserved a better script, the director deserved a better storyline. "Toy Soldiers" had all the makings of a great action film, but just missed its target.

A Writer's Process

Prewriting

Reading, Watching, and Listening

Before McFarland ever sets foot in a movie theater, she does her "research." In part, that means gleaning information from the press kit that film companies send to reviewers and critics.

The press kit is a thick, glossy notebook-sized folder filled with background information, including biographies of the actors, writers, producer, and director. "I read the biographies of the actors so I can see what other work they've done," McFarland explained. "If I'm not familiar with [their work], I'll go out and rent some films."

Watching movies that constitute an actor's body of work is crucial for reviewers. By knowing an actor's skill and range, reviewers can spot new achievements or the lack of them in an actor's current work.

Reviewers begin their real work as they walk into the movie theater. During the film, they look for original writing. "The lines should be imaginative," McFarland said. "They should make the actors glow." Reviewers also watch for strong directing and acting that's natural, not contrived. In a comedy, McFarland notes how much of the audience is laughing—"the entire audience, not just the [person] in front of you." In a drama or action film, she considers the "grip factor"—how much the film grabs your emotions.

Melanie McFarland

Like every good persuasive writer, McFarland tries to understand a differing point of view. She makes a point of taking a friend to the movies "to get another opinion of the film," she said.

After the film, McFarland jots down notes about key scenes, dialogue, and acting, plus her insights and reactions. These prewriting notes will help McFarland to focus her ideas when she sits down to write.

Persuasive Writing

Teach

Reading Media

Have students preview the title and focus of the Media Connection on page 284. Discuss the purpose and audience of a movie review, pointing out that every review is targeted to a specific audience. Remind students that the goal of reviewers is to persuade an audience whether they should attend the screening of a new movie. Have students read the article.

Discussion Prompts

- Have you ever read a movie, theater, or book review that tried to persuade you to see or to read something?
- What audience is Melanie McFarland addressing in her review? (teenagers) How might this review have been different if it were aimed at an older audience? (more formal writing, word choice; less of a focus on stars, more emphasis placed on historical context of film)
- What type of information can reviewers obtain from a press kit? (background information about movie; biographies of actors, director, producers; titles of other relevant films) Should reviewers rely solely on press kits to write their reviews? Why or why not? (No; the press kit would probably contain favorable opinions and misleading information about the film.)
- What different types of movie genres are there? (comedy, adventure, action, mystery, horror, science fiction, westerns, drama, fantasy)

Real World Connection

Considering Expenses

Some people read or listen to a movie reviewer for economic reasons. Ask students what it costs to see a movie, including any snacks they usually consume. Point out that many people do not want to waste money on a bad film; thus, they prefer to get an expert's assessment first.

Teach

Discussion Prompts

- Read aloud this sentence: "Laura's homecoming is one of the most heart-wrenching scenes in cinema." Then read this statement: "On returning home, Laura cannot escape her mother's hawklike intuition. In a devastating close-up, we see Laura withdraw inside herself—perhaps forever." Why is the second statement more convincing? (It describes the scene, detailing the drama of the relationship. Readers can feel the scene's power.)
- If you were writing a movie review, what steps do you think you would take and in what order? **L2**

Additional Resources

 *Writing Process Transparencies* 12, 28–32

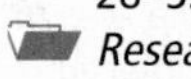 *Research Paper and Report Writing,* p. 42

 *Writing in the Real World,* pp. 21–24

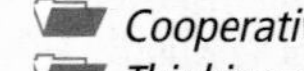 *Cooperative Learning Activities*

Thinking and Study Skills, pp. 13, 25

Drafting
Writing for a Specific Audience

Before McFarland writes her review, she mulls over her reactions for a day. She jots down any important insights and reviews her background information and press kits.

When she's ready to write, McFarland imagines her audience—a few teenagers who want an intelligent opinion of the film she's seen. "I imagine what I would say to an audience right in front of me," McFarland said. "And then I write it down."

Revising
Polishing the Draft

Like professional critics and reviewers, McFarland puts extra time and effort into writing a strong lead that will grab readers. "I tend to set up scenarios in the opening paragraphs that lead into the actual critique."

While revising, she pays special attention to her tone. "Never gush" is a key rule for strong persuasive writing. McFarland realizes that proof of her viewpoints—quoted dialogue, colorful descriptions—gets readers to listen.

Editing
Working with Editors

Once McFarland finishes her review, she checks spelling, grammar, and punctuation. Then she gives the review to one of her peer editors or supervising editors. In addition to proofreading, the peer editor checks the review for completeness, logic, and style. The supervising editor usually makes minor copyediting changes and, if there are major revisions needed, returns the manuscript to McFarland.

Publishing
Going to Press

After McFarland finishes her final draft, the copy is imported from one computer system to another, and dummy electronic pages are created. McFarland is always curious to see the layout and often returns to the office for one last check. A common error, she says, occurs when the copy is imported; text can "disappear" during the process, and she wants one last chance to proofread before press time.

Real World Connection

Using Community Resources

Point out that full-time professional reviewers may view several movies every week, as well as interview film personalities, write articles, and report on special events such as the Academy Awards. Professional reviewers have to work to keep their viewpoints objective and their insights fresh. Encourage students to practice their skills as movie reviewers. Have them select a local movie, watch it in a theater, and then write a review using what they have learned in the Media Connection. If possible, have students post their reviews on a class Web site.

Examining Writing in the Real World

Analyzing the Media Connection

Discuss these questions about the movie review on pages 284–285.

1. How does the first paragraph draw readers into the article and encourage them to read further?
2. What does the reviewer consider the major weakness in the film? What evidence or reasons does she offer to support her opinion?
3. What does the reviewer consider the strengths of the film? What evidence or reasons does she offer to support her opinion?
4. What does the reviewer assume her audience will know?
5. Would this review inspire you to see the film? Why or why not?

Analyzing a Writer's Process

Discuss these questions about Melanie McFarland's writing process.

1. How does McFarland prepare to see a movie?
2. What elements does McFarland look for when she goes to a movie?
3. How does audience reaction influence McFarland's reviews?
4. How might using a strong lead in a review help McFarland persuade her readers to accept her opinion?
5. How do editors help McFarland with her reviews?

Grammar*Link*

Use the correct word of a confusing pair.

Some confusing pairs of words are *homophones*—words like *their* and *there* that sound alike but have different meanings and spellings. Other words, such as *accept* and *except*, are easily confused simply because they sound similar.

Rewrite each sentence below, completing it with the correct word in parentheses. If you are in doubt, use your dictionary.

1. The theater reviewer was (formally, formerly) a movie critic.
2. Her opinion had no (affect, effect) on my decision.
3. Do you like horror movies better (then, than) comedies?
4. The scene was set in the lobby of the state (capital, capitol).
5. The group went to the movies (altogether, all together).

See Lesson 26.2, pages 833–835.

Take 2

'All I Want for Christmas'

Promises, Promises

Cliche 'Christmas'

Assess

Analyzing the Media Connection

1. McFarland mentions her high expectations for a film. The reader wants to find out if the film lived up to them.
2. The script is "lackluster" because the characters lack dimension and the dialogue lacks spark.
3. The film's strengths were excellent cinematography, good casting, great execution of scenes, and fine acting. She cites actors in specific roles.
4. Answers will vary. Possible answer: The reviewer assumes her audience will know references to popular films such as *Star Trek: The Next Generation.*
5. Answers will vary. Possible answer: No, because the weak story line undermines the overall impact of the movie.

Analyzing a Writer's Process

1. McFarland reads information from the press kit and sometimes watches other movies to become familiar with an actor's body of work.
2. original writing; strong directing; acting that's natural, not contrived
3. McFarland uses audience reaction to judge the impact and quality of a movie.
4. Setting up a strong scenario in the lead can convince readers that McFarland's opinion is worthwhile.
5. Editors check her reviews for completeness, logic, and style.

Enrichment

Challenge students to select a target audience for a film. Have students solicit audience reaction to the movie by creating, presenting, testing, and revising a feedback form or questionnaire that the audience can complete after viewing the film. After the data is collected and organized, invite students to present their analysis to the class.

Close

Have students discuss how to use the process described in the Media Connection to review a book or stage play.

Grammar*Link*

Answers

1. formerly
2. effect
3. than
4. capitol
5. all together

Focus

Lesson Overview

Objectives
- To identify the components of a logical argument
- To construct a logical argument that persuades others to accept an idea, adopt a point of view, or take an action

Skills
- using persuasive writing; constructing a logical argument

Critical Thinking
- synthesizing; categorizing; evaluating; summarizing; identifying

Listening and Speaking
- note taking; discussing; listening to a persuasive speech; explaining a process

Bellringer

Daily Language Activity

When students enter the classroom, have this assignment on the board: *Do you think that penalties for drunk drivers should be increased—yes or no?*

Grammar Link to the Bellringer

Have students expand their responses to the Bellringer, making sure they avoid the use of double negatives.

See also  *Daily Language Practice*

Motivating Activity

Discuss students' responses to the Bellringer activity. Then have students choose another current issue of interest, identify at least two viewpoints, and take a class opinion poll. Give students five minutes to come up with arguments on both sides of the issue. Have the class rank the arguments from most persuasive to least persuasive. Encourage students to draw conclusions about the characteristics of a persuasive argument (logical, based on sound evidence).

Persuasive Writing

LESSON 6.1

Writing Persuasively

Persuasive writing is writing that tries to influence a reader to accept an idea, adopt a point of view, or perform an action. Effective persuasive writing uses strong, relevant evidence to support its claims.

Use Persuasive Writing

Newspaper and magazine advertisements, as well as posters announcing events such as the concert pictured, are examples of persuasive writing. You might use persuasive writing to do any or all of the tasks in the following list:

- convince your principal to relax the school's dress code
- persuade others to see a movie or play
- advertise lawn-care services you can provide
- apply for a summer job

Construct a Logical Argument

An argument contains the body of evidence used to support a point of view. The purpose of the argument is to persuade readers to accept your point of view. When you present your evidence logically, you take your readers step by step through your argument.

The chief stages in the construction of a logical argument are detailed on pages 289–290.

Resource Manager

Planning Resources
- *Lesson Plans*

Transparencies
- *Bellringer*
- *Daily Language Practice*
- *Fine Art* 29–32
- *Two-Minute Skill Drill*
- *Writing Process* 12, 28–32

Other Print Resources
- *Composition Enrichment,* p. 46
- *Composition Practice,* p. 46
- *Composition Reteaching,* p. 46
- *Cooperative Learning Activities,* pp. 25–28
- *Listening and Speaking Activities,* pp. 17, 22–23
- *Sentence-Combining Practice,* pp. 34–35
- *Thinking and Study Skills,* pp. 5, 11, 13
- *Writing Across the Curriculum*
- *Writing Assessment and Evaluation Rubrics*

Identify Your Purpose Before you begin constructing your argument, decide what you want your persuasive piece to accomplish. For instance, if you want to write a letter to your principal about the lack of sports opportunities for girls at your school, your purpose might be to ask the principal to help develop a girls' soccer team.

State Your Central Claim A claim is a statement that asserts something. In persuasive writing, your central claim usually clarifies your main purpose for writing, and this claim will often begin your argument. For example, the letter requesting increased sports opportunities for girls might begin, "Our school should organize a girls' soccer team." Identifying your claim at the beginning will help focus your argument.

Identify Supporting Evidence One way to start identifying evidence to support your claim is to ask yourself questions that begin, "What evidence do I have that . . . ?" Then look for answers to your questions.

For example, to support the claim that her school should organize a girls' soccer team, one writer asked herself, What evidence do I have that

- enough girls are interested in joining a soccer team?
- the team would benefit the girls and the school?
- there is a need for additional sports activities for girls?
- the school can provide the necessary staff?

To answer these questions, the writer then conducted a survey of the girls at her school. As a result, she discovered overwhelming interest in a soccer team. She also talked to the coach of the girls' soccer team at a nearby high school and some of the gym teachers at her own school. As authorities on the subject, these people supplied the writer with expert testimony to support her claim. By using these kinds of sound evidence in her persuasive writing piece, the writer will improve her chances of persuading her audience.

Drafting Tip

As you draft, use transitions to show relationships between ideas and to lead your readers step by step through your evidence.

Journal Writing

Identify a situation in which you were persuaded to do something. In your journal, note the evidence and tactics that were most effective in persuading you to take action. Then explain why these tactics may have been so effective.

Teach

Learning Cooperatively

Have students form small groups to identify various purposes for persuasive writing. Mention a current school policy issue (such as allowing an open campus or changing graduation requirements). Ask the class to name different individuals or groups whose support would help to resolve the issue (the school board, principal, teachers, students). Each group member should decide on a position and assign the members to plan a persuasive piece and write a purpose statement to a particular group or individual. The plan and purpose should indicate a good way to reach the audience and a specific action to recommend in regard to the issue. **L2**

Writing Persuasively

Ask students to think of more examples of persuasive writing. (For example, lawyer's argument, letter to the editor, college or job application letter, advertising copy, and political oration.) **L1**

Two-Minute Skill Drill

Have students write four sentences describing a favorite book or TV program. Tell them to use the skills discussed under "Drafting Tip" to assist with their draft.

See also *Two-Minute Skill Drill Transparency 6.1*

Journal Writing Tip

Activating Prior Knowledge
Encourage students to identify evidence and tactics that were not persuasive.

Teach

Using the Model

Use the model to show how to reaffirm a central claim without repeating it. This stage of a logical argument is considered the "clincher," designed to convince the reader of the argument's worth. As in the model, something more should be added to the central claim to reaffirm it: a key transition (A soccer team would be of equal benefit), a means of implementation (Ms. Jordan's willingness to be coach), or additional information (availability of the playing field). **L2**

Applying Logic

Tell interested students that the rules for constructing a logical argument—the use of logic and deductive reasoning in particular—apply when proving geometric theorems. A "proof" begins with true statements (axioms, definitions, or previously proven theorems), orders them logically, and then presents a conclusion. If the premises are true and the logic is sound, the conclusion will also be true. **L3**

Additional Resources

- For further stimuli for persuasive writing, see *Fine Art Transparencies* 29–32.
- *Writing Process Transparencies* 12 28–32
- *Writing Across the Curriculum*
- *Cooperative Learning Activities*
- *Thinking and Study Skills,* pp. 5, 11, 13
- *Sentence-Combining Practice,* pp. 34–35
- *Listening and Speaking Activities,* pp. 17, 22–23
- *Composition Practice,* p. 46

Persuasive Writing

Explain How the Evidence Supports Your Claim If the link between your claim and the evidence you use to support it is obvious, you don't need to state it. If, however, the connection is not clear, you must explain how the evidence supports your claim and why the reader should accept your evidence.

Read the following model in which the writer presents her case for a girls' soccer team in a letter to her high school principal. Notice how the evidence supports her claim.

Model

The link between the survey results and the claim for a soccer team is obvious. The connection does not need to be stated.

What is the logical link between the girls at Fairfax High and the writer's claim?

Dear Mr. Lopez,

I strongly believe that our school should organize a girls' soccer team, and I am not alone in this belief. After conducting a survey among the junior and senior girls at our school, I found that fifty girls would be interested in trying out for a soccer team.

To discover how similar teams have worked out at other schools, I talked to Ms. Young, the girls' soccer coach at Fairfax High. When I asked her how the team has benefited the girls and the school, she said: "The girls on my team have become close friends. They help each other with everything—homework, personal problems." She added, "Their grades have improved—they've become all-around better students—and that's always good for a school."

A soccer team would be of equal benefit to the girls at our school. Just like the girls at Fairfax, many of the girls here would enjoy making close friends. A soccer team might enrich their lives at school.

Moreover, it would be simple to start a team. I've already talked to my gym teacher, Ms. Jordan. She's willing to take on the responsibility of coaching the team. The question of where to practice isn't a problem either, since the playing field isn't used after three o'clock on Tuesdays and Thursdays. All we need now is your support.

Reaffirm Your Claim Conclude your argument by reaffirming your claim. You might suggest that, given the evidence you have presented, your claim is the logical conclusion. You might also explain how your claim could be put into action. In the model above, for example, the writer explains where and when the soccer team could meet and identifies a teacher who is willing to coach it.

English Language Learners

Identifying Evidence

Help students with English language difficulties focus on content, not errors in grammar, spelling, or punctuation. Ask them to focus instead on presenting evidence and developing their arguments. Have pairs of students check each other's drafts for content that supports the claim the writer makes. Emphasize to students that they are not to point out other errors. Direct students to additional resources where they can read about their chosen issue. Suggest that students search the resources for vocabulary that will help them write about their issue.

6.1 Writing Activities

Write a Letter to the Editor

Write a letter to the editor of your school newspaper about some aspect of school life that you would like to see changed. Be sure to construct a logical argument.

PURPOSE To make a case for change in some aspect of school life
AUDIENCE Teachers and other students
LENGTH 1–2 paragraphs

WRITING RUBRICS To write an effective letter to the editor, you should

- identify your purpose
- state your central claim clearly
- present evidence in a logical sequence
- explain how your evidence supports your claim
- conclude by reaffirming your claim

Bronze plaque from Benin

Grammar*Link*

Double negatives, such as *can't. . .no*, cancel each other out. Avoid them.

Rewrite the sentences below, eliminating the double negatives.

[1]There isn't no reason why the school can't sponsor a computer club. [2]We don't have none now, but we could easily organize one. [3]People who don't have no computer games could share them. [4]People who don't know nothing about using a computer could get help. [5]Since we don't need no more computers, we aren't going to need no new printers either.

See Lesson 18.6, page 668.

Cross-Curricular Activity

ART In a small group, discuss whether the plaque at left should be shown in a school exhibit for students to view. Consider the subject and design of the work, as well as how students might react to it. Then write a paragraph stating why the work should or should not be exhibited in the school.

Listening and Speaking

In a small group, choose three letters to the editor from a recent edition of your local newspaper. Analyze the letters for effective persuasive writing by identifying each letter's purpose, central claim, and supporting evidence. Discuss which of the three letters is the most persuasive and give reasons for your choice.

LOG ON **Writing** Online | For more writing and grammar practice, go to **glencoe.com** and enter QuickPass code WC97727p1.

Assess

Evaluation Rubrics

Write a Letter to the Editor

Use these criteria when evaluating your students' writing. The letter should contain

- an identifiable purpose
- a clearly stated central claim
- a logical sequence of evidence
- a strong conclusion that reaffirms the claim

See also *Writing Assessment & Evaluation Rubrics*

Cross-Curricular Activity

Use these criteria when evaluating the results of this activity. Teams should

- produce well-researched evidence on the art and possible student reaction to it
- use logical evidence to state their opinions
- address the possible causes and effects of the final decision

Reteaching

Composition Reteaching, p. 46

Enrichment

Composition Enrichment, p. 46

Fine Art Transparencies 29–32

Close

Ask students to write a letter to the editor of a local newspaper. The letter should express an opinion on an issue that interests the student. Students should follow submission guidelines and use published letters as models. Interested students can submit their revised letters for publication.

Grammar*Link*

Answers

Answers will vary.

1. There is no reason why . . .
2. We don't have one now, but . . .
3. People who don't have computer games could share them.
4. People who don't know anything . . .
5. . . . don't need more computers, we aren't going to need new . . .

Viewing the Art

Bronze plaque, Benin
Bronze casting in Benin is thought to have developed in the early fourteenth century. Most bronze objects from Benin are art works that were displayed for the glorification of the rulers. This plaque is 15⅝ inches high and is in the collection of The Field Museum of Natural History in Chicago.

Focus

Lesson Overview

Objectives

- To identify the most common kinds of evidence used in persuasive writing
- To learn how to assess the accuracy and relevance of evidence

Skills

- identifying and evaluating evidence; writing a review and a letter

Critical Thinking

- establishing and evaluating criteria for a logical argument

Listening and Speaking

- discussing; questioning; evaluating

Bellringer

Daily Language Activity

When students enter the classroom, have this assignment on the board: *What might be the criteria for judging whether evidence is admissible in a court of law?*

Grammar Link to the Bellringer

Correct the verb tenses in the following sentence: *Her jewels had been stole, but the defendant said, "I did not stole nothing."*

See also  *Daily Language Practice*

Motivating Activity

Discuss students' responses to the Bellringer activity. Ask what students already know from newspapers, television, documentaries, or personal experiences about court cases and evidence allowed in court. Discuss that evidence must be relevant, reliable, and directly verifiable by a witness to prove a case. Explain that in this lesson they will learn the criteria to use to evaluate evidence needed for writing a persuasive claim.

LESSON 6.2

Using Evidence Effectively

Just as an attorney must present sound evidence in a courtroom, you must use strong, reliable, and relevant evidence to prove your claim in a piece of writing.

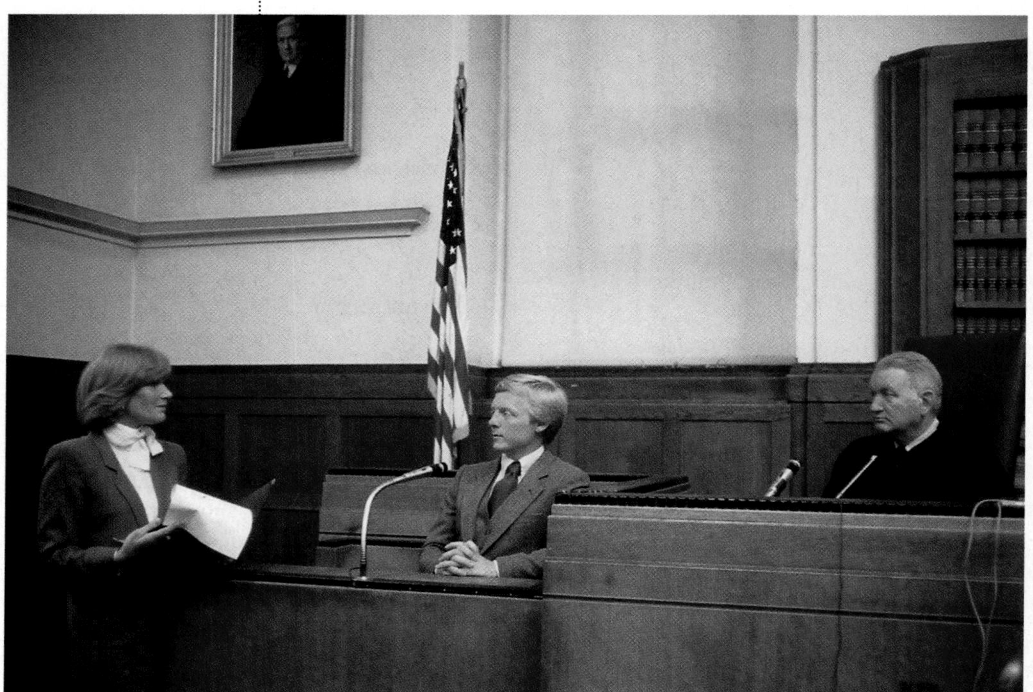

Identify the Evidence

The most common kinds of evidence used in persuasive writing include the following: facts, statistics, examples or incidents, opinions, and reasons. To collect these kinds of evidence, try freewriting, clustering, or making a list about your issue. You can also gather evidence by reading about your issue and by interviewing people. The more kinds of evidence you use to support your claim, the stronger your argument will be.

Resource Manager

Planning Resources

- *Lesson Plans*

Transparencies

- *Bellringer*
- *Daily Language Practice*
- *Fine Art* 29–32
- *Two-Minute Skill Drill*
- *Writing Process* 12, 28–32

Other Print Resources

- *Composition Enrichment,* p. 47
- *Composition Practice,* p. 47
- *Composition Reteaching,* p. 47
- *Cooperative Learning Activities,* pp. 25–28
- *Listening and Speaking Activities,* pp. 17, 22–23
- *Sentence-Combining Practice,* pp. 34–35
- *Thinking and Study Skills,* p. 25
- *Writing Across the Curriculum*
- *Writing Assessment and Evaluation Rubrics*

Evidence Used in Persuasive Writing		
Kind	**Definition**	**Example**
Fact	Something that is known to be true	Prehistoric dancers pictured on rock surfaces in Africa and southern Europe prove that dancing is one of the oldest forms of human expression.
Statistic	A fact that is expressed in numbers	When the musical *A Chorus Line* finally closed on Broadway in 1990, it had achieved a record of 6,137 performances.
Example or Incident	A particular case or event	In some societies, dancing plays a role in courtship. For example, in the U.S., many high school students get to know one another at school dances.
Opinion	A personal judgment based on what the person believes or feels to be true	A famous dancer once claimed, "The dance is a poem of which each movement is a word."
Reason	A logical argument	Many ballet dancers protest the use of toe shoes because the shoes cause permanent damage to the wearer's feet.

Assess the Accuracy of the Evidence

To assess the accuracy of your evidence, verify it in up-to-date sources. Check facts and statistics by consulting current encyclopedias, atlases, and other reference sources. Consult an expert on your subject to clarify something you don't understand or to obtain information that printed sources cannot provide. If you cannot verify a statement, or if the only source available to you is out-of-date, you may want to omit the statement from your argument. Your position will be greatly weakened if your readers spot inaccuracies in your argument.

Journal Writing

What do you think are the most reliable kinds of evidence you can use to support a claim? Why do you think this may be so? Write down your ideas in your journal.

Persuasive Writing

Teach

Locating Experts

Discuss how to find experts on particular subjects by asking students if they know anyone personally who might be considered an expert in his or her field. You might list other means of finding an expert, such as reading articles on the subject and noting the experts mentioned, scanning library references that list likely organizations, or asking universities or local and state agencies. **L2**

Identifying the Evidence

Ask students for examples of each kind of evidence described in the chart on page 293 to support the following claim: Teenagers make up a sizable proportion of the shopping public. (Students may suggest factual findings from recent consumer studies, a relevant statistic, an incident at a shopping mall, a consumer expert's opinion, and a reasonable argument based on teenagers' expendable income.) **L3**

Two-Minute Skill Drill

Write the following on the board. *Write the correct verb form:* rise, rose, *or* risen *to complete the sentences.*

The sun __ at 6:00 A.M., long before the defendant had __.

The bailiff said, "All __," when the judge entered.

The first witness __ and walked forward.

He had __ when his name was called.

See also *Two-Minute Skill Drill Transparency 6.2*

Teach

Using the Model

Ask students to identify the evidence that is relevant in supporting Lewis's claim that cigarette smoking is a serious addiction. (The opinion of an authority, Dr. Koop, supports that cigarette smokers become dependent on the habit. Lewis adds a statistic establishing similar addiction patterns of heroin and cigarettes. A direct quote from Koop provides a reason for the comparison. The final paragraph cites statistics showing that the mortality rate for nicotine users is greater than that of heroin users.) **L2**

Identifying Opinions

Discuss the use of celebrity spokespeople in commercials. What spokespeople can students name? Who are the authorities on the products they endorse? (For example, a basketball player may be an expert on basketball shoes, but probably not on automobiles.) For each nonexpert, students should think of a more authoritative spokesperson for the product. **L1**

Additional Resources

For further stimuli for persuasive writing, see *Fine Art Transparencies* 29–32.

Writing Process Transparencies 12, 28–32

Writing Across the Curriculum

Cooperative Learning Activities

Thinking and Study Skills, p. 25

Listening and Speaking Activities, pp. 17, 22–23

Sentence-Combining Practice, pp. 34–35

Composition Practice, p. 47

Persuasive Writing

Grammar Tip

If you use statistics or number amounts in your evidence, be sure to check the subject-verb agreement. See Lesson 16.4, page 614.

Be sure that the people whose opinions you include are authorities on your subject. Resist using the opinions of well-known persons who have no connection to your subject. So-called testimonials do not have the validity of opinions supplied by authorities.

Evaluate the Relevance of the Evidence

To assess the relevance of your evidence, examine each detail and ask yourself if it helps to develop the point you want to make. If not, you should probably discard the detail as irrelevant to your argument. For example, if you were writing to convince your audience that Spike Lee is a great movie director, you probably wouldn't include a statement naming his favorite restaurant. The statement has nothing to do with Lee's ability as a director and would only distract your readers from your central point.

Now read the following selection by editorial columnist Anthony Lewis. Notice that Lewis uses sound, relevant evidence to support his claim that the nicotine in cigarettes is as addictive as heroin or cocaine.

Literature Model

Lewis cites facts and statistics from a highly respected source, the U.S. Surgeon General, to support his claim.

In what way is each point Lewis uses in his argument relevant to his claim?

Dr. C. Everett Koop, the Surgeon General, was only spelling out in scientific terms what we all have observed about cigarette smoking. Users become dependent on the habit, and breaking it can be extremely difficult.

Of those who try to give up smoking, 80 percent have relapsed by the end of a year. Heroin users who try to give up their addiction have the same rate of failure.

"The pharmacologic and behavioral processes that determine tobacco addiction," the Koop report concluded, "are similar to those that determine addiction to drugs such as heroin and cocaine."

There is one profound difference between heroin and nicotine addiction. Tobacco kills 80 times as many people in this country. About 320,000 Americans die every year as a result of using tobacco products, while 4,000 die from the effects of heroin and related drugs.

Anthony Lewis, "Merchants of Death," *New York Times*

MEETING INDIVIDUAL NEEDS

English Language Learners

Identifying Experts

Students whose native language is not English might identify experts on particular subjects by looking at photo essays in magazines. The photo essay might focus on a professional athlete or someone who had made news recently, such as an astronaut, scientist, or inventor. Students could then discuss what products this expert might be qualified to evaluate in his or her field.

6.2 Writing Activities

Evaluate an Editorial

Find an editorial in a local or school paper and evaluate the evidence it uses to make its case. Write a brief review explaining why you think the editorial is or is not effective. Give clear reasons to support your opinion of the editorial's argument.

PURPOSE To evaluate the evidence in an editorial
AUDIENCE Your teacher and classmates
LENGTH 1–2 paragraphs

WRITING RUBRICS To write an evaluation of an editorial, you should

- summarize the opinion expressed
- identify the evidence
- explain whether the evidence is accurate
- decide whether the evidence is relevant

Using Computers

Using a search engine, find several Web sites that contain editorials about a topic currently in the news. Evaluate the editorials for their use of evidence, effectiveness, and overall appearance. In one or two paragraphs, explain what factors contribute to the persuasiveness of a good online editorial.

Viewing and Representing

COLLABORATIVE WRITING In a small group, watch and discuss three television shows that feature teenagers. Identify ways you think each show could be improved. Then have each group member choose one show and write a letter to its producers in which he or she proposes ideas for change. Finally, take turns presenting each letter to the rest of the group, who will act as the show's producers and assess the relevance of the evidence.

Grammar*Link*

Use verb forms correctly.

Past forms of verbs, such as *went,* should not be used with helping verbs; past participle forms like *done* should not be used alone.

Write the correct verb form to complete each sentence below.

1. The trial (began, begun) six weeks ago.
2. The judge had (gave, given) very clear instructions.
3. The lawyers had (chose, chosen) a jury in about three weeks.
4. They had (took, taken) their time because this trial was so important.
5. Both lawyers (did, done) their best to persuade the jury.
6. The defendant has (wrote, written) notes to her lawyer during the trial.
7. The newspapers said that the trial has (gone, went) on too long.
8. The courtroom (was, been) filled with spectators every day.
9. Has the foreman (spoke, spoken) for a unanimous jury?
10. The defense has (win, won) an acquittal.

See Lessons 15.1 and 15.2, pages 581–585.

Writing Online | For more writing and grammar practice, go to **glencoe.com** and enter QuickPass code WC97727p1.

Assess

Evaluation Rubrics

Evaluate an Editorial

Use these criteria to evaluate your students' writing:

- Are clear reasons given for any opinions stated?
- Is a logical argument developed to explain whether the evidence presented is accurate and/or relevant?

See also *Writing Assessment & Evaluation Rubrics*

Viewing and Representing

Answers will vary, but letters should support the reasons listed with statistical information, examples of incidents in the industry, and opinions of experts.

Reteaching

Composition Reteaching, p. 47

Enrichment

Composition Enrichment, p. 47

Close

Have students identify a situation in which they might want to use persuasive writing. (For example, a situation in which a student is expected to explain why he or she should be hired for a job or accepted by a college.) Ask students why it would be important to present evidence that is factual, relevant, and verifiable. The discussion then might lead to what might happen if the evidence were inaccurate or irrelevant.

Grammar*Link*

Answers

1. began	6. written
2. given	7. gone
3. chosen	8. was
4. taken	9. spoken
5. did	10. won

Focus

Lesson Overview

Objectives

- To identify three types of faulty logic
- To evaluate the logic of the arguments presented in a piece of persuasive writing

Skills

- analyzing the logic of arguments; recognizing faulty logic; recognizing convincing arguments

Critical Thinking

- analyzing; evaluating; identifying logical errors; using cause-and-effect relationships

Listening and Speaking

- discussing

Bellringer

Daily Language Activity

When students enter the classroom, have this assignment on the board: *Should the age at which a person can obtain a driver's license be raised to 18? Write two arguments for or against this idea.*

Grammar Link to the Bellringer

Write the following sentence on the board and ask students to add punctuation if necessary: *Because most teenagers are mature enough to drive before they are eighteen the age for driving should not be raised.*

See also  *Daily Language Practice*

Motivating Activity

Discuss students' responses to the Bellringer activity. Then write the following argument on the board: *"Young people today are irresponsible. They're never on time. That's why the driving age should be raised. If you can't vote until you're eighteen, why should you be able to drive sooner? The money students earn should be saved for college, not spent on cars."* Students can discuss how the argument is illogical.

LESSON 6.3

Checking Reasoning

Learning to recognize the logical flaws in an argument can help you eliminate these flaws from your own writing. There are several types of faulty logic that you should be able to recognize.

Eliminate Faulty Logic

Once you've chosen the evidence to support an argument, you need to make sure that the conclusions you draw from that evidence are logical or follow sound reasoning. Suppose, for example, that you try to persuade your parents to buy you an outfit because it's on sale and they could save by buying it now. Their logical response to this argument could be that they'd save even more money if they didn't buy it at all. If your conclusions are illogical, or include logical fallacies, your readers may reject your entire argument—no matter how compelling your evidence or how well written your argument. As you write, watch out for three of the most common errors in reasoning: red herrings, either/or thinking, and cause-and-effect errors.

Red Herrings The term *red herring* derives from the practice of dragging a strong-smelling fish across a trail to confuse hunting dogs and throw them off the scent. In writing, a red herring is a topic or statement that distracts the reader's attention from the central issue or that hides a weak argument.

Read over your argument to check for red herrings. Make sure that each of your points is directly related to your claim. Anything that sends your reader in a different direction may be a red herring.

Resource Manager

Planning Resources

- *Lesson Plans*

Transparencies

- *Bellringer*
- *Daily Language Practice*
- *Fine Art* 29–32
- *Two-Minute Skill Drill*
- *Writing Process* 12, 28–32

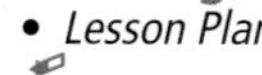

Other Print Resources

- *Composition Enrichment,* p. 48
- *Composition Practice,* p. 48
- *Composition Reteaching,* p. 48
- *Cooperative Learning Activities,* pp. 25–28
- *Listening and Speaking Activities,* pp. 17, 22–23
- *Sentence-Combining Practice,* pp. 34–35
- *Thinking and Study Skills,* pp. 14, 17–18
- *Writing Across the Curriculum*
- *Writing Assessment and Evaluation Rubrics*

Either/Or Thinking Either/or thinking results from oversimplifying your argument by assuming that the issue has only two sides. For example, a writer might make the following claim: "Schools should eliminate computer instruction and return to teaching students the basics—reading, writing, and arithmetic." This position, however, fails to take into account the possibility that computers may aid in teaching these basic subjects.

To make sure that you have not used either/or thinking in your writing, look for other reasonable positions between the two sides you have presented in the argument. If you find them, you are probably oversimplifying the issue.

Cause-and-Effect Errors The fact that one event precedes another in time does not necessarily mean that the first event is the cause of the second. To make sure that you have identified true cause-and-effect relationships, plot your evidence on a cause-and-effect diagram. Check to be sure that each effect is the direct result of the cause you have listed.

In the cause-and-effect diagram shown below, one writer plots some evidence supporting the argument that the demand for ivory jewelry has endangered African elephants. Is each effect the direct result of its preceding cause? Remember that one way to check an argument for cause-and-effect errors is to use the "*because* test": if you can use the word *because* to show the relationship between events or facts, the relation is causal, not just sequential.

Consumers want ivory carvings and jewelry.

Hunters kill elephants to supply ivory.

Because old elephants with larger tusks have been killed, younger ones are hunted.

Younger elephants have smaller tusks, so more are killed to meet demand for ivory.

The killing of elephants accelerates, leading to possible extinction.

Grammar Tip

If you decide to present your argument orally, be sure it does not contain sentences with dangling modifiers, which will distract your audience. See Lesson 18.7, pages 670–675.

Journal Writing

Select an argument you have begun to write. In your journal, plot its evidence on a cause-and-effect diagram like the one shown above. Then ask yourself if each effect you have listed is the direct result of the preceding cause. If it is not, correct your argument.

Teach

Identifying Logical Errors

Students can learn to recognize red herrings by examining letters to the editor in the school or local newspaper, or other media sources. Direct students to identify each letter's main idea first. Make the point that, to be logical, the argument's supporting ideas must all support the main idea. Next, students should look for red herrings—ideas that do not support the main idea. **L2**

Cooperative Learning

To help students recognize either/or thinking, conduct this partners activity. Partners should decide on an issue and identify two extreme positions, such as "No new highways should be constructed, because highways always harm the environment," and "Solving traffic problems is always more important than protecting the environment." The two students should work together to develop some middle-ground statement. ("Highways can be constructed if they do not create major environmental problems.") **L2**

Journal Writing Tip

Clarifying Cause and Effect
Before students begin writing, help them see that just because events usually or always occur together, one does not necessarily cause the other. For example, migrating birds called warblers usually reappear in northern states when early spring flowers blossom, but the returning birds do not cause the flowers to bloom.

6.3

Teach

Using the Model

Help students see that McDonough concedes people's right to object to the killing of animals for their fur. She uses this concession to point out the inconsistency in her opponents' argument: If people think it's cruel to kill animals for their fur, why don't they protest the killing of animals for their skins and refuse to wear leather? **L2**

Two-Minute Skill Drill

Write the following on the board:
Don't vote for Donna for Class President. She isn't planning to go to college!
Have students identify the type of logical error (red herring) and explain why the sentence shows faulty reasoning.

See also *Two-Minute Skill Drill Transparency 6.3*

Additional Resources

For further stimuli for persuasive writing, see *Fine Art Transparencies* 29–32

Writing Process Transparencies 12, 28–32

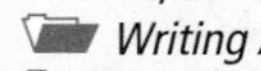
Writing Across the Curriculum
Cooperative Learning Activities
Thinking and Study Skills, pp. 14, 17–18
Sentence-Combining Practice, pp. 34–35
Listening and Speaking Activities, pp. 17, 22–23
Composition Practice, p. 48

Persuasive Writing

Analyze Your Opponent's Logic

Often you can strengthen your position in an argument by pointing out flaws in the opposing argument. To find the logical flaws in an argument, evaluate the information presented, point by point. Look for and identify any red herrings, oversimplifications, or faulty cause-and-effect relationships.

If, upon close examination, you find points in the opposing argument that are difficult to disprove, you may need to concede their worth or admit that those points are valid. Frequently, making reasonable concessions can strengthen your position and give readers the impression that they are reading a well-researched, unbiased argument.

In the following selection, Yona Zeldis McDonough points out some logical flaws in the argument against wearing fur coats. However, she also concedes some points to the opposition. Is her argument strengthened by the concessions she makes?

Literature Model

As I walked along 57th Street in Manhattan, a woman hissed, "A lot of animals were tortured to make that coat!" I was surprised, not by her sentiment, which I understood and even respected, but by her need to express it, unsolicited, in public. In the following weeks, I discovered that my outspoken critic was not alone. . . . Like it or not, I realized I was going to have to defend my coat against detractors.

I understand the arguments against wearing fur and have decided to wear one anyway. Not only does fur solve, more efficiently than any other substance known to man, the need for warmth, it has also been with us for hundreds if not thousands of years.

Since I eat meat, I find the distinction between wearing and eating arbitrary. Animals don't care whether their flesh is consumed or their skins are worn; the point is, they have died and we have killed them. This may sound cruel, but it is honest.

I would like to ask those women who keep shouting at me just how consistent they are: What about wearing leather and suede? Animals must be killed for those skins, too. Do all these women wear only sneakers and carry canvas bags?

Yona Zeldis McDonough, "Sisters Under the Skin,"
The *New York Times*

Notice that McDonough points out a key flaw in the opposing view.

What point does McDonough concede? How does she use it to expose weaknesses in her opponents' argument?

Meeting Individual Needs

English Language Learners

Choosing Words

Students learning English may have difficulty with some of the vocabulary in the Literature Model. Have each student write a list of words from the selection that he or she doesn't understand. Encourage students to try to figure out the meanings of these words by using context clues and dictionaries. Then pair each student with one who is proficient in English to help with the meanings of the words and to provide examples of their use in context.

6.3 Writing Activities

Write a Persuasive Argument

Write a brief report arguing to accept or reject each of these statements about relaxing a school's dress code. Evaluate each statement using sound logic.

1. The way students dress is one of the few things teenagers can control, and that independence shouldn't be restricted.
2. After the dress code at a nearby school was relaxed, the students' grade averages rose.
3. The dress code should be stricter because too many students concentrate on their looks rather than on their schoolwork.
4. Some students' dress expresses their ethnic and cultural diversity.
5. In addition to determining the dress code, students should also have a voice in choosing the books they read in class.

PURPOSE To write a persuasive argument evaluating the logic of certain statements
AUDIENCE A panel composed of teachers and school administrators
LENGTH 1 page

WRITING RUBRICS To write a persuasive argument, you should

- identify the kind of error or logical fallacy in each faulty statement
- explain how each faulty statement weakens the argument

Viewing and Representing

Review a popular television commercial and analyze the reasoning presented. Is the reasoning sound, or are red herrings, either/or thinking, cause-and-effect errors, or other logical fallacies presented? Write a paragraph explaining your findings, and share it with the class.

Using Computers

Some software programs can search writing for errors in grammar, usage, and mechanics. You might want to use such a program as you write. The program can aid the revising process, but you are still responsible for finding and correcting errors in reasoning.

Grammar Link

Use commas to set off parenthetical expressions and long introductory elements in sentences.

Rewrite the following sentences, adding commas where needed.

1. As you watch popular television programs you may ask yourself if they include too much violence.
2. During the course of the past few weeks a group has been monitoring programs to count the violent incidents.
3. The group's report shows that for the most part violence is depicted during prime time.
4. Although viewing violence may have no negative effects on older people constant exposure to violence may have a negative effect on young children.
6. Many parents as a matter of fact are convinced that they see evidence of violent behavior in their children.

See Lesson 21.6, pages 738–748.

LOG ON **Writing** Online — For more writing and grammar practice, go to **glencoe.com** and enter QuickPass code WC97727p1.

Persuasive Writing

Assess

Evaluation Rubrics

Write a Persuasive Argument

Use these criteria when evaluating your students' writing:

- Students' reports should present reasonable analyses of the logic of each of the statements.
- Statement 1 is an either/or error.
- Statement 2 is a cause-effect error.
- Statement 3 is an either/or error.
- Statement 4 is reasonable.
- Statement 5 is a red herring.

See also *Writing Assessment & Evaluation Rubrics*

Using Computers

Point out that when students use spelling checkers on their computers, they should always check to make sure that the suggested corrections are, in fact, warranted.

Reteaching

Composition Reteaching, p. 48

Enrichment

Composition Enrichment, p. 48

Close

Have students write an argument supporting their position on an issue such as extending the school year. Students should then exchange papers and evaluate each other's arguments.

Grammar Link

Answers

1. . . . television programs, you may . . .
2. . . . few weeks, a group . . .
3. . . . shows that, for the most part, violence . . .
4. . . . older people, constant . . .
5. . . . parents, as a matter of fact, are convinced . . .

Using Commas to Set Off Elements Have students check the drafts of their reports for correct comma usage. Where necessary, students should insert commas to set off introductory elements or parenthetical expressions.

Focus

Lesson Overview

Objectives

- To identify three criteria for making writing more precise and effective
- To define and use limiting words to avoid glittering generalities and oversimplifications
- To learn how to replace general words with more specific ones
- To improve word choice by selecting words with the right connotations

Skills

- using limiting words; using specific words; choosing connotations

Critical Thinking

- analyzing; categorizing; classifying; contrasting; evaluating; identifying

Listening and Speaking

- introducing; evaluating; questioning

Bellringer

Daily Language Activity

When students enter the classroom, have this assignment on the board: *Do you agree or disagree with the following statement? Teenagers are irresponsible.*

Grammar Link to the Bellringer

Tell students to use specific nouns and vivid modifiers to persuade others of their point of view. (Example: *Teens are actively involved in community affairs; many have focused, positive career goals.*)

See also *Daily Language Practice*

Motivating Activity

Tell students that overgeneralizations are most often all-inclusive statements. Such statements make sweeping claims without making exceptions. Invite students to suggest personal responses to the Bellringer statement. (Example: *I am extremely responsible, and so are my best friends.*)

Persuasive Writing

LESSON 6.4

Using Language to Advantage

You can make your writing more precise by using limiting words, by replacing general words with specific ones, and by understanding the connotations of the words you use.

You can't always persuade an audience to accept your argument. Empty adjectives and wild promises such as those in the cartoon fool no one. However, using words that precisely express your meaning will give you a better chance of persuading your readers.

Use Limiting Words

Limiting words are words that allow you to account for exceptions when you state your point of view. Use limiting words to avoid glittering generalities, oversimplifications, or gross exaggerations of the facts. For example, if you said, "Today's rock singers depend on sophisticated sound equipment to make up for their lack of musical talent," many of your readers would recognize that your point of view is a gross overstatement. On the other hand, if you said, "Some of today's rock

Resource Manager

Planning Resources
- *Lesson Plans*

Transparencies
- *Bellringer*
- *Daily Language Practice*
- *Fine Art* 29–32
- *Two-Minute Skill Drill*
- *Writing Process* 12, 28–32

Other Print Resources
- *Composition Enrichment,* p. 49
- *Composition Practice,* p. 49
- *Composition Reteaching,* p. 49
- *Cooperative Learning Activities,* pp. 25–28
- *Listening and Speaking Activities,* pp. 17, 22–23
- *Sentence-Combining Practice,* pp. 34–35
- *Thinking and Study Skills,* pp. 15, 18, 25
- *Writing Across the Curriculum*
- *Writing Assessment and Evaluation Rubrics*

singers depend on sophisticated sound equipment to make up for a lack of musical talent," you'd narrow your statement and allow for exceptions to it. *Some* is a limiting word. The chart below lists some common limiting words that you can use to avoid making overgeneralizations.

Limiting Words		
almost never	in most cases	occasionally
a minority of	less than half	often
as a rule	many	rarely
certain	more than half	seldom
few	most	several
frequently	mostly	some
half	nearly all	sometimes
hardly ever	nearly always	the majority of
in general	not all	usually

Use Specific Words

Make your persuasive writing more precise by replacing general words with specific ones whenever you can. For example, compare the following two sentences:

"Certain types of television programs have really bad effects on young children."
"Violent television shows cause violent behavior and nightmares in young children."

Because the second sentence provides more definite information and brings more vivid thoughts and images to mind, it is more likely to hold the reader's attention. You'll never convince your readers of anything if you can't hold their attention.

Revising Tip

During revising, try using a thesaurus to help you find precise words that express your meaning exactly. See Lesson 24.2, page 816.

Journal Writing

What strategies might you use to help identify glittering generalities, oversimplifications, or gross exaggerations of the facts? What strategies might you use to help you identify general words that could be replaced with more specific ones? Write your ideas in your journal.

Using Specific Words

Write on the board these words describing a concert: *great, dumb, wild, dull.* Mention that these are overused, vague words with many meanings and are therefore not persuasive because they leave the reader unsure of what the writer really means. Ask students to think of more precise words (for example, *outstanding, amateurish, exciting, unimaginative*). Discuss how more precise words could help persuade people to adopt the writer's opinion of the concert. (By specifying meanings, they suggest that the writer's perceptions are accurate.) **L1**

Two-Minute Skill Drill

Suggest that students write three or four sentences choosing some limiting words from the chart on this page. Then have them rewrite their sentences by substituting specific words for the limiting ones.

See also *Two-Minute Skill Drill Transparency 6.4*

Journal Writing Tip

Identifying Hierarchical Relationships Help students identify general words by noting the hierarchical distinctions used in dictionaries. If a dictionary lists several definitions for a word, the word is usually a general one. For example, *great* has several definitions, including *immense, extreme, important, outstanding,* and *noble.* Hierarchically, *great* is the more general word, and the others are more specific.

Teach

Using the Model

The phrase *make petty allegations* suggests Badenough's claims are trivial and unfounded. *Level charges* would connote legitimate criticism. Words such as *heroic* and *tirelessly* ennoble Edwards. *Gentleman* and *statesman* imply that he is above mere politics and indeed "will not lower himself" to that level. On the other hand, words such as *notorious* and *vicious* characterize Badenough as low and unscrupulous; *waffling* mocks his indecisiveness. **L2**

Promoting Discussion

To reinforce the concept of denotation and connotation, write these word pairs on the board: *group* and *mob, adequate* and *mediocre, friendly* and *chummy.* Explain that the words in each pair have similar denotations but differing connotations. Ask which word of each pair has the stronger connotation (*mob, mediocre, chummy*). Discuss the words' connotations. (A *mob* is an unruly group; *mediocre* is barely adequate; *chummy* connotes a close relationship that may put off others). **L1**

Additional Resources

For further stimuli for persuasive writing, see *Fine Art Transparencies* 29–32.

Writing Process Transparencies 12, 28–32

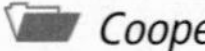

Cooperative Learning Activities

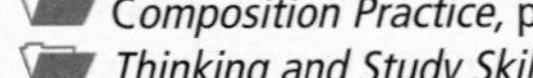

Writing Across the Curriculum

Composition Practice, p. 49

Thinking and Study Skills, pp. 15, 18, 25

Sentence-Combining Practice, pp. 34–35

Persuasive Writing

Consider Connotations

Choose words that not only express your specific meaning but also have the right connotation. *Connotation* refers to an emotion or an underlying value that accompanies a word's *denotation,* or dictionary meaning. Suppose, for instance, that you describe the famous smile in Leonardo da Vinci's painting, the *Mona Lisa,* as "weird." The word *weird* implies that there is something negative—not just unusual—about the smile. If, on the other hand, you refer to Mona Lisa's smile as "mysterious," you suggest that it is interesting and attractive.

Leonardo da Vinci, *Mona Lisa,* 1503–1505

Words with highly emotional connotations cause strong negative or positive responses. Consider the words *bold* and *reckless.* Although they have similar denotations, these words prompt very different emotional responses. *Bold* excites positive feelings because it suggests a daring, confident spirit. *Reckless* stirs up negative feelings because it implies irresponsibility.

In the following model, the writer uses the connotations of words to praise the candidate he supports and to establish arguments against the opposition.

Model

I heartily encourage you to vote for Don "Bud" Edwards for mayor. He is a man of action and notable accomplishments. As a former alderman, Bud battled tirelessly against the bureaucrats on the city council to guarantee inexpensive housing for the underprivileged. Furthermore, his heroic efforts on behalf of the elderly have been chronicled by prominent journalists across the country.

In contrast to Bud, his opponent, Gus Badenough, is notorious for his waffling stands on the issues and for his vicious opposition to Bud. In fact, he has attempted to obstruct Bud's valiant work for the homeless more than once. Now Gus has begun to make petty allegations, which our candidate will not lower himself to address.

Are we going to allow these smear tactics to succeed? I hope not. On election day, I believe that there will still be enough upstanding citizens to vote for a true gentleman and statesman, Bud Edwards.

Words such as "heroic" imply that Edwards nobly defends lost causes.

How would the tone of the piece be affected if you substituted the phrase "level charges" for "make petty allegations"?

What other words used in the model convey particular notions about Edwards and the candidate opposing him?

MEETING INDIVIDUAL NEEDS

English Language Learners

Using Language Effectively

A limited vocabulary may make it difficult for some students to use language effectively. Explain unfamiliar words in the model, paying attention to connotations of words such as *valiant, petty,* and *waffling.*

Viewing the Art

Leonardo da Vinci, *Mona Lisa,* 1503–1505

Leonardo da Vinci's *Mona Lisa,* (30¼ by 21 inches; in the Louvre, Paris) is a study of a woman, epitomizing the Renaissance interest in the individual. The Renaissance was an era of great cultural growth in Europe.

6.4 Writing Activities

Write a Positive Description

Write a paragraph describing the painting below, Pablo Picasso's *Two Acrobats with a Dog,* for your museum's newsletter. Try to inspire museum visitors to come to see the painting.

PURPOSE To write an appealing description of a painting
AUDIENCE Potential art museum visitors
LENGTH 1 paragraph

WRITING RUBRICS To write a positive description, you should

- use limiting words to prevent overgeneralizations
- choose precise words
- choose words with accurate denotations and positive connotations

Cross-Curricular Activity

MUSIC Write a brief review of a song you have heard recently. Use connotative words to evoke either a positive or a negative reaction in your readers and to persuade them to accept your opinion of the song.

Pablo Picasso, *Two Acrobats with a Dog,* 1905

Grammar*Link*

Use specific nouns and modifiers.

The sentences below describe a new cereal. Rewrite the sentences using specific nouns and vivid modifiers that will persuade readers to try this product. Consider the connotations of the words you substitute. Each sentence can be revised in more than one way.

1. You should buy this brand of breakfast cereal because it tastes good.
2. This cereal contains many things that are good for you.
3. The shapes of the flakes are interesting.
4. The flakes have a nice texture.
5. The cereal is more nutritious when served with different kinds of fruits.

See Lesson 10.1, page 439, and Lesson 10.4, page 461.

Using Computers

Compile a list of ten general terms of description. Using the thesaurus function on your computer, find at least three richer, more specific words for each general term. Create an accurately spelled list of the richer terms and keep it posted near your computer, in your journal, or wherever you do your writing.

LOG ON **Writing** Online | For more writing and grammar practice, go to **glencoe.com** and enter QuickPass code WC97727p1.

Assess

Evaluation Rubrics

Write a Positive Description

Use these criteria when evaluating your students' writing. Do students

- provide a clear description of the painting?
- choose precise words instead of general ones?
- avoid overgeneralizations?
- use vivid connotative words evoking reader reaction consistent with their opinion?

See also *Writing Assessment & Evaluation Rubrics*

Cross-Curricular Activity

Evaluate students' music reviews on the persuasiveness of the connotative words they chose and the clarity of their opinions.

Reteaching

Composition Reteaching, p. 49

Enrichment

Composition Enrichment, p. 49

Fine Art Transparencies 29–32

Close

Suggest students write an essay in support of a teacher-of-the year award for a school contest. Warn them to avoid overgeneralizations and to use specific words with positive connotations.

Grammar*Link*

Answers

Answers will vary:

1. . . . because it's naturally sweet without added sugar.
2. . . . is fortified with calcium and iron.
3. The flakes come in animal shapes.
4. . . . have a crunchy, chewy texture.
5. . . . served with your favorite fruits.

Viewing the Art

Pablo Picasso, *Two Acrobats with a Dog,* 1905

Two Acrobats with a Dog, 41½-by-29½ inches, is in the Museum of Modern Art in New York. Circus performers were a favorite subject of Picasso before he developed his Cubist style. Here he shows two young acrobats away from the glamour of the circus.

Focus

Lesson Overview

Objectives

- To identify criteria that make an editorial effective
- To select a contemporary issue as the topic of an editorial
- To learn how to craft a persuasive appeal by using striking images and humor
- To learn how to end an editorial by using a strong conclusion

Skills

- choosing an issue; appealing to one's audience; drawing a conclusion

Critical Thinking

- analyzing; synthesizing; categorizing; classifying; contrasting; identifying main idea; evaluating; summarizing; comparing; making inferences; establishing and evaluating criteria; defining and clarifying

Listening and Speaking

- discussing

Bellringer

Daily Language Activity

When students enter the classroom, have this assignment on the board: *List two political or social issues that are important to you. Write a sentence explaining how you feel about each issue.*

Grammar Link to the Bellringer

Tell students to underline the subject and verb in each sentence they have written.

See also  *Daily Language Practice*

Motivating Activity

Have students take turns reading their opinions from the Bellringer activity. Tell them to be prepared to defend their position in a class discussion.

LESSON 6.5

Writing an Editorial

Persuasive Writing

In an editorial, such as the one below, a writer expresses an opinion about a current news event or issue. An effective editorial is direct and absorbing and can move its readers to take action or to believe something. Do you think the argument in the model is effective?

Literature Model

Yesterday's announcement of a plan for U.S. and Soviet Olympic committees to test athletes for drugs is welcome news. It's also overdue. Sports organizations are fighting a losing battle against anabolic steroids, and the reason is that most don't have their hearts in the struggle. Only a handful of competitors, including Ben Johnson, the Canadian sprinter, were expelled from the Seoul Olympics for using the forbidden drugs. Yet, according to *The Times*'s recent series on drug use, probably half or more of the 9,000 athletes at Seoul had used steroids or similar drugs during training.

Steroid use has long been rampant, yet sports bodies from Olympic committees downward have been failing in their responsibility to deter it. Drug-using athletes set a dispiriting example to a society trying to fight drug abuse, especially to young people who are at grave risk of injury from the drugs. "The system is saying, do whatever it takes to win," says Bill Curry, football coach at Alabama.

. . . [D]iet and exercise are accepted ways of enhancing physical ability; drugs are not. Many athletes apparently take steroids not because they want to but from peer pressure or fear of losing to others who do. . . . Once the message is out that sports organizations are really serious about steroids, most athletes will probably abandon them with relief.

"Winking at Steroids in Sports," November 22, 1988,
The *New York Times*

The writer uses comments such as "It's also overdue" to express an opinion on the use of steroids.

What pieces of evidence does the writer use to support his opinion?

Resource Manager

Planning Resources

- *Lesson Plans*

Transparencies

- *Bellringer*
- *Daily Language Practice*
- *Fine Art* 29–32
- *Two-Minute Skill Drill*
- *Writing Process* 12, 28–32

Other Print Resources

- *Composition Enrichment,* p. 50
- *Composition Practice,* p. 50
- *Composition Reteaching,* p. 50
- *Cooperative Learning Activities,* pp. 25–28
- *Listening and Speaking Activities,* pp. 17, 22–23
- *Sentence-Combining Practice,* pp. 34–35
- *Thinking and Study Skills,* pp. 1, 5–7
- *Writing Across the Curriculum*
- *Writing Assessment and Evaluation Rubrics*

The New Television Season: Another Winning Lineup

What's Right with Rap

Fair Fare for Films

Whatever it is, it isn't art

Why do dancers always have to be on their toes?

Captive Audiences

Support your local drama club

Choose an Issue

Choose one issue about which you feel strongly and state it in the form of a question. If you don't have an issue in mind, get a sense of controversial topics in your community by reading local newspapers, talking to people, and listening to local talk shows on radio or television. Then brainstorm to generate evidence that supports your viewpoint. In the following example, two writers with opposing viewpoints answered this question: "Are rock musicians who lip-sync at live concerts cheating their fans?"

Yes, because . . .	Fans who pay high prices for concert tickets deserve to hear live music. People go to live concerts to hear live music. It's not as exciting for the fans; they might as well listen to a record.
No, because . . .	Today's concerts offer more than just singing. It's exciting just to be there at a live performance. The audience gets more for its money because shows are so extravagant.

Prewriting Tip

If you are having trouble coming up with evidence to support your argument, try to imagine a conversation on the subject with someone who holds an opposing view.

Journal Writing

In your journal, generate a list of currently controversial issues that interest you, and choose one that could be the topic of an editorial you might write. Then brainstorm to generate evidence that you could use to support your viewpoint.

Persuasive Writing

Teach

Using the Model

Ask students to identify examples of limiting words that the writer uses to avoid overgeneralizations or exaggerations in the editorial excerpt on page 304. (most, only a handful, probably half or more, especially, many) To support his opinion, the writer uses facts ("Only a handful of competitors, including Ben Johnson . . ."), statistics ("half or more of the 9,000 athletes at Seoul. . ."), and expert opinions (Bill Curry's statement). **L2**

Choosing an Issue

Some students may not be interested in controversial issues. Ask them to write a sentence about a personal issue that they feel strongly about, such as staying up late or being allowed more privileges at home. Then have them write and present an argument to support their viewpoint. **L1**

Two-Minute Skill Drill

Write the following sentences on the board. Then have students write the verb that completes each sentence.

No one (has, have) ever been able to convince me of that. Of all the people who read the editorial, only a few (was, were) persuaded by its argument.

See also *Two-Minute Skill Drill Transparency 6.5*

Journal Writing Tip

Categorizing Students might find it helpful to group their topics under different categories, such as political issues or the environment.

Teach

Using the Model

Discuss the image with which the student model begins—the list of banned books. Ask students why this is an effective opener. (It focuses the reader's attention and helps the reader identify with the writer. Picturing the list also reinforces the reality of the issue and leads directly to the discussion of what titles are on it and why.) Encourage students to come up with their own images for underscoring a viewpoint on a censorship issue. **L2**

Writing to an Official

Suggest that students write persuasive letters to government officials expressing their opinions and providing supporting evidence on issues that concern them. **L3**

Additional Resources

For further stimuli for persuasive writing, see *Fine Art Transparencies* 29–32.

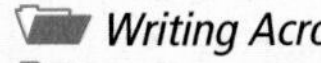

Writing Process Transparencies 12, 28–32

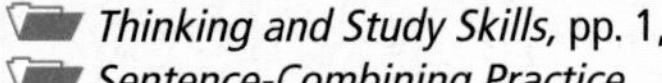

Writing Across the Curriculum
Cooperative Learning Activities
Thinking and Study Skills, pp. 1, 5–7
Sentence-Combining Practice, pp. 34–35
Listening and Speaking Activities, pp. 17, 22–23
Composition Practice, p. 50

Persuasive Writing

Appeal to Your Audience

Select evidence that will persuade your audience to take your stand. Keep in mind that a striking image can often speak more powerfully than a list of facts and statistics. For example, rather than saying "Thousands of people thronged the concert," you might say, "So many people attended the concert that the crowd that night formed the third largest city in the state."

You might also consider injecting some humor into your editorial. When you make your readers laugh, they may feel that they share common ground with you and, therefore, be more disposed to agree with what you're saying.

Draw a Conclusion

A good conclusion sums up the argument and spurs the reader to action. In the editorial below, Eugene Weresow makes his strongest point at the end.

Student Model

Hanging on my classroom wall is a long list of books that have been banned from certain schools. As I scanned the list, I recognized several that were among the best I've ever read, including *Catcher in the Rye, 1984,* and *Brave New World.* Although these books contain controversial language and situations, I believe it would be a mistake to ban them.

Admittedly, some of the characters in *Catcher in the Rye* use words that would be inappropriate in the classroom. But real people often swear and use slang expressions; the author is just trying to make his book realistic. Similarly, *1984* and *Brave New World* portray situations that some may consider unacceptable for political or social reasons. But the authors mean to convey a message with these works; the extreme situations they use make a more lasting impression upon the reader than would more acceptable situations.

I don't believe it is dangerous to expose students to the controversial material in these books. On the contrary, I believe the books should be valued for the ideas they express. Rather than protect impressionable students, those who ban these books do us a disservice: they deny us access to ideas.

Eugene Weresow, Edison High School, Edison, New Jersey

Weresow makes concessions to his opponents but counters their objections by discussing the intentions of the authors.

What is Weresow's strongest point?

Exploring Language

Choosing Words

Before students begin writing their editorials, have them list words related to their chosen issue. For example, if the topic is the environment, they might include words like *pollution, waste, recycling,* and so on. Allow students time to create useful definitions of their words.

6.5 Writing Activities

Write an Editorial for a TV Program

You have been asked to deliver a written editorial on *Teen Say,* a television program for teenagers, on the issue "Should the academic year be extended through July?"

PURPOSE To persuade your audience to accept your views on extending the school year
AUDIENCE Teenage TV viewers
LENGTH 2–3 paragraphs

WRITING RUBRICS To write an effective editorial, you should

- establish your position on the issue
- select evidence to persuade your audience
- summarize your argument with a strong conclusion

Using Computers

Suppose you want to send copies of your television editorial to several different teen magazines. Instead of typing multiple copies of your piece, use the Mail Merge feature of your word-processing program. Just type a list of the addresses to which you want to send the editorial. Then use Mail Merge to print as many copies as you want, each to a different address. Be sure you check your editorial for correct spelling and grammar before sending your copies.

Grammar*Link*

Make verbs agree with indefinite pronoun subjects.

A verb must agree with an indefinite pronoun subject, such as *each* or *several*:

***Each** (singular) **was** satisfactory.*
***Several** (plural) **were** tested.*

Rewrite each sentence, choosing the correct form of the verb in parentheses.

1. I inquired about certain books and was told that some (was, were) not available in the school library.
2. All (is, are) literary classics and (has been, have been) in print for a long time.
3. No one in the library (has, have) time to help me use the computer catalog to locate other books by that author.
4. Most (is, are) in different editions and (has been, have been) reprinted several times.
5. Though there are two copies, neither (is, are) on the shelf.

See Lesson 16.7, page 619.

Listening and Speaking

COOPERATIVE LEARNING In a small group, take turns reading aloud your editorials. After each person has presented his or her views, evaluate the editorial. Which part of the argument was the most persuasive? The least persuasive? What might have made the argument stronger? After you have read and discussed all of the editorials, decide what characteristics strong editorials have in common.

LOG ON **Writing** Online — For more writing and grammar practice, go to glencoe.com and enter QuickPass code WC97727p1.

Assess

Evaluation Rubrics

Write an Editorial for a TV Program

Use these criteria when evaluating your students' writing:

- Does the editorial take a definite position on the issue of extending the school year?
- Does it include evidence?
- Does it appeal to a teenage audience?
- Does it sum up the argument and call the reader to action?

See also *Writing Assessment & Evaluation Rubrics*

Using Computers

Before printing, make sure students proofread the list of addresses they typed in the Mail Merge feature.

Reteaching

Composition Reteaching, p. 50

Enrichment

Composition Enrichment, p. 50

Close

Pair up students who share strong feelings about a particular issue and direct them to state the issue in the form of a pro/con question. To brainstorm for evidence and opinions, both pro and con, each student should arbitrarily adopt one position and debate the issue with a partner, who adopts the other position.

Grammar*Link*

Answers

1. were
2. are; have been
3. has
4. are; have been
5. is

Focus

Lesson Overview

Objectives
- To identify six elements of a movie
- To learn how to evaluate a movie critically and write an effective review

Skills
- evaluating critically; writing a review

Critical Thinking
- providing background; developing criteria; comparing and contrasting

Listening and Speaking
- discussing movies in comparison to real life; listening to opinions of movies

Bellringer
Daily Language Activity
When students enter the classroom, have this assignment on the board: *What criteria do you use to judge the quality of a movie?*

Grammar Link to the Bellringer
Correct the modifiers underlined in the following sentences:
Claustrophobia was the worse movie I have ever seen.
Was it worst than *Arachnophobia*?

See also *Daily Language Practice*

Motivating Activity
Discuss students' responses to the Bellringer activity. Then talk about movies that students have seen recently, and encourage them to share their opinions of the movies. Ask if students read movie reviews. Discuss the role of persuasive writing in a movie review. (A reviewer tries to convince the reader either that the movie is worth seeing or that it is not. The reviewer supports the claim with reasons and evidence.)

Persuasive Writing

LESSON 6.6

Writing About Literature

Writing a Movie Review

A movie review is one person's evaluation of a film. Although critics may differ in their opinions, most critics go through a similar process in writing their reviews.

Scene from *Dances with Wolves*

Provide Background Information

Most critics begin a movie review by stating an opinion about a film. A reviewer, then, may provide background information on the film by briefly summarizing the plot and identifying the characters, actors, director, and scriptwriter. When you review a film, determine how much background information to include. Ask yourself what your audience already knows about the film and what they need to know to understand your review.

Examine the Movie's Elements

Reviewers often evaluate certain elements of the film and measure the film's success by specific criteria. These criteria differ somewhat for

Resource Manager

Planning Resources
- *Lesson Plans*

Transparencies
- *Bellringer*
- *Daily Language Practice*
- *Fine Art* 29–32
- *Two-Minute Skill Drill*
- *Writing Process* 12, 28–32

Other Print Resources
- *Composition Enrichment,* p. 51
- *Composition Practice,* p. 51
- *Composition Reteaching,* p. 51
- *Cooperative Learning Activities,* pp. 25–28
- *Listening and Speaking Activities,* pp. 17, 22–23
- *Sentence-Combining Practice,* pp. 34–35
- *Thinking and Study Skills,* pp. 21, 24
- *Writing Across the Curriculum*
- *Writing Assessment and Evaluation Rubrics*

different types of films. For example, a comedy can be judged according to how funny it is; an action film can be judged by how exciting it is. However, some criteria are useful for judging most movies. These are outlined in the chart below.

The Elements of a Movie	
Plot What happens in the film	Does it hold your interest? Does it seem plausible or contrived?
Theme The main idea or message that the film conveys.	Is the movie's theme significant? Does the film develop the theme, or does it oversimplify a complex subject?
Characterization The way the characters are developed by the scriptwriter and the director	Do the characters seem real? Believable? Are their motivations and actions true to their backgrounds and personalities?
Acting The way the actors portray their characters	Do the actors create believable characters? Do they evoke the intended responses in the audience—laughter, fear, sorrow?
Special Effects Techniques used to create illusions	Do special effects create the desired illusions? Do they enhance or overpower the story?
Sound Track The music that accompanies the visuals	Is the music appropriate to the scene in which it is used? What is the quality of the music? Is the sound track well recorded? Clear?

Journal Writing

Choose a movie that you have seen recently. Use the questions in the chart above to deconstruct, or analyze, the movie's elements and help you generate details that you could use in a movie review. Record the details in your journal.

Persuasive Writing

Teach

Understanding Movies

When Louis Lumière, an early French filmmaker, projected his footage of an approaching train, some moviegoers got out of the way, thinking the train was real. Ask students to identify similarities and differences between movies and real life. Ask what makes a character or plot believable. **L2**

Developing Movie Criteria

Suggest that students create a "top ten" list of movies. First, they might want to list candidates. Then they should list criteria for outstanding movies and apply these criteria to their top ten. **L3**

Two-Minute Skill Drill

Write the following sentences on the board and have students complete them, using the correct modifier —*more* or *(the) most.*

No one is ____ afraid of horror movies than I. Jane is ____ afraid than Kerry, but I am always the ____ afraid. I am ____ afraid of monster movies and ____ afraid of Frankenstein than of any other monster.

See also *Two-Minute Skill Drill Transparency 6.6*

Journal Writing Tip

Generating Details Some students may enjoy writing a review of a film that they disliked. Suggest that students begin with a movie they found boring or unbelievable.

Teach

Using the Model

The reviewer mentions special effects in the first paragraph and examines plot and character in the second. Students should note that she finds the movie interesting and entertaining, but less thoughtful and more conventional than the original *Terminator.* She compares *T2* to the original because many readers may have seen or read about the earlier film. **L2**

Conducting a Joint Review

Suggest that students who have seen and reviewed the same movie conduct a joint review for the class. They can give collaborating or contrasting views and respond to each other's points. Their classmates could evaluate each argument's persuasiveness. **L3**

Additional Resources

For further stimuli for persuasive writing, see *Fine Art Transparencies* 29–32.

Writing Process Transparencies 12, 28–32

Thinking and Study Skills, pp. 21, 24

Sentence-Combining Practice, pp. 34–35

Listening and Speaking Activities, pp. 17, 22–23

Composition Practice, p. 51

Persuasive Writing

Editing Tip

When you edit your review, set off the movie title by underlining it. If you use a computer, input the title in italic type. Capitalize the movie title correctly. Refer to Lesson 20.2, page 713, to review capitalization rules.

Evaluate the Movie Critically

Although you can approach a movie review in many ways, using the questions in the chart below may help you develop your own perspective to evaluate a movie. Read the checklist, then study student Lina Chern's review.

A Critic's Checklist

1. Can I compare or contrast this film with another that explores the same theme?
2. Is this film adapted from a written work, such as a novel or a play? If so, can I compare the film to the original work?
3. Can I compare my reactions with those of the audience?
4. Can I critique the film from a particular social or political perspective? Am I well informed enough to do so?

Student Model

I must admit that I was not expecting terrific results from *Terminator 2: Judgment Day,* the most eagerly awaited sequel of the summer. After all, its predecessor was one of the most thoughtful, understated action movies ever made, while *T2* was promising to be a typical overblown summer blockbuster. I was only half-correct—the story has lost some thought and subtlety and gained a great deal of special effects, but is still interesting and definitely entertaining.

What elements of *T2* does Chern examine in her review?

Arnold Schwarzenegger (too marketable now to play the bad guy) stars as a reprogrammed Terminator cyborg that is ordered to go back in time to protect the still-adolescent John Connor (Edward Furlong); the boy is to become a key figure in the future war between humans and machines. After John and the Terminator rescue John's mother, Sarah (Linda Hamilton)—now a tough, hell-bent warrior—from a mental hospital, the three set out to prevent the coming nuclear holocaust, or Judgment Day. Meanwhile, they have to deal with another, more advanced Terminator that has been sent back to kill John.

What is Chern's opinion of the movie? Why do you think she compares *T2* with the original *Terminator* to express her opinion?

In general, *Terminator 2* is engaging and creative, but in a more conventional way than the original. It is a clean, slick moneymaker, which should not deter anyone from seeing it.

Lina Chern, Maine East High School, Park Ridge, Illinois

MEETING INDIVIDUAL NEEDS

English Language Learners

Reviewing a Movie

Students whose first language is not English might do their prewriting orally, using a tape recorder. Ask students to work in pairs. Partners can ask each other questions from the charts and boxes in this lesson, helping each other develop examples to use in their reviews. Students may wish to review movies from their native countries. Students might also like to discuss American films from their own cultural perspectives, perhaps commenting on the character types portrayed or the values expressed.

6.6 Writing Activities

Write a Movie Review

Select a film known for its special effects and review it for the readers of your school newspaper. Base your review on an evaluation of the movie's use of special effects.

PURPOSE To write a movie review
AUDIENCE Readers of your school newspaper
LENGTH 1–2 paragraphs

WRITING RUBRICS To write an effective movie review, you should

- provide background information
- discuss whether special effects enhance or overpower the movie
- explain whether the special effects create the desired illusions
- compare the special effects to those in another movie
- explain the audience's response

Cross-Curricular Activity

LITERATURE Choose one of the films listed below or another you have seen that is based on a work of literature. Then prepare a written review of the film in which you compare it with the original work of literature. If you like, submit the review for publication in your school's literary journal or newspaper.

- *Wuthering Heights*
- *A Raisin in the Sun*
- *The Grapes of Wrath*
- *Great Expectations*
- *The Age of Innocence*
- *Beauty and the Beast*
- *Howards End*
- *Out of Africa*
- *Elmer Gantry*
- *A Passage to India*
- *The Color Purple*
- *Mansfield Park*

Grammar*Link*

Use comparative and superlative forms of modifiers correctly.

more conventional, one of the most thoughtful

Rewrite the following sentences. Use the correct degree of comparison of the modifiers in parentheses.

1. *The Nightmare Before Christmas* is one of the _______ films I have ever seen. (good)
2. It is ________ than other animated films. (thought provoking)
3. My little brother thought that the creatures in this movie sang _______. (beautifully)
4. The special effects in *Nightmare* are _______ than those in *E.T.* (imaginative)
5. The words of the songs are the _______ I have ever heard. (witty)

See Lesson 18.1, pages 659–660.

Using Computers

Analyze the way an online movie reviewer and a movie critic for a print newspaper or magazine evaluate the same film. What do the two reviews have in common? What differences do you notice? How do you account for those differences? Write a one-page essay comparing and contrasting the reviews. Share your essay with a partner.

Persuasive Writing

LOG ON **Writing** Online For more writing and grammar practice, go to glencoe.com and enter QuickPass code WC97727p1.

Assess

Evaluation Rubrics

Write a Movie Review

Use the following criteria to evaluate your students' movie reviews:

- Is background information provided to help readers understand the film?
- Is there supporting evidence for the evaluation of special effects?
- Have special effects been compared to those in another movie?
- Is the audience response to the movie included?

See also *Writing Assessment & Evaluation Rubrics*

Cross-Curricular Activity

The review should

- compare a movie with the literary work on which it is based
- use specific examples from both written and film versions
- evaluate each version's comparative success

Reteaching

Composition Reteaching, p. 51

Enrichment

Composition Enrichment, p. 51

Close

Have students discuss why a movie review is effective when it compares two movies. Then discuss how important the analysis of character development and other elements is to the success of a movie review.

Grammar*Link*

Answers

1. best
2. more thought provoking
3. beautifully *or* the most beautifully
4. more imaginative
5. wittiest

Focus

Lesson Overview

Objective

- To use persuasive writing techniques in a short editorial

Skills

- using the five stages of the writing process: prewriting, drafting, revising, editing/proofreading, and publishing/presenting; using supporting evidence; stating a central claim; using limiting words, specific words, and connotations

Critical Thinking

- establishing and evaluating criteria; defining and clarifying; analyzing; summarizing

Listening and Speaking

- discussing; evaluating, questioning; interviewing; listening to a persuasive argument

Bellringer
Daily Language Activity

When students enter the classroom, have this assignment on the board: *Describe a situation when you tried very strongly to persuade others to adopt your point of view. What were your most convincing pieces of evidence?*

Grammar Link to the Bellringer

Have students check each other's work for specific nouns and modifiers. Were they used with appropriate connotations? If not, what revisions can students suggest?

See also *Daily Language Practice*

Motivating Activity

Discuss students' responses to the Bellringer activity. Was it easy or difficult to be convincing? Tell students that this lesson will help them apply the information in Unit 6 in order to make their written arguments more effective.

UNIT 6

Writing Process in Action

Persuasive Writing

Persuasive Writing

In this unit you've learned about writing to persuade and about the logical considerations that contribute to presenting a strong and well-supported argument. You've learned how to write reviews, articles, and editorials. Now it's time to apply what you've learned. In this lesson you will select a problem in your school or community and take a stand in favor of whatever corrective action you think is appropriate.

Assignment

Context

You are an editor of *Student Voices,* a monthly newsletter with a broad circulation in your school and community. You have been asked to write an editorial about a problem situation or an injustice you want to see changed. This is your opportunity to reach people who make policies and decisions that affect your life, but who might not listen to you otherwise.

Purpose

To write an editorial that exposes a problem or injustice and encourages readers to take corrective action

Audience

Teenagers, teachers, school administrators, and community members

Length

2 paragraphs

Planning to Write

The following pages can help you plan and write your editorial. Read through them and then refer to them as you need to. But remember, you're in charge of your own writing process. As always, give yourself a time frame for completing this editorial. This helps you to plan your writing and pace yourself. Be sure to keep in mind the controlling idea: to write an editorial that exposes a problem or injustice and encourages readers to take corrective action.

LOG ON **Writing Online**

For prewriting, drafting, revising, editing and publishing tools, go to **glencoe.com** and enter QuickPass code WC97727p1.

Resource Manager

Planning Resources
- *Lesson Plans*

Transparencies
- *Bellringer*
- *Daily Language Practice*
- *Writing Process* 12, 28–32

Other Print Resources
- *Composition Enrichment,* p. 52
- *Composition Practice,* p. 52
- *Composition Reteaching,* p. 52
- *Grammar Workbook,* Lessons 98–105
- *Sentence-Combining Practice,* pp. 34–35
- *Thinking and Study Skills,* pp. 5, 23
- *Writing Assessment and Evaluation Rubrics*

Web Site
- *glencoe.com*

Writing Process in Action

Prewriting

What problems or injustices are on your mind? The suggestions in Prewriting Options may help you explore your thoughts.

Choose two or three problems that you have identified. Using lists or questions, explore the problems you've identified (see Lesson 2.2, page 62). Write down everything you can think of related to each problem. Think about your purpose and the best way to influence your audience. Read what you have written about each problem. Then ask yourself the following questions, and use the answers to narrow your choices to one topic:

- What problem do I care about the most?
- What claim do I feel the most confidence in making?
- About which topic are my readers most likely to share my concern?

Once you've narrowed your choice down to one topic, review your purposes—to persuade your readers that your claim is valid and to rouse them to take corrective action. Then take some time to think about your audience. Are your readers likely to agree or disagree with you? Do they already care about the issue, or must you persuade them to care? Persuading readers to act upon your argument may require meeting their needs and addressing or changing their attitudes.

Finally, begin to gather and evaluate statistics, opinions, examples, and other evidence that will help you back up your central claim.

Prewriting Options

- Review your journal writing.
- Check school and community newspapers.
- Freewrite; complete the sentence "It bothers me that . . . "
- Brainstorm to list and classify problems and injustices.

TIME

For more about the writing process, see **TIME Facing the Blank Page**, pp. 121-131.

Drafting

When you write persuasively, you want to present information in a way that will have a strong impact on your readers. To achieve this goal, use language that is forceful and direct. Choose specific words with strong connotations, as Clara Spotted Elk does in the excerpt on page 314.

Drafting Tip

For help in writing an editorial, see Lesson 6.5, pages 304–307.

Teach

Prewriting

Choosing an Issue

To help students choose an issue, discuss the questions on this page. If they choose an issue they care deeply about, they will need to sort out their feelings in order to use them effectively in an argument. If they have a well-supported claim, they should use the most convincing evidence (facts, statistics, expert opinions). If reader appeal is their main concern, they should concentrate on humor, expression of commonly held values, and the use of examples. **L2**

Developing Ideas for Persuasive Writing

To help students get ideas for an editorial topic, tell the class that they have the chance to speak out now about local issues that concern them. Start the discussion by bringing up school issues currently under consideration, such as changing the dress code or eliminating a particular extracurricular activity. Let students suggest other controversial local issues as you write them on the board. **L1**

Drafting

Using the Model

Students may require help dealing effectively with the connotative language in the model on page 314. Ask why the author used *outraged* instead of *upset.* (*Outrage* connotes moral indignation and deeply felt anger in response to a violation of decency.) Why did she choose *desecrated* instead of *dug up?* (*Desecrated* connotes a violation of the graves' spiritual sanctity.) **L2**

Teach

Revising

Peer Editing

Students can work in writing conferences with peer editors before they revise their work. You may want to duplicate the Peer Response forms in *Writing Assessment & Evaluation Rubrics.* Suggest that peer editors respond to the following questions:

- What is the writing trying to persuade the reader to believe?
- Do logical reasons back up the argument?
- Can I understand the argument and the reasons behind it?
- Does the writer use a variety of kinds of evidence to support the main claim (facts, statistics, examples, opinions, reasons)?
- Is each piece of evidence convincing or not convincing, and why? **L2**

Cooperative Learning

Have students work together in groups. Each member can read aloud his or her persuasive argument. Listeners should notice whether the argument flows smoothly, transitions are clear, and the logic is understandable. Readers should try to use appropriate posture and eye contact, as well as pitch and tone of voice to help persuade the listeners. **L2**

Additional Resources

 *Writing Process Transparencies* 12, 28–32

 *Thinking and Study Skills,* pp. 5, 23

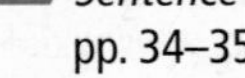 *Sentence-Combining Practice,* pp. 34–35

Composition Practice, p. 52

 *Grammar Workbook,* Lessons 98–105

Persuasive Writing

Literature Model

We are outraged that our religious views are not accepted by the scientific community and that the graves of our ancestors are desecrated. Many tribes are willing to accommodate some degree of study for a limited period of time—provided that it would help Indian people or mankind in general. But how many "specimens" are needed? We will not accept grave robbing and the continued hoarding of our ancestors' remains.

Clara Spotted Elk, "Skeletons in the Attic"

Revising Tip

For suggestions on checking the logic of your arguments, see Lesson 6.3, pages 296–299.

You might choose to state your claim forcefully at the start, then present the evidence and reinforce it with a strong conclusion. Alternatively, you can build up to your central claim, which you state last. As you present your evidence, address opposing arguments. Prove the arguments to be false, or concede them in some way.

Once you've built your case, write a conclusion that will leave a strong impression. Summarize your main points, state or restate your central claim, and urge readers to take action.

Revising Checklist

- Have I presented my central claim clearly?
- Is my evidence accurate and relevant?
- Is my reasoning sound?
- Have I presented my case in a way that will appeal to my audience?

Revising

To begin revising, read over your draft to make sure that what you've written fits your purpose and audience. Then have a writing conference. Read your draft to a partner or small group. Use your audience's reactions to help you evaluate your work.

Enrichment and Extension

Follow-up Ideas

- Set aside time for students to celebrate the conclusion of their writing projects. Encourage them to share their finished pieces with the whole class or in small groups.
- Help students organize their work for public display.

Extending Persuasion

- Help students brainstorm ways they can use their skills in persuasive writing in other areas, such as convincing the school administration to allow a new student activity or writing an editorial for a local newspaper.
- Let students write letters persuading the public to start new health habits.

Editing/Proofreading

At this stage, look closely at your writing, paying special attention to your use of language. As you **proofread,** check for errors in grammar, spelling, usage, and mechanics. Use the questions in the checklist as a guide. Then use the self-evaluation list below to make sure that your editorial satisfies your purpose and communicates your message exactly as you want it to.

Self-Evaluation

Make sure your editorial—

- ✔ focuses on a school or community injustice
- ✔ contains a central claim and identifies a main purpose for writing
- ✔ supports the central claim with accurate and relevant evidence
- ✔ uses sound reasoning and addresses counter-arguments
- ✔ uses limiting words, specific words, and connotations to advantage
- ✔ uses correct grammar, spelling, usage, and mechanics

Editing/Proofreading Checklist

- Have I chosen the correct word of a confusing pair?
- Have I used commas to separate introductory and parenthetical elements from the rest of a sentence?
- Have I used specific nouns and modifiers with appropriate connotations?
- Have I checked the spelling of any unfamiliar words?

Persuasive Writing

Publishing/Presenting

You can submit your editorial to the student newspaper, or you might consider using your article as the starting point for a campaign in support of your position. You can rework your editorial into a petition or a leaflet, or even present it as a speech.

Proofreading Tip

For proofreading symbols, see pages 98 and 411. You can use a computerized spelling or grammar checker to help you edit and proofread your work.

Journal Writing: Write to Learn

Reflect on your writing process experience. What do you like best about your editorial? What was the hardest part of writing it? What did you learn in your writing conference? What new things have you learned as a writer? Write your answers in your journal.

Editing/Proofreading

Peer Editing

After students have edited their own work, have them edit another student's writing. Remind them to refer to the Editing Checklist on page 315. **L2**

Publishing/Presenting

Before students present their persuasive writing, discuss how to prepare their papers for publication. Emphasize the importance of the final draft, which must be legible and free of errors.

Journal Writing Tip

Reflecting on the Experience

Ask students to think about what, if anything, they would change if they were to write another persuasive essay.

Assess

Evaluation Rubric

Use the following questions to evaluate the students' finished writing.

Does it

- focus on one problem or injustice?
- clearly state one central claim?
- support its claim with evidence?
- use sound reasoning?
- address counterarguments and make concessions?
- follow correct grammar, usage, and mechanics?

See also *Writing Assessment & Evaluation Rubrics*

Reteaching

Composition Reteaching, p. 52

Enrichment

Composition Enrichment, p. 52

Close

Inform students that as young people they may think they have little influence on community decision makers, but in fact teenagers can be very powerful. Invite students to think about how they can take their persuasive argument to community leaders.

About the Author

Clara Spotted Elk is one of the Northern Cheyenne people. The group's reservation is in southeastern Montana, approximately 40 miles from the site of the Battle of Little Bighorn ("Custer's Last Stand"). Spotted Elk is a college teacher, consultant, and lobbyist. She worked for five years in Washington, D.C., to promote the enactment of the "Bones Bill."

Focus

Lesson Overview

Objectives

- To evaluate the use of persuasive evidence by a published author whose work effected change
- To observe the quality of voice in professional writing
- To write a problem-solution essay

Skills

- questioning; connecting; clarifying

Critical Thinking

- evaluating

Listening and Speaking

- discussing ideas; questioning; listening to persuasion

Bellringer

Daily Language Activity

When students enter the classroom, have this assignment on the board: *Have you ever had to persuade a parent or another adult to agree with a proposed action? What did you do to convince him or her?*

See also  *Daily Language Practice*

Motivating Activity

Discuss students' responses to the Bellringer activity. How might kinds of arguments differ if students were trying to convince a large group of people? In this lesson, students will learn about persuasion in writing.

UNIT 6

Literature Model

Persuasive Writing

SKELETONS IN THE ATTIC

by Clara Spotted Elk

Clara Spotted Elk has worked to help her fellow Native Americans regain the skeletal remains of their ancestors from museums, collectors, and federal agencies. In September of 1989, thanks in part to persuasive efforts such as hers, the Smithsonian Institution began returning some of these remains to their Native American descendants. As you read the following article, note how Spotted Elk expresses her point of view on this cultural issue. Then try the activities in Linking Writing and Literature on page 320.

Resource Manager

Planning Resources

- *Lesson Plans*

Transparencies

- *Bellringer*
- *Daily Language Practice*
- *Fine Art* 29–32

Other Print Resources

- *Listening and Speaking Activities,* pp. 17, 22–23
- *Thinking and Study Skills,* p. 25
- *Writing Assessment and Evaluation Rubrics*

Web Sites

- *writerschoice.glencoe.com*
- *lit.glencoe.com*

Literature Model

Millions of American Indians lived in this country when Columbus first landed on our shores. After the western expansion, only about 250,000 Indians survived. What happened to the remains of those people who were decimated by the advance of the white man? Many are gathering dust in American museums.

In 1985, I and some Northern Cheyenne chiefs visited the attic of the Smithsonian's[1] Natural History Museum in Washington, D.C., to review the inventory of their Cheyenne collection. After a chance inquiry, a curator[2] pulled out a drawer in one of the scores of cabinets that line the attic. There were the jumbled bones of an Indian. "A Kiowa,"[3] he said.

Subsequently, we found that 18,500 Indian remains—some consisting of a handful of bones, but mostly full skeletons—are unceremoniously stored in the Smithsonian's nooks and crannies. Other museums, individuals, and federal agencies such as the National Park Service also collect the bones of Indian warriors, women, and children. Some are on display as roadside tourist attractions. It is estimated that another 600,000 Indian remains are secreted away in locations across the country.

The museum community and forensic[4] scientists vigorously defend these grisly[5] collections. With few exceptions, they refuse to return remains to the tribes that wish to rebury them, even when grave robbing has been documented. They want to maintain adequate numbers of "specimens" for analysis and say they are dedicated to "the permanent curation of Indian skeletal remains."

Indian people are tired of being "specimens." The Northern Cheyenne word for ourselves is "tsistsistas"—human beings. Like people the world over, one of our greatest responsibilities is the proper care of the dead.

Other museums, individuals, and federal agencies . . . also collect the bones of Indian warriors, women, and children. . . . It is estimated that another 600,000 Indian remains are secreted away in locations across the country.

We are outraged that our religious views are not accepted by the scientific community and that the graves of our ancestors are desecrated.[6] Many tribes are willing to accommodate some degree of study for a limited period of time—provided that it would help Indian people or mankind in general. But how many "specimens" are needed? We will not accept grave robbing and the continued hoarding of our ancestors' remains.

---

1 **Smithsonian** the Smithsonian Institution, a research organization administered by the United States government
2 **curator** (kyoo rā´ tər) a person in charge of a museum
3 **Kiowa** (kī´ ə wä) a Plains people formerly of what is now Colorado, Oklahoma, Kansas, New Mexico, and Texas
4 **forensic** (fə ren´ sik) able to apply medical knowledge to legal matters
5 **grisly** (griz´ lē) horrible; ghastly
6 **desecrate** (des´ ə krāt´) to treat something considered holy in an inappropriate manner

Persuasive Writing

Teach

Active Reading Strategies

Connect Ask students how they might feel if they discovered that the remains of their great-grandparents were kept in a drawer at the Smithsonian. *(Students may express a variety of responses, including shock, sadness, or outrage.)*

6+1 Trait® Writing

Voice Ask students: "Whose voice are you listening to in this essay?" *(the voice of the author, Clara Spotted Elk, and probably other Native Americans)* Ask students whether they can hear this voice loud and clear. If so, why? *(The voice is loud and clear. Word choices like* unceremoniously stored, specimens, *and* outraged *all help to create a strong and angry tone. Beginning the essay with the mention of loss of millions of American Indian lives also helps establish the theme of injustice. The reader senses the voice of an emotionally involved author.)*

For more information on voice and the 6+1 Trait® model, see **Writing and Research Handbook,** pages 947–949.

Active Reading Strategies

Question

Tell students that *questioning* what they read can help them understand a selection. Suggest that students ask these questions as they read:

- Is this idea important? Why?
- Do I understand what this is about?
- What questions can I ask about the selection to test my understanding?

Model questioning this way: "The author begins one of her paragraphs with 'Indian people are tired of being "specimens."' I ask myself if this is a main idea. After rereading, I think it is. The author doesn't want so many Indian remains to be locked in drawers. This is one of her main points."

Practice After students read this page, ask them to formulate and answer a question about what they read. Students can then share their questions and answers.

Teach

Active Reading Strategies

Clarify Ask students to state the writer's argument. *(The remains of Indians should not be regarded as scientific specimens. Indians should have the right to determine how the bones of their ancestors are treated.)*

Critical Thinking

Evaluate Ask students: "Does the author do a good job of persuading you? Why?" *(Students may say Clara Spotted Elk achieves her purpose by citing the fact that one of the greatest responsibilities of Native American peoples is the care of the dead. Clara Spotted Elk's use of a religious context for her argument may also sway students.)*

Additional Resources

For further stimuli for persuasive writing, see *Fine Art Transparencies* 29–32.

Listening and Speaking Activities, pp. 17, 22–23

Thinking and Study Skills, p. 25

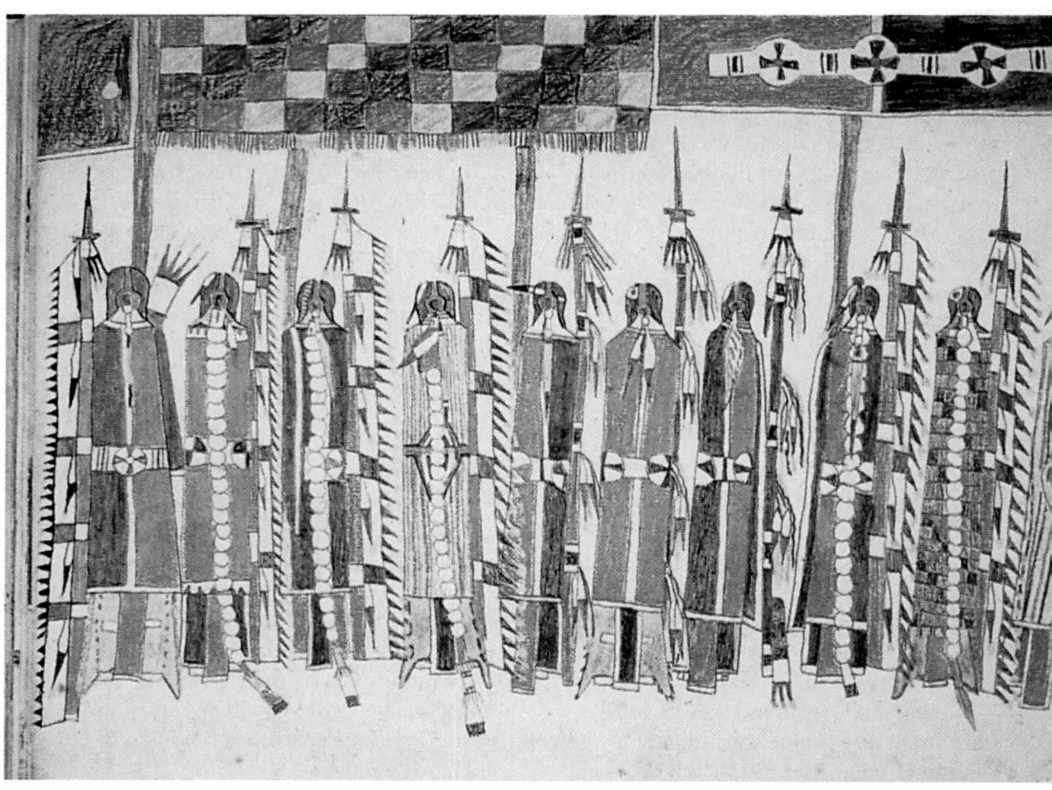

Howling Wolf, Untitled drawing, 1876

Would this be tolerated if it were discovered that it affected other ethnic groups? (Incidentally, the Smithsonian also collects skeletons of blacks.) What would happen if the Smithsonian had 18,500 Holocaust victims in the attic? There would be a tremendous outcry in this country. Why is there no outcry about the Indian collections?

Indians are not exotic creatures for study. We are human beings who practice living religions. Our religion should be placed not only on a par with science when it comes to determining the disposition of our ancestors, but on a par with every other religion practiced in this country.

To that end, Sen. Daniel K. Inouye (D.-HI)[7] will soon reintroduce the "Bones Bill" to aid Indians in retrieving the remains of their ancestors from museums. As in

7 **(D.-HI)** Democrat, Hawaii

Viewing the Art

Howling Wolf, Untitled drawing, 1876

Howling Wolf, a Southern Cheyenne, was among the seventy-two Native Americans from five Plains nations taken hostage by U.S. authorities in 1875. Some of the captives had fought to defend their rights guaranteed by government treaties; others, including Howling Wolf, were rounded up arbitrarily. The drawing, 8⅜ by 11 inches, comes from a sketchbook the artist kept while a prisoner and is now in the archives of the New York State Library, Albany. This drawing is a stylized depiction of dancers.

the past, the "Bones Bill" will most likely be staunchly resisted by the collectors of Indian skeletons—armed with slick lobbyists,[8] lots of money, and the mystique[9] of science.

Scientists have attempted to defuse this issue by characterizing their opponents as radical Indians, out of touch with their culture and with little appreciation of science. Armed only with a moral obligation to our ancestors, the Indians who support the bill have few resources and little money.

Indians are not exotic creatures for study. We are human beings who practice living religions.

But, in my view, the issue should concern all Americans, for it raises very disturbing questions. American Indians want only to reclaim and rebury their dead. Is this too much to ask?

8 **lobbyists** (lob′ ē ists) people who work to influence laws and government decisions in favor of one special-interest group
9 **mystique** (mi stēk′) a set of mysterious feelings and attitudes surrounding a person, group, or activity

Active Reading Strategies

Question Ask students to frame a question about the main idea on this page. *(Sample response: According to the author, what is the view of the scientists in this matter?)* Have students answer their own question. *(Sample response: Scientists don't want to face this issue. They try to defuse the issue by calling the Indians who pose it "radical" and "out of touch with their culture.")*

6+1 Trait® Writing

Voice

Explain to students that persuasive writing often features a forceful voice. When a writer feels strongly about an argument and incorporates emotional word choices, engaging ideas, or even risky content, his or her personality comes through. Read aloud the first full paragraph on this page. Note how the emphasis in the first sentence could fall on *radical* and point out how negative that sounds. Similarly, note how sympathetically, or even sadly, one might read the last words of the paragraph: "few resources and little money."

Practice Write the last sentence from the essay on the board: "Is this too much to ask?" Ask how students hear it. Call for volunteers to create the tone aloud. Then have students discuss how this sentence shows the writer's strong commitment to her topic.

For more information on voice and the 6+1 Trait® model, see **Writing and Research Handbook,** pages 947–949.

Linking Writing and Literature

Assess

Evaluation Rubrics

Talk About Reading

Possible responses to the questions:

1. Answers will vary but should be supported with details from the selection.
2. Students may suggest, for example, that people who have felt the sting of prejudice due to their ethnic background or any other reason may side with the author. They may also suggest that some scientists might argue against the author's position.
3. Yes, because it strikes a meaningful and critical tone right at the outset of the essay. Skeletons in the attic (or closet) are not good things.
4. Clara Spotted Elk mentions the "Bones Bill" as a solution but does not explain it. She wants the remains returned but doesn't suggest a timeline or other compromise by which a difficult issue could be worked out. Students might suggest that interested readers could band together and send letters to the relevant authorities.

Write About Reading

The essay should do the following:

- suggest a reasonable solution
- reflect knowledge of both sides of the issue
- present solutions in a moderate, reasonable voice

Close

Hold a brief point/counterpoint debate responding to the views expressed in this article. One side can represent people who support the bill and the other side, people opposed to it. Have the class vote on the persuasiveness of the arguments.

Linking Writing and Literature

Learning to Learn

Think about the problem Clara Spotted Elk describes. Jot it down, along with some possible solutions.

Talk About Reading

With a group, discuss "Skeletons in the Attic." Appoint a leader to keep your discussion focused and someone to take notes. Use the questions below to guide you.

1. **Connect to Your Life** Is this an issue you could see yourself becoming personally involved in? Why or why not?
2. **Critical Thinking: Evaluate** Different people will judge the ideas in this essay in different ways. Comment on how you think a person's age, ethnic background, gender, occupation, or other characteristics might influence his or her response.
3. **6+1 Trait®: Voice** "Skeletons in the Attic" is a phrase that refers to embarrassments and unpleasant things that have been hidden from view. Do you think this title helps the author create her unique voice in this essay? Why or why not?
4. **Connect to Writing** Does Clara Spotted Elk do a good job of suggesting a solution to the problem she outlines? Find places in the essay where she suggests or hints at a solution. Then decide how willing you think a general audience might be to work on her proposed solutions.

Write About Reading

Write a Solution to the Problem
Write an essay in which you suggest a reasonable solution to the problem discussed in "Skeletons in the Attic." Be sure to consider both the writer's point of view and the opposing point of view.

Focus on Voice Use your voice to show that you are involved in the issue and take a moderate approach to it. When you have completed a draft, read your essay aloud to be sure you sound both reasonable and informed.

For more information on voice and the 6+1 Trait® model, see **Writing and Research Handbook,** pages 947–949.

UNIT 6 Review

Reflecting on the Unit: Summarizing What You Learned

Focus on the following questions to summarize what you learned in this unit.

1. What are the most important elements of persuasive writing?
2. What are some steps to take in constructing a logical argument?
3. What are some criteria for selecting, evaluating, and using evidence?
4. How can choice of words make an argument more persuasive?
5. What are the purpose and the elements of an editorial?
6. What criteria might you use to judge and review a movie?

Adding to Your Portfolio

CHOOSE A SELECTION FOR YOUR PORTFOLIO Look over the persuasive writing you have done during this unit. Select a completed piece to put into your portfolio. The piece you choose should show some or all of the following:

- logical, accurate, relevant evidence to support a claim
- limiting words, specific words, and words with appropriate connotations
- strong evidence, a striking image, or humor to appeal to an audience

REFLECT ON YOUR CHOICE Attach a note to the piece you chose, explaining briefly why you chose it and what you learned from it.

SET GOALS How can you improve your writing? What skill will you focus on the next time you write?

Writing Across the Curriculum

MAKE A CIVICS CONNECTION How do you feel about the large percentage of the population that does not vote in elections? Is voting a citizen's responsibility that should be encouraged? Is not voting a positive way to express dissatisfaction with the candidates? Develop an argument in which you define your position on this topic. Be sure to identify your purpose, state your central claim, and support it with relevant and logical evidence.

Review

Reflecting on the Unit

You may have students respond to Reflecting on the Unit by writing a summary of what they've learned or through discussion.

Adding to Your Portfolio

As students decide what to include in their portfolios, remind them to choose pieces that show them most in command of the persuasive writing skills covered in this unit, including use of logical arguments, substantiated evidence, and logical reasoning.

Portfolio Evaluation

If you grade the portfolio selections, you may want to award two marks—one each for content and form. Explain your assessment criteria before students make their selections.

Commend
- experimentation with creative prewriting techniques
- clear, concise writing in which the main idea, audience, and purpose are evident
- successful revisions
- work that shows a flair for language

Writing Across the Curriculum

Remind students to avoid oversimplification when presenting their arguments. Encourage them to check their reasoning for either/or thinking and cause-and-effect errors.

ASSESSMENT OPTIONS

Tests with Answer Key & Rubrics
Unit 6 Choice A Test, p. 21
Unit 6 Choice B Test, p. 22
Unit 6 Composition Objective Test, pp. 23–24

Testmaker
Unit 6 Choice A Test
Unit 6 Choice B Test
Unit 6 Composition Objective Test

You may wish to administer one of these tests as a mastery test.

MindJogger Videoquizzes

UNIT 7

Viewing the Art

This photograph of a winding path through a misty forest is both mysterious and inviting. The viewer (and the lone traveler) doesn't know what lies ahead, and yet the path beckons. The image may be seen to represent the process of writing a research paper; like the traveler in the mist, students will travel the road of research—following through on leads, taking turns when necessary, and retracing steps when they hit dead ends in order to begin anew.

Interpret and Analyze Use the following questions for discussion:

- How would you describe the mood of this scene? What effect does the fog have on the mood?
- Imagine that you are hiking on this road. What questions come to mind? What information can you uncover simply by focusing your attention on the environment?

Discussing the Quotation

This quotation is the first three lines of the poem "Ithaca" by Greek poet C. P. Cavafy (1863–1933). Discuss the quotation with the class, and ask students how they would interpret these lines of poetry. What literary elements does Cavafy use in these lines? Have students replace the words *to Ithaca* with *of writing a research paper.* Why would Cavafy's words seem like good advice?

Writing Prompt Write a brief explanation of how Cavafy's words, coupled with the image of the road, can be seen to connect to the process of writing a research paper.

"When you start on your journey to Ithaca, then pray that the road is long, full of adventure, full of knowledge."

—C.P. Cavafy, "Ithaca"

322

Resource Manager

Planning Resources
- *Lesson Plans*
- *Block Scheduling*

Transparencies
- *Bellringer*
- *Daily Language Practice*
- *Two-Minute Skill Drill*

Other Print Resources
- *Grammar and Composition Handbook*
- *Research Paper and Report Writing*
- *Style and Documentation Sourcebook for Writers*
- *Tests with Answer Key and Rubrics*
- *Thinking and Study Skills*
- *Writing Across the Curriculum*
- *Writing Assessment and Evaluation Rubrics*

UNIT 7

Research Paper Writing

Objectives

- To learn the stages of writing a research paper and to successfully complete each of those stages
- To demonstrate an understanding of the importance of such strategies as careful note taking, outlining, and time management
- To conduct research and to write and revise a research paper

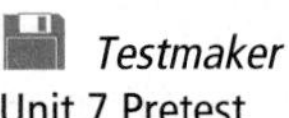

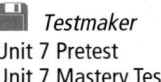

ASSESSMENT OPTIONS

Tests with Answer Key & Rubrics
Unit 7 Pretest, pp. 25–26
Unit 7 Mastery Test, pp. 27–28

Testmaker
Unit 7 Pretest
Unit 7 Mastery Test

You may wish to administer the Unit 7 Pretest at this point.

Key to Ability Levels

L1 Level 1 activities are within the basic ability range of students.

L2 Level 2 activities are within the ability range of average students.

L3 Level 3 activities are more challenging activities.

 Video
- *MindJogger Videoquizzes*

 Software
- *Presentation Plus!*
- *Revising with Style*
- *Testmaker*

- *glencoe.com*

Focus

Lesson Overview

Objective
- To gather information and draft plans for a research paper

Skills
- choosing a topic; gathering information; note taking

Critical Thinking
- analyzing; synthesizing; classifying; evaluating; summarizing; comparing; combining

Listening and Speaking
- discussing; interviewing; note taking

Bellringer
Daily Language Activity

When students enter the classroom, have this assignment on the board: *Write down a topic you would like to learn more about.*

Grammar Link to the Bellringer

Ask students to write their Bellringer topic as a complete sentence. Have them identify as many parts of the sentence as possible (subject, verb, noun, and so on). Then let students review and discuss their sentences.

See also *Daily Language Practice*

Motivating Activity

Explain to students that they would probably need to do some planning before they could write about their Bellringer topic. Ask the class to imagine what safety features might have been planned for the first Ferris wheel. (seats secured to keep passengers from falling; regulation of the wheel's speed) Reinforce the idea that planning is as critical for a successful research paper as for a Ferris wheel.

LESSON 7.1

Research Paper Writing

Prewriting: Planning and Researching

George W. G. Ferris, the man who dreamed up the Ferris wheel, had a great challenge ahead of him: he had to turn his idea into a solid, working structure. After quite a bit of sketching and planning and a step-by-step approach, Ferris finally created this fantastic new contraption, the likes of which the world had never seen before. In much the same way—with careful planning and a step-by-step approach—you can create a successful and engaging research paper.

Evaluation Rubric

By the time you complete Lesson 7.1, you will have
- chosen a research paper topic that interests you and that is neither too broad nor too narrow
- identified a central idea for your paper and written research questions that will help focus your information search
- identified appropriate authoritative sources of information
- created complete and accurate source cards
- taken notes from your sources in a way that will help you avoid plagiarism

What Is a Research Paper?

The research paper differs from many other kinds of writing because it includes factual information from a variety of sources. These sources may be **primary** (records of the people who took part in the event or period you are studying, such as journals, documents, or photos) or **secondary** (books and articles written about the event or period). Whatever the sources, you can write one of four basic kinds of research paper.

Four Types of Research Paper	
Summary	The writer explores a topic by summing up the opinions of other writers and researchers.
Evaluative	The writer states an opinion and backs it up with evidence found in primary and/or secondary resources.
Original	The writer does original research on a topic and reports on his or her findings.
Combination	The writer combines approaches in one paper, such as summarizing opinions, then conducts original research.

Resource Manager

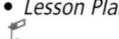

Planning Resources
- *Lesson Plans*

Transparencies
- *Bellringer*
- *Daily Language Practice*
- *Two-Minute Skill Drill*

Other Print Resources
- *Research Paper and Report Writing,* pp. 1–12
- *Style and Documentation Sourcebook for Writers*
- *Thinking and Study Skills,* pp. 2, 6, 7
- *Writing Across the Curriculum*
- *Writing Assessment and Evaluation Rubrics*

Choose a Good Topic

One of your first decisions is what to write about. Try to find a topic that interests you, one that you really want to learn about. If your teacher assigns a subject area, go to the library and skim some general articles covering that area in an encyclopedia. Look for any aspects of the subject that relate to your own interests and activities, or any personalities or events that sound intriguing and exciting. These can become topics to explore in the paper.

Refine Your Topic Also, keep in mind how much information will be manageable given the length of your research paper. If the topic is very broad, you'll have too much information and too many ideas to cover. On the other hand, if the topic is very narrow, you won't be able to uncover enough material. If you write about such a topic, your paper will probably lack substance (unless you do original research). If you can only find one or two articles on the topic, for example, and if the encyclopedia doesn't cover it, you will almost certainly not have enough to write about.

Choose Your Focus Do some preliminary reading on your topic to help you find an appropriate focus for your paper. Keep an open mind as you review encyclopedia articles or books and articles on your topic. Depending on your findings—and the amount and type of information you're able to uncover—your preliminary research may lead you to change or refine your topic.

Brainstorm for Ideas Britta Waller, who wrote the model paper in Lesson 7.6, on pages 350–356, was instructed to write about technology in history. She wanted to avoid run-of-the-mill topics but had to choose a subject on which there was enough information to write an adequate paper. After some brainstorming and a trip to the library, she decided to write about the construction of the first Ferris wheel. It seemed an appropriate topic, since authors have devoted sections of books to it, and since she found articles on different aspects of the topic.

Prewriting Tip

You may wish to discuss your topic ideas with a classmate to get some feedback about the size and scope of your plans. Also, be sure to ask your teacher to approve your final topic.

Too narrow: The gear mechanisms of a Ferris wheel

Appropriate: The history of the Ferris wheel

Too broad: Amusement parks and carnivals

Research Paper Writing

Teach

Using the Model

Direct students to the photo on this page and point out that the labels indicate whether or not possible topics are too narrow, too broad, or appropriate. Too much information means too much to cover in a paper; too little means scraping for enough material to write about or relying on only a few sources. Ask students how they can find out how much information is available on a given topic. (by conducting preliminary research) **L2**

Choosing a Topic

Suggest that students set a goal of selecting a topic that is of interest to them and can be readily researched. An appropriate topic is one for which they can find six to eight good resources (primary as well as secondary). Good secondary resources mean an article or book chapter, not a whole book on the topic (which would be impractical to read). **L1**

Researching Science

Point out to interested students that research papers done in science courses are typically a combination of the types described in the chart on page 324. They include a summary of previous research in the area, an evaluative assessment of it (usually indicating something lacking), and original research (extending the previous research or filling in what is lacking). **L3**

Teach

Using Library Resources

Discuss with students what resources they would investigate for choosing a topic. Suggest that they make use of the school library and discuss what they would find there to help them. (books arranged by subject, encyclopedias, the *Readers' Guide to Periodical Literature* indexing magazines by article topics, and many specialty reference books) Students can use these resources to search for specific subtopics suitable for papers. **L2**

Cooperative Learning

Students working in pairs can help each other define guidelines for topic research by asking *what, why,* and *how* questions about each other's chosen topic. If a student's topic were "the invention of the wireless phone," for example, the partner might ask why the wireless phone is considered important. The student may then research the broader topic of "telecommunications" to put the invention in perspective. **L1**

Using Primary Sources

Tell students that primary sources are usually found outside the classroom and school. They may include oral interviews with people who were participants in or witnesses to an event, accounts written by such people, or graphic representations (photos, sketches, architectural drawings, fine art). Suggest that students conduct interviews in person, on the telephone, or via e-mail if appropriate to their topic. **L2**

Research Paper Writing

Prewriting Tip

For information on library resources, see Unit 23, pages 798–810.

Researching Tip

For information about exploring and evaluating sources, see **Writing and Research Handbook,** pages 950–951.

Find Information on Your Topic

Once you have a topic, you need to decide on your paper's central idea—the idea that will guide your thinking and your selection of research questions. In your learning log, write three to seven research questions, each question focusing on one aspect of the topic. Ask the *why's, what's,* and *how's* about your topic (for example, "Why was it considered important? What effect did it have? How did it come into being?"). As you find answers, you'll have new questions. Feel free to modify your central idea as you learn more about the topic.

The chart below lists and describes various sources of information that can help you answer your research questions in the area of science and technology. Note that most of the examples listed have their own Web sites, and you may conduct research on the Internet.

Basic Sources of Science and Technology Information

Type	Description	Examples
Periodicals	Newspapers, magazines, journals, and other sources that are published on a regular basis, either for general readers or for more specialized audiences	*Washington Post* *Scientific American* *National Geographic* *Science Digest* *Discover*
Government Agencies	Branches of federal, state, and local governments that publish reports, statistics, and other information on scientific topics	National Aeronautics and Space Administration U.S. Fish and Wildlife Service State and local departments of health
Nonprofit Organizations	Private groups that study certain scientific areas or topics and publish reports and statistics	World Wildlife Fund American Cancer Society American Dental Association Sierra Club
Computer Databases	General science information available through computer linkup for a fee	*Applied Science and Technology Index* *General Science Index* *Magazine Index*

TIME

For more information about prewriting, see **TIME Facing the Blank Page,** pp. 124-125.

Create Source Cards or a Computer File for Your Working Bibliography For each suitable source of information you find, record the publication information in a computer file or on a three-by-five-inch index card. Be sure to assign a number to each source, as shown in the upper left corner of the model cards on page 327. You will refer to the information as you complete the process of writing a research paper. For example, when you take notes, you'll jot down the number of the source in which you found each piece of information.

MEETING INDIVIDUAL NEEDS

English Language Learners

Finding Resources

Encourage students who can read another language to use resources in that language to gain information on their topics. Advise them to consult a school or college library for topic indexes that list pertinent periodicals and books in their language. Remind students that the bibliographical information for a book—title, author, publisher, copyright date—is on the title page and the copyright page. Be sure students understand how to avoid plagiarizing the material they translate.

You'll also refer to your source cards or computer file when preparing your works-cited list at the end of your paper.

Different sources require that you record different information, as the samples below illustrate. Look for publication information on the title and copyright pages of books and magazines, and use the works-cited entries on pages 341 and 342 to help you see what information to include for a wider variety of source types.

Sample Source Cards

Book

3
7500.B1B3
Badger, Reid. The Great American Fair.
Chicago: Nelson-Hall, 1979.

Library call number
Author, title
City of publication, publisher, year of publication

Encyclopedia

6
"World's Columbian Exposition."
Encyclopedia Americana. 1999 ed.

Entry title
Source, year of edition

Magazine article

2
Fincher, Jack. "George Ferris Jr. and the Great Wheel of Fortune."
Smithsonian, July 1983: 109–112+.

Comprehensive; systematically traces Ferris's life and the history of his wheel design

Author
Article title
Magazine, issue date
Page numbers
Brief description of information in article

Take Notes

Taking notes is a good way to help you clarify and remember information, and is one of the most important steps in writing a good research paper. You will probably take many more notes than you will end up using, but don't worry—so do professional writers and researchers.

Prepare Note Cards Read your sources for information that relates to your paper's central idea. As you find answers to your research questions, take notes on four-by-six-inch index cards, with one piece of information per card, and record the corresponding number of the source card. On a separate page, jot down new questions that arise as you learn more about your topic. When taking notes, you can paraphrase, summarize, or quote the source directly. Note the differences in note-taking strategies as you study the sample cards on page 328.

Prewriting Tip

Be sure that all words, names, and titles are legible and spelled correctly on your source cards or in your electronic file. Follow the conventions of punctuation shown in the chart on page 341 and in the model works-cited list on page 342.

Summarizing Tip

When summarizing, briefly state the main points in your own words. Focus on the key details that support the main points. Be sure to use key words and phrases.

Taking Notes

Direct students' attention to the bibliography cards and ask why each piece of information is important and helpful to a writer. Why is the library call number important for a book card? (It enables the writer to quickly find the source again if necessary.) Why are the author and publication information important? (They will be part of the bibliographic citation.) Why is the brief description important for the magazine article card? (It tells the writer what kind of information the article includes.) **L2**

Identifying Sources

Remind students that identifying sources is a scholarly responsibility. If such information is not accurate, others could be misled, and confusion will result. Eventually, the integrity of the person supplying the information will be called into question. For the benefit of others and themselves, responsible citizens and scholars try to make all information that they supply as accurate as possible. **L3**

Two-Minute Skill Drill

Have students write a summary of the information in the first paragraph on page 324, the one that begins *George W. G. Ferris . . .*

See also *Two-Minute Skill Drill Transparency 7.1*

Cultural Connections

Choosing Diversity

Encourage students to choose a research topic that connects with their own cultural background or a culture that interests them. Culturally related topics can be found for all subject areas. In science, for example, students could investigate a researcher or inventor with a cultural background that interests them, such as Louis Pasteur (French), Marie Curie (Polish/French), George Washington Carver (African American), Karl Benz and Gottlieb Daimler (German), and Guglielmo Marconi (Italian).

Teach

Searching Databases

Point out that searching computer databases is an efficient means of gaining current information on various topics. Searches of periodicals can be structured to list the title, author(s), and source and to print out a summary of all pertinent articles. In this way, students can find out quickly how much information is available on their topics. **L2**

Gathering Information

Tell students that careful research and note taking play an important role in practically every business and profession. Discuss why this is so. One reason is that new information is continually being generated in all fields and that research and note taking are required to keep abreast of it. Another reason is that the amount of knowledge in most fields is too large to be remembered precisely and therefore must be researched as needed for particular projects. **L1**

Additional Resources

- *Writing Across the Curriculum*
- *Research Paper and Report Writing,* pp. 1–12
- *Thinking and Study Skills,* pp. 2, 6, 7

Source

International expositions are of recent origin. The first was the Great Exhibition held in London in 1851 which was the scene of Joseph Paxton's Crystal Palace—the first large-scale, prefabricated iron and glass building—which alone attested that fair's significance. From then until 1893 there were several European expositions, probably the most famous being that held in Paris in 1889, celebrated for its Eiffel Tower. The United States had hosted several trade fairs but only one full-scale international exposition, that held in Philadelphia in 1876, the celebration of the centennial of American inde-...dence. The World's Columbian Exposition would be the ...and the second American one. But it was ...pe than any of its predecessors. Early ...isted simply of one large exhibition hall, ...bition, or of such a hall augmented with ...heds. The main hall might be artfully de-...empt was made to lay out the surround-... embellish the buildings with sculpture ...Paris Exhibiti... of 1867 originated both

A summary includes only the main ideas and key supporting details. Always use your own words.

Previous fairs 6
1. London, Great Exhibition, 1851
2. Philadelphia, 1876
3. Paris, 1889
Columbian Exposition was of a much larger scale.
Summary

Previous fairs 6
While it was built on the model of the other world's fairs, the 1893 Columbian Exposition was the grandest fair yet.
Paraphrase

This is the number of a source; it corresponds to a source card containing bibliographic information.

A paraphrase is a restatement of the information in your own words.

Previous fairs 6
"The World's Columbian Exposition would be the fifteenth world's fair and the second American one. But it was of vastly greater scope than any of its predecessors."
Quotation *page xii*

To use a passage exactly as written, write the direct quotation as it appears, and put it in quotation marks on your card.

Read Sources Critically As you conduct research, think critically about your sources. Make sure that they are authoritative, reliable, and up-to-date, reflecting the most current thinking on your topic. Newspaper tabloids, for example, are not considered appropriate sources for reliable information. If your topic is scientific or technical in nature, you'll want to be especially sure that your data has been recently published because the field changes so rapidly. Also watch for author bias. Ask yourself whether the author might have a hidden purpose in presenting his or her point of view. Is the author a qualified expert?

MEETING INDIVIDUAL NEEDS

English Language Learners

Recording Information

Some students learning English may have difficulty taking notes. Suggest that they tape-record salient information when possible and transcribe what seems most relevant later on. As students transcribe their notes, they can stop, start, and replay sections. This technique will enable them to clarify and remember information. Remind them to carefully record bibliographic information (such as page numbers) and the wording of exact quotations.

Does the author fail to give evidence for certain claims? Is the author reliable on some points but not others? These are questions to consider as you read and evaluate your sources.

Avoid Plagiarism Presenting someone else's ideas or expressions as your own is plagiarism, a form of cheating. Therefore, you must always acknowledge the source of any information you use in your paper. There are two exceptions to this rule, however. You do not need to credit your own ideas, and you do not need to credit information that is considered common knowledge or that can be found in many sources.

The first step in avoiding plagiarism is to indicate on each note card whether an idea is your own or common knowledge or whether it is a paraphrase, summary, or quotation that comes from one of your sources. Notice how Britta Waller labeled her note cards on page 328. When she uses these cards during the drafting process, she will know to give credit to source number 6. See Lesson 7.4 for information about how to cite your sources properly in your research paper.

Vocabulary Tip

On your note cards, write the definition of any technical or unfamiliar terms. When you draft your paper, include the definition the first time you use one of these terms.

7.1 Writing Activities

Skills Practice

1. Write a brief explanation of why each topic below is too broad, too narrow, or about right for a five-page research paper:
- effects of the car on the United States
- 3-D movies—invention and refinement
- building the Great Pyramid at Giza
2. If you were writing a paper about the development of high-definition television (HDTV), which of the following sources would you turn to for information, and which would you avoid? Explain.
- *Newsweek* magazine
- *Encyclopaedia Britannica*, 1965
- *TV Guide*
- *Scientific American*
- *The Great Old Movies on TV*
- *Video Technology Review*, this year's annual edition

Your Research Paper

Begin your research paper by following these directions:

- Select a research paper topic that interests you, and do some preliminary reading so that you can narrow the topic appropriately.
- Write at least five research questions.
- Conduct library research and prepare source cards, using the *MLA Handbook for Writers of Research Papers* and the examples on pages 327 and 342 as a guide to recording publication information accurately.
- Take legible notes from the sources you've gathered, and make sure to give proper attribution for each idea that is not your own.

Writing Online | For more writing and grammar practice, go to **glencoe.com** and enter QuickPass code WC97727p1.

Assess

Evaluation Rubrics

Skills Practice

1. The topic is too broad. (The car has had many pervasive effects.)
   The topic is about right.(3-D movies, while staging a comeback, have had limited refinements.)
   The topic is too narrow. (Not much is known about the building of this particular pyramid.)
2. *Scientific American* and *Video Technology Review* are likely to have the most specific, current information. *Newsweek* would also be a good source.
   Encyclopaedia Britannica, 1965 and *The Great Old Movies on TV* should not be used; they would not contain current, appropriate information.

Your Research Paper

Use these criteria when evaluating your students' writing:

- topics should be neither too broad nor too narrow
- information on the topic should be readily available
- research questions should focus on important issues
- bibliography cards should contain relevant sources and all necessary data
- each note should be attributed to a source

See also *Writing Assessment & Evaluation Rubrics*

Close

Tell students to choose a paragraph from a newspaper or periodical and try rewriting the passage in their own words—being careful to cite sources and to avoid plagiarism.

Focus

Lesson Overview

Objective

- To create a working outline and a thesis statement for a research paper

Skills

- creating an outline; developing a thesis statement

Critical Thinking

- analyzing; categorizing; classifying; identifying main idea; evaluating; summarizing; making inferences; establishing and evaluating criteria; defining and clarifying

Listening and Speaking

- interviewing; note taking; questioning

Bellringer

Daily Language Activity

When students enter the classroom, have this assignment on the board: *Write an explanation of why using an outline is helpful in writing a report or a research paper.*

Grammar Link to the Bellringer

Have students circle any predicate adjectives in their Bellringer explanations. If there are no predicate adjectives, have students write a sentence containing one.

See also *Daily Language Practice*

Motivating Activity

Begin a class discussion by asking students how they organize their own collections of books, tapes, or compact discs. (Organization may be alphabetical or by genre, such as *rock* and *jazz.*) Point out that an outline organizes information. Let students know that the next step in the writing process is to arrange their notes in outline form.

LESSON 7.2

Prewriting: Outlining

WHAT PURE CHAOS! might be your thought, facing your mounds of research notes. But your notes are probably not any more impossible to sort out than is the pile of hardware shown here. All you need to bring order to the chaos is an organizing principle. For example, if you examine the hardware with the idea of function in mind, you might see that you could place all the items that hold things together in one pile, all the items that prevent leaks in another, and so on. Not only can an organizing principle help you bring order to your notes, it can help you develop an outline, which is a particularly useful tool for writing a research paper.

Evaluation Rubric

By the time you complete Lesson 7.2, you will have

- made a formal outline or graphic organizer that reveals an appropriate method of organization for your paper
- drafted a thesis statement and revised it until it provides a clear focus for your writing

You may also find that you need to return to the stages covered in Lesson 7.1.

Create an Outline

A working outline—one that you continue to write and revise as you conduct your research—helps you think about your topic critically and makes your research efficient. The following tips will help you create such an outline.

Tips on Outlining

1. Look for similarities among notes: group together note cards on similar topics. Use each group as a main topic in your outline.
2. Within groups cluster similar note cards into subgroups that elaborate on the larger and more general main topic. Use these subgroups as the subtopics in your outline.
3. Arrange main topics to build on your central idea. And, under each main topic, arrange subtopics so they elaborate on the main topic in a logical way.
4. As you continue your research and learn more, revise and elaborate in your outline. Subdivide information in subtopics into outline entries as well.
5. Set aside note cards that don't fit under any heading.
6. Before you begin your first draft, prepare a final outline.

Resource Manager

Planning Resources

- *Lesson Plans*

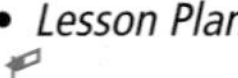

Transparencies

- *Bellringer*
- *Daily Language Practice*
- *Two-Minute Skill Drill*

Other Print Resources

- *Research Paper and Report Writing,* pp. 13–17
- *Style and Documentation Sourcebook for Writers*
- *Thinking and Study Skills,* pp. 13, 17
- *Writing Across the Curriculum*
- *Writing Assessment and Evaluation Rubrics*

```
Title of Paper
   I. Main Topic
      A. Subtopic
         1. Division of a subtopic
            a. Subdivision of a subtopic
            b. Subdivision of a subtopic
         2. Division of a subtopic
            a. Subdivision of a subtopic
            b. Subdivision of a subtopic
      B. Subtopic
  II. Main Topic
```

Number main topics with Roman numerals.

Notice the lettering, numbering, and indentation systems for subtopics and their divisions and subdivisions.

A subtopic doesn't have to have any subdivisions. But if you list any at all, you must list at least two.

Try creating your outline on a computer so you can easily add information and rearrange details as you continue researching. But what is the best way to arrange the ideas in your notes? Because ideas can be divided up many different ways, you have a number of options, depending on the nature of your information. In a history paper you might arrange ideas chronologically. In a science paper you might arrange ideas in causal order to show how one idea or event directly determines another. Britta Waller, writing on a topic that combines history and technology, creates an outline that proceeds from general to specific.

```
              George W. G. Ferris
      The Man Who Reinvented the Wheel

 I.  Background of 1893 Columbian Exposition
     A. Continued tradition of big fairs
        1. Previous world's fairs
           a. London and the Crystal Palace,
              1851
           b. Philadelphia, 1876
           c. Paris and the Eiffel Tower, 1889
        2. Chicago fair to be larger than
           earlier fairs
     B. Emphasized cultural achievements
        1. Planners D. H. Burnham and
           F. L. Olmsted
        2. Nation's top artists, inventors,
           industrialists
     C. Reflected values of the era
II. Background of George W. G. Ferris
```

Waller provides a chronological account of the years leading up to the 1893 fair.

In what order does Waller present her topics? Is this a good way to arrange this paper?

Research Paper Writing

7.2

Teach

Using the Model

After reading Britta Waller's outline, ask students to read Britta's paper from page 350 to page 356 to see how she followed her plan. Suggest that students use Britta's outline as a model. **L2**

Determining the Principle

Suggest that students use the Think-Pair-Share procedure to determine the organizing principle for their papers. Each student should organize his or her note cards in chronological, logical, or general-to-specific order. Students then pair up, exchange cards, and try to guess the other's organizing principle. If one student guesses incorrectly, then the other should probably revise the organization. The pair should discuss the possibilities and then share with the class why they made their final choices. **L3**

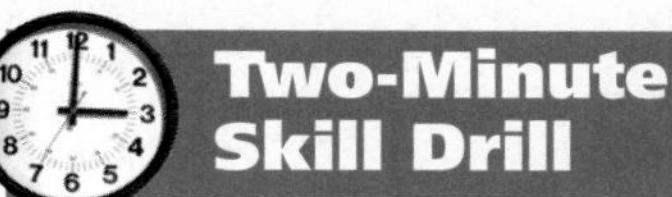

Two-Minute Skill Drill

Students may enjoy mapping out their information and representing their data graphically. Have them practice by creating a cluster or other diagram of Britta Waller's outline shown on this page.

See also *Two-Minute Skill Drill Transparency 7.2*

Teach

Choosing a Statement Type

Direct students' attention to the Four Types of Thesis Statements chart on page 333. Point out that students should choose the type of thesis statement that corresponds to their paper. Make a further point that people use original, evaluative, and summary thinking (and the combination of them) to process all kinds of information. Ask students for examples. (original—getting an idea; evaluative—choosing a movie; summary—making a shopping list; combination—planning a party) **L2**

Finding the Main Idea

Some students may have trouble finding the main idea for their thesis statement. Suggest that they lay out their note cards so that they can see the relationship between the main idea and subtopics. **L1**

Additional Resources

- *Writing Across the Curriculum*
- *Research Paper and Report Writing,* pp. 13–17
- *Thinking and Study Skills,* pp. 13, 17

Drafting Tip

Thesis statements are often compound sentences. To review how to create compound sentences, see Lesson 13.3, pages 541–542.

Develop a Thesis Statement

So far, you have guided your research and outline according to your central idea, or the basic questions you've been exploring. You've probably rethought this idea as you have learned about the topic. Now, as you get ready to begin your first draft, it's time to turn that central idea into a thesis statement—that is, a concise idea that you try to prove, expand on, or illustrate in your writing. This statement gives your writing a focus from start to finish.

To create a thesis statement, look at your central idea critically. Is it as clear as it can be? Does it include all important aspects of your topic? Does it include historical background or new developments if these are relevant? Does it make the significance of your topic clear?

After asking these and other similar sorts of questions, write the idea again as a single sentence that describes your topic more precisely. This time include a mention of your approach to the topic. Are you comparing one topic with another, exploring a single topic in depth, or trying to prove or disprove any common notions?

The chart below progresses from central idea to thesis statement. The chart on page 333 gives four basic kinds of thesis statements.

Example of a central idea:
The Ferris wheel was a unique engineering feat when it was constructed.

Examples of revising a central idea:

1. The Ferris wheel, a unique engineering feat in its day, came on the scene in time to help assert American superiority over Europe and became the most popular attraction at the Columbian Exposition.
2. The Ferris wheel, a unique engineering feat, was conceived at a time when America needed to show its superiority over Europe, and the wheel became the most popular attraction at the Columbian Exposition, overshadowing the many cultural exhibits.

Example of a thesis statement:
The unique engineering feat of the Ferris wheel was one of many assertions of American pride at the World's Columbian Exposition, and its huge popularity overshadowed the fair's cultural attractions.

MEETING INDIVIDUAL NEEDS

Learning Disabled

Developing Outlines

Students with certain kinds of learning disabilities will benefit from careful guidance through all stages of outline development. Have them pair up with other students who can help them create an outline and organize information into main topics, subtopics, and divisions and subdivisions of the subtopics.

Four Types of Thesis Statements		
Type	**Description**	**Example**
Original	Describes the background and results of original research to be presented in the paper	My survey of students and teachers at Lincoln High School has uncovered a desire for more and better computers and more instruction in computer science.
Evaluative	Identifies an issue and evaluates opinions on the issue that the writer will convey through the paper	Solar power provides our best option for future energy needs, taking into account both economic and environmental concerns.
Summary	Introduces the different perspectives on a topic for a paper that primarily summarizes the work of others	High-speed trains, traveling at speeds greater than 125 miles per hour, have revolutionized intercity travel in both France and Japan.
Combination	Combines any two or all three of the above approaches	Interviews with music-store salespeople and compact disc owners lead me to believe that the CD has replaced the record once and for all.

7.2 Writing Activities

Skills Practice

1. Organize the following pieces of information into outline form. Write headings and subheadings as necessary.

- Laser stands for *l*ight *a*mplification by *s*timulated *e*mission of *r*adiation.
- Lasers can be used in surgery.
- Compact discs are "read" by lasers.
- A laser creates a narrow beam of monochromatic and coherent light.
- Holograms rely on laser technology.
- Stores use lasers to ring up purchases.
- Laser light is the result of a chain reaction of atoms discharging photons.
- Manufacturing industries use lasers to inspect the quality of their products.

2. Rewrite the following into a concise, single-sentence thesis statement:

The race to put an astronaut on the moon had numerous motivations. Many people thought it was a waste of money. Yet the space program has resulted in many inventions that improve our lives.

Your Research Paper

Continue working on your research paper. Complete the following steps:

- Arrange your note cards in groups according to subject.
- Identify main ideas and use those as the main headings in a formal outline or graphic organizer.
- Complete your outline or graphic, adding subheadings and details.
- Write a thesis statement that reveals the main idea you will develop in your paper.

For more writing and grammar practice, go to **glencoe.com** and enter QuickPass code WC97727p1.

Assess

Evaluation Rubrics

Skills Practice

Use these criteria when evaluating your students' responses:

1. Does the outline have an opening definition (first point)?
   Does the outline discuss a laser's uses (second, third, fifth, sixth, and eighth points)?
   Does it discuss how a laser works (fourth and seventh points)?
2. The thesis statement should
   eliminate extraneous ideas (sentence one)
   combine sentences two and three with an appropriate conjunction
   be similar to this: *Although many people thought the space program was a waste of money, it is responsible for inventions that improve our lives.*

Your Research Paper

Evaluate outlines and thesis statements on the basis of their clarity of organization and conciseness of expression.

See also *Writing Assessment & Evaluation Rubrics*

Close

Discuss with students whether using note cards proved helpful in organizing their outlines.

Focus

Lesson Overview

Objective

- To draft the initial version of a research paper by elaborating on outlined points

Skills

- organizing information; adding supporting details to main ideas

Critical Thinking

- synthesizing; analyzing; categorizing; evaluating

Listening and Speaking

- discussing; note taking; explaining the steps in a process

Bellringer

Daily Language Activity

When students enter the classroom, have this assignment on the board: *What special things do you do to get yourself ready to begin writing?*

Grammar Link to the Bellringer

Ask students to use at least one infinitive or infinitive phrase in their response to the Bellringer. Invite volunteers to share their phrases with the class.

See also  *Daily Language Practice*

Motivating Activity

To reinforce the main idea of the opening paragraph of the lesson, tell students that Edison is credited with saying that the invention process requires "one percent inspiration and 99 percent perspiration." Ask students to discuss how the quote applies to writing research papers. What part of the research project is inspiration? What part is perspiration?

Research Paper Writing

LESSON 7.3

Drafting

Think of the simple light bulb—something we take for granted. Yet the light bulb was once just an idea in the mind of Thomas Edison. To turn his idea into a reality, Edison had to do research, examine the research of others, make some original observations, and then refine his work. A research paper requires much the same effort. Even as you turn your outline and notes into a draft, you still need to experiment, ask new questions, and refine your ideas.

Use Your Outline and Notes

Look at your outline again to be sure you're satisfied with the flow of ideas from one to the next. Then, using your outline and your note cards, begin drafting. If your keyboarding skills are good, you may want to type your paper directly into a computer file. Keep in mind that even though you are writing a formal research paper, your goal at this point is to get down on paper your ideas and information. You can make adjustments to your voice and style when you revise your draft. The drafting tips in the chart on the next page may help you get started.

Sources 

Fincher, Jack. "George Ferris Jr. and the Great Wheel of Fortune." Smithsonian July 1983: 109–118.

Anderson, Norman D., and Walter R. Brown. Ferris Wheels. New York: Pantheon, 1983.

Valenti, Michael. "100 Years and Still Going Around in Circles." Mechanical Engineering June 1993: 70+. ProQuest Direct. Chicago Public Lib., Chicago. 29 Nov. 1999 <http://proquest.umi.com>.

Notes 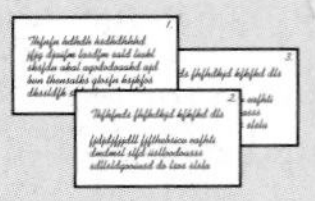

Admission 50 cents, the same as admission to fair. Still, 1.5 million rode it.
—Fincher, p. 114

Twenty-minute ride for 50 cents; two revolutions, six stops each time around; ran 8 A.M.–11 P.M.
—Anderson and Brown, p. 24

Lit by 3,000 electric bulbs at night, powered by generator in boiler house
—Valenti

Resource Manager

Planning Resources

- *Lesson Plans*

 Transparencies

- *Bellringer*
- *Daily Language Practice*
- *Two-Minute Skill Drill*

Other Print Resources

- *Research Paper and Report Writing,* pp. 18–24
- *Style and Documentation Sourcebook for Writers*
- *Thinking and Study Skills,* pp. 22–24
- *Writing Across the Curriculum*
- *Writing Assessment and Evaluation Rubrics*

Some Tips on Drafting

1. Set aside a couple of hours to begin writing. Find a quiet place where you won't be distracted.
2. Try to draft smoothly and quickly without getting stalled on details. Don't worry about finding the "perfect" word or phrase; you can revise later.
3. Write at least one paragraph for each heading in your outline. Each paragraph should have a topic sentence and supporting details.
4. Write the number of each note card as you use it. Later you will replace the numbers with information about your sources.

You don't have to include information from every note card in your draft. In fact, as the diagram below shows, you are likely to develop the ideas from several note cards into one or two outline entries, and likewise into one or two ideas in your paper. As you put these ideas into your paper, identify the source of every borrowed idea, and try to use your own words wherever possible.

As you draft, use your outline as a "map" to help guide you in your writing. The outline should remind you of what comes before or after a particular idea. Furthermore, the outline should suggest the links, or transitions, you might use in your writing. After all, you have already begun linking ideas in your outline; now simply carry on that process, as the diagram below illustrates.

Evaluation Rubric

By the time you complete Lesson 7.3, you will have

- drafted your research paper, making sure that your ideas logically progress from one to the next
- written an interesting introduction that includes your thesis
- created a conclusion that brings your paper to a satisfying close

Outline

III. Specifics of Ferris Wheel
- A. Dimensions
- B. Built on principle of bicycle wheel
- C. Riding
  1. Admission
  2. Hours
  3. Huge number of people riding
  4. Enthusiastic public response

IV. Early Criticism

Paragraph

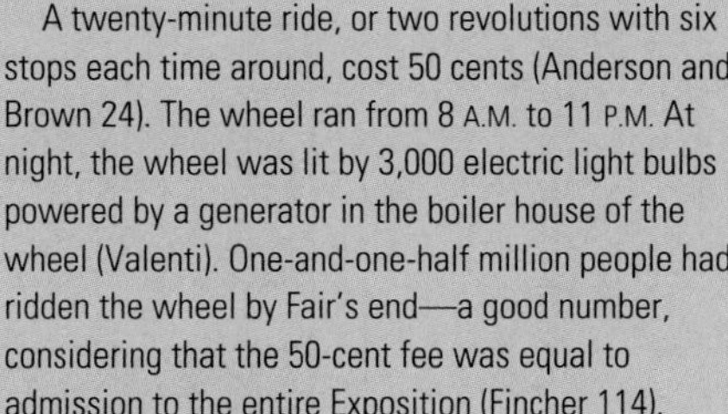

A twenty-minute ride, or two revolutions with six stops each time around, cost 50 cents (Anderson and Brown 24). The wheel ran from 8 A.M. to 11 P.M. At night, the wheel was lit by 3,000 electric light bulbs powered by a generator in the boiler house of the wheel (Valenti). One-and-one-half million people had ridden the wheel by Fair's end—a good number, considering that the 50-cent fee was equal to admission to the entire Exposition (Fincher 114).

Teach

Developing Main Topics

Beginning researchers may feel overwhelmed by the prospect of "boiling down" their research data into one coherent paper. Suggest that students make each main topic a "mini-paper," devoting at least a paragraph to each subhead. Point out the outline segment and corresponding paragraph at the bottom of page 335 as an example. Ask students to identify the subhead that the paragraph refers to. (C. Riding) Encourage students to choose a subhead from their own outline to work on. Some students might wish to write the mini-paper sections at separate sittings or on different days. **L2**

Organizing Information

Some students need help drafting from their note cards and outlines. Ask these students to make a separate stack of cards for each main topic. Then tell them to go through the cards, highlighting the information they want to include in their paper and putting the cards in an order that seems right to them. Suggest that students write an introductory paragraph for each main topic and a sentence for each subhead. Help students add transitional sentences between completed paragraphs. **L1**

Two-Minute Skill Drill

Have students describe how they plan to organize their note cards before they begin writing the first draft of their research papers.

See also *Two-Minute Skill Drill Transparency 7.3*

7.3

Teach

Modeling Introductions

Have students read introductions to feature articles or columns in newspapers and magazines. Challenge them to devise three introductions to their research papers, each with a different strategy gleaned from a professional model. Encourage students to share their introductions and to discuss what they learned from imitating the styles of different professional writers. **L2**

Additional Resources

- *Writing Across the Curriculum*
- *Research Paper and Report Writing,* pp. 18–24
- *Thinking and Study Skills,* pp. 22–24

Research Paper Writing

Vocabulary Tip

For examples of transitions to link paragraphs, see Lesson 2.8, pages 88–91.

Prepare the First Draft

Now that you're ready to write your first draft, read the chart below for solutions to some common drafting problems.

Solving Drafting Problems

Problem	Solution
How can I overcome "writer's block" on my first draft?	Just begin writing and get the ideas down. Try writing for five minutes on whatever comes into your mind. Then, you'll be looser and ready to write your draft.
Do I have to write the first part of the paper first, the second part second, and so on?	Write any way that is easiest for you. If you write out of sequence, pay close attention to the transitions between sections as you revise.
What can I do with all these notes I have?	Set aside any note that duplicates another, or is irrelevant to the main headings or subdivisions in your outline. Sort the others into groups according to topic.
I have many notes on some aspects of my topic but few on others. What should I do?	Do more research, or look at your outline to see if you can write a good paper with the notes you now have. If so, revise your outline.
How can I avoid running out of time before I get very far into my writing?	Set aside at least three hours just for writing your paper. Eliminate distractions by going to a quiet place.
How can I best create transitions between my paragraphs?	Identify one major similarity or difference between the paragraphs. Try linking the paragraphs with a short phrase or sentence describing how they are similar or different.
What can I do to avoid being bogged down correcting spelling and grammar?	Ignore these problems until you are ready to revise.

MEETING INDIVIDUAL NEEDS

English Language Learners

Discussing Drafting Problems

Students whose first language is not English may have drafting problems that are somewhat different from those of other students. Encourage these students to bring specific examples of their writing problems to small-group discussions so that peers can suggest possible solutions. Students who are proficient at writing in English may be particularly helpful in these situations.

Write the Introduction and Conclusion

A good introduction should present your topic and approach, along with your thesis statement. It should grab the attention of your readers and make them want to read on. Britta Waller begins her paper on the Ferris wheel with an intriguing quotation.

Your conclusion should alert the reader that you are wrapping up. You might summarize your main points or mention any new questions your paper raises. Waller concludes by recounting the "true achievement" of Ferris's magnificent wheel.

7.3 Writing Activities

Skills Practice

Write a few paragraphs about the elimination of yellow fever, using the outline and the notes that follow. Your audience is a high school history class.

Outline

I. Eradication of yellow fever
  A. Walter Reed sent to Cuba
    1. Knows about Carlos Finlay's theories
    2. Sets up experiments
  B. William Gorgas establishes mosquito control measures around Havana.

Notes

- 1881: Cuban physician Carlos Finlay suggested that a certain breed of mosquito carried the yellow fever disease.
- 1900: U.S. Army surgeon Walter Reed was sent to Cuba to investigate an epidemic of yellow fever among the U.S. troops there.
- Reed's fellow doctors and a number of soldiers volunteered for rather unconventional experiments:
  - Each was injected with yellow fever so Reed could study how the disease proceeds through the body.
  - All those intentionally injected contracted the disease but survived.
  - Two people who were infected accidentally came down with the disease and died.
- Reed's experiments proved that the disease was transmitted by the mosquito rather than by casual contact.
- 1905: William Gorgas developed and implemented measures to control mosquitoes, eliminating the disease as a major threat in Havana, Cuba.

Your Research Paper

Draft your research paper, completing the following steps:

- Begin by writing the section with which you feel most comfortable.
- Use the main and subordinate headings in your outline as a guide. Pull information from your note cards, providing strong transitions from one idea to the next.
- Craft an introduction that captures readers' attention and includes a thesis statement that reveals the direction your paper will take.
- Write a conclusion that reinforces your thesis and the paper's main points.

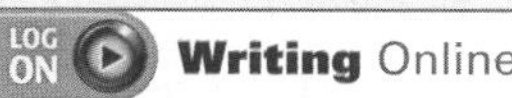

For more writing and grammar practice, go to glencoe.com and enter QuickPass code WC97727p1.

Assess

Evaluation Rubrics

Skills Practice

Use these criteria when evaluating your students' writing:

- Do the paragraphs adhere to the outline?
- Did the writer make selective use of notes?
- Is there a strong introduction?
- Are there smooth transitions between sentences and paragraphs?
- Did the writer treat the information in an interesting way?

Your Research Paper

Use these criteria when evaluating your students' writing:

- Does the draft have an attention-grabbing introduction that contains a thesis statement?
- Are the details clearly organized?
- Are there smooth transitions?
- Is there a conclusion that summarizes important points?

See also *Writing Assessment & Evaluation Rubrics*

Close

Ask students to write a few sentences describing a problem they had during the drafting stage. Have students exchange papers and suggest solutions to each other's problems.

Listening and Speaking

Cooperative Learning

Ask students to take turns reading aloud the first drafts of their research papers to one or two other people. Encourage readers to elicit suggestions for improving any passages with which they are having difficulty. Remind students that people often know what they want to say but don't always know the best way to express their thoughts. Reading your words aloud and sharing ideas with others can be especially helpful in these situations.

Focus

Lesson Overview

Objective

- To document sources accurately, using appropriately formatted citations

Skills

- formatting citations properly; formatting lists of works cited

Critical Thinking

- analyzing; establishing and evaluating criteria; defining and clarifying; decision-making; identifying

Listening and Speaking

- discussing

Bellringer

Daily Language Activity

When students enter the classroom, have this assignment on the board: *List a few sources you are using as sources of information for your research paper.*

Grammar Link to the Bellringer

Have students review the sources they listed in the Bellringer activity for proper capitalization and punctuation of titles, names, and dates. Point out that punctuating sources correctly is an important part of writing a research paper.

See also  *Daily Language Practice*

Motivating Activity

Ask students if someone else has ever claimed credit for their work or ideas. How did they feel? Point out that the authors of their sources also expect to be credited for their work. Discuss your or your school's policies on plagiarism or improper documentation. Emphasize that acknowledging others' contributions will give papers added credibility.

Research Paper Writing

LESSON 7.4

Citing Sources

While Ferris developed his wheel, others worked on some of the earliest automobiles. Yet unlike the Ferris wheel, the automobile has gone through amazing changes. The photo below and to the left shows Henry Ford's early Model T, while the one below and to the right shows a "car of the future."

Evaluation Rubric

By the time you complete Lesson 7.4, you will have

- learned what information in your paper does and does not need to be documented
- chosen an appropriate method for citing your sources
- correctly cited your sources in the body of your paper

Suppose you're writing a research paper about cars and you read that Ford was one of the auto's early developers. You don't have to cite such common knowledge in your paper. But if you read about features planned for future cars, and you include that information in your paper, then you need to document the source.

Document Information

In a research paper, you don't need to document your own original ideas or common knowledge. You do need to document the source of data gleaned from tables, charts, or other graphs, as well as quotations, paraphrases, or summaries that you include in your paper. Such sources include books, magazines, newspapers, encyclopedias, online sources, CD-ROMs, interviews, TV programs, letters, and song lyrics. Proper documentation enables readers to find the source if they want to learn more about your topic; it also enables you to avoid plagiarism, as discussed in Lesson 7.1, page 329.

What to document? You should document your information whenever you use someone's exact words, or whenever you paraphrase or summarize a particular idea or series of ideas. The chart on page 339 offers tips on when to document your information. The rest of this lesson shows you *how* to document, or cite, your sources.

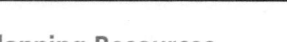

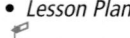

Resource Manager

Planning Resources

- *Lesson Plans*

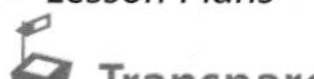

Transparencies

- *Bellringer*
- *Daily Language Practice*
- *Two-Minute Skill Drill*

Other Print Resources

- *Research Paper and Report Writing,* pp. 25–27
- *Style and Documentation Sourcebook for Writers*
- *Thinking and Study Skills,* p. 235
- *Writing Across the Curriculum*
- *Writing Assessment and Evaluation Rubrics*

Documenting Your Information		
INFORMATION	**CITATION?**	**EXPLANATION**
"No single enterprise on the Midway or the grounds proper approached it either in patronage or in wonderment."	Yes	Direct quotations reflect an author's opinion. Readers may want to check the source for bias.
The fair signified economic ambition, the rise of the city, and rapid change.	Yes	This is a paraphrase of another author's opinion or research.
Ironically, there was a focus on cultural enlightenment and achievement.	No	This is a paraphrase of general information found in many sources.
The Ferris wheel cost about $400,000 to build and turned a total profit of $733,086.	Yes	Specific cost and profitability of Ferris's wheel are not common knowledge.
The Columbian Exposition commemorated the four hundredth anniversary of Columbus's first historic voyage.	No	This is common knowledge that would appear in most sources on the fair.
Ferris's name was forever matched with later machines.	No	Most people are aware that such rides are referred to as Ferris wheels.

Format Citations Properly

Documenting your sources will be easy as long as you accurately completed and numbered your source cards and note cards during the prewriting stage. All the information you need should be right at your fingertips. (If it isn't, you'll need to return to the library to find your sources again!)

You can cite your sources in one of three ways: footnotes, endnotes, or parenthetical documentation, which is recommended by the Modern Language Association of America (or MLA). Because parenthetical documentation is generally preferred, the instruction and models in this unit conform to the MLA guidelines. Check with your teacher, however, and use the method that he or she prefers.

Parenthetical Documentation with a Works-Cited List

A works-cited list is an alphabetized list of sources that you used in writing your research paper. In your paper, after each quotation, summary, or paraphrase of information from a source, you must include within parentheses a reference to a source and a page number, when appropriate. This citation points readers to the corresponding entry in your works-cited list.

Teach

Documenting Material

Students will probably know to document direct quotes but may be unsure about unquoted use of source material. Ask students to explain what constitutes common knowledge that does not need documentation. If they seem confused, suggest that they discuss a specific case with a peer or someone who is one grade above or below them in school. If that person is acquainted with the information, citation is probably not required. The most problematic instances occur when students paraphrase an author's material. Emphasize that if they didn't think of the idea themselves, they must give the original author credit. **L2**

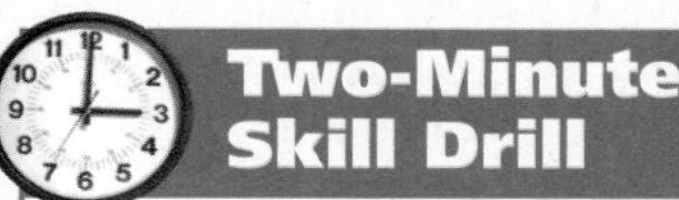

Have students list different kinds of information for which they might need documentation (quotations, statistics, paraphrases of another author's ideas or statements).

See also *Two-Minute Skill Drill Transparency 7.4*

Teach

Checking Spelling

Remind students to carefully check the spelling of all names in their citations. In addition, they should note accents in names and handwrite these marks into their typed or printed copy. Stress that the scholarly community is worldwide, embracing a wide variety of cultures, and that all scholars share the responsibility of properly spelling their source names. **L1**

When you drafted your paper, taking information from your note cards, you jotted down the corresponding number of the source from which you took the information. Now it's time to replace those numbers with proper parenthetical documentation. Place the citation as close as possible to the borrowed information. Generally, the parenthetical reference should be positioned where a pause would naturally occur, such as after a comma or at the end of a sentence (but before the final period):

Ferris sold stock to wealthy Chicago businessmen (Fincher 112).

The examples that follow and Britta Waller's final draft of her research paper on pages 350–356 provide guidance and models for how to reference sources in text, giving credit in parentheses.

Parenthetical Documentation Guidelines

1. **(Fincher 110)** Put the author's last name and the page reference in parentheses. If you're using two or more works by different authors with the same last name, include the author's first name or initial.
2. **(Anderson and Brown 18)** For a work by two or three authors, put the authors' last names and the page reference in parentheses. If a work has more than three authors, use the last name of the first author, followed by *et al.,* and the page reference: (Davis et al. 21).
3. **(Dream City)** When a source does not have an author, use a shortened form of the title in parentheses. Provide a page reference if possible.
4. **(Holliday, "Big Wheels" 229)** If you use more than one source by the same author, include the author's last name followed by a comma, the source title or a shortened form of it, and a page reference.
5. **(Badger 157; Burg 224)** If you use a piece of information that you found in more than one source, cite each work as you normally would, inserting a semicolon between the entries.
6. **(25)** If you use the author's name in the sentence that includes the information you need to document, you need only provide a page reference in parentheses, as shown in this example: *Howells accused the wheel of being a mere money-making contrivance—an exploitation of the visitors (25).*
7. **("Circus")** If you use a nonprint source, such as a videocassette, interview, film, or an article published online (the example above is for an article published by *Britannica Online*), name the work in running text or, in parentheses, give readers the information they need to find the complete citation in the works-cited list.

Writing Tip

For more information about citing sources, see **Writing and Research Handbook,** pages 952–955.

Format Your List of Works Cited

Whether you cite your sources with parenthetical documentation, footnotes, or endnotes, your paper should include a complete list of the sources you used. This is your list of works cited, and, unlike your working bibliography, it contains only those sources that you use in your final paper. While you may have consulted many additional sources for background and other general information, these sources shouldn't be included on this final list unless you use and cite ideas or data from the sources in your paper.

From your source cards, record the publishing information, following the formats shown here and in Britta Waller's works-cited list on page 356. If you use a source that is not modeled in this unit, consult your teacher or the *MLA Handbook for Writers of Research Papers.* Be sure to take note of the side-column explanations on pages 342 and 356.

When you prepare your final works-cited list, alphabetize each source by the last name of the author or editor (use the first name listed on the title page, if there is more than one). If you use more than one work by the same author, you need not repeat the author's name for each entry; use three hyphens followed by a period instead. If the source has no author or editor, alphabetize it by the title of the book or article. The chart below shows the proper style for various sources.

Editing Tip

Remember to underline or italicize titles of books, periodicals, and pamphlets. For more information see Lesson 21.10, pages 757–758.

Formats for Work-Cited Entries

SOURCE	ENTRY
Book with Single Author	Badger, Reid. The Great American Fair. Chicago: Nelson-Hall, 1979.
Book with Multiple Authors	Anderson, Norman D., and Walter R. Brown. Ferris Wheels. New York: Pantheon, 1983.
Book with No Author Named	The Dream City: A Portfolio of Photographic Views. St. Louis: Thompson, 1893. N. pag.
Magazine Article	Fincher, Jack. "George Ferris Jr. and the Great Wheel of Fortune." Smithsonian July 1983: 109–118.
Encyclopedia Article	"World's Columbian Exposition." Encyclopedia Americana. 1999.
Newspaper Article	"The Rays Take in the Columbian Exposition." Chicago Tribune 26 July 1984, sec. 5:2.
Online Encyclopedia	"World's Columbian Exposition." Britannica Online. 1994–1999. Encyclopaedia Britannica. 8 Nov. 1999 <http://www.britannica.com/bcom/eb/article/2/0,5716,79582+1,00.html>.
CD-ROM	Wilmeth, Don B. "Ferris Wheel." World Book Multimedia Encyclopedia. CD-ROM. Chicago: World Book, 1999.
A Professional or Personal Web Site	Rose, Julie K. The World's Columbian Exposition: Idea, Experience, Aftermath. 1 Aug. 1996 <http://xroads.virginia.edu/~ma96/wce/title.html>.

Confirming Accuracy

The entry examples on this page will help students confirm the accuracy of their documentation. Students can use the examples as stylistic models as they proofread their work. **L2**

Acting Out Formatting

Students who are experiencing difficulty formatting their lists of sources may benefit from "acting out" the process. Divide students into groups of four and assign students the following roles: author/editor, title, publisher, periodical. Using their own sources, the groups should piece together problematic citations for the class, each group member writing his or her portion on the board and explaining why it should be formatted in that way.

For example, the student who plays the author/editor role needs to know that if no author is listed, the name of the editor (or translator) should be used first. Since not all group members will take part in each citation, tell groups to vary the kinds of entries they perform. **L3**

MEETING INDIVIDUAL NEEDS

English Language Learners

Understanding Abbreviations

Abbreviations might be difficult for learners whose first language is not English. On the board list the abbreviations on page 341 and spell out the words for which they stand. List all the months in the year with the corresponding abbreviations; students will likely need to use these in their citations.

Teach

Using the Model

Point out that bibliography items consist of two or three components, each ending with a period: the author, title, and publisher. Ask students to note that components can be made up of several subparts. Suggest that students refer to the chart to find the exact order and format for each component, including quotation marks or italics for a title and punctuation between elements. **L2**

Editing Citations

To help students discriminate among the various citation categories on the chart, instruct them to highlight in a different color each citation type on their note cards or in their papers. Students then should edit their references one citation type at a time following the format on the graphic organizer. To make the task even more manageable, suggest that students limit their citation-editing time to only one or two types per session. **L1**

Additional Resources

- *Writing Across the Curriculum*
- *Research Paper and Report Writing,* pp. 25–27
- *Thinking and Study Skills,* p. 25

How to Format a Works-Cited List The following works-cited excerpt shows proper format, indentation, and punctuation. Notice that all entries are alphabetized by author's name or by title, excluding words such as *A* and *The* at the beginning of a title.

Begin your works-cited list on its own page following the last text page of your research paper. Place your name and the page number in the top right corner, as on all other pages. Center the title, *Works Cited,* one inch from the top of the page, and double-space to begin the first entry. Double-space all entries and between the entries as well.

As you examine the works-cited model, take note of the explanations in the margin. Also notice that proper formats are used for a variety of sources not shown in the chart on page 341.

For works with more than one author, reverse the first and last names of the first author only.

No author was given for this weekly magazine article.

Use this format for a face-to-face interview, citing the date on which the interview took place. You may also specify *Telephone interview* or *Online interview,* depending on which method you use.

This is the proper format for a transcribed radio interview that was found online.

Include the publication date of the encyclopedia.

Model

Your name & the page number

Works Cited

Anderson, Norman D., and Walter R. Brown. Ferris Wheels. New York: Pantheon, 1983.

Badger, Reid. The Great American Fair. Chicago: Nelson-Hall, 1979.

"From Ferris Wheels to Virtual Reality." U.S. News & World Report 26 July 1993: 19.

Gomez, Maria. Personal interview. 12 Oct. 1999.

Holliday, Kate. "Big Wheels of the Fun Business." Popular Mechanics Mar. 1969: 144–146+.

Miller, Donald. "Professor Donald Miller Speaks About the History of the Opening of the World's Columbian Exposition." Interview with Neal Conan. Weekend Edition. Natl. Public Radio. 1 May 1993 <http://www.elibrary.com>.

"World's Columbian Exposition." Encyclopedia Americana. 1999.

English Language Learners

Using Models

Students whose first language is not English may be accustomed to a different sequencing of names and dates from that dictated by English documentation. Have peers who speak the same native language identify the differences between book, magazine, and encyclopedia citations in English. Help students to set up models to follow. For easy reference, the models should be labeled *first name, last name, title,* and so on. Be aware that in some languages the name that comes first is the family name.

7.4 Writing Activities

Skills Practice

1. For each of the following pieces of information, tell whether you think source documentation is necessary and explain why.
- Many more calls can be handled by cellular mobile phone service than were handled by earlier systems.
- The first licenses to build and operate mobile telephone systems were granted in 1982.
- Many advances in telephone technology have taken place since Alexander Graham Bell invented the receiver in 1876.
- One author laments, "Cellular phone technology eliminates one more place—inside your own car—where you can be free from interruptions."
- Most Americans probably cannot conceive of life without the telephone.
- As a car equipped with a phone travels from cell to cell, the call is transferred via computer from one transmitter and receiver to another without interrupting the call.

2. Write proper entries for a list of works cited for the following sources:
- an article from the 1990 edition of the *World Book Encyclopedia* called "Jet Propulsion Engines"
- an article entitled "The Concorde Tests the Skies," written by Janet Feldman, which appeared on page 30 of *Newsweek* on August 14, 1975
- an article by John Simons entitled "Breakthroughs in Jet Technology," which appeared on pages 70–84 of the book *Aviation and Space,* edited by M. W. Wister and published in New York by Little, Brown in 1982
- a book written by Richard Samson entitled *Jet Engine Basics,* published by MIT Press in Boston in 1975

Your Research Paper

Continue working on your research paper by successfully completing the following steps.
- Insert proper documentation within the body of your paper. If you're using parenthetical documentation, replace the note card numbers that correspond to your source cards with a proper citation in parentheses.
- Create a draft of your works-cited page.
- Ensure the accuracy of your documentation and of your works-cited list by following the formats outlined in this lesson and in the *MLA Handbook for Writers of Research Papers.*

Research Paper Writing

LOG ON Writing Online | For more writing and grammar practice, go to **glencoe.com** and enter QuickPass code WC97727p1.

Assess

Evaluation Rubrics

Skills Practice

1. Responses should be based on the chart explanations on page 339:
   no, because the comparison is common knowledge
   yes, year of licenses is not common knowledge
   no, common knowledge
   yes, direct quotation
   no, common knowledge
   yes, probably a paraphrased authoritative explanation of a complex process
2. Entries should be listed and alphabetized as follows:
   Feldman, Janet. "The Concorde Tests the Skies." *Newsweek* 14 Aug. 1975: 30.
   "Jet Propulsion Engines." *World Book Encyclopedia.* 1990 ed.
   Samson, Richard. *Jet Engine Basics.* Boston: MIT Press, 1975.
   Simons, John. "Breakthroughs in Jet Technology." *Aviation and Space.* Ed. M. W. Wister. New York: Little, Brown, 1982. 70–84.

Your Research Paper

Evaluate each student's bibliography for consistency with the chart and model on pages 341 and 342.

Close

Cite specific material from models in this text as both direct and indirect quotes as well as general-knowledge facts. Ask the class if each statement should be documented or not. Then ask students to supply examples of parenthetical documentation and lists of works cited, including citations from professional journals, if available. Examine a variety of citations: those with a sole author, more than one author, or no author or editor; those with more than one work by the same author; and those with more than one source for the same information.

Focus

Lesson Overview

Objective

- To revise a research paper draft for word choice, transitions, and effective presentation of ideas

Skills

- analyzing and revising information in a research paper

Critical Thinking

- identifying problems in a first draft and solving these problems

Listening and Speaking

- discussing; evaluating; questioning

Bellringer

Daily Language Activity

When students enter the classroom, have this assignment on the board: *Write an answer to this question: If you could revise any school regulation, what would it be?*

Grammar Link to the Bellringer

Invite students to rewrite an original school regulation using a double negative. Point out how the double negative can cause a regulation to mean the opposite of what was intended—*Don't do no running,* for example, means *Do run.*

See also  *Daily Language Practice*

Motivating Activity

Use the Bellringer to initiate a discussion about revising. Compare revising a research paper to buying clothes. Just as some clothes need alterations to fit perfectly, a first draft may contain good ideas, relevant facts, and authoritative opinions but may still need to be revised to create a better "fit" for the reader.

LESSON 7.5

Revising

"Mr. Watson, come here. I want you!" said Alexander Graham Bell—the first sentence ever uttered over his new invention, the telephone. Bell continued to work on his invention and refine it so that it would communicate even better. Likewise, the first draft of your research paper will also "communicate" even better after you revise it.

Improve Your Paper

When you revise your first draft, work on improving your choice of words, your transitions, and your presentation of ideas. Remember that in a formal research paper, you should write in a voice and style that is appropriate to your audience and purpose. The chart below describes problems you may face at this point—and offers possible solutions to them.

Evaluation Rubric

By the time you complete Lesson 7.5, you will have

- evaluated your research paper draft for both content and mechanics
- reviewed the paper's organization and reorganized the content to ensure coherence, logical progression, and support for ideas
- refined your writing style to suit the requirements of the research paper and to meet the needs of your audience

Solving Revision Problems

PROBLEM	SOLUTION
How can I give my first draft a clearer focus?	Review your thesis statement; delete or rewrite anything in the paper that doesn't support it.
How can I make my argument easier to follow?	Add transitions, rearrange sentences, and include new ideas to make the paper more coherent. Delete irrelevant information.
How can I make my paragraphs flow smoothly from one to another?	Add or change transitions between paragraphs; rearrange paragraphs in a more logical order.
What if my introduction doesn't connect well with the rest of the paper?	Add transitions or rewrite introduction to conform with the purpose and main idea.
What can I do if my sentences sound repetitive?	Vary sentence structure. Use precise, lively language. Find synonyms for repeated words.

Resource Manager

Planning Resources

- *Lesson Plans*

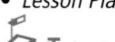

Transparencies

- *Bellringer*
- *Daily Language Practice*
- *Two-Minute Skill Drill*

Other Print Resources

- *Grammar and Composition Handbook*
- *Grammar Workbook*
- *Research Paper and Report Writing,* pp. 28–31
- *Style and Documentation Sourcebook for Writers*
- *Thinking and Study Skills,* pp. 1, 18
- *Writing Across the Curriculum*
- *Writing Assessment and Evaluation Rubrics*

Take a look at some samples of the kind of revising you might need to do on your own research paper. First, look at the model below, which shows the revision of two paragraphs. Consider the reasons for each revision. Next, on page 346, follow the stages in the smaller-scale revision of one particular passage from another part of the same paper.

The Ferris wheel's ~~was very~~ popularity ~~This~~ was due to the ~~popularity of the Midway.~~ The Midway provided escape both from ~~the pressure and pains of~~ real life and from the culture ~~that was so~~ overwhelming ~~in~~ of the rest of the Fair. Couples ~~went~~ rushed to be married at the top of the wheel, but the closest they got was the superintendent's office on the ground below. ~~Rumors were started in the~~ Newspapers started rumors of the wheel losing parts that then hurtled to the ground below. ~~Other rumors~~ or they told of the mechanism locking in place, ~~with~~ trapping the wheel's passengers ~~trapped~~ up in the air with no help. As this never happened, such publicity made the gigantic toy ~~wheel~~ only more popular. (Howells 25). "No single enterprise on the Midway or the grounds proper approached it either in patronage or in wonderment" (Fincher 114).

The wheel did have its critics. Howells accused the wheel of being a mere money-making contrivance--an

Change redundant sentence structures to make the paragraph more concise.

Does this change improve the paper? Why or why not?

Combine sentences that have the same subjects.

Why move this quotation?

A transition helps shift the tone between the two paragraphs.

Research Paper Writing

Teach

Using the Model

The margin notes and questions help students understand the reasons for the revisions made:

- Using both *popular* and *popularity* is redundant.
- The change is an improvement because it makes the two phrases parallel ("real life" and "overwhelming culture").
- The word *rumors* does not need to be repeated; the change combines the two sentences.
- Moving the quotation provides an effective transition between the description of the Midway's popularity and the details supporting the Ferris wheel's popularity.
- The shift from positive tone (describing the wheel's popularity) to critical tone (discussing criticism of the wheel) is jolting. The transition sentence prepares the reader. **L2**

Peer Editing Strategies

Students may wish to share their drafts with a peer to get some feedback about what aspects of the paper are working well and what needs to be improved. Peer editors should describe specifically what they find confusing and, if possible, make suggestions about how to solve the problems. **L2**

Two-Minute Skill Drill

Have students write five or six specific synonyms for each of the following words.

walk	*sad*
vehicle	*occasion*

See also *Two-Minute Skill Drill Transparency 7.5*

7.5

Teach

Revising

To help students understand the revising process, direct their attention to the three revisions of the paragraph.

- After students read the first version, ask: What is the "era"? What is the "better world"? What are the "grand engineering projects"? Why is there an interest in building things other than weapons? Students will see that the first draft gives no clear answers.
- Repeat this exercise with the second version. Answers to the first and third questions should be clear.
- In the third version, the remaining answers become clear: The better world is one without war. In addition, *universal* more vividly characterizes the era's widely shared hope embodied in the fair. Reorganizing the second sentence creates a dramatic image: "Steel and iron were shaped" is more vivid than "engineering projects focused on." **L2**

Cooperative Learning

Use the partners approach to assist students in revising their papers. Direct pairs to read their papers aloud to each other while keeping the checklist questions on page 347 in mind. If the listener has trouble following or does not understand something, he or she calls it to the other's attention. Students should take their partners' comments into consideration when revising. **L2**

Additional Resources

Writing Across the Curriculum

Research Paper and Report Writing, pp. 28–31

Thinking and Study Skills, pp. 1, 18

Research Paper Writing

Draft sentence contains a basic fact, but the specific topic isn't clear.

In an era hoping for a better world, grand engineering projects concentrated on building things other than weapons.

First revision sets off the topic sentence and explains the era, with the modern reader in mind. Supporting details add color and connect sentence ideas to the paper's topic.

The 1890s and early 1900s were marked by a general wish for a better world. Engineering projects focused on new marvels of iron and steel, such as the Ferris wheel, instead of weapons.

How does the choice of words and quotations improve this passage? What does revising the organization accomplish?

The 1890s and early 1900s were marked by a universal wish for a better world, and most of all, "a world without war" (Fincher 109). Steel and iron were shaped into engineering marvels, such as the Ferris wheel, rather than weapons.

Revise Your Paper

When you write a research paper on a scientific subject, you need to pay particularly close attention to certain questions. Presenting scientific data requires precision, so double-check any data you cite. Make certain that you use the most up-to-date information possible. Look for journal, magazine, and newspaper articles for late-breaking developments on your topic. Be sure you use specialized terms precisely and copy direct quotations from sources very carefully.

If you are using the research of others to draw your own conclusions on a topic, you have to be sure that the research is valid. Look closely at your sources to be sure that they are free from possible bias and that they have made logical, convincing arguments. Also, look at your own argument to be sure it is logical and complete. Think about ways your information could be misinterpreted, and revise to make your meaning clearer.

If you wish, exchange papers with a partner to get another perspective on your work and to provide your partner with feedback. Be sure to review the points in the checklist on the next page as you revise your paper.

Revising Tip

If you drafted your paper on a word processor, experiment with organization by cutting and pasting sections of your draft. Save each new version under a new name so that you can track your progress and go back to earlier versions if you wish.

Cooperative Learning

Editing by Peers

Have students trade papers with a peer and comment on incorrectly or awkwardly phrased passages. If many revisions are required in the first drafts, the peer editors may re-read the papers after they are revised. If students receive separate grades for form and content, you may wish to assign a greater-than-usual weight to content to compensate for difficulties that students who are learning English may encounter.

Checklist for Revising a Research Paper

1. How can you strengthen your thesis statement so that it provides a clear focus for the paper?
2. How can your main ideas be better organized to ensure coherence and logical progression? What irrelevant or repetitious ideas can you delete?
3. Which points could be better supported with information from sources?
4. How can you strengthen transitions between ideas and paragraphs?
5. Have you written in a voice and style that is consistent throughout—and is appropriate, given your audience and purpose?
6. Have you varied your sentence structures and used lively verbs so that your paper isn't dull and boring to read?
7. What technical terms still need to be defined?
8. Which frequently used words can be replaced with appropriate synonyms?
9. Have you cited your sources correctly in the body of your paper?
10. Is your works-cited list accurate, complete, and properly formatted?

Revising Tip

For help with revising your research paper, see **Writing and Research Handbook,** pages 947–949.

Research Paper Writing

7.5 Writing Activities

Skills Practice

Revise the following passage for clarity, coherence, and readability.

Compact discs are made of plastic coated with aluminum so that the signals can be read by a laser. Then they are coated in more plastic to protect the pits. Music is recorded on a compact disc in a series of minute pits of varying depths in an outward spiral. In the CD player a low-intensity laser is directed at the pits in their track. As the laser is alternately reflected or scattered off the pits, an optical sensor picks up these signals and converts the signals into sound impulses. The laser never touches the CD, so the CD doesn't wear down or scratch. Also, dust and fingerprints do not distort the laser beam. This results in almost no distortion in the playback. Not surprisingly, CD recordings have become more popular than vinyl records.

Your Research Paper

Revise your research paper. Complete these steps, and use the Checklist for Revising a Research Paper above to guide you.

- Clarify your thesis if necessary, making sure that it adequately sets a purpose and direction for the paper.
- Evaluate the organization of your draft and decide how you can improve the flow of ideas.
- Conduct additional research if necessary to bolster your data in one or more sections of your paper.
- Strengthen your transitions to ensure that your paper is coherent.

For more writing and grammar practice, go to **glencoe.com** and enter QuickPass code WC97727p1.

Assess

Evaluation Rubrics

Skills Practice

Use these criteria when evaluating your students' revisions:

- Do students explain that *pits* are *signals*?
- Do students divide the passage into two paragraphs?
- Do students begin the second paragraph with the sentence "Music is recorded . . . "?

Your Research Paper

Consider basing your evaluation of student revisions on the degree of improvement and the application of the guidelines in the text.

See also *Writing Assessment & Evaluation Rubrics*

Using the Checklist

Encourage students to use the checklist on page 347 as they read and revise their drafts.

Close

Ask students to compare treatments of the same topic in different sources. Have them look for logic errors, such as drawing a conclusion not supported by evidence or letting bias alter the interpretation of the facts. Students should revise any similar questionable material in their first drafts.

Focus

Lesson Overview

Objective

- To use criteria for checking the quality of the research paper before presenting it in its final form

Skills

- writing a summary statement; editing, completing, and presenting a research paper

Critical Thinking

- synthesizing; analyzing; identifying main idea; evaluating; summarizing

Listening and Speaking

- discussing; informal speaking

Bellringer

Daily Language Activity

When students enter the classroom, have this assignment on the board: *List three ways in which you might share your completed research paper with other people.*

Grammar Link to the Bellringer

Have students use a colon when they list their Bellringer ideas. Remind students to include *these, the following,* or *as follows* in the introductory statement that precedes the colon.

See also *Daily Language Practice*

Motivating Activity

Ask students to share their ideas from the Bellringer. If necessary, point out that students might exhibit their finished papers in the library or another prominent spot. Enlist volunteers to help set up the exhibit so the papers can be read. Encourage students to review each other's papers. Suggest that for each paper they read, they give the author at least one written comment.

LESSON 7.6

Editing and Presenting: A Model Paper

George W. G. Ferris's marvelous wheel was at last a reality. After much planning and research, construction and testing, Ferris put the finishing touches on his wheel and opened it to the public. And his efforts truly paid off—the Ferris wheel became a symbol of nineteenth-century technological ingenuity and the world-renowned centerpiece of Chicago's 1893 Columbian Exposition.

In the same way, after much planning, research, and writing, you are about to put the finishing touches on your paper. With these final touches you should have a complete and clean research paper, one that is free of errors and ready for presentation to your teacher and classmates.

Evaluation Rubric

By the time you complete Lesson 7.6, you will have

- proofread your paper, identifying and correcting errors in grammar, punctuation, and spelling
- confirmed that every summary, paraphrase, or quotation is properly credited to a source and checked that every source you used is listed in a properly formatted works-cited list
- created a clean final copy that is free of errors and ready to present to your audience

Prepare the Final Copy

After revising your draft, type or print a new copy of it with your corrections included. Then you can give your paper one final proofreading, checking citations, grammar, spelling, punctuation, and word use. The checklist below can help you catch any remaining problems or errors.

Final Copy Checklist
1. Have I organized my ideas clearly?
2. Have I explained or defined any words that may be unfamiliar to the reader?
3. Have I discussed my topic completely and fairly?
4. Have I corrected all grammar and spelling mistakes?
5. Have I documented my sources properly?
6. Have I considered the proper meaning(s) of the words I've used?
7. Have I spelled and capitalized everything correctly?
8. Have I prepared a neat and easy-to-read final copy?

Editing Tip

For additional editing tips, refer to Lesson 2.10, pages 96–99, and Unit 9, pages 388–411.

Present the Complete Paper

You may want to create a cover for your paper or enclose it in a special folder. If you have a separate title page, it should include the title of your paper, your name, your teacher's name, the course name, and the date on which you submit the paper to your teacher. If you don't have

Resource Manager

Planning Resources

- *Lesson Plans*

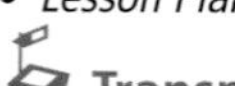

Transparencies

- *Bellringer*
- *Daily Language Practice*

Other Print Resources

- *Research Paper and Report Writing,* pp. 32–35
- *Style and Documentation Sourcebook for Writers*
- *Writing Across the Curriculum*
- *Writing Assessment and Evaluation Rubrics*

a separate title page, put this information on the first page of your paper, as shown here. The last page of your paper is always the list of works cited.

Give some thought to whether your paper would be enhanced by the use of any visuals, such as copies of photographs or works of art, diagrams, time lines, or charts. These materials may be attached to the end of your paper, before the works-cited list.

Keep in mind that your teacher may ask you to submit other materials along with your final paper. For example, you may be asked to submit your note cards, your final outline (which should not include your introduction and conclusion), or a summary statement. Make sure that you know what's expected of you well in advance of the due date! You don't want any last-minute surprises.

Britta C. Waller
Mr. Bruce Dzeda
English Composition
18 April 2000

Waller 1

George W. G. Ferris:
The Man Who Reinvented the Wheel

"Ferris is a crackpot.
He has wheels in his head."
(McGuire)

Even officials of the famous World's Columbian Exhibition of 1893, such as the one quoted above, seemed to think that George Washington Gale Ferris's idea for an industrial monument to rival the Eiffel Tower was far-fetched, if not downright insane. Yet, when it was finally finished, Ferris's colossal wheel embodied the "can-do optimism" of the Exhibition (Fincher 109), America's industrial dominance, the

Writer's last name, and page number, should appear on each page, one-half inch from the top and one inch from the right edge of the paper.

Writer's name, teacher's name, course name, and date should appear flush left on a one-inch margin and one inch from the top of the page.

The title should be centered on the page.

7.6 Writing Activities

Skills Practice

1. Identify the grammatical mistakes in each of the following sentences, and correct them.
   - Scientists should be sure that experiments do not merely reinforce his preconceived ideas.
   - Henry Ford is aware of the European experiments in creating a "horseless carriage." He knew about them for many years before he began his work.
   - People are often unaware of the scientific advance that take place in the era they live in.
2. Edit the following entries for a final list of works cited. You may need to refer to Lesson 7.4, pages 338–343, to review the proper forms of different types of entries.
   - Encyclopaedia Britannica, 1999 ed., Cardiovascular System Diseases and Disorders.
   - Cooke, Alistair. Alistair Cooke's America. Alfred A. Knopf, New York: 1973
   - John Molinari, Hurricane Prediction: Catching the Waves, Science News, 21 October 1989, p. 262
3. Read the research paper by Britta Waller on pages 350–355. Then write a summary statement, about two sentences long, explaining the topic and purpose of her paper.

Your Research Paper

Use what you have learned in this lesson to complete and present the final version of your own research paper.

Teach

Writing Abstracts

Ask students to annotate their list of works cited, critically evaluating each source in terms of scholarship, usefulness, and quality of writing. **L3**

Assess

Evaluation Rubrics

Use these criteria when evaluating your students' writing:

Skills Practice

1. Students should make corrections such as these:
   Noun-pronoun agreement
   Scientists . . . their
   Tense shift
   . . . Ford was aware . . .
   Noun-verb agreement and wordiness
   . . . advances . . . taking place in their era.
2. These are the correct entries:
   "Cardiovascular System Diseases and Disorders." *Encyclopaedia Britannica.* 1991 ed.
   Cooke, Alistair. *Alistair Cooke's America.* New York: Alfred A. Knopf, 1973.
   Molinari, John. "Hurricane Prediction: Catching the Waves." *Science News* 21 Oct. 1989: 262.
3. The summary statement should be one to two sentences long and include a brief restatement of the thesis statement.

Your Research Paper

Evaluate student papers based on items covered in the Final Copy Checklist on page 348.

Teach

Using the Model

Direct students to answer the questions in the margin boxes as a means of analyzing the student model:

- The opening quotation catches the reader's attention.
- The thesis statement is effective because it previews the main topic. **L2**

Cooperative Learning

Divide the class into small groups and ask students to work together to analyze the model research paper. Each group could focus on one of the following: the thesis statement's preview of the paper, the organization's structuring of information, and the evidence's persuasive power. Each group should evaluate the paper's effectiveness in its designated area and give an analytical report to the class. **L2**

Looking at the Author

Explain to students that Britta Waller wrote this paper during her junior year at Theodore Roosevelt High School in Kent, Ohio. Ask students what they think Waller did for her final presentation. Then tell them that the paper was published in *The Concord Review.* **L2**

Why do you suppose Waller includes a quotation here?

Is the thesis statement effective? Why or why not?

Paper should be typed double-spaced, with one-inch margins on all sides.

Parenthetical documentation

Student Model

George W. G. Ferris: The Man Who Reinvented the Wheel

Britta C. Waller

"Ferris is a crackpot. He has wheels in his head."
(McGuire)

Even officials of the famous World's Columbian Exhibition of 1893, such as the one quoted above, seemed to think that George Washington Gale Ferris's idea for an industrial monument to rival the Eiffel Tower was far-fetched, if not downright insane. Yet, when it was finally finished, Ferris's colossal wheel embodied the "can-do optimism" of the Exhibition (Fincher 109), America's industrial dominance, the American dream, and the flexibility of a capitalistic society. This paper will discuss turn-of-the-century America, how these times inspired the World's Columbian Exposition, and the birth, demise, and significance of the great Ferris wheel.

The 1890s and early 1900s were marked by a universal wish for a better world, and most of all, "a world without war" (Fincher 109). Steel and iron were shaped into engineering marvels, such as the Ferris wheel, rather than weapons. Chicago's World's Columbian Exposition of 1893 commemorated the 400th anniversary of Columbus's historic voyage and was the largest, most elaborate, and most magnificent World's Fair ever (Rose). The first international exposition was London's Great Exhibition of 1851, boasting Joseph Paxton's Crystal Palace—the first large scale iron and glass building and the ancestor of the modern skyscraper. The first American exposition was held in Philadelphia in 1876 to celebrate the country's centennial. However, it was the Paris Exhibition of 1889 that inspired the World's Columbian Exhibition (Burg xii). Paris had produced the world-famous Eiffel Tower. America couldn't let Europe have all the limelight. In fact, this national rivalry was one of the prime moving forces behind the Fair. In addition, the Fair signified economic ambition, the rise of the city, and rapid progressive change (Badger 10). Ironically, there was a focus on cultural enlightenment and achievement. Buildings were in the "Greco-Roman-Oriental" style (Fincher 110). Under the direction of Chicago architect Daniel H. Burnham and

Less Proficient Readers

Using the Model

Some students may have difficulty with the vocabulary and the writing style of the model paper. Pair these students with stronger readers and have them analyze the student model together. Suggest that students use a dictionary if neither partner is able to determine a word's meaning from its context. Tell them to be sure to study the annotations in the side column.

landscape architect Frederick Law Olmsted, the nation's best sculptors, architects, painters, writers, and musicians joined with industrialists and inventors to put their best work into the Exposition. Its achievement in the arts far surpassed its historical significance: "We have put aside individual taste and have united in an effort to carry out the several parts of a design which . . . was dominated by one idea," wrote Professor Halsey C. Ives, the Chief of the Department of Fine Arts (Dream City). The dual nature—industry and culture combined—of the Fair was a direct reflection of the era. Henry Steele Commager called the decade of the 1890s a watershed in American history:

> On the one side lies an America predominantly agricultural; concerned with domestic problems; conforming, intellectually, at least, to the political, economic, and moral principles inherited from the 17th and 18th centuries. . . . On the other side lies the modern America, predominantly urban and industrial; inextricably involved in world economy and politics . . . experiencing profound changes in population, social institutions, economy, and technology; and trying to accommodate its traditional institutions and habits of thought to conditions new and in part alien (Burg xiii).

The cultural idealism of the Fair was embodied in its alternate title—"The White City," so named because of a substance called "staff" which covered many of the buildings. Composed of plaster of Paris and jute fibers, staff closely resembled white marble ("World's Columbian Exposition" 533). Author William Dean Howells praised the Fair as "the perfect embodiment of human ingenuity and Christian brotherhood—the ideal of Grecian democracy in industrial America" (vii–viii). Howells saw the Fair as a glimpse of the future of America, and as a departure from the "Age of Accumulation"—a term he used to denounce the period before World War I (xii).

However, Howells's altruistic ideals were pushed aside in favor of the Midway Plaisance, and its Queen—the Ferris wheel.

Early in 1892, Ferris sat quietly at Burnham's planning session for the fabulous Exposition. A tunnel and trestle engineer

(continued)

Set off any quotations longer than three lines by indenting the entire passage.

Use ellipses to indicate that material has been omitted from quotations.

Including the author's name in the text lets Waller use only the page number in the parenthetical note.

Research Paper Writing

Using the Model

Direct students' attention to the margin boxes:

- Discuss why a quotation longer than three lines is indented rather than set off with quotation marks. (The indentation clearly shows where the quotation begins and ends, a distinction that would be more difficult with quotation marks for a long quotation.)
- Reinforce the economy of the parenthetical note, which includes only the page number when the author's name appears in the text. **L2**

Promoting Discussion

Challenge students to identify one paragraph on this page that provides a transition between two major topics. (the one that begins *However, Howells's altruistic . . .*) For what main topics does the paragraph provide a transition? (The paragraph indicates the shift from the Fair's embodiment of turn-of-the-century ideals to Ferris's great wheel.) Point out that *However* signals the reader that what follows is different from the preceding paragraph. Ask students to name some other phrases that can introduce a shift in thought. (*on the other hand, instead of, in contrast*) **L2**

Selecting Long Quotations

To help students who may be uncertain about when or to what extent sources should be directly quoted, point out the quotation of Henry Steele Commager. Such a lengthy quotation is appropriate for explaining a single key idea (here, the dual nature of the United States at the turn of the century). Because the quoted author is an expert and his writing is clear and concise, the quotation is efficient and effective. **L1**

Cultural Connections

Analyzing Cultural Events

World fairs are forums for cultural intermingling as well as international competition. Ask students how the Columbian Exhibition was motivated by national rivalry. (It allowed America to compete with fairs held in Europe, and, in particular, to devise a structure to compete with the Eiffel Tower, which had been produced for the Paris Exhibition of 1889.) Point out that the Olympic Games are also an event in which cultures both intermingle and compete with one another.

Teach

Using the Model

Refer students to the margin boxes for analyzing the model:

- Each sentence is the logical result of the one preceding it—Ferris's design carries out Burnham's instruction.
- The Boeing 747 analogy gives the modern reader a sense of the wheel's immense size and weight.
- This is a comparison organization. Waller probably chose it because it explains the principle of the Ferris wheel in terms of the more familiar bicycle wheel. **L2**

Promoting Discussion

Point out the sentence: *An evening soon after, Ferris sketched the design for his famous amusement ride on a scrap of paper at a Chicago restaurant.* Ask students why Waller mentioned the scrap of paper and the restaurant. Help students see that these details help characterize Ferris and his method of doing things—his brilliance and his spur-of-the-moment inventiveness. **L2**

Logical organization shows how the combination of Ferris's personality and the standards set for the fair produced the Ferris wheel.

Interesting analogy about the wheel's weight puts it in perspective for modern readers.

What kind of organization does Waller use here? Why might she have made this particular choice?

and bridge builder from Pittsburgh, Ferris was 33 years old, tall, slim, and pale, with a bushy black moustache and a "resolute face" (Fincher 110). Born the eighth child of a Nevada farmer, Ferris attended military school in Oakland, California, at age 16 and attended college at Rensselaer Polytechnic Institute (RPI) in Troy, New York. Graduating in 1881, Ferris was said to have a great ability to meet a challenge. Burnham told those who assembled at the planning session: "Mere bigness is not what is wanted. . . . something novel, original, daring and unique must be designed and built if American engineers are to retain their prestige and standing" (Fincher 110). An evening soon after, Ferris sketched the design for his famous amusement ride on a scrap of paper at a Chicago restaurant. He determined all aspects of the wheel—size, number of passengers, price of admission—in his original sketch. He had "re-invented the wheel . . . big" (Fincher 110).

Ferris's wheel was 264 feet high and supported by two 140-foot pyramid-shaped steel towers (Burg 224). The wheel was 26 stories high, taller than any building on the grounds. It weighed, fully loaded, approximately 1,200 tons, or as much as three Boeing 747s (Fincher 111–112). Thirty-six passenger cars were suspended between two steel rims. Made of wood and iron, paneled with plate glass windows, and furnished with swivel chairs, the cars were approximately the size of train passenger cars (Burg 224). The wheel had a total capacity of 2,160 people (Valenti).

The wheel was built on two 20-foot square, 35-foot deep concrete blocks. Plans were approved by the end of 1892. The thousands of parts needed for the steam-powered wheel were built by five different steel companies. In late March of 1893, five trains, each thirty cars long, brought all these parts to Chicago (Anderson and Brown 18). The most crucial was the huge axle—45½ feet long, 33 inches in diameter, weighing 46½ tons. Made by Bethlehem Iron Works of Bethlehem, Pennsylvania, the axle was the largest single piece of steel ever forged in the United States (Valenti; Anderson and Brown 18).

Ferris based his ride on the principle of the bicycle wheel. Heavy steel rods acted as the spokes and pulled toward the axle to keep the wheel's shape. By using tension, Ferris was able to build a lighter, stronger, and vastly larger structure than was ever before possible (Anderson and Brown 17).

Exploring Language

Introductory Phrases

Review the following introductory phrases on page 352:

- *Born the eighth child of a Nevada farmer,* Ferris attended . . .
- *An evening soon after,* Ferris sketched the design . . .
- *Made of wood and iron, paneled with plate-glass windows, and furnished with swivel chairs,* the cars . . .

Discuss the effect of introductory phrases on the readability of the paper. (The use of a variety of sentence structures makes the paper more interesting to read and helps the writer to avoid repetition.)

A twenty-minute ride, or two revolutions with six stops each time around, cost 50 cents. The wheel ran from 8 A.M. to 11 P.M. At night, the wheel was lit by 3,000 electric light bulbs powered by a generator in the boiler house of the wheel (Valenti). One-and-one-half-million people had ridden the wheel by Fair's end—a good number considering that the 50-cent fee was equal to admission to the entire Exposition (Fincher 114). One North Dakota farmboy wrote in a letter home: "Do whatever you have to do—even sell the kitchen stove—come to Chicago and ride the Ferris wheel!" (Anderson and Brown 26). A ride on the wheel, it was said, "may truly be called a round trip" (Lee).

Though an engineering milestone when completed, the wheel was not so well accepted in the early stages of its development. Burnham said it was not strong enough to withstand Lake Michigan winds, and even if it could, the public would be afraid to ride such a "rickety-looking contraption" (Fincher 112). Others doubted the wheel, too, but Ferris was finally allowed to build it if he could finance it. The Exposition had no better match for the Eiffel Tower. Ferris sold stock to wealthy Chicago businessmen (Fincher 112). The wheel cost about $400,000 to build and turned a total profit of $733,086 (Holliday 229).

The Exposition was opened on May 1, 1893, by President Grover Cleveland, but the wheel was not completed. Work was done around the clock, but safety was still ensured. The wheel was powered by two 1,000-horsepower steam engines, one being held as a back-up (Anderson and Brown 21). It also had a huge air brake worked by two 10-foot steel bands that would tighten to stop the wheel in case it began to spin free (Fincher 111). With these features, the wheel was tested extensively. Wrote Ferris's partner and fellow RPI graduate William F. Gronau: "So perfect is the machinery that we did not feel the wheel move" (Fincher 114).

The Ferris wheel had its grand opening on Wednesday, June 21, 1893. Among the invited first riders were Mr. and Mrs. Ferris, the mayor of Chicago, and a 40-piece band, squeezed into one car (Anderson and Brown 23).

The Ferris wheel, and the Midway Plaisance where it was located, were both immediate successes. The Midway was a grand street of international displays and buildings meant

(continued)

What does this quotation contribute to the paragraph?

Presenting Tip

Graphics, such as a labeled diagram of the Ferris wheel, will enhance a reader's understanding of a technical topic.

Using the Model

Refer students to the margin question. Before they respond, you might ask them to determine the paragraph's main idea. (the Ferris wheel's lack of acceptance in its early stages of its development) In response to the question, students may say that the quotation supports the writer's claim, provides some humor, and creates suspense about whether the wheel will actually come into being. Make the point that the humor and suspense offered by the quotation are ironic, since readers already know about the success of the Ferris wheel. The irony involves readers with the wheel's story because they can anticipate seeing the misgivings discussed in the paragraph disappear. **L2**

7.6

Teach

Using the Model

Refer to the margin boxes. Have students discuss how important transitions are in moving a paper along logically from topic to topic, making it easy for the reader to follow and understand the writer's message. **L2**

Promoting Discussion

Discuss organization by referring to the paragraph that begins *The wheel did have its critics.* Ask students the purpose of that first sentence. Students should discern that it is a transition sentence. It indicates a topic change from the preceding paragraph, which discussed the wheel's popularity. Direct students to read through to the sentence *The criticism over the wheel's originality began the wheel's decline* on page 355. Ask them to reread the thesis statement on page 350 to determine at what point in its organization the paper is now. (The writer is beginning to discuss the Ferris wheel's demise.) Point out that the paragraph under discussion is a transition paragraph between discussion of the wheel's beginning and discussion of the wheel's decline. **L2**

Research Paper Writing

to show the everyday life and oddities of all countries (Rose). The Midway was designed to "popularize" the Exposition, which it did very well, because many visitors enjoyed its atmosphere much more than the cultural attractions (Badger 109). Ironically, Jackson Park, the location of the Midway, not the cultural Court of Honor, became the entrance to the University of Chicago, or the "Grey City," as it was known at the time (Badger 90). One anonymous limerick showed the true, educational value of the Fair to the University:

> Oh, there were more Profs than students,
> but then we didn't care;
> They spent their days in research work,
> their evenings at the Fair.
> and life upon the Campus
> was one continual swing,
> We watched the Ferris wheel go round
> and didn't do a thing.
> (Badger 157)

The Ferris wheel's popularity was due to the escape the Midway provided, both from real life and the overwhelming culture of the rest of the Fair. "No single enterprise on the Midway or the grounds proper approached it either in patronage or in wonderment" (Badger 108). Couples rushed to be married at the top of the wheel, but the closest they got was the superintendent's office on the ground below. Newspapers started rumors of the wheel losing parts that then supposedly hurtled to the ground below; or they told of the mechanism locking in place, trapping the wheel's passengers up in the air with no help. As this never happened, such publicity made the gigantic toy only more popular (Fincher 114).

Transitional sentence introduces the controversy surrounding the wheel.

The wheel did have its critics. Howells accused the wheel of being a mere money-making contrivance—an exploitation of the visitors (25). Others said Ferris had plagiarized the idea for the wheel, and that American, Asian, and European history was filled with similar, if less complex, models. This is true, but it was the design that made Ferris's creation unique (Anderson and Brown 37–38).

Transition shows the connection between the original wheel and those that followed.

Though not the first to build such rides, Ferris was forever associated with later machines. British engineer W. B. Basset sought to outdo Ferris's wheel in size and scope. American William Sullivan was also among those inspired by Ferris.

MEETING INDIVIDUAL NEEDS

English Language Learners

Working with a Partner

Shortly before the papers are due, pair each student learning English with a partner more proficient in English. Have partners read each other's draft and critique it. The reviewer should focus on one or two aspects of the paper, such as organization and vocabulary. The reviewer should be sure to point out the paper's strengths as well as its problems.

Sullivan started the Eli Bridge Company in 1906 in Jacksonville, Illinois, the largest current manufacturer of Ferris wheels. Sullivan, after riding the great wheel at the Exposition as many times as possible, capitalized on the commercial possibilities of the wheel. He made smaller, portable versions of about 45 feet in diameter which could be built in quantity (Anderson and Brown 41). George and Mary Tilyou wanted to buy Ferris's wheel and take it to their newly built Brooklyn amusement park—Coney Island, which was modeled after the Midway. The Tilyous couldn't afford the ride and instead built a 125-foot diameter "Wonder Wheel," which still stands. Though it wasn't the first or largest, as the signs claimed, Coney Island's Wonder Wheel established Ferris wheels and their many variations as a permanent fixture in modern American amusement parks (Fincher 117).

The criticism over the wheel's originality began the wheel's decline. Ferris's assets collapsed over lawsuits with the Exposition about the wheel's profits. During the winter of 1893–94, the wheel was left deserted. With a brief appearance at the North Clark Street Fair beginning in early 1895, the wheel regained some of its original standing, but it had simply lost its novelty. Neighbors in Clark Street campaigned to remove the wheel, ironically, complaining of its "undesirable industrialism" (Fincher 117). The wheel then appeared at the Louisiana Purchase Exposition of 1904 in Saint Louis and was still running perfectly. However, it remained unsuccessful. In 1906, following the Louisiana Exposition, the great wheel was brought tumbling down with 100 pounds of dynamite. The *Chicago Tribune* reported, "Within a few minutes, it was a tangled mass of steel and iron forty feet high" (Fincher 118). However, Ferris was not there to see its end. In November 1896, George W. G. Ferris had died unexpectedly in a Pittsburgh hospital at the age of 37. The cause was diagnosed as several different ailments, but mostly Ferris's death was due to depression over his potential bankruptcy and loss of hope (Fincher 118).

The true achievement of the Ferris wheel lay not in how long it stood, but in its combination of pleasurable enjoyment and industrial achievement. It symbolized the ideals of the World's Columbian Exposition. Moreover, the Ferris wheel signified the industrial advancement of the times and provided an escape in the peaceful period before World War I.

(continued)

Story of wheel's demise is presented in chronological order.

What does Waller do in her conclusion?

Using the Model

Point out that Britta Waller succinctly recaps her paper in the final paragraph. Ask students to compare this paragraph with the thesis statement in the opening paragraph of the paper. Mention that introductions (including the thesis statement) and conclusions may include rephrasings of the same essential information. In her conclusion, Waller has elaborated on her topic's significance. **L2**

Listening and Speaking

Taking Notes

Invite as a guest speaker to your class someone who is currently writing or has recently completed a major research paper, such as a doctoral dissertation or master's thesis. Ask the visitor to bring examples of materials that he or she used at various stages of the research process and, if available, the final product. Ask students to prepare questions regarding the stages of the visitor's writing process. Tell students to think of questions that would be most useful to them in writing their own papers.

Teach

Using the Model

Discuss with students the citation formats used in the final Works Cited list. Ask students what questions they have about the information included in the citations or about the punctuation and order of that information. Also discuss the annotations in the side margin. Remind students that they can find proper abbreviations for publishers' names in the *MLA Handbook for Writers of Research Papers* and in *The Chicago Manual of Style*.

Additional Resources

- *Research Paper and Report Writing,* pp. 32–35
- *Writing Across the Curriculum*

Close

After students turn in their papers, encourage them to reflect on the project in a class discussion. Ask them which stages of the writing process were most enjoyable, time-consuming, difficult, enriching, or surprising. What would they do differently next time they are assigned to write a research paper? What procedures and strategies would they like to remember and use again? Suggest that they write down their thoughts in their journals.

Abbreviate publishers' names appropriately. *UP* stands for *University Press.* Also note that the first line of an entry is flush left; indent all other lines five spaces or one-half inch.

This particular book is not paginated. The abbreviation *N. pag.* explains the absence of page references in parenthetical citations of the book.

Works Cited

Anderson, Norman D., and Walter R. Brown. Ferris Wheels. New York: Pantheon, 1983.

Badger, Reid. The Great American Fair. Chicago: Nelson-Hall, 1979.

Burg, David F. Chicago's White City of 1893. Lexington: UP of Kentucky, 1976.

The Dream City: A Portfolio of Photographic Views. St. Louis: Thompson, 1893. N. pag.

Fincher, Jack. "George Ferris Jr. and the Great Wheel of Fortune." Smithsonian July 1983: 109–118.

Holliday, Kate. "Big Wheels of the Fun Business." Popular Mechanics Mar. 1969: 144–146+.

Howells, William Dean. Letters of an Altrurian Traveller (1893–1894). Gainesville: Scholars' Facsimiles and Reprints, 1961.

Lee, William H. Beautiful Scenes of the White City: A Portfolio of Original Copper-plate Half-tone Engravings of the World's Fair. Chicago: Laird and Lee, 1894. N. pag.

McGuire, John M. "Ferris Invented His Big Wheel for Chicago's 1893 Exposition." St. Louis Post-Dispatch 3 May, 1999. ProQuest Direct. Chicago Public Lib. Chicago. 9 Nov. 1999 <http://proquest.umi.com>.

Rose, Julie K. The World's Columbian Exposition: Idea, Experience, Aftermath. 1 Aug. 1996 <http://xroads.virginia.edu/~ma96/wce/title.html>.

Valenti, Michael. "100 Years and Still Going Around in Circles." Mechanical Engineering June 1993: 70+. ProQuest Direct. Chicago Public Lib. Chicago. 9 Nov. 1999 <http://proquest.umi.com>.

UNIT 7 Review

Reflecting on the Unit: Summarize What You Learned

Focus on the following questions to help summarize what you learned in this unit.

1. What does prewriting involve in research paper writing?
2. What does drafting involve when writing a research paper?
3. What does documentation include when writing a research paper?
4. What steps are involved in preparing your paper for its audience?

Adding to Your Portfolio

CHOOSE A SELECTION FOR YOUR PORTFOLIO Look over the research paper you prepared during this unit, and put it into your portfolio. Your research paper should show the following:

- a topic that interests you and is neither too broad nor too narrow
- a strong thesis statement and a logical outline
- an introduction that presents a topic and approach
- a conclusion that wraps it all up
- proper citations for all sources
- careful revision and proofreading

REFLECT ON YOUR CHOICE Attach a note to your research paper, explaining what you learned from writing it.

SET GOALS How can you improve your writing? What skill will you focus on the next time you write?

Writing Across the Curriculum

MAKE A SOCIAL STUDIES CONNECTION One type of research paper is a summary. Look through a newspaper or weekly news magazine. Choose a controversial issue that interests you. Look for different people's opinions on the topic. You can start with the editorial page. Then write a one-page report stating the issue, your position, and evidence supporting your position. Include a thesis statement and an effective conclusion, and be sure to cite your sources correctly.

Reflecting on the Unit

Ask students which of the four stages was most challenging or difficult for them to master. Discuss how students solved any problems they encountered.

Adding to Your Portfolio

Encourage students to be thorough when completing the Reflect on Your Choice activity. The observations they record can teach them about themselves as well as about the process of writing a research paper.

Portfolio Evaluation

If you grade the portfolio selections, you may want to award two marks—one each for content and form. Explain your assessment criteria before students make their selections.

Commend

- experimentation with creative prewriting techniques
- clear, concise writing in which the main idea, audience, and purpose are evident
- successful revisions
- work that shows a flair for language

Writing Across the Curriculum

Suggest that students review the four types of thesis statements before they begin writing. Remind them that a position statement reflects an opinion.

ASSESSMENT OPTIONS

Tests With Answer Key & Rubrics
Unit 7 Pretest, pp. 25–26
Unit 7 Mastery Test, pp. 27–28

Testmaker
Unit 7 Pretest
Unit 7 Mastery Test

You may wish to administer the Mastery Test at this point.

 *MindJogger Videoquizzes*

UNIT 8

Viewing the Art

This photograph of a man in a horse-drawn two-wheeled cart riding along the shore projects a sense of calm against a backdrop of crashing waves. The details in the picture may be combined to create a complex story, in much the same way that writers combine simple sentences into longer ones in order to express more complex thoughts.

Interpret and Analyze Use the following questions for discussion:

- How would you describe the setting of this photograph? What effect does the presence of a buggy have on the setting?
- How might the combination of details in this image be used to generate a story?

Discussing the Quotation

The quotation comes from "A Christmas Memory" by Truman Capote (1924–1984). Discuss the quotation with the class, and ask students how they interpret the author's meaning. How might the author's two short sentences be combined into one longer sentence?

Writing Prompt Write a brief explanation of how Capote's words, coupled with the image of the horse-drawn two-wheeled buggy, can be seen to connect to sentence combining.

"Fetch our buggy. Help me find my hat."

—Truman Capote, "A Christmas Memory"

358

Resource Manager

Planning Resources
- *Lesson Plans*
- *Block Scheduling*

Transparencies
- *Bellringer*
- *Two-Minute Skill Drill*

Other Print Resources
- *Grammar Workbook*
- *Sentence-Combining Practice*
- *Tests with Answer Key and Rubrics*

Video
- *MindJogger Videoquizzes*

UNIT 8

Sentence Combining

Objectives

- To help students, through example and instruction, develop skills in sentence combining
- To learn how to combine short sentences into longer sentences that express more complex thoughts

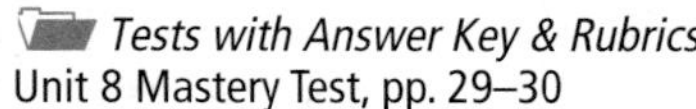

ASSESSMENT OPTIONS

 *Tests with Answer Key & Rubrics*
Unit 8 Mastery Test, pp. 29–30

Testmaker
Unit 8 Mastery Test

Key to Ability Levels

L1 Level 1 activities are within the basic ability range of students.

L2 Level 2 activities are within the ability range of average students.

L3 Level 3 activities are more challenging activities.

Software

- *Presentation Plus!*
- *Revising with Style*
- *Testmaker*

Web Site

- *glencoe.com*

Focus

Unit Overview

Objectives

- To understand and appreciate how sentence combining helps to develop a personal writing style
- To identify two kinds of sentence combining
- To apply various sentence combining techniques to write a longer, more complex sentence

Skills

- combining sentences; exploring writing styles

Critical Thinking

- analyzing writing styles; comparing and contrasting styles

Listening and Speaking

- discussing; questioning; evaluating

Bellringer

Daily Language Activity

When students enter the classroom, have this assignment on the board: *Look at the following short sentences. Write them as one longer sentence.*

I went.

Marie went.

Bill went.

We all went yesterday morning.

Motivating Activity

Discuss students' responses to the Bellringer activity. Explain that one purpose of sentence combining is to learn to write longer, more complex sentences. By combining sentences, students will find they have more stylistic options. In this unit, they will practice sentence combining in different types of writing.

UNIT 8

Style Through Sentence Combining

Skillful writing is partly a matter of habit, just like skillful shooting on the basketball court. Both require practice. You can practice some aspects of sentence writing so that they become habit. The ability to write sentences smoothly frees your mind for other important tasks—like getting your ideas right.

Practice in Sentence Combining

This unit focuses on combining short sentences into longer, more complex ones. Remember that the goal is clear writing, not merely long sentences. Practice in sentence combining reveals your stylistic options, the choices you can make as you write. Long sentences are not always the best option. This unit teaches you how to add variety and interest to your writing by varying your sentence patterns. It also helps you to understand sentence structure.

Regular practice in sentence combining enables you to find clear ways to express your ideas. To write effectively, you must form good sentences consistently. Sentence combining can help you achieve that goal. By making you aware of writing choices, sentence combining also develops your writing style. As you try new types of sentence structures, your personal style will emerge naturally.

Develop Your Style

One way to develop a personal style, as you already know, is by writing regularly in a journal. Such writing helps you unlock your ideas and find your own voice as a writer. Sentence combining is a second approach that has worked for millions of students.

Sentence combining presents you with clusters of short sentences and invites you to express their meanings in more interesting ways. It also helps you make logical connections to ideas for clearer expression in your writing and, at the same time, cures choppiness. Here's an example of a cluster:

Writing is a game.
It is full of challenges.
It requires regular practice.
It leads to personal rewards.

Resource Manager

Planning Resources
- *Lesson Plans*

Transparencies
- *Bellringer*
- *Two-Minute Skill Drill*

Other Print Resources
- *Sentence-Combining Practice,* pp. 1–35

Scanning those four simple sentences, you can probably see different ways of combining them into a longer, more complex statement. Basically, there are four strategies for combining:

- deleting repeated words
- using connecting words
- rearranging words
- changing the form of words

The example below shows one way of combining these sentences.

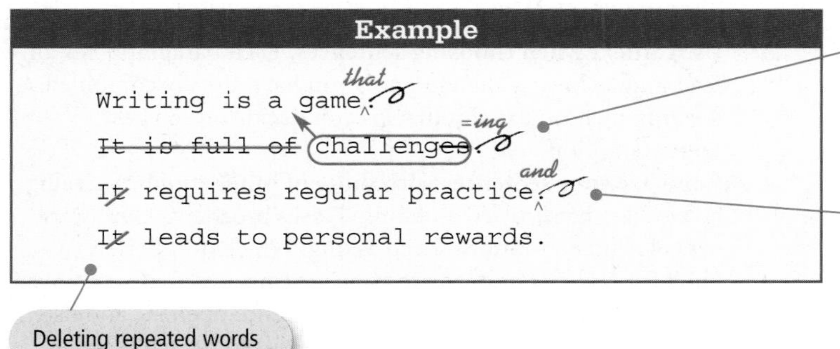

Rearranging words; changing the form of words

Using connecting words

Notice that this editing example produces sentence **1** below. Try reading it and the other variations aloud, listening to differences in style.

1. Writing is a challenging game that requires regular practice and leads to personal rewards.
2. Writing, a game full of challenges, leads to personal rewards through regular practice.
3. Requiring regular practice, the challenging game of writing leads to personal rewards.
4. The challenges of the writing game require regular practice but lead to personal rewards.
5. Writing is a game that leads to personal rewards; overcoming its challenges, however, requires regular practice.

All of these sentences say basically the same thing, but they do so in different ways. In other words, each has a different emphasis. As a skilled writer, you choose the stylistic emphasis that best expresses your aims in the context of an emerging paragraph.

Teach

Using Sentence Combining

In *Creative Approaches to Sentence Combining* (published by NCTE/ERIC in 1986), William Strong stresses that good sentences are not necessarily long. Students may need to be reminded that the point of sentence combining is to improve the quality of sentences, not to increase their length. Even as students combine short sentences, they can look for opportunities to eliminate wordiness from their prose. **L2**

Discussing Decisions

In *Creative Approaches to Sentence Combining,* Strong cautions that students can feel bored or burdened when sentence-combining activities lack instructional focus or are presented too often. Students will benefit most if they spend time discussing their decisions about their writing style. It is important that students understand that sentence combining improves revision skills, not composing skills. Students can use the activities as springboards for real writing, however. Strong suggests that teachers introduce sentence-combining activities for brief periods a couple of times per week. **L2**

Two-Minute Skill Drill

Combine the following short sentences into a longer, more complex sentence.

She sat in a chair.

It had a green cushion.

It was a rocking chair.

It squeaked when she rocked.

See also *Two-Minute Skill Drill Transparency 8.1*

Teach

Taking Risks

In *Creative Approaches to Sentence Combining,* William Strong recommends that teachers present sentence combining as an opportunity for taking risks with language. He points out that mistakes in writing are not only unavoidable and natural but also valuable. Errors provide a writer with opportunities for feedback and improvement. Students will become better writers if they explore how different syntactic choices produce sentences of varying quality. **L2**

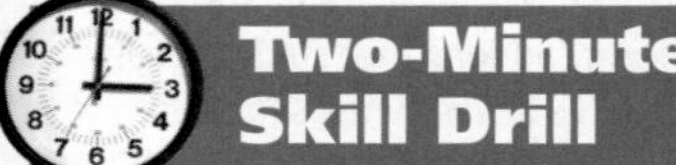

Two-Minute Skill Drill

Combine the following short sentences into longer, more complex sentences:

We stopped.

We froze.

We heard a cracking noise.

A twig snapped.

We dove for cover.

See also *Two-Minute Skill Drill Transparency 8.2*

Sentence-Combining Hints

Sentence combining is easy and fun. Here are some basic suggestions you might try as you explore style.

1. **Whisper sentences to yourself.** As you work with clusters of sentences, try combining them aloud. This process is faster than writing and helps you decide on a "best sentence" to write down.
2. **Work with a partner.** By trying out sentences on a partner—and hearing your partner's ideas—you often discover new, interesting ways to solve specific challenges. Don't be afraid to borrow ideas.
3. **Use context when choosing sentences.** Each paragraph has an emerging context—the sentences you have already combined. Reading this context aloud helps you decide on the best sentence option.
4. **Compare your sentences with those of other students.** Seeing how others have solved combining tasks broadens your awareness of sentence options. Keep asking: Which do I prefer?
5. **Look for stylistic patterns in your writing.** Calculate your average words per sentence, study your sentence openers, and listen to rhythms in your style. Try new patterns to stretch yourself.
6. **Take risks.** Learning to make clear, effective sentences also means taking risks and making mistakes. So, strange as it may sound, it actually makes sense to accept mistakes—even *welcome* them—as you combine sentences. After all, mistakes provide feedback for your language learning. As you learn from them, you develop an expressive style, a voice of personal authority. You come to know yourself as a writer.

As you can see, sentence combining involves skills of talking to yourself, making judgments, and holding what you say in short-term memory so that you can transcribe it. These are oral skills as much as writing skills. Good writers trust an "inner voice."

A Workshop on Style

Looking ahead in this unit, you will find two kinds of sentence combining. The exercises in Lessons 8.1 through 8.4 present clusters of short sentences, with spaces between the clusters. The exercises in Lesson 8.5, drawn from literature selections in this book, are set up in an unclustered format.

Lessons 8.1 to 8.4 give you practice in writing descriptive, narrative, expository, and persuasive paragraphs. You can combine each cluster into a single sentence, leave a cluster partially combined, or combine clusters together. The idea, always, is to take risks and create the best sentences you can. Exercises on facing pages deal with the same topic or situation. Think of these exercises as "bookends" for the writing you will do. After you have combined sentences, your task is to connect the paragraphs into a longer essay or story. Doing so will help you transfer sentence-combining skills to your own writing.

Lesson 8.5 invites you to test your skills against those of a professional writer. As you do these unclustered exercises, you will need to figure out the ideas that logically belong together. After you have done the sentence combining, you can check your version against the author's original. By studying similarities and differences between the two passages, you will learn a great deal about your own style. Sometimes you will prefer the professional writer's sentences. Why, specifically, are they "better" than yours? But sometimes you will prefer your own style. Can you build on this writing skill, trying it out in your own stories and essays? Either way, you learn to write better.

Explore Your Own Style

The whole point of sentence-combining practice is to improve your revising and editing skills—to help you see that sentences are flexible instruments of thought, not rigid structures cast in concrete. The simple fact that you feel confident in moving sentence parts around increases your control of the writing process. To acquire this sense of self-confidence in combining and revising sentences, you can try strategies like those shown below.

1. **Vary the length of your sentences.** Work for a rhythmic, interesting balance of long and short sentences, remembering that brevity often has dramatic force.
2. **Vary the structure of your sentences.** By using different kinds of introductory clauses—and by sometimes tucking information into the middle of a sentence—you can create stylistic variety.

Example

```
Children, were curled in balls,
The balls were little
Children slept on the straw.
The straw was scattered on wagon beds.
```

Tuck a participial phrase in the middle of the sentence by deleting the verb *were.*

Rearrange the position of the adjective.

Delete repeated words.

End the sentence with a participial phrase describing the straw.

Author's Original Version:
Children, curled in little balls, slept on the straw scattered on wagon beds.

from *Winesburg, Ohio* by Sherwood Anderson

Cooperative Learning

Sentence combining is an excellent opportunity for students to work in pairs or small groups. In *Creative Approaches to Sentence Combining,* William Strong notes that it is sometimes helpful to have pairs begin working orally and then write down each other's solutions. Oral work helps students hear how clusters of short sentences can be combined to good effect. Students can also work orally in groups, with students taking turns transcribing the group's solutions. **L2**

UNIT 8

Assess

Evaluation Rubric

Sentence combining practice helps students improve their revising and editing skills. Check to see that students are confidently moving sentence parts around and experimenting with different styles. Use the following questions:

- Are sentences of varying lengths?
- Is sentence structure varied?
- Is parallelism employed?
- Do sentences use colons, dashes, semicolons, commas, and parentheses effectively?
- Are sentence patterns sometimes reversed?

Additional Resources

Sentence-Combining Practice, pp. 1–35

Close

After students have completed the unit, encourage them to discuss how they think they can apply what they have learned about sentence combining to their own writing. When do they think sentence combining efforts will be most useful? (Students will probably consider it to be most useful during the revision stage.) Have students list rules (similar to those on pages 363–364) that work especially well for them when they are combining sentences. Post the ideas on a classroom chart or bulletin board.

Sentence Combining

3. **Use parallelism for emphasis.** Experiment with repeating items in a series—words, phrases, and clauses—to help you understand how structural patterns work and how you can use them to your advantage.

Example

We shall pay any price.
~~We shall~~ bear any burden.
~~We shall~~ meet any hardship.
~~We shall~~ support any friend.
~~We shall~~ oppose any foe.
~~This will~~ *to* assure the survival and success of liberty.

Delete repeated words.

Use **parallelism,** or similar grammatical structure, in the remaining phrases. Note how the repeated use of the pattern *(verb) + any + (noun)* creates a consistent, distinctive rhythm.

Use commas to separate phrases in a series.

Delete *This will* and place *to* before the verb *assure* to form an infinitive phrase.

Author's Original Version:
We shall pay any price, bear any burden, meet any hardship, support any friend, oppose any foe to assure the survival and success of liberty.

from "First Inaugural Address" by President John F. Kennedy

4. **Use interruption for emphasis.** Colons, semicolons, dashes, commas, parentheses—all of these are useful tools in your stylistic tool kit; knowing how to use them well is important.
5. **Use unusual patterns for emphasis.** Reversing normal sentence patterns may never have occurred to you, but such a strategy can work—if you know how to use it.

Writing Tip

For more information about writing good sentences, see **Writing and Research Handbook,** pages 940–943.

LESSON 8.1

Description

Exercise A First Date

Directions Combine each cluster of numbered items into one or more sentences. Combine clusters, if you wish.

1.1 Tony sat on the edge of a sofa.
1.2 The sofa was plush.
1.3 The sofa was mauve.
1.4 He waited for his date to appear.

2.1 The room felt like a funeral parlor.
2.2 The room looked like a funeral parlor.
2.3 This seemed only fitting.
2.4 Her father was a mortician.

3.1 A gas log burned in the fireplace.
3.2 Its burning was cheerless.
3.3 It bathed the room with warmth.
3.4 The warmth was antiseptic.

4.1 Next to it stood a TV console.
4.2 Its screen reflected the firelight.
4.3 The firelight was flickering.

5.1 Gold draperies extended along one wall.
5.2 The draperies were heavy.
5.3 They were like a dark shroud.
5.4 A painting depicted fading sunlight.
5.5 The sunlight was over an ocean shore.

6.1 The quietness of the room seemed eerie.
6.2 Its suggestions of death seemed eerie.
6.3 Its suggestions of dying seemed eerie.

7.1 In front of him was a marble table.
7.2 It had networks of veins.
7.3 It had networks of capillaries.
7.4 The networks were polished.

8.1 He traced its lines with his eye.
8.2 He listened to a mantle clock.

Continue the Story Whom does Tony meet—Mom, Dad, or the family pet? Writing further description will help you link "First Date" to "Ready to Party."

Revising Tip

In cluster 4, try changing *reflected* to *reflecting* as you combine. A connector such as *with* may be useful in cluster 6.

Sentence Combining

Resource Manager

Planning Resources

- *Lesson Plans*

Other Print Resources

- *Sentence-Combining Practice,* pp. 1–35

Focus

Lesson Overview

Objectives

- To identify various options for combining short sentences into longer ones
- To practice combining clusters of short sentences into longer and more complex sentences

Skills

- combining sentences; synthesizing information; evaluating descriptions

Critical Thinking

- identifying; synthesizing; evaluating; summarizing

Listening and Speaking

- informal speaking; explaining process; discussing; note taking

Practice and Assess

Answers: Exercise A

Answers will vary, but some suggestions are given below.

1. Sitting on the edge of a plush mauve sofa, Tony waited for his date to appear.
2. It seemed only fitting that the room looked and felt like a funeral parlor, because her father was a mortician.
3. In the fireplace a gas log burned cheerlessly, bathing the room with antiseptic warmth.
4. Next to it stood a TV console, its screen reflecting the flickering firelight.
5. Heavy gold draperies extended along one wall like a dark shroud. A painting depicted fading sunlight over an ocean shore.
6. The quietness of the room, with its suggestions of death and dying, seemed eerie.
7. In front of him was a marble table with polished networks of veins and capillaries.
8. Tracing its lines with his eye, he listened to a mantle clock.

Practice and Assess

Answers: Exercise B

Answers will vary, but some suggestions are given below.

1. At school she was pretty, but tonight—with her hair pulled back—she looked gorgeous.
2. She had olive skin and finely chiseled facial features.
3. Combed past her ears, her shoulder-length hair was black and lustrous. Her dark eyes sparkled with laughter.
4. She wore gold loop earrings, a denim jacket over a red blouse, and faded blue jeans.
5. Even her boots, with their pointed toes, looked ready for serious dancing.
6. At school her image was low-key and conservative, yet tonight's outfit showed an outgoing, fun-loving personality.
7. Tony felt awkward in his stiff white shirt, his sport coat, and his carefully pressed slacks.

Revising Tip

In clusters 1 and 6, try different connectors—*but, yet, however, while, although*—before settling on one; then check punctuation.

Exercise B Ready to Party

Directions Combine each cluster of numbered items into one or more sentences. Combine clusters, if you wish.

1.1 At school she was pretty.
1.2 Tonight she looked gorgeous.
1.3 Tonight she wore her hair pulled back.

2.1 She had olive skin.
2.2 She had facial features.
2.3 Her features were finely chiseled.

3.1 Her hair was combed past her ears.
3.2 Her hair was shoulder-length.
3.3 Her hair was black and lustrous.
3.4 Her eyes sparkled with laughter.
3.5 Her eyes were dark.

4.1 She wore earrings.
4.2 The earrings were gold loops.
4.3 She wore a denim jacket.
4.4 The jacket was over a red blouse.
4.5 She wore blue jeans.
4.6 The jeans were faded.

5.1 Even her boots looked ready for dancing.
5.2 The boots had pointed toes.
5.3 The dancing would be serious.

6.1 At school her image was low-key.
6.2 At school her image was conservative.
6.3 Tonight's outfit showed a personality.
6.4 The personality was outgoing.
6.5 The personality was fun-loving.

7.1 Tony felt awkward in his white shirt.
7.2 The white shirt was stiff.
7.3 He felt awkward in his sport coat.
7.4 He felt awkward in his slacks.
7.5 The slacks were carefully pressed.

Continue the Story Describe the scene that you see happening *after* this scene. Then share your text—"First Date" plus "Ready to Party"—with a writing partner.

Exercise C Student Teacher

Directions Combine each cluster of numbered items into one or more sentences. Combine clusters, if you wish.

1.1 The day was only half over.
1.2 The student teacher was frustrated.
1.3 She was completely discouraged.

2.1 Morning classes had not cooperated.
2.2 This was despite her best efforts.
2.3 This was despite her planning.
2.4 Her planning was careful.

3.1 Now her mouth was tense.
3.2 It sagged with fatigue.

4.1 Her desk looked like a disaster.
4.2 It was cluttered with announcements.
4.3 It was cluttered with office notes.
4.4 It was cluttered with tardy slips.
4.5 It was cluttered with late papers.
4.6 The disaster was educational.

5.1 A buzzer echoed in the hallway.
5.2 It signaled a class change.
5.3 She still had not found the planner.
5.4 It contained her lecture notes.

6.1 She wore a badge of resignation.
6.2 The resignation was weary.
6.3 She watched the room fill with students.
6.4 They wanted lunchtime to continue.

7.1 The clock's second hand swept toward twelve.
7.2 She searched for a friendly face.
7.3 The face might help her through the period.

8.1 It was there near the back of the room.
8.2 This was much to her surprise.
8.3 This was much to her relief.

Continue the Story Describe yourself as the person who saves the student teacher's day. Link this description to "Thunderstorm."

Revising Tip

In cluster 4, try *cluttered* at the beginning, in the middle, and toward the end of the sentence. Which approach does *not* work?

Answers: Exercise C

Answers will vary, but some suggestions are given below.

1. With the day only half over, the student teacher was frustrated and completely discouraged.
2. Morning classes had not cooperated, despite her best efforts and careful planning.
3. Now her tense mouth sagged with fatigue.
4. Her desk—cluttered with announcements, office notes, tardy slips, and late papers—looked like an educational disaster.
5. A buzzer echoed in the hallway to signal a class change, but she still had not found the planner that contained her lecture notes.
6. Wearing a badge of weary resignation, she watched the room fill with students who wanted lunchtime to continue.
7. As the clock's second hand swept toward twelve, she searched for a friendly face that might help her through the period.
8. Much to her surprise and relief, it was there near the back of the room.

Practice and Assess

Answers: Exercise D

Answers will vary, but some suggestions are given below.

1. Moving to the half-open windows, the class waited for the show to begin.
2. Swirling up from the west, wind-blown dust had turned the sky beige.
3. Above the hills were shades of gray, the color of gunmetal. The gray darkened to an ominous purple.
4. Lightning splintered the turbulent horizon, its flash followed by a heavy boom that rumbled like boxcars in the train yard.
5. Then the wind came up, and the atmosphere seemed strangely luminous.
6. As rain began to fall in fat drops, trees swayed and jerked like frantic dancers.
7. They splattered the concrete, punching tiny craters in the thirsty earth, and washed the air clean.

Additional Resources

Sentence-Combining Practice, pp. 1–35

Close

Ask students to outline a topic that can be drafted in three or four stages. (Possible choices: baking cookies; getting from home to school; taking photographs.) Then have them combine their cluster of numbered items into one or more sentences.

Exercise D Thunderstorm

Directions Combine each cluster of numbered items into one or more sentences. Combine clusters, if you wish.

1.1 The class moved to the windows.
1.2 The windows were half open.
1.3 The class waited for the show to begin.

2.1 Dust had turned the sky beige.
2.2 The dust was wind-blown.
2.3 The dust swirled up from the west.

3.1 Above the hills were shades of gray.
3.2 The gray was the color of gunmetal.
3.3 The gray darkened to purple.
3.4 The purple was ominous.

4.1 Lightning splintered the horizon.
4.2 The horizon was turbulent.
4.3 Its flash was followed by a boom.
4.4 The boom was heavy.
4.5 The boom rumbled.
4.6 The boom was like boxcars.
4.7 The boxcars were in the train yard.

5.1 Then the wind came up.
5.2 The atmosphere seemed luminous.
5.3 Its luminescence was strange.

6.1 Trees swayed like dancers.
6.2 Trees jerked like dancers.
6.3 The dancers were frantic.
6.4 Rain began to fall in drops.
6.5 The drops were fat.

7.1 They splattered the concrete.
7.2 They punched craters in the earth.
7.3 The craters were tiny.
7.4 The earth was thirsty.
7.5 They washed the air clean.

Continue the Story Describe what happens next in this classroom scene. Share the text—"Student Teacher" plus "Thunderstorm"—with a writing partner.

LESSON 8.2

Narration

Exercise A Waking Up

Directions Combine each cluster of numbered items into one or more sentences. Combine clusters, if you wish.

1.1 The alarm rang at 6:30 A.M.
1.2 It brought Gary out of bed.
1.3 He had slept only a few hours.

2.1 He had thrashed about.
2.2 He had been unable to sleep.
2.3 He was worried about an interview.
2.4 The interview was for employment.

3.1 Now he blinked heavily.
3.2 He leaned against squares of tile.
3.3 The squares were smooth.
3.4 The tile was in the shower.
3.5 He tried to wake himself.

4.1 Warm spray stung his back.
4.2 It prickled his shoulders.
4.3 He only wanted to close his eyes.
4.4 He only wanted to go back to bed.

5.1 His brain had become sludge.
5.2 The sludge was thick.
5.3 The sludge was viscous.

6.1 He worked shampoo into his hair.
6.2 He turned under the showerhead.
6.3 The shower head was hissing.
6.4 He hoped to revive himself.

7.1 He finally shut off the shower.
7.2 Cold drops spattered his back.
7.3 The drain sucked at his feet.

8.1 Then he pulled a towel from the rack.
8.2 He wrapped it around his waist.
8.3 He stumbled forward to meet the day.

Continue the Story What happens next? Narrate a transition from "Waking Up" to "Job Interview," perhaps using humor to build interest and tension.

Revising Tip

In cluster 1, use a *who* connector, making sure that sentence 1.3 follows *Gary*. Use a pair of commas for this relative clause.

Sentence Combining

Resource Manager

Planning Resources
- *Lesson Plans*

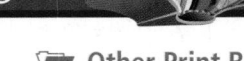

Other Print Resources
- *Sentence-Combining Practice*, pp. 1–35

Focus

Lesson Overview

Objectives
- To use adjective clauses and participial phrases to help combine clusters of short sentences into longer ones
- To develop narrative writing styles by applying sentence combining skills

Skills
- combining sentences; developing a personal narrative style

Critical Thinking
- analyzing; synthesizing; patterning; evaluating; decision making

Listening and Speaking
- discussing; evaluating; questioning

Practice and Assess

Answers: Exercise A

Answers will vary, but some suggestions are given below.

1. At 6:30 A.M. the alarm rang and brought Gary, who had slept only a few hours, out of bed.
2. He had thrashed about, unable to sleep, because he was worried about an employment interview.
3. Now he blinked heavily in the shower, leaning against the smooth square tiles, trying to wake himself.
4. Warm spray stung his back and prickled his shoulders; he only wanted to close his eyes and go back to bed.
5. His brain had become thick, viscous sludge.
6. Working shampoo into his hair and turning under the hissing showerhead, he hoped to revive himself.
7. As he finally shut off the shower, cold drops spattered his back, and the drain sucked at his feet.
8. Then he pulled a towel from the rack, wrapped it around his waist, and stumbled forward to meet the day.

Practice and Assess

Answers: Exercise B

Answers will vary, but some suggestions are given below.

1. The waiting area, which looked like a large broom closet, was noisy, cramped, and poorly lit.
2. Gary sat with two other applicants and tried to relax, but his insides felt tense.
3. He touched his fingers to his face and noticed they were ice cold—a sure sign of nervousness.
4. His plan was to sell himself straightforwardly and without arrogance.
5. He would emphasize his adaptability, his friendliness, and his responsible work habits.
6. When the secretary called his number, he wiped his palms dry, adjusted his new tie, and arranged his face into an upbeat smile.
7. Telling himself he had nothing to lose, he strode into the interview room.
8. It was after shaking hands with the interviewer and settling into an armchair that he noticed his mismatched shoes—one light brown, the other black.

Exercise B Job Interview

Directions Combine each cluster of numbered items into one or more sentences. Combine clusters, if you wish.

1.1 The waiting area was noisy.
1.2 The waiting area was cramped.
1.3 The waiting area was poorly lit.
1.4 It looked like a large broom closet.

2.1 Gary sat with two other applicants.
2.2 He tried to relax.
2.3 His insides felt tense.

3.1 He touched his fingers to his face.
3.2 He noticed they were ice cold.
3.3 This was a sure sign of nervousness.

4.1 His plan was to sell himself.
4.2 The selling would be straightforward.
4.3 It would be without arrogance.

5.1 He would emphasize his adaptability.
5.2 He would emphasize his friendliness.
5.3 He would emphasize his work habits.
5.4 His work habits were responsible.

6.1 The secretary called his number.
6.2 He wiped his palms dry.
6.3 He adjusted his new tie.
6.4 He arranged his face into a smile.
6.5 The smile was upbeat.

7.1 He strode into the interview room.
7.2 He told himself he had nothing to lose.

8.1 He shook hands with the interviewer.
8.2 He settled into an armchair.
8.3 He noticed his mismatched shoes.
8.4 One was light brown.
8.5 The other was black.

Revising Tip

In cluster 1, use *which* to create an adjective clause for sentence 1.4. For more on punctuating adjective clauses, see Lesson 21.6, page 741.

Continue the Story Narrate an interesting conclusion for this story. Then share your text—"Waking Up" plus "Job Interview"—with a writing partner.

Exercise C Breakup

Directions Combine each cluster of numbered items into one or more sentences. Combine clusters, if you wish.

1.1 Sabrina lay on a blanket.
1.2 The blanket was in the backyard.
1.3 Her jacket was off.
1.4 Her sunglasses were on.

2.1 She had tried to study for an exam.
2.2 Last night's breakup was on her mind.
2.3 The breakup was sudden.

3.1 She had been sharing a pizza.
3.2 The pizza was after school.
3.3 She was with her boyfriend.
3.4 They had begun to argue.

4.1 Their voices grew louder.
4.2 Their voices grew more angry.
4.3 He had clenched a fist.
4.4 He had slammed it on the table.
4.5 This caused a stir in the restaurant.

5.1 He had leaned forward.
5.2 He had tried to hold her hand.
5.3 She had turned away.

6.1 Her rejection had been unexpected.
6.2 It had been a sharp blow.
6.3 The blow was to his pride.
6.4 His pride was masculine.

7.1 She had said he was immature.
7.2 He was unable to control his temper.

8.1 She had made her decision.
8.2 Her decision was not to see him again.
8.3 His apologies had been weak.
8.4 His apologies had been pathetic.

Continue the Story Narrate what you imagine Sabrina to be thinking about. Is she having second thoughts? Use your narration as a link from "Breakup" to "The Spider."

Sentence Combining

Answers: Exercise C

Answers will vary, but some suggestions are given below.

1. With her jacket off and her sunglasses on, Sabrina lay on a blanket in the backyard.
2. She had tried to study for an exam, but last night's sudden breakup was on her mind.
3. She had been sharing a pizza with her boyfriend after school when they began to argue.
4. As their voices grew louder and more angry, he had clenched a fist and slammed it on the table, causing a stir in the restaurant.
5. He had leaned forward and tried to hold her hand, but she had turned away.
6. Her rejection had been unexpected— a sharp blow to his masculine pride.
7. She had said he was immature, unable to control his temper.
8. She had made her decision not to see him again because his apologies were weak and pathetic.

Practice and Assess

Answers: Exercise D

Answers will vary, but some suggestions are given below.

1. Grassy spears cushioned her notebook; a long-legged spider moved up a page.
2. Threatened by a pencil, the spider hesitated and then changed direction.
3. Its delicate legs scurried for safety, but Sabrina grabbed one and picked up the thrashing spider.
4. Amused by its frantic dance, she made a two-fingered vise and moved in for the kill.
5. Death hung merciless, poised above the spider's silent scream.
6. She thought about her boyfriend and considered her own impulsiveness in the warm, breathless afternoon.
7. Feeling the sun's warmth on her back and arms, Sabrina rolled over on her side, smiled to herself, and let the spider go.

Additional Resources

Sentence-Combining Practice, pp. 1–35

Close

Have each student create a sentence-combining cluster that includes at least two kernel sentences. Ask volunteers to record their clusters on the board. Have students write a combined sentence for each cluster, and invite them to read their sentences aloud. Use students' responses to explore different syntactic choices. Ask students at what point in narrative writing sentence combining might be most useful. (the revision process)

Revising Tip

In clusters 4 and 7, try participial phrases to open the sentences. For more on participles, see Lesson 12.3, pages 523–524.

Exercise D The Spider

Directions Combine each cluster of numbered items into one or more sentences. Combine clusters, if you wish.

1.1 Spears cushioned her notebook.
1.2 The spears were grassy.
1.3 A spider moved up a page.
1.4 The spider was long-legged.

2.1 The spider hesitated.
2.2 It then changed direction.
2.3 It was threatened by a pencil.

3.1 Its legs scurried for safety.
3.2 Its legs were delicate.
3.3 Sabrina grabbed one.
3.4 She picked up the spider.
3.5 The spider was thrashing.

4.1 She was amused by its dance.
4.2 The dance was frantic.
4.3 She made a two-fingered vise.
4.4 She moved in for the kill.

5.1 Death hung merciless.
5.2 Death hung poised.
5.3 It was above the spider's scream.
5.4 The scream was silent.

6.1 The afternoon was breathless.
6.2 The afternoon was warm.
6.3 She thought about her boyfriend.
6.4 She considered her own impulsiveness.

7.1 Sabrina felt the sun's warmth.
7.2 It was on her back.
7.3 It was on her arms.
7.4 Sabrina rolled over on her side.
7.5 She smiled to herself.
7.6 She let the spider go.

Continue the Story Narrate a conclusion to this story. Then share your text—"Breakup" plus "The Spider"—with a writing partner.

LESSON

8.3 Exposition

Exercise A **Dealing with Acne**

Directions Combine each cluster of numbered items into one or more sentences. Combine clusters, if you wish.

1.1 Acne is a common skin condition.
1.2 It affects mostly teenagers and young adults.
1.3 Both males and females can be affected.
1.4 It may last from five to ten years.

2.1 You may have acne or fear getting it.
2.2 Gaining knowledge should be your first line of defense.
2.3 You should learn about its causes.
2.4 You should learn about its possible cures.

3.1 Information about acne is available.
3.2 You can learn from a physician or dermatologist.
3.3 You can learn from books on the topic.
3.4 You can learn from numerous Internet sites.

4.1 Simple steps can help you deal with acne.
4.2 They are mostly a matter of common sense.

5.1 Wash daily with soap and water.
5.2 Don't waste money on cleansers.
5.3 The cleansers are medicated.
5.4 Don't waste money on granular scrubs.

6.1 Use a drying lotion or cream.
6.2 This should contain benzoyl peroxide.

7.1 Wear your hair off your face.
7.2 This keeps it free of scalp oils.
7.3 Avoid hair dressings.
7.4 Hair dressings are greasy.

8.1 Don't pick at your face.
8.2 This increases inflammation.
8.3 This heightens your risk of pitting.
8.4 This heightens your risk of scarring.

Introduce the Article Introduce the hygiene advice in "Dealing with Acne" by explaining why people need to understand this skin condition.

Revising Tip

In cluster 2, try starting the sentence with the word *if*. In that same cluster, try using a semicolon to divide your sentence into two main parts.

Sentence Combining

Focus

Lesson Overview

Objective
- To combine short sentences into more complex expository sentences

Skills
- developing writing style

Critical Thinking
- analyzing clusters

Listening and Speaking
- discussing sentence combinations; listening to sentence revisions

Practice and Assess

Answers: Exercise A

Answers will vary, but some suggestions are given below.

1. Acne is a common skin condition that affects mostly teenagers and young adults, both males and females, and may last as long as five to ten years.
2. If you have acne or fear getting it, gaining knowledge should be your first line of defense; you should learn about its causes and its possible cures.
3. Information about acne is available from various sources, including a physician or dermatologist, books on the topic, and numerous Internet sites.
4. Simple steps, mostly a matter of common sense, can help you deal with acne.
5. Wash daily with soap and water, but don't waste money on medicated cleansers or granular scrubs.
6. Use a drying lotion or cream that contains benzoyl peroxide.
7. Wear your hair off your face to keep it free of scalp oils; also, avoid greasy hair dressings.
8. Don't pick at your face, because doing so increases inflammation and heightens your risk of pitting and scarring.

Resource Manager

Planning Resources
- *Lesson Plans*

Other Print Resources
- *Sentence-Combining Practice,* pp. 1–35

Practice and Assess

Answers: Exercise B

Answers will vary, but some suggestions are given below.

1. Although suntans may suggest good health, they seriously damage your skin by destroying its elastic fibers.
2. No one wishes for the consequence, premature aging, which leaves skin dry and wrinkled.
3. Even less desirable are the health risks, which include basal cell carcinoma and malignant melanoma.
4. These skin cancers, which are a result of sun exposure, develop cumulatively and irreversibly.
5. Early suntans and sunburns can result in cancers during adult years.
6. Many suntan salons promise safe tans without burns, but actually they pose real health hazards.
7. Tanning booths use ultraviolet radiation, which penetrates the skin deeply, causing premature aging and increased susceptibility to cancers.
8. Protecting your skin requires that you reduce direct exposure to sunlight, use sunscreens rated at SPF 15 or higher, and wear protective clothing in the sun.
9. Avoiding suntan salons is common sense and saves you money.

Exercise B Protecting Your Skin

Directions Combine each cluster of numbered items into one or more sentences. Combine clusters, if you wish.

1.1 Suntans may suggest good health.
1.2 They seriously damage your skin.
1.3 They destroy its elastic fibers.

2.1 Their consequence is premature aging.
2.2 No one wishes for the consequence.
2.3 This leaves skin dry and wrinkled.

3.1 Even less desirable are the health risks.
3.2 The risks include basal cell carcinoma.
3.3 The risks include malignant melanoma.

4.1 These skin cancers develop cumulatively.
4.2 These skin cancers develop irreversibly.
4.3 They are a result of sun exposure.

5.1 Early suntans can result in cancers.
5.2 Early sunburns can result in cancers.
5.3 The cancers are during adult years.

6.1 Many suntan salons promise safe tans.
6.2 They promise tans without burns.
6.3 They actually pose real health hazards.

7.1 Tanning booths use ultraviolet radiation.
7.2 This penetrates the skin deeply.
7.3 This causes premature aging.
7.4 This increases susceptibility to cancers.

8.1 Protecting your skin requires something.
8.2 You reduce direct exposure to sunlight.
8.3 Use sunscreens rated at SPF 15 or higher.
8.4 Wear protective clothing in the sun.

9.1 Avoiding suntan salons is common sense.
9.2 It also saves you money.

Continue the Article Create a transition paragraph after "Dealing with Acne" that links to "Protecting Your Skin." Share your text with a writing partner.

Revising Tip

In clusters 2, 3, 4, 7, and 8, you can practice writing adjective clauses. For help on punctuating adjective clauses, see Lesson 21.6, page 741.

Exercise C Taking Notes

Directions Combine each cluster of numbered items into one or more sentences. Combine clusters, if you wish.

1.1 There are many systems for note taking.
1.2 Two have proved popular with students.
1.3 The students dislike traditional plans.

2.1 One system develops a spiderweb of words.
2.2 The system is sometimes called "webbing."
2.3 The system is sometimes called "mapping."
2.4 The words are from the reading.

3.1 Responses to reading trigger words.
3.2 The responses are personal.
3.3 Words are jotted down as "webs of meaning."

4.1 These webs may not make sense to someone else.
4.2 The webs speak clearly to us.
4.3 We are their authors.
4.4 We know what they are trying to say.

5.1 A second system also uses personal meaning.
5.2 The system is popular.
5.3 It is called the "dialogue journal."

6.1 The journal consists of two facing pages.
6.2 One page is for notes in outline form.
6.3 The other is for thoughts about the notes.

7.1 The notes record information objectively.
7.2 The facing page processes the information.
7.3 It provides emotional reactions.
7.4 It makes summaries.
7.5 It gives examples.
7.6 It asks questions.

8.1 A basic principle underlies both systems.
8.2 We bring unique experiences to reading.
8.3 We take away personal meanings.

Introduce the Article Develop a character sketch or dramatic incident that involves a student with poor study habits; use this sketch to introduce "Taking Notes."

Revising Tip

In cluster 7, try using parallelism to make your sentence clear and coherent. For help with parallelism, see **Writing and Research Handbook,** pages 941–942.

Answers: Exercise C

Answers will vary, but some suggestions are given below.

1. Although there are many systems for note taking, two have proved popular with students who dislike traditional plans.
2. One system—sometimes called "webbing," or "mapping"—develops a spiderweb of words from the reading.
3. Personal responses to reading trigger words that are jotted down as "webs of meaning."
4. Although these webs may not make sense to someone else, they speak clearly to us because we are their authors and know what they are trying to say.
5. A second popular system, called the "dialogue journal," also uses personal meaning.
6. The journal consists of two facing pages—one for notes in outline form and the other for thoughts about the notes.
7. The notes record information objectively, whereas the facing page processes the information by providing emotional reactions, making summaries, giving examples, and asking questions.
8. A basic principle underlies both systems: we bring unique experiences to reading and take away personal meanings.

Practice and Assess

Answers: Exercise D

Answers will vary, but some suggestions are given below.

1. Because they have not discovered certain principles that make it easy and fun, many students have trouble studying and therefore get discouraged.
2. One approach that works for many students is to get an overview by flipping through a text, skimming major headings, and reading the chapter summary.
3. Like a road map, this overview provides "the big picture"; moreover, it triggers personal knowledge and leads to questions.
4. A person turns headings into questions, arousing a sense of curiosity and providing a focus for reading that will follow in a few moments.
5. Because questions engage one's thinking processes, they are an indispensable tool for preparing the mind to remember ideas.
6. Many highly successful students take notes as they read, jotting down answers to questions or challenging the author.
7. Students who are active readers cannot help but learn the material; they recite key points to themselves, discuss ideas with others, and review their notes.

Additional Resources

Sentence-Combining Practice, pp. 1–35

Close

Discuss with students how the practice in revising expository writing has improved their revising skills. Then ask why scientists might find the need to use revising techniques in their writing. (Their data and results may appear in short sentences that need to be combined to form a clear conclusion or summary.)

Revising Tip

In cluster 5, try *because* as a sentence opener; then try an appositive, with dashes, after the word *questions*. Choose the sentence you prefer.

Exercise D Study Strategy

Directions Combine each cluster of numbered items into one or more sentences. Combine clusters, if you wish.

1.1 Many students have trouble studying.
1.2 They have not discovered certain principles.
1.3 The principles make it easy and fun.
1.4 They therefore get discouraged.

2.1 One approach is to get an overview.
2.2 The approach works for many students.
2.3 This is done by flipping through a text.
2.4 This is done by skimming major headings.
2.5 This is done by reading the chapter summary.

3.1 This overview is like a road map.
3.2 This overview provides "the big picture."
3.3 This overview triggers personal knowledge.
3.4 This overview leads to questions.

4.1 A person turns headings into questions.
4.2 Questions arouse a sense of curiosity.
4.3 Questions provide a focus for reading.
4.4 Reading will follow in a few moments.

5.1 Questions engage one's thinking processes.
5.2 They are a tool for preparing the mind.
5.3 The tool is indispensable.
5.4 The preparation is to remember ideas.

6.1 Many students take notes as they read.
6.2 The students are highly successful.
6.3 They jot down answers to questions.
6.4 They challenge the author.

7.1 These students are active readers.
7.2 The readers recite key points to themselves.
7.3 The readers discuss ideas with others.
7.4 The readers review their notes.
7.5 They cannot help but learn the material.

Continue the Article Write a conclusion for "Taking Notes" and "Study Strategy." Then share your text with a writing partner.

LESSON 8.4

Persuasion

Exercise A Diet Myths

Directions Combine each cluster of numbered items into one or more sentences. Combine clusters, if you wish.

1.1 Most Americans worry about their weight.
1.2 Our society says that "thin is in."
1.3 Advertisers sell us images of bodies.
1.4 The bodies are lean and handsome.

2.1 Forty percent of us are on diets.
2.2 This is at any given moment.
2.3 We are trying to shed excess pounds.

3.1 Helping people to lose weight is a major industry.
3.2 Promoters make a variety of claims.
3.3 The promoters seek quick profits.
3.4 The claims are given wide circulation.

4.1 One such myth centers on grapefruit.
4.2 It contains enzymes.
4.3 The enzymes are supposed to burn fats away.

5.1 No scientific evidence supports these claims.
5.2 Dozens of diets are based on this myth.

6.1 A second myth centers on diet pills.
6.2 The pills are touted as "sure cures."
6.3 The cures are for weight loss.

7.1 Pills sometimes have short-term effects.
7.2 No evidence supports long-term weight loss.

8.1 A third myth centers on electric stimulators.
8.2 These claim to provide "passive exercise."
8.3 These claim to trim fat in specific areas.

9.1 Scientific studies show something.
9.2 Such devices provide no change in body weight.
9.3 Such devices provide no change in body fat.
9.4 Such devices do not improve muscle tone.

Introduce the Article To introduce "Diet Myths," find an actual advertisement (from a Sunday supplement magazine, perhaps) and make it part of your paragraph.

Revising Tip

In cluster 1, try rearranging sentences to achieve emphasis; in cluster 9, delete *something* and use *that* as a connector.

Sentence Combining

Resource Manager

Planning Resources
- *Lesson Plans*

Other Print Resources
- *Sentence-Combining Practice*, pp. 1–35

Focus

Lesson Overview

Objectives
- To combine clusters of short sentences into longer ones by rearranging sentences, using connectors, or adding ellipses
- To develop persuasive writing styles by applying sentence combining skills

Skills
- combining multiple ideas in various stylistic constructions

Critical Thinking
- analyzing; relating; patterning; identifying

Listening and Speaking
- discussing

Practice and Assess

Answers: Exercise A

Answers will vary, but some suggestions are given below.

1. Most Americans worry about their weight because our society says that "thin is in" and advertisers sell us images of lean, handsome bodies.
2. At any given moment forty percent of us are on diets, trying to shed excess pounds.
3. Helping people to lose weight is a major industry, and promoters who seek quick profits make a variety of claims that are given wide circulation.
4. One such myth centers on grapefruit, which contains enzymes that are supposed to burn fats away.
5. Although dozens of diets are based on this myth, no scientific evidence supports these claims.
6. A second myth centers on diet pills, which are touted as "sure cures" for weight loss.
7. Although pills sometimes have short-term effects, no evidence supports long-term weight loss.
8. A third myth centers on electric stimulators, which claim to provide "passive exercise" and to trim fat in specific areas.
9. Scientific studies show that such devices provide no change in body weight or body fat and do not improve muscle tone.

Practice and Assess

Answers: Exercise B

Answers will vary, but some suggestions are given below.

1. Whereas some diet myths result from promotion, others seem to grow out of our folklore and are passed on by word of mouth.
2. A widely believed myth that the stomach shrinks when you eat less is simply untrue; your stomach cannot shrink.
3. Another myth, also quite common, is that potatoes are a fattening food.
4. Without butter, gravy, or melted cheese, a baked potato contains only 130 calories.
5. Potatoes are a high-carbohydrate food with no fat or cholesterol; moreover, they have fewer calories than brown rice.
6. Yet another myth surrounds toast, which is listed in many diets and may seem less fattening than untoasted bread.
7. Toasting bread removes only moisture; contrary to popular belief, it does not remove any calories.
8. A fourth myth concerns celery: some say that because it takes so much work to chew it, celery has "negative calories."
9. Chewing celery does not use up extra calories; celery is a high-fiber vegetable and has only about six calories per stalk.

Revising Tip

In either cluster 3 or cluster 4, try dashes to achieve additional emphasis.

Exercise B More Diet Myths

Directions Combine each cluster of numbered items into one or more sentences. Combine clusters, if you wish.

1.1 Some diet myths result from promotion.
1.2 Others seem to grow out of our folklore.
1.3 They are passed on by word of mouth.

2.1 There is a widely believed myth.
2.2 The stomach shrinks when you eat less.
2.3 This is simply untrue.
2.4 Your stomach cannot shrink.

3.1 Another myth is also quite common.
3.2 Potatoes are a fattening food.

4.1 A baked potato contains only 130 calories.
4.2 The potato is without butter.
4.3 The potato is without gravy.
4.4 The potato is without melted cheese.

5.1 Potatoes are a high-carbohydrate food.
5.2 The food has no fat or cholesterol.
5.3 The food has fewer calories than brown rice.

6.1 Yet another myth surrounds toast.
6.2 It is listed in many diets.
6.3 It may seem less fattening than untoasted bread.

7.1 Toasting bread removes only moisture.
7.2 It does not remove any calories.
7.3 This is contrary to popular belief.

8.1 A fourth myth concerns celery.
8.2 Some say it has "negative calories."
8.3 It takes so much work to chew celery.

9.1 Celery is a high-fiber vegetable.
9.2 It has only about six calories per stalk.
9.3 Chewing it does not use up extra calories.

Continue the Article Draw conclusions from "Diet Myths" and "More Diet Myths" that will persuade your reader. Then share your text with a writing partner.

Exercise C Destroying History

Directions Combine each cluster of numbered items into one or more sentences. Combine clusters, if you wish.

1.1 Homolovi is an ancestral home.
1.2 Homolovi means "Place of the Mounds."
1.3 The home is for many Hopi people.
1.4 The Hopi live in the American Southwest.

2.1 This area has been plundered by looters.
2.2 The area covers 10,000 acres in Arizona.
2.3 The area is protected by federal and state laws.
2.4 The looters are in search of pottery.
2.5 The pottery is Native American.

3.1 The "pot hunters" use backhoes.
3.2 The "pot hunters" use other machinery.
3.3 The "pot hunters" leave a wake of destruction.

4.1 Hundreds of craters now scar the landscape.
4.2 Many buildings once stood there.
4.3 Two thousand people once lived there.
4.4 Two thousand people once worked there.
4.5 This was about 700 years ago.

5.1 The "pot hunters" rip the land.
5.2 The "pot hunters" gouge the land.
5.3 They destroy historical evidence.
5.4 The destruction is thoughtless.

6.1 Wealthy collectors support a black market.
6.2 The collectors are mainly from the United States.
6.3 The collectors are mainly from Japan.
6.4 The collectors are mainly from Germany.
6.5 The black market is flourishing.

7.1 Looters do the dirty work.
7.2 Private collectors are equally guilty.
7.3 They underwrite historical destruction.
7.4 They violate the heritage of Native Americans.

Continue the Article Should every culture have the right to record and document its own heritage? Make your case in a follow-up paragraph.

Revising Tip

In clusters 2 and 4, try *which* and *where* as connectors; in cluster 6, try a pair of dashes for stylistic emphasis.

Sentence Combining

Answers: Exercise C

Answers will vary, but some suggestions are given below.

1. Homolovi, which means "Place of the Mounds," is an ancestral home for many Hopi people who live in the American Southwest.
2. This area, which covers 10,000 acres in Arizona and is protected by federal and state laws, has been plundered by looters in search of Native American pottery.
3. Using backhoes and other machinery, the "pot hunters" leave a wake of destruction.
4. Hundreds of craters now scar the landscape where many buildings once stood and where two thousand people lived and worked about 700 years ago.
5. The "pot hunters" rip and gouge the land, thoughtlessly destroying historical evidence.
6. Wealthy collectors—mainly from the United States, Japan, and Germany—support a flourishing black market.
7. Although looters do the dirty work, private collectors are equally guilty: they underwrite historical destruction and violate the heritage of Native Americans.

Practice and Assess

Answers: Exercise D

Answers will vary, but some suggestions are given below.

1. Because many Native Americans believe in spirits, they deeply value ancient burial sites and ancestral dwellings.
2. They see the continuity in life and regard themselves as caretakers with sacred duties.
3. Pots, beads, baskets, and projectile points have significance to them because these objects help spirits find eternal peace.
4. When Alaskan totem poles are cut up and shipped overseas, Native Americans shudder in disgust.
5. When someone tries to sell a mummified Native American infant for $30,000, Native Americans' jaws clench tight.
6. When Anasazi pots bring nearly $100,000 and Anasazi baskets bring over $150,000, Native Americans shake their heads sadly.
7. Desecrating their past and insulting their values, the black market in relics angers Native Americans—and understandably so.
8. They look forward to a happier time, when the black market, now supported by looting, collapses, and their heritage is accorded respect.

Additional Resources

Sentence-Combining Practice, pp. 1–35

Close

Have students list several reasons they have for engaging in a sport or hobby. Then let them combine the reasons into a persuasive sentence that convinces others to participate in the sport or hobby.

Exercise D Black Market

Directions Combine each cluster of numbered items into one or more sentences. Combine clusters, if you wish.

1.1 Many Native Americans believe in spirits.
1.2 They deeply value ancient burial sites.
1.3 They deeply value ancestral dwellings.

2.1 They see the continuity in life.
2.2 They regard themselves as caretakers.
2.3 The caretakers have sacred duties.

3.1 Pots have significance to them.
3.2 Beads have significance to them.
3.3 Baskets have significance to them.
3.4 Projectile points have significance to them.
3.5 These objects help spirits find eternal peace.

4.1 Alaskan totem poles are cut up.
4.2 Alaskan totem poles are shipped overseas.
4.3 Native Americans shudder in disgust.

5.1 Someone tries to sell a Native American infant.
5.2 The Native American infant is mummified.
5.3 The price is $30,000.
5.4 Native Americans' jaws clench tight.

6.1 Anasazi pots bring nearly $100,000.
6.2 Anasazi baskets bring over $150,000.
6.3 Native Americans shake their heads sadly.

7.1 The black market in relics angers Native Americans.
7.2 The black market desecrates their past.
7.3 The black market insults their values.
7.4 Their anger is understandable.

8.1 They look forward to a happier time.
8.2 Their heritage is accorded respect.
8.3 The black market collapses.
8.4 The black market is now supported by looting.

Revising Tip

Try using *when* as an opener in clusters 4, 5, and 6. This effect is called *parallelism.*

Continue the Article Imagine finding an arrowhead while hiking. Does it go into your pocket? Write about the personal reasons behind your decision.

LESSON 8.5

Literature Exercises

Exercise A

Directions Some of the sentences below come directly from *The Crystal Cave* by Mary Stewart. The numbered sentences are adapted from Stewart's original. Combine the numbered sentences. Then compare your sentences with the Literature Model on page 165.

Next moment I stopped short, brought up by a shock which spilled the excitement through my bowels like water. Something had moved in the murk, just to my right.

1. I froze still.
2. I strained my eyes to see.
3. There was no movement.
4. I held my breath.
5. I listened.
6. There was no sound.
7. I flared my nostrils.
8. I tested the air round me.
9. My testing was cautious.
10. There was no animal or human smell.
11. I thought something.
12. The cave smelt of smoke.
13. The cave smelt of damp rock.
14. The cave smelt of the earth itself.
15. The cave had a scent.
16. The scent was musty.
17. The scent was queer.
18. I could not identify it.

I knew, without putting it into words, that had there been any other creature near me the air would have felt different, less empty. There was no one there.

19. I tried a word in Welsh.
20. My try was soft.
21. The word was "Greetings."
22. The whisper came back at me in an echo.
23. The whisper came back so quickly.
24. I knew I was very near the wall of the cave.
25. Then it lost itself.
26. It was hissing in the roof.

Revising Tip

Whisper possible combinations aloud to try them out as you revise.

Sentence Combining

Focus

Lesson Overview

Objectives

- To apply sentence combining techniques to various literature exercises
- To study literature passages that illustrate effective sentence combining techniques

Skills

- combining sentences to make them more effective

Critical Thinking

- analyzing and synthesizing information

Listening and Speaking

- discussing; evaluating information; questioning

Practice and Assess

Answers: Exercise A

Answers will vary, but a sample is given below. When students have completed the exercise, ask how they think their responses compare with Mary Stewart's writing on page 165.

I froze still and strained my eyes to see, but there was no movement. I held my breath and listened. There was no sound. I flared my nostrils to cautiously test the air round me. I thought that there was no animal or human smell. The cave had a scent: it smelt of smoke, damp rock, and the earth itself. The scent was musty and queer, so I could not identify it.

Softly, I tried a Welsh word: "Greetings." The whisper quickly came back at me in an echo and then lost itself, hissing in the roof. I knew I was very near the wall of the cave.

Resource Manager

Planning Resources

- *Lesson Plans*

Other Print Resources

- *Sentence-Combining Practice,* pp. 1–35

Practice and Assess

Answers: Exercise B

Answers will vary, but a sample is given below. When students have completed the exercise, ask how they think their responses compare with Barry Lopez's writing on page 278.

It is now late in the afternoon, and the wolf has stopped traveling. He has lain down to sleep on cool earth beneath a rock outcropping. Mosquitoes rest on his ears, which flicker as he begins to waken. He rolls on his back and lies motionless. His front legs, folded like wilted flowers, are pointed toward the sky. His back legs are splayed. His nose and tail are curved toward each other on one side of his body.

A few minutes pass, and he bolts suddenly into the woods at full speed (almost forty miles per hour) for forty or fifty yards. He begins to skid and to lunge at a lodgepole pine cone. He trots away with the cone inert in his mouth. His head and tail are erect. His hips are slightly to one side, out of line with his shoulders, as if hindquarters were impatient with forequarters.

Exercise B

Directions Scan the sentences below. Some come directly from *Of Wolves and Men* by Barry Lopez. The numbered sentences are adapted from Lopez's original. Decide which of the numbered sentences belong together, and combine them in your own way. Then compare your sentences with the Literature Model on pages 276–279.

1. It is now late in the afternoon.
2. The wolf has stopped traveling.
3. He has lain down to sleep on cool earth.
4. The earth is beneath a rock outcropping.
5. Mosquitoes rest on his ears.
6. His ears flicker.
7. He begins to waken.
8. He rolls on his back.
9. He lies motionless.
10. His front legs are pointed toward the sky.
11. They are folded like wilted flowers.
12. His back legs are splayed.
13. His nose and tail are curved toward each other.
14. They are on one side of his body.

After a few moments he flops on his side, rises, stretches, and moves a few feet to inspect—minutely, delicately—a crevice in the rock outcropping and finds or doesn't find what draws him there. And then he ascends the rock face, bounding and balancing momentarily before bounding again, appearing slightly unsure of the process—but committed.

15. A few minutes pass.
16. He bolts suddenly into the woods.
17. He achieves full speed.
18. This is almost forty miles per hour.
19. This is for forty or fifty yards.
20. He begins to skid.
21. He begins to lunge at a lodgepole pine cone.
22. He trots away with it.
23. His head is erect.
24. His tail is erect.
25. His hips are slightly to one side.
26. They are out of line with his shoulders.
27. It's as if hindquarters were impatient with forequarters.
28. The cone is inert in his mouth.

Exercise C

Directions Scan the sentences below. Some come directly from *How the García Girls Lost Their Accents* by Julia Alvarez. The numbered sentences are adapted from Alvarez's original. Decide which of the numbered sentences belong together, and combine them in your own way. Then compare your sentences with the Literature Model on pages 212–219.

"Go away," Yoyo wailed, but they both knew she was glad her mother was there, and needed only a moment's protest to save face.

1. Together they concocted a speech.
2. There were two brief pages of compliments.
3. The compliments were stale.
4. There were two brief pages of commonplaces.
5. The commonplaces were polite.
6. The commonplaces were on teachers.
7. It was a speech wrought by necessity.
8. It was a speech without much invention.
9. It was wrought by mother and daughter.
10. It was wrought late into the night.
11. It was wrought on one of the pads of paper.
12. Laura had once used the pads for her own inventions.
13. The speech was drafted.
14. Laura typed it up.
15. Yoyo stood by.
16. She corrected her mother's misnomers and mis-sayings.

Finally, her mother came up and pleaded with Yoyo to go down and reconcile with him [her father].

17. Yoyo found her father downstairs.
18. He was setting up a brand new typewriter.
19. The typewriter was on the kitchen table.
20. The typewriter was electric.
21. It was even better than her mother's.
22. He had outdone himself with all the extra features.
23. There was a plastic carrying case.
24. Yoyo's initials were decaled below the handle.
25. There was a brace to lift the paper upright while she typed.
26. There was an erase cartridge.
27. There was an automatic margin tab.
28. There was a plastic hood like a toaster cover.
29. The hood was to keep the dust away.

Answers: Exercise C

Answers will vary, but samples are given below. When students have completed the exercise, ask how they think their responses compare with Julia Alvarez's writing on pages 212–219.

Together they concocted a speech: two brief pages of stale compliments and polite commonplaces on teachers. It was a speech wrought by mother and daughter out of necessity and without much invention. They worked late into the night on one of the pads of paper Laura had once used for her own inventions. The speech was drafted, and then Laura typed it up as Yoyo stood by, correcting her mother's misnomers and mis-sayings.

Yoyo found her father downstairs setting up a brand new electric typewriter on the kitchen table. It was even better than her mother's. He had outdone himself with all the extra features: a plastic carrying case, Yoyo's initials decaled below the handle, a brace to lift the paper upright while she typed, an erase cartridge, an automatic margin tab, and a plastic hood like a toaster cover to keep the dust away.

Practice and Assess

Answers: Exercise D

Answers will vary, but a suggestion is given below. When students have completed the exercise, ask how they think their responses compare with those of Maya Angelou's writing on pages 40–49.

Browned photographs threatened and leered from the walls. The white, freshly done curtains pushed against themselves in the wind. I wanted to gobble up the entire room and take it to Bailey. He would help me analyze it and enjoy it.

They were flat, round wafers, butter-yellow in the center and slightly browned on the edges. They came with the cold lemonade and were sufficient for childhood's lifelong diet. I remembered my manners: I took nice little lady-like bites off the edges. She said she had made them expressly for me and that she had a few in the kitchen I could take home to my brother.

Exercise D

Directions Scan the sentences below. Some come directly from *I Know Why the Caged Bird Sings* by Maya Angelou. The numbered sentences are adapted from Angelou's original. Decide which of the numbered sentences belong together, and combine them in your own way. Then compare your sentences with the Literature Model on pages 40–49.

She took the bags from me and disappeared through the kitchen door. I looked around the room that I had never in my wildest fantasies imagined I would see.

1. Photographs leered from the walls.
2. Photographs threatened from the walls.
3. The photographs were browned.
4. The curtains pushed against themselves.
5. The curtains pushed against the wind.
6. The curtains were white.
7. The curtains were freshly done.
8. I wanted to gobble up the room entirely.
9. I wanted to take it to Bailey.
10. He would help me analyze it.
11. He would help me enjoy it.

"Have a seat, Marguerite. Over there by the table." She carried a platter covered with a tea towel. Although she warned that she hadn't tried her hand at baking sweets for some time, I was certain that like everything else about her the cookies would be perfect.

12. They were wafers.
13. The wafers were flat.
14. The wafers were round.
15. They were slightly browned on the edges.
16. They were butter-yellow in the center.
17. They came with the cold lemonade.
18. They were sufficient for childhood's lifelong diet.
19. I remembered my manners.
20. I took nice little bites.
21. The bites were lady-like.
22. The bites were off the edges.
23. She said something.
24. She had made them expressly for me.
25. She had a few in the kitchen.
26. I could take them home to my brother.

Exercise E

Directions Scan the sentences below. Some come directly from "Skeletons in the Attic" by Clara Spotted Elk. The numbered sentences are adapted from Spotted Elk's original. Decide which of the numbered sentences belong together, and combine them in your own way. Then compare your sentences with the Literature Model on page 317.

After a chance inquiry, a curator pulled out a drawer in one of the scores of cabinets that line the attic. There were the jumbled bones of an Indian. "A Kiowa," he said.

1. We subsequently found 18,500 Indian remains.
2. Some consisted of a handful of bones.
3. Most were full skeletons.
4. They were stored in the Smithsonian's nooks.
5. They were stored in the Smithsonian's crannies.
6. Their storage was unceremonious.
7. Other museums also collect the bones.
8. Other individuals also collect the bones.
9. Other federal agencies also collect the bones.
10. The agencies include the National Park Service.
11. The bones are of Indian warriors.
12. The bones are of Indian women.
13. The bones are of Indian children.
14. Some are on display as attractions.
15. The attractions are for tourists.
16. The attractions are by the roadside.

It is estimated that another 600,000 Indian remains are secreted away in locations across the country.

17. The museum community defends these collections.
18. Forensic scientists defend these collections.
19. Their defense is vigorous.
20. The collections are grisly.
21. There are few exceptions.
22. They refuse to return remains to the tribes.
23. The tribes wish to rebury them.
24. This is even when grave robbing has been documented.

They want to maintain adequate numbers of "specimens" for analysis and say they are dedicated to "the permanent curation of Indian skeletal remains."

Answers: Exercise E

Answers will vary, but a sample is given below. When students have completed the exercise, ask how they think their responses compare with Clara Spotted Elk's writing on page 317.

We subsequently found, stored unceremoniously in the Smithsonian's nooks and crannies, 18,500 Indian remains: some consisted of a handful of bones, but most were full skeletons. Other museums, individuals, and federal agencies, including the National Park Service, also collect the bones of Indian warriors, women, and children. Some are on display as roadside tourist attractions.

The museum community and forensic scientists vigorously defend these grisly collections. With few exceptions, they refuse to return remains to the tribes that wish to rebury them, even when grave robbing has been documented.

Additional Resources

Sentence-Combining Practice, pp. 1–35

Close

Discuss with students how sentence combining can by useful when they write. Why is it useful to be able to vary sentence length and to combine short sentences in a variety of ways? (Students may say it makes the work more engaging to read and sounds more professional.) Invite students to write paragraphs of their own and consider how they can apply what they have learned about sentence combining.

ASSESSMENT OPTIONS

Tests With Answer Key & Rubrics
Unit 8 Mastery Test, pp. 29–30

Testmaker
Unit 8 Mastery Test

You may wish to administer the Unit 8 Mastery Test at this point.

MindJogger Videoquizzes

UNIT 9

Viewing the Art

This photograph of an alpine explorer descending a snow-covered mountain conveys a sense of adventure and isolation. The cold, barren, landscape suggests excitement and fearfulness at the same time. Similarly, student writers may sometimes fear and dread revising their work, even though the revision process itself often reveals pleasant surprises.

Interpret and Analyze Use the following questions for discussion:

- How would you describe the mood of this photograph? What effect does the landscape have on the mood?
- Where do you imagine the explorer might be, and what might be his or her reason for being there?

Discussing the Quotation

The quotation comes from "Field Trip," an essay by Naomi Shihab Nye (b. 1952). Discuss the quotation with the class, and ask students how they interpret the author's meaning. Is worrying about an upcoming event useful or counterproductive? Why?

Writing Prompt Write a brief explanation of how Nye's words relate to the explorer in the photograph.

"... the things we worry about are never the things that happen."

—Naomi Shihab Nye, "Field Trip"

Resource Manager

Planning Resources
- *Lesson Plans*
- *Block Scheduling*

 **Transparencies**
- *Bellringer*
- *Two-Minute Skill Drill*

Other Print Resources
- *Grammar and Composition Handbook*
- *Grammar Workbook*
- *Sentence-Combining Practice*

 **Video**
- *MindJogger Videoquizzes*

 **Software**
- *Presentation Plus!*

 **Web Site**
- *glencoe.com*

UNIT

9

Troubleshooter

Use Troubleshooter to help you correct common errors in your writing.

387

Objectives

- To help students correct common errors they might make in their writing
- To help students become more independent and competent writers and language users

Using the Models

As students review their written work, have them mark errors using the abbreviations shown in the problem boxes throughout the **Troubleshooter**. These abbreviations can be especially useful when students share their writing during peer review.

About the Troubleshooter

Teachers know that they mark some grammar, usage, and mechanics errors more often than others. Current research corroborates this experience. The *Writer's Choice* **Troubleshooter**, Grades 9–12,was prepared by Glencoe editors after they consulted one such study by Robert J. Connors and Andrea Lunsford, reported in "Frequency of Formal Errors in Current College Writing, or Ma and Pa Kettle Do Research" (*College Composition and Communication,* Vol. 39, No. 4, December, 1988), but neither Connors nor Lunsford participated in *Writer's Choice.*

Focus

Lesson Overview

Objectives

- To identify the four most common types of sentence fragments
- To learn how to avoid or correct sentence fragments in writing

Bellringer
Daily Language Activity

When students enter the classroom, have this assignment on the board: *What is wrong with the following sentences, and how would you correct them?*

Went to the store yesterday.

Because my mother asked me to go.

Bought two loaves of bread. A quart of milk. Then went home.

Motivating Activity

Discuss students' responses to the Bellringer activity. Explain that using sentence fragments instead of complete sentences is a common error in writing. This lesson will help students learn how to recognize sentence fragments and how to correct them.

Teach

Cross-reference: Grammar

For instruction and practice of the material in problems 1 and 2, refer students to Lesson 13.9, pp. 553–554.

Troubleshooter

9.1 Sentence Fragment

Problem 1

Fragment that lacks a subject

frag *Sal put his best effort into his painting. Hoped it would win a prize.*

SOLUTION Add a subject to the fragment to make it a complete sentence.

Sal put his best effort into his painting. He hoped it would win a prize.

Problem 2

Fragment that lacks a complete verb

frag *We heard a loud noise. The fire alarm across the street.*

frag *The reviews are enthusiastic. The critics encouraging us to put on future shows.*

SOLUTION A Add a complete verb or a helping verb to make the sentence complete.

We heard a loud noise. The fire alarm across the street was wailing.

The reviews are enthusiastic. The critics are encouraging us to put on future shows.

SOLUTION B Combine the fragment with another sentence.

We heard a loud noise—the fire alarm across the street.

The reviews are enthusiastic, with the critics encouraging us to put on future shows.

Resource Manager

Planning Resources
- *Lesson Plans*

Transparencies
- *Bellringer*
- *Two-Minute Skill Drill*

Other Print Resources
- *Grammar Workbook*, Lesson 31
- *Sentence-Combining Practice*, pp. 1–2

Problem 3

Fragment that is a subordinate clause

frag *Maria was relieved. (Because she found her notebook.)*

frag *The restaurant is out of melon. (Which I wanted for dessert.)*

SOLUTION A Combine the fragment with another sentence.

Maria was relieved because she found her notebook.

The restaurant is out of melon, which I wanted for dessert.

SOLUTION B Rewrite the fragment as a complete sentence, eliminating the subordinating conjunction or the relative pronoun and adding a subject or other words necessary to make a complete thought.

Maria was relieved. She found her notebook.

The restaurant is out of melon. I wanted it for dessert.

Problem 4

Fragment that lacks both a subject and a verb

frag *Paul finally finished his homework. (At ten o'clock.)*

SOLUTION Combine the fragment with another sentence.

Paul finally finished his homework at ten o'clock.

If you need more help in avoiding sentence fragments, turn to Lesson 13.9, pages 553–554.

Troubleshooter

Cross-reference: Grammar

For instruction and practice of the material in Problems 3 and 4, refer students to Lesson 13.9, pp. 553–554.

Two-Minute Skill Drill

List these fragments on the board and have students use them in complete sentences.

Because I already ate. Went home early. The dark room. A terrific book.

See also *Two-Minute Skill Drill Transparency 9.1*

Additional Resources

Sentence-Combining Practice, pp. 1–2

Grammar Workbook, Lesson 31

Close

Initiate a discussion in which students consider how being able to recognize and avoid sentence fragments in writing can help them when they write papers in their other classes. You may want to have students write down their ideas.

Focus

Lesson Overview

Objectives

- To identify three types of run-on sentences
- To learn how to avoid or correct run-on sentences in writing

Bellringer
Daily Language Activity

When students enter the classroom, have this assignment on the board: *Explain and correct what is wrong with the following sentences:*

You go ahead, I'll be along in a minute. Jamal told them to dive in the water was warm. She didn't want to be late however she was running behind.

Motivating Activity

Discuss students' responses to the Bellringer activity. Explain that using run-on sentences instead of complete sentences is a common error in writing. This lesson will help students learn to recognize run-on sentences and how to correct them.

Troubleshooter

9.2 Run-on Sentence

Problem 1

Comma splice—two main clauses separated only by a comma

run-on *On vacation Luisa enjoys hiking in the mountains, Leon prefers swimming at the beach.*

SOLUTION A Replace the comma with an end mark of punctuation, such as a period or a question mark, and begin the new sentence with a capital letter.

On vacation Luisa enjoys hiking in the mountains. Leon prefers swimming at the beach.

SOLUTION B Place a semicolon between the two main clauses.

On vacation Luisa enjoys hiking in the mountains; Leon prefers swimming at the beach.

SOLUTION C Add a coordinating conjunction after the comma.

On vacation Luisa enjoys hiking in the mountains, but Leon prefers swimming at the beach.

Problem 2

Two main clauses with no punctuation between them

run-on *Kim plays the guitar she writes music too.*

SOLUTION A Separate the main clauses with an end mark of punctuation, such as a period or a question mark, and begin the second sentence with a capital letter.

Kim plays the guitar. She writes music too.

Resource Manager

Planning Resources
- *Lesson Plans*

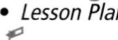

Transparencies
- *Bellringer*
- *Two-Minute Skill Drill*

Other Print Resources
- *Grammar Workbook*, Lesson 32

SOLUTION B Separate the main clauses with a semicolon.

Kim plays the guitar; she writes music too.

SOLUTION C Add a comma and a coordinating conjunction between the main clauses.

Kim plays the guitar, and she writes music too.

Problem 3

Two main clauses with no comma before the coordinating conjunction

run-on *Carla is planning to visit Yellowstone National Park next summer and her sister may join her.*

run-on *The main course was boring but the dessert was magnificent.*

SOLUTION Add a comma before the coordinating conjunction to separate the two main clauses.

Carla is planning to visit Yellowstone National Park next summer, and her sister may join her.

The main course was boring, but the dessert was magnificent.

If you need more help in avoiding run-on sentences, turn to Lesson 13.10, pages 555–557.

Troubleshooter

Teach

Cross-reference: Grammar

For instruction and practice of the material in Lesson 9.2, refer students to Lesson 13.10, pp. 555–557.

Two-Minute Skill Drill

Write these run-on sentences on the board and have students correct them.

Except for me everyone liked the movie I thought it was terrible.

You said we would win the game, you were right.

Since the age of 12, Consuelo hasn't liked running she has loved race walking.

See also *Two-Minute Skill Drill Transparency 9.2*

Additional Resources

Grammar Workbook, Lesson 32

Close

Initiate a discussion in which students consider how being able to recognize and avoid run-on sentences in writing can help them in their other classes.

Cross-reference: Usage

For instruction and practice of the material in Problem 4, refer students to Lesson 16.4, pp. 614–615.

Cross-reference: Usage

For instruction and practice of the material in Problem 5, refer students to Lesson 16.4, pp. 614–615.

Two-Minute Skill Drill

Write these sentences on the board. Ask students to correct the subject-verb errors and to explain why the originals were incorrect.

Two weeks are the time for finishing the project. The class elect officers today.

See also *Two-Minute Skill Drill Transparency 9.3*

Troubleshooter

9.3 Lack of Subject-Verb Agreement

Problem 1

A subject that is separated from the verb by an intervening prepositional phrase

agr *The sound of the nightingales fill the air.*

agr *The storms in winter seems severe.*

SOLUTION Ignore a prepositional phrase that comes between a subject and a verb. Make the verb agree with the subject, which is never the object of a preposition.

The sound of the nightingales fills the air.

The storms in winter seem severe.

Problem 2

A predicate nominative that differs in number from the subject

agr *Bicycle races was his passion.*

SOLUTION Ignore the predicate nominative, and make the verb agree with the subject of the sentence.

Bicycle races were his passion.

Problem 3

A subject that follows the verb

agr *Off the reef lies three sunken ships.*

agr *Here comes the first three volunteers.*

Resource Manager

Planning Resources
- *Lesson Plans*

Transparencies
- *Bellringer*
- *Two-Minute Skill Drill*

Other Print Resources
- *Grammar Workbook,* Lessons 44–51
- *Sentence-Combining Practice,* p. 16

SOLUTION In an inverted sentence look for the subject *after* the verb. Then make sure the verb agrees with the subject.

Off the reef lie three sunken ships.

Here come the first three volunteers.

Problem 4

A collective noun as the subject

agr *The chorus (sing) splendidly.*

agr *The jury (disagrees) among themselves.*

SOLUTION A If the collective noun refers to a group as a whole, use a singular verb.

The chorus sings splendidly.

SOLUTION B If the collective noun refers to each member of a group individually, use a plural verb.

The jury disagree among themselves.

Problem 5

A noun of amount as the subject

agr *Ten months (are) the usual school year.*

agr *Ten dimes (makes) a dollar.*

SOLUTION Determine whether the noun of amount refers to one unit and is therefore singular or whether it refers to a number of individual units and is therefore plural.

Ten months is the usual school year.

Ten dimes make a dollar.

Troubleshooter

Focus

Lesson Overview

Objectives

- To identify sentence constructions that lead to lack of subject-verb agreement
- To learn how to avoid or correct subject-verb errors in writing

Bellringer

Daily Language Activity

When students enter the classroom, have this assignment on the board: *Decide which of the following sentences is incorrect, and then write a correct version:*

Either Mike or his twin brothers has a model car collection.

Each of the girls loves mystery novels.

Motivating Activity

Inform students that the second sentence is the correct one, and note that the verb in the first sentence should be changed to *have.* Ask volunteers to guess why the first sentence takes a plural verb and the second a singular verb. Tell students they will learn more about subject-verb agreement in this lesson.

Teach

Cross-reference: Usage

For instruction and practice of the material in Problems 1, 2, and 3, refer students to Lessons 16.1–16.3, pp. 609–613.

Teach

Cross-reference: Usage

For instruction and practice of the material in Problem 6, refer students to Lesson 16.5, pp. 616–617.

Cross-reference: Usage

For instruction and practice of the material in Problem 7, refer students to Lesson 16.5. pp. 616–617.

Cross-reference: Usage

For instruction and practice of the material in Problem 8, refer students to Lesson 16.5, pp. 616–617.

Troubleshooter

Problem 6

A compound subject that is joined by *and*

agr *Oxygen and hydrogen (is) essential to life.*

agr *Oil and vinegar (are) my favorite salad dressing.*

SOLUTION A If the parts of the compound subject do not belong to one unit or if they refer to different people or things, use a plural verb.

Oxygen and hydrogen are essential to life.

SOLUTION B If the parts of the compound subject belong to one unit or if both parts refer to the same person or thing, use a singular verb.

Oil and vinegar is my favorite salad dressing.

Problem 7

A compound subject that is joined by *or* or *nor*

agr *Neither hardships nor danger (deter) him.*

agr *Either soup or sandwiches (makes) a good lunch.*

SOLUTION Make the verb agree with the subject that is closer to it.

Neither hardships nor danger deters him.

Either soup or sandwiches make a good lunch.

Problem 8

A compound subject that is preceded by *many a, every,* or *each*

agr *Every nook and cranny (were) searched.*

SOLUTION Use a singular verb when *many a, each,* or *every* precedes a compound subject.

Every nook and cranny was searched.

Problem 9

A subject that is separated from the verb by an intervening expression

agr *Carlos, as well as Dana, love baseball.*

Certain expressions, such as *as well as, in addition to,* and *together with* do not change the number of the subject.

SOLUTION Ignore an intervening expression between a subject and its verb. Make the verb agree with the subject.

Carlos, as well as Dana, loves baseball.

Problem 10

An indefinite pronoun as the subject

agr *Each of the climbers carry a rope.*

Some indefinite pronouns are singular, some are plural, and some can be either singular or plural, depending upon the noun to which they refer. (See page 451 for a list of indefinite pronouns.)

SOLUTION Determine whether the indefinite pronoun is singular or plural, and make the verb agree.

Each of the climbers carries a rope.

If you need more help with subject-verb agreement, turn to Lessons 16.1 through 16.7, pages 609–621.

Troubleshooter

Cross-reference: Usage

For instruction and practice of the material in Problem 9, refer students to Lesson 16.6, p. 618.

Cross-reference: Usage

For instruction and practice of the material in Problem 10, refer students to Lesson 16.7, pp. 619–621.

Additional Resources

Sentence-Combining Practice, p. 16

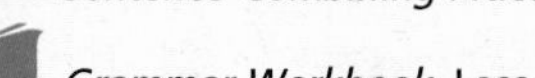

Grammar Workbook, Lessons 44–51

Close

Have each student write two or three sentences demonstrating the correct verb usage for a subject-verb agreement problem. Encourage students to choose problems with which they themselves have difficulty.

Focus

Lesson Overview

Objectives

- To identify sentence constructions that lack pronoun-antecedent agreement
- To learn how to avoid or correct pronoun-antecedent errors in writing

Bellringer
Daily Language Activity

When students enter the classroom, have this assignment on the board: *In the following sentence, underline the pronouns and draw an arrow to their antecedents:*

The ring is too big, but Ms. Galleno says that she can make it smaller.

Motivating Activity

Discuss students' responses to the Bellringer activity. Make sure students understand what a pronoun antecedent is. Then ask students to discuss why the pronoun in the following sentence is confusing: *Each of the candidates gave his speech.*

Teach

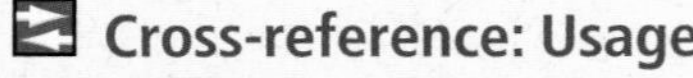

Cross-reference: Usage

For instruction and practice of the material in Problems 1 and 2, refer students to Lesson 17.5, pp. 640–644.

9.4 Lack of Pronoun-Antecedent Agreement

Problem 1

A singular antecedent that can be either male or female

ant *A good athlete must practice (his) routine daily.*

ant *A parent and (his) child form a special bond.*

Traditionally a masculine pronoun was used to refer to an antecedent that might be either male or female. This usage ignores or excludes females.

SOLUTION A Reword the sentence to use *he or she, him or her,* and so on.

A good athlete must practice his or her routine daily.

A parent and his or her child form a special bond.

SOLUTION B Reword the sentence so that both the antecedent and the pronoun are plural.

Good athletes must practice their routines daily.

Parents and their children form special bonds.

SOLUTION C Reword the sentence to eliminate the pronoun.

Good athletes must practice routines daily.

A parent and child form a special bond.

Problem 2

A second-person pronoun that refers to a third-person antecedent

ant *Carlos and Jane love hiking because (you) benefit from vigorous exercise in peaceful, natural surroundings.*

Resource Manager

Planning Resources
- *Lesson Plans*

Transparencies
- *Bellringer*
- *Two-Minute Skill Drill*

Other Print Resources
- *Grammar Workbook,* Lessons 55–57

Be sure not to refer to an antecedent in the third person using the second-person pronoun *you.*

SOLUTION A Use the appropriate third-person pronoun.

Carlos and Jane love hiking because they benefit from vigorous exercise in peaceful, natural surroundings.

SOLUTION B Use an appropriate noun instead of a pronoun.

Carlos and Jane love hiking because hikers benefit from vigorous exercise in peaceful, natural surroundings.

Problem 3

A singular indefinite pronoun as an antecedent

ant *Each of the women had their own goal.*

ant *Neither of the men showed their surprise at the vote.*

Each, everyone, either, neither, and *one* are singular and therefore require singular personal pronouns.

SOLUTION Don't be fooled by a prepositional phrase that contains a plural noun. Determine whether the indefinite pronoun antecedent is singular or plural, and make the noun agree.

Each of the women had her own goal.

Neither of the men showed his surprise at the vote.

If you need more help with pronoun-antecedent agreement, turn to Lesson 16.7, pages 619–621, and Lesson 17.5, pages 640–644.

Troubleshooter

Cross-reference: Usage

For instruction and practice of the material in problem 3, refer students to Lesson 16.7, pp. 619–621.

Two-Minute Skill Drill

Ask students to number four lines on their papers, from one to four. Then read aloud four sentences that contain pronouns. If the pronoun agrees with its antecedent, students should put a check by the number of that sentence. If the pronoun does not agree with its antecedent, students should rewrite the sentence correctly.

 **See also** *Two-Minute Skill Drill Transparency 9.4*

Additional Resources

Grammar Workbook, Lessons 55–57

Close

Ask students to discuss the pronoun-antecedent problems covered in the lesson and to share specific examples of how the lesson has helped them improve a piece of their own writing. What strategies do they use when they are unsure whether the pronoun they have selected is in agreement with its antecedent?

Focus

Lesson Overview

Objectives

- To identify sentence constructions that produce unclear pronoun references
- To learn how to avoid or correct unclear pronoun references in writing

Bellringer
Daily Language Activity

When students enter the classroom, have this assignment on the board: *Tell what is confusing about the following sentences and then write them correctly:*

(1) Ben and John were late for the movie, but he didn't mind.
(2) When the snowflakes hit our faces, they melted.
(3) In some schools, you have free periods every day.

Motivating Activity

Discuss with students why the sentences in the Bellringer are confusing. Explain that such unclear pronoun references can make written material hard to understand. This lesson will teach students how to create clear pronoun references in their writing.

Teach

Cross-reference: Usage

For instruction and practice of the material in Problem 1, refer students to Lesson 17.6, pp. 645–647.

Troubleshooter

9.5 Lack of Clear Pronoun Reference

Problem 1

A pronoun reference that is weak or vague

ref *The traffic was snarled, which was caused by an accident.*

ref *The room was stuffy and dimly lighted, and that made studying difficult.*

ref *Some astronomers think the black holes are very numerous, but it is difficult to prove.*

Be sure that *this, that, which,* and *it* have clear antecedents.

SOLUTION A Rewrite the sentence, adding a clear antecedent for the pronoun.

The traffic was snarled in a massive tie-up, which was caused by an accident.

SOLUTION B Rewrite the sentence, substituting a noun for the pronoun.

The room was stuffy and dimly lighted, and those conditions made studying difficult.

Some astronomers think that black holes are numerous, but that theory is difficult to prove.

Resource Manager

Planning Resources
- *Lesson Plans*

Transparencies
- *Bellringer*
- *Two-Minute Skill Drill*

Other Print Resources
- *Grammar Workbook,* Lesson 58

Problem 2

A pronoun that could refer to more than one antecedent

ref *My sister always beats Susan at chess, but she still enjoys the game.*

ref *When the dancers performed for the children, they were pleased.*

SOLUTION A Rewrite the sentence, substituting a noun for the pronoun.

My sister always beats Susan at chess, but Susan still enjoys the game.

SOLUTION B Rewrite the sentence, eliminating the pronoun.

The children were pleased when the dancers performed.

Problem 3

The indefinite use of *you* or *they*

ref *In Japan you go to school on Saturday mornings.*

ref *In that school they have a fine music program.*

SOLUTION A Rewrite the sentence, substituting a noun for the pronoun.

In Japan students go to school on Saturday mornings.

SOLUTION B Rewrite the sentence, eliminating the pronoun entirely.

That school has a fine music program.

If you need more help in making clear pronoun references, turn to Lesson 17.6, pages 645–647.

Troubleshooter

Cross-reference: Usage

For instruction and practice of the material in Problem 2, refer students to Lesson 17.6, pp. 645–647.

Cross-reference: Usage

For instruction and practice of the material in Problem 3, refer students to Lesson 17.6, pp. 645–647.

Two-Minute Skill Drill

Write this sentence on the board and have students rewrite it so the pronoun reference is clear: *The lunch line moves slowly on Monday, but it is not easy to solve.*

See also *Two-Minute Skill Drill Transparency 9.5*

Additional Resources

Grammar Workbook, Lesson 58

Close

Have students recap the three kinds of unclear pronoun references presented in this lesson. Ask them to check current writing assignments for similar situations and to fix any unclear pronoun references.

Focus

Lesson Overview

Objectives

- To identify sentence constructions that produce incorrect pronoun shifts
- To learn how to avoid incorrect pronoun shifts in writing

Bellringer
Daily Language Activity

When students enter the classroom, have this assignment on the board: *List the plurals of the following singular pronouns: I, you, he, she, it.*

Motivating Activity

As part of a whole-class activity, make a pronoun chart. List all first, second, and third person singular pronouns. Then repeat the process for each pronoun's corresponding plural.

Teach

Cross-reference: Usage

For instruction and practice of the material in Lesson 9.6, refer students to Lesson 17.5, pp. 640–644.

Additional Resources

Grammar Workbook, Lesson 56

Close

Write a sentence on the board that contains an incorrect shift in person between two pronouns. Ask students to list the steps they would take to determine if an incorrect shift in person had occurred and how to rewrite the sentence correctly.

Troubleshooter

9.6 Shift in Pronoun

Problem

An incorrect shift in person between two pronouns

pro *They are going to the international fair, where you can sample foods from many nations.*

pro *I think life was easier when you had fewer possessions.*

pro *After one runs a marathon, you are exhausted yet exhilarated.*

Incorrect pronoun shifts occur when a writer or speaker uses a pronoun in one person and then illogically shifts to a pronoun in another person.

SOLUTION A Replace the incorrect pronoun with a pronoun that agrees with its antecedent.

They are going to the international fair, where they can sample foods from many nations.

I think life was easier when I had fewer possessions.

After one runs a marathon, one is exhausted yet exhilarated.

SOLUTION B Replace the incorrect pronoun with an appropriate noun.

They are going to the international fair, where people can sample foods from many nations.

I think life was easier when people had fewer possessions.

If you need more help in eliminating incorrect pronoun shifts, turn to Lesson 17.5, pages 640–644.

Resource Manager

Planning Resources
- *Lesson Plans*

Transparencies
- *Bellringer*

Other Print Resources
- *Grammar Workbook,* Lesson 56

9.7 Shift in Verb Tense

Problem 1

An unnecessary shift in tense

shift t *Victor reads the newspaper and noted the sports scores.*

shift t *Nan arrived just as the play begins.*

When two or more events occur at the same time, be sure to use the same verb tense to describe both events.

SOLUTION Use the same tense for both verbs.

Victor reads the newspaper and notes the sports scores.

Nan arrived just as the play began.

Problem 2

A lack of correct shift in tenses to show that one event precedes or follows another

shift t *By the time the fire broke out, we were asleep for hours.*

When events being described have occurred at different times, shift tenses to show that one event precedes or follows another.

SOLUTION Shift from the past tense to the past perfect tense to indicate that one action began and ended before another past action began. Use the past perfect tense for the earlier of the two actions.

By the time the fire broke out, we had been asleep for hours.

If you need more help with shifts in verb tenses, turn to Lesson 15.4, pages 589–591, and Lesson 15.6, pages 594–595.

Troubleshooter

Focus

Lesson Overview

Objectives

- To identify sentence constructions that produce incorrect shifts in verb tenses
- To learn how to avoid incorrect shifts in verb tenses in writing

Bellringer
Daily Language Activity

When students enter the classroom, have this assignment on the board: *Change the underlined verb to make its meaning clear. "Shalewa left before the birthday cake is cut."*

Teach

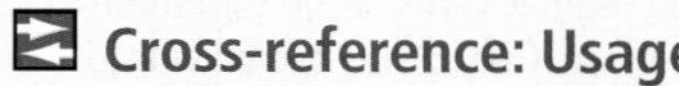

Cross-reference: Usage

For instruction and practice of the material in Problems 1 and 2, refer students to Lesson 15.6, pp. 594–595.

Additional Resources

Grammar Workbook, Lesson 42

Close

Ask students to write one paragraph about two events that occurred at different times. Have students exchange completed paragraphs with a partner and check for incorrect shifts in verb tenses.

Resource Manager

Planning Resources
- *Lesson Plans*

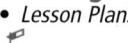

Transparencies
- *Bellringer*

Other Print Resources
- *Grammar Workbook,* Lesson 42

Focus

Lesson Overview

Objectives

- To identify common errors in verb tense
- To identify common errors in verb form
- To learn how to avoid or correct errors in verb tenses or verb forms in writing

Bellringer

Daily Language Activity

When students enter the classroom, have this assignment on the board: *Write the past tense of the following verbs—shout, hurry, swim, follow, try, ride.*

Motivating Activity

Discuss students' responses to the Bellringer activity. Review the difference between regular and irregular verbs in the formation of the past tense. Then divide the class into two teams. In the style of a spelling bee, give each team member a verb and ask him or her to give its past tense. Use both regular and irregular verbs.

9.8 Incorrect Verb Tense or Form

Problem 1

An incorrect or missing verb ending

tense *Yesterday I walk four miles in the morning.*
tense *Have you ever watch a soccer match?*

SOLUTION Add *-ed* to a regular verb to form the past tense and the past participle.

Yesterday I walked four miles in the morning.

Have you ever watched a soccer match?

Problem 2

An improperly formed irregular verb

tense *Mike teared his pants on a nail.*
tense *Angela has sweeped every room.*

Irregular verbs form their past tense and past participle in some way other than by adding *-ed.* Memorize these forms, or look them up.

SOLUTION Use the correct past or past participle form of an irregular verb.

Mike tore his pants on a nail.

Angela has swept every room.

Problem 3

Confusion between the past form and the past participle

tense *Mr. Yei has often spoke about life in China.*

Resource Manager

Planning Resources

- *Lesson Plans*

Transparencies

- *Bellringer*
- *Two-Minute Skill Drill*

Other Print Resources

- *Grammar Workbook,* Lessons 36–37

SOLUTION Use the past participle form of an irregular verb, not the past form, when you use the auxiliary verb *have.*

Mr. Yei has often spoken about life in China.

Problem 4

Improper use of the past participle

tense We (rung) the doorbell several times.

tense Jolene (swum) faster than anyone else on the team.

tense We (begun) the trip without much advance planning.

The past participle of an irregular verb cannot stand alone as a verb. It must be used with the auxiliary verb *have.*

SOLUTION A Add the auxiliary verb *have* to the past participle to form a complete verb.

We have rung the doorbell several times.

Jolene has swum faster than anyone else on the team.

We have begun the trip without much advance planning.

SOLUTION B Replace the past participle with the past form of the verb.

We rang the doorbell several times.

Jolene swam faster than anyone else on the team.

We began the trip without much advance planning.

If you need more help with correct verb forms, turn to Lessons 15.1 and 15.2, pages 581–585.

Troubleshooter

Teach

Cross-reference: Usage

For instruction and practice of the material in Lesson 9.8, refer students to Lessons 15.1 and 15.2, pp. 581–585.

Additional Resources

Grammar Workbook, Lessons 36–37

Write the verbs *speak* and *choose* on the board. Have students write sentences that use each verb in its present tense, in its past tense, and in the form of a past participle.

See also *Two-Minute Skill Drill Transparency 9.8*

Close

Tell students to imagine that a new student has just arrived in class and wants to know what they have been studying. Have students write a short paragraph to help the new student, summarizing what they have learned about using the correct verb tenses or forms.

Focus

Lesson Overview

Objectives

- To identify the most common types of misplaced or dangling modifiers
- To learn how to avoid or correct misplaced or dangling modifiers in writing

Bellringer
Daily Language Activity

When students enter the classroom, have this assignment on the board: *Correct the following headlines so that they mean what the writer intended:*

Complaints About Referees Becoming Ugly

New Housing for Elderly Dead

Fish Biting off the Coast

Car Reported Stolen by Police

Motivating Activity

Discuss students' responses to the Bellringer activity. Explain that the sentences contain misplaced modifiers that change the intended meaning of the sentences. Tell students that this lesson will help them recognize and avoid using misplaced or dangling modifiers.

Troubleshooter

9.9 Misplaced or Dangling Modifier

Problem 1

A misplaced modifier

mod *I got fine pictures of the puppies with my new camera.*

mod *Dented and scratched, Marta found her bicycle.*

mod *We took a backpack on the train stuffed with sandwiches and fruit.*

Modifiers that modify the wrong word or seem to modify more than one word in a sentence are called misplaced modifiers.

SOLUTION Move the misplaced phrase as close as possible to the word or words it modifies.

With my new camera, I got fine pictures of the puppies.

Marta found her bicycle dented and scratched.

We took a backpack stuffed with sandwiches and fruit on the train.

Problem 2

The adverb *only* misplaced

mod *Carlos only eats spaghetti with clam sauce.*

The meaning of your sentence may be unclear if *only* is misplaced.

SOLUTION

Only Carlos eats spaghetti with clam sauce.

Carlos eats only spaghetti with clam sauce.

Carlos eats spaghetti only with clam sauce.

Resource Manager

Planning Resources
- *Lesson Plans*

Transparencies
- *Bellringer*
- *Two-Minute Skill Drill*

Other Print Resources
- *Grammar Workbook, Lesson 64*

Place the adverb *only* immediately before the word or group of words it modifies. Note that each time *only* is moved in the sentence, the meaning of the sentence changes.

Problem 3

A dangling modifier

mod *After working feverishly for days,* the science project was completed.

mod *Watching television,* the screen suddenly went blank.

mod *Hoping for a break from the heat,* a Canadian cold front brought relief.

Dangling modifiers do not logically seem to modify any word in the sentence.

SOLUTION Rewrite the sentence, adding a noun to which the dangling phrase clearly refers. Often you will have to add other words to complete the meaning of the sentence.

After working feverishly for days, Jan completed her science project.

Watching television, Yoshiko saw the screen suddenly go blank.

Hoping for a break from the heat, we were relieved when a Canadian cold front moved in.

If you need more help with misplaced or dangling modifiers, turn to Lesson 18.7, pages 670–675.

Troubleshooter

Teach

Cross-reference: Usage

For instruction and practice of the material in Lesson 9.9, refer students to Lesson 18.7, pp. 670–675

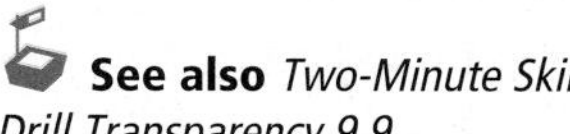

Two-Minute Skill Drill

List these sentences containing misplaced modifiers on the board and have students correct them:

She soaked the toe she injured in a bucket of ice water.

The car hit the telephone pole going 30 miles per hour.

I gave to my brother the car.

I returned the book to the library that I read.

See also *Two-Minute Skill Drill Transparency 9.9*

Additional Resources

Grammar Workbook, Lesson 64

Close

Initiate a discussion in which students consider how being able to recognize and avoid misplaced or dangling modifiers in writing can help them in their other classes.

Focus

Lesson Overview

Objectives

- To identify common instances in which possessive apostrophes are missing or misplaced
- To learn how to avoid or correct missing or misplaced possessive apostrophes in writing

Bellringer
Daily Language Activity

When students enter the classroom, have this assignment on the board: *Do you think the following sentences refer to one or more than one person or thing? Why?*

The soldiers boots were shiny.

The dogs fur was wet.

The cars tires were bald.

Motivating Activity

Discuss students' responses to the Bellringer activity. Explain that the sentences contain missing possessive apostrophes that would clarify the meaning. This lesson will help students recognize and correct missing or misplaced possessive apostrophes.

Teach

Cross-reference: Mechanics

For instruction and practice of the material in Problems 1, 2, and 3, refer students to Lesson 21.11, pp. 759–761.

Troubleshooter

9.10 Missing or Misplaced Possessive Apostrophe

Problem 1

Singular nouns

poss *The waitress wallet held that days tips.*

SOLUTION Use an apostrophe and an *-s* to form the possessive of a singular noun, even one that ends in *-s.*

The waitress's wallet held that day's tips.

Problem 2

Plural nouns ending in *-s*

poss *The soldiers tents dotted the field.*

SOLUTION Use an apostrophe alone to form the possessive of a plural noun that ends in *-s.*

The soldiers' tents dotted the field.

Problem 3

Plural nouns not ending in *-s*

poss *The childrens bookstore is on Broadway.*

SOLUTION Use an apostrophe and an *-s* to form the possessive of a plural noun that does not end in *-s.*

The children's bookstore is on Broadway.

Resource Manager

Planning Resources
- *Lesson Plans*

Transparencies
- *Bellringer*
- *Two-Minute Skill Drill*

Other Print Resources
- *Grammar Workbook,* Lesson 89
- *Sentence-Combining Practice,* p. 10

Problem 4

Pronouns

poss *I found (somebodys) watch.*
poss *The best idea was (her's).*

SOLUTION A Use an apostrophe and an *-s* to form the possessive of a singular indefinite pronoun.

I found somebody's watch.

SOLUTION B Do not use an apostrophe with any of the possessive personal pronouns.

The best idea was hers.

Problem 5

Confusion between *its* and *it's*

poss *The boat has slipped (it's) mooring.*
poss *(Its) a great day for a picnic.*

The possessive of *it* is *its*. *It's* is the contraction of *it is*.

SOLUTION Do not use an apostrophe to form the possessive of *it*. Use an apostrophe to form the contraction of *it is*.

The boat has slipped its mooring.

It's a great day for a picnic.

If you need more help with apostrophes and possessives, turn to Lesson 17.1, pages 633–634, and Lesson 21.11, pages 759–761.

Troubleshooter

Teach

Cross-reference: Usage and Mechanics

For instruction and practice of the material in Problem 4, refer students to Lesson 17.1, pp. 633–634, and Lesson 21.11, pp. 759–761.

Cross-reference: Usage

For instruction and practice of the material in Problem 5, refer students to Lesson 17.1, pp. 633–634.

Two-Minute Skill Drill

List these sentences or phrases with missing or incorrect possessive apostrophes on the board and have students write them correctly:

It is their's.

Franks watch

Its raining today.

one weeks wages

See also *Two-Minute Skill Drill Transparency 9.10*

Additional Resources

Sentence-Combining Practice, p. 10

Grammar Workbook, Lesson 89

Close

Have students write briefly about how being able to recognize and avoid misplaced possessive apostrophes in writing can improve their writing in other classes.

Focus

Lesson Overview

Objectives

- To identify sentence constructions in which commas should be used
- To learn how to avoid or correct comma errors in writing

Bellringer
Daily Language Activity

When students enter the classroom, have this assignment on the board: *Read the following sentences and add commas where you think they are needed.*

Mario running caught up with me.

Bob one of my brothers helped me.

The store normally open on weekends was closed.

Motivating Activity

Discuss students' responses to the Bellringer activity. Elicit from them that the meaning of each sentence becomes clearer when commas are inserted.

Teach

Cross-reference: Mechanics

For instruction and practice of the material in Problems 1 and 2, refer students to Lesson 21.6, pp. 738–748.

9.11 Missing Commas with Nonessential Element

Problem 1

Missing commas with nonessential participles, infinitives, and their phrases

com *Claude watched delighted as Cheryl accepted the award.*

com *Marla finishing her work set out for a late afternoon jog.*

com *To repeat the bus will leave promptly at five.*

SOLUTION Determine whether the participle, infinitive, or phrase is truly not essential to the meaning of the sentence. If it is not essential, set off the phrase with commas.

Claude watched, delighted, as Cheryl accepted the award.

Marla, finishing her work, set out for a late afternoon jog.

To repeat, the bus will leave promptly at five.

Problem 2

Missing commas with nonessential adjective clauses

com *César who is also a licensed pilot is a certified scuba diver.*

SOLUTION Determine whether the clause is truly not essential to the meaning of the sentence. If it is not essential, set off the clause with commas.

César, who is also a licensed pilot, is a certified scuba diver.

Resource Manager

Planning Resources

- *Lesson Plans*

Transparencies

- *Bellringer*
- *Two-Minute Skill Drill*

Other Print Resources

- *Grammar Workbook,* Lessons 76–83
- *Sentence-Combining Practice,* pp. 6–9, 17

Problem 3

Missing commas with nonessential appositives

com *Margaret Donelly our letter carrier is on vacation.*

SOLUTION Determine whether the appositive is truly not essential to the meaning of the sentence. If it is not essential, set off the appositive with commas.

Margaret Donelly, our letter carrier, is on vacation.

Problem 4

Missing commas with interjections and parenthetical expressions

com *Gosh I enjoyed that game.*

com *You know of course that the office is closed on Saturdays.*

SOLUTION Set off the interjection or parenthetical expression with commas.

Gosh, I enjoyed that game.
You know, of course, that the office is closed on Saturdays.

If you need more help with commas and nonessential elements, turn to Lesson 21.6, pages 738–748.

Troubleshooter

Teach

Cross-reference: Mechanics

For instruction and practice of the material in Problems 3 and 4, refer students to Lesson 21.6, pp. 738–748.

Two-Minute Skill Drill

List these sentences or phrases on the board and have students rewrite them if they seem incorrect.

Again class will be postponed next week.

Bill, my dog is terrific.

My mother who is not feeling well didn't work today.

 **See also** *Two-Minute Skill Drill Transparency 9.11*

Additional Resources

Sentence-Combining Practice, pp. 6–9, 17

Grammar Workbook, Lessons 76–83

Close

Initiate a discussion in which students consider how being able to avoid misusing commas in writing can help them improve their grades in other classes. You may want to have students write down their ideas.

Focus

Lesson Overview

Objectives

- To identify when commas should be used to separate items in a series of words, phrases, or clauses
- To learn how to avoid or correct comma errors in writing

Bellringer
Daily Language Activity

When students enter the classroom, have this assignment on the board: *Add commas to this sentence to change the meaning:*

My younger brother likes to eat candy corn and mashed potatoes.

Motivating Activity

Discuss the differences in meaning for the sentence in the Bellringer activity above when it contains commas and when it doesn't. Explain that by learning to use serial commas when needed, students will produce writing that is less likely to be misread or misinterpreted.

Teach

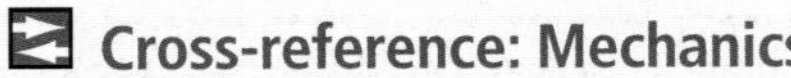

Cross-reference: Mechanics

For instruction and practice of the material in Lesson 9.12, refer students to Lesson 21.6, pp. 738–748.

Additional Resources

- *Sentence-Combining Practice,* p. 3

- *Grammar Workbook,* Lesson 77

Troubleshooter

9.12 Missing Commas in a Series

Problem 1

Missing comma in a series of words, phrases, or clauses

com *The garden was a riot of zinnias hollyhocks marigolds and lilies.*

com *Reggie stopped bent down and picked up the quarter he had dropped.*

com *Yuki ran down the street around the corner and into the Murphys' garage.*

com *We watched the kites soaring into the sky swooping back and forth and gliding to earth.*

com *Angela plays the guitar Bill sings and José accompanies them on the drums.*

SOLUTION When there are three or more items in a series, use a comma after each item that precedes the conjunction.

The garden was a riot of zinnias, hollyhocks, marigolds, and lilies.

Reggie stopped, bent down, and picked up the quarter he had dropped.

Yuki ran down the street, around the corner, and into the Murphys' garage.

We watched the kites soaring into the sky, swooping back and forth, and gliding to earth.

Angela plays the guitar, Bill sings, and José accompanies them on the drums.

If you need more help with commas in a series, turn to Lesson 21.6, pages 738–748.

Resource Manager

Planning Resources
- *Lesson Plans*

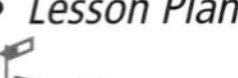

Transparencies
- *Bellringer*

Other Print Resources
- *Grammar Workbook,* Lesson 77
- *Sentence-Combining Practice,* p. 3

Use the proofreading symbols below to mark corrections in your writing.

Proofreading Symbols

Symbol	Example	Meaning
⊙	Lieut Brown	Insert a period.
^	No one came the party.	Insert a letter or a word.
^;	The bell rang the students left for home.	Insert a semicolon.
≡	I enjoyed paris.	Capitalize a letter.
/	The Class ran a bake sale.	Make a capital letter lowercase.
⁀‿	The campers are home sick.	Close up a space.
(sp)	They visited N.Y. (sp)	Spell out.
^,	Sue please help.	Insert a comma.
∿	He enjoyed feild day.	Transpose the position of letters or words.
#	alltogether	Insert a space.
℘	We went to to Boston.	Delete letters or words.
ᵛ ᵛ	She asked, Who's coming?	Insert quotation marks.
/=/	mid January	Insert a hyphen.
¶	"Where?" asked Karl. "Over there," said Ray.	Begin a new paragraph.
ᵛ	She liked Sarahs glasses.	Insert an apostrophe.

Troubleshooter

Close

Have students write a list of tips that will help them remember comma rules. For example: Serial commas are as easy as one comma, two comma, and three period.

Objectives

- To understand the characteristics, styles, and parts of a business letter
- To evaluate different types of business letters
- To learn how to write effective business letters
- To understand the purpose and format of memos, e-mail messages, and application forms
- To compose effective memos and e-mail messages
- To complete application forms properly
- To learn how to use the computer as a writing tool to create appropriate tables, graphs, and charts
- To understand the requirements of effective technical writing
- To write effective abstracts and clear, meaningful instructions
- To understand how to work effectively in a group
- To work in a small group and complete a group activity

ASSESSMENT OPTIONS

Tests with Answer Key & Rubrics
Business and Technical Writing Pretest

Testmaker
Business and Technical Writing Pretest

You may wish to administer the Business and Technical Writing Pretest at this point.

Key to Ability Levels

L1 Level 1 activities are within the basic ability range of students.

L2 Level 2 activities are within the ability range of average students.

L3 Level 3 activities are more challenging activities.

Business and Technical Writing

Contents

Resource Manager

Planning Resources
- *Lesson Plans*

Transparencies
- *Writing Process*

Other Print Resources
- *Business and Technical Writing Activities*
- *Grammar and Composition Handbook*
- *Guide to Using the Internet and Other Electronic Resources*
- *Tests with Answer Key and Rubrics*
- *Writing Assessment and Evaluation Rubrics*

Business Letters

Why Write Business Letters?

Knowing how to write a business letter is a valuable skill—one that you will use while you are in school and throughout your life. Business letters are written not only by people of every age who are engaged in the business world but also by those who want to request help or information and to express their opinions.

Business writing is a special form of expository writing. The most important thing to know about business writing is that it must be efficient communication. The reader should be able to grasp the meaning of a business letter quickly with a minimum of effort. A long, complicated letter simply will not be read. A brief, clearly written letter is more likely to result in a positive response.

The impression a business letter makes on its reader will certainly influence the nature of his or her response. Correct grammar, spelling, and punctuation are musts. While a business letter should employ formal language, its tone may be conversational.

A business letter is usually single-spaced and written on only one side of a page. However, you may double-space a very short business letter so that it fills up more of the page. If the letter is longer than one page, begin each page after the first with the name of the recipient, the date, and the page number, each on its own line flush with the left margin, as shown in the sample below.

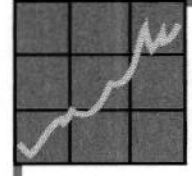

Activity

Bring a copy of a business letter to class. It may be a letter from a charity asking for a donation, a bank explaining a change in policy, your parents asking for information about a coming event, or a civic group seeking support for its policies. Work in small groups to analyze the letters. What do the letters have in common? For what purposes were they written? Share your observations with the rest of the class.

R. Garcia
10/23/--
page 2

Business and Technical Writing

Business Letters

Focus

Objectives

- To understand the purpose and form of an effective business letter
- To analyze two acceptable styles for business letters
- To identify six parts of a business letter
- To evaluate several types of business letters, including request, complaint, apology, and opinion
- To write an effective business letter

Skills

- analyzing styles; identifying components; evaluating writing; selecting a topic

Critical Thinking

- analyzing; identifying; evaluating

Listening and Speaking

- evaluating; questioning; discussing; explaining

Bellringer
Daily Language Activity

When students enter the classroom, have this assignment on the board: *List five different kinds of business letters that you or members of your family have received or have been required to write.*

Grammar Link to the Bellringer

Have volunteers share their lists with the class. Then discuss the different ways in which business letters are punctuated.

Motivating Activity

Discuss students' responses to the Bellringer activity. Display examples of several different types of business letters around the room. Encourage students to identify the audience and purpose of each sample business letter. Which letters seem to be the most effective? The least effective?

Software
- *Presentation Plus!*
- *Revising with Style*
- *ExamView Assessment Suite*

Web Site
- *glencoe.com*

Teach

Using the Model

Have students note and discuss the placement and punctuation of the block style of business letter shown on page 414. If possible, ask students to examine the other business letters on display in the room and point out those letters that are written in the block style. **L2**

Styles of Business Letters

The two main styles of business letters are block style and modified block style.

Block Style The use of conventional styles in business writing lets readers know exactly what to expect and where to look for relevant information. The block style is the most commonly used style today. In this style, all parts of the letter are aligned with the left margin. Paragraphs are not indented. They are separated by a line space.

The letter shown below uses block style. Notice that the letter is brief, clear, and carefully organized. The writer asks for what he wants in the first sentence and provides his reader with more detail in the sentences that follow.

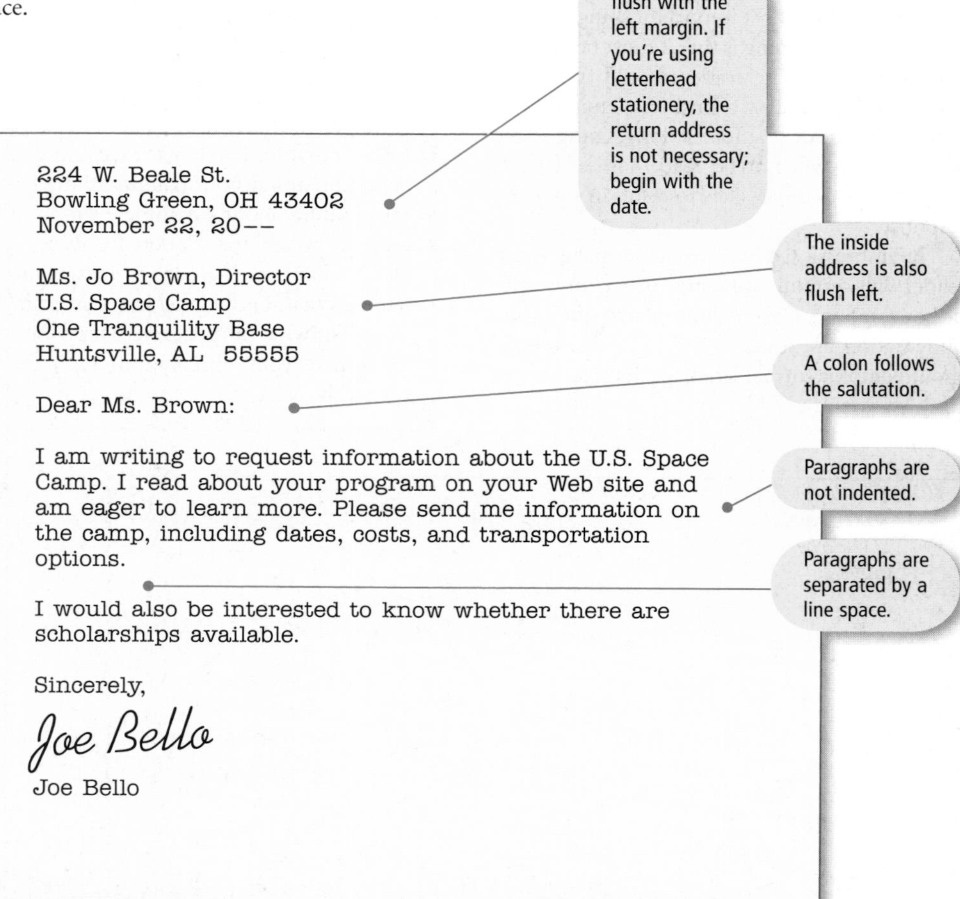

224 W. Beale St.
Bowling Green, OH 43402
November 22, 20--

Ms. Jo Brown, Director
U.S. Space Camp
One Tranquility Base
Huntsville, AL 55555

Dear Ms. Brown:

I am writing to request information about the U.S. Space Camp. I read about your program on your Web site and am eager to learn more. Please send me information on the camp, including dates, costs, and transportation options.

I would also be interested to know whether there are scholarships available.

Sincerely,

Joe Bello

Joe Bello

The heading is flush with the left margin. If you're using letterhead stationery, the return address is not necessary; begin with the date.
The inside address is also flush left.
A colon follows the salutation.
Paragraphs are not indented.
Paragraphs are separated by a line space.

Modified Block Style In the modified block style modeled below, the heading, the closing, the signature, and the typed name begin about three to four inches to the right. Paragraphs are indented and do not have a line space between them.

Parts of a Business Letter

A business letter has six parts.

Heading The heading contains three lines:

- your street address
- your city, state, and ZIP code
- the date

Inside Address The inside address has four or more lines:

- the name and title of the person to whom you are writing
- the name of the business or organization
- the address of the business or organization
- the city, state, and ZIP code

Salutation The salutation begins with the word *Dear* and is followed by a courtesy title (such as *Ms., Mr.,* or *Dr.*) and the last name of the person to whom you are writing. If you don't know the person's name and title, call the company and request that information. Be sure to ask for the correct spelling. If you cannot learn the person's name but know his or her title, you can use the title in the salutation, as in "Dear Manager," or you can use "To whom it may concern." Place a colon after the salutation.

224 West Beale Street
Bowling Green, OH 43402
November 22, 20--

Ms. Jo Brown, Director
U.S. Space Camp
One Tranquility Base
Huntsville, AL 55555

Dear Ms. Brown:

I am writing to request information about the U.S. Space Camp. I read about your program on your Web site and am eager to learn more. Please send me information on the camp, including dates, costs, and transportation options.

I would also be interested to know whether there are scholarships available.

Sincerely,

Joe Bello

Joe Bello

The heading, the closing, and the signature are indented.

Paragraphs are indented.

There is no extra space between paragraphs.

Using the Model

Have students note and discuss the placement and punctuation of the modified block style of business letter shown on page 415. If possible, ask students to examine the other business letters on display in the room and point out those letters that are written in the modified block style. **L2**

Understanding Tone

Remind students that although the tone of a business letter may be conversational, slang of any sort should be avoided. In addition, point out that being businesslike does not mean using long words and sentences, or stilted words and phrases such as *herewith* and *the aforementioned.* Encourage students to suggest ways of achieving the right tone in a business letter. **L3**

Civic Literacy

Writing to an Official

Suggest that students write business letters to government officials. The letters should be formatted in either of the two main styles of business letters, as in the models on pp. 414–415, and request specific information on a subject of interest. **L2**

Teach

Comparing Letter Types

After students have read page 416, discuss the differences between personal letters and business letters. (purpose, audience, tone, format) Note each difference, and offer possible reasons for the differences. **L2**

Using Personal Letter Style

After students read the introduction and model on page 416, have them discuss when it would be appropriate to combine business-letter content with personal letter style. Ask students to think of at least three different occasions when such a letter would be appropriate. **L2**

Business and Technical Writing

Body The body contains your message. Be sure to put the most important information in the first paragraph of your letter or as close to the beginning as possible. Tell your reader clearly and simply what you want. Because you want your letter to be easy to read, break a long message into several short paragraphs and leave as much white space as possible.

Closing The closing is a final word or phrase, such as *Yours truly*, *Sincerely*, *Sincerely yours*, *Best regards*, or *Respectfully*. The second word of a closing is not capitalized. The closing is followed by a comma.

Signature and Name Type your name four lines below the closing. Sign your name in the space between the closing and your typed name. If your first name could belong to either a male or a female, include *Miss*, *Mrs.*, *Ms.*, or *Mr.* in parentheses before your typed name and your signature.

Personal Letter

A business letter is usually written to a stranger. A personal letter is written to someone you know personally, such as a friend or a relative. Its language is less formal than that in a business letter. It differs from a business letter also in its use of indentation, spacing, and punctuation following the salutation. Following is an example of a personal letter written for business purposes.

224 West Beale Street
Bowling Green, OH 43402
November 22, 20--

Bart Hopkins
2150 Richmond Rd.
Toledo, OH 43605

Dear Uncle Bart,

It was great to see you last week. I really enjoyed our conversation. As you suggested, I am looking into several specialty camps for this summer. One of the programs requires that I submit the names of two references. One of those can be a relative. Would you be willing to serve as a reference for me?

I'll call you next week to find out your decision. Thanks so much.

Love,

Joe

The heading, the closing, and the signature are indented to the right.

A comma follows the salutation.

The language is less formal than that used in a business letter.

The writer's name is not repeated following the signature.

Writing in the Real World

Researching Letters

Writers and Writing Encourage students to research one business or personal letter written by a famous author or celebrity such as Charles Dickens, Willa Cather, F. Scott Fitzgerald, Groucho Marx, or Richard Wright. Invite students to present their selection before the class, and discuss the purpose of the letter, the audience for which it was written, the tone used, and the effect the letter may have had on the recipient. **L2**

Types of Business Letters

There are several types of business letters. For example, you can use a business letter to request information or assistance, to make a complaint, to apologize for an error, to express an opinion, or to apply for a job. Although their basic form is always the same, the bodies of the various types of business letters differ in organization, structure, and style, depending on their purpose.

Request The key to writing an effective letter of request is to ask for what you want in the first paragraph. Then, in the paragraphs that follow, point out how you wish the recipient to respond. If you are requesting several items, indicate in a bulleted list what you want, as modeled in the first box below.

> Please send the following items:
> - two 20 pound bags of dog food
> - one 5 pound bag of dog treats
> - one 6 foot leash, black

A request for assistance requires an approach that is different from placing an order or asking for information. The tone of the letter should be respectful but not pleading or demanding. To write a request for assistance, use this approach:

1. Acquaint the reader with the basics of the situation.
2. Provide details.
3. Make it easy for the reader to do as you ask.

> I am writing to ask a favor of you. Would you lend me your video camera for one month so that I can complete a project I am working on at school?
>
> I will be extremely careful with the equipment and will make sure that no one else has access to it.

Discussing the Models

After students have read the material on page 417, ask them to review the two business letters on pp. 414–415. What type of business letters do these two models represent? (request) **L2**

Cross-reference: Punctuation

For instruction and practice in punctuating business letters, refer students to Lesson 21.4, pp. 733–734, and Lesson 21.6, pp. 738–748.

Teach

Writing a Letter of Complaint

Have students read and review the model on page 418. Discuss the purpose of a letter of complaint, and offer the following tips:

- Provide all the necessary information about the problem in the letter. Include details such as the date and time of purchase, the store visited, the stock number of the item, and the price paid.
- Describe the problem objectively. Clearly explain what happened with the item, and why you are dissatisfied with your purchase.
- Request a specific solution to the problem that is fair to both sides. Remind students that most companies will do anything reasonable to keep their customers happy.
- Be polite; avoid personal attacks and insults. In most instances, the person reading the letter is not the one who caused the mistake.
- Keep a copy of the letter until the complaint is resolved to your satisfaction. If necessary, attach a copy of the letter to any follow-up correspondence. **L2**

Practice and Assess

Evaluation Rubrics

To evaluate the letters of request written for the Activity, see the Writing Rubrics on student page 418.

See also *Writing Assessment & Evaluation Rubrics*

Business and Technical Writing

Complaint When writing to complain about a product or service, first decide what you want the company to do. Do you want an apology, a replacement, or a refund, or would you like the company to change a product or service it provides?

In the first paragraph, explain the problem and ask for exactly what you want. When your tone is polite but firm, you are more likely to get a positive response. The formality of your letter conveys the idea that your complaint is to be taken seriously. Note the writer's approach in the sample letter of complaint shown below.

> Recently I ordered the enclosed sweatshirt from your catalogue. When the sweatshirt was washed according to the directions on the label, the logo dyed the whole shirt pink. I would like a full refund.

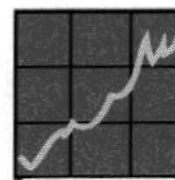

Activity

Use the Internet and the library to find information on summer-camp experiences for teenagers. Choose one camp that you think you might like to attend and write a business letter to request information about its activities, fees, requirements, and dates of operation. Use either block or modified block format.

PURPOSE To write a business letter requesting information
AUDIENCE Camp director
LENGTH 1 page

WRITING RUBRICS When writing a letter of request, you should

- write clearly and succinctly
- state your request in the first paragraph of the letter
- use polite but conversational language
- proofread your letter for errors in grammar, spelling, and mechanics
- use correct spacing and alignment

Apology There are two keys to writing an effective apology. First, be sure not to trivialize the concern of the person who made the complaint. Too often people who write apologies say things such as "I'm very sorry for any inconvenience you experienced." To the person who bothered to complain, *inconvenience* is probably much too weak a word to describe the experience.

Second, do not make excuses. The person who complained does not want to hear about how "the computer was down" or how "we were really busy." Apologize simply and directly. Note that the writer of the sample below takes the complaint seriously and doesn't offer excuses for the error.

> Thank you for alerting us to the fact that the dye used on the logo of your sweatshirt was not colorfast. We are enclosing a check for the full price of the shirt and are returning our entire stock of the item to the manufacturer. We can assure you that this will not happen again. Please bring the enclosed gift certificate with you the next time you come in, and we'll be happy to take $5.00 off your next purchase.

Using the Model

After students read the introduction and the model on page 419, have them discuss instances in which a letter of apology would be helpful, as well as situations where a simple apology would not be enough. **L2**

Cooperative Learning

Effective Business Letters

Have students form small groups to discuss any occasions when they either wrote or received business letters. Students should share whether they considered each letter effective and the criteria they used to judge the letter's effectiveness, including any response given or received. **L2**

Teach

Discussing Letters of Opinion

Point out that when writing letters of opinion, students should also evaluate the audience they are hoping to persuade. Ask students to review the following questions before writing their letters of opinion:

- Is the issue relevant to the audience?
- Is the audience likely to agree or disagree with your opinion?
- How much background information does the audience need to understand your opinion?
- What types of evidence will most likely persuade the audience? Offend the audience? **L2**

Practice and Assess

Evaluation Rubrics

To evaluate the opinion letters written for the Activity, see the Writing Rubrics on student page 420.

See also *Writing Assessment & Evaluation Rubrics*

Close

Direct students to keep samples in their portfolio of the business letters they have written. Discuss the value of knowing how to write an effective business letter.

Opinion When you write to state your opinion, you are doing so in the hope of persuading others to adopt your point of view. Begin by expressing what you believe. If you are disagreeing with another point of view, state the opposing position clearly and correctly. This strategy avoids giving the impression that you are attacking a point of view you do not appreciate or understand. In the sample below, note the effort the writer makes to show an understanding of the other point of view.

Whenever you express an opinion, be sure that your facts are correct and your writing is error free. Your credibility as a writer is important, and mistakes in your letter will negatively affect the impact of your letter.

> I believe we should adopt block scheduling at Witmore High. Block schedules permit more in-depth study of a subject, and lengthened class times permit more discussion and participation than in standard class schedules. Although the traditional schedule has the advantage of providing a full year's worth of exposure, I believe the more concentrated effort required in a block schedule will eventually result in greater learning and improved retention.

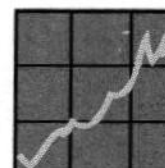

Activity

Select an issue that concerns you and write a letter to the editor of your local or school newspaper expressing your opinion on that issue. Before you write, take time to investigate and understand the other position or positions on the issue. Be sure to find out the publisher's guidelines for the length of your letter. Use either the block or the modified block format.

PURPOSE To write a letter to the editor

AUDIENCE Readers of your local or school newspaper

LENGTH 1 page

WRITING RUBRICS To write an effective letter of opinion, you should

- state your opinion clearly in a reasonable tone
- provide evidence or reasons to support your opinion
- give a fair picture of the opposing points of view
- make sure your statements are accurate

Real World Connection

Planning a Career Day

Have students plan a career day for your school. Divide students into groups, and assign groups different tasks. Tasks might include writing permission letters to school administrators; creating a list of local businesspeople who might be willing to participate; requesting pamphlets, brochures, and other information from local business organizations; extending formal invitations to speakers; organizing the schedule of activities; and writing thank you letters after the occasion. **L2**

Memos, E-mail, and Applications

For most workers, memos and e-mail messages are far more common in their business life than letters. Applications are a form of communication almost everyone will come across sooner or later.

Memos

A memo (short for *memorandum*) is a letter that is written and distributed within a school, a business, or an organization. It shares many of the characteristics of the business letter but is less formal.

The memo is designed for maximum efficiency. Typically, it is one page or less in length, and all text aligns flush with the left margin. The heading is double-spaced and indicates to whom the memo was sent, who wrote it, the date it was sent, and what it is about. The body of the memo is single-spaced with a line space between paragraphs. The content is direct and to the point. Because the writer has already been identified in the heading, there is no closing or signature.

One of the advantages of the memo format is that the recipient can write a response on the memo itself before returning it. If you choose, you can end the memo with the word *Response:* or *Comment:* to make clear that you expect only a quick, handwritten reply.

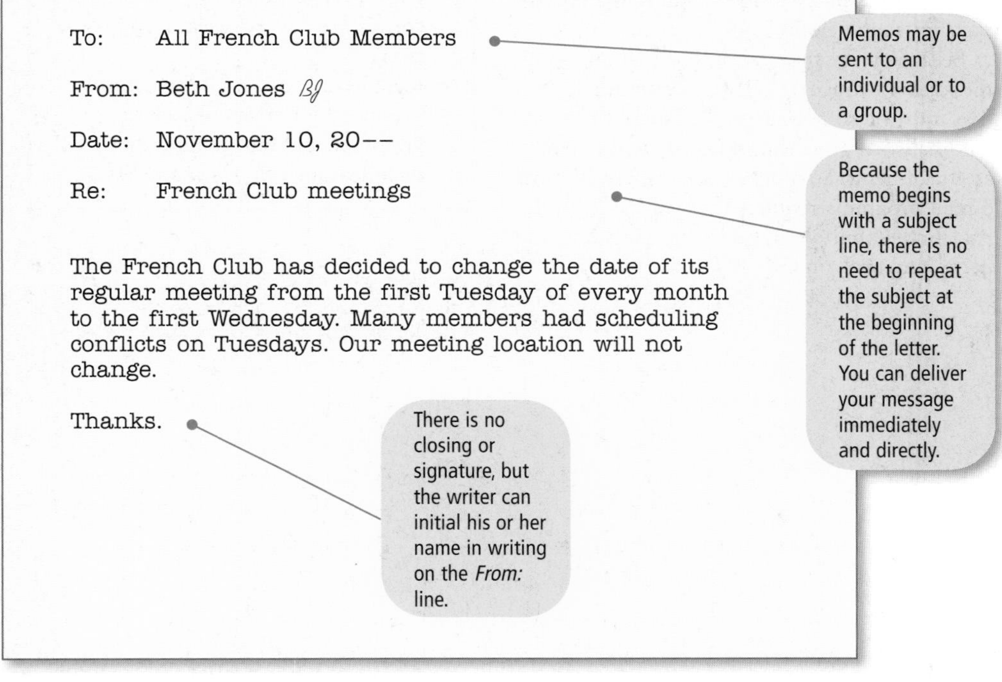

To: All French Club Members

From: Beth Jones BJ

Date: November 10, 20--

Re: French Club meetings

The French Club has decided to change the date of its regular meeting from the first Tuesday of every month to the first Wednesday. Many members had scheduling conflicts on Tuesdays. Our meeting location will not change.

Thanks.

Memos may be sent to an individual or to a group.
Because the memo begins with a subject line, there is no need to repeat the subject at the beginning of the letter. You can deliver your message immediately and directly.
There is no closing or signature, but the writer can initial his or her name in writing on the *From:* line.

Memos, E-mail, and Applications

Focus

Objectives

- To understand the purpose and proper format for writing memos
- To compose an effective memo
- To understand the elements of e-mail messages
- To master the guidelines for filling out application forms
- To complete a sample application form

Skills

- analyzing models; mastering guidelines; identifying essential information

Critical Thinking

- analyzing; identifying

Listening and Speaking

- discussing; explaining

Bellringer

Daily Language Activity

When students enter the classroom, have this assignment on the board: *List five kinds of memos that may be sent. Place a star by those memos that may also be sent as e-mail messages.*

Motivating Activity

Discuss students' responses to the Bellringer activity. Explain that the memo is a common form of business communication. Tell students that e-mail messages are more informal than memos, but they are still used in business to communicate with specific audiences. In this lesson, students will learn how to write concise and informative memos and e-mail messages.

Teach

Using the Model

Have students read and discuss the introduction to memos on page 421. After students have reviewed the sample memo, point out the standard elements in the model. Then assign the Activity on page 422, and answer any questions that students may have about the assignment. **L2**

Using Computers

Remind students that memos may be written in different forms. Point out that word processing programs often include various templates, or patterns, to create memos from scratch. To access these templates, have students use the File pull-down menu, select New, and then choose the Memos option. Some typical memo formats are contemporary, cosmopolitan, and traditional. Have students investigate each format, and discuss any differences they observe. **L2**

Practice and Assess

Evaluation Rubrics

To evaluate the memos written for the Activity, see the Writing Rubrics on student page 422.

See also *Writing Assessment & Evaluation Rubrics*

Business and Technical Writing

E-mail

Of all the forms of business communication, e-mail is by far the most informal. E-mail often reads like the transcript of a conversation.

Writers of e-mail need to analyze their audiences. Sentence fragments, colloquial language, and abbreviations may be fine in notes to friends, but they are not appropriate for many business exchanges.

For anyone other than a close friend, an e-mail message should be similar to a memo in format and style. The subject line is very important, because many readers use it to decide whether to open the message immediately.

When answering an e-mail, repeat enough of the original message to remind its writer of the context so that he or she doesn't have to guess what you are replying to. For example, answering "Sure, anytime" to an e-mail may be more puzzling than helpful.

Because you cannot always format an e-mail message as you can a letter, communications that must be somewhat formal should be written in a word processing program and e-mailed as attachments. Sending an attachment in most e-mail programs requires that you click on the Attachment button, type in the path and file name, and click on OK.

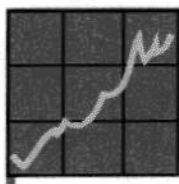

Activity

Imagine that as a member of the drama club, you have been asked to write a memo to all students requesting the donation of items to be used as props in plays. Mention the kinds of items you need and where and when they can be dropped off.

PURPOSE To write a memo

AUDIENCE All students in the school

LENGTH 1 or 2 paragraphs and a list

WRITING RUBRICS To write an effective memo, you should

- use the correct format
- convey the message clearly and concisely
- include all necessary information
- proofread for errors in spelling, grammar, and information that includes dates, times, or addresses

Real World Connection

The First E-mail

In 1971, computer engineer Ray Tomlinson wrote the first e-mail program that allowed two computers, hooked up through a common network, to communicate with each other by means of messages delivered electronically to their mailboxes. Tomlinson selected the @ symbol as a means of separating the user's name from the computer's address. The first e-mail message sent was QWERTYUIOP, the top row of letters found on a computer keyboard.

Applications

In your lifetime, you will complete many application forms. You may apply for library cards, credit, a driver's license, a marriage license, bank accounts, a social security card, memberships in organizations, and various jobs. There may also be forms to fill out for attending camps, colleges, and trade schools and for renting or buying a place to live.

It is important that an application form be completed accurately and neatly. A form that is incomplete or that contains incorrect information can cause problems and delays. In the hiring process, many employers use the application form as an indicator of a person's aptitude for a job. If the application form is incomplete or looks sloppy, the person may not be considered for the position. It is a good idea to ask for more than one copy of any application form that you are going to complete. You can fill out one copy in pencil, making changes until you are sure all the information is correct and in the right place. Then you can transfer the information in ink onto the copy that you will submit.

There are four important things to remember when filling out an application form:

1. Read the instructions, if any, and the entire form carefully before writing anything.
2. Use your best printing or handwriting. Neatness counts.
3. Fill in all the blanks. If the information asked for does not apply to you, write *n/a* (not applicable) in the blank. Leaving the blank empty suggests that you have something to hide or that you did not read the form carefully.
4. Complete the form in ink, preferably blue or black.

Study the sample application shown on page 424.

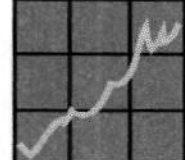

Activity

Obtain an application form for one of the following: organization membership, library card, apartment rental, credit card, savings account, loan, driver's license, volunteer work. Print two copies of the form. Complete a practice copy in pencil. Then complete a final copy in ink. Work with a partner to evaluate each other's work.

PURPOSE To complete a sample application

AUDIENCE Your classmates

LENGTH 1 or 2 pages

WRITING RUBRICS To prepare an application form properly, you should

- read the instructions and the entire form before you begin writing
- use a duplicate form as your draft version
- answer every question; leave no blanks
- place information on the form correctly
- print (preferably) or write neatly and legibly
- proofread for spelling and punctuation errors
- transfer the revised information in blue or black ink to the final form

☑ Teaching Tip

Have students review the four guidelines on page 423 for filling out an application form. Remind them that although application forms vary from company to company, the same guidelines usually apply.

Practice and Assess

Evaluation Rubrics

To evaluate the application forms completed for the Activity, see the Writing Rubrics on student page 423.

See also *Writing Assessment & Evaluation Rubrics*

Teach

Using the Model

Have students discuss the Volunteer Application Form on page 424. Review the format, the items called for, and the information supplied. If possible, bring in sample employment application forms from local businesses. Divide students into groups, and ask each group to analyze two of the application forms. Discuss any similarities or differences among forms. **L2**

Close

Encourage students to discuss actual forms they may have completed (e.g., job applications or library card applications). Have them compare and contrast the formats of the applications, the items called for, and the kind of information they supplied. How did those application forms compare with the sample on page 424?

Business and Technical Writing

Sample Application

Volunteer Application Form

Thank you for considering volunteer work at the Beckwith Library.

Name: Quinn Peterson Date January 20, 20--

Address: 3532 11th Avenue North

City: Grand Forks State: ND Zip: 58203

Phone: 701-555-1212 Fax: 701-555-5510

DOB: 11/29/87 SSN: 123-45-6789

Best times to reach you: After 3:30 p.m. weekdays

Education *(circle highest level completed)*:

7 (8) 9 10 11 12

Is this experience for school credit? Yes (No)

School name and address: Lake Agassiz School

Why do you want to volunteer?

I have good organization skills and I know I would be an asset to the library staff. In addition, I am already very familiar with the layout of the library because I spend a lot of time there. I enjoy reading aloud to my little brother; I would especially like to be a volunteer reader during the story hour.

Describe previous volunteer experience.

n/a

Signature: *Quinn Peterson*

Note that the form is filled out neatly in blue ink.

Abbreviations commonly used on applications include DOB (date of birth) and SSN or SS# (social security number).

Include hyphens in your social security number.

If the information asked for does not apply to you, write *n/a* in the blank.

MEETING INDIVIDUAL NEEDS

English Language Learners

Application Forms

Pair students who are learning English with students who are proficient in English. Ask students to examine the Volunteer Application Form on page 424, and discuss with one another any unfamiliar words or sections. **L2**

Using the Computer as a Writing Tool

A computer is useful in researching information, creating and formatting documents, and presenting data graphically. Instructions that are given in this section for these functions are quite general. Every word processing, desktop publishing, or spreadsheet program works somewhat differently. To learn to use the capabilities of your computer software, read the instruction manual that comes with it or use the Help menu.

Making Tables and Graphs

You can use your word processing program to display information and data in tables or graphs. Keep in mind that in many software programs, tables and graphs are referred to as charts.

Tables Tables organize information into columns and rows. Columns are the vertical elements in a table, and rows are the horizontal elements. Cells are the individual boxes that contain data.

To make a table in most word processing programs, use the Table pull-down menu and then select the number of rows and columns you need. After you have created the table, you can insert or delete rows and columns as often as you wish. The table below was created with fifteen rows and five columns.

Many options allow you to customize a table. You can change the width of columns and the height of rows, add or alter borders, add color to the table, and change the way you align numbers within cells. Some table menus have a Quick Sum function that allows you to calculate sums by placing your cursor in the box where you want the sum to appear and clicking on the Quick Sum key.

Data entered in a table can be aligned right or left, centered in a cell, or aligned on a decimal point (as shown below). As you enter data, use the Tab key to move from cell to cell. By hitting the Enter key, you can create an additional row for data.

Income for Year				
Month	**Lawn Mowing**	**Snow Shoveling**	**Paper Route**	**Total for Month**
January	$0.00	$37.75	$26.55	$64.30
February	$0.00	$42.50	$29.90	$72.40
March	$0.00	$22.00	$27.75	$49.75
April	$30.75	$0.00	$23.00	$53.75
May	$75.00	$0.00	$27.00	$102.00
June	$70.00	$0.00	$28.95	$98.95
July	$65.75	$0.00	$28.55	$94.30
August	$60.00	$0.00	$29.00	$89.00
September	$55.00	$0.00	$27.00	$82.00
October	$0.00	$0.00	$22.00	$22.00
November	$0.00	$0.00	$27.00	$27.00
December	$0.00	$34.75	$29.50	$64.25
Total	$356.50	$137.00	$326.20	$819.70

Using the Computer as a Writing Tool

Focus

Objectives

- To learn how to use a word processing program to display information and data
- To identify the purpose and format of three types of graphs
- To recognize the difference between two types of charts
- To use a computer to create effective tables, graphs, and charts

Skills

- presenting information; identifying components; recognizing differences; creating computer graphics

Critical Thinking

- organizing; identifying; analyzing

Listening and Speaking

- discussing; questioning; analyzing

Bellringer
Daily Language Activity

When students enter the classroom, have this assignment on the board: *When might it be more efficient to present information in a visual format, such as a table, graph, or chart? Do you prefer to study data presented in a visual format or in running text?*

Motivating Activity

Discuss students' responses to the Bellringer activity. Explain that graphics are found in newspapers, magazines, books, and other media sources, including TV and the Internet. Point out that graphics are a useful learning tool because they present information, such as statistics, quantities, and other data, in a condensed visual form.

Teach

Using Computers

Have students review the table on page 425. Tell students that most word processing programs have a Format pull-down menu they can use to customize a table. Point out that all of the cells in the first row were combined to form a single cell for the table title, while the cells in the remaining rows were arranged into five columns. Review the data entries and emphasize that data can also be entered as whole numbers, percentages, exponents, or decimals with multiple digits after the decimal point. **L2**

Reading Graphics

Have students study the bar graph on page 426. Point out that graphs may not always include enough information to make useful comparisons. Ask students which class has the most students on the honor roll. (seniors) Then tell students that there are 110 freshmen, 150 sophomores, 120 juniors, and 180 seniors in the school. Based on this information, ask students which class has the greatest percentage of students on the honor roll. (Each class has exactly 50% of its students on the honor roll.) Discuss how this new information affects the way in which the bar graph is interpreted. **L3**

Graphs While a table helps readers find, compare, and contrast data quickly, a graph highlights a comparison or contrast by showing it pictorially. Use the following information to help you choose the appropriate format in which to display data.

A **bar graph** usually shows numbers or quantities and is used to showcase comparisons or contrasts. It plots data along a vertical line called the y-axis and a horizontal line called the x-axis. The vertical or y-axis includes a scale showing the numbers involved. Both axes should be labeled.

The bar graph below compares the numbers of a school's freshmen, sophomores, juniors, and seniors on the honor roll at the end of a school year. Note that the bar graph does not provide information about the total number of students in the school. Therefore, comparisons should be made with caution.

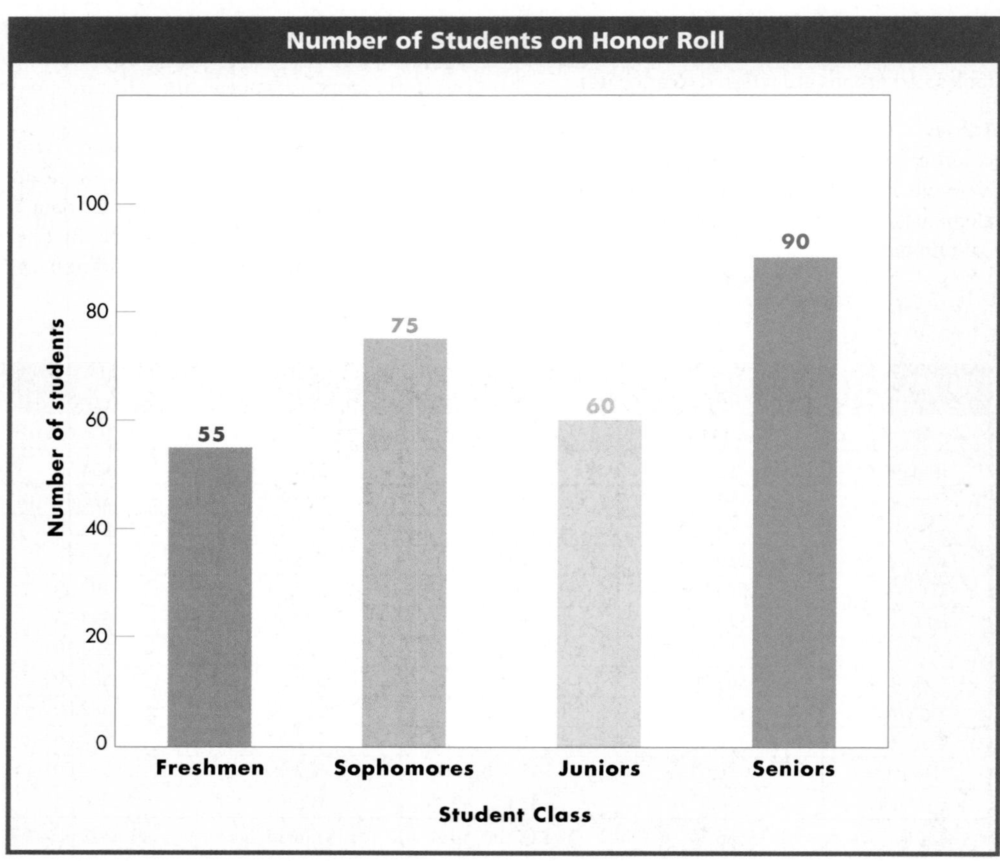

Enrichment and Extension

Data-gathering Techniques

Have students work in groups to select a topic of interest in their school and then collect data about that topic from a representative sample of the four student classes. Groups might use questionnaires, polls, or feedback forms to collect their data. When the data is collected, have students organize and plot their results on a bar graph similar to the one shown on page 426. Groups should then present their data to the rest of the class, where the results can be analyzed and discussed. **L3**

A **circle graph** or **pie chart** shows the relationship of parts to a whole. Each part can be expressed as a number or a percentage. The whole is always 100 percent. The circle graph below shows the distribution of elements within Earth's crust.

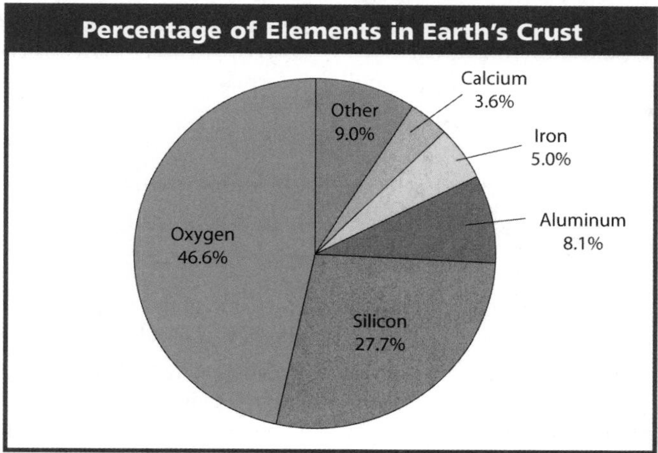

A **line graph** shows changes in numbers or quantities over time or by group or category. This line graph shows which technological devices Americans can't live without.

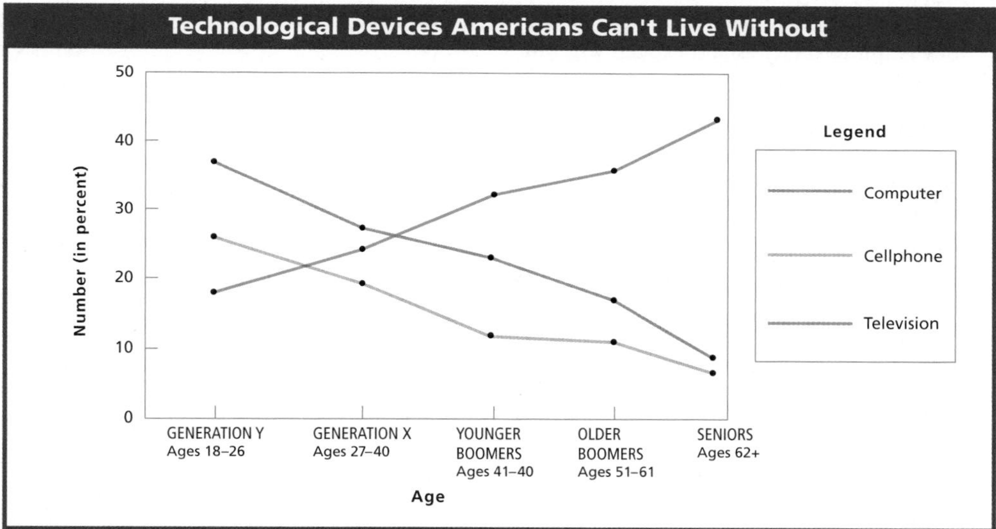

Source: *Forrester Research, The New York Times*

Interpreting Visuals

Have students study the circle graph on page 427. Point out that smaller slices of a circle graph are often combined into one larger slice for convenience. Which slice on the graph has been combined? (Other, 9.0%) Tell students that this slice has the following composition: Sodium, 2.8%; Potassium, 2.6%; Magnesium, 2.1%; and All Other Elements, 1.5%. Draw the main circle graph on the board, and then show how a smaller circle graph positioned next to it can be used to reveal the composition of the *Other* slice on the main graph. **L3**

Reading Graphics

Have students study the line graph on page 427. Point out that color is often used on line graphs to distinguish one series of data from another, and the legend explains how colors are assigned. What is the message of this graph? Among 18–26 year olds, cell phones are more important than television; among people over 62, the opposite is true. Which technology ranks the highest with Generation X? (computers) What do the dots on each line represent? (percentage of people who favor a particular technology) **L2**

Viewing and Representing

Creating Media Texts

Interpreting Visuals Have students work in small groups to create a magazine article that uses at least one bar graph, one circle graph, and one line graph. Students might search newspapers, magazines, and the Internet for sample graphs, or create graphs on their own, using the information presented in this lesson. Students should take turns analyzing and discussing which graphs best match their written text, and help one another if there is any problem with interpretation. When the projects are complete, have groups present their magazine articles to the class. **L2**

Teach

Using Computers

Point out that many word processing programs enable users to create more advanced graphics than the ones shown in this lesson. For example, bar graphs may be drawn as clusters, in stacks, or with bars oriented horizontally rather than vertically. Circle graphs may be drawn with exploded slices, or as combinations of two separate circle graphs. Line graphs may be drawn in stacks, with markers for each data value, or with visual effects (such as dashes, rather than colors). In addition, all three types of graphs may be drawn as 3-D models rather than in 2-D. **L3**

Practice and Assess

Evaluation Rubrics

To evaluate the graphs generated for the Activity, see the Writing Rubrics on student page 428.

See also *Writing Assessment & Evaluation Rubrics*

Using the Computer as a Writing Tool

To create a graph in a word processing program that includes a graphing feature, you enter data directly into a table (called a worksheet) designed to work with the graphing function. Once the data has been entered, choose the kind of graph you want, enter titles, labels, and a legend, and click on OK. The word processor will create the graph for you and insert it into your document. If you discover an error in your graph after it has been inserted into the document, simply double click on the graph to return to the editing function. In some programs, you can switch between one kind of graph and another once the data has been entered to see which best conveys your information.

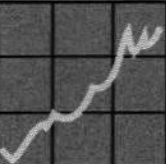

Activity

Gather statistical data about a school topic of interest to you. You might investigate how often tacos are served for lunch in a given month, how many people in each of your classes are absent on a given day, or how often the football team has won in each year of the last five years. Once you have collected the data, use your word processing program to convert it into a graph. Select the format that you think best showcases your information, insert the data, and print the graph. Present your graph to the class and explain why you chose that format.

PURPOSE To gather and present data in a graph
AUDIENCE Classmates
LENGTH 1 page

WRITING RUBRICS To prepare an effective graph, you should

- choose data that can be presented pictorially
- select a format that is appropriate for the audience
- present the data, using the most effective format for conveying your message
- include a descriptive title, labels, and (if needed) a legend
- proofread for accuracy

Creating Organization Charts

Many word processing programs have an Organization Chart function under the Draw menu. An **organization chart** shows the relative standings or rankings of individuals or positions in an organization. Check your Help menu to see if your program has an Organization Chart function. Even if your program does not come with a template for creating organization charts, you may be able to use the drawing tools to create them.

To make an organization chart, click on the appropriate icon and then select the type you want. You can choose a vertical or a horizontal orientation. You can use the ready-made chart structure or alter it by changing the placement of boxes or modifying the branching structure. Once you have designed the structure, simply type in the names, titles, steps, or other information you need. The example below shows the basic organization of the federal government.

The Government of the United States

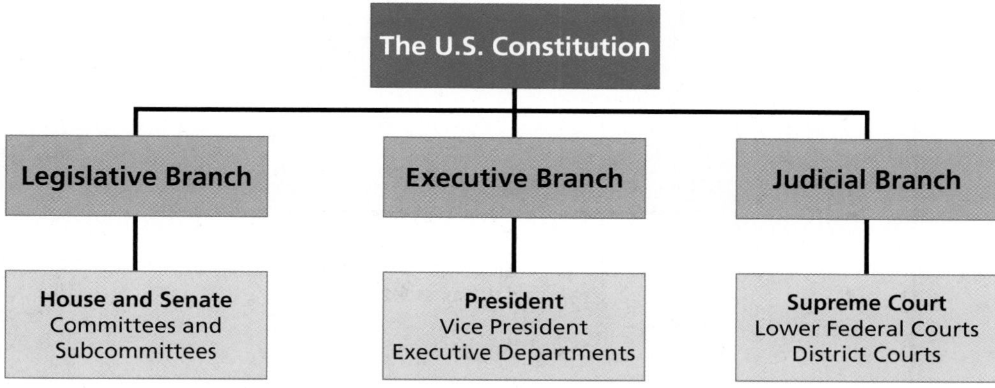

Business and Technical Writing

Discussing Organization Charts

After students read the introduction on page 429, have them discuss places in the community where organization charts might be used. (village hall, police department, fire department, department stores) **L2**

Reading Graphics

Have students study the organization chart on page 429. Point out that all boxes on the same level have equal standing, while branches indicate relative standings. How many equal branches are there in the federal government? (three) Who is the head of the Executive Branch? (president) In which branch would a congressman belong? (legislative) Which courts have the lowest standing within the judicial branch? (district courts) **L2**

Cultural Connections

Foreign Governments

Have students select a country of their choice and then research the government of that country. With the information they find, students should create an organization chart that clearly shows how the foreign government is organized. Encourage students to illustrate their charts with appropriate graphics and then post their finished work around the classroom for other students to view. **L3**

Teach

Understanding Flowcharts

Help students understand flowcharts by discussing the flowchart on page 430. What do the arrows on the flowchart represent? (points where a decision must be made) Point out that once a decision is made, the same path should be followed until another choice is called for. For example, what should a person invest in who is interested in long-term growth but can't afford to take any risks? (money market or short-term bonds) Have students follow the correct arrows for each choice until they understand the final answer. **L1**

Practice and Assess

Evaluation Rubrics

To evaluate the flowcharts created for the Activity, see the Writing Rubrics on student page 430.

See also *Writing Assessment & Evaluation Rubrics*

Close

Have students create a classroom display where several examples of the tables, graphs, or charts they have created can be posted. Encourage students to share strategies that worked well for them in creating graphics.

Creating Flowcharts

A **flowchart** highlights a different kind of relationship—the steps in a process. The flowchart example below shows the steps in making an investment decision. Remember always to include a descriptive title for any table, chart, or graph you create.

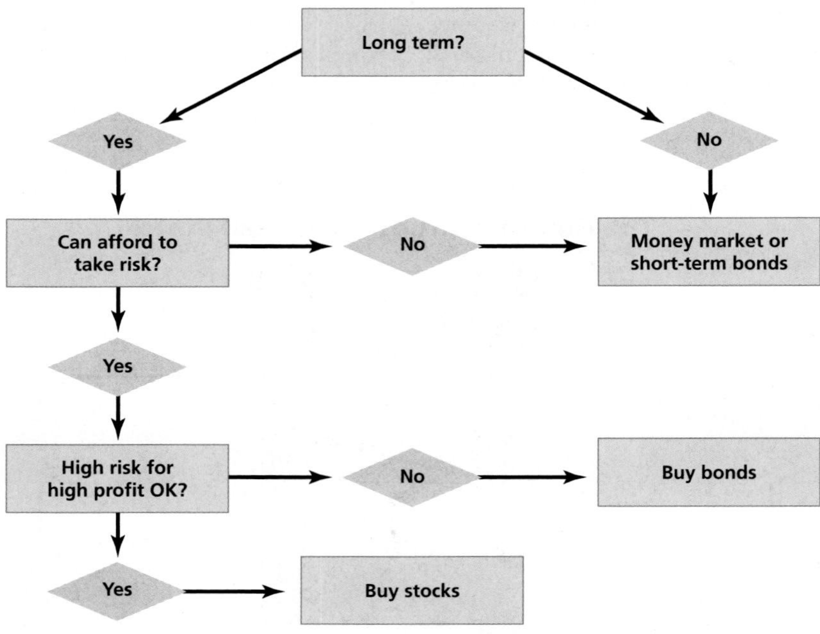

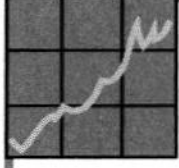

Activity

Use your computer to create a flowchart that outlines the steps in a process. Select a simple process with several steps. For example, it might be how to install software on a hard drive, change a tire, or study for a test.

PURPOSE To create a flowchart
AUDIENCE Your teachers and classmates
LENGTH 1 page

WRITING RUBRICS To create an effective flowchart, you should

- identify each step and its place in the process
- write a title for the chart
- be consistent in labeling
- check for accuracy

Real World Connection

Scientific Flowcharts

Scientists use flowcharts in a variety of ways to indicate the steps in a process. For example, inorganic chemists use flowcharts in qualitative analysis to show how to separate ions in solution. Geologists use flowcharts to separate minerals based on qualities such as hardness, color, luster, and streak. Botanists use flowcharts to classify and sort specimens of plants. Encourage students to research ways in which other scientists such as astronomers, engineers, and physicists might use flowcharts in their work. **L3**

Technical Writing

Technical writing translates technical and scientific information into language that is easy to read and understand. The style of technical writing is simple and direct.

Elements of Technical Writing

Accuracy, consistency, clarity, and brevity are the most important elements of technical writing.

Accuracy Although errors in any kind of writing are undesirable, errors in technical writing must be avoided at all costs. For example, consider that merely substituting the word *left* for the word *right* in directions for the assembly of parts can lead to disaster if the item being assembled is an airplane or an industrial boiler.

Consistency Technical writers and copyeditors use a uniform style in their final drafts. Most companies that issue technical documents and reports use a manual of style to help establish consistency in the use of such matters as capitalization, abbreviations, and punctuation. For your purposes, you can use a standard style guide such as *The Chicago Manual of Style*.

Clarity In technical writing, the goal is to translate scientific or technical information into language that is easy to read and understand. Thus, a technical writer must be aware of his or her audience. Language appropriate for an audience of engineers may baffle nontechnical readers. On the other hand, if a document is intended for engineers, translating its technical terms into everyday language may complicate the writing unnecessarily.

Brevity Readers should not be hindered by long, convoluted sentences and poor organization. Therefore, a technical writer should use short sentences, bulleted lists, and brief paragraphs to convey information. Long reports should include a table of contents, and the text should be divided into chapters or sections. Presenting information in graphs, tables, or other pictorial forms is another way to communicate complex data in an easy-to-understand format.

A technical report or paper often begins with an abstract that summarizes the document in one tightly written paragraph. Many readers rely on the abstract to help them decide whether the document is one they need to read in its entirety. At the end of a technical report, there is often an appendix that contains details that are too cumbersome to include in the body of the report.

Technical Writing

Focus

Objectives

- To identify four important elements of technical writing
- To compose an abstract of an article
- To learn how to write clear, meaningful directions

Skills

- identifying components; presenting information concisely

Critical Thinking

- identifying; organizing; clarifying; drawing conclusions

Listening and Speaking

- active listening; discussing; evaluating; explaining

Bellringer
Daily Language Activity

When students enter the classroom, have this assignment on the board: *What would you include if you were writing instructions on how to download a file from the Internet to your hard drive?*

Motivating Activity

Discuss students' responses to the Bellringer activity. In reviewing responses, remind students how difficult it might be to explain something technical to someone who has never used a computer. Encourage students to recognize and discuss how qualities such as accuracy, consistency, clarity, and brevity are most important in technical writing.

Practice and Assess

Evaluation Rubrics

To evaluate the abstracts written for the Activity, see the Writing Rubrics on student page 432.

See also *Writing Assessment & Evaluation Rubrics*

Teach

Analyzing Instructions

Have students recall any experience they may have had with assembling an item such as a bicycle, a piece of furniture, or a toy. How difficult were the instructions to follow? Did the manual list all the equipment needed for assembly, or were some steps left out? Encourage students to identify potential problems in writing directions, as well as to suggest possible solutions for those problems. **L2**

Activity

Read an article from *Discover*, *National Geographic*, *Psychology Today*, or *Nature*. Write an abstract of no more than 250 words that provides a summary of the article. Attach a copy of the original article to the abstract. Exchange abstracts with a partner and critique each other's work. Evaluate how well you summarized the articles.

PURPOSE To write an abstract of an article
AUDIENCE A partner
LENGTH 250 words or less

WRITING RUBRICS To write an effective abstract, you should

- summarize the major points of the original article
- write simply and succinctly
- state the conclusion clearly

Writing Instructions

Giving directions is a form of technical writing. To write meaningful instructions, you must thoroughly understand the process you are describing. Then you must recall what it was like not to understand it, so that you can explain it fully to others. You must reacquaint yourself with those steps in the process that have become automatic. For example, when parents teach their children to drive, they often have to stop to think about exactly how they execute a particular maneuver that has become automatic over time.

When writing instructions, remember to list all the tools and equipment needed to perform a task first, just as you would list the ingredients for a recipe before the instructions for putting them together. You do not want to send the reader to the basement or to the store in the middle of a project because you forgot to mention that it requires a socket wrench or a staple gun. Divide the process for which you are writing instructions into clearly defined steps. Then put those steps in the correct order so that a person who performs the process does not have to repeat steps or backtrack. It is important to define terms in the instructions that may be unfamiliar to some people. For example, someone who has never used a computer may not know what a cursor is.

Listening and Speaking

Using Manuals

Have students bring to class as many different owners' manuals as they can find. Divide students into groups, and distribute the manuals evenly among the groups. Ask one volunteer to select a manual and begin reading the instructions aloud while the other members of the group listen. Encourage group members to interrupt if any instruction sounds unclear. Once the reading is finished, have students analyze and evaluate the writing in the manual according to the elements listed on page 431. **L2**

Include Visuals Use drawings and illustrations to supplement your text and to help a reader picture particularly complicated steps. A flowchart can help the reader visualize the process.

As you write instructions, remember that people approach tasks in different ways. Some will read the directions thoroughly; others will look only at illustrations; and still others will take a more experimental approach, resorting to directions and illustrations when all else fails. The best instructions are flexible and can be used easily no matter how a person approaches a task.

Hints for Technical Writing

Technical writers of instruction manuals recommend the following:

- Show or describe the finished product so that the reader knows the goal.
- List all required parts and tools at the outset.
- Label each step clearly: *Step One—Open the box.*
- Use imperative sentences: *Sort the parts by color.*
- Spell out even those steps that seem obvious: *Open the hood of the car.*
- Check for any errors or omissions. Try to follow the directions exactly as they are written and then ask someone else to follow them. This will help you to identify instructions that are confusing or difficult to understand.

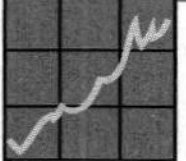

Activity

Select a task that can be performed in the classroom with readily available materials. It can be something as simple as sharpening a pencil or opening a window, as long as it has at least five steps. Write step-by-step instructions for performing the task. Assume that the person who will be following the directions has never performed the task. When your instructions are complete, ask a classmate to use them to perform the task. Have the classmate follow your instructions to the letter and then evaluate them for clarity and precision.

PURPOSE To write a set of clear instructions

AUDIENCE Your teacher and your classmates

LENGTH 1 page

WRITING RUBRICS To write effective instructions, you should

- list the tools and equipment needed
- identify the steps in the process
- put the steps in chronological order
- label each step
- write with clarity
- use helpful visuals
- consider the level of knowledge of the audience
- proofread for spelling and grammatical errors and vague language
- test for omissions

☑ Teaching Tip

Remind students that "a picture is worth a thousand words." Point out that even the most fluent writing is enhanced by the presence of diagrams and photographs. If possible, have on hand examples of instruction manuals with pictures included. Make transparencies of the pictures, and display the transparencies on an overhead projector while reading the instructions in the manual aloud.

Practice and Assess

Evaluation Rubrics

To evaluate the instructions written for the Activity, see the Writing Rubrics on student page 433.

See also *Writing Assessment & Evaluation Rubrics*

Close

Have students keep samples of their abstracts and written instructions in their portfolio for future reference.

Collaborative Writing in the Business World

Focus

Objectives
- To learn how to work collaboratively as part of a team
- To work in a small group to create a new game

Skills
- Observing group performance; listening closely; asking open-ended questions

Critical Thinking
- relating; synthesizing; evaluating; organizing; decision making; summarizing

Listening and Speaking
- active listening; discussing; questioning

Bellringer
Daily Language Activity

When students enter the classroom, have this assignment on the board: *How can group members who disagree with one another still work together?*

Motivating Activity

Discuss students' responses to the Bellringer activity. Have students recall any experience they may have had working in groups. Point out that belonging to a group requires special skills that you don't utilize when you are working alone. The ability to listen, to cooperate, and to compromise on issues help determine whether a group project is successful.

— Collaborative Writing in the Business World —

Today, most organizations stress collaboration and teamwork. People analyze and solve problems in groups, evaluate one another's performances, and report to management, customers, or clients as a team. Many businesses rely on the team approach because a group generates more and better ideas than its members do individually, and creativity is enhanced when people share ideas in open discussion.

Collaborating on a project can be frustrating and time consuming unless those involved know how to work together effectively. When people work in a group, there is always a risk that the more outgoing members may make it difficult for those who are more reserved to contribute. Some group members may be reluctant to challenge ideas and will go along with the majority even when they disagree. In fact, sometimes an entire group will follow a course of action that few individuals in the group actually think is a good idea.

On the other hand, there are few experiences more satisfying than a team experience in which everyone participates to create a first-class product. The key to working effectively in a group is active listening. To listen actively, you should

- make sure that everyone's point of view is not only heard but also understood
- pay attention to what others say and paraphrase their ideas to be sure that you have understood them
- avoid interrupting and try not to disagree with someone before he or she has fully expressed a point of view
- ask open-ended questions

Members of a group that is assigned a project should use the following approach. Begin by discussing the project and coming to an agreement on its purpose and its audience. Be as concrete and specific as possible: *The purpose of this report is to convince the administration of Central High to restore senior privileges for the coming year.* Do not assume that every member of the group understands or agrees on the purpose or the audience. Discuss both thoroughly and record the statements with which everyone is in agreement.

Don't try to create the project as a group. Assign sections of the document to individuals in the group. Then have the entire group evaluate each section, suggest revisions, and proofread the final document. In making the assignments, use the strengths of group members. One person may be especially good at research on the Internet; another may be more knowledgeable about library reference sources; still another may be able to create professional-looking graphics.

Be aware of potential interpersonal problems. If someone is not pulling his or her weight or is refusing to participate, meet as a group to discuss the problem. Use active listening skills. Don't accuse. Don't interrupt. Do try to find a mutually agreeable solution.

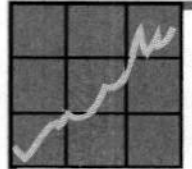

Activity

Work in a small group to create a new game—a board game, a computer game, or any other type of game. You can even base it on an existing game, as long as it is sufficiently changed to constitute something new. Work together to create game parts and packaging, a rules booklet for the game, a print advertisement (newspaper, magazine, poster, billboard), and a radio or TV commercial.

PURPOSE To create a new game as a group
AUDIENCE Game players
LENGTH As needed

PROJECT RUBRIC To complete the group game project, you should

- work effectively as a group
- create an original game
- write effective rules for playing the game
- create game parts and packaging
- create advertising for both print and electronic media

Business and Technical Writing

Teach

Working in a Group

Review with students certain basic rules for group work. Point out that effective group work includes allowing group members to speak without interruption, staying on task, giving all members an equal chance to talk, and responding politely to suggestions and ideas. **L2**

Practice and Assess

Evaluation Rubrics

To evaluate the group game project completed for the Activity, see the Project Rubrics on student page 435.

See also *Writing Assessment & Evaluation Rubrics*

Close

Have students write a short evaluation of the section on Business and Technical Writing. Discuss with students which lessons were the most practical.

ASSESSMENT OPTIONS

Tests with Answer Key & Rubrics
Business and Technical Writing Mastery Test

Testmaker
Business and Technical Writing Mastery Test

You may wish to administer the Business and Technical Writing Mastery Test at this point.

MindJogger Videoquizzes

PART 2

Grammar, Usage, and Mechanics

Objectives

The units in Part 2 continue to guide students in their development toward becoming effective, confident writers. Throughout these units, students will be asked

- to write clearly and effectively using the conventions and mechanics of English
- to identify parts of speech such as nouns, pronouns, verbs, adjectives, adverbs, prepositions, conjunctions, and interjections
- to analyze sentence construction, including phrases and clauses
- to understand, through sentence diagramming, how the various words and parts of a sentence function together
- to demonstrate control over grammatical elements such as verb tenses, verb forms, subject-verb agreement, pronoun-antecedent agreement, and modifiers
- to accurately demonstrate the rules of capitalization and punctuation
- to compose more complex sentences that contain gerunds, infinitives, and participles

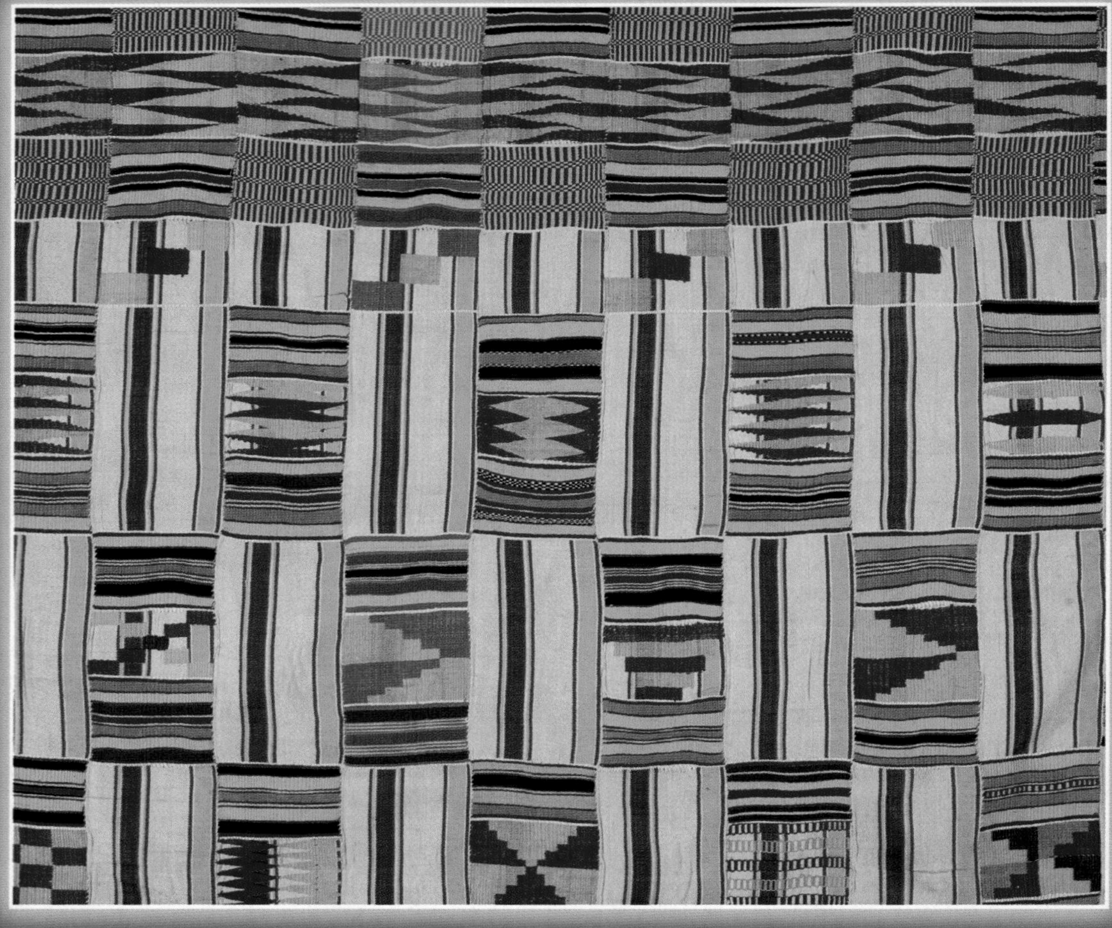

Kente Cloth, Asante People, Ghana, 20th Century

"As usual, in the towns of Ghana, the streets were filled with vendors selling their wares."

—Maya Angelou
All God's Children Need Traveling Shoes

Viewing the Art

Kente cloth, pictured in the photograph, is a ceremonial cloth produced by the Asante people of Ghana. It is hand-woven on a loom and is created by sewing together four-inch strips of cloth to form a larger cloth. Kente cloth comes in various colors and patterns and is worn during important social and religious occasions. It represents the history, beliefs, and culture of the Ghanaian people.

Interpret and Analyze Use the following questions for discussion:

- For Americans, quilting is an art that also carries cultural significance. What are similarities between quilt making and creating Kente cloths?
- How might the order, pattern, and similarity of these sections of the Kente cloth relate to proper sentence construction?

Resource Manager

Planning Resources
- *Lesson Plans*
- *Block Scheduling*

Transparencies
- *Bellringer*
- *Daily Language Practice*
- *Two-Minute Skill Drill*

Other Print Resources
- *Dinah Zike's Foldables™ for Writer's Choice*
- *Grammar and Composition Handbook*
- *Grammar Enrichment*
- *Grammar Practice*
- *Grammar Reteaching*
- *Grammar Workbook*
- *Sentence-Combining Practice*
- *Spelling Power*
- *Taking Standardized Tests*
- *Tests with Answer Key and Rubrics*
- *Vocabulary Power*

PART 2

Grammar, Usage, and Mechanics

Discussing the Quotation

The quotation comes from *All God's Children Need Traveling Shoes,* an autobiographical book by Maya Angelou (b. 1928). Angelou spent four years living and working in Ghana. Discuss the quotation with the class, and ask students how they interpret the author's meaning.

Writing Prompt Write a brief explanation of how Angelou's words, coupled with the image of the Kente cloth, can be seen to connect to grammar, usage, or mechanics.

Video
- *MindJogger Videoquizzes*

Software
- *Interactive Grammar and Language Workbook*
- *Presentation Plus!*
- *Revising with Style*
- *Sentence Diagraming*
- *Testmaker*
- *Vocabulary Power Puzzlemaker*

Web Site
- *glencoe.com*

INTRODUCING

UNIT 10

Objectives

- To develop an understanding of the parts of speech
- To demonstrate control over the parts of speech by identifying their uses and by writing sentences using them effectively

ASSESSMENT OPTIONS

Tests with Answer Key & Rubrics
Unit 10 Pretest, pp. 35–36
Unit 10 Mastery Test, pp. 37–38

Testmaker
Unit 10 Choice A Pretest
Unit 10 Choice B Test

You may wish to administer the Unit 10 Pretest at this point.

Key to Ability Levels

L1 Level 1 activities are within the basic ability range of students.

L2 Level 2 activities are within the ability range of average students.

L3 Level 3 activities are more challenging activities.

UNIT 10

Parts of Speech

438

Resource Manager

Planning Resources
- *Lesson Plans*
- *Block Scheduling*

Transparencies
- *Bellringer*
- *Daily Language Practice*
- *Two-Minute Skill Drill*

Video
- *MindJogger Videoquizzes*

Other Print Resources
- *Grammar and Composition Handbook*
- *Grammar Enrichment*
- *Grammar Practice*
- *Grammar Reteaching*
- *Grammar Workbook*
- *Sentence-Combining Practice*
- *Tests with Answer Key and Rubrics*

Software
- *Interactive Grammar and Language Workbook*
- *Presentation Plus!*
- *Revising with Style*
- *Testmaker*

Web Site
- *glencoe.com*

10.1 Nouns

- A **noun** is a word that names a person, a place, a thing, or an idea.

PERSON	teacher, uncle, niece, sister-in-law
PLACE	garage, city, park, school
THING	paw, giraffe, bicycle, ice cream, doorknob
IDEA	democracy, fame, love, disappointment

Exercise 1 Identifying Nouns

On your paper, list the twenty-five nouns that appear in the following literary passage.

Literature: In a New Country

Hanging from a cord attached to the middle of the ceiling there was an electric bulb, low enough for an adult to reach and turn the black switch. I realized that this was our own electric light for us to turn on and off as we pleased. I pushed a chair under it and after some instruction from my mother proceeded to create lightning in the room by turning the switch as fast as I could.

Next I discovered the bedsprings. When I sat on the bed it sank deliciously. Jumping on it in my stocking feet, I held my balance dangerously as I made the bed creak and the mattress bounce. The head and foot of the bed were made of iron scrollwork in loops and rosettes painted white.

From *Barrio Boy* by Ernesto Galarza

Exercise 2 Completing Sentences with Nouns

On your paper, write nouns to complete the following sentences. Be sure that your completed sentences make sense.

1. The _____ galloped by on her _____.
2. Ten of her _____ waved their blue _____.
3. The other _____ of her _____ cheered.
4. Her yellow _____ blew off her _____.
5. The _____ made her _____ fly wildly.
6. Three miniature _____ sat on the _____.
7. Their _____ were brushing their _____.
8. The _____ and her _____ approached the _____.
9. They walked their _____ and held their _____.
10. Everyone gathered around the tiny _____.

Parts of Speech

Resource Manager

Planning Resources
- *Lesson Plans*

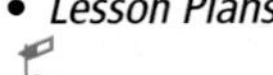

Transparencies
- *Bellringer*
- *Daily Language Practice*
- *Two-Minute Skill Drill*

Other Print Resources
- *Grammar and Composition Handbook*
- *Grammar Enrichment,* p. 1
- *Grammar Practice,* p. 1
- *Grammar Reteaching,* p. 1
- *Grammar Workbook,* Lessons 1–2

Focus

Lesson Overview

Objective
- To identify the major types of nouns and use them effectively

Bellringer
Daily Language Activity

When students enter the classroom, have this assignment on the board: *Identify the nouns in the following sentence:*

In the old garage, the mechanic's feet stuck out from under the body of the pickup truck.

Ask students to explain how they identified the nouns.

See also *Daily Language Practice*

Teach

Vocabulary Link

The term *noun* comes from the Latin word for name. This root is also the basis for the word *anonymous,* "without a name."

Practice and Assess

Answers: Exercise 1

cord, middle, ceiling, bulb, adult, switch, light, chair, instruction, mother, lightning, room, switch, bedsprings, bed, feet, balance, bed, mattress, head, foot, bed, scrollwork, loops, rosettes

Answers: Exercise 2

Answers will vary, but some suggestions are given.

1. girl, horse **2.** friends, banners **3.** members, group **4.** hat, head **5.** wind, hair **6.** dogs, lawn **7.** owners, coats **8.** girl, friends, area **9.** horses, reins **10.** dogs

10.1

Teach

Singular and Plural Nouns

☑ Grammar Tip

Some nouns ending in *-f* form their plurals by adding *-s*. (*reefs*). Since words ending in *-f* and *-fe* follow no set of rules, students will have to remember whether their plurals are formed by adding *-s* or by changing the *-f* or *-fe* to *-v* and adding *-es* or *-s*.

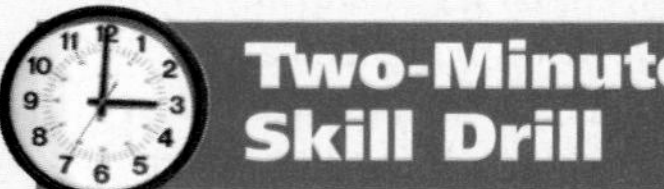

Two-Minute Skill Drill

Have students write the plurals of the following nouns: *wolf (wolves), daisy (daisies), fish (fish), solo (solos), rush (rushes), fox (foxes), latch (latches).* Ask volunteers to explain the rule they used to form each plural.

See also *Two-Minute Skill Drill Transparency 10.1*

Practice and Assess

Answers: Exercise 3

1.	victories	**11.**	businesses
2.	moose	**12.**	batches
3.	lunches	**13.**	galaxies
4.	boxes	**14.**	radios
5.	mice	**15.**	lenses
6.	videos	**16.**	chiefs
7.	men	**17.**	feet
8.	halves	**18.**	deer
9.	geese	**19.**	children
10.	valleys	**20.**	persons/people

Answers: Exercise 4

Answers will vary, but some suggestions are given below.

1. city
2. people, scenery
3. industries
4. river, city
5. houses, sight
6. area, land, climate
7. population
8. buildings, landmarks
9. houses, stores, streets
10. citizens, heritage

Parts of Speech

Singular and Plural Nouns

■ **Nouns** can be singular or plural, depending upon whether they name *one* person, place, thing, or idea or *more than one.*

To form the plural of most nouns, add *-s*. Other plural nouns are formed in different ways. For nouns ending in *-s*, *-ch*, *-sh*, *-x*, or *-zz*, add *-es* to form the plural. For nouns ending in -y preceded by a consonant, change the *-y* to *-i* and add *-es*. For most nouns ending in *-f* or *-fe*, change *-f* to *-v* and add *-es*. Other nouns have irregular plurals (e.g., *woman, women*). Some nouns do not change form from singular to plural (e.g., *sheep, sheep*).

SINGULAR boy, body, watch, wife, ox
PLURAL boys, bodies, watches, wives, oxen

Exercise 3 Forming the Plurals of Nouns

Write the plural form of each noun below on your paper. Consult a dictionary if you need help.

1.	victory	**6.**	video	**11.**	business	**16.**	chief
2.	moose	**7.**	man	**12.**	batch	**17.**	foot
3.	lunch	**8.**	half	**13.**	galaxy	**18.**	deer
4.	box	**9.**	goose	**14.**	radio	**19.**	child
5.	mouse	**10.**	valley	**15.**	lens	**20.**	person

Exercise 4 Completing Sentences with Singular and Plural Nouns

On your paper, write singular or plural nouns to complete the following sentences. Be sure that your completed sentences make sense.

Heidelberg

1. The _____ of Heidelberg, Germany, is neither very large nor strategically important.
2. However, the _____ who live there boast of its beautiful _____.
3. Among the city's _____ are textiles, leather goods, and precision instruments.
4. A wide _____ flows through the _____.
5. Even the gabled _____ are an impressive _____.
6. The _____ is blessed with fertile _____ and a mild _____.
7. In the nineteenth century, the _____ of Heidelberg tripled.
8. Many modern _____ were constructed next to historic _____.
9. New _____ and _____ dotted the _____.
10. Nevertheless, the _____ remain committed to preserving their _____.

MEETING INDIVIDUAL NEEDS

English Language Learners

Using Noncount Nouns

Explain to students that nouns that can be counted are called count nouns—for example, *potatoes.* Nouns that cannot be counted are called noncount nouns—for example, *flour.* One can say *I have two potatoes* but not *I have two flours.* Tell students that noncount nouns cannot be used with *a* or *an,* and they must be used with *much* rather than *many.* Give students a list of words, such as *idea, water, flour, rain, computer, lunch, carrots, orange juice.* Ask them to identify the count and noncount nouns and to use them in sentences.

Possessive Nouns

The possessive form of a noun can show possession, ownership, or the general relationship between two nouns. Add an apostrophe and *-s* to form the possessive of a singular noun, even one that already ends in *-s*. Use an apostrophe alone to form the possessive of a plural noun that ends in *-s*.

SINGULAR POSSESSIVE	PLURAL POSSESSIVE
the **car's** hood	the **cars'** hoods
a **baby's** bottle	the **babies'** bottles
the **dish's** pattern	the **dishes'** patterns
a **valley's** towns	the **valleys'** towns
the **calf's** mother	the **calves'** mother
the **business's** payroll	the **businesses'** payrolls

Add an apostrophe and *-s* to form the possessive of a plural noun that does not end in *-s*.

the **women's** decision
the **children's** toys
the **sheep's** wool

Exercise 5 Forming Possessive Nouns

Rewrite each phrase below, using the possessive form of the italicized noun.

1. the *cat* food
2. the *wagons* wheels
3. the *mice* cage
4. the *parents* advice
5. the *child* toy
6. the *oxen* horns
7. the *book* cover
8. the *family* car
9. the *trolleys* whistles
10. the *boys* homework
11. the *cities* facilities
12. the *states* rights
13. the *mattress* springs
14. the *people* choice
15. the *wives* party
16. the *churches* steeples
17. the *deer* food
18. the *region* climate
19. the *fox* den
20. the *factories* smokestacks

Exercise 6 Completing Sentences with Possessive Nouns

On your paper, write singular or plural possessive nouns to complete the following sentences. Be sure that your completed sentences make sense.

1. The _____ hearts began to pound as the chair lift brought them to the top of the _____ highest peak.
2. In the group behind them, their _____ face had a nervous look.
3. Only the young _____ voices sounded excited.
4. It had been the _____ idea to ski the _____ most challenging moguls.
5. Judy, the _____ most experienced skier, talked about the previous _____ trips.

Parts of Speech

Teach

Possessive Nouns

☑ Grammar Tip

The possessive pronouns *her, his, its,* and *their* can be used as substitutes for possessive nouns. Tell students to try substituting a possessive pronoun to see if a noun is possessive. If a possessive pronoun can replace the noun, then the noun is possessive.

Practice and Assess

Answers: Exercise 5

1. the cat's food
2. the wagons' wheels
3. the mice's cage
4. the parents' advice
5. the child's toy
6. the oxen's horns
7. the book's cover
8. the family's car
9. the trolleys' whistles
10. the boys' homework
11. the cities' facilities
12. the states' rights
13. the mattress's springs
14. the people's choice
15. the wives' party
16. the churches' steeples
17. the deer's food
18. the region's climate
19. the fox's den
20. the factories' smokestacks

Answers: Exercise 6

Answers will vary, but some suggestions are given below.

1. girls', mountain's
2. friend's
3. children's
4. instructor's, area's
5. group's, years'

Cooperative Learning

Recognizing Possessives

Students have a better chance of remembering the spelling of the possessive form if they think of the apostrophe as standing for something. Explain that in the possessive form, the apostrophe can be thought of as standing for the phrases *belongs to, owns,* or *is part of.* Use these phrases as you go over Exercise 5. After you analyze each phrase, encourage students to rewrite the phrase using the apostrophe and to discuss and evaluate their work with a partner. **L2**

Teach

Concrete and Abstract Nouns

Vocabulary Link

A thesaurus is an excellent resource for students to use to find the exact word they are looking for. If students find that the nouns they are using are too vague, encourage them to look in a thesaurus for a word that is more specific.

Practice and Assess

Answers: Exercise 7

1. abstract
2. concrete
3. concrete
4. abstract
5. abstract
6. concrete
7. concrete
8. concrete
9. abstract
10. concrete

Answers: Exercise 8

Answers will vary, but some suggestions are given below.

1. travel
2. humor
3. fear
4. victory
5. peace
6. memories
7. roundness
8. motion
9. excitement
10. sadness
11. alarm
12. fire
13. pennies
14. teacher
15. tears
16. smile
17. gift
18. noise
19. dessert
20. cotton

Answers: Exercise 9

Answers will vary, but some suggestions are given below.

Five of the most important things in my life can be summed up in the following five sentences: (1) Share a dream with family and friends. (2) Bring integrity to all that you do. (3) Have a sense of wonder about the world in which you live. (4) Respect the uniqueness of every living thing. (5) Bring a sense of humor to your struggles.

Concrete and Abstract Nouns

- A **concrete noun** names an object that occupies space or that can be recognized by any of the senses.

  petal smoke cough orange nook

- An **abstract noun** names an idea, a quality, or a characteristic.

  motion humor quantity tact rudeness

Exercise 7 Identifying Nouns as Concrete or Abstract

On your paper, identify each noun as *concrete* or *abstract*.

1. wisdom
2. sunshine
3. book
4. bravery
5. attitude
6. library
7. music
8. guitar
9. happiness
10. electricity

Exercise 8 Using Abstract and Concrete Nouns

For each concrete noun in items 1–10, write an abstract noun that names an idea associated with the concrete noun. For each abstract noun in items 11–20, write a concrete noun that has the quality of the abstract noun.

SAMPLE ANSWERS rocket—power taste—salt

1. bicycle
2. laughter
3. itch
4. home run
5. snow
6. summer
7. apple
8. in-line skates
9. applause
10. sundowns
11. haste
12. warmth
13. poverty
14. insight
15. sadness
16. joy
17. gratitude
18. distraction
19. eagerness
20. softness

Exercise 9 Writing Sentences with Abstract Nouns

On your paper, write five sentences about what you think is important in life. In each sentence, use at least one abstract noun to identify a goal, idea, or personal trait you admire. Underline each abstract noun.

Special Needs

Identifying Nouns

Word association games can be a good way to help students familiarize themselves with the use of concrete and abstract nouns. Ask students to number a sheet of paper from 1 to 10. Then show pictures of ten objects. Tell students to write the name of the object (for example, *tree*). This will be a concrete noun. Then have students discuss how the object makes them feel. This will probably be an abstract noun (for example, *happiness*).

Proper and Common Nouns

■ A **proper noun** is the name of a particular person, place, thing, or idea.

Proper Nouns	
Person	Sean Connery, Uncle Peter, Emily Dickinson
Place	Mexico, Lake George, Grand Canyon
Thing	Statue of Liberty, *Great Expectations,* Thanksgiving
Idea	Romanticism, Baroque Age, Judaism

■ A **common noun** is the general—not the particular—name of a person, place, thing, or idea.

Common Nouns	
Person	actor, uncle, poet
Place	country, lake, canyon
Thing	statue, book, holiday
Idea	movement, era, religion

Proper nouns are capitalized; common nouns are usually not capitalized.

Exercise 10 Matching Proper Nouns with Common Nouns

On your paper, match each proper noun on the left with the corresponding common noun on the right.

1. Middle Ages	**a.** city
2. *New York Times*	**b.** mountains
3. Cuba	**c.** building complex
4. *The Wizard of Oz*	**d.** team
5. Renoir	**e.** painter
6. Rocky Mountains	**f.** newspaper
7. Chicago Cubs	**g.** river
8. San Francisco	**h.** country
9. Nile River	**i.** era
10. Houston Space Center	**j.** motion picture

Exercise 11 Naming Proper Nouns

On your paper, add one more proper noun to each category that follows.

1. Wisconsin, North Dakota, New York, Georgia, _____
2. Atlantic, Antarctic, Indian, Arctic, _____

Teach

Proper and Common Nouns

Vocabulary Link

The term *proper* comes from the Latin word *proprius.* It is related to the words *private* and *property.* Thus, a proper noun is a special noun; it is not a common, or "public," noun.

Parts of Speech

Practice and Assess

Answers: Exercise 10

1. Middle Ages / **i.** era
2. *New York Times* / **f.** newspaper
3. Cuba / **h.** country
4. *The Wizard of Oz* / **j.** motion picture
5. Renoir / **e.** painter
6. Rocky Mountains / **b.** mountains
7. Chicago Cubs / **d.** team
8. San Francisco / **a.** city
9. Nile River / **g.** river
10. Houston Space Center / **c.** building complex

Answers: Exercise 11

Answers will vary, but some suggestions are given below.

1. Texas
2. Pacific
3. Jamal
4. *Miami Herald*
5. Turkey

Cooperative Learning

Listing Nouns

Have small groups of students pick a category, such as music or sports, and make a list of proper nouns that are appropriate to the category. Then tell them to match each proper noun with a common noun.

For example, if they chose sports, they might write the following:

Proper Nouns	Common Nouns
Grant Hill	basketball player

Have groups share their lists and identify the people, places, and things on their lists. Encourage classmates to provide effective feedback.

Teach

Collective Nouns

Grammar Tip

Some collective nouns have regular plural forms—for example, *navy, navies.* Context determines which form to use: *The navy is launching a new battleship today. Navies from several countries are marching in the parade.*

Cross-reference: Usage

For additional practice in deciding whether to use a singular or a plural verb with a collective noun, refer students to Lesson 16.4, pp. 614–615.

Practice and Assess

Answers: Exercise 12

Porgy and Bess
1. chorus
2. cast
3. orchestra
4. audience
5. population

Animal Life in Africa
1. team
2. family
3. herd
4. flock
5. collection

The Power of the Press
1. press
2. audience
3. society
4. team
5. public

3. Michael, Pedro, Gregory, Joel, _____
4. *Chicago Tribune, New York Times, Milwaukee Journal, Trumptown Herald,* _____
5. France, Ghana, Malaysia, Argentina, _____

Collective Nouns

■ A **collective noun** names a group.

family	(the) senate
(the) public	(a) gaggle (of geese)
team	(an) audience
(the) press	(the) board (of directors)

A collective noun is sometimes considered singular and sometimes considered plural. You consider a collective noun singular when you talk about a group as a whole. You consider a collective noun plural when you talk about the individual members of a group.

SINGULAR The audience shouts its approval.
PLURAL The audience have arrived in small groups.

Exercise 12 Identifying Collective Nouns

On your paper, list five collective nouns from each of the following paragraphs.

Porgy and Bess

[1]The Metropolitan Opera's 1985 production of George Gershwin's *Porgy and Bess* had a chorus of seventy voices. [2]The cast included such noted stars as Grace Bumbry and Simon Estes. [3]The orchestra was conducted by James Levine. [4]The audience had bought their tickets well in advance for all sixteen performances. [5]The huge stage was filled with people representing the population of Catfish Row.

Animal Life in Africa

[1]In Africa a team of zoologists can observe many kinds of wild animals. [2]In a western forest might be seen a family of chimpanzees. [3]In the eastern grasslands, quiet watchers might spy a herd of roaming zebras. [4]In the northern desert, a flock of ostriches is not an uncommon sight. [5]The African continent has an extraordinary collection of animal life.

The Power of the Press

[1]The press plays an important and powerful role in contemporary life. [2]Television news programs, newspapers, periodicals, and Web publications reach a large and eager audience. [3]As a result, journalists have a strong influence on society. [4]Sometimes a team of reporters can make or break a candidate's campaign for office. [5]To make an informed choice, the public must separate fact from opinion.

Meeting Individual Needs: English Language Learners

Teaching Collective Nouns

Remind students that collective nouns are usually considered singular. Sometimes this leads to sentences that look as if they contain an error in subject-verb agreement. Write this sentence on the board: *The equipment that we need are bats, balls, and bases.* Explain that in this sentence the writer has mistakenly treated *equipment* as a plural noun instead of a singular one. The verb should be *is.* Have students look through textbooks and magazines for examples of sentences with collective nouns as subjects. Tell them to check for subject-verb agreement.

Exercise 13 Identifying Nouns

On your paper, identify each underlined noun as *common, proper,* or *collective,* depending upon how the noun is used in the sentence. Some nouns may belong in more than one category.

The Trail of Tears

In 1838 sixteen thousand Cherokee were forced from their [1]homes in the [2]Old South. Under armed guard, the [3]mass of Native Americans was pushed west across the [4]Mississippi River to Oklahoma's [5]Indian Territory. Other [6]cultures, including the Creek, Choctaw, and Chickasaw nations, were included in the removal [7]program. Many historians refer to this [8]journey west as the [9]Trail of Tears. They estimate that as many as a quarter of the [10]group may have died during the long and arduous migration.

Some [11]Native Americans rebelled against the removal program, while others fled to Canada or [12]Mexico. The Cherokee led the most organized [13]resistance. They had their own written language; their own [14]newspaper, the [15]*Cherokee Phoenix*; tax-supported schools; and a written [16]constitution. The Cherokee [17]nation also had the sympathy of some members of [18]Congress and of other government [19]officials. Although the Cherokee took legal action, they never were able to regain their [20]homelands.

Exercise 14 Creating Sentences with Nouns

On your paper, write five sentences about a shop in your town or neighborhood. Use concrete nouns to convey a vivid picture of the place.

Exercise 15 Completing Sentences with Nouns

On your paper, complete the paragraphs below by filling in each of the twenty blanks with the kind of noun specified in *italic* typeface. Be sure that your completed sentences make sense.

Thanksgiving Day

The festive [1]*abstract* of the Thanksgiving [2]*concrete* filled our [3]*concrete*. [4]*proper and concrete* told us the [5]*common* of the [6]*proper* who prepared the first Thanksgiving feast. All of the young [7]*common* listened. The table, set with our best [8]*concrete*, held steaming platters of [9]*concrete* and [10]*concrete*. For [11]*common* each of us had a generous [12]*common* of [13]*concrete*.

After dinner we sat by the blazing [14]*concrete*, and [15]*proper and concrete* told us that it was President Lincoln who declared Thanksgiving an official holiday. Then we turned on the [16]*concrete* and watched [17]*proper and concrete*. Later that [18]*common*, we agreed that we had had so much good [19]*abstract* we wished that [20]*proper* came more than once a year.

Parts of Speech

Practice and Assess

Answers: Exercise 13

1. common
2. proper
3. collective, common
4. proper
5. proper
6. collective, common
7. common
8. common
9. proper
10. collective, common
11. proper
12. proper
13. common
14. common
15. proper
16. common
17. collective, common
18. collective, proper
19. common
20. common

Answers: Exercise 14

Answers will vary. Here is a sample: My favorite neighborhood shop is DJ's Produce. It has the best Bartlett pears I have ever eaten.

Answers: Exercise 15

Answers will vary, but some suggestions are given below.

1. atmosphere
2. party
3. house
4. Aunt Sally
5. story
6. Pilgrims
7. children
8. china
9. turkey
10. dressing
11. dessert
12. portion
13. pie
14. fire
15. Uncle Max
16. television
17. *Fantasia*
18. evening
19. fun
20. Thanksgiving

Additional Resources

Grammar Practice, p. 1
Grammar Reteaching, p. 1
Grammar Enrichment, p. 1

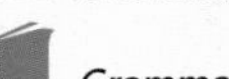
Grammar Workbook, Lessons 1–2

Close

Ask students to list things they would pack in their luggage if they were going to a tropical island. They should work in small groups to use and identify at least one of each of the types of nouns they have learned, with the exception of abstract nouns.

MEETING INDIVIDUAL NEEDS **English Language Learners**

Analyzing Noun Usage

Invite students to select a passage from a magazine or newspaper. Ask students to underline the nouns. Encourage them to pay special attention to concrete nouns, which are nouns they could draw a picture of, such as *school* or *dog*. Explain that abstract nouns are ideas or emotions that are harder to draw (for example, *wisdom* or *fear*). Encourage them to pay particular attention to the use of abstract nouns. Challenge students to try to translate the abstract nouns into specific examples.

Focus

Lesson Overview

Objective

- To identify pronouns and categories of pronouns: personal and possessive; reflexive and intensive; demonstrative; interrogative and relative; and indefinite

Bellringer
Daily Language Activity

When students enter the classroom, have this assignment on the board: *Find and list the pronouns in the passage below.*

> "They" were very kind and bade me come again. Why have I never been taken among the Monkey-People? They stand on their feet as I do. They do not hit me with hard paws. They play all day. Let me get up! I will play with them again.
>
> —Rudyard Kipling, *The Jungle Book*

See also 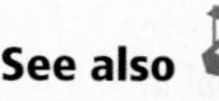 *Daily Language Practice*

Motivating Activity

Discuss the pronouns students listed. Encourage students to ask questions and provide useful feedback. Explain that in this lesson, students will learn to identify different types of pronouns and use them effectively in writing.

Teach

Vocabulary Link

The *pro-* in *pronoun* comes from a Latin preposition that means "for" or "in place of." A pronoun, therefore, is a word used in place of a noun.

Parts of Speech

10.2 Pronouns

- A **pronoun** is a word that takes the place of a noun, a group of words acting as a noun, or another pronoun. The word or group of words to which a pronoun refers is called its **antecedent**. A pronoun must agree in number and gender with its antecedent.

When James Baldwin was fourteen years old, **he** became a preacher. [The pronoun *he* takes the place of its proper noun antecedent, *James Baldwin*.]

When Georgia O'Keeffe and Alfred Stieglitz were married in 1924, **both** were famous artists. [The pronoun *both* takes the place of the nouns *Georgia O'Keeffe* and *Alfred Stieglitz*.]

Although Georgia O'Keeffe **herself** was a painter, **her** husband was a photographer. [The pronouns *herself* and *her* take the place of the noun *Georgia O'Keeffe*.]

English pronouns fall into these categories: personal and possessive pronouns, reflexive and intensive pronouns, demonstrative pronouns, interrogative pronouns, relative pronouns, and indefinite pronouns.

Personal and Possessive Pronouns

- A personal pronoun refers to a specific person or thing by indicating the person speaking (the first person), the person being addressed (the second person), or any other person or thing being discussed (the third person).

Personal pronouns also express number; they are either singular or plural.

Personal Pronouns		
	Singular	**Plural**
First Person	I, me	we, us
Second Person	you	you
Third Person	he, him, she, her, it	they, them

FIRST PERSON **I** kept the dog. [*I* refers to the person speaking.]

SECOND PERSON The dog was afraid of **you**. [*You* refers to the person being addressed.]

THIRD PERSON **It** ran away. [*It* refers to the dog mentioned in the previous sentence.]

Third-person pronouns also express **gender.** *He* and *him* are masculine; *she* and *her* are feminine; *it* is neuter (neither masculine nor feminine).

Resource Manager

Planning Resources
- *Lesson Plans*

Transparencies
- *Bellringer*
- *Daily Language Practice*
- *Two-Minute Skill Drill*

Other Print Resources
- *Grammar and Composition Handbook*
- *Grammar Enrichment,* p. 2
- *Grammar Practice,* p. 2
- *Grammar Reteaching,* p. 2
- *Grammar Workbook,* Lessons 3–4, 52–57

The personal pronouns include several forms that indicate possession or ownership.

■ A **possessive pronoun** takes the place of the possessive form of a noun.

Possessive Pronouns		
	Singular	**Plural**
First Person	my, mine	our, ours
Second Person	your, yours	your, yours
Third Person	his, her, hers, its	their, theirs

Some possessive forms are used before nouns. Other possessive forms can be used by themselves. Notice that possessive pronouns do not contain an apostrophe.

USED BEFORE A NOUN Take **your** bathing suit.

USED ALONE That bathing suit is **yours.**

Exercise 16 Using Personal and Possessive Pronouns

Improve the following paragraph by replacing the underlined words or groups of words with personal or possessive pronouns. Write your answers on your paper.

Isamu Noguchi, Sculptor

Isamu Noguchi is famous for [1]Noguchi's striking abstract sculptures. [2]These sculptures can be seen in museums everywhere. Noguchi's father was a Japanese poet, and [3]Noguchi's mother was an American writer. As a young man in Paris, Noguchi studied with the sculptor Constantin Brancusi, who encouraged [4]Noguchi to work in abstract forms. In the 1930s, Noguchi settled in New York. Soon, [5]Noguchi's spare and elegant sculptures were being exhibited, and many people went to see [6]the sculptures. One admirer, Martha Graham, invited [7]Noguchi to create sets for [8]Martha Graham's dance company. [9]Noguchi also designed sculpture gardens, as well as furniture and lamps. Noguchi's later interest in architectural forms and design is reflected in the monumental *Red Cube* (1968). [10]*Red Cube* stands outside the Marine Midland Building in New York.

Exercise 17 Creating Sentences with Personal and Possessive Pronouns

On your paper, write five sentences about someone or something that is special to you. Be sure to describe what you consider to be important or unique about the person or item. Use at least five personal or possessive pronouns. Then underline all the personal and possessive pronouns in your sentences.

Personal and Possessive Pronouns

Teaching Tip

The term *personal pronoun* has two meanings. It may refer to the complete family of pronouns that includes the personal pronouns listed on p. 446 and the possessive pronouns listed on p. 447. Alternatively, the term may refer only to the subgroup of pronouns listed on p. 446. Accordingly, when we use the term *personal pronoun,* we need to be clear whether we mean the whole family (including possessive pronouns) or just the subgroup (excluding possessive pronouns).

Two-Minute Skill Drill

Write this on the board: *Use the following personal pronouns in sentences of your own:*

we *them*
you *it*
her

See also *Two-Minute Skill Drill Transparency 10.2*

Practice and Assess

Answers: Exercise 16

1. his
2. They
3. his
4. him
5. his
6. them
7. him
8. her
9. He
10. It

Answers: Exercise 17

Answers will vary, but personal and possessive pronouns should be used correctly.

Writing in the Real World

Writing as a Tool for Learning

Invite students to look through current magazines and newspapers for pictures of people. Have students use personal pronouns to create sentences about these people. Then let students rephrase the sentences without using personal pronouns.

Teach

Reflexive and Intensive Pronouns

Vocabulary Link

Reflexive means "directed or turned back on itself." Reflexive pronouns "turn back" to refer to the subject of a sentence.

☑ Grammar Tip

Pronouns are often misused, as in the sentence *Tomás played the guitar for Edna and myself.* This use of the reflexive pronoun *myself* is incorrect because the subject of the sentence and *myself* do not refer to the same person. The sentence should be *Tomás played the guitar for Edna and me.*

Reflexive and intensive pronouns have identical forms but different functions. Reflexive pronouns are part of the basic grammar of their sentence: they are objects.

Intensive pronouns, like appositives, can be deleted without changing the grammar of the sentence.

Cooperative Learning

Have groups of students work together to write sentences using reflexive pronouns. One person in the group can start a sentence using a personal pronoun, such as *you.* Then other members can work together to finish the sentence using a reflexive pronoun, such as *yourself.* Groups may want to share sentences with other groups.

Cross-reference: Listening and Speaking

We tend to use pronouns less carefully in speaking than in writing, often ignoring a pronoun's antecedent. For more information about listening and speaking, see Unit 29, pp. 884–890.

Parts of Speech

Reflexive and Intensive Pronouns

Reflexive and intensive pronouns are formed by adding *-self* or *-selves* to certain personal and possessive pronouns.

Reflexive and Intensive Pronouns		
	Singular	**Plural**
First Person	myself	ourselves
Second Person	yourself	yourselves
Third Person	himself, herself, itself	themselves

- A **reflexive pronoun** refers, or reflects back, to a noun or pronoun earlier in the sentence.

  A reflexive pronoun always adds information to a sentence.

  You outdid **yourself** when you wrote that song.

  Cathy always timed **herself** when jogging.

  In dancing class we watch **ourselves** in the mirror.

  The basketball players prepared **themselves** for the game.

- An **intensive pronoun** adds emphasis to another noun or pronoun in the same sentence.

  I **myself** ate the pizza.

  The team **itself** chose the captain.

  Maria **herself** opened the door.

  George and Pedro planned the party **themselves.**

An intensive pronoun does not add information to a sentence. If the intensive pronoun is left out, the sentence still has the same meaning. An intensive pronoun usually comes immediately after its antecedent.

Meeting Individual Needs: English Language Learners

Using Reflexive Pronouns

Reflexive pronouns are more common in some languages, such as Spanish, than they are in others. If students have difficulty understanding how to use them, you may want students to write pronouns and corresponding reflexive pronouns on index cards. Help students work with the cards to create sentences that use reflexive pronouns.

Demonstrative Pronouns

■ A **demonstrative pronoun** points out specific persons, places, things, or ideas.

Demonstrative Pronouns		
Singular	this	that
Plural	these	those

This is your homeroom.

These are your classmates.

That will be your seat.

Carla's desk is cleaner than **those.** [*Those* refers to other desks.]

A demonstrative pronoun can come before or after its antecedent. Sometimes the antecedent is understood.

Exercise 18 Using Reflexive, Intensive, and Demonstrative Pronouns

Supply the appropriate reflexive, intensive, or demonstrative pronoun for each blank. Write your answers on your paper.

An Orchestra Performance

1. He reminded __________ to watch the conductor's baton.
2. The string, woodwind, brass, and percussion sections had prepared ________ during rehearsals.
3. Even the conductor ________ seemed nervous.
4. The air ________ seemed motionless in expectation.
5. We positioned ________ for the opening note.
6. Soon we found ________ listening anxiously for our cues.
7. ________ is a very moving piece of music.
8. We were so inspired by the occasion that our instruments seemed to play ________.
9. Afterward we all felt very proud of ________.
10. "Take ________," the concert manager said, handing several bouquets to the conductor.

Teach

Demonstrative Pronouns

☑ Teaching Tip

Point out that the demonstrative adjectives *this, that, these,* and *those* always come before a noun.

Students often confuse demonstrative pronouns with the same words used as adjectives. The following example may clarify the difference:

a. *I didn't read that book.*
b. *I didn't read that.*

In sentence *a, that* is a demonstrative adjective because it modifies the noun *book.* In sentence *b, that* is a demonstrative pronoun because it takes the place of a noun.

Practice and Assess

Answers: Exercise 18

1. himself
2. themselves
3. himself/ herself
4. itself
5. ourselves
6. ourselves
7. This/That
8. themselves
9. ourselves
10. these

Enrichment and Extension

Identifying Demonstrative Pronouns

A good way to distinguish between demonstrative pronouns and the same words used as adjectives is to see whether the word in question can be replaced by the word *the.* If it can, then the word is an adjective. If it cannot, then it is probably a demonstrative pronoun. For example, in *I didn't read that book, that* can be replaced by *the,* so *that* is an adjective. In *I didn't read that, that* cannot be replaced by *the,* so *that* is a demonstrative pronoun. Encourage students to ask questions for clarification. **L2**

Teach

Interrogative and Relative Pronouns

Vocabulary Link

Interrogative pronouns are pronouns used to ask questions. They often are the first word in a question. *Interrogative* is related to the verb *interrogate,* meaning "to question," as in *The lawyer interrogated the witness.*

Grammar Tip

Relative pronouns are used to begin subordinate clauses. They are seldom the first word in a sentence. A common error in student writing is the confusion of *whose* and *who's*. *Whose* is an interrogative pronoun or a relative pronoun; *who's* is a contraction of *who is.*

Cross-reference: Usage

For instruction and practice in choosing between *who* and *whom,* refer students to Lesson 17.4, pp. 638–639.

Practice and Assess

Answers: Exercise 19

1. who—relative
2. Who—interrogative
3. whose—relative
4. that —relative
5. Which—interrogative
6. which—relative
7. What—interrogative
8. Whatever—relative
9. Whom—interrogative
10. whom—relative

Parts of Speech

Interrogative and Relative Pronouns

■ An **interrogative pronoun** is used to form questions.

who? whom? whose? what? which?

Who will lead the way?
Whom would you choose?
Whose is the lightest pack?
What makes a good leader?
Which of these paths is easiest?

The interrogative pronouns include the forms *whoever, whomever, whichever,* and *whatever.*

Whoever could have made such a mistake?

■ A **relative pronoun** is used to begin a special subject-verb word group called a subordinate clause (see Unit 13).

who	whoever	which	that
whom	whomever	whichever	what
whose	whosoever	whatever	

The people **who** invented Monopoly were surprised by its success. [The relative pronoun *who* begins the subordinate clause *who invented Monopoly*.]

Dominoes is a game **that** many Texans play. [The relative pronoun *that* begins the subordinate clause *that many Texans play*.]

Exercise 19 Distinguishing Between Interrogative and Relative Pronouns

On your paper, list the relative and interrogative pronouns that appear in the following sentences, and label each pronoun as *relative* or *interrogative.*

Harriet Tubman, a Courageous Woman

1. Harriet Tubman, who was born an enslaved person in 1820, became a leader of the antislavery movement.
2. Who would have anticipated her development into one of the most powerful speakers in the United States?
3. Tubman, whose maiden name was Greene, married John Tubman.
4. She led hundreds of fugitive slaves along the Underground Railroad, a secret route that led from the South to Canada.
5. Which of her many talents did she use during the Civil War?
6. She did many jobs for the Union army, which fought to abolish slavery.
7. What did her fellow abolitionists call her?
8. Whatever she did, she lived up to her nickname, General Tubman.
9. Whom did she look after in the years following the Civil War?
10. She looked after orphans and old people, whom she loved dearly.

Cooperative Learning

Using Pronouns

Have groups of students work together to create questions using interrogative pronouns. Then have student groups create sentences containing subordinate clauses in which the words *who, whose, which, that,* and *what* are used. If students still have difficulty distinguishing between interrogative and relative pronouns, you may want to help them write some sentences. Have students discuss the sentences with peers and write, on their own, sentences using the two types of pronouns.

Indefinite Pronouns

- An **indefinite pronoun** refers to persons, places, or things in a more general way than a noun does.

Everyone needs food. [The indefinite pronoun *everyone* refers to people in general.]

Did you get **enough** to eat? [The indefinite pronoun *enough* refers to a general, not a specific, amount.]

After two hamburgers he did not want **another.** [The indefinite pronoun *another* has the antecedent *hamburger*.]

Some Indefinite Pronouns				
all	each	many	nothing	somebody
another	either	most	one	someone
any	enough	much	other	something
anybody	everybody	neither	others	
anyone	everyone	nobody	plenty	
anything	everything	none	several	
both	few	no one	some	

Exercise 20 Creating Sentences with Indefinite Pronouns

On your paper, write ten sentences with indefinite pronouns. Use at least eight different indefinite pronouns; refer to the chart if you need help. Underline the indefinite pronouns in your sentences.

Exercise 21 Identifying Pronouns

(a) On your paper, list in order the twenty-five pronouns that appear in the following paragraph. (b) Identify each pronoun as *personal, possessive, reflexive, intensive, demonstrative, interrogative, relative,* or *indefinite.*

A Great Magician

[1]Harry Houdini, a great magician who was born Erik Weisz, used a stage name borrowed from an earlier French magician called Houdin. [2]Whereas many of Houdin's illusions were optical ones, those that made Harry Houdini famous were daring escapes from complex traps—most of them designed by Houdini himself. [3]The most famous escape of all was the water-torture trick, in which Houdini, whose hands and feet were bound, was locked in a water-filled tank, only to emerge safe and free a moment later. [4]Audiences would ask themselves, What does Houdini do to free himself? [5]Wouldn't you wonder about this yourself? [6]Actually, Houdini created much of his magic by practicing yoga techniques, learning to survive on less oxygen than most of us need. [7]Whose name is synonymous with magic? [8]That is a question everyone can answer: it is Houdini's.

Parts of Speech

Teach

Indefinite Pronouns

☑ Teaching Tip

Students can distinguish indefinite pronouns from the same words used as adjectives with this simple example:

a. *I didn't order another book.*

b. *I didn't order another.*

In sentence *a, another* is an adjective because it modifies the noun *book.* In sentence *b, another* is an indefinite pronoun because it takes the place of a noun.

Practice and Assess

Answers: Exercise 20

Answers will vary. Check that all pronouns are used correctly.

Answers: Exercise 21

1. who—relative
2. many—indefinite; ones—indefinite; those—demonstrative; that—relative; most—indefinite; them—personal; himself—intensive
3. all—indefinite; which—relative; whose—possessive
4. themselves—reflexive; What—interrogative; himself—reflexive
5. you—personal; this—demonstrative; yourself—intensive
6. much—indefinite; his—possessive; most—indefinite; us—personal
7. Whose—interrogative
8. That—demonstrative; everyone—indefinite; it—personal

Additional Resources

Grammar Practice, p. 2

Grammar Reteaching, p. 2

Grammar Enrichment, p. 2

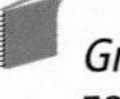

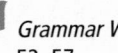

Grammar Workbook, Lessons 3–4, 52–57

Close

Invite students to consider how understanding pronouns can help them write more effectively in their other classes. Encourage them to write definitions of personal, possessive, reflexive, intensive, demonstrative, interrogative, and relative pronouns.

Focus

Lesson Overview

Objectives

- To identify verbs
- To distinguish between action and linking verbs
- To distinguish between transitive and intransitive verbs
- To identify verb phrases
- To use appropriate verbs in writing

Bellringer
Daily Language Activity

When students enter the classroom, have this assignment on the board: *Copy the following sentences and fill in each blank with a verb:*

1. *Lilla ______ down the street toward the bus stop.*
2. *The hungry campers ______ the food.*

See also *Daily Language Practice*

Motivating Activity

Ask volunteers to share the verbs they supplied for the blanks. Then challenge the class to think of additional verbs that will work in each sentence.

Practice and Assess

Answers: Exercise 22

1. include
2. change
3. attract
4. offers
5. provide

10.3 Verbs

- A **verb** is a word that expresses action or a state of being and is necessary to make a statement.

The violinists **begin.**	Rehearsals **are** important.
A flutist **entered** late.	The conductor **seems** enthusiastic.

The primary characteristic of a verb is its ability to express time—present, past, and future. Verbs express time by means of *tense* forms.

PRESENT TENSE	They **walk** home together.
PAST TENSE	They **walked** home together.
FUTURE TENSE	They **will walk** home together.

Exercise 22 Identifying Verbs in Sentences

On your paper, write the verbs that appear in each of the following sentences.

1. National parks in the American Southwest include Bryce Canyon, Zion, Mesa Verde, and Grand Canyon.
2. Over the centuries, water and wind erosion change the land dramatically.
3. Each park's natural features attract people of all ages.
4. An information center at the entrance to the park offers exhibits, maps, and publications.
5. Park rangers provide little-known facts about the history of the park.

Exercise 23 Completing Sentences with Verbs

On your paper, write a verb to complete each of the following sentences.

The American Southwest

1. The Southwest ______ some of the most spectacular scenery in the country.
2. Deep canyons and tall mesas ______ the landscape.
3. Several Native American nations, including the Navajo and Hopi, ______ in the Southwest.
4. Many Native Americans still ______ the customs of their ancestors.
5. Some communities ______ in houses made of adobe (sun-dried earth and straw).
6. Even today, many people in the Southwest ______ their own adobe homes.
7. Navajo women still ______ rugs on handmade looms.
8. The Hopi people still ______ ancient rain dances.
9. The Native Americans of the Southwest ______ proud of their heritage.
10. Despite modern intrusions, many of their traditions ______ unchanged.

Resource Manager

Planning Resources
- *Lesson Plans*

Transparencies
- *Bellringer*
- *Daily Language Practice*
- *Two-Minute Skill Drill*

Other Print Resources
- *Grammar and Composition Handbook*
- *Grammar Enrichment,* pp. 3–4
- *Grammar Practice,* pp. 3–4
- *Grammar Reteaching,* pp. 3–4
- *Grammar Workbook,* Lessons 5–7

Action Verbs

- An **action verb** tells what someone or something does.

  Some action verbs express physical action; others express mental action.

  PHYSICAL ACTION The catcher often **signals** to the pitcher.
  MENTAL ACTION A good catcher **understands** the batter's technique.

- A **transitive verb** is an action verb that is followed by a word or words that answer the question *what?* or *whom?*

  Cats **see** their prey in the dark. [The action verb *see* is followed by the noun *prey,* which answers the question *see what?*]

- An **intransitive verb** is an action verb that is not followed by a word that answers the question *what?* or *whom?*

  Cats **see** well in the dark. [The action verb may be followed by words that tell *how* and *where* or by no words at all.]

Exercise 24 Identifying Action Verbs

On your paper, write the action verbs that appear in the following sentences. Indicate whether each action verb is used as a *transitive* or an *intransitive verb.*

Sacajawea, an Intrepid Woman

1. After President Thomas Jefferson bought the Louisiana Territory from France, he arranged for its exploration.
2. In 1804 Meriwether Lewis and William Clark launched a search for an overland route to the Pacific Ocean.
3. Lewis and Clark hired a French Canadian fur trapper, Toussaint Charbonneau, as guide and interpreter.
4. Charbonneau's wife, Sacajawea, a Shoshone, also joined the expedition.
5. With her linguistic skills, Sacajawea helped Lewis and Clark's communication with Native American tribes.
6. Four years earlier, hostile Native Americans had abducted Sacajawea and later had sold her to Charbonneau.
7. In 1805 Lewis and Clark encountered a group of Shoshone, among them Sacajawea's brother, a chief.
8. He gave Lewis and Clark the horses they needed.
9. Sacajawea, her husband, and their infant son stayed with the expedition until Lewis and Clark had explored the Pacific Coast and returned to Wyoming.
10. Sacajawea and Charbonneau later returned to the Dakota Territory, where, some historians believe, Sacajawea died in 1812.

Teach

Action Verbs

☑ Teaching Tip

Except for the two dozen or so linking verbs, all verbs are action verbs. Consequently, it is next to impossible to define the class of action verbs except negatively: action verbs are not linking verbs. In other words, students may find it easier to first learn the characteristics of linking verbs. Then any verb that doesn't fit the definition of a linking verb is, by definition, an action verb.

Practice and Assess

Answers: Exercise 23

Answers will vary, but some suggestions are given below.

1. offers
2. dot
3. live
4. practice
5. dwell
6. build
7. weave
8. perform
9. remain
10. survive

Answers: Exercise 24

1. bought—transitive; arranged—intransitive
2. launched—transitive
3. hired—transitive
4. joined—transitive
5. helped—transitive
6. had abducted—transitive; had sold—transitive
7. encountered—transitive
8. gave—transitive; needed—intransitive
9. stayed—intransitive; had explored—transitive; returned—intransitive
10. returned—intransitive; believe—intransitive; died—intransitive

MEETING INDIVIDUAL NEEDS **Learning Disabled**

Pantomiming Verbs

Students may benefit from acting out or paraphrasing the concepts of the example sentences on this page. Such an exercise will help students visualize the difference between transitive and intransitive verbs. After students have pantomimed, have them summarize in their journals the difference between transitive and intransitive verbs. **L1**

Teach

Two-Minute Skill Drill

Write the following sentences on the board, or read them aloud. Have students identify each verb and decide whether it is transitive or intransitive.

Emilio will speak at the banquet.

Mrs. Sakata speaks three languages.

The racers ran around the track.

Sue ran the dishwasher after lunch.

See also *Two-Minute Skill Drill Transparency 10.3*

Practice and Assess

Answers: Exercise 25

Answers will vary, but some suggestions are given below.

1. published
2. attended
3. relates
4. hired
5. sank
6. described
7. demonstrates
8. portrayed
9. praise
10. welcomed

Answers: Exercise 26

Answers will vary, but some suggestions are given below.

1. hears the calls of birds (tr.); hears poorly (intr.)
2. studies math and science (tr.); studies every day (intr.)
3. eats oatmeal (tr.); hardly eats (intr.)
4. practices her trumpet (tr.); practices with several other musicians (intr.)
5. play basketball (tr.); play well together (intr.)

Parts of Speech

Exercise 25 Completing Sentences with Action Verbs

On your paper, write an action verb to complete each of the sentences below.

Stephen Crane

1. Stephen Crane ______ his first novel under the pen name Johnston Smith.
2. He ______ Syracuse University for a brief time, where he distinguished himself as a baseball player.
3. Crane's popular novel *The Red Badge of Courage* ______ the story of a young soldier during the Civil War.
4. The novel was widely acclaimed, and syndicated newspapers ______ Crane as a war correspondent.
5. The steamer on which Crane was traveling to Cuba, *The Commodore,* ______ off the coast of Florida.
6. He ______ his nearly fatal experience in "The Open Boat."
7. Crane's natural writing style ______ an understanding of the realities of combat.
8. Crane ______ his varied life experiences in his writings.
9. Critics often ______ Crane's portrayal of war as realistic and powerful.
10. English writer Joseph Conrad ______ Crane when he moved to England in 1897.

Exercise 26 Distinguishing Between Transitive and Intransitive Verbs

On your paper, complete the following sentences using the action verb in *italics*. In one sentence, use it as a transitive verb. In the other sentence, use it as an intransitive verb. Add any other words that are necessary.

1. *hears*
   When hiking through the forest, Alicia ______. (transitive)
   When she pulls her hat over her head, she ______. (intransitive)
2. *studies*
   In the afternoon, the class ______. (transitive)
   In order to do well in school, Paul ______. (intransitive)
3. *eats*
   For breakfast the baby ______. (transitive)
   When the baby is sick, she ______. (intransitive)
4. *practices*
   Before the concert, Susan ______. (transitive)
   Because she wants to be in the band, she ______. (intransitive)
5. *play*
   In the afternoon, the children ______ (transitive)
   Despite their age difference, the children ______. (intransitive)

Enrichment and Extension

Identifying Transitive Verbs

Tell students that an excellent test of a transitive verb is to see whether the sentence can be turned into a *whom* or *what* question whose answer is the object. For example, the sentence *She answered the question* can be rephrased as *What did she answer? the question* (the object of the verb *answered* in the original sentence). Since only transitive verbs have objects, any sentence that can be changed into such a question must contain a transitive verb. **L2**

Linking Verbs

- A **linking verb** links, or joins, the subject of a sentence (often a noun or pronoun) with a word or expression that identifies or describes the subject.

Be in all its forms—*am, is, are, was, were*—is the most commonly used linking verb.

I **am** an athlete.	The players **are** fast.
Squash **is** an indoor sport.	They **were** hockey fans.

Several other verbs besides the forms of *be* can act as linking verbs.

Other Linking Verbs			
look	remain	seem	become
stay	grow	appear	sound
taste	smell	feel	

Exercise 27 Completing Sentences with Linking Verbs

On your paper, write a linking verb to complete each of the following sentences. Try to use as many different verbs as you can.

Georgia

1. The air at higher altitudes in Georgia ______ cool in the summer.
2. Georgia ______ one of the southern states.
3. Azaleas and other colorful plants______ good in the summer.
4. The saws of the lumber mills in the mountains ______ loud and screechy.
5. The Okefenokee National Wildlife Refuge and Stone Mountain Park ______ two popular attractions.
6. The Civil War______ a topic of great interest, especially in Atlanta.
7. Fishing, hunting, and golfing ______ popular with many Georgians.
8. The population of Georgia ______ more diverse every year.
9. With its many different industries and attractions, Georgia ______ ready for a bright future.
10. Atlanta ______ the site of the 1996 Summer Olympics.

Exercise 28 Writing Sentences with Linking Verbs

On your paper, write five sentences about yourself, your family, or your day at school. Use a different form of the verb *be* in each sentence.

Parts of Speech

Teach

Linking Verbs

Teaching Tip

Only linking verbs can be followed by a predicate adjective. Thus a simple test for linking verbs is to see whether you can place an adjective immediately after the verb. For example, *look* can function as a linking verb because it passes this test: *The yard looks beautiful.*

Cross-reference: Composition

Point out that exact, vivid action verbs make narrative writing more compelling. Writers should make a special effort to use action verbs, rather than linking verbs, whenever possible in narrative writing. For instruction and practice with narrative writing, direct students' attention to Unit 4, pp. 180–207.

Practice and Assess

Answers: Exercise 27

Answers will vary, but some suggestions are given below.

1. feels
2. is
3. smell
4. sound
5. are
6. remains
7. are
8. becomes
9. appears
10. was

Answers: Exercise 28

Answers will vary. Here is a sample: *My family is a large one. There are six of us: Mom, Dad, and four children. I am the oldest son. My sisters and I will be visiting our grandparents. My grandparents were farmers.*

MEETING INDIVIDUAL NEEDS

English Language Learners

Identifying Linking Verbs

Explain that *be* is the most common linking verb. Moreover, *be* can replace most of the other linking verbs and will still produce a grammatical sentence with roughly the same meaning. Thus a quick and highly reliable test of linking verbs is to see whether the verb in question can be replaced with a form of *be*. To help students understand this, copy several simple sentences, leaving a blank space where the verb should be. Have students try to fill in a form of *be* in the blank space. If they can do so, then the verb is a linking verb.

Practice and Assess

Answers: Exercise 29

1. presented—action
2. was—linking
3. is—linking
4. know—action
5. commemorated—action
6. celebrated—action
7. holds—action
8. reads—linking (Do not count *action* as a wrong answer, but explain to students that, since *inscription = July 4, 1776, reads* is a linking verb here.)
9. made—action
10. created—action
11. was—linking
12. dismantled—action
13. arrived—action
14. donated—action
15. collected—action
16. found—action
17. was—linking
18. remains—linking
19. became—linking

Answers: Exercise 30

Answers will vary, but some suggestions are given below.

1. are—linking
2. live—action
3. is—linking
4. beats—action
5. sounds—linking
6. are—linking
7. lets—action
8. inserts—action
9. drinks—action
10. eat—action

Exercise 29 Identifying Action and Linking Verbs

On your paper, make a list of the nineteen verbs that appear in the following paragraphs. Identify each verb as either *action* or *linking.*

The Statue of Liberty

[1]In 1884 France presented the United States with a gift as a dramatic gesture of friendship. [2]This spectacular gift was a huge copper statue. [3]Its official name is *Liberty Enlightening the World.* [4]Most people, however, know it simply as the Statue of Liberty. [5]The gift commemorated the hundredth anniversary of the American Revolution. [6]It also celebrated the alliance of France with the colonists during their fight for independence from England. [7]The immense figure of Liberty holds a torch in her right hand. [8]The inscription on the cover of her book reads "July 4, 1776."

[9]Artist Frédéric Auguste Bartholdi first made a nine-foot model of the statue. [10]Gustave Eiffel, a pioneer in the use of metal as an architectural material, created the iron framework for the full-size statue. [11]The completed statue was too large for delivery in one piece. [12]Workers in France dismantled it. [13]The pieces of the statue arrived in the United States in 214 cases.

[14]The French people donated the money for the construction of the statue. [15]Grateful, the people of the United States collected the funds for the massive granite and concrete pedestal. [16]This impressive monument found a permanent home on Liberty Island in New York Harbor. [17]The dedication of the statue by President Grover Cleveland on October 28, 1886, was a great ceremonial occasion.

[18]At 151 feet and 1 inch high, the Statue of Liberty remains one of the largest statues in the world. [19]The monumental lady with the torch quickly became a symbol of American democracy.

Exercise 30 Completing Sentences with Action and Linking Verbs

On your paper, write a verb to complete each of the sentences below. Identify each verb as an *action* or a *linking* verb.

Those Amazing Hummingbirds

1. Hummingbirds _____ the smallest birds in the world.
2. About nineteen different kinds of hummingbirds _____ in the United States.
3. The ruby-throated hummingbird _____ approximately 3 1/2 inches in length.
4. The hummingbird _____ its wings between fifty and seventy times per second.
5. The rapid wing beating _____ soft and low, like the whirring of a distant motorboat.
6. The bird's wings _____ a blur to the human eye.
7. This rapid wing beating _____ the hummingbird hover in midair.
8. While hovering, the hummingbird _____ its long, slender bill into a flower.
9. The bird _____ the flower's nectar through its long, tubelike tongue.
10. Hummingbirds also _____ insects and may even steal them away from spider webs.

Meeting Individual Needs: English Language Learners

Filling in Appropriate Verbs

On ten separate index cards, write an appropriate verb for each sentence in Exercise 30. Scramble the cards. Then invite students to fill in each blank in the exercise with an appropriate verb from one of the cards. Have students discuss their choices. Remind students to ask questions for clarification and to provide effective feedback.

Verb Phrases

■ The verb in a sentence may consist of more than one word. The words that accompany the main verb are called **auxiliary,** or helping, **verbs.**

Auxiliary Verbs			
Forms of *Be*	am, is, are, was, were, being, been		
Forms of *Have*	has, have, had		
Other Auxiliaries	can, could do, does, did	may, might shall, should	must will, would

■ A **verb phrase** consists of a main verb and all its auxiliary, or helping, verbs.

The most common auxiliary verbs are the forms of *be* and *have*. They help the main verb express the various tenses.

We **are working** in the yard.

We **have worked** for the past two weeks.

We **had been working** for an hour before the storm.

The other auxiliary verbs are not used primarily to express time. They are often used to emphasize meaning.

I **should be leaving.**

Could he **have finished?**

Luisa **may** already **be waiting.**

Exercise 31 Using Auxiliary Verbs

On your paper, write two revisions of each sentence below by changing the italicized verb phrase. Remember that you will probably have to change the main verb as well as the auxiliary verb. Underline the verb phrase in each sentence you write.

SAMPLE I *am going*.
ANSWER I <u>have gone</u>. I <u>might go</u>.

1. Jerry and Sue *will eat* dinner.
2. The rest of the family *has left*.
3. When *did* the Murrays *call*?
4. Janice *has been* waiting.
5. Who *should set* the table?

Parts of Speech

Teach

Verb Phrases

Teaching Tip

A verb phrase contains more than one verb. No matter how many verbs make up a verb phrase, it will consist of two components: the main verb (which is always the last verb in the phrase) and one or more helping, or auxiliary, verbs preceding the main verb. A good way to illustrate this point is to write on the board a number of different verb phrases that use the same main verb. After students read these sentences, elicit a generalization about the placement of the main verb: it is always the last verb.

Two-Minute Skill Drill

Write these sentences on the board and have students identify the main verb or verbs and auxiliary verbs in each:

Did the basketball team win last night's game?

Rose will never forget that picnic.

The children have been playing for about an hour.

See also *Two-Minute Skill Drill Transparency 10.3*

Practice and Assess

Answers: Exercise 31

Answers will vary, but some suggestions are given below.

1. Jerry and Sue <u>are eating</u> dinner. Jerry and Sue <u>must eat</u> dinner.
2. The rest of the family <u>may leave</u>. The rest of the family <u>is leaving</u>.
3. When <u>will</u> the Murrays <u>call</u>? When <u>can</u> the Murrays <u>call</u>?
4. Janice <u>must have been waiting</u>. Janice <u>could be waiting</u>.
5. Who <u>has set</u> the table? Who <u>will set</u> the table?

Enrichment and Extension

Scrambling Verb Phrases

The word order of verb phrases is completely fixed. To illustrate this point, take a sentence with a relatively long verb phrase—for example: *John should have been working.* Scramble the order of words in the verb phrase: *John been should working have.* Ask students to put the sentence back in its correct order. There is only one possible correct answer no matter what verb phrase you pick. Then have students write their own sentences with long verb phrases and scramble them as a puzzle for other students. **L2**

Practice and Assess

Answers: Exercise 32

1. (has been) called
2. (could) compose, sing, play
3. (has been) recorded
4. (was) playing
5. (had been) taught
6. (had) felt; (should) follow
7. (had) decided; (would be) dedicated
8. (was) earning; (had) written
9. (must have) appreciated
10. (Can) believe
11. (had) become
12. (had) become known
13. (had) composed; (would) become
14. (has) remained; (was) written
15. (may be) recalled; (had) performed
16. (had) become
17. (were) buying
18. (was) declared
19. (have) seen; (will) forget
20. (will) have
21. (can) enjoy
22. (have) been
23. (should) know
24. (has) benefited
25. (has been) enriched

Exercise 32 Identifying Verb Phrases

On your paper, write each verb phrase that appears in the following sentences. (Some sentences have more than one verb phrase.) Put parentheses around the auxiliary verbs in each phrase. (A word or words that interrupt a verb phrase are not considered part of the verb phrase.)

Fats Waller, a Great Jazz Pianist

1. Fats Waller has been called one of the greatest jazz musicians of the twentieth century.
2. A versatile musician, he could compose, sing, and play several instruments with equal skill.
3. Fortunately, most of his music has been recorded.
4. Waller was already playing the piano at the age of six.
5. He had been taught by his mother, a musician herself.
6. Waller's father, a church deacon, had felt that his son should follow in his footsteps.
7. Nevertheless, young Waller had decided that his life would be dedicated to music.
8. By the age of sixteen, he was earning $23 a week as a theater organist and had already written his first instrumental composition, "Boston Blues."
9. People must have appreciated Waller's talents.
10. Can you believe that Waller's first song, "Squeeze Me," became a jazz classic?
11. A recording of the song by Louis Armstrong and Earl Hines had already become popular by 1928.
12. By the beginning of the 1930s, Waller had become known not only as a major composer, bandleader, and jazz vocalist but also as the greatest jazz organist of his time.
13. By 1932 he had already composed the song that would become his most famous work, "Ain't Misbehavin'."
14. An earlier Waller song, "Honeysuckle Rose" (1928), has remained a favorite ever since the time it was written.
15. It may not be widely recalled today that Waller had performed for several years on radio before becoming a recording artist.
16. By the mid-1930s, Waller had become famous as a recording star for RCA Victor.
17. At that time, people were buying more records by Waller than by any other African American musician.
18. *Ain't Misbehavin'*, a Broadway show with many of Waller's songs, was declared a hit in 1978, more than three decades after Waller's death.
19. Those people who have seen *Ain't Misbehavin'* will surely never forget the experience.
20. Waller will always have a special place in the history of American jazz.
21. Today we can still enjoy his exuberant style of piano playing.
22. Few musicians have been able to imitate Waller's humorous vocal renditions.
23. Fans should know that Fats's real name was Thomas.
24. Waller's lasting popularity has benefited from new recording technologies.
25. Our musical heritage has been greatly enriched by Fats Waller's talents, despite his death at an early age.

MEETING INDIVIDUAL NEEDS

English Language Learners

Emphasizing Auxiliary Verbs

Point out that speakers can often clarify the meaning of a sentence by emphasizing an auxiliary verb rather than a main verb. For example, in reply to the question *Are you going to the park,* someone might say, *I **might** go later.* For the benefit of students who are learning English, say several sentences that demonstrate this principle and explain what the emphasis implies. Encourage students to ask questions for clarification. For more information about listening and speaking, see Unit 29, pp. 884–892.

Exercise 33 Creating Verb Phrases

On your paper, write auxiliary verbs to create a verb phrase for each sentence. Be sure that your completed sentences make sense.

Satellites

1. Satellites ______ defined as artificial objects that orbit celestial bodies.
2. The first satellite, *Sputnik I,* ______ launched in 1957 by the Soviet Union.
3. Satellites ______ study solar radiation, magnetic fields, and atmospheric temperature.
4. Crewed satellites ______ include food, air, and life-support systems for astronauts.
5. One of the earliest crewed satellites ______ named *Skylab.*
6. Astronauts ______ performed experiments in space to find out more about the materials we use on Earth.
7. The Hubble Telescope ______ enabled astronomers to learn more about our universe.
8. Many scientists and engineers ______ work long hours to prepare the next satellite for its mission into space.
9. More advanced satellites ______ help meteorologists predict the weather more accurately.
10. Telecommunications companies ______ financing future experiments in space.

Exercise 34 Completing Sentences with Verb Phrases

On your paper, write a verb phrase to complete each of the following sentences. Be sure that your completed sentences make sense.

James Herriot, Veterinarian and Author

1. Many children and adults _____ a friend in James Herriot.
2. A country veterinarian in Yorkshire, England, Herriot decided after his fiftieth birthday that he _____ books.
3. His first book _____ *If Only They Could Talk.*
4. Herriot had hoped that someone would publish his book and a few people _____ it.
5. It soon became apparent that his book _____ a bestseller.
6. His first two books _____ in the United States in 1972 as one volume entitled *All Creatures Great and Small.*
7. By the time Herriot died in February 1995, his fifteen books _____ more than fifty million copies in twenty countries.
8. Critics _____ Herriot's stories as "fresh, clear, pure, and good."
9. Each of his stories features animals that _____ by the country veterinarian himself.
10. *James Herriot's Treasury for Children* _____ a wonderful gift for readers of all ages.

Parts of Speech

Practice and Assess

Answers: Exercise 33

Answers will vary, but some suggestions are given below.

1. are
2. was
3. can
4. must
5. was
6. have
7. has
8. will
9. may
10. will be

Answers: Exercise 34

Answers will vary, but some suggestions are given below.

1. have found
2. would write
3. is called
4. might read
5. would become
6. were combined
7. had sold
8. have praised
9. were treated
10. can make

Enrichment and Extension

Crystallizing Images

Verbs can help make imagery more powerful. Share these guidelines with students:

1. Try to reduce a group of words to one action verb.
2. Instead of beginning sentences with *There is* or *There were*, begin each sentence with a noun and follow up with a colorful action verb.
3. Whenever possible, use action verbs rather than linking verbs.
4. Replace general verbs with more precise action verbs.

Have students compose a short poem and revise their drafts using these guidelines. **L2**

Practice and Assess

Answers: Exercise 35

Answers will vary. Here is a sample:
As the baseball is zooming through the air, the batter swings her arms in one powerful motion.

Answers: Exercise 36

Answers will vary, but some suggestions are given below.

1. is	**11.** folds
2. began	**12.** provides
3. donated	**13.** displays
4. constructed	**14.** contains
5. designed	**15.** are
6. is	**16.** give
7. is	**17.** visited
8. shields	**18.** opened
9. opens	**19.** brought
10. is	**20.** symbolizes

Answers: Exercise 37

Answers will vary, but some suggestions are given below.

1. has—action verb. The pangolin and the lizard are similar in some ways.
2. cover—action verb. The back of this insect-eating mammal is scaly.
3. feel—linking verb. Some people have likened these scales to a razor in the mouth of a predator.
4. curls—action verb. The pangolin can curl itself into a tight ball for protection.
5. lives—action verb. This toothless anteater is native to Asia and Africa.

Additional Resources

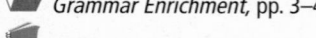

Grammar Practice, pp. 3–4
Grammar Reteaching, pp. 3–4
Grammar Enrichment, pp. 3–4

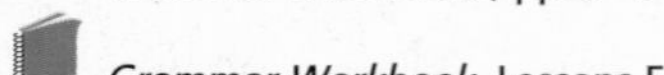

Grammar Workbook, Lessons 5–7

Close

Have students copy two or three sentences from one of their other textbooks, such as a science or social studies textbook. Students should underline all the verbs and verb phrases in the sentences and label the verbs *action* or *linking*. They might also label the action verbs either *transitive* or *intransitive*. Have students share their work with a partner. Remind students to provide effective feedback and to ask questions as needed.

Exercise 35 Using Vivid Verbs

Write five sentences about one of your favorite sports. Choose very specific action verbs and verb phrases to convey a vivid sense of the sport.

Exercise 36 Completing Sentences with Verbs and Verb Phrases

On your paper, complete each of the following sentences as indicated in italic typeface. Be sure that your completed sentences make sense.

The Milwaukee Art Museum

The Milwaukee Art Museum [1]*linking verb* located in Milwaukee, Wisconsin, on the shores of Lake Michigan. Its collection [2]*action verb* in the 1880s when Frederick Layton, owner of a meat packing business, [3]*action verb* $115,000 for an art gallery. In 2001, the museum [4]*action verb* a new, white, concrete pavilion [5]*action verb* by noted architect Santiago Calatrava. The brise soleil, French for "sun breaker," [6]*linking verb* its most notable feature. This [7]*linking verb* a moveable, wing-like mechanism that [8]*action verb* the sun. During the day, the wingspan [9]*action verb* to two hundred and seventeen feet. This [10]*linking verb* wider than a Boeing 747 airplane. In the evenings, at night, or during inclement weather, however, the mechanism [11]*action verb* the wings down over the arched structure of the museum. The beautiful new facility [12]*action verb* thirty percent more gallery space, too. This larger space [13]*action verb* more of the museum's works. The museum's collection primarily [14]*action verb* nineteenth and twentieth century art. However, there [15]*linking verb* ancient collections, too, which [16]*action verb* perspective to the history of Western art. More than five hundred thousand people [17]*action verb* the new Milwaukee Art Museum the first year it [18]*action verb*. Beautiful and dramatic, the new structure [19]*action verb* the museum international recognition. For many people, the building [20]*action verb* the city of Milwaukee.

Identifying Action Verbs, Linking Verbs, and Verb Phrases

On your paper, identify the verb in each of the following sentences as an *action verb* or a *linking verb*. If the verb is a verb phrase, write *verb phrase* as well. Then use the information in the sentence to write a new sentence, using the italicized verb form in parentheses.

SAMPLE The pangolin and the lizard look similar. (*action verb phrase*)
ANSWER look; linking verb The pangolin and the lizard do have similar qualities.

The Pangolin

1. The pangolin has some of the characteristics of a lizard. (*linking verb*)
2. Overlapping scales instead of hair cover the back of this insect-eating mammal. (*linking verb*)
3. These scales feel sharp, similar to a razor, in the mouth of a predator. (*action verb phrase*)
4. The pangolin curls itself into a tight ball for protection. (*action verb phrase*)

10.4 Adjectives

■ An **adjective** is a word that modifies a noun or pronoun by limiting its meaning. An adjective tells *what kind, which one, how many,* or *how much.*

round window	**six** oranges	**that** hat	**adult** cat
romantic story	**many** ideas	**these** books	**Scottish** wool
interesting book	**enough** cups	**third** time	**no** reason

Nouns can also be used as adjectives. They tell *what kind* or *which one* about the noun modified.

afternoon class   **music** lesson   **football** practice

Possessive pronouns, such as *our* and *his,* can be considered adjectives because they modify nouns in addition to their usual function as pronouns.

our book   **his** watch   **their** house   **my** hands

Similarly, possessive nouns can be considered adjectives.

Julia's dream   the **knight's** castle   the **Bowers'** car

Adjectives may be used in various positions in relation to the words they modify.

How **obedient** the poodle is!
That **obedient** poodle belongs to her.
The poodle is **obedient.**
The judges considered the poodle **obedient.**
The poodle, always **obedient,** waited by the door.

Many adjectives have different forms to indicate degree of comparison.

POSITIVE	COMPARATIVE	SUPERLATIVE
light	lighter	lightest
heavy	heavier	heaviest
funny	funnier	funniest
sad	sadder	saddest
practical	more practical	most practical
good	better	best
much	more	most
bad	worse	worst

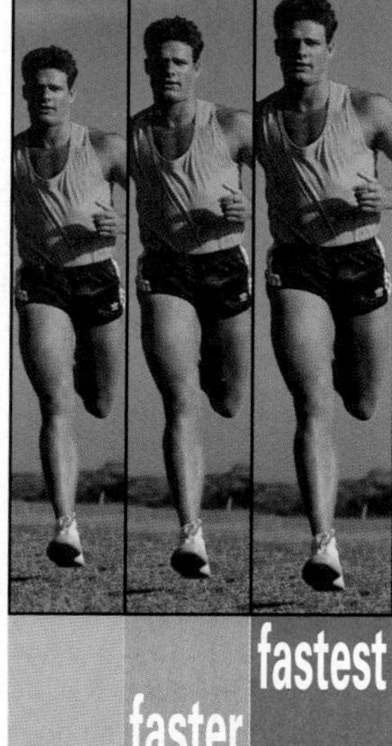

Focus

Lesson Overview

Objective
- To identify adjectives
- To discover how adjectives are formed
- To form proper adjectives
- To create sentences with adjectives

Bellringer
Daily Language Activity

When students enter the classroom, have this assignment on the board: *Read this passage from "Cecilia Rosas" by Amado Muro. Write down the five adjectives or main words that describe Miss Rosas.*

> Miss Rosas was an exemplary saleslady. She could be frivolous, serious or demure, primly efficient too, molding herself to each customer's personality.

See also  *Daily Language Activity*

Motivating Activity

Discuss with students what the words *exemplary, frivolous, serious, demure,* and *efficient* have in common (they all describe Miss Rosas or the word *saleslady*). Then discuss how they are different from *primly.* (*Primly* describes the word *efficient;* the other words describe Miss Rosas.)

Teach

☑ Teaching Tip

A helpful tip for identifying adjectives is to see whether the word in question describes a characteristic of something or someone. For example: The *large* man, the *large* building, the *noisy* crowd.

Resource Manager

Planning Resources
- *Lesson Plans*

Transparencies
- *Bellringer*
- *Daily Language Practice*
- *Two-Minute Skill Drill*

Other Print Resources
- *Grammar and Composition Handbook*
- *Grammar Enrichment,* p. 5
- *Grammar Practice,* p. 5
- *Grammar Reteaching,* p. 5
- *Grammar Workbook, Lesson* 8
- *Sentence-Combining Practice,* pp. 4, 11

Teach

☑ Grammar Tip

Tell students that one way to identify adjectives that modify nouns is to ask a question (typically beginning with *whose, how many,* or *what kind of*) about the noun. Only an adjective can answer this kind of question. See *Grammar Reteaching,* p. 5.

Vocabulary Link

The articles *a* and *an* come from the Old English word *an,* meaning "one." The *n* was dropped before words starting with a consonant: an owl, a peacock.

Practice and Assess

Answers: Exercise 38

long, laborious, dry, empty, white; open, each, that, vast, dark; old, his; long, moving; Its, slow; ordinary, singular; his, red

Answers: Exercise 39

Answers will vary, but some suggestions are given below.

1. grassy
2. gray-green
3. patient
4. lightweight
5. red

Answers: Exercise 40

1. literary
2. grammatical
3. declarative *or* declaratory
4. residential
5. parental
6. scientific
7. intentional
8. mighty, mightier, *or* mightiest
9. idealistic
10. noisy

Exercise 38 Identifying Adjectives

On your paper, list the twenty adjectives that appear in the following fictional passage, which describes a scene on a British heath during the nineteenth century. Count possessive pronouns as adjectives, but do not count the words *a, an,* and *the.*

Literature: A Long Road

Before him stretched the long, laborious road, dry, empty, and white. It was quite open to the heath on each side, and bisected that vast, dark surface. . . . The old man frequently stretched his eyes ahead to gaze over the tract that he had yet to traverse. At length he discerned, a long distance in front of him, a moving spot. . . . Its rate of advance was slow. . . . When he drew nearer he perceived it to be a . . . van, ordinary in shape, but singular in color. . . . The driver walked beside it; and, like his van, he was completely red.

From *The Return of the Native* by Thomas Hardy

Exercise 39 Completing Sentences with Adjectives

On your paper, write an adjective to complete each of the following sentences. Be sure that your completed sentences make sense.

1. The sheepdog trial was held on a _____ field.
2. It was near the edge of a _____ river.
3. The dogs, always _____, waited for the trial to begin.
4. Wearing _____ jackets, the trainers leaned on their long crooks.
5. Soon the judge waved his _____ handkerchief to begin the trial.

Exercise 40 Discovering How Adjectives Are Formed

Use your dictionary to discover the adjective form that is most closely related to each of the following nouns.

1. literature
2. grammar
3. declaration
4. residence
5. parent
6. science
7. intention
8. might
9. idealism
10. noise

Meeting Individual Needs — English Language Learners

Using Articles

The use of articles is often challenging for most students learning English. Here are some basic guidelines for such students: 1. Use *a* or *an* the first time a new topic is introduced: *I saw a mouse this morning.* 2. Use *a* or *an* for generalizations about count nouns: *A stamp costs thirty cents.* 3. Use *the* when the reader already knows the thing or person referred to: *I saw a mouse. The mouse ran away.* 4. Use *the* when the person or thing referred to is unique: *The library is not open on Sundays.*

Exercise 41 Using Forms of Adjectives

On your paper, complete the sentences in each group by writing the correct positive, comparative, and superlative forms of the given adjective.

sample **tall**

answers The basketball player is **tall.**
Other players are **taller** than he is.
The captain of the team is the **tallest** player of all.

bright

1. The male mandrill is a type of baboon that has a very _____ face.
2. Scientists think that the colors become even _____ when the baboon gets angry.
3. During a fight between mandrills, the male with the _____ color usually wins.

good

4. Most people agree that milk is _____ for you.
5. Others argue that water is even _____ for you than milk.
6. Personally, I think fruit juices are the _____.
7. I like orange juice _____ than grapefruit juice.

tasty

8. Last night's dinner was _____.
9. It was _____ than any other meal he has served this week.
10. Thanksgiving dinner is my candidate for our family's _____ meal.
11. Is Jack's cooking ______ than Minna's?

large

12. Compared to Mercury, Earth is a fairly _____ planet.
13. Saturn is much _____ than Earth.
14. Jupiter, however, is the _____ planet.
15. Which is _____, Neptune or Mars?

slow

16. The tortoise was very _____.
17. It was much _____ than the hare.
18. In fact, the tortoise was the ______ animal around.

curious

19. The detective is _____ about the case.
20. Her assistant is even _____.
21. The police captain is the_____ of all.

many

22. Jack won _____ awards at the sports banquet.
23. Did he win the_____ awards?
24. He won _____ awards than he did last year.
25. The team was surprised that Jack won _____ awards than the quarterback.

Answers: Exercise 41

1. bright
2. brighter
3. brightest
4. good
5. better
6. best
7. better
8. tasty
9. tastier
10. tastiest
11. tastier
12. large
13. larger
14. largest
15. larger
16. slow
17. slower
18. slowest
19. curious
20. more curious
21. most curious
22. many
23. most
24. more
25. more

MEETING INDIVIDUAL NEEDS Gifted and Talented

Using Comparative and Superlative Adjectives

Ask students to discuss three favorite books—either read recently or read earlier. Compare such features as characters, plot, and the nature of their appeal. Use comparative and superlative adjectives. **L3**

10.4

Teach

Articles

☑ Grammar Tip

Articles are a special subclass of adjectives. True adjectives typically have comparative forms (*quick, quicker, quickest; beautiful, more beautiful, most beautiful*) and become adverbs of manner when the suffix *-ly* is added (*quickly, beautifully*). Articles have no comparative forms and no comparable adverb form. Articles always precede adjectives: *a tall building,* not *tall a building.*

Practice and Assess

Answers: Exercise 42

Answers may vary, but some suggestions are given below.

1. the; definite
2. A; indefinite
3. the; definite
4. A; indefinite
5. the; definite
6. the; definite
7. the; definite
8. The; definite
9. an; indefinite
10. an; indefinite

Answers: Exercise 43

Answers may vary, but some suggestions are given below.

1. the
2. A
3. its
4. elephant's
5. its
6. their
7. elephant's
8. The
9. their
10. the

Articles

- Articles are the adjectives *a, an* and *the. A* and *an* are called indefinite articles. They can refer to any one of a kind of person, place, or thing. *A* is used before consonant sounds and *an* is used before vowel sounds. *The* is called a definite article. It refers to a specific person, place, or thing.

INDEFINITE	She found **a** ring.	They spotted **an** iceberg.
	I bought **a** used mask.	He was **an** honorable choice.
DEFINITE	She found **the** ring.	They spotted **the** iceberg.
	I bought **the** used mask.	He was **the** honorable choice.

Exercise 42 Completing Sentences with Articles

On your paper, write an article to complete each of the following sentences. Then identify each article as *indefinite* or *definite*.

Coral Reefs

1. Coral reefs are land features formed in ______ ocean.
2. ______ fringing reef extends from the shore of an island or mainland.
3. No body of water comes between ______ fringing reef and land.
4. ______ channel or lagoon comes between a barrier reef and shore.
5. Charles Darwin first explained ______ formation of coral reefs.
6. Darwin's theory is ______ one accepted by modern geologists.
7. Many coral reefs are in ______ Atlantic, Pacific, and Indian oceans.
8. ______ most famous barrier reef is in Australia.
9. The Bikini Atoll was the site of ______ underwater atomic explosion in 1946.
10. The coral that forms ______ atoll can be more than one thousand feet thick.

Exercise 43 Writing with Different Kinds of Adjectives

On your paper, write an adjective to complete each sentence. The kind of modifier to use in each case is indicated in italics. Be sure that your completed sentences make sense.

The African Elephant

The African elephant is [1]*article* largest of all land animals. [2]*article* mature elephant eats about three hundred pounds of plants every day. Some of [3]*possessive pronoun* favorite foods include grass, leaves, roots, bark, and fruit. The [4]*possessive noun* long trunk is actually a nose that serves as a hand. With [5]*possessive pronoun* trunk, the elephant can pick up a small berry or a heavy log. Most African elephants are dark gray with a little pink on the edges of [6]*possessive pronoun* ears. The [7]*possessive noun* big ears brush away flies and other pesty insects. [8]*article* African elephant also has two long, ivory tusks. Elephants use [9]*possessive pronoun* tusks to dig for food, fight, and carry heavy loads. Wild African elephants are found in areas south of [10]*article* Sahara.

MEETING INDIVIDUAL NEEDS

English Language Learners

Choosing Articles

To reinforce students' mastery of articles, remind them that the choice of article (or of not using any article at all) largely depends on the nature and meaning of the noun that the article modifies. Use no article when making a generalization about a plural noun (***Parents** usually choose different music than their children do*) or a mass noun (***Architecture** is an interesting field of study*). When making a generalization about a singular noun, use *a* or *an* (***An architect** must know how to draw plans*).

Proper Adjectives

■ A **proper adjective** is formed from a proper noun and begins with a capital letter.

Rembrandt was a **Dutch** painter.

The **Berlin** Wall came down in 1989.

The following suffixes are often used to create proper adjectives: *-an, -ian, -n, -ese,* and *-ish*. Sometimes there are other changes as well. In some cases, the noun and adjective forms are the same.

PROPER NOUNS	PROPER ADJECTIVES
Alaska	Alaskan
Queen Victoria	Victorian
Vietnam	Vietnamese
Denmark	Danish
Navajo	Navajo

Exercise 44 Identifying Proper Adjectives

On your paper, list the ten proper adjectives that appear in the following passage.

The Early Colonization of the Americas

[1]The Spanish colonization of the Americas began in the late 1400s after Christopher Columbus, an Italian explorer, sailed westward from Europe until he reached some Caribbean islands. [2]The great Columbian drama unfolded as hundreds of Native American cultures, including the Aztec and Incan civilizations, collided violently with conquistadors and colonists. [3]A century later, England and France joined in the quest for a North American empire. [4]Some Europeans hoped to acquire great wealth, while others hoped to spread the Christian faith. [5]Still others sought freedom from oppressive European laws and customs.

Exercise 45 Forming Proper Adjectives from Proper Nouns

On your paper, write a proper adjective formed from each of the following proper nouns. Consult a dictionary if you need help.

1. Africa
2. China
3. Mexico
4. Thomas Jefferson
5. William Shakespeare
6. Dakota
7. Spain
8. Confucius
9. Hawaii
10. Senegal

Parts of Speech

Teach

Proper Adjectives

Cross-reference: Grammar

For guidelines and practice in using the various forms of adjectives, refer students to Lessons 18.1–18.5, pp. 659–667.

Two-Minute Skill Drill

Write the proper noun from which each of these proper adjectives has been formed:

Southern	Chinese
Norwegian	Danish
Tasmanian	Spartan

See also *Two-Minute Skill Drill Transparency 10.4*

Practice and Assess

Answers: Exercise 44

1. Spanish, Italian, Caribbean
2. Columbian, Native American, Aztec, Incan
3. North American
4. Christian
5. European

Answers: Exercise 45

1. African
2. Chinese
3. Mexican
4. Jeffersonian
5. Shakespearean or Shakespearian
6. Dakotan
7. Spanish
8. Confucian
9. Hawaiian
10. Senegalese

MEETING INDIVIDUAL NEEDS

Learning Disabled

Adding Adjectives

Have students read aloud the following: *The lights in the ______ theater dimmed, and the ______ crowd fell silent. Slowly the ______ curtain rose. A(n) ______ spotlight picked out a(n) ______ corner of the stage, where a(n) ______ actress dressed in overalls and a(n) ______ hat sat quietly on a(n) ______ bench.* Then ask them to work in small groups to improve the passage by adding adjectives where indicated. (Possible answers: *bright, young, velvet, amber, far, plump, straw, park.*)

Practice and Assess

Answers: Exercise 46

1. Recent, new, the, ancient, the, oldest
2. impressive, original
3. a, northern, fortunate, the, unmistak-able, an, early
4. This, remarkable, significant, the, Mayan

Answers: Exercise 47

Answers will vary, but some suggestions are given below:

> My aged great-grandfather's bushy white eyebrows nearly hide his piercing gray eyes.

Answers: Exercise 48

Answers will vary, but some suggestions are given below:

1. farm
2. corn
3. leading
4. Midwestern
5. farm
6. high
7. long
8. a
9. silk
10. many
11. main
12. popular
13. Halloween
14. many
15. rusty
16. these
17. an
18. first
19. generous
20. early

Additional Resources

Grammar Practice, p. 5
Grammar Reteaching, p. 5
Grammar Enrichment, p. 5
Sentence-Combining Practice, pp. 4, 11

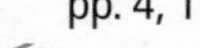
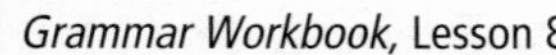
Grammar Workbook, Lesson 8

Close

Tell students to imagine that they are interior designers. Suggest that they write a paragraph describing how they would furnish a house. They should use adjectives in their writing.

Exercise 46 Identifying Adjectives

On your paper, write the twenty adjectives, including articles, that appear in the following paragraph.

Mayan Culture

[1]Recent discoveries have revealed new facts about the ancient Maya, who formed one of the oldest societies in Central America. [2]By A.D. 1000, they had already made impressive and original advancements in art and science. [3]Recently, at a site in northern Belize, fortunate archaeologists unearthed the unmistakable remains of an early civilization. [4]This discovery was remarkable and significant, for it pushed back the origins of Mayan culture to 2400 B.C.

Exercise 47 Creating Sentences with Adjectives

On your paper, write five sentences about someone you know and can picture clearly. In your description, include details about the person's appearance, voice, behavior, and personality. Choose adjectives that are especially descriptive to convey a vivid image of the person.

Exercise 48 Using Adjectives in Writing

On your paper, complete the paragraphs below by replacing each blank with an adjective, including definite and indefinite articles. Be sure that your completed sentences make sense.

Corn

Corn is an important [1]______ crop in the United States. The country's annual [2]______ production is more than six billion bushels, accounting for almost half the total world production. Illinois is a(n) [3]______ producer, along with several other [4]______ states. Most of the corn grown in the United States is used as feed for [5]______ animals such as hogs, cattle, and chickens. Although corn is a(n) [6]______ source of energy, it is low in protein.

Each corn plant has a(n) [7]______ stem, averaging eight feet in height. The ear of corn is protected by [8]______ husk. The [9]______ tassels at the tip of the ear of corn contain pollen.

There are [10]______ different types of corn, and all of them have a specific use. Sweet corn is often served as a(n) [11]______ dish at meals. Popcorn is a(n) [12]______ snack throughout the United States. During the fall, many people use pod corn as a(n) [13]______ decoration. Even the other parts of the corn plant have [14]______ uses. For example, corncobs are ground to make abrasives for cleaning [15]______ engines.

No one knows where or when [16]______ plants were first farmed, but corn was [17]______ important staple in the diet of Native Americans by the 1600s. When the [18]______ colonists arrived in the Massachusetts Bay Colony, Squanto taught them how to grow and harvest corn. Without his [19]______ help, the [20]______ colony might not have survived.

10.5 Adverbs

■ An **adverb** is a word that modifies a verb, an adjective, or another adverb by making its meaning more specific.

The following sentences illustrate the use of adverbs to modify verbs, adjectives, and adverbs.

She **always** waited **patiently.**
verb

The waiting room was **very** noisy and **overly** crowded.
adjective adjective

Rather oddly, we have **almost** never visited his farm.
adverb adverb

Adverbs modify by answering the questions *when? where? how?* and *to what degree?*

I will call **tomorrow.**
His phone rings **often**.
The speaker will stand **here.**
Kim **carefully** polished the car.
We were **truly** sorry.

When an adverb modifies a verb, it may be placed in various positions in relation to the verb. When an adverb modifies an adjective or another adverb, it usually comes directly before the modified word.

MODIFYING A VERB	**Finally** the storm is ending.
	The storm **finally** is ending.
	The storm is **finally** ending.
	The storm is ending **finally.**
MODIFYING AN ADJECTIVE	The snow was **quite** heavy.
	Driving was **very** hazardous.
MODIFYING AN ADVERB	It **almost** never snows this heavily.
	I **hardly** ever need to wear my boots.

Parts of Speech

Focus

Lesson Overview

Objectives

- To define adverbs
- To use negative words as adverbs
- To identify degrees of comparison
- To position adverbs; to follow models
- To use adverbs appropriately in writing

Bellringer
Daily Language Activities

When students enter the classroom, have this assignment on the board: *Write short questions using each of the following words—when, where, how.*

See also  *Daily Language Practice*

Motivating Activity

Explain that adverbs modify by answering the questions *when? where? how?* Invite students to answer the questions they asked in their sentences for the Bellringer activity and to identify an adverb in each answer.

Teach

Adverbs

☑ Grammar Tip

Explain to students that sometimes the *when* and *where* question tests are the only way of identifying adverbs. For example, in the sentence *The train comes Monday, Monday* is an adverb because it answers the question *when.* ***When** does the train come? It comes Monday.* In the sentence *I went home, home* is an adverb because it answers the question *where:* ***Where** did I go? (I went home.)*

Resource Manager

Planning Resources
- *Lesson Plans*

Transparencies
- *Bellringer*
- *Daily Language Practice*
- *Two-Minute Skill Drill*

Other Print Resources
- *Grammar and Composition Handbook*
- *Grammar Enrichment,* p. 6
- *Grammar Practice,* p. 6
- *Grammar Reteaching,* p. 6
- *Grammar Workbook, Lesson* 9
- *Sentence-Combining Practice,* p. 13

Teach

Negative Words as Adverbs

Cross-reference: Usage

For instruction and practice in avoiding double negatives, refer students to Lesson 18.6, pp. 668–669.

Practice and Assess

Answers: Exercise 49

1. opened
2. did intend
3. always
4. clean
5. tiny
6. go
7. is visited
8. difficult
9. bright
10. attracts

Exercise 50

1. often—is considered
2. extremely—poor
3. Hardly—fourteen; already—was touring
4. more—matter-of-factly; matter-of-factly—have sung
5. rhythmically—adventurous
6. commercially—successful
7. very—famous
8. probably—came
9. today—remains
10. not—did survive

Negative Words as Adverbs

The word *not* and the contraction *n't* are considered adverbs. Other negative words can function as adverbs of time and place.

The plane has **not** landed.	They have **hardly** boarded.
The plane is **nowhere** in sight.	I have **never** flown.

Exercise 49 Identifying Words Modified by Adverbs

On your paper, write the word or words that are being modified by the adverb in italics in each sentence.

The Cleaner Wrasse

1. The eel *instinctively* opened its mouth to let the small fish enter.
2. Surprisingly, the eel did *not* intend to eat the small fry.
3. The cleaner wrasse, a tropical fish, is *almost* always welcome to inspect the eel's teeth.
4. Some wrasses, such as blueheads, *thoroughly* clean the teeth of larger fish.
5. They eat the *extremely* tiny creatures and pieces of dead skin that cling to the bigger fish's teeth.
6. *Sometimes* snappers and groupers also go to the "cleaners."
7. One cleaner wrasse is *often* visited by as many as three hundred fish in a period of six hours.
8. Finding customers is *never* difficult for the bluehead wrasse.
9. Its *especially* bright neon color acts as a kind of undersea advertising.
10. Its dancelike swimming motion attracts customers *also*.

Exercise 50 Identifying Adverbs

On your paper, write all the adverb(s) that appear in each sentence below. Then write the word or words each adverb modifies.

A Great Blues Singer

1. Bessie Smith is often considered a great blues singer.
2. She was born into an extremely poor family in Chattanooga, Tennessee.
3. Hardly fourteen, she was already touring with Ma Rainey and her Rabbit Foot Minstrels.
4. Others have sung songs more matter-of-factly than she.
5. Jazz writers have called her style rhythmically adventurous.
6. In 1923 Smith began to make commercially successful records.
7. Louis Armstrong was one very famous jazz musician with whom she sang.
8. Her greatest fame probably came in the years from 1923 to 1928.
9. Her record *Nobody's Blues but Mine,* which covers the period from 1925 to 1927, remains popular today.
10. Bessie Smith did not survive a tragic car accident in 1937.

Parts of Speech

MEETING INDIVIDUAL NEEDS

English Language Learners

Understanding Negative Adverbs

Particularly difficult for some students new to English is the shift from *some* to *any* in negative sentences—for example: *I have **some** money. I **don't** have **any** money.* A common error is *I **don't** have **some** money.*

Recognizing Adverbs

To help students understand how to recognize adverbs, write these sentences on the board: *For babies, nutrition is important. Babies need care and attention.* Ask students to add an adverb to each sentence. (Example: *For babies, nutrition is vitally important. Babies desperately need care and attention.*) **L1**

Adverbs That Compare

Like adjectives, some adverbs have different forms to indicate degree of comparison. The comparative form of an adverb compares two actions. The superlative form of an adverb compares more than two actions. For adverbs of only one syllable, add *-er* to make the comparative form and *-est* to make the superlative form.

POSITIVE	COMPARATIVE	SUPERLATIVE
runs **fast**	runs **faster**	runs **fastest**
arrived **late**	arrived **later**	arrived **latest**
works **hard**	works **harder**	works **hardest**

When an adverb ends in *-ly* or has more than one syllable, use the word *more* to form the comparative and *most* to form the superlative.

POSITIVE	COMPARATIVE	SUPERLATIVE
walks **quickly**	walks **more quickly**	walks **most quickly**
reads **carefully**	reads **more carefully**	reads **most carefully**
calls **often**	calls **more often**	calls **most often**

Some adverbs do not form the comparative and superlative in the regular manner.

POSITIVE	COMPARATIVE	SUPERLATIVE
feels **well**	feels **better**	feels **best**
behaves **badly**	behaves **worse**	behaves **worst**
cares **little**	cares **less**	cares **least**
throws **far**	throws **farther**	throws **farthest**

Exercise 51 Forming Comparative and Superlative Adverbs

On your paper, write the comparative and superlative forms of each of the following adverbs. Consult a dictionary if you need help.

1. high
2. bravely
3. early
4. surprisingly
5. thoroughly
6. easily
7. low
8. far
9. happily
10. foolishly
11. near
12. softly
13. poorly
14. little
15. close
16. eagerly
17. well
18. fearfully
19. strangely
20. speedily

Parts of Speech

Enrichment and Extension

Using Adverbs in Writing

Have students work with a partner to write a short biography of a favorite athlete or musician. Tell them to use adverbs modifying all three parts of speech (verbs, adjectives, and other adverbs) in their writing. **L3**

Substituting Adverbs

Have students take a page from a weekly newsmagazine and then locate and circle all the comparative and superlative adverbs they can find. Suggest that students provide their own adverb(s) to replace each example found in the periodical. **L2**

Teach

Adverbs That Compare

☑ Teaching Tip

Tell students that adverbs are easy to identify if they remember the following: First, the vast majority of adverbs modify verbs. Most of these adverbs are movable—unlike adjectives and other kinds of adverbs. For example, ***Eagerly*** *Anne answered the phone* can be recast as *Anne* ***eagerly*** *answered the phone* or as *Anne answered the phone* ***eagerly.*** Second, the adverbs that modify adjectives and other adverbs are limited in both number and meaning. They are intensifiers (***very*** *accurate;* ***quite*** *dangerous*) or qualifiers (***almost*** *always late;* ***nearly*** *ready*).

Practice and Assess

Answers: Exercise 51

1. higher, highest
2. more bravely, most bravely
3. earlier, earliest
4. more surprisingly, most surprisingly
5. more thoroughly, most thoroughly
6. more easily, most easily
7. lower, lowest
8. farther, farthest
9. more happily, most happily
10. more foolishly, most foolishly
11. nearer, nearest
12. more softly, most softly
13. more poorly, most poorly
14. less, least
15. closer, closest
16. more eagerly, most eagerly
17. better, best
18. more fearfully, most fearfully
19. more strangely, most strangely
20. more speedily, most speedily

Teach

Cross-reference: Grammar

For instruction and practice in forming the degrees of comparison with adverbs, refer students to Lessons 18.1–18.2, pp. 659–662.

Two-Minute Skill Drill

Have students write a negative adverb for each of the following statements:

The bear ______ slept. *(hardly)*

The bear ______ sleeps. *(never)*

The bear did ______ sleep. *(not)*

The bear ______ eats. *(scarcely)*

See also *Two-Minute Skill Drill Transparency 10.5*

Practice and Assess

Answers: Exercise 52

1. easily
2. higher
3. longer
4. more carefully
5. far
6. fastest
7. faster
8. carefully
9. harder
10. more often

Answers: Exercise 53

Answers will vary, but some suggestions are given below:

1. generally
2. never
3. almost
4. especially
5. proudly
6. most
7. often
8. frequently
9. obviously
10. solemnly

Parts of Speech

Exercise 52 Using Adverbs That Compare

On your paper, write the form of the adverb specified in parentheses.

Balloons

1. The highest recorded plastic balloon flight ______ reached an altitude of more than 150,000 feet. (positive form of *easily*)
2. Seven years later, a rubber balloon went 18,000 feet ______. (comparative form of *high*)
3. The longest superpressured balloon flight on record lasted ______ than three hundred days. (comparative form of *long*)
4. The ______ the pilot computes the atmospheric pressures, the better is the chance of a successful flight. (comparative form of *carefully*)
5. A balloon can travel so ______ into the atmosphere because its skin can stretch. (positive form of *far*)
6. The balloon that rises ______ is the one that is the lightest. (superlative form of *fast*)
7. In general, a hot-air balloon will rise ______ if the air in it is heated to a higher temperature. (comparative form of *fast*)
8. Some of the earliest balloons were ______ tethered to the earth. (positive form of *carefully*)
9. Scientists are now working even ______ to improve balloon technology. (comparative form of *hard*)
10. Helium is used ______ than hydrogen because it is safer. (comparative form of *often*)

Exercise 53 Completing Sentences with Adverbs

On your paper, write an adverb to complete each sentence below.

The United States Capitol

1. The hill where the United States Capitol has stood since 1800 is ______ called Capitol Hill.
2. After many delays in construction, some feared that the Capitol would ______ be completed.
3. During the War of 1812, the inside of the Capitol was ______ destroyed by British troops.
4. The dome is ______ impressive, reaching a height of 188 feet.
5. A statue symbolizing freedom stands ______ on top of the Capitol dome.
6. Tourists consider the Capitol a ______ important sight in Washington, D.C.
7. Tourists ______ visit the Library of Congress and the Supreme Court, which are within walking distance of the Capitol.
8. They also see members of Congress, who ______ walk through the corridors on their way to one of the legislative chambers.
9. Statuary Hall ______ contains statues of some famous Americans.
10. Every four years, a new president is ______ sworn in at the Capitol.

Meeting Individual Needs — English Language Learners

Using Negative Words

While students may not have difficulty using the negative words *no, not,* and *never* or the contraction *-n't* in their speech and writing, they may be unsure of when to use the negatives *barely, hardly,* and *scarcely.* Review the meanings of these words and help students understand that they are synonyms.

Exercise 54 Completing Sentences with Adverbs

On your paper, rewrite each sentence, adding the adverb in parentheses. Be sure that you place each adverb in an appropriate position.

Historically Speaking

1. The Greek writer Herodotus is considered to be the first historian. (generally)
2. A practical-minded individual, Herodotus did not worry about the purposes or goals of history. (much)
3. He wondered about the past. (simply)
4. He also asked some intriguing questions about past events. (very)
5. Then he recorded what he had discovered. (carefully)
6. Some people study history for its own sake. (still)
7. They are interested in the past. (truly)
8. Many historians find it challenging to make history relevant to others. (extremely)
9. Students of history learn when they are given the chance to draw their own conclusions about past events. (best)
10. Public officials use the lessons of the past to help find solutions to contemporary problems. (sometimes)

Exercise 55 Positioning Adverbs

On your paper, rewrite each sentence adding an appropriate verb-modifying adverb. Then rewrite the sentence again, placing the adverb in a different position.

SAMPLE Track-and-field star Florence Griffith-Joyner accepted her gold medal.
ANSWER (a) Track-and-field star Florence Griffith-Joyner proudly accepted her gold medal.
(b) Proudly, track-and-field star Florence Griffith-Joyner accepted her gold medal.

An Olympic Race

1. Another group of Olympic runners waited for the signal.
2. The starting shot rang out.
3. All eight racers leaped from their starting blocks.
4. The runner from Kenya began to lag.
5. The French contestant was pulling ahead of her.
6. The Kenyan runner exerted her last ounce of strength.
7. The two women were running neck and neck.
8. The Kenyan spectators jumped to their feet as their favorite crossed the finish line.
9. To the strains of her national anthem, the Kenyan runner accepted the gold medal.
10. The French runner shook her opponent's hand.

Answers: Exercise 54

Answers will vary, but some suggestions are given below:

1. The Greek writer Herodotus is generally considered . . .
2. A practical-minded individual, Herodotus did not worry much about . . .
3. He simply wondered . . .
4. He also asked some very intriguing . . .
5. Then he carefully recorded . . .
6. Some people still study history . . .
7. They are truly interested . . .
8. Many historians find it extremely challenging . . .
9. Students of history learn best when . . .
10. Sometimes public officials . . .

Answers: Exercise 55

Answers will vary, but some suggestions are given below:

1. Another group . . . waited impatiently . . . Impatiently another group . . . waited. . . .
2. The starting shot rang out sharply. Sharply the starting shot rang out.
3. All eight racers leaped quickly. . . . Quickly all eight racers leaped. . . .
4. The runner from Kenya soon began to lag. Soon the runner from Kenya began to lag.
5. Unexpectedly the French contestant was pulling. . . . The French contestant was pulling ahead of her unexpectedly.
6. Deliberately the Kenyan runner exerted . . . strength. The Kenyan runner deliberately exerted. . . .
7. The two women were running tenaciously. . . . Tenaciously the two women were running. . . .
8. The Kenyan spectators jumped to their feet spontaneously. . . . Spontaneously the Kenyan spectators jumped. . . .
9. To the strains of her national anthem, the Kenyan runner proudly accepted. . . . To the strains . . . the Kenyan runner accepted the gold medal proudly.
10. The French runner shook . . . graciously. The French runner graciously shook. . . .

Writing in the Real World

Writing as a Tool for Learning

Have students identify the adverbs in the following passage: *"It may be," I said to myself, "that this bird will carry me away to a civilized land; wherever I am set down, it will surely be better than an uninhabited island."* —From *The Thousand and One Nights,* retold by N. J. Nawood. Then ask students to use the same adverbs in a short paragraph of their own writing and to review one anothers' papers. Remind students to provide effective feedback.

Practice and Assess

Answers: Exercise 56

Answers will vary, but some suggestions are given below:

1. "Please turn on the light," requested Sara brightly.
2. "I need the sandpaper," said the carpenter roughly.
3. "The temperature is rising," said the weather forecaster hotly.
4. "Be careful with that knife!" warned Hiroshi sharply.
5. "My arm is aching," complained the pitcher stiffly.
6. "The freezer is fine now," said the repairperson coldly.
7. "Pick up that load," the mover said heavily.
8. "Squeeze the lemons first," said the cook sourly.
9. "Fasten your coat," the tailor said snappily.
10. "I hate to work," the loafer said idly.

Answers: Exercise 57

(Adverbs are in italics.)

1. severe, strong; *extremely*
2. this, northern; *always*
3. same, western; *not*
4. such; *generally*
5. seventy-five; *officially*
6. Such; *usually, westward*
7. Mexican; *Sometimes, northeastward*
8. ten; *approximately, gradually*
9. mature, circular; *fully, almost*
10. Air, its, low; *extremely*
11. calm, blue; *barely, strangely, often*
12. violent, torrential; *rapidly, outside, quickly*

Additional Resources

Grammar Reteaching, p. 6
Grammar Practice, p. 6
Grammar Enrichment, p. 6
Sentence-Combining Practice, p. 13

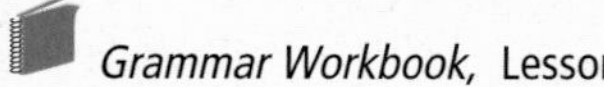
Grammar Workbook, Lesson 9

Close

Ask students to choose one of their papers and add adverbs that modify verbs, adjectives, and other adverbs. Ask them to discuss with a small group how the addition of adverbs changed the paper.

Parts of Speech

Exercise 56 Following Models

A Tom Swifty is a sentence in which an adverb comments in a humorous way on an action or object mentioned in a quotation. Note the relationship between each adverb and quotation in the following examples:

"Will you hang up these wet clothes?" asked Ben dryly.

"I've never seen such flat land," said the farmer plainly.

(a) For items 1–5, write each Tom Swifty on your paper, completing it with an adverb that comments in a humorous way on the quotation. (b) For items 6–10, write a Tom Swifty of your own, using the adverb provided. Consult a dictionary if you need help.

1. "Please turn on the light," requested Sara ________.
2. "I need the sandpaper," said the carpenter ________.
3. "The temperature is rising," said the weather forecaster ________.
4. "Be careful with that knife!" warned Hiroshi ________.
5. "My arm is aching," complained the pitcher ________.
6. coldly
7. heavily
8. sourly
9. snappily
10. idly

Exercise 57 Identifying Adjectives and Adverbs

On your paper, write each of the twenty adjectives and twenty adverbs that appear in the following paragraph. (Do not include *a, an,* and *the.*)

Hurricanes

[1]Hurricanes are severe storms with extremely strong winds. [2]Storms with this name are always limited to the northern Atlantic Ocean. [3]The same storm in the western Pacific Ocean is not called a hurricane; it is a typhoon. [4]In the Indian Ocean, such storms generally are known as cyclones. [5]A hurricane is defined officially as a storm with winds of seventy-five miles an hour. [6]Such storms usually start in the North Atlantic and move westward. [7]Sometimes they progress northeastward from the Mexican coast. [8]They move at approximately ten miles an hour in the beginning and gradually gain speed. [9]A fully mature hurricane is almost circular. [10]Air pressure in its center, or eye, can be extremely low. [11]In the eye the air barely moves, the atmosphere seems strangely calm, and the sky often looks blue. [12]Clouds that swirl rapidly outside quickly bring violent winds and torrential rains.

10.6 Prepositions

- A **preposition** is a word that shows the relationship of a noun or pronoun to some other word in a sentence.
- Prepositions begin phrases that end with a noun or pronoun that is called the **object of the preposition.**

The silverware is **inside** the cabinet. [*Inside* shows the spatial relationship of the silverware and the object of the preposition, *cabinet.*]

All the guests arrived **before** dinner. [*Before* tells the time relationship between the guests' arrival and the object of the preposition, *dinner.*]

He brought a gift **for** the host. [*For* relates *gift* to the object of the preposition, *host.*]

Commonly Used Prepositions

aboard	beneath	in	regarding
about	beside	inside	since
above	besides	into	through
across	between	like	throughout
after	beyond	near	to
against	but*	of	toward
along	by	off	under
amid	concerning	on	underneath
among	despite	onto	until
around	down	opposite	unto
as	during	out	up
at	except	outside	upon
before	excepting	over	with
behind	for	past	within
below	from	pending	without

*meaning "except"

- A **compound preposition** is made up of more than one word.

Compound Prepositions

according to	aside from	in addition to	next to
ahead of	as to	in front of	on top of
along with	because of	in spite of	out of
apart from	by means of	instead of	owing to

Parts of Speech

Focus

Lesson Overview

Objective

- To identify prepositions and their objects

Bellringer
Daily Language Activity

When students enter the classroom, have this assignment on the board: *Look for a pattern in the sentences below. Write a sentence or two that describes the pattern.*

- *The cat is under the bed.*
- *My keys are in my pocket.*
- *He bought popcorn before the show.*
- *They went walking after dinner.*

See also  *Daily Language Activity*

Motivating Activity

Ask volunteers to share their assessments of the sentences in the Bellringer activity. Point out that each sentence includes a phrase that describes a relationship of time or space between a noun or pronoun and some other word. Explain that such phrases, called *prepositional phrases,* are useful in descriptive writing. Suggest that students search a favorite book or story for a descriptive passage that makes use of prepositions.

Teach

Prepositions

Vocabulary Link

The term *preposition* comes from a Latin word meaning "to put in front."

Resource Manager

Planning Resources
- *Lesson Plans*

Transparencies
- *Bellringer*
- *Daily Language Practice*

Other Print Resources
- *Grammar and Composition Handbook*
- *Grammar Enrichment,* p. 7
- *Grammar Practice,* p. 7
- *Grammar Reteaching,* p. 7
- *Grammar Workbook, Lessons* 10, 18
- *Sentence-Combining Practice,* p. 22

10.6

Practice and Assess

Answers: Exercise 58

1. in New York, in 1920, to musical parents
2. Instead of the usual piano, for his instrument
3. Like many jazz musicians, on themes, within the music
4. at the top, of his profession
5. During the late fifties, into the sixties, for its energy
6. out of its usual locations, beyond the usual limits, of the saxophone
7. instead of indoors
8. of his experiments, from his saxophone, off walls
9. with music, throughout his long career
10. In addition to his experimental work, for the movie *Alfie*

Answers: Exercise 59

1. after; Sample: The basketball game started before seven o'clock.
2. onto; Sample: The players eagerly ran out of the locker room.
3. In spite of; Sample: Despite the snowstorm, attendance was high.
4. during; Sample: The pep band played loudly at halftime.
5. Aside from; Sample: Except for a few minor injuries, the game went well.
6. for; Sample: My brother is a cheerleader at the games.
7. during; Sample: He and the other cheerleaders perform throughout the game.
8. throughout; Sample: They have attended games since the beginning of the year.
9. with; Sample: They will attend the state tournament along with the team members.
10. In addition to; Sample: Besides cheering, they also like winning.

Additional Resources

Grammar Practice, p. 7
Grammar Reteaching, p. 7
Grammar Enrichment, p. 7
Sentence Combining Practice, p. 22
Grammar Workbook, Lessons 10, 18

Exercise 58 Identifying Prepositional Phrases

On your paper, list the prepositional phrases that appear in each of the following sentences. Remember that some prepositions are made up of more than one word. (The numeral in parentheses at the end of each item indicates the number of prepositional phrases in that sentence.)

Sonny Rollins, a Great Jazz Saxophonist

1. The great jazz musician Sonny Rollins was born in New York in 1920 to musical parents. (3)
2. Instead of the usual piano, Rollins chose the tenor saxophone for his instrument. (2)
3. Like many jazz musicians, he often improvised on themes within the music. (3)
4. His exceptional album *Moving Out* put him at the top of his profession. (2)
5. During the late fifties and into the sixties, his work became notable for its energy. (3)
6. Rollins took music out of its usual locations and went beyond the usual limits of the saxophone. (3)
7. Sometimes he would play his saxophone outdoors instead of indoors. (1)
8. Another of his experiments involved making the sound from his saxophone bounce off walls. (3)
9. Rollins continued experiments with music throughout his long career. (2)
10. In addition to his experimental work, Rollins played the music for the movie *Alfie*. (2)

Exercise 59 Identifying and Replacing Prepositions in Phrases

On your paper, write the preposition that appears in each sentence below. Then rewrite each sentence using a different preposition. You may also need to change the object of the preposition.

1. The basketball game started after seven o'clock.
2. The players eagerly ran onto the court.
3. In spite of the snowstorm, attendance was high.
4. The pep band played loudly during halftime.
5. Aside from a few minor injuries, the game went well.
6. My brother is a cheerleader for the team.
7. He and the other cheerleaders perform during the game.
8. They have attended games throughout the year.
9. They will attend the state tournament with the team members.
10. In addition to cheering, they also like winning.

Parts of Speech

Close

Ask students to write a short paragraph about a favorite topic and to circle the prepositions they use. Then invite volunteers to read their paragraphs aloud. After each reading, ask the class to identify the prepositions. Encourage students to provide effective feedback.

10.7 Conjunctions

■ A **conjunction** is a word that joins single words or groups of words.

Coordinating Conjunctions

■ A **coordinating conjunction** joins words or groups of words that have equal grammatical weight in a sentence.

Coordinating Conjunctions						
and	but	or	so	nor	for	yet

Two **and** two are four.
She is good at algebra **but** not at arithmetic.
We must leave now, **or** we will be late.
The bell rang, **yet** everyone remained seated.
He could not sleep, **nor** would he eat.

When used as a coordinating conjunction, **for** means "for the reason that" or "because."

The children were tired, **for** they had run a long distance.

Exercise 60 **Identifying Coordinating Conjunctions**

On your paper, write the coordinating conjunctions that appear in the following sentences.

A Monument to Civil Rights

[1]The civil rights leaders of the 1960s strove to win greater respect, dignity, and political freedom for African Americans. [2]Martin Luther King Jr. was the most famous civil rights leader, but he was not the only person to participate in the struggle. [3]Ordinary citizens, such as Rosa Parks, who refused to sit at the back of a segregated bus, contributed to the fight for justice and equality. [4]Taunts did not deter the civil rights demonstrators, nor did physical abuse.

[5]A new monument in Alabama commemorates the famous heroes of the movement, yet it does not ignore its anonymous heroes. [6]The monument is in the city of Montgomery, for it was there that many famous civil rights demonstrations took place. [7]Made of smooth black granite, the monument is simple, yet it is remarkably powerful. [8]Water flows gently over the flat surface of the stone and collects in a pool. [9]The names of civil rights leaders and the dates of famous events in the struggle are engraved on the stone. [10]The monument was designed by the Chinese American architect Maya Lin, who is famous for her bold and austere monument to the veterans of the Vietnam War.

Parts of Speech

Focus

Lesson Overview

Objective

- To relate ideas by using coordinating, correlative, or subordinating conjunctions or conjunctive adverbs

Bellringer
Daily Language Activity

When students enter the classroom, have this assignment on the board: *Finish these sentences:*

I like math but. . .
Neither she nor. . .
We went home because. . .

See also *Daily Language Practice*

Teach

Coordinating Conjunctions

☑ Teaching Tip

Conjunctions are like glue that joins similar things: words to words, phrases to phrases, and clauses to clauses. Coordinating conjunctions join elements as equal partners.

Practice and Assess

Answers: Exercise 60

1. and
2. but
3. and
4. nor
5. yet
6. for
7. yet
8. and
9. and
10. and

Resource Manager

Planning Resources
- *Lesson Plans*

Transparencies
- *Bellringer*
- *Daily Language Practice*
- *Two-Minute Skill Drill*

Other Print Resources
- *Grammar and Composition Handbook*
- *Grammar Enrichment,* p. 8
- *Grammar Practice,* p. 8
- *Grammar Reteaching,* p. 8
- *Grammar Workbook, Lesson* 11

Teach

Correlative Conjunctions

Teaching Tip

Correlative conjunctions are like coordinating conjunctions, except that they always come in pairs. A correlative conjunction—for example, *either . . . or*—joins words of equal weight in a sentence.

Cross-reference: Usage

For instruction and practice of the material in Exercise 61, refer students to Lesson 16.5, pp. 616–617.

Two-Minute Skill Drill

Ask students to use these sets of correlative conjunctions in sentences:

neither . . . nor
whether . . . or
both . . . and
just as . . . so
either . . . or

See also *Two-Minute Skill Drill Transparency 10.7*

Practice and Assess

Answers: Exercise 61

1. Just as/so
2. not only/but also
3. Both/and
4. whether/or
5. Neither/nor
6. Both/and
7. not only/but also
8. Neither/nor
9. both/and
10. not only/but also

Correlative Conjunctions

■ **Correlative conjunctions** work in pairs to join words and groups of words of equal weight in a sentence.

Correlative Conjunctions		
both . . . and	just as . . . so	not only . . . but (also)
either . . . or	neither . . . nor	whether . . . or

Correlative conjunctions make the relationship between words or groups of words a little clearer than do coordinating conjunctions.

COORDINATING CONJUNCTIONS	CORRELATIVE CONJUNCTIONS
She **and** I were there.	**Both** she **and** I were there.
She **or** I can go.	**Either** she **or** I can go.
	Neither she **nor** I can go.
I met Jean **and** Ed.	I met **not only** Jean **but also** Ed.

Exercise 61 Identifying Correlative Conjunctions

On your paper, write both parts of the correlative conjunctions that appear in the following sentences.

Weather Forecasting

1. Just as people are interested in the weather forecast today, so people thousands of years ago tried to predict weather conditions.
2. Methods of predicting the weather have grown not only more complicated but also more accurate.
3. Both modern and ancient cultures have looked to the sky for signs of change in the weather.
4. The predictions of the ancients, whether correct or incorrect, were based on very different methods from those of today.
5. Neither the seemingly essential thermometer nor the equally useful barometer was invented until a few hundred years ago.
6. Both the modern telegraph and the even more recent satellite have made it possible to exchange weather information more rapidly.
7. Satellites are used for early spotting not only of hurricanes but also of tornadoes.
8. Neither high-speed computers nor other advanced technological breakthroughs have revealed all we need to know to predict the weather accurately.
9. The National Oceanic and Atmospheric Administration is responsible for both studying the weather and forecasting it.
10. Weather forecasting is an activity not only of government agencies but also of private companies.

MEETING INDIVIDUAL NEEDS

English Language Learners

Using Conjunctions in English

The correlative conjunction *not only . . . but also* has a feature that confuses most students learning English. When *not only . . . but also* joins clauses, the first verb in the first clause precedes the subject (for example, *Not only can Mary sing, but she can also dance*). Have students join clauses with other correlative conjunctions and then substitute *not only . . . but also* to show the difference.

Subordinating Conjunctions

■ A **subordinating conjunction** joins two clauses, or ideas, in such a way as to make one grammatically dependent upon the other.

The idea, or clause, that a subordinating conjunction introduces is said to be "subordinate," or dependent, because it cannot stand by itself as a complete sentence.

We raked the leaves **because** so many had fallen.
We raked the leaves **before** we had lunch.
When more leaves fall, we will rake again.

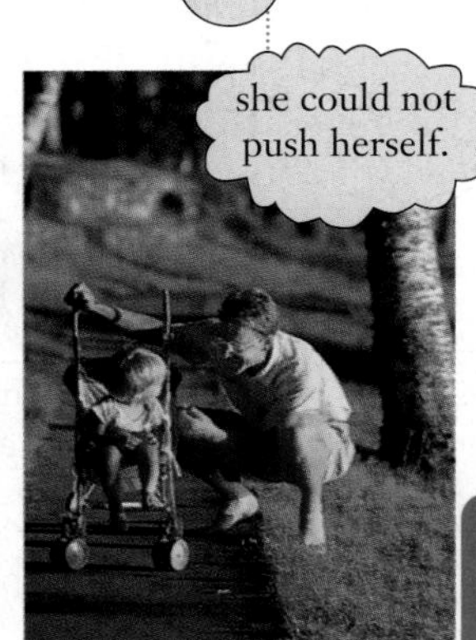

The father pushed the baby...
because
she could not push herself.

Common Subordinating Conjunctions

after	as soon as	inasmuch as	than	where
although	as though	in order that	though	whereas
as	because	provided (that)	unless	wherever
as far as	before	since	until	while
as if	considering (that)	so long as	when	
as long as	if	so that	whenever	

Exercise 62 **Identifying Subordinating Conjunctions**

On your paper, write the subordinating conjunction that appears in each sentence below. Remember that some subordinating conjunctions are made up of more than one word.

The Art of Mural Painting

1. Although they are found in many cultures around the world, murals have always been a particularly important art form in Mexico.
2. Some of the murals painted by Mayan artists in ancient Mexico still survive, though many are in poor condition.
3. Before the Mexican painter Diego Rivera came on the scene, twentieth-century Mexican murals were relatively unknown.
4. Rivera designed extraordinary murals before he died in 1957.
5. Many of Rivera's murals depict scenes from Mexican history because Rivera believed that Mexicans are defined by their past.
6. After Rivera died, many Mexican American muralists took up his style and themes.
7. Some Mexican American artists in Los Angeles paint murals wherever they can find space.
8. They paint on public buildings so that their work can be enjoyed by many people.
9. So that the murals can be easily seen, the muralists use bright colors and bold, eye-catching designs.
10. As long as Hispanic culture continues to thrive in the United States, we will surely have many colorful and exciting murals to enjoy.

Parts of Speech

Teach

Subordinating Conjunctions

☑ Teaching Tip

A subordinating conjunction joins two clauses unequally; that is, the dependent clause is subordinated to the main clause. (*I brought in the clothes before the storm hit.*) When a subordinate clause precedes a main clause, we use a comma after the subordinate clause. (*Before the storm hit, I brought in the clothes.*)

Cross-reference: Grammar

For instruction and practice of the material in Exercise 62, refer students to Lesson 13.6, pp. 548–549.

Practice and Assess

Answers: Exercise 62

1. Although
2. though
3. Before
4. before
5. because
6. After
7. wherever
8. so that
9. So that
10. As long as

MEETING INDIVIDUAL NEEDS

Gifted and Talented

Using Conjunctions

Help students to categorize the following subordinating conjunctions: *after, although, as, as if, as soon as, as though, because, before, even though, if, inasmuch as, since, so that, though, unless, until, when, whenever, where, wherever, while.*

These subordinating conjunctions may be classified in the following categories of meaning: time (*after, as, as soon as, before, since, until, when, whenever, while*); place (*where, wherever*); manner (*as, as if, as though*); cause (*as, because, inasmuch as, since, so that*); concession (*although, even though, though*); condition (*if, unless*). **L3**

Practice and Assess

Answers: Exercise 63

Answers will vary, but some suggestions are given below.

1.	because	**6.**	Because
2.	when	**7.**	in order that
3.	Although	**8.**	whenever
4.	As	**9.**	Because
5.	so that	**10.**	Although

Answers: Exercise 64

Answers will vary, but some suggestions are given below.

1. In the winter, young humpback whales sometimes feed off the coast of Virginia and the coast of North Carolina.
2. Although it looks like a fish, the whale is a warm-blooded animal.
3. Because it needs oxygen to breathe, the whale will drown if submerged too long.
4. Both porpoises and dolphins are considered whales.
5. Whereas most whales dive for an average of three to ten minutes, some of the toothed whales can remain submerged for more than thirty minutes.
6. Not only is the rib cage of a whale very flexible, but it also can withstand great pressure.
7. Though no one has seen whales mate, scientists think whales mate once a year.
8. Blue whales are both the largest and the fastest whales.
9. Although they are rare, blue whales can be found in all oceans of the world.
10. Because they are a valuable catch, finback whales are the mainstay of the whaling industry.

Exercise 63 Completing Sentences with Subordinating Conjunctions

On your paper, write a subordinating conjunction to complete each of the following sentences. Be sure that your completed sentences make sense.

Early Painters

1. We can't name the earliest painters _____ they did not sign their work.
2. The art of painting began as early as the Paleolithic Age, _____ prehistoric hunters decorated the walls of their caves.
3. _____ some ancient Greek painters are known, their works have not survived.
4. _____ images covered walls, gates, palaces, and temples, it seems likely that professional painters lived in Sumeria and ancient Egypt.
5. Decorations on Greek pottery were baked permanently into the surface _____ they could be preserved.
6. _____ they could not be baked, many paintings on wood or walls have been lost.
7. Roman painters used a heating process _____ their paintings might be preserved.
8. They discovered that paints weathered better _____ they were mixed with boiling wax, resin, and vegetable oils.
9. _____ wealthy Roman citizens admired art, fresco paintings covered the walls of their houses.
10. _____ Roman painters were very skillful, few of their works have endured.

Exercise 64 Adding Conjunctions to Make Sentences

On your paper, revise the sentences below. Use a coordinating conjunction, correlative conjunction, or subordinating conjunction to join the two sentences in each item. Try to use a variety of conjunctions. Make sure your completed sentences make sense.

SAMPLE It was such a hot day. I rested in the shade.
ANSWER *Because* it was such a hot day, I rested in the shade.

SAMPLE Whales are interesting. They are mysterious creatures.
ANSWER Whales are interesting *and* mysterious creatures.

Whale Watching

1. In the winter, young humpback whales sometimes feed off the coast of Virginia. They also feed off the coast of North Carolina.
2. The whale is a warm-blooded animal. It looks like a fish.
3. The whale needs oxygen to breathe. It will drown if submerged too long.
4. Porpoises are considered whales. Dolphins are considered whales.
5. Most whales dive for an average of three to ten minutes. Some of the toothed whales can remain submerged for more than thirty minutes.
6. The rib cage of a whale is very flexible. It can withstand great pressure.
7. No one has seen whales mate. Scientists think whales mate once a year.
8. Blue whales are the largest whales. Blue whales are the fastest whales.
9. Blue whales are rare. They can be found in all oceans of the world.
10. Finback whales are a valuable catch. They are the mainstay of the whaling industry.

Meeting Individual Needs: Learning Disabled

Understanding Conjunctions

If a student has trouble using conjunctions in these exercises, you might pair him or her with another student. The pair can discuss and practice using conjunctions that work in each situation. Then they can talk about why others would not work.

Conjunctive Adverbs

■ A **conjunctive adverb** is used to clarify the relationship between clauses of equal weight in a sentence.

Conjunctive adverbs are usually stronger, more precise, and more formal than coordinating conjunctions.

COORDINATING CONJUNCTION	Most people think of deserts as very hot places, **but** desert nights can be quite cool.
CONJUNCTIVE ADVERB	Most people think of deserts as very hot places; **however,** desert nights can be quite cool.

There are many conjunctive adverbs, and they have several uses, as the following examples show:

TO REPLACE *AND*	also, besides, furthermore, moreover
TO REPLACE *BUT*	however, nevertheless, still, though
TO STATE A RESULT	consequently, therefore, so, thus
TO STATE EQUALITY	equally, likewise, similarly

Exercise 65 Identifying Conjunctive Adverbs

On your paper, write the conjunctive adverb in each sentence.

Toltec Civilization

1. The Toltec civilization of ancient Mexico was advanced in arts and architecture; moreover, it produced impressive stonework.
2. Toltec religion centered on Quetzalcoatl; consequently, he appeared in many images.
3. Quetzalcoatl was the name of a deity; furthermore, it was the name of a legendary ruler.
4. Quetzalcoatl was identified with the planet Venus; likewise, he was linked with the wind.
5. Usually he was depicted as a plumed serpent; however, he was often shown as a wind god.
6. The people wished to please Quetzalcoatl; therefore, they built circular temples that presented no sharp obstacles to the wind.
7. There were many different religious ceremonies and rituals; moreover, people played a sacred ball game called *tlatchi* that resembled basketball.
8. The Toltec civilization expanded southward during the tenth century; therefore, the Toltecs dominated the Mayas of the Yucatan.
9. Other nomadic Mexican groups conquered the Toltecs; thus, their civilization declined.
10. The Aztecs soon built their own empire; consequently, art continued to flourish.

Parts of Speech

Teach

Conjunctive Adverbs

☑ Teaching Tip

Clauses beginning with subordinating conjunctions require no preceding punctuation (*I put the clothes back in the dryer because they were still damp*); clauses beginning with a conjunctive adverb follow a comma or a semicolon (*I took the clothes out of the dryer; however, they were still damp*).

Two-Minute Skill Drill

Have students explain whether the following words are conjunctions or conjunctive adverbs:

and	however
although	wherever
consequently	either . . . or

See also *Two-Minute Skill Drill Transparency 10.7*

Practice and Assess

Answers: Exercise 65

1. moreover
2. consequently
3. furthermore
4. likewise
5. however
6. therefore
7. moreover
8. therefore
9. thus
10. consequently

Enrichment and Extension

Using Conjunctions and Adverbs

Conjunctive adverbs and subordinating conjunctions are easily confused. One way to tell them apart is to examine the position of the word in its clause. Subordinating conjunctions must always be the first word in their clause. Conjunctive adverbs, however, can be moved to the middle or the end of their clause:

a. *Jon was in an accident; however, it was not his fault.*
b. *Jon was in an accident; it was, however, not his fault.*
c. *Jon was in an accident; it was not his fault, however.*

L2

Practice and Assess

Answers: Exercise 66

1. After—subordinating
2. where—subordinating
3. and—coordinating
4. Neither . . . nor—correlative
5. because—subordinating

Answers: Exercise 67

Answers will vary.

Answers: Exercise 68

Answers may vary, but some suggestions are given below.

1. moreover
2. Although
3. Not only . . . but also
4. but
5. consequently
6. and
7. and
8. Not only . . . but also
9. whenever
10. Before

Additional Resources

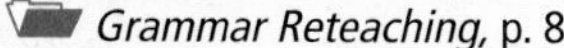
Grammar Practice, p. 8
Grammar Reteaching, p. 8
Grammar Enrichment, p. 8

Grammar Workbook, Lesson 11

Close

Encourage small groups of students to devise a strategy for applying the information they have learned about conjunctions in their writing for other classes. Have students summarize their strategy in their journal for future reference and then discuss their strategy with the rest of the class.

Exercise 66 Identifying Kinds of Conjunctions

On your paper, write the conjunction that appears in each sentence below. Indicate whether the conjunction is a *coordinating, correlative,* or *subordinating* conjunction.

The Galápagos Tortoise

1. After they have mated, adult female Galápagos tortoises lay their eggs on the beach.
2. Each tortoise finds a spot of bare soil where she digs a foot-wide pit.
3. She lays fifteen to twenty eggs inside the pit and covers them with soil.
4. Neither the male nor the female tortoises watch over the eggs.
5. Baby tortoises are on their own after birth because they are able to find their own food.

Exercise 67 Creating Sentences with Conjunctions

Think of a day in which several interesting and varied events happened to you. On your paper, write five sentences about that day, using as many conjunctions as possible.

Exercise 68 Completing Sentences with Conjunctions

On your paper, replace each blank in the following sentences with a conjunction that makes sense. The kind of conjunction to use is stated in parentheses at the end of each sentence.

Modern Tunnel Construction

1. Modern tunnel building is a complicated process; ________, it is a very costly process, involving millions of dollars. (conjunctive adverb)
2. ________ it costs considerably more than a bridge, a tunnel under a river may have certain advantages. (subordinating conjunction)
3. ________ does it allow the unhindered passage of ships, ________ it is less vulnerable. (a pair of correlative conjunctions)
4. A tunnel is a marvelous construction, ________ building one is extremely hazardous. (coordinating conjunction)
5. There are basically three ways to build a tunnel; ________, tunnels may be divided into three types. (conjunctive adverb)
6. A "true" tunnel is dug horizontally through earth ________ rock. (coordinating conjunction)
7. For the cut-and-cover tunnel, a large ditch is dug, a tube is built in the ditch, ________ the tube is covered over. (coordinating conjunction)
8. ________ the first subway in the world, in London, ________ the first on the European continent, in Budapest, were built in this way. (a pair of correlative conjunctions)
9. The trench tunnel involves a kind of cut-and-cover method used ________ the tunnel is dug underwater. (subordinating conjunction)
10. ________ a route is chosen for any tunnel, a careful geologic study is made of the type of earth and rock along the way. (subordinating conjunction)

10.8 Interjections

■ An **interjection** is a word or phrase that expresses emotion or exclamation. An interjection has no grammatical connection to other words.

Oh, I didn't know that.
Ouch! That hurts!
Whew, it's hot.
Why, children!

Exercise 69 Identifying Interjections

On your paper, write the interjection that appears in each item.

1. Dear me! Whatever shall we do?
2. Oh, don't ask me.
3. Alas! The ship was doomed.
4. This box is heavy. Ugh!
5. Yuck! What a disgusting thought!
6. Phooey! I give up.
7. Wow, it's really snowing out there.
8. Whee! We're sliding all over.
9. Well! This is a surprise.
10. Hey, what's that noise?

Exercise 70 Using Interjections

On your paper, replace each blank below with an appropriate interjection from the following list. Remember to add punctuation.

Wow	Oops	Ssh	Ah	Whew
Well	Psst	Yipes	Alas	Ouch

1. ________ That was an amazing catch!
2. ________ I dropped the plate.
3. ________ you are here at last.
4. ________ The stove is hot!
5. ________ the concert is beginning.
6. ________ That was pretty close!
7. ________ it is finally over.
8. ________ come here a second, but do not let anyone see you.
9. ________ That is the wildest thing I have ever heard!
10. ________ It is pouring, and I forgot to shut the windows.

Parts of Speech

Focus

Lesson Overview

Objective

- To use interjections in writing to add emphasis and emotion

Bellringer
Daily Language Activity

When students enter the classroom, have this assignment on the board: *Finish these sentences:*

Whew! I'm_____.
Oops! I_____.
Ouch! That_____.

See also  *Daily Language Activity*

Teach

Grammar Tip

Students often confuse interjections with imperatives. The difference is that interjections never contain a verb, whereas imperatives always contain a verb. (*Go!* is an imperative; *Hey!* is an interjection.)

Practice and Assess

Answers: Exercise 69

1. Dear me!
2. Oh
3. Alas!
4. Ugh!
5. Yuck!
6. Phooey!
7. Wow
8. Whee!
9. Well!
10. Hey

Answers: Exercise 70

Answers may vary, but some suggestions are given below.

1. Wow!
2. Oops!
3. Ah,
4. Ouch!
5. Ssh,
6. Whew!
7. Well,
8. Psst,
9. Yipes!
10. Alas!

Resource Manager

Planning Resources
- *Lesson Plans*

Transparencies
- *Bellringer*
- *Daily Language Practice*

Other Print Resources
- *Grammar and Composition Handbook*
- *Grammar Enrichment,* p. 8
- *Grammar Practice,* p. 8
- *Grammar Workbook, Lesson* 11

Teach

About the Literature

Explain that the Unit 10 Review contains a passage from Marilynne Robinson's novel *Housekeeping,* followed by exercises on related topics. After students read the passage, discuss the characters, setting, and mood. Then ask students to determine which words are, or are not, essential to the meaning of the passage.

Linking Grammar and Literature

Critical Thinking

Ask students to identify some of the nouns, verbs, and adjectives not highlighted in the passage. Remind them that *-ing* forms can sometimes function as nouns or as adjectives, that past participles can function as adjectives, and so on. In the fourth sentence of the first paragraph of the passage, for instance, the word *living* is a noun, not a verb. In the second sentence of the second paragraph, the word *frozen* is an adjective, not a verb.

Cooperative Learning

Have students form an even number of groups. Each group should write a paragraph consisting of very simple sentences composed primarily of nouns and verbs. Then have groups exchange paragraphs to write a second version. The second version should contain not only nouns and verbs but also a variety of pronouns, adjectives, and adverbs, as well as a few prepositions and conjunctions. Ask groups to take turns reading both versions to the class. Discuss how writers can add color, nuance, and precision to their prose by using all of the parts of speech.

ASSESSMENT OPTIONS

Tests with Answer Key & Rubrics
Unit 10 Mastery Test, pp. 37–38

Testmaker
Unit 10 Mastery Test

UNIT 10 Grammar Review

Parts of Speech

Parts of Speech

This passage from Marilynne Robinson's novel *Housekeeping* has been annotated to show some of the parts of speech covered in this unit. Read the passage and do the exercises that follow.

Literature Model

from Housekeeping

by Marilynne Robinson

Common noun · Proper noun · Abstract noun · Adjective · Concrete noun · Linking verb · Relative pronoun · Coordinating conjunction · Personal pronoun

It was a hard winter, too. The snow crested, finally, far above our heads. It drifted up our eaves on one side of the house. Some houses in Fingerbone simply fell from the weight of snow on their roofs, a source of grave and perpetual anxiety to my great-aunts, who were accustomed to a brick building, and to living below ground. Sometimes the sun would be warm enough to send a thick sheet of snow sliding off the roof, and sometimes the fir trees would shrug, and the snow would fall with surprisingly loud and earthy thuds, which would terrify my great-aunts. . . .

For some reason the lake was a source of particular pleasure to Fingerbone that year. It was frozen solid early and long. Several acres of it were swept, for people brought brooms to tend and expand it, till the cleared ice spread far across the lake. Sledders heaped snow on the shore into a precipitous chute that sent them sailing far across the ice. There were barrels on the shore for fires to be built in, and people brought boxes to sit on and planks and burlap bags to stand on around the barrels, and frankfurters to roast, and clothespins to clip frozen mittens to the lips of barrels. A number of dogs began to spend most of their time at the ice. They were young, leggy dogs, affable and proprietary, and exhilarated by the weather. They liked to play at retrieving bits of ice which sped fantastically fast and far across the lake. The dogs made a gallant and youthful joke of their own strength and speed,

Resource Manager

Planning Resources

- *Lesson Plans*

Other Print Resources

- *Grammar and Composition Handbook*
- *Grammar Workbook,* Lessons 1–11, Unit 1 Review

and flaunted an utter indifference to the safety of their limbs. Lucille and I took our skates to school, so that we could go to the lake directly and stay there through the twilight. Usually we would skate along the edge of the swept ice, tracing its shape, and coming finally to its farthest edge, we would sit on the snow and look back at Fingerbone.

We felt giddily far from shore, though the lake was so solid that winter that it would certainly have supported the weight of the entire population of Fingerbone, past, present, and to come. Nevertheless, only we and the ice sweepers went out so far, and only we stayed.

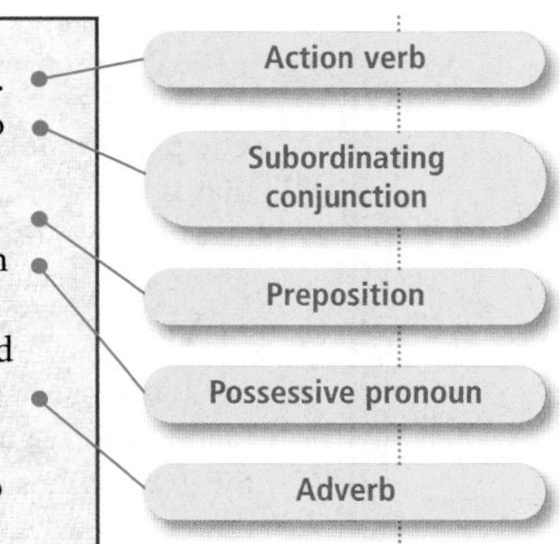

Review: Exercise 1 Identifying Nouns

The following sentences elaborate on ideas from *Housekeeping*. On your paper, write each of the nouns in these sentences. After each noun, write *common, proper,* or *collective,* depending upon how the noun is used in the sentence.

SAMPLE *Housekeeping* is about two sisters and their family.
ANSWER *Housekeeping* (proper), sisters (common), family (common, collective)

1. The village of Fingerbone, Idaho, endured severe winters.
2. During a particularly bad winter, Fingerbone was nearly buried by a fierce storm.
3. The snowfall was heavy, and temperatures were low.
4. Half of the roof was covered with snow.
5. According to Aunt Lily and Aunt Nona, the house might collapse from the weight.
6. The idea that the house could fall made the aunts nervous.
7. Lily and Nona were even startled by the noise made by huge clumps of falling snow.
8. A crowd of local residents gathered daily at Fingerbone Lake.
9. The lake froze early, well before Thanksgiving Day.
10. A team of sweepers cleared the snow from the icy surface.
11. People packed the snow into a steep chute for sledders to use.
12. The public enjoyed many activities on the ice.
13. One crowd of merrymakers roasted wieners.
14. Another group rode sleds down a snowy hill.
15. Gleefully, a pack of dogs scampered among the throng.
16. Ruth and Lucille were among the throng of townspeople at the festivities.
17. After school the pair of girls went straight to the lake.
18. The sisters skated to the boundary of the swept ice.
19. Later, the two skaters rested on a snowbank and looked at the village.
20. Ruth and her sister returned to their home after hours of fun.

Parts of Speech

Practice and Assess

Answers: Exercise 1

1. village (common), Fingerbone (proper), Idaho (proper), winters (common)
2. winter (common), Fingerbone (proper), storm (common)
3. snowfall (common), temperatures (common)
4. Half (common), roof (common), snow (common)
5. Aunt Lily (proper), Aunt Nona (proper), house (common), weight (common)
6. idea (common), house (common), aunts (common)
7. Lily (proper), Nona (proper), noise (common), clumps (common), snow (common)
8. crowd (common, collective), residents (common), Fingerbone Lake (proper)
9. lake (common), Thanksgiving Day (proper)
10. team (common, collective), sweepers (common), snow (common), surface (common)
11. People (common), snow (common), chute (common), sledders (common)
12. public (common, collective), activities (common), ice (common)
13. crowd (common, collective), merry-makers (common), wieners (common)
14. group (common, collective), sleds (common), hill (common)
15. pack (common, collective), dogs (com-mon), throng (common, collective)
16. Ruth (proper), Lucille (proper), throng (common, collective), townspeople (common), festivities (common)
17. school (common), pair (common, col-lective), girls (common), lake (common)
18. sisters (common), boundary (common), ice (common)
19. skaters (common), snowbank (com-mon), village (common)
20. Ruth (proper), sister (common), home (common), hours (common), fun (common)

Practice and Assess

Answers: Exercise 2

Answers will vary, but some suggestions are given below.

1. Ruth and her sister, Lucille, lived in the small town of Fingerbone, Idaho.
2. Their grandfather was originally from the Midwest, but he had come to Idaho years ago and built his home there.
3. Ruth did not remember him, since he had died before she was born.
4. Ruth had been raised by her grandmother until the grandmother died.
5. Then Ruth's great-aunts came to Fingerbone to take care of the two girls.
6. The great-aunts were unfamiliar with rural life and did not really enjoy it.
7. They felt isolated in Fingerbone because of its small population.
8. The heavy snowfall troubled them, and they also worried about their nieces.
9. Ruth did not mind the harsh winter, since she had lived in Fingerbone all her life.
10. She often took her ice skates with her to school and afterward went to Fingerbone Lake to skate on its frozen waters.

Answers: Exercise 3

Answers will vary, but some suggestions are given below.

1. Many
2. themselves
3. Everyone
4. her
5. They
6. Nothing
7. themselves
8. their
9. Who
10. that

Grammar Review

Parts of Speech

Review: Exercise 2 Using Pronouns Effectively

The paragraph below elaborates on ideas suggested by a passage from *Housekeeping* that is not reprinted in this textbook. On your paper, write each sentence in the paragraph, substituting pronouns for nouns when a pronoun would make good sense. Do not substitute a pronoun for a noun if the pronoun would make the sentence unclear.

[1]Ruth and Ruth's sister, Lucille, lived in the small town of Fingerbone, Idaho. [2]Ruth's and Lucille's grandfather was originally from the Midwest, but the grandfather had come to Idaho years ago and built the grandfather's home there. [3]Ruth did not remember the grandfather, since the grandfather had died before Ruth was born. [4]Ruth had been raised by Ruth's grandmother until the grandmother died. [5]Then Ruth's great-aunts came to Fingerbone to take care of the two girls. [6]The great-aunts were unfamiliar with rural life and did not really enjoy rural life. [7]The great-aunts felt isolated in Fingerbone because of Fingerbone's small population. [8]The heavy snowfall troubled the great-aunts, and the great-aunts also worried about the great-aunts' nieces. [9]Ruth did not mind the harsh winter, since Ruth had lived in Fingerbone all Ruth's life. [10]Ruth often took Ruth's ice skates with Ruth to school and afterward went to Fingerbone Lake to skate on Fingerbone Lake's frozen waters.

Review: Exercise 3 Completing Sentences with Pronouns

The following sentences elaborate on ideas suggested by a passage from *Housekeeping* that is not reprinted in this textbook. On your paper, write the type of pronoun specified in italics for each sentence. Be sure that your completed sentences make sense.

1. *Indefinite* of the winters in Fingerbone, Idaho, were severe.
2. During a particularly harsh winter, the people found simple ways to amuse *reflexive*.
3. *Indefinite* seemed to enjoy sledding down snowy hills and skating on Fingerbone Lake.
4. Ruth and *possessive* sister enjoyed skating on the frozen lake after school.
5. *Personal* were certain that the frozen ice was solid enough to hold them.
6. *Indefinite* seemed to stop the girls from enjoying the great outdoors.
7. Of course, the girls' great-aunts needlessly worried *reflexive* about the weather.
8. The great-aunts also worried about *possessive* nieces.
9. *Interrogative* could blame them?
10. The aunts were not accustomed to rural living, and *demonstrative* was an especially severe winter.

Review: Exercise 4 **Identifying Verbs and Verb Phrases**

The following sentences are adapted from the passage. Write on your paper any verbs and verb phrases that appear in the sentences, and label them accordingly.

SAMPLE Ruth's great-aunts had lived in brick houses all their lives.
ANSWER had lived—verb phrase

1. The snow had been falling for days.
2. It piled into drifts and covered the eaves of the house.
3. Finally the sun returned to the sky.
4. Sometimes the fir trees would shudder under a heavy load of snow.
5. A dense layer of snow often slid to the ground with an earthy thud.
6. Many weeks of cold weather had frozen the waters of Fingerbone Lake to its very depths.
7. There must have been a dozen children among the skaters.
8. Townspeople had cleared several acres of ice with their brooms.
9. After school Lucille and Ruth skated until twilight, and they would have stayed even later.
10. They would venture farther out than anyone else onto the frozen surface of the lake.

Review: Exercise 5 **Identifying Transitive and Intransitive Verbs**

The following sentences contain verbs that appear in the passage from *Housekeeping*. For each item, write *transitive* or *intransitive* on your paper, depending upon the way the italicized verb is used in the sentence.

SAMPLE Mounds of snow *crested* as high as the windows.
ANSWER intransitive

SAMPLE The skaters *brought* extra mittens.
ANSWER transitive

1. Snow *drifted* against the fence.
2. A child *fell* in the deep snow.
3. The howling blizzard *terrified* the small children.
4. Some neighbors *brought* snowshoes with them.
5. Children *heaped* snow into small hills to build igloos.
6. An expert skier *sped* through the countryside.
7. Ice skaters *flaunted* their skills before crowds.
8. They *skated* around the lake at dizzying speeds.
9. Toddlers *traced* patterns with their feet in the cold, sparkling snow.
10. The frozen lake *supported* hundreds of skaters.

Answers: Exercise 4

1. had been falling—verb phrase
2. piled—verb; covered—verb
3. returned—verb
4. would shudder—verb phrase
5. slid—verb
6. had frozen—verb phrase
7. must have been—verb phrase
8. had cleared—verb phrase
9. skated—verb; would have stayed—verb phrase
10. would venture—verb phrase

Answers: Exercise 5

1. intransitive
2. intransitive
3. transitive
4. transitive
5. transitive
6. intransitive
7. transitive
8. intransitive
9. transitive
10. transitive

Practice and Assess

Answers: Exercise 6

1. Few—aspects; unremarkable—aspects
2. lofty—Rocky Mountains; spectacular—sights
3. large—portion; remote—wilderness
4. Its—streams; icy—streams; suitable—habitat; many—varieties
5. early—peoples; Native American—peoples; expert—hunters; mighty—buffalo
6. many—settlers; European—settlers; their—homes
7. Hardy—miners; prominent—miners; these—settlers; hardworking—settlers; northern—sections
8. hostile—landscape; difficult— life; most—people
9. Primitive—conditions; generous—spirit
10. major—industry; large—state

Answers: Exercise 7

Answers will vary, but some suggestions are given below.

1. In the small village the air was frosty and crisp.
2. The town of Fingerbone looked for a few days like a pale and icy wonderland.
3. When the warm sun returned, weary neighbors dug paths from their homes.
4. Ruth's elderly aunts worried about the fragile roof.
5. Fingerbone Lake became a solid sheet of ice, perfect for skating.
6. The local townspeople took great pleasure in the lake.
7. Bold sledders built a steep chute of snow.
8. Frisky dogs raced across the ice at reckless speeds.
9. Ruth and Lucille skated on the sparkling ice and looked back at the small town.
10. Tired but happy, the girls trudged home in the dim twilight.

Review: Exercise 6 Identifying Adjectives

The following sentences are about Idaho. On your paper, write the adjectives that appear in each sentence. Include pronouns and proper adjectives, but not the words *a, an,* and *the.* After each adjective, write the word that the adjective modifies.

SAMPLE Idaho is an unusual setting for a novel about ordinary life.
ANSWER unusual—setting; ordinary—life

1. Few aspects of life in the state are unremarkable.
2. The lofty Rocky Mountains provide spectacular sights.
3. A large portion of Idaho remains a remote wilderness.
4. Its icy streams provide a suitable habitat for many varieties of trout.
5. The early Native American peoples of the region were expert hunters of the mighty buffalo.
6. After the discovery of gold in the 1860s, many European settlers came to make their homes in Idaho.
7. Hardy miners were prominent among these hardworking settlers in northern sections of Idaho.
8. Because of the hostile landscape, life was difficult for most people.
9. Primitive conditions fostered a generous spirit of cooperation, however.
10. Today, farming is a major industry in this large state.

Review: Exercise 7 Expanding Sentences with Adjectives

The following sentences elaborate on the passage from *Housekeeping*. On your paper, write adjectives that would make sense in the places indicated by carets. Although there are no specific correct answers, base your choices on the passage.

SAMPLE Temperatures were ∧, and a ∧ layer of snow blanketed the town.
ANSWER low, thick

1. In the ∧ village the air was frosty and ∧ .
2. The town of Fingerbone looked for a few days like a ∧ and ∧ wonderland.
3. When the ∧ sun returned, ∧ neighbors dug paths from their homes.
4. Ruth's ∧ aunts worried about the ∧ roof.
5. Fingerbone Lake became a ∧ sheet of ice, ∧ for skating.
6. The ∧ townspeople took ∧ pleasure in the lake.
7. ∧ sledders built a ∧ chute of snow.
8. ∧ dogs raced across the ice at ∧ speeds.
9. Ruth and Lucille skated on the ∧ ice and looked back at the ∧ town.
10. Tired but ∧, the girls trudged home in the ∧ twilight.

Review: Exercise 8 Identifying Adverbs

The following sentences are about ice skating. On your paper, write each adverb that appears in these sentences and the word that the adverb modifies.

SAMPLE Skilled ice skaters twirl quite gracefully.
ANSWER quite—gracefully; gracefully—twirl

1. Experienced skaters move rather rapidly on the ice.
2. Frequently they form special patterns, or figures.
3. In cold climates they often skate outside.
4. Sometimes they glide on frozen lakes and ponds.
5. Safety is very important for all skaters.
6. Wise skaters never skate alone.
7. Professional figure skaters generally perform indoors.
8. Special equipment creates the ice mechanically.
9. Have you ever seen a professional ice show?
10. The skaters dress beautifully and usually perform to music.

Review: Exercise 9 Using Adverbs

Each of the following sentences is based on the information in the passage from *Housekeeping*. On your paper, write an appropriate adverb to take the place of the prepositional phrase in italics. The adverb should express the same idea as the prepositional phrase.

SAMPLE That year winter descended with much harshness on Fingerbone.
ANSWER harshly

1. The snow fell *in heavy masses* for many days.
2. *In a sudden motion* a heavy slab of snow slid from a tree.
3. Ruth's great-aunts looked *with anxiety* at their own snow-laden roof.
4. *To everyone's amazement* the dilapidated roof held up under the weight of the snow.
5. The villagers walked *with eagerness* to the frozen lake.
6. Some sledded *in a reckless way* down a steep chute of snow.
7. The dogs chased pieces of ice that slid *in a quick manner* across the frozen lake.
8. Dogs scampered *in an exuberant fashion* across the ice.
9. For hours Ruth and Lucille skated *with swiftness* on the frozen lake.
10. After twilight the girls returned home *in a weary manner.*

Answers: Exercise 8

1. rather—rapidly; rapidly—move
2. Frequently—form
3. often—skate; outside—skate
4. Sometimes—glide
5. very—important
6. never—skate; alone—skate
7. generally—perform; indoors—perform
8. mechanically—creates
9. ever—have seen
10. beautifully—dress; usually—perform

Answers: Exercise 9

Answers will vary, but some suggestions are given below.

1. The snow fell heavily for many days.
2. Suddenly a heavy slab of snow slid from a tree.
3. Ruth's great-aunts looked anxiously at their own snow-laden roof.
4. Amazingly, the dilapidated roof held up under the weight of the snow.
5. The villagers walked eagerly to the frozen lake.
6. Some sledded recklessly down a steep chute of snow.
7. The dogs chased pieces of ice that slid quickly across the frozen lake.
8. Dogs scampered exuberantly across the ice.
9. For hours Ruth and Lucille skated swiftly on the frozen lake.
10. After twilight the girls returned home wearily.

Practice and Assess

Answers: Exercise 10

1. about; in
2. by; of
3. to; through; on; to
4. After; of; to; for
5. from; with; in; like
6. to; in spite of; for
7. During; in; of
8. of; in; in; for
9. to; of; in; as
10. According to; about

Answers: Exercise 11

Answers will vary, but some suggestions are given below.

1. Because temperatures had remained below the freezing point, Fingerbone Lake had turned to solid ice.
2. Townspeople with brooms steadily swept the snow from acres of ice.
3. They dumped snow from sleds into huge mounds along the shore.
4. Some villagers skated across the frozen surface almost to the far shore.
5. Sledders raced down a steep hill of snow.
6. People roasted meat over barrels on shore.
7. Frozen mittens were clipped with clothespins to the rims of the barrels.
8. Some of the townsfolk brought boxes to use as chairs.
9. Dogs scampered playfully among the crowd.
10. The lake assumed the aspect of an impromptu festival.

Review: Exercise 10 Identifying Prepositions

The following sentences are based on passages from *Housekeeping* not reprinted in this book. On your paper, list the prepositions that appear in each sentence. Remember that some prepositions are made up of more than one word. (The numeral in parentheses at the end of each item indicates the number of prepositions the sentence contains.)

1. *Housekeeping* is about two orphaned sisters in Idaho. (2)
2. The novel is narrated by Ruth, one of the sisters. (2)
3. Ruth's grandmother brought order to the household through her insistence on strict attention to chores. (4)
4. After the death of Ruth's grandmother, Ruth's great-aunts came to Idaho and cared for the girls. (4)
5. The great-aunts came from Spokane, Washington, and were unfamiliar with life in a small town like Fingerbone. (4)
6. They moved to Fingerbone in spite of their preference for city life. (3)
7. During crises the aunts took refuge in the repetition of familiar chores. (3)
8. The normal needs of adolescents in the home caused too many changes in routine for the aunts' liking. (4)
9. They fled to the safety of a hotel and left Aunt Sylvie in charge as the girls' guardian. (4)
10. According to Sylvie, life is about change and surprises, not housekeeping. (2)

Review: Exercise 11 Using Prepositions

Each of the sentences below elaborates on the passage from *Housekeeping*. On your paper, write a preposition that completes the word or phrase in italics and makes sense in the sentence. More than one preposition may make sense.

SAMPLE The cold spell lasted ___________ *weeks.*
ANSWER for

1. Because temperatures had remained ___________ *the freezing point,* Fingerbone Lake had turned to solid ice.
2. Townspeople ___________ *brooms* steadily swept the snow from acres of ice.
3. They dumped snow from sleds into huge mounds ___________ *the shore.*
4. Some villagers skated ___________ *the frozen surface* almost to the far shore.
5. Sledders raced ___________ *a steep hill* of snow.
6. People roasted meat ___________ *barrels* on shore.
7. Frozen mittens were clipped ___________ *clothespins* to the rims of the barrels.
8. Some of the townsfolk brought boxes to use ___________ *chairs.*
9. Dogs scampered playfully ___________ *the crowd.*
10. The lake assumed the aspect ___________ *an impromptu festival.*

Review: Exercise 12 Using Conjunctions

The following sentences tell more about Idaho, the setting for *Housekeeping.* On your paper, complete each sentence by writing an appropriate conjunction according to the direction in parentheses. Choose your conjunctions from the list below, which has more conjunctions than you will need.

CONJUNCTIONS

and	or	but	yet		
neither . . .	nor	not only . . .	but also		
although	because	before	if	when	wherever

SAMPLE Idaho is located in the Rocky Mountains, ___________ it is very beautiful. (Add a coordinating conjunction.)

ANSWER and

1. ___________ you go in Idaho, you are likely to find spectacular scenery. (Add a subordinating conjunction.)
2. ___________ you visit the Snake River Canyon, be sure to see Shoshone Falls. (Add a subordinating conjunction.)
3. You might fish in one of Idaho's two thousand lakes in the summer ___________ visit the state during the skiing season. (Add a coordinating conjunction.)
4. ___________ Idaho is far from the coast, it has the cold winters typical of the North American interior. (Add a subordinating conjunction.)
5. Winter temperatures often dip below freezing, ___________ several feet of snow fall each year. (Add a coordinating conjunction.)
6. ___________ Idaho is the thirteenth largest state in area, it is sparsely populated. (Add a subordinating conjunction.)
7. ___________ Boise, Idaho's capital city, ___________ the even smaller city of Twin Falls has a population of over 150,000. (Add a pair of correlative conjunctions.)
8. Native American communities had inhabited Idaho for centuries ___________ the first white explorers arrived in 1805. (Add a subordinating conjunction.)
9. ___________ gold was discovered in Idaho in the 1860s, thousands of prospectors flocked to the state. (Add a subordinating conjunction.)
10. Today Idaho is famous for its potatoes, ___________ few people know that it also has the largest silver mine in the nation. (Add a coordinating conjunction.)

Parts of Speech

Answers: Exercise 12

Answers will vary, but some suggestions are given below.

1. Wherever
2. If
3. or
4. Because
5. and
6. Although
7. Neither . . . nor
8. before
9. When
10. yet

Practice and Assess

Answers: Exercise 13

Answers will vary, but some suggestions are given below.

1. Boy!
2. Well,
3. Wow!
4. Yikes!
5. Alas,
6. Oops!
7. Whee!
8. Uh-oh!
9. Ssh!
10. Ah,

Answers: Exercise 14

Proofreading

This proofreading activity provides editing practice with (1) the current or previous units' skills, (2) the **Troubleshooter** errors, and (3) spelling errors. Students should be able to complete the exercise by referring to the units, the **Troubleshooter,** and a dictionary. Answers may vary but some suggestions are given below. (Note: A run-on sentence counts as one error.)

Error (Type of Error)

1. (1860–1961), (nonessential adjective clause)
   Irish (proper adjective)
   descent (spelling)
2. began (verb form)
3. life. She *or* life; she *or* life, and (run-on sentence)
4. father, (nonessential participial phrase)
   her (possessive pronoun)
5. Moses, (nonessential appositive)
6. New York (proper noun)
7. began (verb form)
8. an Eagle (article before a vowel sound)
   were (subject-verb agreement)

Review: Exercise 13 Using Interjections

Each of the sentences below relates to the theme of the passage from *Housekeeping*. On your paper, replace each blank below with an appropriate interjection from the following list. Remember to add punctuation.

Yikes	Wow	Boy	Well	Ssh
Ah	Whee	Alas	Oops	Uh-oh

1. _____ That was a hard winter.
2. _____ the snow finally crested.
3. _____ Some houses fell from the weight of snow on their roofs!
4. _____ The clumps of falling snow almost hit me!
5. _____ the great-aunts are very nervous.
6. _____ I slipped on some ice!
7. _____ Skating is so much fun!
8. _____ We are really far from shore!
9. _____ Can you hear the snow falling?
10. _____ what a winter wonderland!

Review: Exercise 14

Proofreading

The following passage describes the artist Grandma Moses, whose painting appears on the opposite page. Rewrite the passage, correcting the errors in spelling, capitalization, usage, and grammar. Add any missing punctuation. There are twenty-five errors.

Grandma Moses

[1]Anna Mary Robertson Moses (1860–1961) who was known as Grandma Moses, was born in Greenwich, New York, to a family of Scottish and irish desent. [2]She begun painting at the age of seventy-seven. [3]During the last two decades of her life, Moses painted hundreds of scenes of rural farm life, she became perhaps the most famous folk painter in America.

[4]Encouraged by her father Moses developed her talent for drawing; she, however, had little time to pursue hers interest in art. [5]She married a farmer, Thomas Salmon Moses and bore ten children. [6]She spent much of her life on a dairy farm in the tiny community of Eagle Bridge in upstate new york. [7]She begun to paint seriously only after her arthritis became so crippling that she could no longer work on the farm. [8]A few of her paintings on display at a Eagle Bridge drugstore was discovered by an art collector who happened to pass

Anna Mary Robertson ("Grandma") Moses, *Early Skating,* 1951

through town. [9]Somewhat taken aback by her sudden fame, Moses was scandalized when both dealers or tourists began to offer large sums for paintings that she thought were worth only a few dollars'.

[10]Moses paintings are remarkable for their harmony and detail. [11]Although she had no formel training, Moses had a strong intuitive grasp of color, pattern, and design. [12]Recorded the landscapes and customs of her rural countryside with the sensitivity of a poet. [13]Every detail is careful observed: the gray cast of the sky on a snowy morning the steam rising from a locomotive, and the straining muscles of a horse pulling a sleigh. [14]Moses's *Early Skating,* like the passage from Marilynne Robinson's novel *Housekeeping,* capture the atmosphere of a small community on a winter day. [15]Although the painting depict New York, whereas the novel is set in Idaho, the mood are the same. [16]There are a playfulness about the two scenes of children cavorting on the ice. [17]There is also a feeling of isolation, as if these two small towns were seperated from the outside world by time and winters snowy blanket.

Parts of Speech

Answers: Exercise 14 *(continued)*

Error (Type of Error)

9. both dealers and tourists (correlative conjunctions)
dollars (plural noun)
10. Moses's (singular possessive)
11. formal (spelling)
12. She recorded (sentence fragment)
13. carefully (adverb form)
morning, (commas in a series)
14. captures (subject-verb agreement)
15. depicts (subject-verb agreement)
is (subject-verb agreement)
16. is (subject-verb agreement)
17. separated (spelling)
winter's (singular possessive)

Viewing the Art

Anna Mary Robertson ("Grandma") Moses, *Early Skating,* 1951

Many folk painters create vivid and accurate documents of the world around them. While their paintings may be technically naive, their vision of the world is rich and nuanced. Grandma Moses was such an artist.

Marilynne Robinson also has a painter's eye for detail. The lives of the villagers of Fingerbone, so vividly portrayed in her novel, in some ways resemble those of the villagers in *Early Skating.*

Practice and Assess

Answers: Exercise 15
Mixed Review

Answers will vary, but some suggestions are given below.

1. The American author Marilynne Robinson was born in 1947.
2. Robinson published her novel *Housekeeping* in 1981.
3. Although *Housekeeping* was only a first novel, it received much critical attention.
4. *Housekeeping* takes place in a remote community in the Rocky Mountains of Idaho.
5. The novel was praised for its poetic language and keen understanding of human nature.
6. Critics also warmly applauded its finely drawn and well-developed characters.
7. *Housekeeping* was a winner of the Hemingway Foundation/PEN Award.
8. The movie based on the novel was also critically acclaimed.
9. Robinson has published a second novel and has won a Pulitzer Prize for Fiction.
10. Some of Robinson's short stories have appeared in *Harper's*, the noted literary magazine, as well as other major publications in the United States.

Grammar Review

Review: Exercise 15

The following biography of Marilynne Robinson is followed by ten sentences. On your paper, write an appropriate word to complete each sentence. Use the directions in parentheses as a guide. You will need to consult the biography in order to fill in some of the blanks properly.

Marilynne Robinson

Born in 1947, Marilynne Robinson is a highly regarded contemporary American writer. Her first novel, *Housekeeping* (published in 1981), was widely acclaimed for its poetic language, its vivid characterizations, and its keen understanding of human nature. Set in an isolated Rocky Mountain community in Idaho, *Housekeeping* describes two orphaned sisters who are cared for by a number of different guardians, each with her own ideas about what is important in life. This touching story about small-town life earned Robinson the Hemingway Foundation/PEN Award. The book was the basis of a critically acclaimed motion picture. Robinson's second novel *Gilead* won the Pulitzer Prize for Fiction in 2005.

1. The ____________ author Marilynne Robinson was born in 1947. (Add a proper adjective.)
2. Robinson ____________ her novel *Housekeeping* in 1981. (Add an action verb.)
3. ____________ *Housekeeping* was only a first novel, it received much critical attention. (Add a subordinating conjunction.)
4. *Housekeeping* takes place in a remote community in the ____________ of Idaho. (Add a proper noun.)
5. The novel was praised for its ____________ language and keen understanding of human nature. (Add an adjective.)
6. Critics also ____________ applauded its finely drawn and well-developed characters. (Add an adverb.)
7. *Housekeeping* ____________ a winner of the Hemingway Foundation/PEN Award. (Add a linking verb.)
8. The ____________ based on the novel was also critically acclaimed. (Add a common noun.)
9. Robinson has published a second novel ____________ has won a Pulitzer Prize for Fiction. (Add a coordinating conjunction.)
10. Some of Robinson's short stories have appeared ____________ *Harper's*, the noted literary magazine, as well as other major publications in the United States. (Add a preposition.)

Writing Application

Nouns in Writing

Amy Tan uses nouns in this passage from *The Joy Luck Club* to convey the bustle and confusion a California girl feels traveling in a foreign country for the first time. Examine the passage, focusing especially on the italicized nouns.

> Before the *train* even comes to a *stop, people* are bringing down their *belongings* from above their *seats.* For a *moment* there is a dangerous *shower* of heavy *suitcases* laden with *gifts* to *relatives,* half-broken *boxes* wrapped in *miles* of *string* to keep the *contents* from spilling out, plastic *bags* filled with *yarn* and *vegetables* and *packages* of dried *mushrooms,* and camera *cases.* And then we are caught in a *stream* of *people* rushing, shoving, pushing us along, until we find ourselves in one of a dozen *lines* waiting to go through *customs.* I feel as if I were getting on the number 30 Stockton *bus* in *San Francisco.* I am in *China,* I remind myself. And somehow the *crowds* don't bother me. It feels right. I start pushing, too.

Techniques with Nouns

Try to apply some of Amy Tan's writing techniques when you write and revise your own work.

TIME For more about the writing process, see **TIME Facing the Blank Page**, pp. 121–131.

1. Whenever possible, replace general words with precise concrete nouns. Compare the following:

   GENERAL WORDS bags filled with *things*

   TAN'S VERSION plastic bags filled with *yarn* and *vegetables* and *packages* of dried *mushrooms*, and camera *cases*

2. Use proper nouns to help make your writing more specific.

   GENERAL WORDS I am in a foreign *country*. . . . a crowded bus in a *city*. . . .

   TAN'S VERSION I am in *China*. . . . the number 30 Stockton bus in *San Francisco*. . . .

3. Expand single nouns into longer groups of specific words when you wish to provide more details.

   SINGLE NOUN suitcases

   TAN'S VERSION heavy suitcases laden with gifts to relatives

Parts of Speech

Practice Practice these techniques by revising the following passage, using a separate sheet of paper. Pay particular attention to the underlined words.

By seven o'clock on that snowy morning, the park was a scene of great activity. A group of dogs was racing across the area, putting birds to flight. Frantic owners followed, shouting the names of their dogs. Squirrels flicked their tails and scampered to safety. Along the pathway, the dog owners stamped their feet in the snow and chatted about things. Others fed birds that chirped and hopped nervously on the path. Before long, children came running through the park, dragging their toys behind them. Their voices blended with all the other sounds. In a moment, the usually serene park had become quite a hectic place.

Writing Online — For more grammar practice, go to glencoe.com and enter QuickPass code WC97727p2.

Nouns in Writing

Have students read aloud the passage from *The Joy Luck Club.* Go over the italicized noun choices in the passage. Discuss these noun choices in relation to the Techniques with Nouns section below.

Techniques with Nouns

Have students turn back to page 482 and choose ten nouns from the first paragraph of the passage from *Housekeeping.* Compare the use of nouns—proper, common, collective, and so on—to their use in *The Joy Luck Club.*

Practice

The answers to this challenging and enriching activity will vary. Refer to Techniques with Nouns as you evaluate student choices.

Close

Have students write one paragraph on any subject. In their paragraph, ask them to underline and identify at least one example of each of the following parts of speech: noun, pronoun, verb, adjective, adverb, preposition, and conjunction. Have students work in small groups to share and evaluate their assignment.

ASSESSMENT OPTIONS

Tests with Answer Key & Rubrics
Unit 10 Mastery Test, pp. 37–38

Testmaker
Unit 10 Mastery Test

You may wish to administer the Unit 10 Mastery Test at this point.

MindJogger Videoquizzes

INTRODUCING

UNIT 11

Objectives

- To learn about the various parts of sentences, including simple and compound subjects and predicates and various kinds of complements
- To demonstrate control over the uses of various kinds of subjects, predicates, and complements by identifying them and writing sentences using them correctly

ASSESSMENT OPTIONS

Tests with Answer Key & Rubrics
Unit 11 Pretest, pp. 39–40
Unit 11 Mastery Test, pp. 41–42

Testmaker
Unit 11 Pretest
Unit 11 Mastery Test

You may wish to administer the Unit 11 Pretest at this point.

Key to Ability Levels

L1 Level 1 activities are within the basic ability range of students.

L2 Level 2 activities are within the ability range of average students.

L3 Level 3 activities are more challenging activities.

UNIT 11

Parts of the Sentence

494

Resource Manager

Planning Resources
- *Lesson Plans*
- *Block Scheduling*

Transparencies
- *Bellringer*
- *Daily Language Practice*
- *Two-Minute Skill Drill*

Other Print Resources
- *Grammar and Composition Handbook*
- *Grammar Enrichment*
- *Grammar Practice*
- *Grammar Reteaching*
- *Grammar Workbook*
- *Tests with Answer Key and Rubrics*

Video
- *MindJogger Videoquizzes*

Software
- *Interactive Grammar and Language Workbook*
- *Presentation Plus!*
- *Testmaker*

Web Site
- *glencoe.com*

11.1 Simple Subjects and Simple Predicates

- A **sentence** is a group of words expressing a complete thought.

Every sentence has two basic parts, a *subject* and a *predicate.*

- The **subject** is the part of the sentence about which something is being said.
- The **predicate** is the part that says something about the subject.
- The **simple subject** is the key noun or pronoun (or word or group of words acting as a noun) that tells what a sentence is about.

The simple subject may be a compound noun consisting of more than one word.

- The **simple predicate** is the verb or verb phrase that expresses the essential thought about the subject of the sentence.

A simple predicate that is a verb phrase consists of the verb and any helping verbs.

SIMPLE SUBJECT	SIMPLE PREDICATE
Kelly Clarkson	will perform.
Owls	were hooting.
Alex Rodriguez	ran.
Things	change.

The simple subject is found by asking *who?* or *what?* about the verb.

Exercise 1 Identifying Simple Subjects and Predicates

Write each simple subject and each simple predicate. Underline the simple predicates.

The Yo-Yo

1. Donald Duncan was an American inventor.
2. He founded a toy company in the 1920s.
3. A popular Duncan toy was the yo-yo.
4. The yo-yo is a double disc with a string between the discs.
5. The yo-yo moves up and down the string.
6. Duncan used a yo-yo from the Philippines as a model.
7. Prehistoric Filipino hunters used yo-yos as weapons.
8. *Yo-yo* means "to return" in Filipino.
9. The ancient Filipino people had made their yo-yos of stone.
10. Since the 1950s, Duncan has been making yo-yos out of plastic.

Parts of a Sentence

Resource Manager

Planning Resources
- *Lesson Plans*

Transparencies
- *Bellringer*
- *Daily Language Practice*

Other Print Resources
- *Grammar and Composition Handbook*
- *Grammar Enrichment,* p. 9
- *Grammar Practice,* p. 9
- *Grammar Reteaching,* p. 9
- *Grammar Workbook,* Lesson 12

Focus

Lesson Overview

Objective

- To use simple subjects and simple predicates correctly

Bellringer
Daily Language Activity

When students enter the classroom, have this assignment on the board: *Write these sentences, circling the simple subject and underlining the simple predicate.*

I walked.	*Fido howled.*
March arrived.	*Ice floats.*

Encourage students to ask questions for clarification and to explain their answers.

See also *Daily Language Practice*

Teach

Teaching Tip

The predicate is a comment on the subject of a sentence.

Practice and Assess

Answers: Exercise 1

1. Donald Duncan <u>was</u>; **2.** He <u>founded</u>; **3.** toy <u>was</u>; **4.** yo-yo <u>is</u>; **5.** yo-yo <u>moves</u>; **6.** Duncan <u>used</u>; **7.** hunters <u>used</u>; **8.** *Yo-yo* <u>means</u>; **9.** people <u>had made</u>; **10.** Duncan <u>has been making</u>

Close

Discuss how understanding subjects and predicates can help students in their writing. Have students summarize their ideas in their journal.

Focus

Lesson Overview

Objective

- To identify and create complete subjects and complete predicates

Bellringer

Daily Language Activity

As students enter the classroom, have this assignment on the board: *Write a sentence using the word* truck *as the subject and the word* chugged *as its verb.*

See also *Daily Language Practice*

Teach

Two-Minute Skill Drill

Have students identify the complete predicate: *The music on the radio was so loud that it rattled our windows.*

See also *Two-Minute Skill Drill Transparency 11.2*

Practice and Assess

Answers: Exercise 2

1. The . . . Virginia—has . . . system.
2. Virginia . . . parks—offer . . . Bay.
3. Virginia's lakes—contain . . . bream.
4. Boats—can . . . months.
5. Canoes—are . . . places.
6. . . . visitors—can . . . parks.
7. The . . . trails—gives . . . terrain.
8. Hilly . . . areas—can . . . trails.
9. Some trails—lead . . . Trail.
10. Many families—explore . . . horseback.
11. Certain parks—have . . . rental.
12. The . . . system—provides . . . facilities.
13. Campgrounds—are . . . settings.
14. Some parks—have . . . history.
15. Parents—enjoy . . . children.

11.2 Complete Subjects and Complete Predicates

. . .was hooting in the night?

Parts of a Sentence

In most sentences the meaning of the simple subject and the simple predicate is expanded or modified by the addition of other words and phrases.

- The **complete subject** consists of the simple subject and all the words that modify it.
- The **complete predicate** consists of the simple predicate, or verb, and all the words that modify it or complete its meaning.

COMPLETE SUBJECT	COMPLETE PREDICATE
Talented Kelly Clarkson	will perform her biggest hits.
Large owls with bright eyes	were hooting loudly in the dark forest.
The speedy Alex Rodriguez	ran all the way home from first base on a double.
Many things	change daily.

Exercise 2 Identifying Complete Subjects and Predicates

Write the following sentences on your paper. Underline each complete subject once and each complete predicate twice.

Virginia State Parks

1. The state of Virginia has a fine park system.
2. Virginia state parks offer access to lakes, rivers, and the Chesapeake Bay.
3. Virginia's lakes contain largemouth bass, trout, and bream.
4. Boats can be rented only in the summer months.
5. Canoes are available in many places.
6. Frequent visitors can purchase season tickets for state parks.
7. The variety of trails gives hikers access to many different kinds of terrain.
8. Hilly and flat areas can be reached on the various trails.
9. Some trails lead to the Appalachian Trail.
10. Many families explore the Virginia countryside by horseback.
11. Certain parks have facilities for horse rental.
12. The Virginia state park system provides numerous camping facilities.
13. Campgrounds are located in many different settings.
14. Some parks have on-site exhibits about Virginia's rich history.
15. Parents enjoy these exhibits with their children.

Resource Manager

Planning Resources

- *Lesson Plans*

Transparencies

- *Bellringer*
- *Daily Language Practice*
- *Two-Minute Skill Drill*

Other Print Resources

- *Grammar and Composition Handbook*
- *Grammar Reteaching,* p. 9
- *Grammar Workbook,* Lesson 13

Exercise 3 Identifying Complete and Simple Subjects and Predicates

Copy each of the following sentences, and draw a vertical line between the complete subject and the complete predicate. Then underline the simple subject once and the simple predicate twice.

SAMPLE ANSWER An important event | sparked the civil rights movement in the United States.

Rosa Lee Parks, a Woman of Courage

[1]Rosa Lee Parks made history in Montgomery, Alabama, in 1955. [2]She boarded a bus there late one December day. [3]Parks took a seat at the front of the African American section of a segregated bus. [4]More people entered the crowded bus. [5]The driver ordered Parks to give her seat to a white man. [6]She ignored his orders courageously. [7]The police arrested Parks for her action. [8]The African American community of Montgomery conducted a year-long boycott of the city buses in protest. [9]A Supreme Court decision in November 1956 made segregation on all public transportation illegal. [10]Many people consider Parks the catalyst of the modern civil rights movement.

Exercise 4 Expanding Subjects and Predicates

Expand each of the following sentences by adding words and phrases to both the simple subject and the simple predicate. Write your sentence. Then underline the simple predicate in each sentence.

SAMPLE Sky darkened.
ANSWER The blue sky darkened slowly to indigo.

1. Sun set.
2. Night fell.
3. Darkness descended.
4. Frogs croaked.
5. Stars shone.
6. Moon rose.
7. Owls hooted.
8. Possums skulked.
9. People slept.
10. Wind howled.
11. Leaves rustled.
12. Curtains fluttered.
13. Train rattled.
14. Baby cried.
15. Sky lightened.
16. Rooster crowed.
17. Dog barked.
18. Workers left.
19. Cars honked.
20. Day began.

Parts of a Sentence

MEETING INDIVIDUAL NEEDS English Language Learners

Using Pictures

Write *The bird was flying* on the board.Tell students to draw the subject (the *bird*). Then add descriptors, such as *The red bird with the worm.* As students draw their pictures, point out that the subject is still the *bird* and that the complete subject is the *bird* plus the details.

Practice and Assess

Answers: Exercise 3

1. Rosa Lee Parks—made
2. She—boarded
3. Parks—took
4. people—entered
5. driver—ordered
6. She—ignored
7. police—arrested
8. community of Montgomery—conducted
9. decision in November 1956—made
10. people—consider

Answers: Exercise 4

Answers will vary, but some suggestions are given below.

1. The bright sun set in the west.
2. In winter, night fell very early.
3. Total darkness descended on our camp.
4. Each night, frogs croaked a hoarse hello.
5. Millions of stars shone in the sky.
6. The moon rose over the trees.
7. The brown owls hooted loudly.
8. The possums skulked away empty-handed.
9. Few people slept that night.
10. A blustery wind howled outside.
11. Brown leaves rustled in the wind.
12. Lace curtains fluttered in the breeze.
13. The huge train rattled over the tracks.
14. The little baby cried uncontrollably.
15. The morning sky lightened quickly.
16. The proud rooster crowed noisily.
17. The frisky dog barked at cars.
18. All the workers left early.
19. The stalled cars honked noisily.
20. Another day began unceremoniously.

Additional Resources

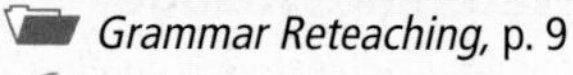
Grammar Reteaching, p. 9

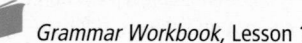

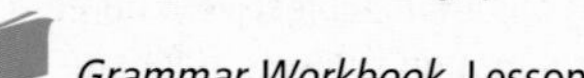
Grammar Workbook, Lesson 13

Close

Ask students to write a paragraph explaining how to embellish their simple subjects and simple predicates to make their writing more powerful.

Focus

Lesson Overview

Objectives

- To identify compound subjects and compound predicates
- To use compound subjects and compound predicates correctly in writing

Bellringer
Daily Language Activity

When students enter the classroom, have this assignment on the board: *Underline the simple subjects once and the simple predicates twice in the following sentences: Steve and George are on the baseball team. They bat and pitch during practice.*

See also *Daily Language Practice*

Motivating Activity

After volunteers share their answers to the Bellringer, challenge students to think of other sentences with two subjects or two verbs.

Teach

Compound Subjects

Teaching Tip

A good way to help students identify compound subjects joined with *and* is by pronoun substitution. Compound subjects joined with *and* can always be replaced by plural subject pronouns—for example: *Eagles and owls* hunt for food. *They* hunt for food.

Cross-reference: Usage

For information about subject-verb agreement with compound subjects, refer students to Lesson 16.5, pp. 616–617.

11.3 Compound Subjects and Compound Predicates

A sentence may have more than one simple subject or more than one simple predicate.

Compound Subjects

■ A **compound subject** is made up of two or more simple subjects that are joined by a conjunction and have the same verb.

The conjunctions most commonly used to join the subjects in a compound subject are *and* and *or.*

Peas and **carrots** are colorful vegetables.

Peas or **carrots** are my favorite vegetable.

Correlative conjunctions may be used to join compound subjects.

Neither the **tomato** nor the **pepper** grows underground.

Both the **tomato** and the **pepper** are rich in vitamin C.

When more than two words are included in the compound subject, the conjunction is usually used only between the last two words, and the words are separated by commas.

Tomatoes, carrots, and **peppers** are healthful.

Exercise 5 Identifying Compound Subjects

Write the compound subject in each of the following sentences.

The Planets in Our Solar System

1. Jupiter and Saturn are the largest planets.
2. Mercury, Venus, and Earth are the warmest planets in our solar system.
3. Mars or one of Jupiter's moons could harbor life forms.
4. Both Jupiter and Saturn have many moons.
5. Neither Mercury nor Venus has moons.

Exercise 6 Expanding Subjects

(a) Write five sentences. In each one use a simple subject and a simple predicate.
(b) Expand each sentence by making the subject compound.

SAMPLE ANSWER **a.** John Hancock signed the Declaration of Independence.
b. John Hancock and John Adams signed the Declaration of Independence.

Resource Manager

Planning Resources

- *Lesson Plans*

Transparencies

- *Bellringer*
- *Daily Language Practice*

Other Print Resources

- *Grammar and Composition Handbook*
- *Grammar Enrichment,* p. 9
- *Grammar Practice,* p. 9
- *Grammar Workbook,* Lesson 14

Compound Predicates

- A **compound predicate** (or **compound verb**) is made up of two or more verbs or verb phrases that are joined by a conjunction and have the same subject.

Horses **gallop** and **charge.**

Nina **inserted** the memory card, **looked** through the viewfinder, and **snapped** the first photograph.

In compound verbs that contain verb phrases, the helping verb may or may not be repeated before the second verb.

Sea gulls **will glide** or **swoop** down to the ocean.

A sentence may have both a compound subject and a compound predicate.

S S P P

Butterflies and **hummingbirds dart** and **dip** in the air.

Exercise 7 Identifying Compound Predicates

Write the compound predicate in each of the following sentences.

Dogs and Water

1. Some dogs swim and play in the water as a recreational activity.
2. Other dogs jump into water but then immediately return to shore.
3. Fearful dogs may scratch or whine.
4. Confident dogs can sit quietly in a canoe and enjoy the scenery.
5. I have swum and played in the water with many dogs.
6. Retrievers jump into the water readily and fetch objects for their owners.
7. Some dogs climb up ladders, dive off docks, or rescue people from the water.
8. Water play relaxes dogs and offers them excellent exercise.
9. Exercise increases energy and improves the dog's health.
10. Many dogs may not recognize polluted water and, unfortunately, may drink it.

Exercise 8 Expanding Predicates

(a) Write five sentences. In each one use a simple subject and a simple predicate.
(b) Expand each sentence by making the predicate compound.

SAMPLE ANSWER **a.** A businessperson bought the Nettlehurst Company.
b. A businessperson bought and sold the Nettlehurst Company.

Compound Predicates

Teaching Tip

Use the following sentence to point out the difference between *compound* predicates and *complete* predicates: *Sam made coffee and poured it.* The compound predicate is *made, poured;* the complete predicate is *made coffee and poured it.*

Practice and Assess

Answers: Exercise 5

1. Jupiter, Saturn
2. Mercury, Venus, Earth
3. Mars, one
4. Jupiter, Saturn
5. Mercury, Venus

Answers: Exercise 6

Answers will vary, but a sample is given below:

a. Snow fell on the ground.
b. Snow and sleet fell on the ground.

Answers: Exercise 7

1. swim, play
2. jump, return
3. may scratch, whine
4. can sit, enjoy
5. have swum, played
6. jump, fetch
7. climb, dive, rescue
8. relaxes, offers
9. increases, improves
10. may recognize, may drink

Answers: Exercise 8

Answers will vary, but a sample is given below:

a. The wind roared.
b. The wind roared and shook the house.

MEETING INDIVIDUAL NEEDS **Learning Disabled**

Separating Compounds

To help students understand that the parts of a compound predicate are grammatically parallel, you might have them rewrite a sentence with a compound predicate as two individual sentences. For example, *Horses gallop and charge* could be rewritten as *Horses gallop* and *Horses charge.* **L1**

Practice and Assess

Answers: Exercise 9

1. Nez Percé—lived, flourished
2. government—ordered, assigned
3. government—wanted
4. leader—was
5. Chief Joseph, men, women, children—packed, left
6. group—encountered, killed
7. Chief Joseph, advisers—foresaw
8. Chief Joseph—sought
9. He, people—fought, surrendered
10. Nez Percé—accepted, settled

Answers: Exercise 10

Answers will vary. Some suggestions follow.

1. American history and literature are taught and tested in schools.
2. Boys and girls in kindergarten learn and practice simple mathematical concepts.
3. Both adults and young children play and enjoy word games.
4. The school lunch period and recess never start soon enough or last long enough.
5. Coaches and team captains will encourage players and teach them useful strategies.
6. Basic algebra and science are introduced in middle school and continued in high school.
7. Special projects and papers improve students' research skills and writing.
8. Computers and cell phones will be smaller and faster in the future.
9. Geography and history teach about other cultures and people.
10. A longer school year and dress codes remain controversial topics and cause much discussion.

Additional Resources

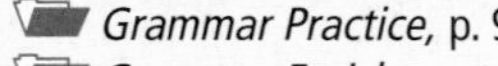
Grammar Practice, p. 9

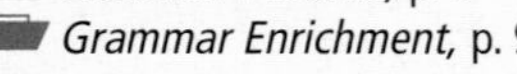
Grammar Enrichment, p. 9

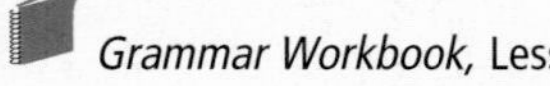
Grammar Workbook, Lesson 14

Close

One half of the class can write sentences with compound subjects, and the other can write sentences with compound predicates. Students can exchange papers and underline the compound subjects and predicates.

Exercise 9 Identifying Subjects and Predicates

Copy each of the following sentences on your paper. For each sentence, underline the simple subject(s) once and the simple predicate(s) twice. Note that some subjects and predicates are compound.

Chief Joseph

1. The Nez Percé lived and flourished for centuries in the Northwest.
2. The federal government ordered them away from their lands in 1877 and assigned them to a reservation in Oregon.
3. The government wanted land for many new white settlers and their families.
4. The leader of the Nez Percé at the time was Chief Joseph, a wise and compassionate man.
5. Chief Joseph and the Nez Percé men, women, and children packed their belongings and left their homes.
6. A small group of Nez Percé encountered and killed several white settlers during their journey.
7. Chief Joseph and his advisers foresaw a long and bloody battle with the United States Army as a result of this incident.
8. Chief Joseph therefore sought freedom for the Nez Percé in Canada.
9. He and his outnumbered people fought courageously but finally surrendered to the United States Army just forty miles from the Canadian border.
10. The Nez Percé accepted land from the United States government on a reservation in Oklahoma and settled there in 1878.

Exercise 10 Writing Compound Subjects and Predicates

On your paper, expand each of the following sentences by making both the subject and the predicate compound. (You may need to make other changes, too.)

SAMPLE Birds fly.
ANSWER Birds and bats fly and eat insects.

School Subjects

1. American history is taught in schools.
2. Children in kindergarten practice simple mathematical concepts.
3. Young children play word games.
4. The school lunch period never lasts long enough.
5. Coaches will teach players useful strategies.
6. Basic algebra is introduced in middle school.
7. Special projects improve students' research skills.
8. Computers will be smaller in the future.
9. Geography teaches about other cultures.
10. A longer school year remains a controversial topic.

11.4 Order of Subject and Predicate

In most sentences in English, the subject comes before the predicate. There are exceptions, however, to this usual word order.

Commands

In commands and requests, the subject is usually not stated. The predicate is the entire sentence. The pronoun *you* is understood to be the subject.

[You] **Run**!   [You] **Give** it to me.   [You] Please **be** careful.

Questions

Questions frequently begin with a verb or helping verb or the words *who, whom, what, when, where, why* or *how.*

Was she right?

Have you **read** Gary Soto's stories?

Whom did he invite?

In both of these cases, the subject generally follows the verb or helping verb. To find the subject of a question, rearrange the words to form a statement.

SUBJECT	PREDICATE
She	was right.
You	have read Gary Soto's stories.
He	did invite whom.

Exercise 11 **Identifying Subjects and Predicates in Questions and Commands**

Write the simple subject and the simple predicate of each of the following sentences. (Remember that the simple predicate may include one or more helping verbs.) If the sentence is a command, write (*You*) as the subject.

Drivers' Licenses

1. Where are drivers' licenses issued?
2. Go to the Department of Motor Vehicles.
3. What kind of preparations should I make?
4. Study the manual carefully.
5. Practice good driving skills every day for about four months before taking the test.

Focus

Lesson Overview

Objective

- To recognize and use normal subject-predicate word order unless there is a valid reason for deviating from that order

Bellringer
Daily Language Activity

When students enter the classroom, have this assignment on the board: *Write the subject and predicate of each of these sentences:*

Look out!
What is this?
Here is my ring.
Up the stairs we raced.

See also *Daily Language Practice*

Motivating Activity

Discuss students' answers to the Bellringer activity. Encourage students to ask questions to clarify understanding. Explain that in this lesson, they will learn about the order of subjects and predicates in commands, questions, and inverted sentences.

Teach

Commands and Questions

☑ Grammar Tip

Often questions that begin with *who* or *what* follow normal word order: *Who answered the question?* The words *who* or *what* are pronouns that may function as subjects.

Practice and Assess

Answers: Exercise 11

1. licenses are issued
2. (You) go
3. I should make
4. (You) study
5. (You) practice

Resource Manager

Planning Resources
- *Lesson Plans*

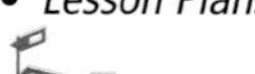

Transparencies
- *Bellringer*
- *Daily Language Practice*

Other Print Resources
- *Grammar and Composition Handbook*
- *Grammar Enrichment,* p. 9
- *Grammar Workbook,* Lesson 15

Teach

Inverted Order

☑ Grammar Tip

The use of the word *there* is the most common deviation from the normal subject-predicate word order. *There* points out the existence of something, for example: *There is a fly in my soup.* The verb *is* comes in front of the subject *fly. There* sentences are a major source of subject-verb agreement error. In spoken language many tend to use a singular verb—*there is*—even with a plural subject. Many speakers think of *there is* or *there was* as a fixed unit, so the plural form—*there are* or *there were*—sounds wrong. Have students review a recent writing assignment for *There* sentences that may have subject-verb agreement problems. Ask students to revise as needed.

Practice and Assess

Answers: Exercise 12

1. The coral snake crawled from under a rock.
2. A water moccasin swam around the bend.
3. Six small water snakes wiggled in the stream.
4. A dozen were hiding along the shore.
5. Only two types of poisonous snakes live in the United States.
6. Coral snakes and pit vipers are included in the poisonous category.
7. The deadly coral snake lives on the low-lying plains of the American Southeast.
8. Circular bands of different colors are on the coral snake's body.
9. Similar but incomplete color bands are on some nonpoisonous snakes.
10. The notorious rattlesnake is among the pit vipers in the United States.

Inverted Order

At times a sentence is written in **inverted order**—that is, with the predicate before the subject. This reversal of the usual order can add emphasis to the subject.

PREDICATE	SUBJECT
Across the field **galloped**	the three **horses.**
In the distance **ran**	a **river.**

Remember, a word in a prepositional phrase is never the subject.

When the word *there* or *here* begins a sentence and is followed by a form of the verb *be,* the subject follows the verb. The words *there* and *here* are almost never the subject of a sentence.

PREDICATE	SUBJECT
There **is**	a **chill** in the air.
Here **are**	my **thoughts** on the subject.

To find a subject in an inverted sentence, ask "Who?" or "What?"

What galloped across the field? The three horses galloped.
What is in the air? A chill is in the air.

Exercise 12 Reordering Inverted Sentences

On your paper, rewrite each of the following sentences so that the complete subject comes before the predicate. Then underline the simple subject once and the simple predicate twice. (Remember that both subjects and predicates may be compound.)

Poisonous Snakes of the United States

1. From under a rock crawled the coral snake.
2. Around the bend swam a water moccasin.
3. In the stream wiggled six small water snakes.
4. There were a dozen hiding along the shore.
5. In the United States live only two types of poisonous snakes.
6. Included in the poisonous category are coral snakes and pit vipers.
7. On the low-lying plains of the American Southeast lives the deadly coral snake.
8. There are circular bands of different colors on the coral snake's body.
9. On some nonpoisonous snakes are similar but incomplete color bands.
10. Among the pit vipers in the United States is the notorious rattlesnake.

MEETING INDIVIDUAL NEEDS English Language Learners

Understanding Word Order

To help students understand inverted sentences, place each word in the following sentence on a card: THE BOAT SAILED DOWN THE RIVER. Then ask students to rearrange the words to form a second sentence that means the same thing, for example: DOWN THE RIVER SAILED THE BOAT.

Exercise 13 Recognizing the Order of Subject and Predicate

Copy each of the following sentences. For each sentence, draw a vertical line between the complete subject and the complete predicate, and label each.

SAMPLE ANSWERS

(P) | Look at that painting.

(P) On the opposite wall is | (S) another work of art.

(P) There is | (S) the loveliest statue in the museum.

An African Art Exhibit

1. A visit to an African art exhibit can be a fine educational experience.
2. Many museums offer temporary shows in addition to their permanent collections.
3. Call ahead for information about special displays of African art.
4. Where are the best examples of beadwork, basketry, woodwork, leatherwork, and metalwork?
5. In some museums are beautiful displays of African textiles.
6. Excellent craftsmanship is found in decorative ornaments and ceremonial objects.
7. Here is a Nigerian bronze sculpture of a priest-king.
8. This ancient civilization used sculptures of former kings in memorial rites for the dead.
9. Look at this elaborately carved ceremonial mask.
10. Dancers wore such masks as these at coronations and royal funerals.
11. There are still more African artifacts of great complexity.
12. On the shelf to the left sits a seventeenth-century ivory bracelet from the kingdom of Benin.
13. Notice the intricate carvings of kings on the antique bracelet.
14. From the workshops of Benin came some of Africa's finest bronze figures.
15. Among the most ancient African art objects are masks and ancestor figures.
16. Terra-cotta is a kind of earthenware.
17. Superb bronze and terra-cotta heads were made in Nigeria from the tenth to the fifteenth centuries.
18. In the museum's exhibit there are even older examples of African art.
19. Prehistoric cave paintings were discovered in the Tassili Plateau in the Sahara.
20. African people of today still create many such exquisite art objects.

Exercise 14 Writing Sentences

Write five sentences about a topic of your choice. Make at least one sentence a question, one a command, one a statement beginning with *here* or *there,* and one a statement in which a prepositional phrase and the verb precede the subject.

Answers: Exercise 13

1. (S) A visit to an African art exhibit | (P) can be . . .
2. (S) Many museums | (P) offer temporary shows . . .
3. (S) (You) | (P) Call ahead for information . . .
4. (P) Where are | (S) the best examples . . .
5. (P) In some museums are | (S) beautiful displays . . .
6. (S) Excellent craftsmanship | (P) is found . . .
7. (P) Here is | (S) a Nigerian bronze . . .
8. (S) This ancient civilization | (P) used sculptures . . .
9. (S) (You) | (P) Look at this . . .
10. (S) Dancers | (P) wore . . .
11. (P) There are | (S) still more African . . .
12. (P) On the . . . sits | (S) a . . . bracelet . . .
13. (S) (You) | (P) Notice the intricate . . .
14. (P) From the workshops of Benin came | (S) some . . .
15. (P) Among the most . . . objects are | (S) masks and ancestor figures.
16. (S) Terra-cotta | (P) is a kind of earthenware.
17. (S) Superb bronze . . . heads | (P) were made . . .
18. (P) In . . . are | (S) even older examples . . .
19. (S) Prehistoric cave paintings | (P) were . . .
20. (S) African people of today | (P) still create many . . .

Answers: Exercise 14

Answers will vary. Check that students use correct word order and that they have one question, one command, one *here* or *there* statement, and one statement in which a prepositional phrase and the verb precede the subject.

Additional Resources

Grammar Enrichment, p. 9

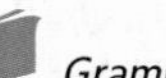

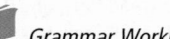

Grammar Workbook, Lesson 15

Close

Have students work together to write a paragraph that begins with a *There* sentence, contains a command, and ends with a question. Then discuss the word order in the sentences.

Focus

Lesson Overview

Objective

- To identify and use correctly the four types of complements

Bellringer
Daily Language Activity

When students enter the classroom, have this assignment on the board: *Write down what was given and to whom in the following sentences: I gave you my book. We gave assistance to the motorist.* Discuss the function in the sentence of each word the students identify.

See also *Daily Language Practice*

Teach

Direct Objects

☑ Grammar Tip

A direct object occurs only after a transitive action verb. The direct object answers the questions *what?* or *whom?*

Practice and Assess

Answers: Exercise 15

1. copied; style **2.** see; vaqueros **3.** wore; sombrero **4.** kept; snow, rain, sun **5.** modeled; hat **6.** roped; cows **7.** lassoed; cows **8.** protected; shins, thighs **9.** put; chaps **10.** roam; plains, *pampas* **11.** provide; food **12.** share; qualities **13.** wear; hats, and chaps **14.** do; sorts **15.** would tell; tales

11.5 Complements

■ A **complement** is a word or group of words that completes the meaning of a verb.

There are four kinds of complements: *direct objects, indirect objects, object complements,* and *subject complements.*

Direct Objects

■ A **direct object** answers the question *what?* or *whom?* after an action verb.

The subject of a sentence usually performs the action indicated by the verb. That action may be directed toward or received by someone or something—the direct object. Nouns, pronouns, or words acting as nouns may serve as direct objects. Only transitive verbs have direct objects.

Carlos served **dinner.** [Carlos served *what?*]

Marie admires **him** deeply. [Marie admires *whom?*]

Carlos served a Mexican **dinner** and a fabulous **dessert.** [Carlos served *what?*]

Exercise 15 Identifying Direct Objects

Write the action verb in each sentence. Then write any direct objects and underline them.

U.S. Cowboys

1. U.S. cowboys copied the style of Mexican cowboys.
2. Historians see the Mexican vaqueros as the first real cowboys.
3. At all times of the year, the vaquero wore a floppy sombrero.
4. This large hat kept snow, rain, or sun off his face.
5. The U.S. cowboy modeled his own hat on the Mexican sombrero.
6. During branding season the vaqueros roped cows with a sturdy riata.
7. Cowboys in the United States lassoed cows with a lariat (from the Spanish word *la riata*).
8. Mexican cowboys protected their shins and thighs with leather chaparejos.
9. In a similar fashion, U.S. cowboys put leather chaps over their pants.
10. Cowboys also roam the grassy plains, or *pampas,* of Argentina and Uruguay.
11. These plains provide excellent food for cattle or sheep.
12. The cowboys, or *gauchos,* of these areas share many qualities with U.S. cowboys.
13. For example, *gauchos* wear hats and chaps for protection against the elements.
14. Cowboys in any country do the same sorts of jobs.
15. Cowboys from North and South America would probably tell very similar tales.

Resource Manager

Planning Resources
- *Lesson Plans*

Transparencies
- *Bellringer*
- *Daily Language Practice*
- *Two-Minute Skill Drill*

Other Print Resources
- *Grammar and Composition Handbook*
- *Grammar Enrichment,* pp. 10–12
- *Grammar Practice,* pp. 10–12
- *Grammar Reteaching,* pp. 10–12
- *Grammar Workbook,* Lesson 16

Indirect Objects

- An **indirect object** answers the question *to whom? for whom? to what?* or *for what?* after an action verb.

In most cases, a sentence may have an indirect object only if it has a direct object. The indirect object will always come between the verb and the direct object.

Tyrone served his **sisters** dinner. [Tyrone served dinner *to whom?*]

Greta saved **him** a seat. [Greta saved a seat *for whom?*]

Kim saved **Rosa** and **José** seats. [Kim saved seats *for whom?*]

The children gave the worthy **charity** all their savings. [The children gave all their savings *to what?*]

Marsha gave the **game** her best effort. [Marsha gave her best effort *for what?*]

Kim saved Rosa

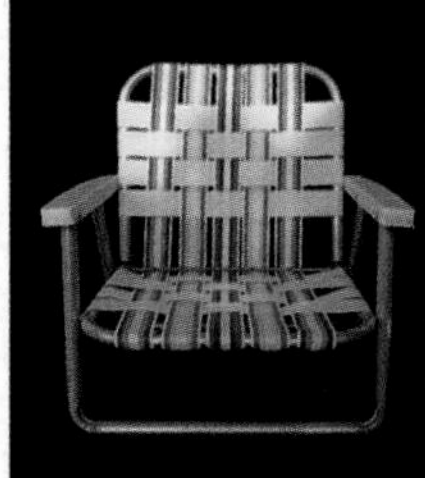

a seat.

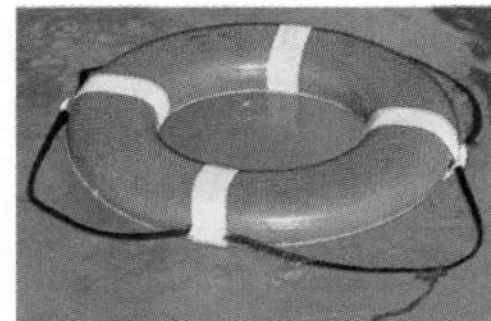

Kim saved Rosa.

Exercise 16 Identifying Indirect Objects

For each sentence, write the direct object, and list any indirect object(s). (Not all sentences have an indirect object.) Label the objects *DO* and *IO* for *direct object* and *indirect object.*

Careers in Sports

1. Professional sports offer many careers.
2. Television or radio sportscasters broadcast sports events.
3. A good sports announcer gives fans play-by-play descriptions of the game.
4. The announcer tells them anecdotes.
5. Reporters and photographers also cover athletic competitions.
6. Newspapers give their readers sports coverage.
7. Teaching may give a person satisfaction.
8. Managers, coaches, and trainers all bring teams success.
9. Sports also give referees, umpires, and doctors jobs.
10. Athletic events even give hot-dog and peanut vendors work.
11. Some boys and girls contemplate sports careers at a very young age.
12. They give famous basketball stars attention.
13. They show their coaches their dedication to their sports.
14. They tell their friends endless stories about their skill on the court or field.
15. Unfortunately, few young athletes will achieve success as professionals.

Enrichment and Extension

Identifying Indirect Objects

A good way to identify an indirect object is to see whether it can be paraphrased as a prepositional phrase beginning with *to* or *for*. For example, you can show that *cat* is the indirect object in the sentence *I gave the cat some water,* because you can replace *cat* with the prepositional phrase *to the cat: I gave some water to the cat*. See *Grammar Reteaching,* p. 10. **L2**

Teach

Indirect Objects

Grammar Tip

A sentence with a transitive verb usually has a direct object. A transitive verb can be followed by both a direct object and an indirect object.

Cross-reference: Grammar

For a review of how to identify action verbs and transitive verbs, refer students to Lesson 10.3, pp. 452–460.

Two-Minute Skill Drill

Write these sentences on the board and have students list the indirect objects. Discuss students' answers. Remind students to provide effective feedback.

Ernesto fed his dog a meal.

Mia saved me a space.

I gave the canvasser money.

We offered aid to the hiker.

You asked me questions.

See also *Two-Minute Skill Drill Transparency 11.5*

Practice and Assess

Answers: Exercise 16

1. careers DO
2. events DO
3. descriptions DO; fans IO
4. anecdotes DO; them IO
5. competitions DO
6. coverage DO; readers IO
7. satisfaction DO; person IO
8. success DO; teams IO
9. jobs DO; referees, umpires, and doctors IO
10. work DO; vendors IO
11. careers DO
12. attention DO; stars IO
13. dedication DO; coaches IO
14. stories DO; friends IO
15. success DO

11.5

Teach

Object Complements

Grammar Tip

Object complements differ from indirect objects in two ways: First, object complements can be nouns or adjectives, whereas indirect objects must be nouns or pronouns. Second, unlike indirect objects, object complements can never be replaced with a prepositional phrase beginning with *to* or *for.*

Practice and Assess

Answers: Exercise 17

1. president
2. extraordinary
3. composer
4. stupendous
5. priority
6. composer; genius
7. (no object complement)
8. sublime
9. favorite
10. exquisite

Answers: Exercise 18

Answers will vary, but some suggestions are given below:

1. terrifying—adj.
2. theirs—pron.
3. their home—n.
4. limitless—adj.
5. a playground—n.

Object Complements

■ An **object complement** answers the question *what?* after a direct object. That is, it *completes* the meaning of the direct object by identifying or describing it.

Object complements occur only in sentences with direct objects *and* only in those sentences with action verbs that have the general meaning of "make" or "consider," such as the following:

appoint	elect	render	consider	name
declare	make	call	find	think

An object complement usually follows a direct object. It may be an adjective, a noun, or a pronoun.

Residents find the park **peaceful.** [adjective]

Katie appointed me **treasurer** and **cook.** [nouns]

My grandmother considers the property **hers.** [pronoun]

Exercise 17 Identifying Object Complements

Write the object complement(s) that appear in the following sentences. (Not every sentence has an object complement.)

Musical Tastes

1. The Music Club has appointed Felipe president.
2. He finds that honor extraordinary.
3. One member, Maya, thinks Mozart the best composer.
4. Another member, Diane, considers Bach stupendous.
5. Felipe, Maya, and Diane make music a priority.
6. Diane calls Verdi a great composer and a musical genius.
7. Felipe likes chamber music better than opera.
8. Maya thinks opera sublime.
9. Diane names the basso singer Justino Díaz her favorite.
10. Maya finds the voice of Kiri Te Kanawa exquisite.

Exercise 18 Using Object Complements

On your paper, complete the following sentences by writing object complements. Then write the letter *A, N,* or *P* to identify the object complement as an *adjective, noun,* or *pronoun.*

1. The fearful swimmers found the ocean _____.
2. Generations of fishers consider the ocean _____.
3. Sailors make the ocean _____.
4. Early explorers thought the ocean _____.
5. Surfers call the ocean _____.

Enrichment and Extension

Identifying Object Complements

One of the ways that object complements can be identified is by a paraphrase test. Most object complements can be paraphrased as an infinitive phrase. Here are two examples: *We elected her* ***president*** becomes *We elected her* ***to be president.*** *I consider the plan* ***risky*** becomes *I consider the plan* ***to be risky.*** Encourage pairs of students to work together to write sentences with object complements. Encourage them to make the sentences as hard as possible. Then they can exchange papers with other pairs and identify the complements the others have written. **L3**

Subject Complements

- A **subject complement** follows a subject and a linking verb and identifies or describes the subject.

There are two kinds of subject complements: *predicate nominatives* and *predicate adjectives.*

- A **predicate nominative** is a noun or pronoun that follows a linking verb and points back to the subject to rename it or to identify it further.

Sopranos are **singers.**

Clearly the star of the opera was **she.**

Many current opera stars are **Italians** or **Spaniards.**

Predicate nominatives are usually found in sentences that contain forms of the linking verb *be*. A few other linking verbs (for example, *become* and *remain*) can be followed by a predicate nominative.

Julia became both a **musician** and an **actress.**

That experience remains a cherished **memory** for me.

- A **predicate adjective** follows a linking verb and points back to the subject and further describes it.

Ballerinas are **graceful.**

Ballerinas must be extremely **dedicated.**

Most ballerinas seem **intense** and **hardworking.**

Predicate adjectives may follow any linking verb.

I felt very **carefree.**

Only a few marathoners appear **fresh** even now.

The water tasted **delicious.**

I grew increasingly **tired.**

My sister appeared **weary.**

My friend Tanya looked **exhausted** but **happy.**

The musty room smelled **bad.**

The band sounded **loud.**

The noise became **louder** as we approached the finish line.

Teach

Subject Complements

Grammar Tip

The complements that follow linking verbs are called subject complements. If the subject complement is a noun or a pronoun, the noun or pronoun is called a predicate nominative. If the subject complement is an adjective, the adjective is called a predicate adjective.

Teaching Tip

Explain that direct objects, indirect objects, and object complements are all complements of action verbs; they follow transitive verbs. Subject complements, on the other hand, are used after linking verbs.

Cross-reference: Grammar

For a review of how to identify linking verbs, refer students to Lesson 10.3, pp. 452–460.

MEETING INDIVIDUAL NEEDS

English Language Learners

Identifying Predicate Nominatives

Predicate nominatives (unlike objects) always refer back to the subject. One way to identify a predicate nominative is to see whether the noun following the verb "equals" the subject. For example in the sentence *Biology is a science, Biology* is the same thing, or equals, *science*. If it does, then it is a predicate nominative. If the noun following a verb does not equal the subject, then it is a direct object. See *Grammar Reteaching,* pp. 10–12. Have students verify this method, using the example sentences on this page. **L1**

Practice and Assess

Answers: Exercise 19

1. one
2. student
3. (none)
4. (none)
5. word
6. candidate
7. victory
8. proponent
9. advocate
10. supporter

Answers: Exercise 20

1. gym; <u>ready</u>
2. tables; <u>beautiful</u>
3. portraits; <u>alive</u>
4. gazes; <u>lifelike</u>
5. music; <u>romantic</u>
6. All; <u>ravenous</u>
7. soup; <u>good</u>
8. food; <u>excellent</u>
9. students; <u>talkative</u>
10. chaperones; <u>sleepy</u>

Answers: Exercise 21

Answers will vary, but some suggestions are given below.

1. basketball—PN
2. glamorous—PA
3. highly paid stars—PN
4. poor—PA
5. the same—PN

Exercise 19 Identifying Predicate Nominatives

On your paper, write the predicate nominatives that appear in the following sentences. (Not all sentences contain predicate nominatives.)

Dwight D. Eisenhower

1. Dwight Eisenhower was one of seven sons.
2. Eisenhower was a student at West Point.
3. He graduated from the academy with the class of 1915.
4. During World War II, he rose to the rank of Supreme Allied Commander in Europe.
5. After that, Eisenhower's name became a household word.
6. He was the Republican presidential candidate in 1952.
7. His election was the first presidential victory for the GOP in twenty-four years.
8. Eisenhower was a proponent of "Modern Republicanism."
9. He remained an advocate of reducing the federal government's power.
10. He also was a supporter of higher minimum wages.

Exercise 20 Identifying Predicate Adjectives

On your paper, write each simple subject and each predicate adjective. Underline the predicate adjectives.

Dinner Is Served

1. The gym was ready for the class banquet.
2. The tables looked beautiful in the soft candlelight.
3. On the walls, portraits of the class members appeared almost alive.
4. Their unwavering gazes seemed lifelike.
5. The music of the combo sounded romantic.
6. All of the students felt ravenous.
7. The onion soup smelled especially good.
8. The food tasted excellent to all of the elegantly dressed diners.
9. The students remained unusually talkative throughout the meal.
10. The chaperones, however, grew sleepy rather early.

Exercise 21 Using Subject Complements

On your paper, complete the following sentences with nouns, pronouns, or adjectives. Write *PN* or *PA* to indicate if the complement you wrote is a *predicate nominative* or a *predicate adjective.*

1. The most popular sport, in my opinion, is _____.
2. The lifestyles of many prominent players seem _____.
3. Very few athletes become _____.
4. The great majority of athletes are _____.
5. Their lives remain _____.

Enrichment and Extension

Using Complements

This activity may help students sort out the kinds of complements: (1) direct object only; (2) indirect object plus direct object; (3) direct object plus object complement; (4) subject complement (either predicate adjective or predicate nominative). Have students match the following sentences to these complement patterns and discuss the reasons for their choices. *Mary knows the answer.* (pattern 1) *Mary told me the answer.* (pattern 2) *We found Mary's answer correct.* (pattern 3) *We considered her answers a gift.* (pattern 3) *Her answers were correct.* (pattern 4) **L2**

Exercise 22 **Identifying Subject Complements**

On your paper, write all the subject complements that appear in the following sentences. Write *predicate nominative* or *predicate adjective* to identify each. (Five sentences have more than one predicate nominative or predicate adjective.)

Japanese Flower Arrangements

[1]Flower arrangement is an ancient Japanese art. [2]This tradition grew popular in the sixth century. [3]Early flower arrangements were decorations for Buddhist temple altars. [4]Over the centuries the art of flower arrangement became increasingly specific. [5]Important materials in Japanese floral arrangement are leaves, stems, and branches. [6]The lines of the branches should be graceful and sleek. [7]In Western countries blossoms are generally the only important features. [8]The best Japanese floral arrangements look natural and colorful. [9]A Japanese florist must be a designer and an artist. [10]The art of Japanese flower arrangement is both simple and complex.

Exercise 23 **Identifying Complements**

On your paper, write the complements that appear in the following sentences. Next to each complement, write the kind of complement it is: *direct object, indirect object, object complement, predicate nominative,* or *predicate adjective.*

A Jazz Musician

1. Davenport, Iowa, was the hometown of Leon Bix Beiderbecke.
2. Mississippi riverboats passing by Davenport gave Bix Beiderbecke a taste for jazz.
3. Bix Beiderbecke played the cornet and the piano.
4. The cornet's sound is mellow and rich.
5. Bix Beiderbecke carried his cornet with him.
6. Beiderbecke's music attracted attention and praise.
7. Louis Armstrong called Beiderbecke's "In a Mist" immortal.
8. No one gave Bix any financial assistance for his musical career.
9. Beiderbecke's reputation is still great in music circles today.
10. In fact, many musicians consider him a true classic of American jazz.

Exercise 24 **Writing Sentences with Complements**

Write five sentences about a natural phenomenon, such as an eclipse, a thunderstorm, or a sunset. In each sentence, use at least one of the four kinds of complements: direct object, indirect object, object complement, or subject complement. Label the complements for each sentence that you write.

Answers: Exercise 22

1. art—PN
2. popular—PA
3. decorations—PN
4. specific—PA
5. leaves, stems, branches—PN
6. graceful, sleek—PA
7. features—PN
8. natural, colorful—PA
9. designer, artist—PN
10. simple, complex—PA

Answers: Exercise 23

1. hometown—PN
2. Bix Beiderbecke—IO; taste—DO
3. cornet, piano—DO
4. mellow, rich—PA
5. cornet—DO
6. attention and praise—DO
7. "In a Mist"—DO; immortal—OC
8. Bix—IO; assistance—DO
9. great—PA
10. him—DO; classic—OC

Answers: Exercise 24

Answers will vary. Sample:
The approaching thunderstorm made the sky [DO] dark [OC] and ominous [OC].

Additional Resources

Grammar Practice, pp. 10–12
Grammar Reteaching, pp. 10–12
Grammar Enrichment, pp. 10–12

Grammar Workbook, Lesson 16

Close

Remind students that varied sentence structure and length make the language in a passage more dramatic. Have them return to Exercise 22 and revise the *Japanese Flower Arrangements* paragraph, changing basic sentence patterns. Ask them to read aloud their revised versions and compare them to the original.

Teach

About the Literature

Explain that the unit Review features a passage from *Things Fall Apart,* a novel by the Nigerian writer Chinua Achebe. Also explain that the literature is followed by exercises based on the novel and on related topics. After students read the passage, initiate a discussion of the characters, the setting, and the mood of the excerpt. Then ask students to focus on the annotated elements of the passage. Discuss how each highlighted element functions within the sentence in which it appears, and ask students to determine which ones are or are not essential to the meaning of the passage.

Linking Grammar and Literature

Critical Thinking

Ask students to write a paragraph about life in a small village or town or about another theme of their choice. Direct them to use a variety of sentence elements: simple and compound subjects, simple and compound predicates, and a variety of objects and complements. Then have them read their paragraphs to the class. Ask students to discuss how using a variety of sentence structures can give rhythm and interest to their writing.

Listening and Speaking

Read aloud from the literary passage five sentences that do not contain subordinate clauses. Ask students to identify the simple subject and the simple predicate in each of the sentences. Encourage students to discuss any clues they could hear in the speaker's voice that made the simple subject and simple predicate easy to identify.

ASSESSMENT OPTIONS

Tests with Answer Key & Rubrics
Unit 11 Mastery Test, pp. 41–42

Testmaker
Unit 11 Mastery Test

UNIT 11

Grammar Review

Parts of the Sentence

A member of the Ibo tribe of eastern Nigeria, Chinua Achebe writes about his people in *Things Fall Apart.* Set in the Ibo village of Umuofia around the turn of the century, the novel chronicles the life of a proud young wrestler named Okonkwo. In this passage Okonkwo is just about to go to bed when he hears the town crier, who beats his metal drum and summons the men of the village to a meeting. The passage has been annotated to show some of the parts of sentences covered in this unit.

Literature Model

from Things Fall Apart

by Chinua Achebe

Okonkwo had just blown out the palm-oil lamp and stretched himself on his bamboo bed when he heard the *ogene* of the town crier piercing the still night air. *Gome, gome, gome, gome,* boomed the hollow metal. Then the crier gave his message, and at the end of it beat his instrument again. And this was the message. Every man of Umuofia was asked to gather at the market place tomorrow morning. Okonkwo wondered what was amiss, for he knew certainly that something was amiss. He had discerned a clear overtone of tragedy in the crier's voice, and even now he could still hear it as it grew dimmer and dimmer in the distance.

The night was very quiet. It was always quiet except on moonlight nights. Darkness held a vague terror for these people, even the bravest among them. Children were warned not to whistle at night for fear of evil spirits. Dangerous animals became even more sinister and uncanny in the dark. A snake was never called by its name at night, because it would hear. It was called a string. And so on this particular night as the crier's voice was gradually swallowed up in the distance, silence returned to the world, a vibrant silence made more intense by the universal trill of a million forest insects.

Direct object
Compound predicate
Subject complement (predicate nominative)
Subject complement (predicate adjective)
Complete predicate
Simple subject
Simple predicate

Resource Manager

Planning Resources
- Lesson Plans

Other Print Resources
- *Grammar and Composition Handbook*
- *Grammar Workbook,* Lessons 12–17

On a moonlight night it would be different. The happy voices of children playing in open fields would then be heard. And perhaps those not so young would be playing in pairs in less open places, and old men and women would remember their youth. As the Ibo say: "When the moon is shining the cripple becomes hungry for a walk."

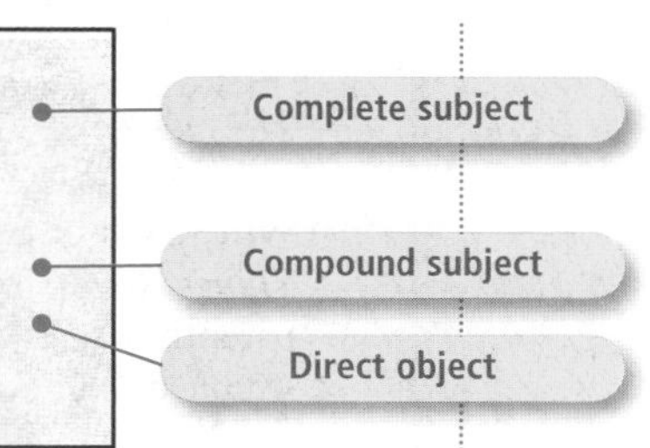

Review: Exercise 1 **Identifying Complete Subjects and Complete Predicates**

Copy each of these sentences, which are based on the content of *Things Fall Apart.* Draw a line between the complete subject and complete predicate.

1. Okonkwo was going to bed for the night.
2. His palm-oil lamp had been blown out.
3. The comfort of his bamboo bed beckoned him.
4. The hollow metal sound of the town crier's drum aroused everyone from sleep.
5. His message of a morning meeting surprised Okonkwo.
6. A clear note of tragedy in the crier's voice made Okonkwo fearful.
7. Nights without moonlight, such as this one, were always very quiet and sinister.
8. The vibration from the crier's voice could be sensed long after his departure.
9. Children were always silenced on dark, moonless nights.
10. The absence of moonlight changed the outlook of the community completely.

Review: Exercise 2 **Writing Sentences with Complete Subjects and Complete Predicates**

These sentences draw on ideas from *Things Fall Apart.* On your paper, write a complete subject or a complete predicate, without repeating the novel's exact words.

SAMPLE The town crier __________.
ANSWER The town crier beat his metal drum.

1. The voice of the crier __________.
2. __________ listened in the darkness.
3. The dark, moonless night __________.
4. Even the bravest villagers __________.
5. __________ roamed the jungle on dark nights.
6. A string __________.
7. __________ trilled in the darkness.
8. Moonlight __________.
9. __________ went outside in the moonlight.
10. Even the older people __________.

Practice and Assess

Answers: Exercise 1

1. Okonkwo / was going to bed for the night.
2. His palm-oil lamp / had been blown out.
3. The comfort of his bamboo bed / beckoned him.
4. The hollow metal sound of the town crier's drum / aroused everyone from sleep.
5. His message of a morning meeting / surprised Okonkwo.
6. A clear note of tragedy in the crier's voice / made Okonkwo fearful.
7. Nights without moonlight, such as this one, / were always very quiet and sinister.
8. The vibration from the crier's voice / could be sensed long after his departure.
9. Children / were always silenced on dark, moonless nights.
10. The absence of moonlight / changed the outlook of the community completely.

Answers: Exercise 2

Answers will vary, but some suggestions are given below.

1. disturbed the silence of the night
2. The villagers
3. was absolutely silent
4. felt afraid on such nights
5. Wild animals and evil spirits
6. was a snake at night
7. Millions of insects
8. made the night less frightening
9. Villagers
10. enjoyed a moonlit night

Practice and Assess

Answers: Exercise 3

Answers will vary, but some suggestions are given below.

1. Okonkwo (ss) / extinguished his light and lay (cp) on his bed.
2. The sound of the drum and the crier's voice (cs) / broke (sp) the silence of the night.
3. Okonkwo (ss) / listened to the message and wondered (cp) about it.
4. The terrifying darkness and unnerving silence (cs) / made (sp) the crier's message all the more ominous.
5. Dangerous animals and evil spirits (cs) / were (sp) troublesome to villagers on a dark night.
6. Villagers (ss) / never whistled or called (cp) a snake by name in the dark.
7. The sound (ss) of the crier's voice / faded and disappeared (cp) into the night.
8. The villagers (ss) / relaxed and played (cp) on moonlit nights.
9. Children, adults, and old people (cs) / would go (sp) outside in the moonlight.
10. Elderly men and women (cs) / would reminisce (sp) about the past.

Answers: Exercise 4

1. On the bamboo bed lay Okonkwo.
2. Down the road came the town crier.
3. There were tragic overtones in the crier's voice.
4. There was many a scary creature out and about.
5. In the darkness lurked dangerous animals.
6. Within any shadow might hide a snake.
7. Into the distance faded the drum.
8. There were millions of insects in the dark jungle.
9. There were no children outside on this moonless night.
10. On a moonlit night appeared people of all ages.

Review: Exercise 3 Writing Sentences with Compound Subjects and Predicates

Write on your paper a complete sentence answering each of these questions about *Things Fall Apart.* Begin your sentence with the subject, and follow the directions in parentheses. Then underline and label the simple or compound subject and the simple or compound predicate.

SAMPLE What two kinds of nights had opposite effects on the people of Umuofia? (Use a compound subject.)

	COMPOUND SUBJECT	SIMPLE PREDICATE
ANSWER	Dark nights and moonlit nights	had opposite effects on the people of Umuofia.

1. What did Okonkwo do to prepare for sleep? (Use a compound predicate.)
2. What sounds broke the silence of the night? (Use a compound subject.)
3. What did Okonkwo do as the crier gave his message? (Use a compound predicate.)
4. What qualities of the night made the crier's message all the more ominous to the villagers? (Use a compound subject.)
5. What things were troublesome on a dark night? (Use a compound subject.)
6. What did the villagers never do in the dark? (Use a compound predicate.)
7. What happened to the sound of the crier's voice? (Use a compound predicate.)
8. What did the villagers do on moonlit nights? (Use a compound predicate.)
9. What groups of villagers would go outside on a moonlit night? (Use a compound subject with three different nouns.)
10. Who would reminisce about the past? (Use a compound subject.)

Review: Exercise 4 Writing Inverted Sentences

The following sentences develop an image or idea suggested by the passage from *Things Fall Apart.* On your paper, rewrite each sentence in inverted order, following the instructions in parentheses and making any needed changes.

SAMPLE A fear of darkness was in the hearts of the villagers. (Begin the sentence with *There was.*)

ANSWER There was a fear of darkness in the hearts of the villagers.

1. Okonkwo lay on the bamboo bed. (Begin the sentence with *On the bamboo bed.*)
2. The town crier came down the road. (Begin the sentence with *Down the road.*)
3. Tragic overtones were in the crier's voice. (Begin the sentence with *There were.*)
4. Many a scary creature was out and about. (Begin the sentence with *There was.*)
5. Dangerous animals lurked in the darkness. (Begin the sentence with *In the darkness.*)
6. A snake might hide within any shadow. (Begin the sentence with *Within any shadow.*)
7. The drum faded into the distance. (Begin the sentence with *Into the distance.*)

8. Millions of insects were in the dark jungle. (Begin the sentence with *There were.*)
9. No children were outside on this moonless night. (Begin the sentence with *There were.*)
10. People of all ages appeared on a moonlit night. (Begin the sentence with *On a moonlit night.*)

Review: Exercise 5 **Writing Sentences with Predicate Nominatives and Predicate Adjectives**

The pairs of words that follow are derived from the passage from *Things Fall Apart.* For each pair, write a sentence that uses the first word as the subject and the second word as a predicate adjective or a predicate nominative. Do not use Achebe's exact words, and add more than just a verb to the pair of words. After you have written the sentence, indicate whether the second word from the pair is acting as a *predicate adjective* or a *predicate nominative.*

SAMPLE Umuofia, village
ANSWER Umuofia was Okonkwo's village in Africa. predicate nominative

1. *Things Fall Apart,* novel
2. Nigeria, country
3. villagers, members
4. Okonkwo, wrestler
5. *ogene,* drum
6. sound, loud
7. message, worrisome
8. morning, time
9. overtone, tragic
10. night, silent
11. people, fearful
12. darkness, time
13. animals, danger
14. string, name
15. trill, persistent
16. silence, extreme
17. villagers, lively
18. children, happy
19. fields, playgrounds
20. elderly, thoughtful

Review: Exercise 6 **Identifying Direct Objects and Object Complements**

The sentences below are based on the content of *Things Fall Apart.* On your paper, write the direct object and object complement from each sentence. Write *direct object* and *object complement* to identify each.

1. The town crier's message made Okonkwo fearful.
2. He considered the crier's tone of voice ominous.
3. The people of his village thought moonless nights menacing.
4. In contrast, the people found moonlit nights comfortable and friendly.
5. The light made their worst fears more bearable.

Answers: Exercise 5

Answers will vary, but some suggestions are given below.

1. *Things Fall Apart* is a novel by Chinua Achebe. (predicate nominative)
2. Nigeria is the country of Achebe's birth. (predicate nominative)
3. The villagers are members of the Ibo tribe. (predicate nominative)
4. Okonkwo is a youthful wrestler. (predicate nominative)
5. An *ogene* is a metal drum. (predicate nominative)
6. The sound of the ogene is loud. (predicate adjective)
7. The crier's message is worrisome. (predicate adjective)
8. Morning is the time for the village meeting. (predicate nominative)
9. The overtone of the crier's voice is tragic. (predicate adjective)
10. After the crier leaves, the night is silent. (predicate adjective)
11. The people are fearful on moonless nights. (predicate adjective)
12. Darkness is a time of terror for the villagers. (predicate nominative)
13. Animals seem a danger on moonless nights. (predicate nominative)
14. A string is a name for a snake. (predicate nominative)
15. The trill of the insects is persistent. (predicate adjective)
16. The silence seems extreme on moonless nights. (predicate adjective)
17. The villagers become lively on moonlit evenings. (predicate adjective)
18. The children are happy on brightly lit nights. (predicate adjective)
19. Open fields are the children's playgrounds. (predicate nominative)
20. The elderly are thoughtful on clear nights. (predicate adjective)

Answers: Exercise 6

1. Okonkwo—DO, fearful—OC
2. tone—DO, ominous—OC
3. nights—DO, menacing—OC
4. nights—DO, comfortable, friendly—OC
5. fears—DO, bearable—OC

Practice and Assess

Answers: Exercise 7

Answers will vary, but some suggestions are given below.

1. The town crier gave his drum a thump.
2. Okonkwo heard the sound of the drum.
3. The crier played his instrument with urgency.
4. The crier brought the villagers a message.
5. Okonkwo sensed tragedy in the crier's voice.
6. Darkness gave the townspeople uneasy feelings.
7. A whistle in the dark could bring trouble.
8. Distance stilled the crier's voice.
9. The trill of insects broke the silence of the night.
10. Moonlight gave the villagers courage.

Answers: Exercise 8 Proofreading

This proofreading activity provides editing practice with (1) the current or previous units' skills, (2) the **Troubleshooter** errors, (3) spelling errors. Students should be able to complete the exercise by referring to the unit, the **Troubleshooter,** and a dictionary. (Note: A run-on sentence counts as one error.)

Error (Type of Error)

1. is (subject-verb agreement)
   Africa. It *or* Africa; (run-on sentence)
2. inhabit (subject-verb agreement)
   modern (spelling)
3. Fulani, (nonessential adjective clause)
4. has (subject-verb agreement)
   its (pronoun-antecedent agreement)
   language, (run-on sentence)
   is (subject-verb agreement)
5. achieved (spelling)
   its (possessive pronoun)
6. Africa's (singular possessive)
7. sculptures, (run-on sentence)

Grammar Review

Review: Exercise 7 Writing Sentences with Direct and Indirect Objects

The following groups of words describe incidents related to the passage from *Things Fall Apart.* Each word is labeled *S* (for *subject*), *DO* (for *direct object*), or *IO* (for *indirect object*). On your paper, write a sentence using these words as those parts of the sentence, but do not use the exact wording from the novel. Try to add modifiers or prepositional phrases.

SAMPLE lamp (S), Okonkwo (IO), light (DO)
ANSWER A palm-oil lamp gave Okonkwo light at night.

1. town crier (S), drum (IO), thump (DO)
2. Okonkwo (S), sound (DO)
3. crier (S), instrument (DO)
4. crier (S), villagers (IO), message (DO)
5. Okonkwo (S), tragedy (DO)
6. darkness (S), townspeople (IO), feelings (DO)
7. whistle (S), trouble (DO)
8. distance (S), voice (DO)
9. trill (S), silence (DO)
10. moonlight (S), villagers (IO), courage (DO)

Review: Exercise 8

Proofreading

The following passage describes the people and the art of Nigeria. (An example of Nigerian sculpture appears on the opposite page.) Rewrite the passage, correcting the errors in spelling, grammar, and usage. Add any missing punctuation. There are twenty-five errors.

The Art of Nigeria

[1]The country of Nigeria are the most populous nation in West Africa it is more than twice the size of California. [2]Perhaps four hundred native tribes inhabits modren Nigeria. [3]The largest tribes are the Hausa and the Fulani who live mainly in the north; the Yoruba, in the southwest; the Ibo, in the south-east; and the Ijo, on the southern coast. [4]Each of the tribal groups have their own language but the common language of all the groups are English, reflecting Nigeria's century-long domination by Great Britain. [5]Nigeria finally acheived it's independence from Great Britain in 1960.

[6]Nigerian cultures have produced some of Africas' most impressive art. [7]The Yoruba fashioned magnificent bronze sculptures and the people of

western Nigeria produced fine ivory figures. [8]Many of these sculptures and figures was used during the religious ceremonies of the people.

[9]The Ijo who live in the warm and humid region of the Niger River delta, are closely related to their neighbors, the Ibo, who live nearby. [10]The Ijo traditionally venerated many gods, each god was thought to control a particular aspect of everyday life. [11]Some of the Ijo people continues to practice the religion of their ancestors.

[12]On this page are pictured a shrine that is typical of the sacred objects of the Ijo culture. [13]It is made of highly polished wood and showed a figure—possibly a tribal ancestor—sitting on a throne. [14]Generally, such an image was not displayed every day, it was probably created for a special ritual, such as a marriage or a funeral.

[15]In recent years many Nigerians have abandoned their native villages and migrate to large cities. [16]Those who remain in the country still lives close to nature. [17]The Ibo villagers described by Chinua Achebe in *Things Fall Apart* is aware of every sound heard on a moonless night. [18]They attribute some of those sounds to animals and insects; they attributes others to the supernatural. [19]Such sacred objects as this shrine may have symbolized a bridge between the natural and the supernatural world's.

Artist unknown, Ijo shrine, Nigeria

Answers: Exercise 8 *(continued)*

Error (Type of Error)

8. were (subject-verb agreement)
9. Ijo, (nonessential adjective clause)
10. gods. Each *or* gods; *or* gods, and (run-on sentence)
11. continue (subject-verb agreement)
12. is (subject-verb agreement)
13. shows (unnecessary shift in tense)
14. day. It *or* day; (run-on sentence)
15. migrated (unnecessary shift in tense)
16. live (subject-verb agreement)
17. are (subject-verb agreement)
18. they attribute others (subject-verb agreement)
19. worlds (plural noun)

Viewing the Art

Artist Unknown, *Ijo Shrine,* Nigeria

In the European art tradition, sculptures are objects of beauty intended for display. African sculptures, however, such as this Ijo shrine, were not meant for display. Some African sculptures portray gods or ancestors and are thought to have magical powers. They were probably brought out during ceremonies to serve as a reminder of a village's heritage and beliefs. Many Africans express their beliefs through stories, proverbs, and myths. Ask students to reread the passage from *Things Fall Apart* and identify some of the beliefs of the people in the village. Have them suggest ways the Ijo shrine could be used in a story.

Practice and Assess

Answers: Exercise 9

Mixed Review

Answers will vary, but some suggestions are given below.

1. . . . are insightful and educational.
2. . . . Ogidi and graduated from the University College at Ibadan.
3. . . . first but learned English as a child.
4. . . . an eager reader.
5. Achebe's mother and father . . .
6. Achebe's powerful themes have come from his experiences . . .
7. . . . give readers a sense . . .
8. There are numerous examples . . . rule in . . .
9. . . . awards and honorary doctorates.
10. . . . people and has been praised for his eloquent writings.
11. . . . describe rural African life.
12. The Ibo had lived in the southeast section of Nigeria for hundreds of years.
13. . . . Nigeria and provided a language for communication with the West.
14. . . . provides his audience detailed pictures.
15. Achebe's works present vivid images of life in Nigeria during colonial times and engage readers with their rich descriptions of aspects of Nigerian culture.
16. Did the long presence of the British government in Nigeria provide many of Achebe's themes?
17. There are many stories about religion in Achebe's work.
18. . . . a rare and important voice in Nigerian literature.
19. . . . is an important literary figure . . .
20. . . . people of all ages everywhere.

Close

Select an engaging passage from a novel or magazine article. Ask students to read the passage and label examples of complete subjects and predicates, direct and indirect objects, and complements. Have students compare their answers and provide appropriate feedback.

Review: Exercise 9

Mixed Review

The following sentences describe the life of Chinua Achebe. Rewrite each sentence on your paper according to the instructions that appear after each item.

Chinua Achebe

1. According to many critics, Chinua Achebe's works are insightful. (Add *and educational* to create a second predicate adjective.)
2. A member of the Ibo tribe of Nigeria, Achebe grew up in the village of Ogidi. (Add *and graduated from the University College at Ibadan* to expand the complete predicate.)
3. He spoke the Ibo language first. (Add *but learned English as a child* to expand the complete predicate.)
4. A member of a large family, Achebe was always a reader. (Add *eager* as a modifier of the subject complement.)
5. Achebe's mother insisted on the best education possible for the family's children. (Add *and father* to create a compound subject.)
6. From his experiences with African life have come Achebe's powerful themes. (Rewrite the sentence so that it begins with the complete subject.)
7. Many of his books give a sense of the effects of colonialism on African culture. (Add *readers* to the complete predicate so that it functions as an indirect object.)
8. Numerous examples of problems caused by colonial rule are in Achebe's works. (Rewrite the sentence so that it begins with *There are.*)
9. Over the years the popular Nigerian author has received many awards. (Add *and honorary doctorates* to the direct object.)
10. Chinua Achebe has become an important spokesperson for African people. (Add *and has been praised for his eloquent writings* to expand the complete predicate.)
11. Achebe's writings describe African life. (Add *rural* to modify the direct object.)
12. In the southeast section of Nigeria had lived the Ibo for hundreds of years. (Rewrite the sentence so that the complete subject comes before the complete predicate.)
13. English helped the unification of Nigeria. (Add *and provided a language for communication with the West* to expand the predicate.)
14. Achebe provides detailed pictures. (Add *his audience* to serve as an indirect object.)
15. Achebe's works present vivid images of life in Nigeria during colonial times. (Add words to create a compound predicate.)
16. Many of Achebe's themes were provided by the long presence of the British government in Nigeria. (Rewrite the declarative sentence as a question.)
17. Many stories about religion are in Achebe's work. (Rewrite the sentence as an inverted sentence that begins with *There are.*)
18. His readers and followers consider Achebe a rare voice in Nigerian literature. (Add *and important* to the object complement.)
19. Achebe is an important figure in twentieth-century African history. (Add *literary* to the predicate nominative.)
20. Achebe's works speak to people everywhere. (Add *of all ages* to the predicate.)

Writing Application

Sentence Elements in Writing

Jack London uses a variety of sentence elements and patterns in this passage from *The Call of the Wild* to create a lively, engaging prose rhythm. As you read the passage, focus especially on the italicized words.

Buck's first day on the Dyea beach was like a nightmare. Every hour was filled with shock and surprise. He *had been* suddenly *jerked* from the heart of civilization and *flung* into the heart of things primordial. *No lazy, sun-kissed life was this,* with nothing to do but loaf and be bored. Here was neither peace, nor rest, nor a moment's safety. All was confusion and action, and every moment life and limb were in peril. There was imperative need to be constantly alert; for *these dogs and men were not town dogs and men.* They were savages, all of them, who knew no law but the law of club and fang.

Techniques with Sentence Elements

Try to use various sentence elements and patterns, as London does, when you write and revise your work.

❶ Vary sentence length and rhythm by using compound subjects and predicates. Compare the following:

BORING PATTERN He *had been* suddenly *jerked* from the heart of civilization. *He had* been *flung* into the heart of things primordial.

LONDON'S PATTERN He *had been* suddenly *jerked* from the heart of civilization and *flung* into the heart of things primordial.

❷ Occasionally use repetition for effect in sentences with predicate nominatives.

BORING PATTERN These dogs and men weren't from towns.

LONDON'S PATTERN These dogs and men were not town dogs and men.

❸ Achieve sentence variety by sometimes using inverted word order.

USUAL ORDER This was no lazy, sun-kissed life . . .

LONDON'S ORDER No lazy, sun-kissed life was this . . .

TIME

For more about the writing process, see **TIME Facing the Blank Page**, pp. 121-131.

Parts of a Sentence

Practice Practice these techniques by revising the following passage, adapted from *The Call of the Wild*, combining ideas to expand the basic sentence patterns. Try to write one sentence in inverted order.

Then an old wolf, gaunt and battle-scarred, came forward. Buck writhed his lips into the preliminary of a snarl. He sniffed noses with him. Whereupon the old wolf sat down. He pointed his nose at the moon. He broke out the long wolf howl. The others sat down, too. They howled. Then the call came to Buck in unmistakable accents. He, too, sat down. He howled. . . . And the story of Buck may well end here.

LOG ON **Writing** Online | For more grammar practice, go to **glencoe.com** and enter QuickPass code WC97727p2.

Sentence Elements in Writing

Ask a volunteer to read aloud the paragraph from *The Call of the Wild.* Remind the reader to emphasize the italicized words. Go back and discuss the manner in which the italicized words add specific meaning to the passage. Discuss these elements in relation to the Techniques with Sentence Elements mentioned in the next section.

Techniques with Sentence Elements

Discuss how the sentences as written by London are more interesting. Ask students to find and to list examples of these techniques in the passage called "The Art of Nigeria," Exercise 8. (For example, students might note sentences 2 and 3 as examples of varying sentences' length and rhythm. Many sentences use a pattern other than the regular S–V pattern.) Discuss students' findings.

Practice

The answers to this challenging and enriching activity will vary. Refer to Techniques with Sentence Elements as you evaluate student revisions. A sample revised passage follows.

Then an old wolf, gaunt and battle-scarred, came forward. Writhing his lips into the preliminary of a snarl, Buck sniffed noses with him. The old wolf sat down, pointed his nose at the moon, and broke out the long wolf howl. The others sat down, too, and howled. In unmistakable accents, the call then came to Buck. He too sat down and he howled . . . and here may well end the story of Buck.

ASSESSMENT OPTIONS

Tests with Answer Key & Rubrics
Unit 11 Mastery Test, pp. 41–42

Testmaker
Unit 11 Mastery Test

You may wish to administer the Unit 11 Mastery Test at this point.

MindJogger Videoquizzes

INTRODUCING

UNIT 12

Objectives

- To learn about the various kinds of phrases, including prepositional, appositive, and verbal phrases
- To demonstrate control over the uses of various kinds of phrases by identifying them and writing sentences using them effectively

ASSESSMENT OPTIONS

Tests with Answer Key & Rubrics
Unit 12 Pretest, pp. 43–44
Unit 12 Mastery Test, pp. 45–46

Testmaker
Unit 12 Choice A Test
Unit 12 Choice B Test

You may wish to administer the Unit 12 Choice A Test or the Choice B Test as a pretest.

Key to Ability Levels

L1 Level 1 activities are within the basic ability range of students.

L2 Level 2 activities are within the ability range of average students.

L3 Level 3 activities are more challenging activities.

UNIT 12 Phrases

Resource Manager

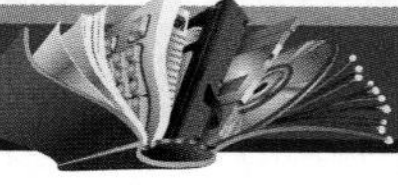

Planning Resources
- *Lesson Plans*
- *Block Scheduling*

Transparencies
- *Bellringer*
- *Daily Language Practice*
- *Two-Minute Skill Drill*

Other Print Resources
- *Grammar and Composition Handbook*
- *Grammar Enrichment*
- *Grammar Practice*
- *Grammar Reteaching*
- *Grammar Workbook*
- *Sentence-Combining Practice*
- *Tests with Answer Key and Rubrics*

Video
- *MindJogger Videoquizzes*

Software
- *Interactive Grammar and Language Workbook*
- *Presentation Plus!*
- *Revising with Style*
- *Testmaker*

Web Site
- *glencoe.com*

12.1 Prepositional Phrases

■ A **prepositional phrase** is a group of words that begins with a preposition and ends with a noun or a pronoun called **the object of the preposition.**

> The stairs lead **to the attic.** [*Attic* is the object of the preposition *to.*]
>
> The staircase is too steep **for her.** [*Her* is the object of the preposition *for.*]
>
> They laid carpeting **on the stairs.** [*Stairs* is the object of the preposition *on.*]

For lists of common prepositions, see page 473.

Adjectives and other modifiers may be placed between the preposition and its object. A preposition may have more than one object.

> The staircase leads **to the crowded, dusty attic.** [adjectives added]
>
> The staircase leads **to the attic and the roof.** [two objects]

A prepositional phrase acts in the same way an adjective or an adverb does. Used as an adjective, a prepositional phrase modifies a noun or a pronoun. Used as an adverb, it modifies a verb, an adjective, or an adverb.

> They used the staircase **on the left.** [adjective phrase modifying the noun *staircase*]
>
> Which **of the staircases** leads downstairs? [adjective phrase modifying the pronoun *which*]
>
> **At midnight** you can come downstairs **to the kitchen.** [adverb phrases modifying the verb phrase *can come*]
>
> My grandfather explained that a daily walk is healthful **for him.** [adverb phrase modifying the adjective *healthful*]
>
> She walks very quickly **for a young baby.** [adverb phrase modifying the adverb *quickly*]

Focus

Lesson Overview

Objectives

- To classify prepositional phrases by function—adjective or adverb
- To use prepositional phrases as modifiers

Bellringer
Daily Language Activity

When students enter the classroom, have this assignment on the board: *Write two sentences using the following phrases:*

on Walnut Street

in the car

See also *Daily Language Practice*

Motivating Activity

Ask students to discuss their phrases from the Bellringer activity. Then have them identify the two kinds of phrases in these sentences: *They work inside the library.* (adv.) *The girl in the blue dress yawned.* (adj.)

Teach

☑ Teaching Tip

Tell students that prepositional phrases have a distinctive structure: a preposition plus the object of the preposition. The object of the preposition is a noun or a pronoun. The object itself can be modified by a prepositional phrase: *The book is on the shelf near the window. Near the window* is a prepositional phrase modifying *shelf,* which is the object of the preposition *on.*

Resource Manager

Planning Resources
- *Lesson Plans*

Transparencies
- *Bellringer*
- *Daily Language Practice*

Other Print Resources
- *Grammar and Composition Handbook*
- *Grammar Enrichment,* p. 13
- *Grammar Practice,* p. 13
- *Grammar Reteaching,* p. 13
- *Grammar Workbook,* Lesson 18
- *Sentence-Combining Practice,* pp. 11, 13

Practice and Assess

Answers: Exercise 1

1. of . . . Revolution **2.** of five men; in 1770; during . . . Massacre **3.** At the time; in Boston **4.** of Boston; around . . . group; of . . . soldiers **5.** at the British **6.** into . . . crowd **7.** by a bullet; beside . . . men **8.** by the British; during the attack; from their wounds **9.** throughout the city; over the incident **10.** At a trial; for punishment; on their thumbs **11.** in Boston; of Crispus Attucks and the others; with him; in . . . Massacre

Answers: Exercise 2

1. hero—adj. **2.** one—adj.; died—adv.; died—adv. **3.** were stationed—adv.; were stationed—adv. **4.** inhabitants—adj.; gathered—adv.; group—adj. **5.** threw—adv. **6.** fired—adv. **7.** was hit—adv.; died—adv. **8.** were shot—adv.; were shot—adv.; died—adv. **9.** Bostonians—adj.; shock, outrage—adj. **10.** were found—adv.; were branded—adv.; were branded—adv. **11.** monument—adj.; memory—adj.; perished—adv.; perished—adv.

Answers: Exercise 3

Answers will vary. Possible answers:
1. The candle flame near the window flickers with a red glow. **2.** Someone in class should have asked me for help. **3.** The comedian performed in a suit with pink stripes. **4.** In no time the gardener pulled the weeds in the yard. **5.** The children from next door brought flowers to us. **6.** The classroom near the exit emptied quickly because of smoke. **7.** For your information, I have used a shovel many times in the past. **8.** The woman in the pickup truck was buying cat food by the ton. **9.** The farmers from Boone County drove their tractors to the meeting. **10.** Her cousin will send a letter with the information by next Friday.

Answers: Exercise 4

Answers will vary. Suggestion:
1. Many people *at work* use computers *on a daily basis.* (adj.; adv.)

Exercise 1 Identifying Prepositional Phrases

On your paper, write each prepositional phrase that appears in the following sentences. (You will find a total of twenty-five prepositional phrases.)

Crispus Attucks

[1]Crispus Attucks, a former enslaved person, is a hero of the American Revolution. [2]He was one of five men who died in 1770 during the historic Boston Massacre. [3]At the time, British troops were stationed in Boston. [4]Approximately four hundred inhabitants of Boston gathered around a small group of British soldiers. [5]They shouted insults and threw snowballs at the British. [6]Suddenly the soldiers fired into the unruly crowd. [7]Attucks was hit instantly by a bullet and died beside two other men. [8]Later two more men, who were also shot by the British during the attack, died from their wounds. [9]Bostonians throughout the city expressed shock and outrage over the incident. [10]At a trial, however, only two soldiers were found guilty, and for punishment they were branded on their thumbs. [11]A monument in Boston honors the memory of Crispus Attucks and the others who perished with him in the Boston Massacre.

Exercise 2 Identifying Adjective and Adverb Phrases

On your paper, write the word or words each prepositional phrase in Exercise 1 modifies. Then indicate whether each phrase is acting as an adjective or an adverb in the sentence.

Exercise 3 Expanding Sentences with Prepositional Phrases

Copy and expand the following sentences by adding at least one adjective phrase and one adverb phrase to each.

SAMPLE The new equipment arrived.
ANSWER The new equipment for the office arrived by truck.

1. The candle flame flickers.
2. Someone should have asked me.
3. The comedian performed.
4. The gardener pulled the weeds.
5. The children brought flowers.
6. The classroom emptied quickly.
7. I have used a shovel many times.
8. The woman was buying cat food.
9. The farmers drove their tractors.
10. Her cousin will send a letter.

Exercise 4 Writing with Prepositional Phrases

Write five sentences that include two or more prepositional phrases. Then underline each prepositional phrase and tell whether it is being used as an *adjective* or an *adverb.*

SAMPLE ANSWER Most students in my grade watch television on weekends. (adjective; adverb)

Close

Tell students to compose two sentences to describe a concert or other performance. Students should use prepositional phrases as adjectives and as adverbs in their sentences.

Meeting Individual Needs: English Language Learners

Using Modifiers

Students learning English may have trouble determining whether prepositional phrases are adjectival or adverbial. Explain that adverb phrases that modify verbs can usually be moved to the beginning or the end of a sentence. (*My grandmother is very active for a woman of ninety. For a woman of ninety, my grandmother is very active.*) Adjective phrases, however, can never be moved. They appear next to the nouns they modify. (*That dog with the black spots snarled and chased us.*)

12.2 Appositives and Appositive Phrases

- An **appositive** is a noun or pronoun that is placed next to another noun or pronoun to identify or give additional information about it.

  My friend **Paulo** sends me long letters from Brazil. [The appositive *Paulo* identifies the noun *friend*.]

- An **appositive phrase** is an appositive plus any words that modify the appositive.

  He is living and working in Brasília, **the capital city.** [The appositive phrase, in bold type, identifies *Brasília*.]

Use commas to set off any appositive or appositive phrase that is not essential to the meaning of a sentence.

Paulo's brother **Ernesto** also lives there. [The appositive **Ernesto** is essential because Paulo has more than one brother.]

Dora, **Paulo's only sister,** lives in New York. [The appositive phrase is not necessary to identify Dora.]

Usually an appositive or appositive phrase follows the noun or pronoun it identifies or explains. Occasionally an appositive phrase precedes the noun or pronoun.

A skilled mechanic, Paulo could probably find work anywhere.

Exercise 5 Identifying Appositives and Appositive Phrases

Write the appositives and appositive phrases in the sentences below.

1. Our neighbor Katie Rosenfeld organized the dance.
2. The most tickets were sold by Mia and Vanessa, two tenth graders.
3. After a long search, Greg finally found and booked the band, a fantastic group.
4. A clever class president, Juan Lopez talked his cousin into performing one of the opening comedy acts.
5. Two of Mr. Swanson's art classes, the third and the fifth periods, began work on the decorations a month in advance.

Phrases

Focus

Lesson Overview

Objective

- To recognize and use appositives and appositive phrases

Bellringer
Daily Language Activity

When students enter the classroom, have this assignment on the board: *Explain the difference between these two sentences:*

My daughter is at school.

My daughter Mabel is at school.

(The appositive *Mabel* identifies the noun *daughter.*)

See also Daily Language Practice

Teach

Teaching Tip

Demonstrate for students how appositives can enhance their writing. In this sentence from *Barrio Boy*, Ernesto Galarza uses an appositive phrase to heighten the sense of tension: *We walked into a frightening scene, a huge barn filled with smoke and noise and the smell of burnt oil.*

Practice and Assess

Answers: Exercise 5

1. Katie Rosenfeld
2. two tenth graders
3. a fantastic group
4. a clever class president
5. the third and the fifth periods

Resource Manager

Planning Resources
- *Lesson Plans*

Transparencies
- *Bellringer*
- *Daily Language Practice*

Other Print Resources
- *Grammar and Composition Handbook*
- *Grammar Enrichment,* p. 14
- *Grammar Practice,* p. 14
- *Grammar Reteaching,* p. 14
- *Grammar Workbook,* Lesson 20
- *Sentence-Combining Practice,* p. 9

Practice and Assess

Answers: Exercise 6

1. an innovative choreographer—Alvin Ailey **2.** Carson McCullers—author **3.** Marian Anderson—contralto **4.** one of the most brilliant violinists of her generation—Midori **5.** a collection of poems—*Annie Allen* **6.** the famous modern American architect—Frank Lloyd Wright **7.** one of the most influential twentieth-century American painters—Georgia O'Keeffe **8.** Billie Holiday—vocalist **9.** the daughter of a Spanish dancer—Rita Hayworth **10.** James Baldwin—author

Answers: Exercise 7

Answers will vary, but some suggestions are given below:
1. The film *Forrest Gump* was . . . **2.** The local newspaper, the *Falmouth Enterprise,* printed . . . **3.** Robert Frost, my favorite poet, wrote . . . **4.** Alaska, the forty-ninth state, entered . . . **5.** . . . Mardi Gras, "Fat Tuesday." **6.** The novel *One Hundred Years of Solitude* is my favorite. **7.** In Washington, our nation's capital, are . . . trees. **8.** My favorite singer, Neil Young, will be appearing . . . in July. **9.** Our team, the Huskies, . . . **10.** The principal of the school, Ms. Davis, . . .

Additional Resources

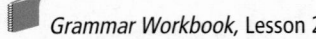

- *Grammar Practice,* p. 14
- *Grammar Reteaching,* p. 14
- *Grammar Enrichment,* p. 14
- *Sentence-Combining Practice,* p. 9

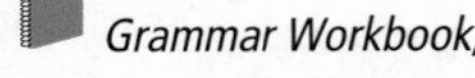

- *Grammar Workbook,* Lesson 20

Close

Tell students to write a short sentence and add an appositive phrase to it to improve the flow or create a dramatic effect.

Phrases

Exercise 6 Identifying Appositives and Appositive Phrases

Write the appositive or the appositive phrase that appears in each sentence. Then write the noun or pronoun that is identified or explained by the appositive.

Stars of American Culture

1. Alvin Ailey, an innovative choreographer, founded a lively modern dance company.
2. *The Heart Is a Lonely Hunter* is a novel by the acclaimed twentieth-century author Carson McCullers.
3. The great contralto Marian Anderson was the first African American singer to perform leading roles at the Metropolitan Opera in New York City.
4. Midori, one of the most brilliant violinists of her generation, launched her career as a very young girl.
5. The Pulitzer Prize was awarded to Gwendolyn Brooks for *Annie Allen,* a collection of poems.
6. The Guggenheim Museum in New York was one of the last projects of Frank Lloyd Wright, the famous modern American architect.
7. Georgia O'Keeffe, one of the most influential twentieth-century American painters, lived in New Mexico from 1949 to 1986.
8. Fans admired the jazz vocalist Billie Holiday for the emotionally charged quality of her singing.
9. Rita Hayworth, the daughter of a Spanish dancer, starred in many American films in the 1940s.
10. *Nobody Knows My Name* is a collection of personal essays by the author James Baldwin.

Exercise 7 Expanding Sentences with Appositive Phrases

On your paper, expand the following sentences by adding an appositive phrase to each sentence. Be sure to use commas where necessary.

SAMPLE Vitus Bering was the first European to chart the Alaskan coast.
ANSWER Vitus Bering, a Danish explorer, was the first European to chart the Alaskan coast.

1. The film was nominated for an Academy Award.
2. The local newspaper printed my letter on its editorial page.
3. Robert Frost wrote the poem.
4. Alaska entered the Union in 1959.
5. Every year New Orleans celebrates Mardi Gras.
6. The novel is my favorite.
7. In Washington are many cherry trees.
8. My favorite singer will be appearing here in concert in July.
9. Our team won.
10. The principal of the school has resigned.

MEETING INDIVIDUAL NEEDS

English Language Learners

Practicing with Appositives

Students learning English may be familiar with other ways to identify or give more information about nouns. Have students discuss methods with which they are familiar and practice writing appositive phrases by completing sentences like the ones that follow.

- My best friend, ______, helps me with my homework.
- Her sister ______ is older than I am.
- Kim was surprised to win the 200-meter race, ______.

Have students write their own sentences.

12.3 Verbals and Verbal Phrases

- A **verbal** is a verb form that functions in a sentence as a noun, an adjective, or an adverb.
- A **verbal phrase** is a verbal plus any complements and modifiers.

There are three kinds of verbals: *participles, gerunds,* and *infinitives.* All three types can be expanded into phrases.

Participles and Participial Phrases

- A **participle** is a verb form that can function as an adjective.
- A **present participle** is made up of the base form of the verb plus *-ing: falling.* A past participle is usually made up of the base form plus *-ed: burned.* Some past participles are irregularly formed.

Participles are often used as adjectives.

No one would eat the **burned** toast.

We were warned to watch out for **falling** rocks.

The **fallen** tree blocked the **winding** road.

A participle may also be used as part of a verb phrase. When a participle is part of a verb phrase, it is not acting as an adjective.

PARTICIPLE AS ADJECTIVE	The **growing** child was curious.
PARTICIPLE IN VERB PHRASE	They saw that he **was growing** stronger.

- A **participial phrase** contains a participle plus any complements and modifiers.

Participial phrases can be placed in various positions in a sentence.

We watched the best teams **playing baseball.**

The **badly defeated** team accepted its fate with grace.

The victors, **elated by the victory,** shook hands with the losers.

Throwing their hats into the air, the fans of the victorious team let out a great roar.

A participial phrase at the beginning of a sentence is usually followed by a comma.

Phrases

Focus

Lesson Overview

Objectives

- To identify verbals and verbal phrases
- To demonstrate how verbals and verbal phrases can be used to express complex ideas

Bellringer

Daily Language Activity

When students enter the classroom, have this assignment on the board: *Is the underlined word in the following sentence a verb, a noun, or an adjective? Explain.*

A barking dog greeted me at the door.

See also  *Daily Language Practice*

Motivating Activity

Tell students that when a verb like *barking* is used as an adjective, as in the Bellringer activity, it is called a verbal. Write some verbs on the board and let students take turns creating sentences using the verb as an adjective. Encourage students to ask questions for clarification.

Teach

Participles and Participial Phrases

Teaching Tip

Remind students that irregular verbs do not form the past tense or past participle by adding *-ed* to the base word. To find out what the participle of an irregular verb is, they should consult a dictionary.

Resource Manager

Planning Resources
- *Lesson Plans*

Transparencies
- *Bellringer*
- *Daily Language Practice*
- *Two-Minute Skill Drill*

Other Print Resources
- *Grammar and Composition Handbook*
- *Grammar Enrichment,* pp. 15–17
- *Grammar Practice,* pp. 15–17
- *Grammar Reteaching,* pp. 15–17
- *Grammar Workbook,* Lessons 19–22
- *Sentence-Combining Practice,* pp. 9, 13, 28, 30

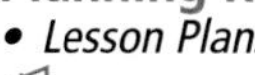

12.3

Teach

Teaching Tip

Write these sentences on the board: *Ernie was laughing at my joke. He could not speak.* Combine the sentences: *Laughing at my joke, Ernie could not speak.* Explain to students that the participial phrase comes from the predicate (verb phrase) of the first sentence. Have students practice combining sentences.

Listening and Speaking

Read aloud the following sentence: *Watching the band members take their seats, the audience became anxious for the concert to begin.* Ask students to identify the participial phrase. (*Watching the band members take their seats*) Use the sentence to point out that participial phrases that end with a slight rise in pitch can effectively set off the rest of the sentence. Ask students to listen for the rise in pitch in other sentences.

Practice and Assess

Answers: Exercise 8

1. blowing
2. broken
3. closed
4. gathering
5. Shivering

Answers: Exercise 9

1. extending . . . California—coast
2. inhabited . . . groups—forests
3. caught in streams—Salmon
4. Knowing . . . well—groups
5. built of wood—houses
6. Prepared for battle—they; made . . . copper—shields
7. decorated with carvings—totem poles
8. Displaying great artistic skill—Northwest Native Americans
9. established . . . years—cultures
10. Determined . . . resources— Europeans

Answers: Exercise 10

Answers will vary, but a suggestion is given below.

Wanting to make a good impression, Keith wore a new shirt. Keith

Exercise 8 Identifying Participles in Sentences

Write the participle that functions as an adjective in each of the following sentences.

1. The blowing trees were etched against the sky.
2. A broken branch scratched against the window.
3. The closed barn doors rattled in the strong wind.
4. Everywhere was evidence of the gathering storm.
5. Shivering, the young boy returned to his chair near the fireplace.

Exercise 9 Identifying Participles and Participial Phrases

Write the participial phrase that acts as an adjective in each of the following sentences. Then identify the word each phrase modifies.

Early Native Americans of the Northwest

1. The northwestern coast of North America, extending from southern Alaska to northern California, was the home of many Native American groups.
2. The dense forests inhabited by these groups have a temperate climate and plentiful rainfall.
3. Salmon caught in streams was an important source of food.
4. Knowing the woodlands well, the groups gathered wild fruit.
5. Northwest Native Americans ordinarily lived in houses built of wood.
6. Prepared for battle, they carried shields made of copper.
7. Some of the groups had totem poles decorated with carvings.
8. Displaying great artistic skill, the Northwest Native Americans produced baskets, rattles, masks, and other artifacts.
9. Native Americans of the Northwest had distinctive cultures established over hundreds of years.
10. Determined to find furs and other natural resources, Europeans came into the area in the late 1700s.

Exercise 10 Writing Sentences with Participial Phrases

Write five sentences with participial phrases. Then underline each phrase and write what noun or pronoun the phrase modifies.

SAMPLE ANSWER Determined to be the next class president, Kevin began his campaign the first day of school. Kevin

MEETING INDIVIDUAL NEEDS

English Language Learners

Understanding Participles

Before teaching verbal phrases, review what students have learned about past and present verb tenses and about adjectives. Make sure they understand that a participle is formed from a verb. Then give students some sentences that use participles as adjectives.

Gerunds and Gerund Phrases

- A **gerund** is a verb form that ends in *–ing* and is used in the same way a noun is used.

Eating is something I enjoy. [gerund as subject]

My grandfather likes **strolling.** [gerund as direct object]

Tony gives **baking** his best effort. [gerund as indirect object]

How much enthusiasm do you feel for **bowling?** [gerund as object of preposition]

Rachel's favorite pastime is **painting.** [gerund as predicate nominative]

My hobbies, **writing** and **reading,** are quiet activities. [gerunds as appositives]

Bowl + ing is fun!

- A **gerund phrase** is a gerund plus any complements and modifiers.

Dancing the tango is not as easy as it looks.

Fred Astaire's marvelous dancing will always be considered superb.

The difference between a present participle and a gerund is that a present participle is used as a verb or an adjective and a gerund is used as a noun.

Running around the track, Yuki felt exhilarated. [present participle]

Running gives Yuki a sense of well-being. [gerund]

Exercise 11 Identifying Gerunds and Gerund Phrases

List on your paper the gerunds and gerund phrases that appear in the following sentences. The number of gerunds or gerund phrases in each sentence is given in parentheses.

A Spanish Conqueror

1. Conquering was the goal of the ruthless Spanish adventurer Hernando Cortés. (1)
2. His greatest accomplishment was claiming for Spain land in central and southern Mexico. (1)
3. Capturing territory was a challenging experience, Cortés found. (1)
4. The famous Spaniard enjoyed discovering and exploring new places. (2)
5. Cortés was adept at gaining the trust of some Native Americans. (1)
6. The result was his winning the Aztec capital, Tenochtitlán, through the overthrow of Emperor Montezuma. (1)
7. By 1521 several of Cortés's goals—finding gold, claiming Mexican lands, and conquering native groups—were fulfilled. (3)
8. For several years, Cortés was famous for controlling much of present-day Mexico. (1)
9. His trip to Spain in 1528 resulted in his receiving the title of *marquis.* (1)
10. Cortés sailed back to Mexico in 1530 and began building his palace and exploring the Pacific region. (2)

Phrases

Teach

Gerunds and Gerund Phrases

Teaching Tip

Remind students that although gerunds and present participles both end in *-ing,* they function differently. Gerunds act as nouns, whereas present participles act as adjectives.

Two-Minute Skill Drill

List these verbs on the chalkboard.

capture	*play*
drive	*shake*
hold	*think*

Have students write each verb in the form of a gerund and then use it in a sentence.

See also *Two-Minute Skill Drill Transparency 12.3*

Practice and Assess

Answers: Exercise 11

1. Conquering
2. claiming for Spain . . . Mexico
3. Capturing territory
4. discovering, exploring new places
5. gaining the trust of some Native Americans
6. winning the Aztec . . . Montezuma
7. finding gold, claiming Mexican lands, conquering native groups
8. controlling much of present-day Mexico
9. receiving the title of *marquis*
10. building his palace, exploring the Pacific region

Enrichment and Extension

Testing for Gerunds

Discuss gerunds and gerund phrases with students. Explain that since gerunds and gerund phrases always act as nouns and are always singular, you can identify them by using the *it* test. If you can replace the phrase with *it,* you are looking at a gerund or gerund phrase. Tell students to try the *it* test on the sentences in Exercise 11. Then have them try the sentences in Exercise 9. Note that the *it* test is a good way to distinguish between gerunds and present participles, both of which end in *-ing.* **L2**

Teach

Infinitives and Infinitive Phrases

☑ Teaching Tips

A split infinitive occurs when an adverb is placed between the word *to* and the verb that follows it.

Students sometimes confuse infinitives with prepositional phrases that begin with *to*. Tell students that a simple way to tell infinitives and prepositional phrases apart is to see whether the word following the *to* can be used (without the *to*) with the helping verb *will*. If it can, then that word is a verb and the *to* phrase is an infinitive phrase; if it cannot, then the *to* phrase is a prepositional phrase.

Practice and Assess

Answers: Exercise 12

1. to paint in the Impressionist style
2. to study at the Pennsylvania Academy of the Fine Arts
3. to live in France
4. to influence her work
5. to master her drawing techniques
6. to paint portraits of mothers and children
7. to exhibit paintings with other Impressionists
8. to purchase the paintings of the French Impressionists
9. to influence a growing American interest in contemporary art
10. to appreciate Cassatt's work for its own remarkable qualities

Infinitives and Infinitive Phrases

■ An **infinitive** is a verb form that is usually preceded by the word *to* and is used as a noun, an adjective, or an adverb.

When you use the word *to* before the base form of a verb, *to* is not a preposition but part of the infinitive form of the verb.

To stand can be uncomfortable. [infinitive as subject]
Infants first learn **to crawl.** [infinitive as direct object]
Her aim is **to walk.** [infinitive as predicate nominative]
Birds have an instinct **to fly**. [infinitive as adjective]
I am happy **to run.** [infinitive as adverb]

■ An **infinitive phrase** contains an infinitive plus any complements and modifiers.

We decided **to sail across the lake.**
They wanted **to drive slowly around the park.**
To run in a marathon someday is my secret ambition.
A triathlon requires athletes **to train diligently.**
To complete a triathlon is a success in itself.

Exercise 12 Identifying Infinitives and Infinitive Phrases

Write the infinitive phrase that appears in each of the following sentences.

Mary Cassatt

1. Mary Cassatt was one of the foremost American artists to paint in the Impressionist style.
2. Cassatt spent much of her childhood in Europe but decided to study at the Pennsylvania Academy of Fine Arts.
3. In 1866 she went to live in France.
4. The great French painter Edgar Degas began to influence her work.
5. Degas helped Cassatt to master her drawing techniques.
6. Cassatt often chose to paint portraits of mothers and children.
7. Degas invited Cassatt to exhibit paintings with other Impressionists.
8. Cassatt encouraged her American relatives and friends to purchase the paintings of the French Impressionists.
9. In so doing, Cassatt helped to influence a growing American interest in contemporary art.
10. Today art lovers are able to appreciate Cassatt's work for its own remarkable qualities.

Enrichment and Extension

Using Verbals in Writing

Encourage students to write a short essay or personal narrative in which they use the three kinds of verbals they learned in this lesson. Suggest that students use a computer to work through each step of the writing process. Have students underline the verbals and explain to a classmate which kind of verbal each one is. Remind students to provide effective feedback.

Exercise 13 **Identifying Verbal Phrases**

On your paper, write each of the verbal phrases that appears in the following sentences. Write whether each phrase is a *participial phrase, a gerund phrase,* or an *infinitive phrase.*

Elephants

1. Elephants have the distinction of being the largest land mammals.
2. Living in the tropical regions of Asia and Africa, they may reach a height of 13 feet.
3. Their tusks, weighing as much as 200 pounds each, can be more than 10 feet long.
4. The distinctive ears of the African elephant are huge, measuring up to 4 feet in width.
5. Elephants use their fingerlike trunks to pick up objects.
6. Elephants browse all day, feeding on a variety of plants.
7. Elephants can learn to carry logs and to perform in circuses.
8. Training young elephants takes great skill.
9. Handling the elephants may be difficult for the trainers.
10. Hunted for ivory and often deprived of their natural surroundings, elephants now must struggle for their survival.
11. An adult elephant needs to eat about 300 pounds of food a day.
12. The elephant needs to search almost constantly for food.
13. Weighing over 200 pounds, a newborn elephant stands about 3 feet tall.
14. The adults form a circle around their offspring to protect them from predators.
15. Young elephants amuse themselves by playing with each other.
16. Traveling to water holes each day, elephants spend a lot of time in and around water.
17. Splashing themselves with muddy water keeps elephants cool.
18. Elephants love to bathe in fresh water and are excellent swimmers.
19. Most wild Asian elephants, protected by regional governments, live on preserves.
20. Large predators avoid attacking adult elephants because of their size.

Exercise 14 **Using Verbal Phrases**

On your paper, use each of the following verbal phrases in an original sentence. Write whether each phrase is a *participial phrase, a gerund phrase,* or an *infinitive phrase.*

1. blaming us for the loud music
2. to test the speakers
3. playing the drums
4. to annoy the neighbors
5. turning down the speakers
6. listening at the door
7. to play more softly
8. upset by all the commotion
9. to make everyone happy
10. putting pads on the floor

Phrases

Answers: Exercise 13

1. being . . . mammals—gerund
2. Living . . . Africa—participial
3. weighing . . . each—participial
4. measuring . . . width—participial
5. to . . . objects—infinitive
6. feeding . . . plants—participial
7. to . . . logs—infinitive; to . . . circuses—infinitive
8. Training young elephants— gerund
9. Handling the elephants—gerund
10. Hunted . . . ivory—participial, deprived . . . surroundings— participial
11. to . . . day—infinitive
12. to . . . food—infinitive
13. Weighing . . . pounds—participial
14. to . . . predators—infinitive
15. playing . . . other—gerund
16. Traveling . . . day—participial
17. Splashing . . . water—gerund
18. to . . . water—infinitive
19. protected . . . governments—participial
20. attacking . . . size—gerund

Answers: Exercise 14

Answers will vary, but one suggestion is given below.

1. Blaming us for the loud music, the neighbors asked that our guests leave. participial phrase

Additional Resources

Sentence-Combining Practice, pp. 9, 13, 28, 30
Grammar Practice, pp. 15–17
Grammar Reteaching, pp. 15–17
Grammar Enrichment, pp. 15–17

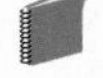
Grammar Workbook Lessons 19–22

Close

Ask students to discuss the impact that the addition of verbal phrases adds to a written piece. What impressed them most about the manner in which verbal phrases were used in the lesson? Have students summarize their impressions in their journal.

Enrichment and Extension

Unmarked Infinitives

Some verbs have as their complement an unmarked infinitive rather than the *to* form—for example, *I made him do it* may be mistakenly written as *I made him to do it.* Explain that sensory verbs, such as *see, hear,* and *feel,* use unmarked infinitives. **L2**

Teach

About the Literature

Explain that the review contains a passage from *Picture Bride*, a novel by the Japanese-American writer Yoshiko Uchida. After students have read the passage, discuss its characters, setting, and mood. Then ask students to consider how the sentences in which the phrases appear would sound if the phrases were eliminated. The exercises that follow are based on this passage and related topics.

Linking Grammar and Literature

Critical Thinking

Ask students to identify some of the prepositional and participial phrases not highlighted in the passage. You might ask students to identify the only sentence in the passage that does not contain a prepositional phrase. (*Why did I ever leave Japan, she wondered bitterly.*)

Cooperative Learning

Ask students to work in pairs to write two versions of a paragraph about leaving home or about a related theme. Tell them to use as few phrases as possible in the first version. The second version should contain a variety of phrases, particularly prepositional phrases, participial phrases, and appositive phrases. Ask pairs of students to exchange paragraphs, read them, and discuss ways in which phrases can add color and detail to their writing. Have students summarize their ideas in their journals.

ASSESSMENT OPTIONS

Tests with Answer Key & Rubrics
Unit 12 Mastery Test, pp. 45–46

Testmaker
Unit 12 Mastery Test

UNIT 12 Grammar Review

Phrases

The passage below is taken from a novel by the Japanese American writer Yoshiko Uchida. The novel tells of a young Japanese woman who arrives in San Francisco in 1917 to marry a man whom she has never met. In this passage, she contemplates her fate. The passage has been annotated to show many of the kinds of phrases covered in this unit.

Literature Model

from Picture Bride

by Yoshiko Uchida

Hana Omiya stood at the railing of the small ship that shuddered toward America in a turbulent November sea. She shivered as she pulled the folds of her silk kimono close to her throat and tightened the wool shawl about her shoulders.

She was thin and small, her dark eyes shadowed in her pale face, her black hair piled high in a pompadour that seemed too heavy for so slight a woman. She clung to the moist rail and breathed the damp salt air deep into her lungs. Her body seemed leaden and lifeless, as though it were simply the vehicle transporting her soul to a strange new life, and she longed with childlike intensity to be home again in Oka Village.

She longed to see the bright persimmon dotting the barren trees beside the thatched roof, to see the fields of golden rice stretching to the mountains where only last fall she had gathered plump white mushrooms, and to see once more the maple trees lacing their flaming colors through the green pine. If only she could see a familiar face, eat a meal without retching, walk on solid ground and stretch out at night on a *tatami* mat instead of in a hard narrow bunk. She thought now of seeking the warm shelter of her bunk but could not bear to face the relentless smell of fish that penetrated the lower decks.

Prepositional phrase (adjective phrase): of her silk kimono

Prepositional phrase (adverb phrase): about her shoulders

Infinitive Phrase: to be home again in Oka Village

Participial phrase (adjective phrase): dotting the barren trees beside the thatched roof

Gerund phrase (object of preposition): seeking the warm shelter of her bunk

Resource Manager

Planning Resources
- *Lesson Plans*

Other Print Resources
- *Grammar and Composition Handbook*
- *Grammar Workbook,* Lessons 18–22, Unit 3 Review, Cumulative Review: Units 1–3

> Why did I ever leave Japan, she wondered bitterly. Why did I ever listen to my uncle? And yet she knew it was she herself who had begun the chain of events that placed her on this heaving ship. It was she who had first planted in her uncle's mind the thought that she would make a good wife for Taro Takeda, the lonely man who had gone to America to make his fortune in Oakland, California.

Appositive phrase

Review: Exercise 1 **Expanding Sentences with Prepositional Phrases**

The following sentences describe an imaginary journey on a boat. Read through the sentences quickly to get an idea of the scene. Then rewrite each sentence, adding at least one prepositional phrase—either an adjective phrase or an adverb phrase—to the sentence. You can imagine any scene that you wish.

1. The ship rocked violently.
2. The boy watched the dark waves.
3. His hair was tossed.
4. He wore a long scarf.
5. The breeze flushed his cheeks.
6. He carried a small suitcase.
7. He was taking a long trip.
8. The previous night he had slept poorly.
9. The boy ate little.
10. Memories flooded his mind.
11. He felt intense longing.
12. He had left his family.
13. All his friends had stayed behind.
14. The ship was crowded.
15. Many people were traveling.
16. Some men sang songs.
17. Small children played games.
18. Young women chatted.
19. Sailors came and went.
20. The captain appeared only once.
21. The boy sat quietly.
22. He had a faraway look.
23. The ship arrived late.
24. A man greeted the boy.
25. The boy's new life had begun.

Phrases

Practice and Assess

Answers: Exercise 1

Answers will vary, but some suggestions are given below.

1. The ship rocked violently in the stormy sea.
2. The boy on the deck watched the dark waves.
3. His hair was tossed by the wind.
4. He wore a long scarf around his neck.
5. The breeze from the sea flushed his cheeks.
6. He carried a small suitcase with a broken handle.
7. He was taking a long trip to America.
8. The previous night he had slept poorly on his hard bunk.
9. The boy ate little of his food.
10. Memories of the past flooded his mind.
11. He felt intense longing for his homeland.
12. He had left his family in Norway.
13. All his friends from Oslo had stayed behind.
14. The ship was crowded with poor immigrants.
15. Many people were traveling to their new home.
16. Some men sang songs about love and adventure.
17. Small children in tattered clothes played games.
18. Young women chatted with each other.
19. Sailors came and went throughout the day.
20. The captain appeared on deck only once.
21. The boy sat quietly in a corner.
22. He had a faraway look in his eyes.
23. The ship arrived late at night.
24. A man greeted the boy at the gate.
25. The boy's new life had begun at last.

Practice and Assess

Answers: Exercise 2

1. A solitary figure, a small woman with a shawl, stood on the open deck.
2. The woman, Hana Omiya, was traveling to America.
3. She had left her home, a small village in Japan, and was traveling to meet her future husband.
4. Her father, a prosperous landowner, had died, leaving four daughters and a wife behind.
5. Of the four sisters, Hana, the youngest, was the only one without a husband.
6. Hana's mother, a practical woman, was determined to find a match for her.
7. The idea that Hana should go to America was suggested by another relative, Uncle Oji.
8. Oji knew a Japanese man, Taro Takeda, who had gone to California to seek his fortune.
9. Taro Takeda, the son of a friend of Oji's, had opened a small shop in Oakland.
10. Oji said that Taro, a hardworking and honest man, would make a good husband.
11. Hana's dark eyes were fixed on the horizon, a barely perceptible line of blue.
12. The bracing scene contrasted with her mood, a heavy feeling of dread.
13. Familiar faces, now only distant memories, filled her mind.
14. She yearned to see not the ocean but the graceful persimmons and maples, the trees of home.
15. The discomforts of the trip, seasickness and unpleasant odors, were becoming unbearable.
16. Even more unbearable was her fear, a constant companion on the voyage.
17. Another land, a country with strange people and an unfamiliar language, was to be her new home.
18. A man totally unknown to her was to be her husband, her companion for the rest of her life.
19. His picture, a faded photograph, offered few clues to his character.
20. She was overwhelmed by bitterness, an emotion unfamiliar to her.
21. She longed for familiar customs, the simple ceremonies of her homeland.
22. She longed as well for the familiar landmarks, the carefully cultivated gardens and flaming maple trees, of her village.
23. Yet she was being hurled toward America, an unknown wilderness.
24. Would she ever again see her old home, Oka Village?
25. Tears, drops of sorrow, streamed from her brimming eyes.

Phrases

Review: Exercise 2 **Expanding Sentences with Appositives and Appositive Phrases**

The following sentences describe Hana Omiya, the main character of *Picture Bride.* Each sentence is followed by a group of words in parentheses. Rewrite each sentence, incorporating the words in parentheses as an appositive or appositive phrase. Use a comma or commas to set off the appositive or appositive phrase from the rest of the sentence.

SAMPLE The ship sailed toward San Francisco. (a small steamer)
ANSWER The ship, a small steamer, sailed toward San Francisco.

1. A solitary figure stood on the open deck. (a small woman with a shawl)
2. The woman was traveling to America. (Hana Omiya)
3. She had left her home and was traveling to meet her future husband. (a small village in Japan)
4. Her father had died, leaving four daughters and a wife behind. (a prosperous landowner)
5. Of the four sisters, Hana was the only one without a husband. (the youngest)
6. Hana's mother was determined to find a match for her. (a practical woman)
7. The idea that Hana should go to America was suggested by another relative. (Uncle Oji)
8. Oji knew a Japanese man who had gone to California to seek his fortune. (Taro Takeda)
9. Taro Takeda had opened a small shop in Oakland. (the son of a friend of Oji's)
10. Oji said that Taro would make a good husband. (a hardworking and honest man)
11. Hana's dark eyes were fixed on the horizon. (a barely perceptible line of blue)
12. The bracing scene contrasted with her mood. (a heavy feeling of dread)
13. Familiar faces filled her mind. (now only distant memories)
14. She yearned to see not the ocean but the graceful persimmons and maples. (the trees of home)
15. The discomforts of the trip were becoming unbearable. (seasickness and unpleasant odors)
16. Even more unbearable was her fear. (a constant companion on the voyage)
17. Another land was to be her new home. (a country with strange people and an unfamiliar language)
18. A man totally unknown to her was to be her husband. (her companion for the rest of her life)
19. His picture offered few clues to his character. (a faded photograph)
20. She was overwhelmed by bitterness. (an emotion unfamiliar to her)
21. She longed for familiar customs. (the simple ceremonies of her homeland)
22. She longed as well for the familiar landmarks of her village. (the carefully cultivated gardens and flaming maple trees)
23. Yet she was being hurled toward America. (an unknown wilderness)
24. Would she ever again see her old home? (Oka Village)
25. Tears streamed from her brimming eyes. (drops of sorrow)

Review: Exercise 3 **Expanding Sentences with Participial Phrases**

The following sentences relate to Hana Omiya and her life. Each sentence is followed by another sentence in parentheses. Combine the sentences, changing the sentence in parentheses into a participial phrase. Be sure to place the participial phrase near the word that it modifies. Note that some of the sentences may be expanded in more than one way.

SAMPLE Hana stood on the deck of the ship. (She was shivering in her thin clothes.)
ANSWER Shivering in her thin clothes, Hana stood on the deck of the ship.

1. The woolen shawl offered little warmth. (The shawl was draped over her shoulders.)
2. Her silk kimono made her look like a bird. (Her kimono was fluttering in the wind.)
3. The sea air was damp and cheerless. (The air was rushing past her face.)
4. Hana recalled the warm colors of her village. (She was gazing absently at the sea.)
5. The memory of familiar faces haunted her. (The faces were filled with goodwill.)
6. She recalled the rice fields. (The rice fields were rustling in the breeze.)
7. She longed to see the orange persimmons. (The persimmons were hanging from the bare trees.)
8. Why was she going to America to marry a man? (The man was unknown to her.)
9. Her uncle had described Taro as decent and hardworking. (Her uncle was speaking eagerly.)
10. Hana had decided to leave Japan. (Hana had been longing for a different kind of life.)
11. Her sisters lived in big cities. (Her sisters were married to merchants.)
12. Their lives were monotonous. (Their lives were filled with routine.)
13. Hana did not want to be a bored wife. (A bored wife is trapped in a dull marriage.)
14. At first Hana had looked forward to a new life. (Her life would be filled with excitement.)
15. She dreaded the future now. (She was plagued with uncertainty.)
16. She had reluctantly boarded the ship. (She was leaving her family behind.)
17. Many passengers had stayed in their quarters. (They were exhausted by the trip.)
18. Hana remained on the deck. (She was not accompanied by even a single friend.)
19. She listened to some Russian travelers. (The Russians were singing of home.)
20. The loneliness was as endless as the sea. (The loneliness was stretching before her.)
21. Family members would have made the journey less terrifying. (They would have provided companionship.)
22. Hana would be alone in America too. (She would be isolated by language.)
23. She listened to the cries of sea gulls. (The gulls followed the ship.)
24. The cries tore at her heart. (The cries reminded her of abandoned infants.)
25. Hana cried. (She lowered her head.)

Phrases

Answers: Exercise 3

Answers will vary, but some suggestions are given below.

1. Draped over her shoulders, the woolen shawl offered little warmth.
2. Fluttering in the wind, her silk kimono made her look like a bird.
3. The sea air rushing past her face was damp and cheerless.
4. Gazing absently at the sea, Hana recalled the warm colors of her village.
5. The memory of familiar faces filled with goodwill haunted her.
6. She recalled the rice fields rustling in the breeze.
7. She longed to see the orange persimmons hanging from the bare trees.
8. Why was she going to America to marry a man unknown to her?
9. Speaking eagerly, her uncle had described Taro as decent and hardworking.
10. Longing for a different kind of life, Hana had decided to leave Japan.
11. Her sisters, married to merchants, lived in big cities.
12. Their lives, filled with routine, were monotonous.
13. Hana did not want to be a bored wife trapped in a dull marriage.
14. At first Hana had looked forward to a new life filled with excitement.
15. Plagued with uncertainty, she dreaded the future now.
16. Leaving her family behind, she had reluctantly boarded the ship.
17. Exhausted by the trip, many passengers had stayed in their quarters.
18. Not accompanied by even a single friend, Hana remained on deck.
19. She listened to some Russian travelers singing of home.
20. Stretching before her, the loneliness was as endless as the sea.
21. Providing companionship, family members would have made the journey less terrifying.
22. Isolated by language, Hana would be alone in America too.
23. She listened to the cries of sea gulls following the ship.
24. The cries, reminding her of abandoned infants, tore at her heart.
25. Lowering her head, Hana cried.

Practice and Assess

Answers: Exercise 4

Answers will vary, but some suggestions are given below.

1. In the late nineteenth century, earning a living was difficult in Japan.
2. Moving to the United States seemed like a good idea.
3. Signing a work contract was a first step for many poor immigrants.
4. Becoming an American citizen was impossible for early Japanese immigrants.
5. Many Japanese immigrants found living in California practical.
6. Picking grapes was a common job for Japanese families who moved to California.
7. Many Japanese immigrants had to accept working for low wages.
8. Owning property was a goal for many of them.
9. Many Japanese immigrants survived by applying skills learned in their native land.
10. One Japanese immigrant began growing rice on wasteland.
11. Cultivating rice is now an important industry in California.
12. Other Japanese immigrants earned a living by fishing for abalone, tuna, and sardines.
13. Some Japanese families in California developed the enterprise of extracting salt from sea water.
14. Many Japanese businesspeople survived by banding together in associations.
15. Lending money to members was one goal of the associations.
16. As more Japanese families arrived, maintaining a sense of their cultural heritage became a part of their lives.
17. Segregating Japanese schools and communities became prevalent in many parts of the West.
18. Wearing traditional dress for special occasions helped keep their heritage alive.
19. Practicing the ancient tea ceremony was one particularly important tradition.
20. Singing traditional songs was another means of preserving cultural ties.
21. Traveling by boat was the only way to cross the ocean before the invention of the airplane.
22. Fishing the ocean waters provided the Japanese with a healthy supply of protein.
23. Living near an ocean enabled Japanese immigrants to continue to enjoy seaweed, a Japanese staple.
24. Some Japanese young people in the United States began to disagree with their elders over keeping to the traditional ways.
25. Working hard has enabled many Japanese Americans to succeed.

Grammar Review

Phrases

Review: Exercise 4 Writing Sentences with Gerund Phrases

The exercise that follows focuses on the lives of immigrants who came from Japan to the United States. Each item consists of a question followed by a phrase in parentheses that answers the question. For each item, write a sentence that answers the question, using the words in parentheses as a gerund phrase.

SAMPLE What is painful? (leaving one's homeland)
ANSWER Leaving one's homeland is painful.

1. In the late nineteenth century, what was difficult in Japan? (earning a living)
2. What seemed like a good idea? (moving to the United States)
3. What was a first step for many poor immigrants? (signing a work contract)
4. What was impossible for early Japanese immigrants? (becoming an American citizen)
5. What did many Japanese immigrants find practical? (living in California)
6. What was a common job for Japanese families who moved to California? (picking grapes)
7. What did many Japanese immigrants have to accept? (working for low wages)
8. What was a goal for many of them? (owning property)
9. How did many Japanese immigrants survive? (applying skills learned in their native land)
10. What did one Japanese immigrant begin doing? (growing rice on wasteland)
11. What is now an important industry in California? (cultivating rice)
12. How did other Japanese immigrants earn a living? (fishing for abalone, tuna, and sardines)
13. What enterprise did some Japanese families in California develop? (extracting salt from sea water)
14. How did many Japanese businesspeople survive? (banding together in associations)
15. What was one goal of the associations? (lending money to members)
16. As more Japanese families arrived, what became a part of their lives? (maintaining a sense of their cultural heritage)
17. What became prevalent in many parts of the West? (segregating Japanese schools and communities)
18. What helped keep their heritage alive? (wearing traditional dress for special occasions)
19. What was one particularly important tradition? (practicing the ancient tea ceremony)
20. What was another means of preserving cultural ties? (singing traditional songs)
21. What was the only way to cross the ocean before the invention of the airplane? (traveling by boat)
22. What provided the Japanese with a healthy supply of protein? (fishing the ocean waters)
23. What enabled Japanese immigrants to continue to enjoy seaweed, a Japanese staple? (living near an ocean)
24. Over what issue did some Japanese young people in the United States begin to disagree with their elders? (keeping to the traditional ways)
25. What is one value that has enabled many Japanese Americans to succeed? (working hard)

Review: Exercise 5 **Writing Sentences with Infinitive Phrases**

The exercise that follows describes some cultural characteristics and practices of Japanese immigrants to the United States early in the twentieth century. Each of the items consists of a question followed by a phrase in parentheses that answers the question. For each item, write a sentence that answers the question, using the words in parentheses as an infinitive phrase.

SAMPLE What did many Japanese immigrants to the United States hope to do? (to start a new life in the new land)

ANSWER Many Japanese immigrants to the United States hoped to start a new life in the new land.

1. What did many Japanese men want to do? (to get married)
2. What was difficult in the United States? (to find a Japanese bride)
3. What did some men return to Japan to do? (to seek a wife)
4. What did other men ask their parents in Japan to do? (to send them a suitable woman for a wife)
5. What did a friend usually agree to do? (to arrange the marriage)
6. What was the young wife forced to do? (to face her frightening and uncertain future with courage)
7. What did the wife need to do? (to travel to America alone)
8. What was wrenching for the picture brides? (to leave their families and their familiar villages behind)
9. What did most wives expect to do in the United States? (to work hard)
10. What did most wives hope to do? (to find economic security)
11. What were Japanese taught as small children? (to control their feelings)
12. What was considered to be proper public conduct for Japanese women? (to be shy and retiring)
13. How was a Japanese wife supposed to act toward her husband? (to act quiet and obedient)
14. What was considered to be a fate worse than death? (to be disgraced)
15. What did Japanese farmers expect their children to do? (to work in the fields)
16. What was the purpose of the large bowl-like hats worn by Japanese fishers? (to protect the head from the sun and the ocean spray)
17. What was the reason behind the Japanese custom of removing shoes upon entering the home? (to avoid damaging the floor mats)
18. What did the large windows in Japanese living rooms allow the members of the family to do? (to view the garden outside)
19. What was one thing that Japanese girls liked to do on holidays? (to wear brightly colored kimonos)
20. What was the purpose of cultivating the silkworm in Japan? (to make silk fabric)

Phrases

Answers: Exercise 5

Answers will vary, but some suggestions are given below.

1. Many Japanese men wanted to get married.
2. To find a Japanese bride was difficult in the United States.
3. Some men returned to Japan to seek a wife.
4. Other men asked their parents in Japan to send them a suitable wife.
5. A friend usually agreed to arrange the marriage.
6. The young wife was forced to face her frightening and uncertain future with courage.
7. The wife needed to travel to America alone.
8. To leave their families and their familiar villages behind was wrenching for the picture brides.
9. Most wives expected to work hard in the United States.
10. Most wives hoped to find economic security.
11. Japanese were taught as small children to control their feelings.
12. To be shy and retiring was considered to be proper public conduct for Japanese women.
13. A Japanese wife was supposed to act quiet and obedient toward her husband.
14. To be disgraced was considered to be a fate worse than death.
15. Japanese farmers expected their children to work in the fields.
16. The purpose of the large bowl-like hats worn by Japanese fishers was to protect the head from the sun and the ocean spray.
17. The reason behind the Japanese custom of removing shoes upon entering the home was to avoid damaging the floor mats.
18. The large windows in Japanese living rooms allowed the members of the family to view the garden outside.
19. One thing that Japanese girls liked to do on holidays was to wear brightly colored kimonos.
20. To make silk fabric was the purpose of cultivating the silkworm in Japan.

Practice and Assess

Answers: Exercise 6

Answers will vary, but some suggestions are given below.

1. Standing at the ship's railing, Hana Omiya shivered.
2. To protect herself from the cold sea winds, she pulled both her silk kimono and her woolen shawl more tightly around her.
3. Transported to a new country, she expected to encounter a strange new life.
4. Wishing desperately for her home consumed all her waking hours.
5. Remembering the beauty of the trees and fields, she longed for home.
6. To see the face of someone she knew would make her happier.
7. Smelling the strong fish odors made her not want to return to her bunk.
8. Anguished about her decision to leave, she knew she was the one who had started this chain of events.
9. Influenced by her uncle's words, she unhappily took the trip to America.
10. To meet her husband-to-be was an experience she was having second thoughts about.

Answers: Exercise 7
Proofreading

This proofreading activity provides editing practice with (1) the current or previous units' skills, (2) the **Troubleshooter** errors, and (3) spelling errors. Students should be able to complete the exercise by referring to the units, the **Troubleshooter,** and a dictionary. (Note: A run-on sentence counts as one error.)

Error (Type of Error)

1. (1797–1858), (nonessential appositive phrase)
   Tokyo. He (run-on sentence)
   planned (unnecessary shift in tense)
   father's (singular possessive)
2. began (verb form)
3. painter's (singular possessive)
4. themes, (introductory participial phrase)
   landscapes, (commas in a series)
5. subjects, (introductory participial phrase)
6. progress, (introductory participial phrase)

Review: Exercise 6 **Writing Sentences with Verbal Phrases**

Use each phrase below in an original sentence about the excerpt from *Picture Bride.* Forms ending with *-ing* may be used in either participial or gerund phrases.

1. standing at the ship's railing
2. to protect herself from the cold sea winds
3. transported to a new country
4. wishing desperately for her home
5. remembering the beauty of the trees and fields
6. to see the face of someone she knew
7. smelling the strong fish odors
8. anguished about her decision to leave
9. influenced by her uncle's words
10. to meet her husband-to-be

Review: Exercise 7

Proofreading

The following passage describes the artist Andō Hiroshige, whose work appears on the opposite page. Rewrite the passage, correcting the errors in spelling, grammar, and usage. Add any missing punctuation. There are twenty-five errors.

Andō Hiroshige

[1]Andō (or Ichiyu-sai) Hiroshige (1797–1858) the son of a fire warden, was born in Edo, a city later called Tokyo and he plans to follow in his fathers footsteps. [2]However, he soon begun to study painting with the famous painter Utagawa Toyohiro.

[3]At first Hiroshige followed another painters practice of using human subjects, but he was soon recognized as a landscape artist. [4]Trying a number of pictorial themes Hiroshige finally settled on landscapes birds, and flowers. [5]Abandoning portraiture and historical subjects he focused on nature themes throughout his life.

[6]Making steady artistic progress Hiroshige experimented with printmaking. [7]Began to make wood-block prints in a style called *ukiyo-e,* which, literally translated, means "floating world." [8]These prints was inexpensively mass-produced for popular consumption. [9]Following an artists instructions craftspeople made the prints.

[10]The subject matter of the *ukiyo-e* prints were historical events portraits, and landscapes. [11]Sometimes the prints was even used to teach people, mainly

Andō Hiroshige, *The Compound of the Tenjin Shrine at Kameido,* 1856

children about some of the elements of Japanese culture. [12]Enabling the populace to have art in their homes printmakers produced countless numbers of such prints. [13]These prints popular and inexpensive works at the time, today are quite valuable.

[14]The artwork on this page, a typical wood-block print is made in the *ukiyo-e* style. [15]Applied with a separate wood block each color is clear and vivid. [16]Hiroshige combined plants, birds, water, and figures crossing a bridge to form a subtly poetic atmosphere in an everyday seen.

[17]To Hana Omiya, the character in Uchida's *Picture Bride* such an image would undoubtedly recall many fond images of Japan and of all things Japanese. [18]Its delicate desine, decorative colors, hanging leaves, and arched bridge would remind her of the world she had left behind.

Phrases

Answers: Exercise 7 *(continued)*

Error (Type of Error)

7. He began (sentence fragment)
8. were (subject-verb agreement)
9. artist's (singular possessive)
   instructions, (introductory participial phrase)
10. was (subject-verb agreement)
    events, (commas in a series)
11. were (subject-verb agreement)
    children, (nonessential appositive phrase)
12. homes, (introductory participial phrase)
13. prints, (nonessential appositive phrase)
14. print, (nonessential appositive phrase)
15. block, (introductory participial phrase)
16. scene (spelling)
17. *Bride,* (nonessential appositive phrase)
18. design (spelling)

Viewing the Art

Andō Hiroshige, *Compound of the Tenjin Shrine at Kameido,* 1856

Japanese art is closely intertwined with literature. Many Japanese prints were inspired by traditional songs, poems, and stories. The written word is also an important part of a Japanese print. Ask students to discuss how beautiful calligraphy that appears in Andō Hiroshige's *Compound of the Tenjin Shrine at Kameido* not only provides information, but also balances visually the composition of the work.

Practice and Assess

Answers: Exercise 8
Mixed Review

Answers may vary, but some suggestions are given below.

1. Yoshiko Uchida, a well-known Japanese American writer, was born in 1921.
2. Her parents came to America to seek a better life.
3. Uchida's mother, an amateur poet, taught her to love words.
4. As a child, Uchida observed many Japanese immigrants struggling to survive.
5. Most of them knew few words of English.
6. Many of the immigrants earned a living running small shops.
7. The immigrants earned a reputation for working hard.
8. The United States entered World War II after Pearl Harbor.
9. When Pearl Harbor was attacked, Uchida was studying for her final exams.
10. The Uchidas were sent to the Tanforan Race Track, a relocation camp.
11. Thousands of Japanese American families were sent to the camps.
12. Uchida's entire family lived in a stall for horses.
13. Uchida lived in the camps for three years.
14. After the war Uchida studied to become a teacher.
15. She taught school in Philadelphia.
16. Later she decided to stop teaching and travel to Japan.
17. She went to Japan to collect folktales.
18. After she returned, she made a decision to write fiction.
19. Most of her work is written for children.
20. *Picture Bride*, her first novel for adults, was published in 1987.

Close

Let groups of students work together to write a paragraph about the most important uses of phrases they have learned in this unit. Ask them to explain how they can apply what they have learned to their other classes. Encourage students to provide effective feedback.

Grammar Review

Phrases

Review: Exercise 8

Mixed Review

Read the brief biography of Yoshiko Uchida. Then use the facts in the biography and the guidelines in parentheses to expand the sentences.

Yoshiko Uchida

Yoshiko Uchida was born in California, in 1921. Her parents, seeking a better life, had moved to the United States several years before Uchida was born. Her mother, who was an amateur poet, taught Uchida to love words. As a child, Uchida witnessed the struggles of many Japanese Americans. Many of them spoke little English but ran their own businesses and earned a reputation as hard workers.

When Uchida was about to begin her final college exams, Japan attacked Pearl Harbor, and the United States entered World War II. Soon afterward the Uchidas, along with thousands of other Japanese Americans, were moved to relocation camps. At the camp at the Tanforan Race Track in California, Uchida's family lived in a horse stall for five months. Uchida spent three years in the grim, dusty camps.

After the war, Uchida studied education and taught in a Philadelphia school. She later left her teaching job and traveled to Japan, where she collected folktales and visited her ancestors' tombs. After learning a great deal about Japanese culture, she returned to California and dedicated herself to writing fiction. Uchida has written mostly for children; *Picture Bride* is her first novel for adults. It appeared in 1987.

1. Yoshiko Uchida was born in 1921. (Add an appositive phrase.)
2. Her parents came to America. (Add an infinitive phrase.)
3. Uchida's mother taught her to love words. (Add an appositive phrase.)
4. As a child, Uchida observed many Japanese immigrants. (Add a participial phrase.)
5. Most of them knew few words. (Add an adjective phrase.)
6. Many of the immigrants earned a living. (Add a participial phrase.)
7. The immigrants earned a reputation. (Add the preposition *for* and a gerund phrase.)
8. The United States entered World War II. (Add an adverb phrase.)
9. When Pearl Harbor was attacked, Uchida was studying. (Add an adverb phrase.)
10. The Uchidas were sent to the Tanforan Race Track. (Add an appositive phrase.)
11. Thousands were sent to the camps. (Add an adjective phrase.)
12. Uchida's entire family lived in a stall. (Add an adjective phrase.)
13. Uchida lived in the camps. (Add an adverb phrase.)
14. After the war Uchida studied. (Add an infinitive phrase.)
15. She taught school. (Add an adverb phrase.)
16. Later she decided to stop and travel to Japan. (Add a gerund or a gerund phrase.)
17. She went to Japan. (Add an infinitive phrase.)
18. After she returned, she made a decision. (Add an infinitive phrase.)
19. Most is written for children. (Add an adjective phrase.)
20. *Picture Bride* was published in 1987. (Add an appositive phrase.)

Writing Application

Phrases in Writing

Note how Mary Stewart uses appositives, participles, and prepositional phrases to enliven this passage from *The Crystal Cave.* As you read, pay particular attention to the italicized words.

Behind me the flow of bats had ceased, and the cave was still. *Reassured*, I stayed where I was, *studying myself with interest in the mirror*. My mother had had one once, *an antique from Egypt,* but then, *deeming such things to be vanity,* she had locked it away. Of course I had often seen my face *reflected in water,* but never my body mirrored, till now. I saw a dark boy, wary, all eyes *with curiosity,* nerves, and excitement. *In that light* my eyes looked quite black; my hair was black, too. . . .

Techniques with Phrases

Try to apply some of Mary Stewart's techniques as you write and revise your own work.

1. Use prepositional phrases to pinpoint location as well as to add specific detail to your sentences. Compare the following:

IMPRECISE VERSION The flow of bats had ceased. My eyes looked quite black.

STEWART'S VERSION *Behind me* the flow of bats had ceased. . . . *In that light* my eyes looked quite black. . . .

2. Use appositives to combine short, choppy sentences.

CHOPPY VERSION My mother had had one once. It was an antique from Egypt.

STEWART'S VERSION My mother had had one once, *an antique from Egypt* . . .

3. Use participles and participial phrases to connect ideas and show the relationships between them.

UNCLEAR VERSION I was reassured. I stayed where I was. I studied myself with interest.

STEWART'S VERSION *Reassured,* I stayed where I was, *studying myself with interest* . . .

TIME

For more about the writing process, see **TIME Facing the Blank Page**, pp. 121-131.

Phrases

Practice Revise the following passage by adding prepositional phrases to show location and by combining choppy sentences with appositives and participles.

Vinland, or Wineland, is an area of North America. It is believed to have been along the coast. The Vikings probably explored this part before other Europeans did. The Vikings were courageous and skillful. The Vikings began to send ships in about the year 1000. They established no settlements. Leif Eriksson was probably sailing from Norway to Greenland. His ship was blown off course. He came to a land. It had first been sighted a few years earlier by another Viking.

LOG ON **Writing** Online | For more grammar practice, go to glencoe.com and enter QuickPass code WC97727p2.

Phrases in Writing

You may want to have students read the paragraph aloud without interruptions and then go back and discuss the italicized phrase choices. Discuss these choices in relation to the Techniques with Phrases section below.

Techniques with Phrases

Discuss the techniques described and then ask students to examine how they are used in a paragraph or two from the Proofreading practice on p. 534.

Practice

The answers to this challenging and enriching activity will vary. Refer to Techniques with Phrases as you evaluate student revisions.

Check to see that students have added prepositional phrases to show locations and have combined choppy sentences using appositives and participles.

ASSESSMENT OPTIONS

Tests with Answer Key & Rubrics
Unit 12 Mastery Test, pp. 45–46

Testmaker
Unit 12 Mastery Test

You may wish to administer the Unit 12 Mastery Test at this point.

MindJogger Videoquizzes

INTRODUCING

UNIT 13

Objectives

- To learn about main and subordinate clauses and about simple, compound, complex, and compound-complex sentences
- To demonstrate control over the use of clauses and the various kinds of sentences by identifying them and employing them effectively in writing

ASSESSMENT OPTIONS

Tests with Answer Key & Rubrics
Unit 13 Pretest, pp. 47–48
Unit 13 Mastery Test, pp. 49–50

You may wish to administer the Unit 13 Pretest at this point.

Testmaker
Unit 13 Pretest
Unit 13 Mastery Test

Key to Ability Levels

L1 Level 1 activities are within the basic ability range of students.

L2 Level 2 activities are within the ability range of average students.

L3 Level 3 activities are more challenging activities.

UNIT 13

Clauses and Sentence Structure

538

Resource Manager

Planning Resources
- *Lesson Plans*
- *Block Scheduling*

Transparencies
- *Bellringer*
- *Daily Language Practice*
- *Two-Minute Skill Drill*

Other Print Resources
- *Grammar and Composition Handbook*
- *Grammar Enrichment*
- *Grammar Practice*
- *Grammar Reteaching*
- *Grammar Workbook*
- *Sentence-Combining Practice*
- *Tests with Answer Key and Rubrics*

Video
- *MindJogger Videoquizzes*

Software
- *Interactive Grammar and Language Workbook*
- *Presentation Plus!*
- *Revising with Style*
- *Testmaker*

Web Site
- *glencoe.com*

13.1 Main Clauses

■ A **clause** is a group of words that has a subject and a predicate and is used as a part of a sentence. A **main**, or **independent**, **clause** has a subject and a predicate and can stand alone as a sentence.

Every sentence must have at least one main clause, but a sentence may have more than one main clause. In each of the following examples, both clauses can stand alone, so both are main, or independent, clauses.

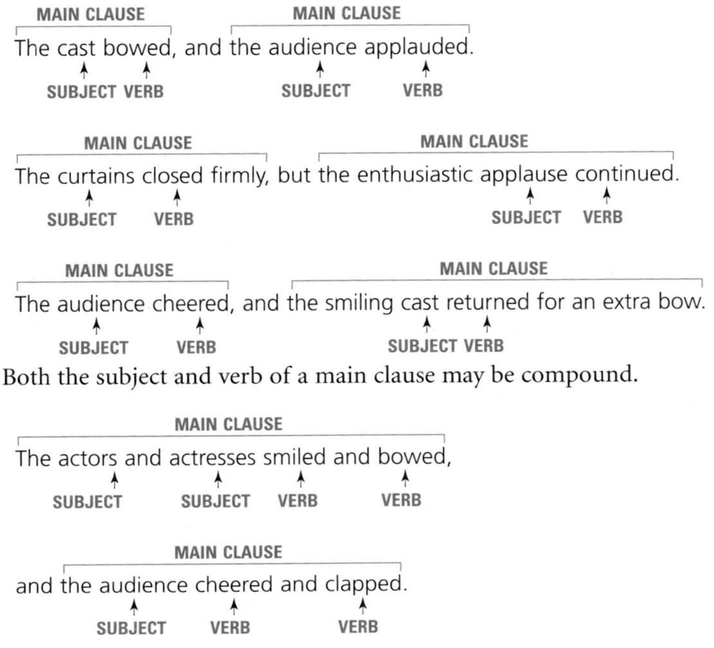

Both the subject and verb of a main clause may be compound.

MAIN CLAUSE

The actors and actresses smiled and bowed,

SUBJECT SUBJECT VERB VERB

MAIN CLAUSE

and the audience cheered and clapped.

SUBJECT VERB VERB

Exercise 1 Identifying Main Clauses

Copy the following sentences and underline each main clause. Then write *S* below each subject and *V* below each verb. Be sure that each clause you mark can stand alone as a sentence.

1. The lights dimmed, and the curtain rose.
2. The setting was a magnificent living room, and the audience applauded the sight.
3. Elegantly dressed people entered and spoke, and the host greeted them.
4. One man sat alone by the fire, and several guests and the host talked with him.
5. The butler announced dinner, but the seated man nodded and slumped in his chair.

Resource Manager

Planning Resources
- *Lesson Plans*

Transparencies
- *Bellringer*
- *Daily Language Practice*

Other Print Resources
- *Grammar and Composition Handbook*
- *Grammar Practice,* p. 18
- *Grammar Workbook,* Lesson 23

Focus

Lesson Overview

Objective
- To understand what a clause is
- To identify main clauses

Bellringer
Daily Language Activity

As students enter the classroom, have this assignment on the board:
Read the following sentences and copy the one that has two main clauses:

1. *Lemons and oranges are both citrus fruits.*
2. *Lemons taste sour, but oranges taste sweet.*

Have students explain their choices. Ask classmates to provide effective feedback and to ask questions for clarification.

See also *Daily Language Practice*

Practice and Assess

Answers: Exercise 1

1. The lights [S] dimmed [V], and the curtain [S] rose [V].
2. The setting [S] was [V] a magnificent living room, and the audience [S] applauded [V] the sight.
3. Elegantly dressed people [S] entered [V] and spoke [V], and the host [S] greeted [V] them.
4. One man [S] sat [V] alone by the fire, and several guests [S] and the host [S] talked [V] with him.
5. The butler [S] announced [V] dinner, but the seated man [S] nodded [V] and slumped [V] in his chair.

Close

Ask students to write a sentence that contains two main clauses. Have volunteers share their sentences with the class, identifying the clauses.

Focus

Lesson Overview

Objective

- To identify subordinate clauses

Bellringer
Daily Language Activity

When students enter the classroom, have this assignment on the board: *Copy the following sentence, underline all clauses, and write* M *above any main clauses:*

Some pine seeds will not sprout unless they have first been heated to a high temperature.

Have students explain their answers. Ask classmates to provide effective feedback and to ask questions for clarification.

See also *Daily Language Practice*

Teach

Listening and Speaking

Point out that speakers can signal the relationship between main and subordinate clauses. For more information about listening and speaking, refer students to Unit 29, pp. 884–892.

Practice and Assess

Answers: Exercise 2

main clause: 1, 3, 10
subordinate clause: 2, 4–9

Close

Write the following sentences on the board: *The school bus arrived late today. It had a flat tire.* Challenge students to rewrite these two sentences as one sentence with a main clause and a subordinate clause.

13.2 Subordinate Clauses

■ A **subordinate**, or **dependent**, clause has a subject and a predicate, but it cannot stand alone as a sentence.

A subordinate clause must be attached to a main clause in order for it to make sense. Subordinate clauses frequently begin with subordinating conjunctions or relative pronouns. When the subordinate clause comes first, a comma separates it from the main clause.

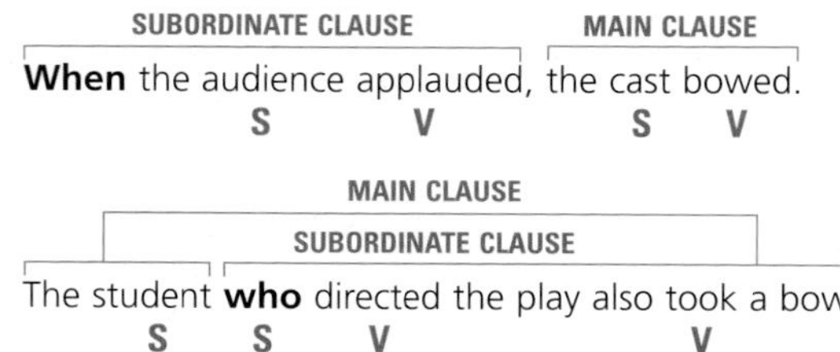

SUBORDINATE CLAUSE
MAIN CLAUSE
When the audience applauded, the cast bowed.
S V S V
MAIN CLAUSE
SUBORDINATE CLAUSE
The student **who** directed the play also took a bow.
S S V V

In the first example, the subordinating conjunction *when* placed before *the audience applauded* creates a word group—*when the audience applauded*—that cannot stand alone as a main clause. Although the clause has a subject and a predicate, it does not express a complete thought.

In the second example, the relative pronoun *who* begins a subordinate clause that comes between the subject and the verb of the main clause. *Who* also serves as the subject of the subordinate clause.

Exercise 2 Identifying Main and Subordinate Clauses

In each of the following sentences, the first clause appears in italics. On your paper, write *main clause* or *subordinate clause* to identify the first clause. (Remember that a subordinate clause cannot stand alone as a sentence.)

Romana Bañuelos, a United States Treasurer

[1]*Romana Acosta Bañuelos was treasurer of the United States from 1971 to 1974,* while Richard Nixon was President. [2]*Though many others have held this position,* Bañuelos was the first Mexican American woman in such a high government post. [3]*Her signature became a familiar sight,* since the treasurer's name is printed on all paper currency. [4]*Because the job of treasurer involves a number of diverse tasks,* the job is a challenging one. [5]*When Bañuelos was in office,* she wrote checks for all government agencies. [6]*Whenever currency became worn out,* she oversaw the destruction and replacement of the bills.

[7]*Although Bañuelos grew up in Mexico,* she was born in Arizona. [8]*After she invested in a small tortilla stand in 1949,* the business grew into a 5-million-dollar food company. [9]*Because her tortilla company had become such a success,* Bañuelos undertook another challenge. [10]*In 1964 she founded the Pan-American National Bank of East Los Angeles,* which was the first bank in the United States run by a Mexican American.

Resource Manager

Planning Resources
- *Lesson Plans*

Transparencies
- *Bellringer*
- *Daily Language Practice*

Other Print Resources
- *Grammar and Composition Handbook*
- *Grammar Reteaching*, p. 18
- *Grammar Workbook*, Lesson 23

13.3 Simple and Compound Sentences

■ A **simple sentence** has only one main clause and no subordinate clauses.

A simple sentence may have a compound subject or a compound predicate or both. The simple subject and the simple predicate may also be expanded in many other ways. Adjectives, adverbs, prepositional phrases, appositives, and verbal phrases may make some simple sentences seem anything but simple. Nevertheless, as long as the sentence has only one main clause and no subordinate clauses, it remains a simple sentence.

Bobcats stalk. [simple sentence]

Bobcats and lynxes stalk. [simple sentence with compound subject]

Bobcats stalk and pounce. [simple sentence with compound predicate]

Bobcats and lynxes stalk and pounce. [simple sentence with compound subject and compound predicate]

Bobcats silently stalk their prey during the night. [simple sentence expanded with modifiers]

■ A **compound sentence** has two or more main clauses and no subordinate clauses.

As the following examples show, each main clause of a compound sentence has its own subject and predicate. Notice that the main clauses of a compound sentence are usually joined by a comma and a coordinating conjunction, such as *and, but, or, nor, yet, so,* or *for*.

MAIN CLAUSE 1 — MAIN CLAUSE 2

Bobcats stalk, and lynxes pursue.

S V — S V

MAIN CLAUSE 1 — MAIN CLAUSE 2 — MAIN CLAUSE 3

Bobcats stalk, and lynxes pursue, but house cats slink.

S V — S V — S V

Two main clauses may also be joined by a semicolon to form a compound sentence.

MAIN CLAUSE 1 — MAIN CLAUSE 2

The frightened rabbit ran swiftly; the lynx followed at a close pace.

Clauses and Sentence Structure

Focus

Lesson Overview

Objective

- To identify simple and compound sentences
- To use them appropriately

Bellringer
Daily Language Activity

When students enter the classroom, have this assignment on the board: *Copy the following sentence and underline each main clause:*

The painter prepared her brushes and chose paints, and she began to paint a forest scene.

Have students trade papers and check each other's sentences. Remind them to provide effective feedback.

See also *Daily Language Practice*

Motivating Activity

Use the Bellringer sentence to show students how a sentence can have two main clauses. Then challenge students to write other sentences with two or more main clauses.

Teach

☑ Teaching Tip

Some students confuse main clauses introduced by the conjunctions *for* and *yet* with subordinate clauses. Point out the difference: Clauses beginning with *for* and *yet* can never be inverted in the way that subordinate clauses can. You can say *I did my homework, yet I failed the test,* but you cannot say *Yet I failed the test, I did my homework.*

Resource Manager

Planning Resources

- *Lesson Plans*

Transparencies

- *Bellringer*
- *Daily Language Practice*

Other Print Resources

- *Grammar and Composition Handbook*
- *Grammar Enrichment,* p. 18
- *Grammar Practice,* p. 18
- *Grammar Reteaching,* p. 18
- *Grammar Workbook,* Lesson 24
- *Sentence-Combining Practice,* p. 1

Practice and Assess

Answers: Exercise 3

1. s
2. c
3. c
4. s
5. s
6. s
7. s
8. c
9. c
10. s

Answers: Exercise 4

Answers will vary, but some suggestions are given below.

1. Robert E. Peary, an arctic explorer, was a brave man.
2. He made his first expedition to Greenland in 1886 and later made several other trips there.
3. In 1898 Peary announced his plans for a trip to the North Pole.
4. He made his trip with his assistant, Matthew Henson, and four Inuit.
5. Peary succeeded in reaching the North Pole on April 6, 1909.

Answers: Exercise 5

Answers will vary, but some suggestions are given below.

1. Robert E. Peary was a brave man; he explored . . .
2. He made his first expedition to Greenland in 1886, and later . . .
3. Peary planned a trip to the North Pole; he . . .
4. Peary's team included four Inuit; his assistant, Matthew Henson, also accompanied him.
5. Peary succeeded in reaching the North Pole, and he arrived . . .

Additional Resources

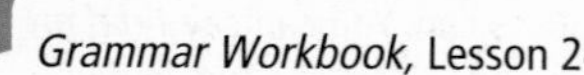

Grammar Practice, p. 18

Sentence-Combining Practice, p. 1

Grammar Workbook, Lesson 24

Close

Ask students to choose a famous person or a character from fiction and to write two sentences about him or her. One sentence should be simple, and the other should be compound.

Exercise 3 Identifying Simple and Compound Sentences

Write *simple* or *compound* to identify each sentence.

Climbing Mount Everest

1. Sir Edmund Hillary and Tenzing Norgay, his Sherpa guide, were the first conquerors of Mount Everest.
2. Norgay was already a well-known mountaineer, but Hillary's experience had been limited to climbing in ice and snow in New Zealand.
3. Norgay was tall and strong, and Hillary liked the Sherpa's friendly attitude.
4. Hillary, Norgay, and all the other members of the expedition looked for the easiest and safest route to the top of Mount Everest.
5. Today climbers look for greater challenges and choose the more difficult routes.
6. Hillary once had traveled overland to the South Pole and also had followed the Ganges River to its source.
7. The public and the media had shown considerable interest in Hillary.
8. Fame came with Hillary's successful ascent of Mount Everest, and afterward he raised money for the Sherpa people of Nepal.
9. They had helped Hillary, and in return he generously helped them.
10. Hillary gave lectures and raised funds for schools, hospitals, clinics, bridges, water pipelines, and airstrips in Nepal.

Exercise 4 Writing Simple Sentences

Combine each pair of ideas below into a simple sentence. Remember that each sentence must have only one main clause, although it may have a compound subject and/or a compound predicate.

SAMPLE Arctic explorers are brave. They must receive special training.
ANSWER Arctic explorers are brave but must receive special training.

1. Robert E. Peary was a brave man. He explored arctic regions.
2. He made his first expedition to Greenland in 1886. Later he made several other trips there.
3. Peary planned a trip to the North Pole. He announced his plans in 1898.
4. He made the trip with his assistant, Matthew Henson. Peary's team also included four Inuit.
5. Peary succeeded in reaching his goal. He arrived at the North Pole on April 6, 1909.

Exercise 5 Writing Compound Sentences

Use the information in each item from Exercise 4 to write a compound sentence. Remember that each sentence must have two or more main clauses joined by a comma and a coordinating conjunction or by a semicolon.

SAMPLE Arctic explorers are brave. They must receive special training.
ANSWER Arctic explorers are brave, but they must receive special training.

MEETING INDIVIDUAL NEEDS English Language Learners

Writing Compound Sentences

Students learning English may have difficulty composing compound sentences in their own writing. Help students go through their journals and identify several simple sentences that could be improved by being combined into a compound sentence. Work with small groups of students to do one or more examples and then have students work on their own to combine sentences.

13.4 Complex and Compound-Complex Sentences

- A **complex sentence** has one main clause and one or more subordinate clauses.

MAIN CLAUSE — SUBORDINATE CLAUSE
Some areas become deforested because people need wood for fuel.
S V S V

SUBORDINATE CLAUSE — MAIN CLAUSE
Because people need fuel, they cut down trees
S V S V

SUBORDINATE CLAUSE
that have grown for many years.
S V

Because people needed fuel
they cut down trees
that had grown for many years.

- A **compound-complex sentence** has more than one main clause and at least one subordinate clause.

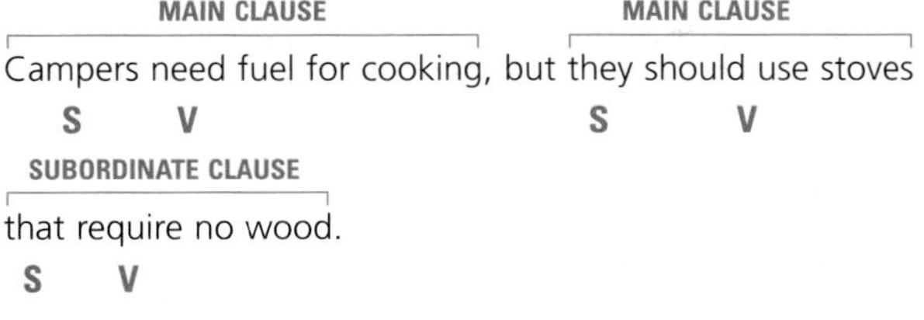
MAIN CLAUSE — MAIN CLAUSE
Campers need fuel for cooking, but they should use stoves
S V S V

SUBORDINATE CLAUSE
that require no wood.
S V

Exercise 6 Identifying Subordinate Clauses

Write the subordinate clause in each of the following sentences. If a sentence has no subordinate clause, write *none*.

1. Since the world's supply of wood is limited, environmentalists encourage conservation of timber resources.
2. The United States government controls large areas of national forest and sets the policy for use of the timber.
3. Many states have set aside land for state forests, which may also be used for recreation.
4. People's ideas about forest conservation differ, and opposing groups present arguments that deserve serious consideration.
5. Because opinions on the subject are so different, no simple solution exists.

Focus

Lesson Overview

Objective

- To identify and create complex and compound-complex sentences

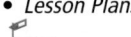

Bellringer
Daily Language Activity

When students enter the classroom, have this assignment on the board: *Write your own definitions of the words* simple *and* complex. Discuss student's answers. Then relate the discussion to sentence structures.

See also *Daily Language Practice*

Teach

Teaching Tip

The terms *complex* and *compound* are easily confused. To help students remember the difference between complex and compound-complex sentences, tell them that a complex sentence has only one main clause.

Practice and Assess

Answers: Exercise 6

1. Since . . . limited
2. none
3. which . . . recreation
4. that . . . consideration
5. Because . . . different

Resource Manager

Planning Resources
- *Lesson Plans*

Transparencies
- *Bellringer*
- *Daily Language Practice*

Other Print Resources
- *Grammar and Composition Handbook*
- *Grammar Enrichment*, p. 18
- *Grammar Workbook*, Lesson 25

Practice and Assess

Answers: Exercise 7

1. because . . . day—complex
2. When . . . homes—complex
3. Although . . . more—compound-complex
4. Because . . . laws—complex
5. When . . . gas—compound-complex
6. Though . . . health—complex
7. Although . . . electricity—complex
8. that . . . goods—compound-complex
9. that . . . us—compound-complex
10. Because . . . forever—complex

Answers: Exercise 8

Answers will vary, but some suggestions are given below.

An electric motor is clean. (simple); It is clean, and it is silent. (compound); Although an electric motor is convenient, it is expensive to manufacture. (complex); Although it is expensive to manufacture, it starts instantly and it stops instantly. (compound-complex)

Answers: Exercise 9

Answers will vary, but some suggestions are given below.

I like movies. (simple); I like movies, and I like books. (compound); Although I like movies, they can be expensive. (complex); Although I like movies and books, movies aren't always easy to get to, and books can be expensive. (compound-complex)

Additional Resources

Grammar Enrichment, p. 18

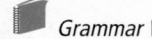

Grammar Workbook, Lesson 25

Close

Ask students to explain in writing the differences between a simple sentence, a compound sentence, a complex sentence, and a compound-complex sentence. Have students share their explanations in small groups. Remind students to respond appropriately and to ask questions for clarification.

Exercise 7 Identifying Complex and Compound-Complex Sentences

Write the subordinate clause that appears in each of the following sentences. Then write *complex* or *compound-complex* to identify each sentence.

Conservation

1. Energy conservation has become extremely important because millions of energy-consuming devices are in use every day.
2. When builders construct new homes, they should install solar panels and other passive solar devices and as many energy-saving appliances as possible.
3. Although energy-efficient appliances cost more, their use results in long-term savings for the owner, and the environment benefits, too.
4. Because legislators have enacted certain laws, all new cars must be energy efficient.
5. When cars use less gas, the air is cleaner, and people may have less trouble breathing.
6. Though sulfur pollution is a threat to human health, it also damages lakes, wildlife, and buildings.
7. Although water power can generate electricity, hydroelectric dams may cause floods on farmland, in forests, and in wildlife areas.
8. We must always find ways of producing more goods, but at the same time we must reduce the amount of energy that we consume in producing those goods.
9. Conservation and solar power are the keys to a safe future, so we must cautiously use the devices that cool, heat, and transport us.
10. Because our natural resources clearly cannot last forever, we must find better ways of conserving them.

Exercise 8 Writing Four Kinds of Sentences

Use your own knowledge and the information below to create four different kinds of sentences about electrical power. Write *simple, compound, complex,* or *compound-complex* to identify each sentence you write.

An electric motor is a source of power.
It is convenient.
It is clean.
It is silent.
It starts instantly.
It stops instantly.
It can be built in almost any size.
It can power a speeding train.
It can run a tiny watch.
Power can come through a wire from an outside source.
Power can come from a battery.
An electric car does not pollute.
It is expensive to manufacture.
It needs frequent recharging.

Exercise 9 Creating Sentences with Various Structures

Write a simple sentence. Then rework it, making it into a compound sentence. Now go back to the simple sentence, and rework it to make it part of a complex sentence. Finally, rework your compound sentence into a compound-complex sentence. Label each sentence.

MEETING INDIVIDUAL NEEDS

English Language Learners

Identifying Clue Words

Tell students to look for clue words, such as subordinating conjunctions and relative pronouns, to identify a subordinate clause. Make a list of subordinating conjunctions and relative pronouns.

13.5 Adjective Clauses

■ An **adjective clause** is a subordinate clause that modifies a noun or a pronoun.

An adjective clause normally follows the word it modifies.

The hikers **who reached the peak** were overjoyed.

The trail, **which was rarely used,** had been a difficult one.

I forgot about the blisters **that covered my feet.**

The hiker **whom we appreciated most** carried the food.

The hikers, who were diverted by the natural splendor, arrived later in the day.

Both relative pronouns (*who, whom, whose, that,* and *which*) and the words *where* and *when* may begin adjective clauses.

I will always remember the time **when I hiked to Pike's Peak.**

That is the spot **where we set up camp.**

Sometimes the relative pronoun is dropped at the beginning of an adjective clause.

Our camp was the place **every hiker loved the most.**
[The relative pronoun *that* has been omitted.]

An adjective clause is sometimes essential to a sentence; that is, it is needed to make the meaning of the sentence clear. This kind of adjective clause is called an *essential clause,* or a *restrictive clause.*

One characteristic **that many Native Americans had in common** was a love of dancing. [essential clause]

An adjective clause that is not needed to make the meaning of a sentence clear is called a *nonessential clause,* or a *nonrestrictive clause.* It adds information to a sentence, but the sentence would be perfectly logical without it. (Note that a nonessential clause must be set off with commas.)

The Iroquois people of the East, **who were farmers,** thanked the spirits for the gift of food. [nonessential clause]

In the Southwest, **where water is scarce,** the Pueblo people performed rain dances. [nonessential clause]

Clauses and Sentence Structure

Focus

Lesson Overview

Objective

- To identify and use adjective clauses appropriately

Bellringer
Daily Language Activity

As students enter the classroom, have this assignment on the board:
Complete each of the following sentences, and underline each adjective clause:

The students who____

The flowers, which____

The classroom that____

See also *Daily Language Practice*

Motivating Activity

Discuss student responses to the sentences in the Bellringer activity above. Explain that students used adjective clauses to complete each of the sentences and that they will learn more about such clauses in this lesson.

Teach

☑ Grammar Tip

One of the features of adjective clauses is the relative pronoun *that* begins the clause. The relative pronoun must always have a noun as its antecedent. Usually the pronoun follows that noun.

Cross-reference: Grammar

For instruction and practice with adjectives and how they modify nouns and pronouns, refer students to Unit 10.4, pp. 461–466.

Resource Manager

Planning Resources
- *Lesson Plans*

Transparencies
- *Bellringer*
- *Daily Language Practice*
- *Two-Minute Skill Drill*

Other Print Resources
- *Grammar and Composition Handbook*
- *Grammar Enrichment,* p. 19
- *Grammar Practice,* p. 19
- *Grammar Reteaching,* p. 19
- *Grammar Workbook,* Lessons 8, 26, 54
- *Sentence-Combining Practice,* pp. 14, 15, 17

Teach

☑ Teaching Tip

The relative pronoun is a distinctive feature of the adjective clause. Sometimes, however, the relative pronoun is deleted from the adjective clause. For example, in *I saw the book I was looking for,* the pronoun *that* is deleted. Restoring the pronoun can help students identify the clause.

Two-Minute Skill Drill

Use these words in sentences containing adjective clauses:

who *that* *where*

which *whom*

See also *Two-Minute Skill Drill Transparency 13.5*

Practice and Assess

Answers: Exercise 10

1. that are deceptively simple—steps
2. which swoops and dives for its food—eagle
3. that require difficult body movements—dances
4. which has been performed for thousands of years—dance
5. each of which represents a different character—layers
6. that is very popular—dance
7. which became popular in George Washington's time—reel
8. [that] the Gypsies in Spain invented—form
9. who is accompanied by a guitarist—dancer
10. that are difficult to learn—steps

Answers: Exercise 11

Answers will vary, but some suggestions are given below.

1. dinner, which I eat at six
2. Francine, who helped me learn algebra
3. robin that flew by
4. book, which is incomprehensible
5. appointment that I made
6. notebook that has the red stars
7. VCR, which is being repaired
8. car that splashed me
9. my brother, who is in college
10. good times that we had shared

When choosing between *that* and *which,* use *that* to introduce an essential clause and *which* to begin a nonessential clause.

The Cheyenne hunted buffalo, **which supplied them with meat and skins for clothing and shelter.** [nonessential clause]

The animal **that was most important to the Cheyenne** was the buffalo. [essential clause]

Exercise 10 Identifying Adjective Clauses and the Words They Modify

On your paper write the adjective clause from each sentence. Then write the word the clause modifies. (In one sentence the relative pronoun has been dropped.)

International Dances

1. The Pueblo rain dancers use dance steps that are deceptively simple.
2. In the eagle dance, the dancers' movements are like those of the eagle, which swoops and dives for its food.
3. Chinese schoolchildren learn dances that require difficult body movements.
4. The Chinese ribbon dance, which has been performed for thousands of years, is often performed by Chinese folk-dance companies.
5. Japanese dancers may wear several layers of kimonos, each of which represents a different character.
6. A lively dance that is very popular is the square dance.
7. Probably the best-known early American dance is the Virginia reel, which became popular in George Washington's time.
8. Flamenco is a dance form the Gypsies in Spain invented.
9. A flamenco dancer, who is accompanied by a guitarist, typically wears bright and colorful clothing.
10. Folk dances often require steps that are difficult to learn.

Exercise 11 Adding Adjective Clauses to Sentences

On your paper complete each sentence below by adding a noun. Then write an adjective clause to modify the noun.

1. My favorite meal is _______.
2. I will always remember _______.
3. Did you see the _______?
4. I really don't like the _______.
5. I had forgotten all about the _______.
6. Where did you get the _______?
7. Tomorrow I will pick up the _______.
8. This is the _______.
9. Last week I visited _______.
10. We laughed about the _______.

Exercise 12 Identifying Essential and Nonessential Clauses

For each sentence in the following pairs, write the adjective clause, and then write *essential* or *nonessential* to identify it.

Maya Lin, Architect

1. **a.** Maya Lin, who was born and raised in Athens, Ohio, designed the Vietnam Veterans Memorial.
   b. The person who designed the Vietnam Veterans Memorial was Maya Lin.
2. **a.** Lin was an architecture student who submitted the once-controversial design.
   b. Lin, who submitted the once-controversial design, was an architecture student at Yale University.
3. **a.** Her simple design consisted of two gleaming black walls that were inscribed with the names of the dead and missing.
   b. The memorial, which has attracted numerous visitors since its unveiling, contains the names of the war's dead and the missing.
4. **a.** In 1988, Maya Lin designed the Civil Rights Memorial, which is in Montgomery, Alabama.
   b. In 1988, Maya Lin designed a memorial that commemorates the Civil Rights Movement.
5. **a.** Maya Lin's parents, who were college professors, emigrated from China in the 1940s.
   b. The college professors who were Lin's parents emigrated from China in the 1940s.

Exercise 13 Identifying Adjective Clauses

Rewrite the sentences below. Underline each adjective clause. If a clause is nonessential, set it off with commas.

1. In most cultures around the world, people have dances that they use to tell stories.
2. Often the dancers who may wear colorful costumes are accompanied by singing, chanting, or playing of special instruments.
3. Many immigrants who moved to the United States from Europe, Africa, Asia, and South America brought their dances with them.
4. The dances that came from England, Ireland, and Scotland became the basis for American square dancing.
5. Native Americans who are descendants of the earliest inhabitants of this continent still perform colorful ceremonial dances of their own.

Answers: Exercise 12

1. **a.** who was born and raised in Athens, *nonessential* **b.** who designed the Vietnam Veterans Memorial, *essential*
2. **a.** who submitted the once-controversial design, *essential* **b.** who submitted the once-controversial design, *nonessential*
3. **a.** that were inscribed with the names of the dead and missing, *essential* **b.** which has attracted numerous visitors since its unveiling, *nonessential*
4. **a.** which is in Montgomery, Alabama, *nonessential* **b.** that commemorates the Civil Rights Movement, *essential*
5. **a.** who were college professors, *nonessential* **b.** who were Lin's parents, *essential*

Answers: Exercise 13

1. that they use to tell stories
2. dancers, who may wear colorful costumes,
3. who moved to the United States from Europe, Africa, Asia, and South America
4. that came from England, Ireland, and Scotland
5. Native Americans, who are descendants of the earliest inhabitants of this continent,

Additional Resources

Grammar Practice, p. 19
Grammar Reteaching, p. 19
Grammar Enrichment, p. 19
Sentence-Combining Practice, pp. 14, 15, 17

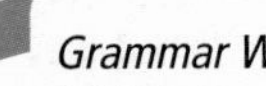

Grammar Workbook, Lessons 8, 26, 54

Close

Have small groups of students formulate a strategy for incorporating what they have learned about adjective clauses into their work in other classes. Ask students to record their strategy in their journal. Then have each group present its strategy to the class. Encourage groups to revise their strategy on the basis of the discussion.

Meeting Individual Needs: English Language Learners

Identifying Essential and Nonessential Clauses

On the board, write sentences with essential and nonessential clauses. After students identify each clause, erase it and have students read the new sentence. Teach students that if the sentence needs the clause, the clause does not need commas.

Focus

Lesson Overview

Objective

- To identify and use adverb clauses in sentences

Bellringer
Daily Language Activity

When students enter the classroom, have this assignment on the board: *Complete these sentences by writing when, where, how, or why:*

The car skidded . . .

No one was hurt . . .

From now on we'll drive . . .

See also *Daily Language Practice*

Motivating Activity

Discuss student answers to the Bellringer activity. Explain that they created adverb clauses. Encourage students to ask questions for clarification.

Teach

Teaching Tip

Like adverbs, adverb clauses can appear in different places in a sentence. When they appear at the beginning or in the middle of a sentence, they must be set off with commas; if they occur at the end of a sentence, a comma is often unnecessary. For example:

Because he was ill, Andy stayed home.

Andy, because he was ill, stayed home.

Andy stayed home because he was ill.

See *Grammar Reteaching,* p. 20.

13.6 Adverb Clauses

- An **adverb** clause is a subordinate clause that modifies a verb, an adjective, or an adverb. It tells *when, where, how, why, to what extent,* or *under what conditions.*

Whenever it rains, the river rises. [The adverb clause modifies the verb *rises.* It tells *when.*]

This canoe can take us **wherever we want to go.** [The adverb clause modifies the verb phrase *can take.* It tells *where.*]

The canoe will be safe **as long as everyone remains seated.** [The adverb clause modifies the adjective *safe.* It tells *under what conditions.*]

You are paddling harder **than I am paddling.** [The adverb clause modifies the adverb *harder.* It tells *to what extent.*]

Subordinating conjunctions, such as those listed on page 477, introduce adverb clauses. Being familiar with those conjunctions will help you recognize adverb clauses.

An adverb clause may come either before or after the main clause. Notice how the comma is used when the adverb clause begins the sentence.

The canoe capsized **when the river got rough.**

When the river got rough, the canoe capsized.

Occasionally words may be left out of an adverb clause. The omitted words can easily be supplied because they are understood, or implied. Such adverb clauses are described as *elliptical.*

You are paddling harder **than I am [paddling].**

Paddling made me more tired **than [it made] him [tired].**

Resource Manager

Planning Resources
- *Lesson Plans*

Transparencies
- *Bellringer*
- *Daily Language Practice*

Other Print Resources
- *Grammar and Composition Handbook*
- *Grammar Enrichment,* p. 20
- *Grammar Practice,* p. 20
- *Grammar Reteaching,* p. 20
- *Grammar Workbook,* Lesson 27
- *Sentence-Combining Practice,* pp. 18-20

Exercise 14 Identifying Adverb Clauses

Write the adverb clauses that appear in the following sentences. (Three sentences have more than one adverb clause.)

Yo-Yo Ma, an Outstanding Cellist

1. Yo-Yo Ma played the cello at Carnegie Hall, when he was only nine years old.
2. Because he had such talent, young Ma already played better than most adults do.
3. When Ma was only four, his father gave him cello lessons.
4. Since Ma's father was a musicologist, he nurtured his son's talent.
5. When he was big enough, Ma switched to a regular cello.
6. After his family moved from Paris to New York, Ma studied at the Juilliard School of Music.
7. Wherever he played, Ma dazzled audiences with his deftness.
8. Ma continued on the cello while he worked on a degree from Harvard.
9. A highlight in his career came in 1978, when Ma received the Avery Fisher Prize for his musical talent.
10. Whenever Ma performs, fans can hardly imagine a cellist more talented than he.
11. When Ma played with the Chicago Symphony recently, I saw him in person.
12. The tickets were more expensive than I had expected.
13. Many people attended that evening because Ma's performance earlier that week had received rave reviews.
14. Before Ma appeared on stage, everyone waited impatiently as the orchestra tuned up their instruments.
15. When the great performer finally made his entrance, the audience jumped to their feet and applauded.

Exercise 15 Using Adverb Clauses in Sentences

Use each of the following adverb clauses in an original sentence. Vary the positions of the clauses in your sentences.

1. whenever the first members of the audience arrive
2. as long as I can hear from the back of the auditorium
3. unless something happens at the last minute
4. although she still used her father's old stereo system
5. because the traffic was so heavy that night
6. although no one was given information beforehand
7. until everyone finds a place to sit down
8. before the master of ceremonies could say a single word
9. since I had decided earlier not to go with them
10. wherever people get together to hear fine music

Practice and Assess

Answers: Exercise 14

1. when he was only nine years old
2. Because he had such talent; than most adults do
3. When Ma was only four
4. Since Ma's father was a musicologist
5. When he was big enough
6. After his family moved from Paris to New York
7. Wherever he played
8. while he worked on a degree from Harvard
9. when Ma received the Avery Fisher Prize for his musical talent
10. Whenever Ma performs; than he
11. When Ma played with the Chicago Symphony recently
12. than I had expected
13. because Ma's performance earlier that week had received rave reviews
14. Before Ma appeared on stage; as the orchestra tuned up their instruments
15. When the great performer finally made his entrance

Answers: Exercise 15

Answers will vary, but some suggestions are given below.

1. The lights come up whenever the first members of the audience arrive.
2. I don't mind arriving later than most as long as I can hear from the back of the auditorium.
3. Unless something happens at the last minute, I plan to be on time for my appointment.
4. She had a new CD player although she still used her father's old stereo system.
5. We were late because the traffic was so heavy that night.
6. We found our way quickly although no one was given information beforehand.
7. The performance won't start until everyone finds a place to sit down.
8. The electricity went off before the master of ceremonies could say a single word.
9. I missed the excitement since I had decided earlier not to go with them.
10. You will find music connoisseurs wherever people get together to hear fine music.

Close

Have small groups of students devise a strategy for applying what they have studied about adverb clauses to another class. Ask each group to write down their strategy and then to discuss it with the class. Encourage students to provide effective feedback. Then have students summarize in their journal the strategy they will use.

Additional Resources

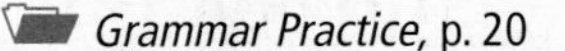 *Grammar Practice,* p. 20

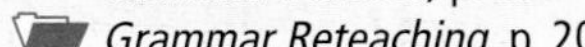 *Grammar Reteaching,* p. 20

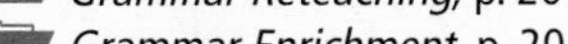 *Grammar Enrichment,* p. 20

Sentence-Combining Practice, pp. 18–20

 *Grammar Workbook,* Lesson 27

Focus

Lesson Overview

Objective

- To identify and use noun clauses correctly in writing

Bellringer
Daily Language Activity

When students enter the classroom, have this assignment on the board: *Complete the following sentences: I know where . . . This is why . . . She believes that . . .*

See also  *Daily Language Practice*

Motivating Activity

Discuss students' sentences from the Bellringer activity. Explain that they used noun clauses when completing the sentences. In this lesson, they will study more about noun clauses.

Teach

Grammar Tip

To identify noun clauses, try replacing them with the pronoun *it* or *somebody.* Because adjective and adverb clauses do not play the role of nouns, they cannot be replaced by pronouns. The pronouns *it* and *somebody* can always replace noun clauses, because noun clauses are always singular.

Unlike adjective and adverb clauses, a noun clause can never be deleted from a sentence without changing its meaning, and it can rarely be moved to another part of the sentence.

Cross-reference: Usage

For more help with using *who* and *whom* in subordinate clauses, refer students to Lesson 17.4, pp. 638–639.

Clauses and Sentence Structure

13.7 Noun Clauses

■ A **noun clause** is a subordinate clause used as a noun.

You can use a noun clause as a subject, a direct object, an indirect object, an object of a preposition, a predicate nominative, or an object complement.

NOUN
Campers enjoy the outdoors.
S

NOUN CLAUSE
Whoever camps enjoys the outdoors.
S

NOUN
Footgear affects hikers.
DO

NOUN CLAUSE
Footgear affects whoever walks often.
DO

In the preceding examples, notice that each noun clause is an inseparable part of the sentence's main clause; the main clause is the entire sentence.

Here are some of the words that can be used to introduce noun clauses:

how	when	who, whom
that	where	whoever
what	which	whose
whatever	whichever	why

Here are additional examples of noun clauses.

I do not know **where my hiking boots are.** [direct object]

That is **why I did not join the others.** [predicate nominative]

We will make do with **whatever camping equipment we can borrow.** [object of a preposition]

Sometimes the introductory word may be dropped at the beginning of a noun clause.

I believe **we can have a great time outdoors.** [The introductory word *that* is omitted.]

Resource Manager

Planning Resources
- *Lesson Plans*

Transparencies
- *Bellringer*
- *Daily Language Practice*

Other Print Resources
- *Grammar and Composition Handbook*
- *Grammar Enrichment,* p. 21
- *Grammar Practice,* p. 21
- *Grammar Reteaching,* p. 21
- *Grammar Workbook,* Lesson 28
- *Sentence-Combining Practice,* p. 24

Exercise 16 Identifying Noun Clauses

Write the noun clauses that appear in each of the following sentences. (Three of the sentences have two noun clauses each. In one sentence the relative pronoun introducing the noun clause has been dropped.)

The Importance of Police Dogs

1. Everyone knows that dogs have a keen sense of smell.
2. What makes their sense of smell valuable is that people can train dogs to sniff out explosives.
3. Specially trained dogs search for whatever explosive device they can find.
4. What the dog finds may save whoever is in danger.
5. Do you believe that police dogs are valuable?
6. Whoever works with a police dog is trained along with the dog.
7. Many police officers say that police dogs make good partners.
8. Whoever says police dogs are vicious animals is misinformed.
9. That these dogs become aggressive upon command is true.
10. Police officers are grateful for whatever help these dogs provide.
11. Most people realize that police dogs will not attack them without cause.
12. They will pay little attention to whomever leaves them alone.
13. The laws of some communities state that police dogs should be muzzled.
14. Another regulation is that they should usually be on leashes.
15. Can you see why their appearance frightens some people?

Exercise 17 Identifying Subordinate Clauses

On your paper write the subordinate clause that appears in each sentence. Then write *adverb clause, adjective clause,* or *noun clause* to identify what kind of clause it is.

Sojourner Truth, a Crusader for Justice

[1]Sojourner Truth was an enslaved person who was born in New York in the late eighteenth century. [2]Isabella is what she was called as a child. [3]Whoever has studied her life understands the importance of her work. [4]She fought against slavery wherever she went. [5]An antislavery law was passed in New York in 1817, which led to Isabella's freedom in 1827. [6]In 1843, after she took the name Sojourner Truth, she began a series of lecture tours throughout New England and the Midwest. [7]Her speeches expressed her strong belief that all people are equal. [8]One source of income was the proceeds from her biography, which was published in 1850. [9]Sojourner Truth campaigned for land where former enslaved persons could establish homes. [10]Sojourner Truth was a woman whom everyone admired.

Exercise 18 Writing Subordinate Clauses in Sentences

Write four original sentences. In the first, use an adverb clause. In the second, use an adjective clause. In the third, use a noun clause as a subject. In the fourth, use a noun clause as a direct object. Label the clauses.

Practice and Assess

Answers: Exercise 16

1. that dogs have a keen sense of smell
2. What makes their sense of smell valuable; that people can train dogs to sniff out explosives
3. whatever explosive device they can find
4. What the dog finds; whoever is in danger
5. that police dogs are valuable
6. Whoever works with a police dog
7. that police dogs make good partners
8. Whoever says [that] police dogs are vicious animals
9. That these dogs become aggressive upon command
10. whatever help these dogs provide
11. that police dogs will not attack them without cause
12. whomever leaves them alone
13. that police dogs should be muzzled
14. that they should usually be on leashes
15. why their appearance frightens some people

Answers: Exercise 17

1. who was born in New York in the late eighteenth century (adjective clause)
2. what she was called as a child (noun clause)
3. Whoever has studied her life (noun clause)
4. wherever she went (adverb clause)
5. which led to Isabella's freedom in 1827 (adjective clause)
6. after she took the name Sojourner Truth (adverb clause)
7. that all people are equal (adjective clause)
8. which was published in 1850 (adjective clause)
9. where former enslaved persons could establish homes (adjective clause)
10. whom everyone admired (adjective clause)

Answers: Exercise 18

Answers will vary, but some suggestions are given below.

1. I am delighted because I can now rent foreign films.
2. The director that I admire most is François Truffaut.
3. Whoever has seen his first film considers it a masterpiece.
4. The film explores what Truffaut felt as a boy growing up.

Close

Discuss with students a strategy for applying what they have learned about noun clauses to writing sentences about history. For example, the president *who inspired the New Deal* is Franklin D. Roosevelt.

Additional Resources

- *Grammar Practice,* p. 21
- *Grammar Reteaching,* p. 21
- *Grammar Enrichment,* p. 21
- *Sentence-Combining Practice,* p. 24

Grammar Workbook, Lesson 28

Focus

Lesson Overview

Objective

- To identify declarative, imperative, interrogative, and exclamatory sentences
- To punctuate them properly

Bellringer
Daily Language Activity

When students enter the classroom, have this assignment on the board: *Copy the following sentences, and punctuate them correctly: (a) Halloween falls on October 31 (b) Is Halloween on Tuesday this year*

See also *Daily Language Practice*

Teach

☑ Grammar Tip

Point out that the term *imperative* literally means "a command." All imperative sentences are commands with an understood "you."

Practice and Assess

Answers: Exercise 19

1. int., ?
2. excl., !
3. decl., .
4. decl., .
5. imp., .

Answers: Exercise 20

Answers will vary, but some suggestions are given below.
1. I was intrigued by our recent school assembly on the art of mime. **2.** Don't miss an opportunity to see an example of this art form. **3.** Have you ever seen a film of the pantomimist Marcel Marceau? **4.** What grace and imagination he displays!

13.8 Four Kinds of Sentences

■ A **declarative sentence** makes a statement.

An owl is hooting.
I cannot see it.

A declarative sentence normally ends with a period. It is the type of sentence used most frequently in speaking and writing.

■ An **imperative sentence** gives a command or makes a request.

Look at that bird.
Please tell me what it is.

An imperative sentence usually ends with a period. The subject "you" is understood.

■ An **interrogative sentence** asks a question.

What kind of bird is that?
Is the hawk hunting for prey?

An interrogative sentence ends with a question mark.

■ An **exclamatory sentence** expresses strong emotion.

Watch out for that hawk's sudden dive!
What a powerful hunter the hawk is!

An exclamatory sentence ends with an exclamation point.

Exercise 19 Identifying and Punctuating Four Kinds of Sentences

On your paper write *declarative, imperative, interrogative,* or *exclamatory* to identify each sentence below. Then give the correct ending punctuation.

1. Have you ever been to Niagara Falls
2. What an awesome sight they are
3. The falls are on the Niagara River between New York State and Ontario, Canada
4. When you go, I hope that you plan to visit both the American and the Canadian sides
5. Don't miss the boat ride on the *Maid of the Mist*

Exercise 20 Writing Four Kinds of Sentences

Write four sentences about a recent school event. Use one declarative, one imperative, one interrogative, and one exclamatory sentence. Remember to punctuate each sentence correctly.

Close

Ask students to imagine that they are sportswriters writing an article about a game or competition. They should write a few sentences about the event, including one example of each kind of sentence. Have students evaluate each other's sentences and provide effective feedback. Ask students to revise their sentences as needed.

Resource Manager

Planning Resources
- *Lesson Plans*

Transparencies
- *Bellringer*
- *Daily Language Practice*

Other Print Resources
- *Grammar and Composition Handbook*
- *Grammar Enrichment,* p. 22
- *Grammar Practice,* p. 22
- *Grammar Reteaching,* p. 22
- *Grammar Workbook,* Lessons 29–30

13.9 Sentence Fragments

■ A **sentence fragment** is an error that occurs when an incomplete sentence is punctuated as though it were a complete sentence. In general, avoid sentence fragments in your writing.

When you check your work for sentence fragments, look for three things. First, be alert for a group of words that lacks a subject. Then, look for a group of words that lacks a verb, especially a group that contains a verbal form rather than a complete verb. Finally, be careful that you have not punctuated a subordinate clause as a complete sentence.

Often you can correct a sentence fragment by joining it to an idea that comes before or after the fragment. Sometimes, however, you may need to add missing words to form a complete sentence.

FRAGMENT	Toshiko and Kenji are happy together. **Seem to be in love.** [lacks subject]
COMPLETE SENTENCE	Toshiko and Kenji are happy together, and they seem to be in love.
FRAGMENT	The two will marry. **Their new life together.** [lacks verb]
COMPLETE SENTENCE	The two will marry, and their new life together will begin.
FRAGMENT	They are planning an out-of-town wedding. **Many of their gifts arriving in the mail.** [lacks complete verb]
COMPLETE SENTENCE	They are planning an out-of-town wedding. Many of their gifts have been arriving in the mail.
FRAGMENT	On their honeymoon they will be traveling to Italy. **Which they both love.** [has subordinate clause only]
COMPLETE SENTENCE	On their honeymoon they will be traveling to Italy, which they both love.

Artist Unknown, *Nike of Samothrace,* 200–190 B.C.

Professional writers sometimes use sentence fragments to create a special effect—to add emphasis to what they are saying or to convey realistic dialogue. Remember that professionals use sentence fragments *carefully* and *intentionally.* In most of the writing you do, however, including your writing for school, you should avoid sentence fragments.

Focus

Lesson Overview

Objectives

- To identify sentence fragments
- To correct sentence fragments in writing

Bellringer
Daily Language Activity

When students enter the classroom, have this assignment on the board: *Identify which of the following is a complete sentence and which is a sentence fragment:*

Clothes tossed all over the room. (sentence fragment) Clothes had been tossed all over the room. (complete sentence)

Ask students to explain how they made the identifications. Remind students to ask questions to clarify understanding as needed.

See also *Daily Language Practice*

Teach

Teaching Tip

Explain that a good test to identify fragments is to put "I know that" in front of the suspected fragment. If it is a fragment, the words won't make any sense.

A common kind of sentence fragment is an adjective clause incorrectly punctuated as a complete sentence. This kind of fragment can be easily corrected by joining the adjective clause to the noun that the clause modifies in the preceding sentence.

Resource Manager

Planning Resources
- *Lesson Plans*

Transparencies
- *Bellringer*

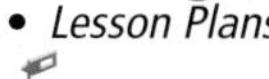

- *Daily Language Practice*

Other Print Resources
- *Grammar and Composition Handbook*
- *Grammar Enrichment,* p. 23
- *Grammar Practice,* p. 23
- *Grammar Reteaching,* p. 23
- *Grammar Workbook,* Lesson 31

Practice and Assess

Answers: Exercise 21

1. complete sentence
2–3. sentence fragment
4–5. complete sentence
6. sentence fragment
7. complete sentence
8–9. sentence fragment
10. complete sentence

Answers: Exercise 22

Answers will vary. Suggestions:
Children in Mexico often celebrate festivals and birthdays with parties at which they break a colorful piñata. An earthenware or papier-mâché container covered with crepe-paper streamers, a piñata is often shaped like an animal or a person. Filled with nuts, candy, and small toys, it is hung by a rope from the ceiling or—if the party is outdoors—from a tree limb. The blindfolded children take turns hitting the piñata with a stick. Hitting it is not always easy because an adult raises and lowers the piñata with a rope. Finally, after many attempts, the piñata breaks, and children rush to collect the treats scattered about.

Answers: Exercise 23

Answers will vary. Suggestions:

1. sentence
2. This usually happens after they get home from school or on the weekends.
3. They often fix soup, pasta, and grilled cheese sandwiches.
4. These are the foods they like the best.
5. Neither Jack nor Kera likes planning the menu or the grocery shopping.
6. The oven and the stove being broken, cooking became more difficult.
7. He finally decided to fix cold foods and use the toaster and microwave.
8. He was too impatient to wait for the electrician.
9. Juice, pancakes, waffles, and muffins are the favorites for Sunday breakfast.
10. Kera enjoys fixing special dishes for birthdays and holidays.
11. sentence
12. The twins especially like to make dinner for their parents.
13. They are delighted when their parents let them prepare the whole meal.
14. Whenever they have a chance, they help make the refreshments for a party.
15. sentence

Exercise 21 Identifying Sentence Fragments

Write on your paper *complete sentence* or *sentence fragment* to identify each of the items below.

The Piñata Game

[1]Children in Mexico often celebrate festivals and birthdays with parties. [2]By breaking a colorful piñata. [3]An earthenware or papier-mâché container covered with crepe-paper streamers. [4]A piñata is often shaped like an animal or a person. [5]Filled with nuts, candy, and small toys, it is hung by a rope from the ceiling. [6]Or—if the party is outdoors—from a tree limb. [7]The blindfolded children take turns hitting the piñata with a stick. [8]Not always easy, because an adult raises and lowers the piñata with a rope. [9]Finally, after many attempts, the break. [10]Children rush to collect the treats scattered about.

Exercise 22 Correcting Sentence Fragments

Revise the preceding paragraph by correcting each fragment. Whenever possible, combine the fragments with other sentences in the paragraph.

Exercise 23 Identifying and Correcting Sentence Fragments

Add your own words and phrases to rewrite each item that is not a sentence as a complete sentence. Change wording if you need to. For any item that is already a sentence, write *sentence.*

1. Jack and Kera help with the cooking for the family.
2. After they get home from school or on the weekends.
3. Soup, pasta, and grilled cheese sandwiches.
4. Which they like the best.
5. Planning the menu or the grocery shopping.
6. The oven and the stove being broken.
7. To fix cold foods and use the toaster and microwave.
8. Because he was too impatient to wait for the electrician.
9. Juice, pancakes, waffles, and muffins, the favorites for Sunday breakfast.
10. Enjoys fixing special dishes for birthdays and holidays.
11. They both enjoy cooking together.
12. Especially like to make dinner for their parents
13. When their parents let them prepare the whole meal.
14. Whenever they have a chance to help make the refreshments for a party.
15. The twins are especially happy after cleaning up.

Close

Have students write a paragraph about how avoiding the use of sentence fragments can enhance a writing project by making thoughts seem complete and coherent.

Enrichment and Extension

Combining Sentence Fragments

Tell students to correct a sentence fragment by combining it with another sentence that comes before or after the fragment: *The first person on the moon.* (fragment) *It was Neil Armstrong.* (sentence) *Neil Armstrong was the first person on the moon.* (complete sentence) **L2**

13.10 Run-on Sentences

- Avoid run-on sentences in your writing. A **run-on sentence** is two or more complete sentences written as though they were one sentence.

There are three basic kinds of run-on sentence.

1. A **comma splice,** probably the most common type of run-on sentence, occurs when two main clauses are separated by a comma rather than a period or a semicolon. To correct this type of run-on, replace the comma with a period (or other end mark of punctuation), and start the new sentence with a capital letter. You can also correct this error by changing the comma to a semicolon or by inserting a coordinating conjunction after the comma.

   RUN-ON Luis and Fredericka are going to Washington, D.C., with their school, they are very excited.

   CORRECT Luis and Fredericka are going to Washington, D.C., with their school. They are very excited.

   CORRECT Luis and Fredericka are going to Washington, D.C., with their school, **and** they are very excited.

2. Another kind of run-on sentence occurs when two main clauses are written with *no* punctuation between them. To correct this type of run-on, separate the main clauses with a semicolon, or insert an end mark of punctuation after the first clause and begin the second one with a capital letter. Still another way to correct the error is to insert a comma and a coordinating conjunction between the main clauses.

   RUN-ON They hope to see many famous sights the Lincoln Memorial will surely be among them.

   CORRECT They hope to see many famous sights; the Lincoln Memorial will surely be among them.

   CORRECT They hope to see many famous sights, **and** the Lincoln Memorial will surely be among them.

3. Still another kind of run-on sentence occurs when the comma is omitted before a coordinating conjunction joining two main clauses. To correct this error, simply add the comma before the coordinating conjunction.

   RUN-ON Fredericka and Luis will need to take notes for a written report on their Washington trip but they plan to have fun anyway.

   CORRECT Fredericka and Luis will need to take notes for a written report on their Washington trip, but they plan to have fun anyway.

Focus

Lesson Overview

Objective

- To identify and correct run-on sentences

Bellringer
Daily Language Activity

When students enter the classroom, have this assignment on the board: *Copy the following sentence. If it is correct, don't change it. If it is incorrect, try to make it correct.*

Stalactites are composed of minerals these mineral deposits form on the ceilings of caves.

See also *Daily Language Practice*

Teach

Grammar Tip

Although the simplest way to correct a run-on sentence is to join the two independent clauses with a comma and a coordinating conjunction, other solutions may make the relationship between the ideas more explicit. First, you can insert a semicolon with or without a conjunctive adverb. Second, you can change one of the independent clauses to an adverb clause. Third, you can change one of the independent clauses to an adjective clause, a noun clause, or even a phrase.

Resource Manager

Planning Resources

- *Lesson Plans*

Transparencies

- *Bellringer*
- *Daily Language Practice*
- *Two-Minute Skill Drill*

Other Print Resources

- *Grammar and Composition Handbook*
- *Grammar Enrichment,* p. 24
- *Grammar Practice,* p. 24
- *Grammar Reteaching,* p. 24
- *Grammar Workbook,* Lesson 32

Teach

Two-Minute Skill Drill

Write the following run-on sentence on the board:

The first runner nears the finish line she is ahead of all the other racers.

Have each student correct the run-on in two different ways. Ask students to discuss their sentences in small groups.

See also *Two-Minute Skill Drill Transparency 13.10*

Practice and Assess

Answers: Exercise 24

1. run-on
2. correct
3. correct
4. run-on
5. run-on
6. correct
7. correct
8. run-on
9. correct
10. correct
11. correct
12. run-on
13. run-on
14. correct
15. run-on

Answers: Exercise 25

1. . . . in 1867, and his . . .
2. . . . together, and then . . .
3. . . . aeronautics, and they . . .
4. . . . dunes, and the winds . . .
5. . . . Kitty Hawk, and in 1903 . . .

Exercise 24 **Distinguishing Between Run-ons and Correct Sentences**

On your paper write *correct* or *run-on* to identify each sentence below.

The Amazon River and the Nile River

1. The Amazon River is 3,900 miles (6,280 km) long it is the second longest river in the world.
2. The river flows generally eastward across northern South America and into the Atlantic Ocean through a wide delta in northern Brazil.
3. The Amazon is formed by the junction of two rivers in Peru, the Ucayali and the Marañón.
4. The Amazon has more than 500 tributaries and its river system drains half of South America.
5. Ships can travel almost the entire length of the river, it has no rapids or waterfalls to obstruct traffic.
6. The Nile is the world's longest river; it flows about 4,145 miles (6,905 km) from its headwaters in Burundi to the Mediterranean Sea.
7. The main part of the river is formed by the joining of two rivers, the Blue Nile and the White Nile.
8. The Blue Nile begins at Lake Tana it flows 1,000 miles to Khartoum.
9. The White Nile is 1,600 miles long, and its source is Lake Victoria.
10. The Blue and the White Nile converge at the city of Khartoum, which is the capital of Sudan.
11. Khartoum was founded as a camp for the Egyptian army in 1821 and developed into a major trading center.
12. Above Khartoum the Nile makes a huge S-curve and then it flows north through Egypt.
13. The Nile valley in Egypt was the location of a great ancient civilization, the tombs of kings and many other historic monuments are preserved there.
14. Dams on the Nile in Egypt have created a water supply for irrigating crops; the dams also produce hydroelectric power for the region.
15. Beyond Cairo the river forms an enormous triangular delta, here the river slows and drops much of its load of sediment before it flows into the sea.

Exercise 25 **Correcting Run-on Sentences by Adding Commas**

Correct each run-on sentence below by adding a comma before the coordinating conjunction.

1. Wilbur Wright was born in Dayton, Ohio, in 1867 and his brother Orville was born in 1871.
2. They ran a weekly newspaper together and then they started a bicycle manufacturing business.
3. The brothers read about aeronautics and they experimented with gliders.
4. Kitty Hawk, North Carolina, had long expanses of rolling sand dunes and the winds there were quite steady and dependable.
5. The Wright brothers tested their gliders on the dunes of Kitty Hawk and in 1903 they made the first powered flight.

MEETING INDIVIDUAL NEEDS

English Language Learners

Listening for Run-Ons

Students learning English may use commas incorrectly or not at all when they write. Encourage students to read sentences aloud to a partner to see if the sentence makes sense as it is written. If they find that they need to pause between parts of the sentence for it to make sense, have students read each part aloud to determine if it is a complete sentence. If so, students can choose a method of punctuating or combining the sentences to correct them.

Exercise 26 Correcting Run-on Sentences with a Period or a Semicolon

Correct each run-on sentence below by adding a period or a semicolon.

1. Benjamin Franklin was an important political figure during the period of the American Revolution, he was a man of many other talents as well.
2. He lived in Boston as a young man, there he learned the printing trade.
3. Franklin published an almanac he also experimented with electricity.
4. Franklin started a university, in Philadelphia he also started a lending library.
5. Franklin helped draft the Declaration of Independence he was also one of the signers of the peace treaty that in 1783 formally ended the American Revolution.

Exercise 27 Correcting Run-on Sentences

Rewrite the following paragraph, correcting the run-on sentences.

Animal Care in Zoos

[1]The earliest known zoo was the Park of Intelligence in the province of Hunan it was started by a Chinese ruler about 1150 B.C. [2]Today zoo facilities are limited and zookeepers cannot keep every animal on display year-round. [3]In the winter in colder climates, most birds must be brought indoors but zookeepers cannot always keep each bird on view for the public. [4]Many visitors are surprised to see that some animals remain outside all year, penguins, polar bears, and timber wolves are happy outdoors in wintertime. [5]Some animals are always indoors in northern areas, reptiles and small desert animals always have indoor displays. [6]Zookeepers must provide indoor shelters for large animals such as elephants how large those shelters must be! [7]Today zoologists understand much more about animal behavior and zoos are being designed that are similar to the animals' natural habitats. [8]Viewers can closely observe animals at animal parks, animals roam free. [9]Zoo kitchens keep a wide variety of foods and these are used to prepare meals that meet each animal's nutritional needs. [10]Zoos contribute to wildlife conservation, they nurture species that are in danger of becoming extinct.

Exercise 28 Correcting Sentence Fragments and Run-on Sentences

Rewrite this paragraph, correcting all sentence fragments and run-on sentences.

Chinese New Year

[1]The biggest and most popular of all Chinese festivals. [2]The Chinese New Year, an exciting and colorful holiday. [3]Falling anywhere between January 21 and February 19. [4]The New Year is celebrated by Chinese people all over the world, they parade through the streets and set off fireworks. [5]People pay visits to friends they wish them luck and prosperity with a greeting that means "happy greetings, and may you gather wealth." [6]On the final day of the year, preparations are made for a great New Year's Eve supper. [7]All doors are sealed with paper strips and no one may leave or enter until the next morning. [8]Businesses are closed. [9]For days after the new year begins. [10]Children receive presents of money in red envelopes no wonder they look forward to this festival.

Close

Have students discuss the ways to identify sentence fragments. What techniques do they find most useful to correct them? Ask students to record the most useful techniques in their journal for future reference.

Additional Resources

- *Grammar Practice,* p. 24
- *Grammar Reteaching,* p. 24
- *Grammar Enrichment,* p. 24
- *Grammar Workbook,* Lesson 32

Answers: Exercise 26

1. . . . Revolution. He . . . *or* . . . Revolution; he . . .
2. . . . young man. There . . . *or* . . . young man; there . . .
3. . . . almanac. He . . . *or* . . . almanac; he . . .
4. . . . university. In Philadelphia . . . *or* . . . university; in Philadelphia . . .
5. Independence. He . . . *or* Independence; he . . .

Answers: Exercise 27

Answers will vary, but some suggestions are given below.

1. The earliest known zoo was the Park of Intelligence in the province or Hunan. It was started by a Chinese ruler about 1150 B.C. **2.** Today zoo facilities are limited, and zookeepers cannot keep every animal on display year-round. **3.** In the winter in colder climates, most birds must be brought indoors, but zookeepers cannot always . . . **4.** Many visitors are surprised to see that some animals remain outside all year. Penguins, polar bears, and timber wolves . . . **5.** Some animals are always indoors in northern areas; reptiles and small desert animals . . . **6.** Zookeepers must provide indoor shelters for large animals such as elephants. How large those shelters must be! **7.** Today zoologists understand much more about animal behavior, and zoos are being designed . . . **8.** Viewers can closely observe animals at animal parks, where animals roam free. **9.** Zoo kitchens keep a wide variety of foods; these are used to prepare meals that meet . . . **10.** Zoos contribute to wildlife conservation, for they nurture species that are in danger of becoming extinct.

Answers: Exercise 28

Answers will vary, but some suggestions are given below.

1–2. The biggest . . . festivals, the Chinese New Year is an exciting and colorful holiday. **3–4.** Falling . . . February 19, the New Year . . . all over the world. They parade . . . fireworks. **5.** People . . . friends; they wish . . . wealth." **6.** On the final day . . . supper. **7.** All doors . . . strips, . . . next morning. **8–9.** Businesses are closed for days . . . begins. **10.** Children . . . envelopes. No wonder . . .

Teach

About the Literature

Explain that the review features a passage from Eudora Welty's *Delta Wedding,* followed by exercises based on the novel and on related topics. Have students read the passage, and then initiate a discussion about the characters, the setting, and the mood of the passage. Ask students to discuss the highlighted clauses. Ask: *Do the highlighted clauses sharpen a reader's view of the scene or detract from it? Are they essential to understanding the scene, or could they be eliminated?*

Linking Grammar and Literature

☑ Teaching Tip

Point out that most of the sentences in the passage consist of a main clause and one or more subordinate clauses. Remind students that every clause must contain a verb. Ask students to identify some of the simple sentences, which consist of only one main clause. (Example: *Its real name was the Yazoo-Delta.*) Then ask the students to identify some subordinate clauses that have not been highlighted. (Examples: *. . . before the lamp would be lighted; . . . for whom, she could not know.)*

Listening and Speaking

Ask students to write a paragraph about a journey, using some short sentences that consist of only one main clause and some longer sentences with two or more main or subordinate clauses. Then have them read their paragraphs to the class. Ask the class to listen to the rhythm of the sentences and to discuss whether a writer should always use longer, more complex sentences.

ASSESSMENT OPTIONS

Tests with Answer Key & Rubrics
Unit 13 Mastery Test, pp. 49–50

Testmaker
Unit 13 Mastery Test

UNIT 13 Grammar Review

Clauses and Sentence Structure

As Eudora Welty's novel *Delta Wedding* begins, young Laura McRaven is on her way from her home in Jackson, Mississippi, to Shellmound, the plantation where her cousin Dabney is to be married. It is Laura's first trip alone, and she savors every minute of it. The passage has been annotated to show the types of sentences and clauses covered in this unit.

Literature Model

from Delta Wedding

by Eudora Welty

The nickname of the train was the Yellow Dog. Its real name was the Yazoo-Delta. It was a mixed train. The day was the 10th of September, 1923—afternoon. Laura McRaven, who was nine years old, was on her first journey alone. She was going up from Jackson to visit her mother's people, the Fairchilds, at their plantation named Shellmound, at Fairchilds, Mississippi. . . .

In the passenger car every window was propped open with a stick of kindling wood. A breeze blew through, hot and then cool, fragrant of the woods and yellow flowers and of the train. The yellow butterflies flew in at any window, out at any other, and outdoors one of them could keep up with the train, which then seemed to be racing with a butterfly. Overhead a black lamp in which a circle of flowers had been cut out swung round and round on a chain as the car rocked from side to side, sending down dainty drifts of kerosene smell. The Dog was almost sure to reach Fairchilds before the lamp would be lighted by Mr. Terry Black, the conductor, who had promised her father to watch out for her. Laura had the seat facing the stove, but of course no fire was burning in it now. She sat leaning at the window, the light and the sooty air trying to make her close her eyes. Her ticket to Fairchilds was stuck up in her Madge Evans straw hat, in imitation of the

Simple sentence

Complex sentence

Compound-complex sentence

Adverb clause

Adjective clause

Compound sentence

Clauses and Sentence Structure

Resource Manager

Planning Resources
- *Lesson Plans*

Other Print Resources
- *Grammar and Composition Handbook*
- *Grammar Workbook,* Lessons 44–49, Unit 13 Review, Cumulative Review, Units 1-13

> drummer [salesman] across the aisle. Once the Dog stopped in the open fields and Laura saw the engineer, Mr. Doolittle, go out and pick some specially fine goldenrod there—for whom, she could not know. Then the long September cry rang from the thousand unseen locusts, urgent at the open windows of the train. . . .
>
> From the warm window sill the endless fields glowed like a hearth in firelight, and Laura, looking out, leaning on her elbows with her head between her hands, felt what an arriver in a land feels—that slow hard pounding in the breast.

Noun clause

Review: Exercise 1 **Identifying Main and Subordinate Clauses**

The following sentences are based on the passage from *Delta Wedding.* Each sentence contains a clause that appears in italics. On your paper write *main clause* or *subordinate clause* to identify the italicized clauses.

1. *Although she was only nine years old,* Laura was traveling alone.
2. The conductor, *who was watching out for Laura,* would soon light the lamp.
3. *The ticket* that was stuck in Laura's hat *would take her to Fairchilds, Mississippi.*
4. Laura was traveling to Fairchilds *so that she could attend her cousin's wedding.*
5. *She would stay at her cousin's plantation,* which was named Shellmound.
6. *The train was called the Yellow Dog,* although its name was really the Yazoo-Delta.
7. *While the train moved along,* Laura sat quietly in her seat.
8. *The car had a faint smell of kerosene,* which came from the swinging lamp overhead.
9. As the car rocked from side to side, *the lamp swung in a big circle.*
10. Laura could see the unlighted stove just opposite *where she sat.*
11. *Even though it was September,* the weather in the delta was still summery.
12. Because it was a warm day, *all the windows of the train were open.*
13. *Since the windows would not stay open by themselves,* they were propped up with sticks.
14. In the car were yellow butterflies, *which had flown in through the open windows.*
15. While the train was stopped, *Laura could hear the loud sounds made by locusts in the fields.*
16. Laura saw a field of goldenrod *as she looked out the window.*
17. Where the sun shone on them, *the broad fields glowed like a lighted fireplace.*
18. *After the engineer had picked some goldenrod,* the train started up again.
19. Laura could feel the warmth of the windowsill beneath her elbows *as she sat with her head between her hands.*
20. *Because the sun was bright,* Laura's eyes wanted to close.

Practice and Assess

Answers: Exercise 1

1. subordinate clause
2. subordinate clause
3. main clause
4. subordinate clause
5. main clause
6. main clause
7. subordinate clause
8. main clause
9. main clause
10. subordinate clause
11. subordinate clause
12. main clause
13. subordinate clause
14. subordinate clause
15. main clause
16. subordinate clause
17. main clause
18. subordinate clause
19. subordinate clause
20. subordinate clause

Practice and Assess

Answers: Exercise 2

1. compound
2. compound-complex
3. complex
4. compound
5. compound-complex
6. complex
7. compound
8. complex
9. compound-complex
10. complex
11. compound-complex
12. complex
13. complex
14. simple
15. complex
16. compound
17. simple
18. complex
19. compound-complex
20. complex

Review: Exercise 2 Identifying Simple, Compound, Complex, and Compound-Complex Sentences

The following sentences elaborate on ideas in the passage from *Delta Wedding* and tell something about its author. On your paper write whether each sentence is *simple, compound, complex,* or *compound-complex.*

1. The train's name was the Yazoo-Delta, but people called it the Yellow Dog.
2. It was September 10, 1923, and Laura McRaven was traveling by train to Fairchilds, Mississippi, where her cousin was getting married.
3. Nine-year-old Laura watched the countryside as it passed by.
4. Laura was enjoying the trip, for she was traveling alone for the first time.
5. The car rocked gently as the train hurried along, and the overhead lamp swung round and round.
6. The windows, which were held open with sticks of wood, let breezes into the cars.
7. The train had been traveling for a long time, yet the conductor had still not collected the tickets from Laura and the salesperson across the aisle.
8. Because the day was warm, no fire burned in the stove.
9. Laura watched while the engineer picked some goldenrod, and she noticed that the flowers were especially fine.
10. Though she sat quietly, Laura could feel her heart pounding.
11. While she sat alone on the train, Laura noticed many details inside the railroad car, and she observed the passing landscape as well.
12. Because she was traveling alone for the first time, she was unusually aware of her surroundings.
13. She compared what she was seeing with her hometown.
14. The author of *Delta Wedding,* Eudora Welty, was born in Jackson, Mississippi, in 1909.
15. When she created the character of Laura McRaven in *Delta Wedding,* Welty created a girl whose life was similar to hers.
16. Welty lived in the Mississippi Delta for most of her life, and the delta landscape was familiar to her.
17. Eudora Welty, like Laura, probably traveled by train through the delta as a young girl.
18. Welty says that she had always been aware of words and of the way people speak.
19. As a young girl, she paid attention to the ordinary sights, sounds, and objects of daily life, and they formed vivid sensory images that remained with her.
20. When Welty grew up and became a writer, her store of early impressions and memories provided a wealth of convincing details for her books and stories.

Review: Exercise 3 **Writing Sentences with Adjective Clauses**

Use the passage from *Delta Wedding* to rewrite the sentences below. To each sentence add an adjective clause that answers the question in parentheses. Your clause must begin with one of the relative pronouns below. It must contain a verb, and it must be correctly punctuated. There may be more than one correct answer.

RELATIVE PRONOUNS who whom whose which that

SAMPLE The train was heading toward Fairchilds, Mississippi. (What was the name of the train?)

ANSWER The train, whose name was the Yazoo-Delta, was heading toward Fairchilds, Mississippi.

1. Laura was traveling alone for the first time in her life. (How old was she?)
2. Laura's father had taken her to the train. (How did her father feel about her trip?)
3. Laura was traveling from Jackson, Mississippi. (What was Jackson to Laura?)
4. She was going to visit her mother's family. (Where did Laura's mother's family live?)
5. Laura's journey was taking place on a September afternoon. (What was the weather like?)
6. Laura felt very dressed up for her ride on the train. (What hat was she wearing?)
7. A breeze blew through the open windows. (What did the breeze smell like?)
8. Laura watched the yellow butterflies. (What were the butterflies doing?)
9. One butterfly seemed to be having a race with the train. (Where was the butterfly?)
10. A black lamp swung to the rhythm of the rocking car. (How was the lamp decorated?)
11. The lamp would probably not be lighted during the journey. (What odor did the lamp give off?)
12. The conductor would light the lamp later. (What was the conductor's name?)
13. Mr. Black had not yet collected the tickets. (What promise had he made?)
14. Laura sat in her seat. (Where was her seat?)
15. The stove provided heat for the car in cold weather. (Was the stove being used on this day?)
16. The air made her want to close her eyes. (What was the air like?)
17. Laura imitated the drummer, or traveling salesperson. (Where was his ticket?)
18. Many drummers traveled by train to call on customers. (Where were the customers?)
19. Mr. Doolittle stopped the train. (What was Mr. Doolittle's job?)
20. The engineer picked some goldenrod. (What was the goldenrod like?)
21. Laura wondered to whom Mr. Doolittle would give the goldenrod. (Why did she want to know?)
22. Through the train's open windows Laura heard a cry. (From what did the cry come?)
23. Laura heard locusts. (Where were they?)
24. Laura gazed at the fields. (What did the fields look like?)
25. Laura wanted her journey to end. (How did she feel?)

Clauses and Sentence Structure

Answers: Exercise 3

Answers will vary, but some suggestions are given below.

1. Laura, who was nine years old, was traveling . . . life.
2. Laura's father, who was worried about the trip, had taken her . . . train.
3. . . . Jackson, Mississippi, which was her home.
4. . . . family, who lived in Fairchilds, Mississippi.
5. . . . afternoon that was warm and breezy.
6. Laura, who was wearing a Madge Evans straw hat, felt . . . train.
7. A breeze that smelled like the woods and flowers blew . . . windows.
8. Laura watched . . . butterflies that flew in and out of the windows.
9. One butterfly that stayed outside the window seemed to . . . train.
10. A black lamp that was decorated with cutout flower shapes swung to . . . car.
11. The lamp, which gave off an odor of kerosene, would . . . journey.
12. The conductor, whose name was Mr. Terry Black, would light the lamp later.
13. Mr. Black, who had promised to watch over Laura, had not . . . tickets.
14. . . . seat, which faced the stove.
15. The stove, which was not being used on this day, provided . . . weather.
16. The air, which was sooty, made . . . eyes.
17. . . . salesperson, who had stuck his ticket in his hat.
18. . . . customers who were not nearby.
19. Mr. Doolittle, who was the engineer, stopped the train.
20. . . . goldenrod that was specially fine.
21. Laura, who was naturally curious, wondered to . . . goldenrod.
22. Through. . . cry that came from the locusts.
23. . . . locusts that were outside in the fields.
24. . . . fields, which glowed with a warm light.
25. Laura, who was tired from her trip, wanted . . . end.

Practice and Assess

Answers: Exercise 4

Answers will vary, but some suggestions are given below.

1. . . . because it was her first trip alone.
2. . . . while the train rolled along.
3. . . . because she would be seeing her cousins soon.
4. . . . because that was where her cousins lived.
5. . . . because it all seemed so new.
6. . . . as its speed increased.
7. . . . because the air in the train was hot.
8. . . . because the windows were open.
9. . . . wherever a window was open.
10. . . . as if it were racing with the train.
11. . . . because the car rocked back and forth.
12. . . . when darkness fell.
13. . . . while she was on her journey.
14. . . . if the weather turned cold.
15. . . . because the soot and the sun bothered them.
16. . . . because the salesperson across the aisle had done so.
17. . . . when he asked for them.
18. . . . so that he could pick some goldenrod.
19. . . . where it grew near the train track.
20. . . . because she didn't know whom the flowers were for.
21. . . . because the train windows were open.
22. . . . as if they were on fire.
23. . . . because her arm rested on it.
24. . . . as the train neared its destination.
25. . . . when the train pulled into the station.

Grammar Review

Review: Exercise 4 Writing Sentences with Adverb Clauses

Use the passage from *Delta Wedding* to rewrite each sentence, adding an adverb clause that answers the question in parentheses. Your clause must begin with one of the subordinating conjunctions listed below, and it must contain a subject and a verb. There may be more than one correct answer for each item.

SUBORDINATING CONJUNCTIONS

after	as if	if	so that	when	wherever
as	because	since	than	whenever	while

SAMPLE Laura McRaven was traveling to Shellmound. (Why?)

ANSWER Laura McRaven was traveling to Shellmound because her cousin Dabney was getting married.

1. It was an exciting day for Laura. (Why?)
2. Laura sat looking out the window. (When?)
3. Laura felt excited. (Why?)
4. Laura had a ticket to Fairchilds, Mississippi. (Why?)
5. Laura carefully observed everything that went on around her. (Why?)
6. The passenger car swayed back and forth. (When?)
7. Pieces of kindling were being used at the windows of the passenger car. (Why?)
8. There were butterflies inside the car. (Why?)
9. Butterflies flew into the train. (Where?)
10. One butterfly flew alongside the train. (In what manner?)
11. The black lamp over Laura's head swung in circles on its chain. (Why?)
12. The conductor would finally light the lamp. (When?)
13. Laura's father had asked the conductor to look after her. (When?)
14. A fire would be lighted in the stove opposite Laura. (Under what condition?)
15. Laura almost had to close her eyes. (Why?)
16. Laura put her ticket in her hat. (Why?)
17. The passengers would give the conductor their tickets. (When?)
18. The engineer stopped the train. (Why?)
19. The engineer picked goldenrod. (Where?)
20. Laura found the engineer's actions somewhat mysterious. (Why?)
21. Laura heard the locusts. (Why?)
22. The fields glowed in the daylight. (How?)
23. Laura could feel the warmth of the windowsill. (Why?)
24. Laura's heart pounded. (When?)
25. Laura would see her mother's family. (When?)

Review: Exercise 5 Identifying Noun Clauses

The following sentences describe the Mississippi Delta area, to which Laura McRaven was traveling. On your paper write the noun clauses that appear in the sentences. Two of the sentences have two noun clauses each. In one sentence the relative pronoun before the noun clause has been dropped.

1. Does this book explain what the Mississippi Delta is?
2. Whoever has visited Mississippi is probably familiar with the area.
3. That the Mississippi River periodically floods its banks is the reason for the delta's existence.
4. What we now call the Mississippi Delta was formed by whatever deposits of silt the receding Mississippi River floodwaters left behind.
5. You can easily understand why many farmers live in the delta.
6. What attracts many farmers to the delta is that the soil is so fertile.
7. Do you know what makes the delta so famous?
8. One reason for its fame is that the area produces large crops of cotton.
9. You may also have read that large crops of soybeans are grown in the delta.
10. I know that visitors are also attracted by the area's many beautiful plantations.

Review: Exercise 6 Identifying Adjective, Adverb, and Noun Clauses

The following sentences give information about the author of *Delta Wedding,* Eudora Welty. Write the adjective clauses, adverb clauses, and noun clauses that appear in the sentences. Then write *adjective clause, adverb clause,* or *noun clause* to identify each clause. One sentence has more than one clause.

1. Author Eudora Welty, who was born in Jackson, Mississippi, was well known for her entertaining and insightful novels and short stories.
2. Because everyone in her family loved to read, there were always many books around Welty's home.
3. After Welty attended Mississippi State College for Women in 1926 and 1927, she graduated from the University of Wisconsin.
4. Later Welty studied at Columbia University, which is in New York City.
5. Welty's reason for returning to Jackson in 1931 was that her father died.
6. While Welty had traveled in the United States and Europe, most of her work focused on southern rural life.
7. Welty's stories of human relationships often were about people who live in small towns.
8. *Delta Wedding,* which was Welty's first full-length novel, was published in 1946.
9. The novel describes a comfortable southern world that would soon change forever.
10. Whoever reads Welty's stories realizes that she believed in the importance of change and love in human life.

Clauses and Sentence Structure

Answers: Exercise 5

1. what the Mississippi Delta is
2. Whoever has visited Mississippi
3. That the Mississippi River periodically floods its banks
4. What we now call the Mississippi Delta; whatever deposits of silt the receding Mississippi River floodwaters left behind
5. why many farmers live in the delta
6. What attracts many farmers to the delta; that the soil is so fertile
7. what makes the delta so famous
8. that the area produces large crops of cotton
9. that large crops of soybeans are grown in the delta
10. that visitors are also attracted by the area's many beautiful plantations

Answers: Exercise 6

1. who was born in Jackson, Mississippi (adjective clause)
2. Because everyone in her family loved to read (adverb clause)
3. After Welty attended Mississippi State College for Women in 1926 and 1927 (adverb clause)
4. which is in New York City (adjective clause)
5. that her father died (noun clause)
6. While Welty had traveled in the United States and Europe (adverb clause)
7. who live in small towns (adjective clause)
8. which was Welty's first full-length novel (adjective clause)
9. that would soon change forever (adjective clause)
10. Whoever reads Welty's stories (noun clause); that she believed in the importance of change and love in human life (noun clause)

Practice and Assess

Answers: Exercise 7

1. int.; The train's official name was the Yazoo-Delta.
2. dec.; Call the train the Yellow Dog.
3. dec.; Was the date September 10, 1923?
4. dec.; How very warm it was that September day!
5. int.; All the train windows were open.
6. int.; Open all the train windows.
7. excl.; Were the butterflies delicate?
8. int.; Laura, sit across the aisle from the drummer.
9. imp.; Laura put the ticket in her hat.
10. dec.; Did Laura like the smell of the kerosene from the lamp?
11. dec.; Did cool breezes come from the woods nearby?
12. excl.; The goldenrod was beautiful.
13. imp.; Mr. Doolittle will give her some goldenrod.
14. dec.; Did Mr. Doolittle stop the train in order to pick some goldenrod?
15. excl.; The cries of the locusts were very loud.
16. int.; Laura looked forward to seeing her cousins.
17. dec.; How Laura's heart was pounding!
18. dec.; Mr. Black, promise to look after Laura.
19. dec.; Were Laura's cousins going to meet her train?
20. dec.; What a wonderful time Laura had!

Answers: Exercise 8

Answers will vary, but teachers should make sure that students have used each type of sentence twice and have labeled each sentence.

Grammar Review

Review: Exercise 7 Writing Four Kinds of Sentences

On your paper write *declarative, imperative, interrogative,* or *exclamatory* to identify each of the following sentences. Then rewrite each sentence in the form noted in parentheses.

SAMPLE The engineer stopped the train. (Rewrite as an imperative sentence.)
ANSWER declarative
Engineer, please stop the train.

1. Was the train's official name the Yazoo-Delta? (Rewrite as a declarative sentence.)
2. We call the train the Yellow Dog. (Rewrite as an imperative sentence.)
3. The date was September 10, 1923. (Rewrite as an interrogative sentence.)
4. It was very warm that September day. (Rewrite as an exclamatory sentence.)
5. Were all the train windows open? (Rewrite as a declarative sentence.)
6. Will you open all the train windows? (Rewrite as an imperative sentence.)
7. How delicate the butterflies were! (Rewrite as an interrogative sentence.)
8. Was Laura sitting across the aisle from the drummer? (Rewrite as an imperative sentence.)
9. Laura, put the ticket in your hat. (Rewrite as a declarative sentence.)
10. Laura liked the smell of the kerosene from the lamp. (Rewrite as an interrogative sentence.)
11. Cool breezes came from the woods nearby. (Rewrite as an interrogative sentence.)
12. How beautiful the goldenrod was! (Rewrite as a declarative sentence.)
13. Mr. Doolittle, please give her some goldenrod. (Rewrite as a declarative sentence.)
14. Mr. Doolittle stopped the train in order to pick some goldenrod. (Rewrite as an interrogative sentence.)
15. How loud the cries of the locusts were! (Rewrite as a declarative sentence.)
16. Did Laura look forward to seeing her cousins? (Rewrite as a declarative sentence.)
17. Laura's heart was pounding. (Rewrite as an exclamatory sentence.)
18. Mr. Black promised to look after Laura. (Rewrite as an imperative sentence.)
19. Laura's cousins were going to meet her train. (Rewrite as an interrogative sentence.)
20. Laura had a wonderful time. (Rewrite as an exclamatory sentence.)

Review: Exercise 8 Creating Four Kinds of Sentences

For each topic below, write two different kinds of sentences: declarative, imperative, interrogative, or exclamatory. Within the exercise, use each type of sentence at least twice. Use correct punctuation. Label each sentence *declarative, imperative, interrogative,* or *exclamatory.*

1. things you see in the classroom
2. your trip to school this morning
3. a visit to a new place
4. a person you have talked to today
5. a meal with your friends or family

Review: Exercise 9 **Correcting Sentence Fragments**

The following paragraph describes Uncle Battle, another character from *Delta Wedding.* Revise the paragraph, correcting any sentence fragments. The fragments may be corrected by combining sentences, by adding words (such as a subject or a verb), or by changing the form of a verb.

SAMPLE Laura arrived. Her cousins rushing out to meet her.
ANSWER When Laura arrived, her cousins rushed out to meet her.

[1]At Shellmound, Laura so happy to see Uncle Battle again. [2]A big man, her mother's brother. [3]Always called all the children Skeeta. [4]All of his children exactly like him. [5]Wore tall boots that creaked when he stood up. [6]His hair always combed back over his brow. [7]At mealtime Uncle Battle always carving and serving the turkey. [8]Likely to drive off at any time of the day or night, without a moment's notice. [9]Because he needed to check to see that the plantation work was getting done. [10]Also to protect the plantation's workers from the sheriff.

Review: Exercise 10 **Correcting Run-on Sentences**

The following sentences elaborate on ideas suggested by the passage from *Delta Wedding.* On your paper revise each sentence, correcting any run-ons. Remember that run-on sentences may be corrected in more than one way. For the sentences that do not contain run-ons, write *correct.*

SAMPLE It was September 10, 1923, Laura McRaven was on her way to Fairchilds.
ANSWER It was September 10, 1923. Laura McRaven was on her way to Fairchilds.
ANSWER It was September 10, 1923, and Laura McRaven was on her way to Fairchilds.

1. Laura was only nine years old, nevertheless, she was traveling alone.
2. Laura's cousins lived at Fairchilds Laura was going to visit them.
3. The day was warm and butterflies flew in and out of the open windows.
4. The breeze kept changing, it would be hot for a while and then it would be cool.
5. Laura wanted to catch every detail of the countryside; however, the sooty air from the train's engine kept making her want to close her eyes.
6. Mr. Black was the conductor, Laura's father had asked him to watch out for Laura.
7. Laura wore a straw hat, she had stuck her ticket in it.
8. The train came to a halt and Mr. Doolittle went into the open fields.
9. Laura couldn't wait to get to Fairchilds she was anxious to see her mother's people.
10. Laura tried to stay calm, but her heart kept pounding.

Clauses and Sentence Structure

Answers: Exercise 9

Answers will vary, but some suggestions are given below.

1. At Shellmound, Laura felt so happy to see Uncle Battle again.

2–3. A big man, he was her mother's brother, and he always called all the children Skeeta.

4. All of his children looked exactly like him.

5–6. He wore tall boots that creaked when he stood up, and his hair was always combed back over his brow.

7. At mealtime Uncle Battle always carved and served the turkey.

8–9. He was likely to drive off at any time of the day or night, without a moment's notice, because he needed to check to see that the plantation work was getting done.

10. He also needed to protect the plantation's workers from the sheriff.

Answers: Exercise 10

Answers will vary, but some suggestions are given below.

1. Laura was only nine years old; nevertheless, she was traveling alone.
2. Laura's cousins lived at Fairchilds, and Laura was going to visit them.
3. The day was warm, and butterflies flew in and out of the open windows.
4. The breeze kept changing. It would be hot for a while, and then it would be cool.
5. correct
6. Mr. Black was the conductor, and Laura's father had asked him to watch out for Laura.
7. Laura wore a straw hat, in which she had stuck her ticket.
8. The train came to a halt, and Mr. Doolittle went into the open fields.
9. Laura couldn't wait to get to Fairchilds, for she was anxious to see her mother's people.
10. correct

Practice and Assess

Answers: Exercise 11

Answers will vary, but some suggestions are given below.

Mississippi is bordered on the east by Alabama, on the south by the Gulf of Mexico, on the north by Tennessee, and on the west by Arkansas and Louisiana. The Mississippi River actually forms most of the state's western boundary. Jackson is the capital of Mississippi and its largest city. The Yazoo-Mississippi Delta, in western Mississippi, is a broad, flat plain with rich, dark soil.

Mississippi has a warm climate and long growing season. Its main crops are cotton and soybeans. Much of the southern part of the state is covered by pine forest. The Delta National Forest northwest of Jackson covers 60,000 acres and has facilities for camping, fishing, and picnicking. The Yazoo River borders the forest and flows into the Mississippi River just above Vicksburg.

Answers: Exercise 12

Proofreading

This proofreading activity provides editing practice with (1) the current or previous units' skills, (2) the **Troubleshooter** errors, and (3) spelling errors. Students should be able to complete the exercise by referring to the units, the **Troubleshooter,** and a dictionary. (Note: A run-on sentence counts as one error.)

Error (Type of Error)

1. born (verb form)
2. grandfather's (singular possessive)
3. believing (spelling)
   talent, (nonessential participial phrase)
   lessons. (end punctuation)
4. continued (unnecessary shift in tense)
5. taught. He *or* taught; *or* taught, and (run-on sentence)
6. live (subject-verb agreement)
7. Utah's (singular possessive)
8. Duncan, (nonessential adjective clause)
9. particularly (spelling)
10. young, (introductory adverb clause)
11. Impressionists, who (sentence fragment)

Grammar Review

Review: Exercise 11 Correcting Sentence Structure

The following paragraphs tell about the state of Mississippi. Revise the paragraphs, correcting sentence fragments or run-on sentences. Some sentences are correct, but you may wish to combine them with other sentences. Try to vary your sentence structure, and use correct punctuation.

1Mississippi is bordered on the east by Alabama, its southern border is the Gulf of Mexico. 2On the north by Tennessee, on the west by Arkansas and Louisiana. 3The Mississippi River actually forms most of the state's western boundary. 4Jackson, the capital of Mississippi and its largest city. 5The Yazoo-Mississippi Delta, in western Mississippi, a broad, flat plain with rich, dark soil.

6Mississippi has a warm climate and long growing season, its main crops are cotton and soybeans. 7Much of the southern part of the state covered by pine forest. 8The Delta National Forest northwest of Jackson. 9Covers 60,000 acres, has facilities for camping, fishing, and picnicking. 10The Yazoo River borders the forest and flows into the Mississippi River just above Vicksburg.

Review: Exercise 12

Proofreading

The following passage describes the artist Robert Duncan, whose painting appears on the opposite page. Rewrite the passage, correcting the errors in spelling, grammar, and usage. Add any missing punctuation. There are twenty-five errors.

Robert Duncan

1Robert Duncan was borned in Salt Lake City, Utah, in 1952. 2He spent his summers on his grandfathers' ranch in Wyoming. 3His grandmother, beleiving in Duncan's talent gave the eleven-year-old boy a set of oil paints and arranged for him to take art lessons 4Duncan continues to paint in high school. 5Duncan, however, is largely self-taught he has been painting full-time since 1972. 6He, his wife, and their six children lives in Midway, Utah. 7Utahs citizens and rugged landscapes are frequent subjects in his paintings.

8Duncan who has visited many museums in Europe and the United States, derived his style from his study of traditional figurative and landscape art. 9He was particlarly influenced by the work of painters from the turn of the century, such as John Singer Sargent. 10When Sargent was young he had been influenced by the Impressionists. 11Who created their paintings with rapid strokes of pure color. 12Duncan, who uses naturalistic settings and loose

Robert Duncan, *Mandy's Sunhat,* 1988

brushwork displays his debt to such Realists as Sargent and, indirectly, to the Impressionists. [13]Although his style is at odds with many currents in modren art it has won him modest acclaim.

[14]Duncan portrays many aspects of rural life his goal is to show that all people are fundamentally the same. [15]Often paints outdoors to capture the natural light. [16]He depicts farms gardens, and country people; children are among his favorite subjects [17]Duncan's style, which is romantic and somewhat sentimental is evident in all his paintings.

[18]*Mandy's Sunhat* shows Duncans facility for depicting atmosphere and light. [19]Anyone who has read Eudora Welty's *Delta Wedding* could easily believe that the girl in the painting are Laura McRaven. [20]The youngster in Welty's novel. [21]Can you imagine her stepping off the train and into the open fields

Answers: Exercise 12 *(continued)*

Error (Type of Error)

12. brushwork, (nonessential adjective clause)
13. modern (spelling)
    art, (introductory adverb clause)
14. life. His *or* life; *or* life, and (run-on sentence)
15. He often (sentence fragment)
16. farms, (commas in a series)
    subjects. (end punctuation)
17. sentimental, (nonessential adjective clause)
18. Duncan's (singular possessive)
19. is (subject-verb agreement)
20. Laura is the *or* She is the *or* McRaven, who is the (sentence fragment)
21. fields? (end punctuation)

Viewing the Art

Robert Duncan, *Mandy's Sunhat,* 1988
Robert Duncan tries to depict his subjects accurately and movingly. For *Mandy's Sunhat,* Duncan has chosen bright, warm colors to create a summery mood. Writers create atmosphere through sensory images and vivid description. Have students discuss which of Welty's images could be used to describe the atmosphere of Robert Duncan's painting.

Practice and Assess

Answers: Exercise 13
Mixed Review

Answers will vary, but some suggestions are given below.

1. Was Welty's first book of short stories, *A Curtain of Green*, published in 1941?
2. Her novella *The Robber Bridegroom*, which contains all the virtues of a good fairy tale, was published in 1946.
3. Welty published two collections of short stories between 1949 and 1955.
4. *The Golden Apples* (1949), her next book after *Delta Wedding*, contained seven related stories about a group of families whose lives were intertwined.
5. Like *The Robber Bridegroom*, Welty's novel *The Ponder Heart* (1954), which has been called Welty's comic masterpiece, does not follow Welty's initial pattern.
6. Welty published almost nothing between 1955 and 1970, but 1970 brought the publication of her novel *Losing Battles*, which deals with humorous characters and situations.
7. Welty won the Pulitzer Prize in 1972 for her novel *The Optimist's Daughter;* this event further increased her popularity.
8. One clear reason for Welty's success is that her fiction is often very humorous.
9. Besides novels and short stories, Welty wrote several works of nonfiction, which include a collection of essays and an autobiography.
10. Pay special attention to Welty's gift for vivid detail and to her wry insights into human nature.

Close

Ask students to write a paragraph describing how good writers can build on simple sentences to create an interesting piece of writing. Encourage students to give specific examples of the ideas they are expressing.

Grammar Review

Review: Exercise 13

Mixed Review

The items that follow describe the writing career of Eudora Welty. Revise each item in the manner indicated in parentheses; there may be more than one correct answer.

SAMPLE Eudora Welty was born in Jackson, Mississippi, in 1909. She was well known for her entertaining and insightful novels and short stories. (Rewrite as a complex sentence.)

ANSWER Eudora Welty, who was well known for her entertaining and insightful novels and short stories, was born in Jackson, Mississippi, in 1909.

Eudora Welty's Published Work

1. Welty's first book of short stories, *A Curtain of Green*, was published in 1941. (Rewrite as an interrogative sentence.)
2. Her novella *The Robber Bridegroom* was published in 1946. It contains all the virtues of a good fairy tale.
(Combine the sentences by turning the second sentence into an adjective clause beginning with *which.*)
3. Did Welty publish two collections of short stories between 1949 and 1955? (Write as a declarative sentence.)
4. *The Golden Apples* (1949), her next book after *Delta Wedding*, contained seven related stories about a group of families. The lives of these families were intertwined. (Combine the sentences by turning the second sentence into an adjective clause beginning with *whose.*)
5. Like *The Robber Bridegroom*, Welty's novel *The Ponder Heart* (1954) does not follow Welty's initial pattern. *The Ponder Heart* has been called Welty's comic masterpiece. (Rewrite as a complex sentence.)
6. Welty published almost nothing between 1955 and 1970, but 1970 brought the publication of her novel *Losing Battles*. The novel deals with humorous characters and situations. (Rewrite as a compound-complex sentence.)
7. Welty won the Pulitzer Prize in 1972 for her novel *The Optimist's Daughter*, this event further increased her popularity.
(Eliminate the run-on by writing a compound sentence.)
8. One reason for Welty's success is clear. Her fiction is often very humorous. (Combine the sentences by turning the second sentence into a noun clause beginning with *that.*)
9. Besides novels and short stories, Welty wrote several works of nonfiction. Including a collection of essays and an autobiography.
(Eliminate the fragment by writing a complex sentence.)
10. Many readers pay special attention to Welty's gift for vivid detail and to her wry insights into human nature. (Rewrite as an imperative sentence.)

Writing Application

Clauses and Sentence Structure in Writing

In the following paragraph from "A Day's Pleasure," Hamlin Garland uses a variety of sentence types to capture the reader's interest and to develop a pleasing rhythm and an appropriate mood of relaxation. Notice how the structure of each of Garland's four sentences varies: compound-complex, simple, complex, compound-complex.

They went into the little sitting room, so dainty and lovely to the farmer's wife, and as she sank into the easy chair she was faint and drowsy with the pleasure of it. She submitted to being brushed. She gave the baby into the hands of the Swedish girl, who washed its face and hands and sang it to sleep, while its mother sipped some tea. Through it all she lay back in her easy chair, not speaking a word, while the ache passed out of her back, and her hot, swollen head ceased to throb.

Techniques with Clauses and Sentence Structure

Try to apply some of Garland's techniques when you write and revise your own work.

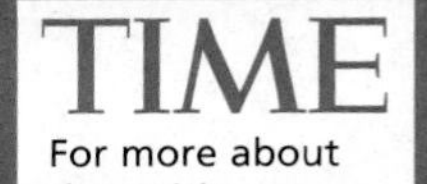

For more about the writing process, see **TIME Facing the Blank Page**, pp. 121-131.

1. Avoid using the same sentence structure repeatedly.

MONOTONOUS STRUCTURE She lay back in her chair. She did not speak. The ache passed out of her back.

GARLAND'S VERSION . . . she lay back in her easy chair, not speaking a word, while the ache passed out of her back. . . .

2. Use subordination to call attention to some ideas and downplay others.

EQUAL ATTENTION TO EACH IDEA She sank into a chair. She was faint and drowsy. She sipped her tea.

GARLAND'S VERSION . . . as she sank into the easy chair, she was faint and drowsy . . . The Swedish girl . . . sang it to sleep, while its mother sipped some tea.

Practice Practice these techniques by revising the following series of simple sentences, using a separate sheet of paper. Decide which ideas should be subordinated, and try to use a variety of sentence structures.

The day grew warmer. A strong wind rose, blowing from the south. They were all thirsty. They had only half a barrel of water left. They knew the next watering place was several hours ahead. The sun rose higher. Dust settled on their hair and clothing. It coated the children's bare feet. The woman sat holding the reins. The deep ruts in the trail jolted the wagon. Her back and neck ached. She shaded her eyes against the glare. Nowhere on the wide horizon could she see a tree or a building. In fact, they had seen no other people for two days. Her husband remained confident. Today, though, even he seemed tired.

LOG ON **Writing Online** For more grammar practice, go to glencoe.com and enter QuickPass code WC97727p2.

Clauses and Sentence Structure in Writing

Ask students to read the passage silently. Elicit their general reactions to the piece. Then ask them how the structure of Garland's sentences helps capture and hold the reader's interest. How does he use clauses to create a mood of relaxation?

Techniques with Clauses and Sentence Structure

Suggest that students reread the essay on Robert Duncan. As students read the essay, remind them to note examples of how the writer uses sentence structure and clauses to establish interest, rhythm, and mood.

Practice

The answers to this challenging and enriching activity will vary. Refer to Techniques with Clauses and Sentence Structure as you evaluate student choices. Sample answer:

As the day grew warmer, a strong wind rose, blowing from the south. They were all thirsty, but they had only half a barrel of water left. They knew the next watering place was several hours ahead. The sun rose higher. Dust, which coated the children's bare feet, also settled on their hair and clothing. The woman sat holding the reins while the deep ruts in the trail jolted the wagon. Her back and neck ached, and she shaded her eyes against the glare. Nowhere on the wide horizon could she see a tree or a building; in fact, they had seen no other people for two days. Her husband remained confident, although today, even he seemed tired.

ASSESSMENT OPTIONS

Tests with Answer Key & Rubrics
Unit 13 Mastery Test, pp. 49–50

Testmaker
Unit 13 Mastery Test

You may wish to administer the Unit 13 Mastery Test at this point.

MindJogger Videoquizzes

INTRODUCING

UNIT 14

Objectives

- To learn how to diagram sentences, including sentences with phrases and sentences with clauses
- To demonstrate understanding of various sentence components by representing them accurately in sentence diagrams

ASSESSMENT OPTIONS

Tests with Answer Key & Rubrics
Unit 14 Pretest, pp. 51–52
Unit 14 Mastery Test, pp. 53–54

Testmaker
Unit 14 Pretest
Unit 14 Mastery Test

You may wish to administer the Unit 14 Pretest at this point.

Key to Ability Levels

L1 Level 1 activities are within the basic ability range of students.

L2 Level 2 activities are within the ability range of average students.

L3 Level 3 activities are more challenging activities.

UNIT 14

Diagraming Sentences

570

Resource Manager

Planning Resources
- *Lesson Plans*
- *Block Scheduling*

Transparencies
- *Bellringer*
- *Two-Minute Skill Drill*

Other Print Resources
- *Grammar and Composition Handbook*
- *Grammar Enrichment*
- *Grammar Practice*
- *Grammar Reteaching*
- *Grammar Workbook*
- *Tests with Answer Key and Rubrics*

Video
- *MindJogger Videoquizzes*

Software
- *Interactive Grammar and Language Workbook*
- *Presentation Plus!*
- *Sentence Diagraming*
- *Testmaker*

Web Site
- *glencoe.com*

14.1 Diagraming Simple Sentences

■ Diagraming is a method of showing how the various words and parts of a sentence function and relate to the sentence as a whole.

You begin to diagram a sentence by finding the simple subject. (Keep in mind that a sentence may have a compound subject.) After you have found the subject, find the action or linking verb that goes with it. Write the subject and the verb on a horizontal line, called a baseline. Separate the subject and the verb with a vertical line that bisects the baseline. This line indicates the division between the complete subject and the complete predicate.

Athletes train.

subject | action verb

Athletes | train

Adjectives and Adverbs

To diagram a simple sentence with adjectives and adverbs, follow the model diagram below.

A very good athlete must train extremely hard.

subject | action verb
adjective, adverb, adjective; adverb, adverb

athlete | must train
A, very, good; extremely, hard

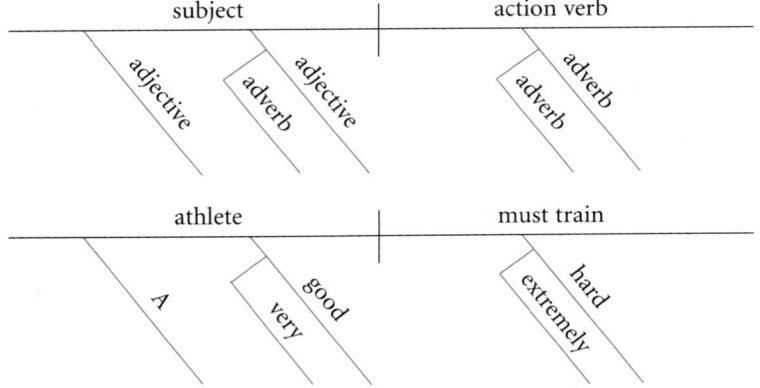

Diagraming Sentences

Focus

Lesson Overview

Objectives

- To identify the components of simple sentences
- To represent the components in sentence diagrams

Bellringer
Daily Language Activity

When students enter the classroom, have this assignment on the board: *Copy the following sentence and underline the subject with one line and the verb with two lines; then circle the direct object.*

Firefighters save lives.

Motivating Activity

Draw the following diagram frame on the board:

(subject) | (verb) | (direct object)

Have volunteers fill in the subject, verb, and direct object from the Bellringer sentence. Help students see how the structure of the diagram helps clarify the relationship between these sentence parts. Encourage students to ask questions to clarify their understanding.

Teach

Adjectives and Adverbs

☑ Teaching Tip

Remind students that introductory adverbs are diagramed beneath the verb, not the subject, despite their position in the sentence.

Resource Manager

Planning Resources
- *Lesson Plans*

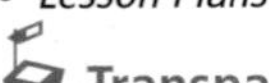

Transparencies
- *Bellringer*

Other Print Resources
- *Grammar and Composition Handbook*
- *Grammar Workbook,* Lesson 33

Teach

Teaching Tip

Tell students that when two or more modifiers modify the same word, the modifiers should appear in the same order in a diagram in which they appear in the original sentence.

Direct Objects and Indirect Objects

Teaching Tip

Emphasize that indirect objects are diagramed beneath the verb rather than the direct object because an indirect object answers the questions *To whom? To what? For whom?* or *For what?* about the action verb.

Object Complements

Cross-reference: Objective Complements

For instruction and practice of objective complements, refer to Lesson 11.5, pp. 504–509.

Subject Complements

Teaching Tip

To contrast the diagraming of direct objects and subject complements, write the following sentences on the board and have students diagram them:

Homemade bread tastes delicious.
They tasted the soup.

Ask volunteers to explain their reasons for diagraming the sentences as they did. Have students clarify and correct as needed.

Direct Objects and Indirect Objects

To diagram a simple sentence with an indirect object and a direct object, follow the model diagram below.

Coaches give players guidance.

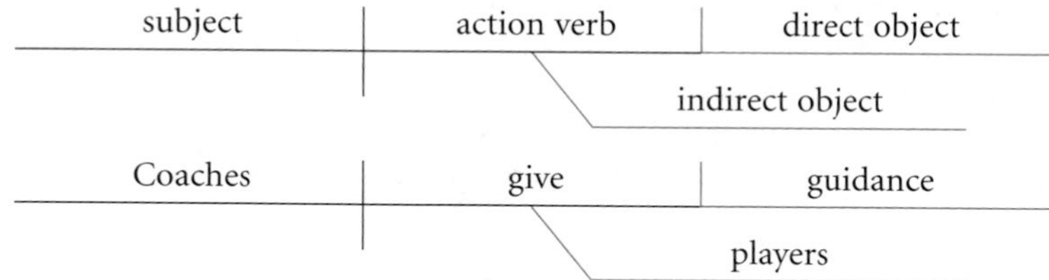

Object Complements

To diagram a simple sentence with a compound subject, a direct object, and an object complement, follow the model diagram below. If the parts of a compound subject are connected by a conjunction, place the conjunction on a dotted vertical line between them. If the parts are connected by a correlative conjunction, such as *both . . . and* or *either . . . or,* place the introductory conjunction on one side of the line and the second conjunction on the other side.

Coaches and players consider practice essential.

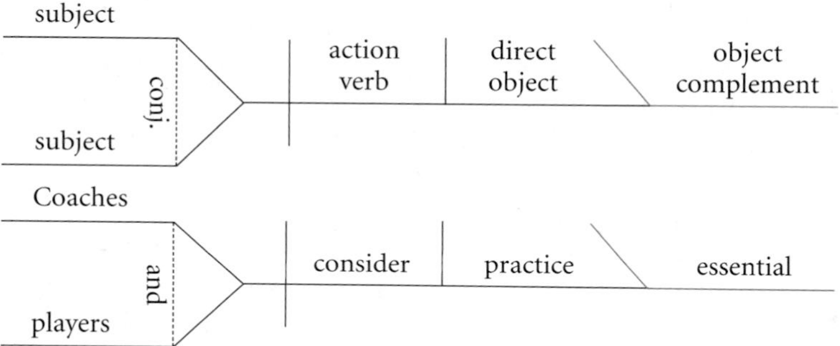

MEETING INDIVIDUAL NEEDS

English Language Learners

Understanding Diagrams

Sentence diagrams can help students understand the parts of English sentences because diagrams graphically show the relationships between different sentence components. Use a sample diagram to explain and point out the parts of a sentence. Emphasize the relationship between modifiers and the words they modify. Have students compare the written sentence with the diagramed sentence. This exercise can be helpful to the student whose primary language differs from English in the placement of modifiers.

Subject Complements

To diagram a simple sentence with a subject complement (a predicate nominative or a predicate adjective), follow the model diagrams below.

Swimmers are athletes.

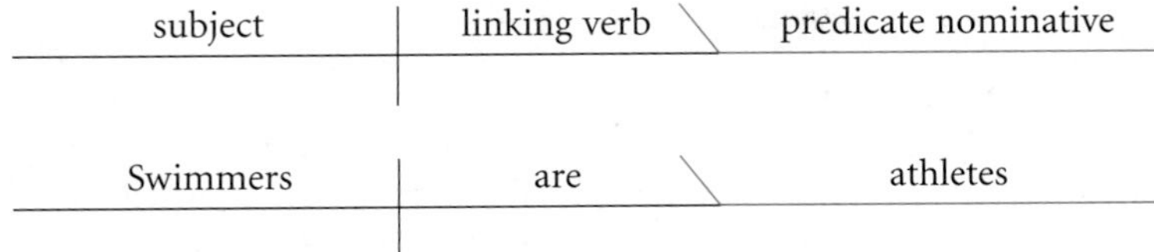

Gymnasts are strong and must be coordinated.

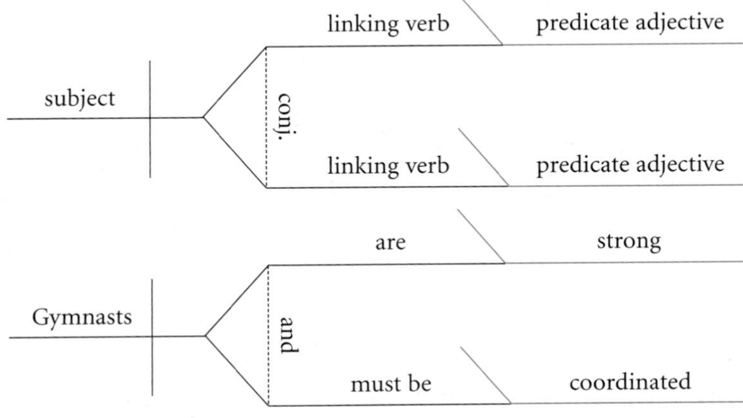

Exercise 1 **Diagraming Simple Sentences**

Using the preceding models as a guide, diagram the following sentences.

1. The muddy field was drying slowly.
2. A coach gave the players instructions.
3. The players and the coach considered the game critical.
4. It was the championship game.
5. The players were ready but felt nervous.
6. They looked calm but felt uneasy.
7. The coach encouraged them.
8. She gave the players a pep talk.
9. The players paid attention and listened silently.
10. They were ready.

Practice and Assess

Answers: Exercise 1

1. 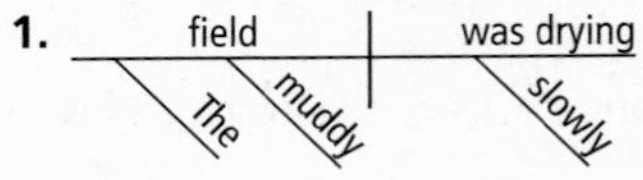

2. 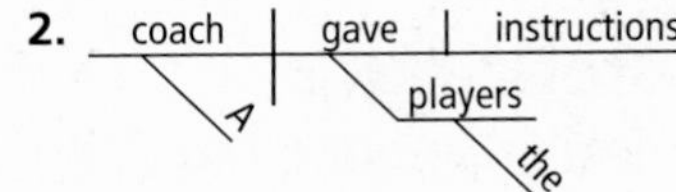

3. 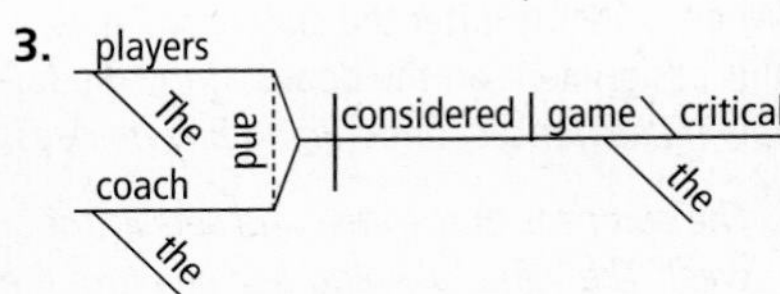

4. 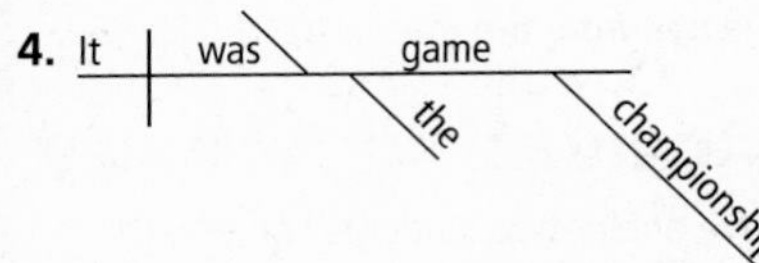

5. 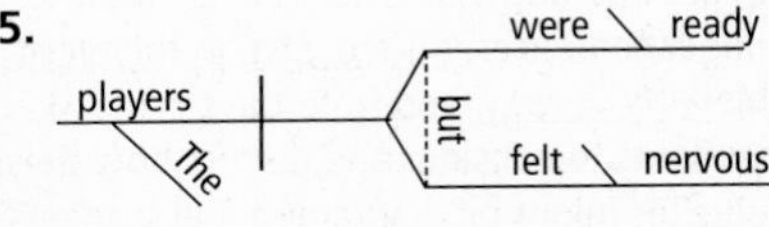

6. 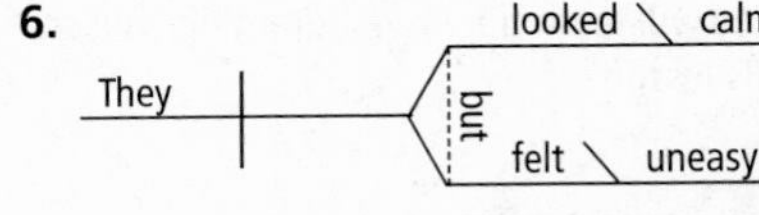

7. 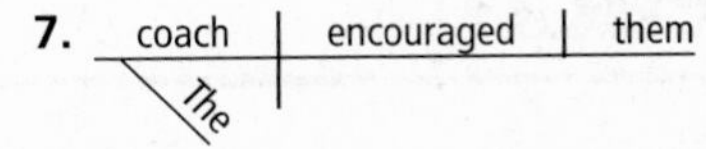

8. 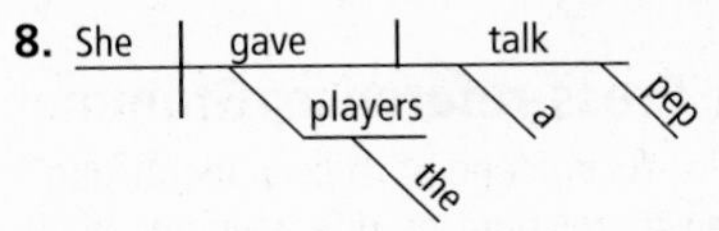

9. 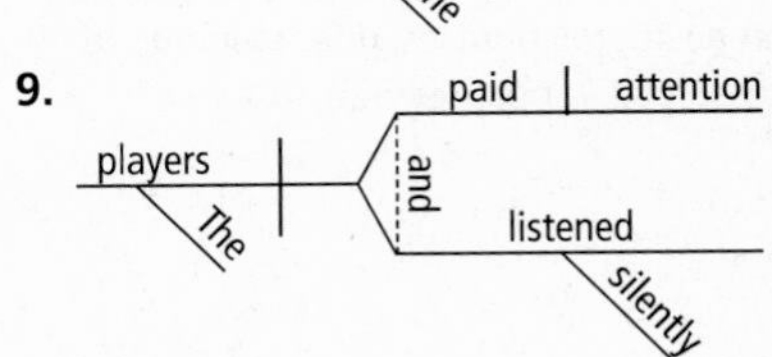

10. 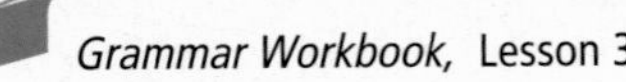

Additional Resources

Grammar Workbook, Lesson 33

Close

Call on three or four volunteers to write some of the diagrams from Exercise 1 on the board. Have students discuss the diagrams, point out mistakes, and suggest and explain corrections.

Focus

Lesson Overview

Objectives

- To identify phrases
- To represent them in sentence diagrams

Bellringer
Daily Language Activity

When students enter the classroom, have this assignment on the board: *Copy the following sentences, underlining any phrases:*

The sun rises in the east and sets in the west. The wind, blowing fiercely, tore the leaves from the trees.

Motivating Activity

Have one or two students come to the board and underline the phrases in the Bellringer sentences. (in the east, in the west, blowing fiercely, and from the trees) Ask students to consider and discuss how these phrases might be diagramed. Tell students they will learn how to diagram phrases in this lesson.

Teach

Prepositional Phrases

Cross-reference: Grammar

For instruction and practice in identifying prepositional phrases, refer students to Lesson 12.1, pp. 519–520.

14.2 Diagraming Simple Sentences with Phrases

Prepositional Phrases

Place the preposition on a diagonal line that descends from the word the prepositional phrase modifies. Place the object of the preposition on a horizontal line that joins the diagonal. The diagonal line on which the preposition is placed should extend somewhat beyond the horizontal on which the object of the preposition is placed, forming a "tail."

Athletes of today set new records at every opportunity during a season.

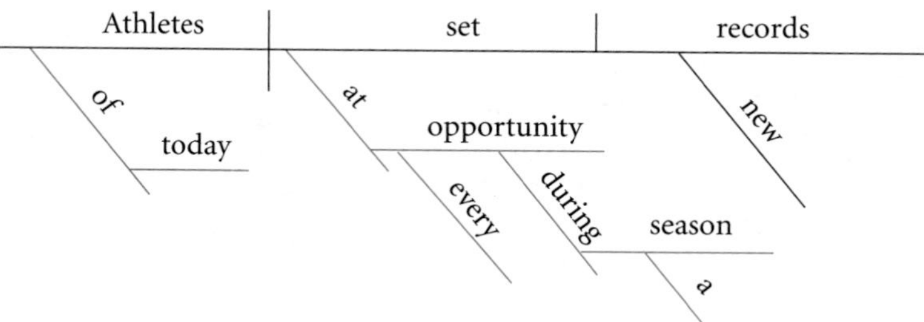

Appositives and Appositive Phrases

Place an appositive in parentheses after the noun or pronoun it identifies. Beneath it add any words that modify the appositive. Any words that modify the noun or pronoun itself, and not the appositive, should be placed directly beneath the noun or pronoun.

The coach, a graduate of the school, preaches team spirit, an important ideal.

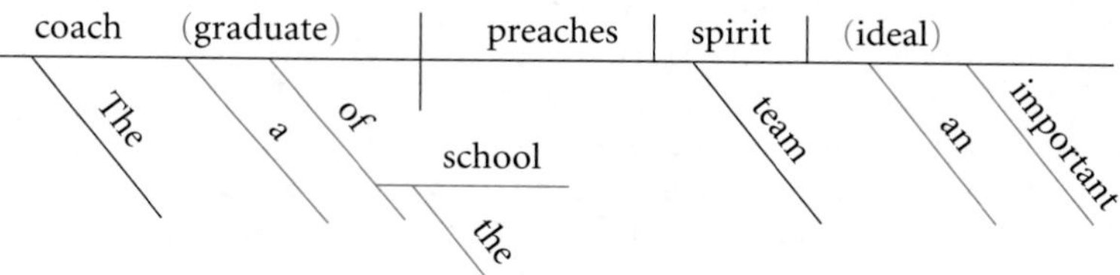

Resource Manager

Planning Resources

- *Lesson Plans*

Transparencies

- *Bellringer*
- *Two-Minute Skill Drill*

Other Print Resources

- *Grammar and Composition Handbook*
- *Grammar Workbook,* Lesson 34

Participles and Participial Phrases

The line on which the participle is placed descends diagonally from the word the participle modifies and then extends to the right horizontally. The participle is written on the curve, as shown below. Add any modifiers and complements to the horizontal line in the same way that you would show the modifiers and complements of an action verb.

Stumbling, the quarterback fell, gracefully completing the pass in midair.

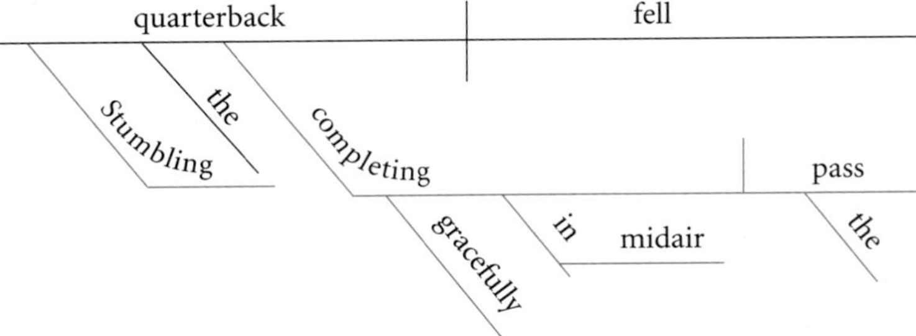

Gerunds and Gerund Phrases

Place a gerund on a "step," adding complements and modifiers in the usual way. Then set the gerund or the gerund phrase on a "stilt" and position the stilt according to the role of the gerund in the sentence. (Remember that a gerund can be a subject, a direct object, an indirect object, a predicate nominative, an object of a preposition, or an appositive.)

Winning is one way of gaining confidence.

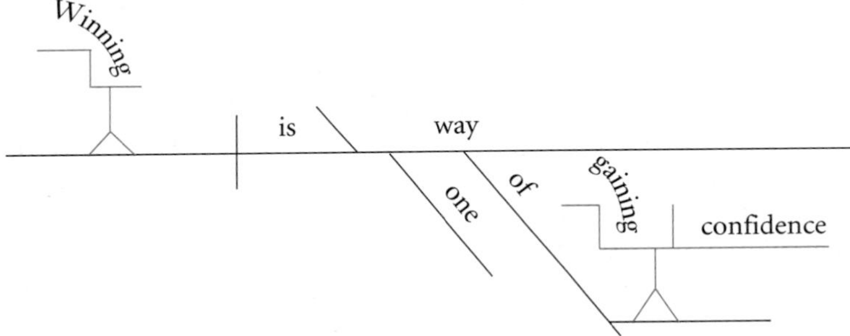

Diagraming Sentences

Teach

Participles and Participial Phrases

Cross-reference: Grammar

For instructions and practice with identifying and using participles and participial phrases, refer students to Lesson 12.3, pp. 523–527.

Gerunds and Gerund Phrases

Cross-reference: Grammar

For instructions and practice with gerunds and gerund phrases, refer students to Lesson 12.3, pp. 523–527.

Infinitives and Infinitive Phrases

Cross-reference: Grammar

For instructions and practice with infinitives and infinitive phrases, refer students to Lesson 12.3, pp. 523–527.

Two-Minute Skill Drill

Write the following sentence on the board for students to diagram:

Roaring, the crowd applauded the racers in the marathon.

When students are finished, have a volunteer draw the diagram on the board. Encourage students to discuss each part of the diagram and to make corrections as needed.

See also *Two-Minute Skill Drill Transparency 14.2*

Meeting Individual Needs

English Language Learners

Distinguishing Between Gerunds and Participles

Explain that participles function as adjectives, whereas gerunds act as nouns. Write the following sentences on the board: *Swimming rapidly, Susan headed for the shore. Swimming is my favorite form of exercise.* Contrast the ways *swimming* is used in the two sentences. Then diagram both sentences. Finally, have students work with a partner who is proficient in English to write and diagram other sentences with participial and gerund phrases.

Practice and Assess

Answers: Exercise 2

1.
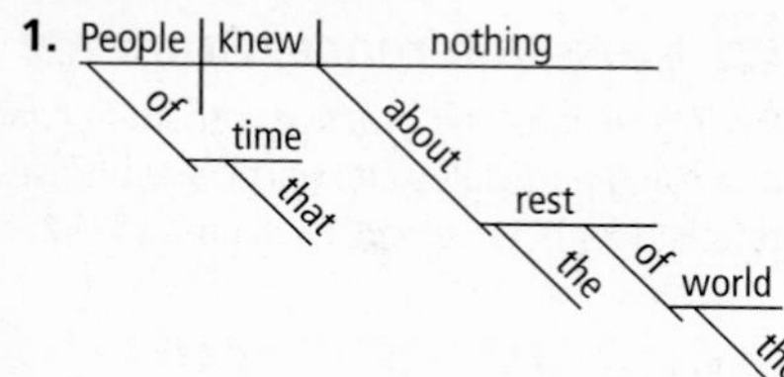

2.
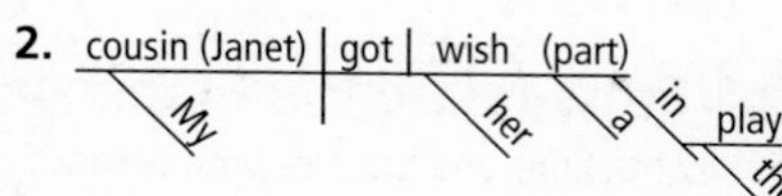

3.
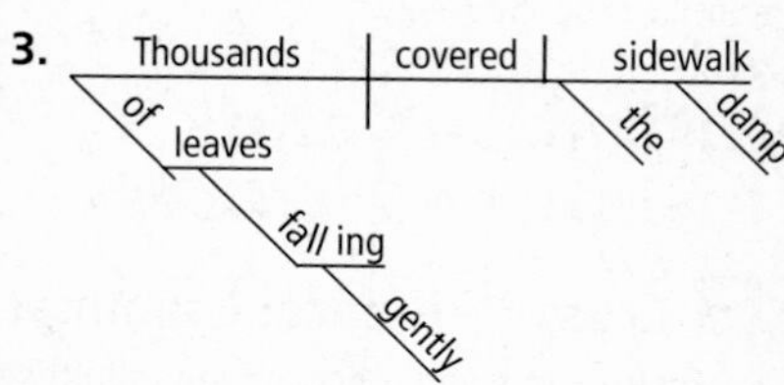

4.
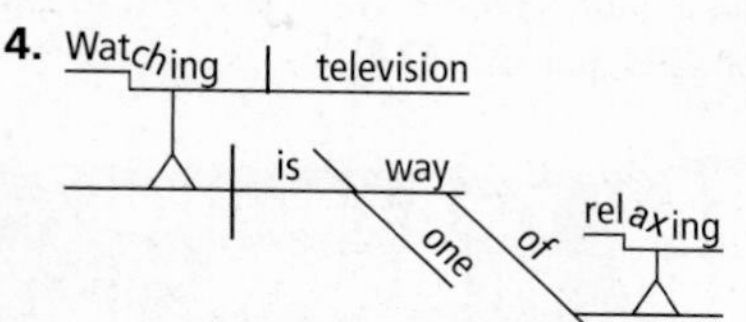

5.
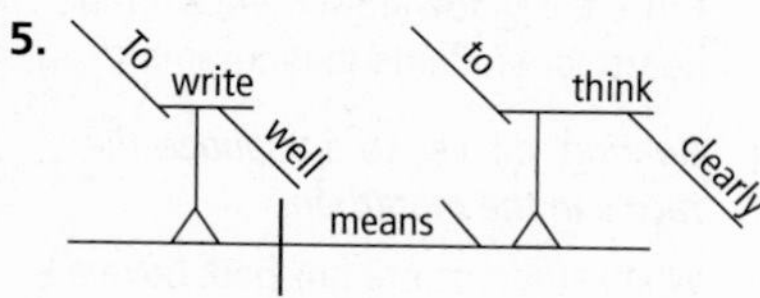

6.
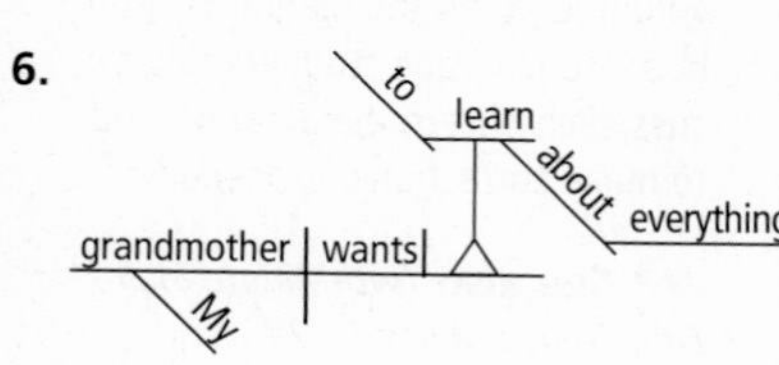

7. **(See next column.)**

8.
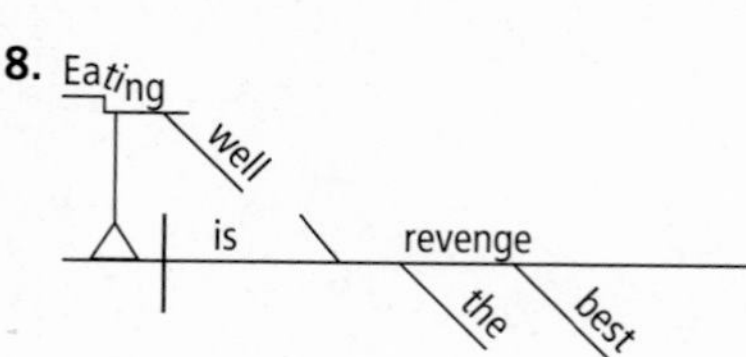

9.
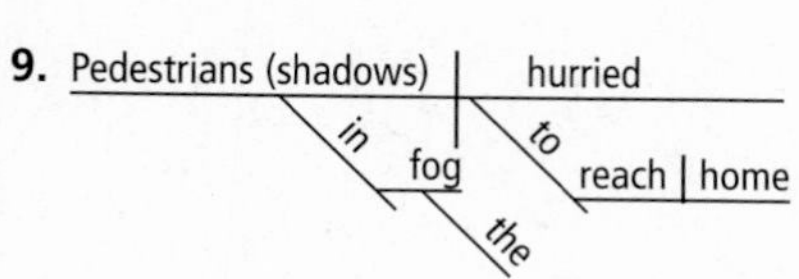

Infinitives and Infinitive Phrases as Adjectives or Adverbs

When an infinitive or an infinitive phrase is used as an adjective or an adverb, it is diagramed as a prepositional phrase is.

Teams have a need to travel frequently.

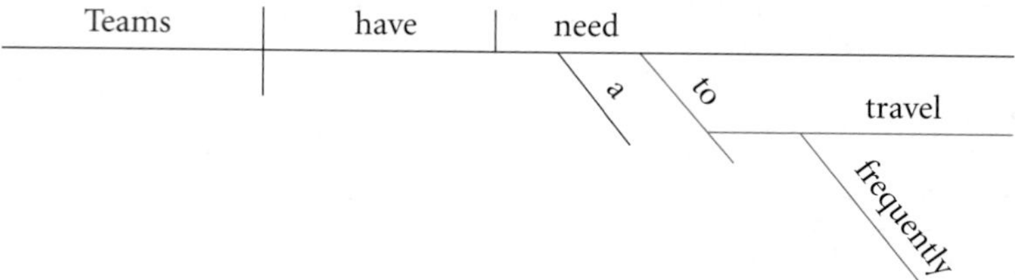

Infinitives and Infinitive Phrases as Nouns

When an infinitive or an infinitive phrase is used as a noun, it is diagramed as a prepositional phrase is and then placed on a "stilt" in the subject, direct object, or predicate nominative position.

To triumph is to taste glory.

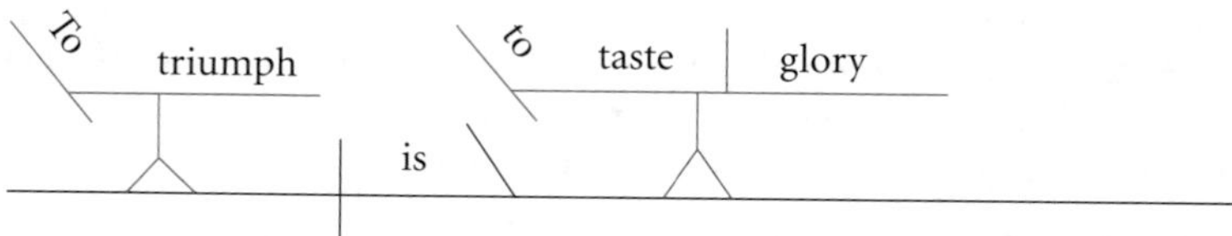

Exercise 2 **Diagraming Simple Sentences with Phrases**

Using the preceding models as a guide, diagram the following sentences.

1. People of that time knew nothing about the rest of the world.
2. My cousin Janet got her wish, a part in the play.
3. Thousands of leaves, falling gently, covered the damp sidewalk.
4. Watching television is one way of relaxing.
5. To write well means to think clearly.
6. My grandmother wants to learn about everything.
7. Roaring, the rapidly widening river raced to cover waiting farmland.
8. Eating well is the best revenge.
9. Pedestrians, shadows in the fog, hurried to reach home.
10. Blinking in bewilderment, I stared at the scene before me.

7.
10.
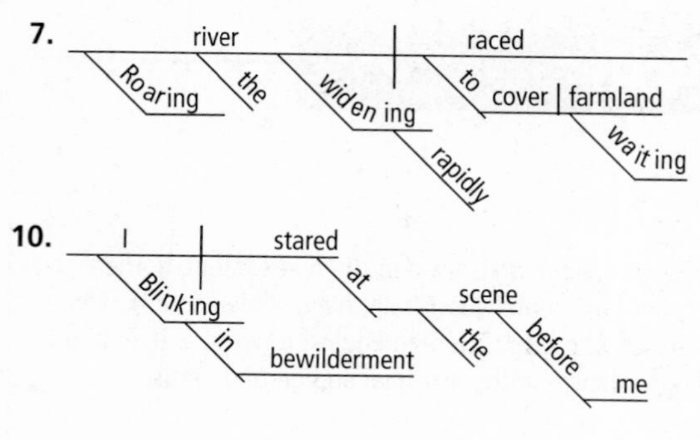

Close

Have volunteers write some of the answers to Exercise 2 on the board. Then review the ways in which the different types of phrases are diagramed.

14.3 Diagraming Sentences with Clauses

Compound Sentences

Diagram each main clause separately. If the clauses are connected by a semicolon, use a vertical dotted line to connect the verbs of each main clause. If the main clauses are connected by a conjunction, place the conjunction on a solid horizontal line and connect it to the verbs of each main clause by vertical dotted lines.

Athletes like to win, but they must also learn to lose.

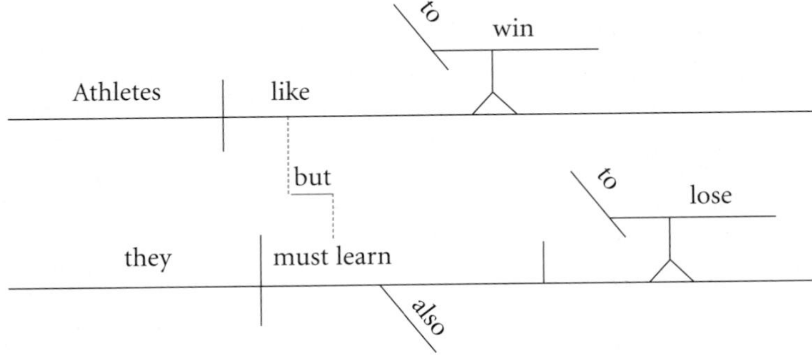

Complex Sentences with Adjective Clauses

Place the main clause in one diagram and the adjective clause beneath it in another diagram. Use a dotted line to connect the relative pronoun or other introductory word in the adjective clause to the modified noun or pronoun in the main clause.

The player whom you like won games that were close.

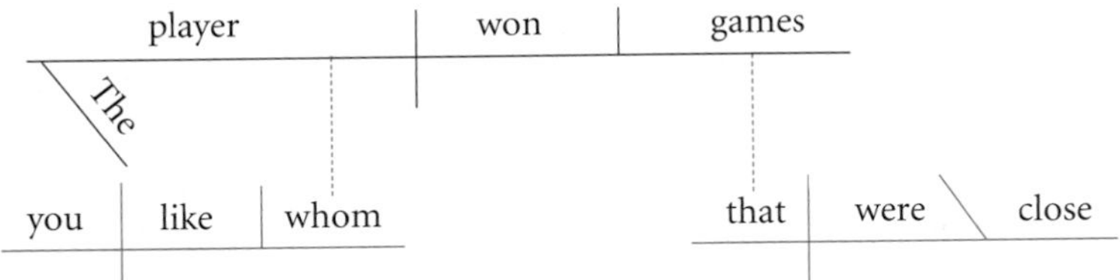

Focus

Lesson Overview

Objectives

- To identify the components of compound and complex sentences
- To represent the components in sentence diagrams

Bellringer
Daily Language Activity

When students enter the classroom, have the following assignment on the board: *Copy the clauses in the following sentence and write whether each is a main clause or a subordinate clause and why:*

Our cousins visited us in September, and we will go to their house in April.

Teach

Compound Sentences

Teaching Tip

After you have explained how to diagram compound sentences, call on a volunteer to diagram the Bellringer sentence on the board. Then ask other students to check the diagram for correctness and to revise as needed.

Complex Sentences with Adjective Clauses

Cross-reference: Grammar

For instruction and practice with adjective clauses, refer students to Lesson 13.5, pp. 545–547.

Diagraming Sentences

Resource Manager

Planning Resources
- *Lesson Plans*

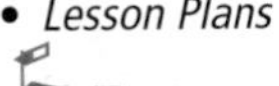

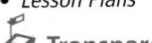

Transparencies
- *Bellringer*
- *Two-Minute Skill Drill*

Other Print Resources
- *Grammar and Composition Handbook*
- *Grammar Workbook*, Lesson 35

Teach

Complex Sentences with Adverb Clauses

Teaching Tip

Point out that clauses, whether subordinate or main, are connected with dotted lines rather than solid lines.

Cross-reference: Grammar

For instruction and practice with adverb clauses, refer students to Lesson 13.6, pp. 548–549.

Complex Sentences with Noun Clauses

Cross-reference: Grammar

For instruction and practice with noun clauses, refer students to Lesson 13.7, pp. 550–551.

Two-Minute Skill Drill

Write the following sentence on the board and have students diagram it:

Nutritionists recommend that people avoid fatty and sugary foods.

Encourage students to discuss the components of this complex sentence. (*noun clause used as a direct object in a main clause*) Then ask a volunteer to draw the diagram on the board. Have students suggest revisions as needed.

See also *Two-Minute Skill Drill Transparency 14.3*

ASSESSMENT OPTIONS

Tests with Answer Key & Rubrics
Unit 14 Mastery Test, pp. 53–54

Testmaker
Unit 14 Mastery Test

You may wish to administer the Unit 14 Mastery Test at this point.

Complex Sentences with Adverb Clauses

Place the main clause in one diagram and the adverb clause beneath it in another diagram. Place the subordinating conjunction on a diagonal dotted line, connecting the verb in the adverb clause to the modified verb, adjective, or adverb in the main clause.

Before a game begins, the coach gives encouragement.

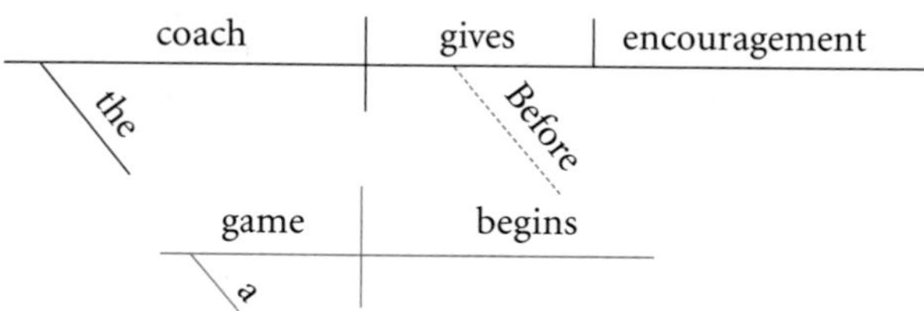

Complex Sentences with Noun Clauses

First decide what role the noun clause plays within the main clause. Is it the subject, direct object, predicate nominative, or object of a preposition? Then diagram the main clause, placing the noun clause on a "stilt" in the appropriate position. Place the introductory word of the clause in the position of subject, object, or predicate nominative within the noun clause itself. If the introductory word merely begins the noun clause, place it on a line of its own above the verb in the noun clause, connecting it to the verb with a dotted vertical line.

NOUN CLAUSE AS SUBJECT

What the coach says is extremely important.

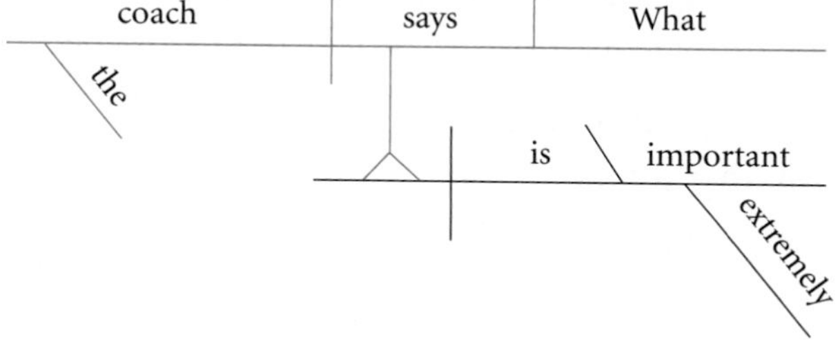

Diagraming Sentences

Cooperative Learning

Working with Diagrams

Have students copy the following sentences: *Mike is a boy who loves sports. Babies cry when they are hungry. You know that I like salads.* Tell them that one of the sentences contains an adjective clause, one a noun clause, and one an adverb clause. Ask students to identify the main clause and the subordinate clause in each sentence, labeling the subordinate clause *adjective, adverb,* or *noun.* Then have them work in small groups to write and diagram sentences with clauses. Check the work of each group.

NOUN CLAUSE AS DIRECT OBJECT

The coach knows that the rival may win.

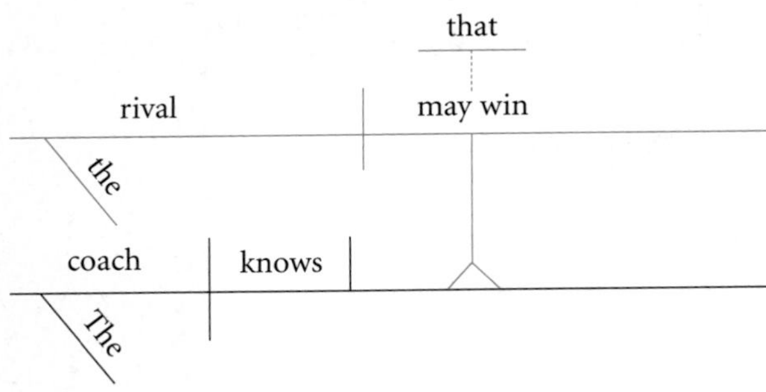

NOUN CLAUSE AS OBJECT OF A PREPOSITION

The coach assigns more practice to whoever needs it.

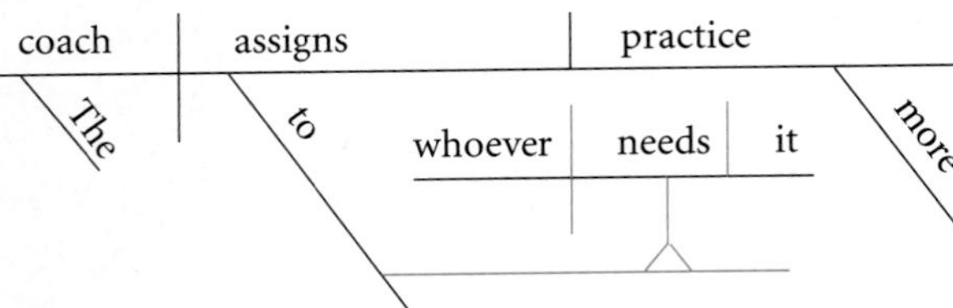

Exercise 3 **Diagraming Sentences with Clauses**

Using the preceding models as a guide, diagram the following sentences.

1. John is the oldest child, and Rebecca is the youngest.
2. The pilot who won last year's competition has sold his airplane.
3. Whenever Manolo remembers, he buys an extra newspaper for Juanito.
4. Whoever wins this game chooses the next one.
5. Everybody knows that Hefflemeyer is the greatest player.
6. After Bettina scored on a jump shot, the score was tied.
7. I liked watching the movie, but the book was better.
8. The team that is better prepared will probably win.
9. Whoever goes first will have the advantage.
10. I want to learn more about what you said.

Diagraming Sentences

Practice and Assess

Answers: Exercise 3

1.
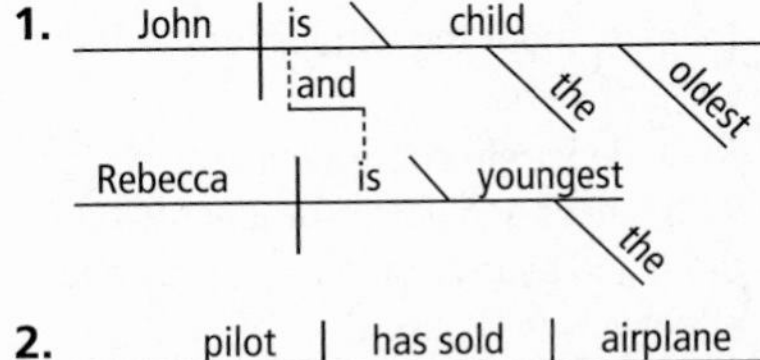

2.
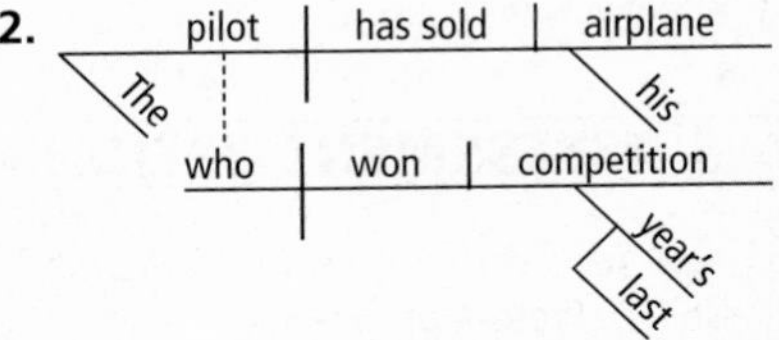

3.
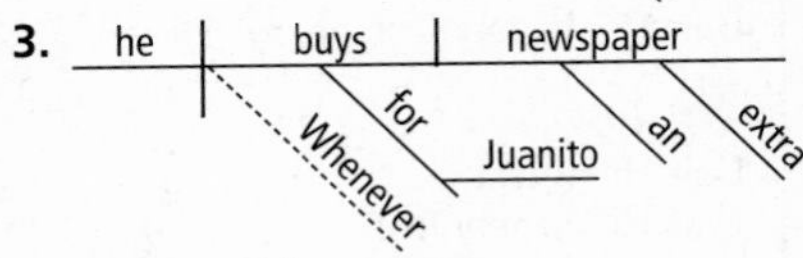

4.
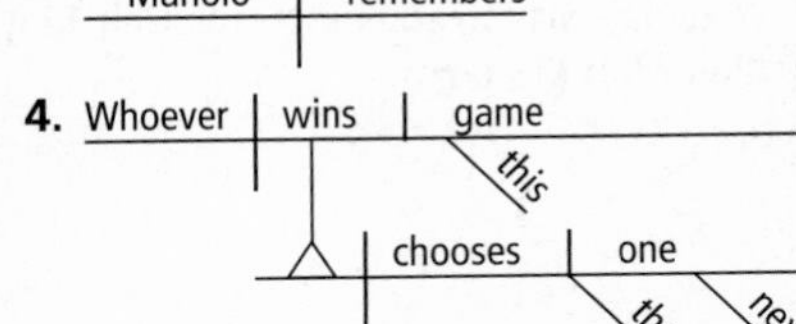

5.
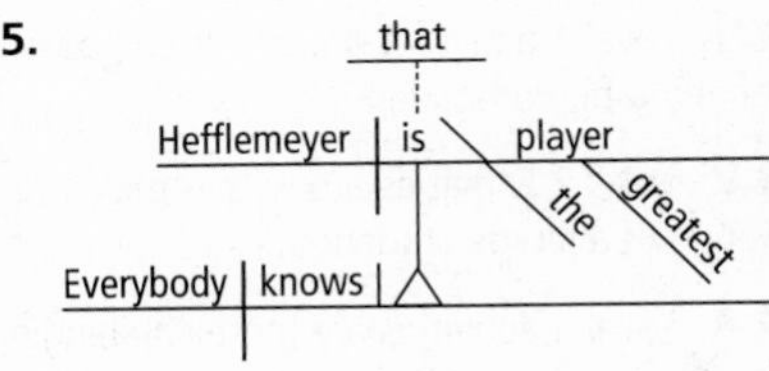

6.
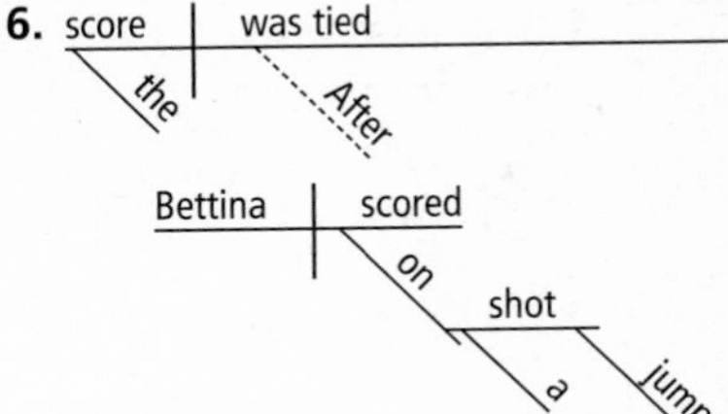

7.
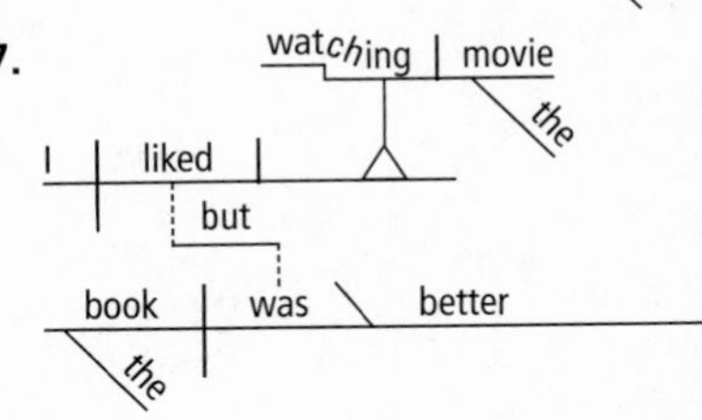

8.
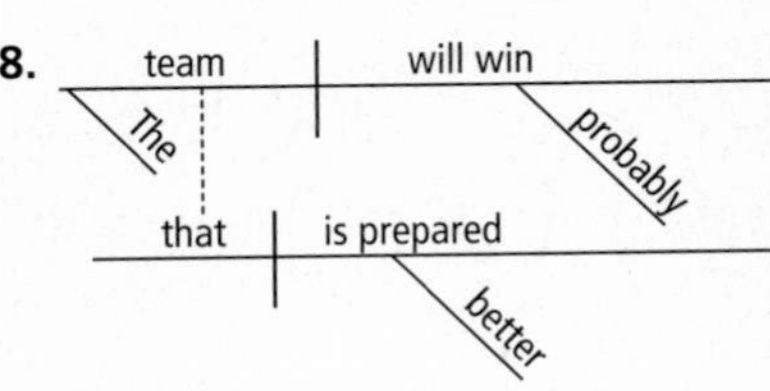

9.
10.
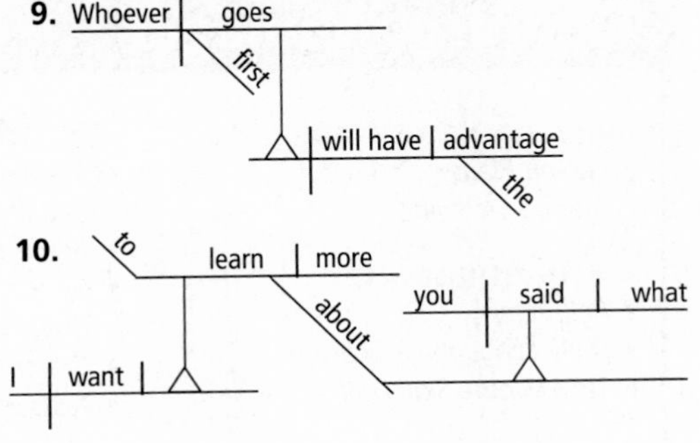

INTRODUCING

UNIT 15

Objectives

- To learn about the various tenses and voice of verbs
- To demonstrate control over the various verb tenses and voices by identifying them and by using them correctly and effectively in writing

ASSESSMENT OPTIONS

Tests with Answer Key & Rubrics
Unit 15 Pretest, pp. 55–56
Unit 15 Mastery Test, pp. 57–58

Testmaker
Unit 15 Pretest
Unit 15 Mastery Test

You may wish to administer the Unit 15 Pretest at this point.

Key to Ability Levels

L1 Level 1 activities are within the basic ability range of students.

L2 Level 2 activities are within the ability range of average students.

L3 Level 3 activities are more challenging activities.

UNIT 15

Verb Tenses and Voice

Resource Manager

Planning Resources
- *Lesson Plans*
- *Block Scheduling*

Transparencies
- *Bellringer*
- *Daily Language Practice*
- *Two-Minute Skill Drill*

Other Print Resources
- *Grammar and Composition Handbook*
- *Grammar Enrichment*
- *Grammar Practice*
- *Grammar Reteaching*
- *Grammar Workbook*
- *Tests with Answer Key and Rubrics*

Video
- *MindJogger Videoquizzes*

Software
- *Interactive Grammar and Language Workbook*
- *Presentation Plus!*
- *Testmaker*

Web Site
- *glencoe.com*

15.1 Principal Parts of Verbs

■ All verbs have four **principal parts:** a *base form,* a *present participle,* a *simple past form,* and a *past participle.* All the verb tenses are formed from these principal parts.

Principal Parts of Verbs			
BASE FORM	**PRESENT PARTICIPLE**	**PAST FORM**	**PAST PARTICIPLE**
nail	nailing	nailed	nailed
carry	carrying	carried	carried
ring	ringing	rang	rung
be	being	was, were	been
sit	sitting	sat	sat

The base form (except the base form of *be*) and the past form can be used by themselves as main verbs. To function as the simple predicate in a sentence, the present participle and the past participle must always be used with one or more auxiliary verbs.

Lions **roar.** [base or present form]

Lions **roared.** [past form]

Lions **are roaring.** [present participle with the auxiliary verb *are*]

Lions **have roared.** [past participle with the auxiliary verb *have*]

Exercise 1 **Using Principal Parts of Verbs**

Write the correct form of the principal part of the verb indicated in parentheses.

1. They ____ for an auto dealership. (base form of *work*)
2. They are ___ up sales of minivans and jeeps. (present participle of *ring*)
3. Last month, he ____ ten people into buying minivans. (past form of *talk*)
4. She is ____ harder than any other salesperson. (present participle of *work*)
5. They have both ____ a bonus and an award. (past participle of *receive*)
6. They are _____ to other salespeople at the award dinner. (present participle of *talk*)
7. They have often _____ techniques with their colleagues. (past participle of *discuss*)
8. Now they _____ a wider audience. (base form of *need*)
9. Their supervisor _____ very proud when they were selected. (past form of *be*)
10. He was actually _____ around in his office. (present participle of *dance*)

Focus

Lesson Overview

Objective

- To identify the principal parts of verbs and their uses

Bellringer
Daily Language Activity

When students enter the classroom, have this assignment on the board: *Write a short paragraph describing something you are doing, have done, or will be doing today.*

See also *Daily Language Practice*

Teach

Grammar Tip

Remind students that the time of the action expressed by a verb is called *tense.*

Practice and Assess

Answers: Exercise 1

1. work
2. ringing
3. talked
4. working
5. received
6. talking
7. discussed
8. need
9. was
10. dancing

Close

Have pairs of students write a paragraph using the four main parts of at least one verb. They should then underline the verbs and tell which tense each is.

Resource Manager

Planning Resources
- *Lesson Plans*

Transparencies
- *Bellringer*
- *Daily Language Practice*

Other Print Resources
- *Grammar and Composition Handbook*
- *Grammar Reteaching,* p. 25
- *Grammar Workbook,* Lesson 36

Focus

Lesson Overview

Objectives

- To identify the forms of regular and irregular verbs
- To use forms of verbs correctly

Bellringer
Daily Language Activity

When students enter the classroom, have this assignment on the board: *Copy each of the following sentences and fill in the blank with the correct form of the verb in parentheses:*

(a) The artist found a pencil and ______ it. *(sharpen)*

(b) Then he ______ a picture. *(draw)*

See also *Daily Language Practice*

Motivating Activity

Point out that the Bellringer sentences both require verbs in the past tense. Have students contrast the ways in which *sharpen* and *draw* form their past tenses. Ask students to think of other verbs besides *draw* that do not form their past tenses by adding *-ed*.

Teach

Cross-reference: Troubleshooter

For instruction and practice in using regular and irregular verbs correctly, refer students to the Troubleshooter.

Cross-reference: Grammar

For instruction and practice in identifying verbs in the predicate of a sentence, refer students to Lessons 11.1–11.4, pp. 495–503.

15.2 Regular and Irregular Verbs

■ A **regular verb** forms its past and past participle by adding *-ed* to the base form.

Regular Verbs		
BASE FORM	**PAST FORM**	**PAST PARTICIPLE**
roar	roared	roared
talk	talked	talked
learn	learned	learned

Some regular verbs undergo spelling changes when a suffix beginning with a vowel is added.

ruffle + **-ed** = ruffl**ed** spy + **-ed** = spi**ed** flop + **-ed** = flop**ped**
argue + **-ed** = argu**ed** tie + **-ed** = ti**ed** refer + **-ed** = refer**red**

■ An **irregular verb** forms its past and past participle in some way other than by adding *-ed* to the base form.

Irregular Verbs		
BASE FORM	**PAST FORM**	**PAST PARTICIPLE**
be	was, were	been
beat	beat	beaten *or* beat
become	became	become
begin	began	begun
bite	bit	bitten or bit
blow	blew	blown
break	broke	broken
bring	brought	brought
buy	bought	bought
catch	caught	caught
choose	chose	chosen
come	came	come
do	did	done
draw	drew	drawn
drink	drank	drunk
drive	drove	driven
eat	ate	eaten
fall	fell	fallen
feel	felt	felt
find	found	found

Resource Manager

Planning Resources
- *Lesson Plans*

Transparencies
- *Bellringer*
- *Daily Language Practice*
- *Two-Minute Skill Drill*

Other Print Resources
- *Grammar and Composition Handbook*
- *Grammar Enrichment*, p. 25
- *Grammar Practice*, p. 25
- *Grammar Workbook*, Lessons 36–37

Irregular Verbs		
BASE FORM	PAST FORM	PAST PARTICIPLE
fly	flew	flown
freeze	froze	frozen
get	got	got *or* gotten
give	gave	given
go	went	gone
grow	grew	grown
hang	hung *or* hanged	hung *or* hanged
have	had	had
keep	kept	kept
know	knew	known
lay*	laid	laid
lead	led	led
leave	left	left
lend	lent	lent
lie*	lay	lain
lose	lost	lost
make	made	made
put	put	put
ride	rode	ridden
ring	rang	rung
rise*	rose	risen
run	ran	run
say	said	said
see	saw	seen
seek	sought	sought
sell	sold	sold
set*	set	set
shrink	shrank *or* shrunk	shrunk *or* shrunken
sing	sang	sung
sink	sank *or* sunk	sunk
sit*	sat	sat
sleep	slept	slept
speak	spoke	spoken
spring	sprang *or* sprung	sprung
steal	stole	stolen
swim	swam	swum
swing	swung	swung
take	took	taken
teach	taught	taught
tear	tore	torn
tell	told	told
think	thought	thought
throw	threw	thrown
wear	wore	worn
win	won	won
write	wrote	written

*For more detailed instruction on *lay* versus *lie* and *raise* versus *rise*, see Unit 19.

*For more detailed instruction on *sit* versus *set*, see Unit 19.

Verb Tenses and Voice

Cross-reference: Writing

For instruction and practice in using verb tenses correctly in writing, refer students to Unit 4, Narrative Writing, pp. 174–211. Since the Case Study focuses on sportswriting and writing about sports involves the use of many verbs to detail action, the accurate use of tense forms is essential for good sportswriting.

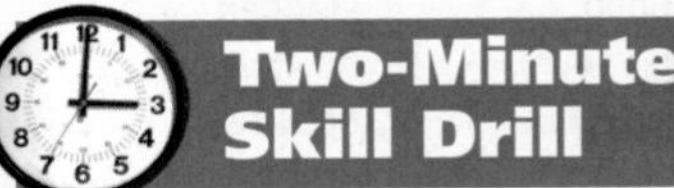

Write the following verbs on the board. Have students write the past and past participle of each verb.

shrink *glance*
move *speak*
give *fall*

See also *Two-Minute Skill Drill Transparency 15.2*

Meeting Individual Needs: English Language Learners

Using Irregular Verbs

Tell students who are learning English that irregular verbs need to be memorized. Have students write all three forms of some of the irregular verbs from the chart on index cards. Let pairs of students work together to pull a card and then create sentences using all the forms of the irregular verb on the card.

Practice and Assess

Answers: Exercise 2

	Past	Past Participle
1.	started	started
2.	thought	thought
3.	climbed	climbed
4.	stopped	stopped
5.	hit	hit
6.	occurred	occurred
7.	grew	grown
8.	skipped	skipped
9.	flew	flown
10.	deterred	deterred
11.	murmured	murmured
12.	prayed	prayed
13.	cried	cried
14.	went	gone
15.	swam	swum
16.	flipped	flipped
17.	insured	insured
18.	stole	stolen
19.	wore	worn
20.	submitted	submitted
21.	wrote	written
22.	ran	run
23.	denied	denied
24.	lent	lent
25.	knew	known

Answers: Exercise 3

1. make
2. rose
3. lying
4. fell
5. chosen
6. sprang
7. been
8. known
9. sank
10. eaten

Exercise 2 Writing Principal Parts of Verbs

Copy and complete the chart. Make sure that you have spelled each form correctly.

BASE FORM	PAST FORM	PAST PARTICIPLE
1. start		
2. think		
3. climb		
4. stop		
5. hit		
6. occur		
7. grow		
8. skip		
9. fly		
10. deter		
11. murmur		
12. pray		
13. cry		
14. go		
15. swim		
16. flip		
17. insure		
18. steal		
19. wear		
20. submit		
21. write		
22. run		
23. deny		
24. lend		
25. know		

Exercise 3 Using Principal Parts of Irregular Verbs

Write the correct form of the principal part of the verb indicated in parentheses.

1. I ____ breakfast for my family every Sunday. (base form of *make*)
2. Last Sunday I ____ late. (past form of *rise*)
3. I was still ____ in bed when a wonderful aroma hit me. (present participle of *lie*)
4. I almost ____ out of bed with excitement. (past form of *fall*)
5. My brother had ____ to give me a present. (past participle of *choose*)
6. I ____ out of bed and sprinted down the stairs. (past form of *spring*)
7. His choice couldn't have ____ a better one. (past participle of *be*)
8. How could he have ____ what I really wanted? (past participle of *know*)
9. I sat and ____ my teeth into my favorite breakfast. (past form of *sink*)
10. I have never ____ better pancakes. (past participle of *eat*)

Enrichment and Extension

Sequencing Principal Parts

Some students have problems with sequencing, and these problems hinder their mastery of tenses and principal parts. Instruct students to review the charts showing principal parts (pp. 582–583). Remind them to look for the appropriate column of the requested form (e.g., past participle) before proceeding down the chart. You might also relate the concept to students' own writing by using a highlighter pen to mark some verbs in students' writing and then helping students identify the tenses and principal parts.

Exercise 4 Using Principal Parts of Verbs

Write the principal part of the verb indicated in parentheses.

Arthur Ashe, a Tennis Pioneer

1. The name Arthur Ashe has ___ to symbolize athletic brilliance and outstanding achievement. (past participle of *come*)
2. Over the past two decades, the name has also ___ personal integrity and grace. (past participle of *signify*)
3. Ashe ___ playing tennis in elementary school. (past form of *begin*)
4. His athletic talent ___ the attention of a local physician, Dr. Robert "Whirlwind" Johnson. (past form of *catch*)
5. Dr. Johnson ____ talented African American youngsters to play for the U.S. Tennis Association. (past form of *teach*)
6. Dr. Johnson had ___ tennis lessons to Althea Gibson. (past participle of *give*)
7. Althea Gibson ___ the first African American to win a championship at Wimbledon, a famous tennis tournament in England. (past form of *be*)
8. By the age of 18, Arthur Ashe had ___ to national prominence. (past participle of *rise*)
9. In 1960 and again in 1961, he ___ the Junior Indoor Singles Championship. (past form of *win*)
10. While he ___ at the University of California in Los Angeles, Ashe was coached by Pancho Gonzales, a tennis champion. (past form of *study*)
11. In 1963 Ashe was ____ for the Davis Cup team. (past participle of *choose*)
12. In 1966 he ____ himself the winner of both the singles and the doubles titles in the National Collegiate Athletic Association Championship. (past form of *find*)
13. In 1968 Ashe's dream of winning at the highest levels of American tennis finally ____ true. (past form of *come*)
14. He ___ first place at the U.S. National Men's Singles Championship. (past form of *take*)
15. By the end of 1968, Ashe had ____ all opponents in the men's singles competition of the first U.S. Open tournament. (past participle of *beat*)
16. Unfortunately, his tournament career ended when he ___ heart surgery. (past form of *undergo*)
17. As a result of a blood transfusion, Ashe ___ HIV. (past form of *contract*)
18. Years later, he ____ a news conference and discussed his illness publicly for the first time. (past form of *hold*)
19. Arthur Ashe ____ in 1993, five months before his fiftieth birthday. (past form of *die*)
20. Friends who ____ at his memorial service praised Ashe for his professional and humanitarian achievements. (past form of *speak*)

Answers: Exercise 4

1. come
2. signified
3. began
4. caught
5. taught
6. given
7. was
8. risen
9. won
10. studied
11. chosen
12. found
13. came
14. took
15. beaten *or* beat
16. underwent
17. contracted
18. held
19. died
20. spoke

Additional Resources

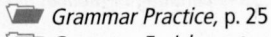

Grammar Practice, p. 25

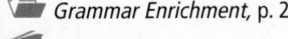

Grammar Enrichment, p. 25

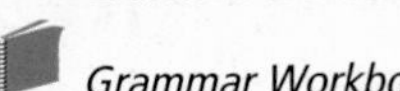

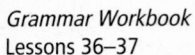

Grammar Workbook
Lessons 36–37

Close

Choose a short passage from a literature selection that the students are reading or have read recently. Ask students to identify the verbs and to write or say aloud the principal parts of each verb.

Meeting Individual Needs: English Language Learners

Pronouncing an Inflection

Students learning English often have trouble pronouncing the regular past-tense ending. Point out that most verbs form the past tense by adding the *d* sound. Help students pronounce a few base forms of verbs and contrast the sound to the sound of the past tense: for example, *help* and *helped*, *enjoy* and *enjoyed*. Then explain that if the base form of a verb ends in *-d* or *-t*, the past tense *-ed* is pronounced with a "schwa" sound, as in *needed* and *roasted*. Once again, contrast the pronunciations: *add* and *added*, *count* and *counted*, and *wait* and *waited*.

Focus

Lesson Overview

Objective

- To identify and use the past, present, and future tenses

Bellringer
Daily Language Activity

When students enter the classroom, have this assignment on the board: *Finish the following sentences using the verbs* teach, taught, *and* will teach.

I ______.
We ______.
You ______.
They ______.

See also *Daily Language Practice*

Motivating Activity

Discuss student responses to the Bellringer activity. Explain that in this lesson, students will learn more about verb tenses.

Teach

Present Tense

☑ Teaching Tip

The term *present tense* is misleading. In fact, we almost never use the present tense to talk about present time. If we want to talk about present time, we normally use the present progressive: *The clock* ***is striking*** *three right now.* The only common use of the present tense for present time is in sports broadcasting: *Jones* ***rounds*** *second base and* ***heads*** *for third.*

15.3 Tenses of Verbs

- **Tense** is the time of the action expressed by a verb.
- There are six tenses in English: *present, past, future, present perfect, past perfect,* and *future perfect.*

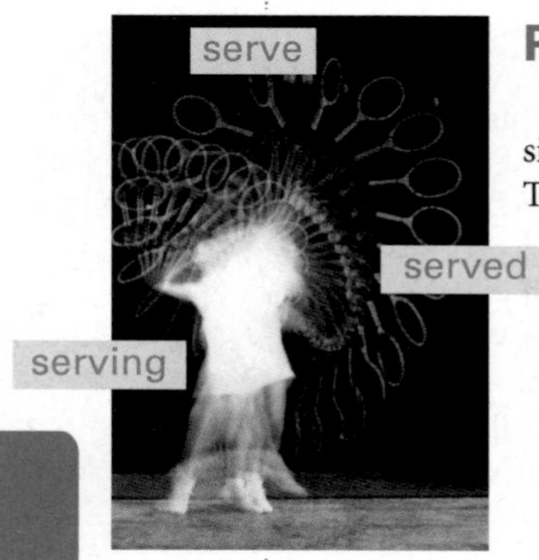

Present Tense

The present-tense form of a verb (excluding the third-person singular, which adds an *-s* or *-es*) is the same as the verb's base form. The one exception is the verb *be.*

THE VERB *STAY*	SINGULAR	PLURAL
FIRST PERSON	I **stay.**	We **stay.**
SECOND PERSON	You **stay.**	You **stay.**
THIRD PERSON	She, he, or it **stays.**	They **stay.**
	Jesse **stays.**	The children **stay.**

THE VERB *BE*	SINGULAR	PLURAL
FIRST PERSON	I **am** sad.	We **are** sad.
SECOND PERSON	You **are** sad.	You **are** sad.
THIRD PERSON	She, he, or it **is** sad.	They **are** sad.
	Sheila **is** sad.	The players **are** sad.

- The **present tense** expresses a constant, repeated, or habitual action or condition. It can also express a general truth.

  My garden **grows** well in the summer. [not just this summer but every summer: a repeated action]

  Helena **bakes** bread well. [always: a habitual action]

  Gold **is** valuable. [a condition that is generally true]

- The **present tense** can also express an action or condition that exists only now.

  Jenny **feels** happy. [not always but just now]

  I **see** a fly on the ceiling. [at this very moment]

- The **present tense** is sometimes used in historical writing to express past events and, more often, in poetry, fiction, and reporting (especially in sports) to convey to the reader a sense of "being there."

  Washington and his troops **spend** the winter at Valley Forge.

  The exhausted runner **seems** to stumble, but in a final spurt he **rushes** over the finish line and **wins.**

Resource Manager

Planning Resources
- *Lesson Plans*

Transparencies
- *Bellringer*
- *Daily Language Practice*

Other Print Resources
- *Grammar and Composition Handbook*
- *Grammar Enrichment,* p. 25
- *Grammar Workbook,* Lesson 38

Past Tense

■ Use the **past tense** to express an action or condition that began and ended in the past.

The orchestra **performed** well.
The musicians **seemed** pleased.
The soloist **sang** beautifully.
The conductor **praised** the musicians.

Nearly all regular and irregular verbs—except *be*—have just one past-tense form, such as *soared* or *began.* The word *be* has two past-tense forms: *was* and *were.*

	SINGULAR	PLURAL
FIRST PERSON	I **was** sad.	We **were** sad.
SECOND PERSON	You **were** sad.	You **were** sad.
THIRD PERSON	She, he, or it **was** sad.	They **were** sad.

Exercise 5 Using the Present Tense

Write a sentence using each of the following present-tense verbs. The content of your sentence should express the kind of present time indicated in parentheses.

SAMPLE does (a repeated action)
ANSWER He does his housecleaning on Saturday.

1. sleeps (a habitual action)
2. feel (just now)
3. is (generally true)
4. hopes (at this moment)
5. takes (constant action)
6. opens (at this moment)
7. am (not always, but just now)
8. practices (a repeated action)
9. need (a condition that is generally true)
10. signs (an event in history)

Exercise 6 Using the Past Tense

Write two paragraphs, one using the past tense of verbs 1 through 5 and one using the past tense of verbs 6 through 10.

1. feel
2. catch
3. freeze
4. eat
5. write
6. be
7. give
8. take
9. wear
10. drink

Verb Tenses and Voice

Meeting Individual Needs: English Language Learners

Understanding Present Tense

Students may be confused about the present tense in English. Explain that a sentence such as *I am eating* refers to an action that is happening right now. A sentence such as *I eat lunch every day at noon* refers to a repeated or habitual action.

Past Tense

Teaching Tip

Narratives, such as anecdotes, short stories, and novels, are usually written in the past tense. The present tense does not convey a sense of past time—it gives the sense of repeated actions and tends to sound "stagey." For example, I **turn on** *the TV to watch the news, and I* **see** *an old friend of mine.* Thus, it is not well suited for storytelling.

Cross-reference: Listening and Speaking

Students should be reminded to enunciate past-tense endings clearly. For instruction and practice in listening and speaking, refer students to Unit 29, pp. 884–892.

Practice and Assess

Answers: Exercise 5

Answers will vary, but some suggestions are given below.

1. Paul sleeps soundly every night.
2. I feel hungry.
3. A good education is important.
4. Frank hopes the rain will stop.
5. Our town takes recycling seriously.
6. He opens the gift.
7. I am ecstatic right now.
8. He practices every evening.
9. I need to study to do well.
10. Washington signs the treaty.

Answers: Exercise 6

Answers will vary, but some suggestions are given below.

I <u>felt</u> happy when I <u>caught</u> the fly ball. I <u>froze</u> briefly in the outfield when I lost the ball in the bright sunlight. Then I made a catch that clinched the game for my team. To celebrate, we <u>ate</u> pizza. Then I <u>wrote</u> my pen pal a letter describing the event.

We <u>were</u> happy that we <u>gave</u> up some time for a good cause. We <u>took</u> the literature door to door. The weather was chilly, so we <u>wore</u> heavy coats. When we finished, we <u>drank</u> hot chocolate to warm up.

Teach

Future Tense

Grammar Tip

At one time in its early history, English had a true future-tense verb form. For some unknown reason, however, that future-tense form completely disappeared from the language. In its place, English has evolved different ways of talking about the future. The most common ways are the following:

1. by means of the modal auxiliary verbs *can, may, must, shall,* and *will*—for example: *We* ***can/may/must/shall/will*** *go there tomorrow.*
2. by means of the present or the present progressive with a future-time adverb—for example: *We* ***go/are going*** *there this afternoon.*
3. by the progressive of the verb plus an infinitive—for example: *We* ***are going to stay*** *there overnight.*

Practice and Assess

Answers: Exercise 7

Answers will vary, but some suggestions are given below.

1. Tomorrow two classmates and I present . . .
2. There will be three parts . . .
3. First, Kate is going to speak . . .
4. She will describe . . .
5. Then Miguel will cover . . .
6. He will focus on . . .
7. I shall be responsible for . . .
8. I shall begin with . . .
9. Then I shall explain the . . .
10. The report is going to conclude with . . .

Answers: Exercise 8

Answers will vary, but a sample sentence is given below.

High-definition television will make our current video system seem primitive.

Future Tense

■ Use the **future tense** to express an action or condition that will occur in the future.

You form the future tense of any verb by using *shall* or *will* with the base form: *I shall study; you will go.*

Roberta **will send** the telegram.

I **shall practice** the piano tonight.

about to...
shall
will
going to

The following are other ways to express future time besides using *shall* or *will:*

1. Use the present tense of *be* with *going to* and the base form of a verb.
   Roberta **is** ***going to*** **send** the telegram.
2. Use the present tense of *be* with *about to* and the base form of the verb.
   Roberta **is** ***about to*** **send** the telegram.
3. Use the present tense of a verb with an adverb or an adverb phrase that shows future time.
   Roberta **leaves** ***tomorrow.***
   Roberta **arrives** ***in the middle of next week.***

Exercise 7 Using Expressions of Future Time

Rewrite each of the following sentences so that the verb is in the future tense. Try to use at least two other ways of expressing future time in addition to *shall* and *will.*

Japan's Classical Theater

[1]Two classmates and I presented a cooperative report on the history of Japanese theater for our literature class. [2]There were three parts to the presentation. [3]First, Kate spoke about the form of medieval theater called No. [4]She described the formality and beauty of No plays. [5]Then Miguel covered the history of Japan's Joruri puppet theater. [6]He focused on the extraordinary realism of the colorful and expressive Joruri puppets. [7]I was responsible for information on Kabuki theater. [8]I began with a description of the typical Kabuki stage with its trapdoors and revolving platforms. [9]I explained the stylized and exaggerated movements of Kabuki actors. [10]The report concluded with a demonstration of Kabuki dance.

Exercise 8 Expressing Future Time in Sentences

Write five statements or predictions about the future. Your sentences may be as realistic or as unrealistic as you wish. Remember to vary the ways in which you express future time.

SAMPLE ANSWER Household robots are going to become a reality.

15.4 Perfect Tenses

Present Perfect Tense

■ Use the **present perfect tense** to express an action that took place or a condition that existed at some *indefinite time* in the past.

Form the present perfect tense by using *has* or *have* with the past participle of a verb: *has stopped, have waited.**

She **has caught** the flu.

They **have brought** a present for us.

The present perfect can refer to completed action in past time only in an indefinite way. Adverbs such as *yesterday* cannot be added to make the time more specific.

Sophia **has completed** her project.

Jack **has wanted** to visit Mexico.

To be specific about completed past time, you would normally use the simple past tense.

Sophia **completed** her project yesterday.

Jack **wanted** to visit Mexico last summer.

The present perfect can also be used to communicate the idea that an action or a condition *began* in the past and *continues* into the present. This use is normally accompanied by an adverb of time or an adverb phrase beginning with *for* or *since*.

The museum **has displayed** the exhibit for months.

We **have kept** the dogs indoors since Sunday.

* Do not be confused by the term *present perfect*; this tense expresses past time. *Present* refers to the tense of the auxiliary verb *has* or *have*.

Verb Tenses and Voice

Exercise 9 Using the Present Perfect Tense

(a) Rewrite each of the following sentences, changing the tense of the verb from past to present perfect. (b) Add adverbs or adverb phrases to each new sentence to communicate the idea that an action or condition began in the past and continues into the present.

SAMPLE We wanted to go to Paris.

ANSWER **a.** We have wanted to go to Paris.
b. We have wanted to go to Paris for two years.

1. Lila gave piano lessons.
2. My parents owned two dogs.
3. The trees were in bloom.
4. My friend wrote poetry.
5. The team played with determination.

Focus

Lesson Overview

Objective

- To use the perfect tenses appropriately

Bellringer
Daily Language Activity

When students enter the classroom, have this assignment on the board: *Complete the following sentences. Explain when the actions occurred.*

I have eaten ______.
We have completed ______.
You will have worked ______.

See also *Daily Language Practice*

Teach

Present Perfect Tense

Grammar Tip

Explain that the perfect tense is used for actions begun at one time and completed at a later time or continuing into another time. Students may forget that the verb *have*, in addition to being the helping verb required in all perfect tenses, can also be a main verb in its own right. *(We have had to work hard.)*

Practice and Assess

Answers: Exercise 9

Answers will vary, but some suggestions are given below.

1. a. Lila has given piano lessons.
   b. Lila has given piano lessons for as long as I can remember.
2. a. My parents have owned two dogs.
   b. My parents have owned two dogs for six years.
3. a. The trees have been in bloom.
   b. The trees have been in bloom since May.
4. a. My friend has written poetry.
   b. My friend has written poetry all her life.
5. a. The team has played with determination.
   b. The team has played with determination all day.

Resource Manager

Planning Resources
- *Lesson Plans*

Transparencies
- *Bellringer*
- *Daily Language Practice*
- *Two-Minute Skill Drill*

Other Print Resources
- *Grammar and Composition Handbook*
- *Grammar Practice,* p. 26
- *Grammar Reteaching,* p. 26
- *Grammar Workbook,* Lesson 39

15.4

Teach

Past and Future Perfect Tenses

☑ Teaching Tips

The past perfect tense is used to show that an action started and was completed before another action, also in the past, started—for example: *I had just opened the door when the phone rang.*

The future perfect is used to show a future action that will begin and end before another future event begins—for example: *At this pace, I will have written the first chapter of my story by Saturday.*

Two-Minute Skill Drill

Write the following words on the board:

work *began*

Have students write the past perfect and future perfect tense of each.

See also *Two-Minute Skill Drill Transparency 15.4*

Practice and Assess

Answers: Exercise 10

1. had held
2. will have become
3. had thrown
4. had driven
5. will have rehearsed

Past Perfect Tense

■ Use the **past perfect tense** to indicate that one past action or condition began *and* ended before another past action or condition started.

You form the past perfect tense by using *had* with the past participle of a verb: *had loved, had written.*

PAST PERFECT — PAST

She **had been** the captain of the team before I **became** captain. [She was captain; she stopped being captain; I became captain.]

PAST — PAST PERFECT

Before I **slipped,** many other pedestrians **had slipped** in the same place. [They slipped; they finished slipping; I slipped.]

PAST PERFECT — PAST

He **had** already **dried** the dishes by the time I **arrived**. [He dried the dishes; he finished drying the dishes; I arrived.]

Future Perfect Tense

■ Use the **future perfect tense** to express one future action or condition that will begin *and* end before another future event starts.

You form the future perfect tense by using *shall have* or *will have* with the past participle of a verb: *shall have walked, will have walked.*

By summertime I **will have lived** here four months. [The four months will be over by the time another future event, the coming of summertime, occurs.]

By the time the astronauts reach the moon, they **will have practiced** the maneuver many times.

Exercise 10 Writing the Past Perfect and Future Perfect Tenses

Write the verb in parentheses in the tense indicated in brackets.

1. When the president resigned, he (hold) office for three years. [past perfect]
2. My father projects that forty years from now the majority of people (become) comfortable with voting by computer. [future perfect]
3. Before she realized it, Janice (throw) away the newspaper with the candidates' statements. [past perfect]
4. Peter learned that he (drive) to the wrong polling place. [past perfect]
5. By the time the candidate makes a speech, she (rehearse) it for weeks. [future perfect]

Meeting Individual Needs — Learning Disabled

Understanding Perfect Tenses

Some students may have difficulty understanding that the perfect tenses refer to actions begun at one time and completed at a later time. You may want to have these students practice telling you about actions they have completed at a specific time, such as *I ate lunch at noon yesterday*, and actions that are habitual, such as *I have eaten lunch at noon for years.* **L1**

Exercise 11 Review: Identifying the Verb Tenses

On your paper, write the tense of each italicized verb. Identify the tense as *present, past, future, present perfect, past perfect,* or *future perfect.*

Reggae Music

1. Perhaps you *listen* to a style of music known as reggae.
2. This intensely rhythmic music *has been* popular in Jamaica for some time.
3. Jamaican and African folk music and American rhythm and blues *had influenced* the reggae star Bob Marley before he *began* to play music himself.
4. Bands *had performed* reggae in Jamaica for twenty years before it was heard in either the United States or Europe.
5. It *has been* popular in the United States since the 1970s.
6. Before the musical style *took* the name reggae, fans *had called* it by various names—including rudie blues, ska, blue beat, and rock steady.
7. Reggae music *gained* international fame as a result of two groups, Bob Marley and the Wailers and Toots and the Maytals.
8. By the time it *became* popular outside Jamaica, reggae *had influenced* such rock musicians as Eric Clapton, John Lennon, and the Police.
9. Reggae *will remain* popular because reggae musicians *tour* frequently.
10. By the time he *completes* his latest tour, Bob Marley's son Ziggy, for example, *will have performed* in dozens of American cities.

Exercise 12 Review: Using Verb Tenses

For each sentence, write the tense of the verb indicated in parentheses.

A Legendary Concert

1. The Woodstock Music and Art Fair ____ to symbolize the hippie culture of the 1960s. (present perfect tense of *come*)
2. By the time Jimi Hendrix played the "Star Spangled Banner," an estimated 500,000 young people ____ in Saugerties, New York, for a weekend of rock and roll. (past perfect tense of *arrive*)
3. At the event, Richie Havens ____ for over two hours. (past tense of *sing*)
4. For years a rumor ____ that Joni Mitchell, known for her rendition of the song "Woodstock," was never at Woodstock. (present perfect tense of *persist*)
5. In August 1994, what some had called the "Reunion at Yasgur's Farm" ____ place on the actual site of Woodstock '69. (past tense of *take*)
6. Rock elders such as Joe Cocker and Bob Dylan, who ____ favor with young audiences, performed at the anniversary concert. (past perfect tense of *gain*)
7. I ____ happy that I had the opportunity to attend. (present tense of *be*)
8. By the fortieth anniversary of Woodstock, many of the "flower children" of the 1960s ____ their sixties. (future perfect tense of *reach*)
9. Do you think they ____ Janis Joplin, Jimi Hendrix, and the other legendary musicians who performed at Woodstock? (future perfect tense of *forget*)
10. I think they ____ still ____ (future tense of *remember*)

Answers: Exercise 11

1. present
2. present perfect
3. past perfect; past
4. past perfect
5. present perfect
6. past; past perfect
7. past
8. past; past perfect
9. future; present
10. present; future perfect

Answers: Exercise 12

1. has come
2. had arrived
3. sang
4. has persisted
5. took
6. had gained
7. am
8. will have reached
9. will have forgotten
10. will . . . remember

Additional Practice

Grammar Practice, p. 26
Grammar Reteaching, p. 26
Grammar Workbook, Lesson 39

Close

Have students write briefly about how they can use the perfect tenses to express time relationships more clearly in their other classes. Have them consider how the perfect tenses might be useful when writing about historical or future events.

Enrichment and Extension

Using the Future Perfect Tense

The future perfect tense is the tense used least frequently. Ask students to write some sentences using the future tense and then rewrite them in the future perfect tense. Example, *I will hide the gift. By the time the party starts, I will have hidden the gift.* Discuss what modifications in a sentence make the future perfect tense necessary. (The tense becomes necessary when the sentence includes a point in the future from which one looks backward.)

Focus

Lesson Overview

Objective

- To identify and use the progressive and emphatic verb forms

Bellringer
Daily Language Activity

When students enter the classroom, have this assignment on the board: *Copy the following sentences, and complete each with the correct form of* walk. *Then underline the complete verb or verb phrase in both sentences.*

Yesterday Linh ______ to school.

Today Linh is ______ to school again.

See also *Daily Language Practice*

Teach

Progressive and Emphatic Forms

Listening and Speaking

Tell students that when they use the emphatic form in speech, they should stress the word *do* or *did.* For instruction and practice in listening and speaking, refer students to Unit 29, pp. 884–892.

Practice and Assess

Answers: Exercise 13

Answers may vary, but some suggestions are given below.

1. are riding
2. has been gaining
3. were working
4. is providing
5. do ride
6. are growing
7. are finding
8. will be trying
9. had been planning
10. do require

15.5 Progressive and Emphatic Forms

■ Each of the six tenses has a **progressive** form that expresses a continuing action.

Make the progressive forms by using the appropriate tense of the verb *be* with the present participle of the main verb:

PRESENT PROGRESSIVE	They ***are*** **reading.**
PAST PROGRESSIVE	They ***were*** **reading.**
FUTURE PROGRESSIVE	They ***will be*** **reading.**
PRESENT PERFECT PROGRESSIVE	They ***have been*** **reading.**
PAST PERFECT PROGRESSIVE	They ***had been*** **reading.**
FUTURE PERFECT PROGRESSIVE	They ***will have been*** **reading.**

■ The present and past tenses have **emphatic forms,** which add special force, or emphasis, to the verb.

Make the emphatic forms by using *do, does,* or *did* with the base form of the verb.

PRESENT EMPHATIC	I ***do*** **read** the newspaper every day.
	Tony ***does*** **read** it occasionally.
PAST EMPHATIC	Inez ***did*** **read** the newspaper yesterday.

Exercise 13 Using the Progressive and Emphatic Forms

For each of the following sentences, write the progressive or the emphatic form of the verb in parentheses that makes sense in the sentence.

The Modern Bicycle

1. Today more than seventy-five million Americans (ride) bicycles.
2. Over the years, bicycling (gain) popularity as a form of both exercise and recreation.
3. Even before bicycles began to be widely used for transportation and exercise, numerous organizations already (work) to promote long-distance trips for experienced riders.
4. Today the bicycle (provide) efficient transportation to and from work for many people.
5. Despite the dangers, many people (ride) bicycles in metropolitan areas.
6. Because of accidents involving bicyclists, safety rules (grow) increasingly important.
7. There is no doubt that bicyclists (find) it difficult to ride on busy streets.
8. We can predict that if environmental conditions don't improve, legislators (try) to pass laws to protect bicyclists.
9. Before the recession, many cities (plan) to create bikeways, special lanes for bicyclists.
10. To ensure safety for all, new traffic laws (require) bicyclists to ride more carefully.

Resource Manager

Planning Resources
- *Lesson Plans*

Transparencies
- *Bellringer*
- *Daily Language Practice*

Other Print Resources
- *Grammar and Composition Handbook*
- *Grammar Enrichment,* p. 28
- *Grammar Workbook,* Lesson 41

Exercise 14 Identifying Verb Tenses and Their Uses

Explain the difference in meaning between the sentences in each of the pairs below. Name the tenses and forms used in each sentence.

SAMPLE **a.** Why was Gloria so secretive?
b. Why has Gloria been so secretive?

ANSWER In sentence *a,* the action occurred and ended (past). In sentence *b,* the action occurred in the past and is still continuing (present perfect).

1. **a.** Do you think Anna is writing a birthday poem for the twins' twenty-first birthday?
   b. Do you think Anna has been writing a birthday poem for the twins' twenty-first birthday?
2. **a.** Anna had finished the poem by the twins' birthday.
   b. Anna did finish the poem by the twins' birthday.
3. **a.** Michael had been painting a picture for the twins before he left town on a business trip to Salt Lake City.
   b. Michael had painted a picture for the twins before he left town on a business trip to Salt Lake City.
4. **a.** The twins had been telling everyone not to make a fuss.
   b. The twins told everyone not to make a fuss.
5. **a.** Nonetheless, the twins' friends planned a surprise party.
   b. Nonetheless, the twins' friends were planning a surprise party.
6. **a.** Last year, they forgot to celebrate the twins' birthday.
   b. Last year, they did forget to celebrate the twins' birthday.
7. **a.** I have been shopping for the perfect gift for weeks.
   b. I had been shopping for the perfect gift for weeks.
8. **a.** Marc and Lydia had been arguing before the twins arrived.
   b. Marc and Lydia were arguing when the twins arrived.
9. **a.** The twins looked happy.
   b. The twins were looking happy.
10. **a.** By this time next week, the twins will have begun their thank-you notes.
    b. By this time next week, the twins will begin their thank-you notes.

Exercise 15 Expressing Past Time in a Paragraph

Write a paragraph of at least eight sentences about an important event in your past. Underline five verbs or verb phrases that you have used. Use some progressive and emphatic forms if possible. (Remember that the perfect tenses, as well as the past tense, can be used to express past action.)

Answers: Exercise 14

Answers will vary, but some suggestions are given below.

1. In sentence *a,* the action begins and continues in the present—present progressive. In *b,* the action began in the past and continues in the present—present perfect progressive. In both sentences the question (*Do you think*) is asked in the present.
2. In *a,* the action began and ended before another event took place—past perfect. In *b,* an action in the past is emphasized—past emphatic.
3. In *a,* the action began in the past and continued—past perfect progressive—until another action occurred—past. In *b,* the action began and ended—past perfect—before the second action occurred—past.
4. In *a,* the action began, continued, and then ended in the past—past perfect progressive. In *b,* the action occurred in the past—past.
5. In *a,* the action happened in the past—past. In *b,* the action began in the past and continued—past progressive.
6. In *a,* the action occurred in the past—past. In *b,* the action in the past is given special emphasis—past emphatic.
7. In *a,* the action began in the past and continues—present perfect progressive. In *b,* the action was ongoing in the past but ended—past perfect progressive.
8. In *a,* an ongoing action in the past ended—past perfect progressive—before another action occurred—past. In *b,* the action began in the past and was continuing—past progressive—at the time the other action occurred—past.
9. In *a,* the action has ended—past. In *b,* the action began in the past and continued—past progressive.
10. In *a,* a future action will have ended by the time specified—future perfect. In *b,* the action takes place in the future—future.

English Language Learners

Using Progressive Forms Correctly

Some students who are learning English may need help in order to use progressive forms correctly. Explain that certain verbs, such as *know, love,* and *smell,* describe a state rather than an action, and these verbs cannot be used in the progressive. Thus it is incorrect to say, for example, *I am knowing the answer, I am loving ice cream,* or *the bread is smelling like honey.*

Answers: Exercise 15

Answers will vary. Sample sentence: While I was attending summer camp last year, I learned an important lesson.

Close

Have students choose an action verb and write sentences that use the six progressive forms, the present emphatic form, and the past emphatic form.

Focus

Lesson Overview

Objectives

- To identify verb tenses
- To use verbs that are compatible within sentences

Bellringer
Daily Language Activity

When students enter the classroom, have this assignment on the board: *Write a sentence that uses the verbs* called *and* had heard.

See also 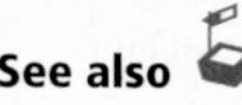 *Daily Language Practice*

Motivating Activity

Ask volunteers to write their sentences from the Bellringer activity on the chalkboard. Have students discuss the verb tenses and how the tenses help to explain when the events in the sentence occurred.

Teach

Compatibility of Tenses

Grammar Tip

Remind students that when a sentence contains a shift in verb tense, the verb form they use must correspond in number to its subject.

Practice and Assess

Answers: Exercise 16

1. had seen
2. opened
3. had gone
4. bought
5. is

15.6 Compatibility of Tenses

- Do not shift, or change, tenses when two or more events occur at the same time.

INCORRECT	During the concert the pianist **forgot** the notes, and she **stops** in the middle of the piece. [The tense needlessly shifts from the past to the present.]
CORRECT	During the concert the pianist **forgot** the notes, and she **stopped** in the middle of the piece. [Now it is clear that both events happened at nearly the same time in the past.]
INCORRECT	The maestro **leaves** the podium. The audience **gave** him a standing ovation. [The tense needlessly shifts from the present to the past.]
CORRECT	The maestro **leaves** the podium. The audience **gives** him a standing ovation. [It is clear that both events are happening at about the same time.]

- Shift tenses to show that one event precedes or follows another.

INCORRECT	By the time we **arrived,** they **ate** dinner. [The two past-tense verbs give the mistaken impression that both events happened at the same time.]
CORRECT	By the time we **arrived,** they **had eaten** dinner. [The shift from the past tense *(arrived)* to the past perfect tense *(had eaten)* clearly indicates that they ate the dinner before we arrived.]

- Keep a statement of universal truth in the present tense even if the main verb is in the past tense.

Columbus proved that the earth is round.

Exercise 16 Choosing Compatible Tenses

Determine which action or condition preceded the other one. Then write the compatible tense of the verb in parentheses.

1. Kim Mason was saving her earnings to buy a CD player she (saw, had seen) in the window of Music World.
2. It had been almost a year since she (opens, opened) her savings account.
3. By the time she saved enough money to buy the CD player, it (had gone, went) on sale.
4. She purchased the CD player and also (buys, bought) some CDs.
5. Kim learned that saving (is, was) a good way to get what you want.

Resource Manager

Planning Resources

- *Lesson Plans*

Transparencies

- *Bellringer*
- *Daily Language Practice*

Other Print Resources

- *Grammar and Composition Handbook*
- *Grammar Enrichment,* pp. 26–27
- *Grammar Workbook,* Lesson 42

Exercise 17 Making Tenses Compatible

First find the two verbs that appear in each of the following sentences. Then rewrite each sentence, making the second verb compatible with the first verb.

Maxine Hong Kingston: A Writer's Heritage

1. Maxine Hong Kingston was born in Stockton, California, in 1940 and was speaking Cantonese as a child.
2. After she had received several scholarships, she attends college at the University of California at Berkeley.
3. Before she switched to English, Kingston studies engineering.
4. Kingston found out in college that she is not a reporter.
5. While she wrote her first book, Kingston supports herself with a full-time job.
6. When *The Woman Warrior: Memoirs of a Girlhood Among Ghosts* was published in 1976, reviewers praise its combination of autobiography, fiction, and history.
7. By the time I finished *The Woman Warrior,* I learned a great deal about Kingston's childhood.
8. Kingston published *China Men* four years after she was writing *The Woman Warrior.*
9. In *China Men,* Kingston described her grandfather, who works on the transcontinental railroad in the early 1900s.
10. After I had completed *The Woman Warrior,* I had decided to read *China Men* as well.
11. *The Woman Warrior* won the National Book Critics Circle Award for nonfiction in 1976; and four years later, *China Men* had received the National Book Award.
12. Kingston made her debut as a novelist when she has written *Tripmaster Monkey: His Fake Book.*
13. This novel tells the story of Wittman Ah Sing, who had been a graduate of Berkeley and a Chinese American hippie.
14. Kingston sets the story in San Francisco in the 1960s and has made Sing a kind of rebel with a cause.
15. The story follows Sing as he will pursue his dream of writing and staging a huge Chinese saga.
16. The novel has been described as surreal and will have been called a bitter and funny tale.
17. In the course of the story, Sing falls in love and also searched for his grandmother in Reno, Nevada.
18. Maxine Hong Kingston is married to Earll Kingston, the actor, and they had had a son, Joseph.
19. Unlike his mother, Joseph Kingston is not a writer; instead, he had been a musician.
20. Maxine Hong Kingston makes her home in Oakland, California, where she continued to write.

Verb Tenses and Voice

Answers: Exercise 17

1. . . . and spoke
2. . . . she attended
3. . . . Kingston had studied
4. . . . that she was not . . .
5. . . . Kingston supported . . .
6. . . . reviewers praised . . .
7. . . . I had learned . . .
8. . . . after she had written . . .
9. . . . who worked . . .
10. . . . I decided . . .
11. . . . *China Men* received . . .
12. . . . when she wrote . . .
13. . . . who is . . .
14. . . . and makes Sing . . .
15. . . . as he pursues . . .
16. . . . has been called . . .
17. . . . and also searches . . .
18. . . . and they have a . . .
19. . . . instead, he is . . .
20. . . . where she continues . . .

Additional Resources

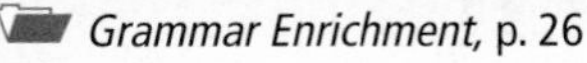
Grammar Enrichment, p. 26

Grammar Workbook, Lesson 42

Close

Ask students to write a paragraph describing a city they have visited or read about. Their paragraphs should demonstrate their understanding of the use of the present tense to make a statement about a universal truth in a past-tense narrative. Have them exchange papers and discuss one another's use of the present tense.

MEETING INDIVIDUAL NEEDS

English Language Learners

Making Tenses Compatible

Have students learning English discuss each of the examples on page 594 with a more fluent partner. Make sure that students are clear about the verb tenses used in each example sentence. Have students discuss the corrections that were made and develop strategies for checking their own writing for shifts in tense.

Focus

Lesson Overview

Objective

- To identify and appropriately use the active and passive voices

Bellringer
Daily Language Activity

When students enter the classroom, have this assignment on the board: *Copy each of the following sentences and underline the verbs:*

Sally planted seeds.

The seeds were planted by Sally.

See also  *Daily Language Practice*

Teach

Voice of Verbs

☑ Teaching Tip

Use the Bellringer sentences to point out that the passive voice may be used to shift emphasis. In the passive version, the focus of attention has been shifted from Sally as the doer of the action to what it was that Sally did.

Practice and Assess

Answers: Exercise 18

1. opened—AV
2. has been labeled—PV
3. was built—PV
4. pushed—AV
5. are designed—PV
6. will operate—AV
7. transport—AV
8. have been corrected—PV
9. is shredded—PV
10. winds—AV

15.7 Voice of Verbs

The woman petted the cat.
The cat was petted by the woman.

- An action verb is in the **active voice** when the subject of the sentence performs the action.

  The student **submitted** her report.

- An action verb is in the **passive voice** when the action is performed on the subject.

  The report **was submitted** by the student.

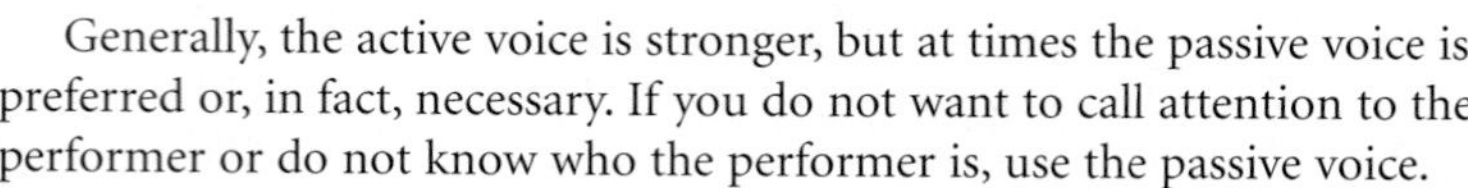

Generally, the active voice is stronger, but at times the passive voice is preferred or, in fact, necessary. If you do not want to call attention to the performer or do not know who the performer is, use the passive voice.

The dinner **was ruined.** [You may not want to identify the culprit.]

The manuscript **was stolen.** [You may not know who the culprit is.]

Form the passive voice by using a form of the auxiliary verb *be* with the past participle of the verb. The tense of a passive verb is determined by the tense of the auxiliary verb.

The child **is pleased** with the dog. [present tense, passive voice]

The child **was pleased** with the dog. [past tense, passive voice]

The child **will be pleased** with the dog. [future tense, passive voice]

Exercise 18 Identifying Active and Passive Voice

Write the verb in each sentence, and tell whether it is *active* or *passive.*

Denver International Airport

1. In 1995 the largest airport (by land area) in North America opened for business.
2. Denver International Airport has been labeled by its supporters as the airport for the twenty-first century.
3. The airport was built on fifty-three square miles of prairie land northeast of the city.
4. Mismanagement and technological mishaps pushed the final cost to almost $5 billion, $3 billion over budget.
5. Three parallel runways are designed to handle ninety-nine aircraft every hour.
6. The control tower, 327 feet tall, will operate even in severe weather.
7. An automated underground transit system and a superhighway of moving sidewalks transport passengers to their gates.
8. Some of the glitches in the $232-million automated baggage system have been corrected.
9. Baggage is no longer shredded by the state-of-the-art system.
10. The baggage system winds for twenty miles beneath the terminal.

Resource Manager

Planning Resources
- *Lesson Plans*

Transparencies
- *Bellringer*
- *Daily Language Practice*

Other Print Resources
- *Grammar and Composition Handbook*
- *Grammar Practice,* p. 27
- *Grammar Reteaching,* p. 27
- *Grammar Workbook,* Lesson 43

Exercise 19 Changing the Voice of Verbs

Rewrite the following sentences, changing active verbs to passive and passive verbs to active. When using passive verbs, drop the performers of the action if they do not need to be identified. Make other wording changes as needed.

SAMPLE Long-distance health care *was made* possible by new technology.
ANSWER New technology *has made* long-distance health care possible.

Explorer Robots

1. The explorer robot has been brought to us by new technology.
2. Human beings operate some of these robots.
3. Areas dangerous to people have been explored by these robots.
4. NASA has tested some explorer robots.
5. Marine biologists expect explorer robots to do underwater research.
6. Endurance superior to that of humans is offered by these robots.
7. Therefore, explorer robots can maintain underwater equipment.
8. Pictures of Mars were relayed to Earth by planetary explorer robots.
9. Engineers have designed some explorer robots to help the physically challenged.
10. Scientists predict a great future for explorer robots.
11. A robotic arm has been constructed by engineers at NASA's Jet Propulsion Laboratory.
12. The device can imitate any action of a surgeon's electronic pointer.
13. The arm provides surgeons access to remote regions of the spine and brain.
14. The robotic arm will be tested on humans by medical researchers.
15. Engineers at MIT are developing a surgical robot for fulfilling a surgeon's commands.
16. Two small cameras have been placed inside the robot's head by engineers.
17. The cameras can continually transmit magnified images back to a video console.
18. A surgeon can direct the robot's movements by manipulating surgical tools mounted on the console.
19. For the next century, long-distance operating rooms with fiber-optic cable connectors are envisioned by researchers.
20. However, many obstacles must first be overcome by medical researchers and electronic engineers.

Exercise 20 Writing Sentences with Active and Passive Voice

Write a paragraph of ten sentences describing a process with which you are familiar. Use a combination of active and passive verbs in your paragraph.

Answers: Exercise 19

Answers may vary, but some suggestions are given below.

1. New technology has brought us . . .
2. Some . . . robots are operated . . .
3. These robots have explored areas . . .
4. Some . . . robots have been tested . . .
5. Explorer robots are expected . . .
6. These robots offer endurance . . .
7. Therefore, underwater equipment can be maintained . . .
8. Planetary explorer robots relayed . . .
9. Some explorer robots have been designed . . .
10. A great future . . . is predicted.
11. Engineers . . . have constructed . . .
12. Any action . . . can be imitated . . .
13. Access to remote . . . is provided . . .
14. Medical researchers will test . . .
15. A . . . robot . . . is being developed . . .
16. Engineers have placed . . .
17. . . . images can be . . . transmitted . . .
18. . . . movements can be directed . . .
19. . . . researchers envision . . .
20. . . . researchers and electronic engineers must first overcome . . .

Answers: Exercise 20

Answers will vary, but two sample sentences are given below.

To build a birdhouse, you must first plan (AV) your work. If a blueprint is made (PV), it may help you later on.

Additional Resources

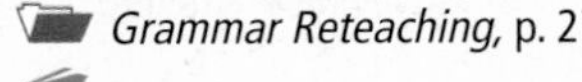

Grammar Practice, p. 27
Grammar Reteaching, p. 27
Grammar Workbook, Lesson 43

Close

Encourage students to discuss the advantages of using the active voice. What techniques can they use to make sure they don't overuse the passive voice?

MEETING INDIVIDUAL NEEDS English Language Learners

Rewriting Sentences

Students who are learning English may need help in identifying active and passive voices. Have them work with a proficient English speaker and identify passive verbs in sentences. Students can then practice orally changing the passive voice to active voice to see which works better.

Teach

About the Literature

This passage appears in Chapter 2 of *Black Boy*, a novel that tells about Richard Wright's coming of age in the southern United States. The exercises that follow are based on this passage and related topics.

Ask a volunteer to read the passage aloud. Have the rest of the class listen, respond, and appropriately evaluate the presentation. In a discussion, students should identify and analyze the characters, the setting, and the mood of the passage. Ask students how the use of different tenses—past, present, progressive, and past perfect—helps the author convey the meaning of the passage.

Linking Grammar and Literature

☑ Teaching Tip

Remind students that some verb forms can function as nouns or as adjectives. In the last sentence of the passage, the words *stealing* and *hoarding* are gerunds, which function as nouns. In the final paragraph, the participle *astonishing* serves as an adjective.

Critical Thinking

Ask students why they think Wright chose to write most of the passage in various forms of the past tense and why he seemed to prefer the active voice to the passive voice.

Listening and Speaking

Ask students to write a paragraph about a childhood memory. Have pairs of students exchange paragraphs and discuss the uses of the active voice and the passive voice.

ASSESSMENT OPTIONS

Tests with Answer Key & Rubrics
Unit 15 Mastery Test, pp. 57–58

Testmaker
Unit 15 Mastery Test

UNIT 15 Grammar Review

Verb Tenses and Voice

The following literary passage is taken from *Black Boy*, Richard Wright's autobiography. Born in Natchez, Mississippi, in 1908, Wright grew up poor, neglected, and hungry. In this passage, he describes a happy memory: the abundant meals that his Aunt Maggie served at her home in Arkansas. The passage has been annotated to show some of the kinds of verbs covered in this unit.

Verb Tenses and Voice

Literature Model

from **Black Boy: A Record of Childhood and Youth**

by Richard Wright

Passive voive

Active voice

Past tense of an irregular verb

Present tense of an irregular verb

Past progressive form

. . . At mealtime Aunt Maggie's table was so loaded with food that I could scarcely believe it was real. It took me some time to get used to the idea of there being enough to eat; I felt that if I ate enough there would not be anything left for another time. When I first sat down at Aunt Maggie's table, I could not eat until I had asked:

"Can I eat all I want?"

"Eat as much as you like," Uncle Hoskins said.

I did not believe him. I ate until my stomach hurt, but even then I did not want to get up from the table.

"Your eyes are bigger than your stomach," my mother said.

"Let him eat all he wants to and get used to food," Uncle Hoskins said.

When supper was over I saw that there were many biscuits piled high upon the bread platter, an astonishing and unbelievable sight to me. Though the biscuits were right before my eyes, and though there was more flour in the kitchen, I was apprehensive lest there be no bread for breakfast in the morning. I was afraid that somehow the biscuits might disappear during the night, while I was sleeping. I did not want to wake up in the morning, as I had so often in the past, feeling hun-

Resource Manager

Planning Resources
- *Lesson Plans*

Other Print Resources
- *Grammar and Composition Handbook*
- *Grammar Workbook,* Lessons 36–43, Unit 6 Review, Cumulative Review: Units 1–6

gry and knowing that there was no food in the house. So, surreptitiously, I took some of the biscuits from the platter and slipped them into my pocket, not to eat, but to keep as a bulwark against any possible attack of hunger. Even after I had got used to seeing the table loaded with food at each meal, I still stole bread and put it into my pockets. In washing my clothes my mother found the gummy wads and scolded me to break me of the habit; I stopped hiding the bread in my pockets and hid it about the house, in corners, behind dressers. I did not break the habit of stealing and hoarding bread until my faith that food would be forthcoming at each meal had been somewhat established.

Past perfect tense

Past tense of a regular verb

Review: Exercise 1 Identifying Principal Parts of Verbs

The following sentences elaborate on ideas suggested by the passage from *Black Boy.* Each sentence contains an italicized verb in one of four forms: (a) the base form, (b) the past form, (c) the present participle, or (d) the past participle. At the end of the sentence is a second verb in parentheses. First, identify the form of the verb in italics. Then write the verb in parentheses in the same form as the original verb.

SAMPLE The family *dined* at Aunt Maggie's. (eat)
ANSWER past form; ate

1. At home in Mississippi, food had often *seemed* scarce. (be)
2. Young Wright *had* the acute, daily ache of hunger. (feel)
3. His stomach frequently was *churning* with discomfort. (growl)
4. Then Wright and his mother *traveled* to his aunt's home in Arkansas. (come)
5. They are *visiting* Wright's Aunt Maggie and Uncle Hoskins today. (see)
6. The kindly pair *welcome* them into their home. (take)
7. Wright *wondered* at the amount of food in the kitchen. (marvel)
8. Later, Wright was *devouring* an abundant dinner. (eat)
9. He had *consumed* the food until his stomach ached. (eat)
10. Aunt Maggie *carried* a lavish platter of hot biscuits to the table. (bring)
11. Wright had *grown* fearful that the biscuits would disappear before breakfast. (become)
12. He was even *concealing* extra food in his pocket. (hide)
13. His mother had *found* gummy wads of bread in his pocket. (discover)
14. For many days, he *feared* that every full meal might be his last. (think)
15. This fear of hunger *remained* with him for months. (stay)

Verb Tenses and Voice

Practice and Assess

Answers: Exercise 1

1. past participle, been
2. past form, felt
3. present participle, growling
4. past form, came
5. present participle, seeing
6. base form, take
7. past form, marveled
8. present participle, eating
9. past participle, eaten
10. past form, brought
11. past participle, become
12. present participle, hiding
13. past participle, discovered
14. past form, thought
15. past form, stayed

Practice and Assess

Answers: Exercise 2

1. On the train to Elaine, Arkansas, Wright becomes aware of racism and segregation.
2. In those days, African Americans and whites rode in separate sections of the train.
3. The naive youngster wants a peek at the whites' part of the train.
4. His mother said, "Quit talking foolishness!"
5. The travelers will go to Aunt Maggie and Uncle Hoskins's home to live.
6. Uncle Hoskins owns a prosperous business in town.
7. Aunt Maggie had plenty of food on the dinner table.
8. Soon a major calamity breaks Wright's mood of contentment.
9. Some white people in town, envious of Uncle Hoskins's success, murdered him one night.
10. Aunt Maggie, Wright, and Wright's mother will flee to safety in another town.
11. Wright's four years at Jim Hill Public School are his only opportunity for formal study.
12. At first, the principal put him in the fifth grade.
13. After studying day and night, Wright will pass to the sixth grade.
14. Flushed with success, Wright thought about studying medicine.
15. In school he tries to deter questions about his home and his life.
16. At noon he will go to the sandwich shop with some of his classmates.
17. One of the boys senses Wright's dilemma.
18. Later, he will suggest that Wright earn some money by selling newspapers published in Chicago.
19. Slowly, Wright collected customers in the African American neighborhoods.
20. Later, he finds out that the newspapers preach the Ku Klux Klan doctrine.

Review: Exercise 2 **Using the Present, Past, and Future Tenses**

The following sentences are based on passages from *Black Boy* that are not reprinted in this textbook. On your paper, write each italicized verb so that it matches the tense in parentheses. Use only the present, past, and future tenses; with the exception of *will* to express the future tense, do not use any helping verbs.

SAMPLE Wright's mother *will bring* her son to Arkansas. (present tense)
ANSWER brings

1. On the train to Elaine, Arkansas, Wright *will become* aware of racism and segregation. (present tense)
2. In those days, African Americans and whites *ride* in separate sections of the train. (past tense)
3. The naive youngster *wanted* a peek at the whites' part of the train. (present tense)
4. His mother *says,* "Quit talking foolishness!" (past tense)
5. The travelers *went* to Aunt Maggie and Uncle Hoskins's home to live. (future tense)
6. Uncle Hoskins *owned* a prosperous business in town. (present tense)
7. Aunt Maggie *will have* plenty of food on the dinner table. (past tense)
8. Soon a major calamity *will break* Wright's mood of contentment. (present tense)
9. Some white people in town, envious of Uncle Hoskins's success, *murder* him one night. (past tense)
10. Aunt Maggie, Wright, and Wright's mother *flee* to safety in another town. (future tense)
11. Wright's four years at Jim Hill Public School *were* his only opportunity for formal study. (present tense)
12. At first the principal *puts* him in the fifth grade. (past tense)
13. After studying day and night, Wright *passes* to the sixth grade. (future tense)
14. Flushed with success, Wright *thinks* about studying medicine. (past tense)
15. In school he *will try* to deter questions about his home and his life. (present tense)
16. At noon he *went* to the sandwich shop with some of his classmates. (future tense)
17. One of the boys *sensed* Wright's dilemma. (present tense)
18. Later, he *suggests* that Wright earn some money by selling newspapers published in Chicago. (future tense)
19. Slowly, Wright *collects* customers in the African American neighborhoods. (past tense)
20. Later, he *found* out that the newspapers preach the Ku Klux Klan doctrine. (present tense)

Review: Exercise 3 **Using the Perfect Tenses**

Each of the following sentences is based on events in Richard Wright's *Black Boy.* On your paper, write the form of the italicized verb that belongs in the place indicated by the caret. Follow the directions in parentheses, using the past participle of the main verb and the appropriate form of the helping verb *have.*

1. By the time he became a teenager, Wright ∧ in several southern states. (past perfect tense of *live*)
2. Wright ∧ the age of four before he moved from his grandparents' home near Natchez, Mississippi. (past perfect tense of *reach*)
3. When Richard's grandmother ∧ ill for some time, a fire nearly destroyed the Wright home. (past perfect tense of *be*)
4. The fire ∧ through several rooms by the time Wright could flee to safety. (past perfect tense of *tear*)
5. When the adults at last put out the blaze, nearly half the house ∧ down. (past perfect tense of *burn*)
6. Wright ∧ to Arkansas to live with his aunt and uncle. (present perfect tense of *come*)
7. Wright ∧ in Memphis, Tennessee, but he had never lived in Arkansas before. (past perfect form of *live*)
8. For most of her life before she decided to leave Memphis, his mother ∧ against exhaustion and despair. (past perfect tense of *struggle*)
9. Her meager wages ∧ her almost no money for food. (present perfect tense of *leave*)
10. Now that his mother ∧ Wright to his aunt's home, he is finally getting enough to eat. (present perfect tense of *bring*)
11. Because he ∧ constant hunger, at first he eats until his stomach hurts. (present perfect tense of *know*)
12. After he ∧ a meal, he hides bread in his pockets. (present perfect tense of *finish*)
13. His mother often finds gummy wads of bread in the clothes that she ∧ . (present perfect tense of *wash*)
14. She realizes what he ∧ and scolds him. (present perfect tense of *do*)
15. In spite of her criticism, she understands why he ∧ the bread. (present perfect tense of *steal*)
16. During his short life, he already ∧ great hardship. (present perfect tense of *endure*)
17. In a month or so, Wright ∧ the habit. (future perfect tense of *break*)
18. By then he ∧ more confident that food will always be available. (future perfect tense of *become*)
19. Violence tears the family apart when they learn that envious whites ∧ Uncle Hoskins. (present perfect tense of *murder*)
20. By the following morning, mother and son ∧ safety in a nearby town. (future perfect tense of *reach*)

Verb Tenses and Voice

Answers: Exercise 3

1. had lived
2. had reached
3. had been
4. had torn
5. had burned
6. has come
7. had lived
8. had struggled
9. have left
10. has brought
11. has known
12. has finished
13. has washed
14. has done
15. has stolen
16. has endured
17. will have broken
18. will have become
19. have murdered
20. will have reached

Practice and Assess

Answers: Exercise 4

1. did teach
2. are sitting
3. is asking
4. will be sleeping
5. did adjust
6. were threatening
7. was waiting
8. did become
9. will be parading
10. will be fighting

Answers: Exercise 5

1. passive voice; The author recounts the events in *Black Boy* with fury and eloquence.
2. active voice; Slavery was ended in the United States by the Civil War.
3. passive voice; Society did little about the plight of African Americans.
4. passive voice; Richard Wright wrote *Black Boy* as a story of protest.
5. active voice; Generations of Americans have been inspired by his forceful voice.

Grammar Review

Review: Exercise 4 Using the Progressive and Emphatic Forms

Each of the following sentences is based on events in Richard Wright's *Black Boy.* On your paper, write the form of the italicized verb that belongs in the place indicated by the caret. Follow the directions in parentheses, using the present participle of the main verb and the appropriate tense of *be*, or the base form of the main verb and the appropriate form of *do.*

SAMPLE The writer ^ about the meaning of his life. (present progressive form of *think*)
ANSWER is thinking

1. A train trip to Arkansas in 1917 ^ Wright about the realities of the Jim Crow laws that limited the rights of African Americans. (past emphatic form of *teach*)
2. He wonders why whites and African Americans ^ in separate sections of the train. (present progressive form of *sit*)
3. During the train ride to Arkansas, Wright ^ about his grandmother's life as a slave before the Civil War. (present progressive form of *ask*)
4. Tonight young Wright ^ in the home of his Uncle Hoskins. (future progressive form of *sleep*)
5. Although startled at first by all the food served by his aunt, eventually Wright ^ to Hoskins's home. (past emphatic form of *adjust*)
6. Envious men in town ^ Uncle Hoskins's life. (past progressive form of *threaten*)
7. One night, Aunt Maggie ^ for Uncle Hoskins's return when a tall boy knocked on the door. (past progressive form of *wait*)
8. The threat ^ a reality: Uncle Hoskins was murdered. (past emphatic form of *become*)
9. Weeks later, a regiment of African American soldiers ^ with rifles on their shoulders. (future progressive form of *parade*)
10. Soon these troops ^ in World War I. (future progressive form of *fight*)

Review: Exercise 5 Identifying and Using Voice of Verbs

The following sentences are about Richard Wright and *Black Boy.* First, identify each sentence as being in either the *passive voice* or the *active voice.* Then rewrite each sentence, changing the active voice to the passive or the passive voice to the active.

SAMPLE *Black Boy* was written by Richard Wright.
ANSWER passive voice; Richard Wright wrote *Black Boy.*

1. The events in *Black Boy* are recounted by the author with fury and eloquence.
2. The Civil War ended slavery in the United States.
3. Little was done by society about the plight of African Americans.
4. *Black Boy* was written by Richard Wright as a story of protest.
5. Wright's forceful voice has inspired generations of Americans.

Review: Exercise 6 **Making Tenses Compatible**

The following sentences elaborate on events in the passage from *Black Boy.* On your paper, correct the tense of the italicized verb so that the tenses are compatible.

SAMPLE Before Wright came to his aunt's home in Arkansas, he *lived* in Memphis, Tennessee.

ANSWER had lived

1. Aunt Maggie was married to Uncle Hoskins, who *runs* a thriving business near their home in Arkansas.
2. In Memphis Wright *is eating* poorly, but at Aunt Maggie's he ate well.
3. He *sits* shyly at the table when Aunt Maggie brought out the first meal.
4. Aunt Maggie was a fine cook, and she *sets* a variety of savory foods on the table.
5. As Wright *bites* into a biscuit, he recalled his many hungry times.
6. The others had not yet finished their first portion when Wright *takes* a second helping of the food.
7. After his meals, Wright *puts* some extra food into a pocket or hid it in the house.
8. Wright's mother *finds* wads of bread when she washed his clothes.
9. Wright controlled his urge to hoard food only after he *becomes* certain of the source of his next meal.
10. In his years in Memphis, Wright *is failing* to gain weight, but in Arkansas, at Aunt Maggie's table, he never went hungry.
11. Wright is hired by a white family who *will want* someone to milk cows, feed chickens, and serve meals.
12. The woman teaches him how to milk and *had shown* him how to gather eggs.
13. When he came into the house, Wright noticed that the dining table *will have been set* for five people.
14. He was appalled that the family habitually *had cursed* each other.
15. When the time came for him to return to school, he *will be* physically tired and emotionally spent.
16. He *clings* to the job, however, because the family never measured how much food he ate.
17. Back home, when he described his meals, his family *feels* envious.
18. In class Wright *will fall* behind with his academic work because he had drifted off to sleep so many times.
19. To keep himself awake and alert, he goes to the water fountain and *ran* cold water over his wrists.
20. Now that he is earning money, he *has bought* sandwiches for lunch.

Verb Tenses and Voice

Answers: Exercise 6

Answers may vary, but some suggestions are given below.

1. ran
2. had eaten
3. was sitting
4. set
5. bit
6. took
7. put
8. found
9. had become
10. had failed
11. wants
12. shows
13. had been set
14. cursed
15. was
16. clung
17. felt
18. fell
19. runs
20. buys

Practice and Assess

Answers: Exercise 7

Paragraphs will vary, but each sentence should contain two verbs that are compatible in tense. The verbs' tenses should be labeled correctly.

Answers: Exercise 8 Proofreading

This proofreading activity provides editing practice with (1) the current or previous units' skills, (2) the **Troubleshooter** errors, and (3) spelling errors. Students should be able to complete the exercise by referring to the units, the **Troubleshooter,** and a dictionary.

Error (Type of Error)

1. Renaissance, (nonessential appositive phrase)
   was born (verb tense)
2. found (verb form)
3. talent, (nonessential participial phrase)
   encouraged (unnecessary shift in tense)
4. Harlem, (nonessential appositive phrase)
5. was accepted (passive voice)
6. went (verb form)
7. spent (verb tense)
8. studied (spelling)
   became (verb form)
9. van Gogh, (nonessential appositive phrase)
10. described (verb tense)
11. came (verb form)
12. deliberately (spelling)
13. workers, (commas in a series)
14. show (subject-verb agreement)

Review: Exercise 7 Using Verb Tenses in Writing

Choose a story you have read recently or seen at the movies or on television. Write ten sentences about the story and the characters. In each sentence, use at least two verbs that are compatible in tense. Write the verbs and label the tenses. Use all six verb tenses in your sentences: present, past, future, present perfect, past perfect, and future perfect.

SAMPLE ANSWER I recently read a story that I had wanted to read for some time. read–past tense; had wanted–past perfect tense

Review: Exercise 8

Proofreading

The following passage describes the artist William H. Johnson, whose painting appears on the opposite page. Rewrite the passage, correcting the errors in spelling, grammar, and usage. Add any missing punctuation. There are twenty-five errors.

William H. Johnson

[1]William H. Johnson (1901–1970), one of the most innovative artists of the Harlem Renaissance is born in Florence, South Carolina. [2]One day, one of his elementary school teachers founded on Johnson's desk a piece of paper with a remarkable likeness of herself. [3]His teachers and his family, recognizing his talent encourage Johnson to develop his skill as a painter.

[4]When he was seventeen, Johnson moved to Harlem a neighborhood in New York City. [5]Three years later, he accepted into the prestigious National Academy of Design, where he won several awards. [6]He gone to Paris in 1926. [7]He was spending twelve years altogether in Europe, nine of them in Scandinavia. [8]There he studyed art and met the Danish woman who become his wife. [9]His painting was influenced by the highly expressive works of Vincent van Gogh the famous Dutch Postimpressionist.

[10]Johnson once describes himself as primitive and cultured at the same time. [11]When he come back to the United States, he had refined his hybrid style. [12]Using vivid colors and a delibreatly primitive technique, he painted scenes of contemporary African American life. [13]Poor farm workers city dwellers, soldiers, convicts, musicians, and preachers appear often in his work. [14]The heightened colors and the strong emotional tone of his paintings shows the influence of the European school of painting known as Expressionism.

William H. Johnson, *Jim,* 1930

[15]Soon after World War II ended, Johnson hospitalized for a nervous disorder. [16]Tragically, his last years was spent in mental institutions. [17]His works has continued to be exhibited and praised despite his career's premature end.

[18]*Jim,* a relatively early portrait is painted in a style that Johnson later abandoned. [19]The vivid colors and loose brush strokes is reminiscent of Expressionist techniques. [20]It is not hard to imagine the young Richard Wright as the boy in Johnsons painting. [21]The gaze in Jim's eyes suggest an inner turmoil that seems akin to the physical and spiritual hunger that Wright feeled as a boy.

Answers: Exercise 8 *(continued)*

Error (Type of Error)

15. was hospitalized (passive voice)
16. were (subject-verb agreement)
17. have (subject-verb agreement)
18. portrait, (nonessential appositive phrase)
19. are (subject-verb agreement)
20. Johnson's (singular possessive)
21. suggests (subject-verb agreement)
felt (verb form)

Viewing the Art

William H. Johnson, *Jim,* 1930

In *Jim,* William Johnson has created a study in contrasts—between the fiery reds and the somber blacks and umbers, and between the static figure and the subtle emotions that animate the young man's expression. The artist seems to have executed the painting confidently; the brush strokes are bold and vigorous. In the passage from *Black Boy*, Richard Wright paints a memorable picture of himself. Ask students to write a description of the young Richard Wright. Then ask them to discuss how their descriptions might apply to the young man in Johnson's painting.

Practice and Assess

Answers: Exercise 9

Mixed Review

1. Richard Wright was born in a rural region of Mississippi, where his grandparents had been enslaved before the Civil War.
2. Wright was living in Memphis when his father abandoned the family to a life of poverty.
3. After he had spent time with relatives in Arkansas and Mississippi, Wright returned to Memphis.
4. In Memphis Wright was working as a postal clerk when he decided to become a writer.
5. He read several books that stimulated his interest in becoming a writer.
6. One of those books was written by the American author H. L. Mencken.
7. The Federal Writers' Project, a government assistance program, gave financial aid to the budding author.
8. Before he moved to New York City in 1937, Wright had lived for a time in Chicago.
9. Wright first won attention with *Uncle Tom's Children*, a collection of short works of fiction that appeared in 1938.
10. His popular novel *Native Son* was published two years later.
11. The noted director Orson Welles adapted *Native Son* for the Broadway stage.
12. Eventually, Hollywood did turn *Native Son* into a film drama.
13. When an Argentine film version of *Native Son* appeared in 1951, Wright himself played the main character, Bigger Thomas.
14. An American studio has recently released a film adaptation of *Native Son*.
15. In fact, the video store in my neighborhood does stock the 1986 version of *Native Son*.

Review: Exercise 9

Mixed Review

The following sentences describe the life and literary achievements of the author Richard Wright. Rewrite each sentence, following the directions in parentheses.

SAMPLE Richard Wright portrayed his childhood and also writes about urban life. (Change the second verb to make the tenses compatible.)

ANSWER Richard Wright portrayed his childhood and also wrote about urban life.

Richard Wright

1. Richard Wright was born in a rural region of Mississippi, where his grandparents were enslaved before the Civil War. (Change the second verb to the past perfect tense.)
2. Wright lived in Memphis when his father abandoned the family to a life of poverty. (Change the first verb to the past progressive form.)
3. After he had spent time with relatives in Arkansas and Mississippi, Wright had returned to Memphis. (Change the second verb to the past tense.)
4. In Memphis Wright worked as a postal clerk when he decided to become a writer. (Change the first verb to the past progressive form.)
5. He reads several books that stimulated his interest in becoming a writer. (Change the first verb to make the tenses compatible.)
6. The American author H. L. Mencken wrote one of those books. (Rewrite the sentence in the passive voice.)
7. Financial aid was given to the budding author by the Federal Writers' Project, a government assistance program. (Rewrite the sentence in the active voice.)
8. Before he moved to New York City in 1937, Wright lived for a time in Chicago. (Change the second verb to the past perfect tense.)
9. Wright first wins attention with *Uncle Tom's Children,* a collection of short works of fiction that appeared in 1938. (Correct the error caused by the use of the present tense.)
10. Two years later he published his popular novel *Native Son.* (Rewrite the sentence in the passive voice.)
11. *Native Son* was adapted for the Broadway stage by the noted director Orson Welles. (Rewrite the sentence in the active voice.)
12. Eventually, Hollywood turned *Native Son* into a film drama. (Change the verb to the past emphatic form.)
13. When an Argentine film version of *Native Son* appeared in 1951, Wright himself plays the main character, Bigger Thomas. (Correct the error caused by the use of the present tense.)
14. An American studio recently released a film adaptation of *Native Son.* (Change the verb to the present perfect tense.)
15. In fact, the video store in my neighborhood stocks the 1986 version of *Native Son.* (Change the verb to the present emphatic form.)

Writing Application

Verbs in Writing

In this passage from her autobiography *I Know Why the Caged Bird Sings,* Maya Angelou describes the relationship between her grandmother and the aristocratic Mrs. Flowers. As you read, concentrate on Angelou's use of verbs, especially the italicized ones.

Mrs. Flowers didn't belong to our church, nor *was* she Momma's familiar. Why on earth *did* she *insist* on calling her Sister Flowers? Shame made me want to hide my face. Mrs. Flowers deserved better than to be called Sister. Then, Momma left out the verb. Why not ask "How *are* you, Mrs. Flowers?" With the unbalanced passion of the young, I hated her for showing her ignorance to Mrs. Flowers. It didn't occur to me for many years that they were as alike as sisters, separated only by formal education.

Techniques with Verbs

When you write and revise your own work, try to use verbs as Angelou does.

1. Do not shift tenses when referring to events in the same time frame.

INCORRECT VERSION Mrs. Flowers doesn't belong to our church, nor was she Momma's familiar.

ANGELOU'S CORRECT VERSION Mrs. Flowers didn't belong to our church, nor was she Momma's familiar.

2. Use the emphatic form and the active voice to make a point.

UNEMPHATIC PASSIVE VERSION Why was Mrs. Flowers called Sister Flowers by her?

ANGELOU'S VERSION Why on earth did she insist on calling her Sister Flowers?

TIME

For more about the writing process, see **TIME Facing the Blank Page**, pp. 121-131.

Verb Tenses and Voice

Practice Revise the following passage on a separate sheet of paper. Keep verb tenses consistent and use active voice as much as possible.

Maya Angelou has enriched American culture with the many books and poems she had written. Perhaps best known for her multivolume autobiography, she also will have been remembered for the poem she wrote to commemorate the inauguration of President William Jefferson Clinton. She completed the poem several days before Clinton was inaugurated.

Interestingly, an experience was shared by President Clinton and this gifted African American writer: They both spent their childhood in Arkansas and were cared for by grandmothers whom they will remember with great affection.

LOG ON **Writing** Online — For more grammar practice, go to glencoe.com and enter Quickpass code WC97727p2

Verbs in Writing

You may have students silently read the passage from *I Know Why the Caged Bird Sings.* Read it without interruption and then go back and discuss the italicized verb choices in relation to the Techniques with Verbs.

Techniques with Verbs

Discuss how to use the techniques described. Then have students see how these techniques are used in the Proofreading exercise on page 604.

Practice

The answers to this challenging activity will vary. Refer to Techniques with Verbs as you evaluate student choices. Sample answer:

Maya Angelou enriches American culture with the many books and poems she writes. Although people know her best for her multivolume autobiography, they also remember her for the poem she wrote to commemorate the inauguration of President William Jefferson Clinton. She completed the poem several days before Clinton's inauguration.

Interestingly, President Clinton and this gifted African American writer share an experience: They both spent their childhood in Arkansas, where their grandmothers cared for them, and they both remember these women with great affection.

Close

Encourage students to work together to write a paragraph about how they could incorporate what they have learned about verbs into their writing for other classes.

✔ ASSESSMENT OPTIONS

Tests with Answer Key & Rubrics
Unit 15 Mastery Test, pp. 57–58

Testmaker
Unit 15 Mastery Test

You may wish to administer the Unit 15 Mastery Test at this point.

MindJogger Videoquizzes

INTRODUCING

UNIT 16

Objectives

- To develop an understanding of subject-verb agreement and how it is achieved in the presence of intervening phrases, linking verbs, compound elements, and other special situations
- To demonstrate control over subject-verb agreement by checking and editing exercises and by writing sentences in which subjects and verbs are used correctly in agreement with each other

✔ ASSESSMENT OPTIONS

Tests with Answer Key & Rubrics
Unit 16 Pretest, pp. 59–60
Unit 16 Mastery Test, pp. 61–62

Testmaker
Unit 16 Pretest
Unit 16 Mastery Test

You may wish to administer the Unit 16 Pretest at this point.

Key to Ability Levels

L1 Level 1 activities are within the basic ability range of students.

L2 Level 2 activities are within the ability range of average students.

L3 Level 3 activities are more challenging activities.

UNIT 16 Subject-Verb Agreement

Resource Manager

Planning Resources
- *Lesson Plans*
- *Block Scheduling*

Transparencies
- *Bellringer*
- *Daily Language Practice*

Other Print Resources
- *Grammar and Composition Handbook*
- *Grammar Enrichment*
- *Grammar Practice*
- *Grammar Reteaching*
- *Grammar Workbook*
- *Sentence-Combining Practice*
- *Tests with Answer Key and Rubrics*

Video
- *MindJogger Videoquizzes*

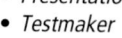

Software
- *Interactive Grammar and Language Workbook*
- *Presentation Plus!*
- *Testmaker*

Web Site
- *glencoe.com*

16.1 Intervening Prepositional Phrases

■ A verb must agree with its subject in number and person.

Number can be singular or plural. Singular words indicate one; plural words indicate more than one. A singular subject takes a singular verb. A plural subject takes a plural verb.

With most verbs, the only change in form to indicate agreement in person occurs in the present tense. An *-s* (or *-es*) is added to the base form of the verb when its subject is third-person singular.

SINGULAR	PLURAL
She **speaks.**	They **speak.**
He **exercises.**	They **exercise.**
She **pitches.**	They **pitch.**

The linking verb *be* changes in both the present and the past tense.

SINGULAR	PLURAL
He **is** there.	They **are** there.
It **was** sweet.	They **were** sweet.

In verb phrases, the auxiliary verbs *be, have,* and *do* change in form to show agreement with third-person subjects.

SINGULAR	PLURAL
He **is going.**	They **are going.**
She **is reading.**	They **are reading.**
She **has seen** a movie.	They **have seen** a movie.
Does he **stay** here?	**Do** they **stay** here?

■ Do not mistake a word in a prepositional phrase for the subject of a sentence.

The simple subject is never within a prepositional phrase. Make sure the verb agrees with the actual subject and not with the object of a preposition.

The ***taste*** of the cherries **surprises** us. [The subject, *taste*, is singular; *of the cherries* is a prepositional phrase; therefore, the verb, *surprises*, is singular.]

ALONG THE ROAD
The signs signal us to yield.

Focus

Lesson Overview

Objective

- To identify prepositional phrases that come between the subject and the predicate

Bellringer
Daily Language Activity

When students enter the classroom, have this assignment on the board:
In the following passage, identify the subject and the verb. Then write the prepositional phrase that intervenes between them.

> The lights of the yacht . . . were blotted out entirely by the night.
>
> —From "The Most Dangerous Game" by Richard Connell

Ask students to explain their answers. Encourage students to ask questions to clarify their understanding.

See also *Daily Language Practice*

Teach

Subject-Verb Agreement

☑ Teaching Tip

Explain that errors in subject-verb agreement occur when a writer makes the verb agree with an object of a prepositional phrase that modifies the simple subject. Point out that a way to help eliminate this kind of error is to delete the prepositional phrase so that the actual subject is placed next to the verb.

Resource Manager

Planning Resources
- *Lesson Plans*

Transparencies
- *Bellringer*
- *Daily Language Practice*

Other Print Resources
- *Grammar and Composition Handbook*
- *Grammar Reteaching,* p. 28
- *Grammar Workbook,* Lesson 45
- *Sentence-Combining Practice,* p. 16

Practice and Assess

Answers: Exercise 1

1. is
2. wants
3. tells
4. are
5. waits

Answers: Exercise 2

1. subject: years; have
2. subject: graduate; was
3. subject: Jordan; has
4. subject: speaker; is
5. subject: Politicians; were
6. subject: abilities; were
7. subject: women; need
8. subject: reputation; was
9. subject: Jordan; was
10. subject: place; seems

Additional Resources

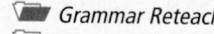

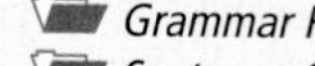 *Grammar Reteaching,* p. 28

 *Sentence-Combining Practice,* p. 16

Grammar Workbook, Lesson 45

Close

To provide extended practice in subject-verb agreement, have each student write a declarative sentence on a piece of paper. Then have them exchange papers and rewrite the sentence they've been given as an interrogative sentence. Next, ask students to rewrite their sentence pairs so that singular subjects and verbs change to the plural form and plural subjects and verbs change to the singular form. Ask partners to check each other's work and to provide effective feedback. Have students make corrections as needed.

Exercise 1 Making Subjects and Verbs Agree

Write on your paper the form of the verb indicated in parentheses that agrees with the subject of each sentence.

A Class Field Trip

1. Don (is/are) looking forward to the field trip.
2. Carol (wants/want) to take the bus.
3. The teacher (tells/tell) the class about the park.
4. They (is/are) going to the zoo after lunch.
5. The bus driver (waits/wait) for the students to return.

Exercise 2 Making Subjects and Verbs Agree When Prepositional Phrases Intervene

Find the simple subject in each of the following sentences. Then write on your paper the form of the verb indicated in parentheses that agrees with the subject of each sentence.

Barbara Jordan: A Prominent Texan

1. Barbara Jordan's years in the U.S. Congress (has/have) given her a unique perspective on American politics.
2. Over thirty years ago, this distinguished graduate of two universities (was/were) first attracted to politics.
3. Jordan, despite many setbacks and difficulties, (has/have) achieved many of her goals.
4. A public speaker with Jordan's exceptional talents (is/are) rare.
5. Politicians from many states (was/were) impressed with Barbara Jordan's address at the 1976 Democratic National Convention.
6. Perhaps Jordan's extraordinary abilities in public speaking (was/were) encouraged by her father, a Baptist minister.
7. African American women, in Jordan's opinion, (needs/need) to make their voices heard in government.
8. Jordan's reputation in political circles (was/were) enhanced by her strong role in the congressional hearings about the impeachment of President Richard Nixon.
9. Jordan, in spite of her popularity among Texas voters, (was/were) prepared to leave politics by 1978 for a teaching career.
10. Barbara Jordan's place in history books clearly (seems/seem) secure.

MEETING INDIVIDUAL NEEDS

English Language Learners

Using Subject-Verb Agreement

Students learning English may have difficulty with subject-verb agreement. Review the first rule and examples on page 609. For practice, write the infinitive form of several common verbs on pieces of paper; have students pick a paper and use that verb in a sentence. First help students with present tense, then have them compose sentences using the auxiliary verbs *be, have,* and *do.* Have students vary the number and person of the subject. Sample infinitives are *to go, to sing, to walk.*

16.2 Agreement with Linking Verbs

■ Do not be confused by a predicate nominative that is different in number from the subject. Only the subject affects the number of the linking verb.

The lightest ***crate* is** two tons. [The singular verb, *is*, agrees with the singular subject, *crate*, not with the predicate nominative, *tons*.]

Recent ***studies*** on the behavior of wild animals **are** his topic for the day. [The plural verb, *are*, agrees with the plural subject, *studies*, not with the predicate nominative, *topic*.]

Exercise 3 Making Linking Verbs Agree with Their Subjects

Find the simple subject or subjects in each of the following sentences. Then write on your paper the form of the verb in parentheses that agrees with the subject of each sentence.

Our Endangered Forests and Wildlife

1. The growing threat to America's wild animals (is/are) a national problem.
2. Another problem (is/are) the many acres of forest land we lose each year.
3. Wildlife (remains/remain) a rich and vital part of our national heritage.
4. Animals (is/are) also an important part of our world.
5. Research on plant and animal life (is/are) the means of much scientific discovery.
6. Our forests (is/are) also a wonderful resource for recreation.
7. Once our forest land (was/were) millions of acres more extensive.
8. Growing cities (is/are) part of the problem.
9. By the 1990s, one result of deforestation (was/were) high numbers of endangered species.
10. Adequate food (is/are) a necessity for animals.
11. The cost of deforestation (is/are) years of floods and damaging soil erosion.
12. Harmful effects on the wild animals that depend on the forest (is/are) a result of deforestation.
13. The long-term effects of excessive hunting and fishing (is/are) another problem.
14. State governments (is/are) important agencies in protecting our endangered forests.
15. The destructive results (is/are) a disturbance in the balance of nature.
16. Our land (is/are) our home, our heritage, and our gift to the future.
17. Protected lands (seem/seems) the only hope for wildlife.
18. Our forests (remains/remain) an important part of their survival.
19. Efforts by government and private citizens (seems/seem) the solution.
20. We (is/are) all part of the solution.

Subject-Verb Agreement

Resource Manager

Planning Resources
- *Lesson Plans*

Transparencies
- *Bellringer*
- *Daily Language Practice*

Other Print Resources
- *Grammar and Composition Handbook*
- *Grammar Enrichment,* p. 28
- *Grammar Practice,* p. 28
- *Grammar Workbook,* Lesson 46

Focus

Lesson Overview

Objectives

- To identify the subject and the predicate nominative
- To ensure that the verb agrees with the subject, not with the predicate nominative

Bellringer
Daily Language Activity

When students enter the classroom, have this assignment on the board: *Rewrite this sentence, using the correct verb from the parentheses. Explain your verb choice. Spotted owls (is, are) the focus of her research. Encourage students to ask questions to clarify their understanding.*

See also *Daily Language Practice*

Teach

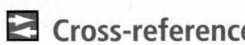

Cross-reference

For more information on predicate nominatives, refer students to Lesson 11.5, pp. 504–509.

Practice and Assess

Answers: Exercise 3

Answers are in subject/verb order.

1. threat, is
2. problem, is
3. Wildlife, remains
4. Animals, are
5. Research, is
6. forests, are
7. land, was
8. cities, are
9. result, was
10. food, is
11. cost, is
12. effects, are
13. effects, are
14. governments, are
15. results, are
16. land, is
17. lands, seem
18. forests, remain
19. Efforts, seem
20. We, are

Focus

Lesson Overview

Objective

- To identify the subject in inverted sentences

Bellringer

Daily Language Activity

When students enter the classroom, have this assignment on the board: *Write the verb you would use in each sentence:*

There (is, are) some people here to see you.

By the house (is, are) two old trees.

Have students explain their answers. Remind students to provide effective feedback and to ask questions for clarification as needed.

See also *Daily Language Practice*

Teach

Teaching Tip

Ask for a show of hands to see how many students chose *is* vs. *are* in the Bellringer activity sentences. Explain to students that in informal situations some speakers use a singular verb form when a sentence begins with *there* and is followed by a linking verb (usually *be*). For these speakers, a sentence like the following one sounds natural: *There's some people here to see you.* A useful first step for finding the subject of this type of sentence is to rephrase the sentence: put the subject back in the initial position and eliminate *there.* For example: *There's some people here to see you* becomes *Some people are here to see you.*

16.3 Agreement in Inverted Sentences

■ In an **inverted sentence**—a sentence in which the subject follows the verb—take care in locating the simple subject and make sure that the verb agrees with the subject.

Inverted sentences often begin with prepositional phrases. Do not mistake the object of the preposition for the subject.

SINGULAR In the jungle **roars** (V) the ***lion.*** (S)

PLURAL In the jungle **roar** (V) the ***lions.*** (S)

SINGULAR In a large cage at the zoo **rests** (V) a noble ***lion.*** (S)

PLURAL In a large cage at the zoo **rest** (V) two noble ***lions.*** (S)

In inverted sentences beginning with *there* or *here,* look for the subject after the verb. The word *there* or *here* is almost never the subject of a sentence.

SINGULAR There **is** (V) a ***lion*** (S) in the jungle.

Here **goes** (V) the ***ambulance.*** (S)

PLURAL There **are** (V) ***lions*** (S) in the jungle.

Here **go** (V) the two ***ambulances.*** (S)

In questions, an auxiliary verb may come before the subject. Look for the subject between the auxiliary verb and the main verb.

SINGULAR **Does** (V) that ***lion*** (S) **live** (V) in the jungle?

PLURAL **Do** (V) those ***jungles*** (S) **contain** (V) lions?

Resource Manager

Planning Resources
- *Lesson Plans*

Transparencies
- *Bellringer*
- *Daily Language Practice*

Other Print Resources
- *Grammar and Composition Handbook*
- *Grammar Enrichment,* p. 28
- *Grammar Workbook,* Lesson 47

Exercise 4 **Making Subjects and Verbs Agree in Inverted Sentences**

Find the simple subject in each of the following sentences. Then write on your paper the form of the verb in parentheses that agrees with the subject of each sentence.

Dining Out

1. There (is/are) three excellent and unusual restaurants in my neighborhood.
2. In the window of one of the restaurants (hangs/hang) an interesting menu.
3. Over the door of another (swings/swing) an old and elaborate sign.
4. Outside the third (stands/stand) two statues representing servers.
5. (Does/Do) the restaurant owners ever cook and bake?
6. (Is/Are) expert chefs brought in to create mouth-watering specialties to please the demanding clientele?
7. There (is/are) a pleasant decor in all three of these restaurants.
8. Into the restaurants (crowds/crowd) the hungry customers.
9. Here (comes/come) the people who want to eat before they go to the theater.
10. There (gathers/gather) the people waiting to be seated.
11. On one menu (is/are) a picture of an unusual animal.
12. On the sign there (is/are) three pictures of the food served.
13. In the lap of one statue in a corner of the restaurant (rests/rest) a knife.
14. How (does/do) the owner find all the foods for the menus?
15. There (is/are) special menus for children in each restaurant.
16. On each table (is/are) a vase of flowers.
17. On a table in the center of the restaurant (is/are) dishes from other countries.
18. There (is/are) a line of three young men outside the door.
19. (Does/Do) the three men have reservations?
20. Here (comes/come) the third delivery of food for today.

Exercise 5 **Writing Inverted Sentences**

On your paper, write the following sentences as inverted sentences. Make sure each verb agrees with its subject.

Team Trophies

1. The prize trophy rests in the office.
2. The members of the team are sitting in the hall.
3. Ten other trophies won by other teams are also in the case.
4. The principal hopes to keep the trophies in the new case. (Write as a question.)
5. The trophy for the basketball tournament is here.

Cross-reference: Grammar

For instruction and practice in the order of subject and predicate, refer students to Lesson 11.4, pp. 501–503.

Subject-Verb Agreement

Practice and Assess

Answers: Exercise 4

1. are **2.** hangs **3.** swings **4.** stand **5.** Do **6.** Are **7.** is **8.** crowd **9.** come **10.** gather **11.** is **12.** are **13.** rests **14.** does **15.** are **16.** is **17.** are **18.** is **19.** Do **20.** comes

Answers: Exercise 5

Answers will vary, but some suggestions are given below.

1. In the office rests the prize trophy.
2. Sitting in the hall are the members of the team.
3. Also in the case are ten other trophies won by other teams.
4. Does the principal hope to keep the trophies in the new case?
5. Here is the trophy for the basketball tournament.

Additional Resources

Grammar Enrichment, p. 28

Grammar Workbook, Lesson 47

Close

Remind the class that keeping the interest of the reader is an important factor in writing. Have students discuss how varying sentence structure can help them avoid writing monotonous and boring prose. Then ask students to summarize their thoughts in their journal.

MEETING INDIVIDUAL NEEDS

English Language Learners

Identifying the Subject

Students who are acquiring English may have difficulty determining the subject and its number in *There is* and *There are* sentences. Write on one poster board *There is* in large letters and write *There are* on another. Mount the poster boards on a bulletin board in the classroom. Have students cut out pictures from magazines and paste them on one of the poster boards. Then have students write captions for the pictures. They can write the words they would use to complete a *There is* or a *There are* sentence about something shown in these pictures.

Focus

Lesson Overview

Objectives

- To identify the number of special subjects
- To ensure that verbs agree with special subjects

Teach

Collective and Special Nouns

☑ Teaching Tip

Students sometimes extend the concept of collective nouns to include nouns that are normally considered plural. For example, the student who writes *The life forms in the tropical rain forest is the richest on earth* is probably thinking—incorrectly—of *life forms in the tropical rain forest* as a total collective entity, like *family*.

Cross-reference: Grammar

For instruction and practice in collective nouns, refer students to Lesson 10.1, pp. 439–445.

Practice and Assess

Answers: Exercise 6

Answers will vary. All nouns in Exercise 6 except *analysis* and *mathematics* can be either singular or plural. In reviewing students' work, first ask them to read their sentences aloud. Then have them reread their sentences, substituting a pronoun for the noun subject to justify their use of a singular or a plural verb.

16.4 Agreement with Special Subjects

Collective Nouns

■ A **collective noun** names a group. Consider a collective noun singular when it refers to a group as a whole. Consider a collective noun plural when it refers to each member of a group individually.

SINGULAR His ***family*** **arrives.**
PLURAL His ***family*** **are** well.

SINGULAR The ***committee*** **decides.**
PLURAL The ***committee*** **sign** their names.

Special Nouns

■ Certain nouns that end in *-s*, such as *mumps, measles*, and *mathematics*, take singular verbs.

SINGULAR ***Mumps*** **is** a disease.

■ Certain other nouns that end in *-s*, such as *scissors, pants, binoculars*, and *eyeglasses*, take plural verbs.

PLURAL The ***scissors*** **were** sharp.
Your ***eyeglasses*** **need** cleaning.

■ Many nouns that end in *-ics* may be singular or plural, depending upon their meaning.

SINGULAR ***Statistics*** **is** an interesting subject. [one subject of interest]

PLURAL ***Statistics*** **show** that women live longer than men. [more than one application of this particular field of study]

Exercise 6 Using Special Subjects in Sentences

Write 10 sentences. In each sentence, use one of the following nouns as the subject. Make sure each subject agrees with a present-tense verb.

SAMPLE measles
ANSWER Measles is a common childhood disease.

1. club
2. politics
3. family
4. fleet
5. audience
6. stairs
7. mathematics
8. news
9. analysis
10. group

Resource Manager

Planning Resources

- *Lesson Plans*

Other Print Resources

- *Grammar and Composition Handbook*
- *Grammar Enrichment*, p. 29
- *Grammar Practice*, p. 29
- *Grammar Workbook*, Lessons 1 and 48

Nouns of Amount

■ When a noun of amount refers to a total that is considered as one unit, the noun is singular. When it refers to a number of individual units, the noun is plural.

SINGULAR	Three ***dollars* is** not too much for that book. [one amount]
PLURAL	Three ***dollars* are** on the table. [three individual bills]
SINGULAR	Ten ***years* is** a decade. [one unit of time]
PLURAL	Ten ***years* have passed.** [ten individual periods of time]

Five players is a team.

Five players are on the court.

Titles

■ A title is always singular, even if a noun within the title is plural.

SINGULAR	***Great Expectations* is** one of the best-loved novels in English literature.

Exercise 7 **Making Verbs Agree with Special Subjects**

Find the subject in each sentence. Then write on your paper the form of the verb in parentheses that agrees with the subject.

Roberto Clemente, a Baseball Hero

1. The first baseball team to hire Roberto Clemente (was/were) the Santurce Cangrejeros of Puerto Rico.
2. When Clemente joined the Pittsburgh Pirates in 1954, fifty thousand dollars (was/were) considered a princely salary.
3. Clemente's family (was/were) eager to show its pride in him.
4. Roberto Clemente's impressive offensive and defensive statistics (shows/show) that he was a versatile player.
5. Professional athletics (is/are) a demanding field.
6. Clemente's eighteen years in major-league baseball (is/are) considered a long career.
7. Five hours (is/are) a long time for a professional baseball game to last.
8. On December 31, 1972, his team (was/were) all very much shocked to hear that Clemente had died in a plane crash while taking supplies to earthquake victims in Nicaragua.
9. Sometimes a professional athlete's second family (is/are) his or her teammates.
10. Our class agrees that *The Great One* (is/are) an appropriate title for a biography of Roberto Clemente.

Teach

Nouns of Amount

☑ Teaching Tip

Point out to students that nouns of amount are surprisingly common. Read these examples to the class: *Three strikes means you're out. Four weeks is the time I have for vacation. Twelve people are on the jury.*

Cross-reference: Mechanics

For instruction and practice with numbers used in the beginning of a sentence, refer students to Lesson 21.14, pp. 768–771.

Practice and Assess

Answers: Exercise 7

1. subject: team; was
2. subject: dollars; was
3. subject: family; was
4. subject: statistics; show
5. subject: athletics; is
6. subject: years; is
7. subject: hours; is
8. subject: team; were
9. subject: family; is
10. subject: *The Great One;* is

Additional Resources

Grammar Practice, p. 29

Grammar Enrichment, p. 29

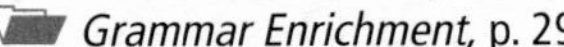

Grammar Workbook, Lessons 1 and 48

Close

Tell students to note any collective or special nouns they see or hear. Encourage them to write out these words and post them on the class bulletin board.

MEETING INDIVIDUAL NEEDS

English Language Learners

Using Collective Nouns

Students who are learning English may have difficulty determining whether to use singular or plural verbs with collective nouns. Provide these students with additional practice by having them work in pairs—a student who is learning English paired with a student fluent in English—to compose two sentences that use one of the following nouns as a singular and as a plural subject.

cast (of a play)	herd
choir	audience
flock	class
group	majority

Focus

Lesson Overview

Objective

- To identify the number (singular or plural) of compound subjects

Bellringer
Daily Language Activity

When students enter the classroom, have the following assignment on the board: *Which of these sentences is incorrect?*

1. *The drama club and the debate team is going on a trip to New York.*
2. *Graham crackers and milk is my favorite snack.*

See also *Daily Language Practice*

Motivating Activity

When discussing answers, make certain students see that graham crackers and milk acts as one unit.

Teach

Compound Subjects Joined by *And*

Cross-reference: Grammar

For instruction and practice of compound subjects, refer students to Lesson 11.3, pp. 498–500.

Practice and Assess

Answers: Exercise 8

1. sing. subj.
2. sing. subj.
3. plural subj.
4. sing. subj.
5. sing. subj.

Subject-Verb Agreement

16.5 Agreement with Compound Subjects

Compound Subjects Joined by *And*

■ A compound subject that is joined by *and* or *both . . . and* is plural unless its parts belong to one unit or the parts both refer to the same person or thing.

PLURAL — The ***lion*** *and* the ***tiger*** **are roaring.**

Both ***skiing*** *and* ***skating*** **are** fun.

SINGULAR — ***Peanut butter*** *and* ***jelly*** **is** a favorite combination. [Compound subject is one unit.]

His ***friend*** *and* ***companion*** **accompanies** him. [One person is both friend and companion.]

Compound Subjects Joined by *Or* or *Nor*

■ With compound subjects joined by *or* or *nor* (or by *either . . . or* or *neither . . . nor*), the verb always agrees with the subject nearer the verb.

PLURAL — *Neither* the ***lion*** *nor* the ***tigers*** **are roaring.**

SINGULAR — *Either* the ***lion*** *or* the ***tiger*** **is roaring.**

Neither the ***lions*** *nor* the ***tiger*** **roars.**

Exercise 8 — **Writing Sentences with Compound Subjects**

Write five sentences. In each sentence, use one of the following items as the compound subject. Make the compound subject agree with a present-tense verb.

1. bread and butter
2. neither the players nor the coach
3. both the climate and the geography of the South
4. Aunt Susan or Uncle Harold
5. either a cat or a dog

Resource Manager

Planning Resources
- *Lesson Plans*

Transparencies
- *Bellringer*
- *Daily Language Practice*

Other Print Resources
- *Grammar and Composition Handbook*
- *Grammar Enrichment,* p. 29
- *Grammar Practice,* p. 29
- *Grammar Workbook,* Lesson 49

Many a, Every, and *Each* with Compound Subjects

- When *many a, every,* or *each* precedes a compound subject, the subject is considered singular.

SINGULAR *Many a* ***giraffe*** and ***elephant*** **lives** in the nature preserve.

Every ***chair, bench,*** and ***table*** **was taken.**

Each ***lion*** and ***tiger*** **is roaring.**

Exercise 9 **Making Verbs Agree with Their Subjects**

On your paper, write the appropriate form of each verb in parentheses.

Leontyne Price, Opera Star

1. The opera expert and the casual listener (agrees/agree) that Leontyne Price is one of the greatest living sopranos.
2. Many people in Price's life (was/were) influential in her decision to pursue a career in music.
3. When Price undertook four demanding years of formal training in New York, neither her talents nor her ambition (was/were) lacking.
4. Before Price became a star, producers Robert Breen and Blevins Davis (was/were) impressed by Price's singing.
5. Price's longtime friend and adviser, vocal coach Florence Page Kimball, probably (feels/feel) that Price's finest role was that of Bess in Gershwin's *Porgy and Bess.*
6. Neither Price's performance in *The Magic Flute* nor her triumphs in Verdi's operas (has/have) given me as much pleasure as her singing in *Madame Butterfly.*
7. Fortunately, neither serious illnesses nor stage fright (has/have) interrupted Price's long career.
8. To be a successful singer like Price, talent and perseverance (is/are) required.
9. Every note, gesture, and facial expression (is/are) crucial to the success of a performance.
10. Many a performer and audience member (feels/feel) excited when the lights in a theater dim.

Subject-Verb Agreement

Teach

Compound Subjects Joined by *Or* or *Nor*

Teaching Tip

To help students quickly see if the verb in an *either . . . or, neither . . . nor* sentence is singular or plural, tell them to drop the *either . . . or* phrase. For example: *Neither Meg nor her parents are going to the concert.* Drop *Neither Meg nor.* When the sentence becomes *Her parents are going to the concert,* it is easy for students to see that the plural verb is correct.

Practice and Assess

Answers: Exercise 9

1. agree
2. were
3. was
4. were
5. feels
6. have
7. has
8. are
9. is
10. feels

Additional Resources

Grammar Practice, p. 29

Grammar Enrichment, p. 29

Grammar Workbook, Lesson 49

Close

Have students write a paragraph about what they and their friends plan to do during the next school vacation. Ask them to include three compound subjects in their paragraphs. Have students exchange papers and check each other's work. Remind students to provide effective feedback so that corrections can be made.

Enrichment and Extension

Diagraming Subject-Verb Agreement

A diagram may help students distinguish between the rules for subject-verb agreement in sentences with compound subjects joined by *and* and the rules for agreement in sentences with compound subjects joined by *or.* **L2**

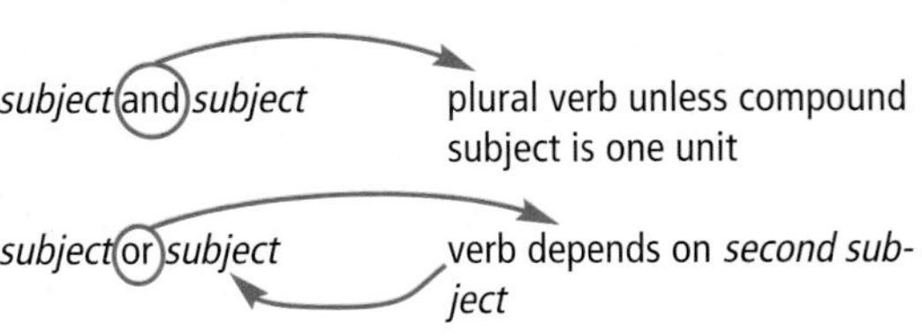

Focus

Lesson Overview

Objective

- To identify intervening expressions such as noun modifiers

Teach

Teaching Tip

Explain that a way to tell that an intervening expression isn't part of a compound subject is to remove the actual subject. What remains cannot stand alone as a subject. *Sleet, in addition to snow, is expected tomorrow* cannot be paraphrased as *In addition to snow is expected tomorrow.*

Grammar Tip

Point out that commas that set off intervening expressions are a clue that what follows the expression is not a second subject; moreover, these commas indicate a pause in speech.

Have students identify the intervening expression *(along with perseverance)* in *To be an opera singer, talent, along with perseverance, is required.*

Practice and Assess

Answers: Exercise 10

1. is
2. makes
3. sings
4. prepare
5. applauds
6. are
7. depart
8. have
9. realizes
10. discusses

Close

Have students describe in a paragraph events that have happened recently. Have them include in their sentences intervening expressions. Ask students to evaluate the sentences for punctuation and for clarity of meaning and to provide effective feedback. Have students revise as needed.

16.6 Intervening Expressions

Certain expressions, such as *accompanied by, as well as, in addition to, plus,* and *together with,* introduce phrases that modify the subject but do not change its number. Although their meaning is similar to that of *and,* these expressions do not create compound subjects.

- If a singular subject is linked to another noun by an intervening expression, such as *accompanied by,* the subject is still considered singular.

SINGULAR ***Margaret,*** *accompanied by* her date, **was** the first girl to dance.

The ***pianist,*** *as well as* the guitarist, the saxophonist, and the lead singer, **is** late.

Her ***course load,*** *plus* her extracurricular activities, **was** a lot to handle.

Sleet, *in addition to* snow, **is expected** tomorrow.

Sports, *together with* band, **is** the most popular extracurricular activity.

Exercise 10 Making Verbs Agree with Intervening Expressions

On your paper, write the appropriate form of each verb in parentheses.

Becoming a Singer

1. A voice teacher, as well as friends and relatives, (is/are) helpful in encouraging a young singer.
2. Talent, together with perseverance and practice, (makes/make) a successful career possible.
3. The student, accompanied by a pianist, (sings/sing) for the first time tonight.
4. Members of the orchestra, plus the soloist and the teacher, (prepares/prepare) for the evening's performance.
5. The teacher, together with family and friends, (applauds/applaud) the students.
6. The students, in addition to the teacher, (is/are) relieved that the performance went so well.
7. The performers, as well as the audience, (departs/depart) satisfied with the evening.
8. Lessons, in addition to practice, (has/ have) proven valuable.
9. Every student, plus the students' parents, (realizes/realize) the importance of rehearsing.
10. The class, together with the teacher, excitedly (discusses/discuss) the performance.

Resource Manager

Planning Resources

- *Lesson Plans*

Other Print Resources

- *Grammar and Composition Handbook*
- *Grammar Enrichment,* p. 29
- *Grammar Workbook,* Lesson 50

16.7 Indefinite Pronouns as Subjects

■ A verb must agree in number with an indefinite pronoun subject.

Indefinite pronouns can be divided into three groups, as shown in the following chart:

Indefinite Pronouns					
ALWAYS SINGULAR	each either neither one	everyone everybody everything no one	nobody nothing anyone anybody	anything someone somebody something	
ALWAYS PLURAL	several	few	both	many	
SINGULAR OR PLURAL	some	all	any	most	none

Plural indefinite pronouns take plural verbs. Singular indefinite pronouns take singular verbs.

SINGULAR ***Everybody*** **is** going to the rodeo.

No one in the audience **looks** upset.

Something in the kitchen **smells** good.

PLURAL ***Both*** of the children **are** in school this morning.

Many of the books **were** donated to the library.

A pronoun from the group labeled singular or plural can be either singular or plural, depending upon the noun to which it refers.

SINGULAR ***Some*** of the dessert **is** left. [*Some* refers to *dessert*, a singular noun.]

PLURAL ***Some*** of the commuters **were caught** in the rainstorm. [*Some* refers to *commuters*, a plural noun.]

Exercise 11 **Making Verbs Agree with Indefinite Pronoun Subjects**

Find the pronoun subject in each sentence and the noun to which it refers. On your paper, write the form of the verb in parentheses that agrees with the subject.

A Night at the Opera

1. All of the performers of the opera (knows/know) their parts.
2. Few of the soloists (was/were) needed for this particular work.
3. Any of the audience who came late (was/were) handed a program by the usher.
4. Each of the programs left after the performance (was/were) recycled.
5. Most of the audience members (was/were) pleased by the performance.

Subject-Verb Agreement

Focus

Lesson Overview

Objective

- To identify the number (plural or singular) of indefinite pronoun subjects

Bellringer

Daily Language Activity

When students enter the classroom, have this assignment on the board: *Write endings to complete the following sentences:*

1. Each of us . . .
2. Some of the food. . .
3. Most of the students. . .

See also  *Daily Language Practice*

Motivating Activity

Discuss students' answers to the Bellringer activity. Ask if the subject of each sentence agrees with the verb. Remind students to ask questions to clarify their understanding.

Teach

Teaching Tip

One way to help students remember that *each, either,* and *neither* are singular is to encourage students to add *one* to them: *each one, either one,* and *neither one.*

Practice and Assess

Answers: Exercise 11

1. know
2. were
3. were
4. was
5. were

Resource Manager

Planning Resources
- *Lesson Plans*

Transparencies
- *Bellringer*
- *Daily Language Practice*

Other Print Resources
- *Grammar and Composition Handbook*
- *Grammar Reteaching,* p. 29
- *Grammar Workbook,* Lesson 51

Practice and Assess

Answers: Exercise 12

Answers will vary, but some suggestions are given below.

1. Each of these patients has an appointment with Dr. Chin.
2. Many schedule morning visits.
3. Few of them have dental insurance.
4. Both of the receptionists are friendly.
5. Neither of my parents knows of a better clinic.
6. Nobody in my family minds going to the dentist.
7. Nothing dentists do bothers us.
8. Everything in the office is interesting.
9. One of my favorite things is the water drill.
10. Several of my friends are nervous about going to the dentist.

Answers: Exercise 13

Answers will vary, but some suggestions are given below.

1. None of your singing sounds amateurish. None of my favorite songs seem to appeal to you.
2. Any of the content is too difficult for me. Any of these books confuse the issue.
3. Most of my wardrobe tends to be casual. Most of my clothes need mending.
4. All of the music is delightful. All of my exercise sessions are enjoyable.
5. Some of the property looks run-down. Some of our trees appear to be dying.

Answers: Exercise 14

1. have
2. excel
3. look
4. have
5. have
6. are
7. is
8. has
9. makes
10. avoid

Exercise 12 Writing Sentences with Indefinite Pronoun Subjects

Write 10 sentences. In each sentence, use one of the following indefinite pronouns as the subject. Make each subject agree with a present-tense verb.

SAMPLE one
ANSWER One of my friends owns a racing bike.

1. each
2. many
3. few
4. both
5. neither
6. nobody
7. nothing
8. everything
9. one
10. several

Exercise 13 Writing Sentences with Indefinite Pronoun Subjects

For each indefinite pronoun listed below, write two sentences, using the pronoun as the subject of both sentences. In the first sentence of each pair, use a singular present-tense verb. In the second sentence, use a plural present-tense verb.

SAMPLE some
ANSWER Some of the work is not finished.
Some of the books are on the shelf.

1. none
2. any
3. most
4. all
5. some

Exercise 14 Making Verbs Agree with Their Subjects

On your paper, write the appropriate form of the verb in parentheses.

Butterflies

1. Almost all of these insects (has/have) some means of protection from enemies.
2. Many of them (excels/excel) at the art of imitation.
3. Some insects, like the walking stick, (looks/look) like inanimate objects when they rest on a plant stem.
4. Some butterflies, like this one, (has/have) special coloration to startle would-be predators.
5. Some of the members of one group (has/have) subdued colors and fly at night.
6. Both of these (is/are) true butterflies.
7. Protective coloration, as well as spiny larvae, (is/are) characteristic of many butterflies.
8. The monarch butterfly, along with its caterpillar, (has/have) a bitter taste.
9. Neither of these insects (makes/make) a tempting meal for a hungry bird.
10. Many of these birds (avoids/avoid) some butterflies.

MEETING INDIVIDUAL NEEDS

English Language Learners

Determining Subject-Verb Agreement

Students learning English may have problems with indefinite pronouns that are plural in meaning but singular in form (particularly the ones beginning with *every-*). List a few of the more difficult indefinite pronouns on the board, *(everybody, any, somebody, none)*. Discuss similar words in other languages. Then pair students learning English with those proficient in English. Have student pairs write a sentence, using correct subject-verb agreement, for each of the words above.

Exercise 15 Correcting Subject-Verb Agreement

The following paragraph contains ten errors in subject-verb agreement. Locate the sentences with errors and rewrite those sentences, using the verb form that agrees with the subject. (Not every sentence contains an error.)

Popular Music

[1]Many people in the cities of Los Angeles, Miami, and New York enjoys several kinds of popular music. [2]While a family in Brooklyn listen to reggae music together, a family in Miami enjoy merengue. [3]Many a music lover, whether young or old, like jazz and blues. [4]Many Americans, as well as people from around the world, dances to the brassy music known as salsa. [5]The syncopated rhythms of calypso music is popular among people who like the steel drum. [6]Very popular in some communities is Mexican folk songs called *rancheras.* [7]From the recording studios come one new popular hit after another. [8]Usually thousands of dollars are the sum needed to record a new song. [9]In many American cities, neither the Motown tunes of the 1960s nor rock-and-roll have gone out of style. [10]Ask whether your family or friends enjoy a special kind of music.

Exercise 16 Making Verbs Agree with Their Subjects

On a separate sheet of paper, rewrite the following paragraphs, replacing each blank with a verb in the present tense.

The boy with black eyes __________ over the rim of the canyon into the valley below. Everything __________ pale, as if the hot midday sun has bleached the colors from the landscape. The boy stands with arms upraised and __________ a stone over the cliff. "One, two, three," __________ the boy as the stone falls, and on "four" he hears it clatter on the rocks. Then he remembers that in one of his pockets __________ the carving of the bird he finished the night before. As polished as river rocks __________ his bird, and as white as sunlight. Quickly, without thinking, the boy from Wide Ruins __________ the bird and __________ it over the cliff. There __________ a brief flash of white, and the bird is gone. Nobody, not even the boy, __________ whether it hits the ground.

The boy listens. No sounds from the valley far below __________ his ears. The silence of his surroundings __________ absolute. Suddenly, faint flutterings __________ a signal to turn his gaze downward. Far below him in the shade of the canyon __________ the valley floor. The boy peers intently, adjusting his gaze from the brightness of sun to the darkness of shadow. In the dimness there __________ a flash of white. __________ his eyes deceive him? Again __________ the white, and then it is gone. Both the valley and the air __________ again still. The boy waits another moment, but there __________ nothing. His family __________. He turns away from the canyon.

Answers: Exercise 15

The corrected verb forms are listed by sentence number.

1. enjoy
2. listens; enjoys
3. likes
4. dance
5. are
6. are
7. comes
8. is
9. has
10. (correct)

Answers: Exercise 16

Answers will vary, but some suggestions are given below.
gazes, looks, throws, chants, rests, glistens, seizes, tosses, is, sees, reach, seems, give, lies, appears, Do, flashes, are, is, calls

Additional Resources

Grammar Reteaching, p. 29

Grammar Workbook, Lesson 51

Close

Have students work in pairs to write a paragraph using at least five indefinite pronouns. Students can exchange their paragraphs with another pair to check for subject-verb agreement. Remind pairs to provide effective feedback. Have students revise their paragraph based on the feedback.

Enrichment and Extension

Checking Subject-Verb Agreement

Have volunteers find examples of indefinite pronouns in magazines, books, or newspapers. Ask volunteers to share an example and identify the indefinite pronoun. Classmates should identify the subject's verb and determine whether it is singular or plural. Remind students that printed items sometimes have mistakes. Have them check for correctness.

Teach

About the Literature

Explain that the review features a passage from Simin Daneshvar's novel *Savushun*. After students have read the passage, initiate a discussion about the setting and mood. The passage from *Savushun* that is reproduced in this review appears in Chapter 5 of the novel. The exercises that follow are based on this passage and related topics.

Linking Grammar and Literature

☑ Teaching Tip

Ask students to discuss the highlighted examples of subject-verb agreement. Point out that careful writers pay attention to subject-verb agreement to make their writing clear and polished. Point out the highlighted inverted sentences. Ask what happens when a sentence begins with the word *there.* Then ask students what effect the inverted subject-verb order has on the passage. Have students summarize the discussion by writing in their journal a generalization about the effect of inverted subject-verb order in writing.

Critical Thinking

Point out to students that proper subject-verb agreement is often masked in the past tense, unless a past-tense verb contains an auxiliary such as *has* or *have* or *was* or *were.* Direct students to the sentence "Mina and Marjan, chirping like birds, followed their mother..." Here the agreement between the compound subject *Mina and Marjan* and the verb *followed* is masked by the use of the past tense. Ask students to identify some other examples in the passage of subject-verb agreement that is masked by the past tense.

ASSESSMENT OPTIONS

Tests with Answer Key & Rubrics
Unit 16 Mastery Test, pp. 61–62

Testmaker
Unit 16 Mastery Test

You may wish to administer the Unit 16 Mastery Test at this point.

UNIT 16 Grammar Review

Subject-Verb Agreement

Simin Daneshvar is from Iran, and her novel *Savushun* describes the fortunes of an Iranian family at the time of the Second World War. The chief characters of the novel are a sensitive young woman named Zari and her husband, Yusof. In this passage, Zari spends a quiet afternoon in her garden with her twin daughters. The passage has been annotated to show some examples of subject-verb agreement covered in this unit.

Subject-Verb Agreement

Literature Model

from Savushun
by Simin Daneshvar
translated from the Persian
by M. R. Ghanoonparvar

Agreement between a singular pronoun subject and a singular past form of *be*

An inverted sentence with agreement between an indefinite pronoun subject (referring to the plural noun *flowers*) and the plural past form of *be*

An inverted sentence with agreement between a plural noun subject and the plural past form of *be*

Agreement between a compound noun subject and the plural past form of *be*

Agreement between a singular noun subject and a singular past form of *be*

Ten days had passed since Yusof had left for the winter pastures, and the weather in the garden wasn't much better than where he was. Summer always hurried in like this, chasing away spring. It was afternoon and Gholam was sprinkling water on the patio in front of the house. Zari, carrying gardening clippers, was looking for flowers to pick. But there were none worth picking in the garden. Mina and Marjan, chirping like birds, followed their mother from one bush to another. By the stream around the patio there were some cockscombs so wilted and dusty that not even an old hen would have looked at them twice. By another stream, the faces and heads of the snapdragons were all covered with dust. Some more humble plants were straining to close their eyes and sleep as the sun set. The only hope was for the tuberoses, which Gholam claimed would "blossom when there is a full moon." The orange-blossom petals had dried up completely and, under the trees, looked like dried and shriveled brown stars. How one missed winter, when the narcissuses opened at the edge of the streams, and gave their reflections to the passing water as a memento. The water flowed

Resource Manager

Planning Resources
- *Lesson Plans*

Other Print Resources
- *Grammar and Composition Handbook*
- *Grammar Workbook,* Lessons 44–51, Unit 7 Review, Cumulative Review: Units 1–7

> on, losing the reflections, pouring into the pool without a witness. One could only hear its current. And when spring came, the white and purple violets gracefully greeted the passing water without promise or memento.

Review: Exercise 1 **Making Subjects and Verbs Agree When Prepositional Phrases Intervene**

Each of the following sentences describes characteristics of the Persian garden. On your paper, rewrite each sentence, following the directions in parentheses. In some cases, you will need to change the form of the verb to make the sentence correct; in other cases, the verb will remain the same.

SAMPLE For Persians, an image of paradise is created by gardens. (Change *an image* to *images.*)

ANSWER For Persians, images of paradise are created by gardens.

1. The scene on ancient Persian pottery often depicts garden images. (Change *scene* to *scenes.*)
2. A pool of water usually plays a role in these scenes. (Change *A pool* to *Pools.*)
3. Often, too, the patterns on Persian rugs suggest a garden. (Change *Persian rugs* to *a Persian rug.*)
4. Persian gardens throughout the years have been laid out in four sections. (Change *the years* to *time.*)
5. Pavilions of cypress trees were often built at the center of the garden. (Change *Pavilions* to *A pavilion.*)
6. In Iran some gardens still follow this plan. (Move the prepositional phrase so that it comes directly after the subject.)
7. The pool in such a garden is still an important feature. (Change *such a garden* to *these gardens.*)
8. Sometimes streams from nearby areas supply the water for these pools. (Change *nearby areas* to *a nearby area.*)
9. In some seasons, water is provided by sloping tunnels called *qanat* lines. (Move the first prepositional phrase so that it comes directly after the subject.)
10. The length of the *qanat* line varies considerably. (Change *line* to *lines.*)
11. Beneath the surface, *qanat* lines connect the valleys to the snow-capped mountains. (Move the first prepositional phrase so that it comes directly after the subject.)
12. Owners of gardens rent the channel for a certain length of time. (Change *gardens* to *a garden.*)
13. From the mountains, melting snow thus becomes a source of water. (Move the first prepositional phrase so that it comes directly after the subject.)

Subject-Verb Agreement

Practice and Assess

Answers: Exercise 1

1. The scenes on ancient Persian pottery often depict garden images.
2. Pools of water usually play a role in these scenes.
3. Often, too, the patterns on a Persian rug suggest a garden.
4. Persian gardens throughout time have been laid out in four sections.
5. A pavilion of cypress trees was often built at the center of the garden.
6. Some gardens in Iran still follow this plan.
7. The pool in these gardens is still an important feature.
8. Sometimes streams from a nearby area supply the water for these pools.
9. Water in some seasons is provided by sloping tunnels called *qanat* lines.
10. The length of the *qanat* lines varies considerably.
11. *Qanat* lines beneath the surface connect the valleys to the snow-capped mountains.
12. Owners of a garden rent the channel for a certain length of time.
13. Melting snow from the mountains thus becomes a source of water.
14. A variety of roses dominates . . .
15. Roses with deep aroma have . . .
16. A gardener . . . presses . . .
17. A flavoring from roses is . . .
18. The songs of a nightingale make . . .
19. Common sights . . . are . . .
20. Plane trees . . . provide . . .

Practice and Assess

Answers: Exercise 2

Answers will vary, but some suggestions are given below.

1. Flowers with different blooming periods offer . . .
2. Some kinds of flowers in some seasons provide . . .
3. Fresh flowers of all fragrances make . . .
4. Flowers in all hues add . . .
5. Fragrant roses in summer delight
6. Lilacs during May are . . .
7. The first crocuses in purples and golds announce . . .
8. A small garden of different flowers needs to be planned carefully.
9. Weeding on a regular basis is . . .
10. Bulbs of tulips, hyacinths, and daffodils are planted long before . . .
11. The rich soil of the region nourishes the flowers.
12. People passing by the garden enjoy the flowers' beauty . . .
13. A birdbath among the flower beds attracts robins and sparrows.
14. A vegetable garden at the rear is practical but not necessarily beautiful.
15. Vegetables of all kinds enhance . . .
16. Fresh vegetables from the garden often taste better than vegetables . . .
17. Surplus crops in large quantities are frozen, dried, or canned.
18. A small herb garden near the kitchen door provides fresh . . .
19. Herb gardens with rosemary, thyme, and sage are . . .
20. Daily watering of the herbs is . . .

Subject-Verb Agreement

14. Varieties of roses dominate Persian gardens. (Change *Varieties* to *A variety.*)
15. A rose with deep aroma has been used in many ways. (Change *A rose* to *Roses.*)
16. Gardeners of certain roses press petals to make fragrant rose water. (Change *Gardeners* to *A gardener.*)
17. A flavoring from the rose is used in a variety of desserts. (Change *the rose* to *roses.*)
18. The song of a nightingale makes a garden even more delightful. (Change *song* to *songs.*)
19. A common sight in Persian gardens is brightly colored tulips. (Change *A common sight* to *Common sights.*)
20. A plane tree of huge proportions often provides shade for the garden. (Change *A plane tree* to *Plane trees.*)

Review: Exercise 2 Writing Sentences with Intervening Prepositional Phrases

The following sentences describe an imaginary garden. Rewrite each sentence, adding an appropriate prepositional phrase in the place indicated by the caret and choosing the correct form of the verb in parentheses.

SAMPLE The flower garden ∧ (is/are) beautiful.
ANSWER The flower garden behind my grandmother's house is beautiful.

1. Flowers ∧ (offers/offer) a spectacle of color throughout the growing season.
2. Some kinds of flowers ∧ (provides/provide) food and nectar for insects.
3. Fresh flowers ∧ (makes/make) the whole house smell good.
4. Flowers ∧ (adds/add) pleasure to your world.
5. Fragrant roses ∧ (delights/delight) all who behold them.
6. Lilacs ∧ (is/are) a charming sight.
7. The first crocuses ∧ (announces/announce) the coming of spring.
8. A small garden ∧ (needs/need) to be planned carefully.
9. Weeding ∧ (is/are) an important part of caring for a garden.
10. Bulbs ∧ (is/are) planted long before they are expected to bloom.
11. The rich soil ∧ (nourishes/nourish) the flowers.
12. People passing ∧ (enjoys/enjoy) the flowers' beauty and fragrance.
13. A birdbath ∧ (attracts/attract) robins and sparrows.
14. A vegetable garden ∧ (is/are) practical but not necessarily beautiful.
15. Vegetables ∧ (enhances/enhance) one's diet.
16. Fresh vegetables ∧ often (tastes/taste) better than vegetables bought in a store.
17. Surplus crops ∧ (is/are) frozen, dried, or canned.
18. A small herb garden ∧ (provides/provide) fresh seasonings for cooking.
19. Herb gardens ∧ (is/are) easy to take care of.
20. Daily watering ∧ (is/are) a must when rainfall is scarce.

Review: Exercise 3 **Making Linking Verbs Agree with Their Subjects**

Each of the following sentences describes the scene from the passage from *Savushun.* On your paper, rewrite each sentence, following the directions in parentheses. If necessary, change the form of the linking verb.

1. Usually Zari's garden is a beautiful sight. (Change *garden* to *flowers.*)
2. Today, however, the main feature of the garden is a cluster of wilted flowers. (Change *a cluster* to *clusters.*)
3. An orange-blossom petal has become a shriveled jumble. (Change *An orange-blossom petal* to *Orange-blossom petals.*)
4. The streams are mirrors for the drooping blossoms. (Change *mirrors* to *a mirror.*)
5. The garden tool is a useless device on such a day. (Change *tool* to *clippers.*)
6. The only animals in the garden are birds. (Change *animals* to *surprising sight.*)
7. In winter a flowering plant is a welcome sight. (Change *a flowering plant* to *flowering plants.*)
8. In spring one image of loveliness is the violet. (Change *the violet* to *violets.*)
9. Water is the key to survival for these fragile plants. (Change *key to* to *means of.*)
10. Irrigation systems are the best solution for dry areas. (Change *Irrigation systems* to *An irrigation system.*)

Review: Exercise 4 **Making Subjects and Verbs Agree in Inverted Sentences**

Each of the following sentences elaborates on an idea suggested in *Savushun.* First write each sentence on your paper, choosing the correct form of the verb in parentheses. Then rewrite each sentence in inverted order, using the correct verb form.

SAMPLE The hot sun (beats/beat) upon the dry plants.
ANSWER The hot sun beats upon the dry plants.
Upon the dry plants beats the hot sun.

1. The clippers (is/are) in Zari's hand.
2. The gardener (stands/stand) among some bushes.
3. A gently curving stream (flows/flow) between the towering trees.
4. Some wilted cockscombs (droops/droop) by the side of the stream.
5. Crumbling orange-blossom petals (lies/lie) in the dry dust.
6. The colorful snapdragons (blooms/bloom) near another stream.
7. The limp blossoms (bends/bend) toward the parched earth.
8. The refreshing water (flows/flow) onto the thirsty plants.
9. New growth (comes/come) with frequent waterings.
10. The white tuberose (appears/appear) on cool moonlit nights.

Answers: Exercise 3

1. Usually Zari's flowers are a beautiful sight.
2. Today, however, the main feature of the garden is clusters of wilted flowers.
3. Orange-blossom petals have become a shriveled jumble.
4. The streams are a mirror for the drooping blossoms.
5. The garden clippers are a useless device on such a day.
6. The only surprising sight in the garden is birds.
7. In winter flowering plants are a welcome sight.
8. In spring one image of loveliness is violets.
9. Water is the means of survival for these fragile plants.
10. An irrigation system is the best solution for dry areas.

Answers: Exercise 4

1. are; In Zari's hand are the clippers.
2. stands; Among some bushes stands the gardener.
3. flows; Between the towering trees flows a gently curving stream.
4. droop; By the side of the stream droop some wilted cockscombs.
5. lie; In the dry dust lie crumbling orange-blossom petals.
6. bloom; Near another stream bloom the colorful snapdragons.
7. bend; Toward the parched earth bend the limp blossoms.
8. flows; Onto the thirsty plants flows the refreshing water.
9. comes; With frequent waterings comes new growth.
10. appears; On cool moonlit nights appears the white tuberose.

Practice and Assess

Answers: Exercise 5

1. mumps is
2. Binoculars help
3. *The Effects of Allied Occupation on Iran* is
4. audience learns
5. panel discuss
6. group disagree
7. years was
8. class hears
9. thousand was
10. Statistics show
11. Committee sponsors
12. committee discuss
13. Nobody arrives
14. months have
15. synopsis is
16. ethics are
17. *World War II Military Occupations* is
18. faculty is
19. hours are
20. class is

Grammar Review

Review: Exercise 5 Making Verbs Agree with Special Subjects

The following sentences are about a panel discussion on the occupation of Iran during the Second World War by Great Britain and the Soviet Union. First write the subject of each sentence and then write the form of the verb in parentheses that agrees with the subject.

SAMPLE A panel of experts (prepares/prepare) for discussions of various aspects of the occupation of Iran.

ANSWER panel prepares

1. Because mumps (is/are) spreading throughout the community, some students will miss the discussion.
2. Binoculars (helps/help) those in the back of the large auditorium to see the speakers.
3. *The Effects of Allied Occupation on Iran* (is/are) a book recommended by one of the speakers.
4. First the audience (learns/learn) about the German influence in Iran at the beginning of World War II.
5. The panel then (discusses/discuss) among themselves the British and Soviet control of Iran in the early 1940s.
6. The group at the podium (disagrees/disagree) about whether that occupation was necessary.
7. Five years (was/were) the length of the Allied occupation of Iran.
8. Our class next (hears/hear) about the economic and social problems in Iran at the time.
9. One panel member claims that thirty thousand (was/were) the approximate number of troops provided by the United States when it joined the occupation in 1942.
10. Statistics (shows/show) that the years of occupation were difficult for Iran.
11. The Committee on International Affairs (sponsors/sponsor) the discussion.
12. The committee (discusses/discuss) the issues thoroughly.
13. Nobody (arrives/arrive) late for the discussion.
14. Six months (has/have) passed since the last panel discussion.
15. A brief synopsis of the events leading to the occupation (is/are) given.
16. The ethics of the occupation (is/are) also discussed.
17. *World War II Military Occupations* (is/are) a book referred to by a speaker.
18. The faculty (is/are) represented by several teachers.
19. The hours spent at the panel discussion (is/are) very productive.
20. Afterwards, our class (is/are) divided on the need for the occupation.

Review: Exercise 6 **Making Verbs Agree with Compound Subjects**

Each of the following sentences elaborates on an idea suggested by the passage from *Savushun*. On your paper, rewrite each sentence, following the directions in parentheses and making any necessary adjustments to the form of the verb.

SAMPLE Every flower needs water. (Add *and shrub* to the complete subject.)
ANSWER Every flower and shrub needs water.

1. Mina scampers from bush to bush. (Add *and her sister* to the complete subject.)
2. Zari and the girls look for flowers. (Delete *and the girls* from the complete subject.)
3. Every cockscomb droops. (Add *and orange blossom* to the complete subject.)
4. Many a violet has faded. (Add *and narcissus* to the complete subject.)
5. Each stem withers. (Add *and blossom* to the complete subject.)
6. Zari and Gholam tend the garden. (Delete *and Gholam* from the complete subject.)
7. The stream and the pond supply water for the garden. (Delete *and the pond* from the complete subject.)
8. Many a dried leaf floats on the still water. (Add *and petal* to the complete subject.)
9. The spring and the winter bring fresh foliage. (Delete *and the winter* from the complete subject.)
10. Now Zari and her children want only the safe return of Yusof. (Delete *and her children* from the complete subject.)

Review: Exercise 7 **Making Subjects and Verbs Agree When Expressions Intervene**

The following sentences describe the situation and characters in *Savushun*. Rewrite each sentence, correcting any errors in subject-verb agreement. If the sentence contains no errors, write *correct.*

1. In the novel *Savushun,* the British army, as well as Soviet troops, occupy Iran.
2. The troops, plus a poor harvest, causes a food shortage.
3. Yusof, as well as Zari, is sympathetic to the hungry nomads and peasants.
4. A tribal leader, accompanied by his brother, bring Yusof news of the peasants' hardships.
5. The peasant population, plus its sheep, is starving.
6. Yusof, accompanied by servants, have gone to his pastures.
7. Yusof, in addition to his foreman, visits the shepherds.
8. Zari, together with Yusof's sister, give food to the poor.
9. Bread, as well as dates, are taken by Zari to hospitals.
10. Famine, together with disease, cause death everywhere.

Answers: Exercise 6

1. Mina and her sister scamper from bush to bush.
2. Zari looks for flowers.
3. Every cockscomb and orange blossom droops.
4. Many a violet and narcissus has faded.
5. Each stem and blossom withers.
6. Zari tends the garden.
7. The stream supplies water for the garden.
8. Many a dried leaf and petal floats on the still water.
9. The spring brings fresh foliage.
10. Now Zari wants only the safe return of Yusof.

Answers: Exercise 7

1. In the novel *Savushun* the British army, as well as Soviet troops, occupies Iran.
2. The troops, plus a poor harvest, cause a food shortage.
3. correct
4. A tribal leader, accompanied by his brother, brings Yusof news of the peasants' hardships.
5. correct
6. Yusof, accompanied by servants, has gone to his pastures.
7. correct
8. Zari, together with Yusof's sister, gives food to the poor.
9. Bread, as well as dates, is taken by Zari to hospitals.
10. Famine, together with disease, causes death everywhere.

Practice and Assess

Answers: Exercise 8

1. A few of the sites . . . feature
2. Each of these poets is . . .
3. Both of their tombs attract . . .
4. Everyone in Iran is familiar . . .
5. Anybody enjoys reading . . .
6. Some . . . have vanished entirely.
7. Many . . . were decorated . . .
8. Someone is able . . .
9. Several . . . have been fully . . .
10. Most . . . is complete.

Answers: Exercise 9 Proofreading

This Proofreading activity provides editing practice with (1) the current or previous units' skills, (2) the **Troubleshooter** errors, and (3) spelling errors. Students should be able to complete the exercise by referring to the units, the **Troubleshooter,** and a dictionary.

Error (Type of Error)

1. were (subject-verb agreement)
2. cherished, (compound sentence)
   written (spelling)
3. divine (spelling)
   were (subject-verb agreement)
4. lends (subject-verb agreement)
   calligraphy, (nonessential appositive phrase)
5. were (subject-verb agreement)
6. were (subject-verb agreement)

Review: Exercise 8 Making Verbs Agree with Indefinite Pronoun Subjects

The following sentences describe gardens around the city of Shiraz, the setting of *Savushun.* Rewrite each sentence, replacing the indefinite pronoun in italics with the pronoun in parentheses. If necessary, change the form of the verb.

SAMPLE *Many* of Iran's historic sites are near Shiraz. (One)
ANSWER One of Iran's historic sites is near Shiraz.

1. *Most* of the sites, such as the tombs of the ancient poets Hafiz and Sadi, feature gardens. (A few)
2. *Both* of these poets are revered in Muslim cultures. (Each)
3. *Either* of their tombs attracts numerous visitors. (Both)
4. *Most* in Iran are familiar with the poems of Hafiz. (Everyone)
5. *Many* enjoy reading his verse in a nearby garden. (Anybody)
6. *Several* of the older gardens have vanished entirely. (Some)
7. *Each* of the area's palaces was decorated with mirrored tile. (Many)
8. *All* are able to imagine the beauty of the palaces. (Someone)
9. *Few* of the ancient gardens have been fully restored. (Several)
10. *Some* of the renovation of the Rose Garden is complete. (Most)

Review: Exercise 9

Proofreading

The following passage describes manuscript illumination; an example by a Persian artist appears on the opposite page. Rewrite the passage, correcting any errors in spelling, usage, and grammar. Add any missing punctuation. There are twenty-five errors.

Persian Illuminated Manuscripts

[1]Illustrated, or illuminated, books was one of the highest art forms in the Islamic world. [2]From the tenth through the sixteenth centuries, manuscript painting was highly cherished for it celebrated the beauty and the power of the writen word. [3]Because in Islam books were considered to be the embodiment of devine revelation, they was treated with reverence. [4]Moreover, written Arabic lend itself to exquisite calligraphy a type of stylized handwriting.

[5]In Persia and in other Middle Eastern countries, the teachings of the sixth-century prophet Mohammed was often illustrated. [6]Similarly, many literary manuscripts was illustrated in the sixteenth century. [7]The illustration above

Habib Allah, from *Mantiq at-Tayr (Language of the Birds)*, c. 1600

date from that time. [8]It is taken from a book entitled *Mantiq at-Tayr (Language of the Birds)* which was written by Farid-Al-Din 'Attar. [9]The image of the birds in the garden are quite small intricate, and carfully painted. [10]Parts of the painting is covered with gold leaf, which was used to brighten the scene. [11]The rich brocade imaje represents the idealized realm of the birds. [12]The birds themselves represents creatures of the heavens.

[13]At the upper right of the picture are the figure of a man. [14]This figure can be interpreted in two ways—as a guardian of the birds sanctuary or as a representation of the human threat to that world. [15]The painting, however, mirror the content of the book in reflecting an ideal world rather than an actual world. [16]Therefore, peace and harmony predominates.

[17]Garden-related themes appears in many Persian literary classics. [18]The richly varied colors and textures of nature is found not only in Persia's art but in it's architecture and in the many complex decorative designs that pervade Persian culture. [19]In the illumination at the top of this page, the colors and sounds of the garden calls up visions of natural beauty.

Answers: Exercise 9 *(continued)*

Error (Type of Error)

7. dates (subject-verb agreement)
8. *Birds),* (nonessential adjective clause)
9. is (subject-verb agreement)
   small, (commas in a series)
   carefully (spelling)
10. are (subject-verb agreement)
11. image (spelling)
12. represent (subject-verb agreement)
13. is (subject-verb agreement)
14. birds' (plural possessive)
15. mirrors (subject-verb agreement)
16. predominate (subject-verb agreement)
17. appear (subject-verb agreement)
18. are (subject-verb agreement)
    its (possessive pronoun)
19. call (subject-verb agreement)

Viewing the Art

Habib Allah, from *Mantiq at-Tayr (Language of the Birds),* c. 1600

Discuss with students how, in the medieval Arab world, books were precious things. Illuminated manuscripts such as *Language of the Birds* were prized by kings and religious leaders and were treated as sacred objects. Hauntingly written and beautifully decorated, such manuscripts are a testament to the Muslim reverence for the written word. Many of these books told allegorical tales about a mythical realm.

Practice and Assess

Answers: Exercise 10

Mixed Review

1. figures
2. criticizes
3. were
4. have
5. are
6. was
7. deal
8. have
9. compose
10. are
11. do
12. is
13. are
14. is
15. is
16. has
17. is
18. give
19. have
20. is

Close

Call on volunteers to share their answers to four or five items from Exercise 10. Each volunteer should explain his or her answer. Classmates should evaluate each answer and provide effective feedback. Discuss students' questions as needed to provide clarification and understanding.

Grammar Review

Subject-Verb Agreement

Review: Exercise 10

Mixed Review

The following sentences describe the life and achievements of Simin Daneshvar [sē mēn′ dä′nesh vär′]. For each sentence, write the appropriate form of the verb in parentheses.

Simin Daneshvar

1. Simin Daneshvar, as well as her husband, (figures/figure) prominently among contemporary Iranian writers.
2. Daneshvar, along with other Iranian writers, (criticizes/criticize) the lack of justice in her homeland.
3. Studies at Tehran University (was/were) the foundation for her doctorate in Persian literature.
4. Daneshvar's lectures at Tehran University (has/have) exposed many scholars to her ideas.
5. All of Iran's social classes (is/are) represented in her fiction.
6. Among the greatest influences on her works (was/were) the famous American author O. Henry.
7. *The Quenched Fire* (1948) and *A City as Paradise* (1961) (deals/deal) with women's roles in society.
8. None of the stories in *The Quenched Fire* (has/have) been reprinted because the author was dissatisfied with the work.
9. In Daneshvar's most widely read novel, *Savushun* (1969), the descriptions of suffering (composes/compose) a portrait of the effects of war on common people.
10. Daneshvar's works (is/are) a realistic depiction of social problems in her country.
11. Politics in Iran (does/do) not generally encourage artistic freedom.
12. In Iran a woman who receives a doctorate, especially in Persian studies, (is/are) unusual.
13. There (is/are) many things Daneshvar wants to do to help her country.
14. One of her concerns (is/are) the needs of the people of Iran.
15. All of Iranian society (is/are) the subject of her work.
16. One of Daneshvar's objectives (has/have) been to help women.
17. Daneshvar (is/are) an author and storyteller who takes pride in her work.
18. Both her clear language and her graceful style (gives/give) a compelling picture of life in Iran.
19. I, as well as my best friend, (has/have) a better understanding of life in Iran after reading her books.
20. Persian, the language of Daneshvar's books, (is/are) an ancient language.

Writing Application

Subject-Verb Agreement

In this passage from *House Made of Dawn,* N. Scott Momaday demonstrates several examples of correct subject-verb agreement. Examine the passage, focusing on the italicized subjects and verbs.

My grandmother lived in a house near the place where Rainy Mountain Creek runs into the Washita River. Once there *was a lot* of sound in the house, a lot of coming and going, feasting and talk. The *summers* there *were* full of excitement and reunion. The Kiowas are a summer people; they abide the cold and keep to themselves, but when the season turns and the land becomes warm and vital they cannot hold still; an old *love* of going *returns* upon them. The old people have a fine sense of pageantry and a wonderful notion of decorum. The aged *visitors* who came to my grandmother's house when I was a child *were* men of immense character, full of wisdom and disdain.

Techniques with Subject-Verb Agreement

Use some of Momaday's techniques when you revise your own work.

TIME For more about the writing process, see **TIME *Facing the Blank Page,*** pp. 121-131.

1. Be alert to prepositional phrases and other expressions that fall between a subject and its verb. Mentally block them out when you check for agreement.

INCORRECT USE *visitors* who came to my house when I was a child *was*

MOMADAY'S CORRECT USE *visitors* who came to my grandmother's house when I was a child *were*

2. When you check for agreement in inverted sentences, remember that the subject follows the verb. In inverted sentences beginning with *there* or *here,* remember that *there* or *here* is almost never the subject.

INCORRECT USE there *were* a *lot* of sound in the house

MOMADAY'S CORRECT USE there *was* a *lot* of sound in the house

Practice Practice these techniques by revising the following passage, using a separate sheet of paper. Rewrite the paragraphs, replacing each blank with a verb in the present tense.

At the tip of a high point overlooking the waves far below ______ the town. The handsome houses of the village ______ me of beautifully bound books on a high shelf. The wide windows facing the sea ______ the curve of book spines.

There, stretching into the distance on three sides, ______ the sea. The light glancing off the waves ______ me squint. The screech of gulls ______ the air. A sloop with billowing sails ______ toward the horizon. A fishing boat laden with crabs ______ toward the safety of harbor. The whole scene—cliff, sea, and houses— ______ so picturesque that it ______ like a watercolor.

For more grammar practice, go to glencoe.com and enter **Quickpass** code WC97727p2

Subject-Verb Agreement

Subject-Verb Agreement

Have students silently read the passage from *House Made of Dawn,* paying close attention to the italicized words. After they have finished reading the passage, discuss it in terms of the points mentioned in the Techniques with Subject-Verb Agreement section below. Ask different volunteers to tell why each italicized word or phrase is a correct example of subject-verb agreement. Have them also explain what rule each example illustrates. Ask classmates to provide effective feedback.

Techniques with Subject-Verb Agreement

Discuss the techniques suggested on this page to help students figure out if a verb agrees with its subject. Then have students reread the Proofreading activity on pages 628–629, applying these techniques to sentences with subject-verb agreement problems.

Practice

The answers to this challenging and enriching activity will vary, but some suggested verbs are given below. Refer to Techniques with Subject-Verb Agreement as you evaluate student choices.

1. lies
2. remind
3. resemble
4. shimmers
5. makes
6. fills
7. glides
8. heads
9. is
10. looks

ASSESSMENT OPTIONS

Tests with Answer Key & Rubrics
Unit 16 Mastery Test, pp. 61–62

Testmaker
Unit 16 Mastery Test

MindJogger Videoquizzes

You may wish to administer the Unit 16 Mastery Test at this point.

INTRODUCING

UNIT 17

Objectives

- To develop an understanding of pronouns
- To demonstrate control over pronoun case and pronoun-antecedent agreement by completing exercises and by writing sentences in which pronoun case is used correctly and pronouns agree with their antecedents

✔ ASSESSMENT OPTIONS

Tests with Answer Key & Rubrics
Unit 17 Pretest, pp. 63–64
Unit 17 Mastery Test, pp. 65–66

Testmaker
Unit 17 Pretest
Unit 17 Mastery Test

You may wish to administer the Unit 17 Pretest at this point.

Key to Ability Levels

L1 Level 1 activities are within the basic ability range of students.

L2 Level 2 activities are within the ability range of average students.

L3 Level 3 activities are more challenging activities.

UNIT 17

Using Pronouns Correctly

Resource Manager

Planning Resources
- *Lesson Plans*
- *Block Scheduling*

Transparencies
- *Bellringer*
- *Daily Language Practice*
- *Two-Minute Skill Drill*

Video
- *MindJogger Videoquizzes*

Other Print Resources
- *Grammar and Composition Handbook*
- *Grammar Enrichment*
- *Grammar Practice*
- *Grammar Reteaching*
- *Grammar Workbook*
- *Tests with Answer Key and Rubrics*

Software
- *Interactive Grammar and Language Workbook*
- *Presentation Plus!*
- *Testmaker*

Web Site
- *glencoe.com*

17.1 Case of Personal Pronouns

- Pronouns that are used to refer to persons or things are called **personal** pronouns.
- Personal pronouns have three **cases,** or forms, called **nominative, objective,** and **possessive.** The case of a personal pronoun depends upon the pronoun's function in a sentence (whether it is a subject, a complement, an object of a preposition, or a replacement for a possessive noun).

Personal Pronouns			
CASE	**SINGULAR PRONOUNS**	**PLURAL PRONOUNS**	**FUNCTION IN SENTENCE**
NOMINATIVE	I, you, she, he, it	we, you, they	subject or predicate nominative
OBJECTIVE	me, you, her, him, it	us, you, them	direct object, indirect object, or object of preposition
POSSESSIVE	my, mine, your, yours, her, hers, his, its	our, ours, your, yours, their, theirs	replacement for possessive noun(s)

Exercise 1 Identifying Pronoun Case and Function

On your paper, write each personal pronoun in the sentences below. Then write what case each is, and how the pronoun functions in the sentence. One pronoun is used in a contraction.

SAMPLE I first met him at our neighbor's party.
ANSWER I—nominative, subject; him—objective, direct object; our—possessive, replacement for possessive noun

1. His parents had just moved into the vacant house next to ours.
2. My mother and father had just been introduced to his mother and father.
3. Maybe they should meet him, too, I thought.
4. We walked up to my mother, and I introduced him to her.
5. She extended her hand and said, "It's certainly a great pleasure to meet any friend of our son's."

Focus

Lesson Overview

Objective
- To use the three cases of personal pronouns correctly

Teach

Cross-reference: Mechanics
For instruction and practice of the material in Lesson 17.1, refer students to Troubleshooter 9.10.

Practice and Assess

Answers: Exercise 1
1. His—possessive, replacement for possessive noun; ours—possessive, replacement for possessive noun
2. My—possessive, replacement for possessive noun; his—possessive, replacement for possessive noun
3. they—nominative, subject; him—objective, direct object; I—nominative, subject
4. We—nominative, subject; my—possessive, replacement for possessive noun; I—nominative, subject; him—objective, direct object; her—objective, object of preposition
5. She—nominative, subject; her—possessive, replacement for possessive noun; It—nominative, subject; our—possessive, replacement for possessive nouns

Using Pronouns Correctly

Resource Manager

Planning Resources
- *Lesson Plans*

Transparencies
- *Two-Minute Skill Drill*

Other Print Resources
- *Grammar and Composition Handbook*
- *Grammar Enrichment,* p. 30
- *Grammar Practice,* p. 30
- *Grammar Reteaching,* p. 30
- *Grammar Workbook,* Lesson 52

Teach

☑ Grammar Tip

A good way to check for pronoun error in compound subjects and objects is to reduce the compound so that only the pronoun remains. Remind students that when they are testing nominative case pronouns, they may need to change the verb to agree with the new subject.

Two-Minute Skill Drill

Have students use each of the following phrases in a sentence:

He and I *you and me*
Juana and her *Raul and I*

See also *Two-Minute Skill Drill Transparency 17.1*

Practice and Assess

Answers: Exercise 2

1. I
2. she
3. her
4. It's
5. my

Additional Resources

Grammar Practice, p. 30
Grammar Reteaching, p. 30
Grammar Enrichment, p. 30

Grammar Workbook, Lesson 52

Close

Have students briefly summarize what they have learned about cases of personal pronouns.

Use these rules to avoid errors with the case of personal pronouns.

1. Use the nominative case for a personal pronoun in a compound subject.

   Paul and **I** play the guitar. **She** and **I** sing duets.

2. Use the objective case for a personal pronoun in a compound object.

   Al's sister visited Al and **her.** This is between you and **me.**

Hint: In a sentence with a compound subject or object, listen for correctness by saying the sentence aloud without the conjunction and the other subject or object.

3. Use the nominative case of a personal pronoun after a form of the linking verb *be.*

   The best guitar player is **he.** The best singer was **she.**

This rule is changing. In informal speech, people often use the objective case after a form of the linking verb *be;* they say, *It's me* or *It was her.* Some authorities even recommend using the objective case in informal writing to avoid sounding pretentious. In formal writing, however, use the nominative case after a form of the linking verb *be.*

4. Do not spell possessive pronouns with apostrophes.

   This sheet music is **hers.** The instruments are **theirs.**

It's is a contraction for *it is.* Do not confuse *it's* with the possessive pronoun *its.*

It's a great day for a walk. Bring me the guitar and **its** case.

5. Use possessive pronouns before gerunds (*-ing* verb forms used as nouns).

   Your dancing bothers me. He wasn't pleased with **my** singing.

Exercise 2 **Choosing the Correct Case Form**

On your paper, write the correct personal pronoun from each pair in parentheses.

Phillis Wheatley, Poet

1. When you and (I/me) think of African American poets, we often forget Phillis Wheatley.
2. Susannah Wheatley, wife of slaveholder John Wheatley, took great interest in Phillis's education, and it was (she /her) who taught Phillis how to read and write English.
3. John Wheatley encouraged Susannah and (she/her) in their studies.
4. (Its/It's) sad that Phillis's health was not good.
5. My knowledge of Phillis Wheatley has increased by (me/my) reading about her.

Meeting Individual Needs: English Language Learners

Learning Pronoun Patterns

For some students who are learning English, the most reasonable learning goal is remembering when to use which case, not remembering the names of the cases. Focus on practicing patterns such as these:

She/He and I <verb> them.
She/He/They <verb> <preposition> me.

17.2 Pronouns with and as Appositives

- Use the nominative case for a pronoun that is in apposition to a subject or a predicate nominative.

  The judges, **she** and **Mrs. Chiu,** will have a difficult task. [*Judges* is the subject of the sentence.]

  The winners were the pianists, **Linda** and **he.** [*Pianists* is the predicate nominative.]

- Use the objective case for a pronoun that is in apposition to a direct object, an indirect object, or an object of a preposition.

  The audience cheered their favorite performers, **Darnell** and **her.** [*Performers* is the direct object.]

  The director gave the stage crew, **Lee** and **him,** special thanks. [*Crew* is the indirect object.]

  The judges explained the rules to both groups, **them** and **us.** [*Groups* is the object of the preposition *to.*]

- When a pronoun is followed by an appositive, choose the case of the pronoun that would be correct if the appositive were omitted.

  We violinists hope one day to play in a concert hall. [*We* is the correct form because *we* is the subject of the sentence.]

  The music teacher handed the scores to **us musicians.** [*Us* is the correct form because *us* is the object of the preposition *to.*]

Exercise 3 **Using Pronouns with and as Appositives**

For each sentence in the following paragraph, write on your paper the correct pronoun from the pair in parentheses.

Making a Movie

[1]The writers, Lawrence Kasdan and (she/her), were willing to revise the script. [2]The director worked well with the leads, Harrison Ford and (she/her). [3]The two cinematographers, Gordon Willis and (him/he), were both efficient and creative. [4](We/Us) young actors were lucky to work with such a fine team. [5]There is no question that working on this film had a positive effect on (we/us) beginners.

Focus

Lesson Overview

Objective

- To use the correct form for pronouns used as or with appositives that identify or clarify nouns

Bellringer
Daily Language Activity

When students enter the classroom, have this assignment on the board: *Write the pronoun that completes each sentence: The students, Bill and (she/her), arrived late. The teacher explained the rules to both students, Maria and (he/him). (We/Us) runners get a lot of exercise.*

See also *Daily Language Practice*

Teach

Grammar Tip

One way to check the case of pronouns in compound appositives is to substitute a plural pronoun for the noun and its appositive. For example, *This rehearsal is for the singers, Maria and him* can be reduced to *This rehearsal is for them* (objective case). *The contestants, Bill and she, entered twice* can be changed to *They entered twice* (nominative case).

Practice and Assess

Answers: Exercise 3

1. she
2. her
3. he
4. We
5. us

Resource Manager

Planning Resources
- *Lesson Plans*

Transparencies
- *Bellringer*
- *Daily Language Practice*

Other Print Resources
- *Grammar and Composition Handbook*
- *Grammar Enrichment,* p. 31
- *Grammar Practice,* p. 31
- *Grammar Reteaching,* p. 31
- *Grammar Workbook,* Lesson 53

Practice and Assess

Answers: Exercise 4

1. I
2. she
3. we
4. he
5. she
6. me
7. he
8. She, us
9. him
10. I

Answers: Exercise 5

1. I
2. he
3. him
4. them
5. their
6. his
7. he
8. theirs
9. he
10. us

Additional Resources

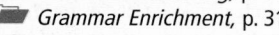

Grammar Practice, p. 31
Grammar Reteaching, p. 31
Grammar Enrichment, p. 31
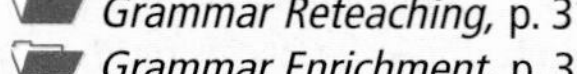
Grammar Workbook, Lesson 53

Close

Invite students to discuss how understanding and using appositives correctly will make their writing more accurate and professional. Have students summarize their discussion in their journals.

Exercise 4 Using Pronouns with and as Appositives

For each of the following sentences, write on your paper the correct personal pronoun from the pair in parentheses.

The Game of Golf

1. The first lecturers, Anna and (I/me), explained to the class that golf was popularized by King James IV of Scotland and his granddaughter, Mary.
2. The two of them, James IV and (she/her), helped to introduce the game to sports enthusiasts in England and France.
3. We then mentioned that (we/us) Americans often do well in professional tournaments.
4. Michelle Wie and (he/him), two very successful contemporary golfers, earn top salaries.
5. Tiger Woods and (she/her), two golf masters, were two recent winners of major golf tournaments.
6. Then the class asked golf experts Anna and (I, me) some questions about the game.
7. Two students, (he/him) and Larry, wanted to know how many Americans actually play the game.
8. (She, Her) and I, the experts, mentioned that the game is enjoyable for all age groups, both older people and (we/us) youngsters, because it emphasizes skill rather than strength.
9. We gave two students, Gayle and (he/him), a putter and a ball.
10. Both of us, Anna and (I, me), felt that our lecture to the class had gone very well.

Exercise 5 Using Pronouns in Sentences

On your paper, complete the following sentences by replacing each blank with a personal pronoun that makes sense.

Impressionism

1. We art lovers, Claire and ______, have learned to appreciate the contribution made by Auguste Renoir to the art style known as Impressionism.
2. Two leaders in Impressionism were Monet and ______ .
3. The first Impressionist exhibit showcased Degas, Cézanne, and ______ .
4. Viewers were highly critical of the work by Renoir and ______ .
5. Critics were not pleased by ______ using mauve shadows.
6. The painters were derisively called Impressionists because of *Impression, Sunrise,* by Monet, which later became one of ______ more famous paintings.
7. The artists, Renoir and ______, were undaunted by the negative criticism.
8. Although Edouard Manet was never part of the group, he was a good friend of ______.
9. Renoir and ______ sometimes painted together.
10. The Impressionists have left a valuable legacy for ______ art lovers.

MEETING INDIVIDUAL NEEDS

Learning Disabled

Using Pronouns

Some students may need to work with pronouns alone before they can understand pronouns in appositives. Help these students use the following pronouns correctly in sentences without appositives: *I, me, you, he, she, it, him, her, my, our.* **L1**

Diagraming Appositives

Some students benefit from diagraming sentences. In explaining the use of pronouns with and as appositives, you may find it helpful to diagram several of the example sentences in order to demonstrate each concept (for example, nominative case versus objective case). **L1**

17.3 Pronouns After *Than* and *As*

■ In elliptical adverb clauses using *than* and *as*, choose the case of the pronoun that you would use if the missing words were fully expressed.

You use a brush more skillfully than **I.** [The nominative pronoun *I* is the subject of the complete adverb clause *than I use a brush.*]

The logic of the problem puzzled Jennifer as much as **me.** [The objective pronoun *me* is the direct object of the complete adverb clause *as much as it puzzled me.*]

Some sentences can be completed with either a nominative or an objective pronoun, depending on the meaning intended.

Art liked Pat more than **I** [liked Pat].

Art liked Pat more than [he liked] **me.**

In informal speech, people often use the objective rather than the nominative form in sentences such as *He is several years older than me.* In your writing, however, you should be careful to use the correct case.

Exercise 6 Using the Correct Pronoun After *Than* and *As*

Each sentence contains an italicized word or group of words. On your paper, rewrite each sentence, substituting the correct pronoun for the words in italics.

Rembrandt van Rijn, Dutch Painter

1. Nobody enjoys Rembrandt's paintings as much as *my family and I.*
2. Few Dutch artists in the seventeenth century could paint as well as *Rembrandt.*
3. Although Rembrandt's father had hoped his son would be a clergyman, few people supported the artist more than *Mr. van Rijn.*
4. It seems Rembrandt's artistic talent astonished his father as much as *his art teachers.*
5. Critics seemed to agree that nobody in Holland could paint better than *Rembrandt.*
6. Rembrandt's rise to fame must have pleased the artist even more than *the leaders of Amsterdam.*
7. As a portrait artist, Rembrandt was sought after much more than *other painters.*
8. Few models seemed as beautiful to Rembrandt as *a girl named Saskia.*
9. On the day of their wedding, it seemed nobody could have been happier than *Rembrandt and Saskia.*
10. Rembrandt's paintings seem to amaze people today even more than *the people of Rembrandt's century.*

Focus

Lesson Overview

Objective

- To use the correct form when a pronoun follows *than* or *as*

Bellringer
Daily Language Activity

When students enter the classroom, have this assignment on the board: *Write a sentence with pronouns for each of these phrases:*

more nervous than

as much as

more curious than

See also *Daily Language Practice*

Teach

Teaching Tip

Remind students that the choice of pronoun case is not determined by whether they use *than* or *as.* Pronoun case is determined solely by the function of the pronoun within the fully expanded adverb clause.

Practice and Assess

Answers: Exercise 6

1. we
2. he
3. he
4. them
5. he
6. them
7. they
8. she
9. they
10. them

Close

Invite students to discuss how they choose the correct case when a pronoun follows *than* or *as.*

Resource Manager

Planning Resources
- *Lesson Plans*

Transparencies
- *Bellringer*
- *Daily Language Practice*

Other Print Resources
- *Grammar and Composition Handbook*
- *Grammar Practice,* p. 32
- *Grammar Workbook,* Lesson 53

Focus

Lesson Overview

Objective

- To use *who* and *whom* appropriately in questions and clauses

Bellringer
Daily Language Activity

When students enter the classroom, have this assignment on the board: *Read the passage below. Why do you think* <u>who</u> *is used?*

> Presently she heard her father go to the door, as if to let in a paper boy who wanted his twenty cents.
>
> —Gwendolyn Brooks, "You're Being so Good, So Kind"

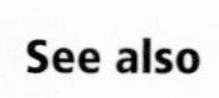
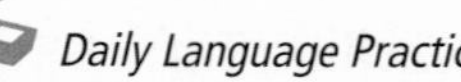

See also *Daily Language Practice*

Teach

☑ Teaching Tip

Whom has virtually disappeared from the spoken language. Consequently, students who write by ear have little awareness of how to use *whom* appropriately. A good way to test for the correct use of *who* and *whom* in subordinate clauses is to turn the clause into a separate sentence and substitute a personal pronoun for *who* or *whom.*

Practice and Assess

Answers: Exercise 7

1. Who
2. whom
3. whom
4. whom
5. who

17.4 *Who* and *Whom* in Questions and Subordinate Clauses

■ Use the nominative pronoun *who* for subjects.

Who won the contest? [*Who* is the subject of the verb *won.*]

Tell me **who** is in your class. [*Who* is the subject of the noun clause *who is in your class.*]

In questions with an interrupting expression, such as *did you say* or *do you think,* it is often helpful to drop the interrupting phrase to determine whether to use *who* or *whom.*

Who do you think will emcee the show? [Think: *Who* will emcee the show? *Who* is the subject of the verb *will emcee.*]

■ Use the objective pronoun *whom* for the direct or indirect object of a verb or verbal or for the object of a preposition.

direct object

Maria invited *them* to the party.
Maria invited *whom* to the party?

Whom are you introducing first? [*Whom* is the direct object of the verb *are introducing.*]

Whom did you say Maria invited to the party? [*Whom* is the direct object of the verb *invited.*]

They told him **whom** he could invite to the show. [*Whom* is the direct object of the verb *could invite* in the noun clause *whom he could invite to the show.*]

Theodore Roosevelt is a president about **whom** I have read quite a bit. [*Whom* is the object of the preposition *about* in the adjective clause *about whom I have read quite a bit.*]

In informal speech, people generally use *who* in place of *whom* in sentences like *Who did you tell?* In writing and in formal speaking situations, however, make the distinction between *who* and *whom.*

Exercise 7 Choosing *Who* or *Whom*

For each sentence, write on your paper the correct pronoun from the pair in parentheses.

Learning About Holography

1. (Who/Whom) did you say gave you the passes to the Museum of Holography?
2. Setsuko Ishii is the holographic artist about (who/whom) I've been reading.
3. Setsuko Ishii, (who/whom) many consider one of Japan's top holographic artists, has put together an exhibit at the museum.
4. The museum director, (who/whom) our teacher knows, will show us a twenty-minute film.
5. The director mentioned several artists (who/whom) he said will exhibit in the future.

Using Pronouns Correctly

Resource Manager

Planning Resources
- *Lesson Plans*

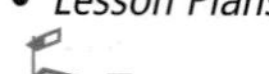

Transparencies
- *Bellringer*
- *Daily Language Practice*

Other Print Resources
- *Grammar and Composition Handbook*
- *Grammar Enrichment,* p. 32
- *Grammar Reteaching,* p. 32
- *Grammar Workbook,* Lesson 54

Exercise 8 Choosing *Who* or *Whom*

For each of the following sentences, write on your paper the correct pronoun from the pair in parentheses.

George Washington Carver, Scientist

1. (Who/Whom) would you say changed forever the way we look at the lowly peanut?
2. George Washington Carver, (who/whom) many consider one of the best scientists of his day, developed hundreds of products from peanuts.
3. Carver, (who/whom) many still admire today, was born on a Missouri plantation in 1861 and left home when he was ten years old.
4. He was accepted by a college in Kansas, but he was barred from attending by faculty members (who/whom) were prejudiced.
5. Carver was later admitted to Simpson College in Iowa and paid his way by ironing laundry for students (who/whom) were attending the college.
6. Carver, (who/whom) every student of agriculture has studied, made several important discoveries about plants.
7. Booker T. Washington, an educator (who/whom) Carver greatly respected, invited Carver to work at the Tuskegee Institute in Alabama.
8. Carver, (who/whom) Washington believed to be hardworking and imaginative, eventually came up with more than three hundred products derived from peanuts, including peanut butter, ink, shampoo, vinegar, and a coffee substitute.
9. For (who/whom) did Carver develop these products?
10. Carver developed them for poor southern farmers, about (who/whom) he was greatly concerned.

Exercise 9 Using *Who* or *Whom* in Sentences

On your paper, complete the following paragraph by replacing each blank with who or whom.

Mary Cassatt, an American Painter

[1]Mary Cassatt, __________ many students of art admire, was a successful nineteenth-century American painter who spent much of her time in France. [2]Her friends, __________ included Edgar Degas, were some of the great French Impressionists. [3]Degas, __________ we know primarily for his paintings of ballerinas, greatly influenced Cassatt. [4]Cassatt also encouraged American collectors to purchase the art of the Impressionists, __________ she considered very important. [5]__________ are some other American artists influenced by the European Impressionists?

Exercise 10 Using *Who* or *Whom* in Writing

Write ten sentences. In five, use the nominative pronoun *who.* In the other five, use the objective pronoun *whom.*

Answers: Exercise 8

1. Who
2. whom
3. whom
4. who
5. who
6. whom
7. whom
8. whom
9. whom
10. whom

Answers: Exercise 9

1. whom
2. who
3. whom
4. whom
5. Who

Answers: Exercise 10

Answers will vary, but some suggestions are given below.

1. Who is your favorite writer?
2. I like writers who write science fiction.
3. Isaac Asimov, who many think is the best science fiction writer ever, has written hundreds of books and articles.
4. If you could read the complete works of any writer, whom would you choose to read?
5. I would choose someone who has stood the test of time.

Additional Resources

Grammar Reteaching, p. 32
Grammar Enrichment, p. 32

Grammar Workbook, Lesson 54

Close

Have students discuss how knowing when to use *who* and *whom* will help them sound more literate in their written work for other classes.

Cooperative Learning

Using *Who* and *Whom*

Students may confuse *who* and *whom.* The use of *who* and *whom* in questions requires a verb in front of the subject (for example, *Who is he?*). Learners often make the mistake of transferring this same word order to noun clauses: *I know who are you.* Students can work with a partner to practice writing these types of sentences and to determine the correct usage of *who* and *whom* in the sentences.

Focus

Lesson Overview

Objectives

- To use correct pronoun agreement
- To learn about gender-neutral wording

Bellringer
Daily Language Activity

When students enter the classroom, have this assignment on the board: *Identify the pronouns and their antecedents:*

> Mrs. Hattori nodded, but she did not say anything because she did not feel her English up to the occasion.
>
> —Hisaye Yamamoti, "The Brown House"

See also *Daily Language Practice*

Teach

Agreement in Number and Gender

Teaching Tip

The term antecedent literally means "the thing that has gone before." In grammar a pronoun's antecedent is a noun, pronoun, or group of words acting as a noun to which the pronoun refers.

In spoken English, people often use the plural pronouns *they, them,* or *their* when talking about one person rather than a gender-specific pronoun, such as *he* or *her: A speaker must capture their listeners' attention.* The simplest solution to this agreement problem is probably to say: *Speakers must capture their listeners' attention.*

17.5 Pronoun-Antecedent Agreement

■ An **antecedent** is the word or group of words to which a pronoun refers or that a pronoun replaces. All pronouns must agree with their antecedents in number, gender, and person.

Agreement in Number and Gender

■ A pronoun must agree with its antecedent in number (singular or plural) and gender (masculine, feminine, or neuter).

A pronoun's antecedent may be a noun, another pronoun, or a phrase or clause acting as a noun. In the following examples, the pronouns appear in bold type and their antecedents in bold italic type. Note how they agree in both number and gender:

Helen Keller did not let an inability to see and hear prevent **her** from graduating *cum laude* from Radcliffe College. [singular feminine pronoun]

Helen Keller and ***Robert Smithdas*** overcame many challenges to earn **their** college degrees. [plural pronoun]

Octavio Paz is one of the greatest poets of **his** era. [singular masculine pronoun]

Walt Whitman and ***Emily Dickinson*** are also famous for **their** poetry. [plural pronoun]

The ***horseshoe crab,*** despite **its** name, is not a true crab but is related to the spider. [singular neuter pronoun]

Oysters and ***clams*** are becoming endangered because of oil spills near **their** breeding grounds. [plural pronoun]

Traditionally a masculine pronoun has been used when the gender of the antecedent is not known or may be either masculine or feminine.

An ***author*** must capture **his** readers' interest.

This usage has changed, however. Many people now prefer to use gender-neutral wording. If you do not wish to use a masculine pronoun when the antecedent may be feminine, you can frequently reword the sentence in one of three ways: (1) by using *he or she, his or her,* and so forth, (2) by using a plural pronoun, or (3) by eliminating the pronoun.

An ***author*** must capture **his or her** readers' interest.

Authors must capture **their** readers' interest.

Authors must capture readers' interest. [no pronoun]

Resource Manager

Planning Resources

- *Lesson Plans*

Transparencies

- *Bellringer*
- *Daily Language Practice*
- *Two-Minute Skill Drill*

Other Print Resources

- *Grammar and Composition Handbook*
- *Grammar Enrichment,* p. 33
- *Grammar Practice,* p. 33
- *Grammar Reteaching,* p. 33
- *Grammar Workbook,* Lesson 55

Agreement in Person

■ A pronoun must agree in person with its antecedent.

Many problems with agreement in person arise when the second-person pronoun *you* is used incorrectly to refer to an antecedent in the third person. Either change *you* to an appropriate third-person pronoun, or replace it with a suitable noun.

POOR Suki and James are going to visit the Everglades, where ~~**you**~~ can see storks and alligators.

BETTER Suki and James are going to visit the Everglades, where **they** can see storks and alligators.

BETTER Suki and James are going to visit the Everglades, where **tourists** can see storks and alligators.

When the antecedent of a pronoun is another pronoun, be sure that the two pronouns agree in person. Avoid unnecessary shifts from *they* to *you*, *I* to *you*, or *one* to *you*.

POOR **They** often visit New Orleans, where ~~**you**~~ can enjoy French cooking.

BETTER **They** often visit New Orleans, where **they** can enjoy French cooking.

POOR **I** hiked on trails that amazed ~~**you**~~ with their beauty.

BETTER **I** hiked on trails that amazed **me** with their beauty.

POOR When **one** travels, ~~**you**~~ can learn a lot.

BETTER When **one** travels, **one** can learn a lot.

BETTER When **you** travel, **you** can learn a lot.

Exercise 11 Making Pronouns and Antecedents Agree

Complete the following sentences by writing an appropriate possessive pronoun in each blank. Then write the antecedent for each pronoun that you supply.

Sarah Winnemucca, a Piute Spokeswoman

[1]Sarah Winnemucca, the daughter of a Piute chief, was taken by ____________ grandfather to California in 1850. [2]Some years later, after she had learned English and Spanish, she moved to Nevada and worked for a stagecoach agent and ____________ wife and family. [3]When several bands of Piutes were forced off their ancestral land in the 1860s, Winnemucca served as ____________ interpreter. [4]After lecturing in the East about the plight of her people, she moved to the town of Vancouver and taught in one of ____________ schools for Native Americans. [5]Winnemucca's book *Life Among the Piutes* was a great success, and it has added to ____________ understanding as Americans of an important chapter in Native American history.

Using Pronouns Correctly

Agreement in Person

Cross-reference: Listening and Speaking

For instruction and practice in using pronouns and antecedents when speaking, refer students to Lessons 29.1–29.3.

Remind students that in speaking, replacing the second-person pronoun with a specific word when the pronoun is used to refer to a third-person antecedent will make the meaning of the sentence clearer.

Cross-reference: Writing

For instruction and practice in using pronouns correctly in writing, refer students to Unit 2: The Writing Process.

Have students check pronoun agreement in their recent writing assignment. Ask them to make sure that *you* is not used to refer to an antecedent in the third person and that two pronouns always agree in person when one is the antecedent of the other. Have students revise as needed.

Two-Minute Skill Drill

Tell students to look at the sentences below and write the antecedent for each pronoun.

Ty and Bill went to their class.

Lei likes her new computer.

The dog ate its food quickly.

Ask volunteers to explain their answers.

See also *Two-Minute Skill Drill Transparency 17.5*

Practice and Assess

Answers: Exercise 11

1. her
2. his
3. their
4. its
5. our

Meeting Individual Needs: English Language Learners

Pronoun-Antecedent Agreement

In teaching pronoun-antecedent agreement to students learning English, begin by making sure that students understand the concepts of gender and person. Then write some example sentences on the board, using the same color for the pronoun and its antecedent. Draw circles and arrows to show the relationship between the pronoun and its antecedent in the following sentence. *A doctor must watch her patients carefully.*

Practice and Assess

Answers: Exercise 12

Answers will vary, but some suggestions are given below.

1. Cooks who like unusual food are in luck these days, for they can . . .
2. Lovers of Japanese food can prepare their own shrimp . . .
3. Even an amateur chef can make his or her own pasta at home . . .
4. People who are partial to Mexican food can concoct their own . . .
5. correct
6. People who crave a North African dish can purchase their own . . .
7. Seafood lovers might want to try their luck . . .
8. While sipping bouillabaisse, a fish stew, Americans can imagine that they are . . .
9. Food lovers can take cooking classes, where they will learn . . .
10. . . . by its different seasonings.

Answers: Exercise 13

Answers will vary, but some suggestions are given below.

1. Visually impaired people face more obstacles than the sighted, for they must be unusually self-reliant and persevering.
2. José Feliciano is a highly respected visually impaired musician. He grew up in Puerto Rico, where he had to struggle hard to get ahead.
3. When Feliciano was five, he and his family moved to New York, where they hoped to find better opportunities.
4. From his idol, Ray Charles, Feliciano learned that visually impaired people can succeed in the music business. They must learn to expect setbacks and disappointment, however.
5. Feliciano's fans praise his skillful guitar playing. They say that they can expect nothing less than the best from this disciplined musician.

Exercise 12 Making Pronouns and Antecedents Agree

In each of the following sentences, find the personal pronoun and its antecedent. If there is an error in agreement, rewrite the sentence in one or more ways to correct the problem. If there is no error, write *correct.*

Ethnic Cuisines

1. A cook who likes unusual food is in luck these days, for they can find plenty of ethnic recipes and special ingredients.
2. A lover of Japanese food can prepare their own shrimp or vegetable tempura.
3. Even an amateur chef can make their own pasta at home, using an electric or hand-cranked machine.
4. A person who is partial to Mexican food can concoct their own hot sauce with tomatoes, onions, and hot green peppers.
5. Shoppers can visit ethnic grocery shops, where they can purchase many hard-to-get ingredients, such as dried Chinese mushrooms, tortilla mix, collard greens, juniper berries, pine nuts, and litchi nuts.
6. People who crave a North African dish can purchase your own couscous and add morsels of meat or fish.
7. A seafood lover might want to try his luck at paella, a delicious Spanish dish that includes shrimp, clams, rice, and vegetables.
8. While sipping bouillabaisse, a fish stew, an American can imagine that they are sitting at a French café.
9. Food lovers can take cooking classes, where you will learn how to prepare lefse and other Norwegian foods.
10. Connoisseurs of ethnic foods know that they can distinguish an Italian meatball from a Swedish one by their different seasonings.

Exercise 13 Making Pronouns and Antecedents Agree in Person

On your paper, rewrite each of the following items, eliminating the inappropriate use of *you* by substituting a third-person pronoun or a suitable noun.

José Feliciano: A Success Story

1. Visually impaired people face more obstacles than the sighted, for you must be unusually self-reliant and persevering.
2. José Feliciano is a highly respected visually impaired musician. He grew up in Puerto Rico, where you had to struggle hard to get ahead.
3. When Feliciano was five, he and his family moved to New York, where you hoped to find better opportunities.
4. From his idol, Ray Charles, Feliciano learned that visually impaired people can succeed in the music business. You must learn to expect setbacks and disappointment, however.
5. Feliciano's fans praise his skillful guitar playing. They say that you can expect nothing less than the best from this disciplined musician.

MEETING INDIVIDUAL NEEDS

English Language Learners

Correcting Errors in Number or Gender

Students may have difficulty noticing errors in number or gender if the pronoun and its antecedent are not close together in a sentence. Help students practice identifying errors in sentences with which they are comfortable and have them gradually work up to identifying errors in longer and longer sentences.

Agreement with Indefinite Pronoun Antecedents

- In general, use a singular personal pronoun when the antecedent is a singular indefinite pronoun, and use a plural personal pronoun when the antecedent is a plural indefinite pronoun.

Indefinite Pronouns				
ALWAYS SINGULAR	each either neither one	everyone everybody everything no one	nobody nothing anyone anybody	anything someone somebody something
ALWAYS PLURAL	several others	few	both	many
SINGULAR OR PLURAL	some none	all	any	most

Each of the boys must buy **his** own uniform.

One of the women has **her** own diving equipment.

Many of the students bring **their** lunch to school.

Note that the plural nouns in the prepositional phrases—*of the boys, of the women*—do not affect the number of the personal pronouns. *His* and *her* are singular because *each* and *one,* their antecedents, are singular. In speaking, however, people often use the plural pronoun *their.*

INFORMAL ***Neither*** of the boys bought **their** own uniforms.

FORMAL ***Neither*** of the boys bought **his** own uniform.

When no gender is specified, use gender-neutral wording.

Everyone must buy **his or her** own uniform.

If you find the sentence above a bit awkward, you may want to reword the sentence. You might substitute a plural indefinite pronoun or a word such as *people* for the singular indefinite pronoun. Or you might eliminate the personal pronoun entirely.

All must buy **their** own uniforms.

People must buy **their** own uniforms.

Everyone must buy a uniform. [no pronoun]

Using Pronouns Correctly

Teach

Agreement with Indefinite Pronoun Antecedents

Teaching Tip

A useful strategy for checking for agreement with indefinite pronoun antecedents is to actually write *S* for singular and *P* for plural over the subject, the verb, and any pronouns to ensure that they are all in agreement. See *Grammar Reteaching,* p. 33.

Cross-reference: Grammar

For instruction and practice in indefinite pronouns, refer students to Lesson 10.2, pp. 446–451.

Cross-reference: Usage

For instruction and practice in singular and plural indefinite pronoun use and subject-verb agreement when indefinite pronouns function as subjects, refer students to Lesson 16.7, pp. 619–621.

Enrichment and Extension

Agreement and Indefinite Pronouns

Many students have a problem with the indefinite pronouns *everyone* and *everybody* because they seem to be plural in meaning but singular in number. Remind students that *every* means "each single individual." Suggest that they think of *every* as meaning "each" rather than "all." Ask students to review a recent writing assignment for verb agreement with indefinite pronouns and to revise as needed. **L2**

Practice and Assess

Answers: Exercise 14

Answers will vary, but some suggestions are given below.

1. correct
2. All of the herbs in the shaman's collection had special curative powers of their own.
3. Many in the Dakota nation drank powdered skunk-cabbage roots to relieve their asthma.
4. Each of the women in the Cheyenne nation would gather her own stock of wild mint . . .
5. Everybody searched for natural remedies for illnesses; the Cree people chewed . . .
6. Among the Kiowa, anybody with dandruff knew that his or her scalp should be washed with soaproot.
7. Some of the Utes treated their cuts and bruises . . .
8. Many who lived on the frontier owed their lives to natural cures.
9. correct
10. correct

Answers: Exercise 15

1. his or her
2. their
3. her
4. his or her
5. their
6. their
7. his or her
8. their
9. their
10. his

Additional Resources

Grammar Practice, p. 33
Grammar Reteaching, p. 33
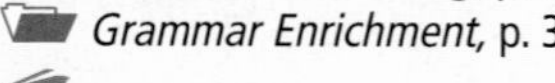
Grammar Enrichment, p. 33

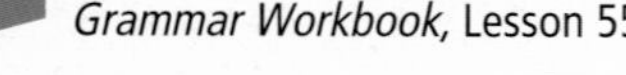
Grammar Workbook, Lesson 55

Close

Discuss with students how they can remember what they have learned about unclear pronoun reference and how they can apply what they have learned to their writing in other classes.

Exercise 14 Making Pronouns Agree with Indefinite Pronoun Antecedents

On your paper, indicate which of the following sentences are correct. Then revise each of the incorrect sentences to make it correct. In some cases, you will need to change a single word; in others you may wish to revise the entire sentence.

Native American Medicine

1. Many of the Native American nations relied on their shaman, or medicine man, to treat anyone who became ill.
2. All of the herbs in the shaman's collection had special curative powers of its own.
3. Many in the Dakota nation drank powdered skunk-cabbage roots to relieve his asthma.
4. Each of the women in the Cheyenne nation would gather their own stock of wild mint, which was used to treat nausea.
5. Everybody searched for natural remedies for their illnesses; the Cree people chewed the cones of the spruce tree to soothe sore throats.
6. Among the Kiowa, anybody with dandruff knew that their scalp should be washed with soaproot.
7. Some of the Utes treated his cuts and bruises with a salve made from the yarrow plant.
8. Many who lived on the frontier owed his life to natural cures.
9. Some of the pioneers ended their bouts with scurvy by eating wild garlic, a plant used by many Native American nations.
10. Today, few doctors question the curative powers of Native American medicines, and their respect for the shaman's remedies continues to grow.

Exercise 15 Using Pronouns in Sentences

On your paper, complete each of the following sentences by writing a personal pronoun that agrees with its indefinite pronoun antecedent.

Early Native American Nations

1. Each of the Native American leaders spoke _____ own language.
2. Few of the Native Americans shared a language with _____ neighbors.
3. Each of the Inuit mothers dressed _____ children in fur parkas, while some children in more southern climates wore little clothing.
4. In some of the Native American nations, everybody carried _____ goods by canoe.
5. Many of the Great Plains groups hunted animals for _____ food.
6. Some of the other Plains nations developed _____ farming skills.
7. Everyone worked hard harvesting _____ crops.
8. Some of the Native Americans in the Southwest foraged for food, and acorns were a mainstay of _____ diet.
9. Many who lived in the Southwest made _____ homes of adobe.
10. In some nations, each of the men had to support _____ own family, while in other nations, resources were shared.

17.6 Clear Pronoun Reference

■ Make sure that the antecedent of a pronoun is clearly stated and that a pronoun cannot possibly refer to more than one antecedent.

Vague Pronoun Reference

Do not use the pronouns *this, that, which,* and *it* without a clearly stated antecedent.

VAGUE She is an excellent singer, and **this** was evident in the performance last night. [What showed in the performance? Her talent showed, but the word *talent* is not specifically mentioned.]

CLEAR She is an excellent singer, and **her talent** was evident in the performance last night.

VAGUE The senator loved public speaking, and **that** greatly helped boost his popularity. [What helped boost his popularity? His speeches did, but the word *speeches* is not specifically mentioned.]

CLEAR The senator loved public speaking, and **his speeches** greatly helped boost his popularity.

VAGUE Last week our garage burned, **which** started from a kerosene heater. [What started from a kerosene heater? A fire started, but the word *fire* is not specifically mentioned.]

CLEAR Last week a fire, **which** started from a kerosene heater, burned our garage.

VAGUE The Supreme Court is deliberating on the question of the death penalty, and **it** will have a great impact on the nation. [What will have a great impact? The Supreme Court's decision will, but the word *decision* is not specifically mentioned.]

CLEAR The Supreme Court is deliberating on the question of the death penalty, and the court's **decision** will have a great impact on the nation.

Using Pronouns Correctly

Resource Manager

Planning Resources
- *Lesson Plans*

Transparencies
- *Bellringer*
- *Daily Language Practice*

Other Print Resources
- *Grammar and Composition Handbook*
- *Grammar Enrichment,* p. 34
- *Grammar Practice,* p. 34
- *Grammar Reteaching,* p. 34
- *Grammar Workbook,* Lesson 56

Focus

Lesson Overview

Objective
- To ensure that pronoun antecedents are clear and unambiguous

Bellringer
Daily Language Activity

When students enter the classroom, have this assignment on the board: *Rewrite these sentences to make them clear:*

1. *They say there were 60,000 people at the concert.*
2. *When my papers got mixed in with the magazines, they were thrown out.*
3. *The raindrops pelted the windows, so they got cleaner.*

See also *Daily Language Practice*

Motivating Activity

Ask volunteers to read aloud and explain their answers to the Bellringer activity above. Point out that in this lesson, they will learn how to make pronoun references clear.

Teach

Vague Pronoun Reference

Teaching Tip

The demonstrative pronouns *this, that, these,* and *those* are often used in a vague way to refer to a previous idea, without making clear which aspect of the idea the writer meant. A good way to avoid this problem is to expand the demonstrative pronoun with a noun or a noun phrase that clarifies the reference.

Cross-reference: Troubleshooter

For instruction and practice in pronoun references, refer students to Unit 9: Troubleshooter.

Teach

Ambiguous and Indefinite Pronoun Reference

☑ Teaching Tip

Point out that using ambiguous pronoun references will distort a speaker's meaning. The listener will very likely be confused and may jump to the wrong conclusion. To avoid any ambiguity, students should always make sure that a pronoun clearly refers to a single antecedent.

Practice and Assess

Answers: Exercise 16

Answers will vary, but some suggestions are given below.

1. France, which is quite beautiful and historic, is the largest country of western Europe.
2. clear
3. France's delicious food and wine are important to the French and are often considered the best in the world.
4. People in France really know how to enjoy life.
5. France also plays an important role in world politics, and this role affects many other countries.
6. Paris, the capital of France, is also the country's largest city.
7. Paris has been home to many of the world's best artists, and this fact is reflected in the number of masterpieces that have been painted there.
8. clear
9. Paris's culture and beauty impressed American writers Ernest Hemingway and Gertrude Stein.
10. In Paris, Hemingway met the popular writer F. Scott Fitzgerald, and Fitzgerald helped Hemingway get his stories published.

Ambiguous and Indefinite Pronoun Reference

If a pronoun seems to refer to more than one antecedent, either reword the sentence to make the antecedent clear or eliminate the pronoun.

UNCLEAR ANTECEDENT	When the tickets slipped between the reports, **they** were lost. [Which word is the antecedent of *they?* Were the tickets or the reports lost?]
CLEAR ANTECEDENT	The tickets were lost when **they** slipped between the reports.
NO PRONOUN	When the tickets slipped between the reports, **the tickets** were lost.

When the tickets slipped between the reports,

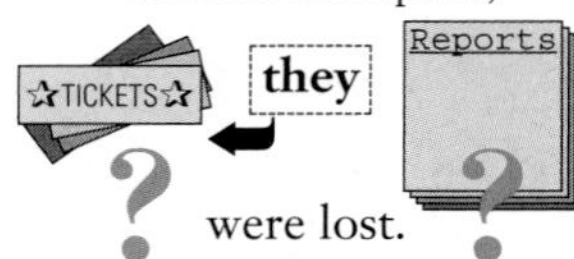

were lost.

Avoid the indefinite use of the pronouns you and they.

INDEFINITE	In Japan **you** bow after saying hello.
CLEAR	In Japan **people** bow after saying hello.
INDEFINITE	In some countries **they** take a nap after lunch.
CLEAR	In some countries **people** take a nap after lunch.

Exercise 16 Making Pronouns References Clear

For each sentence, determine whether the antecedent of the italicized pronoun is clear or unclear. If the antecedent is unclear, rewrite the sentence to make it clear. You may need to reword the sentence or eliminate the pronoun. If the antecedent is clear, write *clear.*

France

1. France is the largest country of western Europe, and *it* is quite beautiful and historic.
2. France has sunny beaches, *which* stretch along the Mediterranean Sea.
3. Their delicious food and wine are important to the French, and *they* are often considered the best in the world.
4. In France *they* really know how to enjoy life.
5. France also plays an important role in world politics, and *this* affects many other countries.
6. Paris is the capital of France, and *it* is also the country's largest city.
7. Paris has been home to many of the world's best artists, and *this* is reflected in the number of masterpieces that have been painted there.
8. When writers and artists arrive in Paris, *they* immediately fall in love with the city.
9. Paris is both cultured and beautiful, *which* impressed American writers Ernest Hemingway and Gertrude Stein.
10. Hemingway met the popular writer F. Scott Fitzgerald in Paris, and *he* helped *him* get his stories published.

MEETING INDIVIDUAL NEEDS — English Language Learners

Avoiding *You*

Remind students with little exposure to formal English that the use of *you,* meaning "everybody" or "people in general," is not acceptable in formal written English. Unfortunately, there is no simple substitute for this meaning of *you.* Usually the entire sentence must be rewritten to avoid the problem.

Exercise 17 Making Pronoun References Clear

On your paper, rewrite each of the following sentences, making sure that all pronoun references are clearly stated.

Politics

1. The governor told the mayor that she would win by a landslide.
2. When the mayor thanked the governor, she was happy.
3. People who wish to vote must get to the polling places before 7:00 P.M., for after that you are turned away.
4. A citizens' group charged that the elections had been fixed, and it angered the officials.
5. The newspaper's editors criticized the politicians, and they argued for full disclosure of the facts.
6. The activists said that some of the politicians in the city had accepted bribes; this was a scandal.
7. Eric's father was mayor of the city, which gave him considerable social status.
8. When several of the newspapers disclosed the mayor's actions, it caused a great decline in his prestige.
9. The city council member told the newspaper reporter that he had manipulated the coverage of the election.
10. The early election returns pleased the senator, which had been widely predicted.

Exercise 18 Using Pronouns Correctly

On your paper, rewrite each of the following sentences by eliminating any mistakes in the use of pronouns. Each sentence has one error.

Sports Jargon

1. Sportscasters and us use sports jargon frequently.
2. A word that means one thing in ordinary conversation sometimes changes it's meaning when applied to sports.
3. Anyone who watches tennis knows that you call an unreturned serve an ace.
4. The same word is used in golf, which refers to a hole in one.
5. In baseball a bean ball is a pitch thrown so near a batter's head that you're in danger of being hit.
6. The batter must watch each ball carefully and determine it's speed and position.
7. We watched Roger Clemens pitch three shutouts in a row, and him pitching so well seemed almost miraculous to us.
8. The word *eagle* is familiar to my friends and I.
9. No one was more surprised than me to learn that in golf the word *eagle* means "two strokes under par."
10. I always thought I knew sports, but it was her who first made me especially aware of sports jargon.

Answers: Exercise 17

Answers will vary, but some suggestions are given below.

1. The governor told the mayor that the mayor would win by a landslide.
2. When she thanked the governor, the mayor was happy.
3. People who wish to vote must get to the polling places before 7:00 P.M., for after that everyone is turned away.
4. A citizens' group charged that the elections had been fixed, and the accusation angered the officials.
5. The newspaper's editors criticized the politicians and argued for full disclosure of the facts.
6. The activists said that some of the politicians in the city had accepted bribes; this corruption was a scandal.
7. Eric's father was mayor of the city, a position that gave Eric considerable social status.
8. When several of the newspapers disclosed the mayor's actions, the news caused a great decline in his prestige.
9. The city council member told the newspaper reporter that the reporter had manipulated the coverage of the election.
10. The early election returns, which had been widely predicted, pleased the senator.

Answers: Exercise 18

Answers will vary, but some suggestions are given below.

1. Sportscasters and we . . .
2. . . . sometimes changes its meaning . . .
3. . . . knows that an unreturned serve is called an ace.
4. The same word used in golf refers to a hole in one.
5. . . . batter's head that the batter is . . .
6. . . . determine its speed . . .
7. . . . and his pitching so well . . .
8. . . . my friends and me.
9. . . . more surprised than I . . .
10. . . . but it was she who . . .

Close

Have students write a paragraph about how they intend to apply what they have learned about clear and unambiguous pronoun references to writing they do for their other classes. Ask volunteers to read their paragraphs aloud. Discuss students' ideas.

Additional Resources

- *Grammar Practice,* p. 34
- *Grammar Reteaching,* p. 34
- *Grammar Enrichment,* p. 34

- *Grammar Workbook,* Lesson 56

Teach

About the Literature

Explain that the Grammar Review contains a passage from Ernest Hemingway's *The Old Man and the Sea,* followed by exercises on related topics. After students have read the literature, initiate a discussion about its characters, setting, and mood. Then ask students which words are, or are not, essential to the meaning of the passage.

Linking Grammar and Literature

☑ Teaching Tip

Ask students to focus on the highlighted pronouns in the passage. Have them determine whether a noun could be substituted for each highlighted pronoun. Discuss why Hemingway might have chosen to use a pronoun rather than a noun.

Critical Thinking

Ask students to identify some of the pronouns not highlighted in the literary passage, particularly personal and indefinite pronouns. Point out that Hemingway chose to use some pronouns for poetic effect: he used feminine pronouns to describe both the skiff and the ocean, and he described the forces of nature or supreme beings with the pronoun *they* in the sentence that begins "Why did they make birds so delicate . . . ?" Have students discuss how pronoun usage can be a matter of style as well as of grammar. Ask students to summarize their thoughts in their journal.

ASSESSMENT OPTIONS

Tests with Answer Key & Rubrics
Unit 17 Mastery Test, pp. 65–66

Testmaker
Unit 17 Mastery Test

UNIT 17 Grammar Review

Using Pronouns Correctly

In this passage from *The Old Man and the Sea,* an aging Cuban fisher named Santiago sets out for his day's work after eighty-four days without a catch. A young boy named Manolín has come to see him off. The passage has been annotated to show examples of the kinds of pronouns covered in this unit.

Literature Model

from The Old Man and the Sea

by Ernest Hemingway

The boy was back now with the sardines and the two baits wrapped in a newspaper and they went down the trail to the skiff, feeling the pebbled sand under their feet, and lifted the skiff and slid her into the water.

"Good luck old man."

"Good luck," the old man said. He fitted the rope lashings of the oars onto the thole pins and, leaning forward against the thrust of the blades in the water, he began to row out of the harbor in the dark. There were other boats from the other beaches going out to sea and the old man heard the dip and push of their oars even though he could not see them now the moon was below the hills.

Sometimes someone would speak in a boat. But most of the boats were silent except for the dip of the oars. They spread apart after they were out of the mouth of the harbor and each one headed for the part of the ocean where he hoped to find fish. The old man knew he was going far out and he left the smell of the land behind and rowed out into the clean early morning smell of the ocean. He saw the phosphorescence of the Gulf weed in the water as he rowed over the part of the ocean that the fishermen called the great well because there was a sudden deep of seven hundred fathoms where all sorts of fish congregated because of the swirl the current made

Pronoun in the possessive case

The pronoun *them* in the objective case is used as a direct object. The pronoun agrees in number with its antecedent, *boats.*

Pronoun in the nominative case used as a subject

The pronoun in the nominative case used as a subject agrees in gender and number with its antecedent, *the old man.*

Resource Manager

Planning Resources
- *Lesson Plans*

Other Print Resources
- *Grammar and Composition Handbook*
- *Grammar Workbook,* Lessons 8.52–8.58, Unit 8 Review, Cumulative Review: Units 1–8

against the steep walls of the floor of the ocean. Here there were concentrations of shrimp and bait fish and sometimes schools of squid in the deepest holes and these rose close to the surface at night where all the wandering fish fed on them.

In the dark the old man could feel the morning coming and as he rowed he heard the trembling sound as flying fish left the water and the hissing that their stiff set wings made as they soared away in the darkness. He was very fond of flying fish as they were his principal friends on the ocean. He was sorry for the birds, especially the small delicate dark terns that were always flying and looking and almost never finding, and he thought, the birds have a harder life than we do except for the robber birds and the heavy strong ones. Why did they make birds so delicate and fine as those sea swallows when the ocean can be so cruel? She is kind and very beautiful. But she can be so cruel and it comes so suddenly and such birds that fly, dipping and hunting, with their small sad voices are made too delicately for the sea.

He always thought of the sea as *la mar* which is what people call her in Spanish when they love her. Sometimes those who love her say bad things of her but they are always said as though she were a woman.

Pronoun in the objective case used as the object of a preposition

The pronoun *they* in the nominative case is used as a subject. The pronoun agrees with its antecedent, the irregular plural *fish.*

The pronoun *who* in the nominative case is used as the subject of *love.*

Review: Exercise 1 **Choosing Nominative and Objective Pronouns**

The following sentences give background information on the passage from *The Old Man and the Sea.* For each sentence, determine whether the italicized nominative or objective pronoun is used correctly. If it is not, on your paper write the pronoun as it should appear. If it is used properly, write *correct.*

1. The boy and Santiago had worked together for many years, but now Santiago and *him* would no longer be able to fish together.
2. The boy's parents had made it clear that *they* disapproved of his working with the unlucky old fisher.
3. It was *him* who had brought supper the previous night for the old man and himself to share.
4. Forgetting his parents, the boy had decided, "It is *us* who will eat supper together this evening."
5. Martin, the owner of a nearby restaurant, had kindly provided the supper for Santiago and *he.*

Practice and Assess

Answers: Exercise 1

1. he
2. correct
3. he
4. we
5. him

Practice and Assess

Answers: Exercise 2

1. he
2. his
3. correct
4. he
5. its
6. him
7. I
8. theirs
9. its
10. correct

Answers: Exercise 3

1. him
2. he
3. he
4. correct
5. them
6. correct
7. they
8. I
9. I
10. they

Grammar Review

Review: Exercise 2 Choosing the Correct Pronoun Case

The following sentences give background information on the passage from *The Old Man and the Sea.* Determine whether the italicized pronoun is used correctly. If it is not, write the correct pronoun on your paper. If it is used correctly, write *correct.*

1. Santiago stood by the boat with the other fishers as the fisher and *him* prepared to leave.
2. By *him* fitting the ropes onto the thole pins, the old man secured the boat's oars.
3. Other fishers were near, and Santiago could hear them rowing, although he could not see their boats or *them.*
4. It was *him* who would catch a fish so huge that it would astonish the other fishers.
5. The ocean suddenly became deep, and *it's* current made a deep swirl over the well in the ocean floor.
6. Santiago seemed to realize the ocean was beautiful, but the ocean was also cruel to wildlife and men like *he.*
7. The old man watched the terns and thought, "The gulls and terns have a harder life than *me.*"
8. He also pitied the sea swallows, and the sad voices he heard were *their's.*
9. Santiago landed a huge marlin, but *it's* size was a challenge.
10. After sharks bit the marlin's head, Santiago thought the fish was now *theirs* and his.

Review: Exercise 3 Using Pronouns Correctly with and as Appositives

The following sentences are based on passages from *The Old Man and the Sea* not reprinted in this textbook. For each sentence, determine whether the italicized pronoun appears in the proper form. If it does not, write the correct pronoun on your paper. If it is used properly, write *correct.*

1. The restaurant owner sometimes fed the two fishers, the boy and *he.*
2. The two early risers, Santiago and *him,* quietly left the hut and went to the boat.
3. Joe DiMaggio was a great athlete; apparently Santiago's idols were two baseball players, Dick Sisler and *him.*
4. While at sea, Santiago caught a dolphin with two fish in its stomach; such catches, *they* and a tuna, were his only food.
5. Santiago loved the terns and often watched two groups of birds, *they* and the swallows.
6. Santiago hooked a marlin that attracted sharks; he had to contend with two powerful species, the marlin and *them.*
7. The other fishers, the boy and *them,* felt sad at the sight of Santiago's poor marlin.
8. The boy might have decided, "Now we will again be partners, Santiago and *me.*"
9. He thought, "The villagers, the other fishers and *me,* have never seen such a fish."
10. Tourists showed interest in the fish, but no onlookers, not *them* or the fishers, could fully understand Santiago's experience.

Review: Exercise 4 Using Pronouns After *Than* and *As*

The following sentences are based on passages from *The Old Man and the Sea.* Each sentence contains an italicized word or group of words. On your paper, rewrite each sentence, substituting the correct pronoun for the word or words in italics.

1. Still, the other fishers caught more fish than *Santiago.*
2. They did not even go as far out as *the old man.*
3. The boy might have concluded, "Santiago is braver than *the other fishers.*"
4. Not caring as much for the other fishers as he did for Santiago, the boy helped Santiago more than *the others.*
5. The old man rowed as steadily as *the younger fishers.*
6. Later Santiago would seem to vow to the marlin, "You are not as strong as *Santiago.*"
7. Although the sea could be cruel to humans, Santiago reflected that it seemed more cruel to birds than to *his fellow human beings.*
8. The sea swallows searched as hard for food as *the terns.*
9. Watching the ocean's ceaseless waves, Santiago wondered whether anything was as cruel as *the ocean.*
10. Did he love anything else as much as *the ocean?*

Review: Exercise 5 Making Pronouns and Antecedents Agree

Each of the following sentences about terns contains an example of pronoun-antecedent agreement. On your paper, rewrite each sentence, replacing the word or words in italics with the word or words in parentheses and changing the pronouns if necessary. In some cases, you will also have to change the form of the verb and other words in the sentence.

1. *These sea birds* make tropical and semitropical islands their habitat. (This sea bird)
2. *The male tern* grooms the female's face as part of his courtship. (Male terns)
3. As *people* watch the terns, their wonder at the birds' behavior increases. (we)
4. Because *females* build no nest, their eggs may appear in odd, even unsuitable, places. (the female)
5. The *mother* often lays her egg on the edge of a roof or in the fork of a tree. (mothers)
6. *Both* of the parent birds take their turn tending the egg. (Each)
7. *Fairy tern eggs* hatch thirty-four days after they are laid. (A fairy tern egg)
8. *Many* of the parents leave their young untended for hours while they search for food. (Some)
9. *A flying fish* sometimes finds itself in the throat of a hungry tern. (Flying fish)
10. *Chicks* may fall while their parents are gone. (A chick)

Answers: Exercise 4

1. he
2. he
3. they
4. them
5. they
6. I
7. them
8. they
9. it (*or* she)
10. it (*or* her)

Answers: Exercise 5

1. This sea bird makes tropical and semitropical islands its habitat.
2. Male terns groom the females' faces as part of their courtship.
3. As we watch the terns, our wonder at the birds' behavior increases.
4. Because the female builds no nest, her eggs may appear in odd,even unsuitable, places.
5. The mothers often lay their eggs on the edge of a roof or in the fork of a tree.
6. Each of the parent birds takes its (*or* his or her) turn tending the eggs.
7. A fairy tern egg hatches thirty-four days after it is laid.
8. Some of the parents leave their young untended for hours while they search for food.
9. Flying fish sometimes find themselves in the throat of a hungry tern (*or* hungry terns).
10. A chick may fall while its (*or* his or her) parents are gone.

Practice and Assess

Answers: Exercise 6

1. who
2. Whom
3. whom
4. whom
5. whom
6. whom
7. who
8. Who
9. whom
10. whom
11. whom
12. Who
13. whom
14. whom
15. whom
16. whom
17. who
18. whom
19. who
20. whom

Review: Exercise 6 Choosing *Who* or *Whom*

On your paper, write the correct pronoun from the pair in parentheses.

1. When Columbus reached Cuba in 1492, he encountered the Taino, (who/whom) he discovered were farmers.
2. (Who/Whom) did the Spanish Crown appoint to conquer Cuba?
3. The mountains helped hide the natives, (who/whom) the Spanish treated harshly.
4. The Taino population, to (who/whom) European diseases proved deadly, became greatly reduced.
5. Enslaved Africans, (who/whom) the Spaniards wished to use for mining gold, were imported in 1524.
6. The enslaved people, (who/whom) the plantation owners bought, toiled long hours in sugarcane and coffee fields.
7. Hernán Cortés, (who/whom) we know conquered Mexico, used Cuba as a base for his expeditions.
8. (Who/Whom) did you say established Havana as an important port?
9. Ports like Havana offered recreation for sailors, (who/whom) the natives entertained with African drums and Spanish guitars.
10. At sea many dangers threatened these sailors, (who/whom) pirates attacked regularly for their ships' gold.
11. Tobacco growers, (who/whom) the Spanish government regulated, rebelled unsuccessfully as early as 1717.
12. (Who/Whom) did you say told you that the name *criollos* refers to people of Spanish descent?
13. In Haiti enslaved people, (who/whom) the American Revolution inspired, rebelled and set up a free republic.
14. Enslaved Cubans, (who/whom) the government freed in 1880, revolted several times between 1812 and 1840.
15. Chinese laborers, (who/whom) nervous landowners recruited, added a new ethnic group to the Cuban population.
16. Cubans, (who/whom) Indian, Spanish, African, and Chinese cultures have influenced, share a colorful heritage.
17. In 1895 revolutionary armies, (who/whom) were led by José Martí, demanded Cuba's independence from Spain.
18. American investors, for (who/whom) an independent Cuba would be profitable, rejoiced when America aided the revolutionaries.
19. Cuban independence in 1898 attracted the attention of American businesspeople, (who/whom) invested heavily in Cuba for nearly sixty years.
20. Nonetheless, peasant classes, to (who/whom) fishers like Santiago belonged, continued to live in poverty.

Review: Exercise 7 Making Pronouns and Antecedents Agree

The following sentences are about Hemingway's characters. Each sentence contains an example of pronoun-antecedent agreement. Rewrite the sentences according to the directions in parentheses, changing the pronouns if necessary. In some cases, you will also have to change the verb and other words.

SAMPLE Sports enthusiasts have compared their true experiences to Santiago's fictional one. (Change *Sports enthusiasts* to *A sports enthusiast.*)

ANSWER A sports enthusiast has compared his or her true experiences to Santiago's fictional one.

1. Cuban fishers have described their own struggles with a large fish. (Change *Cuban fishers* to *A Cuban fisher.*)
2. In these stories, a marlin has fought as long as fifteen hours before it was caught. (Change *a marlin* to *a few marlins.*)
3. Two of Hemingway's skippers have stated their ideas about the true identity of Santiago. (Change *Two* to *Each.*)
4. Are some of the real people who found their way into Hemingway's fiction famous? (Change *some* to *any.*)
5. In fact, readers find themselves drawn to Hemingway's characters because they seem so real. (Change *readers* to *we.*)
6. Have all of Hemingway's wives seen reflections of themselves in his female characters? (Change *all* to *each.*)
7. Any veteran of war might recognize his or her own feelings in Hemingway's soldiers. (Change *Any veteran* to *Veterans.*)
8. All people must fight personal obstacles to maintain their self-respect. (Change *All people* to *Everyone.*)
9. Hemingway characters show their valor amidst violence. (Change *Hemingway characters* to *A Hemingway character.*)
10. The stories, with their familiar conflicts, help us understand real life. (Change *The stories* to *Each story.*)
11. Does any character in the Nick Adams stories take his likes and dislikes from Hemingway's own personality? (Change *any character* to *the characters.*)
12. Did Hemingway's friends in Europe live their lives as desperately as the characters in *The Sun Also Rises*? (Change *friends* to *best friend.*)
13. Did someone like Catherine in *A Farewell to Arms* actually exert her influence on Hemingway's life? (Change *someone* to *women.*)
14. Consider the narrator in *For Whom the Bell Tolls*—does his experience reflect Hemingway's own experiences? (Change *narrator* to *characters.*)
15. It is clear that Hemingway created vivid characters because he wrote about people and situations he knew. (Change *Hemingway* to *both Hemingway and Fitzgerald.*)

Using Pronouns Correctly

Answers: Exercise 7

1. A Cuban fisher has described his or her own struggles with a large fish.
2. In these stories, a few marlins have fought as long as fifteen hours before they were caught.
3. Each of Hemingway's skippers has stated his or her ideas about the true identity of Santiago.
4. Are any of the real people who found their way into Hemingway's fiction famous?
5. In fact, we find ourselves drawn to Hemingway's characters because they seem so real.
6. Has each of Hemingway's wives seen reflections of herself in his female characters?
7. Veterans of war might recognize their own feelings in Hemingway's soldiers.
8. Everyone must fight personal obstacles to maintain his or her self-respect.
9. A Hemingway character shows his or her valor amidst violence.
10. Each story, with its familiar conflicts, helps us understand real life.
11. Do the characters in the Nick Adams stories take their likes and dislikes from Hemingway's own personality?
12. Did Hemingway's best friend in Europe live his or her life as desperately as the characters in *The Sun Also Rises*?
13. Did women like Catherine in *A Farewell to Arms* actually exert their influence on Hemingway's life?
14. Consider the characters in *For Whom the Bell Tolls*—do their experiences reflect Hemingway's own experiences?
15. It is clear that both Hemingway and Fitzgerald created vivid characters because they wrote about people and situations they knew.

Practice and Assess

Answers: Exercise 8

Answers may vary, but some suggestions are provided below.

1. Santiago's wife had died years ago, and her death must have been a source of almost unbearable pain.
2. Removing his wife's picture from the wall made Santiago sad.
3. The boy and the old fisher enjoyed spending time together, and the boy sometimes ignored his parents' objections.
4. One day while Santiago and the boy were talking, the old man spoke of his love of fishing.
5. Santiago finally got the huge marlin into his boat, but the fish had been severely damaged by sharks.

Answers: Exercise 9

Proofreading

This proofreading activity provides editing practice with (1) the current or previous units' skills, (2) the **Troubleshooter** errors, and (3) spelling errors. Students should be able to complete the exercise by referring to the units, the **Troubleshooter,** and a dictionary.

Error (Type of Error)

1. was (subject-verb agreement)
2. he, along with (subject pronoun)
3. country, (nonessential participial phrase)
4. his life (pronoun-antecedent agreement)
5. seventeen (spelling)
6. it was he (pronoun as predicate nominative)
   whom *Harper's Weekly* sent (object pronoun)
   drew (verb form)
7. enabled (verb tense)
8. saw them (pronoun-antecedent agreement)
9. began (verb form)
   they were (subject pronoun)
10. began (verb form)

Review: Exercise 8 Making Pronoun References Clear

The following sentences give background information on the passage from *The Old Man and the Sea.* Each sentence contains an unclear pronoun reference. On your paper, rewrite each sentence to make the pronoun reference clear. In some cases, you will need to reword the sentence or eliminate the pronoun.

1. Santiago's wife had died years ago, and that must have been a source of almost unbearable pain.
2. Santiago removed his wife's picture from the wall, which made him sad.
3. The boy and the old fisher enjoyed spending time together, and he sometimes ignored his parents' objections.
4. One day while Santiago and the boy were talking, he spoke of his love of fishing.
5. Santiago finally got the huge marlin into his boat, but it had been severely damaged by sharks.

Review: Exercise 9

Proofreading

The following passage describes the artist Winslow Homer, whose painting appears on the opposite page. Rewrite the passage, correcting the errors in spelling, grammar, and usage. Add any missing punctuation. There are twenty-five errors.

Winslow Homer

[1]Winslow Homer (1836–1910) were one of America's finest watercolorists. [2]Born in Boston, Massachusetts, him, along with his family, moved to the town of Cambridge when he was six. [3]Growing up with his two brothers in the country Homer learned to love the outdoors. [4]This interest in nature preoccupied him for much of their life.

[5]For the first seventen years of his long career, Homer supported himself by doing illustrations for periodicals, including *Ballou's Pictorial* and *Harper's Weekly.* [6]During the four years of the Civil War, it was him who *Harper's Weekly* sent to the front lines in Virginia, where he drawed many illustrations of battle scenes.

[7]Homer's training in illustration enables him to depict dramatic scenes naturally and unsentimentally. [8]His masterful draftsmanship allowed him to create a clear and honest record of landscapes and people as he saw it.

[9]After the war was over, Homer begun to exhibit his paintings, and them were very well received. [10]When he reached his late thirties, he begun making

Winslow Homer, *Palm Trees, Nassau,* 1898

watercolors directly from nature. [11]His' watercolors are forceful, direct, and saturated with pure color. [12]It was later in life that she began to paint large and powerful canvases of the sea. [13]No American painter is more closely associated with scenes of the sea than him.

[14]*Palm Trees, Nassau* is charateristic of Homers' late watercolors. [15]The casual observer may see an apparently simple nature scene, but looking closer, you can see the tension between the calm setting and the coming storm. [16]The trees bend in the rising wind, clouds scud acros the sky, and a red flag (possibly signaling an oncoming hurricane) flutters near the lighthouse.

[17]*The Old Man and the Sea* is about an old Cuban fisher whom is confronted with the great power of nature. [18]In the passage from the novel reprinted in this textbook, Hemingway hinting at the seas ominous power. [19]He write, "She is kind and very beautiful. But she can be so cruel. . . ." [20]Homers watercolor also evokes this insight.

Answers: Exercise 9 *(continued)*

Error (Type of Error)

11. His (possessive pronoun)
12. he began (pronoun-antecedent agreement)
13. than he (subject pronoun)
14. characteristic (spelling)
Homer's (singular possessive)
15. he or she can see *or* the observer can see (pronoun-antecedent agreement)
16. across (spelling)
17. who is confronted (subject pronoun)
18. hints *or* is hinting (verb tense)
sea's (singular possessive)
19. wrote (verb tense) *or* writes (subject-verb agreement)
20. Homer's (singular possessive)

Viewing the Art

Winslow Homer's *Palm Trees, Nassau,* 1898

Homer's watercolor is a good example of how an artist can use understatement to create a powerful impression. Ask students to discuss the feelings communicated in the painting and the elements of design that Homer used to create these feelings.

Point out, if necessary, that by contrasting the gentle scenery with subtle signs of the oncoming storm, Homer sets up a tension that gives life to his painting.

Practice and Assess

Answers: Exercise 10

Mixed Review

1. who
2. his
3. he
4. he
5. he
6. whom
7. he
8. him
9. their
10. Who
11. their
12. his or her
13. who
14. she
15. their
16. him
17. their
18. whom
19. his
20. its

Close

Each student can select a piece of writing in progress or completed recently. Pairs of students should then exchange papers and note any pronouns with unclear antecedents. When the reviewers return the papers, they should discuss and explain any needed revisions. Then students should revise their writing to eliminate antecedent problems.

Using Pronouns Correctly

Review: Exercise 10

Mixed Review

Each of the following sentences describes aspects of Hemingway's life and work. For each sentence, choose the proper pronoun from the pair in parentheses and write it on your paper.

Ernest Hemingway

1. Ernest Hemingway, (who/whom) we know was one of America's finest writers, was born in Oak Park, Illinois, in 1899.
2. Hemingway's numerous sports activities were balanced by (him/his) playing the cello and writing for his school newspaper.
3. His father was an outdoors enthusiast, and the two of them, (he/him) and Ernest, often took fishing trips to Michigan.
4. It was (he/him) who discouraged Hemingway from enlisting in the army when the United States entered World War I.
5. While driving an ambulance in the war, Hemingway received a wound that might have killed a man who was weaker than (he/him).
6. In Paris after the war, Hemingway met F. Scott Fitzgerald and Gertrude Stein, both of (who/whom) influenced him.
7. These young writers, Fitzgerald and (he/him), were part of what Stein called the Lost Generation.
8. A friendship also grew up between the writer Sherwood Anderson and (he/him).
9. The Lost Generation writers found the politics and morality of (its/their) society destroyed by war.
10. (Who/Whom) would you say is the most admirable character in *The Sun Also Rises,* Hemingway's first novel?
11. Several pieces of Hemingway's writing have found (its/their) way into movies.
12. Everybody has (his or her/their) favorite Hemingway novel.
13. Hemingway, (who/whom) many know was a journalist, wrote in a spare style.
14. He and his third wife bought a home in Cuba in 1940; the couple, Ernest and (she/her), entertained many celebrities.
15. Some of these celebrities remember adventures they had with Hemingway—for example, (their/them) watching bullfights in Spain and hunting in Africa.
16. This lifestyle appealed less to Hemingway's third wife than to (he/him), and the marriage ended.
17. His wartime experiences as an ambulance driver and as a news correspondent had (its/their) own profound effects on Hemingway's fiction.
18. Hemingway, (who/whom) Cuba fascinated, stayed in this tropical country even after Castro gained control in 1958.
19. *The Old Man and the Sea,* a best-seller in 1952, led to (his/him) winning the Pulitzer and Nobel prizes.
20. In the years following Hemingway's death in 1961, the novel has retained (its/it's) immense popularity.

Writing Application

Pronouns in Writing

In the following excerpt from *Great Expectations* by Charles Dickens, the narrator, Pip, is discussing two other characters, Mr. Jaggers and Mr. Pocket. Examine the passage closely, noting the many italicized masculine pronouns. Focus especially on how Dickens avoids unclear pronoun references.

My guardian took me into *his* room, and while *he* lunched, standing, from a sandwich-box and a pocket flask of sherry (*he* seemed to bully *his* very sandwich as *he* ate it), informed me what arrangements *he* had made for me. I was to go to "Barnard's Inn," to young Mr. Pocket's rooms, where a bed had been sent in for my accommodation; I was to remain with young Mr. Pocket until Monday; on Monday I was to go with *him* to *his* father's house on a visit, that I might try how I liked it.

Techniques with Pronouns

Try to apply some of Charles Dickens's writing techniques when you write and revise your own work.

TIME

For more about the writing process, see **TIME *Facing the Blank Page,*** pp. 121-131.

1. Avoid confusion by keeping pronoun references clear. Compare the following:

UNCLEAR REFERENCE I was to remain with *him* . . .

DICKENS'S VERSION I was to remain with *young Mr. Pocket* . . .

2. When you revise sentences containing many pronouns, make sure that each pronoun has a clear antecedent.

UNCLEAR REFERENCE I was to go to "Barnard's Inn," to *his* rooms . . .

DICKENS'S VERSION I was to go to Barnard's Inn, to young *Mr. Pocket's* rooms . . .

Using Pronouns Correctly

Practice Practice these techniques by revising the following passage, using a separate sheet of paper. Eliminate confusion by making the unclear pronoun references clear. Make sure each pronoun has a clear antecedent.

The young child sat cuddled on her grandmother's wide lap, as she rocked the old oak chair back and forth. She loved swaying with her. Wonderful scents wafted past her delicate little nose on the shifting breeze created by the rocking motion. She easily detected the pungent scent of garlic. Had she helped herself to a generous serving of her famous calzones? (Nobody could refuse her spicy creations, and especially not she, who succumbed easily to all cheesy, tomatoey foods.) Less obvious was the almost sterile scent of her heavily starched dress, which she was careful to iron each morning. Her grandmother had an awful impatience with anything less than perfection, a fact that the young girl on her lap knew only too well.

 **Writing** Online — For more grammar practice, go to glencoe.com and enter QuickPass code WC97727p2.

Pronouns in Writing

Direct students to read the passage twice—the first time to understand what it is saying and the second time to pay particular attention to Dickens's use of pronouns. Ask students to examine every pronoun and to decide what its antecedent is.

Techniques with Pronouns

Discuss the examples of clear and unclear referents, as well as clear and unclear antecedents. Be sure students understand both kinds of error. Call on volunteers to identify the antecedents of pronouns in the passage and to explain how they know what the antecedents are. Then have students reread part of the excerpt from *The Old Man and the Sea,* pp. 648–649, and to identify and discuss some pronoun-antecedent relationships and unclear antecedents in that passage.

Practice

The answers to this challenging and enriching activity will vary, but students should clarify the feminine pronouns as referring to the child or the grandmother by changing some of the words.

ASSESSMENT OPTIONS

Tests with Answer Key & Rubrics
Unit 17 Mastery Test, pp. 65–66

Testmaker
Unit 17 Mastery Test

You may wish to administer the Unit 17 Mastery Test at this point.

MindJogger Videoquizzes

INTRODUCING

UNIT 18

Objectives

- To learn how modifiers work, with an emphasis on the three degrees of comparison, irregular comparisons, and the use of *good, well, bad, and badly*
- To demonstrate control over modifiers by completing exercises and writing sentences that employ them effectively and avoid such problems as incomplete comparisons, double negatives, and dangling modifiers

ASSESSMENT OPTIONS

Tests with Answer Key & Rubrics
Unit 18 Pretest, pp. 67–68
Unit 18 Mastery Test, pp. 69–70

Testmaker
Unit 18 Pretest
Unit 18 Mastery Test

You may wish to administer the Unit 18 Pretest at this point.

Key to Ability Levels

L1 *Level 1 activities are within the basic ability range of students.*

L2 Level 2 activities are within the ability range of average students.

L3 Level 3 activities are more challenging activities.

UNIT 18

Using Modifiers Correctly

658

Resource Manager

Planning Resources
- *Lesson Plans*
- *Block Scheduling*

Transparencies
- *Bellringer*
- *Daily Language Practice*
- *Two-Minute Skill Drill*

Other Print Resources
- *Grammar and Composition Handbook*
- *Grammar Enrichment*
- *Grammar Practice*
- *Grammar Reteaching*
- *Grammar Workbook*
- *Tests with Answer Key and Rubrics*

Video
- *MindJogger Videoquizzes*

Software
- *Interactive Grammar and Language Workbook*
- *Presentation Plus!*
- *Revising with Style*
- *Testmaker*

Web Site
- *glencoe.com*

18.1 The Three Degrees of Comparison

Most adjectives and adverbs have three degrees: the positive, or base, form; the comparative form; and the superlative form.

- The **positive** form of a modifier cannot be used to make a comparison. (This form appears as the entry word in a dictionary.)
- The **comparative** form of a modifier shows two things being compared.
- The **superlative** form of a modifier shows three or more things being compared.

POSITIVE	My cousin is **tall.** The cat ran **swiftly.**
COMPARATIVE	My cousin is **taller** than I am. My dog ran **more swiftly** than the cat.
SUPERLATIVE	Of the three cousins, Paula is **tallest.** The rat ran **most swiftly** of all.

The following rules will guide you in forming the comparative and superlative degrees of adjectives and adverbs:

In general, for one-syllable modifiers add *-er* to form the comparative and *-est* to form the superlative.

green, green**er,** green**est**

The neighbor's grass always looks **greener** than ours.

loud, loud**er,** loud**est**

That sonic boom is the **loudest** noise I've ever heard.

fast, fast**er,** fast**est**

Her hair grows **faster** than mine.

In some cases adding *-er* and *-est* requires spelling changes.

big, bi**gger**, bi**ggest** — true, tru**er,** tru**est**

hot, ho**tter,** ho**ttest** — dry, dr**ier**, dr**iest**

With some one-syllable modifiers, it may sound more natural to use *more* and *most.*

just, **more** just, **most** just

Of the three, that judge's ruling was the **most just** of all.

She ran **swiftly.**

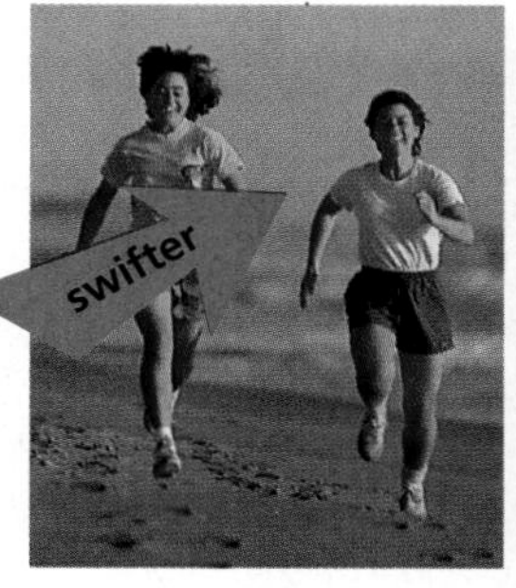

She ran **more swiftly.**

She ran **most swiftly** of all.

Using Modifiers Correctly

UNIT 18

Focus

Lesson Overview

Objective

- To identify the positive, comparative, and superlative forms of adjectives and adverbs

Bellringer
Daily Language Activity

When students enter the classroom, have this assignment on the board: *Look at the sentence below. Write two more sentences, each using a different form of the underlined word to show degrees of comparison.*

He wrote a short essay.

See also *Daily Language Practice*

Motivating Activity

Invite volunteers to share their sentences from the Bellringer. Encourage students to provide effective feedback and to ask questions for clarification. If necessary, identify the three modifiers: *short, shorter,* and *shortest.* Point out that *short* is an adjective that modifies the word *essay.* Lead students to understand that such modifiers are useful in descriptive writing, especially when comparing or contrasting.

Teach

Cross-reference: Grammar

For instruction and practice in the use of adjectives and adverbs, refer students to Lessons 10.4 and 10.5, pp. 461–472.

Resource Manager

Planning Resources
- *Lesson Plans*

Transparencies
- *Bellringer*
- *Daily Language Practice*

Other Print Resources
- *Grammar and Composition Handbook*
- *Grammar Enrichment,* p. 35
- *Grammar Practice,* p. 35
- *Grammar Workbook,* Lesson 59

Practice and Assess

Answers: Exercise 1

1. talented (positive); more softly (comparative)
2. slow (positive); sweetest (superlative)
3. sadder (comparative); more mellow (comparative)
4. most clearly (superlative); less strident (comparative)
5. most emotional (superlative); least fortunate (superlative)

Additional Resources

Grammar Practice, p. 35
Grammar Enrichment, p. 35

Grammar Workbook, Lesson 59

Close

Have students write several sentences describing the three degrees of comparison. Tell them to include and identify the positive, the comparative, and the superlative forms of an adjective or adverb in their sentences. If students need help, write one or more of the following on the board:

- This is a *good* modifier, although it cannot be used to make a comparison. (positive)
- This modifier is *better* than the first because it can show two things being compared. (comparative)
- This modifier is the *best* of the three because it shows three or more things being compared. (superlative)

Discuss students' sentences and have them record the best ones in their journal for future reference.

For most two-syllable adjectives, add *-er* to form the comparative and *-est* to form the superlative.

ugly, ugl**ier,** ugl**iest**
Your mask is **uglier** than mine.
That is the **ugliest** mask I've ever seen.

If *-er* and *-est* sound awkward with a two-syllable adjective, use *more* and *most.*

afraid, **more** afraid, **most** afraid
No one is **more afraid** of spiders than I am.
Of all of us, I was the **most afraid.**

For adverbs ending in *-ly,* always use *more* and *most* to form the comparative and superlative degrees.

clearly, **more** clearly, **most** clearly
Lewis gives directions **more clearly** than most people.
This candidate explains his views **most clearly** of all.

For modifiers of three or more syllables, always use *more* and *most* to form the comparative and superlative degrees.

attractive, **more** attractive, **most** attractive
I think red looks **more attractive** on you than on me.
That watercolor is the **most attractive** one in the exhibit.

Less and *least,* the opposite of *more* and *most,* can also be used with most modifiers to show comparison.

Are prepared foods **less economical** than fresh foods?
I think cabbage is the **least appetizing** of all vegetables.

Exercise 1 Identifying Comparisons

In the following sentences, identify the adjectives and adverbs, and write them on a separate sheet of paper. Then write *positive, comparative,* or *superlative* to indicate the degree of comparison.

The Blues

1. A talented blues band can play more softly than a hard-rock band.
2. The slow blues, to my way of thinking, sound the sweetest of all.
3. The sadder the lyrics, the more mellow the melody becomes.
4. The vocalist tells the tale of woe most clearly when the trumpet's tone becomes less strident.
5. Then the most emotional mood is created out of songs that describe the least fortunate circumstances.

Meeting Individual Needs: English Language Learners

Using *-er* and *-est*

Write some modifiers (for example, *tall, brown, slow, small, cold*) on index cards. Also write *-er* and *-est* on cards. Have students who are learning English combine words and endings. Then help students use the words in sentences. Make sure students use the comparative and superlative form of each modifier. Students might work in groups with fluent speakers of English to think of other regularly formed modifiers and write the comparative and superlative form of each.

18.2 Irregular Comparisons

A few modifiers form their comparative and superlative degrees irregularly. It is most helpful simply to memorize their forms.

Modifiers with Irregular Forms of Comparison		
POSITIVE	COMPARATIVE	SUPERLATIVE
good	better	(the) best
well	better	(the) best
bad	worse	(the) worst
badly	worse	(the) worst
ill	worse	(the) worst
far (distance)	farther	(the) farthest
far (degree, time)	further	(the) furthest
little (amount)	less	(the) least
many	more	(the) most
much	more	(the) most

Exercise 2 Making Correct Comparisons

On another sheet of paper, complete the following sentences by writing the correct degree of comparison of the modifier in parentheses.

SAMPLE Which vegetable tastes the ____________ of all? (good)
ANSWER best

Space and Space Exploration

1. Are there _____ planets in our solar system than the nine we know about? (many)
2. The distance between Venus and Earth is _____ than that between Mars and Earth. (little)
3. Pluto has the _____ mass of all the planets. (little)
4. The _____ planet from the sun is Pluto. (far)
5. *Voyager I* did a _____ job of photographing Jupiter than its predecessor. (good)
6. One of the _____ space catastrophes ever was the destruction of the *Challenger* spacecraft in 1986. (bad)
7. Of all the descriptions of the motion of the planets, that of the seventeenth-century astronomer Johannes Kepler is the _____. (good)
8. There are _____ celestial bodies in the Milky Way than just our solar system. (many)
9. Some asteroids have diameters of _____ than 120 miles. (much)
10. A comet, with its bright head and glowing tail, is one of the _____ astronomical sights you will ever see. (good)

Using Modifiers Correctly

Focus

Lesson Overview

Objectives

- To identify irregular forms of comparison
- To use these comparisons appropriately in writing

Bellringer
Daily Language Activity

When students enter the classroom, have this assignment on the board: *Write three sentences using the words* good, well, *and* bad.

See also *Daily Language Practice*

Motivating Activity

Point out that irregular modifiers usually do not sound right with the suffixes *-er* and *-est.* Say aloud the words *good, well,* and *bad* with incorrect regular suffixes; then use the correct irregular forms of comparison. Discuss students' sentences. Encourage students to provide effective feedback and to ask questions to clarify their understanding.

Teach

☑ Grammar Tip

Tell students that the best way to memorize the correct irregular forms of comparison is to use them in their writing. For example, explain that *worse* and (*the*) *worst* are the comparative and superlative forms of the adjectives *bad* and *ill* and the adverb *badly.*

Practice and Assess

Answers: Exercise 2

1. more
2. less
3. least
4. farthest
5. better
6. worst
7. best
8. more
9. more
10. best

Resource Manager

Planning Resources
- *Lesson Plans*

Transparencies
- *Bellringer*
- *Daily Language Practice*
- *Two-Minute Skill Drill*

Other Print Resources
- *Grammar and Composition Handbook*
- *Grammar Enrichment,* p. 35
- *Grammar Practice,* p. 35
- *Grammar Workbook,* Lesson 60

18.2

Teach

Two-Minute Skill Drill

Have students write sentences using adjectives that do not have comparative or superlative forms, such as *annual* or *seasonal.*

See also *Two-Minute Skill Drill Transparency 18.2*

Practice and Assess

Answers: Exercise 3

1. easier
2. liveliest
3. longer
4. more famous
5. most frequent
6. less
7. more complicated
8. more
9. most challenging
10. more quickly
11. older
12. happier
13. most content
14. farther
15. worst
16. best
17. more remote
18. further
19. more popular
20. farthest

Additional Resources

Grammar Practice, p. 35

Grammar Enrichment, p. 35

Grammar Workbook, Lesson 60

Close

Have students write a paragraph using irregular comparisons. Ask them to use words from the chart on page 661. Have students check each other's work and provide effective feedback.

Using Modifiers Correctly

Exercise 3 Making Correct Comparisons

On another sheet of paper, complete the following sentences by writing the correct degree of comparison of the modifier in parentheses.

SAMPLE *The Joy Luck Club* is one of the ___________ novels I have ever read. (interesting)

ANSWER most interesting

1. *The Joy Luck Club* is an entertaining book, and it is ___________ to read than many other contemporary novels. (easy)
2. The novel is by Amy Tan, perhaps the ___________ voice in contemporary Asian American fiction. (lively)
3. *The Joy Luck Club* is a ___________ book than some that have recently been on the best-seller list. (long)
4. Maxine Wong is another talented Asian American writer, although Amy Tan is ___________ than Wong. (famous)
5. In the book the members of the Joy Luck Club do many things, but their ___________ activity is playing mah-jongg. (frequent)
6. Though she is ___________ experienced than the other club members, June Woo is asked to join the mah-jongg game. (little)
7. Though mah-jongg resembles rummy, it is ___________. (complicated)
8. In my opinion it relies ___________ on strategy than rummy does. (much)
9. Most people believe, however, that chess is still the ___________of all board games. (challenging)
10. Even so, one can play chess ___________ than mah-jongg. (quickly)
11. The club members, who are June's unofficial aunts, are ___________ than June and observe traditional Chinese customs. (old)
12. At first June is ___________ to be with friends her own age than she is to be playing games with her aging aunts. (happy)
13. The aunts are the ___________ of all when they are reminiscing about their years in China. (content)
14. China seems even ___________ away for June than it does for her aunts, for whom China is a distant memory. (far)
15. Eventually, though, June learns that the ___________ decision of all would be to abandon her Chinese heritage completely. (bad)
16. From all the aspects of her Chinese heritage, it seems that June learns to accept only the ___________. (good)
17. The ethnic roots of many Americans are ___________ than June's. (remote)
18. Many of us would have to go much ___________ back in time to recapture information about our ancestors. (far)
19. Researching, tracing, and studying one's genealogy has become a ___________ pursuit than it once was. (popular)
20. There are some people who will travel to the ___________ corners of the earth to trace their family histories. (far)

MEETING INDIVIDUAL NEEDS

Learning Disabled

Using *Much* and *Many*

Some students may have difficulty with *much* and *many,* because both words have the same comparative and superlative forms: *more* and (*the*) *most. Much,* however, is used with noncount nouns, while *many* is used with count nouns. Have students compare the following:

- Do you have much money? (*Money* is a noncount noun.)
- Do you have many bills? (*Bills* is a count noun.)

Explain that a noncount noun always remains singular. A count noun becomes plural when there are more. **L1**

18.3 Double Comparisons

Do not make a double comparison by using both *-er* or *-est* and more or most.

INCORRECT	A redwood grows more taller than an oak.
CORRECT	A redwood grows taller than an oak.
INCORRECT	Aunt Rosa is my most kindest aunt.
CORRECT	Aunt Rosa is my kindest aunt.
INCORRECT	He will visit us more oftener in the fall.
CORRECT	He will visit us more often in the fall.

Exercise 4 Correcting Double Comparisons

Rewrite each of the following sentences, correcting the double comparison.

Thomas Edison, Inventor

1. Many people believe that Thomas Alva Edison was the world's most best inventor.
2. Some people consider him even more greater than Leonardo da Vinci.
3. The phonograph and the electric light are probably Edison's most usefulest creations.
4. Edison was most happiest with his phonograph.
5. He was most proudest of his work on the electric light.
6. Electric light is certainly more safer than candlelight.
7. Edison also took others' inventions, such as the telephone and the typewriter, and made them more better.
8. As a boy, Edison was more curiouser than other children.
9. He worked more harder and longer than his peers.
10. Historians agree that Edison was one of the most fruitfulest inventors of modern times.
11. After electric lights were invented, nights seemed more brighter.
12. People could read or do chores more longer after dark.
13. Before the phonograph was invented, hearing great music was more difficulter.
14. The phonograph and the electric light, though expensive at first, became more cheaper as time went by.
15. Edison was blessed with a more quicker mind than most boys his age.
16. After only a few months of formal schooling, he entered the more wider world of work.
17. An illness caused him to become more harder of hearing than he had been before.
18. One of his most earliest inventions was a stock ticker for printing stock-exchange quotations.
19. A more later invention, the movie projector, aided the development of motion pictures.
20. During his lifetime, Edison patented over 1,000 inventions, the most greatest number ever recorded for one person.

Resource Manager

Planning Resources
- *Lesson Plans*

Transparencies
- *Bellringer*
- *Daily Language Practice*

Other Print Resources
- *Grammar and Composition Handbook*
- *Grammar Enrichment,* p. 36
- *Grammar Workbook,* Lesson 61

Focus

Lesson Overview

Objective
- To avoid using double comparisons

Bellringer
Daily Language Activity

When students enter the classroom, have this assignment on the board: *Copy any incorrect sentences and write your explanation of each error.*

That building is the tallest one.
That building is the most tall.
That building is the most tallest.
That building is the tallest of all.

Discuss students' explanations. Encourage students to provide effective feedback and to ask questions for clarification.

See also  *Daily Language Practice*

Teach

Teaching Tip
Often a word or phrase can be substituted to repair a double comparison. For example, the final sentence in the Bellringer activity corrects the one before it.

Practice and Assess

Answers: Exercise 4

1. world's best inventor
2. even greater
3. most useful creations
4. was happiest
5. was proudest
6. certainly safer
7. them better
8. more curious
9. worked harder and longer
10. most fruitful
11. seemed brighter
12. chores longer
13. more difficult
14. became cheaper
15. a quicker
16. the wider
17. more hard-of-hearing
18. his earliest
19. A later
20. the greatest

18.3

Practice and Assess

Answers: Exercise 5

1. the best experience
2. weighed less
3. most cheerful
4. health was worse
5. worst days
6. more upset
7. The worse he felt
8. go far back
9. to be the best
10. more frequent
11. farther from home
12. better part of the morning
13. less adventurous spirit
14. More (*or* Much) peace
15. The happiest day

Answers: Exercise 6

1. More
2. spicier
3. spiciest
4. most elegant
5. richer
6. less healthy
7. more heavily
8. most popular
9. less common
10. best

Additional Resources

Grammar Enrichment, p. 36

Grammar Workbook, Lesson 61

Close

Encourage students to discuss how using comparisons correctly can help them improve their writing. Then have them write a paragraph comparing several family members. Have students trade paragraphs and check all the comparative and superlative adjectives and adverbs for double comparisons.

Exercise 5 Correcting Irregular and Double Comparisons

Rewrite each of the following sentences, correcting the comparisons.

Twins

1. Mother says that raising twins has been the goodest experience of her life.
2. When they were born, Laura weighed littler than Lonnie, but she soon caught up.
3. All of us children had sunny dispositions, but Lonnie's was the most cheerfulest.
4. Lonnie was always serene, even though his health was worser than it should have been.
5. When he got sick, Mother used to go through some of the baddest days of her life.
6. The higher his temperature rose, the more upsetter she became.
7. The worser he felt, the more time she devoted to him.
8. "Sometimes," she told us, "I would like to go farrer back in history to an era when people had more time to spend with their children."
9. Being the oldest, I tried to be the most good, but I made a lot of mistakes.
10. I could have found more frequenter opportunities to lend a hand.
11. As toddlers, the twins tried to see which one could wander more farther from home.
12. Mother or the baby-sitter would chase them for the gooder part of the morning.
13. We would have appreciated a lesser adventurouser spirit on the twins' part.
14. Mucher peace and quiet was what we wanted.
15. The most happiest day of our lives was the twins' first day of school.

Exercise 6 Writing Correct Comparisons

On your paper, complete the following sentences by writing the correct degree of comparison of the modifier in parentheses. In two sentences you will use *less* or *least.*

Ethnic Cuisine

1. (Many) Americans than ever before are enjoying the pleasures of ethnic cuisine.
2. Mexican dishes are usually (spicy) than those prepared north of the border.
3. Mexican chilies run the gamut in flavor and appearance, but the habañero is the (spicy) one of all.
4. French food, with its emphasis on sauces and careful methods of preparation, is for some people the (elegant) of all the world's cuisines.
5. French recipes often call for (rich) ingredients, such as real butter and whole cream, than do American recipes.
6. Strangely enough, in spite of their eating habits, the French appear to be no (healthy) than Americans.
7. Mediterranean cultures—Italian, Spanish, Greek, Turkish, Moroccan—rely (heavily) on foods low in cholesterol than do other cuisines.
8. For many years Chinese food was the (popular) ethnic cuisine in our town, but now Mexican and Tex-Mex foods have more fans.
9. Chinese delicacies such as dim sum and Peking duck are (common) taste treats than the more ordinary chop suey and chow mein.
10. A quick look at the restaurant listings in the yellow pages will convince you that the (good) words to describe America's food preferences are ethnic and diverse.

Meeting Individual Needs: Learning Disabled

Avoiding Double Comparisons

Although superlative adjectives and adverbs cannot be modified by *most,* they can be modified by the adverb phrase *of all.* Rather than *Aunt Rosa is the most kindest aunt,* have students say *Aunt Rosa is the kindest aunt of all.* Encourage students to practice until they are successful at avoiding double comparisons. **L1**

18.4 Incomplete Comparisons

Do not make an incomplete or unclear comparison by omitting *other* or *else* when you compare a person or thing with the group of which it is a part.

UNCLEAR Mercury is closer to the sun than any planet in our solar system. [*Any planet* includes Mercury.]

CLEAR Mercury is closer to the sun than any **other** planet in our solar system.

UNCLEAR My aunt has more pets than anyone. [*Anyone* includes the aunt.]

CLEAR My aunt has more pets than anyone **else.**

Be sure your comparisons are between like things.

UNCLEAR The grace of a basketball player is more obvious than a baseball player. [The grace of a basketball player is being compared illogically with everything about a baseball player.]

CLEAR The grace of a basketball player is more obvious than **that of a baseball player.**

CLEAR The grace of a basketball player is more obvious **than a baseball player's.**

UNCLEAR The claws of a lion are sharper than a cat. [The claws of a lion are being compared illogically with everything about a cat.]

CLEAR The claws of a lion are sharper than **those of a cat.**

CLEAR The claws of a lion are sharper than **a cat's.**

Using Modifiers Correctly

Exercise 7 **Making Complete Comparisons**

Rewrite the following sentences to correct the incomplete comparison in each.

Historical Native American Dwellings

[1]Native American homes of the past were just as varied as today. [2]The buffalo-skin dwellings of the Plains groups were more portable than the Wichita. [3]The design of the tepees of the Plains peoples was perhaps more ingenious than any design. [4]Women were responsible for erecting the tepees, and they could do this faster than anyone. [5]Many people think that the tepee was more beautiful than any Native American dwelling. [6]The lodges of the Pawnees were warmer and sturdier than the Plains groups. [7]Because the Pawnees did not move frequently, their homes were less portable than Native American dwellings. [8]The Pueblo groups of New Mexico were probably cooler than anyone, for they lived in well-insulated buildings made of adobe. [9]Some Pueblo dwellings were several stories high, like many city dwellers today. [10]If I could, I would rather live in a tepee than any place.

Resource Manager

Planning Resources
- *Lesson Plans*

Transparencies
- *Bellringer*
- *Daily Language Practice*

Other Print Resources
- *Grammar and Composition Handbook*
- *Grammar Enrichment,* p. 36
- *Grammar Practice,* p. 36
- *Grammar Workbook,* Lesson 61

Focus

Lesson Overview

Objective
- To avoid using incomplete and unclear comparisons in writing

Bellringer
Daily Language Activity

When students enter the classroom, have this assignment on the board: *What is wrong with the following sentences? Bill has more CDs than anyone. The ears of a ferret are smaller than a cat.*

See also  *Daily Language Practice*

Teach

Teaching Tip

Have students expand the second part of a comparison to show what is being compared. For example, *The claws of a lion are sharper* can be expanded to *The claws of a lion are sharper than the claws of a housecat.*

Practice and Assess

Answers: Exercise 7

Answers will vary, but some suggestions are given below.

1. varied as homes today
2. than those of the Wichita
3. than any other design
4. faster than anyone else
5. more beautiful than any other Native
6. than those of the Plains groups
7. than other Native
8. cooler than anyone else's
9. like many city dwellers' homes today
10. than any other place

Close

Have students apply what they have learned about incomplete comparisons by writing paragraphs comparing dogs and cats. Ask students to check each other's paragraphs and to provide effective feedback.

Focus

Lesson Overview

Objective

- To use *good, well, bad,* and *badly* appropriately

Bellringer
Daily Language Activity

When students enter the classroom, have this assignment on the board: *Write four sentences using* good, well, bad, *and* badly.

See also *Daily Language Practice*

Motivating Activity

Ask students to hand in their sentences anonymously. Write several of the sentences on the board and discuss each one. How did students decide whether to use *well* or *good? bad or badly?* Have students ask questions to clarify their understanding.

Teach

Teaching Tip

Ask students to identify the difference between these sentences: (a) *Sam is good;* (b) *Sam is well.* (Sentence (*a*) describes Sam's behavior; sentence (*b*) describes how Sam feels.) Have students make note of these differences and example sentences in their journal.

18.5 *Good* or *Well; Bad* or *Badly*

Always use *good* as an adjective. *Well* may be used as an adverb of manner telling how ably or adequately something is done. *Well* also may be used as an adjective meaning "in good health."

Blue is a **good** color for you. [adjective]
You look **good** in blue. [adjective after a linking verb]

You dress **well.** [adverb of manner]
Aren't you feeling **well?** [adjective meaning "in good health"]

Always use *bad* as an adjective. Therefore, *bad* is used after a linking verb. Use *badly* as an adverb. *Badly* almost always follows an action verb.

That was a **bad** idea. [adjective]
The milk tasted **bad.** [adjective following a linking verb]

I feel **bad** about your moving to another state. [adjective following a linking verb]
The faucet is leaking **badly.** [adverb following an action verb]

Exercise 8 Correcting Errors with *Good, Well, Bad,* and *Badly*

If a sentence contains an error with *good, well, bad,* or *badly,* on your paper write the form that should have been used. If a sentence is correct, write *correct.*

SAMPLE Marisa did bad on her algebra test.
ANSWER badly

1. "You'll do good on your tests if you will just remember to study," my mother always tells me.
2. "That's easy for you to say," I always answer. "You were always a good student."
3. I don't feel good enough to study because of this headache.
4. My mother feels badly that I am ill.
5. "Would a little chicken soup taste good to you today?" she inquires kindly.
6. "I'll eat whatever you think will make me well," I respond.
7. "But, really, my head hurts so bad that I don't know that soup will help much," I continue.
8. "I know, but your grandmother always believed that eating good could cure anything," Mom says.
9. "Let's give it a try, then. Maybe it will help me study well for the test, too," I say.
10. "That soup smells so well that I'm starting to feel cured already."

Resource Manager

Planning Resources
- *Lesson Plans*

Transparencies
- *Bellringer*
- *Daily Language Practice*

Other Print Resources
- *Grammar and Composition Handbook*
- *Grammar Enrichment,* p. 36
- *Grammar Workbook,* Lesson 62

Exercise 9 **Using *Good, Bad, Well,* and *Badly***

On your paper complete the following sentences by writing *good, well, bad,* or *badly*.

Taking a Hike

1. No one can hike ____________ without comfortable hiking shoes.
2. Improper equipment can make a hiker or camper feel ____________ .
3. ____________ planning is absolutely essential for a long and difficult hike.
4. A hike that is planned ____________ will not be enjoyable and may be unpleasant.
5. Locating a ____________ trail is one important aspect of planning a hike.
6. A hiker who is not feeling ____________ can become a serious problem on the trail.
7. Hikers feel ____________ if they cannot keep up with their companions.
8. If a hike begins ____________, the hikers may become discouraged and decide to turn back.
9. The views along the Appalachian Trail look as ____________ as the views that one sees in the Rocky Mountains.
10. Hikers should know their capabilities ____________ before they start off on an ambitious hike.
11. I recently took an energetic walk with my friend Arnold, who could not hike _____.
12. Arnold tripped and hurt himself _____ after we had hiked only about a mile and a half.
13. Arnold said that his new hiking boots felt _____, but I thought they looked quite loose on his feet.
14. It also appeared that the soles were too thin to support his weight _____.
15. I felt _____ that he had hurt himself because I had really wanted our hike to go _____.
16. Arnold had been feeling _____ about his girlfriend, but then she suddenly broke up with him.
17. Needless to say, his confidence was _____ shaken.
18. He needed a _____ friend to spend time with him and make him forget his problems.
19. Ever since we were young children, we have gotten along with each other very _____.
20. I will be very disappointed if this misadventure hurts our friendship _____.

Exercise 10 **Writing Paragraphs with Modifiers**

Write two paragraphs, using each of the phrases below. You can use the phrases for each paragraph in any order.

SAMPLE danced badly
SAMPLE SENTENCE Ellie danced badly at her first audition.

Paragraph 1

1. feel well
2. stumbled badly
3. than any other basketball player
4. than those of Patrick Ewing
5. played well

Paragraph 2

6. feel good
7. drove well
8. than any other student
9. failed her driving test badly
10. looked bad

Using Modifiers Correctly

Practice and Assess

Answers: Exercise 8

1. well
2. (correct)
3. (correct)/well
4. bad
5. (correct)
6. (correct)
7. badly
8. well
9. (correct)
10. good

Answers: Exercise 9

1. well
2. bad
3. Good
4. badly
5. good
6. well/good
7. bad
8. badly
9. good
10. well
11. well
12. badly
13. good
14. well
15. bad; well
16. good
17. badly
18. good
19. well
20. badly

Answers: Exercise 10

Answers will vary, but some suggestions are given below.

Maria skipped basketball practice because she did not *feel well* after lunch. On her way home from school, she *stumbled badly* and bruised her knee. In spite of her health, she *played well* in the championship game.

Additional Resources

 *Grammar Enrichment,* p. 36

Grammar Workbook, Lesson 62

Close

Encourage students to create and share mnemonics for remembering the appropriate use of *good, well, bad,* and *badly*. Have students record the best mnemonics in their journal.

Enrichment and Extension

Using Mnemonics

Here is a sentence that students can memorize to help them remember that *good* is an adjective used with linking verbs and *well* is an adverb used with action verbs: *The car is good because it runs well.* **L2**

Focus

Lesson Overview

Objectives
- To identify double negatives
- To learn how to correct them

Bellringer
Daily Language Activity

When students enter the classroom, have this assignment on the board: *Write each of these sentences correctly:*

I can't hardly see the stage.

We don't have no eggs.

They never go nowhere.

Discuss students' corrections. Encourage classmates to provide effective feedback and to ask questions to clarify understanding.

See also *Daily Language Practice*

Teach

Teaching Tip

Tell students who use double negatives to mark each negative word in a sentence with a minus sign. A sentence is nonstandard if it has more than one minus sign in any one clause.

Practice and Assess

Answers: Exercise 11

1. wasn't no
2. didn't want no
3. hadn't never
4. (correct)
5. didn't want nobody
6. never said nothing
7. didn't seem to have no
8. never gets no
9. hardly never
10. (correct)

Using Modifiers Correctly

18.6 Double Negatives

In general, do not use a **double negative,** two negative words in the same clause. Use only one negative word to express a negative idea.

INCORRECT	I don't have no stereo equipment.
CORRECT	I do**n't** have **any** stereo equipment.
CORRECT	I have **no** stereo equipment.
INCORRECT	We haven't seen no concerts this year.
CORRECT	We have**n't** seen **any** concerts this year.
CORRECT	We have seen **no** concerts this year.
INCORRECT	My parrot never says nothing.
CORRECT	My parrot **never** says **anything.**
CORRECT	My parrot says **nothing.**

The words *hardly* and *scarcely* are also negatives. Do not use them with other negative words such as *not.*

INCORRECT	I haven't hardly finished.	He can't scarcely never be on time.
CORRECT	I have **hardly** finished.	He can **scarcely** ever be on time.

Exercise 11 Identifying Double Negatives

On your paper write each double negative in the following sentences. If a sentence is correct, write *correct.*

Working Out

1. I used to think there wasn't no reason for me to exercise.
2. I didn't want no new activity to distract me from my other interests.
3. I hadn't never explored the possibility of joining an aerobics class.
4. Eventually, my friend Ramón convinced me that my negative attitude was neither sensible nor smart.
5. I signed up for an aerobics class at the "Y," but at first I didn't want nobody to watch me make mistakes.
6. The other students never said nothing about my clumsy moves.
7. They didn't seem to have no interest in anything but stepping, jogging, and dancing to the high-energy music.
8. Soon I realized that exercising never gets no harder; it just gets easier.
9. Now I hardly never miss a session.
10. Not even bad weather can keep me from working out.

Resource Manager

Planning Resources
- *Lesson Plans*

Transparencies
- *Bellringer*
- *Daily Language Practice*

Other Print Resources
- *Grammar and Composition Handbook*
- *Grammar Reteaching,* p. 36
- *Grammar Workbook,* Lesson 63

Exercise 12 Correcting Double Negatives

On your paper rewrite the following sentences, eliminating the double negative in each. (Most sentences can be corrected in more than one way.) If a sentence is correct, write *correct.*

Camping

1. When our family goes camping, we like to find a site where there isn't no one around.
2. Don't never pitch your tent on sloping ground, for you will be very uncomfortable.
3. Nobody should never forget to dig a trench around the tent, in case it rains during the night.
4. Can't none of them help us pitch our tent?
5. It's best never to leave no food in your tent, for animals may be attracted to it.
6. One time my sister and I discovered a raccoon in our tent, and after that we didn't leave nothing edible inside.
7. In some wilderness areas, campers aren't allowed to build no fires, and they must cook all their meals on a portable stove.
8. Some campers bring canned food along, but we don't bring none because it is too heavy to carry.
9. My parents always pack dried food because it is light and doesn't never spoil.
10. When it is time to break camp, no one should leave no trash on the ground, and all fires should be put out.
11. Our most memorable camping trip was one I don't never want to repeat.
12. One summer we decided to go to Crater Lake in southern Oregon because we hadn't never been to that site in the Cascade Range.
13. There isn't no more beautiful place in all the world.
14. The lake hasn't no inlet or outlet.
15. Nobody can't see it without being amazed by its sapphire-blue color.
16. However, we didn't have no idea about the area's changeable summer weather when we pitched our tent.
17. We hadn't no sooner gone to bed than it began to rain.
18. We didn't get hardly any sleep as the rain poured down, the wind blew, and the temperature dropped.
19. In the morning when we opened our tent flap, we realized we hadn't had no other camping experience like this before.
20. The rain had turned to snow, leaving not a patch of green grass or a brown tree trunk anywhere to be seen.
21. We had never seen nothing like it before in our lives.
22. We wanted something hot to drink, but we couldn't start no fire.
23. There wasn't scarcely any dry firewood around.
24. We decided that we didn't want to spend no more time there, even though the lake looked beautiful surrounded by the snow-covered trees.
25. We just hadn't no idea that it could snow in the Cascades in the middle of summer.

Answers: Exercise 12

Answers may vary, but some suggestions are given below.

1. When our family goes camping, we like to find a site where there is no one around.
2. Don't ever pitch your tent on sloping . . .
3. Nobody should ever forget to dig . . .
4. Can't any of them help us . . .
5. It's best never to leave any food in your . . .
6. One time my sister and I discovered a raccoon in our tent, and after that we didn't leave anything edible inside.
7. In some wilderness areas, campers aren't allowed to build any fires . . .
8. Some campers bring canned food along, but we don't bring any . . .
9. My parents always pack dried food because it is light and never spoils.
10. When it is time to break camp, no one should leave any trash on the ground . . .
11. Our most memorable camping trip was one I don't ever want to repeat.
12. One summer we decided to go to Crater Lake in southern Oregon because we had never been . . .
13. There is no more beautiful place in all . . .
14. The lake has no inlet or outlet.
15. Nobody can see it without . . .
16. However, we didn't have any idea . . .
17. We had no sooner gone . . .
18. We got hardly any sleep . . .
19. In the morning when we opened our tent flap, we realized we had had no other . . .
20. (correct)
21. We had never seen anything like it . . .
22. We wanted something hot to drink, but we couldn't start a fire.
23. There was scarcely any dry firewood . . .
24. We decided that we didn't want to spend any more time there . . .
25. We just had no idea that it . . .

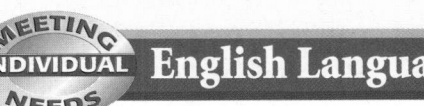

MEETING INDIVIDUAL NEEDS English Language Learners

Avoiding Double Negatives

In some languages, using double negatives is correct. Students who are used to this may need extra practice. Write words such as *no, not, any, much, nothing, don't, haven't, anything,* on index cards. Ask students to make up sentences using the words from two cards; for example, *I don't have any paper.*

Additional Resources

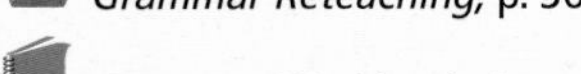

Grammar Reteaching, p. 36

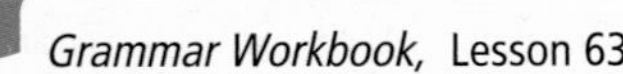

Grammar Workbook, Lesson 63

Close

Have students write a paragraph about an outing or special occasion that did not work out as they had hoped. Have them avoid using double negatives as they describe what the event lacked.

Focus

Lesson Overview

Objective

- To avoid misplaced and dangling modifiers

Bellringer
Daily Language Activity

When students enter the classroom, have this assignment on the board: *Rewrite the following sentences so that the meaning is clear:*

He saw a deer using his binoculars.

Juana only has algebra three days this week.

Walking along the beach, a rock scraped my foot.

See also *Daily Language Practice*

Motivating Activity

Discuss students' responses to the Bellringer activity. Encourage students to provide effective feedback and to ask questions for clarification. Explain that in this lesson, they will study how to avoid writing sentences with misplaced modifiers.

18.7 Misplaced and Dangling Modifiers

Place modifiers as close as possible to the words they modify in order to make the meaning of the sentence clear.

- **Misplaced modifiers** modify the wrong word, or they seem to modify more than one word in a sentence. To correct a sentence with a misplaced modifier, move the modifier as close as possible to the word it modifies.

Soaring over the edge of the cliff, the photographer captured the eagle.

MISPLACED **Soaring over the edge of the cliff,** the photographer captured the eagle. [participial phrase incorrectly modifying *photographer*]

CLEAR The photographer captured the eagle **soaring over the edge of the cliff.** [participial phrase correctly modifying *eagle*]

MISPLACED The photographer easily spotted the eagle **with high-powered binoculars.** [prepositional phrase incorrectly modifying *eagle*]

CLEAR The photographer **with high-powered binoculars** easily spotted the eagle. [prepositional phrase correctly modifying *the photographer*]

Place the adverb *only* immediately before the word or group of words it modifies.

If *only* is not positioned correctly in a sentence, the meaning of the sentence may be unclear.

UNCLEAR Dan **only** has art on Monday. [Does Dan have only one class on Monday, or does he have no class on any day but Monday, or is Dan the only person (in a group) who has one class on Monday?]

CLEAR Dan has **only** art on Monday. [He has no other class.]

CLEAR Dan has art **only** on Monday. [He does not have art on any other day.]

CLEAR **Only** Dan has art on Monday. [No other person has art on Monday.]

Resource Manager

Planning Resources
- *Lesson Plans*

Transparencies
- *Bellringer*
- *Daily Language Practice*
- *Two-Minute Skill Drill*

Other Print Resources
- *Grammar and Composition Handbook*
- *Grammar Enrichment,* p. 37
- *Grammar Practice,* p. 37
- *Grammar Reteaching,* p. 37
- *Grammar Workbook,* Lesson 64

Dangling modifiers seem logically to modify no word at all. To correct a sentence that has a dangling modifier, you must supply a word the dangling phrase can sensibly modify.

DANGLING **Working all night long,** the fire was extinguished. [participial phrase logically modifying no word in the sentence]

CLEAR **Working all night long,** firefighters extinguished the fire. [participial phrase modifying *firefighters*]

DANGLING **After finishing his homework,** it was time to play soccer. [prepositional phrase logically modifying no word in the sentence]

CLEAR **After finishing his homework,** the boy went to play soccer. [prepositional phrase modifying *boy*]

DANGLING **Sleeping soundly,** the raucous alarm startled me into consciousness. [participial phrase logically modifying no word in the sentence, since *me* is an object pronoun]

CLEAR **Sleeping soundly,** I sprang into consciousness at the sound of the raucous alarm. [participial phrase modifying *I*]

Exercise 13 Identifying Misplaced and Dangling Modifiers

On your paper, write the misplaced or dangling modifier from each sentence. If a sentence is correct, write *correct.*

SAMPLE The police officer saw the tire explode in his binoculars.
ANSWER in his binoculars

1. Last night Darnell had a flat tire on the way to his job.
2. A motorcycle rider offered to fix the tire with a friendly grin.
3. Coming out from behind some parked cars, neither Darnell nor his helper could see the police officer.
4. Watching the motorcycle rider work, the tire was soon fixed.
5. "I only have trouble on this road," Darnell lamented.

Teach

Teaching Tip

A participial phrase must modify a noun in the main clause. A participial phrase dangles when there is no noun in the main clause that it can logically modify. For example, in the sentence *Digging in the field, a spoon was found,* the participial phrase *digging in the field* is a dangling modifier because it cannot logically modify the only noun, *spoon.*

Two-Minute Skill Drill

Correct the following sentences:

Digging in the yard, I tried to stop the dog.

Running, we watched the contestants in the race.

Crying, Fred comforted the baby.

Discuss students' corrections. Encourage students to provide effective feedback and to ask questions for clarification.

See also *Two-Minute Skill Drill Transparency 18.7*

Practice and Assess

Answers: Exercise 13

1. (correct)
2. with a friendly grin
3. Coming out from behind some parked cars,
4. Watching the motorcycle rider work,
5. only

Cooperative Learning

Identifying Misplaced Modifiers

Explain that modifiers must be near the words they modify, otherwise they will modify the wrong words.

Have pairs of students move the modifiers in the following sentences close to the word they modify. Then have students explain to their partner the differences in meaning between the two sentences.

Meowing, my brother rescued the cat. *Bigger than most,* Alberto went to a new school. The dog chased the cat *barking loudly.*

Practice and Assess

Answers: Exercise 14

1. The sign at the park entrance said, "Children under eight years of age should be with an adult."
2. A little boy with unmatched shoes was riding around on a bicycle.
3. Marty noticed a baby squirrel scampering around the top rung of the jungle gym.
4. On the way home from school, Helen saw the sand castle her little sister had built.
5. The new paint set that he had received for his birthday was under the porch.

Answers: Exercise 15

Answers will vary, but some suggestions are given below.

1. Waking up in the dark, Pete thought his room seemed mysterious and gloomy.
2. After taking a shower, he noticed that the sun had finally come out.
3. Putting on a short-sleeved shirt, he hoped that the temperature outside was warm.
4. (correct)
5. The school bus pulled up right on time after Pete had eaten a hurried breakfast.

Answers: Exercise 16

Answers will vary, but some suggestions are given below.

1. I wake up early on Saturdays only if there's an emergency. I don't wake up early if there is not an emergency.
2. The only chore I have is mowing the grass. I don't have any other chores.
3. I go to the movies only on Saturday afternoons. I don't go to the movies at any other time except Saturday afternoons.
4. I eat pizza only at my favorite pizzeria, Paul's Place. I don't eat pizza anywhere else.
5. Only I can appreciate how much my Saturdays mean to me. No one else can appreciate it.

Using Modifiers Correctly

Exercise 14 Correcting Misplaced Modifiers

Rewrite each sentence, moving the misplaced modifier closer to the word it modifies.

SAMPLE I noticed the park walking home from school.
ANSWER Walking home from school, I noticed the park.

At the Park

1. The sign at the park entrance said, "Children should be with an adult under eight years of age."
2. A little boy was riding around on a bicycle with unmatched shoes.
3. Scampering around the top rung of the jungle gym, Marty noticed a baby squirrel.
4. Helen saw the sand castle her little sister had built on the way home from school.
5. The new paint set was under the porch that he had received for his birthday.

Exercise 15 Identifying and Correcting Dangling Modifiers

Rewrite each sentence that needs correction, fixing the dangling modifier. If a sentence has no dangling modifier, write *correct*.

SAMPLE Waking to the screech of the alarm, the blankets were pulled up over Pete's head.
ANSWER Waking to the screech of the alarm, Pete pulled the blankets over his head.

Rise and Shine

1. Waking up in the dark, Pete's room seemed mysterious and gloomy.
2. After taking a shower, the sun finally came out.
3. Putting on a short-sleeved shirt, the temperature outside was warm.
4. Shouting from the kitchen downstairs, Pete's dad let him know that juice and cereal were on the table.
5. The school bus pulled up right on time after a hurried breakfast.

Exercise 16 Using the Adverb *Only*

Rewrite each of the following sentences, adding the word *only*. Then explain what *only* means in your sentence.

SAMPLE I sleep late on Saturday.
ANSWER I sleep late only on Saturday. I don't sleep late on any day except Saturday.

Only on Saturday

1. I wake up early on Saturdays if there's an emergency.
2. The chore I have is mowing the grass.
3. I go to the movies on Saturday afternoons.
4. I eat pizza at my favorite pizzeria, Paul's Place.
5. I can appreciate how much my Saturdays mean to me.

Gifted and Talented

Identifying Dangling Modifiers

Some students may already have a good understanding of dangling and misplaced modifiers. Let these students work in pairs to provide several possible answers for the exercises on this page. They might want to present their answers to the rest of the class. Encourage classmates to ask questions to clarify understanding. **L3**

Exercise 17 Correcting Misplaced and Dangling Modifiers

On your paper rewrite the following sentences, correcting any misplaced or dangling modifiers. (Some sentences can be corrected in more than one way.)

Going to the Circus

[1]The Barnum and Bailey circus is a big event, for it comes only to our town once a year. [2]Julio and I arrived early and took our seats inside the tent in high spirits. [3]Dimming the lights, the elephants lumbered into the ring. [4]Swinging their great trunks, the trainers marched the elephants in a circle. [5]On a tightrope high above the ring, we watched the acrobat walk steadily and fearlessly. [6]Three lions were released from a cage growling fiercely. [7]The clown pretended that he had been attacked by the lions, but one girl in the audience only screamed. [8]Galloping around the ring, a woman in a blue sequined dress waved to the crowd on horseback. [9]Julio watched nervously as the trapeze artists leaped through the air clutching his chair. [10]We watched her intently sitting on the bleachers and eating cotton candy.

[11]Facing north, the second ring could be seen quite clearly. [12]The snake charmer only charmed one snake, but it was a big one. [13]A trainer commanded a bear with a chair. [14]Watching the acrobats, the thrills never stopped. [15]Barking furiously, the clowns chased little dogs around the tent. [16]Julio enjoyed photographing the ringmaster with his miniature camera. [17]Knowing what a bad photographer I was, the spectacle itself was enough. [18]The band played a march dressed in star-spangled khaki. [19]Taking their bows, the crowd applauded all the performers. [20]Under the stars our hearts were content as we walked home.

Exercise 18 Review: Correcting Modifiers

The following paragraph contains 10 errors in the use of modifiers. Rewrite the paragraph, correcting the errors.

Ted Williams, Home-Run Ace

[1]Ted Williams is considered one of the most finest baseball players of all time. [2]At the age of 17, a team in San Diego was the team he joined. [3]By 1939 he was playing good enough to start with the Boston Red Sox. [4]From that time until his retirement in 1960, Ted Williams only played baseball with the Red Sox; he never played for no other team. [5]Williams was one of baseball's all-time most greatest hitters. [6]His batting average was higher than most other players. [7]He hit especially good in 1941, when he had a 0.406 batting average. [8]Williams did not play so bad in 1942 either. [9]In both 1941 and 1942, he hit more home runs than any player in the league.

Answers: Exercise 17

Answers will vary, but some suggestions are given below.

1. it comes to our town only once a year
2. In high spirits, Julio and I
3. When the lights dimmed,
4. The elephants, swinging their great trunks, were marched in a circle by the trainers.
5. We watched the acrobat walk . . . on a tightrope high
6. Growling fiercely, three lions
7. but only one girl
8. Galloping on horseback around the ring, a woman
9. Clutching his chair, Julio
10. Sitting on the bleachers and eating cotton candy, we
11. Facing north, we could see the second ring quite clearly.
12. charmed only one snake
13. A trainer with a chair commanded a bear.
14. The thrills never stopped when we watched the acrobats.
15. The clowns chased little dogs, furiously barking, around the tent.
16. With his miniature camera, Julio enjoyed photographing the ringmaster.
17. Knowing what a bad photographer I was, I thought watching the spectacle itself was enough.
18. Dressed in star-spangled khaki, the band played a march.
19. The crowd applauded all the performers taking their bows.
20. As we walked home under the stars, our hearts were content.

Answers: Exercise 18

1. . . . one of the finest baseball players . . .
2. At the age of seventeen, he joined a team in San Diego.
3. . . . he was playing well enough . . .
4. . . . Williams played baseball only with the Red Sox; he never played for any other team.
5. . . . one of baseball's all-time greatest hitters.
6. His batting average was higher than that of most other players.
7. He hit especially well in 1941, when . . .
8. Williams did not play so badly in 1942 either.
9. . . . home runs than any other player . . .

Enabling Strategies

Identifying Dangling Modifiers

Students may need help identifying dangling participles. On the board, write this sentence: *Waking suddenly, Ian's room shook violently.* Tell students they can test for a dangling modifier by turning the participial phrase into a complete sentence. To do this, they make the subject of the main clause the subject of the new sentence and change the verbal to a complete verb. (*Ian's room awoke suddenly.*) As the new sentence is not logical, the participial phrase is not a legitimate modifier and the sentence needs revision. **L2**

Practice and Assess

Answers: Exercise 19

Answers will vary, but some suggestions are given below.

1. Walking along the sidewalk, Winston tripped on a stone and fell.
2. Winston hardly had time to get to Sabah's house without being late.
3. The buzzer rang as Sabah ran to the door in a great hurry.
4. Out for a walk, Winston and Sabah walked farther than they usually did.
5. The yogurt sundaes they stopped to eat tasted good.
6. As they walked to the movies, they saw that a fire had destroyed a neighbor's house and only the chimney was left standing.
7. The next morning Sabah slept too late, and the school bus left her behind.
8. Sabah felt worse than she had felt in a long time.
9. Walking to school, Sabah bought from a vendor a stuffed bear with fuzzy pink fur.
10. Because she was late, Sabah was reprimanded by her teacher.
11. Sabah felt bad that she had overslept.
12. Sabah decided that English grammar was easier than algebra.
13. She liked English class better than any other class.
14. Winston and Sabah had only one class together.
15. Winston, using a ballpoint pen, wrote an essay about his cat.
16. Concentrating deeply, Sabah wrote a paragraph about her dog.
17. The teacher announced that both had done well.
18. Hoping to do well on the pop quiz, students quieted and a silence fell over the classroom.
19. Having fallen asleep, Winston awoke when Sabah threw her pencil at him.
20. It made Winston feel good to know that his friend was looking out for him.
21. correct
22. Sabah waved as their classmates, running in all directions, left for home.
23. Winston and Sabah watched the team practice in the middle of the football field.
24. The best player was not at the practice.
25. correct

Using Modifiers Correctly

Exercise 19 Correcting Modifiers

On your paper rewrite the following sentences, correcting the misplaced, dangling, or other incorrect modifiers in each. (Some sentences can be corrected in more than one way.) If a sentence is correct, write *correct*.

SAMPLE Winston and Sabah only go out together once a week.
ANSWER Winston and Sabah go out together only once a week.

Winston and Sabah

1. Walking along the sidewalk, a stone made Winston trip and fall.
2. Winston hadn't hardly time to get to Sabah's house without being late.
3. In a great hurry, the buzzer rang as Sabah ran to the door.
4. Out for a walk, Winston and Sabah walked more farther than they usually did.
5. The yogurt sundaes they stopped to eat tasted well.
6. As they walked to the movies, they saw that a fire had destroyed a neighbor's house and the chimney was only left standing.
7. Sleeping too late the next morning, the school bus left Sabah behind.
8. Sabah felt worser than she had felt in a long time.
9. Walking to school, Sabah bought a stuffed bear from a vendor with fuzzy pink fur.
10. Because she was late, Sabah's teacher reprimanded her.
11. Sabah felt badly that she had overslept.
12. Sabah decided that English grammar was more easier than algebra.
13. She liked English class better than any class.
14. Winston and Sabah only had one class together.
15. Winston wrote an essay about his cat using a ballpoint pen.
16. Sabah wrote a paragraph about her dog concentrating deeply.
17. The teacher announced that both had done good.
18. Hoping to do well on the pop quiz, a silence fell over the classroom.
19. Having fallen asleep, Sabah threw her pencil at Winston.
20. Winston felt well that his friend was looking out for him.
21. Greeting each other enthusiastically, Winston and Sabah met after school.
22. Running in all directions, Sabah waved as their classmates left for home.
23. In the middle of the football field, Winston and Sabah watched the team practice.
24. The bestest player was not at the practice.
25. Starting for home, Winston and Sabah bid each other a fond farewell.

Exercise 20 Correcting Modifiers

On your paper rewrite any of the following sentences in which there are errors in the use of modifiers, correcting the errors in your revision. (Some sentences may be corrected in more than one way.) Write *correct* for each sentence that does not contain any errors.

Famous Comic Strips

1. In 1896 the first comic strip appeared in the New York *World,* called "The Yellow Kid."
2. The next comic strip to come along was "The Katzenjammer Kids," whose prankster stars, Hans and Fritz, usually behaved bad.
3. Hans and Fritz never gave the Captain and Mama no peace.
4. In "Mutt and Jeff," a strip that started in 1908, Mutt is more taller than Jeff.
5. "Mutt and Jeff" was one of the most early strips to appear in the newspaper.
6. All the comic strips in the early years depended upon slapstick more than any form of comedy.
7. Based on a typical family, the cartoonist of "The Gumps" drew popular characters.
8. The character Andy Gump had a mustache, but he didn't have no chin.
9. First appearing in 1919, Frank King sometimes drew innovative backgrounds for his "Gasoline Alley" strip.
10. People liked this strip very much, especially after the character Uncle Walt adopted little Skeezix.
11. Before "Gasoline Alley" there had been no comic strip in which the characters grew up and aged.
12. Although full of political content, "Little Orphan Annie" also told a good story.
13. The eyes of Little Orphan Annie are larger than most people.
14. For its first ten years, the "Thimble Theatre" comic didn't have no Popeye in it.
15. "Blondie" was more widely circulated than any comic strip.
16. Dagwood, Blondie's husband, only made huge sandwiches when he raided the refrigerator; he never made an average-sized sandwich.
17. In his pursuit of such bizarre criminals as Flattop and Eighty-eight Keys, a yellow hat and square jaw were the trademarks of the cartoon detective Dick Tracy.
18. In "Peanuts," Pigpen is more dirtier than his friends Charlie Brown, Lucy, and Linus.
19. The comic-strip opossum, Pogo, makes philosophical comments on life.
20. In spite of its sometimes controversial political remarks, Garry Trudeau won a Pulitzer Prize for his "Doonesbury" strip.
21. The editorial page only runs political cartoons, not comic strips.
22. Solving one problem, another problem always faces the kindly heroine of "Mary Worth."
23. In the strip "Peanuts," Charlie Brown always feels badly after his baseball team loses.
24. Many people believe that "Calvin and Hobbes" is funnier than any comic strip.
25. The strip "Flash Gordon" is more older than most of the other strips in newspapers today.

Using Modifiers Correctly

Answers: Exercise 20

Answers may vary, but some suggestions are given below.

1. In 1896, the first comic strip, called "The Yellow Kid," appeared in the New York *World.*
2. The next comic strip to come along was "The Katzenjammer Kids," whose prankster stars, Hans and Fritz, usually behaved badly.
3. Hans and Fritz never gave the Captain and Mama any peace.
4. In "Mutt and Jeff," a strip that started in 1908, Mutt is taller than Jeff.
5. "Mutt and Jeff" was one of the earliest strips to appear in the newspaper.
6. All the comic strips in the early years depended upon slapstick more than upon any other form of comedy.
7. The cartoonist of "The Gumps" drew popular characters based on real-life people.
8. The character Andy Gump had a mustache, but he didn't have a chin.
9. Frank King sometimes drew innovative backgrounds for his "Gasoline Alley" strip, which first appeared in 1919.
10. (correct)
11. (correct)
12. (correct)
13. The eyes of Little Orphan Annie are larger than those of most other people.
14. For its first 10 years, the "Thimble Theatre" comic had no Popeye in it.
15. "Blondie" was more widely circulated than any other comic strip.
16. Dagwood, Blondie's husband, made only huge sandwiches when he raided the refrigerator; he never made an average-sized sandwich.
17. In his pursuit of such bizarre criminals as Flattop and Eighty-eight Keys, the cartoon detective Dick Tracy always appeared with his trademarks, a yellow hat and a square jaw.
18. In "Peanuts," Pigpen is dirtier than his friends Charlie Brown, Lucy, and Linus.
19. (correct)
20. In spite of its sometimes controversial political remarks, Garry Trudeau's "Doonesbury" strip won him a Pulitzer Prize.
21. The editorial page runs only political cartoons, not comic strips.
22. Solving one problem, the kindly heroine of "Mary Worth" always faces another problem.
23. In the strip "Peanuts," Charlie Brown always feels bad after his baseball team loses.
24. Many people believe that "Calvin and Hobbes" is funnier than any other comic strip.
25. The strip "Flash Gordon" is older than most of the other strips in newspapers today.

Additional Resources

Grammar Practice, p. 37
Grammar Reteaching, p. 37
Grammar Enrichment, p. 37

 *Grammar Workbook,* Lesson 64

Teach

About the Literature

Explain that the review contains a passage from Annie Dillard's memoir, *An American Childhood,* and that the literature is followed by exercises based on her memoir and on related topics. After students read the passage, discuss its theme and mood. Then ask students to discuss the roles that the highlighted modifiers play. Do they add more information to the sentences? How do they set up a contrast or a comparison? Do they enhance the tone and the rhythm of the writing?

Linking Grammar and Literature

Critical Thinking

Ask students to write two versions of a paragraph about a hobby or another theme of their choice. Suggest that students use a computer to make revisions quicker and easier. Tell students to use as few modifiers as possible in the first version. The second version should contain a variety of modifiers. Ask students to read both of their paragraphs to a partner. Then have partners discuss the ways in which both writers used modifiers to sharpen their writing and enhance the rhythm and tone of their prose. Have students summarize their findings in their journal.

Listening and Speaking

Ask volunteers to take turns reading aloud sentences from the passage. After a sentence is read, have students identify any modifiers that are not highlighted, including adjectives, adverbs, participles, and prepositional and participial phrases. Remind students that pronouns sometimes function as modifiers and that participles can function as adjectives, as nouns, or as verbs.

✓ ASSESSMENT OPTIONS

Tests with Answer Key & Rubrics
Unit 18 Mastery Test, pp. 69–70

Testmaker
Unit 18 Mastery Test

UNIT 18

Grammar Review

Using Modifiers Correctly

The passage in this workshop is taken from *An American Childhood,* a memoir by Annie Dillard. In it Dillard recalls her fascination with books that describe the pleasures and perils of rock collecting, one of her hobbies as a child. The passage has been annotated to show the kinds of modifiers covered in this unit.

Literature Model

from An American Childhood

by Annie Dillard

People who collected rocks called themselves "rockhounds." In the worst of cases, they called their children "pebble pups." Rockhounds seemed to be wild and obsessive amateurs, my kind of people, who had stepped aside from the rush of things to devote themselves to folly. . . .

Some rockhounds had recently taken up scuba diving. These people dove down into "brawling mountain streams" with tanks on their backs to look for crystals underwater, or to pan for gold. The gold panning was especially good under boulders in rapids.

One book included a photograph of a mild-looking hobbyist in his basement workshop: he sawed chunks of Utah wonderstone into wavy, landscapy-looking slabs suitable for wall hangings. Here was a photograph of rockhounds in the field: Two men on a steep desert hillside delightedly smash a flat rock to bits with two hammers. Far below stands a woman in a dress and sensible shoes, doing nothing. Here is their campsite: a sagging black pyramidal tent pitched on the desert floor. A Studebaker fender nudges the foreground. The very hazards of field collecting tempted me: "tramping for miles over rough country," facing cold, heat, rain, cactus, rough lava, insects, rattlesnakes, scorpions, and glaring alkali

Positive form of the adjective *wild*

Positive form of the adverb *recently*

Correct use of *good*

Correctly placed prepositional phrase modifying men

Using Modifiers Correctly

Resource Manager

Planning Resources
- *Lesson Plans*

Other Print Resources
- *Grammar and Composition Handbook*
- *Grammar Workbook,* Lessons 59–64, Unit 9 Review, Cumulative Review: Units 1–9

flats. Collectors fell over boulders and damaged crystals. Their ballpoint pens ran out of ink. . . .

Getting back home alive only aggravated their problems. If you bring home five hundred pounds of rocks from an average collecting trip, what do you do with them? Splay them attractively about the garden, one book suggested lamely. Give them away. Hold yard sales. One collector left five tons of rough rock in his yard when he moved. . . .

On the other hand, rock collecting had unique rewards. For example, the thinner you sliced your specimens when you sawed them up, the more specimens you had. In this way you could multiply your collection without leaving home.

Correct placement of the adverb *only*

Comparative form of the adverb *thin*

Review: Exercise 1 Making Correct Comparisons

The following sentences are about rock collecting. For each sentence, write on your paper the proper comparative or superlative form of the modifier in parentheses.

SAMPLE Rock collecting is ____________ in some areas than in others. (easy)
ANSWER easier

1. Rock hunting in areas where the ground is already broken, such as quarries and building sites, is ____________ than hunting in areas with unbroken ground. (simple)
2. Some rock hunters gather rocks at a local site, whereas others travel ____________ than that for specimens. (far)
3. One of the ____________ practices to engage in while rock hunting is trespassing on private property. (bad)
4. One of the ____________ and most dangerous things a rock hunter can do is to hunt alone on a steep rock wall. (silly)
5. Of the rock hunter's various tools, a rock hammer is the ____________ implement for loosening solid rock. (good)
6. To loosen individual crystals, a chisel works ____________ than a pocketknife. (good)
7. Museum specimens are often larger and ____________ than those kept by amateur rock collectors. (impressive)
8. Minerals can be identified ____________ than rocks because the atoms in minerals are arranged in a regular pattern, resulting in the formation of crystals. (quickly)
9. Rocks and minerals cannot always be identified simply by looking at them; ____________ testing is often required. (far)
10. Of the various testing methods, the one that is probably used ____________ is the streak test. (frequently)

Using Modifiers Correctly

Practice and Assess

Answers: Exercise 1

1. simpler
2. farther
3. worst
4. silliest
5. best
6. better
7. more impressive
8. more quickly
9. further
10. most frequently

Practice and Assess

Answers: Exercise 2

1. The young Annie Dillard liked nothing better . . .
2. She was more curious . . .
3. To Dillard, rock hunting seemed like the liveliest . . .
4. The books she read showed rockhounds hunting for specimens in the wildest . . .
5. Although Dillard obtained her own specimens by less rugged . . .
6. Some plain-looking rocks, when scratched on a rough surface, created streaks of color brighter than greasepaint.
7. correct
8. Of the rocks in Dillard's collection, the prettiest . . .
9. Many minerals have strange names, but chalcopyrite (a brassy yellow mineral) was the hardest for Dillard to pronounce.
10. correct
11. Dillard was impressed with the fact that the earth is older . . .
12. Before she began to read about rocks, she thought they were the drabbest . . .
13. Only with further . . .
14. Once she started her collection, she looked for the fastest . . .
15. With delight she learned that the thinner . . .
16. She realized that sooner . . .
17. With time and training, Dillard developed a stronger . . .
18. One of her greatest . . .
19. All of her latest books, . . .
20. It's interesting to note that the seeds of her talent as an adult author were planted much earlier in a youthful enthusiasm for rock collecting.

Grammar Review

Review: Exercise 2 Correcting Double Comparisons

The following sentences are based on passages from *An American Childhood* that are not reprinted in this textbook. Rewrite the sentences, correcting any errors of double comparison. If a sentence contains no errors, write *correct.*

SAMPLE To outsiders no one seems more crazier than rockhounds.
ANSWER To outsiders no one seems crazier than rockhounds.

1. The young Annie Dillard liked nothing more better than the natural sciences.
2. She was more curiouser about rocks than she was about stamps or coins.
3. To Dillard, rock hunting seemed like the most liveliest of hobbies.
4. The books she read showed rockhounds hunting for specimens in the most wildest places imaginable.
5. Although Dillard obtained her own specimens by less ruggeder methods, she still found the rocks' secrets intriguing.
6. Some plain-looking rocks, when scratched on a rough surface, created streaks of color more brighter than greasepaint.
7. Even the dullest rocks, when cracked open, might reveal lovely crystals inside.
8. Of the rocks in Dillard's collection, the most prettiest was a red one called cinnabar.
9. Many minerals have strange names, but chalcopyrite (a brassy yellow mineral) was the most hardest for Dillard to pronounce.
10. Dillard longed to possess rocks with names even odder than that of chalcopyrite: sillimanite and agaty potch, for example.
11. Dillard was impressed with the fact that the earth is more older than any rock yet discovered.
12. Before she began to read about rocks, she thought they were the most drabbest things imaginable.
13. Only with more further exposure to the subject did she begin to find them fascinating.
14. Once she started her collection, she looked for the most fastest way to expand it.
15. With delight she learned that the more thinner she sliced her specimens, the bigger her collection became.
16. She realized that more sooner or later she would need a larger room for the collection.
17. With time and training, Dillard developed a more stronger descriptive prose than most other authors of her generation.
18. One of her most greatest gifts is her keen eye for detail.
19. All of her most latest books, including her fiction, continue to reflect her strong grounding in nature.
20. It's interesting to note that the seeds of her talent as an adult author were planted much more earlier in a youthful enthusiasm for rock collecting.

Using Modifiers Correctly

Review: Exercise 3 Correcting Incomplete Comparisons

The following sentences are about minerals and gemstones. Rewrite the sentences, correcting any errors of incomplete comparison. Some of the sentences can be revised in more than one way. If a sentence contains no errors, write *correct.*

SAMPLE The value of a diamond is far greater than an amethyst.
ANSWER The value of a diamond is far greater than that of an amethyst.

1. On the Mohs scale, which lists minerals by their hardness, the mineral talc is softer than any mineral.
2. Quartz, a mineral that can cut glass, is much harder than talc.
3. Diamonds, among the world's most valuable minerals, are harder than anything in nature.
4. The facets, or flat surfaces, of a diamond are different from an amethyst.
5. Among the stones called beryls, which come in different colors, green is more valuable than any color.
6. Green beryls are called emeralds, and the value of some emeralds is higher than some diamonds.
7. The emeralds from Colombia are finer than those supplied by any South American country.
8. More fine rubies are found in Southeast Asia than anywhere.
9. The appearance of many synthetic rubies is very close to natural rubies.
10. Unlike most other gemstones, pearls are not minerals but an organic material.
11. A gemologist is more interested in the chemical structure of precious stones than any scientist.
12. Unlike other gemstones, such as lapis and malachite, diamonds are not only polished, but also facet-cut.
13. The aquamarine from Brazil is of better quality than Colombia.
14. In Thailand one can find finer sapphires than anywhere.
15. Unlike any rubies, star-rubies appear to contain six-rayed stars that can be seen in bright light.
16. In ancient China, jade was considered more precious than any gemstone.
17. Chinese collectors often valued a tiny piece of jade sculpture over any artifact.
18. The turquoise jewelry created by a Navajo is different from a Zuni.
19. Native American artisans create more exquisite turquoise jewelry than anyone.
20. Today there is a greater selection of gemstones available than at any time in history.

Answers: Exercise 3

Answers will vary, but some suggestions are given below.

1. . . . the mineral talc is softer than any other mineral.
2. correct
3. Diamonds . . . are harder than anything else in nature.
4. The facets . . . of a diamond are different from those of an amethyst.
5. Among the stones called beryls, . . . green is more valuable than any other color.
6. . . . the value of some emeralds is higher than that of some diamonds.
7. . . . are finer than those supplied by any other South American country.
8. More . . . are found in Southeast Asia than anywhere else.
9. The appearance . . . is very close to that of natural rubies.
10. correct
11. A gemologist is more interested in the chemical structure . . . than is any other scientist.
12. correct
13. . . . is of better quality than that from Colombia.
14. In Thailand one can find finer sapphires than anywhere else.
15. Unlike any other rubies, . . .
16. . . . was considered more precious than any other gemstone.
17. . . . valued a tiny piece of jade sculpture over any other artifact.
18. . . . is different from that of a Zuni.
19. . . . create more exquisite turquoise jewelry than anyone else.
20. . . . than at any other time in history.

Practice and Assess

Answers: Exercise 4

1. well—adv.
2. good—adj.
3. badly—adv.
4. well or good—adj.
5. bad—adj.
6. good—adj.
7. bad—adj.
8. well—adv.
9. badly—adv.
10. good—adj.
11. well—adv.
12. well—adv.
13. good—adj.
14. badly—adv.
15. bad—adj.

Review: Exercise 4 Choosing the Correct Modifier

The following sentences are based on passages from *An American Childhood* not reprinted in this textbook. For each sentence choose the correct form of the modifier in parentheses, and write it on your paper. Then indicate whether the modifier you have chosen is being used as an *adjective* or an *adverb.*

SAMPLE To the young Annie Dillard, few hobbies seemed as (good/well) as rock collecting.

ANSWER good—adjective

1. Dillard obtained the first rocks in her collection from a newspaper boy whom she did not know very (good/well).
2. The newspaper boy had received the rocks as a gift from a (good/well) customer named Mr. Downey.
3. Mr. Downey, an avid rock hunter and collector, could no longer maintain his collection because his health was failing (bad/badly).
4. He had not been feeling (good/well) for several months, so he decided to give the collection to his newspaper boy, one of the few young people he knew.
5. The newspaper boy felt (bad/badly) because he did not have enough time to devote to the rock collection, and eventually he decided to give it to Dillard.
6. Dillard noticed right away that some of the rocks were attractive; others did not look too (good/well).
7. The fact that he could identify only two stalagmites made the newspaper boy feel (bad/badly) about his right to the collection.
8. Dillard herself was not (good/well) informed about the rocks and minerals when she first accepted the collection.
9. Had someone tested her on the names of Mr. Downey's rocks, Dillard would have done quite (bad/badly).
10. It was (good/well) that Dillard was able to borrow and read several books about rocks and minerals.
11. Dillard became more and more interested in rocks, quickly learning how to identify them (good, well).
12. She discovered that "rockhounds" were people that she got along with very (good, well).
13. She felt (good, well) about the amount of information and assistance some of these rockhounds could provide for her.
14. When she went on rock-finding expeditions, Dillard at first was (bad, badly) frustrated about not knowing what to do when she brought her findings home.
15. The rigors of actually looking for the rocks did not seem (bad, badly) by comparison.

Review: Exercise 5 **Correcting Double Negatives**

The following sentences are about precious metals. Rewrite the sentences, eliminating any double negatives. Most sentences can be corrected in more than one way.

SAMPLE Finding precious metals isn't no easy task.
ANSWER Finding precious metals is no easy task.

1. Gold is a very malleable metal; if you hammer it, it won't never break.
2. Because there isn't no more malleable metal, people began using gold for jewelry thousands of years ago.
3. Nobody never has to worry that gold will tarnish, as many other metals do.
4. You can't make no jewelry out of pure gold, however, for it is too soft.
5. Pure gold is hardly never found; usually it is combined with another metal.
6. For centuries there wasn't nothing more valuable than gold.
7. Silver was also deemed valuable, but there wasn't no interest in platinum.
8. Medieval alchemists tried to create gold, but no one could make none.
9. Few early European explorers of the Americas hadn't never heard about the legend of El Dorado.
10. Most prospectors in nineteenth-century America never had no scientific training.

Review: Exercise 6 **Correcting Misplaced Modifiers**

The following sentences elaborate on ideas suggested by the passage from *An American Childhood.* Rewrite the sentences, correcting each misplaced modifier. If a sentence has no errors, write *correct.*

SAMPLES Dillard identified rocks consulting books and visiting local museums.
ANSWER Consulting books and visiting local museums, Dillard identified rocks.

1. Rockhounds seem eccentric to conventional people, having an unusual obsession.
2. Everyday activities seem unimportant to adventurous rockhounds with their dull routines.
3. Divers find some of the most interesting specimens in mountain streams using scuba-diving equipment.
4. Rockhounds often pan for gold in streams leaving no opportunity unexplored.
5. Some hobbyists might find enough gold to turn a tidy profit in the water.
6. Browsing through a book, Dillard noticed a strange photograph of a rockhound.
7. The picture showed a hobbyist sawing a chunk of wonderstone in his workshop destined for use as a wall hanging.
8. Lugging home huge quantities of rock, the question of practicality gnaws at the hobbyist.
9. The rockhound now begins to search for ideas about unloading his bounty in books.
10. One idea is to sell the specimens to friends occupying too much space.

Answers: Exercise 5

Answers will vary, but some suggestions are given below.

1. Gold is a very malleable metal; if you hammer it, it won't ever break.
2. Because there is no more malleable metal, people began using gold for jewelry thousands of years ago.
3. Nobody ever has to worry that gold will tarnish, as many other metals do.
4. You can't make jewelry out of pure gold, however, for it is too soft.
5. Pure gold is hardly ever found; usually it is combined with another metal.
6. For centuries there was nothing more valuable than gold.
7. Silver was also deemed valuable, but there was no interest in platinum.
8. Medieval alchemists tried to create gold, but no one could make any.
9. Few early European explorers of the Americas hadn't heard about the legend of El Dorado.
10. Most prospectors in nineteenth-century America never had any scientific training.

Answers: Exercise 6

Answers will vary, but some suggestions are given below.

1. Rockhounds, having an unusual obsession, seem eccentric to conventional people.
2. The dull routines of everyday activities seem unimportant to adventurous rockhounds.
3. Divers, using scuba-diving equipment, find some of the most interesting specimens in mountain streams.
4. Leaving no opportunity unexplored, rockhounds often pan for gold in streams.
5. Some hobbyists might find in the water enough gold to turn a tidy profit.
6. correct
7. The picture showed a hobbyist sawing in his workshop a chunk of wonderstone destined for use as a wall hanging.
8. The question of practicality gnaws at the hobbyist lugging home huge quantities of rock.
9. The rockhound now begins to search in books for ideas about unloading his bounty.
10. One idea is to sell to friends the specimens occupying too much space.

Practice and Assess

Answers: Exercise 7

1. correct
2. Pausing to reflect, Dillard began to regard rock hunting as a wild obsession.
3. Strapping on their heavy tanks, rock hunters began the hunt for rock crystals in mountain streams.
4. correct
5. Sawed into wavy slabs by one hobbyist, Utah wonderstone became suitable for wall hangings.
6. After climbing a steep hillside, rockhounds smashed the flat rock with two hammers.
7. correct
8. Hunting for unusual rock specimens in wild and isolated places, rock collectors encountered minor problems like running out of ink.
9. Five tons of rock remained in the rockhound's old yard after he moved to a new home.
10. After tramping for miles over rough country, some rockhounds found that their ballpoint pens had run out of ink.

Answers: Exercise 8

Proofreading

This proofreading activity provides editing practice with (1) the current or previous units' skills, (2) the **Troubleshooter** errors, and (3) spelling errors. Students should be able to complete the exercise by referring to the units, the **Troubleshooter,** and a dictionary. (Note: A run-on sentence counts as one error.)

Error (Type of Error)

1. Wisconsin, Georgia O'Keeffe had an early love of art. (dangling modifier)
2. studying (spelling)
3. 1909, (run-on sentence)
4. First she (sentence fragment)
5. Virginia, and (sentence fragment) later (double comparison)

Review: Exercise 7 Correcting Dangling Modifiers

The following sentences elaborate on ideas suggested by the passage from *An American Childhood.* Rewrite the sentences, correcting each dangling modifier by adding appropriate information. Reword the sentence if necessary. Some sentences can be corrected in more than one way. If a sentence has no errors, write *correct.*

SAMPLE Finding rock collectors wildly impractical, their hobby was attractive.
ANSWER Finding rock collectors wildly impractical, Dillard was attracted to their hobby.

1. Calling themselves "rockhounds," rock collectors sometimes called their children "pebble pups."
2. Pausing to reflect, rock hunting began to seem like a wild obsession.
3. Strapping on their heavy tanks, the hunt for rock crystals in mountain streams began.
4. After studying the photographs and reading the anecdotes in books about rock collecting, Dillard decided the hobby was both artistic and adventurous.
5. Sawed into wavy slabs by one hobbyist, its suitability for wall hangings was achieved.
6. After climbing a steep hillside, the flat rock was smashed with two hammers.
7. Pitched in the desert, a tent served as the rockhounds' refuge from the elements.
8. Hunting for unusual rock specimens in wild and isolated places, minor problems like running out of ink arose.
9. After moving to a new home, five tons of rock remained in the rockhound's old yard.
10. Tramping for miles over rough country, their ballpoint pens ran out of ink.

Review: Exercise 8

Proofreading

The following passage describes the artist Georgia O'Keeffe, whose painting appears on the opposite page. Rewrite the passage, correcting the errors in spelling, grammar, and usage. Add any missing punctuation. There are twenty-five errors.

Georgia O'Keeffe

[1]Born in 1887 in Sun Prairie, Wisconsin, art was an early love of Georgia O'Keeffe. [2]She began studing art while still in her teens. [3]She worked in Chicago as an advertising illustrator in 1909 but she resumed her art studies in 1912. [4]First worked as a teacher for the public school system in Amarillo, Texas. [5]She then taught art at the University of Virginia And more later, she returned to Texas to head the art department at West Texas State Normal College.

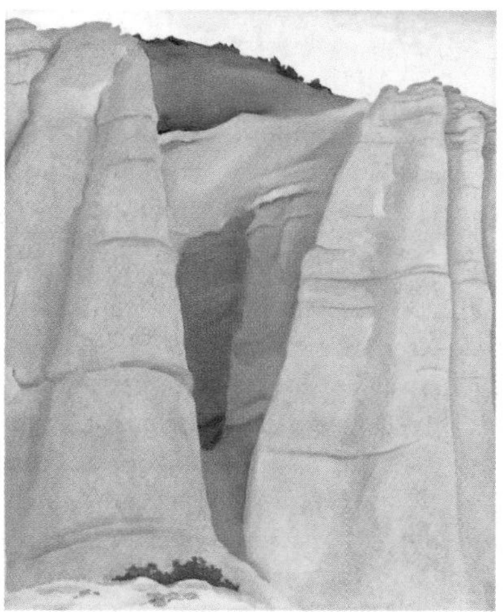

Georgia O'Keeffe, *The White Place in Shadow,* 1940

[6]Although she had been painting good for some years, O'Keeffe did not produce no important works until 1915. [7]They were large charcoal drawings based on elements in nature showing great promise. [8]These works were seen by the photographer and gallery owner Alfred Stieglitz who admired them very much. [9]O'Keeffe's first exhibition was in 1916 at one of Stieglitzs galleries in New York City. [10]Eight years later O'Keeffe and Stieglitz was married. [11]Every year until her husband's death, it had an exhibit at one of Stieglitz's galleries.

[12]After visiting New Mexico in 1929, the dessert landscape became O'Keeffe's main subject. [13]She was more happier painting there than anywhere. [14]In the years after her husband's death, she made Abiquiu, New Mexico, her permanant home.

[15]O'Keeffe belonged to the first generation of American abstract artists and drew on her American roots (particularly the vastest landscape of the arid Southwest) more than many of her compatriots. [16]She was not greatly influenced by no European art. [17]O'Keeffe often used large, simplest forms that combined both soft and vivid colors. [18]In many of her works, she exaggeratted the size of an object.

[19]O'Keeffe painted some of the more dramatic landscapes in all America. [20]In her painting *The White Place in Shadow,* she used subdued tones and massive shapes more than anything to capture the dry, sun-bleached cliffs of northern New Mexico. [21]A setting such as this would perhaps be attractive to the rockhounds described by Annie Dillard than to most people.

Using Modifiers Correctly

Answers: Exercise 8 *(continued)*

Error (Type of Error)

6. painting well (adverb)
did not produce any *or* produced no (double negative)

7. Showing great promise, they (misplaced modifier)

8. Stieglitz, (nonessential adjective clause)

9. Stieglitz's (singular possessive)

10. were (subject-verb agreement)

11. O'Keeffe had (unclear pronoun reference)

12. 1929, O'Keeffe made the desert landscape her main subject. (dangling modifier)
desert (spelling)

13. was happier (double comparison) anywhere else (incomplete comparison)

14. permanent (spelling)

15. the vast landscape (no comparison)

16. by any European (double negative)

17. simple (no comparison)

18. exaggerated (spelling)

19. the most dramatic (superlative degree)

20. anything else (incomplete comparison)

21. be more attractive (incomplete comparison)

Viewing the Art

Georgia O'Keeffe, *The White Place in Shadow,* 1940

Discuss with students how the Southwest was a spiritual place to Georgia O'Keeffe. Her landscapes of northern New Mexico, such as *The White Place in Shadow,* reflect her reverent attitude toward the land. The monumental white cliffs depicted in the painting have all the grandeur and spiritual power of a cathedral.

Practice and Assess

Answers: Exercise 9

Mixed Review

Answers will vary, but some suggestions are given below.

1. Writing vividly about the world of nature and her own experiences, Annie Dillard has produced books that have enjoyed great popularity.
2. Some readers and critics consider her writings about nature as powerful as those of the classic American author Henry David Thoreau.
3. Born in Pittsburgh, Dillard vividly described her youth in the book *An American Childhood,* an autobiography published in 1987.
4. As a child, Dillard was an avid reader and almost never had any trouble with her schoolwork.
5. She later did well at Hollins College in Virginia.
6. After spending a year in rural Virginia, she expanded her journal of that period into her acclaimed best-seller *Pilgrim at Tinker Creek.*
7. *Pilgrim at Tinker Creek* is probably more popular than any other book by Dillard.
8. Although it was Dillard's first book, *Pilgrim at Tinker Creek* won her the 1975 Pulitzer Prize as the year's finest work of nonfiction.
9. Dillard has published only a single volume of poetry.
10. Writing often keeps Dillard cooped up in her office, away from the natural world she loves.

Close

Conclude the review exercises by asking students to write a summary of what they have learned about modifiers. Ask them to use specific examples, including comparative and superlative forms of modifiers and correctly placed modifiers. Invite volunteers to share their summaries with the class. Have students provide effective feedback.

Review: Exercise 9

Mixed Review

Read the following biography of Annie Dillard. Then rewrite the sentences below it, correcting any errors in the use of modifiers. If you need additional information in order to complete any of your sentences, consult the biography.

Annie Dillard

Born and raised in Pittsburgh, Annie Dillard fell in love with nature when, at the age of 10, she discovered *The Field Book of Ponds and Streams* at a local library. Always a fine scholar, Dillard excelled in her studies at Hollins College. For her master's degree, she wrote a paper on Henry David Thoreau, the famous American nature writer to whom she is often compared. Dillard's journal of a year spent alone in rural Virginia became the basis for *Pilgrim at Tinker Creek,* which earned her the 1975 Pulitzer Prize. This vivid and introspective exploration of the natural world remains Dillard's best-known work. She has also published a volume of poetry and several more works of nonfiction, including her fine autobiography, *An American Childhood* (1987).

In 1992 Dillard published her first book of fiction, *The Living,* to great critical acclaim. In this novel she described the harsh life of the pioneers who came to the Pacific Northwest during the nineteenth century. In spite of her successes, Dillard claims to dislike writing because it takes her away from the great outdoors.

1. Writing vividly about the world of nature and her own experiences, Annie Dillard's books have enjoyed great popularity.
2. Some readers and critics consider her writings about nature as powerful as the classic American author Henry David Thoreau.
3. Born in Pittsburgh, her youth is described vividly in the book *An American Childhood,* an autobiography published in 1987.
4. As a child, Dillard was an avid reader and almost never had no trouble with her schoolwork.
5. She later did good at Hollins College in Virginia.
6. After spending a year in rural Virginia, her journal of that period was expanded into her acclaimed best-seller *Pilgrim at Tinker Creek.*
7. *Pilgrim at Tinker Creek* is probably more popular than any book by Dillard.
8. Although it was Dillard's first book, *Pilgrim at Tinker Creek* won her the 1975 Pulitzer Prize as the year's most finest work of nonfiction.
9. Dillard has only published a single volume of poetry.
10. Cooped up in her office, writing often keeps Dillard away from the natural world she loves.

Writing Application

Modifiers in Writing

Good writers are careful about the clear use and placement of modifiers. Notice, for example, the italicized modifiers in the following passage from Flannery O'Connor's *A View of the Woods.*

No one was particularly glad that Mary Fortune looked like her grandfather except the old man himself. He thought it added greatly to her attractiveness. He thought she was the *smartest* and the *prettiest* child he had ever seen and he let the rest of them know that if, IF that was, he left anything to anybody, it would be Mary Fortune he left it to. She was now nine, *short* and *broad* like himself, *with his very light blue eyes, his wide prominent forehead, his steady penetrating scowl, and his rich florid complexion;* but she was like him on the inside too. She had, to a singular degree, his intelligence, his strong will, and his push and drive.

Techniques with Modifiers

Try to apply some of O'Connor's techniques when you write and revise your own work.

TIME
For more about the writing process, see **TIME Facing the Blank Page**, pp. 121-131.

1. Use comparative and superlative forms of modifiers when appropriate.

WEAK VERSION a smart and pretty child

O'CONNOR'S VERSION the *smartest* and the *prettiest* child

2. Place modifiers correctly to make your meaning clear.

CONFUSING PLACEMENT *With his very light blue eyes, his wide prominent forehead, his steady penetrating scowl, and his rich florid complexion,* she was now nine, *short* and *broad* like himself. . . .

O'CONNOR'S VERSION She was now nine, *short* and *broad* like himself, *with his very light blue eyes, his wide prominent forehead, his steady penetrating scowl, and his rich florid complexion.*

Using Modifiers Correctly

Practice Practice using modifiers correctly by revising the following passage on a separate piece of paper.

Margaret watched her friend Linda windsurf sitting on the prow of the small boat. She wondered if she would ever be able to do it as effortlessly. There only was one way to find out. Taking a deep breath, her board was tossed into the water. Then she took another deep breath and plunged in after it. Climbing aboard, her feet were positioned just as Linda had taught her. She began to skim over the water as the wind became stronger. Feeling more freer than a seagull and more playful than a dolphin, suddenly the wind shifted, tossing her off the board. The sea was icy. It had not been icy near the shore. Struggling to the surface, a sobering thought occurred to her. She had a long way to go before she could windsurf in Linda's league.

LOG ON **Writing** Online | For more grammar practice, go to glencoe.com and enter QuickPass code WC97727p2.

Modifiers in Writing

Encourage students to read silently to themselves the passage from Flannery O'Connor's *A View of the Woods.* Then lead a discussion about modifiers that focuses on what students learned in Unit 18. You can initiate discussion by asking students to identify modifiers used in the passage. Discuss these choices in relation to the Techniques with Modifiers section below.

Techniques with Modifiers

Discuss with students the techniques with modifiers used in O'Connor's passage. If necessary, point out that O'Connor's use of comparative and superlative forms of modifiers is more descriptive and provides more information than the weak example.

Continue the discussion by asking students to describe the importance of correctly placed modifiers. Ask volunteers to interpret and compare the meanings of the two examples on page 685. Then invite volunteers to share with the class other examples of misplaced modifiers. What would they do to correct them? Invite the rest of the class to create their own misplaced modifier for classmates to correct. Use examples from Exercise 6 on page 681.

Practice

The answers to this challenging and enriching activity will vary. Refer to Techniques with Modifiers as you evaluate students' choices.

ASSESSMENT OPTIONS

Tests with Answer Key & Rubrics
Unit 18 Mastery Test, pp. 69–70

Testmaker
Unit 18 Mastery Test

You may wish to administer the Unit 18 Mastery Test at this point.

MindJogger Videoquizzes

INTRODUCING

UNIT 19

Objectives

- To develop an understanding of and an ability to recognize and correct common usage problems
- To demonstrate control over usage problems by editing sentences and using the Usage Glossary to find answers to specific usage problems

✓ ASSESSMENT OPTIONS

Tests with Answer Key & Rubrics
Unit 19 Pretest, pp. 71–72
Unit 19 Mastery Test, pp. 73–74

Testmaker
Unit 19 Pretest
Unit 19 Mastery Test

You may wish to administer the Unit 19 Pretest at this point.

Key to Ability Levels

L1 Level 1 activities are within the basic ability range of students.

L2 Level 2 activities are within the ability range of average students.

L3 Level 3 activities are more challenging activities.

UNIT 19

Usage Glossary

686

Resource Manager

Planning Resources
- *Lesson Plans*
- *Block Scheduling*

Transparencies
- *Bellringer*
- *Daily Language Practice*
- *Two-Minute Skill Drill*

Other Print Resources
- *Grammar and Composition Handbook*
- *Grammar Enrichment*
- *Grammar Practice*
- *Grammar Reteaching*
- *Grammar Workbook*
- *Tests with Answer Key and Rubrics*

Video
- *MindJogger Videoquizzes*

Software
- *Interactive Grammar and Language Workbook*
- *Presentation Plus!*
- *Testmaker*

Web Site
- *glencoe.com*

19 Usage Glossary

The glossary that follows presents some particularly troublesome matters of preferred usage. The glossary will give you guidance, for example, in choosing between two words that are often confused. It will also make you aware of certain words and expressions that you should avoid when speaking or writing for school or business.

a, an Use the article *a* when the word that follows begins with a consonant sound, including a sounded *h: a poem, a house.* Use *an* when the word that follows begins with a vowel sound or an unsounded *h: an apple, an heirloom.* Use *a* before a word that begins with the "yew" sound: *a European, a unit.*

a lot, alot This expression is always written as two words and means "a large amount." Some authorities suggest avoiding it altogether in formal English.

> **A lot** of snow fell last night.

a while, awhile *A while* is made up of an article and a noun. *In* and *for* often come before *a while,* forming a prepositional phrase. *Awhile* is an adverb.

> We'll stop in **a while.**
> We'll stop for **a while.**
> We'll stop **awhile** before hiking to the top of the mountain.

accept, except *Accept* is a verb that means "to receive" or "to agree to." *Except* is a preposition, a verb, or a conjunction. As a preposition, *except* means "but."

> Eric will **accept** the trophy for the team.
> Alanna will not **accept** defeat.
> Everyone will be at the ceremony **except** the captain. [preposition]

affect, effect *Affect* is a verb that means "to cause a change in" or "to influence." *Effect* may be a noun or a verb. As a noun, it means "result." As a verb, it means "to bring about" or "to accomplish."

> The mayor's policies have **affected** every city agency.
> The mayor's policies have had a good **effect** on every agency. [noun meaning "result"]
> The mayor has been able to **effect** his goals in every city agency. [verb meaning "to bring about"]

Usage Glossary

Focus

Lesson Overview

Objectives

- To understand the difference between words that are often confused
- To know how to use them correctly

Bellringer

Daily Language Activity

When students enter the classroom, have this assignment on the board: *Look at the two pairs of words below. Write the term in each pair that is spelled correctly.*

a lot / alot; all right / alright

See also *Daily Language Practice*

Motivating Activity

Ask students to share their answers to the Bellringer. *(a lot, all right)* Then ask them to name other word pairs that give them problems. List the words on the board. Ask students which words they think will be discussed in Unit 19 and why.

Teach

Vocabulary Link

Remind students that a dictionary is a good source for discovering correct usage. Sometimes a dictionary answers questions of correct usage by an absence. For instance, because the term *alot* does not appear in most dictionaries, students can infer that it is not a word and that *a lot* is properly spelled as two words.

Resource Manager

Planning Resources

- *Lesson Plans*

Transparencies

- *Bellringer*
- *Daily Language Practice*
- *Two-Minute Skill Drill*

Other Print Resources

- *Grammar and Composition Handbook*
- *Grammar Workbook,* Lessons 65–69

Teach

Listening and Speaking

The words *accept* and *except* sound very much alike. Students who spell by ear will misuse these two words unless they can hear the subtle difference in the initial vowel sounds. Have students practice saying the words *accept* and *except* until they can hear the distinction.

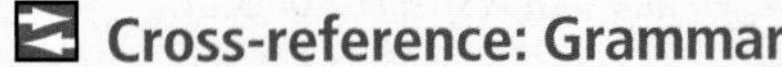

Grammar Tip

Point out that *all together* in the first example sentence functions as an adverb modifying *will be*, whereas *altogether* in the second example sentence functions as an adverb modifying the adjective *delighted*.

Cross-reference: Grammar

For instruction in and practice with adverbs, refer students to Lesson 10.5, pp. 467–472.

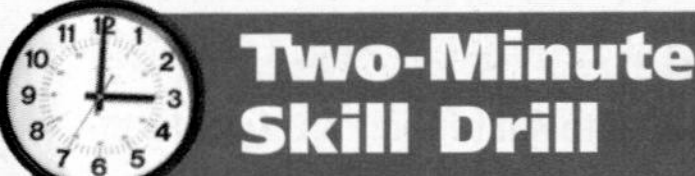

Two-Minute Skill Drill

Rewrite the following sentence correctly:

Ahmad was all ready excited about the trip, so he had alot of trouble excepting the two-day delay.

(Ahmad was already excited about the trip, so he had a lot of trouble accepting the two-day delay.)

See also *Two-Minute Skill Drill Transparency 19*

ain't *Ain't* is unacceptable in speaking and writing unless you are quoting somebody's exact words. Instead of using *ain't,* use *I am not; she is not; he is not;* and so on.

all ready, already The two words *all ready* mean "completely ready." *Already* is an adverb that means "before" or "by this time."

> The band was **all ready** to play its last number, but the fans were **already** leaving the stadium.

all right, alright Always write this expression as two words. Although the expression is often seen in print as one word, most language authorities prefer *all right.*

> She was sick yesterday, but today she feels **all right.**

all the farther, all the faster These are regional expressions. Use *as far as* and *as fast as* in writing.

> We drove **as far as** we could during daylight hours.
>
> I'm pedaling this bike **as fast as** I can.

all together, altogether Use *all together* to mean "in a group." Use the adverb *altogether* to mean "completely" or "on the whole."

> For the holidays, our family will be **all together** at my grandmother's house.
>
> My grandmother is **altogether** delighted to have us with her.

amount, number *Amount* and *number* both refer to quantity. Use *amount* when referring to nouns that cannot be counted. Use *number* when referring to nouns that can be counted.

> Fort Knox contains a vast **amount** of gold.
>
> Fort Knox contains a large **number** of gold bars.

bad, badly See Unit 18.

being as, being that These expressions are sometimes used instead of *because* or *since* in informal conversation. In formal speaking and writing, always use *because* or *since.*

> **Because** their car broke down, they could not get here.
>
> **Since** they did not call, we assumed they were not coming.

Meeting Individual Needs: English Language Learners

Hearing Words

To help students who are learning English to practice hearing and saying words that sound similar, write some words that sound alike on index cards. Cards containing words such as *accept, except, affect,* and *effect* can be used by students to practice speaking and hearing differences between the words.

beside, besides *Beside* means "at the side of." *Besides* usually means "in addition to."

Katrina sat **beside** her mother at the table.

Besides yogurt and fruit, they had homemade muffins.

between, among In general, use *between* to compare one person or thing with one other person or thing or with an entire group.

What is the difference **between** Seattle and Portland? [Two cities are compared.]

What was the difference **between** Pavlova and other ballet dancers? [One dancer is compared with an entire group of dancers.]

In general, use *among* to show a relationship in which more than two persons or things are considered as a group.

The committee members were arguing **among** themselves.

You are **among** friends.

Exercise 1 Making Usage Choices

For each of the following sentences, choose the correct word or expression from the pair in parentheses.

San Francisco

1. When gold was discovered in California in 1848, people seeking their fortune traveled there (all the faster/as fast as) they could.
2. Although most prospectors found no gold, some of them discovered that staying on in California as storekeepers or farmers was quite (all right/alright).
3. During the summer months, San Francisco has everything residents could want (except/accept) a hot, sunny climate, for the weather is often cool and foggy then.
4. In 1906 a terrible earthquake and fire destroyed much of San Francisco, but by 1915 the city had recovered and was (all ready/already) for the Panama-Pacific International Exposition.
5. There are (a lot/alot) of people of Chinese ancestry in San Francisco.
6. Many of them live in (a/an) area known as Chinatown.
7. The buildings in this district, many of which echo traditional Chinese architectural styles, create a picturesque (affect/effect).
8. Many visitors spend quite (a while/awhile) browsing in the shops on Grant Avenue, Chinatown's main thoroughfare.
9. There probably (ain't/is not) another Chinese community in the entire Western Hemisphere that is as large as San Francisco's Chinatown.
10. At first the Chinese families who immigrated to San Francisco lived (all together/altogether) in Chinatown, but now many of them have resettled in other parts of the city.

Usage Glossary

Cross-reference: Grammar

For instruction and practice with prepositions such as *beside* and *besides,* refer students to Lesson 10.6, pp. 473–474.

Grammar Tip

The word *amount* is used with noncount nouns, and the word *number* is used with count nouns. To help students understand the difference, write the following sentences on the board:

I have a huge amount of homework.

I have a large number of lessons.

Grammar Tip

Here are some word associations that might help students remember to use *between* with two items and *among* with more than two items: *between a rock and a hard place; among friends.*

Practice and Assess

Answers: Exercise 1

1. as fast as
2. all right
3. except
4. all ready
5. a lot
6. an
7. effect
8. a while
9. is not
10. all together

Enrichment and Extension

Choosing the Correct Word

Have students choose three or four pairs of words that they find troublesome. Then ask them to think of some word associations or mnemonic devices that will help them remember how to use these words correctly. Have students share their word associations and mnemonic devices in small groups. Encourage students to record the best ones in their journal. **L2**

Teach

Listening and Speaking

Say the phrase *could of danced.* Tell students that sometimes using *of* instead of *have* in verb phrases like *could of danced* is not an error of grammar but an error of spelling. Students who make such mistakes are spelling words by sound, rather than meaning. They are essentially writing down oral language they dictate to themselves. Have students practice saying the phrases *could have, might have, must have, should have,* and *would have.*

Usage Glossary

borrow, lend, loan *Borrow* and *lend* have opposite meanings. *Borrow* is a verb meaning "to take something with the understanding that it must be returned." *Lend* is a verb meaning "to give something with the understanding that it will be returned." *Loan* is a noun. It may be used as a verb, but most authorities prefer *lend.*

May I **borrow** ten dollars till payday? [verb]

Will you **lend** me some money? [verb]

Did the bank give you a **loan?** [noun]

bring, take Use *bring* to mean "to carry from a distant place to a closer one." Use *take* to mean the opposite: "to carry from a nearby place to a more distant one."

Will you **bring** me some perfume when you come back from Paris?

Don't forget to **take** your passport when you go to Europe.

can, may *Can* indicates the ability to do something. *May* indicates permission to do something or the possibility of doing it.

You **can** make hot chocolate by dissolving cocoa in warm milk.

You **may** have a cup of hot chocolate before going to sleep.

can't hardly, can't scarcely These terms are considered double negatives because *hardly* and *scarcely* by themselves have a negative meaning. Therefore, avoid using *hardly* and *scarcely* with *not* or *-n't.*

Eduardo **can hardly** tell the twins apart.

The driver **can scarcely** see through the dense fog.

could of, might of, must of, should of, would of After the words *could, might, must, should,* or *would,* use the helping verb *have,* not the preposition *of.*

Some historians say that the United States **could have** prevented the stock market crash of 1929.

The country **might have** avoided the Great Depression that followed.

The Great Depression **must have** been a difficult time to raise a family.

different from, different than The expression *different from* is generally preferred to *different than.*

The sport of cross-country skiing is **different from** downhill skiing.

English Language Learners

Using Negatives

In some languages, the use of a double negative is acceptable. Remind students that in English the use of double negatives is considered incorrect. Write this sentence on the board: *We can't go nowhere after school.* Ask a volunteer to circle the two negative words *(can't, nowhere)* in the sentence. Then correct the sentence: *We can't go anywhere after school.* Repeat the process using other contractions with *nothing, none, no one, never,* and so on.

Exercise 2 Making Usage Choices

For each of the following sentences, choose the correct word or expression from the pair in parentheses.

Kansas City and Native American History

1. The Missouri River flows (between/among) Kansas City, Missouri, and Kansas City, Kansas.
2. Both cities are situated (beside/besides) the river.
3. If you look at a map, you (can/may) see that the Missouri River forms part of the boundary between Kansas and Missouri.
4. Until the Civil War, Kansas City's economy was based on supplying and outfitting the large (number/amount) of travelers headed west.
5. After the first railroads reached the city in the 1860s, (alot of/a lot of) things changed.
6. One major (affect/effect) was that the city became a busy cattle-trading center.
7. The city was (already/all ready) a railroad hub, and it soon became a great grain center.
8. A large (amount/number) of Native Americans once lived in the area that is now Kansas City.
9. Pioneers who settled in the area established trading posts (being as/because) the river facilitated travel and trade.
10. (Beside/Besides) the Osage nation, the Kansa, Delaware, and Wyandot nations lived in the area where Kansas City now stands.
11. Until the late nineteenth century, visitors to Kansas City (could of/could have) seen people of several Native American nations living around the town.
12. One (can scarcely/can't scarcely) exaggerate the importance of the role played by Native Americans in the history of Kansas City.
13. If you visit Kansas City, carry your camera or (borrow/loan) one from a friend.
14. Years ago Native Americans would (bring/take) furs to Fort Osage from far away to exchange for manufactured goods.
15. Many historians claim that the federal government's resettlement of many Native Americans to Indian Territory in Oklahoma was carried out (bad/badly).
16. (Being as/Because) most of the Native Americans who were resettled had not chosen to move, many people today feel that the mass movement was unjust.
17. The Cherokee, Chickasaw, Creek, Choctaw, and Seminole peoples each had traditions and customs that were quite (different than/different from) those of the others.
18. The history of all of these Native American nations (would of/would have) been quite different had they not been moved forcibly to Indian Territory.
19. Originally, Indian Territory also included a vast (number/amount) of land in Kansas and Nebraska.
20. When Oklahoma became a state in 1907, the last of the Indian Territory was dissolved, leaving Native Americans in Oklahoma to live (between/among) the general population.

Practice and Assess

Answers: Exercise 2

1. between
2. beside
3. can
4. number
5. a lot of
6. effect
7. already
8. number
9. because
10. Besides
11. could have
12. can scarcely
13. borrow
14. bring
15. badly
16. Because
17. different from
18. would have
19. amount
20. among

Enrichment and Extension

Explaining Choices

Have students study the following sentence from *Shakespeare of London* by Marchette Chute: *A major company seldom had more than twelve actors in it and could not afford to hire an indefinite number of extra ones for a single production.* Ask students why *number* is used instead of *amount.* (It refers to items that can be counted.) Invite students to search through books and magazines for other examples of word usage they have studied and to write an explanation of the writer's choice. **L2**

Teach

Cross-reference: Mechanics

For instruction and practice using apostrophes to form contractions such as *doesn't* and *don't,* refer students to Lesson 21.11, pp. 759–761.

doesn't, don't *Doesn't* is a shortened form of *does not,* which is used with *he, she, it,* and all singular nouns. *Don't* is a shortened form of *do not,* which is used with *I, you, we, they,* and all plural nouns. Authorities usually discourage the use of contractions in formal writing.

Our state **doesn't** allow people to drive before the age of seventeen.

Some countries **don't** require their citizens to attend school.

emigrate, immigrate Use *emigrate* to mean "to leave one country and go to another to live." Use *immigrate* to mean "to come to a country to settle there." Use *from* with *emigrate* and *to* or *into* with *immigrate.*

Mr. Roh **emigrated** from South Korea.

He **immigrated** to the United States.

farther, further *Farther* should be used in reference to physical distance. *Further* should be used in reference to degree or time.

San Antonio is **farther** south than Dallas.

She did not question him **further.**

fewer, less Use *fewer* when referring to nouns that can be counted. Use *less* when referring to nouns that cannot be counted. *Less* may also be used with figures that are seen as single amounts or single quantities.

Fewer students have enrolled in physics this year than last year.

This year there is **less** interest in physics among the students.

We traveled to New York City in **less** than two hours. [*Two* is treated as a single period of time, not as individual hours.]

It cost **less** than $20.00 to go by train. [The amount of money is treated as a single sum, not as individual dollars.]

good, well See Unit 18.

had of Do not use *of* between *had* and a past participle.

I wish I **had received** this information earlier.

hanged, hung Use *hanged* when you mean "put to death by hanging." Use *hung* in all other instances.

Were any convicts in our state **hanged** during the twentieth century?

The teacher **hung** the bulletin board above her desk.

in, into Use *in* to mean "inside" or "within" and *into* to indicate movement or direction from the outside to a point within. The preposition *in* suggests a fixed location within a particular area or place. The preposition *into* suggests movement within or between locations.

Jeanine was sitting outdoors **in** a lawn chair.

When it got too hot, she went **into** the house.

Enrichment and Extension

Using Fewer and Less

Review count and noncount nouns with students. Then write the following nouns on the board: *marbles, pudding, ideas, rice, violins, water.* Ask students to identify each as either a count or a noncount noun. Then have them create sentences using *fewer* or *less* before each noun (*fewer marbles, less pudding, fewer ideas, less rice, fewer violins, less water*). Ask students to check each other's work and to provide effective feedback, supporting their answers with specific rules or examples from this glossary. **L2**

irregardless, regardless Use *regardless.* The prefix *ir-* and the suffix *-less* both have negative meanings. When used together, they produce a double negative, which is incorrect.

Regardless of what the critics said, I liked the movie.

Exercise 3 **Making Usage Choices**

For each of the following sentences, choose the correct word or expression from the pair in parentheses.

San Antonio

1. During its early history, San Antonio, Texas, was under the control of no (fewer/less) than three countries.
2. In 1731, fifteen families (emigrated/immigrated) from Spain's Canary Islands and settled in San Antonio.
3. The beautiful mission of San José still looks (good/well) after many years.
4. If you visit San Antonio, (don't/doesn't) miss seeing the Alamo.
5. To see the Alamo, the site of the famous 1836 battle between Texas and Mexico, you must go (in/into) the center of San Antonio.
6. If the Texas garrison (had/had of) been larger, would it have withstood the Mexican attack?
7. (Irregardless/Regardless) of their defeat at the Alamo, the Texans went on to win the war.
8. Do you suppose that officials (hanged/hung) the flag of the independent Republic of Texas in buildings in San Antonio?
9. During the 1800s, pioneers flocked to Texas, pushing the frontier (farther/further) west.
10. The modern city of San Antonio is quite different (from/than) the original Spanish settlement founded hundreds of years ago.
11. (In/Into) the modern city are a number of military bases.
12. The bases (affected/effected) population growth in the region.
13. Because of jobs on the bases, many people (emigrated/immigrated) to the area.
14. It's possible that the military has (less/fewer) economic importance for the region today.
15. The future of the defense industry in San Antonio is open to (farther/further) study.
16. San Antonio has (less/fewer) residents than Houston or Dallas.
17. At the time of the 2006 census, San Antonio's population was (less/fewer) than 2 million.
18. That population figure is (all ready/already) out of date.
19. It (doesn't/don't) take into account the many people who live in the surrounding metropolitan area.
20. Many people think that there (can/can't) hardly be a better place to live than San Antonio.

Vocabulary Link

When the prefix *ir-* is used in conjunction with the suffix *-able*, it does not form a double negative. Words such as *irradicable, irreconcilable, irrecoverable, irredeemable,* and *irremovable* are all acceptable.

Two-Minute Skill Drill

Complete the following sentence with the words in and into:

They were going to take a trip _______ the city _______ a bus.

See also *Two-Minute Skill Drill Transparency 19*

Practice and Assess

Answers: Exercise 3

1. fewer
2. emigrated
3. good
4. don't
5. into
6. had
7. Regardless
8. hung
9. farther
10. from
11. In
12. affected
13. immigrated
14. less
15. further
16. fewer
17. less
18. already
19. doesn't
20. can

Cooperative Learning

Discovering Word Usage

Dictionary entries often provide information about usage. If a word is designated as *slang, dialect, nonstandard,* or *obsolete*, it is best omitted from formal usage. Ask pairs of students to compile a list of slang terms and their definitions. Students may post the results of their research on the bulletin board or present them to the whole class.

Teach

Grammar Tip

One reason for the confusion between *lay* and *lie* is that the present-tense form of *lay* (*lay*) is the same as the past-tense form of *lie* (*lay*). *Lay* is a causative verb; it means "to cause something to lie."

Cross-reference: Usage

For instruction and practice with the correct use of the principal parts of irregular verbs such as *lay* and *lie,* refer students to Lesson 15.2, pp. 582–585.

Usage Glossary

this kind, these kinds *Kind* is singular. Therefore, the singular form *this* or *that* modifies *kind. This* and *that* should also be used with *sort* and *type (this type, that type, this sort, that sort). Kinds* is plural. Therefore, the plural form *these* or *those* modifies *kinds.* Also use *these* and *those* with the plural nouns *sorts* and *types.*

This kind of bulb should be used in your lamp.
These kinds of lamps are very attractive.
This sort of food is found in many ethnic cuisines.
These sorts of foods are nutritious.
That type of exercise is my favorite.
Those types of exercises are considered good for your heart.

lay, lie *Lay* means "to put" or "to place"; it takes a direct object. *Lie* means "to recline" or "to be positioned"; it never takes an object.

Lay your coat on the bed.
I am going to **lie** in the sun now.

Problems arise particularly in using the principal parts of these verbs. Notice, for example, that the past tense of *lie* is *lay.* Learn all the principal parts of these verbs.

BASIC FORM	lay	lie
PRESENT PARTICIPLE	laying	lying
PAST FORM	laid	lay
PAST PARTICIPLE	laid	lain

She **laid** her coat on the bed.
I **lay** in the sun too long and got sunburned.
She had **laid** her coat on the bed before the party started.
I have **lain** in the sun longer without getting as sunburned.

learn, teach *Learn* means "to gain knowledge or understanding," and *teach* means "to give knowledge or instruction."

Jon **learned** to play the piano at the age of nine.
Mrs. Ramos **teaches** American history.

leave, let *Leave* means "to go away," and *let* means "to allow" or "to permit."

When you **leave** next week, I will miss you.
Please **let** me use your dictionary.

Cooperative Learning

Visualizing Usage

To help with word usage, have students form four groups and ask each group to choose one of the following pairs of words or phrases: *this kind* and *these kinds*; *lay* and *lie*; *learn* and *teach*; *leave* and *let.* Then tell students to make a simple chart, writing the words they chose at the top and a summary of their differences below. To use the chart, have them insert words into sample sentences. For example, ask the group that charted *lay* and *lie* to complete the following sentence with the correct verb: *I fell asleep ______ on the grass.* **L2**

like, as *Like* is a preposition and introduces a prepositional phrase. *As* is a subordinating conjunction and introduces a subordinate clause. Many authorities say that it is incorrect to use *like* before a clause.

Phil plays baseball **like** a professional.

Teresa is confident, **as** I am, that everything will go well on the expedition.

loose, lose The adjective *loose* means "free," "not firmly attached," or "not fitting tightly." The verb *lose* means "to have no longer," "to misplace," or "to fail to win."

That ring is so **loose** you are sure to **lose** it.

Which team do you think will **lose** the game?

passed, past *Passed* is the past form and the past participle of the verb *to pass. Past* may be an adjective, a preposition, an adverb, or a noun.

We **passed** your house on the way to school. [verb]

Chris had a cold this **past** week. [adjective]

We drove **past** your house last Sunday. [preposition]

What time did you drive **past?** [adverb]

Louise's grandmother always tells wonderful stories about her **past.** [noun]

precede, proceed *Precede* means "to go before" or "to come before." *Proceed* means "to continue" or "to move along."

Our band **preceded** the homecoming float as the parade **proceeded** through town.

raise, rise The verb *raise* means "to cause to move upward"; it always takes an object. The verb *rise* means "to go up"; it is intransitive and does not take an object.

Raise your hand if you know the answer.

The rocket will **rise** from the launching pad at 9:01 A.M.

reason is, because *Because* means "for the reason that." Therefore, do not use *because* after *reason is.* Use *that* after *reason is* or use *because* alone.

The **reason** I am tired is that I did not sleep last night.

I am tired **because** I did not sleep last night.

Usage Glossary

Listening and Speaking

Students will not misuse *loose* and *lose* if they know the correct pronunciation of each word. Have them listen for the differences in pronunciation as you read aloud the example sentences in the lesson.

Cross-reference: Grammar

For instruction and practice with transitive and intransitive verbs such as *raise* and *rise*, refer students to Lesson 10.3, pp. 452–460.

MEETING INDIVIDUAL NEEDS

Gifted and Talented

Identifying Causative Verbs

Write the verb pairs *lay, lie*; *raise, rise*; and *set, sit* on the chalkboard. Tell students that the first verb in each pair is a causative verb—one whose meaning involves causing something to happen. For example, to raise something is "to cause it to rise." Causative verbs always take an object. Explain that the second verb in each pair is intransitive and does not take an object. Discuss with students how they can use this information to determine if they have used these verbs properly in their writing. Then have students apply the method as they review and revise a recent writing assignment. **L3**

Practice and Assess

Answers: Exercise 4

1. lies
2. that
3. teach
4. emigrated
5. lets
6. as
7. proceed
8. past
9. rises
10. these kinds
11. lose
12. learn
13. lies
14. Proceeding
15. past
16. As
17. raise
18. leave
19. that
20. This kind

Exercise 4 Making Usage Choices

For each of the following sentences, choose the correct word or expression from the pair in parentheses.

New York City

1. New York City (lies/lays) near the mouth of the Hudson River in the southeast corner of New York State.
2. The reason New York is often called a melting pot is (because/that) many ethnic groups have settled there.
3. At the Ellis Island Immigration Museum, exhibits (teach/learn) visitors about the history of European immigration to the United States.
4. More than twelve million people (immigrated/emigrated) from their homelands and passed through the reception center on Ellis Island between 1892 and 1954.
5. The federal government now (lets/leaves) tourists visit Ellis Island.
6. If you wish to learn more about ethnic America, (like/as) our class did, you can visit the Hispanic Society of America, the Japan Society Gallery, the Museum of the American Indian, and the Jewish Museum.
7. You can admire works by African American artists at the Studio Museum in Harlem and then (precede/proceed) to the Schomburg Center for Research in Black Culture.
8. At the Metropolitan Museum of Art, visitors can stroll (past/passed) exhibits of art from around the world.
9. In Chinatown, near an apartment building that (rises/raises) high above the street, is a bronze statue of Confucius, the venerable Chinese philosopher.
10. Tourists and New Yorkers alike enjoy visiting (these kinds/this kind) of places to learn more about our country's multicultural heritage.
11. New York is still a city in which people of many races and ethnic backgrounds can live together and not (lose/loose) their cultural identity.
12. You can (teach/learn) much about New York City's history by visiting the Museum of the City of New York and the New York Historical Society.
13. The South Street Seaport Museum, which (lays/lies) near the East River, specializes in maritime history.
14. (Preceding/Proceeding) from Manhattan to the Bronx, maritime buffs can also visit the City Island Nautical Museum.
15. In 1998 New York City held many festivals to celebrate its (passed/past).
16. (As/Like) they did a century ago, traditional sailing ships moor in New York Harbor.
17. When the time arrives to depart, sailors (raise/rise) the ships' billowing white sails.
18. When the ships set sail, they (let/leave) many admirers gazing after them.
19. What is the reason (because/that) so many people are intrigued by the sea?
20. (This kind/These kinds) of question is hard to answer.

English Language Learners

Hearing Differences

Ask students who are learning English to look at the glossary and select all the word pairs that consist of words that sound alike to them. For example, some students may have difficulty distinguishing *precede* from *proceed.* Write the word pairs on the chalkboard.

Then have students take turns pronouncing the words and using them in sentences. Remind students that the more they hear the words used properly in sentences, the more likely they will be to use the words correctly in their own speech.

respectfully, respectively *Respectfully* means "with respect." *Respectively* means "in the order named."

The audience listened **respectfully** as the poet spoke.

Phoenix and Phoenixville are, **respectively,** in Arizona and Pennsylvania.

says, said *Says* is the third-person singular of the verb *say. Said* is the past tense of *say.* Be careful not to use *says* for *said.*

At dinner last night, Nelson **said** that he wasn't hungry.

He always **says** that, but he eats everything anyway.

sit, set *Sit* means "to place oneself in a seated position." *Sit* rarely takes an object. *Set* means "to place" or "to put" and usually takes an object.

Set is also an intransitive verb when it is used with *sun* to mean "the sun is going down" or "the sun is sinking below the horizon." When *set* is used in this way, it does not take an object.

Grandpa likes to **sit** on the porch.

Lian **set** the pots on the stove after the sun **set.**

than, then *Than* is a conjunction used to introduce the second element in a comparison; it also shows exception.

Elsa is taller **than** Isabel.

Our visitor was none other **than** Uncle Al!

Then is an adverb that means "at that time," "soon afterward," "the time mentioned," "at another time," "for that reason," or "in that case."

My grandmother was a young girl **then.**

Marguerite finished the book and **then** turned out the light.

By **then** the party was almost over.

If it rains, **then** we cannot go.

this here, that there Avoid using *here* and *there* after *this* and *that.* Use *this* and *that* alone.

All of us want to read **this** magazine.

Have you heard **that** story?

where at Do not use *at* after *where.*

Where is Valley Forge?

who, whom See Unit 17.

Teach

Cooperative Learning

Most newspapers will have examples of the types of word usage covered in this glossary. Tell the class that in this activity they will be functioning as teams of editors, checking to make sure the reporters are following the word usage guidelines described in Unit 19.

Begin by asking the class to choose the part of the newspaper they would like to check. Then divide the class into small groups. Each group should choose a section of the glossary as its responsibility and check the paper for sentences that use those words, trying to find at least one example for each word. If students think the word has been used incorrectly, they should note the sentence and how it should be corrected, citing a specific rule from this glossary. Groups should then share their results and any insights they had during the process.

Two-Minute Skill Drill

Have students study the sentence below. Ask them what part of speech *then* is and why it is used instead of *than.* (*Then* is an adverb, whereas *than* is a conjunction. Here, then means "soon afterward," and it modifies an adjective, the participle stacking.)

Mrs. Delahanty watched her husband eat, nibbling up to the edges of the toast, then stacking the crusts about his tea cup in a neat fence-like arrangement.

—Jessamyn West, "Sixteen"

See also *Two-Minute Skill Drill Transparency 19*

Enrichment and Extension

Using *Say* in a Narrative

Ask students to recall an interesting conversation they have had or heard. Then have them write the conversation, making sure to use the verb *say.* Suggest that students exchange papers with a friend. Tell them to check each other's writing to make sure the verb *say* has been used correctly. Remind students to provide effective feedback. Encourage volunteers to share their narratives with the class. **L2**

Practice and Assess

Answers: Exercise 5

1. than
2. then
3. sit
4. This
5. respectfully
6. respectively
7. whom
8. said
9. where
10. This

Answers: Exercise 6

1. Where
2. sits
3. lies
4. badly
5. Between
6. rise
7. Besides
8. Like
9. bring
10. learn

Exercise 5 Making Usage Choices

For each of the following sentences, choose the correct word or expression from the pair in parentheses.

Santa Fe

1. Santa Fe, New Mexico, has more sites of historic interest (than/then) some other American cities.
2. Tourists in Santa Fe can explore the narrow, winding streets and (than/then) visit museums that display Native American crafts.
3. In summer, audiences (set/sit) in the open-air theater of the Santa Fe Opera.
4. (This/This here) opera house is one of the most famous in the world.
5. Audiences listen (respectfully/respectively) as some of the world's greatest opera singers perform.
6. Native Americans and Spanish colonists were, (respectfully/ respectively), the first two groups to reside in the Santa Fe area.
7. Many of the early Spaniards (who/whom) we know about in this area came to search for fabulous riches.
8. These early Spaniards reported hearing of a man who (said/says) he had seen seven cities of gold in the area.
9. Santa Fe is the place (where/where at) the historic Santa Fe Trail ended.
10. (This/This here) trail was used by pioneers traveling west during the 1800s.

Exercise 6 Making Usage Choices

For each of the following sentences, choose the correct word or expression from the pair in parentheses.

Washington, D.C.

1. (Where/Where at) is Washington, D.C., located?
2. The capital of the United States (sets/sits) at what may be considered the dividing line between the North and the South.
3. The city (lies/lays) along the banks of two rivers, the mighty Potomac and its tributary, the Anacostia.
4. When the location was first selected for the capital of the country, some people thought that the choice had been (bad/badly) made.
5. (Between/Among) the two rivers stretched a broad area of what many people considered swamp.
6. They did not believe that a graceful city would (raise/rise) where they saw only bog.
7. (Besides/Beside) the swampy ground, the hot summer climate was a problem.
8. (Like/As) other towns and cities of the time, Washington had streets that were little better than rutted dirt roads.
9. Planes, cars, and trains today (take/bring) about 20 million tourists a year to this beautiful city with a multicultural population.
10. In addition, people from many countries and states move to the capital and (teach/learn) to call it home.

Exercise 7 Making Usage Choices

For each of the following sentences, choose the correct word or expression from the pair in parentheses.

New Orleans

1. New Orleans, Louisiana, has (a/an) average annual rainfall of about fifty-five inches, and much of the city (lays/lies) below sea level, making it vulnerable to hurricanes.
2. (A lot/Alot) of levees were constructed along the banks of the Mississippi River to prevent flooding.
3. Residents have all (taught/learned) the importance of the levees after they failed during Hurricane Katrina.
4. The Mississippi River flows through Baton Rouge and then (precedes/proceeds) southeasterly to New Orleans.
5. New Orleans (ain't/is not) only a shipping center, but it is also a mecca for tourists.
6. (Being that/Because) New Orleans is picturesque, many people enjoy vacationing there.
7. The temperature in the winter months (doesn't/don't) drop below freezing very often.
8. French and Spanish settlers (preceded/proceeded) German and Irish immigrants to the city of New Orleans by more than one hundred years.
9. In addition, people from Italy (emigrated/immigrated) to New Orleans.
10. In some New Orleans restaurants, customers can choose (among/between) French and Creole cuisine.
11. Most visitors enjoy strolling through the streets of the historic French Quarter for quite (a while/awhile), taking in the beautiful architecture.
12. No skyscrapers (raise/rise) above the low skyline of the French Quarter.
12. Visitors need walk no (farther/further) than Bourbon Street to hear jazz.
14. A large (number/amount) of visitors attend concerts at music venues like the famous Preservation Hall.
15. Visitors crowd (in/into) this hall whenever jazz is being played.
16. In Preservation Hall, women (set/sit) their purses on their laps as they (set/sit) on the crowded wooden benches.
17. Here musicians play jazz (like/as) it was played in the early 1900s.
18. This style of jazz is quite (different from/different than) the style of modern jazz.
19. By February of each year, the citizens of New Orleans are (all ready/already) to hold their famous Mardi Gras festival.
20. During Mardi Gras, the city (can scarcely/can't scarcely) accommodate its many visitors.
21. During this celebration, it is (all right/alright) to dress in elaborate costumes and take part in carnivals and parades.
22. Although the heat and humidity of New Orleans may (affect/effect) some visitors, the local inhabitants wouldn't want to live anywhere else.
23. Similarly, they (accept/except) without serious complaint the amount of rainfall.
24. It seems the residents are (altogether/all together) used to the climate.
25. (Between/Among) the inhabitants of New Orleans are Creoles, descendants of early French and Spanish settlers, and Cajuns, descendants of French Canadian refugees from Nova Scotia.

Answers: Exercise 7

1. an; lies
2. A lot
3. learned
4. proceeds
5. is not
6. Because
7. doesn't
8. preceded
9. immigrated
10. between
11. a while
12. rise
13. farther
14. number
15. into
16. set; sit
17. as
18. different from
19. all ready
20. can scarcely
21. all right
22. affect
23. accept
24. altogether
25. Among

Practice and Assess

Answers: Exercise 8

1. altogether
2. might have
3. respectively
4. accept
5. badly
6. set
7. hung
8. than
9. that
10. into
11. bring
12. then
13. these kinds
14. passed
15. beside
16. can
17. fewer
18. teach
19. lose
20. can hardly
21. Besides
22. then
23. fewer
24. Among
25. as

Exercise 8 Making Usage Choices

For each of the following sentences, choose the correct word or expression from the pair in parentheses.

Boston

1. Boston is an (all together/altogether) special place.
2. Do you think that if Boston had been more centrally located, it (might have/might of) become the nation's capital?
3. New York City and Philadelphia were, (respectively/respectfully), the first and second capitals of the United States.
4. In 1773 Bostonians who would not (accept/except) King George III's taxes dumped three shiploads of tea into Boston Harbor.
5. They wanted independence from England (bad/badly).
6. They (set/sit) several demands before the English king.
7. The government of the city of Boston has (hanged/hung) plaques at historic sites.
8. Some people say that Beacon Hill, more (than/then) any other area in Boston, is known for its beauty and historic importance.
9. Boston is a very accessible city. The reason is (because/that) it has an efficient transit system.
10. If you want to get from the suburbs to the city center, just go (in/into) the nearest station of the rapid transit system, and you'll be there in no time.
11. Be sure to (bring/take) a raincoat if you come to Boston in the fall, for the weather can be stormy.
12. A visitor can tour the Boston Museum of Fine Arts and (then/than) visit the Museum of Science.
13. Boston abounds in (this kind/these kinds) of museums.
14. After the Charles River has (passed/past) through the city, the river empties into Boston Harbor.
15. People can picnic in the parks (beside/besides) the river.
16. A visitor who likes to walk (can/may) follow the Freedom Trail to many of Boston's historic sites.
17. Along the one-and-a-half-mile-long trail are no (less/fewer) than 15 historic sites.
18. Guidebooks will (learn/teach) the visitor about places on the trail.
19. The visitor will not (lose/loose) the way because the trail is well marked.
20. Time spent in Boston (can't hardly/can hardly) be forgotten.
21. (Besides/Beside) being a historical treasure trove, Boston is a leader in education.
22. In 1636 Harvard College was founded in what was (than/then) Newtowne.
23. Harvard, the first university founded in the English colonies, had many (less/fewer) students in the 1600s than it does now.
24. (Among/Between) Boston's many institutions of higher learning are Tufts, Boston University, Northeastern University, and the Massachusetts Institute of Technology.
25. If you run, (like/as) I have, along the jogging trail that follows the Charles River, you can glimpse at least three of these universities.

Exercise 9 Making Usage Choices

For each of the following sentences, choose the correct word or expression from the pair in parentheses.

Seattle

1. Recently a report (said/says) that Seattle, Washington, is one of America's most attractive cities.
2. (Irregardless/Regardless) of whether or not people choose to live in Seattle, most agree it is a beautiful place.
3. Many tourists (who/whom) the Century 21 Exposition attracted in 1962 later returned to Seattle to live.
4. Seattle is known as the Emerald City, a name (borrowed/loaned) from *The Wizard of Oz.*
5. The city of Seattle (lays/lies) near the Pacific Ocean.
6. (This/This here) location made Seattle a gateway to the Far East.
7. Many Japanese were (between/among) Seattle's early settlers.
8. Other early settlers (emigrated/immigrated) from Scandinavia.
9. A glance at the beautiful Cascade Mountains east of Seattle can easily (raise/rise) one's spirits.
10. This is the mountain range (where/where at) Mount Saint Helens is located.

Exercise 10 Making Usage Choices

For each of the following sentences, choose the correct word or expression from the pair in parentheses.

Atlanta

1. (Leave/Let) us go to Atlanta, Georgia.
2. Atlanta is a larger city (than/then) Birmingham, Alabama.
3. Today's Atlanta is very (different from/different than) the city portrayed in *Gone with the Wind.*
4. Traces of the Old South (can't hardly/can hardly) be found in Atlanta.
5. A devastated city after the Civil War, Atlanta is more than (alright/all right) now.
6. Other cities seeking Atlanta's success have done (like/as) Atlanta has.
7. Because of its location, Atlanta is (all ready/already) well situated as a transportation crossroads.
8. By promoting itself (good/well), Atlanta has attracted national corporations and federal government offices.
9. Some visitors who (could have/could of) seen the *Cyclorama,* a depiction of the Battle of Atlanta and one of the three largest paintings in the world, (passed/past) up the opportunity.
10. Many of those who see the painting agree that its (affect/effect) is striking.

Answers: Exercise 9

1. said
2. Regardless
3. whom
4. borrowed
5. lies
6. This
7. among
8. emigrated
9. raise
10. where

Answers: Exercise 10

1. Let
2. than
3. different from
4. can hardly
5. all right
6. as
7. already
8. well
9. could have; passed
10. effect

Usage Glossary

Additional Resources

 *Grammar Workbook,* Lessons 65–69

Close

Ask students to write a paragraph in their journals naming those words and expressions they find most difficult. Have them explain how the usage glossary has helped them use these words and expressions correctly in their writing. Then have students exchange papers and discuss one another's explanations.

Teach

About the Literature

Explain that the review contains several quotations about friendship and love, followed by exercises on related topics.

Linking Grammar and Literature

☑ Teaching Tip

Each quotation contains one or more of the usage items covered in the glossary. After students have read the quotations, ask them to discuss the highlighted words and the explanation for each usage.

Critical Thinking

Ask students to look up each term highlighted in the quotations in the glossary of usage items. Discuss with them the rule, if there is one, that governs the usage of each item. Explain that while improper usage may be acceptable in everyday speech, it is usually unacceptable in formal writing. Point out that most writers strive to make proper usage choices.

ASSESSMENT OPTIONS

Tests with Answer Key & Rubrics
Unit 19 Mastery Test, pp. 73–74

Testmaker
Unit 19 Mastery Test

UNIT 19

Grammar Review

USAGE GLOSSARY

The following quotations, which relate to the themes of friendship and love, have been annotated to show usage items covered in this unit.

Usage Glossary

Literature Models

Quotations About Friendship and Love

The relative pronoun *who* in the nominative case because it is the subject of a clause

He who has a thousand friends has not a friend to spare.
And he who has one enemy will meet him everywhere.

From Sentences *by Ali Ibn-Abi-Talib (seventh century), translated from the Arabic*

Can used to suggest ability

To me, fair friend, you never can be old. . . .

From Sonnet 104 by William Shakespeare

The preposition *into* used to suggest movement from one place to another

I breathed a song into the air,
It fell to earth, I knew not where. . . .
And the song, from beginning to end,
I found again in the heart of a friend.

The preposition *in* used to mean "inside"

From "The Arrow and the Song" by Henry Wadsworth Longfellow

"Every man's his own friend."
"Except sometimes some people are nobody's enemies but their own."

Except used as a conjunction meaning "but"

From Oliver Twist *by Charles Dickens*

Like, a preposition, used to introduce a prepositional phrase

For there is no friend like a sister
In calm or stormy weather;
To cheer one on the tedious way,
To fetch one if one goes astray. . . .

From "Goblin Market" by Christina Rossetti

May used to suggest possibility

The process of falling in love at first sight is as final as it is swift . . . , but the growth of true friendship may be a lifelong affair.

From The Country of the Pointed Firs *by Sarah Orne Jewett*

Resource Manager

Planning Resources

- *Lesson Plans*

Other Print Resources

- *Grammar and Composition Handbook*
- *Grammar Workbook,* Lessons 65–69, Unit 10 Review, Cumulative Review: Units 1–10

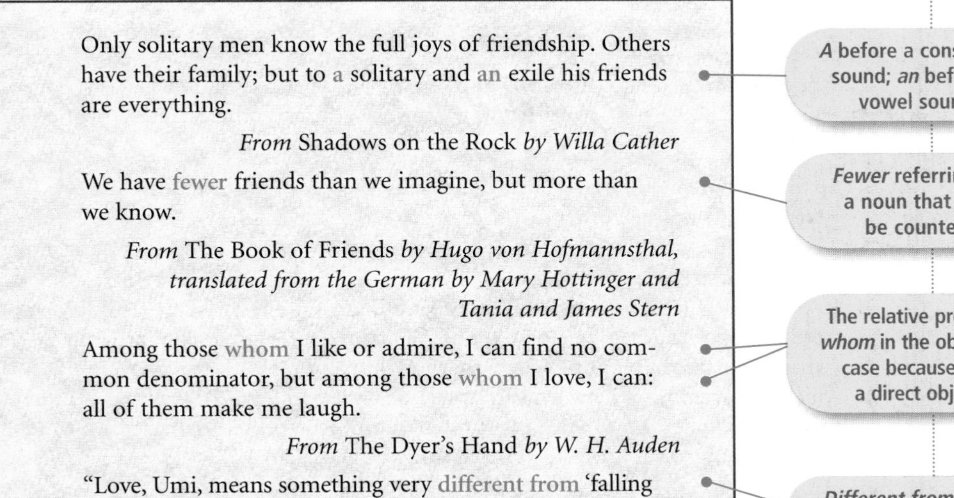

Only solitary men know the full joys of friendship. Others have their family; but to a solitary and an exile his friends are everything.

From Shadows on the Rock *by Willa Cather*

We have fewer friends than we imagine, but more than we know.

From The Book of Friends *by Hugo von Hofmannsthal, translated from the German by Mary Hottinger and Tania and James Stern*

Among those whom I like or admire, I can find no common denominator, but among those whom I love, I can: all of them make me laugh.

From The Dyer's Hand *by W. H. Auden*

"Love, Umi, means something very different from 'falling in love,'" Daddyji said. "It's not an act but a lifelong process. . . ."

From The Ledge Between the Streams *by Ved Mehta*

A before a consonant sound; *an* before a vowel sound

Fewer referring to a noun that can be counted

The relative pronoun *whom* in the objective case because it is a direct object

Different from rather than *different than*

Review: Exercise 1 **Making Usage Choices**

The following sentences describe friendships between famous artists. For each item, choose the correct word or expression in parentheses and write it on your paper.

1. Though they were very (different from/different than) each other in temperament, the Dutch painter Vincent van Gogh and the French painter Paul Gauguin were close friends.
2. The French artist Edgar Degas noted the similarities (between/among) his drawing style and that of his friend, the American artist Mary Cassatt.
3. (Beside/Besides) Degas, Cassatt was also friendly with several other Impressionist painters.
4. (Being as/Since) Berthe Morisot's close friend, fellow French painter Edouard Manet, so admired one of her paintings, she gave it to him as a gift.
5. The friendship may have influenced Morisot's work more (than/then) it influenced that of Manet.

Practice and Assess

Answers: Exercise 1

1. different from
2. between
3. Besides
4. Since
5. than

Practice and Assess

Answers: Exercise 2

1. effect
2. altogether
3. where they taught painting
4. preceded
5. hung

Answers: Exercise 3

1. as
2. This
3. this kind
4. already
5. respectively
6. whom
7. than
8. all right
9. must have
10. immigrate

Grammar Review

Review: Exercise 2 Making Usage Choices

The following sentences describe more friendships between famous artists. For each item, choose the correct word or expression in parentheses and write it on your paper.

1. Spanish artist Pablo Picasso and French artist Georges Braque had a great (affect/effect) on each other's work.
2. They are known as the founders of Cubism, which was an (all together/altogether) new style of art for its time.
3. In the 1920s, the Russian artist Wassily Kandinsky and the Swiss artist Paul Klee were colleagues at the Bauhaus, a school of architecture and design in Berlin, (where they taught painting/where they taught painting at).
4. An artistic friendship between two Americans, the painter Georgia O'Keeffe and the photographer Alfred Stieglitz, (preceded/proceeded) their marriage.
5. Stieglitz (hanged/hung) O'Keeffe's paintings in his gallery.

Review: Exercise 3 Making Usage Choices

The following sentences describe friendships between famous writers. For each item, choose the correct word or expression in parentheses and write it on your paper.

1. In Rome in the first century B.C., the poet Virgil was supported, (like/as) his friend and fellow poet Horace also was, by the patron Maecenas.
2. (This/This here) article says that the writers Edith Wharton and Henry James were friends.
3. The authors Gustave Flaubert and Ivan Turgenev exchanged letters faithfully for two decades; (this kind/these kinds) of long-term correspondence is now rare.
4. Flaubert and Turgenev had (all ready/already) published some of their most famous novels when they met in 1863.
5. *Madame Bovary* and *Fathers and Sons,* by Flaubert and Turgenev, (respectfully/respectively), remain classics.
6. Herman Melville befriended his fellow American writer Nathaniel Hawthorne, (who/whom) he greatly admired.
7. During these authors' lifetimes, Hawthorne's works were more widely read (than/then) Melville's.
8. The novelists Joseph Conrad and Ford Madox Ford thought it was (all right/alright) to collaborate on two novels.
9. In the course of their friendship, the American poets Elizabeth Bishop and Marianne Moore (must of/must have) enjoyed each other's lively wit and humor.
10. The poet Joseph Brodsky received much support from his fellow Russian poet Anna Akhmatova before he was forced to (immigrate/emigrate) to the United States.

Review: Exercise 4 Making Usage Choices

The following sentences describe famous fictional friendships and romances. For each item, choose the correct word or expression in parentheses and write it on your paper.

1. In Arthur Conan Doyle's works, Sherlock Holmes investigates a great (amount/number) of criminal cases with his friend Watson.
2. Horatio tells his dear friend Hamlet, one of Shakespeare's tragic heroes, that he has seen the ghost of Hamlet's father (raise/rise) from the dead.
3. Romeo and Juliet, Shakespeare's famous young lovers, (can't/can't hardly) bear to be apart from each other.
4. By the end of Jane Austen's novel *Pride and Prejudice,* Elizabeth Bennet thinks she (passed/past) judgment on Mr. Darcy much too quickly.
5. In Emily Brontë's *Wuthering Heights,* Cathy's brother, who feels (bad/badly) about her impending marriage, tries to prevent the match and causes a tragedy.
6. In Tolstoy's novel *War and Peace,* Prince Andrei and Pierre are devoted friends, (irregardless/regardless) of their opposing personalities.
7. Huckleberry Finn and Tom Sawyer have (a lot/alot) of adventures together in Mark Twain's novels.
8. At the outset of Herman Melville's *Moby Dick,* Ishmael is terrified to find that he is (laying/lying) beside the bizarre-looking Queequeg, but they later become close friends.
9. Unhappy at school, the orphan Jane Eyre, Charlotte Brontë's main character, finds comfort for (a while/awhile) in a friendship with the sweet but sickly Helen Burns.
10. Although Cervantes's character Don Quixote (looses/loses) touch with reality, his squire and friend, Sancho Panza, maintains common sense.

Review: Exercise 5 Making Usage Choices

The following sentences describe relationships from mythology and folklore. For each item, choose the correct word or expression in parentheses and write it on your paper.

1. In Homer's *Iliad,* Achilles (borrows/lends/loans) his armor to his dear friend Patroclus, who lacks armor of his own, but Patroclus is nevertheless killed in battle.
2. Because Orpheus cannot (accept/except) the death of Eurydice, he enters the underworld to try to retrieve her.
3. In a tale told by Ovid, the parents of Pyramus and Thisbe tell the young lovers they (cannot/may not) marry.
4. The reason Pyramus stabs himself is (that/because) he believes a lioness has killed Thisbe.
5. Orestes, with his friend Pylades, goes (in/into) the palace of Clytemnestra to avenge Orestes' father's death.

Usage Glossary

Answers: Exercise 4

1. number
2. rise
3. can't
4. passed
5. bad
6. regardless
7. a lot
8. lying
9. a while
10. loses

Answers: Exercise 5

1. lends
2. accept
3. may not
4. that
5. into

Practice and Assess

Answers: Exercise 6

1. less
2. beside
3. raise
4. well
5. might have
6. further
7. amount
8. respectively
9. among
10. Altogether

Answers: Exercise 7 Proofreading

This proofreading activity provides editing practice with (1) the current or previous units' skills, (2) the **Troubleshooter** errors, and (3) spelling errors. Students should be able to complete the exercise by referring to the units, the **Troubleshooter,** and a dictionary. Note: A run-on sentence counts as one error.

Error (Type of Error)

1. past (usage)
   century, (nonessential appositive phrase)
2. physician, (nonessential appositive phrase)
   an amateur (usage)
3. spent (verb tense)
   a lot (usage)
   than (usage)
4. began (verb form)
5. fourteen and (sentence fragment)

Grammar Review

Usage Glossary

Review: Exercise 6 Making Usage Choices

The following sentences describe collaborations in science. For each item, choose the correct word or expression in parentheses and write it on your paper.

1. In 1903 the inventors Orville and Wilbur Wright altered aviation history with the first sustained flight; its distance was (fewer/less) than 150 feet.
2. The French chemist Marie Curie, working (beside/besides) her husband, Pierre Curie, discovered the element radium.
3. The Curies' work caused scientists to (raise/rise) their hopes about treating certain medical problems.
4. The Swiss psychologist Carl Jung and the Austrian founder of psychoanalysis, Sigmund Freud, worked (good/well) together for a brief time.
5. Jung (might of/might have) supported Freud's ideas initially, but he later disputed many of Freud's doctrines.
6. The discovery of the DNA double helix by James D. Watson and Francis H. C. Crick (farther/further) advanced our understanding of biology.
7. Their discovery, in turn, spurred a great (amount/number) of research into the role of DNA in the human body.
8. The anthropologists Louis and Mary Leakey and the team of Don Johanson and Tom Gray, working in Tanzania and Ethiopia (respectfully/respectively), made astounding archaeological discoveries.
9. The first lunar landing succeeded through cooperation (between/among) Neil Armstrong, Buzz Aldrin, and Michael Collins of the *Apollo 11* spaceflight.
10. (All together/Altogether) there were sixteen Apollo space missions.

Review: Exercise 7

Proofreading

The following passage describes the artist John Singer Sargent, whose painting is reproduced on the opposite page. Rewrite the passage, correcting any errors in spelling, grammar, and usage. Add any missing punctuation. There are twenty-five errors.

John Singer Sargent

[1]John Singer Sargent, a famous portrait and landscape painter of the passed century was born in Italy in 1856. [2]His father, a physician and his mother, a amateur painter, were wealthy New Englanders. [3]They spend alot more time in Europe then in America, however. [4]Sargent begun his studies in Florence at the age of fourteen. [5]And moved to Paris four years later. [6]He

John Singer Sargent, *Carnation, Lily, Lily, Rose,* 1886

discovered in Paris that he preferred to paint directly on the canvass without making preliminary sketches.

[7]When he was still younger then twenty-one, Sargent made his first trip to the United States. [8]He became instantly popular his portraits were in great demand in Boston and New York for awhile. [9]He quickly made a name for himself in London and emigrated there permenently in 1884.

[10]While living in London, Sargent cultivated influential friends; between these were the painter Edwin Abbey and the writer Henry James. [11]Sargents taste for aristocratic life are reflected in his portraits of upper-class people. [12]Although it may look as if Sargent painted all the faster he could, he actually labored over each piece until he achieved the affect he wanted. [13]He never excepted anything but the best from himself.

[14]As the art world turned increasingly toward modernism and abstraction, Sargent's realistic style gradually fell out of fashion. [15]His great talent as a painter however, was never challenged. [16]The Sargent work above show Sargent's extraordinary technique. [17]This here painting echoes the love and friendship expressed in the quotations that appear in this review.

Usage Glossary

Answers: Exercise 7 *(continued)*

Error (Type of Error)

6. canvas (spelling)
7. than (usage)
8. popular. His *or* popular; *or* popular, and (run-on sentence)
a while (usage)
9. immigrated (usage)
permanently (spelling)
10. among these (usage)
11. Sargent's (singular possessive)
is reflected (subject-verb agreement)
12. painted as fast as he (usage)
effect (usage)
13. accepted (usage)
14. gradually (spelling)
15. painter, (parenthetical element)
16. shows (subject-verb agreement)
17. This painting (usage)

Viewing the Art

John Singer Sargent, *Carnation, Lily, Lily, Rose,* 1886

Paintings, like works of literature, may be interpreted. Ask students to work in small groups to discuss these questions. *Who are the subjects of the painting? What is the mood? Which quotation from the Literature Models on pages 702–703 best describes the painting?*

Practice and Assess

Answers: Exercise 8

Mixed Review

1. who
2. can
3. take
4. Except
5. past
6. a
7. may
8. like
9. like
10. Besides
11. awhile
12. respectively
13. effect
14. that
15. fewer
16. past
17. emigrated
18. respectfully
19. proceeded
20. sits

Close

Ask groups of students to write a paragraph about friendship and love, incorporating at least five of the following pairs of terms: *awhile* and *a while, bad* and *badly, bring* and *take, fewer* and *less, hanged* and *hung, lay* and *lie, loose* and *lose, passed* and *past, sit* and *set,* and *who* and *whom.*

Students may write about anything they wish, providing the sentences form a cohesive paragraph. Have students read their paragraphs to their group and discuss whether the usage items in each paragraph are correct. Have students revise their paragraphs based on the feedback during discussion.

Usage Glossary

Review: Exercise 8

Mixed Review

The following sentences provide information about the authors of the quotations in this review. For each sentence, write the correct word or expression from parentheses.

1. Ali Ibn-Abi-Talib, (who/whom) was married to Mohammed's daughter, became a leader of Islam.
2. The division of Islam between Shia and Sunni (can/may) be traced back to events that occurred during the lifetime of Ali Ibn-Abi-Talib.
3. If you could (bring/take) only one writer's works to a desert island, the plays of William Shakespeare might suffice.
4. (Accept/Except) for *King Lear,* I prefer Shakespeare's comedies to his tragedies.
5. In narrative poems such as *Hiawatha* and *The Courtship of Miles Standish,* Henry Wadsworth Longfellow explored the events and folklore of the American (passed/past).
6. Longfellow combined the epic form of poetry with (a/an) simple and sentimental style that was his own.
7. It (can/may) be fair to say that Charles Dickens ranks among the most popular English writers of all time.
8. Most of Dickens's novels, (as/like) *Nicholas Nickleby,* first appeared in installments in periodicals.
9. Christina Rossetti, (like/as) her brother, Dante Gabriel Rossetti, was an English poet known for vivid imagery.
10. (Beside/Besides) writing lyrical religious poetry, Christina Rossetti specialized in writing verses for children.
11. The stories and novels of Sarah Orne Jewett give readers a sense of lingering (a while/awhile) in the countryside of the author's native Maine.
12. Christina Rossetti and Sarah Orne Jewett died in 1894 and 1909, (respectively/respectfully).
13. Her childhood in Nebraska had a great (affect/effect) on Willa Cather.
14. One reason Willa Cather was able to create strong characters who embody the pioneer spirit is (because/that) she knew many such people when she was growing up.
15. Hugo von Hofmannsthal, an Austrian writer, wrote (fewer/less) lyric poems as he grew older.
16. Von Hofmannsthal, a poet, dramatist, and essayist, wrote the text for some operas composed by Richard Strauss during the (passed/past) century.
17. The poet W. H. Auden (emigrated/immigrated) from England in 1939 and became an American citizen.
18. I listened (respectfully/respectively) when our teacher told us that Auden won the Pulitzer Prize in 1948 for *Age of Anxiety.*
19. Although the Indian-born author Ved Mehta had become completely blind by the age of three, he (preceded/proceeded) to excel in college and in his profession.
20. Ved Mehta owns a summer home on the island of Isleboro, which (sets/sits) in Penobscot Bay off the coast of Maine.

Writing Application

Usage of *Lie* in Writing

In this passage from *Of Wolves and Men,* Barry Holstun Lopez uses several forms of the intransitive verb *lie.* Read the passage, concentrating on the italicized verb forms.

> It is now late in the afternoon. The wolf has stopped traveling, has *lain* down to sleep on cool earth beneath a rock outcropping. Mosquitoes rest on his ears. His ears flicker. He begins to waken. He rolls on his back and *lies* motionless with his front legs pointed toward the sky but folded like wilted flowers, his back legs splayed, and his nose and tail curved toward each other on one side of his body.

Techniques with Usage of *Lie*

Try to use correct principal parts of the verb *lie* when you write and revise your own work.

TIME

For more about the writing process, see **TIME Facing the Blank Page**, pp. 121–131.

1. Learn the difference between *lie* and *lay.* Remember that *lie* means "to recline" or "to be positioned." *Lie* never takes an object. *Lay,* on the other hand, takes a direct object. *Lay* means "to put" or "to place."

INCORRECT USE He rolls on his back and *lays* motionless . . .

CORRECT USE He rolls on his back and *lies* motionless . . .

2. Learn the principal parts of the verb *lie: lie, lying, lay, lain.*

INCORRECT USE The wolf has stopped traveling, has *laid* down . . .

CORRECT USE The wolf has stopped traveling, has *lain* down . . .

Practice Practice these techniques by revising the following passage on a separate sheet of paper. Replace each set of parentheses with the correct form of *lie* or *lay.*

When I got home from school, I was exhausted. I ( ) down my backpack, which felt like a ton of bricks, and wanted nothing more than to ( ) down and lose some of my weariness. First, though, I had to ( ) out the ingredients my father would use to make his famous chicken stew. I trudged to the kitchen, where I found the cat ( ) in its own private patch of sunlight. It has probably ( ) there all day, I thought with resentment. I'd be ( ) there myself if I didn't have to go to school and to work and then home to do chores. "How long have you ( ) there, Hercules?" I demanded. A wheezy purr was its only response, so I picked up the hairy critter and ( ) it outside the kitchen door. Then I quickly ( ) out the food on the counter next to the stovetop before finally ( ) my own weary body to rest on my bed.

LOG ON Writing Online | For more grammar practice, go to glencoe.com and enter QuickPass code WC97727p2.

Usage Glossary

Usage of *Lie* in Writing

You may have students read the paragraph aloud. Read it without interruptions and then go back and discuss the italicized choices. Discuss these choices in relation to the Techniques with Usage of *Lie* in column two.

Techniques with Usage of *Lie*

Discuss the difference between *lie* and *lay.* Encourage students to develop mnemonics to help them remember the correct usage. Have students record the mnemonics in their journal. Then review the usage in the Review exercises.

Practice

Answers:

1. laid
2. lie
3. lay
4. lying
5. lain
6. lying
7. lain
8. laid
9. laid
10. laying

ASSESSMENT OPTIONS

Tests with Answer Key & Rubrics
Unit 19 Mastery Test, pp. 73–74

Testmaker
Unit 19 Mastery Test

You may wish to administer the Unit 19 Mastery Test at this point.

MindJogger Videoquizzes

INTRODUCING

UNIT 20

Objectives

- To learn the rules of capitalization
- To demonstrate control over the rules of capitalization by completing exercises in which those rules must be applied

ASSESSMENT OPTIONS

Tests with Answer Key & Rubrics
Unit 20 Pretest, pp. 75–76
Unit 20 Mastery Test, pp. 77–78

Testmaker
Unit 20 Pretest
Unit 20 Mastery Test

You may wish to administer the Unit 20 Pretest at this point.

Key to Ability Levels

L1 Level 1 activities are within the basic ability range of students.

L2 Level 2 activities are within the ability range of average students.

L3 Level 3 activities are more challenging activities.

UNIT 20

Capitalization

Resource Manager

Planning Resources
- *Lesson Plans*
- *Block Scheduling*

Transparencies
- *Bellringer*
- *Daily Language Practice*
- *Two-Minute Skill Drill*

Other Print Resources
- *Grammar and Composition Handbook*
- *Grammar Enrichment*
- *Grammar Practice*
- *Grammar Reteaching*
- *Grammar Workbook*
- *Tests with Answer Key and Rubrics*

Video
- *MindJogger Videoquizzes*

Software
- *Interactive Grammar and Language Workbook*
- *Presentation Plus!*
- *Testmaker*

Web Site
- *glencoe.com*

20.1 Capitalization of Sentences

■ Capitalize the first word of every sentence, including the first word of a direct quotation that is a complete sentence.

One of the first computers was large enough to fill a two-car garage.

Henry Ford said, "**T**hinking is the hardest work there is, which is the probable reason why so few engage in it."

Do not capitalize the first word of a quotation unless the entire quotation can stand as a complete sentence or it is capitalized in the original text.

Although astronauts must learn how to use computers, experts say most astronauts are "**c**omputer users, not computer wizards."

Do not capitalize an indirect quotation. An **indirect quotation** gives the meaning of an original statement without repeating it word for word. It is often introduced by the word *that.*

This letter from a computer camp states that **s**wimming, hiking, and archery will be offered this summer.

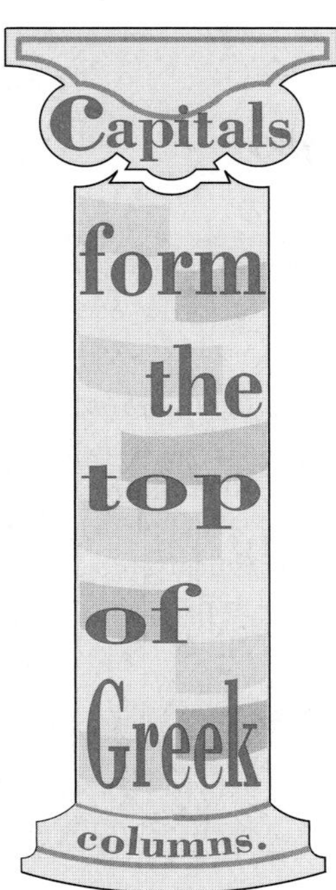
Capitals
form
the
top
of
Greek
columns.

Exercise 1 Capitalizing Quotations

Rewrite any incorrect sentences that follow, correcting any errors in capitalization. If a sentence is correct, write *correct.*

Franklin's Wisdom

1. Writer and publisher Benjamin Franklin observed, "nothing should be expressed in two words that can be as well expressed in one."
2. He advised writers to choose words that were "Smooth, clear, and short, for the contrary qualities are displeasing."
3. Franklin believed that writers should rarely, if ever, use synonyms or words that have almost the same meaning as other words.
4. He said, "words should be the most expressive that the language affords."
5. He recommended that words be so placed "As to be agreeable to the ear in reading."

Capitalization

Focus

Lesson Overview

Objective

- To know when to capitalize the first word in a sentence, a direct quotation, a sentence in parentheses, or an indirect quotation

Bellringer
Daily Language Activity

When students enter the classroom, have this assignment on the board: *Why are the underlined words below capitalized?* Discuss students' answers. Encourage students to ask questions for clarification.

His room was as black as pitch with the thick darkness (for the shutters were close fastened through fear of robbers) . . . . He had been saying to himself, "It is nothing but the wind in the chimney . . . ."

—Edgar Allan Poe, "The Tell-Tale Heart"

See also *Daily Language Practice*

Teach

Cross-reference: Quotation Marks

For instruction and practice with quotation marks, refer students to Lesson 21.9, pp. 752–756.

Practice and Assess

Answers: Exercise 1

1. "Nothing
2. "smooth
3. correct
4. "Words
5. "as

Resource Manager

Planning Resources
- *Lesson Plans*

Transparencies
- *Bellringer*
- *Daily Language Practice*

Other Print Resources
- *Grammar and Composition Handbook*
- *Grammar Enrichment,* p. 38
- *Grammar Practice,* p. 38
- *Grammar Workbook,* Lesson 70

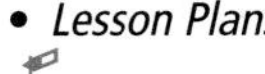

Practice and Assess

Answers: Exercise 2

1. (He hoped no one would notice him.)
2. correct
3. (someone was sneaking up behind him)
4. correct
5. (His wife always knew that it would be.)

Answers: Exercise 3

1. The great Indian leader Mohandas Gandhi said, "Civilization is . . ."
2. The Chinese American novelist Maxine Hong Kingston remarked, "You can. . . . You don't have to . . ."
3. correct
4. The civil rights leader Dr. Martin Luther King Jr. wrote that nonviolence is a powerful weapon. (He described nonviolence as a "sword that heals.")
5. correct
6. The Spanish philosopher and statesman José Ortega y Gasset wrote, "Living is a constant process of deciding . . ."
7. The Native American poet Simon J. Ortiz answered the question "Why do you write?" by saying, "Your children will not survive unless . . ."
8. correct
9. The American abolitionist Frederick Douglass wrote, "If there is no struggle . . ."
10. Margaret Mead (she was an anthropologist) wrote, "Today's children are the first . . ."

Additional Resources

Grammar Practice, p. 38

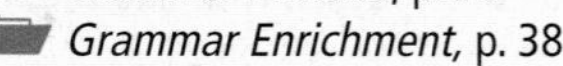

Grammar Enrichment, p. 38

Grammar Workbook, Lesson 70

Close

Initiate a discussion in which students consider how understanding correct capitalization will help them in other areas both inside and outside of school. Have students summarize their thoughts in their journal.

Capitalize the first word of a sentence in parentheses that stands by itself. Do not capitalize a sentence within parentheses that is contained within another sentence.

> Games can be tools for learning about computers. (**M**any programmers think that programming itself is the best game of all.)
>
> They were looking for software (**t**hey hoped to buy no more than three or four programs) that they could use in writing reports.

Exercise 2 Capitalizing Within Parentheses

Rewrite each item that is incorrect, correcting the capitalization. If an item is correct, write *correct.*

1. He went in through the back door. (he hoped no one would notice him.)
2. He expected to be nervous facing a huge crowd (ironically, no one was even in the room).
3. When he heard the noise (Someone was sneaking up behind him), he turned quickly.
4. Eventually the audience filled with young adults (no children were allowed).
5. His speech was very well received. (his wife always knew that it would be.)

Exercise 3 Capitalizing Sentences

Rewrite correctly any of the following sentences that have errors in capitalization. Write *correct* if a sentence has no errors.

Words to Ponder

1. the great Indian leader Mohandas Gandhi said, "civilization is the encouragement of differences."
2. The Chinese American novelist Maxine Hong Kingston remarked, "you can be a writer at any time. you don't have to worry about talent."
3. Eleanor Roosevelt wrote, "No one can make you feel inferior without your consent."
4. the civil rights leader Dr. Martin Luther King Jr. wrote that nonviolence is a powerful weapon. (he described nonviolence as a "sword that heals.")
5. The Russian-born sculptor Louise Nevelson said, "I never liked the middle ground—the most boring place in the world."
6. the Spanish philosopher and statesman José Ortega y Gasset wrote, "living is a constant process of deciding what we are going to do."
7. The Native American poet Simon J. Ortiz answered the question "why do you write?" by saying, "Your children will not survive unless you tell them something about them."
8. Albert Einstein wrote that imagination is more important than knowledge.
9. The American abolitionist Frederick Douglass wrote, "if there is no struggle, there is no progress."
10. Margaret Mead (She was an anthropologist) wrote, "today's children are the first generation to grow up in a world that has the power to destroy itself."

Meeting Individual Needs: Learning Disabled

Using Initial Capital Letters

Create word cards of commonplace nouns—some of which have the first letter capitalized and some of which do not—and have students use the nouns in sentences. The nouns with initial capital letters should always begin a sentence. **L1**

20.2 Capitalization of Proper Nouns

■ Capitalize a proper noun.

Proper nouns name particular persons, places, things, or ideas. In proper nouns composed of several words, capitalize only the important words. Do not capitalize articles, coordinating conjunctions, and prepositions of fewer than five letters.

1. Names of individuals

Seiji **O**zawa	**S**equoya
Sally **R**ide	**S**erena **W**illiams
Mark **T**wain	**J**esse **J**ackson
Charles de **G**aulle	**C**atherine the **G**reat

2. Titles of individuals

■ Capitalize titles used before a proper name and titles used in direct address.

Dr. Henry Ramirez	**C**hief Sitting Bull
Princess Caroline	**P**rime **M**inister Tony Blair
General Robert E. Lee	**S**ecretary of **S**tate Jefferson
Mother **T**eresa	**M**s. **J**ones
Pope John Paul II	**S**enator Durbin
Congresswoman Schroeder	Aye, aye, **C**aptain. [direct address]

■ In general, do not capitalize titles that follow a proper name or are used alone.

Lawton Chiles, the **g**overnor of Florida, met with the **p**resident last evening at the White House.

■ In general, capitalize a title that describes a family relationship when it is used with or in place of a proper name.

Have you met **A**unt Flora?	*but*	Have you met my **a**unt?
Please ask **G**randfather.		Please ask your **g**randfather.
What did you say, **M**other?		What did my **m**other say?
After a moment, **M**other spoke.		After a moment, my **m**other spoke.

Capitalization

Focus

Lesson Overview

Objective

- To identify and capitalize proper nouns when writing

Bellringer
Daily Language Activity

When students enter the classroom, have this assignment on the board: *Capitalize the words that require capitalization in the following sentences.*

My doctor is dr. cooper. He went to medical school at the university of oregon on the west coast.

See also  *Daily Language Practice*

Motivating Activity

Discuss students' responses to the Bellringer activity above. Remind students to provide feedback and to ask questions for clarification. Then explain that in this lesson they will learn to capitalize proper nouns correctly.

Teach

☑ Teaching Tip

Students may be confused by the fact that the same word can be lowercased as a common noun and capitalized as a proper noun in a title, for example: *I saw the principal at noon. I saw Principal Brown at noon. Can you see me now, Principal?* The lowercase form is used when the word stands alone (other than in direct address) or when it follows rather than precedes a proper noun. *(Mr. Brown, the principal, saw me at noon.)* The capitalized form is used in a title or in direct address.

Resource Manager

Planning Resources
- *Lesson Plans*

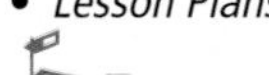

Transparencies
- *Bellringer*
- *Daily Language Practice*
- *Two-Minute Skill Drill*

Other Print Resources
- *Grammar and Composition Handbook*
- *Grammar Enrichment,* p. 39
- *Grammar Practice,* p. 39
- *Grammar Reteaching,* p. 38
- *Grammar Workbook,* Lessons 2, 71

Teach

Cooperative Learning

Have groups of students work together to write a paragraph that uses as many proper nouns as possible. Suggest that students use a computer to draft their paragraph. Then have the groups rewrite the paragraph, lowercasing all the capital letters. Ask groups to exchange paragraphs and list all proper nouns that should be capitalized. Groups should evaluate each other's answers and provide effective feedback.

Practice and Assess

Answers: Exercise 4

1. George Allen, the governor of Virginia
2. Senator Barbara Boxer
3. Aunt Luisa and her mother
4. the Progressive party
5. Mount Vernon College
6. correct
7. Attorney General Janet Reno
8. Securities and Exchange Commission
9. Sign here, General.
10. correct
11. General Motors Corporation
12. Chief Justice John Marshall
13. Scotch Irish
14. Hernando de Soto
15. Bishop John Walker
16. What did you mean, Grandfather?
17. 4-H Club
18. Please respond, Mr. Secretary.
19. Arabic
20. Vietnamese Americans
21. Commodore Matthew C. Perry
22. Mothers Against Drunk Driving
23. correct
24. Secretary of State Albright
25. correct

Capitalization

3. **Names of ethnic groups, national groups, and languages**

Native **A**mericans	**I**talian
Laotians	**S**wahili
Mexicans	**J**apanese
Scots	**L**atin

4. **Names of organizations, institutions, political parties and their members, and firms**

Food and **D**rug **A**dministration
Girl **S**couts of **A**merica
Utah **S**tate **U**niversity
the **C**ongress
the **D**emocratic party
a **R**epublican
Bank of **A**merica
General **E**lectric

The word *party* is not capitalized. Do not capitalize common nouns such as *court* or *university* unless they are part of a proper noun.

She was appointed judge of the **F**irst **D**istrict **C**ourt.
Mr. Tavares was a witness in **t**raffic **c**ourt.
He became interested in science at the **u**niversity.

Exercise 4 Capitalizing Names and Titles

Rewrite the following items if they are incorrect, adding capital letters as necessary. If an item is correct, write *correct.*

1. george allen, the governor of Virginia
2. senator barbara boxer
3. aunt luisa and her mother
4. the progressive party
5. mount vernon college
6. our secretary of the interior
7. attorney general janet reno
8. securities and exchange commission
9. Sign here, general.
10. small claims court
11. general motors corporation
12. chief justice john marshall
13. scotch irish
14. hernando de soto
15. bishop john walker
16. What did you mean, grandfather?
17. 4-h club
18. Please respond, mr. secretary.
19. arabic
20. vietnamese americans
21. commodore matthew c. perry
22. mothers against drunk driving
23. We saw your uncle last night.
24. secretary of state albright
25. the university

Enrichment and Extension

Understanding Capitalization

When teaching capitalization, use each student's own writing. Use a highlighter to emphasize each capitalized letter, and take turns with the student explaining why the capitalization is necessary. You may want to have students work together to create a sheet summarizing the capitalization rules taught in this unit. Such a sheet could be displayed on a bulletin board and would be useful when students edit their work.

5. **Names of monuments, buildings, bridges, and other structures**

the **E**iffel **T**ower
Vietnam **V**eterans **M**emorial
Golden **G**ate **B**ridge
the **P**arthenon
Sears **T**ower
Lincoln **T**unnel
Hoover **D**am
Shea **S**tadium
the **W**hite **H**ouse

6. **Trade names**

Chevrolet	**C**heerios
Kleenex	**F**riskies cat food
Xerox	**L**ifesavers

7. **Names of documents, awards, and laws**

the **C**onstitution	**P**ulitzer **P**rize
Fifth **A**mendment	a **G**rammy
Emancipation **P**roclamation	**B**ill of **R**ights
Treaty of **P**aris	**E**nvironmental **P**rotection **A**ct

Do not capitalize short prepositions that appear as part of the name.

8. **Geographical terms**

■ Capitalize the names of continents, countries, states, counties, and cities, as well as the names of specific bodies of water, topographical features, regions, and streets.

Asia	**L**ake **H**uron
Africa	**B**iscayne **B**ay
Mexico	**G**rand **C**anyon
Virginia	**B**lue **R**idge **M**ountains
Oregon	**C**ape **C**od
Dade **C**ounty	the **S**ahara
Dallas	**M**iddle **E**ast
Atlantic **O**cean	**S**outhern **H**emisphere
Mississippi **R**iver	**M**ain **S**treet
Great **P**lains	**P**rince **E**dward **I**sland

Capitalization

☑ Teaching Tip

In German all nouns—both common and proper—are capitalized, as they were in English centuries ago.

Foreign languages use different rules of capitalization. For example, the names of the months are not capitalized in Spanish.

Cross-reference: Writing

An important part of confirming proofreading is looking for errors in capitalization. Direct students' attention to Unit 2, The Writing Process, for additional support in this area.

Cross-reference: Dictionary

A recent dictionary is an excellent source of information on the capitalization of specific words. For instruction and practice in using a dictionary, refer students to Lesson 24.1, pp. 812–816.

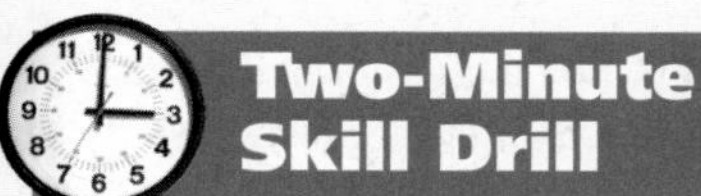

Two-Minute Skill Drill

Have students capitalize the following words correctly:

aunt mary	*my aunt*
a university	*ucla*
dr. miller	*nobel prize*

See also *Two-Minute Skill Drill Transparency 20.2*

Enrichment and Extension

Understanding Family Terms

Tell students that when a family term that is not followed by a proper name is preceded by a possessive personal pronoun *(my, our, your, his, her, their)*, the term is generally not used as a proper noun and thus does not require capitalization *(my mother, her uncle)*. When a family term is not preceded by a possessive pronoun, it is used as a proper noun and should be capitalized *(Uncle Carlos, Cousin Tina, Grandmother)*. See *Grammar Reteaching*, p. 38. **L2**

20.2

Teach

Teaching Tip

The term *capital* comes from the Latin word for "head." In the Middle Ages, oversized decorated letters were used to mark the "heads," or openings, of chapters or sections in hand-copied books.

Cross-reference: Writing

Explain that in writing about social studies and science, the rules on this page will prove especially useful. Refer students to Unit 5, Expository Writing.

Two-Minute Skill Drill

Ask students to capitalize the compass points correctly in the following sentences:

On a tour of the southwest, we visited Arizona. Arizona is southwest of Kansas.

See also *Two-Minute Skill Drill Transparency 20.2*

Capitalization

9. Names of planets and other celestial bodies

Pluto	the constellation **S**corpio	the **S**un
Mars	**N**orth **S**tar	the **M**oon
the **B**ig **D**ipper	the **M**ilky **W**ay	

Earth is capitalized only when the word refers to the planet, but in that case, do not use the definite article, *the.*

Venus and **M**ars are **E**arth's closest planetary neighbors.

The archaeologists dug deep into the hard, sandy **e**arth.

10. Compass points

■ Capitalize the words *north, east, south,* and *west* when they refer to a specific area of the country or the world or when they are part of a proper name. Do not capitalize them when they merely indicate direction.

the **N**orth	*but*	**n**orth of 42nd Street
the **W**est **C**oast		the **w**est **c**oast of Africa
South **P**acific		**s**outh of Bangor
East **L**ansing		**e**ast of the school

11. Names of ships, planes, trains, and spacecraft

U.S.S. ***C**onstitution*	***S**pirit of **S**t. **L**ouis*
***C**hallenger*	***Y**ankee **C**lipper*

12. Names of most historical events, eras, and calendar items

Reconstruction	**W**ashington's **B**irthday
Middle **A**ges	**L**abor **D**ay
Ming **D**ynasty	**W**orld **W**ar **II**
the **C**rusades	**B**attle of **H**astings

Do not capitalize a historical period when it refers to a general span of time.

the **t**wenties

the **t**enth **c**entury

■ Capitalize the days of the week and the months of the year, but do not capitalize the names of the seasons *(spring, summer, autumn, fall, winter).*

We met on a **M**onday in **M**arch; it was the first day of **s**pring.

Enrichment and Extension

Capitalizing Correctly in Writing

Some writers may consistently use the uppercase form of a letter in place of the lowercase form in their handwriting. Thus, they may use an uppercase letter anywhere in a sentence, even within a word. This is a problem in handwriting, not a problem with identifying proper nouns.

You may want to draw students' attention to this problem and let them devise a strategy of their own for correcting the situation. Students may decide to use a computer for important writing, or they may make a conscious effort to write letters correctly. **L2**

13. Religious terms

- Capitalize names of deities, religions and their denominations and adherents, words referring to a supreme deity, and religious books and events.

God	**M**uslims
Allah	**Q**ur'an
Christianity	**N**ew **T**estament
Russian **O**rthodox	the **A**lmighty
Protestants	**H**anukkah
Jews	the **S**econd **C**oming
Buddhism	**F**our **N**oble **T**ruths

14. Names of school courses

- Capitalize only those school courses that are the name of a language or the title of a specific course. Do not capitalize the name of a subject.

Advanced **A**lgebra	*but*	**al**gebra
Spanish		**g**eography
Music 101		**m**usic
World **C**ultures II		**w**orld **h**istory

15. Titles of works

the ***O**dyssey*	[epic poem]
"**T**he **G**ift of the **M**agi"	[story]
the *Los **A**ngeles **T**imes*	[newspaper]
"**H**ome on the **R**ange"	[song]
*Information Please **A**lmanac*	[reference book]

Always capitalize the first and last words of a title or subtitle. Do not capitalize articles, coordinating conjunctions, or prepositions of fewer than five letters unless they appear as the first word of the title itself.

- Capitalize articles (*a, an,* and *the*) at the beginning of a title only when they are part of the title itself. It is common practice not to capitalize (or italicize) articles preceding the title of a newspaper or a periodical. Do not capitalize (or italicize) the word *magazine* unless it is part of the title of a periodical.

"**T**he Fifty-first Dragon"	**t**he *Christian Science Monitor*
"**A** Marriage Proposal"	**a** *Newsweek* **m**agazine

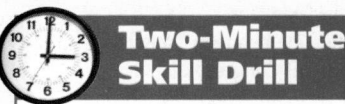

Cross-reference: Mechanics

For instruction and practice on how quotation marks and italics are used with titles, refer students to Lesson 21.9, pp. 752–756, and Lesson 21.10, pp. 757–758.

Two-Minute Skill Drill

Have students capitalize the following words correctly:

algebra
algebra II
the boston globe
history
french 201

See also *Two-Minute Skill Drill Transparency 20.2*

Capitalization

Enrichment and Extension

Checking for Correct Capitalization

Encourage groups of students to use what they have learned about capitalization in this unit to proofread sentences and paragraphs they have written for other classes. Have them pay special attention to proper nouns.

Writing Effectively

Have students write an essay or personal narrative in which they employ the capitalization rules they have learned in this unit. Students may want to explain which rules they used and why.

Practice and Assess

Answers: Exercise 5

1. Antioch College
2. Jacqueline Kennedy Onassis
3. Library of Congress
4. the *Wall Street Journal* and Time magazine
5. Portuguese, Spanish, and Latin
6. the Capitol
7. Aunt Lydia and Uncle Ted
8. the speaker of the house, Denny Hastert
9. the Magna Carta
10. National Urban League
11. Amy Tan's *The Kitchen God's Wife*
12. the Oscars
13. Sunday, March 5
14. the Eastern Hemisphere
15. Hispanics
16. Pikes Peak
17. Aunt Vanessa
18. Venus, Pluto, Mars, and Earth
19. My . . . Calculus II and my history class.
20. *The World Book Encyclopedia*
21. "The Legend of Sleepy Hollow"
22. Ivory soap
23. Fourth of July
24. the USS *Maine*
25. Fifth Avenue in New York City

Answers: Exercise 6

1. name of an institution
2. name of an individual
3. name of a building
4. names of a newspaper and a magazine
5. names of languages
6. name of a building
7. titles of individuals when used with proper nouns
8. title used separately from individual's name
9. name of a document
10. name of an organization
11. names of an individual and of a book
12. name of an award
13. names of day and month
14. name of a specific area of the world
15. name of an ethnic group
16. name of a mountain
17. title of an individual when used with a proper name
18. names of planets
19. first word in a sentence; name of a specific course; name of a subject
20. name of a reference book
21. name of a story
22. trade name
23. name of a holiday
24. name of a ship
25. names of a street and a city

Capitalization

Exercise 5 Capitalizing Proper Nouns

Write the following items, adding capital letters where necessary.

SAMPLE jefferson memorial
ANSWER Jefferson Memorial

1. antioch college
2. jacqueline kennedy onassis
3. library of congress
4. the *wall street journal* and *time* magazine
5. portuguese, spanish, and latin
6. the capitol
7. aunt lydia and uncle ted
8. the speaker of the house, denny hastert
9. the magna carta
10. national urban league
11. amy tan's *the kitchen god's wife*
12. the oscars
13. sunday, march 5
14. the eastern hemisphere
15. hispanics
16. pikes peak
17. aunt vanessa
18. venus, pluto, mars, and earth
19. my favorite classes are calculus II and my history class.
20. *the world book encyclopedia*
21. "the legend of sleepy hollow"
22. ivory soap
23. fourth of july
24. the uss *maine*
25. fifth avenue in new york city

Exercise 6 Identifying Reasons for Capitalization

On your paper, explain why you capitalized or did not capitalize each of the items in Exercise 5.

SAMPLE Jefferson Memorial
ANSWER name of a monument

Exercise 7 Capitalizing Proper Nouns

For each sentence below, find the words with capitalization errors and write them correctly.

Early Settlers in America

1. Early in the Seventeenth Century, king james I of England gave a trading company the right to send settlers to live in what would become north america.
2. The settlers, among them captain John Smith, set sail in the Company's ships, the *godspeed,* the *discovery,* and the *susan constant.*
3. After crossing the atlantic ocean, the Settlers founded jamestown, Virginia, the first permanent British settlement in north america.
4. In 1619 a ship owned by holland brought the first africans to the colonies in america.
5. The pilgrims, a group of English puritans, landed a good distance North of Virginia, in present-day massachusetts, in december of 1620.
6. Squanto, a native american, helped the pilgrims survive their first harsh Winter in the Settlement named plymouth.
7. Wall street in New York city is named after a wall built in 1653 by colonists from holland who feared an attack by the British.
8. In 1681 william penn, the english quaker leader, together with a group of quakers, founded the City of Philadelphia on the Delaware river.
9. In philadelphia members of all religious groups were allowed to worship god and interpret the bible in their own way.
10. In 1704 the first issue of a successful colonial newspaper, the *boston newsletter,* was printed.
11. Samuel de Champlain, who built the first french settlement in north America at quebec, established friendly ties with the powerful algonquian nation.
12. Among the hundreds of french explorers who explored the area around the great lakes was father marquette, a Priest.
13. La salle claimed the entire valley of the mississippi River for France and named the area louisiana in honor of king Louis XIV.
14. The southern section of the carolinas, South Carolina, attracted scots, germans, and emigrants from the west Indies.
15. In the winter of 1634, some 200 settlers, many of them catholics, sailed into the chesapeake bay and established the colony of maryland.
16. In 1649 lord baltimore secured the passage of the toleration act, guaranteeing freedom of worship for all Christians.
17. In 1636 the first colonial college, harvard, was founded in massachusetts.
18. Two of the early Presidents of the college were the reverend increase mather and his son cotton.
19. Among the required subjects were greek, latin, and theology.
20. In the north, schoolchildren were taught not only to read but also to write about god from the *new england primer.*

Capitalization

Answers: Exercise 7

1. seventeenth century; King James I; North America
2. Captain John Smith; company's; the *Godspeed,* the *Discovery,* and the *Susan Constant*
3. the Atlantic Ocean; settlers; Jamestown, Virginia; North America
4. Holland; Africans; America
5. The Pilgrims; English Puritans; north of Virginia; Massachusetts; December of 1620
6. a Native American; the Pilgrims; winter; settlement; Plymouth
7. Wall Street; New York City; Holland
8. William Penn; the English Quaker leader; Quakers; city of Philadelphia; Delaware River
9. Philadelphia; God; the Bible
10. the *Boston Newsletter*
11. first French settlement; North America; Quebec; Algonquian nation
12. French explorers; Great Lakes; Father Marquette; a priest
13. La Salle; Mississippi River; Louisiana; King Louis XIV
14. the Carolinas; Scots; Germans; West Indies
15. Catholics; Chesapeake Bay; colony of Maryland
16. Lord Baltimore; Toleration Act
17. Harvard; Massachusetts
18. presidents; Reverend Increase Mather; Cotton
19. Greek; Latin
20. North; God; the *New England Primer*

Additional Resources

- *Grammar Practice,* p. 39
- *Grammar Reteaching,* p. 38
- *Grammar Enrichment,* p. 39

Grammar Workbook, Lessons 2, 71

Close

Have students briefly write about how they can use these capitalization rules in their other classes. Encourage them to think about science and social studies classes in particular and share conclusions with a partner.

MEETING INDIVIDUAL NEEDS

Learning Disabled

Using Proper Nouns

Suggest that students list places they have been and people they know, being careful as they write to use capital letters when appropriate. Have students discuss their lists with a classmate and explain the capitalization. Remind classmates to provide effective feedback. **L1**

Focus

Lesson Overview

Objectives

- To learn to recognize proper adjectives
- To capitalize them correctly in writing

Bellringer
Daily Language Activity

When students enter the classroom, have this assignment on the board: *Capitalize the words that require capitalization in the following:*

The japanese language uses both chinese characters and japanese characters.

Ask students to explain their answers. Remind classmates to provide effective feedback and to ask questions for clarification.

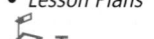

See also *Daily Language Practice*

Teach

Grammar Tip

Remind students that proper adjectives are formed from proper nouns and that they are usually capitalized. The nouns that the proper adjectives modify are not usually capitalized.

Practice and Assess

Answers: Exercise 8

1. Jeffersonian **2.** Guatemalan **3.** Picasso **4.** South American **5.** Alaskan **6.** Japanese **7.** Islamic **8.** Greek **9.** Easter **10.** Navajo **11.** Shakespearean **12.** Australian **13.** Michigan **14.** Parisian **15.** Hanukkah **16.** Middle Eastern **17.** Malaysian **18.** Stalinist **19.** African American **20.** Pacific Ocean

20.3 Capitalization of Proper Adjectives

■ Capitalize proper adjectives (adjectives formed from proper nouns).

Most proper adjectives fit into the following categories:

1. Adjectives formed from names of people

Napoleonic era	**J**acksonian ideals
Victorian customs	**M**arxist revolutionary
Georgian architecture	**D**ickensian character

2. Adjectives formed from place names and names of national, ethnic, and religious groups

Chinese acupuncture	**H**ispanic studies
Saharan winds	**I**sraeli dances
Midwestern accent	**N**orwegian accent
European languages	**B**uddhist temple

Many proper nouns do not undergo a change in form when they are used as adjectives.

United **N**ations calendar	**T**hanksgiving dinner
New **O**rleans cooking	**P**assover meal
Beethoven sonata	**M**onday night
Kodak camera	**R**epublican victory

Capitalization

Exercise 8 Using Proper Adjectives

Form a proper adjective from each of the proper nouns listed below.

SAMPLE Queen Elizabeth I
ANSWER Elizabethan

1. Thomas Jefferson
2. Guatemala
3. Pablo Picasso
4. South America
5. Alaska
6. Japan
7. Islam
8. Greece
9. Easter
10. Navajo
11. William Shakespeare
12. Australia
13. Michigan
14. Paris
15. Hanukkah
16. Middle East
17. Malaysia
18. Joseph Stalin
19. African American
20. Pacific Ocean

Resource Manager

Planning Resources
- *Lesson Plans*

Transparencies
- *Bellringer*
- *Daily Language Practice*

Other Print Resources
- *Grammar and Composition Handbook*
- *Grammar Enrichment,* p. 39
- *Grammar Practice,* p. 39
- *Grammar Reteaching,* p. 39
- *Grammar Workbook,* Lesson 72

Exercise 9 Capitalizing Proper Adjectives and Proper Nouns

For each sentence below, find the words with capitalization errors and write them correctly.

The Triumph of Kathleen Battle

1. Kathleen Battle, a talented contemporary american Opera singer, is celebrated for the purity of her voice.
2. Born in the City of Cleveland, Ohio, she studied at the College Conservatory of music at the university of Cincinnati.
3. In addition to being one of the favorite Sopranos at the Metropolitan Opera House in New York city, she has won ovations in many european Opera Houses.
4. Battle is best known for her roles in mozart operas, including *the magic flute.*
5. She has worked closely in many Concerts and on many Musical Recordings with James Levine, a well-known Conductor.
6. In 1988 Battle sang in New York's central park with the italian star luciano Pavarotti.
7. Later that year, she traveled to the far east and sang in Tokyo with the spanish opera star Placido Domingo.
8. One of her greatest triumphs was her role in *antony and cleopatra,* an opera based on a shakespearean play.
9. The Opera recounts the story of Mark Antony, a Roman Consul, who is bewitched by the charms of queen Cleopatra of Egypt.
10. Although they often appeared in broadway musicals, few african American singers won major roles in opera.
11. In recent years, however, Kathleen Battle, Leontyne price, and Jessye norman have reversed that trend.
12. Battle may perform at the tallest opera house, a 42-story building on wacker drive in Chicago, illinois.
13. She may sing excerpts from italian operas written during the Nineteenth Century.
14. It is unlikely that she will sing one of the long Arias from a wagnerian opera.
15. My Aunt Julia is taking her Mother to the concert as a mother's day present.
16. It is believed that the first opera was *dafne,* written by jacopo Peri and introduced in florence, italy, in 1597.
17. One Winter, Battle's outstanding recording of spirituals was nominated for a grammy.
18. Battle may one day follow in the steps of the Contralto marian anderson and sing at the Lincoln memorial.
19. Do you think the daughters of the american revolution will invite her to perform at constitution hall in Washington, d.c.?
20. I would like Battle to be invited to sing when the democratic party meets to nominate its next Candidate for President.

Teach

Grammar Tip

Capitalization of proper adjectives is not universal. In Italian, for example, proper nouns are capitalized but proper adjectives are not.

Practice and Assess

Answers: Exercise 9

1. American opera singer
2. city of Cleveland; College Conservatory of Music; University of Cincinnati
3. favorite sopranos; New York City; European opera houses
4. Mozart operas; *The Magic Flute*
5. concerts; musical recordings; well-known conductor
6. New York's Central Park; Italian star; Luciano Pavarotti
7. Far East; Spanish opera star
8. *Antony and Cleopatra;* Shakespearean play
9. opera; Roman consul; Queen Cleopatra
10. Broadway musicals; African American singers
11. Leontyne Price; Jessye Norman
12. Wacker Drive; Chicago, Illinois
13. Italian operas; nineteenth century
14. long arias; Wagnerian opera
15. her mother; Mother's Day present
16. *Dafne;* Jacopo Peri; Florence, Italy
17. winter; Grammy
18. contralto Marian Anderson; Lincoln Memorial
19. Daughters of the American Revolution; Constitution Hall; Washington, D.C.
20. Democratic party; candidate, president

Meeting Individual Needs: Learning Disabled

Using Proper Adjectives

Have students list some names of people and places. Make sure these nouns are correctly capitalized. Then ask students to turn these nouns into proper adjectives. (For example, from *Mexico* they might create *Mexican cities.*) Have students share their work. **L1**

Teach

☑ Grammar Tip

In general, the nouns that proper adjectives modify are not capitalized: *African languages, Napoleonic era, Beethoven sonata, Buddhist temple, Chinese tradition.*

Practice and Assess

Answers: Exercise 10

Answers will vary but some suggestions are given below.

"I'd like to visit London, England."

"Why?" asked my friend.

"I hear Trafalgar Square and Kew Gardens are wonderful," I replied.

"I know someone who liked the British Museum. She told me that it has a copy of the Magna Carta on display."

"British food is different from American food, I'm told."

"How true," my friend replied.

The chart below reviews which words should be capitalized.

Summary of Capitalization Rules

CAPITALIZE	DO NOT CAPITALIZE
She gave us thirty pages of reading for homework. (**S**he said we needed to do it.)	For homework (**s**he said we needed to catch up) she gave us thirty pages of reading.
He said, "**L**et me drive."	He said that **h**e would drive.
Then **F**ather smiled at me.	My **f**ather wants to retire.
Captain **A**hab	The **c**aptain paced the deck.
Texas **S**tate **U**niversity	a **u**niversity in Texas
Lawrence **H**all of **S**cience	the **s**cience **m**useum in town
Prell shampoo; **I**vory soap	Bring **s**oap and **s**hampoo.
Bill of **R**ights	an animal **b**ill of **r**ights
Pacific **O**cean; **G**hirardelli **S**quare; **S**anta **C**lara **A**venue	the **s**quare where the two **a**venues meet near the **o**cean
Neptune; **M**ercury; **E**arth	**p**lanets; the **e**arth
the **K**orean **W**ar	the **w**ar in the former Yugoslavia
the **B**ible; **H**alloween	**s**acred **b**ook; **h**olidays
Russian; **E**nglish **L**iterature **I**	**f**oreign **l**anguage; **l**iterature
Third **D**istrict **C**ourt	**s**mall **c**laims **c**ourt
the **F**ar **E**ast	the **f**ar **e**astern tip of **K**orea
the **I**ce **A**ge	the **t**wentieth **c**entury
"**T**he **F**all of the **H**ouse of **U**sher"	the **s**tory
the *Dayton **D**aily **N**ews*	the **b**ook, **n**ewspaper, or **m**agazine
Tuesday; **J**uly	**s**pring; **f**all

Exercise 10 Using Correct Capitalization in a Dialogue

Write several sentences of dialogue between you and a friend about a country you would like to visit and the sights you would like to see. Use a variety of proper nouns and proper adjectives. Capitalize all sentences, quotations, proper nouns, and proper adjectives correctly.

Enrichment and Extension

Using Proper Nouns

Let students look at photos in magazines. For each person or place they choose, have them identify first a proper noun and then a proper adjective to describe it (for example, *New York; New York subway*). **L2**

Checking Capitalization

Have students write a paragraph that has intentional errors in capitalization. Let students exchange papers and correct all the errors they find. Students can then discuss the reasoning behind their corrections. **L2**

Exercise 11 Identifying Correct Capitalization

Write the letter of the one item that is correctly capitalized in each of the following pairs.

1. a. James Baldwin wrote, "one cannot deny the humanity of another without diminishing one's own."
   b. James Baldwin wrote, "One cannot deny the humanity of another without diminishing one's own."
2. a. university of California
   b. University of California
3. a. General George Patton
   b. general George Patton
4. a. The English stage actress Rachel Kempson is the mother of Vanessa and Lynn Redgrave.
   b. The English stage actress Rachel Kempson is the Mother of Vanessa and Lynn Redgrave.
5. a. Georgia O'Keeffe's painting *New York night* is done mostly in dark colors.
   b. Georgia O'Keeffe's painting *New York Night* is done mostly in dark colors.
6. a. *A Raisin In The Sun*
   b. *A Raisin in the Sun*
7. a. European History I and physics
   b. European History I and Physics
8. a. a Buddhist temple on Homan Avenue
   b. a buddhist temple on Homan avenue
9. a. I wished that summer would not fade so quickly.
   b. I wished that Summer would not fade so quickly.
10. a. West of the Colorado River
    b. west of the Colorado River

Georgia O'Keeffe's *New York Night*

New York at night

Cooperative Learning

Using Capitalization Rules

Some students may be interested in working together to create a reference book for other class members to use. The reference book could summarize and clearly explain rules for capitalization of nouns and adjectives. Students may want to create mnemonic devices to help them remember capitalization rules, or they may want to draw charts or diagrams. They could also poll other class members to find out common capitalization problems. Suggest that students use a computer to work through each step of the writing process. **L2**

Answers: Exercise 11

1. b
2. b
3. a
4. a
5. b
6. b
7. a
8. a
9. a
10. b

Additional Resources

Grammar Practice, p. 39
Grammar Reteaching, p. 39
Grammar Enrichment, p. 39

Grammar Workbook, Lesson 72

Close

Invite students to summarize briefly the rules for capitalizing proper adjectives. Have them write a paragraph about a trip that they have been on or would like to take. Encourage them to practice using proper adjectives correctly. Students should exchange paragraphs and check each other's work. Remind students to provide appropriate feedback.

Teach

About the Literature

Explain that the review features a passage from Garrison Keillor's *Lake Wobegon Days.* After students read the passage, initiate a discussion of the characters, the setting, and the mood. Then ask students to discuss the capitalized words. Ask: *Would the meaning be as clear if the writer had not thought carefully about which words needed to be capitalized?* The exercises that follow are based on this passage and related topics.

Linking Grammar and Literature

Teaching Tip

Ask students to focus on some of the capitalized words not highlighted in the passage. Have them find a geographical term (*Main Street, Mist County, Norway*), a trade name (*Pure Oil*), a proper name (*Clint Bunsen*), a religious group (*Catholics*), a railroad (*Great Northern*), and a title (*Mr.*).

Cooperative Learning

Ask students to write a paragraph about a topic of their choice, containing the name and the title of a person, the name of a place, a compass point, the name of an ethnic or religious group, a trade name, and a holiday. Have students write all these terms in lowercase letters.

Next, have each student trade his or her work with another student, who will capitalize the appropriate terms. When students have finished, have partners meet and discuss the revisions. Encourage students to explain their reasons for their corrections. If students cannot agree on a change, have them present their arguments before the class. (You might want to remind students that titles and compass points may or may not be capitalized, according to their use.)

ASSESSMENT OPTIONS

Tests with Answer Key & Rubrics
Unit 20 Mastery Test, pp. 77–78

Testmaker
Unit 20 Mastery Test

UNIT 20 Grammar Review

CAPITALIZATION

Immortalized in Garrison Keillor's radio show *A Prairie Home Companion* is the fictional town of Lake Wobegon. Keillor's book *Lake Wobegon Days* grew out of the radio show. This passage from the book has been annotated to show some of the rules of capitalization covered in this unit.

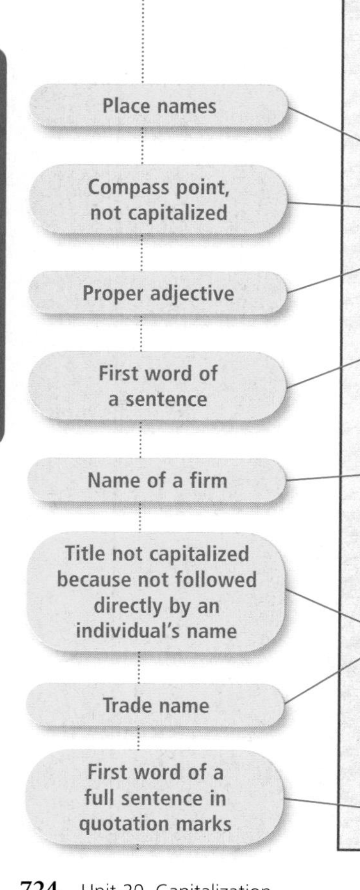

Literature Model

from Lake Wobegon Days

by Garrison Keillor

The town of Lake Wobegon, Minnesota, lies on the shore against Adams Hill, looking east across the blue-green water to the dark woods. From the south, the highway aims for the lake, bends hard left by the magnificent concrete Grecian grain silos, and eases over a leg of the hill past the SLOW CHILDREN sign, bringing the traveler in on Main Street toward the town's one traffic light, which is almost always green. A few surviving elms shade the street. Along the ragged dirt path between the asphalt and the grass, a child slowly walks to Ralph's Grocery, kicking an asphalt chunk ahead of him. It is a chunk that after four blocks he is now mesmerized by, to which he is completely dedicated. At Bunsen Motors the sidewalk begins. . . . The boy kicks the chunk at the curb, once, twice, then lofts it over the curb and sidewalk across the concrete to the island of Pure Oil pumps. He jumps three times on the Bunsen bell hose, making three dings back in the dark garage. The mayor of Lake Wobegon, Clint Bunsen, peers out from the grease pit, under a black Ford pickup.

Incorporated under the laws of Minnesota but omitted from the map due to the incompetence of surveyors, first named "New Albion" by New Englanders who thought it would become the Boston of the west, taking its ultimate name from an Indian phrase that means either "Here we are!"

Resource Manager

Planning Resources
- *Lesson Plans*

Other Print Resources
- *Grammar and Composition Handbook*
- *Grammar Workbook*, Lessons 70–72, Unit 11 Review, Cumulative Review: Units 1–11

or "We sat all day in the rain waiting for [you]," Lake Wobegon is the seat of tiny Mist County, the "phantom county in the heart of the heartland" (Dibbley, *My Minnesota*), founded by Unitarian missionaries and Yankee promoters, then found by Norwegian Lutherans who straggled in from the west, having headed first to Lake Agassiz in what is now North Dakota, a lake that turned out to be prehistoric, and by German Catholics, who, bound for Clay County, had stopped a little short, having misread their map, but refused to admit it.

A town with few scenic wonders such as towering pines or high mountains but with some fine people of whom some are over six feet tall, its highest point is the gold ball on the flagpole atop the Norge Co-op grain elevator south of town on the Great Northern spur, from which Mr. Tollefson can see all of Mist County when he climbs up to raise the flag on national holidays, including Norwegian Independence Day, when the blue cross of Norway is flown. (No flag of Germany has appeared in public since 1917.) Next highest is the water tower, then the boulder on the hill, followed by the cross on the spire of Our Lady, then the spire of Lake Wobegon Lutheran (Christian Synod), the Central Building (three stories), the high school flagpole, . . . etc.

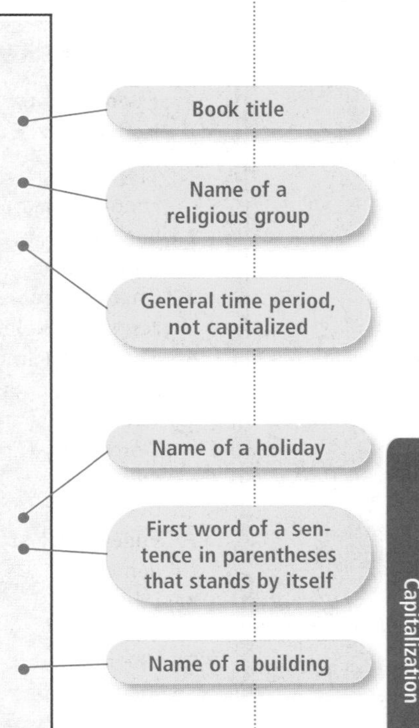

Capitalization

Review: Exercise 1 **Capitalizing Sentences**

For each sentence below, find the words with capitalization errors and write them correctly. If a sentence has no errors, write *correct.*

1. Lake Wobegon has been called "The little town that time forgot."
2. Keillor claims the town is not on any map because of surveying errors. (it is supposedly in central Minnesota.)
3. One explorer thought Lake Wobegon was the headwaters of the Mississippi River.
4. A statue of an unknown Norwegian Settler is a major landmark.
5. There is also a stone carved with Viking runes. (runes are old alphabetical symbols.)
6. A settler from Boston said that no civilized society could find comfort in the town.
7. later she said, "Providence has led us here."
8. The young woman (She had come west as a missionary) married a French trapper.
9. In his broadcasts, Keillor said, "that's the news from Lake Wobegon, where all the women are strong, all the men are good-looking, and all the children above average."
10. he also described the residents of Lake Wobegon as "Skeptical of progress."

Practice and Assess

Answers: Exercise 1

1. Lake Wobegon has been called "the little town that time forgot."
2. Keillor claims the town is not on any map because of surveying errors. (It is supposedly in central Minnesota.)
3. correct
4. A statue of an unknown Norwegian settler is a major landmark.
5. There is also a stone carved with Viking runes. (Runes are old alphabetical symbols.)
6. correct
7. Later she said, "Providence has led us here."
8. The young woman (she had come west as a missionary) married a French trapper.
9. In his broadcasts, Keillor said, "That's the news from Lake Wobegon, where all the women are strong, all the men are good-looking, and all the children above average."
10. He also described the residents of Lake Wobegon as "skeptical of progress."

Practice and Assess

Answers: Exercise 2

1. Lake Wobegon; Americans; Minnesota
2. Nobel Prize; *Babbitt;* Sauk
3. Minnesota; Swedish; Atlantic Ocean
4. correct
5. correct
6. Scandinavian; Dakotas
7. United States; Democratic; president
8. Pillsbury; Republican governor
9. Minnesota-born; World War I
10. Paul Bunyan; Hiawatha; Minnesota

Answers: Exercise 3 Proofreading

This proofreading activity provides editing practice with (1) the current or previous unit's skills, (2) the **Troubleshooter** errors, and (3) spelling errors. Students should be able to complete the exercise by referring to the units, the **Troubleshooter,** and a dictionary.

Error (Type of Error)

1. Anamosa (proper noun)
2. Institute (proper noun)
3. military (spelling)
   decorator, (commas in a series)
4. War (proper noun)
   art (common noun)

Review: Exercise 2 Capitalizing Proper Adjectives and Proper Nouns

For each of the following sentences, find the words that contain errors in capitalization and write them correctly. If a sentence has no errors, write *correct.*

1. Though lake wobegon characters seem ordinary, many famous americans, both real and imaginary, have minnesota roots.
2. Sinclair Lewis, a nobel prize winner, set his novel *babbitt* in a town that resembled his birthplace, sauk Centre.
3. Charles Lindbergh, a minnesota native of swedish descent, made the first solo flight across the atlantic ocean.
4. The Mayo Clinic founders, Drs. Charles and William Mayo, established their famous hospital in Minnesota.
5. The Minnesota-born actress and singer Judy Garland won worldwide popularity as Dorothy in *The Wizard of Oz.*
6. Ole Rölvaag, a Minnesotan of scandinavian ancestry, wrote novels about pioneers in the dakotas.
7. Eugene McCarthy, who was a united states senator from Minnesota, sought the democratic party's nomination for President in 1968.
8. John S. Pillsbury, a founder of pillsbury, a food-products company, served as a republican Governor of Minnesota for three terms.
9. The minnesota-born author F. Scott Fitzgerald depicted the decaying morality of society in the years following world war I.
10. The paul bunyan and hiawatha legends, both based on fictional heroes, are set in the minnesota frontier.

Review: Exercise 3

Proofreading

The following passage describes the artist Grant Wood, whose painting appears on the opposite page. Rewrite the passage, correcting the errors in spelling, capitalization, grammar, and usage. Add any missing punctuation. There are twenty-five errors.

Grant Wood

[1]Grant Wood (1892–1941) was born on a farm outside the small town of anamosa, Iowa. [2]He studied at the Handicraft Guild in Minneapolis and at the Art institute of Chicago. [3]Before he began militery service in 1918, he worked as a schoolteacher, an interior decorator and a metalworker. [4]After World war I ended, he returned to Iowa to teach Art.

Grant Wood, *Stone City, Iowa,* 1930

[5]Wood made several trips to Europe over the next decade, and he studied at a parisian art school. [6]His European travels reflected his discontent with american art, and his early works recall those of the french painters of the late nineteenth century. [7]Wood later had a change of hart and began to concentrate on American subjects. [8]Eventually, he, along with thomas Hart Benton, was ranked as one of America's great regional painters.

[9]Wood is best known for his portrayals of the land and the people of the midwest. [10]His pictures are finely detailed his landscapes are reduced to round shapes, and his people are witty caricatures. [11]His technique was influenced by the lush and detailed paintings of the flemish masters. [12]He was also influenced strangely enough, by the stylized pattern on his Mother's dishes. [13]His best-known work, *American gothic,* is typical of his mature style. [14]The painting, which was completed in the 1930s, show a man holding a pitchfork and standing with his wife in front of a farmhouse.

[15]Wood, who painted very slowly produced relatively few major works during his lifetime. [16]In *Stone City, Iowa,* the painting on this page, neither his skill as an Artist nor his reverence for the rural countryside are missing. [17]Woods gently ironic realism is like that of Garrison Keillor. [18]Each poke fun at the obsesive orderliness—both physical and moral—of the people who live in the small towns of the Midwest. [19]Do so with respect and tenderness.

Answers: Exercise 3 *(continued)*

Error (Type of Error)

5. Parisian (proper adjective)
6. American (proper adjective)
French (proper adjective)
7. heart (spelling)
8. Thomas (proper noun)
9. Midwest (proper noun)
10. detailed, (commas in a series)
11. Flemish (proper adjective)
12. influenced, (parenthetical element)
mother's (common noun)
13. Gothic (proper noun)
14. shows (subject-verb agreement)
15. slowly, (nonessential adjective-clause)
16. artist (common noun)
is missing (subject-verb agreement)
17. Wood's (singular possessive)
18. pokes (subject-verb agreement)
obsessive (spelling)
19. Midwest. They do
or Midwest; they do
or Midwest, but they do
(sentence fragment)

Viewing the Art

Grant Wood, *Stone City, Iowa,* 1930

Late in his life Grant Wood founded an artist's colony in Stone City, Iowa, the subject of the painting reproduced on this page. The painting presents an idealized, almost cartoonlike vision of the town—its immaculate pastel buildings, its orderly rows of crops.

It is difficult to separate fact from fiction in both *Lake Wobegon Days* and *Stone City, Iowa.* Ask students to reexamine *Stone City, Iowa* and to discuss which elements in the painting might have been invented or exaggerated.

Practice and Assess

Answers: Exercise 4

Mixed Review

1. Garrison Keillor was born in 1942 in Anoka County, Minnesota, to parents of Scottish descent.
2. After finishing high school, he entered the University of Minnesota. (He earned a degree in English in 1966.)
3. Keillor had written earlier for the *Anoka Herald,* and he became editor of the literary magazine at the university.
4. Hoping to work as a journalist, Keillor went east to New York after college, but he soon returned to Minnesota.
5. In 1974 he sold a story about the Grand Ole Opry to the *New Yorker* for $6,000 (more money than he had ever seen).
6. In the spring of 1974, Keillor and his wife and son traveled by train through the northern Rockies.
7. In Idaho the Keillor family boarded an old bus heading for Washington. (The train they had been traveling on had derailed.)
8. From Portland they took the southbound train, the *Coast Starlight,* to San Francisco.
9. On the trip, Keillor started a story titled "The Lake Wobegon Memoir," but it was stolen from his briefcase in the train station.
10. Years later, in the eighties, Keillor would write *Lake Wobegon Days,* a book that he insists is not as fine as his lost story.
11. correct
12. In July 1974, Keillor began hosting *A Prairie Home Companion,* a radio show on public radio in Minnesota.
13. Keillor has said that one of his great-uncles, Uncle Lew (his grandmother's brother), inspired some of the show's homespun characters.
14. The imaginary sponsors for the humorous show were Raw Bits cereal and a pet shop called Bertha's Kitty Boutique.
15. On the show, Keillor talked about the Unitarian missionaries who started the town and the arrival of the first settlers, Norwegian Lutherans and German Catholics.
16. He described Albion College and its crazed founder, the Reverend Watt.

Grammar Review

Review: Exercise 4

Mixed Review

For each of the following sentences, find the words that contain errors in capitalization and write the words correctly. If a sentence has no errors, write *correct.*

Garrison Keillor

1. Garrison Keillor was born in 1942 in Anoka county, Minnesota, to parents of scottish descent.
2. After finishing High School, he entered the University of Minnesota. (he earned a degree in english in 1966.)
3. Keillor had written earlier for the *Anoka herald,* and he became Editor of the literary magazine at the University.
4. Hoping to work as a journalist, Keillor went East to New York after college, but he soon returned to minnesota.
5. in 1974 he sold a story about the Grand ole Opry to the *New Yorker* for $6,000 (More money than he had ever seen).
6. In the Spring of 1974, Keillor and his Wife and son traveled by train through the Northern rockies.
7. In idaho the Keillor family boarded an old bus heading for Washington. (the train they had been traveling on had derailed.)
8. From portland they took the southbound train, the *coast starlight,* to San Francisco.
9. On the trip, Keillor started a story titled "the lake wobegon memoir," but it was stolen from his briefcase in the Train Station.
10. Years later, in the Eighties, Keillor would write *Lake Wobegon Days,* a book that he insists Is not as fine as his lost story.
11. The book has been described as an unforgettable portrait of why we "are what we are" and why being smart "doesn't count for much."
12. In july 1974, Keillor began hosting a *Prairie Home Companion,* a radio show on Public Radio in Minnesota.
13. Keillor has said that one of his Great-Uncles, Uncle Lew (his Grandmother's brother), inspired some of the show's homespun characters.
14. The imaginary sponsors for the humorous show were Raw bits Cereal and a pet shop called Bertha's kitty boutique.
15. On the show, Keillor talked about the unitarian missionaries who started the town and the arrival of the first settlers, norwegian lutherans and german catholics.
16. He described albion college and its crazed founder, the reverend watt.
17. Students at the college studied latin, poetry, penmanship, and moral psychology I.
18. On Groundhog Day, the Sons of Knute sponsored an ice melt contest.
19. The radio show was a recipient of the peabody award.
20. At times Garrison Keillor has lived in Wisconsin and in new york city.

Capitalization

17. Students at the college studied Latin, poetry, penmanship, and Moral Psychology I.
18. correct
19. The radio show was a recipient of the Peabody Award.
20. At times, Garrison Keillor has lived in Wisconsin and in New York City.

Close

Have students list the types of capitalization errors that they most commonly make. Using what they have learned in this unit, how can students improve their writing in the future? What strategies can they employ to correct these errors? Help students answer these questions in their journals.

Writing Application

Capitalization in Writing

In "Skeletons in the Attic," Clara Spotted Elk describes how Native Americans regained the skeletal remains of their ancestors. As you read the passage below, pay special attention to the use of capitalization.

> Millions of American Indians lived in this country when Columbus first landed on our shores. After the western expansion, only 250,000 Indians survived. What happened to the remains of these people who were decimated by the advance of the white man? Many are gathering dust in American museums.
>
> In 1985, I and some Northern Cheyenne chiefs visited the attic of the Smithsonian's Natural History Museum in Washington, D.C., to review the inventory of their Cheyenne collection. After a chance inquiry, a curator pulled out a drawer in one of the scores of cabinets that line the attic. There were the jumbled bones of an Indian. "A Kiowa," he said.

Techniques with Capitalization

Like Clara Spotted Elk, you should apply the rules of capitalization when you write and revise your own work.

1. Capitalize proper nouns that name monuments, bridges, buildings, and other structures. Do not capitalize common nouns unless they are part of a proper noun.

PROPER NOUN the attic of the Smithsonian's Natural History Museum

COMMON NOUN the attic of the museum

2. Capitalize adjectives formed from proper nouns but not those formed from common nouns.

PROPER ADJECTIVE Cheyenne collection

COMMON ADJECTIVE chance inquiry

TIME

For more about the writing process, see **TIME Facing the Blank Page**, pp. 121-131.

Capitalization

Practice Practice the rules of capitalization by revising the following paragraph on a separate sheet of paper. (You will need to capitalize twenty-five additional words.)

The explorer christopher columbus landed on what is now the island of san salvador in the late fifteenth century. Although he thought he had landed in india (because he thought so, he mistakenly called the people he found indians), he really landed in the bahamas, a chain of islands, cays, and reefs lying southeast of florida. At the time, the continent of north america was home for a wide array of independent cultural groups. since that time, archaeologists have discovered artifacts left by these pre-Columbian (that is, "before columbus") societies. Some of these artifacts are displayed in natural history museums such as the museum of natural history in new york city. Federal agencies such as the national park service in the department of the interior also house native american collections.

Writing Online | For more grammar practice, go to glencoe.com and enter QuickPass code WC97727p2.

Capitalization in Writing

You may have students read the paragraph aloud, without interruptions. Then go back and discuss the words with boldface capitals. Discuss why, in relation to the Techniques with Capitalization in column two, these words are or are not capitalized.

Techniques with Capitalization

Discuss the capitalization techniques explained in this section. Then have students reread the proofreading activity on pages 726–727. Ask them to write a paragraph describing how these capitalization techniques are employed. Have students read and discuss their paragraphs in small groups.

Practice

Answers

The explorer Christopher Columbus landed on what is now the island of San Salvador in the late fifteenth century. Although he thought he had landed in India (because he thought so, he mistakenly called the people he found Indians), he really landed in the Bahamas, a chain of islands, cays, and reefs lying southeast of Florida. At the time, the continent of North America was home for a wide array of independent cultural groups. Since that time, archaeologists have discovered artifacts left by these pre-Columbian (that is, "before Columbus") societies. Some of these artifacts are displayed in natural history museums such as the Museum of Natural History in New York City. Federal agencies such as the National Park Service in the Department of the Interior also house Native American collections.

ASSESSMENT OPTIONS

Tests with Answer Key & Rubrics
Unit 20 Mastery Test, pp. 77–78

Testmaker
Unit 20 Mastery Test

You may wish to administer the Unit 20 Mastery Test at this point.

MindJogger Videoquizzes

INTRODUCING

UNIT 21

Objectives

- To develop an understanding of the correct use of punctuation, abbreviations, and italics and the writing of numbers and numerals
- To demonstrate control over rules that govern the use of various punctuation marks and other conventions by completing exercises that illustrate those uses and conventions

ASSESSMENT OPTIONS

Tests with Answer Key & Rubrics
Unit 21 Pretest, pp. 79–80
Unit 21 Mastery Test, pp. 81–82

Testmaker
Unit 21 Pretest
Unit 21 Mastery Test

You may wish to administer the Unit 21 Pretest at this point.

Key to Ability Levels

L1 Level 1 activities are within the basic ability range of students.

L2 Level 2 activities are within the ability range of average students.

L3 Level 3 activities are more challenging activities.

UNIT 21

Punctuation, Abbreviations, and Numbers

730

Resource Manager

Planning Resources
- *Lesson Plans*
- *Block Scheduling*

Transparencies
- *Bellringer*
- *Daily Language Practice*
- *Two-Minute Skill Drill*

Video
- *MindJogger Videoquizzes*

Other Print Resources
- *Grammar and Composition Handbook*
- *Grammar Enrichment*
- *Grammar Practice*
- *Grammar Reteaching*
- *Grammar Workbook*
- *Sentence-Combining Practice*
- *Tests with Answer Key and Rubrics*

Software
- *Interactive Grammar and Language Workbook*
- *Presentation Plus!*
- *Revising with Style*
- *Testmaker*

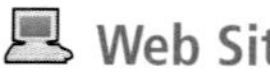

Web Site
- *glencoe.com*

21.1 The Period

- There are three punctuation marks used at the ends of sentences: the period, the exclamation point, and the question mark.
- Use a period at the end of a declarative sentence and at the end of an imperative sentence that is a polite command or request.

DECLARATIVE SENTENCE	Track practice is held twice a week.
IMPERATIVE SENTENCE	Please sign up for two track events.

Exercise 1 **Identifying Use of the Period**

Identify each of the following sentences that should end with a period by writing *declarative* or *imperative* on your paper. If a sentence is neither a declarative sentence nor a polite command, write *no period.*

The Swim Team

1. Our swim team will hold its first meeting next Tuesday
2. The first big swim meet will take place in one month
3. Please sign up in the gym
4. My specialty is the backstroke
5. Do you want to become a winner
6. We won three gold medals at the last swim meet
7. Be sure to wear your goggles
8. To remain on the team, you must maintain good grades
9. We have a lot of fun during practice
10. After practice we often get together at the restaurant across the street
11. Have you heard us sitting there talking about swimming
12. If you learn something about the sport, our conversations will be livelier
13. The ancient Greeks trained their soldiers to swim so they could cross rivers
14. In medieval times, swimming was unpopular because people feared the water might be unhealthful
15. In the nineteenth century, the British discovered that Native Americans used a swimming method similar to the modern crawl
16. Development of the flutter kick inspired the Australian crawl, the most common stroke today
17. Tell me how swimming became part of the modern Olympic games
18. There are four basic categories of Olympic swimming events: freestyle, backstroke, breaststroke, and butterfly
19. Have you heard that some Olympic swimmers have become movie stars
20. John Weissmuller, who won five Olympic gold medals in the 1920s, played Tarzan in the movies in the 1940s

Focus

Lesson Overview

Objective

- To use periods, exclamation points, and question marks correctly in a variety of sentences

Bellringer
Daily Language Activity

When students enter the classroom, have the following assignment on the board: *Rewrite, using periods where appropriate.*

I stayed late at school for basketball practice Please give me a ride home

See also *Daily Language Practice*

Teach

Teaching Tip

Have students identify the need for a period after the words *practice* and *home* in the Bellringer activity. Elicit from volunteers that the first sentence is declarative, the second imperative. Encourage students to ask questions to clarify understanding.

Practice and Assess

Answers: Exercise 1

1. declarative
2. declarative
3. imperative
4. declarative
5. no period
6. declarative
7. imperative
8. declarative
9. declarative
10. declarative
11. no period
12. declarative
13. declarative
14. declarative
15. declarative
16. declarative
17. imperative
18. declarative
19. no period
20. declarative

Resource Manager

Planning Resources
- *Lesson Plans*

Transparencies
- *Bellringer*
- *Daily Language Practice*

Other Print Resources
- *Grammar and Composition Handbook*
- *Grammar Enrichment,* p. 40
- *Grammar Practice,* p. 40
- *Grammar Reteaching,* p. 40
- *Grammar Workbook,* Lesson 73

Teach

☑ Teaching Tip

Explain that many verbs have as their direct object a noun clause beginning with *if, how,* or the *wh-* words. These are called indirect questions. (*I asked myself if I had ever been that tired before.*) True questions, however, always begin with a verb or an interrogative pronoun.

Practice and Assess

Answers: Exercise 2

Answers will vary, but some suggestions are given below.

1. . . . first aid? I think it's crucial.
2. . . . ill or injured person. First aid can save lives.
3. Oh, if only . . . first aid! So many . . . helped!
4. . . . about first aid. Will . . . the library?
5. . . . comfortable as possible. Other . . . less important.
6. . . . right away. Don't panic.
7. . . . to take charge? If . . . one can assist.
8. . . . at a distance. Be firm!
9. . . . attention. Which are less critical?
10. . . . necessary. How vital this is!

Close

Ask students to write examples of sentences that end in an exclamation point or that are direct or indirect questions. Have volunteers read sentences aloud, and then have others identify the appropriate end marks. Have students provide effective feedback.

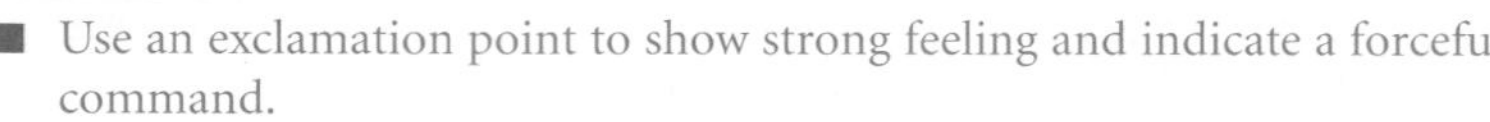

21.2 The Exclamation Point

- Use an exclamation point to show strong feeling and indicate a forceful command.

Oh, no**!**	Look out**!**	What lovely weather**!**
Hurrah**!**	Wake up**!**	Get going**!**

21.3 The Question Mark

- Use a question mark to indicate a direct question.

  Who would like a part-time job**?**

  Which call should I answer first**?**

- Do not place a question mark after an indirect question (one that has been reworded so that it is part of a declarative sentence).

  He asked whether I needed a work permit**.**

  I wondered why such a document was needed**.**

Exercise 2 Using End Punctuation

On your paper, rewrite the following sentences, adding periods, exclamation points, and question marks where necessary. You will add 20 marks in all.

First Aid

1. Don't you think that everyone should learn about first aid I think it's crucial
2. First aid is the immediate medical care given to an ill or injured person First aid can save lives
3. Oh, if only people realized the importance of first aid So many people could be helped
4. An instruction manual by John S. Kelly, published by the U.S. Bureau of Mines, has useful information about first aid Will you get the book from the library
5. The primary goals of first aid are to treat serious injuries, prevent infection, and make the injured or ill person as comfortable as possible Other problems are less important
6. If you come upon an injured person, try to send for medical help right away Don't panic
7. Are you the person best qualified to take charge If two of you know first aid, the one with more experience and training should take charge, and the other one can assist
8. If people are crowding the injured person, make them stand at a distance Be firm
9. Once you have sent for help and the patient is lying still, ask yourself which injuries require immediate attention Which are less critical
10. Because of possible broken bones or internal injuries, move an injured person only if it is absolutely necessary How vital this is

English Language Learners

Using End Marks

Students who are learning English may not be comfortable with end marks used in English or with interrogative sentence inflection. Therefore, write these phrases in a column on the board: *your name; where you were born; the city and the state where you live; the names of your brothers and sisters.* Have students practice writing declarative, imperative, and interrogative sentences based on the phrases. Students can use their written sentences to role-play an interview or an introduction of a classmate.

21.4 The Colon

Colons to Introduce

1. Lists

■ Use a colon to introduce a list, especially after a statement that uses such words as *these, the following,* or *as follows.*

> The science test on Friday will cover **these** areas**:** the circulatory system, the digestive system, and the nervous system.
>
> He requested **the following:** a hammer, a screwdriver, four nails, and a level.

Do not use a colon to introduce a list if the list immediately follows a verb or a preposition.

> The best nonanimal sources of protein **are** soybeans, wheat germ, brewer's yeast, nuts, seeds, and whole grains. [The list follows the verb *are*.]
>
> My sister likes to top her hamburger **with** lettuce, tomato, mustard, ketchup, and relish. [The list follows the preposition *with*.]

2. Illustrations or restatements

■ Use a colon to introduce material that illustrates, explains, or restates the preceding material. A complete sentence following a colon is capitalized.

> I often wish that my parents had had more than one child**:** They worry too much about me.

3. Quotations

■ Use a colon to introduce a long or formal quotation. A formal quotation is often preceded by such words as *this, these, the following,* or *as follows.*

> Mrs. Hopkins asked us to write an essay on **the following** African saying**:** "It is the rainy season that gives wealth."

Poetry quotations of more than one line and prose quotations of more than four or five lines are generally written below the introductory statement and indented on the page.

> In his long poem *The Other Pioneers*, Roberto Félix Salazar describes some of this nation's early settlers**:**
>
> Now I must write
> Of those of mine who rode these plains
> Long years before the Saxon and the Irish came.

Punctuation, Abbreviations, and Numbers

Resource Manager

Planning Resources
- *Lesson Plans*

Transparencies
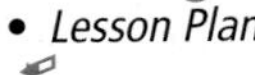

- *Bellringer*
- *Daily Language Practice*
- *Two-Minute Skill Drill*

Other Print Resources
- *Grammar and Composition Handbook*
- *Grammar Enrichment*, p. 41
- *Grammar Practice*, p. 41
- *Grammar Reteaching*, p. 41
- *Grammar Workbook*, Lesson 74

Focus

Lesson Overview

Objectives
- To learn how to use colons to introduce lists, illustrations, explanations, restatements, and quotations
- To learn how to use colons between the hour and minute, between a chapter and verse, and after a salutation

Bellringer
Daily Language Activity

When students enter the classroom, have the following assignment on the board: *Write the sentence that is correct. Tell why it is correct and why the other is not.*

1. *All the tools you need are: paper, pencils, and eraser.*
2. *These are all the tools you need: paper, pencils, and eraser.*

See also *Daily Language Practice*

Motivating Activity

Have students tell why Bellringer sentence number 2 is correct (because the colon is used to introduce a list after a statement). Explain to students that in sentences with lists, people often mistakenly use the colon between the verb and its complement. (*The classes offered this semester include: history, algebra, and music.*) For the colon to be used correctly, what appears before the colon must be a complete sentence.

Teach

Colons to Introduce

Vocabulary Link

The literal meaning of the word *colon* is "limb" or "part." A colon sets off part of a sentence.

Teach

Other Uses of Colons

Two-Minute Skill Drill

Have volunteers insert colons as needed in the letter below.

Dear Dr. Jenkins
I cannot see you next Saturday at 1100 A.M. That morning I have to do the following clean my room, oil my bike, and ice a cake. Could we meet after 300 P.M.?

See also *Two-Minute Skill Drill Transparency 21.4*

Practice and Assess

Answers: Exercise 3

1. games:
2. order:
3. chess:
4. pieces:
5. correct
6. war:
7. follows:
8. war:—Isaiah 2:4
9. times:
   11:00 A.M.
   1:00 P.M.
   5:00 P.M.
   7:30 P.M.
10. correct

Additional Resources

Grammar Practice, p. 41
Grammar Reteaching, p. 41
Grammar Enrichment, p. 41
Grammar Workbook, Lesson 74

Close

Have students recall everyday situations in which colons are used, such as on invitations or in television listings.

Other Uses of Colons

- Use a colon between the hour and the minute of the precise time, between the chapter and the verse in biblical references, and after the salutation of a business letter.

12:30 A.M.	Genesis 7:20–24	Sir:
4:00 P.M.	Ruth 1:16–18	Dear Ms. Snow:

Exercise 3 Using the Colon

For the items below, write each word or number that should be followed by a colon. Then write the colon itself. For any sentence that does not need a colon, write *correct.*

SAMPLE Any of these will work as substitutes ketchup, chili sauce, or salsa.
ANSWER substitutes:

The Game of Chess

1. Many people enjoy playing these board games chess, checkers, and pachisi.
2. Chess may have spread from place to place in the following order India, Persia, and Spain.
3. There are several board games that resemble chess checkers, the Japanese game *go,* and Chinese checkers.
4. In chess each player has the following playing pieces one king, one queen, two bishops, two knights, two rooks, and eight pawns.
5. The qualities essential to a good chess player are a good memory, a quick mind, and foresight.
6. In some ways, chess is like war it pits two "armies" against each other.
7. The *Encyclopaedia Britannica* notes that chess players use strategies of attack and defense aimed at the surrender of the opponent's king. The encyclopedia continues as follows "Nevertheless, the game is only a rather limited simulation of war or, in Freudian terms, a sublimation of that aggressive impulse."
8. The Old Testament has the following to say about war

   They shall beat their swords into plowshares
   and their spears into pruning-hooks;
   nation shall not lift up sword against nation,
   neither shall they learn war anymore.
   —Isaiah 2 4

9. A regional chess tournament typically takes place on a three-day weekend, with two rounds each day at the following times round 1 occurs from 1100 A.M. to 100 P.M. and round 2 from 500 P.M. to 730 P.M.
10. In addition to the type of chess that most people play, other types include blindfold chess, lightning chess, postal chess, and computer chess.

Enrichment and Extension

Using Colons

Students may have difficulty figuring out when to use colons as opposed to semicolons, commas, or periods. To help them, write *the following* on an index card. Let them write this pair of words in their own sentences, adding a colon after the words *the following.* Then let them write other sentences that contain colons. They may want to model their sentences on sentences in the lesson. Return to this exercise regularly until students are at ease using colons. **L2**

21.5 The Semicolon

Semicolons to Separate Main Clauses

- Use a semicolon to separate main clauses that are not joined by a coordinating conjunction (*and, but, or, nor, yet,* and *for*).

  Paul Robeson was an excellent singer and actor**;** he was also a talented football player.

  Paul Robeson was an excellent singer and actor, **and** he was also a talented football player.

- Use a semicolon to separate main clauses joined by a conjunctive adverb (such as *however, therefore, nevertheless, moreover, furthermore,* and *subsequently*) or by an expression such as *for example* or *that is.*

In general, a conjunctive adverb or an expression such as *for example* is followed by a comma.

Robeson appeared in many plays and musicals**;** for example, he starred in *Othello* and *Porgy and Bess.*

Robeson appeared in *Show Boat* in 1926**;** subsequently, he acted in the films *Jericho* and *Song of Freedom.*

Exercise 4 Using Semicolons and Commas in Clauses

On your paper, rewrite the following sentences, adding semicolons and commas where necessary.

Ancient Bridges

1. An early type of bridge was a tree trunk thrown across a stream another type was a primitive suspension span of twisted bamboo.
2. In 500 B.C., the Persian king Xerxes created a "bridge" of boats over the Bosporus Strait his purpose was to rapidly deploy ground troops into ancient Greece.
3. The finest ancient bridges were built by the Romans nearly 2,000 years ago for example the semicircular arch bridge over the Tagus River in Spain is still standing.
4. In the Middle Ages, Europeans began to build bridges with pointed arches however these features had been invented by Persian and Muslim engineers many years earlier.
5. In 1973 the Bosporus Bridge created the first road link between Europe and Asia since King Xerxes's bridge of boats more recently, a second bridge was built across that same waterway.

Focus

Lesson Overview

Objective

- To use semicolons correctly

Bellringer
Daily Language Activity

When students enter the classroom, have the following assignment on the board: *Write two sentences that contain semicolons.*

See also *Daily Language Practice*

Motivating Activity

Have a few students read their examples aloud and write them on the board, especially any containing conjunctive adverbs (such as *however, therefore,* and *nevertheless*).

Teach

Semicolons to Separate Main Clauses

Teaching Tip

Explain that semicolons help show the exact relationship between two main clauses when they are connected with a conjunctive adverb, such as *however, moreover,* or *thus.*

Practice and Assess

Answers: Exercise 4

1. . . . stream; another . . .
2. . . . Bosporus Strait; his . . .
3. . . . ago; for example, the . . .
4. . . . arches; however, these . . .
5. . . . of boats; more . . .

Resource Manager

Planning Resources

- *Lesson Plans*

Transparencies

- *Bellringer*
- *Daily Language Practice*
- *Two-Minute Skill Drill*

Other Print Resources

- *Grammar and Composition Handbook*
- *Grammar Enrichment,* p. 42
- *Grammar Practice,* p. 42
- *Grammar Reteaching,* p. 42
- *Grammar Workbook,* Lesson 75

Teach

Semicolons and Commas

Vocabulary Link

Explain that since *semi-* means "half" and *colon* means "part," a *semicolon* literally means "a half part." It is so called because it is a punctuation mark halfway between a comma and a period. Read aloud the examples, pointing out to students each use of semicolons and commas.

Two-Minute Skill Drill

Use the last sentence in Exercise 4 to have students identify the simple subjects and simple predicates in each of the clauses.

(first clause—subject: Bosporus Bridge; predicate: created; second clause—subject: bridge; predicate: was built)

See also *Two-Minute Skill Drill Transparency 21.5*

Practice and Assess

Answers: Exercise 5

1. . . . Shabako; . . .
2. . . . sun; . . . goddess; . . . underworld; . . .
3. . . . gems; . . .
4. . . . trading; . . .
5. . . . Khartoum, Sudan; Merowe, Sudan; Aswan, Egypt; Luxor, Egypt; . . .

Semicolons and Commas

- Use a semicolon to separate the items in a series when the items contain commas.

  Some of the powerful African kingdoms that flourished before the sixteenth century were Kush**,** which dominated the eastern Sudan**;** Karanga**,** which was located around Zimbabwe in southern Africa**;** Ghana**,** Mali**,** and Songhai**,** which successively controlled the Niger River in West Africa**;** and Benin**,** which had its center in what is now Nigeria.

- Use a semicolon to separate two main clauses joined by a coordinating conjunction when the clauses already contain several commas.

  The rule of Mansa Musa**,** the Moslem emperor of the African kingdom of Mali from 1312 to 1337**,** is remembered for military success**,** trade expansion**,** and Moslem scholarship**;** but this period is probably most noteworthy as a golden age of peace and prosperity.

Exercise 5 **Using Semicolons with Items Containing Commas**

For the following sentences, write each word that should be followed by a semicolon and add the semicolon.

Ancient Kush

1. The heroes of the ancient kingdom of Kush were King Kashta, Prince Piankhi, and Piankhi's brother, Shabako, and they and their Kushite successors ruled Egypt for almost 100 years.
2. The Kushites, like the ancient Egyptians they conquered, worshipped Ra, the god of sky and sun, Isis, the great mother goddess, Osiris, the god of the underworld, and Horus, the son of Isis and Osiris.
3. In early times, Kush was famous for its ebony, ivory, gold, silver, incense, wood, and precious gems, but later its most precious resource became iron.
4. The gifts of the Nile River included rich soil for farming, water for irrigation, and a route for trading, and Kush was one of many societies that benefited from these gifts.
5. On its way to the Mediterranean Sea, the Nile River passes Khartoum, Sudan, Merowe, Sudan, Aswan, Egypt, Luxor, Egypt, and Cairo, Egypt.

English Language Learners

Using Coordinating Conjunctions and Conjunctive Adverbs

Students new to English may need practice using and punctuating coordinating conjunctions and conjunctive adverbs. Have students write a paragraph explaining why they like or dislike a food. Have them use at least one coordinating conjunction (*and, but, or, nor, yet, for*) and one conjunctive adverb (*however, therefore*). Have partners meet so that each student may identify the conjunctions and adverbs in their paragraphs and discuss their use.

Exercise 6 Using Semicolons

For the sentences below, write each word that should be followed by a semicolon and add the semicolon.

Louise Nevelson, Sculptor

1. The sculptor Louise Nevelson lived in a number of places in Europe and the United States, including Kiev, Ukraine, Rockland, Maine, Munich, Germany, and New York City.
2. At the age of five, Nevelson moved to Rockland with her family she lived there for fifteen years.
3. Nevelson's family name was Berliawsky at the age of twenty she married Charles Nevelson and moved to New York.
4. Nevelson studied art under Hans Hofmann, the abstract painter who used primary colors in explosive contrasts she also studied with the muralist Diego Rivera.
5. Many artists are not willing to struggle however, Louise Nevelson worked for years without money or fame.
6. Nevelson's first one-woman sculpture show was in 1940 after that she became world renowned.
7. Nevelson made sculptures with found objects her artworks were large and intricate.
8. Nevelson used many materials in her sculptures nevertheless, her wooden assemblages in black and white are the best known.
9. A pioneer in environmental art, Nevelson created walls of framed sculptures her large-scale works sometimes take up an entire room.
10. Nevelson's art was influenced by multimedia sculpture as well as Cubism and Surrealism in addition, the art of Africa and pre-Columbian America affected her work.
11. Her life spanned most of the twentieth century she was born in 1900 and died in 1988.
12. She collected old parts of furniture subsequently, she used such objects in her famous black-box sculptures.
13. The black boxes are arranged like shelves along a wall however, their effect is almost musical, with changes in tone and rhythm.
14. Nevelson's decorated walls reached the height of their development in the 1950s nevertheless, she continued to explore new artistic avenues.
15. In some of her later works, she employed aluminum, steel, and Plexiglas she became interested in working with these materials as time passed.
16. From an early emphasis on somber blacks and whites, she turned to brighter materials for example, she gave a white and gold finish to the sculpture known as Transparent Sculpture VI.
17. At first the untrained eye may find Nevelson's art difficult to understand however, close attention increases the viewer's appreciation for her imagination.
18. Nevelson's works can be seen in the Whitney Museum in New York City she also created an all-white chapel in Saint Peter's Lutheran Church in New York City.
19. There are several books that describe Nevelson's life and art one is a biography by John Gordon.
20. Other noted twentieth-century sculptors include Henry Moore, Alberto Giacometti, Alexander Calder, and Claes Oldenburg their styles are all fairly distinct from each other.

Answers: Exercise 6

1. Ukraine; Maine; Germany;
2. family;
3. Berliawsky;
4. contrasts;
5. struggle;
6. 1940;
7. objects;
8. sculptures;
9. sculptures;
10. Surrealism;
11. century;
12. furniture;
13. wall;
14. 1950s;
15. Plexiglas;
16. materials;
17. understand;
18. New York City;
19. art;
20. Oldenburg;

Additional Resources

- *Grammar Practice,* p. 42
- *Grammar Reteaching,* p. 42
- Grammar Enrichment, p. 42

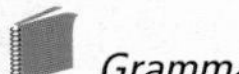

Grammar Workbook, Lesson 75

Close

Remind students that using semicolons to separate the main clauses in sentences provides one way for them to vary the sentence structure in their writing, thus allowing them to make their meaning clearer and their sentence structure more interesting.

Enrichment and Extension

Locating Semicolons

Have students look through magazines and reference books to find examples of the use of semicolons. Have students bring their examples to class and share them with others. Make sure students cite their references appropriately. **L2**

Using Semicolons

Ask students to write a sentence with two main clauses separated by a semicolon and then rewrite it as two separate sentences. Point out that the entities on either side of the semicolon should stand alone and that the second sentence may begin with a conjunctive adverb. **L2**

Focus

Lesson Overview

Objective

- To use commas correctly

Bellringer
Daily Language Activity

When students enter the classroom, have the following assignment on the board: *Rewrite the following sentences, adding commas where necessary:*

I can walk to school but sometimes I sleep late and end up taking the bus. In fact I take the bus often.

Discuss students' answers. Encourage students to provide effective feedback and to ask questions to clarify understanding.

See also *Daily Language Practice*

Teach

Commas and Compound Sentences

Teaching Tip

Tell students they can test whether a comma is required between two clauses by inserting a period after the first clause and omitting the coordinating conjunction from the second clause. If each clause forms a complete sentence, they should use a comma.

Practice and Assess

Answers: Exercise 7

1. Park,
2. Florida,
3. land,
4. toll,
5. Everglades,

21.6 The Comma

As you study the rules for comma usage, keep in mind that to *separate* elements means to place a comma between two equal elements. To *set off* an element means to put commas before and after it.

Commas and Compound Sentences

- Use commas between the main clauses in a compound sentence.

Place a comma before a coordinating conjunction *(and, but, or, nor, yet,* or *for)* that joins two main clauses.

I am not going to the concert, for I am too busy.

Many of the prospectors searched for years, but others struck gold immediately.

You may omit the comma between very short main clauses that are connected by a coordinating conjunction unless the comma is needed to avoid confusion.

Mara washed the dishes and Jim dried them. [clear]

We visited Miami and the Everglades are next. [confusing]

We visited Miami, and the Everglades are next. [clear]

Exercise 7 Using Commas in Compound Sentences

For each sentence below, write the word that should be followed by a comma and add the comma.

The Everglades

1. We wanted to visit the Everglades National Park and we tried to learn as much as possible about the area before taking our trip.
2. These large marshlands are located in southern Florida but they once extended all the way to the Gulf of Mexico.
3. The northern part of the Everglades has been drained to provide more dry land and this area is now used for farming.
4. A hundred years of dredging, draining, and land clearing have taken their toll yet the Everglades have managed to survive.
5. We must work diligently to protect the Everglades or we will lose a unique ecological system.

Resource Manager

Planning Resources

- *Lesson Plans*

Transparencies

- *Bellringer*
- *Daily Language Practice*
- *Two-Minute Skill Drill*

Other Print Resources

- *Grammar and Composition Handbook*
- *Grammar Enrichment,* pp. 43–47
- *Grammar Practice,* pp. 43–47
- *Grammar Reteaching,* pp. 43–47
- *Grammar Workbook,* Lessons 76–83
- *Sentence-Combining Practice,* pp. 1, 3, 5–9, 17–21

Commas in a Series

■ Use commas to separate three or more words, phrases, or clauses in a series.

A chair, a table, and a sofa were the room's only furnishings.

The cat ran out of the house, across the lawn, and down the street.

I rounded third, headed for home, and slid in safely.

Read carefully, take good notes, and outline the chapter.

No commas are necessary when all of the items are connected by conjunctions.

It was a sunny and hot and humid day in July.

Nouns that are used in pairs (*thunder and lightning, table and chairs, bread and butter*) are usually considered single units and should not be separated by commas. If such pairs appear with other nouns or groups of nouns in a series, they must be set off from the other items in the series.

My favorite breakfast is bacon and eggs, toast, and milk.

Exercise 8 **Using Commas in Series**

For each sentence below, write the words that should be followed by commas and add the commas.

Our Scottish Terrier

1. We decided to get a Scottish Terrier to be our family's companion watchdog and friend.
2. At one time, terriers were bred to dig for burrowing rodents chase them from their holes and kill them.
3. Today terriers are prized for their curiosity high spirits and friendliness.
4. Monty likes to take long walks ride in the car and eat all kinds of food.
5. We enrolled Monty in an obedience school where he learned to sit to stay and to heel.
6. The instructor told us that the secret to successful dog training is praise patience and persistence.
7. Sometimes Monty runs across the street sits in the neighbors' yard and watches their cat.
8. When he refuses to come, we try to entice him with a treat toy or ride in the car.
9. Monty's favorite toys are a squeaky soccer ball a rubber hamburger and a rope bone.
10. Everyone in our family agrees that Monty is a good friend valued family member and loving pet.

Punctuation, Abbreviations, and Numbers

Teach

Commas in a Series

☑ Teaching Tip

Explain to students that most authorities recommend using a comma before the word *and* in a series that contains paired nouns, such as *butter, sugar,* and *salt and pepper.*

Two-Minute Skill Drill

Write the following categories on the board. Have students write at least three responses for each category, using commas in a series.

types of music

kinds of stores

species of birds

Have students share their responses and write them on the board. If not everyone in the class is familiar with a student's response, have that student give the meaning of what he or she chose.

See also *Two-Minute Skill Drill Transparency 21.6*

Practice and Assess

Answers: Exercise 8

1. companion, watchdog,
2. rodents, holes,
3. curiosity, spirits,
4. long walks, car,
5. to sit, to stay,
6. praise, patience,
7. street, yard,
8. treat, toy,
9. ball, hamburger,
10. friend, member,

MEETING INDIVIDUAL NEEDS

English Language Learners

Using an Encyclopedia

Students new to English may benefit from using an encyclopedia in order to increase their vocabularies. Have pairs of students use an encyclopedia to research responses to the categories *types of trees, types of dances,* and *types of land formations.* Later, allow time for students to share what they have learned and to explain any of their information that is unfamiliar to other class members.

Teach

Commas and Coordinate Adjectives

Vocabulary Link

Tell students that the words *hatchet* and *comma* are related: Both derive from a Greek verb meaning "to cut." Commas were originally used to "cut" or mark off the ends of sentences; today they mark off sentence parts.

Practice and Assess

Answers: Exercise 9

1. Arthur Schomburg led a long, active, productive life.
2. He grew up in Puerto Rico, studied in the Virgin Islands, and came to the United States in 1891.
3. Schomburg was an author and historian, but he is best known as a collector of literature about African American culture.
4. Schomburg was also an important figure in the literary, artistic, and musical movement known as the Harlem Renaissance.
5. correct
6. The Carnegie Corporation bought the collection, donated it to the New York Public Library, and named it in Schomburg's honor.
7. correct
8. The collection is housed in a tall, modern brick building in the Harlem neighborhood.
9. Users of the collection study African American history, literature, art, or music.
10. correct

Commas and Coordinate Adjectives

■ Place a comma between coordinate adjectives that precede a noun.

Coordinate adjectives modify a noun equally. To determine whether adjectives are coordinate, try to reverse their order or put the word *and* between them. If the sentence still sounds natural, the adjectives are coordinate.

Pepper is a good, obedient, gentle dog.

Do not use a comma between adjectives preceding a noun if they sound unnatural with their order reversed or with *and* between them. In general, adjectives that describe size, shape, age, and material do not need commas between them.

Jelani grew up in a small white frame house.

Commas may be needed between some of the adjectives in a series but not between others.

I like to read in our bright, cozy family room.

In the preceding sentence *and* would sound natural between *bright* and *cozy*, but it would not sound natural between *cozy* and *family*.

Exercise 9 Using Commas in Sentences

On your paper, rewrite the following sentences, adding commas between coordinate adjectives, items in a series, and main clauses. If a sentence needs no comma, write *correct*.

Arthur Schomburg, Collector

1. Arthur Schomburg led a long active productive life.
2. He grew up in Puerto Rico studied in the Virgin Islands and came to the United States in 1891.
3. Schomburg was an author and historian but he is best known as a collector of literature about African American culture.
4. Schomburg was also an important figure in the literary artistic and musical movement known as the Harlem Renaissance.
5. His collection included over 10,000 books and manuscripts and pamphlets.
6. The Carnegie Corporation bought the collection donated it to the New York Public Library and named it in Schomburg's honor.
7. The Schomburg Collection has a wide reputation because it has more books on African American history and literature than any other library in North America.
8. The collection is housed in a tall modern brick building in the Harlem neighborhood.
9. Users of the collection study African American history literature art or music.
10. You may find that your own local library has a collection of books about African American culture or that a nearby historical society has some information about local African American families.

Enrichment and Extension

Using Commas with Coordinate Adjectives

Explain that when coordinate adjectives modify the same noun, it does not matter which adjective comes first. For example, in the sentence *Jeff is a kind, considerate, and thoughtful friend*, the adjectives could be reordered and the sentence would still sound natural. Identify coordinate adjectives by determining whether their positions can logically be reversed. Work orally with students to identify coordinate adjectives in sentences from Exercise 9. **L2**

Commas and Nonessential Elements

1. **Participles, infinitives, and their phrases**

- Use commas to set off participles, infinitives, and their phrases if they are not essential to the meaning of the sentence.

She watched, puzzled, as the man in the yellow hat drove away.

A customer, complaining loudly, stepped up to the counter.

I have no idea, to be honest, what you would like for a graduation present.

Do not set off participles, infinitives, and their phrases if they are essential to the meaning of the sentence.

The man standing by the door is my father. [The participial phrase tells *which* man.]

My mother's car is the one parked in the driveway. [The participial phrase identifies the car.]

She went to medical school to become a doctor. [The infinitive phrase tells *why*.]

To become a doctor had been her goal for years. [The infinitive phrase is used as the subject of the sentence.]

I wanted to go home. [The infinitive phrase is used as the direct object.]

2. **Adjective clauses**

- Use commas to set off a nonessential adjective clause.

A nonessential (nonrestrictive) clause can be considered an extra clause because it gives additional information about a noun. Because an extra clause adds to the basic meaning of a sentence, it is set off by commas.

Atlanta, which is the capital of Georgia, is the transportation center of the Southeast. [*Which is the capital of Georgia* is a nonessential clause.]

Do not set off an essential adjective clause. Because an essential (restrictive) clause gives necessary information about a noun, it is needed to convey the exact meaning of the sentence.

People who are afraid of heights do not like to look down from balconies or terraces. [*Who are afraid of heights* is an essential clause.]

Punctuation, Abbreviations, and Numbers

Teach

Commas and Nonessential Elements

Cross-reference: Grammar

For instruction and practice with participles, infinitives, and their phrases, refer students to Lesson 12.3, pp. 523–527. For instruction and practice with adjective clauses, refer students to Lesson 13.5, pp. 545–547. For instruction and practice with appositives, refer students to Lesson 12.2, pp. 521–522.

Two-Minute Skill Drill

Write the following sentences on the board, and have students write the infinitive form of each of the verbs.

I'm the oldest.

They have two dogs.

She gave one to her neighbors.

Having done that, she went home.

Have volunteers share their answers (*to be, to have, to give, to do, to go*).

See also *Two-Minute Skill Drill Transparency 21.6*

Listening and Speaking

Select a few students to read aloud the Declaration of Independence of the United States. Allow students sufficient time to prepare. As part of their preparation, emphasize that they are to pay special attention to punctuation in order to determine such things as when to pause and what words to emphasize.

After the oral readings, have volunteers comment on any reading techniques used by the speakers that were especially helpful to the listeners.

Meeting Individual Needs

English Language Learners

Recognizing Inflections in English

Explain that speakers usually pause briefly when they come to a comma in writing. Then read aloud from a newspaper or magazine article that contains commas. Ask students to listen for those brief pauses and gently rap on their desks to indicate any words they think are followed by commas. If time permits, ask a few volunteers to select and read excerpts from famous speeches. The rest of the group can try to determine where the commas are placed.

Practice and Assess

Answers: Exercise 10

1. Junior, the oldest male orangutan in the National Zoo in Washington, D.C., is a favorite of visitors.
2. correct *or* The orangutan, whose formal name is Atjeh, is a great red ape.
3. correct
4. correct
5. Being so different from each other, they probably would not interbreed in nature.
6. correct
7. correct
8. Critics of the policy, disagreeing vocally, claim that the hybrids are being treated as second-class apes.
9. correct *or* These critics' argument, that the existence of the great red ape does not endanger the zoos' mission to emphasize conservation, represents a controversial viewpoint.
10. A long-lived animal, the orangutan can survive as long as sixty years.

3. **Appositives**

■ Use commas to set off an appositive if it is not essential to the meaning of a sentence.

A nonessential (nonrestrictive) appositive can be considered an extra appositive; it calls for commas.

Nelson Mandela**,** the president of South Africa**,** was freed from a South African prison in 1990.

My mother lives in Escondido**,** a town near San Diego in southern California.

A nonessential (nonrestrictive) appositive is sometimes placed before the noun or pronoun to which it refers.

An insurance executive**,** Charles Ives wrote music in his spare time. [The appositive, *An insurance executive*, precedes the subject of the sentence, *Charles Ives.*]

An essential (restrictive) appositive gives necessary information about a noun and is not set off.

The word *fiesta* came into English from Spanish. [The appositive, *fiesta*, is needed to identify *word.*]

Exercise 10 Using Commas with Nonessential Elements

On your paper, rewrite the following sentences that need commas, adding commas as necessary. If a sentence needs no commas, write *correct.*

The Great Red Ape

1. Junior the oldest male orangutan in the National Zoo in Washington, D.C., is a favorite of visitors.
2. The orangutan whose formal name is Atjeh is a great red ape.
3. He is a member of a species created by zookeepers who crossbred two subspecies of orangutans.
4. Many scientists have lately been surprised to learn that Sumatran and Bornean orangutans are more genetically different from each other than lions are from tigers.
5. Being so different from each other they probably would not interbreed in nature.
6. The organization overseeing zoo programs in the United States has called a halt to the interbreeding of Sumatran and Bornean orangutans.
7. The hybrids that are now in zoos will not reproduce.
8. Critics of the policy disagreeing vocally claim that the hybrids are being treated as second-class apes.
9. These critics' argument that the existence of the great red ape does not endanger the zoos' mission to emphasize conservation represents a controversial viewpoint.
10. A long-lived animal the orangutan can survive as long as sixty years.

Commas with Interjections, Parenthetical Expressions, Conjunctive Adverbs, and Antithetical Phrases

- Use commas to set off interjections (such as *oh* and *well*), parenthetical expressions (such as *on the contrary, on the other hand, in fact, by the way, to be exact,* and *after all*), and conjunctive adverbs (such as *however, moreover,* and *consequently*).

Well, we'd better be going home.

Oh, I don't know.

We have to leave, unfortunately.

Last night, on the other hand, we could have stayed longer.

We said we'd be home early; consequently, we must leave now.

You might want to come with us, however.

- Use commas to set off an antithetical phrase.

An **antithetical phrase** uses a word such as *not* or *unlike* to qualify what precedes it.

You, not I, deserve this honor.

Bicycles, unlike cars, cause no pollution.

Exercise 11 Using Commas

On your paper, rewrite the following sentences, adding commas where they are needed. If a sentence needs no commas, write *correct*.

Sequoya and the Cherokee Language

1. Most Native American languages unlike European ones were not written down before the eighteenth century; consequently it was difficult for people to learn them.
2. The Cherokees thought that writing was the privilege of certain people.
3. Like many other Native American groups in fact the Cherokees used smoke and drum signals to communicate with people some distance away.
4. Sequoya for example saw the need for a way of writing down his language.
5. Having considered the idea for some time he realized how valuable a written language would be.
6. He had been hurt in a hunting accident; therefore he had the leisure to think about a writing system.
7. Specifically he began to draw marks on twigs and stones.
8. People at first laughed at Sequoya's dream; however they soon began to change their minds about him.
9. Sequoya produced the first Cherokee alphabet making it possible for his people to write messages and record its history.
10. Sequoya who became successful despite the doubts of others was sent to Washington, D.C., in 1828 to represent the Cherokees.

Teach

Commas with Interjections, Parenthetical Expressions, Conjunctive Adverbs, and Antithetical Phrases

☑ Teaching Tip

Explain that parenthetical expressions are often like external commentaries on the truth or the importance of a sentence. These commentaries are also external to the grammar of the sentence; that is, they play no grammatical role within the sentence. One of the characteristics of parenthetical expressions is that they can be moved around the sentence rather freely. Tell students that the word *antithetical* is the adjective form of *antithesis,* meaning "the exact opposite." Antithetical phrases and clauses are usually set off from the rest of a sentence with commas so that readers will understand that what comes next in the sentence is counter to what they would expect.

Practice and Assess

Answers: Exercise 11

1. . . . languages, unlike European ones, were not . . . consequently, . . .
2. correct
3. . . . groups, in fact, the Cherokees . . .
4. Sequoya, for example, . . .
5. . . . some time, he realized . . .
6. . . . therefore, he had . . .
7. Specifically, he began . . .
8. . . . however, they soon began
9. . . . Cherokee alphabet, making it . . .
10. Sequoya, who became successful despite the doubts of others, was sent to . . .

Teach

Commas with Other Phrases and Clauses

Cross-reference: Grammar

For instruction and practice with prepositional phrases, refer students to Lesson 12.1, pp. 519–520. For instruction and practice with verbal phrases, refer students to Lesson 12.3, pp. 523–527. For instruction and practice with adverb clauses, refer students to Lesson 13.6, pp. 548–549.

Teaching Tip

Remind students of the distinction between a clause and a phrase: A clause contains a subject and a verb; a phrase does not.

Remind the class that one kind of adverb phrase is a prepositional phrase that acts as an adverb. Tell students that there is one more difference between an adverb clause and an adverb phrase. An adverb clause that starts a sentence must always be set off from the rest of the sentence with a comma. However, an adverb phrase that starts its sentence needs to be followed by a comma only if the comma would prevent confusion. If there is no possibility of confusion, a comma after an introductory adverb phrase is optional. Have students review a recent writing assignment for incorrect comma usage with phrases and clauses. Encourage students to revise their writing.

Commas with Other Phrases and Clauses

1. Introductory prepositional phrases

- Although a comma after a short introductory prepositional phrase is not incorrect, it is necessary only if the sentence would be misread without the comma.

To those outside**,** the house appeared deserted. [comma needed to prevent misreading]

At the last moment we decided not to go. [comma not needed]

- Use a comma after a long prepositional phrase or after the final phrase in a succession of phrases.

On the extremely steep and rocky cliff**,** the mountain climbers carefully found their footholds.

On the afternoon of the day of the game**,** we made a banner.

Do not use a comma if the phrase is immediately followed by a verb.

On the stone above the front door of the building was the date.

2. Introductory participles and participial phrases

- Use commas to set off introductory participles and participial phrases.

Purring**,** the kitten curled up in my lap.

Sitting in a tree**,** my little sister called down to us.

3. Adverb clauses

- Use commas to set off all introductory adverb clauses.

Although I like country music**,** I did not want to hear his entire collection.

Until she arrived**,** I thought that no one was coming.

- Also use commas to set off internal adverb clauses that interrupt the flow of a sentence.

Evan**,** after he thought about it awhile**,** agreed with our idea.

In general, do not set off an adverb clause at the end of a sentence unless the clause is parenthetical or the sentence would be misread without the comma.

English Language Learners

Using Inflection in Questions

Students learning English may have difficulty with the inflection in spoken questions. Explain that a rise in tone usually indicates a question. Americans tend to place the highest tone on the final word of a question; other English speakers place it earlier.

Write the following questions on the board. Have students work in pairs to ask the questions and to answer them using sentences 1–3 in Exercise 8 on page 739.

a) Why did you get a Scottish Terrier?
b) For what were terriers originally used?
c) Why are terriers prized today?

Exercise 12 **Using Commas with Phrases and Clauses**

On your paper, rewrite the sentences that need commas, adding commas as necessary. If a sentence needs no additional commas, write *correct.*

I. M. Pei

1. To most people the name I. M. Pei means good taste and quality of design.
2. Among contemporary architects throughout the world Pei's name is unquestionably one of the best known and most respected.
3. Because his firm has frequently combined a beautiful and practical design with an affordable budget Pei is considered a gifted architect.
4. Among Pei's most successful designs are the East Building of the National Gallery of Art in Washington, D.C., and the pyramidal entrance to the Louvre in Paris.
5. Architects unlike artists must seek to harmonize appearance with purpose.
6. After a series of problems with the John Hancock Tower in Boston Pei's firm lost some business.
7. Pei and his staff gradually regained their hands-on reputation after the problems with the John Hancock Tower were resolved.
8. For a resort hotel in mainland China Pei created a design that pleased everyone.
9. Having been born in China Pei was happy to design a structure for his native land.
10. Although Pei has become highly successful as an architect he continues to welcome new challenges.

Exercise 13 **Using Commas with Phrases and Clauses**

Rewrite the sentences that need commas adding commas as necessary. If a sentence needs no commas, write *correct.*

Corn in the Americas

1. When it was recently determined that corn was first cultivated in the Americas only 4,700 years ago many scientists were puzzled.
2. Before this discovery they had thought that people in central Mexico started farming corn about 7,000 years ago.
3. Perplexed the scientists are trying to figure out if an earlier example of cultivated corn could have existed.
4. About 9,000 years ago in the Middle East around the Jordan River valley both plants and animals were domesticated.
5. If they do not locate an earlier sample scientists may have to rethink the chronology of civilization in the Western Hemisphere.
6. One famous botanist after he studied the matter cautioned his fellow scientists not to be too hasty.
7. In other parts of Mexico still older corn may be found.
8. Growing wild a plant that is similar to domesticated corn still exists in Mexico.
9. Scientists believe that ancient people once they discovered the wild corn plant began to cultivate it.
10. After it was discovered by the rest of the world corn became very popular.

Practice and Assess

Answers: Exercise 12

1. correct *or* To most people, . . .
2. . . . the world, Pei's name is . . .
3. . . . affordable budget, Pei is considered . . .
4. correct
5. Architects, unlike artists, must seek . . .
6. . . . Tower in Boston, Pei's firm . . .
7. correct
8. . . . China, Pei created a . . .
9. . . . born in China, Pei was . . .
10. . . . an architect, he continues . . .

Answers: Exercise 13

Answers will vary, but some suggestions are given below.

1. . . . years ago, many scientists . . .
2. correct *or* Before this discovery, . . .
3. Perplexed, the scientists . . .
4. . . . Jordan River valley, both . . .
5. . . . sample, scientists . . .
6. . . . botanist, after he studied the matter, . . .
7. . . . Mexico, still older . . .
8. Growing wild, a plant . . .
9. . . . ancient people, once they discovered the wild corn plant, . . .
10. . . . rest of the world, corn . . .

21.6

Teach

Additional Uses of Commas

Cross-reference: Mechanics

For instruction and practice of capitalization rules pertaining to geographical terms and dates, refer students to Lesson 20.2, pp. 713–719.

Teaching Tip

Point out to students that when an address, a date, or a source reference appears in a sentence, a comma (like the ones after *California* and *1995* in the sample sentences) separates the term from the rest of the sentence. This comma is not used, however, with a date that requires no other comma: *September 2005 will mark our tenth year in Evanston.*

Teaching Tip

Tell students that words or names used in direct address are not part of the basic grammar of a sentence. A good test of whether the word or name should be set off with a comma or commas is to ask whether it can be deleted from the sentence. If it can be deleted, then the term is being used in direct address and requires the use of either one or two commas.

Additional Uses of Commas

1. Titles of people

- Use commas to set off titles when they follow a person's name.

Alan Wong, M.D. Maureen O'Connor, mayor of San Diego
Jorge Gonzalez, Ph.D., will speak on Thursday.

2. Addresses, geographical terms, and dates

- Use commas to separate the various parts of an address, a geographical term, or a date.

Anaheim, California, is the home of Disneyland.
Her address is 9 Lee Road, Nome, AK 99762.
Friday, March 15, 1995, was the day I got my driver's license.

Use the following forms for letter writing.

90 Sherwick Road
New Bedford, MA 02745
July 7, 1997

Do not use commas if only the month and the day or only the month and the year are given.

October 31 September 1996

3. References

- Use commas to set off the parts of a reference that direct the reader to the exact source.

Odysseus becomes reunited with his son Telemachus in the *Odyssey*, Book 16, lines 177–219.

4. Direct Address

- Use commas to set off words or names used in direct address.

Nathaniel, do you know where Kathleen is?
I can order the book for you, sir, if you like.

5. Tag Questions

- Use commas to set off a tag question.

A tag question (such as *shouldn't I?* or *have you?*) emphasizes an implied answer to the statement preceding it.

You've already seen this film, haven't you?

Civic Literacy

Using Commas in Writing History

Arrange with the history or civics teacher to have small student groups research and write short papers on the early history of their state. Suggest that students use a computer to work through each step of the writing process. Students should include such information as when, why, and by whom the state was first settled, as well as when it received statehood. Remind students to cite all references used to obtain information. Have students pay particular attention to the punctuation in their papers, especially the use of commas. When all reports are finalized, they can be presented in their history or civics classes. **L3**

6. **Letter Writing**

- Place a comma after the salutation of an informal letter and after the closing of all letters.

Dear Dolores, Very truly yours,

Misuse of Commas

In general, do not use a comma before a conjunction that connects a compound predicate or compound subject.

INCORRECT She started the car, and drove down the hill. [compound predicate]

CORRECT She started the car and drove down the hill.

INCORRECT The adults playing softball, and the children playing soccer argued in the field. [compound subject]

CORRECT The adults playing softball and the children playing soccer argued in the field.

Do not use only a comma to join two main clauses that are not part of a series. Use a coordinating conjunction with the comma, or use a semicolon.

INCORRECT John Wayne worked in Hollywood for almost 50 years, he made more than 200 films.

CORRECT John Wayne worked in Hollywood for almost 50 years, and he made more than 200 films.

Do not use a comma between a subject and its verb or between a verb and its complement.

INCORRECT What you do with your money, is your business.

CORRECT What you do with your money is your business.

INCORRECT For the overnight camping trip, you will need, a sleeping bag, a towel, soap, and a toothbrush.

CORRECT For the overnight camping trip, you will need a sleeping bag, a towel, soap, and a toothbrush.

Misuse of Commas

Teaching Tip

Point out to students that writers sometimes unnecessarily add commas in compound predicates. For example, in the sentence *She started the car, and drove down the hill,* writers may mentally add the understood subject (she) and then mistakenly use a comma before this second implied "main clause."

Practice and Assess

Answers: Exercise 14

1516 Evergreen Road
Bonita, California 92002
October 5, 1997

Dear Belinda,
Your mom told me that you want advice about a good diet. She said you want to lose twenty pounds. I hope that she has misunderstood your goal, Belinda, because you would be quite thin if you lost that much weight, wouldn't you?

I have enclosed a copy of an article about diet and weight loss that was published in the May 6, 1996, issue of *News in America,* page 22. Ruth Smith, M.D., the author, is a specialist in nutrition. In November 1990, I heard Dr. Smith speak at a conference in Washington, D.C., and I have a great deal of respect for her knowledge. You will read this article carefully, won't you?

I am looking forward to visiting your family at Thanksgiving. I haven't seen any of you since I was in San Diego on May 14, 1989, for a convention. When I visit this year, I hope we'll be able to spend some time together, Belinda.

Love,
Aunt Miriam

Practice and Assess

Answers: Exercise 15

Answers will vary, but some suggestions are given below:

1. . . . *Oz,* a cyclone . . . wild, . . . Munchkins.
2. . . . *The Lion King,* haven't you?
3. . . . remembers, Shirley Temple, a famous, adorable, . . . 1930s, appeared in dozens of films.
4. . . . time: . . . *Wind,* . . . *Life,* . . . *Madre.*
5. To be honest, most . . . cold, cruel facts of history.
6. . . . movies, by the way, have . . . characters; *Batman* . . . examples.
7. Robert Redford, best known for his acting, directed *A River Runs Through It.*
8. . . . great-grandfather, who will soon be eighty-five, the comedy . . . *Rush,* . . . Chaplin, . . . May 1925.
9. . . . *Miracle Worker,* both Anne Bancroft, who played Annie Sullivan, and Patty Duke, who played Helen Keller, won Academy Awards.
10. unnecessary, foolish, childish chances.

Additional Resources

Sentence-Combining Practice, pp. 1, 3, 5–9, 17–21

Grammar Practice, pp. 43–47

Grammar Reteaching, pp. 43–47

Grammar Enrichment, pp. 43–47

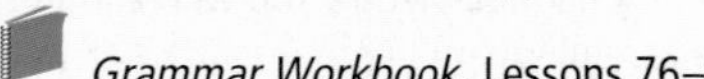

Grammar Workbook, Lessons 76–83

Close

Have volunteers take turns telling about three things they have done today. Let others write about what the volunteers said. Students should work together to check that they used commas correctly in their writing. Encourage students to provide effective feedback and to revise as necessary.

Exercise 14 Using Commas with Various Elements

On your paper, rewrite the following letter, adding twenty commas.

1516 Evergreen Road
Bonita CA 92002
October 5 20--

Dear Belinda

Your mom told me that you want advice about a good diet. She said you want to lose twenty pounds. I hope that she has misunderstood your goal Belinda because you would be quite thin if you lost that much weight wouldn't you?

I have enclosed a copy of an article about diet and weight loss that was published in the May 6 20-- issue of *News in America* page 22. Ruth Smith M.D. the author is a specialist in nutrition. In November 20-- I heard Dr. Smith speak at a conference in Washington D.C. and I have a great deal of respect for her knowledge. You will read this article carefully won't you?

I am looking forward to visiting your family at Thanksgiving. I haven't seen any of you since I was in San Diego on May 14 20-- for a convention. When I visit this year I hope we'll be able to spend some time together Belinda.

Love
Aunt Miriam

Exercise 15 Using End Marks, Colons, Semicolons, and Commas

On your paper, rewrite the following sentences, adding all necessary punctuation.

The Movies

1. In the 1939 movie *The Wizard of Oz,* a cyclone sweeps Dorothy out of rural Kansas and deposits her in the wild wonderful land of the Munchkins
2. You've surely seen and enjoyed *The Lion King* haven't you
3. As my grandmother remembers Shirley Temple a famous adorable and talented child star of the 1930s appeared in dozens of films
4. Movies such as these from the 1930s and 1940s have stood the test of time *Gone with the Wind It's a Wonderful Life* and *Treasure of the Sierra Madre*
5. To be honest most of Hollywood's films about cowboys and pioneers and Native Americans don't reflect the cold cruel facts of history
6. Quite a few movies by the way have been inspired by comic strip characters *Batman* and *Superman* are two outstanding examples
7. Robert Redford best known for his acting directed *A River Runs Through It*
8. According to my great-grandfather who will soon be eighty-five the comedy *The Gold Rush* starring Charlie Chaplin opened in May 1925
9. Because of their acting in *The Miracle Worker* both Anne Bancroft who played Annie Sullivan and Patty Duke who played Helen Keller won Academy Awards
10. Stars who perform their own stunts take unnecessary foolish childish chances

21.7 The Dash

When using a typewriter, indicate the dash with two hyphens (--). Do not place a comma, semicolon, colon, or period before or after a dash.

If you use a computer, you may make a dash with a certain combination of keystrokes. Refer to the manual of your word-processing program for instructions.

1. Dashes to Signal Change

■ Use a dash to indicate an abrupt break or change in thought within a sentence.

A small stand sells sugar loaves—the gift to bring when invited to dinner—sugar for the mint tea and for the sweet pastry, so flaky and light, that they bake.

Anaïs Nin

2. Dashes to Emphasize

■ Use a dash to set off and emphasize supplemental information or parenthetical comments.

It was a shiny new car—the first he had ever owned.

A shiny new car—the first he had ever owned—was his most prized possession.

Do not overuse dashes in your writing.

Exercise 16 Using Dashes

For each sentence below, write the phrase that should be set off with dashes and add the dash or dashes.

SAMPLE He waxed and polished the old car a waste of time before he tried to sell it.
ANSWER —a waste of time—

1. Uncle Raymond by the way, he's my mother's brother-in-law was the proud owner of a new foreign car.
2. He had purchased the sedan at the start of a driving tour of Europe his first visit to the place he called the Old Country.
3. When he brought the car back to the United States, he realized it had a few drawbacks especially the cost of maintenance.
4. Ironically, this car from northern Europe a region of frigid, snowbound winters performed poorly on icy roads in the upper Midwest.
5. The car proved its worth, however, after Uncle Raymond was involved in a major accident a highway pileup on Route 1 that totaled some of the other vehicles but left his car undamaged.

Resource Manager

Planning Resources
- *Lesson Plans*

Other Print Resources
- *Grammar and Composition Handbook*
- *Grammar Enrichment,* p. 48
- *Grammar Practice,* p. 48
- *Grammar Reteaching,* p. 48
- *Grammar Workbook,* Lesson 84
- *Sentence-Combining Practice,* pp. 6–8

Focus

Lesson Overview

Objective
- To use the dash correctly

Teach

Teaching Tip

Explain to students that a test of the correct use of dashes is to delete the information set off by the dashes. If crucial information is lost, then the dashes were incorrectly used.

In the following sentences have students insert dashes as appropriate:

1. *My cousin Cathy(—)my cousin from Minneapolis, not the one from Pierre(—)is coming for a visit in May.*
2. *The speed of the race cars and the cheering of the crowd(—)to say nothing of the heat and dust(—) made my birthday a day I'll remember.*

Discuss students' answers. Encourage students to ask questions to clarify understanding.

Practice and Assess

Answers: Exercise 16

1. —by the way, he's my mother's brother-in-law—
2. —his first visit to the place he called the Old Country.
3. —especially the cost of maintenance.
4. —a region of frigid, snowbound winters—
5. —a highway pileup on Route 1—

Close

Let volunteers write on the board sentences that need dashes.

Focus

Lesson Overview

Objective

- To use parentheses correctly

Bellringer
Daily Language Activity

When students enter the classroom, have the following assignment on the board: *Put parentheses where you think they will help in the following sentence:*

I have 11 pencils red ones, 3 erasers the blue kind, and a new pen it's bright green.

Have students explain their answers. Ask classmates to provide effective feedback and to ask questions for clarification.

See also *Daily Language Practice*

Practice and Assess

Answers: Exercise 17

1. Albuquerque (this fast-growing city is headquarters for a large computer chip manufacturer) . . .
2. The "sky city" of Acoma (Native Americans have lived there for hundreds of years) is a place to view handsome geometric pottery.
3. The altitude of Santa Fe and Taos (5,000 to 7,000 feet) helps to explain the cold winters that these two cities frequently get.
4. Bandelier National Monument contains fascinating cliff dwellings . . . the Anasazi people. (The Anasazi mysteriously disappeared from the pueblo long before the Spanish arrived.)
5. Los Alamos (named after the Spanish word for poplar trees) is where the atomic bomb was developed in the 1940s.

Punctuation, Abbreviations, and Numbers

21.8 Parentheses

Parentheses with Supplemental Material

■ Use parentheses to set off supplemental material.

Commas and dashes as well as parentheses can be used to set off supplemental material; the difference between the three marks of punctuation is one of degree. Use commas to set off supplemental material that is closely related to the rest of the sentence. Use parentheses to set off supplemental material that is not important enough to be considered part of the main statement. Use dashes to set off and emphasize material that interrupts the main statement.

Many contemporary women's fashions **(**business suits and low heels**)** show the influence of Gabrielle "Coco" Chanel.

A complete sentence within parentheses is not capitalized and needs no period if it is contained within another sentence. If a sentence in parentheses is not contained within another sentence (if it stands by itself), both a capital letter and a period are needed.

The unisex trend **(i**t still seems to be popular**)** was started by Chanel, who wore a man's trench coat.

Chanel introduced the world's most famous perfume, Chanel No. 5. **(T**his scent is still in great demand.**)**

Exercise 17 Using Parentheses

Rewrite the following sentences, adding parentheses where needed.

New Mexico

1. Albuquerque this fast-growing city is headquarters for a large computer chip manufacturer has a hot-air balloon fiesta every October.
2. The "sky city" of Acoma Native Americans have lived there for hundreds of years is a place to view handsome geometric pottery.
3. The altitude of Santa Fe and Taos 5,000 to 7,000 feet helps to explain the cold winters that these two cities frequently get.
4. Bandelier National Monument contains fascinating cliff dwellings carved out of the volcanic rock by the Anasazi people. The Anasazi mysteriously disappeared from the pueblo long before the Spanish arrived.
5. Los Alamos named after the Spanish word for poplar trees is where the atomic bomb was developed in the 1940s.

Resource Manager

Planning Resources
- *Lesson Plans*

Transparencies
- *Bellringer*
- *Daily Language Practice*

Other Print Resources
- *Grammar and Composition Handbook*
- *Grammar Enrichment,* p. 47
- *Grammar Workbook,* Lesson 85
- *Sentence-Combining Practice,* pp. 6, 8

Parentheses with Other Marks of Punctuation

1. With a comma, semicolon, or colon

- Place a comma, semicolon, or colon *after* the closing parenthesis.

Despite the simple clothes that Chanel designed and wore (the little black dress became her uniform**),** she became wealthy.

In the early 1950s, women wore long skirts with cinched waists and high heels (the Dior look**);** Chanel helped change that.

2. With a question mark or an exclamation point

- Place a question mark or an exclamation point *inside* the parentheses if it is part of the parenthetical expression.

Chanel believed that simplicity and practicality were more important than obviously expensive, complicated-looking clothes (who would not agree today**?)**.

Chanel exerted little influence on fashion during World War II (1939–1945), but she reopened her fashion house in 1954 (when she was seventy**!)**.

- Place a question mark or an exclamation point *outside* the parentheses if it is part of the entire sentence.

Did you know that Chanel introduced many of today's fashion classics (sweaters, costume jewelry, sling-back shoes**)?**

How amazed I was to find out that it was Chanel who made a suntan fashionable (in the 1930s**)!**

Exercise 18 **Using Parentheses**

Rewrite the following sentences correctly, adding parentheses where they are needed.

1. Roger he lived next door to us for years had a great love for baseball.
2. Amarillo from the Spanish word for "yellow" is a town in the Texas Panhandle.
3. It was a December night the first winterlike night of the month, and snow was falling.
4. That song is it by Handel or Mozart? always reminds me of Paula, for she used to play it constantly when we were in college together.
5. He was aggressive, overbearing, mean, and who would have thought it possible! completely devoted to his dachshund.
6. Anorexia can have serious even tragic consequences if not treated properly.
7. Some people I am not one of them think that Elvis Presley was devastatingly handsome.
8. Do you believe in love at first sight forgive the cliché?
9. It was an extraordinary feat: she threw the javelin 245 feet about 75 meters!
10. Otis was an Air Force pilot during the Persian Gulf War the war against Iraq.

Punctuation, Abbreviations, and Numbers

Teach

Parentheses

Teaching Tip

When parentheses are used to set off lengthy material, students sometimes forget to use the closing parenthesis. Suggest to them that when proofreading, they should always look for the closing parenthesis as soon as they encounter an opening parenthesis.

Practice and Assess

Answers: Exercise 18

1. Roger (he lived next door to us for years) had . . .
2. Amarillo (from the Spanish word for "yellow") is a town . . .
3. It was a December night (the first winterlike night of the month), and snow was falling.
4. That song (is it by Handel or Mozart?) always reminds me of Paula, for she used to play it constantly when we were in college together.
5. He was aggressive, overbearing, mean, and (who would have thought it possible!) completely devoted to his dachshund.
6. Anorexia can have serious (even tragic) consequences if not treated properly.
7. Some people (I am not one of them) think that Elvis Presley was devastatingly handsome.
8. Do you believe in love at first sight (forgive the cliché)?
9. It was an extraordinary feat: she threw the javelin 245 feet (about 75 meters)!
10. Otis was an Air Force pilot during the Persian Gulf War (the war against Iraq).

MEETING INDIVIDUAL NEEDS

English Language Learners

Using Punctuation Marks

Some students may benefit from additional work with commas, dashes, parentheses, exclamation points, and question marks in written English. Write each of these punctuation marks on an index card. Have volunteers choose a card and explain whether that mark exists in their first language. If it does, have the student tell how the mark is used in the language. If it does not, have the student tell whether there is an equivalent mark and what it is. In addition, have students tell what other marks their first language uses.

Focus

Lesson Overview

Objective

- To use quotation marks correctly

Bellringer
Daily Language Activity

When students enter the classroom, have the following assignment on the board: *Write the sentences below, adding quotation marks where they are needed:*

I'll go, Leeza mumbled, but I won't have any fun. The whole group, including Leeza, enjoyed the picnic and the game. Well, I guess watching a baseball game can be entertaining, after all, admitted Leeza with a big grin.

See also *Daily Language Practice*

Motivating Activity

Ask a volunteer to list students' suggestions from the Bellringer activity on the board. Discuss students' suggestions. Encourage students to ask questions to clarify understanding.

Teach

Quotation Marks for Direct Quotations

Vocabulary Link

The word *quotation* comes from a Latin term meaning "how many." The English word was used originally in quoting numbers, and the expression *to quote a price* is still used.

21.9 Quotation Marks

Quotation Marks for Direct Quotations

- Use quotation marks to enclose a direct quotation.

Place quotation marks around the quotation only, not around purely introductory or explanatory remarks. Generally, separate such remarks from the actual quotation with a comma. (For the use of colons to introduce quotations, see page 733.)

A famous poster asks**,** **"**What if they gave a war and nobody came?**"**

A Pawnee poem reminds us of **"**the sacredness of things.**"**

Do not use a comma after a quotation that ends with an exclamation point or a question mark.

"What is the question**?"** Gertrude Stein asked.

- When a quotation is interrupted by explanatory words such as *he said* or *she wrote,* use two sets of quotation marks.

Separate each part of the quotation from the interrupting phrase with marks of punctuation before and after the phrase. If the second part of the quotation is a complete sentence, begin it with a capital letter.

"A thing of beauty**,"** wrote John Keats**,** **"**is a joy forever.**"**

"It wasn't just that Babe Ruth hit more home runs than anybody else**,"** said Red Smith**.** **"**He hit them better, higher, and farther.**"**

Do not use quotation marks in an indirect quotation (a quotation that does not repeat a person's exact words).

ORIGINAL QUOTATION	**"**Dance is life at its most glorious moment**,"** said Pearl Lang.
INDIRECT QUOTATION	Pearl Lang said that dance is life's most glorious moment.

- Use single quotation marks around a quotation within a quotation.

President John F. Kennedy said, "I am one person who can truthfully say, **'**I got my job through the *New York Times.***'**"

- In writing dialogue, begin a new paragraph and use a new set of quotation marks every time the speaker changes.

He looked at me proudly. **"**Was it so hard to do, Daughter?**"**

"Not so hard as I thought.**"** I pinned the brooch on my dress. **"**I'll wear it always,**"** I said. **"**I'll keep it forever.**"**

—Kathryn Forbes

Resource Manager

Planning Resources

- *Lesson Plans*

Transparencies

- *Bellringer*
- *Daily Language Practice*

Other Print Resources

- *Grammar and Composition Handbook*
- *Grammar Enrichment,* p. 49
- *Grammar Practice,* p. 49
- *Grammar Reteaching,* p. 49
- *Grammar Workbook,* Lessons 86–87
- *Sentence-Combining Practice,* p. 27

Exercise 19 **Writing Dialogue Correctly**

Copy the following sentences, setting them up correctly as a dialogue.

[1]"I need help," Robert said. [2]"What happened?" I asked. [3]"I just locked the car keys in the trunk," he responded. [4]"How did you ever happen to do such a thing?" I demanded. [5]"I set them down there while I was looking for my house keys, which are missing too."

Exercise 20 **Using Quotation Marks with Direct Quotes**

Rewrite the following sentences, adding quotation marks where they are needed. For sentences that need no changes, write *correct.*

1. My method for remembering the numbers of days in all twelve months was given by my first-grade teacher, who said, Thirty days hath September, April, June, and November. All the rest have thirty-one, excepting February, and that has twenty-eight.
2. These are the times that try men's souls, warned eighteenth-century American pamphleteer and patriot Tom Paine.
3. Poet Bliss Carman writes, There is something in the autumn that is native to my blood / Touch of manner, hint of mood.
4. According to poet Bliss Carman, there is something about the autumn that is native to her blood—a touch of manner and a hint of mood.
5. Describing the false sense of good days ahead that Indian summer frequently inspires, poet Emily Dickinson writes, These are the days when skies put on the old, old sophistries.
6. If you were coming in the fall, writes Dickinson in another poem, I'd brush the summer by / With half a smile.
7. Poet T. S. Eliot tells us that for him April is the cruelest month.
8. April is the cruelest month, writes Eliot, breeding lilacs out of the dead land, mixing memory and desire.
9. Shall I compare thee to a summer's day? wrote Shakespeare. Thou art more lovely and more temperate.
10. At her sixtieth birthday party, the guest of honor said, This occasion inspires me to repeat the words of that old song, Though it's a long, long time from May to December, the days grow short when you reach September.

☑ Teaching Tip

Students may have difficulty distinguishing between direct and indirect quotations. Point out that a direct quotation represents exact speech and requires quotation marks; for example, *"I like mystery and horror movies,"* said Jean.

An indirect quotation states the general meaning of what a person said or thought and does not require quotation marks: *Jean said that she likes certain kinds of movies.*

Practice and Assess

Answers: Exercise 19

1. "I need help," Robert said.
2. "What happened?" I asked.
3. "I just locked the car keys in the trunk," he responded.
4. "How did you ever happen to do such a thing?" I demanded.
5. "I set them down there while I was looking for my house keys, which are missing too."

Answers: Exercise 20

1. . . . said, "Thirty . . . twenty-eight."
2. "These are the times that try men's souls," warned . . . Paine.
3. . . . writes, "There . . . mood."
4. correct
5. . . . writes, "These . . . sophistries."
6. "If you were coming in the fall," writes . . . poem, "I'd . . . smile."
7. correct
8. "April is the cruelest month," writes Eliot, "breeding . . . desire."
9. "Shall I . . . day?" wrote Shakespeare. "Thou art . . . temperate."
10. . . . said, "This occasion . . . song, 'Though it's a . . . September.'"

Enrichment and Extension

Distinguishing Between Direct and Indirect Quotations

Some students may be confused by the idea that an indirect quotation is a noun clause serving as the direct object of the verb. This kind of noun clause can be recognized by inserting *that* in front of it; for example, *He said they are coming* can be rewritten as *He said that they are coming.* In contrast, *that* cannot be added before direct quotations; one does not say *He said, "That they are coming."* Give students other examples. **L2**

Teach

Quotation Marks with Titles and Unusual Expressions

Teaching Tip

In informal usage, quotation marks around a phrase can also suggest that the writer does not agree with the sentiment expressed: *My grandfather often complains about the "racket" I listen to on the radio.*

Cross reference: Mechanics

For instruction and practice with capitalizing titles of works, refer students to Lesson 20.2, pp. 713–719.

Practice and Assess

Answers: Exercise 21

1. "The Gift of the Magi."
2. "Giving to the Other Person"
3. "Time for Others"
4. "the giving tree"
5. Stephanie remarked, "Your essay is . . . school paper."

Quotation Marks with Titles and Unusual Expressions

■ Use quotation marks to enclose titles of short works, such as short stories, short poems, essays, newspaper and magazine articles, book chapters, songs, and single episodes of a television series.

"The Legend of Sleepy Hollow**"** [short story]
"The Raven**"** [poem]
"On the Duty of Civil Disobedience**"** [essay]
"Steven Spielberg's Newest Film**"** [newspaper article]
"The 1980s in America**"** [chapter]
"If I Had a Hammer**"** [song]
"Division of the Spoils**"** [episode in a television series]

(For the use of italics with titles of longer works, see page 757.)

■ Use quotation marks to enclose unfamiliar slang and other unusual or original expressions.

My cousin uses the expression **"**the cat's meow**"** to describe something she likes.

The 1920s were known as the **"**roaring twenties.**"**

■ Be careful not to overuse quotation marks with expressions like these. Generally, use quotation marks only the first time you use the expression in a piece of writing.

Exercise 21 Using Quotation Marks with Titles and Expressions

Rewrite the following sentences, adding quotation marks where they are needed.

1. Before they began to write their essay, Sara and Miguel read the short story The Gift of the Magi.
2. Sara decided the title Giving to the Other Person would be good.
3. Miguel suggested adding his poem Time for Others at the end.
4. The teacher asked Miguel to explain the term the giving tree in the first paragraph.
5. Stephanie remarked, Your essay is going to be so good that I really think you ought to submit it to the school paper.

Meeting Individual Needs: English Language Learners

Slang and Idioms

Students learning English may be unfamiliar with certain slang words or idioms. Have the whole class brainstorm to think of expressions that they have read or heard that might fit in this category, such as *he's a cool cat, I let the cat out of the bag,* or *the cat's pajamas.* Suggest that students record in their journals a list of expressions and explanations of their meanings.

Quotation Marks with Other Marks of Punctuation

1. With a comma or a period

- Always place a comma or a period *inside* closing quotation marks.

"The frog does not drink up the pond in which it lives**,"** states a Native American proverb.

Henry David Thoreau humorously advises, "Beware of all enterprises that require new clothes**."**

2. With a semicolon or a colon

- Always place a semicolon or a colon *outside* closing quotation marks.

Her father said, "We cannot go**";** her mother said, "Perhaps we can go next year**";** her elder brother just shrugged his shoulders.

This is what I think of Lady Ōtomo's poem "My Heart, Thinking**":** it is romantic and powerful.

3. With a question mark or an exclamation point

- Place the question mark or the exclamation point *inside* the closing quotation marks when it is part of the quotation.

A famous sonnet by Shakespeare begins with these words: "Shall I compare thee to a summer's day**?"**

She said, "I never want to hear from you again**!"**

- Place the question mark or the exclamation point *outside* the closing quotation marks when it is part of the entire sentence.

I've finally memorized all of "Paul Revere's Ride**"!**

Why do you keep saying, "I'm sorry**"?**

If both the sentence and the quotation at the end of the sentence need a question mark (or an exclamation point), use only one punctuation mark, and place it *inside* the quotation marks.

When did he ask, "Would you like to go to the movies**?"**

Punctuation, Abbreviations, and Numbers

Teach

Quotation Marks with Other Marks of Punctuation

Cross-reference: Writing

Explain that in writing dialogue, the rules on this page will prove especially useful. Refer students to Unit 4, Narrative Writing. Emphasize that when revising their work, students should make sure they use quotation marks correctly with other marks of punctuation. Have students review a recent writing assignment for correct usage of quotation marks with other marks of punctuation. Students should revise their writing as needed.

Teaching Tip

Point out that a comma is always used at the end of a sentence in a quotation when the quoted material is followed by an explanatory phrase like *said Jan* or *demanded Paul.* The reason for this is that the explanatory phrase completes the sentence and therefore requires a period. However, when the quotation is an interrogative or exclamatory sentence, the question mark or exclamation point is placed inside the quotation marks; if it followed explanatory phrases like *asked Jan* or *exclaimed Paul,* it would indicate that these phrases, not the quotation, were questions or exclamations.

Learning Disabled

Using Double and Single Quotation Marks Correctly

Help students who are having a difficult time with the use of quotation marks with other marks of punctuation. Write this sentence on the board: *"My favorite poem is Robert Frost's 'Birches,'" Carla told Mike.* Point out the double and single quotation marks. Have students add punctuation marks correctly to the following sentences:

1. How much was that bike? asked Phil.

2. I love the poem Jabberwocky, said Nan. **L1**

Practice and Assess

Answers: Exercise 22

1. correct
2. The poem "Close to Me," which . . .
3. . . . refrain "sleep close to me!" . . .
4. correct
5. "Even when . . . life," writes critic A. Ortiz-Vargas, "there . . . tone."
6. . . . say, "Sometimes . . . heart."
7. . . . writes, "There . . . passionate"; . . .
8. The phrase "a cry from the heart" . . .
9. . . . motherhood, "Song of Virgo"?
10. . . . writes: "Mildred Adams wrote, 'Gabriela's . . . ideals.'"
11. . . . way: "a son . . . destiny."
12. . . . his work, "It is . . . behavior."
13. . . . poem "You Flame-Foot!" Neruda writes, "Those . . . leather!"
14. . . . the critic Montesinos, "Montesinos . . . baroque, 'It . . . nothing.'"
15. "Poetry," to quote Neruda, "is useful . . . virtuous."
16. Have . . . poem "Walking Around"?
17. correct
18. In "Ode with a Lament," Neruda mourns, "Only . . . you."
19. . . . Neruda, "He is . . . bad poet."
20. correct

Additional Resources

Sentence-Combining Practice, p. 27
Grammar Practice, p. 49
Grammar Reteaching, p. 49
Grammar Enrichment, p. 49

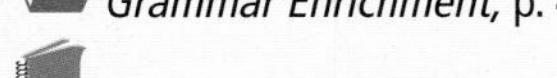

Grammar Workbook Lessons 86–87

Close

Have small groups of students compose brief dialogues about poetry they enjoy. They should decide on the proper punctuation and have a group member write the dialogue. Let groups exchange their dialogues and check each other's work. Each group should provide effective feedback.

Exercise 22 Using Quotation Marks

Rewrite the following sentences, adding quotation marks where they are needed. For the sentences that need no changes, write *correct.*

Gabriela Mistral and Pablo Neruda

1. When Chilean poet Gabriela Mistral received the Nobel Prize for literature in 1945, the Swedish Academy said that Mistral had almost become a legend.
2. The poem Close to Me, which appears in Gabriela Mistral's first book, *Despair,* is a lullaby that is sung by a mother to a young child.
3. The refrain sleep close to me! appears at the end of each verse of the poem.
4. In his introduction to a collection of Mistral's poems, the African American poet Langston Hughes implies that her language is simple and direct.
5. Even when she sings the commonplace in life, writes critic A. Ortiz-Vargas, there is always a restraint, a dignity in her tone.
6. Ortiz-Vargas goes on to say, Sometimes her song soars high as on eagle wings, but more often it is rooted in the fertile region of her own heart.
7. Ortiz-Vargas writes, There is never any gaiety in her poetry—nor lightness—for her emotions are always ardently passionate; many other critics agree with his view.
8. The phrase a cry from the heart could be used to describe many of Mistral's verses.
9. Do you know Mistral's powerful poem about motherhood, Song of Virgo?
10. In his introduction to *Selected Poems of Gabriela Mistral,* Langston Hughes writes: Mildred Adams wrote, Gabriela's clarity and precision, her passion and that characteristic which can only be called her nobility of soul are accepted as ideals.
11. Another Chilean poet, Pablo Neruda, has been described by Luis Monguió in this way: a son of the New World, surging, creating, and coming to be, in quest of his destiny.
12. Neruda, also a Nobel Prize winner, says of his work, It is a poetry impure as the clothing we wear, or our bodies, soup stained, soiled with our shameful behavior.
13. In his poem You Flame-Foot! Neruda writes, Those feet of yours—pint-sized, no bigger than bees, how they eat up the shoe leather!
14. In his introduction to Neruda's *Selected Poems,* Monguió writes this about the critic Montesinos, Montesinos has said of the old Spanish baroque, It is the art of denying oneself nothing.
15. Poetry, to quote Neruda, is useful and usable; true and virtuous.
16. Have you read Neruda's famous poem Walking Around?
17. In it the poet compares Monday morning to an oil slick.
18. In Ode with a Lament, Neruda mourns, Only with waves at my back can I love you.
19. Juan Jiménez has said of Neruda, He is a great poet; a great, bad poet.
20. Neruda, in Monguió's view, seeks his salvation not in fantasy but in realism.

Enrichment and Extension

Identifying Quotation Uses

Have students bring in examples of the various uses of quotation marks discussed in the lesson. Encourage them to bring magazines, newspapers, or books they are reading or to copy down items from these sources. Have students discuss and explain their findings, citing specific rules for punctuation.

21.10 Italics (Underlining)

Italic type is a special slanted type that is used in printing. (*This is printed in italics.*) Indicate italics on a typewriter or with handwriting by underlining. (This is underlined.) When using a computer, find out the special keystrokes or icon needed for italics by referring to the manual for the software you are using.

1. Italics with Titles

- Italicize (underline) titles of books, lengthy poems, plays, films and television series, paintings and sculptures, and long musical compositions. Also italicize the names of newspapers and magazines, ships, airplanes, and spacecraft.

Great Expectations [book]
Romeo and Juliet [play]
Nova [television series]
The Thinker [sculpture]
Sports Illustrated [magazine]
USS *Enterprise** [ship]
Snow-Bound [long poem]
Gone with the Wind [film]
Starry Night [painting]
Grand Canyon Suite [musical work]
the *Oakland Tribune* [newspaper]
Spirit of St. Louis [airplane]
Columbia [spacecraft]

*Do not italicize abbreviations such as USS that precede the name of a ship.

- Italicize (underline) and capitalize articles (*a, an, the*) written at the beginning of a title only when they are part of the title itself. It is common practice not to italicize (underline) the article preceding the title of a newspaper or a magazine. Do not italicize the word *magazine* unless it is part of the title of a periodical.

A Light in the Attic *but* a *National Geographic* magazine
The Red Badge of Courage the *Chicago Tribune*

2. Italics with Foreign Words

- Italicize (underline) foreign words and expressions that are not used frequently in English.

The motto of the U.S. Marine Corps is ***semper fidelis*** ("always faithful").

Do not italicize a foreign word or expression that is commonly used in English.

I eat **croissants** for breakfast.

Punctuation, Abbreviations, and Numbers

Focus

Lesson Overview

Objective

- To use italics (underlining) correctly

Bellringer
Daily Language Activity

When students enter the classroom, have the following assignment on the board: *Some of the following items should be punctuated using italics (underlining) and others using quotation marks. Add the correct punctuation to each item.*

1. the poem If 2. the ship the USS Constitution 3. the song Scarlet Ribbons 4. the newspaper the Boston Globe 5. the German word angst 6. the book Jane Eyre 7. the expression in the pink

See also  *Daily Language Practice*

Motivating Activity

Discuss which items in the Bellringer activity use italics, which use quotations, and what the items in each group might have in common. Encourage students to ask questions for clarification.

Teach

☑ Teaching Tip

Explain that one difference between oral and written language is emphasis. In spoken language, people rely on tone of voice and stress to make their points clear. In written language, however, emphasis is used sparingly. Written English communicates mainly by careful organization and word choice.

Resource Manager

Planning Resources
- *Lesson Plans*

Transparencies
- *Bellringer*
- *Daily Language Practice*
- *Two-Minute Skill Drill*

Other Print Resources
- *Grammar and Composition Handbook*
- *Grammar Enrichment,* p. 50
- *Grammar Practice,* p. 50
- *Grammar Reteaching,* p. 50
- *Grammar Workbook,* Lesson 88

Teach

Two-Minute Skill Drill

Have students tell which of these items take italics (underlining):
1. the play Waiting for Godot (I)
2. a Mozart symphony called Jupiter (I) **3.** the magazine article Homer Epic (Q) **4.** the song Climb Every Mountain (Q) **5.** the motto e pluribus unum (I)

See also *Two-Minute Skill Drill Transparency 21.10*

Practice and Assess

Answers: Exercise 23

1. Golden Girls
2. arete
3. Golden Girls; stade; stadium; stade
4. Olympics
5. One in a Million
6. Pathétique
7. Chicago Tribune; Alsace
8. Olympic Odyssey
9. Time, Life, Newsweek, New York Times, Sports Illustrated
10. Saturday Night Live, 20/20

Additional Resources

Grammar Practice, p. 50
Grammar Reteaching, p. 50

Grammar Enrichment, p. 50
Grammar Workbook, Lesson 88

Close

Have volunteers write examples on the board of a variety of titles and tell whether they should be italicized (underlined) or put in quotation marks. Ask classmates to provide effective feedback.

3. Italics with Words and Other Items Used to Represent Themselves

- Italicize (underline) words, letters, and numerals used to represent themselves.

Do not start a sentence with ***and*** or ***but.***

She was too superstitious to say the number aloud, so she handed the elevator operator a piece of paper on which she had written ***13.***

Replace all of the number signs (**#**'s) with the word ***number.***

Exercise 23 **Using Italics**

Write the words in each sentence below that should be italicized. Underline the words.

Women in the Olympics

1. In the book Golden Girls by Carli Laklan, you will find information about the many women who have won Olympic medals.
2. The ancient Greeks based the first Olympics on the concept of arete, which means "excellence in every area of life—physical, moral, and intellectual."
3. The author of Golden Girls notes that the earliest games featured just one event, the stade, a 200-yard footrace; the English word stadium comes from the Greek word stade.
4. The word Olympics comes from Olympia, the name of the Greek city where the first Olympic games were held in 776 B.C.
5. Sonja Henie, who won three gold medals in figure skating at three successive Olympic games, gained recognition as a movie star with her first film, One in a Million.
6. Peggy Fleming won a gold medal in figure skating at the 1968 Grenoble Olympics; she skated to Tchaikovsky's Pathétique.
7. With the financial backing of the publishers of the Chicago Tribune, Gertrude Ederle, who had won the gold medal for swimming in 1924, became the first woman to swim the English Channel in 1926; the French tug the Alsace followed her with a jazz band on board "to keep up her spirits."
8. Wilma Rudolph, who overcame serious illnesses in childhood, was the first American woman to win three gold medals in track and field; she later became a commentator for the radio series Olympic Odyssey.
9. After the 1984 Olympics, gold-medal winners Florence Griffith-Joyner and Jackie Joyner-Kersee were featured in Time, Life, Newsweek, the New York Times, and Sports Illustrated.
10. Many of the Olympic gold medalists have been on television series ranging from Saturday Night Live to 20/20.

Enrichment and Extension

Deciding When to Use Italics

A test for students having trouble deciding when to use italics or quotation marks is to ask if the title is part of a larger work that requires italics. Write the following titles on the board without punctuation. Have students determine whether they require quotation marks or italics:
1. an article titled "Floral Decoration" in the *Encyclopaedia Britannica*
2. the poem "I Never Saw a Moor" in Emily Dickinson's *Collected Works*
3. "The Swan" in Saint-Saëns's *Carnival of the Animals.*

21.11 The Apostrophe

Apostrophes with Possessives

1. Pronouns

- Use an apostrophe and *-s* for the possessive of a singular indefinite pronoun.

Do not use an apostrophe with other possessive pronouns.

everybody**'s** problem	*but*	**its** owner
each other**'s** parents		**whose** talents
one**'s** beliefs		The bikes are **theirs.**

2. Singular nouns

- Use an apostrophe and *-s* to form the possessive of a singular noun, even one that ends in *-s.*

the woman**'s** team	San Francisco**'s** earthquake
the class**'s** election	Robert Burns**'s** poetry
the princess**'s** career	Cape Hatteras**'s** beauty
the box**'s** lettering	Groucho Marx**'s** biography

There are some exceptions to this rule, however. To form the possessive of ancient proper nouns that end in *-es* or *-is,* and the names *Jesus* and *Moses,* just add an apostrophe.

Euripides' plays	Jesus' teachings
Acropolis' structure	Moses' laws
Hercules' feats	

3. Plural nouns ending in *-s*

- Use an apostrophe alone to form the possessive of a plural noun that ends in *-s.*

the countries' treaty	the Joneses' picnic
the trees' leaves	the Greens' barbecue

4. Plural nouns not ending in *-s*

- Use an apostrophe and *-s* to form the possessive of a plural noun that does not end in *-s.*

women**'s** clubs	Women**'s** Bar Association
oxen**'s** harness	mice**'s** squeaks

Focus

Lesson Overview

Objective

- To use the apostrophe correctly

Bellringer

Daily Language Activity

When students enter the classroom, have the following assignment on the board: *What is missing in the following words?*

1. cant	*4. childrens*
2. youre	*5. each others*
3. xs	*6. lynxs*

See also *Daily Language Practice*

Motivating Activity

Ask students to identify the three uses of the apostrophe in the Bellringer activity (in contractions, in special plurals, and for possession). Encourage students to ask questions to clarify understanding.

Teach

The Apostrophe

Vocabulary Link

The word *apostrophe* comes from a Greek word meaning "to turn away from, to ignore." Apostrophes were originally used only to show missing, or "ignored," letters; their use in showing possession was not firmly established until the early 1900s.

Resource Manager

Planning Resources
- *Lesson Plans*

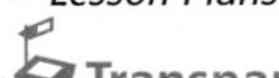

Transparencies
- *Bellringer*
- *Daily Language Practice*
- *Two-Minute Skill Drill*

Other Print Resources
- *Grammar and Composition Handbook*
- *Grammar Enrichment,* p. 51
- *Grammar Practice,* p. 51
- *Grammar Reteaching,* p. 51
- *Grammar Workbook,* Lesson 89

21.11

Teach

Apostrophes with Possessives

Teaching Tip

A good way to tell whether a noun is possessive (and thus requires an apostrophe) is to see whether it can be paraphrased as the answer to a *whose* question. For example, when students see the words *the woman's magazine,* have them ask, "Whose magazine?" The answer is *the woman's.* Any noun answering a *whose* question must be a possessive. An additional benefit of this test is that the answer often makes clear whether the possessive noun is singular or plural. Have students review a recent writing assignment, using this teaching tip to check the possessives and correct punctuation.

Cross-reference: Grammar

For instruction and practice in indefinite and possessive pronouns, refer students to Lesson 10.2, pp. 446–451.

Practice and Assess

Answers: Exercise 24

1. the Smiths' car
2. correct
3. one lawyer's opinion
4. the children's playground
5. Johnson and Goldberg's main office
6. Orestes' father
7. somebody's mistake
8. two weeks' worth of laundry
9. the editor in chief's orders
10. Larry's and Joel's bicycles

5. Compound nouns

- Put only the last word of a compound noun in the possessive form.

  my sister-in-law**'s** office
  the court-martial**'s** effect
  attorney general**'s** job
  the chief of staff**'s** order

6. Joint possession versus individual possession

- If two or more persons (or partners in a company) possess something jointly, use the possessive form for the last person named.

  Claude and Louise**'s** children
  Johnson and Johnson**'s** baby-care products
  Abbott and Costello**'s** antics

- If two or more persons (or companies) possess an item (or items) individually, put each one's name in the possessive form.

  Tina Turner**'s** and the Rolling Stones**'** songs
  Chrysler**'s** and the American Motor Company**'s** cars

7. Expressions of time and money

- Use a possessive form to express amounts of money or time that modify a noun.

The modifier can also be expressed as a hyphenated adjective. In that case, no possessive form is used.

one dollar**'s** increase	*but*	a one-dollar increase
five minutes**'** drive		a five-minute drive
ten days**'** wait		a ten-day wait

Exercise 24 Using Apostrophes with Possessives

Copy the phrases below, adding apostrophes and whatever else is needed to make the italicized parts possessive. If a phrase is correct, write *correct.*

1. the *Smiths* car
2. a book of *hers*
3. one *lawyer* opinion
4. the *children* playground
5. *Johnson and Goldberg* main office
6. *Orestes* father
7. *somebody* mistake
8. two *weeks* worth of laundry
9. the *editor in chief* orders
10. *Larry and Joel* bicycles

Learning Disabled

Using Apostrophes

Some students might have trouble with apostrophes because they cannot hear differences between words such as *boys, boy's,* and *boys'.* Although the three forms have different meanings, they are all pronounced alike.

Write the three words on the board. Have students work in pairs, alternating giving sentences that use each word correctly. Do the same with other nouns they suggest. **L1**

Apostrophes with Special Plurals

- Use an apostrophe and *-s* to form the plural of letters, numerals, symbols, and words used to represent themselves.

Italicize (underline) the letter, numeral, symbol, or word but not the apostrophe and the *-s*.

Your *q*'**s** look like *g*'**s**, and your 5'**s** look like S'**s.**
She told me to replace the *henceforth*'**s** with *therefore*'**s.**

Apostrophes in Contractions

- Use an apostrophe in place of letters omitted in contractions.

A **contraction** is a single word made up of two words that have been combined by omitting letters. Common contractions combine a subject and a verb or a verb and an adverb.

you'd	*formed from*	you had, you would
you're		you are
who's		who is, who has
it's		it is, it has
won't		will not

- Use an apostrophe in place of the omitted numerals of a year.

the class of '94   the '92 campaign

Exercise 25 Using Apostrophes

Write the words from the following sentences that require an apostrophe or an apostrophe *-s*. Mark them as needed.

Women and Literature

[1]Imagine that you were making a list of writers names for a new encyclopedia about female authors. [2]Under the *as* youd include Louisa May Alcott, whos best known for *Little Women,* and Isabel Allende, author of *The House of the Spirits.* [3]Maya Angelou, who wrote *I Know Why the Caged Bird Sings,* would surely be on everyones list. [4]The *bs* would include the names of Toni Cade Bambara and Gwendolyn Brooks. [5]Both Bambaras novels and Brooks poems focus on the lives of African Americans and on womens issues. [6]Nikki Giovanni is a poet whod be listed under the *gs*; her books include *Black Feeling* and *My House.* [7]At least five twentieth-century authors names would be listed under the *ms*: Carson McCullers, Edna St. Vincent Millay, Margaret Mitchell, Marianne Moore, and Toni Morrison. [8]Millays and Moores names would be found on anyones list of talented poets; McCullers and Morrisons names are familiar to lovers of prose. [9]Most people don't know that Margaret Mitchells *Gone with the Wind* took ten years labor to write; it was finally published in 36. [10]In the entry about the novelist Katherine Anne Porter, youd want to mention Porters great-great-grandfathers name: Daniel Boone.

Teach

Apostrophes in Contractions

Teaching Tip

To help students recognize contractions that use apostrophes, have them see if the expression can be expanded into a fuller form. If it can be expanded, then the original word is a contraction. For example, *it's cold* can be expanded into *it is cold,* but *it's foot* cannot be expanded to *it is foot.*

Two-Minute Skill Drill

List these sentences on the board. Have students italicize (underline) and place apostrophes correctly in them: *1. Mind your ps and qs. 2. Youve used too many buts in this paragraph. 3. How many 0s are in the number two million?*

See also *Two-Minute Skill Drill Transparency 21.11*

Practice and Assess

Answers: Exercise 25

1. writers'
2. *a's*; you'd; who's
3. everyone's
4. *b's*
5. Bambara's; Brooks's; women's
6. who'd; *g's*
7. authors'; *m's*
8. Millay's; Moore's; anyone's; McCullers's; Morrison's
9. Mitchell's; years'; '36.
10. you'd; Porter's; great-great-grandfather's

Additional Resources

Grammar Practice, p. 51
Grammar Reteaching, p. 51
Grammar Enrichment, p. 51

Grammar Workbook, Lesson 89

Enrichment and Extension

Using Apostrophes

Have students use newspapers and magazines at home to find examples of apostrophe usage. In class, ask students to categorize the examples according to the uses of apostrophes taught in this lesson. Create a bulletin board on which to place the examples, and give the display a catchy title. **L2**

Close

Ask each student to write one sentence with an apostrophe in it. Have students trade papers and discuss how the apostrophe is used.

Focus

Lesson Overview

Objective

- To use the hyphen correctly

Bellringer
Daily Language Activity

When students enter the classroom, have the following assignment on the board: *Write the following items correctly:*

1. selfeffacing *3. preCivil War*
2. exwife *4. transAtlantic*

See also *Daily Language Practice*

Motivating Activity

Discuss how the hyphen helps readers more easily understand the words in the Bellringer activity.

Teach

Hyphens with Prefixes

Teaching Tip

A prefix usually joins to a word without requiring a hyphen. There are, however, many exceptions. Consult a dictionary to be sure.

Practice and Assess

Answers: Exercise 26

1. pre-Revolutionary; anti-British
2. mid-Atlantic; self-confident
3. ex-indentured; all-out
4. re-sent
5. anti-independence

21.12 The Hyphen

The offensive end recovered the ball.

Hyphens with Prefixes

A hyphen is not ordinarily used to join a prefix to a word. There are a few exceptions, however. If you are in doubt about using a hyphen, consult a dictionary. You should also keep in mind the following guidelines:

- Use a hyphen after any prefix joined to a proper noun or a proper adjective. Use a hyphen after the prefixes *all-*, *ex-* (meaning "former"), and *self-* joined to any noun or adjective.

mid-Atlantic	pre-Renaissance
all-city	trans-Pacific
ex-coach	all-American
self-confidence	post-Elizabethan

- Use a hyphen after the prefix *anti-* when it joins a word beginning with *i-*. Also use a hyphen after the prefix *vice-*, except in *vice president*.

anti-intellectual
vice-mayor
vice president

- Use a hyphen to avoid confusion between words beginning with *re-* that look alike but are different in meaning and pronunciation.

re-cover the couch	*but*	recover the ball
re-store those cans		restore your confidence
re-lease the car		release the brake

Exercise 26 **Using Hyphens with Prefixes**

On your paper, write each word in the following sentences that needs a hyphen and add the hyphen.

Colonial America

1. In the preRevolutionary War era, there was a slow growth of antiBritish sentiment.
2. The average individual living in the midAtlantic colonies, for example, was beginning to feel more selfconfident about taking control of the government.
3. America was a land of opportunity where an exindentured servant could become a property owner, although the transformation sometimes required an allout effort.
4. After the Boston Tea Party, the colonists would have been doubly resentful had the British resent tea shipments into Boston Harbor.
5. The main place in the colonies where antiindependence feelings remained surprisingly strong was New York.

Resource Manager

Planning Resources
- *Lesson Plans*

Transparencies
- *Bellringer*
- *Daily Language Practice*
- *Two-Minute Skill Drill*

Other Print Resources
- *Grammar and Composition Handbook*
- *Grammar Practice,* p. 52
- *Grammar Reteaching,* p. 52
- *Grammar Workbook,* Lesson 90

Hyphens with Compounds and Numbers

1. Compound adjectives

■ Use a hyphen in a compound adjective that precedes a noun.

In general, a compound adjective that follows a noun is not hyphenated.

dark-green eyes	*but*	Her eyes are dark green.
a fifteen-year-old aunt		His aunt is fifteen years old.
a well-liked reporter		That reporter is well liked.

An expression made up of an adverb ending in *-ly* and an adjective is not hyphenated.

a nicely behaved dog	a fairly close race
a slightly rusted exterior	a hastily written report

2. Compound numbers

■ Hyphenate any spelled-out cardinal or ordinal compound number up to ninety-nine or ninety-ninth.

sixty-four	sixty-fourth
eighty-two	eighty-second

3. Fractions used as adjectives

■ Hyphenate a fraction used as an adjective (but not one used as a noun).

one-eighth teaspoon	*but*	one eighth of a teaspoon
one-quarter cup		one quarter of a cup
one-half pound		one half of a pound

4. Connected numerals

■ Hyphenate two numerals to indicate a span.

pages 30-56	1986-1990

Teach

Hyphens with Compounds and Numbers

Vocabulary Link

One of the most confusing areas of English spelling is compound words. Recently coined compounds (such as *home page*) are often spelled as two words. If a compound is not listed in the dictionary, assume that it is spelled as two words. For many years the trend has been away from spelling compound words with a hyphen. Thus, once compounds become established in the language, they are spelled as a single word, not as a hyphenated word (such as *database*). Tell students to use a current dictionary, especially an unabridged dictionary, when in doubt.

☑ Teaching Tip

Hyphens show when words or letters are to be considered as a single unit. There is a big difference, for example, between; *twenty-odd students and; twenty odd students.*

Two-Minute Skill Drill

Tell students to add hyphens where appropriate in these phrases:

1. *twenty four blackbirds*
2. *one half of the class*
3. *pages 305 311*
4. *six year old son*
5. *happily married couple*

See also *Two-Minute Skill Drill Transparency 21.12*

MEETING INDIVIDUAL NEEDS — English Language Learners

Using Hints for Hyphens

The use of hyphens can be confusing to students learning English. Suggest they replace a compound adjective with a single adjective—such as *yellowish shirt* for *yellow-green* shirt. This will help them see that *yellow-green* is a unit, that is, one adjective. Treat fractions in the same manner. Have them substitute the *one-half* in *one-half cup* with the single adjective *one. One half of a cup,* however, is a noun modified by a prepositional phrase and thus is not hyphenated.

Teach

Hyphen, End of Line

Cross-reference: Dictionary and Thesaurus

For instruction and practice with using dictionaries and thesauruses, refer students to Lessons 24.1–24.2, pp. 812–817.

Two-Minute Skill Drill

Have students show where these words would be divided at the end of a line:

dictate	*bookkeeper*
premeditate	*super*
basketball	*supper*

See also *Two-Minute Skill Drill Transparency 21.12*

Practice and Assess

Answers: Exercise 27

1. thirty-one; or-bit
2. young-est
3. col-lege
4. doc-tor-ate
5. one-third; sci-en-tists
6. thirty-four-year-old; or-bit-ed
7. re-source-ful; self-confident
8. com-mon
9. Well-known; ex-astronauts; all-American; mis-sions
10. weight-less; low-gravity

Additional Resources

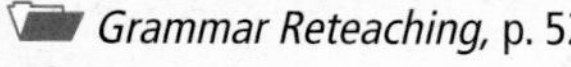
Grammar Practice, p. 52

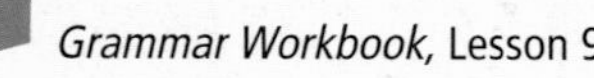
Grammar Reteaching, p. 52

Grammar Workbook, Lesson 90

Close

Have students write sentences needing hyphens, exchange work with a partner, and insert hyphens where needed. Partners should provide effective feedback.

Hyphens to Divide Words at the End of a Line

Words are generally divided between syllables or pronounceable parts. Because it is frequently difficult to determine where a word should be divided, check your dictionary.

- In general, if a word contains two consonants occurring between two vowels or if it contains a double consonant, divide the word between the two consonants.

foun-tain	struc-ture
lin-ger	sup-per
profes-sor	tomor-row

- If a suffix has been added to a complete word that ends in two consonants, divide the word after the two consonants.

pull-ing	point-less
meaning-ful	strong-est

Exercise 27 **Using Hyphens**

Hyphens must be added to five of the following sentences. On your paper, rewrite those sentences, adding the hyphens where they are needed. Then make a list of all the italicized words, showing where each would be divided if it had to be broken at the end of a line.

Sally Ride, Astronaut

1. Sally Ride was thirty one in 1983 when she became the first American woman to *orbit* the earth.
2. She was also the *youngest* American astronaut to go into orbit.
3. At Swarthmore College, where she did her undergraduate work, Sally Ride won a national tennis tournament for *college* students.
4. Astronaut Ride received her *doctorate* from Stanford University.
5. Dr. Ride said that one third of the *scientists* at NASA are women.
6. A thirty four year old Russian woman, Svetlana Savitskaya, *orbited* the earth about eight months before Dr. Ride.
7. Astronauts are *resourceful,* self confident, healthy, highly educated, and experienced in their special fields of study.
8. By the year 2010, space flight may become *common;* within your lifetime, thousands may be taking trips into space every year.
9. Well known ex astronauts such as John Glenn and Neil Armstrong were viewed as all American heroes for years after their space *missions.*
10. Astronaut trainees must learn to live in an almost *weightless,* low gravity environment.

Enrichment and Extension

Hyphenating Homophones

Have groups list strategies for knowing where to hyphenate words. For instance, some words are spelled the same but pronounced differently, such as *present* (gift) and *present* (deliver). Tell students that with the first meaning, *present* is hyphenated after the *-s,* while with the second meaning, it is hyphenated after the first *-e.* Encourage students to devise strategies relating to which syllable is stressed and whether the vowel sound is long or short. **L2**

21.13 Abbreviations

Abbreviations are shortened forms of words. Abbreviations save space and time and prevent unnecessary wordiness. For instance, *M.D.* is more concise and easier to write than *Medical Doctor.* Most abbreviations take periods. If you are unsure of how to write an abbreviation, consult a dictionary.

- Use only one period if an abbreviation occurs at the end of a sentence that would ordinarily take a period of its own.
- If an abbreviation occurs at the end of a sentence that ends with a question mark or an exclamation point, use the period and the second mark of punctuation.

Gerry left at 8:00 **A.M.** Did she leave at 8:00 **A.M.?**

Capitalizing Abbreviations

1. **Abbreviations of proper nouns**

- Capitalize abbreviations of proper nouns.

109-46 Queens **Blvd.**	**Rev.** Martin Luther King Jr.
N. Michigan **Ave.**	**U.S.** Congress

2. **Abbreviations formed from initial letters**

Abbreviations of organizations and government agencies are often formed from the initial letters of the complete name. Such abbreviations, whether pronounced letter by letter or as words, omit periods and are written with capital letters.

YWCA	NAACP	IRS
NASA	UNICEF	CBS

3. **Abbreviations related to dates and times**

Capitalize the following abbreviations related to dates and times:

A.D. (*anno Domini*), "in the year of the Lord" (since the birth of Christ); place before the date: **A.D.** 5

B.C. (before Christ); place after the date: 1000 **B.C.**

C.E. (common era; equivalent to *A.D.*); place after the date: 66 **C.E.**

B.C.E. (before the common era; equivalent to *B.C.*); place after the date: 164 **B.C.E.**

A.M. (*ante meridiem*), "before noon"; place after exact times: 7:45 **A.M.**

P.M. (*post meridiem*), "after noon"; place after exact times: 2:30 **P.M.**

Focus

Lesson Overview

Objective

- To recognize the correct use and form of abbreviations
- To use abbreviations correctly

Bellringer
Daily Language Activity

When students enter the classroom, have the following assignment on the board: *Explain what the underlined items in the following sentences indicate:*

1. *There is a chapter of SADD in my school.*
2. *Socrates was born about 470 B.C.*
3. *Ken Griffey Jr. is Neil's favorite baseball player.*

See also  *Daily Language Practice*

Motivating Activity

Have volunteers explain what the abbreviations in the Bellringer activity stand for. Discuss why abbreviations are useful in everyday life.

Teach

Vocabulary Link

The term *abbreviation* comes from a Latin verb meaning "to shorten." Related English words include *abridge* and *brief.*

☑ Teaching Tip

Certain expressions used in academic writing are abbreviations of Latin expressions and are thus used with periods—for example: *i.e.* is an abbreviation of *id est; e.g.* of *exempli gratia; viz.* of *videlicet; ca.* or *c.* of *circa; cf.* of *confer;* and *etc.* of *et cetera.*

Resource Manager

Planning Resources
- *Lesson Plans*

Transparencies
- *Bellringer*
- *Daily Language Practice*
- *Two-Minute Skill Drill*

Other Print Resources
- *Grammar and Composition Handbook*
- *Grammar Practice,* p. 52
- *Grammar Workbook,* Lesson 91

Teach

Cross reference: Composition

For instruction and practice in abbreviation use, refer students to Unit 1, Personal Writing. Point out that when they are writing a personal letter, students should use zip code abbreviations in the address. In other forms of writing, students should not abbreviate a state's name. For example, in a paper about agriculture in California, students should always spell out *California.*

Two-Minute Skill Drill

Have students write what states' names are indicated by the following abbreviations:

OH	*GA*	*AK*	*KY*
UT	*HI*	*RI*	*MS*

See also *Two-Minute Skill Drill Transparency 21.13*

Practice and Assess

Answers: Exercise 28

1. D.C.
2. IRS *or* correct
3. A.M.; P.M.
4. A.D.
5. correct

Postal Abbreviations

In ordinary prose spell out state names. On envelopes, however, abbreviate state names as shown in the following list.

Alabama	**AL**	Montana	**MT**
Alaska	**AK**	Nebraska	**NE**
Arizona	**AZ**	Nevada	**NV**
Arkansas	**AR**	New Hampshire	**NH**
California	**CA**	New Jersey	**NJ**
Colorado	**CO**	New Mexico	**NM**
Connecticut	**CT**	New York	**NY**
Delaware	**DE**	North Carolina	**NC**
Florida	**FL**	North Dakota	**ND**
Georgia	**GA**	Ohio	**OH**
Hawaii	**HI**	Oklahoma	**OK**
Idaho	**ID**	Oregon	**OR**
Illinois	**IL**	Pennsylvania	**PA**
Indiana	**IN**	Rhode Island	**RI**
Iowa	**IA**	South Carolina	**SC**
Kansas	**KS**	South Dakota	**SD**
Kentucky	**KY**	Tennessee	**TN**
Louisiana	**LA**	Texas	**TX**
Maine	**ME**	Utah	**UT**
Maryland	**MD**	Vermont	**VT**
Massachusetts	**MA**	Virginia	**VA**
Michigan	**MI**	Washington	**WA**
Minnesota	**MN**	West Virginia	**WV**
Mississippi	**MS**	Wisconsin	**WI**
Missouri	**MO**	Wyoming	**WY**

The postal abbreviation for the District of Columbia is **DC.** In ordinary prose, however, use periods to write **Washington, D.C.**

Exercise 28 **Using Abbreviations with Capital Letters**

On your paper, write the abbreviations for the italicized words or phrases in the following sentences. If the terms should not be abbreviated, write *correct.*

1. My aunt lives near Washington, *District of Columbia.*
2. The *Internal Revenue Service* is responsible for collecting federal taxes.
3. The House of Representatives will be in session today from 10:00 *ante meridiem* to 4:00 *post meridiem.*
4. President Franklin Delano Roosevelt took office in *anno Domini* 1933.
5. The senior senators from *Illinois, California,* and *South Carolina* are having lunch together this week.

Meeting Individual Needs: Gifted and Talented

Learning Scientific Abbreviations

Many scientific abbreviations have passed into general usage. Ask if students know what these abbreviations stand for: AC (alternating current), AM (amplitude modulation), Btu (British thermal unit), cc (cubic centimeter), FM (frequency modulation), kw (kilowatt). **L3**

Using Abbreviations

■ Use abbreviations for some personal titles.

Titles such as *Mrs., Mr., Ms., Sr.,* and *Jr.* and those indicating professions and academic degrees (*Dr., Ph.D., M.A., B.S.*) are almost always abbreviated. Titles of government and military officials and members of the clergy are frequently abbreviated when used before a full name.

Mrs. Roosevelt	**Sen.** Dianne Feinstein
Harry Connick **Jr.**	**Gen.** Colin Powell
Rosalyn Ying, **Ph.D.**	Myron Greene, **D.D.S.**

Ken Griffey **Sr.** and Ken Griffey **Jr.**

■ Abbreviate units of measure used with numerals in technical or scientific writing. Do not abbreviate them in ordinary prose.

The abbreviations that follow stand for both plural and singular units:

ENGLISH SYSTEM

ft.	foot	**mi.**	mile	**tbsp.**	tablespoon
gal.	gallon	**oz.**	ounce	**tsp.**	teaspoon
in.	inch	**pt.**	pint	**yd.**	yard
lb.	pound	**qt.**	quart		

METRIC SYSTEM

cg	centigram	**l**	liter
cl	centiliter	**m**	meter
cm	centimeter	**mg**	milligram
g	gram	**ml**	milliliter
kg	kilogram	**mm**	millimeter
km	kilometer		

Exercise 29 **Using Abbreviations of Titles and Measurement Units**

On your paper, write the abbreviations for the italicized words or phrases in the following sentences. If the terms should not be abbreviated, write *correct.*

1. *Senator* John F. Kennedy was elected president in 1960.
2. *Doctor* C. Everett Koop was surgeon general during the administration of President George Bush.
3. Harvey J. McCarthy *Junior* will testify before a Senate subcommittee during the first week of February.
4. I believe that the Washington Monument stands 555 *feet* 5 1/8 *inches* high.
5. Bethesda, Maryland, a suburb of Washington, is located 8 *miles* (14.8 *kilometers*) from the Capitol.

Teach

☑ Teaching Tip

Periods are used with abbreviations in the English system but not with abbreviations in the metric system, which is used in all areas of science. Occasionally, however, you might also see abbreviations in the English system set without periods.

Two-Minute Skill Drill

Have students explain and use each of these abbreviations in a sentence:

mi.	*tsp.*	*kg*	*gal.*
Jr.	*Ph.D.*	*Ms.*	*Rep.*

See also *Two-Minute Skill Drill Transparency 21.13*

Practice and Assess

Answers: Exercise 29

1. Sen. *or* correct
2. Dr.
3. Jr.
4. correct
5. correct

Additional Resources

Grammar Practice, p. 52

Grammar Workbook, Lesson 91

Close

Have volunteers think of an abbreviation and use it in a sentence.

Enrichment and Extension

Exploring Abbreviations

Ask each student to find an organization name that is abbreviated. Have students make a chart of the organizations' abbreviated names and what they stand for. They may wish to expand the chart to include names or terms commonly abbreviated, such as JFK, VCR, or CD. Students may also talk to their parents about words that are abbreviated where they work. Some abbreviations, such as MS (manuscript) in publishing, are jargon, terms usually known only to those who work in that field. Discuss how this shorthand way of writing might be helpful in a work situation. **L3**

Focus

Lesson Overview

Objective

- To recognize the correct use of numbers and numerals

Bellringer
Daily Language Activity

When students enter the classroom, have the following assignment on the board: *Read these sentences. Write how you might change them.*

1. *I have collected one thousand two hundred sixty-one shells.*
2. *Today I learned that one mile is five thousand two hundred eighty feet.*
3. *Jeanette is the 3rd child in a family of 5.*

See also 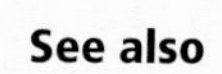 *Daily Language Practice*

Motivating Activity

Have volunteers suggest how they might fix the sentences. Discuss how difficult it is to read a long, spelled-out number. Ask why abbreviated numbers, such as the ones in sentence 3, should not be used in formal writing. Remind students to provide effective feedback.

Teach

Regular Uses of Numbers and Numerals

☑ Teaching Tip

The most commonly followed convention for spelling out numerals is that whole numbers from one to ninety-nine are spelled out, as are these same numbers when followed by the words *hundred, thousand, million,* and so forth: *nine hundred; four thousand; sixty million.*

21.14 Numbers and Numerals

In nontechnical writing, some numbers are spelled out, and some are expressed in figures. Numbers expressed in figures are called *numerals.*

Regular Uses of Numbers and Numerals

- In general, spell out cardinal and ordinal numbers that can be written in one or two words.

  New Hampshire is one of the original **thirteen** states.

  There are **twenty-seven** students in the class.

  Alaska was the **forty-ninth** state to join the Union.

- Spell out any number that occurs at the beginning of a sentence.

  Sixteen hundred fifteen delegates attended.

  Eleven thousand people live in that town.

- In general, use numerals to express numbers that would be written in more than two words.

  Mount Mitchell, the highest mountain in the eastern United States, is **6,684** feet tall.

  In 1790 the total population of the United States (according to the first census) was **3,929,214.**

  In 1984 Joe W. Kittinger covered **3,535** miles in eighty-three hours and fifty-three minutes, setting a new record for balloon flight.

Very large numbers are often written as a numeral followed by the word *million* or *billion.*

  The surface area of the earth is close to **197 million** square miles.

- If related numbers appear in the same sentence and some can be written out while others should appear as numerals, use all numerals.

  Edgar ranked **5th** in the class; his brother ranked **119th.**

  They ordered **38** doll houses and **112** toy robots.

Resource Manager

Planning Resources
- *Lesson Plans*

Transparencies
- *Bellringer*
- *Daily Language Practice*
- *Two-Minute Skill Drill*

Other Print Resources
- *Grammar and Composition Handbook*
- *Grammar Enrichment,* p. 52
- *Grammar Workbook,* Lesson 92

Special Uses of Numbers and Numerals

1. **Money, decimals, and percentages**

■ Use numerals to express amounts of money, decimals, and percentages.

$897 million   **1.2** kilograms   **5** percent

Amounts of money that can be expressed in one or two words, however, should be spelled out.

forty-five cents   **two thousand** dollars

2. **Dates and time**

■ Use numerals to express the year and day in a date and to express the precise time with the abbreviations A.M. and P.M.

The U.S.S.R. launched *Sputnik I* on October **4, 1957.**

She went to the meeting at **4:15 P.M.**

■ Spell out expressions of time that do not use A.M. or P.M.

She set her alarm clock for **five** o'clock.

■ To express a century when the word *century* is used, spell out the number. Likewise, to express a decade when the century is clear from the context, spell out the number.

The **twentieth** century saw great technological advances.

The Great Depression of the **thirties** was an economic crisis.

■ When a century or a decade is expressed as a single unit, use numerals followed by an *-s.*

1930s   **1400s**

3. **Addresses**

■ Use numerals for numbered streets and avenues over ten and for all house, apartment, and room numbers. Spell out numbered streets and avenues of ten or under.

1654 West **66th** Street   **4** North Main Street

Apartment **8C**   **20 Second** Avenue

4. **References**

■ Use numerals for page, line, act, and scene numbers and the like.

Look on pages **20** and **59** for information about Pablo Casals.

Read lines **1–80** in Book **I** of the *Iliad.*

We rehearsed act **2,** scenes **3** and **4,** of the play.

Special Uses of Numbers and Numerals

☑ Teaching Tip

In writing that involves many numbers, numerals may be used instead of numbers. For example, in sportswriting, a numeral is used, often to save space, in terms like *60-yard dash*. Inform students that for the purposes of this unit, they should follow the rules in the text.

☑ Teaching Tip

In scientific writing, numbers are usually expressed in figures rather than words: *5 gallons; 110 volts; 9 kilograms; 15 liters.*

☑ Teaching Tip

Tell students that they should never use the words *morning* or *evening* with *A.M.* or *P.M.* It would be redundant, for example, to write *8 A.M. in the morning*. In expressing time on the basis of a twenty-four hour clock, no colon is used between the hours and the minutes: *0415*, not *04:15*.

☑ Teaching Tip

In a complete street address, numbered streets and avenues are written in numerals if the number is greater than ten: *119 West 57th Street.* When simply referring to a street and not to an address on the street, spell out the name of the street: *Kim works on West Fifty-seventh Street.*

MEETING INDIVIDUAL NEEDS

English Language Learners

Writing Numbers as Words

Students whose first language is not English may have difficulty converting numbers into words. Have students write some dollar amounts, times, and numbers using numerals. Then have them convert these numbers to words in their first language. Finally, help them to convert the numbers to words in English. Have students notice how the word order is different in the two languages.

Teach

Grammar Tip

The name of a century is hyphenated only when it is used as a compound adjective before a noun. As with all compound adjectives, it should be treated as one unit. Thus, it is correct to write *twentieth-century literature,* but the hyphen is dropped when writing *literature of the twentieth century.*

Two-Minute Skill Drill

List these numbers on the board. Have students spell out the numbers that should be written as words.

69 cents	*30,000,000 people*
5:00	*5 teenagers*
2 dollars	

See also *Two-Minute Skill Drill Transparency 21.14*

Cross reference: Usage

For instruction in and practice in using nouns of amount as special subjects, refer students to Lesson 16.4, pp. 614–615.

Cross reference: Mechanics

For instruction in and practice with the rules for capitalizing a historical period that refers to a general span of time, refer students to Lesson 20.2, pp. 713–719.

Exercise 30 Using Numbers and Numerals

On your paper, rewrite each sentence below, correcting the errors with numbers or numerals. If a sentence has no errors, write *correct.*

1. Please come to our meeting on October 4 at eight thirty P.M.
2. It will be held at 153 3rd Street.
3. Our speaker will discuss everyday life in the 16th century.
4. Then two group members will read act One, scenes 1 and 2, from *Hamlet.*
5. The admission charge for tonight only will be $3.50.

Exercise 31 Using Numbers and Numerals

For each sentence below, write correctly any number or numeral that should be changed to a different form.

Althea Gibson, Tennis Star

1. In 1957, the year Althea Gibson turned 30, she became the 1st African American tennis player to win the championship in the annual tennis tournament at Wimbledon in England.
2. Gibson traveled three thousand five hundred miles from her home in New York City to Wimbledon, but the distance that she traveled from being a 13-year-old high school dropout to a renowned tennis champion was even greater.
3. Gibson was born on a farm in South Carolina on August twenty-fifth, 1927; she was the oldest of 5 children.
4. For many years, she lived with her family at 135 West One hundred forty-third Street in Harlem, and she spent her free time playing basketball at the Boys Club.
5. When she was a lanky girl of fifteen (she would eventually be five feet eleven inches tall), she started taking tennis lessons from a 1-armed coach named Fred Johnson.
6. In 1947, when Gibson was 19, she played in 9 tennis tournaments and won the singles title in every single one.
7. Through the late 40s and into the early 50s, Gibson concentrated on both her tennis and her education.
8. She went back to high school, finishing 10th in her class, and then went to college, graduating in 1953 at the age of twenty-five.
9. 49 minutes was all the time it took Gibson to win the championship at Wimbledon in 1957.
10. After Wimbledon she won a one-hundred-thousand-dollar contract to play exhibition tennis matches and, in 1960, the women's professional singles title; she later became a professional golfer.

Punctuation, Abbreviations, and Numbers

Practice and Assess

Answers: Exercise 30

1. . . . 8:30 P.M.
2. . . . 153 Third Street
3. . . . sixteenth century
4. act 1
5. correct

Answers: Exercise 31

1. thirty; first
2. 3,500 miles; thirteen-year-old
3. August 25, 1927; five
4. 143rd Street
5. one-armed
6. nineteen; nine
7. forties; fifties
8. tenth
9. Forty-nine minutes
10. $100,000

Enrichment and Extension

Using Numerals in Publications

Have students find numerals in news magazines, charts, textbooks, and newspapers, such as the *Wall Street Journal.* Have them compare the numbers from different sources to determine whether the sources use different number styles. Discuss when writing numbers as numerals might be more appropriate than writing them out.

Exercise 32 Using Punctuation, Abbreviations, and Numbers

On your paper, rewrite the following sentences, correcting the errors in punctuation, abbreviations, and numbers. There may be several errors in each sentence.

1. In the travel section of Campbells Bookshop, I looked at books about Kenya Switzerland and Mexico.
2. The travel sections most informative book about Mexico I should know because I visited there last year had lavish colorful realistic photographs of people landscapes and architecture
3. Before I took it off the shelf my eyes were drawn to a book titled America bc written by Harvard professor Barry Fell phd.
4. Skimming through it I realized it had been misplaced for its subject was actually archaeology not one of my interests instead of travel.
5. My sights in case you are interested are focused on the people and places of the world as it looks in the 20th century not some mud covered artifacts from over 2,000 years ago.
6. While I looked at travel books Jane and Rafael wandered into other sections.
7. Jane went to the literature section for she wanted a copy of Wuthering Heights.
8. On her way, Jane spied a book of quotations with an attractive bright red cover.
9. Picking it up she thumbed through the thick white pages.
10. Then her eye fell on a familiar saying Ask me no questions and Ill tell you no lies.
11. Oh she said to herself. I didn't know that Oliver Goldsmith first wrote that line in his play She Stoops to Conquer.
12. Rafael in the meantime hurried to the compact disc videotape and audiocassette section.
13. A music student he was hoping to find a videotape of Mozarts Magic Flute.
14. May I help you? inquired Mrs Kato a sales clerk.
15. Rafael who wanted to browse first thanked her and then headed for the neatly arranged video packages.
16. Mozarts opera was not on the shelf but Rafael found twenty one copies of a new release, James Galway Plays Mostly Mozart.
17. With all out enthusiasm he grabbed a copy paid for the tape and came looking for me.
18. Having found the travel books I wanted I had moved to the humor section to find a birthday present for my brother.
19. I thought I might give him a book of cartoons perhaps Gary Larsons The Far Side, but Rafael nixed that idea.
20. Rafael suggested James Thurbers Fables for Our Time.
21. I especially like The Unicorn in the Garden he said referring to his favorite fable. Then he added Your brother will like it.
22. Jane arrived next, having bought Wuthering Heights and the book of quotations.
23. I have no self restraint she explained. I wish I could buy out the whole store.
24. Laughing I admitted that I had found approximately thirty five books I would have liked to buy.
25. With our arms laden with the purchases we had made we left the bookstore and headed for the post office where I mailed the Thurber book to my brother.

Answers: Exercise 32

1. . . . Campbell's (*or* Campbells') Bookshop . . . Kenya, Switzerland, and . . .
2. . . . section's . . . Mexico (I . . . year) had lavish, colorful, realistic . . . people, landscapes, and architecture.
3. . . . shelf, my . . . *America B.C.,* . . . Fell, Ph.D.
4. . . . it, I . . . misplaced, for its . . . archaeology—not one of my interests—instead of travel.
5. My sights—in . . . interested—are. . . twentieth century, not some mud-covered . . . two thousand years ago.
6. . . . travel books, Jane . . .
7. . . . section, for . . . Wuthering Heights.
8. . . . an attractive, bright red cover.
9. . . . up, she . . . thick, white . . .
10. . . . saying: "Ask . . . questions, and I'll . . . lies."
11. "Oh!" she said to herself. "I . . . She Stoops to Conquer."
12. Rafael, in the meantime, hurried . . . disk, videotape, and . . . section.
13. A music student, he . . . Mozart's Magic Flute.
14. "May I help you?" inquired Mrs. Kato, a sales clerk.
15. Rafael, who . . . browse, *or* first, thanked . . .
16. Mozart's . . . shelf, but . . . twenty-one . . . release, James Galway Plays Mostly Mozart.
17. With all-out enthusiasm, he . . . copy, paid for the tape, and . . .
18. Having . . . wanted, I . . .
19. . . . cartoons (perhaps Gary Larson's The Far Side), but . . .
20. Rafael . . . Thurber's Fables for Our Time.
21. "I . . . 'The Unicorn in the Garden,'" he said, referring . . . added, "Your . . . it."
22. Jane . . . Wuthering Heights . . .
23. "I have no self-restraint," she explained. "I wish I could buy out the whole store."
24. Laughing, I . . . thirty-five books . . .
25. With . . . made, we . . . post office, where . . .

Close

Have students write sentences containing numbers. Have students trade papers and check each other's usage of numbers. Remind students to cite specific rules as they provide effective feedback.

Additional Resources

Grammar Enrichment, p. 52

Grammar Workbook, Lesson 92

Teach

About the Literature

Explain that the review contains a passage from Barry Lopez's *Arctic Dreams,* followed by exercises on related topics. Ask a volunteer to read the passage aloud as classmates listen and follow along in their books. Initiate a discussion about the author's main ideas and the manner in which he presents statistics and other information. Then ask students to discuss the sentences that contain highlighted punctuation. Would the meaning be as clear if the writer had not punctuated these sentences properly?

Linking Grammar and Literature

Critical Thinking

Ask students to write a paragraph about an imaginary encounter with a polar bear. The paragraph should contain no marks of punctuation. Tell students to exchange their paragraphs and insert the correct punctuation marks in the proper places. Then discuss which rules of punctuation must be followed and which rules are optional.

Listening and Speaking

Ask students to close their textbooks. Read aloud the passage from *Arctic Dreams* in a steady monotone, as if there were no marks of punctuation in the passage. Then initiate a discussion of the ways in which punctuation marks help readers construct meaning from texts.

ASSESSMENT OPTIONS

Tests with Answer Key & Rubrics
Unit 21 Mastery Test, pp. 81–82

Testmaker
Unit 21 Mastery Test

UNIT 21

Grammar Review

Punctuation, Abbreviations, and Numbers

In *Arctic Dreams,* Barry Lopez describes the landscapes of the North and the people and animals who live there. In the following passages, which have been annotated to show some of the rules of punctuation covered in this unit, he describes the Arctic's most magnificent creature: the polar bear.

Literature Model

from Arctic Dreams

by Barry Lopez

Colon to introduce a sentence that explains the preceding material

Commas to separate elements in a series

Comma to separate two main clauses joined by a coordinating conjunction

Parentheses to set off supplemental material

Hyphen in a compound adjective preceding a noun

Semicolon to separate two main clauses

The polar bear is a creature of arctic edges: he hunts the ice margins, the surface of the water, and the continental shore. The ice bear, he is called. His world forms beneath him in the days of shortening light, and then falls away in the spring.

Polar bears vary in size, and their weights can change dramatically during the year. (Very large polar bears may stand 12 feet on their hind legs and weigh 2000 pounds. The number of 12- and 13-foot bears weighing 2200 or 2400 pounds that have been reported, however, says more about unadjusted scales, stretched hides, and wishful exaggeration than about polar bears.) Bears eat prodigiously in the spring, lightly in late summer, and lightly or not at all (in the case of denning females) during the winter. An adult male might weigh between 550 and 1700 pounds and measure 75 to 100 inches from tip of nose to tip of tail.

The Polar Eskimos of northwest Greenland call the polar bear *pisugtooq,* the great wanderer. On the basis of mark-and-recapture studies and radio-tracking information, scientists have determined that individual bears wander largely within a local area; but some, indeed, are long-distance travelers. A polar bear tagged in Svalbard, for example, showed up a year

Resource Manager

Planning Resources
- *Lesson Plans*

Other Print Resources
- *Grammar and Composition Handbook*
- *Grammar Workbook,* Lessons 73–92, Unit 12 Review, Cumulative Review: Units 1–12

later near Nanortalik, Greenland, 2000 miles to the southwest. Another bear, a female, traveled a straight-line distance of 205 miles in two days. Polar bears have also been found far afield in unlikely places, at the crest of Mount Newton in Svalbard, for example, 6600 feet above sea level, or 30 miles inland on the Greenland ice cap. An American crew on the ice island Alpha saw a female and her cub at 84°N in December 1957.

Thor Larsen, a biologist who has observed polar bears in Svalbard for more than fifteen years, when I asked him about their hunting behavior, said, "Cats. They are like big cats." Fast? "It is absolutely unbelievable how fast they are—oh, do they come fast." Shrewd? "Yes. They are making judgments at every point about what to do. And they are patient."

Period at the end of a declarative sentence

Commas to set off a nonrestrictive appositive

Quotation marks for dialogue

Dash to mark an abrupt break

Question mark to indicate a direct question

Review: Exercise 1 Using End Punctuation

Rewrite each sentence, correcting any errors in end punctuation. If a sentence contains no errors, write *correct.*

1. How is the arctic region commonly defined.
2. Geographers describe it as the region around the North Pole lying north of the Arctic Circle.
3. The Arctic can also be defined as the area north of the tree line, which is the area where trees cannot grow.
4. How the Arctic has always fascinated people?
5. People wonder who first reached the North Pole?
6. Robert E. Peary attained this goal on April 6, 1909.
7. Can you imagine a blizzard that, in Peary's words, "surpasses in fury the sandstorms of the Sahara."
8. Imagine an immense, ice-covered ocean?
9. Water temperatures in the Arctic remain near the freezing point of salt water—about 29 degrees Fahrenheit or minus 1.7 degrees Celsius?
10. "On this great frozen Sahara of the North," wrote Peary, "the wind never ceases to blow."
11. Did you realize that many adventurers besides Peary have explored the Arctic.
12. As recently as 1995, a group began an expedition!
13. Their goal was to traverse the Arctic by going "over the top of the world".
14. They set out from the European side of the Arctic during the winter months.
15. How surprising many people found that departure date?

Punctuation, Abbreviations, and Numbers

Practice and Assess

Answers: Exercise 1

1. How is the arctic region commonly defined?
2. correct
3. correct
4. How the Arctic has always fascinated people!
5. People wonder who first reached the North Pole.
6. correct
7. Can you imagine a blizzard that, in Peary's words, "surpasses in fury the sandstorms of the Sahara"?
8. Imagine an immense, ice-covered ocean.
9. Water temperatures in the Arctic remain near the freezing point of salt water—about 29 degrees Fahrenheit or minus 1.7 degrees Celsius.
10. correct
11. Did you realize that many adventurers besides Peary have explored the Arctic?
12. As recently as 1995, a group began an expedition.
13. Their goal was to traverse the Arctic by going "over the top of the world."
14. correct
15. How surprising many people found that departure date!

Practice and Assess

Answers: Exercise 2

1. . . . regions: Greenland . . .
2. . . . Arctic; others, . . .
3. . . . Arctic: gold . . .
4. . . . harsh; nevertheless, . . .
5. correct

Answers: Exercise 3

1. Caribou, similar to reindeer, migrate in huge herds.
2. No, the caribou might not seem threatened.
3. As a prime resource for the peoples of the Arctic, this animal has, however, been overhunted.
4. Caribou are prized for their meat, which is extremely nutritious.
5. Another arctic animal that lives on the tundra is the musk ox.
6. Wrapped in their dense wool, musk oxen can easily withstand the bitter chill of the Arctic.
7. Snowshoe hares, unlike musk oxen, seek the protection of the taiga, the forests of the Arctic North.
8. The taiga is also the habitat of the hare's archenemy, the lynx.
9. In 1986 the writer Fred Buemmer estimated that fifteen thousand polar bears remained in the Arctic.
10. A remarkable sight along the shoreline is polar bears hunting their favorite prey, the harp seal.

Grammar Review

Review: Exercise 2 Using Colons and Semicolons

Rewrite each sentence, correcting any errors in the use of colons and semicolons. If a sentence contains no errors, write *correct.*

SAMPLE Arctic winters are cold and long: summers are cool and short.
ANSWER Arctic winters are cold and long; summers are cool and short.

1. The Arctic includes parts of the following regions; Greenland, Canada, Alaska, Russia, Finland, Sweden, and Norway.
2. Some geographers include Iceland in the Arctic: others, however, exclude it from the region.
3. These are the minerals that have been discovered in the Arctic; gold, tin, nickel, copper, and coal.
4. The climate is harsh: nevertheless, the Arctic is home to a variety of animals and plants.
5. Two features of the area are permafrost and lack of rainfall.

Review: Exercise 3 Using the Comma

Rewrite each sentence, adding the material in parentheses in the place indicated by the caret. If the material in parentheses is *not* essential to the meaning of the sentence, add commas. If it is essential, do not add commas.

SAMPLE The Arctic ∧ is home to many animals. (a region of extreme cold)
ANSWER The Arctic, a region of extreme cold, is home to many animals.

1. Caribou ∧ migrate in huge herds. (similar to reindeer)
2. ∧ the caribou might not seem threatened. (No)
3. ∧ this animal has, however, been overhunted. (As a prime resource for the peoples of the Arctic)
4. Caribou are prized for their meat ∧. (which is extremely nutritious)
5. Another arctic animal ∧ is the musk ox. (that lives on the tundra)
6. ∧ musk oxen can easily withstand the bitter chill of the Arctic. (Wrapped in their dense wool)
7. Snowshoe hares ∧ seek the protection of the taiga, the forests of the Arctic North. (unlike musk oxen)
8. The taiga is also the habitat of the hare's archenemy ∧. (the lynx)
9. In 1986 ∧ Fred Buemmer estimated that fifteen thousand polar bears remained in the Arctic. (the writer)
10. A remarkable sight along the shoreline is polar bears hunting their favorite prey ∧. (the harp seal)

Review: Exercise 4 **Using the Comma**

Rewrite each sentence, adding or deleting commas where necessary.

1. In general, arctic animals have only two major defenses against the harsh pervasive cold.
2. Voracious eating helps animals to stay warm and insulation minimizes heat loss.
3. A seventy-pound sea otter for example frequently will eat fifteen pounds of food in an average day.
4. An otter's typical diet includes sea urchins mollusks and fish.
5. Life is feast or famine for wolves; consequently a single meal may be 25 percent of a wolf's body weight.
6. Fur, and fat, and feathers are all insulation devices that shield arctic animals from the intense cold.
7. The musk ox's long, glossy skirt of coarse, guard hair is undeniably its most striking feature.
8. Musk oxen will in fact seek shelter during severely cold weather, but their thick fur provides such excellent insulation that they routinely endure extremes of minus forty degrees Fahrenheit in the open air for prolonged periods.
9. Nature insulates many animals, but leaves humans unprotected.
10. For warmth the Inuit dress in animal skins; indeed they have long copied the animals' survival strategies.

Review: Exercise 5 **Using the Dash and Parentheses**

Rewrite each sentence, adding dashes or parentheses where necessary. Use the marks of punctuation indicated in parentheses at the end of each sentence.

SAMPLE Eric the Red he was a Norse chieftain explored Greenland in the tenth century. (parentheses)

ANSWER Eric the Red (he was a Norse chieftain) explored Greenland in the tenth century.

1. The Dutch navigator Willem Barents a sea is named for him led a mission of exploration in 1597. (dashes)
2. Barents's arctic expedition the first in recorded history set out to survive a winter in the Far North. (dashes)
3. The Dutch were looking for a Northeast Passage a northern route from Europe to the Pacific. (dash)
4. Vitus Bering the strait between Asia and North America bears his name was a Dane in service to Russia during the eighteenth century. (parentheses)
5. The strait usually frozen from October to June is a mere fifty-five miles wide. (parentheses)

Answers: Exercise 4

1. . . . harsh, pervasive cold.
2. . . . stay warm, and insulation . . .
3. . . . sea otter, for example, . . .
4. . . . sea urchins, mollusks, and fish.
5. . . . consequently, a single meal . . .
6. Fur and fat and feathers are . . .
7. . . . coarse guard hair . . .
8. Musk oxen will, in fact, seek shelter . . .
9. . . . animals but leaves . . .
10. . . . indeed, they have . . .

Answers: Exercise 5

1. . . . Willem Barents—a sea is named for him—led . . .
2. . . . expedition—the first in recorded history—set out . . .
3. . . . Passage—a northern route . . .
4. Vitus Bering (the strait between Asia and North America bears his name) was a Dane . . .
5. The strait (usually frozen from October to June) is . . .

Practice and Assess

Answers: Exercise 6

1. In his book *Arctic Dreams,* . . .
2. . . . chapter of the book entitled "Lancaster Sound," . . .
3. "We know more about the rings of Saturn," Lopez writes, "than we know about the narwhal."
4. . . . words: *Monodon monoceros.*
5. . . . means "one tooth," and the second part means "one horn."

Answers: Exercise 7

1. Lopez's
2. wolves'
3. correct
4. haven't
5. It's

Answers: Exercise 8

Proofreading

This proofreading activity provides editing practice with (1) the current or previous units' skills, (2) the **Troubleshooter** errors, and (3) spelling errors. Students should be able to complete the exercise by referring to the units, the **Troubleshooter,** and a dictionary.

Error (Type of Error)

1. Heights, (nonessential appositive phrase)
2. three (spell out one-word numbers)
   teachers: (colon before a list)
   Henri, (commas in a series)
3. artists, (nonessential appositive phrase)
4. twenties, he (sentence fragment, introductory adverb clause)
5. landscape, (commas in a series)
6. time, (two or more introductory prepositional phrases)

Grammar Review

Punctuation, Abbreviations, and Numbers

Review: Exercise 6 Using Quotation Marks and Italics

Rewrite each sentence, adding quotation marks or italics (underlining) where necessary. For the sentences that contain no errors, write *correct.*

1. In his book Arctic Dreams, Barry Lopez describes his first encounter with a narwhal.
2. According to the chapter of the book entitled Lancaster Sound, narwhals are very mysterious.
3. "We know more about the rings of Saturn, Lopez writes, than we know about the narwhal.
4. The scientific name of this whale consists of two Greek words: Monodon monoceros.
5. The first part of this name literally means "one tooth, and the second part means one horn."

Review: Exercise 7

Rewrite each sentence, adding or deleting apostrophes where necessary. If a sentence has no errors, write *correct.*

1. Another of Barry Lopezs major books is entitled *Of Wolves and Men.*
2. In this widely acclaimed work, Lopez studies wolve's behavior.
3. Minnesota's and Canada's wolves have drastically declined in number, Lopez reports.
4. Wolves are so shy that some people havent spotted one even after a three-month stay in the woods where wolves live.
5. Its surprising how many myths feature wolves as major characters.

Review: Exercise 8

Proofreading

The following passage describes the artist Rockwell Kent, whose painting appears on the opposite page. Rewrite the passage, correcting the errors in spelling, usage, and grammar. Add any missing punctuation. There are twenty-five errors.

Rockwell Kent

[1]Rockwell Kent (1882–1971) was born in Tarrytown Heights a small town on the Hudson River north of New York City. [2]He was strongly influenced by these 3 teachers William Chase, Robert Henri and Abbott Thayer. [3]These men, all prominent artists portrayed American life with a clear and unsentimental eye.

[4]When Kent was in his early twenties. [5]He developed a strong interest in the landscape people, and culture of the Arctic and the Antarctic. [6]Like many other

Rockwell Kent, *The Trapper,* 1921

young men of his time Kent had become interested in Alaska and the Yukon after reading the novels of Jack London. [7]Kent, like London, lived an adventurous life, spending much of his time in the harsh cold climates that he loves. [8]He trap lobsters in Maine, sailed through treacherous waters off the tip of South America and lived in the hinterlands of Alaska, Newfoundland, and Greenland.

[9]Kent were also a gifted writer. [10]He wrote and illustrated several books, including *Wilderness* (1920), which describes his travels through Alaska and *Voyaging Southward from the Strait of Magellan* (1924), which tells of his seafaring adventures in South America. [11]Kent received wide praise for the powerful evocative wood engravings that appeared in the books he illustrated during the 1920's and 1930s. [12]Developed a boldly graphic style that used strong but simple patterns and decorative designs. [13]His interest in simplicity and stylized forms is apparent in *The Trapper* which depicts a solitary man trudging through a bleak landscape.

[14]Kent would have been the ideal illustrater for Barry Lopez' *Arctic Dreams.* [15]The book was published in 1986, 15 years after Kents death). [16]Both men felt a deep affinity for the harsh landscape of the Arctic and the struggles endured by your inhabitants. [17]Lopez writes in *Arctic Dreams,* "I came to believe that people's desires and aspirations were as much a part of the land as the wind, solitary animals, and the bright fields of stone and tundra.

Punctuation, Abbreviations, and Numbers

Answers: Exercise 8 *(continued)*

Error (Type of Error)

7. harsh, (coordinate adjectives)
   loved (verb tense)
8. trapped (verb tense)
   America, (commas in a series)
9. was (subject-verb agreement)
10. Alaska, (nonessential adjective clause)
11. powerful, (coordinate adjectives)
    1920s (special use of numerals)
12. He developed (sentence fragment)
13. *Trapper,* (nonessential adjective clause)
14. illustrator (spelling)
    Lopez's (singular possessive)
15. (The (parentheses with supplemental material)
    fifteen (spell out one-word numbers)
    Kent's (singular possessive)
16. its inhabitants (unclear pronoun reference)
17. tundra." (quotation marks for direct quotations)

Viewing the Art

Rockwell Kent, *The Trapper,* 1921

Good artists often evoke strong emotions. Ask students to describe the mood of *The Trapper.* (sad, lonely, serene) Ask what elements contribute to this mood. (the cool colors, the solitary figure and single tree stump, the long shadows, the ghostly moon)

Ask students to describe the mood of the passage from *Arctic Dreams.* (cool, objective, distant) Ask students to consider why Lopez chose to adopt this neutral attitude toward his subject. Then have students write a few sentences describing *The Trapper.* Remind students to use correct punctuation, abbreviations, and numbers.

Practice and Assess

Answers: Exercise 9

Mixed Review

1. Barry Lopez, one of America's . . . nature, was born in 1945.
2. He grew up in the postwar world of the 1950s, an . . . history.
3. A precocious child, Lopez . . . observation, careful thought, and precise writing even during grade school.
4. Lopez . . . prestigious, privately funded midwestern university.
5. Soon . . . Dame in 1966, Lopez became a full-time writer.
6. However, most writers (even those with great talent) find . . . necessities: food, shelter, and clothing.
7. Isn't . . . said, "I never . . . writer"?
8. <u>Arctic Dreams</u>, a celebration . . . Arctic, was published in 1986; it . . . nonfiction . . . Arts in 1987.
9. A literary . . . honor; it . . . author.
10. Among . . . are these: polar bears, narwhals, musk ox, and caribou.
11. Most Americans, you should realize, have . . . habitat, and they . . . "armchair travels."
12. <u>Arctic Dreams</u>—the work won a National Book Award—explores human beings' . . . landscape.
13. Like . . . writer Peter Matthiessen (with whom he has been compared), Lopez, of course, has . . . books.
14. Other writers—William Least Heat Moon springs to mind—describe . . . landscapes that . . . home.
15. Nature, which . . . granted, is . . . imagination.

Close

Have students look at something they have written recently and proofread it for the kinds of punctuation errors dealt with in this unit. You may wish to have them do this exercise in pairs. If so, instruct them to trade papers and proofread each other's work. Tell them to consult together if any questions arise and to cite specific rules to support their answers. Encourage students to revise their writing as needed.

Grammar Review

Review: Exercise 9

Mixed Review

The following sentences are about Barry Lopez. Rewrite each sentence, correcting all errors in punctuation. For a sentence that contains no errors, write *correct*.

Barry Lopez

1. Barry Lopez one of Americas' foremost writers on nature was born in 1945.
2. He grew up in the postwar world of the 1950's an optimistic era in American history.
3. A precocious child Lopez began to demonstrate a gift for keen observation careful thought and precise writing even during grade school.
4. Lopez attended a prestigious privately-funded midwestern university.
5. Soon after his graduation from the University of Notre Dame (in 1966), Lopez became a full time writer.
6. However most writers (even those with great talent, find they must hold another job in order to pay for these daily necessities food shelter and clothing.
7. Isnt it ironic that Lopez said, "I never thought I would be able to make a living as a writer?"
8. "Arctic Dreams" a celebration of animals and people in the frozen Arctic was published in 1986, it earned the Francis Fuller Victor Award in nonfiction from the Oregon Institute of Literary Arts, in 1987.
9. A literary award is not simply a great honor, it also helps persuade a publisher to accept future manuscripts from a struggling young author.
10. Among the animals, Lopez describes are these; polar bears, narwhals, musk ox, and caribou.
11. Most Americans you should realize, have never seen these animals in their natural habitat and they enjoy observing them vicariously through "armchair travels
12. Arctic Dreams—the work won a National Book Award explores human being's relationship with the landscape.
13. Like the nature writer, Peter Matthiessen, with whom he has been compared), Lopez of course has traveled widely in search of material for his books.
14. Other writers—William Least Heat Moon springs to mind, describe in great detail the ordinary landscapes, that are closer to home.
15. Nature which most of us take for granted is frequently the springboard that an author uses to exercise the imagination.

Writing Application

Commas and Parentheses in Writing

In the following passage from *Of Wolves and Men*, Barry Lopez gives the reader a palpable sense of the wolf's reality by his attention to detail. His careful use of commas and parentheses clarifies his message and contributes to the effect. Examine the passage, focusing on the commas and the italicized words.

> The wolf weighs ninety-four pounds and stands thirty inches at the shoulder. His feet are enormous, leaving prints in the mud along a creek (*where he pauses to hunt crayfish but not with much interest*) more than five inches long by just over four wide. He has two fractured ribs, broken by a moose a year before. They are healed now, but a sharp eye would notice the irregularity. The skin on his right hip is scarred, from a fight with another wolf in a neighboring pack when he was a yearling.

Techniques with Commas and Parentheses

Try to apply some of Barry Lopez's techniques when you write and revise your own work.

TIME

For more about the writing process, see **TIME Facing the Blank Page**, pp. 121-131.

1. Use commas to set off material not essential to the meaning of a sentence.

CARELESS STYLE He has two fractured ribs broken by a moose a year before.

LOPEZ'S STYLE He has two fractured ribs, broken by a moose a year before.

2. Use parentheses to set off material that is purely incidental to the meaning.

CONFUSING STYLE His feet are enormous, leaving prints . . . along a creek, *where he pauses to hunt crayfish but not with much interest*, more than five inches long . . .

LOPEZ'S STYLE His feet are enormous, leaving prints . . . along a creek (*where he pauses to hunt crayfish but not with much interest*) more than five inches long . . .

Punctuation, Abbreviations, and Numbers

Practice On your paper, practice these techniques by revising the following passage, adding commas, capitalization, parentheses, and other forms of punctuation where appropriate.

The West Highland white terrier commonly known as the Westie is an imaginative hunter of badgers otters, rabbits and rats. It is a "small game" dog weighing twenty pounds or less. Its fur should be double-coated, with the outer coat consisting of straight hard hair about two inches long. The ideal Westie should measure about eleven inches around the withers withers is a term borrowed from horse breeding that refers to the ridge between the shoulder bones. The ears should be small and terminate in a sharp point. Be sure to keep them free of fringes. The tail ideally measuring about six inches in length is the Westie's pride and joy and should be carried gaily.

LOG ON **Writing Online** For more grammar practice, go to glencoe.com and enter QuickPass code WC97727p2.

Commas and Parentheses in Writing

Have students read the passage silently. Then discuss with them how Lopez's use of commas and parentheses makes the passage clearer and easier to understand and contributes to its overall effect.

Techniques with Commas and Parentheses

Discuss the punctuation techniques explained in this section. Have students reread the Proofreading activity on pages 776–777 to notice how these punctuation techniques are used.

Practice

Refer to Techniques with Commas and Parentheses as you evaluate students' choices. Answers will vary. A sample answer is given below.

The West Highland white terrier, commonly known as the Westie, is an imaginative hunter of badgers, otters, rabbits, and rats. It is a "small game" dog, weighing twenty pounds or less. Its fur should be double-coated, with the outer coat consisting of straight, hard hair about two inches long. The ideal Westie should measure about eleven inches around the withers. (*Withers* is a term borrowed from horse breeding that refers to the ridge between the shoulder bones.) The ears should be small and terminate in a sharp point. (Be sure to keep them free of fringes.) The tail, ideally measuring about six inches in length, is the Westie's pride and joy and should be carried gaily.

ASSESSMENT OPTIONS

Tests with Answer Key & Rubrics
Unit 21 Mastery Test, pp. 81–82

Testmaker
Unit 21 Mastery Test

You may wish to administer the Unit 21 Mastery Test at this point.

MindJogger Videoquizzes

PART 3

Resources and Skills

Objectives

The units in Part 3 continue to guide students in their development toward becoming effective, confident writers. Throughout these units, students will be asked

- to develop an appreciation of the richness and diversity of English
- to use the library to organize and compile information from a variety of sources
- to develop vocabulary by analyzing the context of unfamiliar words
- to produce legible work that reflects an understanding of basic spelling rules
- to use writing as a study tool to clarify, organize, and remember information
- to learn strategies for answering a wide variety of objective test questions
- to prepare, organize, and present informative and persuasive oral messages and to analyze, appreciate, and evaluate the presentations of others
- to interpret visual messages
- to analyze and critique media messages
- to use technology in the writing process

Viewing the Art

Mark Ruchlewicz makes a powerful statement with this painting of a single tree in full leaf standing in the middle of a landscape scattered with tree stumps. This form of political art decries the deforestation that is harming our environment. Much of Ruchlewicz's art addresses the negative environmental impact of many of humankind's economic decisions.

Interpret and Analyze Use the following questions for discussion:

- What elements of color, shape, or design affect your reaction to this painting?
- How might Ruchlewicz's picture of a deforested landscape relate to the quotation on this page?

Mark Ruchlewicz, Tree on a deforested landscape

"Ours was rich soil formed by that same Kern river as it ground Sierra granite and turned it into coarse sand."

—Gerald Haslam
"The Horned Toad"

Resource Manager

Use the following resources to customize your teaching of the units in Part 3.

Planning Resources

- *Lesson Plans*
- *Block Scheduling*

Transparencies

- *Bellringer*
- *Daily Language Practice*
- *Two-Minute Skill Drill*

Other Print Resources

- *Dinah Zike's Foldables™ for* Writer's Choice
- *inTime*
- *Listening and Speaking Activities*
- *Spelling Power*
- *Style and Documentation Handbook for Writers*
- *Taking Standardized Tests*
- *Tests with Answer Key and Rubrics*
- *Thinking and Study Skills*
- *Viewing and Representing Activities*
- *Vocabulary and Spelling Strategies and Practice*
- *Vocabulary Power*

PART 3

Resources and Skills

Discussing the Quotation

The quotation is from "The Horned Toad," a short story by Gerald Haslam (b. 1937). Haslam grew up in south central California, where large fortunes were made digging for oil. Discuss the quotation with the class, and ask students how they would interpret the author's meaning. How would you contrast the process that it took to form the rich soil through grinding granite into sand to the process of ridding a landscape of trees? What statement does this make about nature's processes and humankind's respect for it?

Writing Prompt

Write a brief explanation of how Haslam's words, coupled with the image, can be seen to connect to the process of research and study skills.

Video
- *MindJogger Videoquizzes*

Software
- *Presentation Plus!*
- *Testmaker*
- *Vocabulary Power Puzzlemaker*

Web Site
- *glencoe.com*

INTRODUCING

UNIT 22

Objectives

- To learn about the history and adaptability of the English language, including its tradition of borrowing words, blending words, and changing meanings
- To use dictionaries to trace the origins of words and to analyze and consider the use of new words and slang

ASSESSMENT OPTIONS

Tests with Answer Key & Rubrics
Unit 22 Pretest, pp. 83–84

Testmaker
Unit 22 Pretest

You may wish to administer the Unit 22 Pretest at this point.

Key to Ability Levels

L1 Level 1 activities are within the basic ability range of students.

L2 Level 2 activities are within the ability range of average students.

L3 Level 3 activities are more challenging activities.

UNIT 22

Sources of English Words

LOG ON Writing Online — For research tools and additional skills practice, go to glencoe.com and enter QuickPass code WC97727p3.

Resource Manager

Planning Resources
- *Lesson Plans*
- *Block Scheduling*

Transparencies
- *Bellringer*
- *Daily Language Practice*

Other Print Resources
- *Tests with Answer Key and Rubrics*
- *Vocabulary and Spelling Strategies and Practice*

Video
- *MindJogger Videoquizzes*

Software
- *Presentation Plus!*
- *Testmaker*
- *Vocabulary Power Puzzlemaker*

Web Site
- *glencoe.com*

22.1 English in Our Time

Twenty years ago, the following news item probably wouldn't have made much sense to most Americans. Can you imagine why?

> A cyberspace traffic jam as never before—that's what many called the situation on the Internet this Sunday evening between 6 P.M. and midnight. So many people logged on that popular Web sites reported twice the normal number of hits for a Sunday evening. Eventually some e-mail carriers crashed for much of the evening. Many users who tried to go online were furious, calling tech support numbers at record rates.

Most Americans of the 1980s would have been baffled by the above news item. Words like *cyberspace, Internet,* and *e-mail* would have been largely unknown at that time. Yet by 2000, these words were routinely used in conversation and in broadcast, print, and online news. How did these words find their way into English?

A Living Language

Like all living languages, English is continually changing. The creation of new words to describe developments in science and technology is not a new phenomenon. Just think about it; the word *telephone* was once a brand-new word in our language, as were *airplane, automobile,* and *television.*

So when the Internet rose to such great popularity during the latter part of the twentieth century, people simply created the words needed to describe the new technology. The more often such words were used, the less "technological" they sounded, and they came to be used routinely in speech and writing.

As fresh ideas evolve and innovative technologies are developed, new English words are created to describe them. These words may be words borrowed from other languages, existing words taking on new meanings, acronyms, blends, compounds, or newly coined words, as the following examples and the chart on the next page show.

Focus

Lesson Overview

Objective

- To become familiar with the history and adaptability of the English language
- To appreciate the variety and richness of the English language

Skills

- classifying types of words being assimilated into English; defining words being assimilated into English

Critical Thinking

- classifying; using prior knowledge

Listening and Speaking

- discussing

Bellringer
Daily Language Activity

When students enter the classroom, have this assignment on the board: *Write a sentence that contains words that are new to the English language. Exchange papers and identify the new words.*

See also *Daily Language Practice*

Teach

Looking at Lingo

Encourage students to consider how often the English they use—for example, in reference to technology, sports, and music—incorporates words borrowed from other languages, words that have been newly coined, words that have taken on new meanings, or acronyms. Suggest that students make lists of such words, then discuss them. **L2**

Resource Manager

Planning Resources
- *Lesson Plans*

Transparencies
- *Bellringer*
- *Daily Language Practice*

Other Print Resources
- *Vocabulary and Spelling Strategies and Practice,* pp. 79–82

Practice and Assess

Answers: Exercise 1

Answers will vary. Students might encounter words such as *laptop, multiplex, webcast, pad thai, edamame, foie gras,* and *tamale.*

Additional Resources

Vocabulary and Spelling Strategies and Practice, pp. 79–82.

Close

Invite students to discuss which areas of business have produced most of the new words on the chart. (government, military, and communications/computer technology) Why do they think this has happened? (Constant research and invention produce new things and processes that require a new vocabulary.)

Kwanza	borrowing from Swahili: seven-day African American cultural festival
rap	old word, meaning "to knock quickly," taking on a new meaning: a form of music
AIDS	acronym for Acquired Immune Deficiency Syndrome
cineplex	blend of existing words *cinema* + *complex*
download	compound of existing words
cellulite	new word for fatty deposits on the hips and thighs, coined in 1971

In the next four lessons, you'll be introduced to some of the history and mechanisms that continue to shape the language we use. No matter where the words we speak originated, they illustrate a vital feature of English—adaptability. English is alive.

Some Recent Additions to the English Vocabulary	
Borrowed Words	• paparazzi (freelance photographers who aggressively pursue celebrities to take candid photos; from Italian) • feng shui (a Chinese practice of harmonious placement of objects, especially furniture) • tai chi (a Chinese discipline of meditative exercises)
Old Words, New Meanings	• scan (to transfer words and images into electronic files) • mouse (hand-operated device for controlling movement on a computer screen)
Acronyms	• RAM (random-access memory) • MIRV (multiple independently targeted re-entry vehicle—a missile with two or more warheads)
Blends	• modem (modulator/demodulator—device for transferring computer files from one computer to another via telephone lines)
Compounds	• compact disc (a small plastic optical disc containing recorded music or computer data) • e-mail (electronic mail)

Exercise 1

Skim the contents of several popular magazines, looking for words that you think are in the process of being assimilated into English. These might be words from foreign languages (often italicized) or words that have been created, or adapted from existing words, to name new ideas, technologies, events, consumer goods, and so on. Make a list of the words you find and define each word. In a brief oral report, share your findings with the class.

MEETING INDIVIDUAL NEEDS

English Language Learners

Borrowing Words

Provide students with an opportunity to consider how their own primary language has assimilated words from English—or vice versa. Ask if students have ever used an English word, or other foreign-language word, in a sentence in their primary language. Have they used a word from their primary language—or from another language—in an English sentence? Invite volunteers to provide examples.

WORDWORKS

EPONYMS

Making History

Have you ever wondered why men, boys, and sometimes whole groups of people are called *guys*? Well, here's the story. Guy Fawkes was an English traitor who plotted to murder the king. Fawkes was hanged for his treason in 1606, but each year on November 5 (Guy Fawkes Day), the British burn a straw figure of Guy Fawkes in effigy. Originally, any ragged or odd-looking men—men who resembled Fawkes's straw effigy—were called guys. Today the word refers to men, boys, or people in general.

Guy Fawkes is an eponym. An eponym is a person whose name is the source for the name of someone or something. William Penn, for example, is the eponym for Pennsylvania. Madame de Pompadour (pictured at the right) gave her name to a hairstyle.

Some people have become eponyms because of their inventions or achievements. The Ferris wheel is named for George W. G. Ferris, who invented this popular ride. Louis Pasteur gave his name to pasteurization—the process of sterilizing milk and other bacteria-rich liquids.

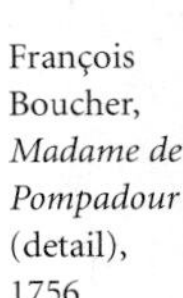

François Boucher, *Madame de Pompadour* (detail), 1756

Other people have become eponyms because their names were associated with a certain thing. Jules Léotard, for example, was a nineteenth-century French circus performer whose costume included a form-fitting body stocking—what we today call a leotard. Similarly, Samuel Maverick was a Texas cattle rancher who, unlike his fellow ranchers, refused to brand his cattle. These unbranded cattle became known as *mavericks,* and the word *maverick* has now come to mean anyone who refuses to go along with the group.

Eponymous Explorations

Look at the list of definitions on the left and match them with their eponyms on the right. If necessary, use a dictionary.

1. a wind instrument	**A.** Rudolf Diesel
2. a type of car engine	**B.** Adolphe Sax
3. a temperature scale	**C.** George Pullman
4. a railroad sleeping car	**D.** James Watt
5. a unit of power	**E.** Gabriel Fahrenheit

Lesson Overview

Objective
- To learn about eponyms

Skills
- using prior knowledge to identify and infer the meanings of eponyms

Critical Thinking
- defining and clarifying; analyzing; categorizing

Listening and Speaking
- discussing; explaining a process

Teach

Discussion

Have students read Wordworks, page 785, and discuss the following question: What are some reasons why people may become eponyms?

Speaking of Eponyms

Invite students to think of people they know who could or perhaps have become eponyms. For example, family members might have invented words based on each other's names: "yurivision" might describe Uncle Yuri's—and other people's—ability to read in the dark; or sayings like Aunt Helen's might be called "helenisms." **L3**

Practice and Assess

Answers: Eponymous Explorations

1. B, Adolphe Sax
2. A, Rudolf Diesel
3. E, Gabriel Fahrenheit
4. C, George Pullman
5. D, James Watt

Close

Invite a volunteer to look up the words *eponymic* and *eponymous* in the dictionary and share the definitions with the class. Challenge students to use the words orally in sentences.

Focus

Lesson Overview

Objective

- To understand how and why English words have been borrowed from other languages

Skills

- using a dictionary to research word origins

Critical Thinking

- analyzing; comparing; defining and clarifying

Listening and Speaking

- discussing

Bellringer

Daily Language Activity

When students enter the classroom, have this assignment on the board: *Write down two or three types of historical events that might have led to one language borrowing words from another.*

See also  *Daily Language Practice*

Teach

Borrowing Words

Refer students to the charts on this and the next page, asking them to identify what part of speech each word is. (*Altar, candle, wine, temple, sky,* and *fellow* are nouns. *School, cup, call, seat, skin,* and *die* can be nouns or verbs. *Master* can be a noun, verb, or adjective. *Both* is an adjective.) Discuss with them why nouns are more often borrowed than other parts of speech. (Nouns name the institutions, practices, or inventions being adopted by one culture from another. Since these things may not exist in both cultures, new words may be needed to name them.) **L2**

22.2 Conquest and Conversion

The year is A.D. 449, and throughout the British Isles the apprehensive mood of the Celtic people is reflected in the low gray clouds of the winter sky. The Roman legions that have enforced the rule of law in this distant outpost of the empire have now withdrawn to Rome in what will prove to be a futile effort to repel invading barbarians from the north. The once-invincible empire is collapsing.

Meanwhile, poised for attack just across the English Channel are three fierce Germanic tribes—the Angles, the Saxons, and the Jutes. (The Celts had enlisted the aid of these tribes to fight off the Picts and Scots, who had been attacking the Celts from the west and the north—the areas we now know as Ireland and Scotland.) The Germanic warriors have routed the Picts and Scots but now will turn on their Celtic hosts, driving the Celts into the mountains of what are today Wales and Scotland. A new culture will take root on the island of Britain, and its principal language will be Anglo-Saxon, or Old English.

Emissaries from the Pope

Almost as soon as Old English was established, it began to change. Many of the language changes were due to foreign influences. Both Celtic and Anglo-Saxon already had been influenced by Latin because of the dominance of the Roman Empire. That influence increased during the sixth century when Pope Gregory, the spiritual leader of the Roman Catholic Church, sent missionaries to Britain to convert the Anglo-Saxons to Christianity.

The monks opened schools where they taught Latin to the Anglo-Saxon people. In addition, religious services were routinely conducted in Latin, and most texts were written in Latin. As you might expect, many Latin words, especially those pertaining to school and religion, became part of the Anglo-Saxon vocabulary.

Latin into English

LATIN	OLD ENGLISH	MODERN ENGLISH
schola	scōl	school
magister	magister	master
altare	altar	altar
candela	candel	candle
vinum	wīn	wine
cuppa	cuppe	cup
templum	tempel	temple

Resource Manager

Planning Resources

- *Lesson Plans*

Transparencies

- *Bellringer*
- *Daily Language Practice*

Other Print Resources

- *Vocabulary and Spelling Strategies and Practice*, p. 37

Invaders from the North

Starting around 800, the conquering Anglo-Saxons were given a taste of their own military medicine. Vikings from the Scandinavian countries to the north began raiding Engla Land (Land of the Angles) much as the Angles, Saxons, and Jutes had invaded Britain four hundred years earlier. This sporadic warfare continued for more than two hundred years. By the eleventh century, many Norse had settled in Engla Land, and again English underwent change with the addition of Scandinavian words.

Significantly, the Scandinavians contributed three Danish words: the personal pronouns *they, their*, and *them.* One language borrowing pronouns from another language is unusual. Generally, pronouns are firmly entrenched in a language, and the native forms are not readily displaced.

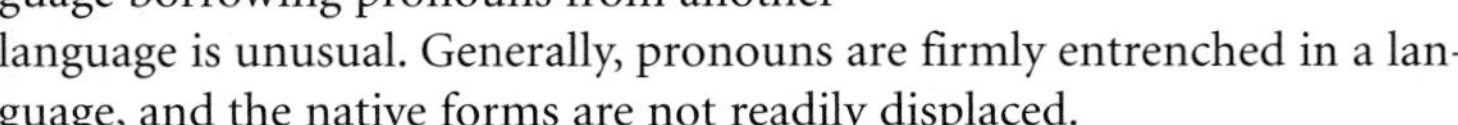

Scandinavian into English

OLD NORSE	MIDDLE ENGLISH	MODERN ENGLISH
kalla	callen	call
sæti	sete	seat
skinn	skin	skin
skȳ	sky	sky
bāthir	bothe	both
deyja	dien	die
fēlagi	felawe	fellow

Exercise 2

Each of the following words from modern English was originally borrowed from either Latin or a Scandinavian language. Use a dictionary to research the origin of each word. Give its Latin or Scandinavian form as well as its Old or Middle English form.

1. discipline
2. low
3. skull
4. priest
5. Sabbath
6. take

Sources of English Words

Practice and Assess

Answers: Exercise 2

In the answers to this activity, abbreviations are used as follows: L for Latin, ME for Middle English, ON for Old Norse, and OE for Old English.

1. L *disciplina;* ME *descepline*
2. ON *lagr;* ME *loue* or *lah*
3. ON *skol, skul;* ME *scolle* or *skulle*
4. L *presbytr* or *prester;* OE *preost* or *prest;* ME *prest*
5. L *sabbatum;* OE *sabbat* or *sabat;* ME *sabath* or *sabat*
6. ON *taka;* OE *tacan;* ME *taken*

Additional Resources

Vocabulary and Spelling Strategies and Practice, p. 37

Close

Invite students to write down five words that they have heard or read and whose language origins they would like to know. Have them look up each word in a dictionary, record for each word the language origins cited there, and share their findings with the class.

Exploring Language

Using Languages Today

By the end of the sixth century A.D., Anglo-Saxon, or Old English, was the dominant language in England. However, the Celtic people who had been driven out retained their languages. Today Gaelic and Welsh, both Celtic languages, are still spoken along with English in some areas of Great Britain—Gaelic in Ireland and Scotland, and Welsh in Wales. **L2**

Lesson Overview

Objective
- To become familiar with spoonerisms

Skills
- using prior knowledge to identify and create spoonerisms; identifying logical errors

Critical Thinking
- analyzing; synthesizing

Listening and Speaking
- discussing

Teach

Discussion

Have students read Wordworks, page 788, and discuss the following questions:

- What makes a spoonerism?
- What are more examples of spoonerisms?
- The article refers to the process of making spoonerisms as an "art." Are readers expected to take this seriously?

Creating Spoonerisms

Guide students in pairs or small groups to create spoonerisms. Suggest some familiar expressions to get them started. Suggest that they transpose words or the beginning sounds of words to make their humorous spoonerisms. Have students take turns reading their spoonerisms aloud. **L2**

Practice and Assess

Answers: Scrambled Sayings

1. Is the dean busy?
2. a crushing blow
3. You have wasted a whole term.
4. Someone is occupying my pew.
5. a well-oiled bicycle

Close

Invite students to consider and discuss why people find spoonerisms funny. (They replace the correct words in a phrase with other words that mean something completely different.)

WORDWORKS

SPOONERISMS

Time Wounds All Heels

Have you ever made some unintentionally humorous or embarrassing slip of the tongue, such as telling someone to "ship up or shape out" when you meant to say "shape up or ship out"? Well, if that's the case, you're in good company.

Around the beginning of the twentieth century, an English clergyman and educator named William Spooner (pictured at left) acquired a reputation for habitually making such humorous blunders. It seems the Reverend Spooner's brain anticipated what his tongue was about to say, and he would often transpose the sounds from one word to another.

For example, when steering a prominent member of his congregation away from a reserved pew, he supposedly offered this assistance: "Let me sew you to another sheet." Another time, to the amusement of his congregation, when Spooner was delivering a sermon about half-formed wishes, he announced, "We all know what it is to have a half-warmed fish within us." The Reverend Spooner became so notorious for these linguistic bungles that people began calling them spoonerisms.

Everyone makes such slips now and then. The technical term for this normal process is *metathesis.* Other practitioners of the art besides Spooner include the meteorologist who forecast "rain and slow, followed by sneet" and the radio announcer who, while describing the audience at a world championship bout at Madison Square Garden, informed his listeners, "I see the beautiful Mrs. DePuyster Van Courtland looking gorgeous in her stunning white gownless evening strap."

Scrambled Sayings

With a partner, unscramble the following spoonerisms.

1. Is the bean dizzy?
2. a blushing crow
3. You have tasted a whole worm.
4. Someone is occupewing my pie.
5. a well-boiled icicle

22.3 A Conqueror from France

The English weren't the only people to be harassed by Scandinavian warriors. Coastal areas of France were also attacked and settled. The French called the invaders Normans, the Old French word for "Northmen." The region of France settled by the Normans became known as Normandy.

In 1066 the seventh Duke of Normandy, William the Conqueror (pictured at right), was embroiled in a dispute for succession to the English throne. The dispute ended when William defeated King Harold II at the Battle of Hastings. William became king, and the Norman Conquest, as William's victory came to be called, altered the English language.

Parlez-vous Français?

Because the conquering Normans were from France, French became the language of the aristocracy in England. The working classes still spoke English, but after several decades of French rule, English was borrowing liberally from the French language. Words relating to religion, the arts and sciences, military affairs, social life, clothing, manners, and food were taken from French.

The vocabulary of food provides an interesting example of how social class influenced the development of English. Farmers and herders were

The Norman Invasion, 1066

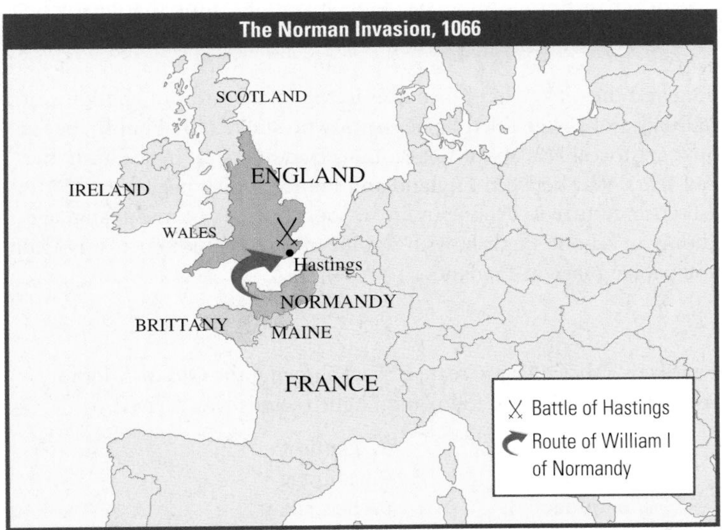

Sources of English Words

Focus

Lesson Overview

Objective
- To understand how and why English words have been borrowed from other languages

Skills
- using a dictionary to research word origins

Critical Thinking
- building background; categorizing

Listening and Speaking
- discussing

Bellringer
Daily Language Activity

When students enter the classroom, have this assignment on the board: *When England was conquered by the French-speaking Normans, the aristocracy adopted the French language, but the peasants did not. Why do you think this happened?*

See also *Daily Language Practice*

Teach

Discussing How Words Become Common Terms

Help students understand that during Norman rule, whether a French or an English word became the common term was determined by who used the word most often. Since most people (the workers, or peasants) spoke English, English words were used to identify aspects of their daily lives. Do students think people's vocabulary today reflects their daily lives? Assign groups each a different occupation for which to list five to ten words used especially in that occupation. **L2**

Resource Manager

Planning Resources
- *Lesson Plans*

Transparencies
- *Bellringer*
- *Daily Language Practice*

Other Print Resources
- *Vocabulary and Spelling Strategies and Practice,* p. 37

Practice and Assess

Answers: Exercise 3

1. Old French *bacon*
2. Old French *porche*
3. Old French *castel*
4. Old French *boillir*
5. Old French *preiere*
6. Old French *juge* or *jugier*
7. Old French *gentil*
8. Old French *corage*
9. Middle French and Old French *lieu* and *tenir*

Additional Resources

Vocabulary and Spelling Strategies and Practice, p. 37

Close

Discuss possible reasons why words on the chart were borrowed from French. (They name items important to French-speaking rulers, but not to English-speaking peasants.) Then ask students whether the following words came from Old English or Old French, and challenge them to explain how they know: *bread* (OE—staple food of common people), *thatch* (OE—roofing material of common people, who lived in cottages unlike the wooden and stone castles of Norman aristocracy), *legal* (OFr—Norman conquerors made and administered laws), *army* (OFr—led by Norman leaders).

part of the working class, so the names of the animals they tended are from Old and Middle English: *cou (cow), cealf (calf), sceap (sheep), deor (deer),* and *swin (swine).* When these animals were prepared as elaborate dishes for the nobility, their names shifted from English to Old and Middle French: *buef (beef), veel (veal), moton (mutton), veneison (venison),* and *porc (pork).*

English Borrowings from French	
Social Life	peasant (paisant), court (court)
Food	roast (rostir), sausage (saussiche)
Government	authority (auctorité), constable (conestable)
Housing	palace (palais), tower (tor)
Religion	chaplain (chapelain), saint (saint)
Arts and Sciences	music (musique), medicine (medicine)
Military	charge (chargier), powder (poudre)

Plague and War

During the fourteenth century, a terrible plague known as the Black Death swept across Europe and Asia. Some historians think that nearly one-fourth of the European and Asian population died from the plague during this period.

In England the plague left businesses in the towns without enough workers. Eventually, jobs were filled by peasants, who spoke only English, because no proper aristocrat was about to become a tradesperson. In addition, the Hundred Years' War between England and France, which began in 1337, caused French culture to decline in favor. Soon French became a language studied only in school. English, with significant French influence, was again the principal language of England.

Exercise 3

Look up these words in a dictionary. Create a chart showing the Old or Middle French word from which each of the following English words was derived.

1. bacon
2. porch
3. castle
4. boil
5. prayer
6. judge
7. gentle
8. courage
9. lieutenant

Meeting Individual Needs: English Language Learners

Using a Dictionary

Students whose first language is not English can benefit from dictionary work. Make sure that students understand the purpose of the pronunciation key on each page. Have students work with a partner to locate the English words from the chart, use the pronunciation key to pronounce the word, and identify its part of speech and word origin if given. Help students with any abbreviations used. Have students write sentences, using the words correctly.

WORDWORKS

PUNS AND TOM SWIFTIES

Ever Seen a Horse Fly?

Remember when you were a kid and loved to tell silly riddles like "What's black and white and red (read) all over?" (Answer: a newspaper) This riddle is an example of a pun, or a play on words.

Shakespeare loved puns. So did Lewis Carroll, author of *Alice in Wonderland.* Here's how the Mock Turtle describes his education to Alice:

> "I only took the regular course."
>
> "What was that?" enquired Alice.
>
> "Reeling and Writhing, of course, to begin with," the Mock Turtle replied; "and then the different branches of Arithmetic—Ambition, Distraction, Uglification, and Derision."

The puns in this passage are double-sound puns—words that sound very similar to other words. Homophone puns are based on different words that sound the same, such as *red* and *read.* Homograph puns are based on words that are spelled and pronounced the same but have different meanings. Benjamin Franklin used this type of pun when, after signing the Declaration of Independence, he told the gathering of revolutionaries, "We must all hang together or, most assuredly, we shall all hang separately!"

Some of the funniest puns are "Tom Swifties." In the Tom Swift stories, created by Edward Stratemeyer, Tom and his cronies never just plain said anything—they said it *happily* or *hurriedly* or *speedily* or in some other adverbial way. The humor in Tom Swifties occurs when the adverb describing how something is said forms a pun on what the speaker is saying, for example: "I love pancakes," said Tom flippantly.

"Try This Game," Said Tom Playfully

Work with a partner to match each quotation with a punning adverb below.

1. "These cherries aren't quite ripe," said Tom _____.
2. "This tire needs repair," said Tom _____.
3. "My dog just had puppies," said Tom _____.
4. "Come in out of the rain," said Tom _____.
5. "We studied the body's circulatory system," said Tom ___

A. literally **B.** tartly **C.** dryly **D.** vainly **E.** flatly

Lesson Overview

Objective

- To become familiar with puns and Tom Swifties

Skills

- using prior knowledge to identify and infer meanings of puns and Tom Swifties; comparing and contrasting puns and Tom Swifties

Critical Thinking

- analyzing; defining and clarifying; comparing; contrasting

Listening and Speaking

- discussing and inventing puns

Teach

Discussion

Have students read Wordworks, page 791, and discuss these questions:

- What is the difference between a pun and a Tom Swifty?
- What makes puns and Tom Swifties funny?

Becoming Punsters

Have students create illustrated, captioned greeting cards based on puns or Tom Swifties. (Provide these examples: thank-you card based on *thin Q* or *ten Q;* card with Tom Swifty caption, *"We're having a geometry test tomorrow," said Rita squarely.*) **L2**

Practice and Assess

Answers: Try This Game

1. B, tartly
2. E, flatly
3. A, literally
4. C, dryly
5. D, vainly

Close

Explain to students that puns and Tom Swifties are examples of wordplay. Invite a volunteer to look up *wordplay* in the dictionary and share its meaning with the class.

Focus

Lesson Overview

Objective

- To learn more of the history of English in order to understand how and why the English language has grown

Skills

- using a dictionary to research word origins

Critical Thinking

- generating new information

Listening and Speaking

- discussing

Bellringer
Daily Language Activity

When students enter the classroom, have this assignment on the board: *Write down the names of three different cultures that you think could have contributed new words to English in North America after the United States became a country.*

See also *Daily Language Practice*

Teach

Learning New Words

Help students understand what happens when language is borrowed from other cultures by asking students if they have ever learned new words by talking to someone from a different place. (For example, *hoagie, hero,* and *sub* are the same kind of sandwich but are used in different parts of the U. S.) Discuss with students other ways that new words have come into their vocabulary. **L1**

22.4 Commerce, Culture, and Settlement

algebra

cipher

sugar

Throughout its early history, English acquired most of its new words from invaders and conquerors. By the Middle Ages, however, trade had led to peaceful contacts with distant cultures whose languages further enriched the English word bank.

When traders came back from the Middle East, their cargoes of exotic imports included sugar. In Middle English, sugar was called *sucre,* originally from the Arabic *sukkar.* Arabic was also the source of the name for the mathematical discipline of algebra, *al-jabr,* and for the numeral cipher, from the Arabic *sifr.* Later, commercial contacts with Spain added *vanilla (vainilla), brocade (brocado),* and *embargo (embargar)* to the English vocabulary.

Cultural Exchange

The exchange of goods between nations led inevitably to an exchange of culture. For example, William Shakespeare's *The Merchant of Venice* (1597) was based on a story written by the Italian author Giovanni Fiorentino. In contrast, Shakespeare's *Othello* (1604), adapted from an Italian story by Cinthio, was itself adapted in 1887 by Italian composer Giuseppe Verdi for his opera *Otello.* Such cultural exchanges, particularly in the field of music, led to cultural word borrowings in English. From Italian, English borrowed *stanza (stanza), studio (studio),* and *violin (violino).* Other English borrowed words are shown in the chart below.

Some English Borrowed Words

Language	Word	Date into English
French	shanty (chantier) depot (dépôt)	1822 1795
Dutch	cookie (koekje) snoop (snoepen)	1786 1832
German	quartz (quarz) nix (nichts)	1631 1789
Yiddish	bagel (beygel) klutz (klotz)	1932 1960
Italian	ravioli (ravioli) piano (pianoforte)	1611 1803
Spanish	alligator (el legarto) cannibal (canibal)	1568 1553

Resource Manager

Planning Resources
- *Lesson Plans*

Transparencies
- *Bellringer*
- *Daily Language Practice*

Other Print Resources
- *Vocabulary and Spelling Strategies and Practice,* p. 37

Settling North America

As English-speaking people settled North America, contact with Native Americans soon added new words to the settlers' vocabularies. From both the Natick and the Narraganset languages came *squash (askootasquash)* and from the Natick came *moccasin (mokussin)*. The chart below shows additional borrowings from Native American languages.

Borrowings from Native American Languages

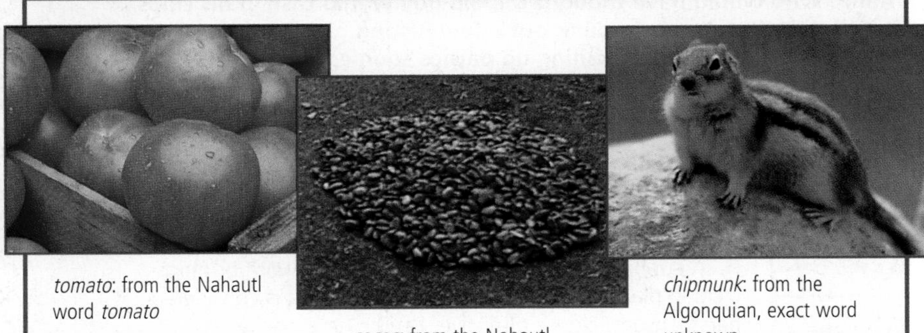

tomato: from the Nahautl word *tomato*

cocoa: from the Nahautl word *cacahautl*

chipmunk: from the Algonquian, exact word unknown

Native American languages were just one influence on the English settlers' speech. The Spanish who settled in what is now the southwestern United States added *corral (corral)* and *rodeo (rodear)*. The Dutch contributed *bakery (bakkerij)* and *sleigh (slee)*. Enslaved Africans brought to America added *gumbo* (from the Bantu *gombo*) and *banjo* (akin to Kimbundu *mbanza*).

Exercise 4

Look up the following words in a dictionary. From what language was each word borrowed?

1. coleslaw
2. afghan
3. delicatessen
4. lariat
5. moose
6. tycoon

Sources of English Words

Practice and Assess

Answers: Exercise 4

1. Dutch, *koolsla*
2. Pashto, *afghani*
3. German, *delikatessen*
4. Spanish, *la reata*
5. Algonquian or Natick, *moos*
6. Japanese, *taikun*

Additional Resources

Vocabulary and Spelling Strategies and Practice, p. 37

Close

Encourage students to continue to take advantage of the cultural richness of the United States to expand their vocabularies. Students might continue to discover interesting words from other languages by talking with one another; by reading cookbooks, menus, or travel literature; or by seeing foreign films with subtitles.

Enrichment and Extension

Borrowing Today

Discuss why English speakers adopted Native American names for the items pictured on this page. (There were no words in the English language to name them, so the settlers used the existing Native American words.) Can students name other items that have names that come from other cultures? (Examples include *bongo, bonsai, boomerang, croissant, falafel, futon, gibbon, gyros, kindergarten, karate, kiwi, koala, kung fu, okapi, panda, piranha, pistachio, sari, serape, sushi, tabouli, tamale, tortilla, tutu, umbrella.*)

Lesson Overview

Objective
- To become familiar with euphemisms

Skills
- using prior knowledge

Critical Thinking
- defining and clarifying; identifying attributes and components of euphemisms

Listening and Speaking
- discussing reasons behind familiar euphemisms

Teach

Discussion

Have students read Wordworks, page 794, and discuss the following question: Why do people invent euphemisms?

Discussing Euphemisms

Initiate a discussion about positive and negative functions that euphemisms serve in society. (positive—to avoid giving offense, to soften unpleasant facts; negative—to mask the truth, to gloss over discriminatory practices or policies) **L2**

Practice and Assess

Answers: Euphemistically Speaking

1. B, terminate
2. E, unhygienic
3. D, strategic withdrawal
4. A, intelligence gathering
5. C, underprivileged

Close

Ask students to name other familiar euphemisms as you list them on the board. (at liberty — unemployed; discomfort — pain; undesirable elements—unpopular people)

WORDWORKS

EUPHEMISMS

Burt's Gone West

"Well," said the young man with a sigh, "Burt bought the farm this morning. Who would have thought the old guy would cash in his chips so soon? His wife's been checking out a few resting places in the memorial park. We'll all be pushing up daisies soon enough."

No, this young man isn't talking about real-estate transactions, a poker game, or gardening. He's talking about death, an unpleasant subject that most people would just as soon avoid mentioning. When people talk about it, they often employ euphemisms to soften this unpleasant fact of life.

A euphemism is an agreeable or neutral word or phrase used in place of another word or phrase that is considered harsh, insensitive, or offensive. People have created euphemisms to cover a wide variety of subjects, especially anything having to do with the human body. The concern to avoid mention of the human body was taken to absurd lengths during the Victorian era.

The Victorian era, named for Queen Victoria of England, was characterized by extreme modesty and propriety. For example, not only was it considered indecent to display one's legs, it was even thought improper to say the word *leg.* Instead, Victorians said *limb. Belly* was another Victorian no-no. Much preferred were *tummy* and *breadbasket*.

At the dinner table, no proper Victorian, eyeing the roast chicken, would dream of shocking the other diners by requesting a breast or a thigh. *White meat* and *dark meat* became the accepted euphemisms.

Euphemistically Speaking

Try to match the words on the left with their euphemisms on the right.

1. fire	**A.** intelligence gathering
2. dirty	**B.** terminate
3. retreat	**C.** underprivileged
4. spying	**D.** strategic withdrawal
5. poor	**E.** unhygienic

Sources of English Words

22.5 New Technology and Ideas

Do you know what a *CAT scan* is? How about a *hantavirus*, a *velociraptor*, or *nanotechnology?* All of these words or phrases are fairly recent additions to the English vocabulary, made necessary by the advance of science and technology and the need to name and describe new things, ideas, and concepts.

As the world changes, so does English. New words are invented to name and describe space exploration, computers, medical science, social movements—any new aspect of any people's culture. The chart on page 796 shows some new words added to the English language.

CAT scan of human brain

Compounds and Blends

These new words arise through a variety of methods. Some are compounds, such as *meltdown*, which describes the uncontrollable burning of the fuel rods in a malfunctioning nuclear reactor. Another new compound is *cross-training,* a physical workout that combines several different types of exercise, such as running, swimming, weight lifting, and rowing.

Blending, another way new words are formed, occurs when parts of two or more words are blended into one. *Simulcast,* the process of broadcasting a program simultaneously on radio and television, is a blend of *simultaneous* and *broadcast*. *Jazzercise,* a popular form of aerobic dance, is a blend of *jazz* and *exercise.*

Acronyms

Acronyms are yet another way new words enter English. *CD,* for example, stands for *c*ompact *d*isc, a thin, round, silver-colored disk that contains laser-etched, digitally coded music and information. In 1963, when the U.S. Postal Service wanted to speed up delivery, the service urged that all mail include a ZIP code, for *z*one *i*mprovement *p*lan.

Focus

Lesson Overview

Objective

- To recognize and understand words that arise because of new technology or ideas

Skills

- recognizing new compounds and blends, acronyms, and new meanings for old words

Critical Thinking

- recalling; relating; analyzing; synthesizing; classifying; contrasting; comparing

Listening and Speaking

- discussing; explaining a process

Bellringer
Daily Language Activity

When students enter the classroom, have this assignment on the board: *Write what you think this sentence means: My laptop had a bug and crashed, so I used a hard copy to work on the spreadsheet.*

See also *Daily Language Practice*

Teach

Examining New Compounds

Help students locate unfamiliar compound words on this page and make the connection between the meaning associated with the parts of the word and the idea the compound represents. Encourage students to create their own compounds and blends to name familiar objects. Did it ever occur to them, for example, that a VCR might have been named an "SVT" (soundvision taper), or a water bed might have been named an "aquasleeper"? **L2**

Resource Manager

Planning Resources

- *Lesson Plans*

Transparencies

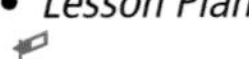

- *Bellringer*
- *Daily Language Practice*

Other Print Resources

- *Vocabulary and Spelling Strategies and Practice,* p. 37

Practice and Assess

Answers: Exercise 5

Responses will vary but should reflect an understanding of how new words are formed. The following list shows how words in certain fields or of specific types are sometimes formed:

- slang—blends of existing words with new meanings, abbreviated versions of existing words
- science fiction (books or movies)—new creations, compounds or blends
- product manufacturers—new creations, compounds or blends, existing words with new meanings
- technological advances—compounds or blends, acronyms, words with new meanings
- medicine and other sciences—acronyms, compounds or blends, eponymous creations

Additional Resources

Vocabulary and Spelling Strategies and Practice, p. 37

Close

Discuss how understanding compounds, blends, acronyms, and new word meanings can help students in their other classes, especially science and technological classes.

ASSESSMENT OPTIONS

Tests with Answer Key & Rubrics
Unit 22 Mastery Test, pp. 85–86

Testmaker
Unit 22 Mastery Test

You may wish to administer the Unit 22 Mastery Test at this point.

MindJogger Videoquizzes

Existing Words with New Meanings

Around the time of World War II, military scientists working with radar discovered short radio waves that travel in straight lines. They called this particular type of radio wave a microwave. Today, however, say *microwave* and most people assume you mean "a small oven that cooks food quickly using microwave radiation." The word has taken on a new meaning.

Launder is another such example. It has always meant "to wash in water." Today it also means "to 'cleanse' money obtained from illegal or disreputable sources." Similarly, *rap* once meant "to knock." Today, rap is a style of music based on rhymed verses spoken to a particular beat.

Words Added to English

	Word	Date	Source
Compounds and Blends	netiquette	1988	net (Internet) + etiquette
	three-peat	1988	three + repeat
	screen saver	1990s	screen + saver
Acronyms	RAM	1957	*r*andom *a*ccess *m*emory
	CD-ROM	1983	*c*ompact *d*isk *r*ead-*o*nly *m*emory
Existing Words, New Meanings	aerobics	1967	physical exercise designed to increase oxygen intake
	net	1990s	shortened form of *Internet,* often capitalized

Exercise 5

Make a list of new words you and your friends use in casual conversation. Most, if not all, of these words will be slang, but chances are they have their roots in other words. Which are completely new creations? Compounds or blends? Are any acronyms? Are any existing words with new meanings?

Cooperative Learning

Finding Words

Divide students into groups and assign each group a field, such as government, food, or electronics. Students can locate in magazines recent words related to their field and then make a card for each word, identifying it as a blend, compound, acronym, or an old word with a new meaning. Have groups meet to see how many different words they have. A spokesperson for each group can report findings to the class.

WORDWORKS

SLANG

Awesome, Daddy-O!

The scene: Lou's Short Orders Deluxe on a rainy Sunday in 1952. A woman walks in and seats herself at the counter. After a quick glance at the menu, she tells the waitress that she'd like two scrambled eggs on toast and some coffee. The waitress turns to the kitchen and yells, "Adam and Eve on a raft—wreck 'em—and a cup of jamoch!"

A young man who's already ordered toast and orange juice decides he'd like a couple of eggs as well. The waitress sighs and shouts to the cook, "Make that toast cackle!" A mother orders a hamburger for her daughter—"Hitch old Dobbin to a bun!" the waitress calls out.

Such colorful and inventive language was once part of the atmosphere in every American diner. The words and phrases are slang, popular, informal, faddish, and nonstandard speech. The use of slang is probably as old as language itself, but early examples of slang are difficult to document because most slang has a very brief life span. What is popular today is often long forgotten by tomorrow.

Consider a case in point. When you're leaving a party today, you might say "Catch you later" or "I'm outta here." In the 1960s, you would have said "Let's split"; in the 1940s, "Let's amscray" (pig Latin for "scram"); and in the Roaring Twenties, the popular expression was "Twenty-three skiddoo!" A few years from now, the expression will change again. That's the nature of slang.

Slang

1920 *the cat's meow* anything desirable

1940 *mess around* to kill time, hang out

1950 *dig* to understand

1960 *groovy* wonderful

1970 *far out* great, wonderful

1980 *excellent* first-rate

1990 *dis, or diss* to treat with disrespect or to criticize

Today

?

Generations of Slang

How have slang expressions changed over the years? You can find out by conducting a slang survey. First, make a list of popular slang expressions that you and your friends use. Assign each word to a category—such as "used when leaving," "means up-to-the-minute," and so on. Ask adults you know of different ages about comparable expressions from their youth. In a brief report, share your findings with the class.

Lesson Overview

Objective

- To become familiar with slang and how it changes over time

Skills

- recognizing and understanding slang expressions and their changes

Critical Thinking

- analyzing; synthesizing; recalling; inferring

Listening and Speaking

- discussing; interviewing; note taking; informal speaking; questioning

Teach

Discussion

Have students read Wordworks, page 797, and discuss the following questions:

- What are some slang expressions from the 1940s and 1960s?
- Why do you think that informal language changes over time but formal language stays much the same?

Using Slang Dictionaries

Students may enjoy browsing through a dictionary of slang. Many libraries have several. Have students find and share with the class outdated slang expressions they find amusing. **L2**

Practice and Assess

Evaluation Rubric: Generations of Slang

Responses will vary, but students should include the following:

- words that are clearly slang, rather than standard vocabulary
- slang with approximately the same meaning from different time periods

Close

Ask students why it's useful to be able to recognize when slang is being used. (It can help students use appropriate vocabulary in their formal speaking and writing.)

INTRODUCING

UNIT 23

Objectives

- To learn how to conduct a search for and locate books, periodicals, reference material, and other resources in a library
- To find sources for research and answers to questions by using library resources, including electronic databases

ASSESSMENT OPTIONS

Tests with Answer Key & Rubrics
Unit 23 Pretest, pp. 87–88

Testmaker
Unit 23 Pretest

You may wish to administer the Unit 23 Pretest at this point.

Key to Ability Levels

L1 Level 1 activities are within the basic ability range of students.

L2 Level 2 activities are within the ability range of average students.

L3 Level 3 activities are more challenging activities.

UNIT 23

Library Resources

LOG ON **Writing** Online — For research tools and additional skills practice, go to **glencoe.com** and enter QuickPass code WC97727p3.

Resource Manager

Planning Resources

- *Lesson Plans*
- *Block Scheduling*

Transparencies

- *Bellringer*
- *Daily Language Practice*

Other Print Resources

- *Tests with Answer Key and Rubrics*
- *Thinking and Study Skills*
- *Vocabulary and Spelling Strategies and Practice*

Video

- *MindJogger Videoquizzes*

Software

- *Presentation Plus!*
- *Testmaker*

Web Site

- *glencoe.com*

23.1 Library Arrangement

Modern libraries offer many resources. You can borrow a book to read for pleasure, or you can research a topic. You can take out DVDs, CDs, videotapes, and other recordings. Public libraries also provide Internet access. Many libraries offer services such as community information, reading programs, and evening classes. While each library is unique, the graphic below shows a typical library organization.

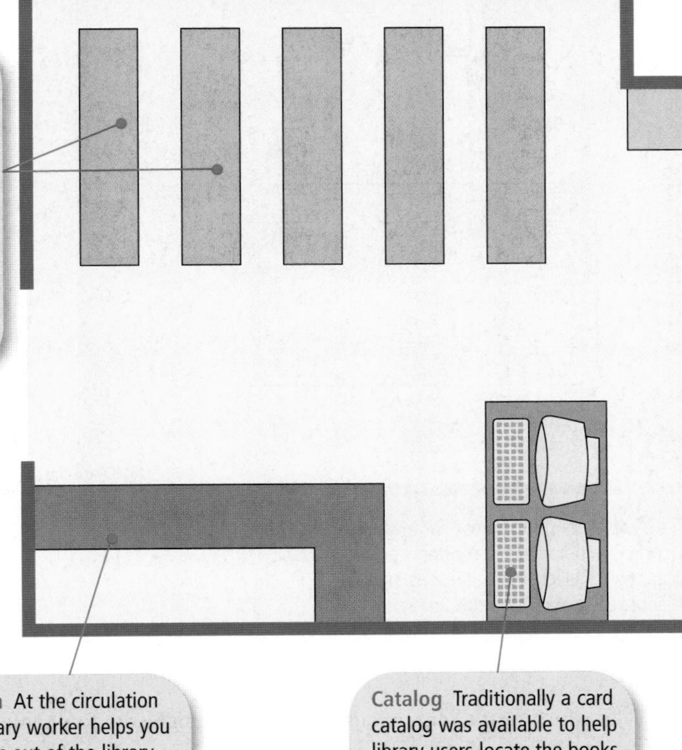

Stacks The stacks, or shelves, hold fiction and nonfiction books. Nonfiction books, which are based on fact, are written about subjects such as history, religion, technology, or literature. Fiction books are works of the imagination. They include novels and short story collections.
Circulation At the circulation desk, a library worker helps you check books out of the library. Generally, this is also the place where you return your materials and apply for a new card.
Catalog Traditionally a card catalog was available to help library users locate the books or materials they needed. Today a computer catalog provides such information.

Focus

Lesson Overview

Objectives

- To become familiar with the organization of libraries
- To become familiar with the use of library resources

Skills

- identifying common library resources; understanding how to locate and access library resources

Critical Thinking

- analyzing; categorizing; classifying; comparing

Listening and Speaking

- discussing; questioning; explaining a process

Bellringer
Daily Language Activity

When students enter the classroom, have this assignment on the board: *List the sections of a library that you would expect to utilize in doing a research project.*

See also  *Daily Language Practice*

Library Resources

Resource Manager

Planning Resources
- *Lesson Plans*

Transparencies
- *Bellringer*
- *Daily Language Practice*

Other Print Resources
- *Thinking and Study Skills,* pp. 6–7, 11
- *Vocabulary and Spelling Strategies and Practice,* pp. 18–22

Teach

Creating a Floor Plan

Help students create a floor plan of the school or local library, using labels such as *Fiction Stacks, Nonfiction Stacks, Reference, Computer Center, Circulation Desk,* and so on. You can ask the librarian for help or work from a map provided by the library. **L2**

Practice and Assess

Answers: Exercise 1

1. audiovisual section
2. reference section
3. periodical section
4. stacks
5. reference section
6. young adult and children's section

You may extend this exercise by naming other items and asking students to explain where in the library the items might be found.

Additional Resources

- *Vocabulary and Spelling Strategies and Practice,* pp. 18–22
- *Thinking and Study Skills,* pp. 6–7, 11

Close

Ask students to describe the school or local library resources and tell where the resource sections are located. Have them give examples of how they might use various resources to prepare a school assignment or personal project.

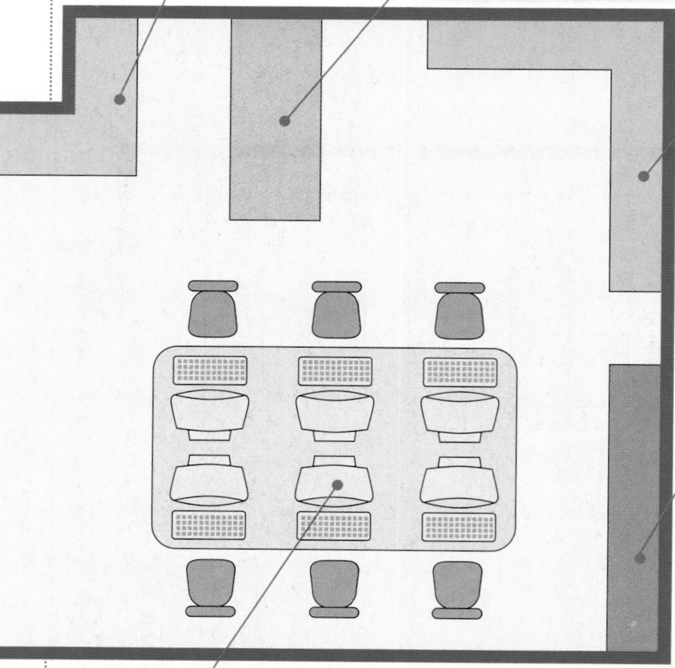

Young Adult and Children's Sections These sections contain books, magazines, and other materials which should appeal to young children and to teenagers.

Audiovisual Materials The library's audiovisual collection includes videos, compact discs, audiocassettes, and even computer software. Many audiovisual departments also have listening rooms.

Reference The reference section holds atlases, encyclopedias, dictionaries, almanacs, and other reference materials. Many of these resources are also available online. Most reference materials cannot be checked out. Reference librarians will answer your questions and help locate materials. They will also teach you how to use the print and online sources.

Periodicals Until the early 1990s, the periodicals section was the primary place in the library in which you could find periodicals—journals, newspapers, and magazines. Now many periodicals can be retrieved electronically. In the periodicals section, you will find current magazines and newspapers, as well as microfilm copies of older magazines and newspapers. Your library may offer computer indexes and electronic databases in this section as well as in the reference section.

Computers Today most libraries provide computers that offer access to electronic databases and indexes, as well as to the Internet.

Exercise 1

In which section or sections of the library might you find these items?

1. *Les Miserables* (a recording of the musical)
2. *Statistical Abstract of the United States*
3. *Newsweek,* an issue from 1969
4. *Ragtime* (a novel)
5. *Readers' Guide to Periodical Literature* (a database)
6. *Cricket* (magazine), an issue from 2008

Listening and Speaking

Exploring Audiovisual Resources

Many libraries contain a variety of audiovisual materials and the equipment needed to use them. Encourage students to explore the audiovisual section of the school or local library. They can use audiovisual materials to learn about life in another part of the world, to learn more about an admired or distinguished person, to practice a foreign language, to listen to a recording of a new or favorite story, and so on.

23.2 Locating Books and Other Resources

When searching for materials in the library, first identify what subject area you would like to research. Unit 7, Research Paper Writing, includes information on choosing an appropriate topic (see page 324). When doing library research, be as specific as possible. Instead of choosing the terms *History* and *War,* choose terms that are more specific to your research, such as *Vietnam War,* for example. Then decide on the best source to use to begin your research. For a general overview of a subject, choose an encyclopedia. For items currently in the news or for newsgroups on a topic, try the Internet first. The Internet often has the most up-to-date material, including daily newspapers, TV and radio transcripts, and current issues of many magazines.

If you have only a vague idea of your topic, try typing several keywords into the library catalog and then carefully read through the records that your search pulls up. When you find a likely book, locate its subject headings. (These will be displayed on the record.) Then search under that term to find more books on that topic.

Using an Online Catalog

Library catalogs allow you to search by author, title, subject, and keyword, among other options. If you know the title, start with that first for the most direct search. However, several books can have the same title. In libraries the word *subject* refers to a specific set of words selected by the Library of Congress. If you type *Texas Cooking* for a subject, you will find nothing because the heading actually should read *Cookery—Texas.* Whenever you come up with no results, try that same term in a keyword search. The keyword search will find many books on your topic; in fact, the keyword search will list all books that use the phrase in a title or a section. The main problem with keyword searches is that they often find too much, and some of what they find is not on target. Scan your results list for something similar to what you want; then open that record and find its Library of Congress subject heading. Now go back and search under that subject. Your results list should now be exactly what you want.

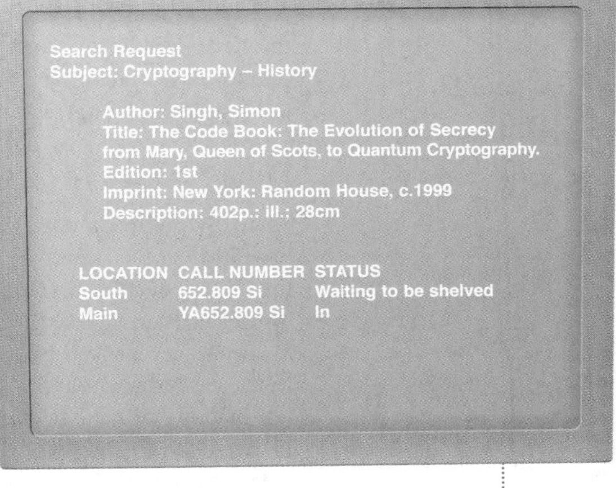

Search Request
Subject: Cryptography – History
Author: Singh, Simon
Title: The Code Book: The Evolution of Secrecy from Mary, Queen of Scots, to Quantum Cryptography.
Edition: 1st
Imprint: New York: Random House, c.1999
Description: 402p.: ill.; 28cm
LOCATION CALL NUMBER STATUS
South 652.809 Si Waiting to be shelved
Main YA652.809 Si In

Library Resources

Focus

Lesson Overview

Objective
- To become familiar with computer catalogs
- To become familiar with the Dewey Decimal System and the Library of Congress Classification System

Skills
- using alphabetical and numerical orders; classifying and categorizing information; identifying topics and main ideas

Critical Thinking
- analyzing; synthesizing; categorizing; classifying; comparing and contrasting; recognizing main ideas; evaluating criteria

Listening and Speaking
- discussing; questioning

Bellringer
Daily Language Activity

When students enter the classroom, have this assignment on the board: *List six categories under which you would expect to find library books classified.*

See also *Daily Language Practice*

Motivating Activity

Have students discuss their last research project. How effectively did they use the library catalog? What other information might they have used if they could have found it? Explain that in this unit, students will learn how to better identify and track down information.

Resource Manager

Planning Resources

- *Lesson Plans*

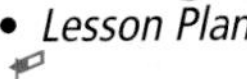

Transparencies
- *Bellringer*
- *Daily Language Practice*

Other Print Resources
- *Thinking and Study Skills,* pp. 6–7, 11
- *Vocabulary and Spelling Strategies and Practice,* pp. 18–22

Teach

Understanding How to Search

Have students choose a topic they might want to research and write it down on a piece of paper. Then ask them to write a list of synonyms for that topic. For a paper about ozone layer depletion, for example, the student might write: *climate, weather changes, global warming, ozone hole,* etc. Encourage them to use their topic as well as their synonyms to search an online catalog. Tell them to try both subject and keyword options. When their search leads them to a book that matches the focus of their report, have them check that book record for its subject headings. They should then add those subject headings to their list of synonyms and continue searching, using the new subject headings as they do so. **L2**

Cross-reference: Research

For more information on using library resources for research, refer students to Lesson 7.1, pp. 324–329.

Hints for a Good Search

1. Make sure that you are spelling the words correctly.
2. If you want only recent books, set your computer to search for books published in the last year or two years only. This is called limiting your search. You can also limit by format; that is, you can choose only books or only videos.
3. Try synonyms for your words.
4. Print out the call number for each record you have found. That way you won't forget the call number by the time you reach the stacks.

The catalog record gives a lot of information in a small space. Besides author, title, and publisher, you are also given the copyright date and the number of pages. The term *ill.* stands for illustrations. If you are searching for photos or drawings on a subject, make sure the book you choose has the symbol *ill.,* for illustrations, in its record. The listing *YA* or *YA Collection* means that the book will be found in the young adult section rather than the regular nonfiction shelf.

The online catalog also lists books in other branches of your library system. These books can probably be delivered for you. If the catalog says that a book is waiting to be shelved, ask a librarian to help you find it. If the book is checked out, you can place a *hold* on it. Then, when the book comes back, a library worker will save it for you.

Understanding Classification Systems

Once you have found the information you need in the catalog, you are ready to look for a specific book in a particular section of the library, often in the stacks. All libraries use a system to categorize their collections and physically organize their materials. Most libraries use either the Dewey decimal system or the Library of Congress classification.

Dewey Decimal System

In 1876 librarian Melvil Dewey created a system that groups books into ten broad categories based on general areas of thought and study. In a library using the Dewey decimal system, books are shelved according to the categories listed in the chart on page 803.

Books are shelved by their Dewey decimal call number and then by author. In the case of anthologies, the letters after the number will come from the title. For instance, for the book *Latino Voices,* the call number will be 860.8 La. The *La* comes from the first two letters of the title because this book has many authors instead of one.

Learning Disabled

Connecting Books and References

Some students may need help to understand the connection between a book and its computer catalog reference. Show students a library copy of Simon Singh's *The Code Book.* This is the book referenced in the model screen on page 801. Point out the book's call number and other bibliographic information. Help students locate the corresponding information on the model screen. **L1**

Dewey Decimal System			
CALL NUMBERS	**CATEGORY**	**EXAMPLES OF SUBCATEGORIES**	**SAMPLE TITLES**
000–099	Computers, information, and general reference	encyclopedias, computer books, journalism	*Outstanding Books for the College Bound* *Doing Documentary Work*
100–199	Philosophy	ethics, logic	*Enduring Issues in Psychology* *The Enigma of Personality*
200–299	Religion	theology, mythology	*Greek Myths* *Tao Te Ching*
300–399	Social Sciences	sociology, economics, education	*The Rise and Fall of the American Teenager* *Investing for Women*
400–499	Language	dictionaries, foreign languages	*American Sign Language* *French Lessons* *Dictionary of Slang*
500–599	Science	biology, math, physics	*Chasing Monarchs* *The Night Sky*
600–699	Technology	medicine, engineering, food technology (cooking)	*The Cake Bible* *Countdown: A History of Space Flight*
700–799	Arts and recreation	painting, photography, dance, recreation, sports	*From Satchmo to Miles* *Backcountry Snowboarding* *Star Trek Encyclopedia and Reference Guide*
800–899	Literature	poetry, plays, essays	*Latino Voices* *The Writer on Her Work*
900–999	History and Geography	ancient history, biography, travel	*Einstein* *The History of Mexico*

Some books will share the same call number. When they do, they will be filed next to each other, alphabetically by the author's last name. For instance, two books about African American Society will both be filed in the 301.45 section, but a book by W. E. B. DuBois would appear before a book by Henry Louis Gates.

Public libraries usually do not use call numbers for fiction books. Instead, they are shelved alphabetically by the author's last name. When the author has more than one book, the titles are shelved alphabetically. Some libraries have special sections for mystery, science fiction, and westerns. If you're not sure what collection the book belongs to, ask a librarian.

Understanding Call Numbers

To clarify how library items are classified (and therefore located), point out that the call numbers of books and other library resources, such as CDs and DVDs, are based on subject matter (as grouped by the Dewey decimal system or the Library of Congress classification system). For example, the Dewey decimal system category for a call number of a book about the moons of Jupiter would be 500–599. Suggest another general subject or specific book title and guide students in using the Dewey decimal system chart on this page to determine the numerical category of its call number. Then show students actual library books or copy the information from their spines onto the board and ask students to use the call numbers to identify the applicable major categories in the Dewey decimal system. **L2**

Discussing Classification

Help students to understand how subjects are classified by discussing why the subjects and books referred to in the Understanding Call Numbers note above were classified as they were. For example, students know that they study the planets in science, so the book about the moons of Jupiter would probably be classified under Sciences. Tell students that they can sometimes guess how a book is classified by determining what the book is probably not about (it is probably not about religion or literature, for example) and then eliminating those categories. **L3**

Connecting to Libraries

Tell students that many libraries make their catalogs available through the Internet. Have students use an Internet search engine to find out whether their local library's catalog is available online. Then have them brainstorm a list of libraries in other communities and search to see whether their catalogs are available online. Remind students that it is possible to borrow books from faraway libraries through the interlibrary loan service. Students can search online for books at other libraries and then ask their librarian to order the books for them from those locations.

Teach

Finding Related Books

Remind students that nonfiction books are shelved in numerical order by call number, based on the subject. Books on similar subjects are, therefore, shelved in the same area. Next to the book *African Roots of Jazz,* for example, will be other books about the general subject of jazz. In a school or local library, have students look up and locate a book on a favorite subject. Then have them look in the same general area for more books on the same subject. Discuss their discoveries with them. **L2**

Investigating the Library

With students, find out whether your school or local library uses the Dewey decimal system or the Library of Congress classification system. Then find out whether the library assigns call numbers to fiction books or labels them with a fiction symbol and organizes them alphabetically by author's last name. Ask students to go to the library and locate a fiction book by one of their favorite authors. **L1**

Library of Congress Classification

Very large libraries that have many books on a specific topic use a different classification scheme. If they did not, they would have hundreds or even thousands of books with the same call number. University libraries use the Library of Congress classification, or LC classification. This system divides books into twenty-one general categories. Each category is assigned a letter, as shown in the chart below.

Like the Dewey decimal system, the LC classification has subcategories, identified by additional letters and numbers. Look at the LC call number for the book *Planets* by Carl Sagan.

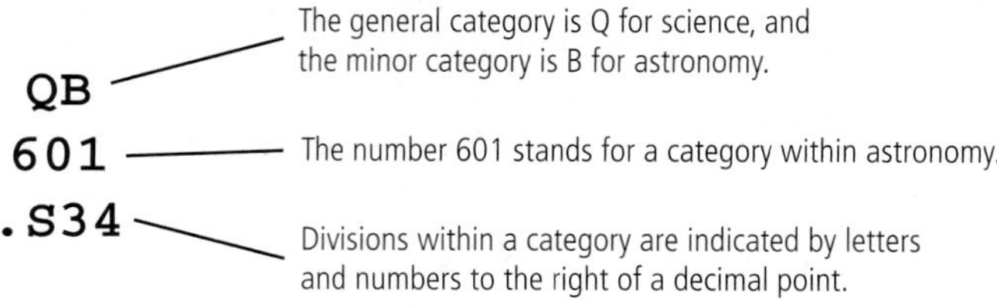
QB
601
.S34
The general category is Q for science, and the minor category is B for astronomy.
The number 601 stands for a category within astronomy.
Divisions within a category are indicated by letters and numbers to the right of a decimal point.

Library of Congress Classification System

CATEGORY LETTER	MAJOR CATEGORY	CATEGORY LETTER	MAJOR CATEGORY
A	General works	N	Fine arts
B	Philosophy, psychology, religion	P	Language and literature
C–F	History	Q	Science
G	Geology, anthropology, recreation	R	Medicine
H	Social sciences	S	Agriculture
J	Political science	T	Technology
K	Law	U	Military science
L	Education	V	Naval science
M	Music and books on music	Z	Bibliography , information resources (general)

Library Resources

Real World Connection

Learning About Cataloging

How do library books get categorized? Tell students that when a new book arrives at a library, it goes to a librarian called a cataloger. The cataloger first checks a list of Dewey decimal numbers prepared by the Library of Congress for newly published books. If no number has been assigned, the cataloger determines a general category number and then uses a detailed list of categories to assign a complete Dewey decimal call number. Since catalogers use personal judgment, the same book may have slightly different Dewey decimal call numbers in different libraries.

Special Sections

Libraries often have special sections for books. The symbols *R* or *REF* stand for reference. Reference books will be found in the reference section. Biographies are shelved in the B's, mysteries in the D's, and science fiction books in the SF section. Many libraries shelf new books in a special section; so if the record says *new* for its location, make sure that you find the stacks for new books and search there.

Exercise 2

Use the computer catalog to find a book for each of the following topics. List the author, title, call number, and publication date of the books you find.

1. How to create your own Web page
2. Black holes
3. Comedy writing
4. Indonesia
5. Ebola virus
6. A book by Gabriel García Márquez
7. An autobiography of Langston Hughes
8. Robots
9. A history of the Vietnam War
10. A book about haiku
11. Speeches by American presidents
12. A science fiction novel by Ursula LeGuin
13. Korean folktales
14. A book of herbal remedies
15. A car repair book
16. A book on pre-algebra
17. A collection of letters
18. A book on how to use the Internet
19. A memoir by a Chinese American
20. A collection of short stories by Edgar Allan Poe

Practice and Assess

Evaluation Rubric: Exercise 2

Answers will vary. Accept all complete answers. In some libraries, works of fiction—such as those by Gabriel García Márquez and Ursula K. LeGuin—may not have call numbers because they are filed alphabetically.

To extend this exercise, have students choose one or two items to locate, check out, and bring to class. Choose assignments that meet your classroom needs.

Additional Resources

- *Vocabulary and Spelling Strategies and Practice,* pp. 18–22
- *Thinking and Study Skills,* pp. 6–7, 11

Close

Ask students to list the steps they would follow to search for and locate a specific item in the library.

Technology Tip

Search Histories

The Search History section on the library's online catalog can be a helpful tool for students. This option compiles a history of the searches just performed, along with all records retrieved by those searches. Remind students to carefully review their search histories. Sometimes students will find helpful leads in them that they missed the first time around. The Search History also provides a quick review of what search terms yielded the best hits, or most successful finds.

Focus

Lesson Overview

Objective

- To become familiar with locating periodicals in a library

Skills

- using electronic databases to find periodicals; using the *Readers' Guide to Periodical Literature* to find periodicals in a library

Critical Thinking

- analyzing; categorizing; understanding main ideas

Listening and Speaking

- discussing; questioning

Bellringer

Daily Language Activity

When students enter the classroom, have this assignment on the board: *List five current-events topics that you think you could learn more about by reading newspapers or magazines.*

See also *Daily Language Practice*

Teach

Magazines Offline

Have students practice using the *Readers' Guide to Periodical Literature* to search for older publications. Ask students to pick a year from the 1980s or earlier and to browse the *Guide's* listings on a particular subject. For example, they may want to browse listings for immigration, space exploration, or fashion for the year they have chosen. Tell students that they will need the title of an article, the title and date of the publication in which it appears, and the page number of the article in order to be able to find it. Encourage students to find a copy of at least one article pertaining to their topic. **L2**

23.3 How to Search for Periodicals

Recent issues of newspapers, magazines, and journals are kept in the periodicals section. Most libraries keep a few years of back issues either bound or stored in folders. Older issues may be kept on microfilm. A microfilm, which looks like a long roll of photographic negatives, can store complete copies of a magazine or newspaper. To read microfilm, you need a special microfilm reader. If you are doing a report on an event that happened fifteen or more years ago, the library's microfilm sources may provide excellent background material. An article in an old magazine will have many details of the time and help you imagine what life was like in that period. Remember that older magazine articles will not be available online. To research older issues, you will need to use a printed index called *Readers' Guide to Periodical Literature.* Readers' Guide is also published as a database product and may be used online to search for articles from the mid-1980s onward.

Often you will search for periodicals online. Most libraries provide two different types of electronic databases: general periodical databases and databases specific to a subject. *eLibrary,* which searches newspapers, general magazines, maps, Web sites, multimedia files, and TV and radio transcripts, is an example of a multimedia database. *Literature Resource Center* is an example of a database that is focused on only one subject.

Although databases differ, they share common features. Most offer a basic search or a more advanced search. Each one will have a query screen where you need to type in your search term(s)—either one word or a search phrase. Sometimes you can search by subject or by keyword, sometimes only by keyword. Other databases allow you to use *natural language;* in other words, you can ask the question the way you would if talking to another person. Most online indexes will allow you to limit by date. This is very helpful when you are searching for only recent articles. Some databases will let you limit your search to *full-text* articles only. *Full text* means that the entire text of the article is available on the computer. Limits may also be applied to formats, for example, maps only.

The results of your search will be displayed either in chronological order or in order of *relevancy. Relevancy* means that the returns that have the closest relationship to your topic will be listed first. Look over your display results carefully. The display screen will tell you many things about the article, including the title, a brief summary of the article, the source, the date of the article, the length of the article, and the availability of photos or graphics.

Resource Manager

Planning Resources

- *Lesson Plans*

Transparencies

- *Bellringer*
- *Daily Language Practice*

Other Print Resources

- *Thinking and Study Skills,* pp. 6–7, 11
- *Vocabulary and Spelling Strategies and Practice,* pp. 18–22

Example of a Periodical Search

Look at the following sample. This search was done on a database called *MasterFILE Premier,* which searches many magazines and newspapers.

Screen 1

Enter subject terms or keywords in dialog box, set the limits you want, such as publication date, and click on "search." A sample search on the role of women in rap music is shown here.

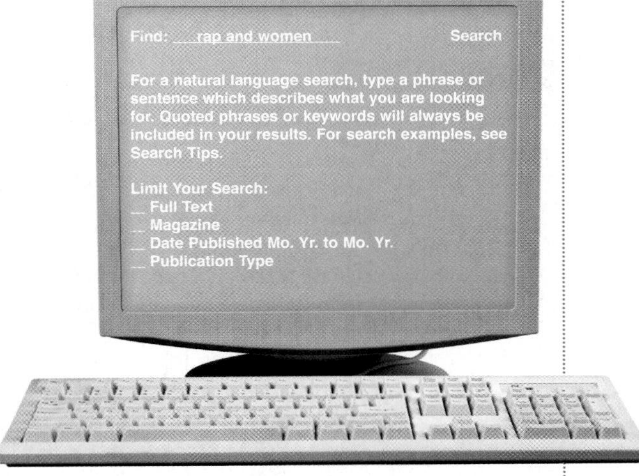

Screen 2

Here are results of the search above. The citations give you authors, article titles, magazine names, and publication dates. Links to the full text of the articles are given below. You may choose from various file formats such as HTML or PDF and may print the articles you want at the library or e-mail them to yourself to use at home.

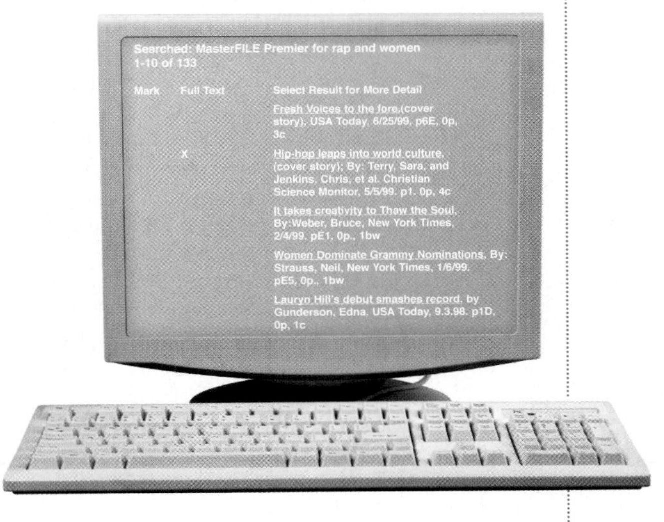

Practice and Assess

Answers: Exercise 3 *(page 808)*

1. Yes. Answers will vary.
2. one, "Hip-hop leaps into world culture"
3. all of them
4. "Hip-hop leaps into world culture" contains four color photographs.
5. "Fresh voices to the fore" and "Hip-hop leaps into world culture"

Additional Resources

- *Thinking and Study Skills,* pp. 6–7, 11
- *Vocabulary and Spelling Practice,* pp. 18–22

Close

Ask students to locate articles about the same subject they selected for the Magazines Offline activity on page 806. This time, however, students should search for articles that have appeared within the last few years, using an electronic periodical database. Ask students to note how many steps it takes to locate the full text of an article using an electronic database. Then ask how many steps it took to locate the full text of an article using the *Readers' Guide to Periodical Literature.* Which way of searching did they feel was most helpful overall?

Library Resources

MEETING INDIVIDUAL NEEDS

English Language Learners

Databases in the Spanish Language

Modern libraries offer a wide selection of databases that index many kinds of magazines and other materials. If you live in an area where Spanish is spoken widely, there is a good chance your public library will carry a database that provides indexing for Spanish language periodicals. A Spanish language database provides access in Spanish to the most popular Spanish language titles, including many Hispanic magazines.

Focus

Lesson Overview

Objectives
- To become familiar with library reference works
- To become familiar with online reference sites

Skills
- using reference works to answer questions; using books and the Internet effectively

Critical Thinking
- analyzing; synthesizing; categorizing; identifying main ideas

Listening and Speaking
- discussing; questioning; explaining process

Bellringer
Daily Language Activity

When students enter the classroom, have this assignment on the board: *Suppose that you are going to write a report on the impact of the speeches of Dr. Martin Luther King Jr. List two types of reference sources you think that you might use.*

See also *Daily Language Practice*

Teach

Using Reference Works

Discuss with students how they might use reference works such as general and biographical encyclopedias, biographies, and newspapers and magazines of Dr. Martin Luther King Jr.'s time to write the report mentioned in the Bellringer activity. Mention that some libraries and Internet sites also have recordings of King's speeches. **L2**

Other Computerized Indexes

Other specialized databases allow you to search for materials on specific subjects, such as biography, sociology, art, science, or literature. *Social Issues Resources Series (SIRS)* allows you to search for a topic from a sociological perspective, such as single parenting, drug abuse, or pollution. *Literature Resource Center* allows you to research authors, literary themes, and information about specific literary works.

Exercise 3

Look at the display results from the search on *rap and women* to answer the following questions:

1. Did the searcher use a natural language query in this search? Give an example of a natural language search you would use for a topic of your choice.
2. How many articles have full text? List the article or articles that have full text.
3. What articles are less than a page long?
4. What article contains the most color photographs? How many does it contain?
5. What article or articles are cover stories?

23.4 Using Reference Sources

General reference works, such as encyclopedias and almanacs, can answer many of your reference questions easily and quickly. Almanacs are good for simple reference questions, such as "Who was the fifteenth president of the United States?" or "How much does it cost to mail a letter to China?" Almanacs also provide good information about events that occurred in the past year. Encyclopedias give a thorough overview of a topic. They also provide bibliographies. A bibliography is a list of books or materials on a specific topic. Online versions of encyclopedias are available at most libraries. In addition to text, online encyclopedias provide film clips, photos, and audio clips. Since online encyclopedias are updated frequently, they provide information that is more current than the print versions.

Internet reference sites also can answer many reference questions. One advantage of these sites is that they are available twenty-four hours a day. You can use them on your home computer if you have Internet access. One disadvantage of these sites is that there are no librarians available to help you find the information you need quickly. Examples of excellent online reference sites include *The Internet Public Library*, sponsored by the School of Information at the University of Michigan, and *Thor: The Virtual Reference Desk +*, the online resource site of Purdue University Library, hosted by the College of Information Science and Technology at Drexel University and the Virtual Reference Shelf maintained by the Library of Congress.

The chart on page 809 gives examples of some widely used reference resources, many of which can be found both in print and online.

Resource Manager

Planning Resources
- *Lesson Plans*

Transparencies
- *Bellringer*
- *Daily Language Practice*

Other Print Resources
- *Thinking and Study Skills*, pp. 6–7, 11
- *Vocabulary and Spelling Strategies and Practice*, pp. 18–22

Using General Reference Works to Answer Questions		
QUESTION	**WHERE TO LOOK FOR AN ANSWER**	**EXAMPLES OF SOURCES TO CHECK**
Were any Civil War battles fought in Indiana?	**Encyclopedias** include general information on a variety of topics.	• *Grolier Online* • *World Book Encyclopedia* • *Encyclopaedia Britannica*
Who were the recipients of Pulitzer Prizes in letters for fiction and for general nonfiction in 1989?	**Almanacs** and **yearbooks** provide statistics, lists, and detailed information on recent issues.	• *Information Please Almanac* • *Guinness Book of World Records*
What is the coldest month of the year in Lima, Peru?	**Atlases** are collections of maps. They often include special maps on climate, land use, history, and other features.	• *Hammond Comparative World Atlas* • *Times Atlas of World History* • *Cambridge Atlas of Astronomy*
Where was Ernest Hemingway born?	**Biographical reference works** include short life histories of noteworthy individuals, both living and deceased.	• *Merriam-Webster's Biographical Dictionary* • *Current Biography* • *Cambridge Dictionary of American Biography*

Specialized Reference Sources

Other reference sources target more specific subject areas. *McGraw-Hill Concise Encyclopedia of Science and Technology*, available both in print and online, is one source for scientific information. *Columbia Granger's Index to Poetry*, available both in print and online, will help you find a specific poem. *Statistical Abstract of the United States* will give you statistics on various topics.

The Internet

The Internet is a valuable resource for doing research. Not only does the Internet provide the most current news, but it also supplies the full text of speeches and laws and excerpts of many books. On the Internet, you can search for the title of a new book. You can also search the catalogs of world-class libraries, such as the Library of Congress and the New York Public Library. You can visit the National Gallery in Washington, D.C., and see portraits of all the presidents.

However, when researching the Internet, you must be very careful to check for accuracy. Information on the Internet may be unreliable. Whenever you are surveying a Web site for information, always evaluate what you see. Ask yourself the following questions:

1. Is the material authoritative? Who sponsors this site? Is the sponsor a government agency, a business promoting its own products, a nonprofit organization, or a private individual? The most reliable sites are sponsored by government agencies, universities, libraries, and similar organizations.
2. How current is the information? A site that has not been updated for three years may be too old for your purposes.

How to Search a Reference Book

Tell students that using a book's index—especially a reference book's index—is vital. The index provides a quick, concise listing of all the pages where information on a topic will be found. If you have one or more reference books available, give them to volunteers. Tell each volunteer to look in the index and describe what he or she notices. Draw students' attention to any bold text or bold page numbers. Tell them that these markers usually indicate where the most relevant information will be found, so students should search those pages first. **L1**

*inter***NET** CONNECTION

Wikipedia

Wikipedia is a free online encyclopedia that accepts contributions by volunteers from around the world. When articles are posted, other readers are invited to review them and suggest corrections and additions. Articles are then revised in collaboration with the original authors. In this way, Wikipedia has grown to be one of the largest and most used sites on the Internet. Users are cautioned against relying solely on Wikepedia as a source, however, because errors sometimes have been discovered in posted articles.

Practice and Assess

Answers: Exercise 4

1. Helen Mirren won the Academy Award for best actress in 2007 for her role in *The Queen.*
2. No, Herod was the name of a ruling family in Palestine during the last century B.C. and the first century A.D. Herod Antipas was the son of Herod the Great. Both were known to be cruel rulers.
3. Mt. Kilimanjaro is located in northern Tanzania about 140 miles south of Nairobi, Kenya, in Africa.
4. Guatemala's chief export crops are coffee, bananas, sugar cane, and a spice called cardamom. Corn is the major domestic crop.
5. T. S. Eliot wrote "The Waste Land."
6. Roger Bannister of Great Britain was the first person on record to run the mile in less than four minutes. He did this in 1954.
7. Pluto was the planet most recently discovered. It was discovered in 1930.
8. Hank Aaron retired as a baseball player in 1976.
9. Yugoslavia, Slovenia, and Macedonia lie in Europe across the Adriatic Sea from Italy.
10. The population of the United States as of July 1, 2007 was estimated by the United States Census Bureau to be 300,913.000.

Additional Resources

Thinking and Study Skills, pp. 6–7, 11

Vocabulary and Spelling Strategies and Practice, pp. 18–22

Close

Ask students to name the types of library materials they might use in gathering information for a report.

3. Look over the screens. Are there many errors, misspellings, typos? If so, the person may have been careless with the accuracy of the information as well.
4. Is the site easy to navigate? Or are you lost in a sea of words and images?
5. Are there links to other helpful sites? Although this isn't absolutely necessary, the linking feature is an important and useful addition.

Online Search Terms	
ABSTRACT	A summary of an article or information source.
DATABASE	A collection of information resources that can be searched electronically. Some databases, such as Biography Index, search only a specific subject; others, such as Nexus/Lexus search all subjects.
DISCUSSION GROUPS	An online location where you can ask questions or discuss problems and current events. Discussion groups exist on almost every topic, such as the environment, pets, music, and sports.
HIT	The term for a successful result after you have searched online.
FULL TEXT	Indication that the entire article is present online. However, sometimes full-text articles do not include charts and graphics.
INTERNET	A computer network that is composed of many smaller computer networks. The Internet is the largest computer network in the world.
RELEVANCY	In computer searching, how closely your search results answer your search query. Many databases and search engines display results in a hierarchy from the most relevant to the least. These relevancy relationships are usually given in percentages.
SEARCH ENGINE	Computer software that browses the Internet for places where your words appear. Examples are Google, MSN, Ask, and Yahoo! Search.
URL	Acronym for Universal Resource Locator. An address for a Web site that contains the domain name, directory name, and Web page name.
WORLD WIDE WEB	The part of the Internet that provides information in various formats, including print, sound, photos, graphics, and video. Links allow you to move within a Web site or from Web site to Web site.

Exercise 4

Use the Internet or a print resource in your school library to answer five of the following questions.

1. Who won the Academy Award for best actress in 2007?
2. Were the historical figures Herod and Herod Antipas (from Roman times) the same person? Explain.
3. Where is Mount Kilimanjaro?
4. What are Guatemala's chief crops?
5. Who wrote the poem "The Waste Land"?
6. Who was the first person on record to run one mile in less than four minutes?
7. Which planet was the most recently discovered?
8. When did Hank Aaron retire as a baseball player?
9. Where are the nations of Yugoslavia, Slovenia, and Macedonia?
10. What was the population of the United States in 2007?

ASSESSMENT OPTIONS

Tests with Answer Key & Rubrics
Unit 23 Mastery Test, pp. 89–90

Testmaker
Unit 23 Mastery Test

You may wish to administer the Unit 23 Mastery Test at this point.

MindJogger Videoquizzes

Meeting Individual Needs: English Language Learners

Understanding Reference Books

Provide and name several examples of general and specific reference works such as those mentioned on page 809. Open each book and display examples of its contents. Then point out and name the various parts of one of the books, such as the title page, copyright page, table of contents, and index. Clearly and simply define what each book part does or contains. Ask students to identify some of the book parts in this textbook.

UNIT 24

UNIT 24 Using Dictionaries

LOG ON Writing Online | For research tools and additional skills practice, go to glencoe.com and enter QuickPass code WC97727p3.

Objectives

- To develop an understanding of the functions and conventions of dictionaries and thesauruses
- To use dictionaries and thesauruses to find definitions, etymologies, usage information, and synonyms

ASSESSMENT OPTIONS

Tests with Answer Key & Rubrics
Unit 24 Pretest, p. 91

Testmaker
Unit 24 Pretest

You may wish to administer the Unit 24 Pretest at this point.

Key to Ability Levels

L1 Level 1 activities are within the basic ability range of students.

L2 Level 2 activities are within the ability range of average students.

L3 Level 3 activities are more challenging activities.

Resource Manager

Planning Resources
- *Lesson Plans*
- *Block Scheduling*

Transparencies

- *Bellringer*
- *Daily Language Practice*

Other Print Resources

- *Tests with Answer Key and Rubrics*
- *Vocabulary and Spelling Strategies and Practice*

Video
- *MindJogger Videoquizzes*

Software

- *Presentation Plus!*
- *Testmaker*
- *Vocabulary Power Puzzlemaker*

Web Site

- *glencoe.com*

Focus

Lesson Overview

Objective

- To understand and be able to use the information in a dictionary

Skills

- using dictionaries to locate word meanings, synonyms, homonyms, syllabication, cross-references, and usage rules

Critical Thinking

- defining and clarifying

Listening and Speaking

- discussing

Bellringer

Daily Language Activity

When students enter the classroom, have this assignment on the board: *List five types of information you can locate in a dictionary.*

See also *Daily Language Practice*

Motivating Activity

Read aloud the following quote from Lewis Carroll's *Alice in Wonderland:* "When I use a word . . . it means just what I choose it to mean." Ask, What might happen if everyone felt this way? (People would have difficulty communicating with one another.) Discuss how dictionaries help people use a common set of definitions to communicate more effectively. Then examine the other types of information found in dictionaries that students listed in the Bellringer activity above.

24.1 General Dictionaries

Through its alphabetical listing of words with their definitions, called entries, dictionaries can tell you about almost everything. Most dictionaries fall into one of the categories below.

Unabridged Dictionaries
250,000 or more entries

Characteristics	Examples
• Extensive word histories • Detailed definitions • May be in several volumes • Found mostly in libraries	• *Random House Webster's Unabridged Dictionary* • *Webster's Third New International Dictionary*

College Dictionaries
About 150,000 entries

Characteristics	Examples
• Detailed enough to answer most questions on spelling or definitions • Widely used in schools, homes, and businesses	• *Random House Webster's College Dictionary* • *American Heritage Dictionary of the English Language* • *Webster's New World College Dictionary*

School Dictionaries
90,000 or fewer entries

Characteristics	Examples
• Definitions based on students' backgrounds • Emphasis on common words	• *Macmillan Dictionary for Students* • *Merriam-Webster's School Dictionary*

The Organization of Entries

With many entries to search through, how do you find the one you want? Guide words, the first and last words listed on the page, can help you locate entries much more quickly than if you simply browse. The sample dictionary page on page 813 shows the organization of word entries and how to use guide words and the pronunciation key.

Resource Manager

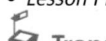

Planning Resources

- *Lesson Plans*

Transparencies

- *Bellringer*
- *Daily Language Practice*

Other Print Resources

- *Vocabulary and Spelling Strategies and Practice*

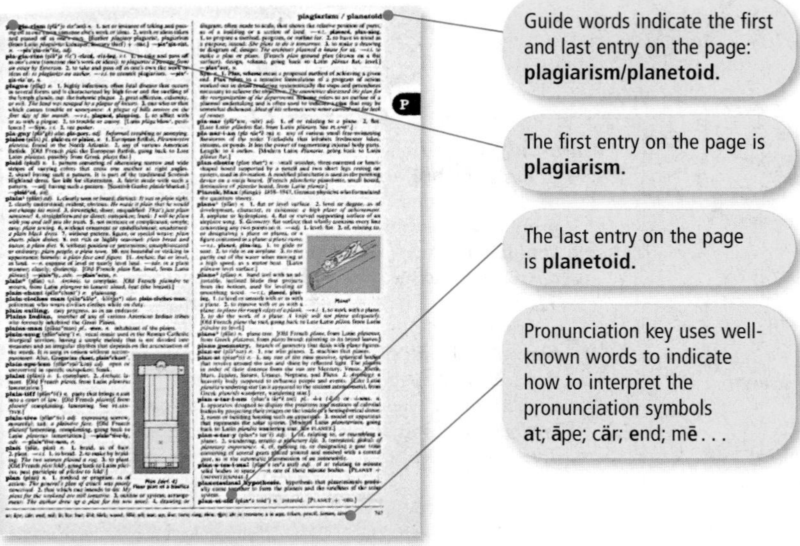
Guide words indicate the first and last entry on the page: **plagiarism/planetoid.**
The first entry on the page is **plagiarism.**
The last entry on the page is **planetoid.**
Pronunciation key uses well-known words to indicate how to interpret the pronunciation symbols **at; āpe; cär; end; mē . . .**

If you do not know how to spell a word, you can usually find it in a dictionary if you try to sound it out. You may also want to look at the tips for improving your spelling presented in Unit 26. The following tips suggest other ways of finding unfamiliar words.

Tips on Finding Unfamiliar Words

1. Consider whether the word contains silent consonants. They might appear at or near the beginning of a word, such as *k* in *knife* and *h* in *rhyme.* Silent consonants may also appear in the middle of a word, such as *b* in *debt* and *gh* in *night.*
2. Consider alternative spellings of consonants. For example, the *sh* sound can be spelled several ways, as in these words: *ocean, tissue, election, chandelier, special, conscious,* and *sugar.*
3. Consider alternative spellings of vowels. Some vowel sounds are formed by combinations of vowels, such as the *ā* sound in *paid, suede, eight, obey,* and *break.*
4. Check a larger dictionary. Even if you have the right spelling in mind, a school dictionary may not contain the word you need. If you can't find the word in a college or unabridged dictionary, try the above tips again.

The Main Entries

The main part of a dictionary consists of word entries and their definitions. Other information is given as well. The entry for *forbid* on the next page shows some of the main information in an entry.

Using Dictionaries

Teach

Using a Dictionary

Say the word *lexicographer* aloud. Explain to students that in order to find this word in a dictionary, they should be able to spell it correctly. But what if they don't know how to spell the word *lexicographer?* Have students discuss possible ways to spell *lex* (*lex, lecs, leks, lecks*), *cog* (*kog, cog*), and *graph* (*graf, graph*). Have students locate *lexicographer* in the dictionary, tell how it is spelled, and give its meaning. ("one who compiles a dictionary") **L2**

Pronouncing New Words

Have each student locate an unusual word in a dictionary. Provide words such as *somatotype* and *ephemeral.* Then tell each student to say the unusual word aloud several times. Have others listen carefully to the pronunciation and then use the pronunciation key to spell the entry for the word. **L1**

Exploring Language

History

In 1604, schoolmaster Robert Cawdrey compiled the first known English dictionary, titled *The Table Alphabeticall of Hard Words.* The dictionary defined only difficult English words, all 3,000 of which had been borrowed from other languages. It wasn't until 1755 that Samuel Johnson published a dictionary that attempted to include all English words.

Teach

Using Specialized Vocabulary

Tell students to choose a subject that they know something about but with which others may be unfamiliar. Offer suggestions such as guitar playing or botany. Ask them to think of specialized words pertaining to that subject and to use those words in sentences. Have others look up the specialized words and explain the meanings of the sentences. **L2**

Understanding Parts of a Dictionary

Write these names of dictionary parts on the board: *entry word, pronunciation, inflected forms, part of speech, etymology, definitions, synonyms.* Referring to the sample entry on this page, discuss with students the information given in each part and its usefulness in various contexts. **L2**

The entry word is listed first.

The pronunciation is indicated by symbols.

Inflected forms, such as past tense and past participle for a verb, are sometimes listed.

The part or parts of speech that the word takes are indicated.

The etymology explains the history of a word.

for•bid (fər bid′, fôr-) **-bade** (-bad′, -bād′) or **-bad** (-bad′), **bid•den** or *(archaic)* **-bid, -bid•ding,** *v.t.* **1.a.** to command (someone) not to do something; refuse to allow: *I forbid you to go out.* **b.** to prohibit (something); ban: *to forbid the wearing of makeup.* **2.** to command to keep away from; bar or exclude from: *I forbid you the car.* **3.** to stand in the way of or make impossible; hinder; prevent: *The snowstorm forbids air travel.* [Old English *forbēodan* to prohibit, restrain.]

Syn. 1. Forbid, prohibit mean to order that something not be done. **Forbid** suggests a direct command from an authority who expects to be obeyed: *The airline forbids smoking on takeoff and landing.* **Prohibit** implies a legal order, as by statute, or a less arbitrary command: *The law prohibits smoking on the subways.*

Syllabication The entry word indicates how to divide, or hyphenate, a word of more than one syllable. Notice how *for•bid* is divided by the dot. A word entry may also indicate when a word is a solid compound, such as *folklore;* a hyphenated compound, such as *follow-up* when used as a noun or an adjective; or two words, such as *folk song.*

Synonyms When an entry includes synonyms, words with similar meanings, it often also includes examples to help you distinguish between the meanings. Compare the synonyms *forbid* and *prohibit* in the example above.

Homographs Words that are spelled the same but have different meanings and histories are called homographs. They are listed separately and identified by small, raised numerals after the word. If pronunciation varies between different homographs, these pronunciations are noted in the entry. Two separate entries are listed below for *meal.*

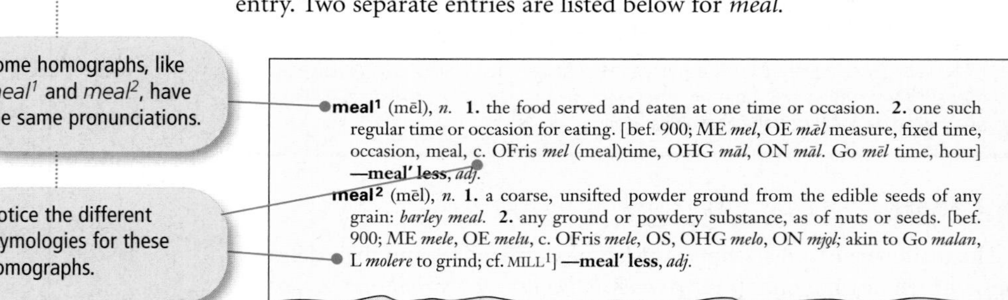
Some homographs, like meal¹ and meal², have the same pronunciations.
Notice the different etymologies for these homographs.

meal¹ (mēl), *n.* **1.** the food served and eaten at one time or occasion. **2.** one such regular time or occasion for eating. [bef. 900; ME *mel,* OE *mǣl* measure, fixed time, occasion, meal, c. OFris *mel* (meal)time, OHG *māl,* ON *māl.* Go *mēl* time, hour] **—meal′ less,** *adj.*

meal² (mēl), *n.* **1.** a coarse, unsifted powder ground from the edible seeds of any grain: *barley meal.* **2.** any ground or powdery substance, as of nuts or seeds. [bef. 900; ME *mele,* OE *melu,* c. OFris *mele,* OS, OHG *melo,* ON *mjǫl;* akin to Go *malan,* L *molere* to grind; cf. MILL¹] **—meal′ less,** *adj.*

Using Dictionaries

MEETING INDIVIDUAL NEEDS

English Language Learners

Using Bilingual Dictionaries

Some students may benefit from instruction in how to use dictionaries that translate words to and from English. Provide several of these dictionaries and help students understand how best to use them. Pair students who are learning English with those who are fluent, and have them take turns offering words that are unfamiliar to their partner and looking up the unfamiliar words.

Cross-references The entry for *depreciate* lists a cross-reference to *deprecate.* The usage information for *deprecate* shows you that *depreciate* and *deprecate* sometimes have the same meaning; however, *deprecate* has almost totally replaced *depreciate* in certain situations.

> **de·pre·ci·ate** (di prē′ shē āt′), *v.*, **-at·ed, -at·ing.** —*v.t.* **1.** to reduce the purchasing value of (money). **2.** to lessen the value or price of. **3.** to claim depreciation on (a property) for tax purposes. **4.** to represent as of little value or merit; belittle. —*v.i.* **5.** to decline in value. [1640–50; < LL *dēpretiātus* undervalued, ptp. of *dēpretiāre* (in ML sp. *dēpreciāre*) = L *dē-* DE- + *-pretiāre*, der. of *pretium* PRICE + *-ātus* -ATE[1]] **—de·pre′ci·at′ing·ly,** *adv.* **—de·pre′ci·a′tor,** *n.* **—Usage.** See DEPRECATE.

Cross-references direct you to other main entries for information that may help you understand a word's meaning and when to use it.

> **dep·re·cate** (dep′ ri kat′), *v.t.*, **-cat·ed, -cat·ing.** . . . **—Usage.** The most current sense of DEPRECATE is "to express disapproval of." In a sense development still occasionally criticized. DEPRECATE has come to be synonymous with the similar but etymologically unrelated word DEPRECIATE in the sense "belittle": *The author deprecated the importance of his work.* In *self-* compounds, DEPRECATE has almost totally replaced DEPRECIATE in modern usage: *She charmed the audience with a self-deprecating account of her career.*

Usage information explains the differences between the uses of certain words.

Usage Information Some definitions may be preceded by usage labels. These labels indicate when to use a particular definition of a word. For example, the label "baseball" appears before a definition of the term *hit-and-run.* The label tells you that the definition that follows is used only when describing a baseball play. The following chart describes different kinds of usage information.

Usage Information in Dictionary Entries

TYPE OF INFORMATION	DESCRIPTION	EXAMPLE
Capitalization	Indicates when a word or a particular meaning of a word needs to be capitalized	**southeast . . . 3. the Southeast.** southeastern part of the United States.
Out-of-date usage	Labels words as obsolete—no longer used—or archaic—once used commonly but now used only in special contexts	**quick . . . 1.** *Archaic.* living; alive.
Special field usage	Indicates with subject labels a definition that is restricted to a particular study or area of reference	**fly^2. . . 8.** *Baseball.* to hit a fly ball.
Regional usage	Indicates how a word is used in a certain geographical area	**tonic . . . 5.** *Chiefly Eastern New Eng.* soda pop.
Usage note	Provides general guides for using (or not using) words in particular situations	**scorcher . . . 2.** *Informal.* an extremely hot day.

Using Dictionaries

Cross–reference: Grammar

For more information on the use of hyphens in compound words and on how to divide words of more than one syllable, refer students to Lesson 21.12, pp. 762–764.

MEETING INDIVIDUAL NEEDS

Learning Disabled

Recognizing How Words Are Used

Help students locate and identify usage notes in a dictionary. Explain that a word may have both a formal and an informal or slang usage. Have students look up the word *bad.* Discuss with students its out-of-date usage, its slang usage, and any other usage notes on the word. If possible, students should use different dictionaries and compare usage notes. **L1**

Practice and Assess

Answers: Exercise 1

1. *heroes*
2. Answers will vary according to the dictionary used.
3. In rugby, *try* is a "scoring play similar to a touchdown in football"; also "the score made on such a play."
4. The definition of "free from bias" or "light in coloring" comes from the Old English *faeger*, meaning "beautiful or pleasing." The definition "an exhibition" comes from the Old French *feire*, meaning "market"; from Late Latin *feria*; and from Latin *feriae*, meaning "holidays."
5. No. The term *Draconian* refers to Draco, an Athenian lawmaker, or his code of laws. The term *draconian* refers to something that is severe or harsh.

Additional Resource

Vocabulary and Spelling Strategies and Practice

Close

Ask students to summarize the kinds of information available in dictionaries. Initiate a discussion about when they might need to know each kind of information. Have them tell where they can find various kinds of dictionaries in your classroom, school, or local library.

Other Information in Dictionaries

In addition to a greater number of word entries, some larger dictionaries include separate biography and geography sections. A biography section alphabetically lists names of important people and provides brief details about them. Names of cities, countries, and other geographical areas and information about them are alphabetically listed in the geography section. These sections usually appear at the back of the dictionary, after the main entries.

Accessing Dictionaries on Computers

You can obtain CD versions of many major dictionaries. You can also access numerous dictionaries on the Internet. Using an online dictionary, you simply enter a search word to find its definition. Often, even an illustration is provided. Online dictionaries may offer features such as help with spelling your search word, word games, audio pronunciations, and amusing facts about words. Some online dictionary services allow access to numerous general and specialized dictionaries in one search.

Exercise 1

Use a school or college dictionary to answer the following questions.

1. What is the plural of *hero?*
2. What are the guide words for the page on which *hakim* is listed?
3. What does *try* mean in the game of rugby?
4. What are the origins of the two homographs of *fair?*
5. Is *Draconian* always capitalized? Explain your answer.

24.2 Thesauruses

One special type of dictionary is a collection of synonyms, also known as a thesaurus. Such a book can help a writer choose just the right word in a given context. Even though a thesaurus is a type of dictionary, it is used in the opposite way from most dictionaries. You usually refer to a dictionary to find the meaning of a certain word. You refer to a thesaurus when you know the meaning you want to convey but need a specific word to express that meaning.

You can also access thesauruses on CDs, on the Internet, and even on some word processing software.

Thesaurus Formats

The best-known thesaurus was first developed by British doctor Peter Mark Roget, in 1852. Roget's *Thesaurus of English Words and Phrases* organized large

Real World Connection

Using Spelling Dictionaries

Electronic handheld dictionaries are available. Using an alphabetical keyboard, the user enters the possible spelling of a word. In response, the device displays a limited dictionary entry of a correctly spelled word, with pronunciation and a short definition. Electronic foreign language dictionaries are available, too. The user enters a word in one language, and the device translates it into another.

lists of words into broad categories, such as *color* and *honor.* He then developed an index to the categories. This original thesaurus format is still used. To use this type of thesaurus, first check the index. Then refer to one of the lists of possible synonyms given in the index.

Dictionary-style Entries

A dictionary-style thesaurus, which organizes words alphabetically, is also widely used. In the dictionary format, each word entry is followed by several synonyms and cross-references to related major categories. A major category includes words that are all related to one main idea. Thus, if you can't find an appropriate synonym under the regular entry, try one of the major categories, which appear in parentheses in the regular entry. Most major category entries also include cross-references to antonyms. The following entry for the major category *generality* shows the main parts of a thesaurus entry.

GENERALITY

Nouns—**1**, generality, generalization; universality, broadness, collectivity; average; catholicity, catholicism; miscellany, miscellaneousness; prevalence; DISPERSION.
2, everyone, everybody [and his brother]; all hands, all the world and his wife; anybody. *Colloq.*, whole kit and caboodle. *Slang*, the works.
Verbs— be general, prevail, be going about; generalize, render general.
Adjectives—general, generic, collective; broad, comprehensive, sweeping; encyclopedic, widespread, dispersed; universal, catholic, common, all-inclusive, worldwide; ecumenical; transcendental; prevalent, prevailing, rife, epidemic, besetting; all over, covered with; every, all; unspecified, impersonal; customary (see HABIT).
Adverbs—generally, in general, generally speaking; always, for better or worse; for the most part, in the long run; whatever, whatsoever; to a man, one and all, all told.

Antonym, see SPECIALITY.

Major categories appear in boldface, capital letters.

In this thesaurus, synonyms are listed by part of speech.

Cross-references to other major categories appear in capital letters.

Antonyms can be located by referring to the cross-reference at the end of an entry.

Exercise 2

Use a thesaurus to find one synonym and one antonym for each word listed below. Then write an original sentence to illustrate the meaning of either the synonym or the antonym for each word listed. You may wish to check the exact meaning of each word in a dictionary before you use it in a sentence.

1. ability (noun)
2. defeat (verb)
3. modesty (noun)
4. move (verb)
5. strong (adjective)
6. fear (noun)
7. courtesy (noun)
8. difficult (adjective)
9. growth (noun)
10. talk (verb)

Using Dictionaries

Focus

Lesson Overview

Objective
- To learn how to use a thesaurus

Skills
- locating synonyms and antonyms in a thesaurus; understanding how words are arranged in a thesaurus

Critical Thinking
- comparing; defining; clarifying

Listening and Speaking
- discussing

Practice and Assess

Answers: Exercise 2

Possible synonyms (S) and antonyms (A) follow:

1. S: skill, talent, competence;
   A: incompetence, inadequacy
2. S: beat, overpower, thwart;
   A: lose, surrender, fail
3. S: humility, propriety, simplicity;
   A: arrogance, impropriety, bravado, vanity
4. S: go, advance, relocate, inspire;
   A: stop, stall, leave untouched
5. S: powerful, intense, vivid;
   A: weak, frail, dull
6. S: anxiety, terror, phobia;
   A: bravery, valor, guts, calm
7. S: politeness, civility, respect;
   A: incivility, disrespect, rudeness
8. S: tough, stubborn, thorny;
   A: easy, manageable, simple
9. S: accumulation, progress, maturity, development;
   A: reduction, shrinkage, decline
10. S: speak, chat, address, converse;
    A: listen, be silent

Close

Have students tell how to find synonyms and antonyms in a thesaurus.

Resource Manager

Planning Resources
- *Lesson Plans*

Other Print Resources
- *Vocabulary and Spelling Strategies and Practice,* pp. 35–37

ASSESSMENT OPTIONS

Tests with Answer Key & Rubrics
Unit 24 Mastery Test, pp. 93–94

 *Testmaker*
Unit 24 Mastery Test

You may wish to administer the Unit 24 Mastery Test at this point.

MindJogger Videoquizzes

INTRODUCING

UNIT 25

Objectives

- To learn how to use context clues and recognize word parts in order to build a vocabulary
- To demonstrate the ability to define words based on context clues and word parts

✓ ASSESSMENT OPTIONS

Tests with Answer Key & Rubrics
Unit 25 Pretest, pp. 95–96

Testmaker
Unit 25 Pretest

You may wish to administer the Unit 25 Pretest at this point.

Key to Ability Levels

L1 Level 1 activities are within the basic ability range of students.

L2 Level 2 activities are within the ability range of average students.

L3 Level 3 activities are more challenging activities.

UNIT 25 Vocabulary

818

LOG ON **Writing** Online | For research tools and additional skills practice, go to glencoe.com and enter QuickPass code WC97727p3.

Resource Manager

Planning Resources
- *Lesson Plans*
- *Block Scheduling*

Transparencies
- *Bellringer*
- *Daily Language Practice*

Other Print Resources
- *Tests with Answer Key and Rubrics*
- *Vocabulary and Spelling Strategies and Practice*
- *Vocabulary Power*

Video
- *MindJogger Videoquizzes*

Software
- *Presentation Plus!*
- *Testmaker*
- *Vocabulary Power Puzzlemaker*

Web Site
- *glencoe.com*

25.1 Building Vocabulary

With Marcie's helpful tips whispered in her ear, Peppermint Patty might yet develop a stronger vocabulary. As with any student, the better she understands words and their meanings, the better equipped she will be to communicate with others.

Developing Your Vocabulary

You hear and read unfamiliar words and phrases every day. Even words you know in one context or subject area can have new meanings when used in a different context or subject area. For example, the word *fare* has multiple meanings, and the word *mouse* has developed a new meaning within the context of technology. You can develop strategies for learning and remembering the new words and phrases you encounter. The following steps suggest ways to strengthen your vocabulary.

Steps for Learning and Remembering a New Word

1. **Notice** new words and phrases while reading or listening. You might want to keep a vocabulary journal in which you record unfamiliar words and their meanings as well as familiar words with unusual meanings in specific contexts.
2. **Understand** the meaning of a new word by studying the context—the surrounding words and sentences that provide clues to the meaning.
3. **Verify** your understanding of a word with someone else. Use a dictionary or ask a teacher or a friend whether you correctly understand the meaning of the word.
4. **Use** the new word or phrase in your speaking and writing. You might want to double-check the meaning to be sure you're using the word appropriately.

Vocabulary

Focus

Lesson Overview

Objective

- To learn and remember new words using specific and general context clues

Skill

- determining the meaning of unfamiliar words from context; using specific strategies to figure out word meanings

Critical Thinking

- analyzing; contrasting; recalling; relating; evaluating; comparing; inferring

Listening and Speaking

- discussing

Bellringer
Daily Language Activity

When students enter the classroom, have this assignment on the board: *Write this sentence: Because the gas was volatile, we had to keep it in an airtight container. Write what you think the underlined word means. Write the clues in the sentence that helped you decide.*

See also  *Daily Language Practice*

Motivating Activity

Tell students that Maya Angelou once said that she had a large vocabulary and had been reading constantly since childhood. Ask students how a large vocabulary and reading might be related. Then have students discuss how reading other parts of the sentence in the Bellringer activity above helped them figure out the meaning of the word *volatile*. Ask students how they think they can enrich their vocabularies.

Resource Manager

Planning Resources
- *Lesson Plans*

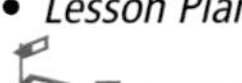

Transparencies
- *Bellringer*
- *Daily Language Practice*

Other Print Resources
- *Vocabulary and Spelling Strategies and Practice*, pp. 18–34

Teach

Finding New Words

Have students look through books or magazines to find unfamiliar words or familiar words that are used in new ways. Encourage students to "claim" several words that appeal to them, perhaps because they like their sounds, because the words are unusual, or because the words refer to something students are interested in. Students should locate definitions of their unfamiliar or multiple-meaning words and write sentences that include the words and context clues to the meanings. Ask students to use their new words in speech or writing at least once a day for a week. **L2**

Using Scientific and Technical Vocabulary

Invite students to increase their working vocabulary in a field that interests them. For example, if they like biology, guide them to list and define words from the biological sciences. Encourage students to use their new words at least once a day for a week. **L3**

Cross-reference: Writing

For more information on how students can use a larger vocabulary to enhance their writing, refer them to Lesson 3.2, pp. 144–147, and Lesson 5.3, pp. 236–239.

Vocabulary

You may also want to study vocabulary with someone—a friend or a small group of classmates. Then you can share your journals, agree to use new words in conversation, and help each other figure out vocabulary meanings. The chart below suggests a few ways to increase your vocabulary, both on your own and with other people.

Tips on Discovering New Words
1. Read extensively in a variety of areas. The more time you spend reading high-quality material, the more new words and phrases you are certain to encounter.
2. Use a thesaurus. Especially when you write, challenge yourself to use new vocabulary. Try to replace "worn out" verbs, such as forms of the verb *to be*, with vivid verbs.
3. Play word games. There are many word games on the market that can be challenging and fun. You might also enjoy inventing a game of your own.

Learning from Context

An unfamiliar word nearly always appears among other words that are familiar to you. These surrounding words provide the context for the new word. Thinking about the meaning of the rest of the phrase, sentence, paragraph, or passage, and analyzing how the unknown word fits into that meaning help you figure out the meaning of the new word.

Analyzing Specific Clues Writers often supply clues that help you figure out the meanings of unfamiliar and multiple-meaning words. Notice how the sentence structure provides clues to the meaning of *mélange*.

> Our last talent show featured a *mélange* of acts: classical vocalists, jugglers, gymnasts, tap dancers, and performance artists.

The colon tells you that examples of the acts follow. Because the examples are diverse, you might guess that *mélange* means "a mixture." In the following sentence, clue words can help you determine the meaning of *impediment*:

> The Postal Service allows no *impediment*, such as bad weather, to prevent the delivery of mail.

The clue phrase is *such as*. Bad weather is an example of an impediment. You can figure out that the Postal Service does not let any obstacle, such as bad weather, get in its way. *Impediment* means "obstacle."

The chart on the next page describes different types of context clues and the specific clue words that help you interpret them. In the Example column, the clue words are in **boldface** type. The unfamiliar words and the context that will help you interpret them are in *italic* type.

English Language Learners

Using Context Clues

Students who are fluent in a language other than English have an extra knowledge base from which to draw when they encounter new words. Ask them to choose some unfamiliar words in a literature selection they have recently read. Work with them to understand the meanings in English of the context clues surrounding the unfamiliar words. Then ask them to think about the meanings of the context clues in their first language as well. Help them use what they know to figure out the meanings of the unfamiliar words.

Interpreting Clue Words		
TYPE OF CONTEXT CLUE	**CLUE WORDS**	**EXAMPLE**
Definition: The meaning of the unfamiliar word is stated in the sentence.	that is in other words or also known as which means	The lecturer was *verbose*; **in other words,** he was *long-winded.*
Example: The meaning of the unfamiliar word is explained through one familiar case.	like for example such as for instance including	The paramedic quickly checked Amy's *vital signs,* **including** her *pulse rate and body temperature.*
Comparison: The unfamiliar word is similar to a familiar word or phrase.	also likewise similarly resembling identical	Joan's friend testified to her *veracity*; **likewise**, her teacher said that Joan's *honesty* was evident to all who knew her.
Contrast: The unfamiliar word is the opposite of a familiar word or phrase.	but on the other hand on the contrary unlike however	Rachel is always *punctual,* **unlike** Brendan, who is usually *late.*
Cause and effect: The unfamiliar word describes a cause in a sentence for which the effects are understood.	because since therefore as a result consequently	Maria felt the stranger was being *intrusive* **because** he *asked too many personal questions.*

Analyzing the General Context What if the context of an unfamiliar or multiple-meaning word has no specific clue words? You can still interpret unfamiliar words when the context clues are more general. After figuring out the part of speech of the unfamiliar word, you can try to figure out the idea of the word from supporting and contrasting details, as shown in the following examples.

Because your friend Jesse was reading a book about the field of *ornithology*, she went to the library to view some of John James Audubon's famous drawings of birds.

How can you figure out the meaning of *ornithology?* You know from the passage that ornithology is a field of study. You also know that Jesse wanted to look at drawings of birds while she was reading about that subject. Therefore, you might deduce that *ornithology* is the study of birds.

Vocabulary

Writing Context Clues

Have students write a paragraph about a sport or hobby. The paragraph should include any specialized vocabulary or terminology relevant to their topic. Students should be instructed to craft their sentences so that each term is defined in context for people unfamiliar with the topic. **L3**

Cooperative Learning

Writing Context Clues

Let small groups choose a new word and define it on one side of a sheet of paper. On the other side of the paper, students should write a sentence containing the new word, underlined, and a type of context clue from the chart on this page. Then have groups exchange papers and use context clues to write a definition of the underlined word. When students have finished with their definition, they can turn the paper over to see how close they came to the definition written there. Groups can then pass the paper to another group and repeat the process.

25.1

Practice and Assess

Answers: Exercise 1

The following pattern is used to give the answer for each item in Exercise 1: *word:* "definition," strategy (*clue words*).

1. *gratis:* "without charge," example (*accepted no payment*)
2. *malleable:* "easily shaped," definition (*that is*)
3. *balmy:* "mild," comparison (*similarly*)
4. *scale:* "climb," cause and effect (*because*)
5. *enshrouded:* "covered," definition (*or*)
6. *immaculate:* "perfectly clean," contrast (*although*)
7. *acrophobia:* "fear of heights," comparison (*also*)
8. *contiguous:* "touching or bordering," example (*such as*)
9. *symmetrical:* "balanced and even," cause and effect/contrast (*before/however*)
10. *philately:* "having to do with the collection of stamps," cause and effect (*because*)

Additional Resources

Vocabulary and Spelling Strategies and Practice, pp.18–34.

Close

Have students discuss current reading assignments in which they can use these vocabulary strategies in the chart on page 821 to figure out the meanings of unfamiliar words.

The satellite was 670 miles from Earth at its *apogee* but only 260 miles away at its *perigee.*

What are the meanings of *apogee* and *perigee?* You know these two words are nouns because they are both objects of a preposition in a prepositional phrase. The particular measurements cited must be significant. You might guess that the *apogee* is the farthest point away from Earth in the satellite's orbit, while the *perigee* is the closest point.

You can see that being a good word detective helps you figure out unfamiliar and multiple-meaning words. Paying attention to all of the surrounding details and to the general tone of a passage can help you learn new vocabulary. Once you begin to notice and interpret new vocabulary, each consecutive experience with those words or phrases will expand and deepen your understanding of them. If you pay attention to context as you read, you can often wait until a more convenient time to consult a dictionary or another reliable source.

Exercise 1

Each of the following passages contains an italicized word that may be unfamiliar to you or may be used in an unfamiliar way. Determine the meaning by examining the context, looking for the different types of context clues described in the chart on page 821. Write the italicized word and its meaning. Then indicate the strategy you used in each case by writing *definition, example, comparison, contrast,* or *cause and effect.* Afterwards, check your work in a dictionary to see how close you came to figuring out the word meanings.

1. Gayle frequently performed *gratis;* for example, last year she accepted no payment for singing the lead in the new community musical.
2. Copper is highly *malleable*, that is, easily shaped.
3. The first day of winter was downright *balmy*, and the days that followed were similarly mild.
4. Because Raoul is afraid of heights, he has no desire to *scale* a mountain.
5. The village was *enshrouded*, or enveloped, in a thick fog.
6. Although Eduardo is an *immaculate* housekeeper, his twin sister, Mercedes, is an untidy person.
7. Michael's *acrophobia* was intense; his father also had an overwhelming fear of heights.
8. *Contiguous* countries, such as the United States and Canada, usually have border patrols.
9. Before the accident, my car bumper was perfectly *symmetrical*; however, it is now uneven.
10. Teresa joined a *philately* club because she enjoyed looking at stamps from different countries.

English Language Learners

Interpreting Context Clues

Some students may need additional support in figuring out words from context clues. Have these students work in pairs with a more proficient reader to complete Exercise 1. Encourage them to use the chart on page 821 to help them locate clue words. Allow them to use a dictionary if neither partner is able to determine a meaning from context, but instruct them to use the dictionary definition to determine what context clues the sentence did contain. **L1**

25.2 Recognizing Parts of a Word

Another way to understand words is by analyzing their parts. The main part of a word is its **root.** When it is a complete word, the root is called a **base word.** A root can be thought of as the "spine" of the word: it gives the word its backbone of meaning. It is often combined with a **prefix** (a part inserted at the beginning), a **suffix** (a part attached to the end), or another root. Prefixes and suffixes often change the direction of a word's meaning. Look at the following example.

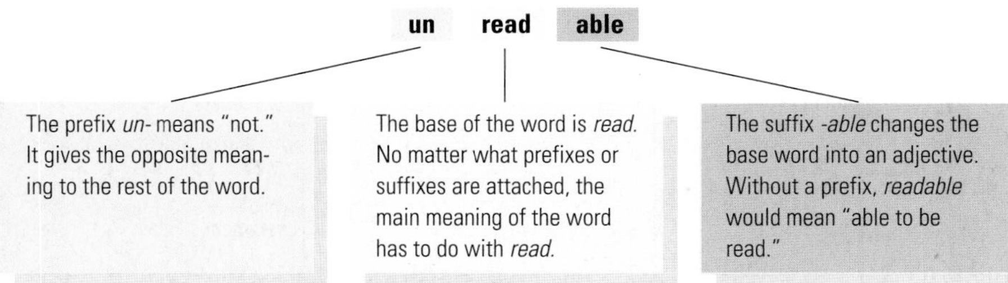

un read able
The prefix *un-* means "not." It gives the opposite meaning to the rest of the word.
The base of the word is *read.* No matter what prefixes or suffixes are attached, the main meaning of the word has to do with *read.*
The suffix *-able* changes the base word into an adjective. Without a prefix, *readable* would mean "able to be read."

Analyzing its parts, you can see that the word *unreadable* means "not possible to read."

Word Roots

Although prefixes and suffixes can change a word's meaning, remember that the root gives the word its central meaning. The following words have the same root.

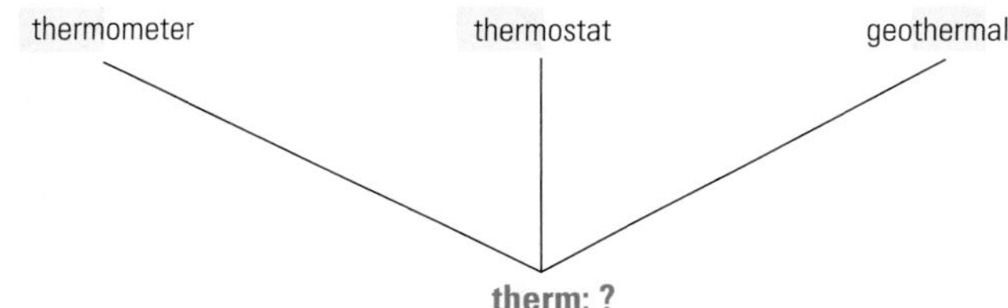

You may know that a meter is a unit of measure and that a thermometer measures temperature. You may also know that *static* can mean "motionless" and that a thermostat is a device that keeps the temperature steady. Finally, you may know that *geo* means "earth" and that *geothermal* means "related to heat produced by the earth." Because all three words in the graphic concern temperature or heat and contain the root *therm,* you can infer that *therm* has a similar meaning. If you didn't know the meaning of one of the words above, you could begin to figure it out by using what you know about *therm.* The table on page 824 shows some words that share roots.

Vocabulary

Focus

Lesson Overview

Objective

- To learn and remember new words using word roots, prefixes, and suffixes

Skills

- using knowledge of roots, prefixes, and suffixes to determine meaning of unfamiliar words

Critical Thinking

- analyzing; contrasting; recalling; relating; comparing; making inferences

Listening and Speaking

- discussing

Bellringer

Daily Language Activity

When students enter the classroom, have this assignment on the board: *Write these three words: import, export, transport. Write a sentence about what the words all have in common. Based on what you already know about the meaning of these words, what could the prefixes* im-, ex-, *and* trans- *mean?*

See also  *Daily Language Practice*

Motivating Activity

Write on the board this quote from Mark Twain: *The difference between the almost right word and the right word is really a large matter—'tis the difference between the lightning bug and the lightning.* Ask how understanding the meaning of word parts can help students use the right word. Discuss how knowing the meaning of *im-*, *ex-*, and *trans-* would help students to understand the words *import, export,* and *transport.*

Resource Manager

Planning Resources

- *Lesson Plans*

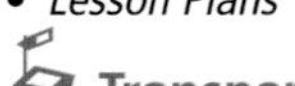

Transparencies

- *Bellringer*
- *Daily Language Practice*

Other Print Resources

- *Vocabulary and Spelling Strategies and Practice,* pp. 18–34

25.2

Teach

Analyzing Word Roots

Assign each student a word from the chart on this page. Ask students to locate the word in the dictionary and identify the original language from which the root is taken. Discuss which languages contributed most of the roots on the chart. (Two are Greek—*arch* and *hydr;* all others are Latin.) Then ask students to look at nearby words in the dictionary to locate and define other words with the same roots. **L2**

Examining Word Roots

Point out that a root can be at the beginning, in the middle, or at the end of a word. Ask students to find examples of roots in each position in the words on the chart. Emphasize that when figuring out the meaning of a word, it's helpful to find the root first and figure out its general meaning by thinking of other words that have the same root. **L3**

Cross-reference: Dictionary and Thesaurus

For more information on checking the etymology of words, refer students to Lesson 24.1, pp. 812–815.

Analyzing Word Roots

WORDS	MEANINGS	ROOTS
animate unanimous	having life being of one mind	*anima* means "mind" or "life"
anarchy archives	without government government records	*arch* means "rule" or "govern"
beneficial benevolent	good, helpful inclined to do good	*bene* means "good"
recede proceed	go back, yield again go forward	*ced* means "go"
contradict dedicate	to say the opposite of to set apart for recognition	*dict* and *dic* mean "say" or "speak"
facsimile factory	a copy or an item similar to a place where goods are made	*fac* and *fact* mean "make"
general generate	affecting a whole class to start or create	*gen* means "class" or "origin"
hydrant dehydrate	a large pipe or water main to remove water from	*hydr* means "water"
manuscript manual	a document written by hand done by hand	*man* means "hand"
portable porter	possible to carry one who carries	*port* means "carry"
science omniscient	knowledge about the natural world knowing everything	*sci* means "know"
stringent unrestricted	binding, severe not bound, free	*string* and *strict* mean "bind"
traction extract	friction that occurs when a load is pulled across a surface to pull out	*trac* means "draw" or "pull"
vivacious revive	full of life, lively to bring back to life	*viv* means "live" or "alive"

Vocabulary

Prefixes

Prefixes are inserted before a root to alter or enhance its meaning. Although the English language does not contain as many prefixes as suffixes, prefixes are still important tools for understanding and learning new words.

Learning Disabled

Understanding Word Parts

To help students understand the concept of word parts, make a set of flash cards on index cards. On one card write the prefix *un-*. On another write the suffix *-able*. On separate cards write the base words *port, break, read,* and *wash*. Demonstrate how the same word parts can be used to form many different words. Allow students to take turns combining cards to make words. Ask them to name other word parts they have seen in words. **L1**

A prefix can sometimes completely change the meaning of a word. For example, the prefix *un-* gives the opposite meaning to any word before which it is inserted. The following chart shows other valuable prefixes and their meanings. Notice that some prefixes have more than one meaning and that sometimes different prefixes can convey the same meaning.

Analyzing Prefixes

WORDS	MEANINGS	PREFIXES
circumstance circumference circumvent	surrounding conditions distance around a circle to avoid by going around	*circum-* means "around" or "about"
demote deduction	to move down in rank conclusion drawn from reasoning	*de-* means "down" or "from"
disapprove disassociate	not to approve not to associate	*dis-* means "not"
hypersensitive hyperbole	overly sensitive great exaggeration	*hyper-* means "excessive"
illegal immortal insignificant irresponsible	not legal not mortal not significant not responsible	*il-*, *im-*, *in-*, and *ir-* mean "not"
misspell misogamy	to spell badly hatred of marriage	*mis-* means "do badly" or "hate"
precede premonition	to go before advance warning	*pre-* means "before"
submarine subhuman	beneath the ocean less than human	*sub-* means "beneath" or "less than"

Suffixes

Suffixes can be added to the ends of base words to create new words with new meanings. Besides having specific meanings, however, suffixes also have grammatical functions. For example, the suffix *-ness* means "state of," "act of," or "quality of." In addition to creating a new meaning, this suffix also turns the base word *deaf*, which is an adjective, into an abstract noun. The word *deafness* is a noun meaning "the state, act, or quality of being deaf." As you study the following chart, notice that the spelling of the root may change when a suffix is added.

Remembering Prefixes

Have students make cards listing a prefix on one side and showing a simple sketch of the prefix's meaning on the other. **L1**

Cross-reference: Spelling

For a discussion of spelling rules that apply when adding prefixes or suffixes to words, refer students to Lesson 26.1, pp. 828–832.

Enrichment and Extension

Noting Words from Latin and Greek

Both Latin and Greek have heavily influenced English. In some cases English contains two words with similar meanings, one originating in Greek and the other in Latin. For example, among words relating to the stars, *astral* and *astronomy* come from the Greek root, and *stellar* comes from Latin. The words *universe* (Latin) and *cosmos* (Greek) are used to refer to the entire realm of space, including Earth and the heavenly bodies.

Practice and Assess

Answers: Exercise 2

Answers to this exercise will be shown as follows:
prefixes = underlined
base words = bold type
suffixes = italic type

1. un/**friend**/*ly;* not in the manner of a friend
2. pro/**cess**/*ion;* the act of going forward
3. dis/**satis**/*fy;* to fail to satisfy; not make sufficient
4. in/**cred**/*ible;* not able to be believed
5. trans/**mis**/*sion;* the act of sending across
6. circum/**navigat**/*ion;* the act of sailing around
7. in/**corrupt**/*ible;* not able to be ruined or contaminated
8. omni/**vor**/*ous;* the characteristic of eating all kinds of food
9. re/**pent**/*ance;* the act of thinking again
10. inter/**media**/*tion;* the act of going between

Additional Resources

Vocabulary and Spelling Strategies and Practice, pp. 18–34

Close

Have students discuss current reading assignments (science or technical subjects, for example) in which knowledge of prefixes, suffixes, and roots would be especially useful.

ASSESSMENT OPTIONS

Tests with Answer Key & Rubrics
Unit 25 Mastery Test, pp. 97–98

Testmaker
Unit 25 Mastery Test

You may wish to administer the Unit 25 Mastery Test at this point.

MindJogger Videoquizzes

Analyzing Suffixes

WORDS	MEANINGS	SUFFIXES	PART OF SPEECH FORMED
movable peaceable visible	capable of being moved inclined to promote peace able to be seen	*-able* and *-ible* mean "capable of," "inclined to," or "able to be"	Adjective
occupant dependent	one who occupies a place one who depends on another for support	*-ant* and *-ent* mean "one who performs an action"	Concrete noun
quicken moisten deepen	make quick or alive make moist make deep	*-en* means "to become"	Verb
parenthood childhood	state of being a parent state of being a child	*-hood* means "condition" or "state"	Abstract noun
dentist scientist	one who repairs teeth one who is knowledgeable about science	*-ist* means "one who works at"	Concrete noun
evenly closely slowly	in an even manner in a close manner in a slow way	*-ly* means "in the manner or way mentioned"	Adverb
joyous courageous	full of joy full of courage	*-ous* means "full of"	Adjective
suspension civilization	state of being suspended process of becoming civilized	*-sion* and *-tion* mean "the state of" or "process of"	Abstract noun

Exercise 2

Copy the words below onto a separate sheet of paper. Then draw one line under the prefix in each of the words. Circle the root or the base word. Draw two lines under the suffix. Then write the meaning of the original word.

1. unfriendly
2. procession
3. dissatisfy
4. incredible
5. transmission
6. circumnavigation
7. incorruptible
8. omnivorous
9. repentance
10. intermediation

Enrichment and Extension

Playing Word Games

Allow class time for students to work on crossword puzzles and acrostics or play hangman and other word games. Initiate a discussion about how knowing word parts enriches their vocabulary and adds to their enjoyment of word games.

UNIT 26 Spelling

LOG ON Writing Online | For research tools and additional skills practice, go to glencoe.com and enter QuickPass code WC97727p3.

827

INTRODUCING UNIT 26

Objectives

- To learn basic spelling rules, strategies for spelling new words, and strategies for spelling difficult words
- To demonstrate the ability to spell words correctly and identify misspelled words

ASSESSMENT OPTIONS

Tests with Answer Key & Rubrics
Unit 26 Pretest, pp. 99–100

Testmaker
Unit 26 Pretest

You may wish to administer the Unit 26 Pretest at this point.

Key to Ability Levels

L1 Level 1 activities are within the basic ability range of students.

L2 Level 2 activities are within the ability range of average students.

L3 Level 3 activities are more challenging activities.

Resource Manager

Planning Resources
- *Lesson Plans*
- *Block Scheduling*

Transparencies
- *Bellringer*
- *Daily Language Practice*

Other Print Resources
- *Listening and Speaking Activities*
- *Spelling Power*
- *Tests with Answer Key and Rubrics*
- *Thinking and Study Skills*
- *Vocabulary and Spelling Strategies and Practice*

Video
- *MindJogger Videoquizzes*

Software
- *Presentation Plus!*
- *Testmaker*

Web Site
- *glencoe.com*

Focus

Lesson Overview

Objectives
- To learn how to spell words that follow basic rules
- To learn how to spell words that are difficult to spell

Skills
- using basic spelling rules to spell words correctly; examining difficult words and remembering how to spell them correctly

Critical Thinking
- analyzing; synthesizing; recalling; identifying patterns; comparing; visualizing

Listening and Speaking
- discussing; listening for the sounds of words

Bellringer

Daily Language Activity

When students enter the classroom, have this activity on the board: *Rewrite the following sentences and correct the errors in spelling: My father recieved a wierd letter. It said that according to a legel judgement, he could have a fantusy cruise if he returned the correct winning number.*

See also *Daily Language Practice*

Motivating Activity

Ask students to discuss how spelling problems affect their work in other classes. Ask: Do you ever struggle with spelling when you should be concentrating on how to answer an essay test question? Are your grades or test scores sometimes lower because of misspelled words? Explain that in this lesson, students will learn some basic rules that will help them improve their spelling. After completing this unit, they should be able to spell the words in the Bellringer activity correctly.

26.1 Improving Your Spelling

One of your goals as a writer is to communicate your ideas clearly to your audience. If your writing is filled with misspelled words, your ideas may be lost. One of the best ways to become a good speller is to be an avid reader.

You can do a number of things to improve your spelling and help others understand what you write. First, you can learn some basic spelling rules. Second, by noticing how words have spelling patterns, you can learn to guess accurately when attempting to spell a new word. Third, you can learn to check your spelling with an authoritative source.

Basic Spelling Rules

The following rules, examples, and exceptions will help you master the spellings of many words.

Spelling *ie* and *ei* Many writers find the rules for certain combinations of letters, such as *ie* and *ei,* difficult to remember. One helpful learning strategy is to develop a rhyme to remember a rule, such as the following rhyme for the *ie* and *ei* rule.

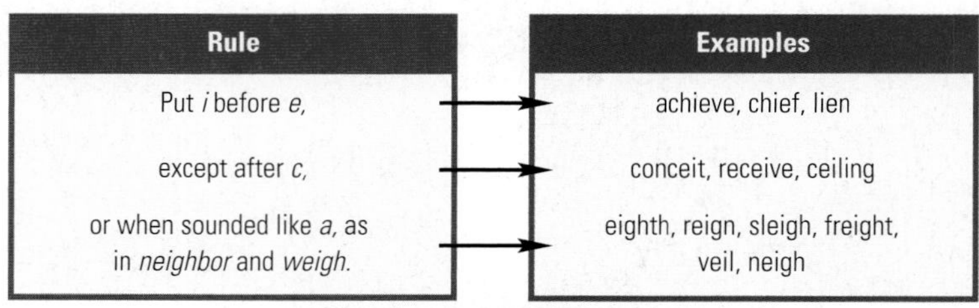

Rule	Examples
Put *i* before *e,*	achieve, chief, lien
except after *c,*	conceit, receive, ceiling
or when sounded like *a,* as in *neighbor* and *weigh.*	eighth, reign, sleigh, freight, veil, neigh

Exceptions
seize, leisure, weird, height, either, forfeit, protein

Spelling *-cede, -ceed,* and *-sede* Because various letters in the English spelling system are sometimes pronounced the same way, it is often easy to make slight spelling errors. The similarity of pronunciation between *c* and *s* accounts for the confusion in spelling words ending in *-cede, -ceed,* and *-sede.* Because there are only four exceptions, however, you should be able to memorize them.

Spelling

Resource Manager

Planning Resources
- *Lesson Plans*

Transparencies
- *Bellringer*
- *Daily Language Practice*

Other Print Resources
- *Listening and Speaking Activities,* pp. 5–6
- *Vocabulary and Spelling Strategies and Practice,* pp. 38–49

Rule	Examples
Spell the *sēd* sound as *cede.* →	concede, recede, intercede

Exceptions
Three words use *-ceed* to spell the *sēd* sound: *proceed, exceed, succeed.* One word uses *-sede* to spell the *sēd* sound: *supersede.*

Spelling Unstressed Vowels Notice the vowel sound in the second syllable of the word *or-i-gin*. This is the unstressed vowel sound, and it can be spelled several ways. Dictionary respellings use the schwa symbol (ə) to represent it. To help spell words with unstressed vowels correctly, try thinking of a related word in which the syllable containing the vowel sound is stressed. The following chart shows examples of this process.

Spelling Unstressed Vowels

UNKNOWN SPELLING	RELATED WORD	SPELLED CORRECTLY
leg_l	le**gal**ity	legal
fant_sy	fan**tas**tic	fantasy
host_le	hos**til**ity	hostile
opp_site	op**pose**	opposite

Adding Prefixes When adding a prefix to a word, keep the original spelling of the word. If the prefix results in a double letter, keep both letters.

dis- + appear = disappear　　ir- + regular = irregular
mis- + direct = misdirect　　co- + operate = cooperate

Suffixes and the Silent *e* Many English words end in a silent letter *e*. Sometimes the *e* is dropped when a suffix is added. The following chart shows when to keep and when to drop the *e*.

Adding Suffixes to Words with Silent *e*

RULE	EXAMPLES
When adding a suffix that begins with a consonant to a word that ends in silent *e*, keep the *e*.	place + -ment = placement rare + -ly = rarely
Common exceptions	*awe + -ful = awful* *judge + -ment = judgment*

(continued)

Spelling

Teach

Identifying Prefixes and Suffixes

With students, brainstorm some common prefixes and suffixes. Then ask a volunteer to select a prefix or suffix and name a word to which it could be added. Work with students to examine the spelling rules for adding prefixes and suffixes to words, select the rule that applies, and then write the new word on the board. **L2**

Cross-reference: Vocabulary

For a discussion of definitions of some common prefixes and suffixes and how they affect the meanings of root words, refer students to Lesson 25.2, pp. 823–826.

English Language Learners

Practicing Schwa

Carefully review the concept of unstressed vowels for students who are less familiar with English pronunciation. Ask students to check several words on the chart in a dictionary, pointing out the schwa in the pronunciation and identifying which vowel spells the sound in each word.

You may wish to point out that there are some regional variations in pronunciations in which the vowel may be stressed. For example, some people pronounce the word *hostile* with a long *i*, not an unstressed vowel.

Teach

Doubling Final Consonants

For students who need help with rules on the doubling of final consonants, review syllabication and accents, allowing students to practice each step separately. List a number of words on the board. Have students divide each into syllables and explain which syllable is accented. Then ask students to explain which syllable is accented after a suffix is added. Finally, ask whether or not they would double the final consonant. **L2**

Using Memory Aids

Ask students to pick a subject such as science, math, or history in which there are difficult words to spell. Provide a few examples to get them started. Then have them make a list of difficult words pertaining to the subject they chose and suggest mnemonic devices or other tricks for remembering how to spell them. Ask students to share their memory aids with others. (Remind students to select words that are not only difficult to spell but also important to remember.) **L3**

Adding Suffixes to Words with Silent *e*

RULE	EXAMPLES
When adding a suffix that begins with a vowel or *y* to a word that ends in silent *e*, usually drop the *e*.	excite + -able = excitable shine + -y = shiny
Common exceptions	*mile + -age = mileage*
When adding a suffix that begins with *a* or *o* to a word that ends in *ce* or *ge*, keep the *e* so the word will retain the soft *c* or *g* sound.	trace + -able = traceable courage + -ous = courageous
When adding a suffix that begins with a vowel to a word that ends in *ee* or *oe*, keep the *e*.	agree + -able = agreeable canoe + -ing = canoeing

Suffixes and the Final *y* When adding a suffix to a word that ends in a consonant + *y*, change the *y* to *i*. Do not change the *y* to *i* when the suffix begins with *i*.

try + -ed = tried copy + -ing = copying

When adding a suffix to a word that ends in a vowel + *y*, keep the *y*.

joy + -ous = joyous convey + -ed = conveyed

Doubling the Final Consonant When adding a suffix to a word, you sometimes need to double the final consonant before adding the suffix. You double the consonant when adding a suffix that begins with a vowel to a word that ends in a single consonant preceded by a single vowel, if the original word

- is a one-syllable word
  dip + -ing = dipping stop + -age = stoppage
- has an accent on the last syllable and the accent remains there after the suffix is added
  occur + -ence = occurrence repel + -ing = repelling
- is a prefixed word based on a one-syllable word
  reset + -ing = resetting

On the basis of the preceding rule, you would not double the final consonant when

- the accent is not on the last syllable
  develop + -ing = developing
- the accent shifts when the suffix is added
  refer + -ence = reference
- the final consonant is preceded by two vowels
  train + -ing = training

Spelling

Technology Tip

Using Spelling Checkers

Many stores carry handheld electronic spelling checkers. On an alphabetical keyboard, the user enters his or her best guess as to the spelling of a word. In response, the correct spelling (or spellings, if several words are similar to the misspelling entered) appears on the display screen. Similar to pocket calculators, these handy "spelling dictionaries" are small enough to be kept in a bookbag or purse.

- the final consonant is preceded by another consonant
  remind + -er = reminder
- the word ends in a consonant and the suffix begins with a consonant
  reck + -less = reckless

Adding *-ly* When adding *-ly* to a word that ends in a single *l*, keep the *l*. When the word ends in a double *l*, drop one *l*. When the word ends in a consonant + *le*, drop the *le*.

real + -ly = really dull + -ly = dully terrible + -ly = terribly

Adding *-ness* When adding *-ness* to a word that ends in *n*, keep the *n*.

sullen + -ness = sullenness keen + -ness = keenness

Forming Compound Words When joining a word that ends in a consonant to a word that begins with a consonant, keep both consonants.

after + noon = afternoon key + board = keyboard

Forming Plurals English nouns form plurals in many ways. Most nouns simply add *-s*. The following chart shows other ways of forming plural nouns and some common exceptions to the patterns.

General Rules for Plurals

IF THE NOUN ENDS IN	THEN GENERALLY	EXAMPLE
ch, s, sh, x, or *z*	add *-es*	crutch → crutches wish → wishes
a consonant + *y*	change *y* to *i* and add *-es*	baby → babies
a vowel + *y*	add *-s*	day → days
a vowel + *o*	add *-s*	studio → studios
a consonant + *o*	generally add *-es*	potato → potatoes cargo → cargoes
Common exceptions	but sometimes add *-s*	silo → silos
f or *ff*	add *-s*	reef → reefs cuff → cuffs
Common exceptions	change *f* to *v* and add *-es*	leaf → leaves
lf	change *f* to *v* and add *-es*	half → halves wolf → wolves
fe	change *f* to *v* and add *-s*	life → lives

A few plurals are exceptions to the rules listed previously (or they present some other special problem) but are easy to remember. The following chart lists these plurals and some examples.

Listing Spelling Rules

Have groups of students work together to compile a list of steps to follow to spell new, unfamiliar words. Groups may want to create flow charts, diagrams, or mnemonic devices. Let groups share their ideas with the class and post their ideas on a bulletin board. **L2**

English Language Learners

Encouraging Students

Some students may feel overwhelmed by the many exceptions to English spelling rules. Encourage these students by reminding them that correct spelling is important only in writing. Explain that the average English speaker can speak or understand about 25,000 words but generally uses far fewer words in writing. Encourage these students to concentrate on learning to spell words they are likely to use in writing before trying to learn the spelling of unusual words.

Teach

Using the Flow Chart

The flow chart on this page illustrates a process for learning to spell difficult words. You may wish to have students practice this process, repeating it until they have mastered several common but difficult words. Encourage students to copy this chart in their notebooks and use it when they encounter difficult spelling words in other classes. **L2**

Cross-reference: Grammar

For additional information on making and using plural nouns, refer students to Lesson 10.1, pp. 439–445.

Special Rules for Plurals	
SPECIAL CASES	**EXAMPLES**
To form the plural of proper names, add either *-s* or *-es.*	D'Amico → D'Amicos Sanchez → Sanchezes
To form the plural of one-word compound nouns, follow the general rules for plurals.	penknife → penknives blackberry → blackberries
To form the plural of hyphenated compound nouns or compound nouns of more than one word, generally make the most important word plural.	father-in-law → fathers-in-law attorney general → attorneys general
Some nouns have irregular forms. These nouns do not follow any rules.	man → men ox → oxen
Some nouns have the same singular and plural form.	series → series deer → deer

Learning to Spell New Words

As you read, note unfamiliar words as well as words that you recognize but that look hard to spell. As you write, pay attention to any words that you have difficulty spelling. Then try the following simple process to learn to spell those words.

1. Say It
Look at the printed word, and say it out loud. Then say it again, pronouncing each syllable.

▶

2. Visualize It
Without looking at the printed word, imagine seeing the word printed or written. Try to picture the word spelled correctly.

▶

3. Write It
Look at the printed word, and write it. Then write it again without looking at the printed word.

▶

4. Check It
Check what you have written against the printed word. Did you spell the word correctly? If not, try the process again.

Remember that the dictionary can help you find the correct spelling of words. You may ask, How can I look up a word if I don't know how to spell it? Many times you will be able to spell enough of the beginning of a word to find it in the dictionary. If you don't find a word in the first place you look, think of other probable spellings, based on sound patterns you know. Once you have located the correct spelling of a word, use the four-step process shown above to help you learn the word.

Cooperative Learning

Spelling New and Old Words

Have groups of students create a spelling rules booklet in which they can list their most common spelling problems and their solutions. Students may want to poll other class members to find out other common spelling problems. Have students organize the information into a usable format and then distribute copies for other class members. **L2**

Exercise 1

In each group of words, find the one word that is misspelled. Write the word correctly. Cite the rule that applies to the spelling of the word. If the word is an exception to a rule, note that as well.

1. biege, conceit, thief
2. exceed, supercede, accede
3. definite, editor, abdumen
4. enjoiment, daily, carriage
5. truly, arguement, brownness

26.2 Spelling Difficult Words

Clearly, some words are more difficult to spell than others. As you have learned, not all words follow basic spelling rules, but you can learn to spell even the most difficult words.

One very useful strategy for learning difficult words is to develop a personal word list. What words are especially difficult for you? What words do you frequently misspell? Include those words in your personal word list. Study the words, using the four-step process you learned in Lesson 26.1, page 832.

Another helpful strategy for learning to spell difficult words involves developing memory devices. For example, if you have trouble remembering whether the word is spelled *cemetery* or *cemetary*, you might think of how we get there with *e*'s (ease). Puns, like this one, can help you remember how to spell difficult words.

Frequently Misspelled Words

Following is a list of words that many people misspell. Which words on the list do you have difficulty spelling?

Words Often Misspelled			
absence	buffet	concede	environment
accidentally	bureau	conscientious	exceed
accommodate	business	convenient	familiarize
adviser	cafeteria	definite	fascinating
allot	canceled	deodorant	foreign
answer	catastrophe	descend	forty
arctic	choir	discipline	genius
attendant	colonel	efficiency	government
ballet	commercial	eligible	guarantee
beautiful	complexion	embarrass	height

(continued)

Spelling

Practice and Assess

Answers: Exercise 1

1. beige. Put *i* before *e,* except after *c,* or when sounded like *a,* as in *neighbor* and *weigh.*
2. supersede. This is the only English word that spells the *sēd* sound *-sede.*
3. abdomen. Use the related word *abdominal* to determine how to spell the unstressed vowel sound. Caution students that while *abdominal* can help determine which letter spells the first unstressed vowel sound (*o*), the unstressed vowel in the third syllable is spelled differently in the two words: *abdomen* and *abdominal.*
4. enjoyment. When adding a suffix to a word that ends in a vowel + *y,* keep the *y.*
5. argument. This is an exception to the general rule to keep the silent *e* when adding a suffix that begins with a consonant.

Additional Resources

- *Vocabulary and Spelling Strategies and Practice,* pp. 38–49
- *Listening and Speaking Activities,* pp. 5–6

Close

Have students discuss writing assignments they currently have or have had in the past in which these spelling strategies would be useful.

Enrichment and Extension

Understanding Spelling

Ask students to speculate about what would happen if English spelling were changed so that spelling reflected pronunciation more precisely (for example, *throo for through, nak for knack*). One problem would be that people who learn to spell this way would have difficulty reading the billions of books and articles printed before the change. Additional problems would result from regional or other alternate pronunciations, making uncertain which pronunciation should determine the spelling of these words. Benefits might be that spelling would be easier and fewer rules would need to be memorized.

Focus

Lesson Overview

Objective

- To learn to spell difficult words as well as words that are easily confused because they sound similar to other words

Skills

- devising helpful strategies for spelling difficult words

Critical Thinking

- recalling; relating; patterning; visualizing; analyzing; contrasting; comparing

Listening and Speaking

- note taking; discussing

Bellringer
Daily Language Activity

When students enter the classroom, have this assignment on the board: *Write these sentences. Choose the correct word from inside the parentheses.*

The (capitol, capital) building is in the state (capitol, capital).

The (affect, effect) of the sad movie was to (affect, effect) her mood.

Dad is (all together, altogether) pleased that we waited (all together, altogether).

See also *Daily Language Practice*

Teach

Listing Different Words

Have groups of students list words from their other classes that they frequently misspell or confuse. Together they can develop memory devices to help remember the words. L2

Words Often Misspelled			
hippopotamus	necessary	pneumonia	supersede
humorous	neighborhood	precede	technique
hygiene	niece	proceed	technology
incidentally	occasion	receipt	theory
jewelry	pageant	recommend	traffic
laboratory	pamphlet	restaurant	truly
leisure	parallel	rhythm	unanimous
license	pastime	schedule	usually
mischievous	permanent	separate	vacuum
misspell	pharmacy	sincerely	variety
molasses	physical	succeed	versatile
muscle	physician	sufficient	Wednesday

Easily Confused Words

Some words are easily confused with others because they contain similar sounds. Other words are confused because they are homophones, words that have the same pronunciation but different meanings and spellings. Study the following list of easily confused words. Are there any words on the list that you find confusing?

Words Often Confused	
Affect	to influence; to act upon: *A sad movie will affect her mood.*
Effect	a result: *What effect did the punishment have on him?*
Altogether	entirely: *Mom is altogether pleased with my report.*
All together	everyone in one place: *We waited all together at the bus stop.*
Capital	a city that is the seat of government: *Jefferson City is the capital of Missouri.*
Capital	wealth: *The company invested its capital.*
Capitol	a building in which a legislature meets: *In the capitol we observed the Senate in session.*
Formally	politely; officially; according to custom or rule: *Because our visitor was so important, we addressed him formally.*
Formerly	previously: *The principal was formerly a teacher.*
Holy	sacred: *Religious travelers make pilgrimages to holy places.*
Holey	having holes: *You should probably stop wearing that holey jacket.*
Wholly	completely; fully: *I am wholly satisfied with your story.*

(continued)

Spelling

Resource Manager

Planning Resources
- *Lesson Plans*

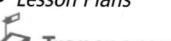

Transparencies
- *Bellringer*
- *Daily Language Practice*

Other Print Resources
- *Listening and Speaking Activities*, pp. 5–6
- *Vocabulary and Spelling Strategies and Practice*, pp. 38–49

Words Often Confused	
Its	possessive pronoun: *The United States celebrated its bicentennial in 1976.*
It's	contraction of *it is: It's not about winning; it's about fair play.*
Lose	to misplace; to drop: *Did you lose your assignment on the way to school?*
Loose	free; not confined; not tight: *My clothes are loose since I lost ten pounds.*
Passed	moved through; elapsed; completed satisfactorily: *I passed you in the hall several times today.*
Past	the time before the present; gone by; ended; over: *You can't change the past.*
Stationary	fixed; unmoving: *For a moment the plane appeared stationary in the sky.*
Stationery	writing paper and envelopes: *Rhonda wrote me a letter on hot pink stationery.*
Than	in comparison with: *You studied harder today than I have ever seen you study.*
Then	at that time; next: *He did his chores, and then he played a computer game.*

Exercise 2

For each sentence below, determine which word in parentheses correctly completes the sentence.

1. The ambulance (passed, past) us.
2. Our teacher was (formerly, formally) a stockbroker.
3. (Its, It's) beginning to snow.
4. (Then, Than) what do you do?
5. I always seem to (loose, lose) my keys.

Spelling

Practice and Assess

Answers: Exercise 2

1. passed
2. formerly
3. It's
4. Then
5. lose

You may wish to extend this exercise by having students write additional sentences, correctly using the "incorrect" alternative from each sentence in the exercise.

Additional Resources

Vocabulary and Spelling Strategies and Practice, pp. 38–49

Listening and Speaking Activities, pp. 5–6

Close

Discuss how keeping personal word lists and developing memory devices can help students in their other classes.

ASSESSMENT OPTIONS

Tests with Answer Key & Rubrics
Unit 26 Mastery Test, pp. 101–102

Testmaker
Unit 26 Mastery Test

You may wish to administer the Unit 26 Mastery Test at this point.

MindJogger Videoquizzes

Enrichment and Extension

Creating a Crossword Puzzle

Students may enjoy working with you to create crossword puzzles using the words in the charts on pages 833–835. Graph paper with large squares makes creating crosswords easier. Classmates may wish to exchange and work the crossword puzzles.

INTRODUCING UNIT 27

Objectives

- To learn strategies and techniques for study skills such as note-taking, reading effectively, evaluating, and using graphics
- To demonstrate the ability to take notes, read effectively, evaluate, and learn from graphics

✔ ASSESSMENT OPTIONS

Tests with Answer Key & Rubrics
Unit 27 Pretest, pp. 103–104

Testmaker
Unit 27 Pretest

You may wish to administer the Unit 27 Pretest at this point.

Key to Ability Levels

L1 Level 1 activities are within the basic ability range of students.

L2 Level 2 activities are within the ability range of average students.

L3 Level 3 activities are more challenging activities.

UNIT 27 Study Skills

836

LOG ON **Writing** Online — For research tools and additional skills practice, go to glencoe.com and enter QuickPass code WC97727p3.

Resource Manager

Planning Resources
- *Lesson Plans*
- *Block Scheduling*

Transparencies
- *Bellringer*
- *Daily Language Practice*

Other Print Resources
- *Listening and Speaking Activities*
- *Tests with Answer Key and Rubrics*
- *Thinking and Study Skills*
- *Vocabulary and Spelling Strategies and Practice*

Video
- *MindJogger Videoquizzes*

Software
- *Presentation Plus!*
- *Testmaker*

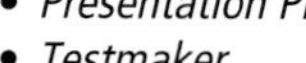

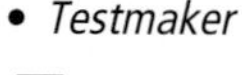

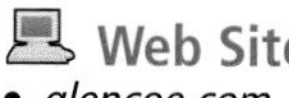

Web Site
- *glencoe.com*

27.1 Taking Notes in Class

Taking notes from classroom lectures can help you review important ideas later on. Jotting down a teacher's directions also can save time and prevent you from making careless mistakes. Whenever you take good notes, you help yourself do the following:

- organize ideas
- recognize relationships among different topics
- remember and evaluate information
- identify points you find confusing

Many students take notes in the form of an outline. For information on outline form, see Lesson 7.2 in Composition, pages 330–333. The following chart lists other suggestions on how to take class notes.

Tips on Taking Notes
1. Write down only key words and phrases. Focusing on main points allows you to continue to listen while you write.
2. Underline or star main ideas. Highlighting the most important points makes reviewing easier.
3. Revise your notes after class. Clarifying your organization and adding details makes your notes more complete.
4. Keep your notes in a folder or notebook. Having a separate folder for each class helps you keep your notes organized.

Life in an ecosystem *Sept. 28 Biology*

Ecosystem: plants, animals, and physical environment of a community

Types of biomes

1. rain forest—Amazon *4. tundra—Arctic*

2. desert—Sahara, Gobi *5. deciduous forest—Europe*

3. grassland—U.S. Plains *6. taiga—northern Asia*

Organize your notes by topic, date, and class for easy reference.

To save time, use symbols, numerals, and abbreviations.

Study Skills

Focus

Lesson Overview

Objective

- To learn how to take notes to record and remember important information

Skills

- note taking to organize information; recognizing relationships between topics; evaluating information; identifying confusing points

Critical Thinking

- analyzing; synthesizing; categorizing; classifying; recalling; recognizing main ideas; evaluating; summarizing

Listening and Speaking

- note taking; evaluating; explaining a process

Bellringer

Daily Language Activity

When students enter the classroom, have this assignment on the board: *List subjects for which you take notes in class. How does taking notes help you remember the material?*

See also *Daily Language Practice*

Teach

Taking Notes

Some students will be better able to master the skill of taking notes by learning in stages. To begin, play a tape, stopping as necessary to point out ideas students should write down. In the second stage, ask students to tell you when to stop; then wait as they write notes. The third stage repeats the second stage, but with shorter waiting times, forcing students to take notes quickly. The final stage allows no waiting time. **L2**

Resource Manager

Planning Resources
- *Lesson Plans*

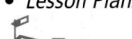

Transparencies
- *Bellringer*
- *Daily Language Practice*

Other Print Resources
- *Listening and Speaking Activities,* pp. 1–2
- *Thinking and Study Skills,* pp. 2, 4–5, 8–9, 12, 14, 17, 34–38
- *Vocabulary and Spelling Strategies and Practice,* pp. 13–17

Practice and Assess

Evaluation Rubrics

Exercise 1

It is not important to grade students on this exercise but to guide them in picking out the most important information presented. In their notes, students should try to identify both main ideas and supporting information. Try to assess how much they can remember by using their notes.

Exercise 2

While comparing notes, each student should identify information that others did not include. Ask students to discuss what standards they used to decide what to write. Point out that their notes on the same material might differ if the notes were taken for a different purpose. For example, notes taken to prepare for a test will be different from notes for a research paper. Evaluation should be based on whether students' notes met their own criteria and whether students could read their notes.

Additional Resources

- *Listening and Speaking Activities,* pp. 1–2
- *Thinking and Study Skills,* pp. 2, 4–5, 8–9, 12, 14, 17, 34–38
- *Vocabulary and Spelling Strategies and Practice,* pp. 13–17

Close

Write the following abbreviations on the board: *hv, impt, w/, w/o.* Can students guess what each means? (*have, important, with, without*) Explain that using abbreviations for common words can help them take notes quickly. Have students brainstorm other abbreviations.

Exercise 1

Watch a television program or listen to a radio broadcast in order to practice taking two-column notes. Divide a piece of paper in half vertically. On the left-hand side, take notes on what you see and hear. On the right-hand side, record comments and questions for later classroom discussion. Two-column notes allow for your own responses to topics and result in better comprehension of materials you study.

Exercise 2

In a small group, have one volunteer read aloud from an encyclopedia article for five minutes. Other students in the group should take notes as the volunteer reads. After the reading, the students taking notes should compare what they have written. What can you learn from your classmates about how to take good notes?

27.2 Studying Outside of Class

Your teacher usually determines what learning activities take place in class. Outside class, though, you're responsible for allocating your study time and learning material. The first step in studying efficiently is to learn how to manage your study time.

Using Study Time Wisely

Proper preparation and organization can help you make the most effective use of your study time. The following suggestions may help you study more efficiently.

Divide large assignments into smaller tasks. Reading four pages of a textbook each night is easier than trying to read twenty pages every fifth night.

Gather necessary materials. If possible, leave study supplies such as pencils and a dictionary at your study place.

Select a place to study. By using the same place for studying each day, you will begin to associate that place with studying.

Make a monthly assignment calendar. By writing down due dates, test dates, and notes about tasks to complete, you can see at a glance what work you need to do and when.

When you sit down to study, follow the tips on page 839 to help you make the best use of your study time.

Meeting Individual Needs: English Language Learners

Using a Tape Recorder

Tape recorders can be useful study tools for recording important classroom lectures. Students can replay and review sections they didn't understand the first time, using a dictionary as necessary to look up any difficult or confusing terminology.

Tips on Studying Effectively
1. Focus on one assignment at a time. Try to stay on task until you accomplish your goal.
2. Take short breaks after reaching a goal. Stretching, walking, or having a light snack can help keep you alert.
3. Write down questions about any material you are studying. This gives you a written record of what to ask during classroom discussions or when speaking with your teacher.
4. Review each major section of material you have studied. Even a short review can greatly increase the amount of information you remember.

Reading Efficiently

To be an efficient reader, you must pay close attention to how well you understand what you are reading. You literally must think about your thinking. Efficient readers have ongoing conversations with themselves as they work through a selection. They also adjust their reading speed with the demands of the task. Can you summarize what you have read? Is anything unclear? What questions do you have about the selection so far? What information do you think will come next? Use appropriate reading strategies for each reading purpose. Look at the three strategies in the chart below.

Hints for Using Three Reading Strategies

STRATEGY	DESCRIPTION	PURPOSE
SKIMMING	Glancing over the text to identify main ideas by reading chapter and lesson titles, words in bold or italic type, and topic sentences	• To preview material and get a general overview of the topic • To determine main ideas and the author's purpose • To decide whether a book covers a subject you are interested in
SCANNING	Glancing over the text to find specific information by looking for key terms	• To review key terms • To look for details to support an opinion • To search for specific information
IN-DEPTH READING	Reading the text carefully to absorb new ideas and facts	• To analyze new concepts or gather new information • To evaluate the information presented • To prepare to explain the information to someone else

Study Skills

Focus

Lesson Overview

Objectives

- To learn to use different reading styles for different kinds of materials
- To apply the SQ3R method
- To interpret figurative language
- To distinguish between facts and opinions

Skills

- organizing study time by setting goals, asking questions, and reviewing material; deciding whether to skim, scan, or read in-depth; using SQ3R; identifying facts and opinions; evaluating figurative language

Critical Thinking

- contrasting; recalling; main idea; summarizing; evaluating criteria; defining and clarifying

Listening and Speaking

- note taking; discussing; questioning; explaining a process

Bellringer

Daily Language Activity

When students enter the classroom, have this activity on the board: *How might you read a book to find out if it covered a particular topic? To look for a specific date? To know as much as possible about something?*

See also *Daily Language Practice*

Motivating Activity

Discuss students' responses to the Bellringer activity. Explain that in this lesson students will learn how to study effectively by reading for different purposes and by setting achievable goals.

Resource Manager

Planning Resources

- *Lesson Plans*

Transparencies

- *Bellringer*
- *Daily Language Practice*

Other Print Resources

- *Listening and Speaking Activities,* pp. 1–2
- *Thinking and Study Skills,* pp. 2, 4–5, 8–9, 12, 14, 17, 34–38
- *Vocabulary and Spelling Strategies and Practice,* pp. 13–17

Teach

Asking Questions

Make sure students understand how to determine what kind of information they are reading for. Encourage them to write down their questions before they begin reading. Suggest that as they learn the answers to their questions, they write these down as well. Ask a volunteer to locate a section in a textbook from another class and briefly explain the topic of the passage. Then have students suggest some questions they might ask before beginning to read the material. **L2**

Organizing Study Time

You may wish to give extra guidance to some students to help them organize their study time. Encourage students to keep a calendar of assignments and study goals. As students receive an assignment, they write it under the due date. Students should then break the assignment into manageable parts, indicating on the calendar the deadline they set for each part. As each portion of the assignment is completed, students cross it off the calendar. Students may find that meeting short-term goals provides satisfaction and builds confidence. **L1**

Cross-reference: Writing

For research and writing situations in which students make use of the three reading techniques, see Lesson 7.1, pp. 324–329.

When you prepare to study, follow the tips on page 839 to help you make the best use of your time.

Skimming
Scanning
In-depth reading

The Quran According to a Muslim tradition, the angel Gabriel revealed divine messages to Muhammad over a twenty-two-year period. Faithful Muslims wrote down or memorized these messages, but they were not compiled into one written collection until after Muhammad died. Then his successor, Abu Bakr, ordered Muslims to retrieve these messages from wherever they could be found, from the ribs of palm-leaves and tablets of white stone and from the breasts of men. It took twenty years before the messages were compiled into the holy book of Islam, the Quran, whose name means recital. For all Muslims, the Quran is the final authority in matters of faith and practice.

Written in Arabic, the Quran is believed to contain God's message as revealed to Muhammad. This message is expressed in stories, legends, and poems. Some of the stories—such as Noah's ark and Jonah in the belly of the whale—are variations of those found in the Bible.

Using the SQ3R Method

One way to increase your efficiency when studying material for the first time is to follow a five-step process known as the SQ3R method. The steps are described below.

1. Survey
Skim the material first. Read heads, highlighted terms, and the first sentence of each paragraph. Look at all pictures and graphs.

2. Question
Ask questions about the material. Your questions might begin with *who, what, when, where, why,* and *how.*

3. Read
Read the selection carefully. Identify the main idea of each section. Take notes, and add questions to your list.

4. Record
Write answers to your questions without looking at the text. Make brief notes about additional main ideas or facts.

5. Review
Check answers in the text. Continue to study the text until you can answer all questions correctly.

Study Skills

MEETING INDIVIDUAL NEEDS

Learning Disabled

Understanding SQ3R

Make sure students understand what *SQ3R* means. Explain that the purpose of the term is to help students remember the steps of the study method. Seeing the connection between the name *SQ3R* and its parts (*S* for "survey," *Q* for "question," and *3R* for "read," "record," and "review") can help students remember the method. Encourage them to memorize these terms and use all parts of the SQ3R method. **L1**

You can apply the SQ3R method to studying any subject. If you use the method regularly, it will become a habit. You may find that this habit brings several benefits, including the following:

- You remember more of what you read.
- You develop specific questions about information that is unclear.
- You are better prepared for class discussions and lectures.

Evaluating What You Read

The more you think about what you read, the better you will remember it. Therefore, if you get in the habit of evaluating material as you read it, you will find that you learn it better.

Identifying Facts and Opinions Most of what you read includes both facts and opinions. A fact is a statement that can be verified or proved to be true. How do you prove that something is true? One way is through direct experience—something you see or experience for yourself. If someone says that it is raining outside, you can step outside and see for yourself.

Proof also might come from an authoritative source, such as a reference book or an expert on the subject. Did the Inca emperor Pachacuti come to power in 1438? You can check the date in an encyclopedia.

An opinion is a personal judgment. Because opinions are expressions of someone's beliefs or feelings, they cannot be proved true or false. A valid opinion, however, is one that is based on accurate information. Opinions are most convincing when supported by evidence.

The following chart shows examples of facts and opinions. Learning how to distinguish between them will help you evaluate what you read.

Distinguishing Between Facts and Opinions

STATEMENT	FACT OR OPINION
1. Computers now do much of the assembly-line work that formerly was performed by factory workers.	**Fact:** Examining factories over the last twenty years would verify this statement.
2. Computerized manufacturing is bad because it causes people to lose their jobs.	**Opinion:** Computerized manufacturing may actually cause some unemployment, but whether it is good or bad is a value judgment.
3. Many kinds of vegetation and wildlife live in areas known as wetlands.	**Fact:** You could check this statement by reading studies done by biologists or by visiting a wetland yourself.
4. The federal government should do more to protect wetlands from pollution.	**Opinion:** Facts could be used to support or oppose this statement, but the statement is an opinion. People often disagree on the role of the federal government in protecting the environment.

Cross-reference: Writing

For pointers on recognizing facts and opinions in the writing of others and making effective use of facts and opinions in their own writing, refer students to Lesson 6.2, pp. 292–295.

Enrichment and Extension

Examining Written Material

Psychologists have identified several methods people can use to help themselves learn. The following methods apply specifically to learning written material: (1) relate the material you are trying to learn to other material you have learned in the past, and (2) underline or highlight important points in the text. It is easier to remember material that is underlined, capitalized, or highlighted. For this reason writers and publishers often use boldface or italic type to make important information stand out. You may want to suggest that students pay special attention to such material as well as to headings.

Practice and Assess

Evaluation Rubrics

Exercise 3

Students should demonstrate an ability to distinguish facts and opinions. In particular, students should point out opinions lacking support or opinions that are presented as facts.

Exercise 4

Students should give accurate literal translations of figurative descriptions. In many cases, a literal description will take many more words. To evaluate which style is more effective, students may need to consider the purpose of a passage, as well as its clarity.

Exercise 5

Look for specific phrases in rewritten passages that must be interpreted in imaginative rather than literal terms. Students will most likely invent figurative, direct, or indirect comparisons.

Additional Resources

- *Listening and Speaking Activities,* pp. 1–2
- *Thinking and Study Skills,* pp. 2, 4–5, 8–9, 12, 14, 17, 34–38
- *Vocabulary and Spelling Strategies and Practice,* pp. 13–17

Cross-reference: Writing

For additional writing situations in which students might use figurative language, see Lesson 3.3, pp. 148–151, and Lesson 3.4, pp. 152–155.

Close

Invite students to discuss their study habits. Which study strategies do they use? What methods do they find work best for them? What new methods would they like to try?

Using Figurative Language Writers use figurative language to make their texts more interesting and to express their ideas more clearly. Figurative language is a word or phrase used in an imaginative way rather than in a literal sense. Similes, metaphors, and idioms are examples of figurative language. The example below includes several examples of figurative language. Do they work to help convey the writer's message?

The dancers, clad in silks of green and blue, took their positions as the curtain rose. The music floated softly upward from somewhere below the stage and gathered like mist about their feet. As the melody swelled, their frozen forms melted into a celebration of movement. They swept across the floor, colorful rivers seeking their own paths along the barren landscape of the stage.

The dancers were not cold enough to be actually "frozen." Rather, they were as motionless as if they were frozen.

The description of how the dancers "melt" into "rivers" suggests their graceful, fluid movements.

Exercise 3

Read a newspaper article, a magazine article, or an editorial. In the piece you have chosen, identify ten statements as being either fact or opinion. If any of the statements are opinions, decide which ones are supported by accurate information. Share your comments with your class.

Exercise 4

Select a short passage from a novel or short story that uses figurative language. Rewrite the passage, changing the figurative language to literal language. How does the passage change? What is the overall effect?

Exercise 5

Find a three- or four-paragraph passage in a history or science textbook. Rewrite the passage, expressing the same information with figurative language. Evaluate the results.

Meeting Individual Needs: English Language Learners

Examining Figurative Language

Some students who are learning English may have difficulty understanding figurative language. You may wish to assign a student who is proficient in English to work with these students to complete Exercises 4 and 5. Encourage students who are learning English to give examples of figurative language from their first language, translating and explaining the examples for the class.

27.3 Learning from Graphics

Read the following sentence quickly: "In 2006, the seasonally adjusted unemployment rate for the United States was 4.6; the rate for Canada was 5.5; the rate for Australia was 4.9; the rate for Japan was the lowest, at 4.2; and the rate for Germany was highest at 10.3." Did you grasp all of that? Probably not. The string of numbers in the sentence makes the information difficult to comprehend at a glance. To present numbers and other facts that are difficult to communicate clearly in sentences, writers often use tables, graphs, flow charts, cluster diagrams, and maps. The rest of this lesson will give you tips on how to interpret each of these types of graphics.

Tables

Tables separate information into categories so that you can compare specific items easily. The following table shows the seasonally adjusted unemployment rates for several countries in 2006. Notice how much more easily you can pick out information from the chart than from the example above.

Seasonally Adjusted Unemployment Rates for 10 Countries in 2006

COUNTRY	1ST QUARTER	2ND QUARTER	3RD QUARTER	4TH QUARTER	YEAR
UNITED STATES	4.7	4.7	4.7	4.5	4.6
CANADA	5.7	5.5	5.5	5.4	5.5
AUSTRALIA	5.0	4.9	4.7	4.6	4.9
JAPAN	4.3	4.2	4.2	4.1	4.2
FRANCE	10.0	9.8	9.6	9.4	9.7
GERMANY	10.9	10.5	10.1	9.6	10.3
ITALY	7.3	6.9	6.7	6.5	6.9
SWEDEN	7.3	7.3	6.	6.5	7.0
NETHERLANDS	4.9	4.4	4.3	4.3	4.5
UNITED KINGDOM	5.3	5.5	5.6	5.5	5.5

Across the top row and down the left-hand column are the categories of information in the chart.

Compare information across columns. Which country had the highest seasonally adjusted unemployment rate?

Compare information between rows. Which country had the same unemployment rate as the United States during the third quarter of 2006?

To find the unemployment rate for the Netherlands for the third quarter of 2006, you would first read down the left-hand column to find *Netherlands.* Then you would read across the top row of the table until you find third quarter. Moving down the column of percentages, you would see that the seasonally adjusted unemployment rate for the Netherlands in the third quarter of 2006 was 4.3.

Resource Manager

Planning Resources

- *Lesson Plans*

Transparencies

- *Bellringer*
- *Daily Language Practice*

Other Print Resources

- *Listening and Speaking Activities,* pp. 1–2
- *Thinking and Study Skills,* pp. 2, 4–5, 8–9, 12, 14, 17, 34–38
- *Vocabulary and Spelling Strategies and Practice,* p. 36

Focus

Lesson Overview

Objectives

- To understand how information is organized in different kinds of graphics
- To make the best use of information presented in graphics

Skills

- comparing information in a table; understanding quantities compared in a bar graph; interpreting sequence in a flow chart; understanding relationships in cluster diagrams; reading maps

Critical Thinking

- analyzing; contrasting; relating; comparing; evaluating data; defining and clarifying; visualizing

Listening and Speaking

- discussing; evaluating; questioning; explaining a process

Bellringer

Daily Language Activity

When students enter the classroom, have this assignment on the board: *Write down the kind of information that you might find represented in a table, in a bar graph, in a flow chart, in a cluster diagram, and on a map.*

See also *Daily Language Practice*

Motivating Activity

Ask students if they've ever read difficult information and thought, "There must be an easier way to explain this." Explain that visuals, such as tables and graphs, present information in a format that is easy to see and understand. Have students discuss their ideas from the Bellringer activity. Do they think it is easier to show these kinds of information visually or to write them in a paragraph? Why?

Teach

Creating a Table

To help students understand how data is organized in tables, assign groups to develop simple tables. Suggest that students survey their classmates to collect data such as month of birth, height, favorite sport, or other information students can readily share. Have each group member poll a certain number of students. The group should then combine the data, divide it into males and females, and develop a table presenting the data. Allow spokespeople for each group to present and discuss their completed table. **L2**

Developing a Flow Chart or Bar Graph

Work with students to develop either a bar graph or a flow chart using material from one of their other classes. For example, for history they could use a bar graph to illustrate the number of bales of cotton exported by the United States in each decade from 1810 through 1870. For science they might use a flow chart to illustrate the life cycle of a butterfly or the process leading to a volcanic eruption. Provide time for students to display their completed charts or graphs and explain them to the class. Ask students to evaluate the presentations. **L3**

Bar Graphs

In bar graphs, each quantity is shown as a bar. The height of the bar reflects the amount. Because the bars are separate and distinct, writers often use bar graphs to compare quantities.

The bar graph shown here compares the consumption of vegetable protein in different world regions. The horizontal axis identifies the five world regions studied, while the vertical axis shows the amount of protein actually consumed (measured in grams per person per day).

The height of the bar represents the amount of vegetable protein consumed.

Each bar represents a different region.

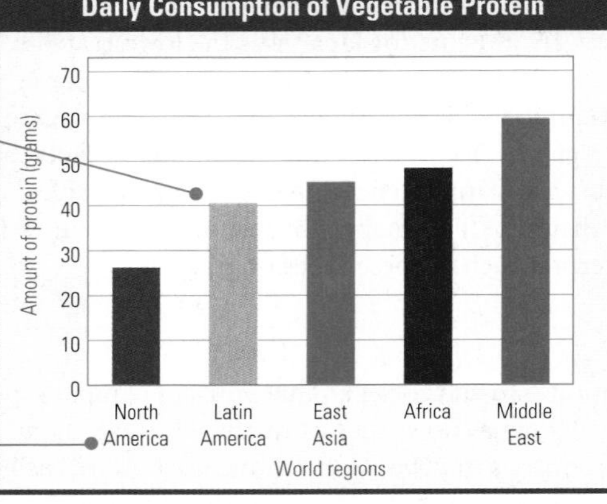
Daily Consumption of Vegetable Protein
Amount of protein (grams)
70
60
50
40
30
20
10
0
North America
Latin America
East Asia
Africa
Middle East
World regions

The bars provide a quick way to see which regions consume the most and the least vegetable protein.

In the bar graph shown here, the bars run vertically. In other bar graphs the bars run horizontally. When bars run horizontally, the vertical axis indicates the categories being compared, and the horizontal axis indicates the quantities being compared.

Flow Charts

Flow charts show relationships among items, ideas, and events. Often they show the steps in a process. Arrows connect the ideas or steps to show how one flows into the next. For example, a flow chart might show the steps a bill goes through in becoming a law or the stages in the life of a frog. The flow chart below shows the selection process for a Supreme Court justice.

Identify where the process begins. Arrows show the steps in the process.

At some stages more than one result may occur.

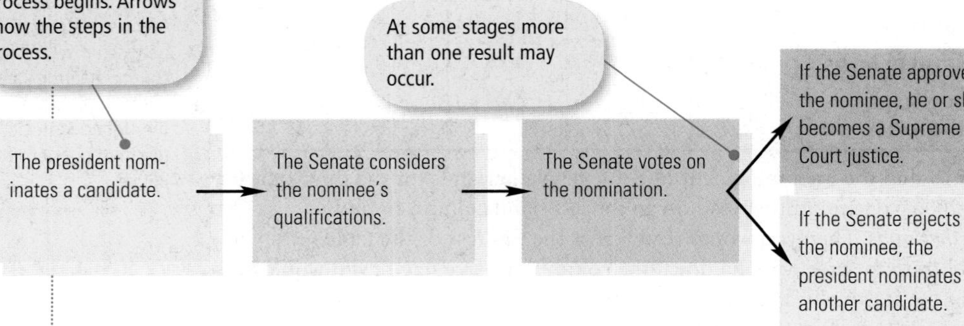
The president nominates a candidate.
The Senate considers the nominee's qualifications.
The Senate votes on the nomination.
If the Senate approves the nominee, he or she becomes a Supreme Court justice.
If the Senate rejects the nominee, the president nominates another candidate.

Study Skills

Meeting Individual Needs: Learning Disabled

Reading Graphs and Flow Charts

Help students read the information on the bar graph and flow chart. Make sure students understand the labels. The labels at the bottom tell what each bar represents—in this case, one region's daily vegetable protein consumption. Ask students what the numbers on the left side of the graph mean. (They provide a scale for measuring the grams of vegetable protein consumed per day.) How many grams per person are consumed in Africa? (nearly fifty) In which region is consumption per person lowest? (North America)

Cluster Diagrams

Another way to show the relationships among ideas is through a cluster diagram. Start by writing a topic or main idea inside a circle in the center of a piece of paper. As you think of ideas related to your topic, add those in circles arranged around the central one. Connect new ideas with related ideas.

Cluster diagrams connect the ideas you learn in class. The example below shows a cluster diagram about South American rain forests. Notice how the diagram shows the relationships among ideas.

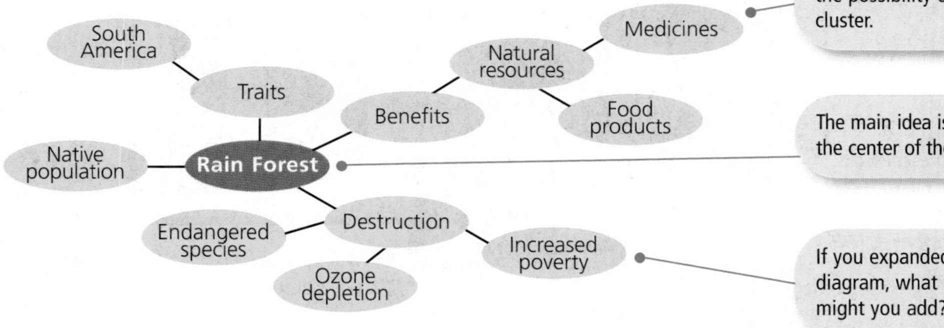

Each new idea creates the possibility of another cluster.

The main idea is listed in the center of the diagram.

If you expanded the diagram, what ideas might you add?

Maps

Maps are a representation of a section of the earth. Political maps show features that are created by people or reflect their cultures, such as countries, cities, or roads. Physical maps show the natural features of the earth, such as mountains, rivers, and plains. The map at right shows both political and physical features.

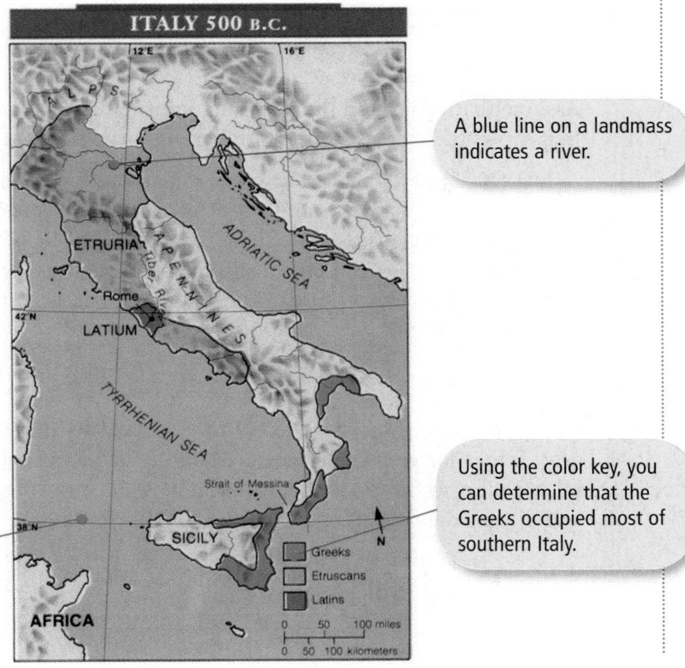

A blue line on a landmass indicates a river.

Using the color key, you can determine that the Greeks occupied most of southern Italy.

Why would you use a map such as this one?

Cross-reference: Writing

For situations in which cluster diagrams can be used to generate writing and research ideas, see Lesson 2.2, Prewriting: Getting Started, pp. 62–67.

Additional Resources

- *Listening and Speaking Activities,* pp. 1–2
- *Thinking and Study Skills,* pp. 2, 4–5, 8–9, 12, 14, 17, 34–38
- *Vocabulary and Spelling Strategies and Practice,* p. 36

Study Skills

interNET CONNECTION

Map Reading

Tell students that Google maps, Mapquest, and Yahoo maps are among the most visited sites on the Internet for providing driving directions. Global positioning sites are even available on the Internet by which they can pinpoint their home's location. Have students log onto one of these map sites. Challenge them to get driving directions from their home to a distant address using two of the sites. Then have students compare which site saves the most time and is the most accurate. Have students report their findings to the class.

Practice and Assess

Evaluation Rubrics

Exercise 6

The table should look similar to the one below.

Percent of Scientists Who Are Women

Category	1970	1986
Social scientists	23	46
Mathematical scientists	17	36
Natural scientists	14	23
Physicians	10	18
Engineers	2	6

Exercise 7

Make sure students start with a broad topic. The diagram should include a main idea in the center, with lines connecting it to several related ideas that branch out into subordinate points. Connections between ideas should be clear.

Close

Have students discuss how graphics are or can be used in some of their other classes—for example, what kind of historical information could be shown on maps, tables, bar graphs, cluster diagrams, and flow charts? What kind of mathematical or scientific information could be shown?

ASSESSMENT OPTIONS

Tests with Answer Key & Rubrics
Unit 27 Mastery Test, pp. 105–106

Testmaker
Unit 27 Mastery Test

You may wish to administer the Unit 27 Mastery Test at this point.

MindJogger Videoquizzes

Political maps and physical maps usually show large land areas: the world, a country, a state, a city. Maps can also show smaller areas: the houses in a neighborhood, the buildings on a college campus, or the location of rooms in a building. Architects use one type of map, a floor plan, to help them visualize their ideas. Below is an example of a floor plan that you might see in a history book. The floor plan shows the layout of a palace built in Morocco about one thousand years ago.

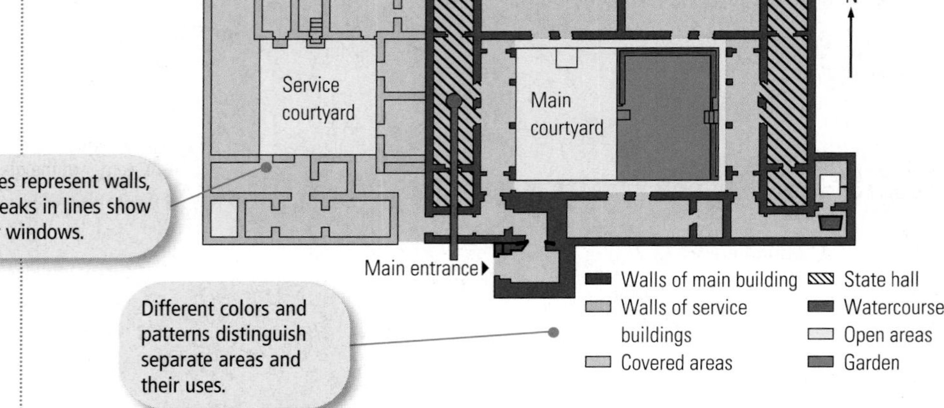

Solid lines represent walls, while breaks in lines show doors or windows.

Different colors and patterns distinguish separate areas and their uses.

Exercise 6

Assume that you found the following information in an encyclopedia. Create a table that shows the increase in the number of female scientists between 1990 and 2006.

> In 1990 about 23 percent of social scientists were women. About 17 percent of mathematical scientists and about 14 percent of natural scientists were women. Among physicians, 10 percent were women. Only 2 percent of engineers were women. By 2006, women constituted 56 percent of social scientists, 36 percent of mathematical scientists, 23 percent of natural scientists, 18 percent of physicians, and 13 percent of engineers.

Exercise 7

In a group of four to six students, develop a cluster diagram. Decide on a broad concept or idea for your center circle. Members of the group should take turns adding related ideas to the diagram. Once you have filled the page, analyze the connections and discuss their meanings.

Study Skills

Enrichment and Extension

Creating a Graphic

Invite students to create a graphic to organize information they are studying in another class. Encourage them to consider a topic they find difficult or confusing. Students should consider what information to show and how best to organize it. When they are finished, have students present their graphic in class and explain the information on it.

INTRODUCING UNIT 28

UNIT 28 Taking Tests

LOG ON Writing Online | For research tools and additional skills practice, go to glencoe.com and enter QuickPass code WC97727p3.

Objectives

- To become familiar with various kinds of test items, including multiple-choice items, true-false items, short-answer items, fill-in items, matching items, vocabulary items, and more
- To learn tips for taking various kinds of tests, including standardized tests
- To apply test-taking strategies by taking practice tests

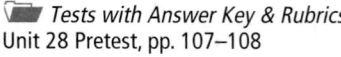

ASSESSMENT OPTIONS

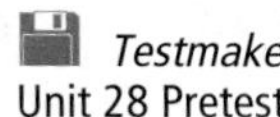

Tests with Answer Key & Rubrics
Unit 28 Pretest, pp. 107–108

Testmaker
Unit 28 Pretest

You may wish to administer the Unit 28 Pretest at this point.

Key to Ability Levels

L1 Level 1 activities are within the basic ability range of students.

L2 Level 2 activities are within the ability range of average students.

L3 Level 3 activities are more challenging activities.

Resource Manager

Planning Resources
- *Lesson Plans*
- *Block Scheduling*

Transparencies
- *Bellringer*
- *Daily Language Practice*

Other Print Resources
- *Taking Standardized Tests*
- *Tests with Answer Key and Rubrics*
- *Thinking and Study Skills*

Video
- *MindJogger Videoquizzes*

Software
- *Presentation Plus!*
- *Testmaker*

Web Site
- *glencoe.com*

Focus

Lesson Overview

Objective

- To develop test-taking confidence by mastering and using strategies to answer various types of objective test questions

Skills

- using test-taking strategies; managing test-taking time

Critical Thinking

- analyzing; synthesizing; classifying; recalling; relating; comparing and contrasting; recognizing main ideas; evaluating criteria; decision making

Listening and Speaking

- discussing; questioning

Bellringer

Daily Language Activity

When students enter the classroom, have this assignment on the board: *Write a sentence or two telling what would make you a better test taker.*

See also *Daily Language Practice*

Motivating Activity

Invite volunteers to discuss how they feel before and during tests. Explain that even though studying is the best way to prepare for a test, knowing the material is not always enough to ensure success—anxiety can undermine the effort. Learning basic test-taking strategies can alleviate test anxiety and increase test takers' confidence.

28.1 Classroom Tests

Careful attention to daily classroom work is the most important step you can take to prepare for a test. In addition, though, you can get ready for an exam by learning how to answer the types of questions your teachers will ask.

This lesson will show you some strategies for answering different types of objective test items. An objective test item is one that asks for very specific information about material that you have studied.

Multiple-Choice Items

A multiple-choice test item includes an incomplete sentence, or a question and a number of responses. You are to pick the response that best completes the sentence or answers the question. Consider the following tips.

Tips on Answering Multiple-Choice Items

1. Read the item carefully. You need to know what information you are looking for.
2. Read all the responses. Even if the first one seems right, another response may be better.
3. Eliminate any responses that are clearly incorrect. Eliminating incorrect responses helps you focus your attention on the responses that may be correct.
4. Be cautious about responses that contain absolute words—*always, never, all,* or *none.* Because many statements have exceptions, absolute statements are often incorrect.

Here is an example of a multiple-choice test item. In this case, you are given a statement with a missing word. You are to choose the response that, when placed in the blank, will make the statement correct.

In *The Thousand and One Nights,* ______________ prevents her execution by telling tales of high adventure to her husband.

a. an Arab writer
b. Sinbad
c. Scheherazade
d. an unnamed man

Though the stories were written by Arab writers, choice *a* does not complete the sentence correctly.

The sentence structure indicates that the answer is a female, so choices *b* and *d* are incorrect. The correct answer is choice *c.*

Taking Tests

Resource Manager

Planning Resources
- *Lesson Plans*

Transparencies
- *Bellringer*
- *Daily Language Practice*

Other Print Resources
- *Taking Standardized Tests*
- *Thinking and Study Skills,* pp. 24, 39–40

Here is another multiple-choice item. This one is phrased as a question. You are to select the best answer to the question.

Which of the following statements concerning the book *Native Son* is accurate?

a. It was written by Richard Wright.
b. It takes place in the North.
c. It is a work of fiction.
d. all of the above.

Though choice *a* sounds correct, read all of the responses before answering.

Select this response only if you are sure that at least two of the responses are correct. In this case, choice *d* is correct.

True-False Items

A true-false item asks you to decide whether a statement is true or not. Many true-false items include some information that is true and some that is false. If any part of a statement is false, the entire statement is considered false. For the answer to be true, the entire statement must be true. Look at the statement on word usage below. Why is it false?

The word *affect* is usually a verb meaning "to influence," and the word *effect* is always a noun meaning "the result."

The first part of this sentence is true, but the second is not because *effect* can also be a verb meaning "to cause." The correct answer is *false.*

Short-Answer Items

Short-answer items ask for specific information. Therefore, they are usually best answered with precisely phrased complete sentences. Also, since these items may ask you to supply several pieces of information, your answers to these items may be worth more than answers to other questions. For example, look at the following question, which might appear on an earth-science test.

Why is soil erosion viewed as both helpful and harmful to people?

The preceding question asks for more than a list of the effects of soil erosion. In your answer, you should clearly distinguish between effects of soil erosion that are viewed as helpful and those that are viewed as harmful. Soil erosion is seen as helpful because it breaks up rocks and earth, moving rich soil to valleys and the mouths of rivers. Erosion is seen as harmful because it often strips farmland of valuable topsoil and threatens crop production.

Taking Tests

Teach

Reading Test Questions

Students may need to be reminded of the critical importance of careful reading in test taking. Point out that multiple-choice questions or answers often contain words such as *not.* If students overlook such key words, they will probably choose the wrong answers. Bring in sample multiple-choice questions from test-taking preparation books or old classroom tests. Ask students to read several questions and possible answers aloud, pointing out key words such as *not, never, both, all, or without.* Explain how these key words should affect one's answer choice. **L2**

Getting Help from Technology

Software programs designed to help users prepare for a variety of tests are now available. If possible, have students obtain copies of such software. Help them prepare a demonstration of the software for the class, and allot class time for students to use the program. **L3**

English Language Learners

Recognizing Test Clues

Help students recognize clues that can help them answer test questions. Read some sample test questions aloud, working with students to identify clues. For example, the first fill-in example on page 850 gives two clues that three planets should be given in the answer (the word *three* and the three blanks). What does the word *both* indicate in the last sample test question on page 849? (The answer should have two parts.) How can students tell that the answer to the sample test question on page 848 is a woman's name? (The word *her* is used.)

Teach

Verbalizing Strategies

To make sure students internalize test-taking strategies, ask them to describe in their own words the strategies given for the five types of test items in this lesson. Also ask them to describe in their own words the best way to allocate their time during test taking. Add to or refocus their responses if necessary. **L2**

Cross-reference: Grammar

For more information on subject-verb agreement, refer students to Lesson 16.2, p. 611; Lesson 16.4, pp. 614–615; Lesson 16.5, pp. 616–617; and Lesson 16.7, pp. 619–621.

Fill-in Items

Fill-in items usually consist of a sentence with one or more blanks for you to fill in. The number of blank spaces provided often indicates the number of words needed in the response. Your answer should make the statement true and also grammatically correct. Consequently, rereading the statement with your answer included will help you check whether your choice is correct. Try to answer the fill-in question below.

Notice that the order of planets is important. The only correct answer is *Mercury, Venus,* and *Earth.*

In our solar system, the first three planets in order from the sun are _______, _______, and _______.

On some tests, you may be given a list of words from which to choose your answers. If so, complete the ones you're sure of first. If answers from the list can be used only once, cross them off as you use them. As you reduce the number of possible answers, you increase your chances of finding the correct answers to the harder items. For example, assume that you can answer the first two items below but not the third.

1. Astronomers believe that the sun is a star in the ________ galaxy.
2. The ________ revolves around the earth about once per month.
3. The second closest star to the earth is ________.

Milky Way	moon
Andromeda	Alpha Centauri
quasar	

After answering *Milky Way* for the first item and *moon* for the second, only three possible responses remain. Because the structure of the sentence suggests that the correct answer is the name of a star, and star names are capitalized, you can eliminate *quasar*. Choosing between only two answers improves your chances of choosing correctly. What is the correct answer? *Alpha Centauri.*

Taking Tests

Real World Connection

The Science of Sleep

Ask students how well they are able to remember information. Share with them that researchers have found that people are more likely to remember information after sleeping for eight hours than they are after spending eight hours engaged in typical daytime activities. It seems that less memory loss occurs during sleep because conscious events do not intervene and interfere with the memory. Getting a good night's sleep before a test is a good idea!

Matching Items

In matching items, you have two sets or lists of items, and you must match those in the first column or group to those in the second. Reading the directions carefully helps you know what type of match you should make. Some common matches are

- terms and their definitions
- events and the dates they occurred
- causes and their effects
- chemical elements and their symbols

Whatever the subject, compare the lists. Do they include the same number of items? Will every item be used exactly once? If so, you can cross out each one as it is used. Just as you used the process of elimination to help you with fill-ins, you can use the same approach again here. In the following example, match each country with its capital. Each city is used only once.

1. ________	Japan	a. New Delhi
2. ________	Uruguay	b. London
3. ________	India	c. Montevideo
4. ________	Great Britain	d. Cairo
5. ________	Egypt	e. Tokyo

As with other test items, answer the ones you're sure of first. Note, however, that if each response is used only once, you'll have to make two changes if you change an answer.

Time Management

Tests usually last no more than one class period. Because time is limited, you need to use it efficiently. The chart that follows gives a few suggestions for using your time wisely.

Tips for Allocating Time During a Test
1. Spend the first few minutes preparing. Reading the directions carefully will help you answer items appropriately.
2. Answer the items you are sure of first. Skipping difficult items will allow you to respond to all of the items you know.
3. Return to the difficult items. Using the strategies learned in this lesson, give the best answers you can.
4. Spend the last few minutes reviewing your answers. Taking time to check your answers will help prevent simple mistakes.

Checking Answers

Warn students against marking answers in the wrong place. Explain that if they skip a difficult question or if they inadvertently overlook a question, they could accidentally mismatch the next question and answer, making all subsequent answers on the test incorrect. On a sample test, guide students through the process of checking test item numbers and answers. Point out that such checking is especially important if answers are written on a separate piece of paper. If necessary, show students how to use a piece of paper or a ruler as a place marker. **L1**

Cooperative Learning

Working with Test-Taking Strategies

Ask small groups to develop a current-events quiz in roundtable format. Each group passes around five sheets of paper, one for each of these format categories: multiple-choice, true-false, short-answer, fill-in, and matching. Students write a test question to fit each format category as they receive the sheet. (Remind them to use what they have learned about test-taking strategies.) Groups then gather the sheets, exchange them with other groups, and answer the questions using their knowledge of test-taking strategies, as well as their knowledge of current events.

Practice and Assess

Answers: Exercise 1

1. d
2. True
3. special effects
4. Government bans seem to have increased Kabuki's popularity.
5. It would be good to have students state each cause-effect relationship rather than just identify the letter of the correct answer:
   c. The rise of a new social class led to a desire for a new form of drama.
   a. Ridicule of political figures was the cause of bans on Kabuki by the government.
   b. Censorship of performances caused an increase in the popularity of Kabuki.

Additional Resources

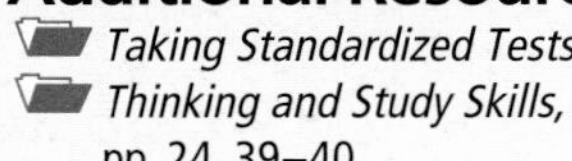

Taking Standardized Tests
Thinking and Study Skills, pp. 24, 39–40

Close

Ask students to list tips for dealing with the following kinds of objective test items: multiple-choice, true-false, short-answer, fill-in, and matching.

Exercise 1

Read the passage below and use the test-taking strategies in this lesson to help you complete the items that follow.

Over the centuries, Japanese kabuki theater has grown and flourished. Continuing a tradition that historians have traced back to the 1600s, kabuki plays are still performed in Japan to large audiences. Kabuki theater seems to have originated as a new form of drama to satisfy the lavish and melodramatic tastes of a new social class in Tokugawa, Japan.

When the lower and middle classes of society began to increase in the urban centers, they sought new forms of entertainment. The name *kabuki* means "to lean in the direction of fashion," reflecting kabuki theater's popular origins.

Kabuki dramatizes subjects ranging from historical events to daily life. With elaborate costumes, exaggerated movements, and amazing special effects (including snowstorms and fires), kabuki theater is a spectacular event. Sometimes the stories make fun of political figures. During the 1600s, government officials banned some performances they felt were too controversial. If anything, this censorship seems to have made kabuki all the more popular.

1. Which of the following is true of kabuki theater?
   a. It is an old art form.
   b. It can be controversial.
   c. It is still performed today.
   d. all of the above
2. True or False: Kabuki has a name appropriate to its origins.
3. Like many popular films today, kabuki theater makes spectacular use of elaborate staging and ________ ________, such as snowstorms and fires.
4. How did the government's ban on certain political plays affect public opinion of kabuki?
5. For each effect in the following list, choose the cause from which that effect most directly resulted.
   a. bans on kabuki by the government
   b. increase in the popularity of kabuki
   c. desire for a new form of drama

   ___ rise of a new social class
   ___ ridicule of political figures
   ___ censorship of performances

Meeting Individual Needs: English Language Learners

Understanding Test Items

Make sure students understand all the terms used in the exercise passage and the questions on this page. Encourage them to ask for help if they don't understand terms used in tests. Before they begin this exercise, have them discuss strategies for answering each question.

28.2 Standardized Tests

To compare large numbers of students, schools often give standardized tests, or examinations that have been given to similar groups of students around the country. By studying these test results, experts develop standards of performance. Most standardized tests fall into one of three categories:

- Ability tests evaluate general learning skills, such as how well you can read, write, or use logic.
- Achievement tests evaluate knowledge in specific content areas, such as how much you know about biology or world history.
- Aptitude tests evaluate individual talents and interests, such as whether you prefer working in groups or alone.

Standardized tests contain several types of items. Becoming familiar with the kinds of test items most often used on standardized tests will improve your chances of scoring well.

Reading-Comprehension Items

How well you understand what you read is measured by reading-comprehension items. These items usually include a long passage about a literature, social studies, or science topic, and several questions about the passage. You should be able to answer all of the questions on the basis of the information in the passage. These questions often require you to

- identify main ideas
- recognize details supporting main ideas
- figure out what is not stated in the passage

The last type of item, also known as an inference item, requires coming to a conclusion that is based on the information in the passage but is not explicitly expressed. As you read the following passage and the items that follow it, notice the suggestions for how to respond to the items.

> Siddhartha Gautama, the founder of Buddhism, began his life as a Kshatriya prince. Born the son of a prince in northern India around 566 B.C., Gautama was raised in luxury. As a young man he continued to live a sheltered life, shielded from sickness and poverty. Tradition states that one day Gautama's charioteer drove him around his estates, and for the first time Gautama saw sickness, old age, and death. Shocked at these scenes of misery, Gautama decided to find out why people suffered and how suffering could be ended. At the age of 29, he left his wife and newborn son and wandered throughout India in what is known as the Great Renunciation.

Taking Tests

Focus

Lesson Overview

Objective

- To become familiar with responding to various kinds of standardized test questions

Skills

- using test-taking strategies; managing test-taking time

Critical Thinking

- analyzing; synthesizing; classifying; recalling; relating; comparing and contrasting; recognizing patterns and main ideas; evaluating criteria; decision-making; inferring

Listening and Speaking

- discussing; questioning

Bellringer
Daily Language Activity

When students enter the classroom, have this assignment on the board: *Write three types of items or questions you would expect to find on standardized tests.*

See also  *Daily Language Practice*

Motivating Activity

Have students discuss the differences between classroom tests and standardized tests. Which do they prefer taking and why? What kinds of items do they have the most trouble with on standardized tests and why? Explain that this lesson will familiarize them with common standardized test questions and the best ways to respond to them.

Resource Manager

Planning Resources
- *Lesson Plans*

Transparencies
- *Bellringer*
- *Daily Language Practice*

Other Print Resources
- *Taking Standardized Tests*
- *Thinking and Study Skills,* pp. 24, 39–40

Teach

Responding to Reading Comprehension Questions

To assist students in answering reading comprehension questions, suggest that they try reading the sample questions at the top of this page before reading the paragraph at the bottom of page 853. Explain that to answer question 1, students will need to think about what ideas are important as they read the passage. Then point out that the words *seemed to be* in question 2 are a clue that the answer is not stated directly in the passage but will have to be inferred from other information that is stated. **L2**

Taking Tests for Fun

Some students may enjoy the challenge of completing the vocabulary or topical tests featured in magazines such as *Reader's Digest.* Provide examples of such tests or invite students to find some and bring them to class. Let students work in groups to answer the questions and discuss strategies that helped them arrive at their answers. **L3**

Cross-reference: Study Skills

For tips on comprehension and retention of information obtained through reading, refer students to Lesson 27.2, pp. 838–842.

Although each sentence is true, choice *d* states the most important point, so it is correct.

This item requires you to infer the correct response, which is choice *b.*

1. Which sentence best summarizes the most important information in this passage?
   a. Gautama was raised in luxury in India.
   b. Gautama was born around 566 B.C.
   c. Gautama left home at the age of 29.
   d. Gautama wanted to know why people suffered.
2. Based on this passage, Gautama seemed to be
   a. proud of his achievements.
   b. concerned about others.
   c. angry about his family's situation.
   d. eager to meet other people.

Vocabulary Items

Standardized tests often evaluate vocabulary knowledge through varieties of multiple-choice items. Sometimes you may be asked to complete a sentence by filling in the meaning of a word, as in the item that follows.

A preliminary step is taken ______.
a. before any other step in a process
b. during the most important steps of a process
c. after all other steps in a process are completed
d. only when necessary to complete a process
e. only if the first step of a process fails

One tip for completing vocabulary items is to analyze the parts of an unknown word. See Unit 25, pages 818–826, for more information on how to build vocabulary. Notice that the word *preliminary* begins with the letters *pre-*. If you recall other words that begin with these letters, such as *precede, preface*, and *prepare*, you may realize that *pre-* often means "in front of" or "before." Using this knowledge, you may correctly determine that the answer is choice *a.*

A different type of vocabulary item, an analogy, tests the ability to analyze the relationships between words, not just an understanding of the meanings of words. Consider the words *healthy* and *robust.* What is the relationship between them? They are synonyms, words that have the same or nearly the same meaning. Now examine the pairs of words at the top of page 855. Which pair has the same relationship as *healthy* and *robust?*

Taking Tests

MEETING INDIVIDUAL NEEDS

Less Proficient Readers

Drawing Inferences

Go over any difficult vocabulary in the passage on page 853 and in the questions on page 854. Guide students in inferring the answer to question 1 on page 854. In this passage, it is "Gautama wanted to know why people suffered." Model how to answer question 2: The passage says that Gautama did not suffer himself, so his decision to find out why people suffered must have been based on his concern for others. Point out that the other choices are not supported by information in the passage. **L1**

```
Healthy is to robust as
   a. sociable is to disagreeable.
   b. haughty is to arrogant.
   c. mumbled is to audible.
   d. scholastic is to readable.
   e. loving is to polite.
```

Sociable is the opposite of *disagreeable*. *Haughty* and *arrogant* are synonyms. *Mumbled* speech is very different from speech that is *audible*. *Scholastic* and *readable* do not have similar meanings, and a *loving* person is not the same as a *polite* person.

None of the choices listed has anything to do with being healthy. However, the relationship you're looking for is one in which the pairs are synonyms. Only in choice *b* are the word meanings nearly the same. Therefore, choice *b* is the correct answer.

Some analogy items are shown in a different format. Each pair of words is separated by a colon, with a double colon used after the first pair. However, this format still requires you to choose the pair of words with the same relationship as the first. What is the relationship below?

```
carpenter : hammer : :
   a. swimmer : athlete
   b. hospital : doctor
   c. waiter : tray
   d. letter : post office
   e. bottle : beverage
```

One strategy for answering analogy items is to create a simple sentence in your mind that states the relationship between the first pair of words—for example, *A carpenter uses a hammer.* Then try each pair of words, using that particular sentence format. For choice *a* you would come up with the statement *A swimmer uses an athlete.* Since this sentence makes no sense, you could conclude that the relationship between *swimmer* and *athlete* is not the same as the relationship between *carpenter* and *hammer*. After trying each pair of words in the sentence, you would find that choice *c* makes the most sense.

Grammar, Usage, and Mechanics Items

Standardized tests often include sections that evaluate the ability to recognize and use standard English. Items may ask you to find grammatical errors in sentences, point out misused words, or choose the best way to correct an awkward or incorrect sentence.

Writing Analogies

On the board, write a sample test question using an analogy. Then ask individual students or groups to write several test items using analogies. Students may wish to brainstorm a number of analogies before beginning the assignment. Allow students to read their work aloud, while their classmates listen carefully and write down answers. Then call on listeners to explain the correct answers. **L2**

Taking Standardized Tests

Work with groups of students to find and practice taking sample standardized tests, such as PSATs or SATs. Let groups work together to answer the questions and then discuss which strategies seem to be most effective. **L3**

Cross-reference: Thesaurus

For further information on how to use a thesaurus to locate synonyms and antonyms in preparation for analogy items, refer students to Lesson 24.2, pp. 816–817.

English Language Learners

Working with Analogies

Help students feel comfortable with analogies in English by developing a chart on the board showing some common analogies. You may choose examples such as the following: quick : rapid :: happy : joyous (synonyms); house : room :: piano : key (whole/part). Ask students to identify the category for each example and to provide additional examples.

28.2

Teach

Cross-reference: Vocabulary

For lists of homonyms and other often confused words that may appear on standardized tests, refer students to Lesson 26.2, pp. 833–835.

English-usage items often show a sentence with several underlined and lettered sections. As you read the sentence, decide whether one of the underlined parts contains an error, and then mark the corresponding letter on your answer sheet. If the sentence contains no error, mark that choice; it usually follows the sentence. Examine the following item.

The error is in *b.* *"I"* should be *"me."*

```
The competition between Michelle and I became more intense
        a                     b                  c
as the school year progressed.  no error
        d                          e
```

Some usage questions test the knowledge of homonyms, or words that sound alike but have different spellings and meanings. Given a list of phrases that contain homonyms, you might be asked to find the one item with a word used incorrectly or the one item with no errors. In the following example, find the response in which all words are used correctly.

The only phrase in which all words are used correctly is choice *b.*

a. a heard of cattle
b. a jury of your peers
c. a steal beam
d. to much sun

Correction items ask you to correct a mistake as well as to recognize it. Usually in such items, only one part of the given sentence is underlined. Each response is a possible correction. You have to choose the response that best corrects the error in the sentence. Often one of the choices will look identical to the underlined section. Choose it if you feel the sentence contains no error. Here is an example of a sentence-correction item.

As you read the sentence, decide if the underlined words are incorrect.

Ms. Hasan is the best of the two candidates running for mayor.
a. is the best of
b. is the more better of
c. is the very best of
d. is the better of

"Best" should be used only in discussing three or more items, so choices *a* and *c* are incorrect. *"More better"* is incorrect usage. The best response is choice *d.*

Taking Tests

*inter*NET CONNECTION

College Placement Tests

Tell students that most colleges and universities require applicants to take one of two standardized tests, the SAT or the ACT. These tests are usually taken in the eleventh or twelfth grade, and the scores are one factor that admissions officers evaluate when they decide whether or not to admit a student to their institution. Students can use the Internet to gain information about these tests, to learn strategies to prepare for them, and to take practice tests. Ask students to use a search engine to locate a useful site about the SAT or ACT. They should share any sites they find with interested classmates. **L3**

Test-taking Strategies

Certain test-taking strategies will help you as you take a test. The chart that follows lists some strategies you might use.

Tips for Taking Standardized Tests
1. Skip difficult items at first. Because standardized tests are usually timed, focus on answering items you know. You can return to skipped items later.
2. Mark only your answers on the answer sheet. Because the test is machine-graded, stray marks may be read as wrong answers.
3. Frequently compare the item numbers on your test and answer sheet. This helps you avoid putting your answers in the wrong spaces.
4. If you have time, check your answers. If the test does not penalize you for wrong answers, guess the answers for all items you did not have time to complete.

Exercise 2

Use the test-taking strategies described in this lesson to help you complete the following items.

1. Choose the phrase that best completes this sentence:
   A transatlantic message is one that _____________.
   a. travels under a body of water
   b. is sent across the ocean
   c. is sent by passengers on a ship
   d. is always about navigation
2. Find the pair of words with the same relationship as the given pair.
   player : team : :
   a. conductor : baton
   b. engineer : bridge
   c. United States : country
   d. soldier : army
   e. cat : pet
3. Where is the error in the following sentence?
   Our teacher was pleased (**a**) that all of us (**b**) have passed (**c**) the exam, and we were happy (**d**) that the test was over. no error (**e**)
4. Which item includes a word that is used incorrectly?
   a. a strong ally
   b. gives good advice
   c. the capital building
   d. the bare facts
5. Correct the underlined section in the following sentence.
   I wanted to remind her that the party starts at seven o'clock, but she had already went out the door.
   a. had already went
   b. had went already
   c. had went
   d. had already gone

Taking Tests

Practice and Assess

Answers: Exercise 2

1. b
2. d
3. c
4. c
5. d

Learning Disabled

Skipping Questions

Discuss ideas for implementing the test-taking tips on this page. To clarify the first tip, suggest that students place a mark next to test questions that they skip. They might use a check mark for difficult questions that they can probably figure out with more time and an *X* for questions that they cannot answer without guessing. **L1**

Practice and Assess

Answers: Exercise 3

1. a
2. c
3. b
4. d

Additional Resources

Taking Standardized Tests
Thinking and Study Skills, pp. 24, 39–40

Close

Ask students to write in their journal about when they might employ the standardized test-taking strategies covered in this lesson. How might these strategies help them on important standardized tests?

Exercise 3

Read the following passage. Then read each question below and choose the best answer. Mark the letter for that answer on your paper.

Dear Neighbor,

I am the Chairman of Troop 597's October Charity Drive. The proceeds of our activities will benefit the Willimet Community Center on Dodd Street. To raise money, we are holding a recycling drive, and you can help!

As you know, state laws require a 5-cent deposit on all aluminum cans sold. When a can is emptied, it may be redeemed at the recycling center for the nickel deposit. However, many people throw their "empties" out with the trash or litter them along our highways and in our parks.

Help us to help the environment and our Community Center at the same time. Troop 597 will set up a collection stall in the Community Center parking lot from October 1st–31st. Please stop by to drop off any empty cans you would like to donate. In addition, Troop 597 will lead volunteer clean-up crews to key sites across town to collect discarded recyclables. If you would like to join us, the crews will meet in the Community Center parking lot every Saturday in October at 9:00 A.M.

On behalf of Troop 597, I'd like to thank you in advance for whatever efforts you can make on behalf of this worthy campaign.

Yours,
David Hafner, Troop 597

1. David's purpose for writing this letter is primarily to __.
a. ask the community for its support in the scout troop's recycling drive
b. explain why members of his scout troop will take up space in the Community Center parking lot during the month of October
c. try to get more boys to join the scout troop
d. request that people not park in the Community Center parking lot on Saturday

2. Which of the following is a concerned member of the community most likely to do after reading David's letter?
a. Buy fewer cans at local stores
b. Discard more cans in local parks and along highways
c. Drop off empty cans at the Community Center parking lot
d. Go to the library to find out more about fund-raising drives

3. David probably thinks that people who throw their empty cans in the parks are __.
a. helpful and concerned
b. careless and wasteful
c. uninformed about state laws
d. likely to volunteer for a clean-up crew

4. David attempts to show that this year's October Charity Drive will not only raise money for the Community Center but also __.
a. allow the scouts to earn a merit badge
b. help restore and maintain buildings on Dodd Street
c. convince the local government to increase the deposit on aluminum cans
d. help clean up local highways and parks

Taking Tests

Critical Thinking

Analyzing Letter Styles

Ask students what kind of letter David Hafner wrote to his neighbors. (a business letter) Have students compare and contrast the style of David's letter with the business letters modeled in Business and Technical Writing, pages 414–415. Be sure that students understand that a true business letter includes a heading and an inside address, as well as a signature above the writer's typed name.

Evaluating Persuasion

In small groups, have students evaluate the persuasiveness of the letter on this page. Would students have responded positively if they had received the letter in the mail? Why or why not?

28.3 Standardized Test Practice

Introduction

The following pages of exercises have been designed to familiarize you with the standardized writing tests that you may take during the school year. These exercises are very similar to the actual tests in how they look and what they ask you to do. Completing these exercises will not only provide you with practice but also will make you aware of areas you might need to work on.

These writing exercises—just like the actual standardized writing tests—are divided into three sections.

Sentence Structure In this section, pages 860 to 867, you will be given a short passage in which some of the sentences are underlined. Each underlined sentence is numbered. After you finish reading the passage, you will be asked questions about each underlined section. The underlined sections will be either incomplete sentences, run-on sentences, correctly written sentences that should be combined, or correctly written sentences that do not need to be rewritten. You will need to select which is best from the four choices provided.

Usage In this section, pages 868 to 875, you will also be asked to read a short passage. However, in these exercises, a word or words in the passage will be omitted and a numbered blank space will be in their place. After reading the passage, you will need to determine which of the four provided words or groups of words best belongs in each numbered space.

Mechanics Finally, in the third section, pages 876 to 883, the short passages will have parts that are underlined. You will need to determine if, in the underlined sections, there is a spelling error, capitalization error, punctuation error, or no error at all.

Writing well is a skill that you will use the rest of your life. You will be able to write more accurate letters to your friends and family, better papers in school, and more interesting stories. You will be able to express yourself and your ideas more clearly and in a way that is interesting and engaging. These exercises should help to improve your writing and to make you comfortable with the format and types of questions you will see on standardized writing tests.

Resource Manager

Planning Resources
- *Lesson Plans*

Other Print Resources
- *Taking Standardized Tests*
- *Thinking and Study Skills*

Standardized Test Practice

One way you may wish to use this section of *Writer's Choice* is to have students complete an exercise or a series of exercises in an environment that resembles a testing environment. Students should be encouraged to work slowly and carefully. After students have completed the assigned exercises, you may want to go over the answers with students. You can explain the correct answers and review the skills being tested.

Not covered in these test practices is the section in many standardized test situations that requires students to write a composition based on a provided topic. In that section, students are tested on their ability to write clear, concise, and persuasive compositions. You may want to assign topics to your students and have them write one- or two-page compositions so that they get practice for the composition section. When assigning a topic, choose subjects that require the student to have an opinion and to write convincingly as to why their opinion is valid. When advising students on how to prepare for the composition section, tell students that the following abilities may earn not only a higher grade on the test, but may also result in good writing skills: use specific examples to illustrate your point, organize your argument in a logical manner, carefully choose words that effectively and descriptively state your thoughts and opinion, and be consistent in style and purpose throughout the composition. These are some of the ways that students can create interesting, persuasive, and clearly written compositions. Students are often anxious about taking standardized tests. Part of a teacher's responsibility is to provide support and instruction and to assure students that thorough preparation will enable them to meet the challenges of the test. The Teacher Edition Wrap Notes should better help you to understand the tests and to approach the instruction and preparation process with confidence and insight.

Standardized Test Practice

Tested Objective

- To recognize appropriate English usage and sentence structure within the context of a written passage

Answers and Analyses

1. A Point out to students that *Not having the tolerance for slavery that their friends and family had* is a sentence fragment, since it does not contain a subject. Who did not have the tolerance? The correct answer creates one complete sentence with the use of a comma.

2. H Explain to students that this is a run-on sentence because it is two complete sentences separated by only a comma. The correct answer removes the unnecessary pronoun *they* and replaces *drew* with the participle *drawing.*

3. B These sentences are correct as is, but are better combined because they both contain the same subject. The pronoun *she* is dropped from the second sentence and the sentences are combined with the use of a comma.

Test-Taking Tip

Remind students to make sure that the answer choice retains the original meaning of the text in the passage. This is one way for them to eliminate incorrect answer choices.

Standardized Test Practice

Read each passage. Some sections are underlined. The underlined sections may be one of the following:

- Incomplete sentences
- Run-on sentences
- Correctly written sentences that should be combined
- Correctly written sentences that do not need to be rewritten

Choose the best way to write each underlined section and mark the letter for your answer.
If the underlined section needs no change, mark the choice "Correct as is" on your paper.

Angelina and Sarah Grimké, sisters born in South Carolina, are known for their contributions to the abolitionist movement. Not having the tolerance for slavery that their friends and family had. The two sisters moved to Philadelphia, and ultimately settled in New York in the early 1830s. (1) The American Anti-Slavery Society sponsored the Grimkés' early public speeches. These lectures were very successful, they drew large audiences. (2)

In 1838, after a lecture tour of New England, Angelina gave testimony to the Massachusetts legislature. She was the first American woman to address a legislative body. She presented thousands of antislavery petitions. (3) Since women did not normally speak like this in public, the sisters faced criticism, even from fellow abolitionists; yet they continued with their crusade.

1 **A** Not having the tolerance for slavery that their friends and family had, the two sisters moved to Philadelphia and ultimately settled in New York in the early 1830s.
B The two sisters did not have the tolerance for slavery that their friends and family had. Moving to Philadelphia, and ultimately settled in New York in the early 1830s.
C The two sisters did not have the tolerance for slavery that their friends and family had, they moved to Philadelphia, and ultimately settled in New York in the early 1830s.
D Correct as is

2 **F** These lectures were very successful and drawing large audiences.
G These lectures were very successful. Drawing large audiences.
H These lectures were very successful, drawing large audiences.
J Correct as is

3 **A** She was the first American woman to address a legislative body, which presented thousands of antislavery petitions.
B Presenting thousands of antislavery petitions, she was the first American woman to address a legislative body.
C Since she was the first American woman to address a legislative body, she presented thousands of antislavery petitions.
D After she presented thousands of antislavery petitions, she was the first American woman to address a legislative body.

Victor's parents sighed as the players walked off the field. The baseball game had been cancelled at the last minute after thunder had rumbled through the sky. Victor had been looking forward to playing his first game of the season, his mom and dad knew that this was a disappointment for him. (1) The team had been practicing hard and were ready to win. But now, with a big storm coming, they would have to wait until next week. (2)

Victor's parents tried to go to every one of Victor's games. They were always the most enthusiastic fans in the bleachers. The first game of the year was usually very crowded. They had arrived early and managed to get good seats. (3) Now everyone was running to their cars as the rain started. Thoughts of attending the next game. This would help Victor's parents to get through the week! (4)

1 **A** Victor had been looking forward to playing his first game of the season. His mom and dad knowing that this was a disappointment for him.
B Victor had been looking forward to playing his first game of the season, and his mom and dad knew that this was a disappointment for him.
C Victor looking forward to playing his first game of the season. And his mom and dad knew that this was a disappointment for him.
D Correct as is

2 **F** But now, with a big storm coming. They would have to wait until next week.
G But now, with a big storm coming, they would have to wait. Until next week.
H But now, with a big storm coming, they would have to wait, until next week.
J Correct as is

3 **A** The first game of the year was usually very crowded, and they had arrived early, and they had managed to get good seats.
B The first game of the year, which was usually very crowded, had arrived early and managed to get good seats.
C The first game of the year was usually very crowded, but they had arrived early and managed to get good seats.
D The first game of the year, which had arrived early, was usually very crowded and they managed to get good seats.

4 **F** Thoughts of attending the next game helping Victor's parents to get through the week!
G Thoughts of attending the next game would help Victor's parents. To get through the week!
H Thoughts of attending the next game would help Victor's parents to get through the week!
J Correct as is

Answers and Analyses

1. B Explain to students that this is a run-on sentence because it is two complete sentences separated only by a comma. The sentences are combined with use of the conjunction *and.*

2. J The answer is *Correct as is* because it is complete. You may want to point out to students that the sentence begins with a dependent clause starting with a conjunction (*but*).

3. C The two original sentences are complete, but they read better when put together into one sentence. The correct answer combines them with a conjunction (*but*).

4. H Students should recognize that the underlined section contains a sentence fragment that is dependent upon the second sentence for its meaning. Who had the thoughts? The correct answer is created by removing the relative pronoun *this* to form one complete sentence.

Test-Taking Tip

It might be useful to review conjunctions. Coordinating conjunctions are words that connect words or parts of sentences. For example: *but, with, because.* Ask your students to use them in a sentence. Correlative conjunctions are always used in pairs (*either—or, both—and, not only—but,* etc.).

Standardized Test Practice

Tested Objective

- To recognize appropriate English usage and sentence structure within the context of a written passage

Answers and Analyses

1. B This is a run-on sentence because it is two complete sentences separated by only a comma. The correct answer creates one sentence through the use of the conjunction *and.* The second subject-verb clause *he could see* is eliminated because it is redundant.

2. F *When the sun came out from behind the clouds* is a subordinate clause and therefore cannot stand on its own. It modifies—and is dependent upon—the second sentence for its meaning. The correct answer simply replaces the period with a comma to form one complete sentence.

3. A When combined, the meaning of these two sentences will become clearer. Note how the object of the first sentence, *the lake,* is the subject of the second sentence. The correct answer replaces the subject (*it*) with *that,* a relative pronoun.

4. J Make sure your students recognize that this sentence is complete and grammatically correct. It uses the word *before* as a conjunction to combine two complete clauses.

Test-Taking Tip

Tell your students not to panic if they don't know the correct answer to a question. They should move on to the next question and come back to the one they skipped later.

Standardized Test Practice

Read each passage. Some sections are underlined. The underlined sections may be one of the following:

- Incomplete sentences
- Run-on sentences
- Correctly written sentences that should be combined
- Correctly written sentences that do not need to be rewritten

Choose the best way to write each underlined section and mark the letter for your answer. If the underlined section needs no change, mark the choice "Correct as is" on your paper.

The hike to this point had been difficult. Alberto could see the peaks of nearby mountains, he could see the treetops for miles around. (1) The view was spectacular. Alberto reached into his backpack and removed the camera that his grandfather had given him. When the sun came out from behind the clouds. He snapped the perfect photo. (2) A great picture, while no substitute for the real thing, would help Alberto describe the hike to his family. He was looking forward to putting together an album. He had already taken some photographs of the lake. It was far below at the foot of the mountain. (3)

Alberto knew it was time to go even before the troop leader gathered everyone together. (4) The sun would be setting soon, and the hike back down to camp was still ahead. Nevertheless, the view had made the entire trip worthwhile.

1 **A** Alberto could see the peaks of nearby mountains, and he could see. The treetops for miles around.
B Alberto could see the peaks of nearby mountains and the treetops for miles around.
C Alberto could see the peaks of nearby mountains. And the treetops for miles around.
D Correct as is

2 **F** When the sun came out from behind the clouds, he snapped the perfect photo.
G The sun came out from behind the clouds, because he snapped the perfect photo.
H The sun. It came out from behind the clouds and he snapped the perfect photo.
J Correct as is

3 **A** He had already taken some photographs of the lake that was far below at the foot of the mountain.
B Far below at the foot of the mountain, he had taken some photographs of the lake, already.
C He had already taken some photographs. Of the lake that was far below at the foot of the mountain.
D He had already taken some photographs of the lake when it was far below at the foot of the mountain.

4 **F** Alberto knew it was time to go. Even before the troop leader gathered everyone together.
G Alberto knowing it was time to go even before the troop leader gathered everyone together.
H Time to go. Alberto knew it even before the troop leader gathered everyone together.
J Correct as is

The high school Young Astronomers club was hoping to see a rare comet tonight. The comet was visible only in February. That's why the group was standing out in the cold waiting for it. (1) Patrick silently thanked his parents for reminding him to bring an extra sweater.

Patrick set up the telescope and gathered the group around. It was hard to believe that what they were about to see became visible only every few years. (2) Everyone looked through the telescope at the comet, which appeared as a bright streak in the sky. Patrick felt proud. The comet had been discovered by his uncle. A former member of the Young Astronomers, who was now a well-known astronomer. (3) The comet would still be visible for the next few nights. Patrick was delighted after seeing it once, they had seen something beautiful. (4)

1 **A** The group was standing out in the cold waiting for the comet because it was visible only in February.
B The comet was visible only in February since the group was standing out in the cold waiting for the comet.
C The comet was visible only in February, the group was standing out in the cold waiting for it.
D The group was standing out in the cold waiting for the comet, which was visible only in February.

2 **F** It was hard to believe. That what they were about to see became visible only every few years.
G It was hard to believe that what they were about to see becoming visible every few years.
H It was hard to believe that what they were about to see. It became visible only every few years.
J Correct as is

3 **A** The comet had been discovered by his uncle, he was a former member of the Young Astronomers, who was now a well-known astronomer.
B The comet had been discovered by his uncle, a former member of the Young Astronomers. Who was now a well-known astronomer.
C The comet had been discovered by his uncle, a former member of the Young Astronomers, who was now a well-known astronomer.
D Correct as is

4 **F** Patrick was delighted after seeing it once. Because they had seen something beautiful.
G After seeing it once, Patrick was delighted that they had seen something beautiful.
H After seeing it once, Patrick was delighted. That they had seen something beautiful.
J Correct as is

Answers and Analyses

1. A The two sentences are complete, but will read more smoothly if combined by using the conjunction *because. That's why* is removed because it is an unnecessary dependent clause.
2. J The answer is *Correct as is* because the sentence is complete and grammatically correct. It is a complex sentence combining a dependent and independent clause with the relative pronoun *that.*

3. C The second item is a fragment because it does not contain a subject. Explain to your students that the relative pronoun *who* refers to the subject of the first sentence, *his uncle.* By replacing the period with a comma, the sentences are combined to form one complete thought.

4. G This is a run-on sentence because it is two sentences separated only by a comma. The correct answer begins with the prepositional phrase *After seeing it once.* Inserting the relative pronoun *that* creates one complete sentence.

Test-Taking Tip

It might be useful to review phrases and clauses with students. A clause contains a subject and a verb. A phrase does not have a subject and a verb. The two main kinds of phrases are prepositional phrases and verbal phrases. Students should be able to identify phrases and understand that they cannot stand on their own.

Standardized Test Practice

Tested Objective

- To recognize appropriate English usage and sentence structure within the context of a written passage

Answers and Analyses

1. B The two sentences are complete but will read better if combined. The correct answer creates a dependent clause beginning with *since* that is set off by commas.

2. H Point out to your students that the two sentences are complete, but they both contain the same subject (the pronoun *they* refers to *printing presses*). The sentences are easily combined with a conjunction (*and*).

3. A The first sentence is a dependent clause and is incomplete unless combined with the second sentence. The correct answer simply replaces the period with a comma.

4. J The answer is *Correct as is* because the sentence is complete and grammatically correct. You may want to point out to students that the sentence begins with a dependent clause starting with a conjunction (*but*).

Test-Taking Tip

Suggest to students that they first try to identify the error in the original text. This will help them understand the answer choices. Is the text a run-on sentence? A sentence fragment? Or are the sentences correct, but better if combined?

Standardized Test Practice

Read each passage. Some sections are underlined. The underlined sections may be one of the following:

- Incomplete sentences
- Run-on sentences
- Correctly written sentences that should be combined
- Correctly written sentences that do not need to be rewritten

Choose the best way to write each underlined section and mark the letter for your answer. If the underlined section needs no change, mark the choice "Correct as is" on your paper.

Today it is simple to get a national newspaper at your local newsstand. <u>However, obtaining a newspaper was very difficult in colonial America. Publishers faced many obstacles.</u> (1) Their equipment was primitive compared to today's equipment. <u>Printing presses had to be operated by hand. They were extremely slow.</u> (2) Distribution was also a problem. <u>Since all the newspapers were delivered on horseback. Subscribers usually lived in the same town where the paper was published.</u> (3) Circulation was low. The largest newspapers published weekly and only printed a few hundred copies. <u>But now, with better printing technology and larger distribution, newspapers can be found on almost any corner in America.</u> (4)

1 **A** However, obtaining a newspaper and publishers facing many obstacles was very difficult in colonial America.
B However, since publishers faced many obstacles, obtaining a newspaper was very difficult in colonial America.
C However, obtaining a newspaper was very difficult in colonial America because publishers faced many obstacles.
D However, publishers faced many obstacles because obtaining a newspaper was very difficult in colonial America.

2 **F** Printing presses had to be operated by hand when they were extremely slow.
G Printing presses having to be operated by hand, they were extremely slow.
H Printing presses had to be operated by hand and they were extremely slow.
J Printing presses had to be operated by hand, and these printing presses were extremely slow.

3 **A** Since all the newspapers were delivered on horseback, subscribers usually lived in the same town where the paper was published.
B All the newspapers were delivered on horseback, so subscribers usually lived in the same town. Where the paper was published.
C All the newspapers were delivered on horseback, subscribers usually lived in the same town where the paper was published.
D Correct as is

4 **F** But now, with better printing technology and larger distribution. Newspapers can be found on almost any corner in America.
G But now, to have better printing technology and larger distribution, newspapers can be found on almost any corner in America.
H Newspapers can be found with better printing technology and larger distribution on any corner in America.
J Correct as is

In the first century, the city of Pompeii was destroyed when Mount Vesuvius, a nearby volcano, erupted. Scientists have studied similar phenomena for centuries. Scientists have created a number of different categories to classify volcanoes. (1) Composite volcanoes are tall and pointy, and are composed of thick lava and ash. Shield volcanoes, such as Kilauea in Hawaii, are made up of sloping layers of rock formed by small eruptions of lava. (2) A third type of volcano is called a cinder cone. This kind of volcano has very steep sides made up of small chunks of solid lava.

When a volcano erupts. Molten rock is forced to the surface by pressure deep inside the earth. (3) The intensity of an eruption varies, but sometimes it can result in a massive explosion. Scientists can learn not only about nature's fury from volcanoes. But also about the materials that can be found under the surface of our planet. (4)

1 A Scientists have studied similar phenomena for centuries but have created a number of different categories to classify volcanoes.
B Scientists have studied similar phenomena for centuries, have created a number of different categories to classify volcanoes.
C Scientists have studied similar phenomena for centuries, creating a number of different categories to classify volcanoes.
D Studying similar phenomena for centuries, scientists have studied a number of different categories to classify volcanoes.

2 F Shield volcanoes, such as Kilauea in Hawaii, are made up of sloping layers of rock. Which are formed by small eruptions of lava.
G Shield volcanoes, such as Kilauea in Hawaii. Are made up of sloping layers of rock formed by small eruptions of lava.
H Shield volcanoes, such as Kilauea in Hawaii, making sloping layers of rock formed by small eruptions of lava.
J Correct as is.

3 A When a volcano erupts, molten rock is forced to the surface by pressure deep inside the earth.
B When a volcano erupts, then molten rock is forced to the surface by pressure deep inside the earth.
C When a volcano. Erupting molten rock is forced to the surface by pressure deep inside the earth.
D Correct as is

4 F Scientists can learn not only about nature's fury. From volcanoes but also about the materials that can be found under the surface of our planet.
G Scientists can learn not only about nature's fury, but also about the materials surfacing under our planet from volcanoes.
H Scientists can learn not only about nature's fury from volcanoes, but also about the materials that can be found under the surface of our planet.
J Correct as is

Answers and Analyses

1. C Students should recognize that the sentences are complete, but should be combined because they both contain the same subject (*scientists*). The past perfect *have created* is replaced with the gerund *creating,* and the period is replaced with a comma.

2. J The answer is *Correct as is* because the sentence is complete and grammatically correct. Make sure your students understand that *Shield volcanoes* is the subject of the sentence, not *Kilauea.*

3. A The relative clause *When a volcano erupts* is a fragment. The sentences must be combined. The correct answer replaces the period with a comma.

4. H The second sentence is incomplete because it does not contain a subject. The correct answer replaces the period with a comma to form a complete sentence. You might want to point out the correlative conjunction (*not only . . . but also*) that is used to connect the parts of the sentence.

Test-Taking Tip

Sentences that are complete but sound better when combined often contain the same subject. The repetition of the subject should be a clue to students.

Standardized Test Practice

Tested Objective

- To recognize appropriate English usage and sentence structure within the context of a written passage

Answers and Analyses

1. C Students should recognize that the second sentence is dependent on the first. A dependent clause cannot stand on its own. The correct answer simply removes the period to combine the sentences.

2. F Point out to your students that these sentences are complete, but work better when combined. The indirect object of the first sentence—*network*—is the subject of the second sentence. To combine the sentences, the correct answer eliminates the noun *This network* and replaces it with the relative pronoun *that.*

3. D This sentence is *Correct as is.* It uses the relative pronoun *who* to further describe how the man constructed the subway.

4. G Explain to students that this is a run-on sentence containing an unnecessary pronoun (*it*). The correct answer removes this pronoun and replaces the present tense *gets* with the gerund *getting.*

Test-Taking Tip

Writing tests of this type follow a standard layout and contain specific content. Ask your students what they have noticed. How many questions does each passage have? How many choices are offered for each question? Finally, what skills are being tested?

Standardized Test Practice

Read each passage. Some sections are underlined. The underlined sections may be one of the following:

- Incomplete sentences
- Run-on sentences
- Correctly written sentences that should be combined
- Correctly written sentences that do not need to be rewritten

Choose the best way to write each underlined section and mark the letter for your answer. If the underlined section needs no change, mark the choice "Correct as is" on your paper.

A visit to New York City may feel overwhelming. To someone who has never been there before. (1) The buildings appear to go on for miles. In fact, Manhattan is only a little more than 22 square miles in area.

Running beneath New York's surface, the subway system is a vast transportation network. This network contains 772 miles of active track. (2) It is the largest underground transportation system in the world. The first subway was constructed in 1870 by Alfred Ely Beach, who was also the inventor of the typewriter. (3) Of course, there are many different ways to get around town in New York. The subway, however, is often the fastest option, it gets you where you need to go without the worry of traffic. (4)

1 A A visit to New York City overwhelming to someone who has never been there before.
B A visit to New York City may feel overwhelming to someone. Who has never been there before.
C A visit to New York City may feel overwhelming to someone who has never been there before.
D Correct as is

2 F Running beneath New York's surface, the subway system is a vast transportation network that contains 772 miles of active track.
G Running beneath New York's surface, the subway system and a vast transportation network contain 772 miles of active track.
H Running beneath New York's surface, the subway system is a vast transportation network, and this transportation network contains 772 miles of active track.
J Running beneath New York's surface, the subway system is a vast transportation network, and the subway system also containing 772 miles of active track.

3 A The first subway was constructed in 1870 by Alfred Ely Beach, he was also the inventor of the typewriter.
B The first subway was constructed in 1870 by Alfred Ely Beach. Who was also the inventor of the typewriter.
C The first subway constructing in 1870 by Alfred Ely Beach, who also the inventor of the typewriter.
D Correct as is

4 F The subway, however, is often the fastest option. Getting you where you need to go without the worry of traffic.
G The subway, however, is often the fastest option, getting you where you need to go without the worry of traffic.
H The subway, however, is often the fastest option getting you where you need to go. Without the worry of traffic.
J Correct as is

On October 2, 1800, Nat Turner was born as an enslaved person, it was in Virginia. (1) Thirty-one years later, he would be known as one of the bravest enslaved people in history when he led the Southampton Slave Revolt.

Nat Turner had grown increasingly angry with the way that his people were treated in the South. It was an early morning in August of 1831. Nat Turner decided to rebel against slavery in his community. (2) He recruited seventy fellow enslaved men and, together, they marched through the streets of Southampton. The revolt lasted two days. Before the Virginia Militia finally put an end to it. (3) Nat Turner escaped, but was captured two months later. Although Nat Turner was not able to put an end to slavery with his revolt, he did make an important contribution toward freedom for enslaved peoples. (4)

1 **A** On October 2, 1800, Nat Turner was born an enslaved person. In Virginia.
B On October 2, 1800, Nat Turner was born an enslaved person in Virginia.
C On October 2, 1800. Nat Turner was born an enslaved person in Virginia.
D Correct as is

2 **F** It was an early morning in August of 1831 if Nat Turner decided to rebel against slavery in his community.
G Nat Turner decided to in 1831 to rebel on an early August morning against slavery in his community.
H It was an early morning in August of 1831, when Nat Turner decided to rebel against slavery in his community.
J Early morning 1831 when Nat Turner in August decided to rebel against slavery in his community.

3 **A** The revolt lasted two days before the Virginia Militia finally put an end to it.
B The revolt lasted. Two days before the Virginia Militia finally put an end to it.
C The revolt lasted two days before. The Virginia Militia finally put an end to it.
D Correct as is

4 **F** Although Nat Turner. Was not able to put an end to slavery with his revolt, he did make an important contribution toward freedom for enslaved peoples.
G He did make an important contribution toward freedom for enslaved peoples, then Nat Turner was not able to put an end to slavery with his revolt.
H Although Nat Turner was not able to put an end to slavery with his revolt. He did make an important contribution toward freedom for enslaved peoples.
J Correct as is

Answers and Analyses

1. B Students should understand that this is a run-on sentence because it is two sentences separated by only a comma. The correct answer eliminates *It was,* which is unnecessary, and the comma to create a complete sentence.

2. H Explain to your students that these sentences can stand on their own independently, but work better when combined. The correct answer removes the period and inserts the preposition *when.*

3. A Identify *Before the Virginia Militia finally put an end to it* as a dependent clause. In order to complete its meaning, it must be combined with the first sentence. Simply remove the period to do so.

4. J The sentence is complete, containing two clauses featuring the same subject (*Nat Turner* and the pronoun *he*). You may want to point out to students that the sentence begins with a dependent clause starting with a conjunction (*although*).

Test-Taking Tip

Help your students to identify dependent clauses. They often begin with words like *since, if, whether,* etc. Ask them to come up with their own dependent clauses. What are they dependent on?

Standardized Test Practice

Tested Objectives

- To recognize appropriate English usage within the context of a written passage

Answers and Analyses

1. B Point out to students that a pronoun is required to complete the sentence. The pronoun must be plural because it refers to *digital recording and analog recording.* The correct answer is the subject pronoun *they* because it is the subject of the sentence.

2. H Students should recognize that a verb in the present tense is needed. The present tense, *is coated,* is correct because it matches the other verb in the sentence, *is magnetized.*

3. B A singular pronoun is needed here because the antecedent is *electromagnet.* Explain to students that the object pronoun *it* is correct because in the sentence *it* functions as an object.

4. F The answer is a verb in the present tense that matches the tense of the other verb in the sentence, *picks up.*

5. D A superlative adjective is needed here. *Significantest* is an incorrectly formed adjective, so the answer is *most significant.*

Test-Taking Tip

Remind students that superlative adjectives are used to describe the best or worst of something. Point out to students that superlatives often end in *-est,* although not always. The word *most* is used with some adjectives to create the superlative. Can students come up with some examples of both?

Standardized Test Practice

Read each passage and choose the word or group of words that belongs in each space. Mark the letter for your answer on your paper.

There are two types of sound recordings: digital recording and analog recording. __(1)__ are both acceptable ways to record effects and music.

Analog tape is made of thin, sturdy plastic. This material __(2)__ with an oxide powder, which is magnetized when exposed to a magnetic field. The record head of a tape recorder is a very small electromagnet. When an audio signal passes through __(3)__, the oxide is magnetized and imprinted with sound. A digital recorder picks up sound at rapid intervals and __(4)__ it into numbers. A compact disc may store as many as 44,000 bits of sound per second. One of the __(5)__ advantages digital technology has over analog technology is that digital recordings do not degrade over time.

1 **A** it
B they
C we
D you

2 **F** will be coated
G was coated
H is coated
J had been coated

3 **A** you
B it
C them
D us

4 **F** converts
G is converting
H has converted
J convert

5 **A** significantly
B significantest
C more significantly
D most significant

Test-Taking Tip

A review of pronouns might be useful. Pronouns act as stand-ins for nouns. There are several different categories of pronouns. Personal pronouns can be either subject pronouns (*I, you, he*), which act as the subject of the verb in the sentence; object pronouns (*me, you, him*), which, as objects, have something done to them (instead of doing the action themselves, which would make them subjects); or ownership pronouns (*my, mine, theirs*), which show possession.

Millions of people across the globe are near-sighted. The __(1)__ way to correct this problem is with the use of eyeglasses or contact lenses.

The inner layer of the eye is called the retina. This light-sensitive membrane __(2)__ to the brain by the optic nerve. When someone is nearsighted, or myopic, the light that enters the eye is focused in front of the retina rather than directly on it. This causes distant objects to appear blurred.

Wearing glasses or contact lenses helps to focus incoming light waves directly onto the retina. This is how corrective lenses allow people who suffer from myopia to see __(3)__. So if you should discover that you have blurred vision, at least you know that you can correct __(4)__ without difficulty.

1 **A** easier
  B more easy
  C easiest
  D most easiest

2 **F** was connected
  G is connected
  H will be connected
  J had been connected

3 **A** more clearly
  B more clearer
  C more clear
  D more clearest

4 **F** they
  G it
  H we
  J you

Answers and Analyses

1. C Explain to students that the sentence is completed with the superlative form of the adjective *easy,* which is *easiest.*

2. G The present tense is needed to match *is called* from the previous sentence. *Is connected* is the correct answer.

3. A This answer requires the comparative form of the adjective *clear,* which is *more clearly.* Explain to your students that the sentence is comparing nearsighted people who don't use corrective lenses to those who do.

4. G The answer requires a singular pronoun because the antecedent is *blurred vision.* The object pronoun *it* is correct, because *it* is the object of the sentence.

Test-Taking Tip

When attempting to identify the appropriate tense for a verb, look at the other verbs in the sentence or in the sentences directly preceding or following. You may want to tell your students that preserving the consistency of tense is called *parallel construction.*

Standardized Test Practice

Tested Objective

- To recognize appropriate English usage within the context of a written passage

Answers and Analyses

1. B The sentence is completed with the singular present tense of the verb *to cause.* The present tense is needed to correspond with *is found* in the following sentence.

2. F Explain to students that a superlative adjective is needed here. The superlative is formed with the word *most,* so the answer is *most effective.*

3. C The correct answer requires a pronoun. Ask your students to identify the pronoun's antecedent. (*Urushiol*) The correct answer is the object pronoun *it.*

4. J The comparative adjective is needed here. *More widely* is the only correct answer, because the other answer choices contain incorrect adjective constructions.

Test-Taking Tip

The comparative adjective is used to compare two or more things. Often, *-er* can be added to an adjective to create the comparative. Ask your students to think of a few. (some examples: *faster, quicker, easier*) The comparative can also be created with the word *more.* Ask your students for some of these. (*more beautiful, more interesting*)

Standardized Test Practice

Read each passage and choose the word or group of words that belongs in each space. Mark the letter for your answer on your paper.

The rash that most people get from poison ivy can be itchy and uncomfortable. This rash __(1)__ by a chemical called urushiol.

Urushiol is found in the sap of the poison ivy plant. When your skin is exposed to poison ivy, an allergic reaction does not occur immediately. The urushiol must penetrate the outer layer of skin before your body's immune system reacts. If you have been exposed to poison ivy, washing your skin immediately is the __(2)__ way to prevent a rash.

Urushiol will rub off onto anything that comes into contact with __(3)__ . That means if you walk through a patch of poison ivy, you can get a rash later by touching your shoes or clothes. Anything that touches the plant will help the urushiol to spread __(4)__ .

1 **A** will be caused
B is caused
C was caused
D had been caused

2 **F** most effective
G effectivest
H more effective
J effective

3 **A** you
B we
C it
D them

4 **F** more wider
G more wide
H more widest
J more widely

Zoos, with __(1)__ diverse array of wildlife, are now a popular destination in cities across America. This was not always the case. Centuries ago, traveling __(2)__ with only one wild animal on display were normal. The first wild animal exhibited in America was a lion, but perhaps the __(3)__ of these early attractions was an elephant. In 1797 an elephant was displayed in Boston's Market Square. Visitors __(4)__ an admission of 25 cents to see the giant animal. At the time, viewing any type of exotic wildlife was a rare treat. Elephants continued to be a popular tourist attraction well into the 1800s.

1 A its
  B your
  C their
  D our

2 F exhibits
  G exhibitor
  H exhibiting
  J exhibited

3 A successest
  B successful
  C most successful
  D more successfully

4 F have paid
  G will pay
  H pay
  J paid

Answers and Analyses

1. C Explain to students that a pronoun is required here. The antecedent is *zoos,* so the answer must be in the plural. The correct response is *their* because the pronoun in this case shows ownership: *their diverse array of wildlife.*

2. F The correct answer is a noun. It is modified by the adjective *traveling.* It must be in the plural form, to match the verb *were. Exhibitor* is singular; *exhibiting* and *exhibited* are verbs. The correct answer is the plural verb *exhibits.*

3. C Point out to students that the superlative adjective is required here. Ask your students to look for the word that identifies a superlative adjective. (*most*) The correct answer is *most successful.*

4. J The correct answer requires a verb in the past tense to correspond with the verb *displayed* in the previous sentence. The correct answer is *paid.*

Test-Taking Tip

If your students get stuck on a question, ask them to try and fill in the blank without referring to the answer choices. Read the sentence aloud. What kind of word is required? A noun? A verb? If a verb is required, what tense? If it is an adjective, is it comparative or superlative? Sometimes students will arrive at the correct answer simply by performing this exercise.

Standardized Test Practice

Tested Objective

- To recognize appropriate English usage within the context of a written passage

Answers and Analyses

1. C Explain to students that a verb is required to complete the sentence. Students should know it will be in the past tense because the text mentions *At the turn of the century.* The answer is *referred.*

2. F The correct answer is a verb in the past tense, corresponding with the tense of the verb in the same sentence (*were*). *Focused* is the past tense of *to focus.*

3. D A pronoun is required. Ask your students to identify the antecedent. (*muckrakers*) The correct answer is a pronoun that shows possession (*their*).

4. J The answer must be a verb in the present tense because the sentence refers to *today.* The subject is plural (*they*), so the answer is plural, *are remembered.*

Test-Taking Tip

One way to attack questions of this type is to use process of elimination. Encourage your students to cross out choices that they know are wrong if they are unsure of the correct answer.

Standardized Test Practice

Read each passage and choose the word or group of words that belongs in each space. Mark the letter for your answer on your paper.

Investigative journalists in America research news stories and try to uncover buried pieces of information. At the turn of the century, President Theodore Roosevelt __(1)__ to investigative journalists as "muckrakers." This name was derived from a character in a John Bunyan novel who always looked down and raked the dirt, or "muck." Muckrakers were writers and reporters who __(2)__ on society's problems. Some of __(3)__ subjects included political corruption in city government and racial discrimination in the South. Today, they __(4)__ as journalists who alerted the public to controversial issues and called for social change.

1 **A** refers
B refer
C referred
D will refer

2 **F** focused
G have been focusing
H had focused
J will focus

3 **A** us
B our
C your
D their

4 **F** have been remembered
G has been remembered
H is remembered
J are remembered

In 1848, the U.S. Army __(1)__ creating a cavalry of soldiers mounted on camels. In 1856, thirty-four camels arrived from various Mediterranean countries. They __(2)__ at Camp Verde in Texas, which some people called "Little Egypt." Camels had a number of advantages over horses. First of all, camels could travel great distances without water, making difficult journeys __(3)__ . Camels were not afraid of gunfire, and the sight of an oncoming camel herd would cause enemy horses to turn and flee. Unfortunately, some soldiers were not able to sit securely on the camels for long periods of time. Ultimately, this project __(4)__ , but not before a few camels had the opportunity to experience military service.

1 **A** consider
B considered
C are considering
D will consider

2 **F** stationed
G is stationed
H was stationed
J were stationed

3 **A** more easiest
B most easiest
C easier
D more easy

4 **F** have been abandoned
G has been abandoned
H is abandoned
J was abandoned

Answers and Analyses

1. B Explain to students that the correct answer is a verb in the past tense because the text refers to something that occurred in 1848. The answer is the past of *to consider—considered.*

2. J A verb in the past tense is also needed here to match the tense of the other verb in the sentence, *called.* The subject is a plural pronoun (*They*), so the answer must also be plural.

3. C The question is asking for a comparative adjective because the sentence is comparing one thing to another (*long journeys with horses* and *long journeys with camels*). The comparative is formed with the suffix *-er—easier.*

4. J The correct answer requires the past tense to correspond with the other verb in the sentence *had.* The correct answer is in the singular, *was abandoned,* because the subject is singular, *this project.*

Test-Taking Tip

Point out to your students that this passage is of the *informational* type. Explain to them that another type of passage is *narrative.* Both are featured on tests like this one. Ask your students to describe the differences between both types of passages.

Standardized Test Practice

Tested Objective

- To recognize appropriate English usage within the context of a written passage

Answers and Analyses

1. C The correct answer requires a plural pronoun because the antecedent is plural, *magazines.* The answer is *their,* the pronoun that shows ownership. Whose pages are they? *Theirs.*

2. J Explain to students that a noun is required to complete the sentence. Who or what does the creating? *Beginners* is the correct answer. Point out to students that to make the answer singular (*beginner*), an "a" would have to precede it (*a beginner*).

3. B The superlative adjective is needed here. Remind your students to identify the superlative with words ending in *-est* or the word *most* and the suffix *-ly. Commonest* is not a word, so the correct answer is *most commonly.*

4. F The subject of this sentence is *you,* so the answer must be a singular verb. It must also be in the present tense to match the verb *can,* the second verb in the sentence. Therefore, the correct answer is *want.*

Test-Taking Tip

Ask students to identify the skills tested in these questions. (*choosing words in context, selecting correct verb tense, using pronouns correctly*) Students will be better prepared to answer questions such as these if they understand what is being asked of them.

Standardized Test Practice

Read each passage and choose the word or group of words that belongs in each space. Mark the letter for your answer on your paper.

Have you ever carried a big pile of magazines to the recycling box? The next time you do, think twice. Those magazines, and the images on __(1)__ pages, can be transformed into a work of art. Even if you don't consider yourself to be an artist, cutting and pasting pictures together from different magazines is a fun way for __(2)__ to create a collage. Advertisements, illustrations, and photographs are just a few of the __(3)__ used images in this type of collage.

If you __(4)__ to be really creative, you can also attach cloth, wood or other materials to your picture. Then you can hang the magazines on your wall instead of putting them in the recycling box.

1 **A** our
B its
C their
D your

2 **F** begin
G beginner
H began
J beginners

3 **A** most common
B most commonly
C common
D commonest

4 **F** want
G wanted
H will want
J had wanted

Many Native Americans of the American Southwest were among the first apartment dwellers. Hundreds of years ago, these __(1)__ people lived in multistory communities not unlike the apartment houses of today. Instead of staircases, the inhabitants moved from floor to floor by using ladders. They __(2)__ these homes out of stone or adobe, which is a type of clay used for construction. They fashioned bricks, reinforced them with straw, and dried them in the sun.

The builders were also skilled craftsmen and known for their pottery and basketwork. Although not aggressive, the people did not hesitate to rise in __(3)__ of their homes when attacked. The Apache and Navaho were legendary enemies of the pueblo dwellers. Today, the unique buildings can still be seen in the Southwest, where they __(4)__ for centuries.

1 **A** invention
B inventions
C inventive
D invent

2 **F** built
G will build
H build
J are building

3 **A** defend
B defends
C defender
D defense

4 **F** stand
G is standing
H have been standing
J has been standing

Answers and Analyses

1. C Students should recognize that the correct answer requires an adjective because the missing word describes the noun *people*. The only choice that contains an adjective is *inventive*. Ask your students to describe the other answer choices. What parts of speech are they?

2. F A verb in the past tense is needed here to match the verb *moved* from the previous sentence. The only choice in the past tense is *built*.

3. D The missing word is a noun: the person or thing that did the rising. Of the two nouns in the answer choices, *defense* is the correct answer. It does not make sense to rise in *defender*.

4. H The correct answer is a verb in the past perfect tense because the sentence describes something that occurred in the past and continues to occur in the present. The subject is plural (*they*), so the correct answer must be *have been standing*.

Test-Taking Tip

Encourage your students to focus on the types of questions with which they have the most difficulty. Mastering just a few skills does not translate to success on the test. Remind your students to practice their trouble spots more often than the questions that come to them easily.

Standardized Test Practice

Tested Objective

- To proofread for spelling, capitalization, and punctuation errors within the context of a written passage

Answers and Analyses

1. B Explain to students that nationalities need to be capitalized.

2. H Explain to students that items in a list must be separated by commas.

3. D Students should recognize that there are no errors. Note that commas are correctly placed after the introductory phrase *for example* and after the subordinate clause starting with *if Melies wanted . . .*

4. F *Innovative* is spelled incorrectly.

Test-Taking Tip

Explain to your students that words with double consonants are often misspelled in these types of writing tests. Try to come up with a short list of words that fits this description. (examples: *disappear, arrival, roommate*)

Test-Taking Tip

A review of other common spelling errors may be useful. For example, forgetting to drop the *e* when adding the *-ing* suffix to some verbs (*abusing, forgiving*).

Standardized Test Practice

Read each passage and decide which type of error, if any, appears in each underlined section. Mark the letter for your answer on your paper.

In today's cinema, it seems that almost any visual trick can be accomplished through the use of special effects. This kind of movie magic, while commonplace today, may not have been possible without the films of french director Georges Méliès. (1) As early as 1896, Méliès was using trick photography in his work. His films featured monsters spaceships, and women vanishing into thin air. (2) While any of these things might be found in a modern science-fiction blockbuster, Méliès was one of the first to develop them for the screen. For example, if Méliès wanted to suggest an underwater scene, he placed (3) a fish tank in front of the camera. His effects may seem crude by today's standards, but without his inovative first attempts at cinematic illusion, (4) the films we see today might not have been made.

1
- A Spelling error
- B Capitalization error
- C Punctuation error
- D No error

2
- F Spelling error
- G Capitalization error
- H Punctuation error
- J No error

3
- A Spelling error
- B Capitalization error
- C Punctuation error
- D No error

4
- F Spelling error
- G Capitalization error
- H Punctuation error
- J No error

It was the first friday in May and it was simply beautiful (1) outside. Mrs. Major thought she would try something new. She decided to hold her English class on the field in front of the school.

All of the students sat in a circle, with Mrs. Major in the center. She began by reciting an elizabethan sonnet. (2) The gorgeous weather only added to the sonnets beauty. The sweet smell in the air (3) complimented the words perfectly. When she was finished reading, Mrs. Major initiated a discusion with (4) a few questions about the poem. The conversation was lively and stimulating. Mrs. Major was very happy with the results of her experiment. She hoped to conduct at least one more class outdoors before the end of spring. (5)

1 **A** Spelling error
B Capitalization error
C Punctuation error
D No error

2 **F** Spelling error
G Capitalization error
H Punctuation error
J No error

3 **A** Spelling error
B Capitalization error
C Punctuation error
D No error

4 **F** Spelling error
G Capitalization error
H Punctuation error
J No error

5 **A** Spelling error
B Capitalization error
C Punctuation error
D No error

Answers and Analyses

1. B Students should recognize that days of the week must be capitalized. Point out to students that the months of the year must also be capitalized (*May*).

2. G *Elizabethan* is a proper noun and must therefore be capitalized.

3. C Explain to students that possessive nouns must always contain an apostrophe.

4. F Students should recognize that *discussion* is spelled incorrectly.

5. D Students should recognize that the sentence contains no errors.

Test-Taking Tip

Suggest to your students that they make a list of the kinds of words that need to be capitalized. Some examples: proper names (people, places, organizations), days of the week, months of the year, book titles.

Standardized Test Practice

Tested Objective

- To proofread for spelling, capitalization, and punctuation errors within the context of a written passage

Answers and Analyses

1. D There are no errors in this sentence. *Mother* does not need to be capitalized because it is not being used as a proper noun in this context. You may want to explain to students that words like *mother* or *father* are only capitalized when they are being used as names.

2. G Places with proper names must be capitalized (*Himalayan Mountains*). Explain that the word *mountain,* when used as a common noun, does not need to be capitalized.

3. C The sentence is missing two commas, after *he liked* and after *Julio said.* Point out to students that without the commas, the sentence is hard to understand. See the Test-Taking Tip on this page for a review of comma rules.

4. F *Nodded* is spelled incorrectly. Many verbs require a double consonant when combined with a suffix.

5. C Point out to students that a quotation mark is required to end Julio's remark.

6. F In this context, *fair* is spelled incorrectly.

Test-Taking Tip

Remind students of the basic rules for commas. Commas are used to separate two independent clauses connected by conjunctions (*and, but, or,* etc.); to separate items in a list or a series of words like adjectives; to separate an introductory phrase or clause from the independent clause; to set off words or phrases that interrupt the flow of the sentence; or to separate a full sentence quotation from surrounding comments.

Standardized Test Practice

Read each passage and decide which type of error, if any, appears in each underlined section. Mark the letter for your answer on your paper.

Mark and Julio wanted to see a movie. Julio's mother promised to take them to the theater and pick them up after the show. (1) The only problem was, they couldn't decide which movie to see.

Mark loved movies with elaborate mystery plots. He wanted to see the movie about an investigator in the himalayan mountains. (2) Julio's main interest was science fiction. He wanted to see the movie about a space alien who lands in Los Angeles, California.

Attempting to convince his friend to pick the movie he liked Julio said "Remember (3) that movie we saw together about the extraterrestrial creature?"

Mark noded his head. "I remember." (4)

"Well, you loved that movie! Julio exclaimed. (5)

Mark thought for a moment. His friend had a point.

"Why don't we see the movie you want this time and the movie I want next time?"

Julio thanked his friend for being so fare. "Your generosity will be returned!" (6)

1 **A** Spelling error
B Capitalization error
C Punctuation error
D No error

2 **F** Spelling error
G Capitalization error
H Punctuation error
J No error

3 **A** Spelling error
B Capitalization error
C Punctuation error
D No error

4 **F** Spelling error
G Capitalization error
H Punctuation error
J No error

5 **A** Spelling error
B Capitalization error
C Punctuation error
D No error

6 **F** Spelling error
G Capitalization error
H Punctuation error
J No error

The Inuit, sometimes called Eskimos, are known for building igloos to provide warmth in sub-zero temperatures. Contrary to popular belief, these dome-shaped shelters are <u>rarely permmanent homes. For the most part, the Inuit</u> (1) use igloos only when they are hunting or traveling. Snow provides remarkable protection from the cold. <u>For instance a candle burning inside an igloo can sometimes</u> (2) raise the <u>Interior temperature 40 degrees.</u> (3) Igloos can be <u>made of snow, earth, sod or stone. These materials</u> (4) are formed into rectangular <u>blocks. A hole is left at the top of the igloo for ventilation.</u> (5)

1 **A** Spelling error
B Capitalization error
C Punctuation error
D No error

2 **F** Spelling error
G Capitalization error
H Punctuation error
J No error

3 **A** Spelling error
B Capitalization error
C Punctuation error
D No error

4 **F** Spelling error
G Capitalization error
H Punctuation error
J No error

5 **A** Spelling error
B Capitalization error
C Punctuation error
D No error

Answers and Analyses

1. A Explain to students that *permanent* is spelled incorrectly. Note that, in this case, a double consonant was added.

2. H A comma is required after the introductory phrase *for instance.*

3. B Explain to students that *interior* does not need to be capitalized.

4. G Students should recognize that *Earth* does not need to be capitalized in this context. Earth is capitalized when it is used as the proper name of our planet.

5. D There are no errors.

Test-Taking Tip

Remind your students not to rush when reading the passages. Simple mistakes may be missed if your students do not read the text carefully. It may be helpful to read each sentence twice.

Standardized Test Practice

Tested Objective

- To proofread for spelling, capitalization, and punctuation errors within the context of a written passage

Answers and Analyses

1. B Student should understand that *Pacific* must be capitalized. Note that *United States, Europe,* and *World War II* all have proper capitalization.

2. H Commas are used to separate items in a list.

3. D Students should recognize that there are no errors.

4. F *Competitive* is spelled incorrectly. Point out to your students that *war,* used here as a common noun, does not need to be capitalized.

5. B The word *country* does not need to be capitalized.

Standardized Test Practice

Read each passage and decide which type of error, if any, appears in each underlined section. Mark the letter for your answer on your paper.

When United States soldiers were deployed to Europe and the pacific during World War II, our country (1) faced a shortage of defense workers. During this time, 5 million women entered the U.S. workforce. They accepted jobs that were traditionally reserved for men.

To aid in the war effort, women worked on production lines in factories in steel mills, and on the docks. (2) The government offered incentives to encourage women to work. For example, government-sponsored day care centers allowed women (3) with children to leave home and go to their jobs. Although women's wages were very low at the start of the war, over time their wages became more competative. (4) These working women and their contributions to our Country helped change the American perception (5) of a woman's position in the workforce.

1 A Spelling error
B Capitalization error
C Punctuation error
D No error

2 F Spelling error
G Capitalization error
H Punctuation error
J No error

3 A Spelling error
B Capitalization error
C Punctuation error
D No error

4 F Spelling error
G Capitalization error
H Punctuation error
J No error

5 A Spelling error
B Capitalization error
C Punctuation error
D No error

Howard was in the highest math class. He had always been good at math. Before a mid-term math test Howard noticed that several (1) of his peers were having trouble studying for the exam. Howard decided that it might be a good idea to offer his services as a tutor. He would (2) post a sign in the school cafeteria.

Howards sign read: "Howard Goldstein: Available (3) to help with math."

About a week later, a girl from Howard's homeroom aproached him in the gym. (4)

The girl explained that she wanted to start a buisness tutoring students (5) in various subjects. "Would you like to be my partner? she asked. (6)

"That's a great idea!" Howard remarked. "We can help each other find students and devise the best ways to explain things."

1 **A** Spelling error
B Capitalization error
C Punctuation error
D No error

2 **F** Spelling error
G Capitalization error
H Punctuation error
J No error

3 **A** Spelling error
B Capitalization error
C Punctuation error
D No error

4 **F** Spelling error
G Capitalization error
H Punctuation error
J No error

5 **A** Spelling error
B Capitalization error
C Punctuation error
D No error

6 **F** Spelling error
G Capitalization error
H Punctuation error
J No error

Answers and Analyses

1. C Students should recognize that a comma is needed after the word *test* because it is the end of an introductory prepositional phrase.

2. J Students should recognize that there are no errors.

3. C The possessive requires an apostrophe. Point out to your students that the quotation marks are used correctly, even though no one is actually speaking. The quotation marks are used to identify the words on a sign.

4. F *Approached* is spelled incorrectly (double consonants are needed). Note that in this sentence, the possessive is constructed properly.

5. A *Business* is spelled incorrectly. Note that because what the girl said is not quoted, but instead mentioned, quotation marks are not needed.

6. H Closing quotation marks are missing. See the Test-Taking Tip below.

Test-Taking Tip

It might be useful to review the rules for quotation marks with students. Quotation marks should be placed around direct quotations. Quotation marks always come in pairs. Make sure your students find an opening and closing quotation mark when someone is speaking in the text.

A comma appears to separate the quote from explanatory words. (For example, "I like chocolate cake," said Francis.) Commas do not appear if the quotation ends with an exclamation point or a question mark. (For example, "Would you like to be my partner?" she asked.)

Standardized Test Practice

Tested Objective

- To proofread for spelling, capitalization, and punctuation errors within the context of a written passage

Answers and Analyses

1. C Students should recognize that a comma is required after the word *thermometers* because it separates two independent clauses joined by the conjunction *but.*

2. F *Temperature* is spelled incorrectly.

3. C Explain to students that commas are needed to separate items in a list.

4. G *Naked eye* should not be capitalized because it is a common noun and not a proper noun.

5. D There are no errors in this sentence.

Test-Taking Tip

On writing tests such as these, there are only three different types of errors to look for: spelling, capitalization, or punctuation. Encourage students to first read the text with only spelling errors in mind. If no error is found, they should reread the text with only capitalization errors in mind. If still no errors are found, they should reread the text one last time for punctuation errors. If your students narrow their focus, these questions may become easier for them.

Standardized Test Practice

Read each passage and decide which type of error, if any, appears in each underlined section. Mark the letter for your answer on your paper.

There are a few different kinds of thermometers but the bulb thermometer (1) is the most common. This type of thermometer contains a liquid, which is usually mercury. Bulb thermometers work because as the temprature rises, the volume (2) of a liquid increases. All liquids, including water oil and milk, take up more space when they are heated. (3) This change is not generally visible to the Naked Eye. The mercury (4) inside a bulb thermometer is encased in a thin, glass, tube. When it is hot, the mercury expands and rises. When it is cold, the mercury takes up less space, and the thermometer indicates that it is cooler. (5)

1 **A** Spelling error
B Capitalization error
C Punctuation error
D No error

2 **F** Spelling error
G Capitalization error
H Punctuation error
J No error

3 **A** Spelling error
B Capitalization error
C Punctuation error
D No error

4 **F** Spelling error
G Capitalization error
H Punctuation error
J No error

5 **A** Spelling error
B Capitalization error
C Punctuation error
D No error

Mail delivery was slow and unreliable during the expansion of the american western territories. This prompted the creation (1) of the Pony Express in 1860, which was established to organize a faster mail service between Missouri and California. The 1,600 mile route took mail carriers through a number of states, including the following, Kansas, Nebraska, Wyoming (2) and Nevada. Pony Express employees, riding on horseback, were expected (3) to travel thirty to seventy miles a day. The journey could take weeks. Close to two hundred relay stations were built along the route, where exausted riders could hand their mail pouches (4) over to the next available courier. In 1861, a telegraph line was completed that connected the East to the west. After only nineteen months of operation, (5) the Pony Express was shut down. It still stands as a reminder of American ingenuity.

1 **A** Spelling error
B Capitalization error
C Punctuation error
D No error

2 **F** Spelling error
G Capitalization error
H Punctuation error
J No error

3 **A** Spelling error
B Capitalization error
C Punctuation error
D No error

4 **F** Spelling error
G Capitalization error
H Punctuation error
J No error

5 **A** Spelling error
B Capitalization error
C Punctuation error
D No error

Answers and Analyses

1. B Point out to students that names of countries must be capitalized even when they are used as adjectives. Note that *western territories* does not need to be capitalized.

2. H A colon is used to introduce a list. See the first Test-Taking Tip on this page.

3. D Students should recognize that there are no errors.

4. F *Exhausted* is spelled incorrectly.

5. B *West* needs to be capitalized just as *East* is. See the second Test-Taking Tip on this page.

Test-Taking Tip

A review of colon usage might be helpful. A colon simply means "as follows." Use a colon to mark the beginning of a list.

Test-Taking Tip

Remind students that compass headings—north, south, east, west, etc.—are capitalized only when they indicate specific regions. The rule is capitalize locations, but not directions.

ASSESSMENT OPTIONS

Tests with Answer Key & Rubrics
Unit 28 Mastery Test, pp. 105–106

Testmaker
Unit 28 Mastery Test

You may wish to administer the Unit 28 Mastery Test at this point.

MindJogger Videoquizzes

INTRODUCING

UNIT 29

Objectives

- To learn strategies for listening effectively, including preparing to listen and evaluating what is heard
- To learn strategies for speaking effectively, including techniques for preparing, giving, and following up on a formal speech
- To learn about how to participate in groups effectively
- To demonstrate the ability to listen effectively by evaluating a persuasive message or dramatic or literary presentation
- To demonstrate the ability to speak effectively by giving a speech

ASSESSMENT OPTIONS

 *Tests with Answer Key & Rubrics*
Unit 29 Pretest, pp. 111–112

Testmaker
Unit 29 Pretest

You may wish to administer the Unit 29 Pretest at this point.

Key to Ability Levels

L1 Level 1 activities are within the basic ability range of students.

L2 Level 2 activities are within the ability range of average students.

L3 Level 3 activities are more challenging activities.

UNIT 29

Listening and Speaking

884

LOG ON **Writing** Online — For research tools and additional skills practice, go to glencoe.com and enter QuickPass code WC97727p3.

Resource Manager

Planning Resources
- *Lesson Plans*
- *Block Scheduling*

- *Bellringer*
- *Daily Language Practice*

- *Listening and Speaking Activities*
- *Tests with Answer Key and Rubrics*
- *Thinking and Study Skills*

- *MindJogger Videoquizzes*

- *Presentation Plus!*
- *Testmaker*

- *glencoe.com*

29.1 Listening Effectively

How well you listen can affect your success in school, sports, jobs, and personal relationships. If you're like most people, however, you understand about half of what you hear and remember only about half of that. In this lesson, you'll learn how to improve your listening comprehension.

Active Listening

Whether you're listening to a friend, a coach, or a teacher, you need to do more than just hear what the person says. Only by listening actively will you be able to understand, interpret, and respond to what you hear. The chart below presents strategies for active listening.

Strategies for Active Listening
PREPARE TO LISTEN
• **Eliminate physical distractions.** Set aside other work and make yourself comfortable.
• **Clear your mind of other thoughts.** Don't think about your schedule for the day or what you're going to do over the weekend.
• **Adopt a positive attitude and keep an open mind.** Be willing to listen to what the speaker has to say, and don't jump to conclusions before the speaker is finished.
LISTEN TO THE MESSAGE
• **Focus your attention on what the speaker is saying.** Don't jump ahead and think about what the speaker may say next.
• **Maintain your concentration by finding something of interest in the message.** Don't doodle, daydream, constantly look around, or become impatient for the speaker to finish.
• **Take notes if the situation calls for it.** Note taking is often useful for classroom presentations, speeches, and interviews.
INTERPRET THE MESSAGE
• **Summarize the message.** Identify the purpose of the message and the main ideas or themes presented.
• **Reflect on what you hear.** Ask yourself: Does this information sound reasonable? Does it conflict with anything else I know?
RESPOND TO THE MESSAGE
• **Ask questions.** Request clarification of ideas and terms you don't understand, and ask questions that relate to the topic.
• **Discuss the message.** Compare your interpretations with those of others.
• **Assess the message.** What significance or consequences does the message have for you or for others?

Focus

Lesson Overview

Objective

- To learn how to listen actively
- To evaluate what is heard

Skills

- listening effectively in class by thinking about what is heard, noticing verbal clues, listening for helpful information, and organizing what is heard; evaluating what is heard on television and radio

Critical Thinking

- analyzing; synthesizing; categorizing; classifying; contrasting; recognizing main ideas; summarizing; comparing; evaluating information

Listening and Speaking

- in-class listening; interviewing; listening to a lecture; evaluating

Bellringer
Daily Language Activity

When students enter the classroom, have this assignment on the board:
List five tips for effective listening.

See also  *Daily Language Practice*

Listening and Speaking

Resource Manager

Planning Resources
- *Lesson Plans*

Transparencies
- *Bellringer*
- *Daily Language Practice*

Other Print Resources
- *Listening and Speaking Activities,* pp. 1–3
- *Thinking and Study Skills,* p. 34

Teach

Listening to a News Program

Ask students to listen to a radio or television commercial and answer the questions posed on page 886. Students may read aloud their answers and discuss them with others who have heard the same commercial. **L2**

Evaluating What You Hear

In all listening situations, you can use the strategies for active listening to help you absorb, understand, and interpret the messages you hear; but, in certain situations, you'll want to do even more with the information you hear. Some situations—such as responding to persuasive messages and performances of poems, short stories, plays, and other literary works—require you to evaluate and to analyze critically what you hear.

Persuasive Messages

Each day you hear many persuasive messages—from your friends, teachers, parents, radio commercials, and other sources. Some of these messages are reasonable and worth following or acting on; others are not. How do you decide when a persuasive message is convincing and worthwhile? You can use the questions in the chart below to help you analyze and evaluate persuasive messages.

Questions for Evaluating Persuasive Messages
• **Purpose:** What is the purpose of the message? In other words, what is the speaker trying to sell or convince people to do?
• **Audience:** To what audience is the message targeted?
• **Facts/opinions:** What are the facts and what are the opinions in the message? Do the facts support the opinions or claims? What facts or opinions are missing?
• **Errors in reasoning:** Does the message contain errors in reasoning, such as overgeneralizations and either/or arguments?
• **Persuasive techniques:** What kinds of persuasive techniques—such as bandwagon appeal, loaded language, celebrity testimonial, and exaggeration—are used in the message? How does the message appeal to people's emotions?
• **Values and biases:** What values or biases does the message reflect? Do these values match yours?
• **Your opinion:** After analyzing the message, what is your opinion of it? Do you agree, disagree, or need more information to make a decision?

Literary Performances

Some literary works, such as poems and plays, are intended to be read aloud or performed. However, even short stories and essays, which are intended for silent reading, can seem to come to life in a performance. You can use the questions in the chart below both to assess literary performances and to improve your own performance of literary works.

Listening Online

Tell students that they can listen to poems being read aloud on the Internet. In some cases, students may even be able to find audio files of poets reading their own work. Ask students to search for an audio file of the work of a favorite poet. (If students have difficulty finding a poetry reading, direct them to look for an audio file of Maya Angelou reading a poem she wrote.) Have students use a dictionary to look up the meaning of any words they hear but do not know. Students should also use their knowledge of language to interpret accurately the speaker's message. Then have students evaluate the reading based on the Questions for Evaluating Literary Performances on page 887.

Questions for Evaluating Literary Performances

- **Voice qualities:** Does the performer effectively use voice qualities such as volume, stress, tone, and pronunciation to present the work?
- **Body language:** Does the performer use body language—including posture, eye contact, facial expressions, gestures, and movements—to engage the audience and bring the work to life?
- **Literary elements:** What element of the literary work (e.g., character development, plot, imagery, rhyme, or figurative language) does the performance emphasize? What is the effect of this element?
- **Your rating:** How would you rate the performer's interpretation of the literary work? Why?

Exercise 1

Work in a small group to practice the Strategies for Active Listening presented on page 885. Brainstorm a list of topics on which each member of the group could give a brief, informative speech. Take turns presenting one- or two-minute impromptu speeches on some of these topics. Listen actively to each speech. Then, as a group, follow the steps outlined in the chart under the headings Interpret the Message and Respond to the Message.

Exercise 2

Listen to a persuasive message on radio or television (such as a commercial or a news editorial), or obtain a videotape or audiotape of a historic persuasive speech. Use the Questions for Evaluating Persuasive Messages presented on page 886 to write an analysis and evaluation of the speech. Then present your analysis and evaluation orally to the class. Be sure to provide concrete support for the points in your analysis.

Exercise 3

Attend a poetry reading or a play in your community or watch the performance of a drama on television. Listen actively to the performance, keeping in mind the Questions for Evaluating Literary Performances presented in the chart above. Use the questions to write an evaluation of the performance.

Exercise 4

Schedule an artistic-performance week in your class. Working alone, with a partner, or in a small group, select and perform a poem or scene from a play. Use the Questions for Evaluating Literary Performances above both as you practice your own performance and as you listen to the performances of others. After your performance, ask for the audience's evaluation. Use their comments to help you write your own performance evaluation, including goals for future presentations.

Practice and Assess

Evaluation Rubrics

Exercise 1

To demonstrate that they have listened closely to each speech, students should be able to summarize, discuss, and ask informed questions about the material presented.

Exercise 2

In their analyses and evaluations, students should identify what they listened to, the purpose of the message, the targeted audience, and the facts and opinions given. Students should also identify any errors in reasoning, the persuasive techniques used, and the values or biases reflected in the message. They also should give their opinion of the message and support their opinion with reasons.

Exercise 3

In their evaluations, students should identify the performance they listened to, rate the performance, and give reasons for their rating. Their reasons should focus on voice qualities, body language, and one or more literary elements in the performance.

Exercise 4

Students should demonstrate that they listened attentively to the performance of other students by giving effective feedback. In their written evaluations of their own performances, students should incorporate the feedback they received by setting goals that address their individual weaknesses.

Additional Resources

- *Thinking and Study Skills,* p. 34
- *Listening and Speaking Activities,* pp. 1–3

Close

Encourage students to discuss how listening skills can help them in other classes. When are good listening skills useful? How can good listening skills improve their grades?

Real World Connection

Targeting Audiences

Tell students that advertisers and politicians conduct extensive analyses of their audiences in order to create messages that will reach and affect the people with whom they want to communicate. Researchers identify the age, sex, educational background, income, area of residence, and other factors of target audiences. Then they gather information about the group's beliefs, tastes, and feelings by conducting surveys, polls, focus groups, and other kinds of research. Ask students to identify and discuss advertisements or public service messages that are directed at teenagers their age.

Focus

Lesson Overview

Objective

- To learn to speak effectively in both formal and informal situations and to practice before presenting a speech

Skills

- speaking clearly in informal situations; identifying a clear purpose for a speech; tailoring a speech to an audience; conducting research; organizing, drafting, and revising a speech; using verbal and nonverbal techniques effectively in delivering a speech; listening actively to the speeches of peers and evaluating their persuasive messages; providing feedback to speakers

Critical Thinking

- analyzing; synthesizing; evaluating; recognizing main ideas; summarizing; classifying; categorizing; comparing

Listening and Speaking

- informal speaking; formal speaking; listening actively to speeches; evaluating persuasive speeches; providing verbal feedback to others

Bellringer
Daily Language Activity

When students enter the classroom, have this assignment on the board: *Write about a time when you gave an oral report, speech, or dramatic reading. What was the experience like? What would you do differently?*

See also  *Daily Language Practice*

Motivating Activity

Read aloud this statement by Adam Clayton Powell: "Never let anyone keep you contained and never let anyone keep your voice silent." Encourage students to discuss speeches they have heard that moved them or that were unusually effective. Ask, How might believing strongly in what you have to say help you deliver an effective speech? Discuss students' ideas from the Bellringer activity, and explain that in this lesson students will learn how to present information orally in an engaging manner.

29.2 Speaking Effectively

The way you speak can influence your relationships with other people and your success in groups. In this lesson, you'll gain important advice on how to speak effectively in both informal and formal situations.

Speaking Informally

Most of the speaking you do is informal. You talk with friends, family, teachers, and others. You speak on the phone, introduce people to others, give directions. Keep in mind, though, that even in such casual situations it is important to communicate effectively.

In all informal speaking, be sure to communicate clearly and in a lively tone. Don't mumble or talk too loudly or too softly. Be careful about "filler" words that have no real meaning, such as *like* ("He was, like, studying"), *um,* and *you know.* Finally, always be polite to your audience.

In most instances of informal speaking, common sense and consideration are the best guides to effective communication. For example, when you are on the telephone, identify yourself and explain your reason for calling. Be sure to call people at times that are convenient for them, and keep the call to a reasonable length.

When giving directions or instructions, present your points as a series of logical steps. Speak slowly and be sure the listener understands. Encourage the listener to ask questions. You might even ask questions yourself to help your listener understand.

Making Formal Speeches

Unlike informal speaking, formal speeches are prepared, rehearsed, and then delivered at a prearranged place and time. Preparing a formal speech is similar to writing a research paper or a persuasive essay, but involves more steps.

Consider Purpose and Audience Once you have a topic, focus on your purpose for making the speech. Do you want to inform, persuade, or entertain your audience? You may end up doing all three—an audience that is entertained is more likely to listen attentively, and an audience that hears solid evidence is more likely to be persuaded. But as you start out, write a clear statement of your main purpose, such as *I want to persuade my audience to donate money to disaster relief efforts that help flood victims in North Carolina.*

After clearly defining the purpose of the speech, identify your audience. Is it made up of urban high school students with diverse backgrounds? Suburban middle-class parents? Evaluate what your audience

Resource Manager

Planning Resources
- *Lesson Plans*

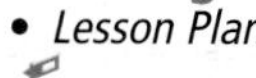

Transparencies
- *Bellringer*
- *Daily Language Practice*

Other Print Resources
- *Listening and Speaking Activities,* pp. 14–17
- *Thinking and Study Skills,* p. 34

already knows about your topic, even interviewing some of them if possible. What concerns or biases do they have? What misinformation might you need to correct? Then think about the level of language that is suitable for your audience. For a formal speech, you'll use standard English, but you may need to tailor your vocabulary to your audience and explain any technical terms you use.

Research the Topic Gather facts, examples, and experts' opinions on your topic by conducting library and Internet research—even polls and interviews, if appropriate. After studying the information you gather, write a clear statement of your thesis. Then select accurate, relevant evidence and examples from reliable sources to support your thesis.

Create an Outline Choose a pattern of organization that fits your information and your purpose. Outline your information, using your thesis as the controlling idea. At this point, consider whether visual aids might be useful in presenting your topic.

Draft and Revise Use your outline as a guide to drafting your speech, following the standard structure of an introduction, a body, and a conclusion. If you are preparing a persuasive speech, you may want to review Unit 6, Persuasive Writing, pages 282–321.

In your introduction, think of a way to attract your audience's attention. Consider one of the methods listed in the following chart.

Getting Your Audience's Attention	
STRATEGY	**EXAMPLE**
Tell a story	When my family's home was washed away in a flood three years ago, I felt as though my whole past had been swept away.
Ask a question	Why should you care about the possible extinction of gorillas?
Use a quotation	Mark Twain wrote, "Civilizations proceed from the heart rather than from the head."
State an amazing fact or statistic	A bolt of lightning is five times hotter than the surface of the sun.

For your conclusion, you might refer to the method you used in your introduction and provide a twist that sums up your speech. For example, if you began with a question, you might pose it again and then give the answer. Whatever method you use, strive for a strong finish that drives home your message. Your last words are the ones your audience will be most likely to remember.

Revise your speech, just as you would any other work of informative or persuasive writing. Then read your speech out loud and make further changes so that it flows smoothly. You have to be able to say what you write.

Teach

Choosing a Topic

Encourage students to look to their own experiences and interests in choosing a topic for a speech. Guide the class in brainstorming a list of possible topics by asking leading questions, such as

- What could make your school, community, or country a better place for everyone?
- What do you spend most of your time doing? What would you like to spend most of your time doing?
- What social or political issue affects your life the most?

Write responses on the board and ask students how they could turn some of the responses into a topic for a speech. **L1**

Discussing Outlines and Drafts

Review students' outlines and drafts and offer suggestions for improvements. Advise students that it is appropriate to use personal stories and personal pronouns in their speeches. A speaker wants the audience to identify with him or her, and people like to hear about the personal experiences of others. These stories should make a point, though, and support the students' theses. **L2**

MEETING INDIVIDUAL NEEDS

English Language Learners

Practicing a Speech

Suggest that students use tape recorders to practice their speeches, replaying the recording and then repeating their speeches to make appropriate adjustments. If possible, make a tape recorder available for students to use during any free class periods they may have.

Teach

Discussing Relaxation Techniques

Share with students some standard techniques for relaxing before giving a speech, such as tensing and then relaxing different muscle groups, doing knee bends, and taking a few slow, deep breaths. Suggest that speakers keep in mind that their audience is on their side. An audience typically wants the speaker to succeed. Mention also an added benefit of visual aids—they take the audience's eyes off the speaker, which may help the speaker relax. **L1**

Discussing Delivery Methods

List the different methods of delivering a speech on the board and ask students to identify the advantages and disadvantages of each method. For example, memorizing a speech ensures that the content and wording are exact, but it is time-consuming and difficult. Reading from a manuscript also ensures that the content and wording are exact, but the reader may have difficulty maintaining eye contact with the audience. Using an outline or note cards requires the speaker to rely on memory but can result in a fresher delivery. Take a poll to see how many students prefer each method. **L2**

Practice and Assess

Evaluation Rubrics

Exercise 5

Divide your evaluation of each student's presentation into three parts: content of the speech, verbal techniques, and nonverbal techniques. A speech should have a clear thesis, be organized logically, contain solid supporting evidence, and use appropriate appeals. Students should speak audibly and clearly at a moderate pace and in a lively tone, stressing important words. Students should maintain good posture, look at the audience, and use facial expressions and gestures to reinforce ideas.

Additional Resources

Listening and Speaking Activities, pp. 10–11

Thinking and Study Skills, p. 34

If your sentences are too long, shorten them. If you stumble over a group of words, change them.

Prepare Materials Unless you choose to memorize your speech, you'll need to prepare materials to use during your delivery. Some speakers read from manuscript pages; others speak from an outline or note cards. If you are not required to use a particular method, choose the method that works best for you and your situation. If you read your speech, prepare a double- or triple-spaced manuscript with wide margins. If you choose to speak from an outline or note cards, use your written speech to prepare these materials. Underline topic sentences, number supporting points, and transfer the ideas to an outline or note cards. Be sure to number your manuscript pages, outline pages, or note cards at the top.

Practice and Deliver Your Speech Practice your speech a few times in front of a mirror. Then ask a friend or relative to listen to your speech or to videotape it. As you rehearse, pay attention to the points listed in the chart below. Even if you read your speech, be sure to look up often and make eye contact with your audience, especially at the beginning and the end of sentences.

Techniques for Giving a Speech

VERBAL TECHNIQUES
- **Volume:** Speak loudly enough so that everyone in the audience can hear you.
- **Pronunciation:** Speak clearly, pronouncing all the words.
- **Pace:** Speak at a moderate speed, but vary the rate; use pauses to convey your meaning.
- **Tone:** Speak in a lively tone.
- **Emphasis:** Stress important words and ideas.

NONVERBAL TECHNIQUES
- **Posture:** Stand up tall with your head straight.
- **Eye contact:** Make eye contact with people throughout your audience.
- **Facial expressions and gestures:** Vary your facial expressions to reflect what you are saying, and use natural gestures to reinforce your ideas.
- **Visual aids:** If appropriate for your topic, use charts, diagrams, graphs, or video clips to enhance your speech and to convey important information.

Audience questions and comments At the end of your speech, allow your audience to respond by asking for any questions or comments. Answer your listeners' questions honestly and respectfully. Use this question-and-answer period to correct misunderstandings, to repeat points that your listeners may have missed, and to learn what you may need to make clearer in your speech.

Close

Have students summarize what they learned from giving and listening to formal speeches. What were the characteristics of the most effective speakers?

Technology Tip

Using a Video Camera

If your school has a video camera, you may wish to allow some class time for students to work in small groups, rehearsing the speeches and videotaping the performances. A video recording allows students to evaluate their use of gestures, eye contact, and other delivery techniques.

Exercise 5

Follow the process described in this lesson to prepare, practice, and present a ten-minute informative or persuasive speech. Choose from the following topics, or come up with a topic of your own:

- safety and security measures at your school
- censorship of books in public schools
- high school students' working at part-time jobs
- sports programs at your school

As you listen to the speeches of your classmates, apply the Strategies for Active Listening presented on page 885. Use the Questions for Evaluating Persuasive Messages on page 886 as you offer comments on the persuasive speeches to the presenters.

29.3 Participating in Groups

Throughout your life, you'll participate in many groups—families, classes, study groups, teams, clubs or organizations, and work groups. To be an active member who contributes in positive ways to any of these groups, you need good listening and speaking skills as well as an understanding of how to function in, and contribute to, a group.

In a typical study or discussion group, the members have roles such as group leader, recorder, and participants. The group leader guides the discussion and keeps the group focused on the topic or task. The recorder takes notes on ideas and records final decisions. The participants contribute ideas, respond to the ideas of others, and vote on decisions. A study group operates most effectively if all members follow the guidelines listed in the chart below.

Guidelines for Participating in a Study Group

- **Be prepared:** Complete any assigned reading or research before the group meets.
- **Focus on the issue:** Don't bring up unrelated topics.
- **Listen actively:** Make an effort to understand each person's viewpoint. Don't interrupt when anyone is speaking. Make a note of any word you might not understand. Try to define the word in context. Later, you can look up any word or, if possible, ask the speaker to define the word.
- **Show respect:** Recognize that each person has something worthwhile to contribute. An effective group draws upon the different strengths of its members.
- **State your ideas clearly and concisely:** Don't talk on and on so that others have little chance to speak.
- **Respond constructively to the ideas of others:** Explain why you agree or disagree with someone's idea, providing reasons or evidence for your position.
- **Encourage everyone to participate:** If someone has not spoken, ask for his or her opinion.

Resource Manager

Planning Resources
- *Lesson Plans*

Other Print Resources
- *Listening and Speaking Activities,* pp. 10–11
- *Thinking and Study Skills,* p. 34

Focus

Lesson Overview

Objective:
- To learn roles and procedures for group participation

Skills
- observing group performance; listening to group members; summarizing group experience

Critical Thinking
- relating; synthesizing; evaluating; summarizing; decision making

Listening and Speaking
- discussing; questioning

Bellringer
Daily Language Activity

When students enter the classroom, have this assignment on the board: *Write one rule to help group members who are in disagreement to have an effective discussion.*

See also  *Daily Language Practice*

Practice and Assess

Evaluation Rubrics

Exercise 6 *(page 892)*
Observers' evaluations should be specific and cover the criteria given. Encourage students to use the evaluations to improve their future participation in groups.

Close

Stress the importance of being able to work effectively in a group by noting that almost all occupations require working in groups at least part of the time.

Focus

Lesson Overview

Objective:

- To learn how to conduct an effective interview

Skills

- researching; formulating questions; asking and responding to questions; listening actively; taking notes

Critical Thinking

- questioning; synthesizing; recognizing main ideas

Listening and Speaking

- asking questions; listening actively

Bellringer
Daily Language Activity

When students enter the classroom, have this assignment on the board: *Describe an interview you have read, heard, or seen. How effective was the interviewer?*

See also  *Daily Language Practice*

Practice and Assess

Evaluation Rubrics

Exercise 7

Students' evaluations of each other's work should focus on how well prepared the interviewer was, on how clear the questions were, and on how accurate and complete the written account of the interview was.

Close

Remind students that interviewing skills may be useful in other classes, in extracurricular activities, and in job searches.

Exercise 6

In a group of five or six students, discuss the following question: What is the most crucial problem facing high school students today? Choose a group leader and a recorder. In addition, select an observer, a person to keep track of how well the group is functioning. The observer should note whether all group members participate, stay focused, listen actively, and respond constructively. After the discussion concludes, the observer should give an evaluation of how well the group functioned, providing specific examples of each observation.

29.4 Conducting Interviews

Good listening and speaking skills are also useful in conducting interviews, a valuable way of gathering information for reports and projects. The following guidelines will help you conduct an effective interview.

Guidelines for Conducting Interviews	
Prepare for the interview	• Research the subject and learn a little about the person you will interview. • Prepare a list of five or more *who, what, where, when, why,* and *how* questions. Avoid questions that require just a yes or no answer. For example, instead of *Do you enjoy your work?* ask *What do you enjoy most about your work?* • If you plan to tape the interview, make sure your tape recorder works. If you plan to take notes, make sure you bring along two pens that work and a pad of paper as well as your list of interview questions.
Listen actively during the interview.	• Take notes or tape-record the interview. Ask for the correct spelling of the person's name and of any unfamiliar places or terms the person uses. If necessary, ask the person to explain or repeat statements you do not understand. • Ask intelligent follow-up questions. • At the end of the interview, be sure to thank the person.
Follow up after the interview.	• As soon as possible after the interview, write a full account of everything you remember, referring to your notes or your tape. • If necessary, ask the person interviewed to clarify any points of confusion. • Write the person a thank-you letter.

Exercise 7

With a partner, take turns conducting an interview about each other's favorite interests and activities, following the guidelines in this lesson. Check each other's written accounts of the interview for accuracy and completeness. Then offer each other observations on how well the interview was conducted.

Listening and Speaking

ASSESSMENT OPTIONS

Tests with Answer Key and Rubrics
Unit 29 Mastery Test, pp. 113–114

Testmaker
Unit 29 Mastery Test

You may wish to administer the Unit 29 Mastery Test at this point.

MindJogger Videoquizzes

Resource Manager

Planning Resources

- *Lesson Plans*

Other Print Resources

- *Listening and Speaking Activities*

UNIT 30 Viewing and Representing

LOG ON Writing Online | For research tools and additional skills practice, go to glencoe.com and enter QuickPass code WC97727p3.

893

Objectives

- To learn how to examine and evaluate visual images and media messages
- To demonstrate an understanding of visual and film elements and persuasive techniques by analyzing a media message
- To produce a video and a web page

ASSESSMENT OPTIONS

Tests with Answer Key & Rubrics
Unit 30 Pretest, pp. 115–116

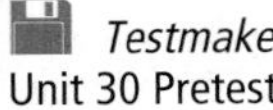
Testmaker
Unit 30 Pretest

You may wish to administer the Unit 30 Pretest at this point.

Key to Ability Levels

L1 Level 1 activities are within the basic ability range of students.

L2 Level 2 activities are within the ability range of average students.

L3 Level 3 activities are more challenging activities.

Resource Manager

Planning Resources
- *Lesson Plans*
- *Block Scheduling*

Other Print Resources
- *Tests with Answer Key and Rubrics*
- *Viewing and Representing*

Video
- *MindJogger Videoquizzes*

Software
- *Presentation Plus!*
- *Testmaker*

Web Site
- *glencoe.com*

Focus

Lesson Overview

Objective

- To develop effective skills for identifying, understanding, and interpreting the visual images and messages of mass media

Skills

- identifying and analyzing visual elements; describing and understanding how meanings are communicated through such elements of visual design as shape, line, color, and texture; analyzing relationships, ideas, and cultures as represented in various media; distinguishing and comparing the purposes of various media forms; recognizing how visual and sound techniques contribute to the overall message

Critical Thinking

- interpreting; describing; analyzing; comparing; drawing conclusions; classifying; speculating

Listening and Speaking

- discussing; asking and answering questions; informal speaking; interpreting and explaining various visual techniques

Bellringer

Daily Language Activity

When students enter the classroom, have this assignment on the board: *Write a definition of* mass media *and of* media literacy. *Then list types of mass media and cite specific examples of each type.* (Mass media: "a form of communication that is widely available to many people;" media literacy: "the ability to understand, interpret, analyze, and critique media messages.")

Motivating Activity

Lead students to understand that many verbal and visual messages sent by mass media are carefully constructed to affect the reader or viewer in predetermined ways. Therefore, becoming media literate is crucial for empowering oneself to make wise decisions about the validity of information and the value of various commercial products. Point out that in this lesson students will learn how to develop skills for media literacy.

30.1 Examining Visual Messages

Television and the other mass media have an immense influence on your life. They keep you informed and entertained; in many cases, what you see and hear in mass media presentations will attempt to persuade you in one way or another. Whether you are aware of it or not, media presentations help shape your attitudes, values, and behavior. Media presentations not only reflect your culture, they help create it. Developing *media literacy*—the ability to understand, interpret, analyze, and critique media messages, as well as the ability to create your own media messages—will help you recognize the ways media messages might influence your thinking and your life. The goal of this unit is to help you gain such media literacy.

Except for radio, all mass media send visual messages. Being aware of the techniques used in developing visual messages will help you to interpret the messages you see and to understand and analyze the ideas being presented.

Interpreting Visual Design

To understand the design of a visual image such as a photograph or illustration, you examine its *composition*, or arrangement of elements. The following chart lists some basic elements in the composition of a photograph or illustration and describes effects that can be achieved by manipulating these elements. The actual effect of an element depends on the overall context of the picture, however.

Elements of Visual Design

ELEMENT	EXAMPLE	POSSIBLE EFFECTS
SHAPE	Circle Square Triangle	Suggests wholeness, lovableness Suggests firmness, stability Suggests unity, balance; tension
LINE Lines can be real or implied. An example of a real line is the edge of a building; a person's gaze can create an implied line.	Straight lines Curved lines Vertical lines Horizontal lines Diagonal lines	Direct the eye to something Suggest motion, warmth Suggest dignity, status, power Suggest peace, stillness Suggest tension, action, energy

(continued)

Resource Manager

Planning Resources
- *Lesson Plans*

Other Print Resources
Viewing and Representing

Elements of Visual Design		
ELEMENT	**EXAMPLE**	**POSSIBLE EFFECTS**
COLOR OR TONE	Cool colors (blue, green, gray) Warm colors (red, yellow, orange) Bright colors Subdued or pastel colors Light tones Dark tones	Convey calm, emotional distance Convey energy, vibrancy, warmth Convey joy, action, excitement Suggest innocence, softness, serenity Create a happy, playful mood Convey sadness, mystery, dullness
TEXTURE	Smooth, flat Rough, woven Silky, shiny	Suggests emptiness; something modern, streamlined Conveys wholesomeness, naturalness, homeliness Creates sense of luxury
POSITIONING OF SUBJECTS The positions of figures grouped together can show how the artist views the relationships to one another.	Top of frame Center of frame Bottom of frame	Conveys importance, power Conveys stability Conveys inferiority, weakness
LIGHT A viewer's eye naturally travels to the most lighted area.	Bright light Dim light or shadows	Draws the eye to a specific area; creates a cheerful mood Creates a sense of mystery, doom
SPACE	Large space around subject Little space around subject	Draws attention to the subject; isolates details; creates a sense of openness, emptiness, loneliness. Makes the subject seem dominating, overwhelming

To understand how elements of visual design work together in a photograph, study this picture of a section of an ocean shoreline. The curving lines and rounded shapes of the mountains, hills, and ocean waves create a soothing, warm mood. The pale color of the ocean water and mist fills most of the frame, giving the picture a soft look. The hazy light adds to the soft, wispy feel of the picture. All these elements combine to convey a warm, soothing portrait of the meeting of water and land.

Viewing and Representing

Teach

Using the Chart

Discuss the *Elements of Visual Design* chart. Then call on volunteers to use the chart to identify and interpret the visual message of the photograph on this page. Use the text relating to the photograph as a starting point. Have students speculate how the visual message might be altered if the photographer had taken the picture under different weather conditions, at a different time of day, with different positions of the subjects, with a different amount of light and shadows, and so on. **L2**

Cooperative Learning

Analyzing Visual Elements

Have students work in small groups to select an image from a media source of their choice and to analyze the image's visual elements. They should use the chart on these two pages as a guide. Tell students that they may not always agree on the effect of each element, and that they should explain and explore their different interpretations in order to arrive at a richer analysis. Have each group present its analysis to the class. After each presentation, encourage classmates to ask questions about any part of the analysis that remains unclear.

Teach

Interpreting Film Techniques

Emphasize that film and video directors rely on many of the elements of visual design listed on the chart on pages 894–895. In addition, they have other techniques that are not available to artists and still photographers, such as movement of the camera, angle of the shot, special effects, and so on. They also have the advantages of sound, both in the form of background music, which can influence a viewer's emotions, and in the form of dialogue. Ask students to consider whether the use of these additional techniques always makes film and video more effective than still photography. **L2**

Practice and Assess

Evaluation Rubric: Exercise 1

Students' descriptions should focus on three of the following elements: color or tone; texture; shape; line; positioning of subjects; light; or space. Their summaries should discuss one or more ideas communicated by the relationship between the people and the landscape. For example, students may discuss the smallness and vulnerability of humans compared to the vastness, strength, and permanence of mountain, earth, and sky.

The photograph on page 895 presents one view of an ocean shoreline at a particular place and time and from a particular perspective. If this were the only picture of a shoreline that you had ever seen, you would probably develop a single impression of coastlines. However, many other photographs could be taken of the same location under varying conditions and from varying perspectives to create radically different impressions. Similarly, different photographs of a foreign environment would probably give you different impressions of its culture. Every photograph presents just one view of a subject from a particular perspective.

Exercise 1

Use the Elements of Visual Design chart to describe the effects of at least three elements in this photograph of rock climbers in the Central Asian country of Kyrgyzstan. Summarize the ideas that the photograph conveys about the relationship between the people and the landscape.

Interpreting Film Techniques

The basic elements of visual design apply to the media of motion pictures and videos as well as to photographs and illustrations. Motion picture and television directors also use a wide variety of film techniques to tell stories and to convey messages. The chart on page 897 describes some of these techniques and the effects they can have.

Enrichment and Extension

Analyzing Characters and Film Techniques

Have students analyze the character traits of specific movie characters, as well as the film techniques used to represent and extend the messages embodied in such characters. You might start the activity by showing film clips from movies featuring such strong screen presences as John Wayne, Humphrey Bogart, Paul Newman, Robert Redford, Katharine Hepburn, Meryl Streep, and Bette Davis. Have students draw conclusions regarding the qualities and values typically embodied by the characters such actors have played.

Basic Film Techniques		
TECHNIQUE	**EXAMPLE**	**POSSIBLE EFFECTS**
CAMERA ANGLE	High (looking down)	Minimizes importance or status of subject
	Straight on (eye level)	Puts viewer on equal level with subject; promotes identification with subject
	Low (looking up)	Emphasizes importance or power of subject
CAMERA SHOTS	Close-up (magnified view)	Promotes identification with subject
	Long shot (wide view)	Establishes relationship between characters and a setting
	Reaction shot	Shows effect of one character on another, or of an event on a character
LIGHTING	High key (bright, even)	Creates cheerful, optimistic mood
	Low key (producing shadows)	Creates gloomy, eerie mood
	Light from above	Allows subject to glow with significance
	Light from below	May raise audience apprehension
MOVEMENT	Slow motion	Emphasizes movement and heightens drama
	Blurred motion	Suggests speed, confusion, or dreamlike state
EDITING (selection and arrangement of scenes)	Sequence of short shots	Builds tension; creates a rushed mood
	Sequence of long shots	Conveys a feeling of stability
SPECIAL EFFECTS	Artwork and miniature models	Appear real when filmed
	Computer enhancement	Creates composite images; distorts qualities of a character or scene
BACKGROUND MUSIC		Evokes audience's emotional response, sets mood, reinforces theme

Examine the elements of visual design and the film techniques used in the still on page 898 from the movie *Star Wars: Episode 1—The Phantom Menace* (1999). In the scene, the Sith Lords, Darth Sidious and Darth Maul, are making a report to the trade federation leaders after the invasion of Naboo. The

Teach

Using the Chart

Invite students to discuss their favorite television program in terms of the elements listed in the chart on this page. Ask such questions as *How does the director want you to respond to the show? Is it supposed to be funny? Scary? Suspenseful? Dramatic? What techniques does the director use to get you to respond this way? What kinds of camera shots and angles are used to encourage a particular response? How does the background music encourage a particular response? To what purpose are special effects used?*

Then encourage students to break into small groups and agree on a television show to watch at home, taking notes about the basic film techniques used. Then allow students to meet with their group, compare notes, and present their findings to the class. **L2**

English Language Learners

Visual Language

Once students who are learning English are familiar with the basic film techniques explained in the chart, they should be able to analyze English language commercials, television shows, or movies, since most film techniques and visual elements do not rely on language to communicate their message. Similarly, students who speak only English should be able to analyze a foreign-language commercial, television show, or movie. In fact, doing so may highlight their understanding of visual and film techniques. Ask a volunteer who is learning English to videotape a television show in his or her native language. Show the video to the class. Then have students work together to analyze the purpose of the show and some of the film techniques used to achieve that purpose.

Practice and Assess

Evaluation Rubric: Exercise 2

Students' analyses should: include details concerning the film director's use of lighting, camera angle, and position of characters; indicate an accurate interpretation of the director's intended visual message; contain thoughtful speculation regarding how the effects might be different if Lucas had made other creative and technical decisions.

Close

Call on volunteers to identify specific visual techniques used by still photographers and film directors. Which techniques do they feel are particularly effective in getting across messages? Why is it helpful for readers and viewers to be aware of these techniques? Share ideas in a class discussion.

diagonal lines of the table draw the viewer's gaze into the picture to focus on Darth Sidious and Darth Maul. The outline of the body of each character forms a triangle, conveying tension. Dark colors dominate the picture, suggesting evil and menace. The viewer's sense of fear is heightened when Darth Maul seems to be looking down upon him or her. This scene was created with special effects. Darth Sidious and Darth Maul appear as holographic images, which are produced with lasers. This technique makes them seem even more menacing and otherworldly. All the elements in this scene reinforce the idea that these characters represent evil and are dangerous.

Exercise 2

Study the still below from the movie *Star Wars: Episode 1—The Phantom Menace* (1999). Use the Elements of Visual Design and Basic Film Techniques charts to help you identify at least three elements or techniques used in the scene and to analyze their effects. Share your analysis in a brief oral report to the class.

Enrichment and Extension

About George Lucas

Star Wars director George Lucas has been a great success as a filmmaker. When the Academy of Motion Picture Arts and Sciences awarded him the Irving G. Thalberg Award in 1992 for his exceptionally high standard of filmmaking, he responded, "I've always tried to be aware of what I say in my films, because all of us who make motion pictures are teachers; teachers with very loud voices." Lucas may serve as a role model for students not only for his outstanding achievements in filmmaking and his technical expertise in computer graphics, games, and special effects but also for his unexpected rise to prominence. No one in his high school class in Modesto, California, ever dreamed that the George Lucas they knew then would become a media mogul. In fact, a former classmate said Lucas was often teased and disrespected by his peers. Students interested in George Lucas may wish to research his life and career.

30.2 Evaluating Media Messages

Many photographs, movies, and television programs seem to capture realistic, believable scenes from life. Media messages are constructed for a purpose, which is typically to inform, entertain, or persuade. As a result, the presentation may show only one particular view of life.

Think about a music video that has been designed to entertain teen viewers. The creators of the video might feature clothing, hair styles, or music that appeal to a very specific portion of teen culture. However, the styles and music do not necessarily represent the tastes of all teenagers in the country. Even in a documentary that you would consider to be strictly factual, a director may have made many decisions about how to shoot scenes, what information to include and exclude, and what effects to strive for to achieve his or her purpose. The purpose or goal may or may not be worthwhile—that is for you to decide. To make an informed decision, you need to be able to **deconstruct,** or analyze, media messages. This lesson will help you develop that skill.

Recognizing Media Genres

Media messages reach you in a wide variety of forms. These forms, or genres, can be grouped into four main types: print, broadcast, film, and the Internet. *Print media* include newspapers, magazines, billboards, books, product packaging, and other materials that convey messages through printed words and images. In *Broadcast media,* consisting of radio and television, sounds alone or both sounds and moving images are transmitted to a wide public audience. *Film media,* including movies and videotapes, also consist of sounds and moving images. The *Internet* contains a wide variety of Web sites that consist of some combination of printed words, still and moving images, and sounds.

The form of a media message can affect its meaning or your interpretation of or response to the message. For information on a specific topic, you might choose between several types of presentations, depending on the kind and amount of information you need. For example, for a quick rundown of a current news story, such as a recent earthquake, you might read a newspaper or a newsmagazine. However, you could gain a fuller appreciation of the effects of an earthquake from watching a live television newscast. The sounds and moving images on television have a strong impact and often arouse a stronger emotional response than print does. To learn more about earthquakes in general, you could refer to a book, an in-depth magazine article, or you might view a film documentary. Imagine learning from the newspaper that the United States was involved in aiding earthquake victims in a foreign country. How might your view of events and your reactions be different than if you watched the television news coverage?

Resource Manager

Planning Resources
- *Lesson Plans*

Other Print Resources
- *Viewing and Representing*

Focus

Lesson Overview

Objective
- To develop effective skills for analyzing and critiquing the significance of visual images, messages, and meanings

Skills
- investigating the source and purpose of a media presentation or production; deconstructing media to identify and understand the main idea of a message; evaluating and critiquing persuasive techniques; recognizing how visual and sound techniques contribute to the overall message; creating a short editorial

Critical Thinking
- interpreting; analyzing; critiquing; evaluating; drawing conclusions; classifying; speculating; comparing and contrasting

Listening and Speaking
- discussing; asking and answering questions; informal speaking

Bellringer
Daily Language Activity

When students enter the classroom, have this assignment on the board: *Write about a time when you tried to inform, entertain, or persuade someone. What helped you to succeed in achieving your goal?*

Motivating Activity

Tell students that the primary purpose of most media messages is to either inform, entertain, or persuade. Ask volunteers to cite examples of specific types of media, matching each to a purpose. Then ask students to consider who creates these media types, and why they might make the choices they do. Explain to students that in this lesson they will learn how to deconstruct, or analyze, media messages in order to evaluate and critique them.

Practice and Assess

Evaluation Rubric: Exercise 3

Students should note the unique properties of four of the following: magazines, newspapers, radio, Internet sites, television. They should identify a current event. Their Venn diagrams should reflect the similarities and differences between the coverage given, the impressions created, and the impact achieved.

Teach

Using the Chart

Discuss each entry in the *How to Analyze a Media Message* chart. Remind students that the three main purposes behind media messages are to inform, to entertain, and to persuade. Point out that often a message that aims to persuade, such as an advertisement, may seem to aim to entertain or to inform. Ask students why it is crucial for consumers to deconstruct the message to get to its actual purpose.

Then go over each of the persuasive techniques shown in the chart on page 901. Call on volunteers to suggest examples of the use of each technique. Lead students to understand how each technique can cleverly persuade viewers and readers to buy the product. **L2**

Exercise 3

List four kinds of media presentations that provide information on current events, and identify the unique properties of each genre. Then watch a television newscast for coverage of an important news event and take notes on what you learn. Follow the coverage of the same event in one of the other kinds of presentations on your list. Create a Venn diagram comparing and contrasting the coverage in the two media, the impressions you gain from each, and the impact that each has on you.

Examining Media Messages

Before you form an opinion about a media message—whether it's a television commercial, an informational Web site, or a popular movie—you need to think about how and why the message was created. The following chart describes how to deconstruct a media message.

How to Analyze a Media Message

IDENTIFY	BY ASKING YOURSELF	EXAMPLE
SOURCE	Who made this? How does the source affect the message?	A television commercial says, "Our athletic shoes are the best ever made." The source of the ad is the shoe manufacturer. This company would want viewers to think their shoes are the best because they want people to buy them.
PURPOSE	Why was the message made? Is it meant to inform, entertain, or persuade?	The commercial seems made to inform people about the benefits of these particular shoes. But really, it is meant to persuade viewers to buy the shoes.
TARGET AUDIENCE	For whom is the message intended? How has the content been shaped to appeal to the intended audience?	The message is intended for preteens in middle school. The commercial shows groups of attractive, stylish eleven- and twelve-year-olds winning a foot race and a basketball game as well as walking around a mall.
MAIN IDEA OR THEME	What is the intended message?	The intended message is that buying the shoes will make you a winner and will also make you popular and stylish.
DESIGN ELEMENTS AND/OR FILM TECHNIQUES	How are design elements or film techniques used to communicate a message or manipulate a viewer's response?	Bright lighting, vivid colors, and sleek, popular styles all suggest energy and success. Actors moving diagonally across the screen convey a sense of energy and action. The eye-level camera angle helps viewers identify with the children in the commercial.

(continued)

Viewing and Representing

Enrichment and Extension

Exploring Language Connotations

Discuss advertisers' common use of emotionally loaded words and phrases, such as *dazzling, elite, unforgettable, unmatched, exceptional, best value,* and *for the 21st century.* Find examples of magazine advertisements that use connotative language. Discuss how such language is "loaded," carrying positive or negative connotative values. For example, an advertiser's toothpaste might be described as producing a *gleaming smile* (positive) that cannot be achieved by using an *ordinary* (negative) toothpaste. Have students study advertisements and television commercials to find examples of "loaded" language containing positive or negative values. **L2**

How to Analyze a Media Message		
IDENTIFY	**BY ASKING YOURSELF**	**EXAMPLE**
ELEMENTS THAT REFLECT A SPECIFIC CULTURE	What cultural values and assumptions are reflected in this presentation?	The presentation suggests that athletic ability and winning are important; preteens are portrayed as carefree, energetic, and stylish, with plenty of time for fun.
PERSUASIVE TECHNIQUES		
• glittering generalities	Does the message make sweeping claims that are impossible to support?	Yes, because the message suggests that the winner of the race will *always* be the one wearing our shoes.
• logical fallacies	Are the statements in the message logical, or are there errors in logic?	The message is illogical because it suggests that all you need to be a winner is to buy the shoes.
• symbols	Does the message use symbols that stand for popular ideas or values?	The company logo, a bird in flight, appears on all the sports gear that the actors use. The bird symbolizes independence and freedom.
• celebrity testimonial	Do admired celebrities add to the message or endorse the product?	A famous soccer player, wearing the company's shoes, is seen jogging with a group of young people.

Exercise 4

Select a television advertisement targeted to teenagers and analyze it by answering the questions in the How to Analyze a Media Message chart. Then create a billboard advertisement, promoting the same product or service but using techniques that are different from the ones in the advertisement you found. Write an explanation of the techniques used in your ad.

Exercise 5

Write a short editorial stating your opinion on how media shape the perceptions and habits of people in your age group. Consider, for example, how magazines, television, and movies influence your buying habits and the style of clothes you wear. Share your editorial with other members of your class, and then conduct a poll to find out which of your classmates allow the media to influence the purchases they make.

Using the Chart

Have students study the chart on pp. 900–901. Explain to students that advertisements often use techniques such as glittering generalities (attractive claims based on insufficient evidence) or logical fallacies (errors in reasoning) to persuade people to buy specific products. Ask students to select an advertisement that uses one of these techniques and then to critique the effect of the ad's message.

Practice and Assess

Evaluation Rubric: Exercise 4

Students should answer each of the questions in the *How to Analyze a Media Message* chart. Their billboards could employ persuasive techniques listed on the chart but not used in the original ad or avoid persuasive techniques and aim for a more straightforward approach.

Evaluation Rubric: Exercise 5

Students' editorials should demonstrate an understanding of the persuasive techniques, visual design elements, and film techniques presented in the charts in this unit. The editorials should specify the way advertising reaches and affects teenagers, including themselves.

Close

Have students use their journals to reflect on whether and how the information in this lesson has affected the way that they view mass media. Encourage them to consider specific shows, sites, or advertisements in their journal entries.

interNET CONNECTION

Evaluating Advertisements

Discuss advertisements and commercial offers that appear on the Internet. Ask students to work in small groups to devise a set of guidelines for how viewers and readers can evaluate advertising on the Internet. They may want to begin by searching the Internet and categorizing the different kinds of ads they encounter. Tell them that as they devise their guidelines, they should consider how Internet advertising is both similar to and different from advertising in other mediums and analyze how Internet ads influence their perceptions of reality. Groups should present their finished guidelines to the class. If possible, they should enhance their presentation by displaying screen captions of Internet advertisements. **L3**

Focus

Lesson Overview

Objective

- To produce visual representations that communicate with others

Skills

- examining the effect of media on constructing his/her own perception of reality; using a variety of forms and technologies to communicate specific messages; using a range of techniques to plan and create media texts and to reflect critically on the work produced; identifying and reaching a target audience; creating, presenting, testing, and revising a project and analyzing public response by creating forms to gather feedback

Critical Thinking

- establishing goals; considering audience and purpose; organizing; drawing conclusions; classifying; adapting techniques and concepts to fit purpose and goals; working cooperatively

Listening and Speaking

- discussing; asking and answering questions; informal speaking; interpreting, analyzing, and evaluating various visual techniques; presenting work to others; listening to others' presentations

Bellringer

Daily Language Activity

When students enter the classroom, have this question on the board: *Have you ever been involved with producing a media message? If so, what techniques did you use?* Ask students to discuss their answers.

Motivating Activity

Call on volunteers to summarize various techniques used by photographers, filmmakers, television producers, and advertisers to create effective media messages. (Students might review the charts in lessons 30.1 and 30.2.) Then ask students to offer their opinions on which techniques seem particularly interesting and effective. Point out that in this lesson, they will use what they have learned to produce their own media messages.

30.3 Producing Media Messages

Another way to increase your understanding of media messages and the decisions that go into their creation is to produce your own media presentation. This lesson provides guidelines for producing two forms of media messages: videos and Web pages.

Making a Video

The creation of a video requires the skills and cooperation of a group of people. Each group member should take on one or more of the following roles, based on his or her skills and interests. For example, creating a video documentary that features interviews with people might include these roles:

- **Director:** coordinates the activities of the group members and supervises the filming of the video
- **Researcher:** finds background information on the topic and the interviewees
- **Scriptwriter:** writes and revises the script
- **Storyboard designer:** prepares a series of simple sketches of each video scene to go along with the dialogue or narration
- **Interviewer:** prepares questions to ask the interviewees and conducts the interviews
- **Narrator:** reads the script during the filming
- **Camera operator:** films the interviews and other shots

Depending on the size of the group, some members may take on two or more roles. For example, the scriptwriter might also function as the researcher and narrator. Making a video provides an opportunity to try out different roles and learn new skills.

As you plan and produce your video, consider the elements of visual design and the film techniques described in the first section of this unit. Be sure you can clearly summarize the focus of your video in a paragraph. The following chart provides guidelines for completing a video project.

Tips on Producing a Video

1. **Begin by brainstorming.** In your group, discuss these questions: Who are the intended viewers? What do they already know or think about the subject? What is the purpose of the video? What information do we need to find out? Who will we interview? What scenes will we shoot? You may want to have a group member write down these questions and the answers that come up in the discussion.
2. **Plan your video by creating a storyboard.** A storyboard provides a blueprint for shooting your video. It consists of simple sketches of the sequence of scenes you will shoot, with the dialogue or narration for each scene. You want your video to tell a story—so create a beginning, a middle, and an end. Include scenes that set the stage, show the location, or provide details that enrich the story.

(continued)

Resource Manager

Planning Resources
- *Lesson Plans*

Other Print Resources
- *Viewing and Representing*

Tips on Producing a Video

3. **When you shoot, vary your scenes.** Mix long shots that show a location with closer shots that focus on a single subject. Shoot from different angles and heights to achieve different effects. Vary the length of the shots you take as well.
4. **Pay attention to lighting.** Shoot in strong light—outside during daylight or inside near windows and with all the lights on. Set up your own lights if necessary.
5. **Shoot to edit.** To make it easier to edit scenes later, leave a little room before and after each scene by letting the camera run. Reshoot scenes that don't turn out well.
6. **Edit to create a polished final product.** At the editing stage, you can eliminate bad footage, add music and sound effects, and insert titles. You also can mix short cuts and long cuts to achieve the pacing you want.
7. **Ask for viewer feedback.** After you present your video, ask the audience to fill out a questionnaire or to participate in a discussion to give you feedback. Ask viewers to state the main idea of your video and to comment on how effectively the main idea was conveyed. In addition, elicit viewers' comments on the pacing, the camera techniques, and the audio and visual quality.

Exercise 6

Working in a small group, choose one of the following video projects to undertake:

- a three-minute documentary on training for a sport
- a public-service advertisement on the importance of staying in school
- a demonstration of designing a cereal box targeted to teenagers

Decide on a topic and agree on roles for each group member. Then work together to plan, write, shoot, and edit your video. After presenting the video to the class, hold a discussion to gather feedback from your audience.

Developing a Web Page

Using a software program or hypertext mark-up language (HTML), you can create a Web page, like the one shown on page 904, that incorporates photographs, graphics, text, and even sound. A good Web page is attractive, informative, and easy to follow. The following guidelines will help you design a Web page that has all of these qualities.

Guidelines for Developing a Web Page

1. **Begin with a clear purpose.** Identify your intended audience and make sure that you have something useful to share. Create a title that tells visitors what your page is about.
2. **Plan your page before you build it.** View other pages on your topic, or on similar topics, for ideas about what to include and how to make the presentation. Design a layout for the page that is logical, easy to follow, and attractive.

(continued)

Teach

Building Production Teams

Divide the class into production teams based on the roles suggested in the Making a Video text on page 902. As you compose teams, make sure that each group contains students of all talents and interests. Encourage students to use established Cooperative Learning procedures to delegate tasks, work independently to complete their tasks, and then collaborate on the final production. Additionally, encourage them to refer back to the charts earlier in this unit for ideas regarding effective techniques. **L2**

Practice and Assess

Evaluation Rubric: Exercise 6

Final videos should reflect comprehension and application of elements from the *Basic Film Techniques* chart; reflect adherence to at least most of the tips covered on pp. 902–903; cover one of the topics assigned in Exercise 6; and reflect the equal participation of all members of the production team.

Enrichment and Extension

Show Videos

Students will benefit from seeing an example of the kind of video they are going to create. Consider showing part of a video documentary, such as *The Story of Babe Ruth,* and a public service announcement, such as one by the American Lung Association. Discuss with students the characteristics of each type of video as well as the techniques used in each specific example you show.

Teach

Introduce Web Page Project

Go over the Guidelines for Developing a Web Page on page 904, making sure that students understand each step. Advise students to follow these steps to make effective and attractive web pages. Encourage them to use the model shown on this page for ideas, but encourage them to be creative and original in the design and function of their own web pages. **L1**

Practice and Assess

Evaluation Rubric: Exercise 7

Web pages should: reflect comprehension and application of elements from the Elements of Visual Design chart on pp. 894–895; follow the guidelines listed on pp. 903–904; be attractive, informative, and easy to use; and reflect the equal participation of both partners.

Close

Discuss the results of both media projects, inviting students to share their ideas about the steps they followed and the results they accomplished. Point out that they have now experienced, analyzed, and evaluated media messages from "both sides of the street"—as critical viewers and thoughtful consumers and as creators of their own media messages. Tell students to reflect in their journals about how having produced a media message affects the way they view messages presented to them.

ASSESSMENT OPTIONS

Tests with Answer Key & Rubrics
Unit 30 Mastery Test, pp. 117–118

Testmaker
Unit 30 Mastery Test

You may wish to administer the Unit 30 Mastery Test at this point.

MindJogger Videoquizzes

Guidelines for Developing a Web Page

3. **Keep the design simple.** Pick a few colors and fonts (or styles of type) for your page. Avoid a busy background that detracts attention from your message.
4. **Be sure the page is quick to download.** Viewers avoid pages that take too long to download. Keep the images small in size and few in number so that your page downloads quickly.
5. **Consider including links.** Links enable visitors to reach related sites.
6. **Keep the text short and easy to read.** Use a font that is easy to read and a background color that provides enough contrast for your text. Carefully proofread and correct all text.
7. **Test your page and revise it.** Ask your friends or classmates to visit your page and test how well it works. Make an evaluation form and ask them to complete it.

Exercise 7

Work with a partner to design a Web page that analyzes how teenage culture is portrayed in a particular medium, such as a teen magazine, a television sitcom, or a movie. Ask classmates to visit your page and complete an evaluation form. Study the responses you receive, and then revise and improve your page as necessary.

interNET CONNECTION

Learning from Models

If possible, call up, or display printouts of, web pages that you feel are particularly effective and appropriate as models. Call on volunteers to suggest other models and ask them what they consider to be leading features of particularly attractive, informative, and user-friendly web pages. **L2**

UNIT 31 Electronic Resources

LOG ON Writing Online | For research tools and additional skills practice, go to glencoe.com and enter QuickPass code WC97727p3.

INTRODUCING UNIT 31

Objectives

- To learn how to use technology to prepare for, draft, and revise written material
- To learn how to use technology to compile and organize information and to represent information visually
- To develop strategies for analyzing information in visual media
- To demonstrate a familiarity with technology by researching, drafting, revising, and designing material
- To create, revise, and evaluate multimedia projects

ASSESSMENT OPTIONS

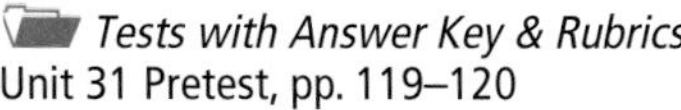

Tests with Answer Key & Rubrics
Unit 31 Pretest, pp. 119–120

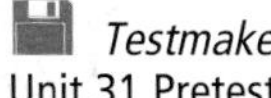

Testmaker
Unit 31 Pretest

You may wish to administer the Unit 31 Pretest at this point.

Key to Ability Levels

L1 Level 1 activities are within the basic ability range of students.

L2 Level 2 activities are within the ability range of average students.

L3 Level 3 activities are more challenging activities.

Resource Manager

Planning Resources
- *Lesson Plans*
- *Block Scheduling*

Other Print Resources
- *Tests with Answer Key and Rubrics*

Video
- *MindJogger Videoquizzes*

Software
- *Presentation Plus!*
- *Testmaker*

Web Site
- *glencoe.com*

Focus

Lesson Overview

Objective
- To use technology to organize, draft, and revise an article

Skills
- brainstorming; gathering information; planning; drafting; editing; revising

Critical Thinking
- analyzing; synthesizing; evaluating

Listening and Speaking
- collaborating to generate ideas and publish texts; discussing

Bellringer
Daily Language Activity

When students enter the classroom, have this assignment on the board: *Describe the similarities and differences between writing with pen and paper and writing on a word processor.*

Motivating Activity

Ask students to share the similarities and differences they identified in the Bellringer activity. Then work with the class to summarize the benefits of word processing. Tell students that word processing is more than typing words into a computer—it is a skill that can continuously be improved upon and adapted to meet the needs of individuals' writing processes.

31.1 Word Processing and the Writing Process

Almost anything you can write on paper with a pen or pencil can be done more efficiently on a computer with word processing software. When you work on a computer, you don't have to copy something over and over again from one sheet to another as you write and revise. You can cut and paste words, sentences, or an entire draft from one file to a new file in a few seconds. If you prefer, you can simply keep your work on the same file—adding, deleting, correcting, and revising until you're satisfied with what you've written.

Prewriting

You might begin a writing project by freewriting or by brainstorming for ideas or topics—either alone or in collaboration with one or more other students. Brainstorming may start with a list of random thoughts on a sheet of paper. Try listing your ideas on an electronic file instead. You might find starting a special file for your writing ideas to be useful. You can add to the file whenever you get a new idea, or look through the file when you're searching for something to write about.

At the prewriting stage, you should also consider your purpose and your audience. Thinking about purpose and audience will help define the kinds of ideas you hope to generate. For example, if your purpose is to entertain and your audience is your fellow students, you will brainstorm for ideas that will meet that purpose and appeal to those readers.

Finding Information

Once you have a topic, you may need to find out more about it. This, too, can be done with your computer, especially if the computer is connected to the Internet. Almost any writing topic you can think of has probably generated at least a few Web sites, if not hundreds of them. Newspapers, magazines, and standard references like dictionaries and encyclopedias are also available on the Web. Information from Internet sources can be downloaded to your hard drive or printed out directly from the source to your printer.

Planning and Organizing

As you begin planning and organizing a piece of writing, word processing comes into its own. You can easily take your prewriting ideas or pieces of information and reorganize them into an outline. You might start by looking for your main ideas. For a brief essay, for example, identify three or four

Resource Manager

Planning Resources
- *Lesson Plans*

main ideas. Then look through the remaining information. Drag and drop each detail under the main idea it relates to. As you work, you may think of other details you can add. If a piece of information doesn't fit, you can either drop it or revise your main ideas so that the information does fit under one of the main ideas.

Your word processing program probably allows you to use an outline format. After you've identified the main ideas and the details that support each idea, you can add the headings *Introduction* and *Conclusion* above and below the main ideas and the supporting details that will make up the body of your essay.

At this point, your outline should be set in the following format:

I. Introduction
II. Body
  A. [First main idea]
    1. [Detail]
    2. [Detail]
  B. [Second main idea]
. . . .
III. Conclusion

You can then think about what you might want to do in your introduction and conclusion. Will you start by simply stating a thesis and end by restating it? Or is there an attention-catching anecdote or example that would make a better introduction? The computer frees you to play with different ideas.

Drafting

When you're satisfied with your outline, you can begin drafting your essay by simply expanding the outline. Try turning each main idea and supporting detail into a sentence (or more, if necessary). Then keep expanding as needed. Each main idea might be expanded into a paragraph. Anything that doesn't work can be easily replaced or revised. You can also save any part of your work-in-progress, duplicate it on another file, and try a new version. In fact, you can save as many versions as you like, so that all of your thoughts remain available as you continue drafting and revising your work.

Revising and Editing

Your word processing program probably has tools that will help you in the revising and editing stages. The most common tool is a spelling checker. In a few seconds, this tool will check the spelling of every word in a file. Be careful, however. A computer spelling checker can only identify words that are in its memory as correctly spelled words. Proper names and foreign words may be questioned by the program even though they're correctly

Teach

Avoiding Plagiarism

Explain to students that while cutting and pasting text from their notes and other sources may make the writing process easier, it also makes it easier to plagiarize unintentionally. Remind students that plagiarism is not only academically unacceptable, it is also illegal. Review with them the definition of plagiarism and discuss the necessity of citing sources of information. **L2**

Cross-reference

For more information on citing sources, have students refer to Lesson 7.4, pp. 338–343.

Using a Spelling Checker

Have students use a word processor to draft an opinion piece suitable for their school newspaper. After the students have completed their first draft, have them exchange printouts of their papers with a partner to check the spelling of their partner's paper. Then have students run a spelling check of their first drafts on the word processor and compare the results. They should notice that while the word processor may be more consistent in catching some mistakes, people can catch mistakes the word processor can't. Suggest to students that by learning the word processor's limits, they can become better proofreaders. **L1**

Gifted and Talented

Freewriting

Tell students that while word processing is very useful for researching, outlining, drafting, and revising papers for school, it can also be used as a creative tool. Give students a time limit, and suggest that they use their word processor to freewrite a story or journal entry. Direct them to use a variety of functions–cut and paste, delete, use color, change type sizes and typefaces–whatever helps them express themselves. **L3**

Practice and Assess

Evaluation Rubrics

Exercise 1

Students may cite such features as the following:

- cut and paste, which allows users to delete highlighted text and move it elsewhere
- insert hyperlink, which allows users to instantly link to another document or web site
- page layout, which allows users to see how their text will fall on the page

Exercise 2

Students' essays should focus on a current events topic; demonstrate some basic knowledge of that topic; contain a beginning, middle, and end; and be free of spelling and usage errors.

Close

Ask students to summarize the word processing features that helped them with their writing in this lesson. Then ask them to speculate about word processing features they didn't use in this lesson but might find useful in the future.

spelled. The program cannot distinguish between homonyms, so if you type *their* when you should have typed *they're,* the word will not be identified as misspelled. Always proofread your writing carefully in addition to using a computer spelling check.

A grammar checker may also be available on your word processor. This function checks for problems like sentence fragments, capitalization, and the overuse of passive voice. Usually you can choose which grammar and usage items you want checked. A word processor's grammar checker can be time-consuming and frustrating if you ask it to check everything, so use it sparingly. Don't depend on it to discover every problem in your writing. The programs are not foolproof. Read your work carefully yourself for grammar and usage problems even if you use a computer grammar checker.

Exercise 1

Check out the word processing program on your computer at home or at school. Find out what writing tools the program includes and what each item does. Look at the menu bar, tool bar(s), and rules.

Technology Tip

Specialized software programs are available to help you produce different writing projects. Some CD-ROM programs, such as Glencoe's *Writer's Assistant,* will take you step-by-step through various specific writing projects from prewriting through the publishing stage. These programs may include such features as writing models and help in revising and editing a project.

Publishing

Word processing programs offer you many options for publishing your writing projects. You can experiment with different fonts, make type **bold** or *italic* or ***bold and italic,*** change the size of the type, adjust spacing, and set different types of margins. In fact, you can make your printed work look every bit as good as something published professionally. Most programs also allow you to add illustrations—such as photos, artwork, graphs, and maps—to your work.

Your word processing program may include some of the features of more-complex desktop publishing programs. These features will allow you to design professional-looking newsletters, brochures, and booklets. They may include pre-designed templates with attractive layouts you can use or adapt as you see fit. Working with classmates, you can collaborate to put together an attractive collection of writings, including full-color illustrations.

Exercise 2

Think of a topic that is currently in the news. Use a computer to learn more about the topic from Internet sources. (For more about researching topics on the Internet, see pages 909–911.) Then, using word processing software, explore your own feelings about the topic and write a brief essay expressing your opinion.

English Language Learners

Grammar Checker

Like all students, students who are learning English must already have an understanding of English grammar if they are to benefit from the grammar checker feature on their word-processing program. Make sure students know that the criteria computers use to identify grammar problems and suggest solutions are not always appropriate for all sentences. Have students experiment with a grammar checker. When the computer identifies a sentence that may have problems, tell students to consider these questions before deciding whether they should revise the sentence: *Do I understand why the computer has suggested a change for this sentence? What does this textbook say about the grammar rule in question? Am I sure the computer's suggestion is correct? Is there another way to fix this sentence?*

31.2 Learning with Technology

In the not-so-distant past, if you needed information on a topic you had only one choice. You would have visited a library and searched through various books, encyclopedias, magazines, and newspapers to find out what you needed to know. You might have chosen to write a letter and send away for information. Libraries are still important resources, but the growth of the Internet means that you do not always have to leave your computer in order to find information.

The Internet

The Internet allows you to travel to distant places and communicate with people around the world. You can often get information directly from the source. For example, even if you are not able to visit Washington, D.C., you can tour the White House via the Internet. The Internet includes both sources of information and ways of communicating with people in other places.

Sources of Information There are millions of Web sites dealing with nearly any topic you can think of. The chart below lists a few sites you might use for help with your homework. These sites will not do your work for you, but they will lead you to Internet sources of information and help you find answers to your questions.

Helpful Internet Sites

SITE	URL (Uniform Resource Locator, or Web site address)
Answers.com	http://www.answers.com
Discovery School Homework Help	http://school.discovery.com/students/
Homework Center	http://www.infoplease.com/homework
Homework Spot	http://www.homeworkspot.com
Infoplease	http://www.infoplease.com

E-mail and Instant Messaging Electronic mail, or e-mail, and instant messaging are a ways of reaching out to people via of the Internet. E-mail allows you to keep in touch with friends, write to pen pals in foreign countries, and ask questions of NASA scientists. E-mail is available twenty-four hours a day, seven days a week, and can be sent and received almost instantaneously. Many people use it more often than the telephone or regular mail. If you want to communicate with people even more quickly, you can send them an instant message. If the person is online, he or she can send you back an answer immediately. Instant messaging is as fast as having a telephone conversation. You can conduct interviews via e-mail as part of

Electronic Resources

Focus

Lesson Overview

Objective

- To use the Internet and other electronic resources to gather information

Skills

- collaborating; compiling information using technology

Critical Thinking

- analyzing; comparing and contrasting; evaluating

Listening and Speaking

- discussing

Bellringer

Daily Language Activity

When students enter the classroom, have this assignment on the board: *Write down the quickest way to find the answer to each of these questions: What is the population of Tucson, Arizona? Who is the author of the book* The Secret Garden? *What Congressional district do you live in? Who is the Congressperson for your district?*

Motivating Activity

Have volunteers tell where they would look for fast answers to the questions in the Bellringer activity. Have students explain why they think their method would be faster than another method. Lead students to realize the Internet is often, but not always, the fastest and most convenient way to find basic information.

Resource Manager

Planning Resources

- *Lesson Plans*

Teach

Evaluating Search Engines

Ask students to search for Web sites on a topic of interest to them by using each of the five search engines listed in the chart on this page. Tell students that as they search, they should consider questions such as the following:

- Which search engines yield the most useful results?
- Which search engines are easiest to use and why?
- Which search engines yield similar results?

Encourage students to do some additional searching to find alternative search engines and compare them to those listed in the chart. Then have students write an evaluation of the additional search engines, specifying which ones they felt were the best and the worst. **L2**

your research for a writing project. In addition, the information you get will often be the most up-to-date that you can find.

Chat Rooms Chat rooms are Internet links with people who have similar interests. You can join people in real-time discussions in chat rooms. When you type comments or questions, chat room visitors anywhere in the world can respond via their computers. Visiting a chat room is like to having a telephone conversation, except you write rather than talk and can communicate with more than one person at a time.

Newsgroups Newsgroups are similar to e-mail chat rooms.They also bring together people interested in a particular topic, but they do so by way of e-mail. When you e-mail a comment or question to the group, your it goes to all group members—and they, in turn, can respond to the entire group. Thus, everyone shares in the exchange of information.

Blogs Many people have blogs, or Web logs, on the Internet. Blogs are online journals that many people use to record their day-to-day activities and observations. Most blogs invite readers to post their own comments. Blogs may also feature pictures, music, and video alongside the text.

Finding What You Want

Often the best way to find information on the Internet is to start with a search engine or a subject directory. These sites provide you with lists of Web pages on a topic. A search engine seeks out sites from keywords that you type into it. For example, typing in the keyword *armadillo* would send you to many Web sites with information about that animal. A subject directory is a list of general topics that you use to narrow your search. Below are popular search engines and subject directories.

Useful Search Engines

SEARCH ENGINES	URL
Ask	http://www.ask.com
Excite	http://www.excite.com
Google	http://www.google.com
Infoseek	http://www.infoseek.com
Lycos	http://www.lycos.com

Sample Subject Directories

SUBJECT DIRECTORIES	URL
About.com	http://www.about.com
Google Directory	http://directory.google.com
Magellan	http://www.mckinley.com
Yahoo! Search Directory	http://dir.yahoo.com/

Enrichment and Extension

Reviews on the Internet

Have students use the Internet to locate reviews of a movie they have seen recently. Ask students to compare the opinions of at least two reviewers who have seen the same movie as they have seen. Then have them present to the class a brief oral report summarizing their comparisons of the two reviews. Students should be encouraged to use partners more familiar with the Internet to guide them in their search.

Tracking Web Sites

As you find different interesting sites, you will want to keep track of them. Internet browsers let you keep track of useful sites you might want to go back to again and again by creating a bookmark, sometimes referred to as a favorite. Your collection of bookmarks or favorites is a kind of Internet address book. As you come across a site of interest, you need only to pull down a menu on your browser and select the bookmark (or favorite).

Using Keywords to Search

When you use a search engine, think carefully about the keywords you use. For example, if you used *armadillo* as your only keyword, a search engine would list sites about that animal. However, it might also list sites for a real-estate office, a softball club, and a country-western band—all of which use the animal's name somewhere on their site. By adding a second keyword, such as *mammal* or *animal*, you would narrow your search and avoid some of those unusable sites. On most search engines, you can use the command AND between two keywords to tell the engine to find only sites that contain both words, or the command OR to find sites that include either keyword.

CDs and DVDs

While the Internet is filled with information, getting the information can sometimes be slow. Information can also be gathered from specific software packages on CDs or DVDs. CDs and DVDs, which you insert into the computer's CD drive, can hold large amounts of information, including video clips, animation, photos, and sound clips as well as text. Encyclopedias, atlases, dictionaries, and other useful references are available on CDs and DVDs. You can't alter the information on a CD, but you can copy and paste information from the disks into your writing. After you do so, however, be sure to use quotation marks around it and note the source from which you've taken it. (For more about citing sources, see Lesson 7.4 on pages 338–343.)

DVDs (*d*igital *v*ideo *d*iscs) represent a more advanced storage technology. A DVD can hold far more information than a CD. A single DVD can hold an entire full-length, wide-screen motion picture that you can view on your computer monitor. Dual-layer DVDs record on both sides of the disc, thus doubling the storage capacity of a standard DVD.

Exercise 3

Use an Internet source mentioned in this lesson to find the answer to at least one of the following questions or a question of your own.

- **a.** What is the difference between a band and an orchestra?
- **b.** What happened on this day in history?
- **c.** How many Mexican pesos will a dollar buy today?
- **d.** What is today's weather forecast in Cape Town, South Africa?
- **e.** What online English-language newspaper is published in Hong Kong, China?

Exercise 4

Think of a topic you want to research. Enter the most general keyword into your search engine and see how many sites come back. Then narrow or expand the search by using the commands AND or OR (for example, "armadillo AND mammal AND Texas"), and compare the quantity and quality of the information returned.

Electronic Resources

MEETING INDIVIDUAL NEEDS

Special Needs

Visually Impaired Students

Although using the Internet may present some challenges to visually impaired students, awareness about accessibility has risen, and many sites make an effort to ensure that their design allows the greatest number of people to take advantage of their offerings. In order to be accessible to visually impaired users, Web site designs should avoid the use of multi-column presentations or tables; include an alternative, short text description for all images on the web page; and provide plain-text format alternatives to graphically based file formats, among other things. The Web site WebXACT (webxact.watchfire.com) provides a tool that analyzes Web pages for accessibility to people with disabilities.

Practice and Assess

Answers: Exercise 3

- **a.** A band tends to be smaller than an orchestra and, unlike an orchestra, does not have a large string section.
- **b.** Answers will vary. Many newspapers' Web sites, such as the *New York Times'*, tell what happened on this day in history.
- **c.** Answers will vary. As of this printing the rate was approximately 9.5 Mexican pesos to a U.S. dollar.
- **d.** Answers will vary. An online South African or international newspaper or a weather forecast Web site such as *The Weather Channel* are good sources for this information.
- **e.** *South China Morning Post*

Evaluation Rubric

Exercise 4

Students will probably note that using a general keyword yields a large number of results, many of which do not look promising. Introducing the terms *and* or *or* should narrow the results but yield a higher percentage of promising Web sites.

Close

Ask students to once again consider the questions you wrote on the board for the Bellringer activity on page 909. (What is the population of Tucson, Arizona? Who is the author of the book *The Secret Garden?* What Congressional district do you live in? Who is the Congressperson for your district?) Based on what they have learned about using technology as a research tool, how would they go about finding the answers to those questions?

Focus

Lesson Overview

Objectives

- To learn about design elements
- To learn about and explore the graphics capabilities of a computer
- To communicate data using graphic explanations
- To use technology to enhance written work with graphics and graphic explanations

Skills

- gathering information; representing information visually; interpreting visual data; revising

Critical Thinking

- analyzing; evaluating

Listening and Speaking

- discussing

Bellringer

Daily Language Activity

As students enter the classroom, have this assignment on the board: *Where have you seen a chart, table, or other graphic appear in a piece of writing? What information did the graphic convey?*

Motivating Activity

Have students discuss the graphics they have seen. Ask them what type of information graphics typically contain. (statistical information) Do students think their own writing could benefit from the use of graphics? Tell them that in this lesson they will learn how to use technology to enhance their own writing with graphics.

31.3 Communicating Visually

While words are the building blocks of most writing, design plays an important part as well. Everything from the size and style of the font, to the spacing between lines and the size of the margins contributes to the readability of a document.

Design Elements

As you already know, there are many different forms of writing, each with its own peculiarities of style. Essays and reports may include headings and subheadings that help organize the ideas presented. A drama looks different on the page than a novel or a short story. A screenplay will include camera directions as well as directions for the actors. A science report may contain diagrams, graphs, and other pictorial elements, while a history paper may include maps, time lines, and photos. All these and other design elements help determine how your writing will look on the page.

Many design elements can be found on the pull-down menus of the menu bar and on the tool bars and ruler at the top of your word processing window. Some design elements are shown in the following picture of a typical tool bar. If you are not familiar with these features of your word processing program, experiment with them the next time you're at the computer. Find out what each one does and consider how it can help you format your own writing.

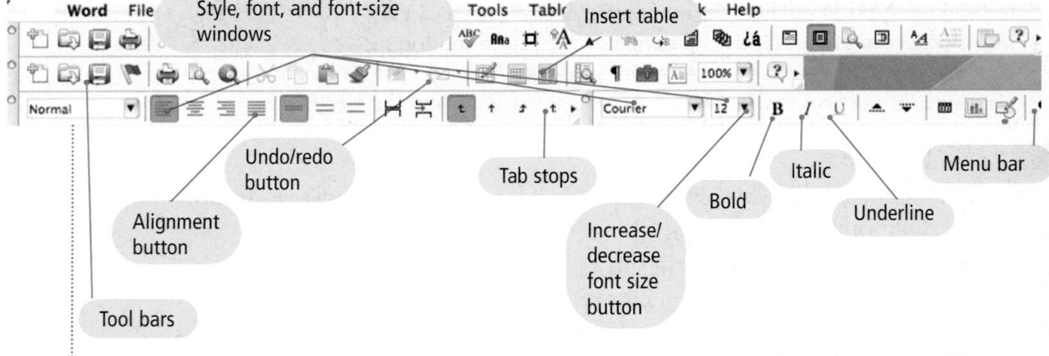

Each design element contributes to the document. By making a word **bold** or by underlining it, you indicate that it has extra importance. *Italics* are also used for emphasis as well as for other reasons—indicating book titles, for example. A list can be bulleted or numbered to make the list items stand out. You can use pictures, graphs, or other pictorial matter. Word processing software makes adding any of these elements to your writing as easy as pressing a button or pulling down a menu.

Electronic Resources

Resource Manager

Planning Resources

- *Lesson Plans*

Graphics and Writing

As your writing becomes more sophisticated, you will want to become more skilled at presenting your work. Graphic images can help. You can write about how world population grew in the twentieth century, but a graph showing the growth pictorially can be more powerful. You can describe the devastation that a flood has caused, but a photo of a car floating down the street will add to the impact of your words. Describing a complicated route between two places is much better done on a map than in a wordy description. Visual images do not take the place of good writing, but they can enhance it.

The computer allows you to include all these elements. Just as you can cut and paste text, you can create and paste visual elements into your writing. Various graphing, drawing, photo editing, and publishing software programs are available. Your word processing software probably includes some of these features. All graphic programs have similar tools, with icons that help show what the tools do. The bar graph, below, for example, was created to show how sales of a product rose in three regions of the country over two quarters.

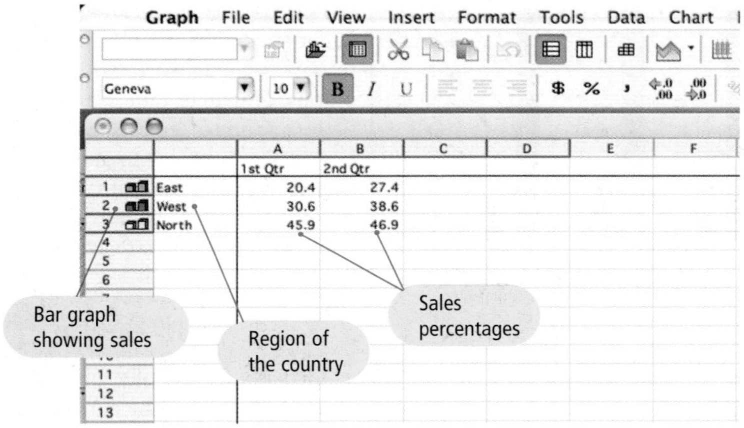

Exercise 5

Experiment with the drawing tools included with your word processing software (or with a separate drawing program if you have access to one). Learn to use the various drawing tools. Then discuss with a group how these tools could be used to enhance your writing assignments.

Teach

Emphasizing Healthy Work Habits

Tell students that people who spend a great deal of time at a computer are susceptible to Repetitive Stress Injuries if their work space is not set up correctly and if their work habits are not healthy. Define the word *ergonomics* for students (an applied science concerned with designing and arranging things people use so that people and things interact more efficiently and safely) and tell them that an ergonomically designed work space can help prevent injury. Suggest that students search the Internet for guidelines about how to set up an ergonomic work space and how to avoid Repetitive Stress Injuries.

Practice and Assess

Evaluation Rubric

Exercise 5

Students should note possibilities such as the following:

- tables and charts can help organize certain kinds of information and help make the information clear at a glance
- text boxes can set off text in order to draw attention to it and let it stand on its own
- lines can be used to separate different parts of a composition
- bullets can make the separation between related pieces of information clear

Meeting Individual Needs: Less Proficient Readers

Spatial Learners

Some students who have difficulty with reading may be able to excel at computer work that involves the use of images, graphics, and programming. Some examples include drawing programs and the diagraming and graphing functions of a word processing program. Encourage these students to experiment with the graphics capabilities of the computer and then to share what they know with other students. After their presentations, they should ask their audience for feedback about how effectively they communicated their information. They should then set goals for future informational presentations.

Practice and Assess

Evaluation Rubrics

Exercise 6

Students should communicate the same data using two of the following: bar graph, line graph, pie graph, pictograph, cone graph. The information on their graphs should be easy to understand and should include a legend, or key, if necessary.

Exercise 7

Students should identify an appropriate place for a graphic, use the technology available to them to produce the graphic, and provide a graphic that is relevant and easy to understand.

Close

Review with students when it is helpful and appropriate to use graphic explanations in their writing. Then ask students to discuss situations when it is not helpful or appropriate to use graphic explanations. (Writing with too many graphics may be distracting; graphics may interrupt the flow of narrative or expository prose; graphics may reduce a complicated situation or trend to a falsely simple level.)

Graphic Explanations

Once you become comfortable with a graphing program, you can begin to experiment with different types of charts and graphs. The number of earthquakes that took place over a period of five years might be represented in a bar graph like the one on this page.

From this graph, you can tell at a glance that an overwhelming majority of the earthquakes were of low magnitude. You can also easily see that there was a dramatic increase in 4.0–4.9 earthquakes between 2004 and 2005, followed by a dramatic decrease between 2006 and 2007.

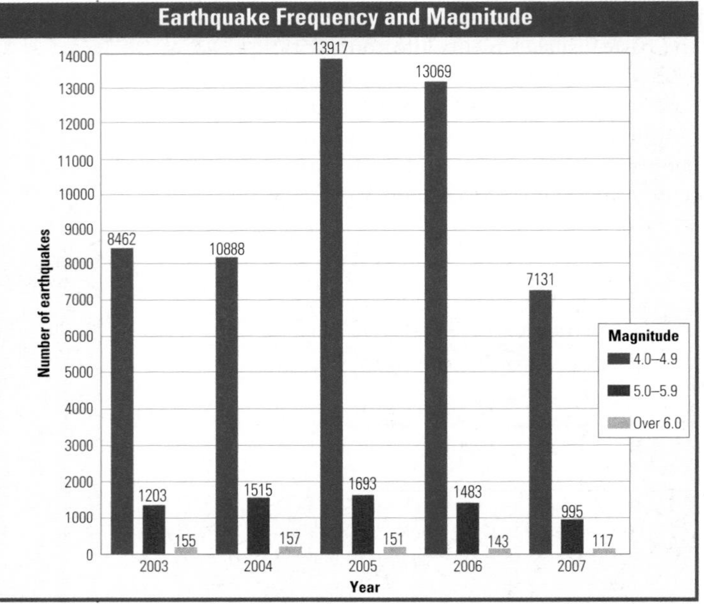

A graph allows you to present information in an easy-to-understand manner. The use of colors helps to distinguish among the different elements of the graph. The legend, or key, on the side tells what each color represents. A graphing program makes it easy to create and revise such illustrations.

Computer software allows a writer to construct or manipulate many forms of graphic representation—artwork, photographs, drawings, tables, and various kinds of graphs and charts. The best way to gain a better understanding of the power of graphics is to experiment with the software available to you.

Exercise 6

If you have access to graphing software (it may be included as a feature of your word processing program), try creating a few graphs of your own. Either use the data on the bar graph or find some data of your own. Use the same data to create two different kinds of graph—for example, a bar graph and a line graph. Consider which type of graph best suits your data, or your purpose, and explain why.

Exercise 7

Look through your portfolio for a piece of your writing that would benefit from the addition of graphics. Work with a partner or small group to revise your writings to make greater use of graphic representation.

Enrichment and Extension

Collect Graphics

Tell students that newspapers, magazines, Web sites, and television news programs all frequently use graphic aids to communicate information. For example, three- and five-day weather forecasts are often given in the form of a pictograph. Assign students the task of searching newspapers and magazines outside of class for graphic aids. Tell them to bring in at least one such aid, using a photocopier to reproduce any material they might find in a library. Students should be able to explain their graphic to the class.

31.4 Producing in Multimedia

In the recent past, multimedia productions required very expensive equipment and expertise that few people had. Now almost anyone with a desktop computer and presentation software can create multimedia productions.

Types of Multimedia Productions

Multimedia is the merging of text (written words), sound (speech, music, sound effects) and images (photos, art, video clips, animation) into a single presentation. Multimedia can be as low-tech as a slide show with a tape recorder or as high-tech as your own Web page with video and audio clips. Some multimedia productions are created to be viewed in a linear fashion—that is, from beginning to end along a particular path as the author assembled it. Other productions include hyperlinks that allow users to choose the paths they want to follow.

The following chart shows three easy ways to create a multimedia production.

Technology Tip

Complex projects like Web site design with full-motion video require additional computer hardware and software. Images (photos and video clips) and audio clips take up an enormous amount of hard drive space. However, with enough computer memory, a reasonably fast processing speed, a digital camera, and the right software, you can use your computer to make a movie.

Creating Multimedia Productions

HARDWARE	SOFTWARE
Computer with speakers, monitor, and a microphone Also useful: digital camera, video camera, scanner (to scan and digitalize images)	Use presentation software to create a computer-based "slide show" combining text, graphics, images, and sound.
Computer with speakers, monitor, and a microphone Also useful: digital camera, video camera, scanner (to scan and digitalize images)	Use a html program to combine text, graphics, images, and sound to create a series of "cards" containing hyperlinks that can make different sequences possible.

Electronic Resources

Focus

Lesson Overview

Objectives

- To learn about different types of multimedia productions
- To learn multimedia techniques and how to apply writing skills and visual techniques to multimedia productions
- To create a multimedia production

Skills

- planning; analyzing; outlining/storyboarding

Critical Thinking

- analyzing; evaluating

Listening and Speaking

- discussing

Bellringer
Daily Language Activity

As students enter the classroom, have this assignment on the board: *If you could use images, music, and words to communicate something, what would that "something" be?*

Motivating Activity

Have students write down their answers to the Bellringer question in their journal. Then tell them that while once most people did not have access to the technology needed to complete multimedia projects, today many more people have the opportunity to express themselves by combining images, sound, and language. In this lesson they will have their own chance to create a multimedia work.

Resource Manager

Planning Resources

- *Lesson Plans*

Teach

Use the Web

If you want to familiarize yourself with multimedia software, check the Web pages for HyperStudio and HyperCard. Training materials and workshop materials for Hyper-Studio can also be accessed from its site, as can sample works by students of various ages. If you feel these sites may be helpful for your class, direct students to investigate them.

Encourage Brainstorming

After students have done some initial thinking about the subject of their multimedia projects, encourage them to form small workshop groups in order to brainstorm the best way to use various media in their presentations. Group members can explain their ideas to each other and give and receive creative and technical advice. Suggest that the groups meet periodically to review each other's progress and provide feedback.

Multimedia Techniques

The power of multimedia is its ability to provide you with additional tools with which to communicate. Describing in an essay your recent trip through a national park is great. But creating a multimedia project with pictures you took, postcards you bought, audio clips of remarks by park rangers, and perhaps a short film clip you downloaded from the Internet can make the experience much more alive.

In multimedia, as in writing, different subjects lend themselves to different forms. If you are demonstrating how to build a bicycle, you will want to start at point A and follow the instructions point-by-point to point Z. This is a linear progression that ensures that the bike will be put together properly and operate well when it is finished. The author is in charge of how the user navigates through the production.

However, if you are informing people about six favorite bike trails in your area, you may want to let them choose how they view these trails. You provide all the pieces and the hyperlinks, but the viewers are in control of their own experience. Part of the fun is letting viewers explore and discover what you have discovered before them. Both of these examples work well in a multimedia format; the experiences are richer when you add images and sound to the text.

Creating a Project

Perhaps the best way to start a multimedia project is by creating an outline or storyboard for what you want to do. A storyboard describes what is going to take place in each segment of the presentation. For example, if your project is a documentary on a neighborhood bakery, the storyboard might begin like the one below.

Storyboard: How Sweet It Is

Segment	Text	Sounds	Images
1	Title: How Sweet It Is A Multimedia Presentation by Olivia Sugar	Song: "If I Knew You Were Comin' I'd've Baked a Cake"	Beautiful cake
2	This bakery was first opened at the end of the nineteenth century.	None	Picture of bakery storefront
3	Hans and Gretchen Sacher came from Austria to the city's Lower West Side.	Kitchen noises—pots and pans clanging	Photo of old kitchen counter with equipment

Electronic Resources

Exploring Language

Old Terms for New Concepts

Most multimedia presentations rely on new digital technology, but the vocabulary associated with the technology is not always new. Often, old words are used to describe new things or processes. For example, many multimedia software programs refer to a single screen as a *card* or a *slide*. Similarly, designers who work on the computer still discuss text using terms (such as *font*, *type*, and *leading*) that were familiar to the printers who set type by hand a hundred and more years ago.

Remember not to overload the production with extras (too much information, too many colors, too many different things happening in each segment) and thus lose the story. Have each segment make a single point, and support that point with sounds and images. You may want to use a spoken narration for your presentation. In that case, you may need little or no written text except for titles and credits. Similarly, if the images are particularly powerful, a segment may not need text. At the end of the presentation, include a segment to credit your sources.

Keep the audience in mind, as you would if you were writing an essay. If your audience is familiar with the topic, include more specifics and assume the audience knows the basics. If your audience is likely to know nothing about the topic, start with the basic ideas and explain everything carefully.

In creating your multimedia project, use some of the skills you learned in Unit 30: Viewing and Representing, found on pages 893–904 of this book. In addition, try to view other multimedia presentations, both amateur and professional, and note what you like or dislike. Look for techniques that you can adapt for your project. Mostly, though, have fun being creative and expressing yourself.

Evaluating a Project

You have spent many hours creating a multimedia project that you think is wonderful. How can you be sure? Following is a checklist to ensure that the project works.

- ✓ Turn the sound off. Do the written text and the images tell the story?
- ✓ Is the information easy to understand?
- ✓ Are the visual elements powerful and relevant?
- ✓ Are the look and tone appealing?
- ✓ Do the sounds and visuals work together, each supporting the other?
- ✓ Does the organization make sense?

Ask a friend to go through your presentation to see if it is understandable. Because a multimedia presentation is ultimately viewed by an audience, working with a friend is probably the best way to make sure that you have accomplished your goal. Often what an author thinks is obvious is not obvious to the viewer. You may have left out information or provided too much information. Ask a friend to help you revise the project until it is as good as it can be.

Exercise 8

Think about various forms of communication—writing, video, movie, multimedia—and consider how some ideas are better suited to one form than another. Make a list of other examples—like the bicycle and bike trails examples—where one presentation should be controlled by the multimedia author while the other should be controlled by the user/viewer.

Electronic Resources

Practice and Assess

Evaluation Rubric

Exercise 8

Students should note at least one instance when each media mentioned—writing, video, movie, and multimedia—would be the best way to communicate. Their lists should state at least two examples of multimedia presentations that should be controlled by the author (how-to presentations, linear narratives) and those that should be controlled by the user/viewer (virtual tours, guides).

✓ ASSESSMENT OPTIONS

Tests with Answer Key & Rubrics
Unit 31 Mastery Test, pp. 121–122

Testmaker
Unit 31 Mastery Test

You may wish to administer the Unit 31 Mastery Test at this point.

MindJogger Videoquizzes

Cooperative Learning

Presenting and Revising

Suggest that students make a feedback form that can be used to respond to a multimedia presentation. They can use the checklist on this page as a start and then add other questions and spaces for comments. Encourage students to ask reviewers to tell what they think is the purpose of the presentation. They can give a copy of this form to one or more student reviewers, who should use it to respond to the author's multimedia presentation. The author should take into account the reviewers' comments in order to revise the presentation.

Writing and Language Glossary

This glossary will help you quickly locate grammatical and other terms useful for writers.

Abstract noun. *See* Noun.

Active voice. A verb is in the **active voice** if the subject of the sentence performs the action.

Adjective. A word that modifies a noun or pronoun by limiting its meaning. An adjective may tell *what kind, which one, how many,* or *how much.*

The **positive degree** is the simple form of the adjective.

The **comparative degree** compares two persons, places, things, or ideas.

The **superlative degree** compares more than two persons, places, things, or ideas.

Adjective clause. A dependent clause that modifies a noun or pronoun. *See also* Clause.

Adverb. A word that modifies a verb, an adjective, or another adverb by making its meaning more specific. Adverbs tell *how, when, where,* and *to what degree.*

The **comparative** form of an adverb compares two actions. *(more quickly, better)*

The **superlative** form compares three or more actions. *(most quickly, best)*

Adverb clause. A dependent clause that modifies a verb, an adjective, or an adverb. *See also* Clause.

Allusion. A reference in a composition to a well-known character, place, or situation from a work of literature, music, or art or from history.

Analysis. The act of breaking down a subject into its separate parts to determine its meaning.

Anecdote. A short story or incident, usually presented as part of a longer narrative.

Antecedent. *See* Pronoun.

Appositive. A noun or a pronoun placed next to another noun or pronoun to identify or give additional information about it. (My cousin *Lonnie* is going to Guatemala this summer.)

Argument. A statement, reason, or fact for or against a point; a composition intended to persuade.

Article. The adjectives *a, an,* and *the.* **Indefinite articles** *(a* and *an)* refer to one of a general group of persons, places, or things. The **definite article** *(the)* indicates that the noun is a specific person, place, or thing.

Audience. The person(s) who reads or listens to what the writer or speaker says.

Auxiliary verb. *See* Verb.

Bias. A tendency or inclination that prevents impartial consideration of an idea; a quality to consider when producing or evaluating persuasive writing.

Bibliography. A list of the books, articles, and other sources used as reference sources in a research paper.

Body. The central part of a composition that communicates the main idea identified in the introduction.

Bookmarks/Favorites. The feature on many Web browsers that allows the user to save addresses of Internet sites so that the sites can be accessed quickly.

Brainstorming. A group activity in which people generate as many ideas as possible without stopping to judge them.

C

Case. The form of a noun or pronoun that is determined by its use in a sentence. A noun or pronoun is in the **nominative case** when it is used as a subject or after a linking verb, in the **objective case** when it is used as an object, and in the **possessive case** when it is used to show possession.

Cause-and-effect development. A kind of organization that involves examining the reasons for actions or events and the results of those actions.

Character. An individual involved in the plot of a work of fiction. **Round characters** have different traits, some of which may be contradictory. **Flat characters** are those which display one dominant trait. **Static characters** do not change. **Dynamic characters** show development in the course of a story.

Characterization. The techniques a writer uses to reveal character. Characterization may be **direct,** revealed through the description of the character and the character's own words and actions, or **indirect,** revealed through what other characters think and say about the character.

Chronological order. The arrangement of events in order of time.

Clarity. The quality of a piece of writing that makes it easy to understand.

Clause. A group of words that has a subject and a predicate and is used as part of a sentence. Clauses fall into two categories: **independent clauses,** which are also called **main clauses,** and **dependent clauses,** which are also called **subordinate clauses.**

An **independent clause** has a subject and a predicate and can stand alone as a sentence.

A **dependent clause** is one that cannot stand alone as a sentence. It may be restrictive or nonrestrictive.

A **nonrestrictive clause,** also called a **nonessential clause,** is one that is not needed to make the meaning of a sentence clear. (Mae Jemison, *who comes from Chicago,* gained fame as an astronaut.)

A **restrictive clause,** also called an **essential clause,** is essential to the meaning of a sentence. (A free doughnut will be given to everyone *who arrives before 9 A.M.*)

Cliché. An overused expression. *(quiet as a mouse)*

Climax. The point of greatest emotional intensity, interest, or suspense in the plot of a narrative.

Clustering. A technique for generating writing ideas, which involves writing a word, circling it, and surrounding it with other words and phrases.

Coherence. The quality of a paragraph or composition in which sentences are clearly and logically connected; also called cohesiveness.

Cohesive writing. A type of writing in which sentences and paragraphs are logically connected to one another.

Collaboration. The process of working with others on writing or other projects.

Collective noun. *See* Noun.

Colloquialism. A casual, colorful expression used in everyday conversation.

Common noun. *See* Noun.

Comparative degree. *See* Adjective; Adverb.

Compare-and-contrast development. A type of organization used in expository writing that examines similarities and differences in order to find relationships and draw conclusions.

Complement. A word or phrase that completes the meaning of a verb. The four basic kinds of complements are **direct objects, indirect objects, object complements,** and **subject complements.**

Conceptual map. A graphic device that develops a central concept by surrounding it with examples or related ideas in a weblike arrangement.

Conclusion. A restatement or summing up of the ideas in a composition that brings it to a definite close.

Conflict. The struggle between opposing forces that lies at the center of the plot in a story or drama.

Conjunction. A word that joins single words or groups of words.

Coordinating conjunctions *(and, but, or, nor, for, yet)* join words or groups of words that are equal in grammatical importance.

Correlative conjunctions work in pairs to join words and groups of words of equal importance.

Subordinating conjunctions join a dependent idea or clause to a main clause.

Conjunctive adverb. An adverb used to clarify the relationship between clauses of a compound sentence. (The team lost the game last night; *consequently*, they will not play in the tournament.)

Connotation. The thoughts and feelings associated with a word, rather than its dictionary definition.

Constructive criticism. Comments on another person's writing made with the intention of helping the writer improve a particular draft.

Context. The words and sentences that come before and after a specific word and help to explain its meaning.

Conventions. Correct spelling, grammar, usage, and mechanics.

Coordinating conjunction. *See* Conjunction.

Correlative conjunction. *See* Conjunction.

Credibility. The quality of a speaker or writer that makes that person's words believable.

Critical analysis. The consideration of the elements of a literary work to examine, organize, evaluate, or draw conclusions about them.

D

Declarative sentence. A sentence that makes a statement.

Deconstructing. Breaking down into component parts, or analyzing.

Deductive reasoning. A way of thinking or explaining that begins with a general statement or principle and applies that principle to specific instances.

Definite article. *See* Article.

Denotation. The dictionary definition of a word.

Dependent clause. *See* Clause.

Descriptive writing. Writing that uses sensory details to convey a dominant impression of, for example, a setting, a person, an animal, and so on.

Desktop publishing. The use of computer programs to format and produce a document that may include written text, graphics, and/or images.

Dialect. A variation of a language spoken by a particular group of people. A dialect may be regional (based on location) or ethnic (based on cultural heritage).

Dialogue. The conversation between characters in a story, play, or novel.

Diction. A writer's choice of words and the arrangement of those words in phrases, sentences, or lines of a poem.

Documentation. Identification of the sources used in writing research or other informative papers, usually in the form of endnotes or footnotes, or using parenthetical documentation.

Drafting. One of the steps in the writing process; the transforming of thoughts, words, and phrases into sentences and paragraphs.

E

Editing. One of the steps in the writing process in which a revised draft is checked for standard usage, varied sentence structure, and appropriate word choice.

Editorial. An article in a newspaper or other form of media that expresses a personal opinion about a subject of current or general interest.

Either-or reasoning. A logical fallacy that limits possibilities to two opposite choices, ignoring other valid possibilities.

Elaboration. The support or development of a main idea with facts, statistics, sensory details, incidents, examples, or quotations.

Ellipsis. A mark of punctuation, consisting of three spaced periods, that indicates the omission of one or more words.

E-mail. Short for electronic mail; messages, usually text, sent from one person to another by way of computer.

Emphatic form. *See* Verb tense.

Essential clause. A subordinate clause that cannot be omitted without changing the intended meaning of a sentence.

Evaluation. Making a judgment about the strengths and weaknesses of a draft in content, organization, and style.

Evidence. Facts or examples from reliable sources that can be used to support statements made in speaking or writing.

Exclamatory sentence. A sentence that expresses strong or intense emotion.

Explanatory writing. *See* Expository writing.

Expository writing. A kind of writing that aims at explaining an idea or presenting a process; also called informative or explanatory writing.

Expressive writing. Writing that emphasizes and conveys the writer's feelings.

F

Fact. A piece of information that can be verified from direct experience or from an authoritative source.

Feedback. The response a listener or reader gives a speaker or writer about his or her work.

Fiction. Literature in which situations and characters are invented by the writer.

Figurative language. Words used for descriptive effect that express some truth beyond the literal level. Figures of speech such as similes, metaphors, or personification are examples of figurative language.

921

Foreshadowing. Clues that hint at events that will occur later in the plot.

Formal language. Language that uses correct grammar and omits slang expressions and contractions. It is especially common in nonfiction writing that is not personal.

Freewriting. Writing for a specific length of time without stopping or limiting the flow of ideas.

Future perfect tense. *See* Verb tense.

Future tense. *See* Verb tense.

G

Generalization. A statement that presents a conclusion about a subject without going into details or specifics.

Genre. A division of literature. The main literary genres are prose, poetry, and drama. Each of these is further divided into subgenres.

Gerund. A verb form that ends in *-ing* and is used as a noun.

Glittering generality. An attractive claim based on insufficient evidence.

Graphic organizer. A visual way of organizing information; types of graphic organizers include clustering, graphs, tables, time lines, and tree diagrams.

H

Home page. The location on a Web site by which a user normally enters the site. A typical home page may explain the site, summarize the content, and provide links to other sites.

Hyperlink. A highlighted or underlined phrase or word on a Web page that, when clicked, moves the user to another part of the page or to another Web page.

Hypertext. Links in some text that can be clicked with a mouse to take the user to another document or to a different section in the same document.

I

Idea map. *See* Clustering.

Ideas. In writing, the message or theme and the details that elaborate upon that message or theme.

Idiom. A word or phrase that has a special meaning different from its standard or dictionary meaning. *(In the same boat* is an idiom that means "having the same problem.")

Imagery. Language that emphasizes sensory impressions that can help the reader of a literary work to see, hear, feel, smell, and taste the scenes described in the work.

Imperative sentence. A sentence that makes a request or gives a command.

Indefinite article. *See* Article.

Independent clause. *See* Clause.

Inductive reasoning. A way of thinking or explaining that arrives at a conclusion by examining a series of examples.

Infinitive. A verb form that usually begins with the word *to* and functions as a noun, adjective, or adverb in a sentence.

Informative writing. *See* Expository writing.

Intensifier. An adverb that emphasizes an adjective or another adverb. (*very* important, *quite* easily)

Interjection. A word or phrase that expresses emotion or exclamation. An interjection has no grammatical connection to other words.

Internet. A worldwide computer network that allows users to link to any computer on the

922

network electronically for social, commercial, research, and other uses.

Interpretation. An explanation of the meaning of a piece of writing, a visual representation, or any other type of communication.

Interrogative sentence. A sentence that asks a question.

Interview. A question-and-answer dialogue that has the specific purpose of gathering up-to-date or expert information.

Intransitive verb. *See* Verb.

Introduction. The beginning part of a composition, in which a writer identifies the subject and gives a general idea of what the body of the composition will contain.

Inverted order. The placement of a predicate before the subject in a sentence.

Irregular verb. *See* Verb tense.

J–L

Jargon. Specialized language used by a particular trade, profession, or other group of people.

Journal. A personal notebook for freewriting, collecting ideas, and recording thoughts and experiences.

Learning log. A journal for clarifying ideas about concepts covered in various classes.

Lexicon. A wordbook or dictionary.

Listing. A technique used in generating ideas for writing.

Literary analysis. The act of examining the different elements of a piece of literature in order to evaluate it.

Logical fallacy. An error in reasoning often found in advertising or other persuasive writing. *See* Glittering generalities; Either-or reasoning.

Main clause. *See* Clause.

Main idea. *See* Thesis statement.

Media. The forms of communication used to reach an audience; newspapers, radio, TV, and the Internet reach large audiences and so are known as mass media.

Memoir. A type of narrative nonfiction that presents an account of an event or period in history, emphasizing the narrator's personal experience.

Metaphor. A figure of speech that compares seemingly unlike things without using the word *like* or *as.* (The girl's aloof *manner* was her *armor* against snubs.)

Mood. The feeling or atmosphere that a writer creates.

Multimedia presentation. The presentation of a piece of writing accompanied by other media, such as music, video, and visual art.

Narrative writing. A type of writing that tells about events or actions as they change over a period of time and often includes story elements such as character, setting, and plot.

Nominative pronoun. *See* Pronoun case.

Nonessential clause. A clause that adds information but is not absolutely needed to express the meaning of the sentence.

Nonfiction. Prose writing about real people, places, and events.

Nonrestrictive clause. *See* Nonessential clause.

Noun. A word that names a person, a place, a thing, an idea, a quality, or a characteristic.

An **abstract noun** names an idea, a quality, or a characteristic.

A **collective noun** names a group of people or things.

A **common noun** names a general type of person, place, thing, or idea, characteristic, or quality.

A **proper noun** names a particular, person, place, thing, or idea.

Noun clause. A dependent clause that functions as a noun.

Number. The form of a noun, pronoun, or verb that indicates whether it refers to one (**singular**) or to more than one (**plural**).

O

Objective pronoun. *See* Pronoun case.

Onomatopoeia. A word with a sound that suggests its meaning. *(buzz, clink, pop)*

Opinion. A belief or attitude that cannot be proven true or false. Readers and writers should clearly distinguish opinion from fact.

Oral tradition. Literature that passes by word of mouth from one generation to the next. Oral tradition often reflects the cultural values of a people.

Order of importance. A way of organizing details in a paragraph or composition from least to most or most to least important.

Organization. The arrangement of main points and supporting details in a piece of writing; the internal structure of a piece of writing.

Outline. A systematic arrangement of main and supporting ideas, using Roman numerals, letters, and numbers for a written or an oral presentation.

Paragraph. A unit of writing that consists of related sentences.

Parallelism. The use of a series of words, phrases, or sentences that have similar grammatical form.

Paraphrase. A restatement of an idea in different words that retains the meaning, tone, and general length of the original.

Parenthetical documentation. A specific reference to the source of a piece of information; it is placed in parentheses directly after the information appears in a piece of writing.

Participle. A verb form that can function as an adjective. Present participles always end in *-ing*. Although past participles often end in *-ed,* they can take other forms as well.

Passive voice. The form of a verb used when the subject of the sentence receives the action of the verb.

Peer response. The suggestions and comments provided by peers, or classmates, about a piece of writing or another type of presentation.

Personal writing. Writing that expresses the writer's own thoughts and feelings.

Personification. A figure of speech that gives human qualities to an animal, object, or idea.

Perspective. *See* Point of view.

Persuasive writing. Writing that aims at influencing a reader's opinion and actions.

Phrase. A group of words that acts as a single part of speech in a sentence.

A **prepositional phrase** consists of a preposition, its object, and any modifiers of the object. A **verb phrase** consists of one or more auxiliary verbs followed by a main verb.

Plagiarism. The dishonest presentation of another's words or ideas as one's own.

Plot. The series of events that follow one another in a story, novel, or play.

Poetry. A form of literary expression that emphasizes the line as the unit of composition. Traditional poetry contains emotional, imaginative language and a regular rhythm.

Point of view. The perspective, or angle, from which a story is told. Most writing is done from a first-person, third-person limited, or third-person omniscient point of view.

Portfolio. A collection of various pieces of writing, which may include finished pieces and works in progress.

Positive degree. *See* Adjective.

Possessive pronoun. *See* Pronoun case.

Predicate. The verb or verb phrase and any of its modifiers that make an essential statement about the subject of a sentence.

Preposition. A word that shows the relationship of a noun or pronoun to some other word in the sentence.

Presentation. The way words and design elements look on the page.

Presenting/Publishing. The last step in the writing process, which involves sharing the final writing product with others.

Prewriting. The first step in the writing process, which includes deciding what to write about, collecting ideas and details, and making an outline or a plan. Prewriting strategies include brainstorming, clustering, word webs, and freewriting.

Prior knowledge. The facts, ideas, and experiences that a writer, reader, or viewer brings to a new activity.

Progressive form. *See* Verb tense.

Pronoun. A word that takes the place of a noun, a group of words acting as a noun, or another pronoun. The word or group of words that a pronoun refers to is called its **antecedent.**

Pronoun case. A personal pronoun refers to a specific person or thing. Personal pronouns have three **cases**—nominative, objective, and possessive. *See also* Case.

Proofreading. The last part of the editing process that involves checking work to discover typographical and spelling errors.

Propaganda. Information aimed at influencing thoughts and actions; it is usually of a political nature and may contain distortions of truth.

Prose. Writing that is similar to everyday speech and written language, as opposed to poetry and drama.

Publishing. The preparation of a finished piece of writing, often using available technology, so that it can be presented to a larger audience.

Purpose. The aim of writing, which may be to express, discover, record, develop, reflect on ideas, problem solve, entertain, influence, inform, or describe.

R

Regular verb. *See* Verb tense.

Representation. A way in which information or ideas are presented to an audience.

Research. Locating information on a topic from a variety of sources.

Restrictive clause. *See* Essential clause.

Review. An analysis and interpretation of a subject presented through the mass media.

Revising. The stage of the writing process in which a writer goes over a draft, making changes in content, organization, and style in order to improve it. Revision techniques include adding, elaborating, deleting, combining, and rearranging text.

Root. The part of a word that carries the main meaning.

Run-on sentence. Two or more sentences or clauses run together without appropriate punctuation.

S

Sensory details. Words that appeal to the senses—sight, hearing, taste, smell, and feeling; important element of descriptive writing, especially of poetry.

Sentence. A group of words expressing a complete thought. Every sentence has a **subject** and a **predicate.** Sentences can be classified by function or by structure.

A **simple sentence** has only one main clause and no subordinate clauses.

A **compound sentence** has two or more main clauses.

A **complex sentence** has one main clause and one or more subordinate clauses.

A **compound-complex sentence** has two or more main clauses and at least one subordinate clause. *See also* Declarative sentence; Exclamatory sentence; Imperative sentence; Interrogative sentence.

Sentence fluency. The smooth rhythm and flow of sentences that vary in length and style.

Sentence variety. The use of different types of sentences to add interest to writing.

Setting. The time and place in which the events of a story happen.

Simile. A figure of speech that compares two unlike things, using the word *like* or *as.* (The clouds looked *like* melted marshmallows.)

Spatial order. The arrangement of the details of a setting according to their location—for example, from left to right or from top to bottom.

Standard English. The most widely used and accepted form of the English language.

Style. The writer's choice and arrangement of words and sentences.

Subordinate clause. *See* Clause.

Subordinating conjunction. *See* Conjunction.

Summary. A brief statement of the main idea of a composition.

Superlative degree. *See* Adjective, Adverb.

Supporting evidence. *See* Evidence.

Suspense. A literary device that creates growing interest and excitement leading up to the climax or resolution of a story. A writer creates suspense by providing clues to the resolution without revealing too much information.

Symbol. An object, a person, a place, or an experience that represents something else, usually something abstract.

Tense. *See* Verb tense.

Theme. The main idea or message of a piece of writing.

Thesis statement. A one- or two-sentence statement of the main idea or purpose of a piece of writing.

Time line. A line, usually horizontal, divided into equal segments, each of which represents a specific interval of time; a helpful device for organizing events in chronological order.

Time order. The arrangement of details based on when they occurred.

Tone. A reflection of a writer's or speaker's attitude toward a subject.

Topic sentence. A sentence that expresses the main idea of a paragraph.

Transition. A connecting word or phrase that clarifies relationships between details, sentences, or paragraphs.

U–V

Unity. The quality of a composition in which all the sentences and paragraphs support one main idea.

URL. The standard form of an Internet address; stands for Uniform Resource Locator.

Venn diagram. A graphic organizer consisting of two or more overlapping circles; used to compare items that have both similar and different traits.

Verb. A word that expresses action or a state of being and is necessary to make a statement. An auxiliary verb, or helping verb, accompanies the main verb of a sentence. An intransitive verb does not take a direct object. (Horses *run* across the plains.)

Verbal. A verb form that functions in a sentence as a noun, an adjective, or an adverb. The three kinds of verbals are gerunds, infinitives, and participles. *See* Gerund; Infinitive; Participle.

Verb phrase. *See* Phrase.

Verb tense. The tense of a verb indicates when the action or state of being occurs. The **present tense** names an action that happens regularly. The **past tense** names an action that has happened, and the **future tense** names an action that will take place in the future.

All verb tenses are formed from the four principal parts of a verb: a base form *(swim),* a present participle *(swimming),* a simple past form *(swam),* and a past participle *(swum).* A **regular verb** forms its simple past and past participle by adding *-ed* to the base form. *(jump, jumped, jumped)* An **irregular verb** forms its past and past participle in some other way. *(drive, drove, driven; begin, began, begun)* In addition to present, past, and future tense, there are three perfect tenses: present perfect, past perfect, and future perfect. The **progressive form** of a verb expresses a continuing action with any of the six tenses. To make the progressive forms, use the appropriate tense of the verb *be* with the present participle of the main verb. The **emphatic form** adds special force, or emphasis, to the present or past tense of a verb. For the emphatic form, use *do, does,* or *did* with the base form.

Voice. A writer's unique way of using tone and style to communicate with the audience.

W

Web site. A location on the World Wide Web that can be reached through links or by accessing a Web address, or URL. *See* URL.

Word choice. The vocabulary a writer chooses to convey meaning.

Word processing. The use of a computer for the writing and editing of written text.

World Wide Web. A global system that uses the Internet and allows users to create, link, and access fields of information. *See* Internet.

Writing process. The series of stages or steps that a writer goes through to develop ideas and to communicate them.

GLOSARIO
DE ESCRITURA Y LENGUAJE

Este glosario permite encontrar fácilmente definiciones de gramática inglesa y términos que usan los escritores.

A

Abstract noun/Nombre abstracto. *Ver Noun.*

Active voice/Voz activa. Forma verbal usada cuando el sujeto de la oración realiza la acción.

Adjective/Adjetivo. Palabra que modifica, o describe, un nombre (*noun*) o pronombre (*pronoun*), limitando su significado. Un adjetivo indica *qué tipo, cuál, cuántos* o *cuánto.* Los adjetivos aparecen en varias posiciones en la oración.

Positive degree/Grado positivo. Forma simple del adjetivo.

Comparative degree/Grado comparativo. Adjetivo que compara a dos personas, lugares, cosas o ideas.

Superlative degree/Grado superlativo. Adjetivo que compara más de dos personas, lugares, cosas o ideas.

Adjective clause/Proposición adjetiva. Proposición dependiente que modifica un nombre o pronombre. *Ver también Clause.*

Adverb/Adverbio. Palabra que modifica a un verbo, adjetivo u otro adverbio, haciendo que su significado sea más específico. Los adverbios responden a las preguntas *cómo, cuándo, dónde, de qué manera* y *qué tan seguido* sucede algo.

Comparative/Comparativo. Compara dos acciones (*more quickly, better*; en español: *más rápido, mejor).*

Superlative/Superlativo. Compara tres o más acciones (*most quickly, best;* en español: *el más rápido, lo mejor).*

Adverb clause/Proposición adverbial. Proposición dependiente que modifica un verbo, un adjetivo o un adverbio. *Ver Clause.*

Allusion/Alusión. Referencia en un texto escrito a un personaje, lugar o situación muy conocidos de una obra literaria, musical, artística o histórica.

Analysis/Análisis. Acción de descomponer un tema o escrito en distintas partes para encontrar su significado.

Anecdote/Anécdota. Narración breve o incidente que se presenta como parte de una narrativa más larga.

Antecedent/Antecedente. *Ver Pronoun.*

Appositive/Apositivo. Nombre colocado junto a otro para identificarlo o agregar información sobre él. (Mi prima *Lupe* va a ir a Guatemala este verano.)

Argument/Argumento. Afirmación, razón o hecho en favor o en contra de algún comentario; texto escrito que trata de persuadir.

Article/Artículo. Nombre dado a las palabras *a, an* y *the* (en español: *un, uno/a, el, la*). *A* y *an* son artículos **indefinidos** (*indefinite articles*), que se refieren a cualquier cosa de un grupo. *The* es un artículo **definido** (*definite article*); indica que el nombre al que precede es una persona, lugar o cosa específica.

Audience/Público. Persona (o personas) que lee o escucha lo que dice un escritor o un hablante.

Auxiliary verb/Verbo auxiliar. *Ver Verb.*

B

Bias/Tendencia. Inclinación a pensar de cierta manera que impide la consideración imparcial de una idea; importante de considerar al producir o evaluar un texto persuasivo.

Bibliography/Bibliografía. Lista de los libros, artículos y otras fuentes que se utilizan como referencia en una investigación.

Body/Cuerpo. Parte central de una composición que comunica la idea principal identificada en la introducción.

Bookmarks/favorites/Marcadores/favoritos. Característica de muchos buscadores de red que permiten guardar direcciones de Internet para entrar a ellas rápidamente.

Brainstorming/Lluvia de ideas. Actividad de grupo por medio de la cual se generan ideas a hacer una lista de todo lo que se les ocurre sin evaluarlo.

C

Case/Caso. Forma de un nombre o pronombre que se determina por su uso en la oración. El nombre o pronombre está en caso **nominativo** (*nominative case*) cuando se utiliza como sujeto o después de un verbo copulativo; en caso **acusativo** y **dativo** (*objective case*) cuando recibe la acción del verbo; y en caso **posesivo*** (*possessive case*) cuando se utiliza para indicar posesión o propiedad.

Cause and effect development/Desarrollo de causa y efecto. Técnica de organización que examina las razones y los resultados de las acciones.

Character/Personaje. Individuo presentado en la trama de una obra de ficción.

Round character/Personaje redondeado. El que tiene una variedad de características, algunas de las cuales pueden ser contradictorias.

Flat character/Personaje plano. El que tiene una característica dominante.

Static character/Personaje estático. El que no cambia.

Dynamic character/Personaje dinámico. El que se desarrolla a lo largo de la narración.

Characterization/Caracterización. Técnicas que utiliza un escritor para crear sus personajes. Puede ser **directa,** por medio de descripción y de las palabras del personaje, o **indirecta,** por medio de lo que dicen de él otros personajes.

Chronological order/Orden cronológico. Organización de detalles de acuerdo con el tiempo en que sucedieron los acontecimientos o acciones.

Clarity/Claridad. Cualidad de un escrito que lo hace fácil de entender.

Clause/Proposición. Grupo de palabras que consta de sujeto y predicado y que se usa como parte de una oración.

Independent clause/Proposición independiente. También llamada **proposición principal** (*main clause*); tiene sujeto y predicado y hace sentido por sí misma.

Dependent clause/Proposición dependiente. También llamada **proposición subordinada** (*subordinate clause*); tiene sujeto y predicado pero depende de la proposición principal. La proposición dependiente puede ser:

Restrictive o **essential clause/ Proposición restrictiva** o **esencial,** que es necesaria para el significado de la oración. **Nonessential** o **nonrestrictive clause/Proposición no esencial** o **no restrictiva,** que no es necesaria para entender el significado de la oración.

Cliché/Cliché. Expresión usada con demasiada frecuencia *(blanco como la nieve).*

Climax/Clímax. Momento donde ocurre la mayor intensidad emocional, interés o suspenso en la trama de una narración.

Clustering/Agrupamiento. Técnica para generar ideas que consiste en escribir una palabra, ponerla dentro de un círculo y rodearla con otras palabras y frases.

Coherence/Coherencia. Cualidad de un párrafo o composición en que las oraciones tienen una relación clara y lógica; también se llama cohesión.

Cohesive writing/Escritura coherente. Tipo de escritura en que las oraciones y párrafos están lógicamente relacionados entre sí.

Collaboration/Colaboración. Proceso de trabajar en equipo para escribir un texto o realizar un proyecto.

Collective noun/Nombre colectivo. *Ver Noun.*

Colloquialism/Expresión coloquial. Expresión informal y pintoresca que se utiliza en la conversación diaria.

Common noun/Nombre común. *Ver Noun.*

Comparative degree/Grado comparativo. *Ver Adjective; Adverb.*

Comparison-and-contrast development/ Desarrollo por comparación y contraste. Técnica de organizar ideas, señalando sus similitudes y diferencias a fin de ver relaciones y sacar conclusiones.

Complement/Complemento. Palabra o frase que completa el significado de un verbo en una oración. En inglés hay cuatro clases básicas de complementos: **directo** (*direct object*), **indirecto** (*indirect object*), **de objeto** (*object complement*) y **predicativo (atributo)** (*subject complement*).

Conceptual map/Mapa conceptual. Recurso gráfico que desarrolla un concepto central rodeándolo con ejemplos o ideas relacionadas a manera de red.

Conclusion/Conclusión. Afirmación que resume las ideas de una composición, antes de ponerle punto final.

Conflict/Conflicto. Lucha entre dos fuerzas opuestas que constituye el elemento central de la trama en un cuento u obra de teatro.

Conjunction/Conjunción. Palabra que une dos palabras o grupos de palabras.

Coordinating conjunction/Conjunción coordinante. Las palabras *and, but, or, nor, for, yet* (*y, pero, o, no, para, aun*) unen palabras o grupos de palabras que tienen igual importancia gramatical.

Correlative conjunction/Conjunción correlativa*. Las palabras *both . . . and, just as . . . so, not only . . . but also, either . . . or, neither . . . nor* (*tanto . . . como, así como, no sólo . . . sino, o . . . o*) son palabras en pares que vinculan palabras o frases de igual importancia.

Subordinate conjunction/Conjunción subordinante. Une una idea u proposición subordinada con la proposición principal.

Conjunctive adverb/Adverbio de coordinación. Adverbio para aclarar la relación entre las proposiciones de una oración compuesta. (El equipo perdió anoche; *por lo tanto,* no jugará en las finales.)

Connotation/Connotación. Pensamientos y sentimientos relacionados con una palabra, más que con su definición de diccionario.

Constructive criticism/Crítica constructiva. Comentario sobre lo que escribe otra persona, con la intención de ayudar a que mejore el borrador.

Context/Contexto. Palabras y oraciones que vienen antes y después de una palabra y ayudan a explicar su significado.

Conventions/Reglas de escritura. Normas que regulan la ortografía, la gramática, el uso y la puntuación de un escrito.

Coordinating conjunction/Conjunción coordinante. *Ver Conjunction.*

Correlative conjunction/Conjunción correlativa*. *Ver Conjunction.*

Credibility/Credibilidad. Cualidad de un hablante o escritor que hace creer sus palabras.

Critical analysis/Análisis crítico. Consideración de los elementos de una obra literaria para examinarlos, organizarlos, evaluarlos o sacar conclusiones sobre ellos.

Declarative sentence/Oración afirmativa. Oración que declara algo.

Deconstructing/Desensamblar. Separar en componentes o analizar.

Deductive reasoning/Razonamiento deductivo. Pensamiento o explicación que parte de una afirmación o principio generales y los aplica a casos específicos.

Definite article/Artículo definido. *Ver Article.*

Denotation/Denotación. Definición de una palabra que da el diccionario.

Dependent clause/Proposición dependiente. *Ver Clause.*

Descriptive writing/Escritura descriptiva. Tipo de escritura que da detalles sensoriales para comunicar una impresión predominante de un escenario, persona, animal, etcétera.

Desktop publishing/Edición por computadora. Uso de programas de computadora para formar un documento con texto escrito, gráficas y/o imágenes.

Dialect/Dialecto. Variedad de lenguaje hablado que usa un grupo particular. Un dialecto puede ser regional (de un lugar) o étnico (de un grupo cultural).

Dialogue/Diálogo. Conversación entre personajes en un cuento, obra o novela.

Diction/Dicción. Palabras que escoge un escritor y cómo las utiliza en frases, oraciones o versos.

Documentation/Documentación. Identificación de las fuentes que se emplean para escribir un documento u otros textos informativos; generalmente se ponen como notas al pie, al final del texto o entre paréntesis.

Drafting/Borrador. Paso del proceso de escritura; transformación de ideas, palabras y frases a oraciones y párrafos.

E

Editing/Edición. Paso del proceso de escritura en que se revisa que el borrador corregido tenga un lenguaje estándar, una estructura sintáctica variada y la elección adecuada de palabras.

Editorial/Editorial. Artículo en un periódico u otro medio que expresa las ideas personales y la opinión del escritor.

Either-or reasoning/Razonamiento excluyente. Falacia lógica que limita las posibilidades a dos alternativas opuestas sin tomar en cuenta otras posibilidades válidas.

Elaboration/Elaboración. Sustento o desarrollo de una idea principal con hechos, estadísticas, detalles sensoriales, incidentes, anécdotas, ejemplos o citas.

Ellipsis/Puntos suspensivos. Signo de puntuación que consiste en dejar tres puntos con espacios iguales para indicar que se están suprimiendo una o varias palabras.

E-mail/Correo electrónico. Abreviatura de correo electrónico; mensajes, generalmente textos, que se envían por computadora.

Emphatic form/Forma enfática. *Ver Verb tense.*

Essential clause/Proposición esencial. Proposición subordinada que no puede omitirse sin cambiar el significado de una oración.

Evaluation/Evaluación. Juicio sobre las fallas y los aciertos de un texto en borrador en cuanto a contenido, organización y estilo.

Evidence/Evidencia. Datos o ejemplos de fuentes confiables que sirven para sustentar afirmaciones escritas o habladas.

Exclamatory sentence/Oración exclamativa. Oración que expresa una emoción fuerte o repentina.

Explanatory writing/Texto explicativo. *Ver Descriptive text.*

Expository writing/Texto descriptivo. Tipo de escritura que informa al público presentando información y explicando conceptos e ideas; también llamada escritura informativa o explicativa.

Expressive writing/Texto expresivo. Texto que realza y transmite los sentimientos del escritor.

F

Fact/Hecho. Información que puede comprobarse a partir de la experiencia directa o de una fuente reconocida.

Feedback/Retroalimentación. Respuesta del escucha o lector al mensaje de un hablante o escritor.

Fiction/Ficción. Literatura donde las situaciones y los personajes son inventados por el escritor.

Figurative language/Lenguaje figurado. Palabras usadas con un efecto descriptivo que expresa una verdad más allá del nivel literal. Los tropos, como el símil, la metáfora y la personificación, son ejemplos de lenguaje figurado.

Foreshadowing/Presagio. Pistas o claves que utiliza un autor para advertir a los lectores de los acontecimientos que ocurrirán más adelante en la narración.

Formal language/Lenguaje formal. Lenguaje que utiliza una gramática correcta y omite contracciones y expresiones coloquiales. Es adecuado para textos de no ficción, que no son de carácter personal.

Freewriting/Escritura libre. Búsqueda de ideas escribido durante un tiempo determinado, sin detenerse ni limitar el flujo de ideas.

Future tense/Tiempo futuro. *Ver Verb tense.*

Generalization/Generalización. Afirmación que presenta una conclusión acerca de un tema sin entrar en detalles específicos.

Genre/Género. Clasificación literaria o de otro medio. Los principales géneros literarios son la prosa, la poesía y el drama. Cada uno se divide en subgéneros.

Gerund/Gerundio. Verboide que termina en *-ing* y se usa como nombre (en inglés).

Glittering generality/Generalización deslumbrante. Afirmación atractiva sin pruebas suficientes.

Graphic organizer/Organizador gráfico. Manera visual de organizar la información, como el agrupamiento, las tablas, las gráficas, las redes y los árboles de ideas.

932

H

Home page/Página principal. Página por medio de la cual un usuario entra normalmente a un sitio de Web. Por lo general, explica el sitio, resume el contenido y proporciona vínculos con otros sitios.

Hyperlink/Hipervínculo. Oraciones o palabras sombreadas o subrayadas en una página en red que al activarse con un clic conectan al usuario con otra parte de la página o con otra página de la red.

Hypertext/Hipertexto. Vínculos en algunos textos que con el clic del ratón el usuario llega a otro documento o a una sección distinta del mismo documento.

I

Idea map/Mapa de ideas. *Ver Cluster.*

Ideas/Ideas. En composición, el mensaje o tema y los detalles que lo elaboran.

Idiom/Modismo. Palabra o frase cuyo significado es diferente del significado estándar o de diccionario. (*Hacer la vista gorda* es un modismo que significa "pasar por alto".)

Imagery/Imaginería. Lenguaje que describe impresiones sensoriales para que el lector de un texto literario pueda ver, oír, sentir, oler y gustar las escenas descritas.

Imperative sentence/Oración imperativa. Oración que exige u ordena algo.

Indefinite article/Artículo indefinido. *Ver Article.*

Independent clause/Proposición independiente. *Ver Clause.*

Inductive reasoning/Razonamiento inductivo. Pensamiento o explicación que parte de varios ejemplos para llegar a una afirmación general.

Infinitive/Infinitivo. Verboide que comienza con la palabra *to* (en español termina en *-ar*, *-er* o *-ir*). En inglés se usa como sustantivo, adjetivo o adverbio en la oración.

Informative writing/Texto informativo. *Ver Descriptive text.*

Intensifier/Intensificador. Adverbio que refuerza un adjetivo u otro adverbio (*very* important, *quite* easily; *muy* importante, *bastante* fácil).

Interjection/Interjección. Palabra o frase que expresa emoción o exclamación. No tiene relación gramatical con las demás palabras.

Internet/Internet. Red mundial computarizada que permite comunicarse electrónicamente con cualquier computadora de la red para buscar información social, comercial, de investigación y de otro tipo.

Interpretation/Interpretación. Explicación del significado de un texto, de una representación visual o de cualquier otro tipo de comunicación.

Interrogative sentence/Oración interrogativa. Oración que hace una pregunta.

Interview/Entrevista. Diálogo a base de preguntas y respuestas cuyo propósito es obtener información actualizada o de expertos.

Intransitive verb/Verbo intransitivo. *Ver Verb.*

Introduction/Introducción. Sección inicial de un texto en la que el escritor identifica el tema y da la idea general de lo que contendrá el cuerpo del mismo.

Inverted order/Orden invertido. Colocación del predicado antes del sujeto. En la mayoría de las oraciones en inglés, el sujeto va antes del predicado.

Irregular verb/Verbo irregular. *Ver Verb tense.*

J-L

Jargon/Jerga. Terminología peculiar de una profesión, comercio u otro grupo de personas.

Journal/Diario. Libreta personal en la que con toda libertad se anotan ideas, pensamientos y experiencias.

Learning log/Registro de aprendizaje. Diario para aclarar ideas sobre conceptos tratados en varias clases.

Lexicon/Léxico. Diccionario.

Listing/Lista. Técnica para generar ideas a partir de las cuales se escribe un texto.

Literary analysis/Análisis literario. Examen de las diferentes partes de una obra literaria a fin de evaluarla.

Logical fallacy/Falacia lógica. Error de razonamiento que se encuentra con frecuencia en publicidad o en escritos persuasivos. *Ver Glittering generality; Either or reasoning.*

M

Main clause/Proposición principal. *Ver Clause.*

Main idea/Idea principal. *Ver Thesis statement.*

Media/Medios. Formas de comunicación usadas para llegar a un público. Los periódicos, la radio, la televisión y la Internet llegan a públicos muy grandes, por lo que se conocen como medios de comunicación masiva.

Memoir/Memoria. Tipo de narrativa de no ficción que presenta el relato de un hecho o período de la historia, resaltando la experiencia personal del narrador.

Metaphor/Metáfora. Tropo que compara dos cosas aparentemente distintas sin usar las palabras *like* o *as* (*como*). *(Él es una roca.)*

Mood/Atmósfera. Sentimiento o ambiente de un texto escrito.

Multimedia presentation/Presentación multimedia. Uso de una variedad de medios como video, sonido, texto escrito y artes visuales para presentar ideas e información.

Narrative writing/Narrativa. Tipo de escritura que narra sucesos o acciones que cambian con el paso del tiempo; por lo general tiene personajes, escenario y trama.

Nominative pronoun/Pronombre nominativo. *Ver Pronoun case.*

Nonessential clause/Proposición no esencial. Proposición que agrega información pero que no es absolutamente necesaria para expresar el significado de la oración.

Nonfiction/No ficción. Literatura que trata sobre personas, sucesos y experiencias reales.

Nonrestrictive clause/Proposición no restrictiva. *Ver Nonessential clause.*

Noun/Nombre (o sustantivo). Palabra que nombra a una persona, lugar, cosa, o a una idea, cualidad o característica.

- **Abstract noun/Nombre abstracto.** Nombra una idea, una cualidad o una característica.
- **Collective noun/Nombre colectivo.** Nombra un grupo de personas o cosas.
- **Common noun/Nombre común.** Nombra a cualquier persona, lugar, cosa o idea.
- **Proper noun/Nombre propio.** Nombra a una persona, lugar, cosa o idea específica.

Noun clause/Proposición nominal. Proposición dependiente que se usa como nombre.

Number/Número. Forma del nombre, pronombre o verbo que indica si se refiere a uno (**singular**) o a más de uno (**plural**).

Objective pronoun/Pronombre personal de complemento directo o indirecto. *Ver Pronoun case.*

Onomatopoeia/Onomatopeya. Palabra o frase que imita o sugiere el sonido que describe (*rattle, boom;* en español: *pum, zas*).

Opinion/Opinión. Creencia o actitud; no puede comprobarse si es falsa o verdadera.

Oral tradition/Tradición oral. Literatura que se transmite de boca en boca de una generación a otra. Puede representar los valores culturales de un pueblo.

Order of importance/Orden de importancia. Forma de acomodar los detalles en un párrafo o en otro texto escrito según su importancia.

Organization/Organización. La disposición y el orden de los puntos principales y los detalles de apoyo en un escrito; estructura interna de un escrito.

Outline/Esquema. Organización sistemática de ideas principales y secundarias con números romanos, letras y números arábigos para una presentación oral o escrita.

Paragraph/Párrafo. Una unidad de texto que consta de oraciones relacionadas.

Parallelism/Paralelismo. Uso de una serie de palabras, frases y oraciones que tienen una forma gramatical similar.

Paraphrase/Parafrasear. Reformulación de un pasaje en palabras diferentes que conservan el significado, el tono y la longitud general del original.

Parenthetical documentation/Documentación parentética. Referencia específica a la fuente de la información que se pone entre paréntesis directamente después de ésta.

Participle/Participio. Verboide que se usa como adjetivo. El participio presente siempre termina en *-ing* y el participio pasado por lo general termina en *-ed.*

Passive voice/Voz pasiva. Forma verbal usada cuando el sujeto de una oración recibe la acción del verbo.

Peer response/Respuesta de compañeros. Sugerencias y comentarios que dan los compañeros de clase sobre un texto escrito u otro tipo de presentación.

Personal writing/Escritura personal. Texto que expresa los pensamientos y sentimientos del autor.

Personification/Personificación. Tropo que da cualidades humanas a un animal, objeto o idea.

Perspective/Perspectiva. *Ver Point of view.*

Persuasive writing/Texto persuasivo. Tipo de escritura, generalmente de no ficción, encaminado a llevar al lector a aceptar el punto de vista del escritor mediante la lógica, la emoción, la súplica o la sugestión.

Phrase/Frase. Grupo de palabras que funcionan como unidad en una oración.

Prepositional phrase/ Frase preposicional. Consta de una preposición, su objeto y cualquier modificador del objeto; puede funcionar como adjetivo o adverbio.

Verb phrase/ Frase verbal. Consta de uno o más **verbos auxiliares** (*auxiliary verbs*) seguidos del verbo principal (*main verb*).

Plagiarism/Plagio. Presentación deshonesta de palabras o ideas ajenas como si fueran propias.

Plot/Trama. Serie de sucesos en secuencia en un cuento, novela u obra de teatro.

Poetry/Poesía. Forma de expresión literaria compuesta por versos. La poesía tradicional contiene un lenguaje emotivo e imaginativo y un ritmo regular.

Point of view/Punto de vista. Relación del narrador con la historia. La mayoría de las obras están escritas en primera persona, tercera persona, o tercera persona omnisciente.

Portfolio/Portafolio. Colección de obras creativas que representan el logro de un artista o escritor.

Positive degree/Grado positivo. *Ver Adjective.*

Possessive pronoun/Pronombre posesivo. *Ver Pronoun case.*

Predicate/Predicado. Verbo o frase verbal y sus modificadores que hacen una afirmación esencial sobre el sujeto de la oración.

Preposition/Preposición. Palabra que muestra la relación de un nombre o pronombre con otra palabra en la oración.

Presentation/Presentación. La forma en que se ven en una página las palabras y los elementos de diseño.

Presenting/Publishing/Presentación/ Publicación. Último paso del proceso de escritura que implica compartir con otros lo que se ha escrito.

Prewriting/Preescritura. Primer paso del proceso de escritura: decidir sobre qué se va a escribir, reunir ideas y detalles, y elaborar un plan para presentar las ideas; usa estrategias como lluvia de ideas, organizadores gráficos, notas y registros.

Prior knowledge/Conocimiento previo. Hechos, ideas y experiencias que un escritor, lector u observador lleva a una nueva actividad.

Progressive form/Durativo. *Ver Verb tense.*

Pronoun/Pronombre. Palabra que va en lugar del nombre; grupo de palabras que funcionan como un nombre u otro pronombre. La palabra o grupo de palabras a que se refiere un pronombre se llama **antecedente** (*antecedent*).

Pronoun case/Caso del pronombre. Forma del pronombre que se determina por su uso en la oración. El pronombre está en caso **nominativo** (*nominative case*), en caso **acusativo** y **dativo** (*objective case*) y en caso **posesivo*** (*possessive case*), dependiendo de su función en la oración. *Ver también Case.*

Proofreading/Corrección de pruebas. Último paso del proceso editorial en que se revisa el texto en busca de errores tipográficos y de otra naturaleza.

Propaganda/Propaganda. Información encaminada a influir en los pensamientos o acciones; en general es de naturaleza política y puede distorsionar la verdad.

Prose/Prosa. Escritura que se diferencia de la poesía por su similitud con la dicción y los ritmos del lenguaje común.

Publishing/Publicación. Presentación de una obra escrita terminada mediante el uso de la tecnología, para darla a conocer a un público amplio.

Purpose/Finalidad. Objetivo de la escritura: expresar, descubrir, registrar, desarrollar o reflexionar sobre ideas, resolver problemas, entretener, influir, informar o describir.

R

Regular verb/Verbo regular. *Ver Verb tense.*

Representation/Representación. Forma en que se presenta información o ideas al público.

Research/Investigación. Proceso de localizar información sobre un tema.

Restrictive clause/Proposición restrictiva. *Ver Essential clause.*

Review/Reseña. Análisis e interpretación de un tema presentado por lo general a través de los medios de comunicación masiva.

Revising/Revisión. Paso del proceso de escritura en que el autor repasa el borrador, cambia el contenido, la organización y el estilo para mejorar el texto. Las técnicas de revisión son agregar, elaborar, eliminar, combinar y reacomodar el texto.

Root/Raíz. Parte de una palabra que contiene el significado principal.

Run-on sentence/Oración mal puntuada. Dos o más oraciones o proposiciones seguidas, cuyo significado es confuso debido a su inadecuada puntuación.

S

Sensory details/Detalles sensoriales. Lenguaje que apela a los sentidos; los detalles sensoriales son elementos importantes de la escritura descriptiva, sobre todo en la poesía.

Sentence/Oración. Grupo de palabras que expresa un pensamiento completo. Cada oración tiene **sujeto** (*subject*) y **predicado** (*predicate*). Las oraciones se clasifican según su función o según su estructura:

Simple sentence/Oración simple. Consta de una sola proposición principal y no tiene proposiciones subordinadas.

Compound sentence/Oración compuesta. Tiene dos o más proposiciones principales.

Complex sentence/Oración compleja. Formada por una proposición principal y una o más proposiciones subordinadas.

Compound-complex sentence/Oración compuesta-compleja. Consta de dos o más proposiciones principales y por lo menos una proposición subordinada. *Ver también Declarative sentence; Exclamatory sentence; Imperative sentence; Interrogative sentence.*

Sentence fluency/Fluidez oracional. El ritmo suave y suelto de las oraciones que varían en longitud y estilo.

Sentence variety/Variedad de oraciones. Uso de diferentes tipos de oraciones para agregar interés al texto.

Setting/Escenario. Tiempo y lugar en que ocurren los sucesos de un cuento, novela u obra de teatro.

Simile/Símil. Tropo que compara dos cosas esencialmente distintas, usando las palabras *like* o *as* (*como*).

Spatial order/Orden espacial. Forma de presentar los detalles de un escenario según su ubicación: de izquierda a derecha o de arriba hacia abajo.

Standard English/Inglés estándar. La forma más ampliamente usada y aceptada del idioma inglés.

Style/Estilo. Forma en que un escritor elige y organiza las palabras y oraciones.

Subordinate clause/Proposición subordinada. *Ver Clause.*

Subordinating conjunction/Conjunción subordinante. *Ver Conjunction.*

Summary/Resumen. Breve explicación de la idea principal de una composición.

Superlative degree/Grado superlativo. *Ver Adjective; Adverb.*

Supporting evidence/Sustento. *Ver Evidence.*

Suspense/Suspenso. Recurso literario que genera interés y emoción para llegar al clímax o desenlace de una historia. Un escritor crea suspenso al proporcionar pistas sobre el desenlace pero sin revelar demasiada información.

Symbol/Símbolo. Objeto, persona, lugar o experiencia que representa algo más, por lo general, abstracto.

937

T

Tense/Tiempo. *Ver Verb tense.*

Theme/Tema. Idea o mensaje principal de una obra escrita.

Thesis statement/Exposición de tesis. Exposición de la idea principal o finalidad de una obra en una o dos oraciones.

Time order/Orden temporal. Organización de detalles en un texto escrito según el momento en que ocurrieron.

Tone/Tono. Reflejo de la actitud del escritor o hablante hacia un sujeto.

Topic sentence/Oración temática. Oración que expresa la idea principal de un párrafo.

Transition/Transición. Palabra o frase de enlace que aclara las relaciones entre los detalles, oraciones o párrafos.

U-V

Unity/Unidad. Integridad de un párrafo o composición; coherencia entre todas las oraciones o párrafos para expresar o sustentar una idea principal.

URL/URL. Forma estándar de una dirección de Internet. (Son iniciales de *Uniform Resource Locator.*)

Venn diagram/Diagrama de Venn. Representación visual que consta de dos círculos que se traslapan, usado para comparar dos cosas con características comunes y diferentes.

Verb/Verbo. Palabra que expresa acción o estado y que es necesaria para hacer una afirmación.

Verbal/Verboide. Forma del verbo que funciona como nombre, adjetivo o adverbio en la oración. Los verboides son: participio *(participles)*, gerundio *(gerunds)* e infinitivo *(infinitives). Ver Gerund; Infinitive; Participle.*

Verb phrase/Frase verbal. *Ver Phrase.*

Verb tense/Tiempo verbal. El tiempo de un verbo indica cuándo ocurre la acción.

Present tense/Presente. Indica una acción que sucede regularmente.

Past tense/Pasado. Indica una acción que ya sucedió.

Future tense/Futuro. Indica una acción que va a suceder.

En inglés todos los tiempos verbales están formados por las cuatro partes principales del verbo: base derivativa (*base form*) *(swim, nadar)*, participio presente (*present participle*) *(swimming, nadando)*, pretérito simple (*simple past form*) *(swam, nadó)* y participio pasado (*past participle*) (*swum, nadado*).

Un **verbo regular** (*regular verb*) forma su pretérito simple y su participio pasado agregando la terminación *-ed* al infinitivo. Los verbos que forman su pretérito y participio pasado de otra forma se llaman **verbos irregulares** (*irregular verbs*).

Además de los tiempos presente, pasado y futuro hay tres tiempos perfectos: presente perfecto (*present perfect*), pretérito perfecto (*past perfect*) y futuro perfecto (*future perfect*).

Cada uno de los seis tiempos tiene una forma **durativa** (*progressive form*) que expresa acción continua.

Emphatic form/Forma enfática. Agrega fuerza especial, o énfasis, al tiempo presente o pasado de un verbo. Para la forma enfática se usa *do, does*, o *did* con el infinitivo.

Voice/Voz. La forma única que tiene un escritor o escritora de usar el tono y el estilo para comunicarse con los lectores.

Web site/Sitio Web. Sitio de World Wide Web que puede ser alcanzado mediante vínculos o una dirección Web o URL. *Ver también* URL; *World Wide Web.*

Word choice/Léxico. El vocabulario que selecciona una escritora o escritor para presentar un significado.

Word processing/Procesador de palabras. Programa de computadora para escribir y editar un texto.

World Wide Web/World Wide Web. Sistema global que usa Internet y permite a los usuarios crear, vincularse y entrar a campos de información. *Ver también Internet.*

Writing process/Proceso de escritura. Serie de pasos o etapas por los que atraviesa un escritor para desarrollar sus ideas y comunicarlas.

*Este término o explicación solamente se aplica a la gramática inglesa.

Writing and Research Handbook

What are some basic tools for building strong sentences, paragraphs, compositions, and research papers? You'll find them in this handbook—an easy-to-use "tool kit" for writers like you. Check out the helpful explanations, examples, and tips as you complete your writing assignments.

Writing Effective Sentences

A sentence is a group of words that expresses a complete thought. Every sentence has a subject and a predicate. An effective sentence communicates an idea clearly and reads smoothly. Try these strategies as you write and revise your sentences.

Varying Sentence Structure and Length

Even when the subject matter is interesting, many sentences in a row that sound alike or that have the same grammatical structure can be dull. You can make your writing lively and interesting by varying the structure, or pattern, of your sentences. You can give your writing impact by varying the length of your sentences.

Varying Sentence Openers A sentence doesn't always need to begin with the subject. Vary your sentence openers with these techniques.

- **Start a sentence with a descriptive word.**
  Outside, the line to enter the theater stretched around the block.
  Eager and expectant, the crowd waited for the concert to start.
  Nervous, the sound crew rechecked the microphones.
  Suddenly the lights in the auditorium dimmed.
- **Start a sentence with a phrase.**
  Behind the curtain, the performer waited for his cue.
  Looking into the crowd, the entertainer spotted his brother and smiled.
  Dressed in a shiny suit, the rock star strutted onstage.
- **Start a sentence with a clause.**
  While the crowd cheered, the band began to play.
  As the lead vocalist sang his greatest hits, backup singers provided perfect harmony.
  After the concert came to an end, the band filed offstage.

Varying Sentence Structure Use a variety of sentence patterns to make your writing more effective and more interesting to read.

- **Use a simple sentence to state an idea directly. A simple sentence has only one main clause.**

  Marian Anderson was an African American opera singer.
  She sang for a huge crowd at the Lincoln Memorial in 1939.

- **Use a compound sentence to show two or more ideas of equal importance. A compound sentence has at least two main clauses.**

  Marian Anderson worked hard to develop her voice, but she was refused admission to a music school.
  She was a pioneer in the performing arts, and she never let prejudice stand in her way.

- **Use a complex sentence to show the relationship between two ideas. A complex sentence has at least one main clause and one subordinate clause.**

  Because Europeans would accept an African American opera singer, Marian Anderson performed in Europe for ten years.
  In 1955 she became the first African American singer to perform at New York's Metropolitan Opera House, where she received a standing ovation.

Varying Sentence Length Many short sentences in a row make writing sound choppy. Add style, rhythm, and emphasis by varying the length of your sentences.

- **Combine short sentences into longer ones.**

  Short The country-and-western song was sad. It told the story of a lonely man. The man missed his family.

  Combined The sad country-and-western song told the story of a lonely man who missed his family.

- **Alternate shorter sentences with longer ones.**

  The singer strummed his guitar. He sang about the troubles of a poor farmer, the power of a kind woman, and the pride of a patriotic soldier.

Using Parallelism

Parallelism is the use of a pair or a series of words, phrases, or sentences that have the same grammatical structure. Use parallelism to call attention to the items in the series and to create unity in writing.

Not Parallel A pulled muscle can feel stiff, sore, and cause pain.
Parallel A pulled muscle can feel stiff, sore, and painful.
Parallel A pulled muscle can cause stiffness, soreness, and pain.

Not Parallel The average person uses fourteen muscles to smile and forty-three muscles for frowning.
Parallel The average person uses fourteen muscles to smile and forty-three muscles to frown.
Parallel The average person uses fourteen muscles for smiling and forty-three muscles for frowning.

Check It Out

To learn more about clauses and sentence structure, see Unit 13, pages 538–569.

Check It Out

For more on how to improve your style by varying sentence length and structure, review Unit 8, Sentence Combining, pages 358–385.

941

Not Parallel Lifting weights builds strong muscles; do stretches to develop flexible muscles.

Parallel Lifting weights builds strong muscles; doing stretches develops flexible muscles.

Parallel Lift weights to build strong muscles; do stretches to develop flexible muscles.

Not Parallel Riding leisurely on a bike burns about three hundred calories per hour, but seven hundred calories are burned when you race on a bike for an hour.

Parallel Riding leisurely on a bike burns about three hundred calories per hour, but racing on a bike burns about seven hundred calories per hour.

Parallel Three hundred calories are burned when you leisurely ride a bike for an hour, but seven hundred calories are burned when you race on a bike for an hour.

Drafting Tip

You can expand the power of parallelism beyond the reach of a single sentence or pair of sentences. Try using parallel structure throughout a paragraph or an entire composition by repeating similar words, phrases, or clauses for emphasis and rhythm.

Remember to use parallel structure in charts, graphic organizers, or visual aids you include in a composition. Also use parallelism in the formal outline you create when writing a research report. Study this portion of an outline for a report on the Olympic Games.

Not Parallel

A. History of Olympic Games
   1. In 776 B.C. first Olympic Games in Ancient Greece
   2. Greece—site of first modern Olympic Games in 1896
   3. 1900 was the first year women athletes competed in the Olympic Games

Parallel

A. History of Olympic Games
   1. First Olympic Games held in Ancient Greece in 776 B.C.
   2. First modern Olympic Games held in Greece in 1896
   3. First Olympic Games opened to women athletes in 1900

Revising Wordy Sentences

Have you ever listened to a friend tell a two-minute story in ten minutes? You probably wanted to interrupt to say, "Get to the point!" The same is true with writing. You don't want to wade through extra words to find the writer's point. Be sure to show your readers the same consideration by getting to the point and making every word count. Here are some tips for revising wordy sentences.

- **Cut needless words.**

  Wordy I believe that all the high school students who go to Willow High School should really make every effort to volunteer in community service programs.

  Concise Students at Willow High School should volunteer in community service programs.

- **Rewrite sentences beginning with empty phrases such as *there are* and *it is important to note that.***

Wordy There are some students already working on a homework help line for younger kids.

Concise Some students already work on a homework help line for younger kids.

- **Change verbs in passive voice to active voice.**

Wordy Plays at nursing homes are being performed by drama club members.

Concise Drama club members perform plays at nursing homes.

- **Reduce clauses to phrases and phrases to words.**

Wordy Students who act as volunteers make a choice to help improve the community.

Concise Student volunteers choose to help improve the community.

- **Reduce the number of prepositional phrases.**

Wordy Four of the students in my class are teaching senior citizens who are unable to leave their homes how to use a computer.

Concise Four classmates are teaching computer skills to homebound senior citizens.

TRY IT OUT

Write five sentences about music, sports, or another topic that interests you. Use what you've learned about writing effective sentences.

- Use a variety of sentence types, lengths, and structures.
- Use parallelism.
- Be concise.

Writing Effective Paragraphs

A paragraph is a group of sentences that relate to one main idea. An effective paragraph develops a single idea and brings that idea into sharp focus. All the sentences flow smoothly from the beginning to the end of the paragraph.

Writing Unified Paragraphs

A paragraph has **unity** when the sentences belong together and center on a single main idea. Here is a helpful strategy for building a unified paragraph: State the main idea in a topic sentence and then add related details.

Writing Topic Sentences A **topic sentence** is a concise expression of your most important idea. It gives your readers the "big picture"—a general view of what you want them to know. A topic sentence can appear anywhere in the paragraph—at the beginning, middle, or end. A topic sentence at the beginning of an expository paragraph (a paragraph that conveys information) can communicate the key point right away. A topic sentence in the middle can unify the sentences that come before and after it. A topic sentence at the end can summarize the essential details of a paragraph, leaving your readers with a strong statement of your main idea.

Revising Tip

To unify a paragraph, omit details that do not relate to the topic sentence.

Elaborating Topic Sentences Elaboration gives your readers a more detailed picture of the main idea stated in your topic sentence. Elaboration is a technique you can use to include details that develop, support, or explain the main idea. The following chart shows various kinds of elaboration you might try.

Topic sentence: Zoo animals need protection during hurricanes.	
Facts and statistics	In 1992 a devastating hurricane killed more than fifty birds at the Miami Metrozoo.
Anecdotes	One animal panicked during the storm; it ran around in circles and yelped.
Reasons	During a hurricane, an open-air habitat is a dangerous place for a zoo animal, so plans are now in place to move animals to safer enclosures in case of emergency.
Descriptions	Zookeepers herd the long-legged pink flamingos into the rest room, where they safely stand, quietly waiting for the storm to pass.
Examples	Mammals such as lions, tigers, bears, and monkeys are kept safe in concrete pens.
Quotations	One zoo director said, "The animals just have to ride out the storm like everyone else."

Writing Coherent Paragraphs

A paragraph has **coherence** when all the sentences flow smoothly and logically from one to the next. All the sentences *cohere,* or "stick together," sensibly. To make your writing coherent, choose a pattern of organization that is appropriate for your topic and use transitions to link ideas.

Check It Out

For more about organizing your writing, see pages 84–86.

Organizing Paragraphs A few basic patterns of organization you can use to arrange the sentences of a paragraph are listed below. Choose the pattern that helps you meet your writing goal.

- Use **chronological order,** or time order, to tell a story or to explain a process.
- Use **spatial order** to order your description of places, people, and things. You might describe the details in the order you see them—for example, from top to bottom or from near to far.
- Use **order of importance** to show how you rank opinions, facts, or details—for example, from most to least important or the reverse.

Using Transitions Linking words and phrases, called **transitions,** act like bridges between sentences or between paragraphs. Transitions, such as the ones shown below, can make the organization of your paragraphs stronger by showing how ideas are logically related.

To show time order or sequence
after, before, finally, first, last year, later, meanwhile, next, now, second, sometimes, soon, yesterday

To show spatial relationships
above, ahead, around, beyond, down, here, inside, near, on top of, opposite, under, within

To show importance or degree
above all, first, furthermore, in addition, least important, mainly, moreover, most important, second

Using Repetition Another transitional device is the repetition of key words or phrases. To make connections between sentences stronger, you can repeat identical or similar words. Note the repeated key words in these two closely linked sentences.

Rosa Parks's *political actions* strongly *influenced* the Civil Rights movement of the 1950s and 1960s. What is the legacy of her *political influence* today?

Check It Out

For more about transitions, see pages 89 and 142.

Paragraph Unity and Coherence Checklist

- ✔ Is the main idea stated clearly in a topic sentence?
- ✔ Do all the sentences relate to the main idea?
- ✔ Are all the sentences arranged in an order that makes sense?
- ✔ Do transitions link the sentences together and help show the order of your thoughts?

TRY IT OUT

Copy the following paragraph on your paper. Underline the topic sentence. Cross out the sentence that interrupts the unity and is unrelated to the topic sentence. Add a transition to make a clear connection between two of the sentences.

Here is how to use an incredible Japanese invention that supposedly translates the sounds your dog makes into words. First fasten this tiny gadget to your dog's collar. Then Encourage your dog to woof, bark, snarl, or howl. Finally press a button that interprets the dog sounds and plays them back as phrases or sentences. ~~Dogs also use body language to communicate their feelings~~.

Writing & Research Handbook

945

Writing Effective Compositions

A composition is a short paper made up of several paragraphs, with a clear introduction, body, and conclusion. An effective composition presents a clear, complete message about a specific topic. Ideas flow logically from one sentence to the next and from one paragraph to the next.

Making a Plan

The suggestions in the chart below can help you shape the information in each part of your composition to suit your writing purpose.

Drafting Tip

You may need two paragraphs to introduce your topic. For example, the first can tell an anecdote; the second can include a thesis statement that expands the point of the anecdote.

Introductory Paragraph

Your introduction should interest readers in your topic and capture their attention. You may

- give background
- use a quotation
- ask a question
- tell an anecdote, or brief story

Include a **thesis statement,** a sentence or two stating the main point or central idea you will develop in the composition.

Body Paragraphs

Elaborate on your thesis statement in the body paragraphs. You may

- offer proof
- give examples
- explain ideas

Stay focused and keep your body paragraphs on track. Remember to

- develop a single idea in each body paragraph
- arrange the paragraphs in a logical order
- use transitions to link one paragraph to the next

Drafting Tip

Be sure that you do not introduce new or unrelated material in the conclusion.

Concluding Paragraph

Your conclusion should bring your composition to a satisfying close. You may

- sum up main points
- tie the ending to the beginning by restating your main point or thesis in different words
- make a call to action if your goal is to persuade readers

Using the 6+1 Trait® Model

What are some basic terms you can use to discuss your writing with your teacher or classmates? What should you focus on as you revise and edit your compositions? Check out the following seven terms, or traits, that describe the qualities of strong writing. Learn the meaning of each trait and find out how using the traits can improve your writing.

Ideas **The message or the theme and the details that develop it**

Writing is clear when readers can grasp the meaning of your ideas right away. Check to see whether you're getting your message across.

- ✔ Does the title suggest the theme of the composition?
- ✔ Does the composition focus on a single narrow topic?
- ✔ Is the thesis—the main point or central idea—clearly stated?
- ✔ Do well-chosen details elaborate your main point?

Organization **The arrangement of main ideas and supporting details**

An effective plan of organization points your readers in the right direction and guides them easily through your composition from start to finish. Find a structure, or order, that best suits your topic and writing purpose. Check to see whether you've ordered your key ideas and details in a way that keeps your readers on track.

- ✔ Are the beginning, middle, and end clearly linked?
- ✔ Is the order of ideas easy to follow?
- ✔ Does the introduction capture your readers' attention?
- ✔ Do sentences and paragraphs flow from one to the next in a way that makes sense?
- ✔ Does the conclusion wrap up the composition?

Voice **A writer's unique way of using tone and style**

Your writing voice comes through when your readers sense that a real person is communicating with them. Readers will respond to the **tone** (or attitude) that you express toward a topic and to the **style** (the way that you use language and shape your sentences). Read your work aloud to see whether your writing voice comes through.

- ✔ Does your writing sound interesting?
- ✔ Does your writing reveal your attitude toward your topic?
- ✔ Does your writing sound like you—or does it sound like you're imitating someone else?

Revising Tip

Use the cut-and-paste features of your word processing program to experiment with the structure—the arrangement of sentences or paragraphs. Choose the clearest, most logical order for your final draft.

Word Choice **The vocabulary a writer uses to convey meaning**

Words work hard. They carry the weight of your meaning, so make sure you choose them carefully. Check to see whether the words you choose are doing their jobs well.

- ✔ Do you use lively verbs to show action?
- ✔ Do you use vivid words to create word pictures in your readers' minds?
- ✔ Do you use precise words to explain your ideas simply and clearly?

Revising Tip

Listen carefully to the way your sentences sound when someone else reads them aloud. If you don't like what you hear, revise for sentence fluency. You might try adding variety to your sentence openers or combining sentences to make them less choppy.

Sentence Fluency **The smooth rhythm and flow of sentences that vary in length and style**

The best writing is made up of sentences that flow smoothly from one sentence to the next. Writing that is graceful also sounds musical—rhythmical rather than choppy. Check for sentence fluency by reading your writing aloud.

- ✔ Do your sentences vary in length and structure?
- ✔ Do transition words and phrases show connections between ideas and sentences?
- ✔ Does parallelism help balance and unify related ideas?

Conventions **Correct spelling, grammar, usage, and mechanics**

A composition free of errors makes a good impression on your readers. Mistakes can be distracting, and they can blur your message. Try working with a partner to spot errors and correct them. Use this checklist to help you.

- ✔ Are all words spelled correctly?
- ✔ Are all proper nouns—as well as the first word of every sentence—capitalized?
- ✔ Is your composition free of sentence fragments?
- ✔ Is your composition free of run-on sentences?
- ✔ Are punctuation marks—such as apostrophes, commas, and end marks—inserted in the right places?

Check It Out

See the Troubleshooter, pages 386–411, for help in correcting common errors in your writing.

Presentation **The way words and design elements look on a page**

Appearance matters, so make your compositions inviting to read. Handwritten papers should be neat and legible. If you're using a word processor, double-space the lines of text and choose a readable font. Other design elements—such as boldfaced headings, bulleted lists, pictures, and charts—can help you present information effectively as well as make your papers look good.

Evaluating a Composition Read this sample composition, which has been evaluated using the 6+1 Trait® model.

Overcoming the Odds

"Why me?" Those are two words you will never hear Heather say. Heather faced many difficulties, such as childhood pneumonia and the death of her grandfather. But she has never complained or felt sorry for herself. Her positive attitude and strong spirit have helped her succeed despite hardships. Even when she had a tragic skiing accident, she worked hard to make the best of her situation. In fact, she worked so hard that she ended up achieving more than she ever imagined.

On the day of her accident, everyone on the ski team had called it quits after a hard day of training, but Heather wanted one more run. She was unhappy with her last slalom time and was determined to end with a good run. Standing at the top of the slope, she focused on the course and then sped through the starting gate. Just as she passed the halfway mark, the tip of her ski caught the stake of a gate. The sudden collision and her great force brought her tumbling down the mountain under a giant spray of snow.

Heather was rushed to the hospital, where she learned that she would need two operations on her knee over the next two years. She would not be able to take part in any strenuous physical activity until her knee was repaired, and she would probably never downhill ski again. In one brief moment, all her hopes and dreams of joining the downhill ski team in college ended. Later she stood on the sidelines and watched a teammate take away the state title she had wanted so much.

However, Heather never felt sorry for herself, and she never lost hope. After surgery, she endured emotional and physical pain. Though she was heartbroken that she could no longer downhill ski, she worked with her physical therapist as if she were training for an athletic event. She relearned simple things, like climbing stairs. Many people would be frustrated and depressed under similar circumstances, but Heather approached the therapy as a challenge. What she learned about muscles, bones, and coordination helped her when she started training for a new sport—cross-country skiing.

Three years after her accident, Heather glided past her opponents in the last race of the season—the state finals. As she crossed the finish line, hundreds of people cheered for the new state champion. Because of Heather's positive attitude and strong spirit, she overcame what seemed unbeatable physical odds to achieve her goal as a cross-country skier—a goal she was unable to achieve as a downhill skier.

Organization The opening paragraph captures readers' attention with vivid background information.

Ideas The thesis statement clearly states the central idea.

Organization Key moments of the incident are arranged in chronological order.

Sentence Fluency Sentences vary in length and structure, and the rhythm is smooth and effortless.

Word Choice Words such as *hope, heartbroken, frustrated,* and *depressed* vividly convey emotion.

Voice The writer's tone shows respect and admiration.

Conventions The composition is free of errors in grammar, spelling, and mechanics.

949

Writing Effective Research Papers

A research paper reports facts and ideas gathered from various sources about a specific topic. An effective research paper blends information from reliable sources with the writer's original thoughts and ideas. The final draft follows a standard format for presenting information and citing sources.

Exploring a Variety of Sources

Once you've narrowed the topic of your research paper, you'll need to hunt for the best information. You might start by reading an encyclopedia article on your topic to learn some basic information. Then widen your search to include both primary and secondary sources.

- **Primary sources** are records of events by the people who witnessed them. Examples include diaries, letters, speeches, and historical documents (such as the Declaration of Independence). Primary sources also include photographs, posters, interviews, and radio and TV news broadcasts that include eyewitness interviews.
- **Secondary sources** contain information that is often based on primary sources. The creators of secondary sources often conduct original research and then report their findings, shaping the information they've gathered in their own way. Examples include encyclopedias, textbooks, biographies, magazine articles, Web site articles, and educational films.

Research Tip

Look for footnotes at the bottom of a page. Look for endnotes at the end of a chapter or a book. Look for a bibliography at the end of a book.

When you find a secondary source that you can use for your report, check to see whether the author has given credit to his or her sources of information in **footnotes, endnotes,** or a **bibliography.** Tracking down such sources may lead you to more information you can use for your report.

If you're exploring your topic on the Internet, look for Web sites that are sponsored by government institutions, famous museums, and reliable organizations. If you find a helpful site, check to see whether it contains links to other Web sites you can use.

Evaluating Sources

As you conduct your research, do a little detective work and investigate the sources you find. Begin by asking some key questions to help you decide whether you've tracked down reliable resources that are suitable for your purpose. Some important questions to ask about your sources are listed in the box on the next page.

950

Ask Questions About Your Sources

✔ **Is the information useful?**
Look for sources that are closely related to your research topic. Dig deep; you may find a single chapter that pertains to your topic within a longer work.

✔ **Is the information easy to understand?**
Look for sources that are written at a reading level that's right for you.

✔ **Is the information up to date?**
Look for sources that were recently published if you need the most-current facts and figures.

✔ **Is the information trustworthy and accurate?**
Check to see whether the authors document their sources of facts and support their opinions with reasons and evidence. Also check out the background of the authors. They should be qualified experts on the topic that you're researching.

✔ **Is the information balanced and fair?**
Read with a critical eye. Does the source try to persuade readers with a one-sided presentation of information? Or is the source balanced, approaching a topic from various perspectives? Be on the lookout for **propaganda** and for sources that reflect an author's **bias,** or prejudice. Make sure that you learn about a topic from more than one angle by reviewing several sources of information.

Giving Credit Where Credit Is Due

When you write a research paper, you support your own ideas with information that you've gleaned from your primary and secondary sources. But presenting someone else's ideas as if they were your own is **plagiarism,** a form of cheating. You can avoid plagiarism by citing, or identifying, the sources of your information within the text of your paper. The following chart tells what kinds of information you do and don't need to cite in the body of your paper.

DO credit the source of . . .	DON'T credit the source of . . .
• direct quotations • summaries and paraphrases, or restatements, of someone else's view-points, original ideas, or conclusions • photos, art, charts, and other visuals • little-known facts or statistics	• information found in many sources—dates, facts, and ideas considered common knowledge • your own unique ideas

Writing & Research Handbook

Citing Sources Within Your Paper The most common method of crediting sources is with parenthetical documentation within the text. Generally a reference to the source and page number is included in parentheses at the end of each quotation, paraphrase, or summary of information borrowed from a source. An in-text citation points readers to a corresponding entry in your **works-cited list**—a list of all your sources, complete with publication information, that will appear as the final page of your paper. The Modern Language Association (MLA) recommends the following guidelines for crediting sources in text. You may wish to refer to the *MLA Handbook for Writers of Research Papers* by Joseph Gibaldi for more information and examples.

- **Put in parentheses the author's last name and the page number where you found the information.**

  As *Time* magazine once noted, "Gorbachev seemed eager to stop talking about change and to begin making it happen" (Moody 41).

- **If the author's name is mentioned in the sentence, put only the page number in parentheses.**

  Time magazine journalist John Moody once noted, "Gorbachev seemed eager to stop talking about change and to begin making it happen" (41).

- **If no author is listed, put the title or a shortened version of the title in parentheses. Include a page number if you have one.**

  Mikhail Gorbachev won the Nobel Peace Prize in 1990 "for his leading role in the peace process which characterizes important parts of the international community" *(Nobel)*.

Check It Out

Read a model of a research paper on pages 350–356.

Preparing the Final Draft

Ask your teacher how he or she wants you to format the final draft of your paper. Most English teachers will ask you to follow the MLA guidelines listed below.

- Create a heading in the upper left-hand corner of the first page with your name, your teacher's name, and the date on separate lines.
- Center the title on the line below the heading.
- Number the pages one-half inch from the top in the right-hand corner. After page one, put your last name before the page number.
- Set one-inch margins on all sides of every page; double-space the lines of text.
- Include an alphabetized, double-spaced works-cited list as the last page of your final draft. All sources noted in parenthetical citations in the paper must be listed.

On the next three pages, you'll find sample style sheets that can help you prepare your list of sources—the final page of the research paper. Use the one your teacher prefers.

MLA Style

MLA style is most often used in English and social studies classes. Center the title *Works Cited* at the top of your list.

Source	Style
Book with one author	Witham, Barry B. *The Federal Theatre Project: A Case Study.* New York: Cambridge UP, 2003. ["UP" is an abbreviation for "University Press."]
Book with two or three authors	Hoy, Pat C., II, Esther H. Schor, and Robert DiYanni. *Women's Voices: Visions and Perspectives.* New York: McGraw-Hill, 1990. [If a book has more than three authors, name only the first author and then write "et al." (Latin abbreviation for "and others").]
Book with editor(s)	Komunyakaa, Yusef, and David Lehman, eds. *The Best American Poetry 2003.* New York: Scribners, 2003.
Book with an organization or a group as author or editor	Smithsonian Institution. *Aircraft of the National Air and Space Museum.* Washington: Smithsonian Institution Press, 1998.
Work from an anthology	Cofer, Judith Ortiz. "Tales Told Under the Mango Tree." *Hispanic American Literature.* Ed. Nicolas Kanellos. New York: HarperCollins, 1995. 34–44.
Introduction in a published book	Weintraub, Stanley. Introduction. *Great Expectations.* By Charles Dickens. New York: Signet, 1998. v–xii.
Encyclopedia article	"Jazz." *Encyclopaedia Britannica.* 15th ed. 1998.
Weekly magazine article	Franzen, Jonathan. "The Listener." *New Yorker* 6 Oct. 2003: 85–99.
Monthly magazine article	Quammen, David. "Saving Africa's Eden." *National Geographic* Sept. 2003: 50–77.
Newspaper article	Dionne, E. J., Jr. "California's Great Debate." *Washington Post* 26 Sept. 2003: A27. [If no author is named, begin the entry with the title of the article.]
Internet	"Visit Your Parks." *National Park Service.* 1 Oct. 2003. National Park Service, U.S. Dept. of the Interior. 3 Nov. 2003 <http://www.nps.gov/parks.html>.
Online magazine article	Martin, Richard. "How Ravenous Soviet Viruses Will Save the World." *Wired Magazine* 11.10 (Oct. 2003). 17 Oct. 2003 <http://www.wired.com/wired/archive/11.10/phages.html>.
Radio or TV program	"Orcas." *Champions of the Wild.* Animal Planet. Discovery Channel. 21 Oct. 2003.
Videotape or DVD	Hafner, Craig, dir. *The True Story of Seabiscuit.* DVD. A & E Home Video, 2003. [For a videotape (VHS) version, replace "DVD" with "Videocassette."]
Interview	Campeche, Tanya. E-mail interview. 25 Feb. 2004. [If an interview takes place in person, replace "E-mail" with "Personal"; if it takes place on the telephone, use "Telephone."]

CMS Style

CMS style was created by the University of Chicago Press to meet its publishing needs. This style, which is detailed in *The Chicago Manual of Style* (CMS), is used in a number of subject areas. Center the title *Bibliography* at the top of your list.

Source	Style
Book with one author	Witham, Barry B. *The Federal Theatre Project: A Case Study.* New York: Cambridge University Press, 2003.
Book with multiple authors	Hoy, Pat C., II, Esther H. Schor, and Robert DiYanni. *Women's Voices: Visions and Perspectives.* New York: McGraw-Hill, 1990. [If a book has more than ten authors, name only the first seven and then write "et al." (Latin abbreviation for "and others").]
Book with editor(s)	Komunyakaa, Yusef, and David Lehman, eds. *The Best American Poetry 2003.* New York: Scribners, 2003.
Book with an organization or a group as author or editor	Smithsonian Institution. *Aircraft of the National Air and Space Museum.* Washington, DC: Smithsonian Institution Press, 1998.
Work from an anthology	Cofer, Judith Ortiz. "Tales Told Under the Mango Tree." *Hispanic American Literature*, edited by Nicolas Kanellos, 34–44. New York: HarperCollins, 1995.
Introduction in a published book	Dickens, Charles. *Great Expectations.* New introduction by Stanley Weintraub. New York: Signet, 1998.
Encyclopedia article	[Credit for encyclopedia articles goes in your text, not in your bibliography.]
Weekly magazine article	Franzen, Jonathan. "The Listener." *New Yorker,* October 6, 2003, 85–99.
Monthly magazine article	Quammen, David. "Saving Africa's Eden." *National Geographic,* September 2003, 50–77.
Newspaper article	Dionne, E. J., Jr. "California's Great Debate." *Washington Post,* September 26, 2003, A27. [Credit for unsigned newspaper articles goes in your text, not in your bibliography.]
Internet	U.S. Dept. of the Interior. "Visit Your Parks." *National Park Service.* http://www.nps.gov/parks.html.
Online magazine article	Martin, Richard. "How Ravenous Soviet Viruses Will Save the World." *Wired Magazine* 11.10 (October 2003). http://www.wired.com/wired/archive/11.10/phages.html.
Radio or TV program	[Credit for radio and TV programs goes in your text, not in your bibliography.]
Videotape or DVD	Hafner, Craig, dir. *The True Story of Seabiscuit.* A & E Home Video, 2003. DVD. [For a videotape (VHS) version, replace "DVD" with "Videocassette."]
Interview	[Credit for interviews goes in your text, not in your bibliography.]

APA Style

The American Psychological Association (APA) style is commonly used in the sciences. Center the title *References* at the top of your list.

Source	Style
Book with one author	Witham, B. B. (2003). *The federal theatre project: A case study.* New York: Cambridge University Press.
Book with multiple authors	Hoy, P. C., II, Schor, E. H., & DiYanni, R. (1990). *Women's voices: Visions and perspectives*. New York: McGraw-Hill. [If a book has more than six authors, list the six authors and then write "et al." (Latin abbreviation for "and others").]
Book with editor(s)	Komunyakaa, Y., & Lehman, D. (Eds.). (2003). *The best American poetry 2003*. New York: Scribners.
Book with an organization or a group as author or editor	Smithsonian Institution. (1998). *Aircraft of the National Air and Space Museum*. Washington, DC: Smithsonian Institution Press.
Work from an anthology	Cofer, J. O. (1995). Tales told under the mango tree. In N. Kanellos (Ed.), *Hispanic American literature* (pp. 34–44). New York: HarperCollins.
Introduction in a published book	[Credit for introductions goes in your text, not in your references.]
Encyclopedia article	Jazz. (1998). In *Encyclopaedia Britannica*. (Vol. 6, pp. 519–520). Chicago: Encyclopaedia Britannica.
Weekly magazine article	Franzen, J. (2003, October 6). The listener. *The New Yorker,* 85–99.
Monthly magazine article	Quammen, D. (2003, September). Saving Africa's Eden. *National Geographic, 204,* 50–77.
Newspaper article	Dionne, E. J., Jr. (2003, September 26). California's great debate. *The Washington Post,* p. A27. [If no author is named, begin the entry with the title of the article.]
Internet	U.S. Dept. of Interior, National Park Service. (2003, October 1). *National Park Service*. Visit your parks. Retrieved October 17, 2003, from http://www.nps.gov/parks.html
Online magazine article	Martin, R. (2003, October). How ravenous Soviet viruses will save the world. *Wired Magazine, 11.10*. Retrieved October 17, 2003, from http://www.wired.com/wired/archive/11.10/phages.html
Radio or TV program	Orcas. (2003, October 21). *Champions of the wild* [Television series episode]. Animal Planet. Silver Spring, MD: Discovery Channel.
Videotape or DVD	Hafner, C. (Director). (2003). *The true story of Seabiscuit* [DVD]. A & E Home Video. [For a videotape (VHS) version, replace "DVD" with "Videocassette."]
Interview	[Credit for interviews goes in your text, not in your references.]

INDEX

A

956

958

D

M

N

964

O

P

965

966

967

968

970

T

U

Y

973

Acknowledgments

Text

Unit One Letter to Gwendolyn Brooks by Sandra Cisnero, reprinted by permission of Susan Bergholz Literary Services, New York. All rights reserved.

From *Selected Poems* by Langston Hughes. Copyright © 1926 by Alfred A. Knopf, Inc., and renewed 1954 by Langston Hughes. Reprinted by permission of Random House, Inc.

"Reflection" from *A Light in the Attic* by Shel Silverstein. Copyright © 1981 by Shel Silverstein. Reprinted by permission of HarperCollins Publishers.

From *I Know Why the Caged Bird Sings* by Maya Angelou. Copyright © 1969 and renewed 1997 by Maya Angelou. Reprinted by permission of Random House, Inc.

Unit Two "The Quest for Hispanic Roots" by Lorenzo Chavez. Reprinted by permission of the author.

From *The Kitchen God's Wife* by Amy Tan. Copyright © 1991 by Amy Tan. Used by permission of G.P. Putnam's Sons, a division of Penguin Group (USA) Inc.

Unit Three From *The Crystal Cave* by Mary Stewart. Copyright © 1970 by Mary Stewart. Reprinted by permission of HarperCollins Publishers, Inc.

Unit Four Reprinted courtesy of *Sports Illustrated*: "Salute to an Amazing Ironman" by Lisa Twyman Bessone, July 2, 1990. Copyright © 1990, Time Inc. All rights reserved.

From *How the Garcia Girls Lost Their Accents,* by Julia Alvarez. Copyright © 1991 by Julia Alvarez. Published by Plume, an imprint of Dutton Signet, a division of Penguin USA, Inc., and originally in hardcover by Algonquin Books of Chapel Hill. Reprinted by permission of Susan Bergholz Literary Services, New York. All rights reserved.

Unit Five From "Counting Cacti" by Suzanne Winckler. *Audubon,* November 1985. Reprinted by permission.

From *Of Wolves and Men* by Barry Lopez. Copyright © 1978 by Barry Holstun Lopez. Reprinted by permission of Sterling Lord Literistic, Inc.

Unit Six "Petrie's 'Toy Soldiers' Has Glitches" by Melanie McFarland. *New Expression,* May 1991. Reprinted by permission of the author.

Unit Seven From *The Concord Review,* Copyright © 1991 by The Concord Review, P.O. Box 661, Concord, Massachusetts 01742. Reprinted by permission.

Photo

1 Art Resource, NY; **2-3** Art Kowalsky/Alamy; **4** (t) John Dyer, (b) David Moench; **5** Ralph J. Brunke; **6** John Dyer; **8** The Estate of John Lennon; **14** Ralph J. Brunke; **19** Boston Athenaeum; **24** D. Taylor/H. Armstrong Roberts; **27** Courtesy Fundacion Rufino Tamayo/Art Resource, NY; **29** (t) *Lord of the Flies* courtesy of Castlerock Entertainment/Colombia Pictures, (b) Eric Futran; **32** Bettmann/Corbis; **41** Bequest of Maxim Karolik. Courtesy, Museum of Fine Arts, Boston; **43** Courtesy Bernice Stienbaum Gallery, New York; **45** Courtesy of the Evan-Tibbs Collection, Washington DC; **47** Courtesy of the collection of the B. R. Brazeal Family, Atlanta, Georgia; **52-53** © CuboImages srl/Alamy; **55** Manuel Chavez/The Houston Post; **58** Nippon Television Network, Japan; **62** Matthew Naythons/Stock Boston; **70** Eric Futran; **72** Private Collection; **74** Dorothy Gallagher/ The Estate of Hannah Lambertson Nesbitt; **78** The Metropolitan Museum of Art, Gift of Frederic H. Hatch; **79** Collection of the Chase Manhattan Bank, NA; **81** The Bridgeman Art Library/Art Resource, NY; **85** SCALA/Art Resource, NY; **87** Iran, late 12th-early13th-century. Ceramic 3 3/8 x 8. The Brooklyn Museum 86.227.61. Gift of the Ernest Erickson Foundation; **91** Carl Van Vechten Gallery of Fine Arts, Fisk University, Nashville, TN; **92** © Antar Dayal/Illustration Works/Corbis; **100** The Peninsula Outlook; **102** Bob Daemmrich/The Image Works; **106** Paramount Pictures Corporation. All Rights Reserved; **114** Tomie Aral; **117** Courtesy Bluett and Sons, London/Bridgeman Art Library, London; **132-133** Fabio Cardoso/zefa/Corbis; **134** John Dugan; **135** Eric Futran; **136** Photofest; **138** Frank Siteman/Stock Boston; **141** Budd Symes, Budd Symes, Superstock; **142** Nancy Thrill; **144** Collection Grimaldi, Monaco/Superstock; **147** Marc Chagall, *Paris Through the Window.* 1913. Oil on Canvas, 53 1/2 x 55 3/4". Solomon R. Guggenheim Museum, NY, Gift, Solomon Guggenheim, 1937. Photo: David Heald. Copyright Solomon R. Guggenheim Foundation; **150** Masahiro Sano/The Stock Market; **152** Courtesy Holly Solomon Gallery, NY; **156** David Wenzel; **167** The Academy of Natural Science/Corbis; **170** Francis G. Mayer/Corbis; **174-175** Paul Souders/Getty Images; **176** Eric Futran; **177** Tracy Frankel; **178** Eric Futran; **181** Bob Daemmrich/The Image Works; **184** Photofest; **187** Courtesy the artist and J. Cacciola Gallery; **188** Calvin and Hobbes © 1985 Universal Press Syndicate; **195** Courtesy Frumkin/Adams Gallery, NY, private collection; **196** Nicholas Foster/Getty Images; **200** Grant Wood, *Death on Ridge Road,* 1935 oil on masonite, 32 x 39" Collection Williams College Museum of Art, Williamstown, MA; **201** Eric Futran; **204** Sherry Rayn Barnett/Michael Ochs Archives; **215** Courtesy the Chapingo Chapel of the National School of Agriculture and the Instituto Nacional de Bellas Artes, Mexico; **218** Thames and Hudson, Ltd. London, photo by David Lavendar; **222-223** Robert Michael/CORBIS; **225** David Smart; 226 David Smart, Art Wolfe; **228** Ralph J Brunke; **232** Obremski/Getty Images; **240** NASA; **241** Scott Anger/ Liaison International; **247** Reprinted with permission from Clear Light Publishers from Old Father Story Teller by Pablita Velarde; **251** Spaulding Collection. Courtesy Museum of Fine Arts, Boston; **252** Andrew Christie/ © Discover Magazine; **256** Mike Mazzaschi/Stock Boston; **261** Jake Rajs/Getty Images; **262** Slug Signorino; **276** file photo; **277** Nancy Schutt; **279** Courtesy of the Thomas Burke Memorial Washington State Museum; **282-283** Andre Gombert/Reuters/CORBIS; **285** Scott Raffe; **286** Tetra Images/Alamy; **287** Morray Alcosser/Getty Images; **288** Camera Five; **291** Field Museum of Natural History, Chicago; **292** Julie Houck/Stock Boston; **296** David P. Hall/CORBIS; **300** For Better or Worse © 1990 Lynn Johnston. Reprinted with permission of Universal Press Syndicate; **302** SCALA/Art Resource, NY; **303** The Museum of Modern Art, NY; **308** Photofest; **318** Collection New York State Museum; **324** Chicago Historical Society; **325** P and G Bowater/Getty Images; **330** Stephen Kennedy; **334** Courtesy of the US Department of the Interior, National Park Service, Edison National Historical Site, West Orange, New Jersey; **338** (l)

974

Photoworld/Getty Images, (r)Courtesy of General Motors Corp; **344** Bettmann/Corbis; **358-359** Alain Le Garsmeur/CORBIS; **386-387** Galen Rowell/CORBIS; **436-437** The Newark Museum/Art Resource, NY; **461** The Telegraph Colour Library/Getty Images; **477** Steve Woit/Stock Boston; **491** Anna Mary Robertson Moses (Grandma Moses) 1860-1961 *Early Skating.* (1951) tempera or oil on masonite 17 7/8 x 24" The Brooklyn Museum 83.122.1. Bequest of R. Thorton Wilson; **505** (t)Shawn Weiner/Lifestyles, (b)Kent Flemming 1991/Lifestyles; **515** The Metropolitan Museum of Art, The Michael C. Rockefeller Memorial Collection, Gift of the Matthew T. Mellon Foundation, 1960 ; **535** The Metropolitan Museum of Art, Rogers Fund, 1936 (JP2517) **553** Giraudon/Art Resource, NY; 567 Robert Duncan; **586** The Estate of Harold Edgerton, courtesy of Palm Press, Inc; **596** Don Smetzer/Getty Images; **605** National Museum of American Art, Washington DC/Art Resource, NY; **615** Jerry Wachter/Focus on Sports; **629** The Metropolitan Museum of Art, Fletcher Fund, 1963 (63.210.11) **655** The Metropolitan Museum of Art, Amelia B. Lazarus Fund, 1910; **659** (t)Benn Mitchell/Getty Images, (c) David Brownell/Getty Images, (b)Janeart Ltd./Getty Images; **683** Courtesy of the Phillips Collection, Washington DC; 707 Tate Gallery, London/Art Resource, NY; 723 NAA-Thomas C Woods Memorial Collection, Sheldon Memorial Art Gallery, University of Nebraska-Lincoln. Joseph Pobereskin/Getty Images; **727** Joslyn Art Museum, Omaha, Nebraska; **752** Gino Beghe Encore Art Prints, NY; **762** Elyse Lewin/Getty Images; **767** Chuck Solomon/Focus on Sports; **777** Rockwell Kent, The Trapper, 1921. Oil on canvas, 34 x 44" Collection of Whitney Museum of American Art. Purchase 31.258; **780-781** Mark Ruchlewicz/SuperStock; **785** The Bridgeman Art Library/Art Resource, NY; **787** Bettmann/Corbis; **788** The Hulton Deutsch Collection, London; **789** Bettmann/Corbis; **791** Courtesy of the Lilly Library, Indiana University, Bloomington, IN; **793** John Feingersch/Stock Boston, Robert Frerck/Odyssey Productions, Andre Gallant/Getty Images; **794** By permission of Johnny Hart and Creators Syndicate, Inc.; **795** Jay Freis/Getty Images; **796** Bill Horsman/Stock Boston; **801 807** DIL/Jupiterimages; **812** Ralph J. Brunke; **813** File photo; **819** PEANUTS reprinted by permission of UFS, Inc.; **838** Stephen Kennedy; **845** Courtesy of Collier, Macmillan Publishers, London. Photo by Ralph J. Brunke; **895** Terry Donnelly/Getty Images; **896** Panos; **898** Digital work by Industrial Light & Magic. © Lucasfilm Ltd. & tm. All rights reserved. Used under authorization; **904** file photo